Federal Income Taxation of Business Enterprises

CASES, STATUTES, RULINGS

RICHARD A. WESTIN
Professor of Law
University of Houston Law Center

JOHN K. McNULTY
Roger J. Traynor Professor of Law
University of California at Berkeley

RICHARD C. E. BECK
Professor of Law
New York Law School

MICHIE
Law Publishers
CHARLOTTESVILLE, VIRGINIA

COPYRIGHT © 1995
BY
MICHIE
A Division of Reed Elsevier Inc.

Library of Congress Catalog Card No. 95-81415
ISBN 1-55834-289-3

Printed in the United States of America
All rights reserved.

Preface

Albert Einstein, to whom we do not compare ourselves, once said that "things should be as simple as possible, but no simpler." That wise observation applies to the teaching of federal income taxation, among other things. In recent years, the Internal Revenue Code has become ever more complex, as has the teaching of the taxation of business enterprises. The practical problem is that the law student who plans a career in business law is in an unpleasant predicament. He or she must either avoid federal income tax courses, and bear the guilty knowledge that a large area of relevant law has been overlooked, with significant implications in terms of personal feelings of inadequacy, or face the burden of taking a large dose of notoriously difficult courses in corporate and partnership taxation. This book is designed to alleviate that Hobson's choice. Whether it has succeeded is for the instructor and student to decide. We feel it has, although we must admit that we had to make some disagreeable decisions about where to perform surgery on the subject matter. One thing we did not do is put the study of S corporations at the very end of a long book, with the insidious implication that one need not really get to the subject and that "the other course" probably would anyway.

To put it another way, we designed this book in the hope that we could use it to attract students planning a career in business law back to take a course in the taxation of business enterprises without the fear of facing something worse than death.

This book provides teaching materials for a basic income taxation course dealing with the taxation of partnerships, corporations, S corporations, and limited liability companies. In addition, it alludes to a short list of other business enterprises. It can definitely be completed in the usual three hours assigned to such courses, on the assumption that students will spend two hours of preparation for each hour in the classroom.

The book begins with the study of partnerships, moves to C corporations, then to S corporations, then to limited liability companies, and closes with an optional review of some unusual forms, such as cooperatives, regulated investment companies, and real estate investment trusts. In general, we take a cradle-to-grave approach to each subject. Our teaching of the course out of these materials convinces us that the order is realistic and effective.

The cases have been extensively edited, and most footnotes in the original cases have been eliminated without any explicit reference to the fact of their elimination, other than the words in this paragraph. Case and statute citations of the court and commentators, as well as footnotes, have been omitted without so specifying; numbered footnotes are from the original materials but do not retain the original numbering, except by accident. We have reviewed each other's materials.

The book is fairly rich with problems that are scattered along the way, rather than at the end of each chapter. They are not especially difficult and are designed to build confidence while at the same time forcing at least some review of the central Code provisions and pertinent regulations. We do not view this as a "problems" book, and we advise students that if they find themselves struggling unduly with a problem, to drop it, but always at least take a crack at the problems, because if they do not, the colloquy in class in which the answer is revealed will pass over their heads.

We wish to acknowledge with thanks the careful outside reviews of prior drafts by Gray Jennings, Esq., of Baker & Botts, Professor Ira Shepard and Gina Carnino Thomas, Esq., of Houton. We are grateful for the secretarial assistance and invaluable contribution of Mrs. Beverly Jones, Mrs. Susan Evangelist, and Mr. Brian Hope at the University of Houston Law Center and that of Kenneth Matthews and Stefanie Tokiyama of Berkeley. We also wish to thank David Adams and Laurie Babich, both of whom are students at the University of Houston Law Center, as well as Robert C. Calandra of New York Law School, for their contribution to the preparation of this book.

Richard A. Westin
John K. McNulty
Richard C.E. Beck

Houston, Texas
Berkeley, California
New York City, New York
1995

Introduction Regarding Outside Readings

Students taking this course tend to seek out other readings, believing that only the unwise rely on reading the casebook and attending class. In fact, they can do fine without investing in outside hornbooks, outlines, and the like. However, we believe there are certain solid treatises that can be helpful in clarifying areas that students found confusing in class or in preparing a foundation for materials they have not yet covered. The following is a list of such treatises and study aids, with a brief comment about the nature of each of them.

General References

A. Corporations:

   1. B. Bittker & J. Eustice, Federal Income Taxation of Corporations & Shareholders (5th ed., Warren, Gorham & Lamont 1987). This is the bedrock book, used by practitioners, students and teachers. It is superbly written, but perhaps too long. It is available in a student edition, which is more than adequate.

   2. B. Bittker & L. Lokken, Federal Taxation of Income, Estates and Gifts (Warren, Gorham & Lamont 1991). Volume 3 contains an abbreviated version of the Bittker & Eustice book, and it includes materials on partnerships.

   3. H. Abrams & R. Doernberg, Federal Corporate Taxation (3d ed., Foundation Press 1995). This is a short, popular book which combines a nuts-and-bolts approach to the tax law rules with explanations of the rationales for the rules.

   4. P. Weidenbruch & K. Burke, Federal Income Taxation of Corporations and Shareholders (West Publishing Co., Nutshell Series, 3d ed. 1989).

   5. R. Stanley, Dimensions of Law in the Service of Order: Origins of the Federal Income Tax, 1861-1913 (Oxford University Press 1993). This is a fine historical writing, but it is unlikely to be practical from the perspective of the harried law student.

   6. S. Schwartz & D. Lathrope, Corporate and Partnership Taxation (West Black Letter Series, regularly updated). This thorough outline provides both the basic rules and many details, as well as examples.

7. J. McNulty, Federal Income Taxation of S Corporations (Foundation Press 1992). A succinct introduction to the taxation of S corporations.

B. Partnerships

1. W. McKee, W. Nelson, & R. Whitmire, Federal Income Taxation of Partners and Partnerships (2d ed., Warren, Gorham & Lamont 1992). An extensive multivolume series on the minutiae of partnership taxation.

2. A. Willis, J. Pennell, & P. Postlewaite, Partnership Taxation (4th ed., Shepard's/McGraw Hill 1989). An extensive multivolume series on the minutiae of partnership taxation.

3. K.C. Burke, Federal Income Taxation of Partners and Partnerships (West, Nutshell Series 1992).

4. A. Gunn, Partnership Income Taxation (Foundation Press, Second Edition 1991).

5. H.E. Abrams, Federal Income Taxation of Partnerships and Other Pass-Thru Entities (1993).

6. C. Bishop & J. Brooks, Federal Partnership Taxation (West Publishing Co. 1994). A fairly extensive survey of partnership tax law.

7. A. Willis, Partnership Taxation (2d ed, McGraw Hill 1976). This is the earlier version of "2" immediately above. It is especially well written and concise, but clearly dated.

In addition, there are references to germane law review articles and government publications in the text and at the ends of the chapters, in the form of references to related readings.

FEDERAL INCOME TAXATION OF BUSINESS ENTERPRISES

**CONTEMPORARY
LEGAL EDUCATION SERIES**

LAW SCHOOL ADVISORY BOARD

CO-CHAIRS

Howard P. Fink
*Isadore and Ida Topper Professor
of Law
Ohio State University
College of Law*

Stephen A. Saltzburg
*Howrey Professor of Trial Advocacy,
Litigation and Professional
Responsibility
George Washington University
National Law Center*

MEMBERS

Charles B. Craver
*Leroy S. Merrifield Research Professor
of Law
George Washington University
National Law Center*

Jane C. Ginsburg
*Morton L. Janklow Professor of
Literary and Artistic
Property Law
Columbia University School of Law*

Edward J. Imwinkelried
*Professor of Law
University of California at Davis
School of Law*

Daniel R. Mandelker
*Howard A. Stamper Professor of Law
Washington University
School of Law*

Mark V. Tushnet
*Professor of Law
Georgetown University
National Law Center*

Summary Table of Contents

	Page
Preface	v
Introduction Regarding Outside Readings	vii
Table of Contents	xv

CHAPTER 1. THE TAX CHARACTER OF PARTNERSHIPS ... 1
    A. Introduction ... 1
    B. The Growing Popularity of Partnerships ... 3
    C. Partnership Status ... 4
    D. IRS Audits ... 30

CHAPTER 2. PARTNERSHIP FORMATION ... 31
    A. Contributions of Capital ... 31
    B. Contributions of Services ... 42
    C. Assignment of Income Principles ... 56
    D. Foreign Partnerships ... 56

CHAPTER 3. PARTNERSHIP OPERATIONS ... 59
    A. Taxation of Partnership Operations ... 59

CHAPTER 4. TRANSACTIONS BETWEEN PARTNERS AND PARTNERSHIPS ... 81
    A. Limitations on Losses in Transactions Between Partners and Partnerships ... 81
    B. Conversion of Character of Assets ... 82
    C. Limitations on Current Deductions on Transactions Between Partners and Partnerships ... 82
    D. Guaranteed Payment ... 83
    E. Disguised Transactions ... 92
    F. Fringe Benefits ... 94

CHAPTER 5. PARTNERSHIP ALLOCATION ... 95
    A. Allocation of Profits and Losses Generally ... 95
    B. Apportioning Partnership Liabilities ... 111
    C. Varying Intra-Year Capital Shares ... 118
    D. Family Partnerships ... 120

CHAPTER 6. SALES AND EXCHANGES OF PARTNERSHIP INTERESTS ... 127
    A. Taxation of the Seller: The General Rule ... 128
    B. Exception for § 751 ... 129
    C. Tax Impact on Buyer ... 140

CHAPTER 7. OPERATING DISTRIBUTIONS ... 145
    A. Effect on Partner ... 145
    B. Effect on Partnership ... 153
    C. Foreign Partners ... 156
    D. Disproportionate Distributions Involving "Hot Assets" ... 156

	Page
CHAPTER 8. LIQUIDATION OF A PARTNERSHIP INTEREST	159
A. Introduction	159
B. Sale Versus Liquidation	159
C. Taxing the Partner: Section 736	163
D. Liquidating the Two-Person Partnership	176
E. Taxation of the Partnership	176
F. Selecting Between a Sale or a Liquidation of the Partnership Interest	176
G. The Partnership Anti-Abuse Rule Regulations	182
CHAPTER 9. TERMINATION OF A PARTNERSHIP	187
A. Introduction	187
B. Termination by Cessation of Business	187
C. Technical Terminations	193
CHAPTER 10. MERGER AND DIVISION OF PARTNERSHIPS	205
A. Merger of Partnerships	205
B. Division of a Partnership	210
CHAPTER 11. DEATH OF A PARTNER	211
A. Partnership Income	211
B. Estate Taxes	213
C. Other Estate Tax Issues	219
CHAPTER 12. INTRODUCTION TO THE CORPORATE INCOME TAX	227
A. Incidence of the Income Tax	229
B. Integration of Corporate and Shareholder Level Taxes	229
C. Corporate Taxes and Tax Rates	231
D. Operating Via Overseas Subsidiaries	233
CHAPTER 13. RECOGNITION OF THE CORPORATE FORM	235
A. Background	235
B. Other Bases for Attacking the Corporation Form	240
CHAPTER 14. ORGANIZATION OF A CORPORATION	251
A. Introduction	251
B. Taxation of the Corporation	251
C. Taxation of the Shareholder	252
D. Transfer of Property in Exchange for Stock	252
E. Stock	253
F. Control Immediately After the Transaction	257
G. Accommodation Transferors	260
H. The Impact of "Boot"	260
I. Assumption of Liabilities	263
J. The Control Requirement	271
K. Property Transferred in Exchange and Transferors' Control	274
L. Basis of Transferor's Stock	278
M. Corporation's Basis for Property It Receives	280
N. Special Problems of Midstream Incorporation	282
O. Contributions to Capital Distinguished	293

SUMMARY TABLE OF CONTENTS

Page

    P. Organizational and Syndication Expenditures 294

CHAPTER 15. PLANNING THE CORPORATION'S CAPITAL STRUCTURE 297
    A. The Debt-Equity Problem 298
    B. The Section 1244 Stock Opportunity 309
    C. Section 1202 and 1044 Opportunities 310

CHAPTER 16. DISTRIBUTIONS FROM CORPORATIONS TO SHAREHOLDERS ("WITH RESPECT TO THEIR SHARES") 313
    A. Introduction 313
    B. Basic Structure 314
    C. "Dividend" Defined 314
    D. Chronological Aspects of Dividends 315
    E. "Earnings and Profits" Explained 316
    F. Disguised and Constructive Distributions 318
    G. Distributions of Property 320
    H. Distribution of Corporate Obligations 324
    I. Dividends Received Deduction 324
    J. Leveraged Dividends 325
    K. Holding Periods 326
    L. Restrictions of Deductions for Extraordinary Dividends 326
    M. Stock Dividends 326
    N. Basis and Holding Period of Stock 331
    O. Section 306 Stock 331

CHAPTER 17. REDEMPTIONS OF CORPORATE STOCK 335
    A. Constructive Ownership 335
    B. Redemption Not Essentially Equivalent to a Dividend 337
    C. Substantially Disproportionate Redemptions 346
    D. Complete Termination of the Shareholder's Interest 355
    E. Redemptions in Partial Liquidation of the Corporation 365
    F. Redemptions to Pay Death Taxes 367
    G. Redemptions Through Related Corporations 370

CHAPTER 18. LIQUIDATIONS 373
    A. State Law Background 373
    B. Complete Liquidations 373
    C. Recognition of Losses Under § 336 378
    D. Section 332 Liquidations 382

CHAPTER 19. TAXABLE ACQUISITIONS 387
    A. Introduction 387
    B. Types of Taxable Acquisitions 389
    C. Asset Purchases 390
    D. Overview of § 197 399
    E. Stock Purchases 403
    F. Anti-Loss Realization Rule for Consolidated Subsidiaries 408

	Page
CHAPTER 20. TAX-FREE CORPORATE DIVISIONS	411
A. Tax-Free Corporate Divisions Under Current Law	417
B. Spin-Off Followed by a Taxable Acquisition	441
C. Tax Treatment of Distributees in a Corporate Division	442
D. Tax Treatment of Distributing Corporation	446
E. Distributions in Connection with Taxable Divisions	447
CHAPTER 21. CORPORATE REORGANIZATIONS	449
A. Introduction	449
B. Code Structure	450
C. Statutory Mergers and Consolidations	451
D. Type B Reorganizations	472
E. Type C Reorganizations	477
F. Triangular Mergers	481
G. Acquisitive Type D Reorganizations and § 356(b)	485
H. Type E Reorganizations	488
I. Type F Reorganizations	494
J. Type G Reorganizations	495
K. Treatment of the Parties to a Reorganization	495
L. Contingent Payouts	507
CHAPTER 22. CARRYOVERS OF TAX ATTRIBUTES AND RESTRICTIONS ON CARRYOVERS	511
A. Section 269: The Subjective Approach to Denying Losses	512
B. Section 382: The Objective Approach to Losses	517
C. Section 384: Limitation on Use of Preacquisition Losses to Offset Built-in Gains	526
CHAPTER 23. SPECIAL CORPORATE PENALTY OR REGULATORY TAXES	529
A. Introduction	529
B. Accumulated Earnings Tax	529
C. Calculating the Tax	535
D. Personal Holding Companies	535
E. Collapsible Corporations	539
F. Limitations on the Use of Multiple Corporations	540
CHAPTER 24. S CORPORATIONS: DEFINITION AND QUALIFICATIONS	541
A. Introduction	541
B. Eligibility to Elect Status	543
C. Loss of Status via Termination or Revocation of the Election	563
CHAPTER 25. TAXATION OF THE ENTITY AND ITS OWNERS	567
A. Conduit Model	567
B. Computation of Corporate Tax Base	567
C. Elections	568
D. Built-in-Gains Tax on S Corporations that Formerly Were C Corporations	569
E. Tax on Excess Net Passive Income	572
F. Pass-Through of Income and Loss: Timing of Pass-Through and Character	

SUMMARY TABLE OF CONTENTS

Page

      of Income 574
   G. Limits on Use of Losses and Deductions 585
   H. Current Distributions: Introduction 593
   I. Relationship of Subchapter S to Rest of Code 598

CHAPTER 26. LIMITED LIABILITY COMPANIES 625
   A. Background 625
   B. The Wyoming Response 625
   C. Current Status 631
   D. Selected Complications 634
   E. Possible Optional Federal Income Tax Classification of
      Unincorporated Entities 635

CHAPTER 27. TAX POLICY: ISSUES IN THE TAXATION OF CORPORATIONS AND
OTHER BUSINESS ENTITIES 639
   A. The Problem of Corporate and Individual Income Tax 639
   B. Corporate Tax Incidence 643
   C. Possible Justifications for a Separate Corporate Income Tax 646
   D. Incorporating the Corporate and Individual Income Taxes:
      Possible Techniques 647
   E. The January 1992 U.S. Treasury Department Study 658
   F. The December 1992 U.S. Treasury Legislative Recommendations 664
   G. The May 1993 American Law Institute "Reporter's Study" 667
   H. Evaluation of the Merits and Deficiencies of the A.L.I. and
      Treasury Proposals 674
   I. Important Themes: Rate Relationships and Stock Basis 679
   J. Corporate Tax Integration While Retaining Two Taxes 683
   K. The Superiority of Complete Integration, Partnership or
      S Corporation Style Over Other Methods 686

Appendix. IRS Forms 693
Table of Cases 703
Table of Authorities 707
Index 731

Table of Contents

	Page
Preface	v
Introduction Regarding Outside Readings	vii
Summary Table of Contents	ix

CHAPTER 1. THE TAX CHARACTER OF PARTNERSHIPS 1
   A. Introduction 1
      1. State Law Characteristics 1
      2. Tax Background 1
   B. The Growing Popularity of Partnerships 3
   C. Partnership Status 4
      Larson v. Commissioner 4
      Notes 15
      Problem 1-1 17
      Partner or Lender? 17
      Dorzback v. Collison 17
      Notes 21
      Publicly Traded Partnerships 22
      Election Against Partnership Status 22
      Madison Gas & Electric Co. v. Commissioner 23
      Notes 28
      Problem 1-2 29
      Retroactive Amendments of Partnership Agreement 30
   D. IRS Audits 30
   Outside Readings 30

CHAPTER 2. PARTNERSHIP FORMATION 31
   A. Contributions of Capital 31
      1. Nonrecognition of Gain 31
         United States v. Stafford 32
         Notes 38
      2. Basis Effects 38
         a. Impact of Section 704(c) on Contributed Property 39
         b. Holding Periods 40
      3. Impact of Debt on Outside Basis 41
         Problem 2-1 41
      4. Capital Accounts 41
      5. Section 724: Closing Loopholes 42
   B. Contributions of Services 42
      1. Capital Interest Received for Services 42
         a. Impact on the Service Partner 43
            McDougal v. Commissioner 43
         b. Impact on the Partnership 48

Page

    2. Receipt of a Profits Interest for Services 48
        Campbell v. Commissioner 51
        Rev. Proc. 93-27 55
        Problem 2-2 56
C. Assignment of Income Principles 56
D. Foreign Partnerships 56
Outside Readings 56

CHAPTER 3. PARTNERSHIP OPERATIONS 59
A. Taxation of Partnership Operations 59
    1. Computing Partnership Income 59
        a. Separately Stated Items 60
            Gershkowitz v. Commissioner 60
        b. Disallowed Deductions 64
        c. Organization, Syndication and Start-Up Expenditures 64
            Problem 3-1 65
    2. Partnership Level Elections 65
        a. Accounting Method 66
        b. Selection of Taxable Year 66
            Notes 68
            Problem 3-2 69
    3. Tax Consequences to Partners 69
        a. Timing of Distributive Shares 69
            Commissioner v. Goldberger's Estate 69
            Notes 71
        b. Character of Distributive Shares 72
        c. Adjustments to Basis 72
            (1) Partner's (Outside) Basis and Partnership's (Inside) Basis   72
            (2) Impact of Income and Loss on a Partner's Basis 73
            (3) Impact of Distributions on a Partner's Basis 74
            (4) Outside Basis Adjustments for Partnership Income That Is
                Tax-Exempt 74
            (5) Basis Adjustments for Partnership Expenses That Are
                Nondeductible 74
            (6) Basis Adjustments for Partnership Expenditures That Are
                Capitalized 74
            (7) Symmetry Between Inside and Outside Basis 75
        d. General Deferral Limitation on Flow-Through of Losses 75
            Sennett v. Commissioner 75
            Questions 78
        e. Other Restrictions on Losses 78
            (1) At-Risk Rules 78
            (2) Hobby Losses 79
            (3) Passive Activity Losses 79
                Problem 3-3 80
Outside Readings 80

TABLE OF CONTENTS

Page

CHAPTER 4. TRANSACTIONS BETWEEN PARTNERS AND PARTNERSHIPS 81
    A. Limitations on Losses in Transactions Between Partners and Partnerships   81
    B. Conversion of Character of Assets 82
    C. Limitations on Current Deductions on Transactions Between
        Partners and Partnerships 82
        Problem 4-1 82
    D. Guaranteed Payment 83
        1. Impact on Recipient 83
            Pratt v. Commissioner 83
            Note 88
            Rev. Rul. 81-300 88
            Notes 91
            Problem 4-2 91
        2. Guaranteed Payment Plus Allocation 91
            Problem 4-3 92
        3. Impact on the Partnership 92
    E. Disguised Transactions 92
        1. Compensation Disguised as a Distribution 92
            Problem 4-4 93
            Problem 4-5 93
        2. Property Purchases Disguised as Distributions 93
    F. Fringe Benefits 94
    Outside Readings 94

CHAPTER 5. PARTNERSHIP ALLOCATION 95
    A. Allocation of Profits and Losses Generally 95
        Orrisch v. Commissioner 97
        Note 101
        1. Special Allocations Versus "Bottom-Line" Allocations 102
        2. Post-1985 Approach to Partnership Allocations 102
            a. Economic Effect 103
            b. Illustration of an Economic Effect 105
            c. Substantial 106
                (1) General Rule 106
                (2) Shifting and Transitory Allocations 107
                    (a) Shifting Allocations 107
                        Problem 5-1 107
                    (b) Transitory Allocations 107
                        Problem 5-2 108
            d. Amendment of the Partnership Agreement 109
            e. Partner's Interest in the Partnership 109
                Problem 5-3 110
    B. Apportioning Partnership Liabilities 111
        1. Apportioning Recourse Liabilities 111
            Problem 5-4 113
        2. Apportioning Nonrecourse Liabilities 113

	Page
Problem 5-5	114
3. Allocating Deductions Attributable to Nonrecourse Debt	115
a. Background	115
b. The Four-Part Test	116
C. Varying Intra-Year Capital Shares	118
1. Varying Capital Interests	118
2. Admission of New Partner	119
3. Sale, Exchange, or Liquidation of Entire Interest	119
Problem 5-6	119
4. Cash-Method Items Limit	119
D. Family Partnerships	120
1. Recognition of the Family Partnership	120
Ballou v. United States	120
Notes	124
2. Limits on Allocations	124
Problem 5-7	125
Outside Readings	125
CHAPTER 6. SALES AND EXCHANGES OF PARTNERSHIP INTERESTS	127
A. Taxation of the Seller: The General Rule	128
Problem 6-1	128
B. Exception for § 751	129
1. Contract Interests as Unrealized Receivables	129
Ledoux v. Commissioner	130
Note	137
Problem 6-2	137
2. Traditional Recapture Items	138
3. Substantially Appreciated Inventory	138
Problem 6-3	138
4. Calculating Gains and Losses from Sale or Exchange of Partnership Interests	139
C. Tax Impact on Buyer	140
1. Introduction	140
2. Section 743(b) Optional Basis Adjustment	140
Problem 6-4	142
3. Section 755: Allocating Section 743 Basis Adjustment	142
Problem 6-5	143
CHAPTER 7. OPERATING DISTRIBUTIONS	145
A. Effect on Partner	145
1. Introduction	145
2. Distributions of Cash	146
Problem 7-1	146
3. Distributions of Property	147
a. Distributee's Basis in Distributed Property and Partnership Interest	147
Problem 7-2	148

TABLE OF CONTENTS

Page

   b. Character and Holding Period of Distributed Property 148
    Problem 7-3 149
   c. Section 732(d) Election 149
   d. Distributions of Encumbered Property 150
    Rev. Rul. 79-205 150
  B. Effect on Partnership 153
   1. Section 734 Election 154
    a. Timing: Section 734(b)(1)(A) 154
    b. Basis: Section 734(b)(1)(B) 155
     Problem 7-4 156
  C. Foreign Partners 156
  D. Disproportionate Distributions Involving "Hot Assets" 156
   Problem 7-5 158
 Outside Readings 158

CHAPTER 8. LIQUIDATION OF A PARTNERSHIP INTEREST 159
 A. Introduction 159
 B. Sale Versus Liquidation 159
  Foxman v. Commissioner 159
  Note 163
 C. Taxing the Partner: Section 736 163
  1. Modified Distribution Rules for Partnership Liquidations 163
  2. Role of § 736 164
  3. Payments for Partner's Share of Property: Section 736(b) 165
  4. Treatment of Payments for Partner's Share of Unrealized Receivables and Goodwill 166
  5. Treatment of Payments for Partner's Share of Goodwill 166
  6. Treatment of § 736(a) Payments 166
  7. Timing of a § 731(a) Gain 167
   Estate of Thomas P. Quirk v. Commissioner 168
   Question 174
  8. Losses on Distribution 174
   Problem 8-1 175
 D. Liquidating the Two-Person Partnership 176
 E. Taxation of the Partnership 176
 F. Selecting Between a Sale or a Liquidation of the Partnership Interest ... 176
  Kinney v. United States 177
  Notes 181
 G. The Partnership Anti-Abuse Rule Regulations 182
  General Anti-abuse Rule 183
  Abuse of Entity Treatment 185

CHAPTER 9. TERMINATION OF A PARTNERSHIP 187
 A. Introduction 187
 B. Termination by Cessation of Business 187
  Neubecker v. Commissioner 188
   Problem 9-1 192

Page

C. Technical Terminations 193
    Evans v. Commissioner 193
    Note 202
    Problem 9-2 202
Outside Readings 203

CHAPTER 10. MERGER AND DIVISION OF PARTNERSHIPS 205
  A. Merger of Partnerships 205
    Rev. Rul. 68-289 205
    Notes 206
    Rev. Rul. 90-17 206
    Note 209
    Problem 10-1 209
  B. Division of a Partnership 210

CHAPTER 11. DEATH OF A PARTNER 211
  A. Partnership Income 211
    1. Generally 211
    2. Problem of Lost Deductions 212
  B. Estate Taxes 213
    Quick's Trust v. Commissioner 214
    Notes 217
    Rev. Rul. 79-124 218
  C. Other Estate Tax Issues 219
    1. Estate Freeze 219
    2. Buy-Sell Agreement 220
        St. Louis County Bank, Executor v. United States of America . . 221
        Notes 225
        Problem 11-1 226
Outside Readings 226

CHAPTER 12. INTRODUCTION TO THE CORPORATE INCOME TAX 227
  A. Incidence of the Income Tax 229
  B. Integration of Corporate and Shareholder Level Taxes 229
  C. Corporate Taxes and Tax Rates 231
  D. Operating Via Overseas Subsidiaries 233
    Comparison of the Tax Systems of the United States,
      the United Kingdom, Germany, and Japan, July
      20, 1992 (Joint Committee Print) 233
Outside Readings 234

CHAPTER 13. RECOGNITION OF THE CORPORATE FORM 235
  A. Background 235
    Commissioner v. Bollinger 236
    Notes and Questions 240
  B. Other Bases for Attacking the Corporation Form 240
    Achiro v. Commissioner 240
    Problem 13-1 250

TABLE OF CONTENTS

Page

Outside Readings	250
CHAPTER 14. ORGANIZATION OF A CORPORATION	251
A. Introduction	251
B. Taxation of the Corporation	251
Problem 14-1	252
C. Taxation of the Shareholder	252
D. Transfer of Property in Exchange for Stock	252
E. Stock	253
Hamrick v. Commissioner	253
F. Control Immediately After the Transaction	257
Fahs v. Florida Machine & Foundry Co.	257
Problem 14-2	259
G. Accommodation Transferors	260
H. The Impact of "Boot"	260
Rev. Rul. 68-55	261
I. Assumption of Liabilities	263
Lessinger v. Commissioner	265
Problem 14-3	271
J. The Control Requirement	271
Rev. Rul. 59-259	271
Problem 14-4	273
K. Property Transferred in Exchange and Transferors' Control	274
James v. Commissioner	274
Notes	278
L. Basis of Transferor's Stock	278
M. Corporation's Basis for Property It Receives	280
Problem 14-5	280
Problem 14-6	281
Problem 14-7	281
Problem 14-8	281
N. Special Problems of Midstream Incorporation	282
Hempt Bros., Inc. v. United States	282
Notes	287
Rev. Rul. 84-111	288
O. Contributions to Capital Distinguished	293
Senate Report No. 1622	293
Notes	294
P. Organizational and Syndication Expenditures	294
Outside Readings	294
CHAPTER 15. PLANNING THE CORPORATION'S CAPITAL STRUCTURE	297
A. The Debt-Equity Problem	298
Plantation Patterns, Inc. v. Commissioner	301
Notes	307
Problem 15-1	308
B. The Section 1244 Stock Opportunity	309

	Page
Problem 15-2	309
C. Section 1202 and 1044 Opportunities	310
Outside Readings	311

CHAPTER 16. DISTRIBUTIONS FROM CORPORATIONS TO SHAREHOLDERS ("WITH RESPECT TO THEIR SHARES") ... 313
    A. Introduction ... 313
    B. Basic Structure ... 314
    C. "Dividend" Defined ... 314
    D. Chronological Aspects of Dividends ... 315
    E. "Earnings and Profits" Explained ... 316
        Problem 16-1 ... 317
        Problem 16-2 ... 317
    F. Disguised and Constructive Distributions ... 318
        Stinnett's Pontiac Service, Inc. v. Commissioner ... 318
        Problem 16-3 ... 320
    G. Distributions of Property ... 320
        Notes and Problems ... 322
        Rev. Rul. 84-71 ... 323
        Notes ... 324
    H. Distribution of Corporate Obligations ... 324
    I. Dividends Received Deduction ... 324
    J. Leveraged Dividends ... 325
    K. Holding Periods ... 326
    L. Restrictions of Deductions for Extraordinary Dividends ... 326
    M. Stock Dividends ... 326
        1. Optional Distributions to Shareholders ... 327
            Problem 16-4 ... 328
        2. Distributions of Common and Preferred Stock ... 328
            Problem 16-5 ... 328
        3. Distributions on Preferred ... 328
            Problem 16-6 ... 329
        4. Distributions of Convertible Preferred Stock ... 329
            Problem 16-7 ... 329
        5. Disproportionate Distributions ... 329
            Problem 16-8 ... 329
        6. Constructive Distributions ... 330
            Problem 16-9 ... 330
            Problem 16-10 ... 330
    N. Basis and Holding Period of Stock ... 331
    O. Section 306 Stock ... 331
        Problem 16-11 ... 332
        Problem 16-12 ... 333
    Outside Readings ... 333

CHAPTER 17. REDEMPTIONS OF CORPORATE STOCK ... 335
    A. Constructive Ownership ... 335

	Page
B. Redemption Not Essentially Equivalent to a Dividend	337
United States v. Davis	337
Notes and Questions	343
Problem 17-1	346
C. Substantially Disproportionate Redemptions	346
Patterson Trust v. United States	347
Notes	354
Problem 17-2	355
Problem 17-3	355
D. Complete Termination of the Shareholder's Interest	355
Priv. Rul. 9041005	356
Notes	360
Grove v. Commissioner	362
E. Redemptions in Partial Liquidation of the Corporation	365
Problem 17-4	366
Problem 17-5	366
Problem 17-6	366
Problem 17-7	367
F. Redemptions to Pay Death Taxes	367
Rev. Rul. 87-132	368
Problem 17-8	370
G. Redemptions Through Related Corporations	370
Problem 17-9	371
Outside Readings	372
CHAPTER 18. LIQUIDATIONS	373
A. State Law Background	373
B. Complete Liquidations	373
1. Shareholder Level Effects	373
Problem 18-1	374
2. Corporate Level Effects	375
Problem 18-2	375
Priv. Ltr. Rul. 9428006	376
Notes	378
C. Recognition of Losses Under § 336	378
House of Representatives Report No. 841	379
Problem 18-3	381
Problem 18-4	382
Problem 18-5	382
Problem 18-6	382
D. Section 332 Liquidations	382
1. Requirements Imposed by § 332	383
2. Minority Shareholders	384
Rev. Rul. 70-106	385
Notes	385
Problem 18-7	386

	Page
Problem 18-8	386

CHAPTER 19. TAXABLE ACQUISITIONS ... 387
A. Introduction ... 387
B. Types of Taxable Acquisitions ... 389
C. Asset Purchases ... 390
    Newark Morning Ledger Co. v. United States ... 392
    Note ... 399
D. Overview of § 197 ... 399
    Abandonment of Intangibles ... 400
    Problem 19-1 ... 402
    Problem 19-2 ... 402
    Problem 19-3 ... 403
E. Stock Purchases ... 403
    1. The Section 338 Election ... 403
    2. Deemed Elections Under § 338 ... 405
        Problem 19-4 ... 405
    3. Section 338(h)(10) Election ... 406
    4. Section 336(e) Election ... 407
F. Anti-Loss Realization Rule for Consolidated Subsidiaries ... 408
    Problem 19-5 ... 408
Outside Readings ... 409

CHAPTER 20. TAX-FREE CORPORATE DIVISIONS ... 411
Illustrative Problem ... 412
Gregory v. Helvering ... 415
A. Tax-Free Corporate Divisions Under Current Law ... 417
    1. Control ... 417
    2. Distribution Threshold ... 417
    3. Business Purpose ... 418
        Rafferty v. Commissioner ... 418
        Notes ... 422
    4. Device for Distributing Earnings and Profits ... 423
    5. Active Trade or Business Requirement ... 423
        Problem 20-1 ... 424
    6. Vertical Division of a Single Business ... 424
    7. Horizontal Division of a Single Business ... 425
        Nielsen v. Commissioner ... 425
        Notes and Questions ... 429
        Problem 20-2 ... 430
        Problem 20-3 ... 430
    8. Spin-Off of Unwanted Assets Followed by Tax-Free Acquisition ... 431
        Commissioner v. Morris Trust ... 431
        Note ... 439
    9. Spin-Off of Wanted Assets Followed by Tax-Free Acquisition ... 439
        Rev. Rul. 70-225 ... 440
        Questions ... 441

TABLE OF CONTENTS

Page

  B. Spin-Off Followed by a Taxable Acquisition 441
  C. Tax Treatment of Distributees in a Corporate Division 442
    1. Boot in a Spin-Off 443
    2. Split-Off or Split-Up 443
     Rev. Rul. 93-62 443
     Note 446
     Problem 20-4 446
  D. Tax Treatment of Distributing Corporation 446
    Impact on Tax Attributes 447
  E. Distributions in Connection with Taxable Divisions 447

CHAPTER 21. CORPORATE REORGANIZATIONS 449
  A. Introduction 449
  B. Code Structure 450
  C. Statutory Mergers and Consolidations 451
    Minimum Continuity of Proprietary Interest 451
    G.C.M. 39404 452
    Notes 458
    McDonald's Restaurants of Illinois, Inc. v. Commissioner 460
    Notes 467
    Estate of Mose Silverman v. Commissioner 467
    Note 472
  D. Type B Reorganizations 472
    Notes 473
    1. Creeping "B" Reorganizations 474
     Problem 21-1 475
     Problem 21-2 475
    2. Acquiring Company's Basis in Target Company Stock 476
     Problem 21-3 476
     Problem 21-4 476
     Problem 21-5 477
  E. Type C Reorganizations 477
    1. Substantially All the Properties 477
     Rev. Rul. 57-518 478
    2. Permissible Consideration 480
    3. Overlaps 481
     Problem 21-6 481
  F. Triangular Mergers 481
    1. Forward Triangular Mergers 482
    2. Reverse Triangular Mergers 483
     Forced B Reorganization 484
     Problem 21-7 484
  G. Acquisitive Type D Reorganizations and § 356(b) 485
    Problem 21-8 487
    Problem 21-9 487
    Notes 487

Page

H. Type E Reorganizations	488
Bazley v. Commissioner	488
Notes	491
Rev. Rul. 55-112	492
Notes	494
I. Type F Reorganizations	494
Notes	495
J. Type G Reorganizations	495
K. Treatment of the Parties to a Reorganization	495
1. Impact on Corporations	496
a. As to the Transferor ("Target") Corporation	496
b. As to the Transferee (Acquiring) Corporation	496
c. The Acquiring Company's Basis in Acquired Assets	497
d. Foreign Corporations	497
2. Taxation of Shareholders and Security Holders	497
Commissioner of Internal Revenue v. Clark	498
Notes	507
L. Contingent Payouts	507
Rev. Proc. 77-37	507
Outside Readings	509

CHAPTER 22. CARRYOVERS OF TAX ATTRIBUTES AND RESTRICTIONS ON

CARRYOVERS	511
A. Section 269: The Subjective Approach to Denying Losses	512
Canaveral International Corp. v. Commissioner	512
Question	517
B. Section 382: The Objective Approach to Losses	517
1. Introduction	518
a. Ownership Change	519
b. Owner Shift Involving 5% Shareholders	519
c. Equity Structure Shift	520
d. Constructive Ownership	521
2. Limits on the Use of NOL After an Ownership Change	522
a. Business Continuity Requirement	522
b. Annual Income Limitation	522
c. Anti-Stuffing Rules	524
d. Built-in Gains and Losses	524
Problem 22-1	525
Problem 22-2	526
Problem 22-3	526
C. Section 384: Limitation on Use of Preacquisition Losses to Offset Built-in Gains	526
Problem 22-4	527
Problem 22-5	527
Problem 22-6	527
Outside Readings	528

TABLE OF CONTENTS

Page

CHAPTER 23. SPECIAL CORPORATE PENALTY OR REGULATORY TAXES 529
  A. Introduction 529
  B. Accumulated Earnings Tax 529
    Myron's Enterprises v. United States 530
  C. Calculating the Tax 535
    Problem 23-1 535
  D. Personal Holding Companies 535
    1. Introduction 535
    2. Determination of Personal Holding Company Status 536
      a. The Incorporated Talent 537
        Rev. Rul. 75-67 537
      b. The Incorporated Pocketbook 538
      c. The Incorporated Yacht 538
      d. Miscellany 539
        (1) In the Foreign Sphere 539
        (2) Overlap 539
        (3) Deficiency Dividends 539
  E. Collapsible Corporations 539
  F. Limitations on the Use of Multiple Corporations 540
    Problem 23-2 540

CHAPTER 24. S CORPORATIONS: DEFINITION AND QUALIFICATIONS 541
  A. Introduction 541
  B. Eligibility to Elect Status 543
    1. Affiliated Groups 543
      Problem 24-1 544
    2. Thirty-five Shareholder Limit 544
    3. Limits on Types of Shareholders 544
      a. Nonresident Aliens 544
      b. Trusts 545
        (1) Trusts Other Than Qualified Subchapter S Trusts 545
        (2) Qualified Subchapter S Trusts 545
      c. Estates 546
    4. One Class of Stock 546
      a. General Rule 546
        Paige v. United States 546
        Portage Plastics Co. v. United States 549
      b. Straight Debt Safe Harbor 556
      c. Treasury Views on Debt and Hybrid Instruments 557
        Problem 24-2 561
    5. Election Procedure 562
      a. Effect of Election 562
      b. Shareholder Consents for Obtaining S Corporation Status 562
      c. Corporate Election 563
  C. Loss of Status via Termination or Revocation of the Election 563
    1. Revocation 563

	Page
2. Termination	564
a. By Cessation of Small Business Corporation Status	564
Problem 24-3	564
b. By Violating Passive Income Limitation	565
3. S Termination Year	565
4. Relief for Inadvertent Terminations	566
Outside Readings	566

CHAPTER 25. TAXATION OF THE ENTITY AND ITS OWNERS 567

A. Conduit Model	567
B. Computation of Corporate Tax Base	567
1. Accounting Method	567
2. Taxable Year	568
3. Taxable Income and Distributive Shares	568
C. Elections	568
D. Built-in-Gains Tax on S Corporations that Formerly Were C Corporations	569
Problem 25-1	571
Problem 25-2	571
E. Tax on Excess Net Passive Income	572
Problem 25-3	573
Problem 25-4	573
F. Pass-Through of Income and Loss: Timing of Pass-Through and Character of Income	574
1. Pro Rata Share Rule	574
Problem 25-5	574
Problem 25-6	575
Priv. Ltr. Rul. 9026005	575
Notes	578
2. Basis of Stock	579
Problem 25-7	579
3. Reallocation Among Family Groups	579
Davis v. Commissioner	580
Notes	585
G. Limits on Use of Losses and Deductions	585
1. General Limitation	585
2. Manipulation of Debt and Guarantees	586
Estate of Leavitt v. Commissioner	586
Questions	592
H. Current Distributions: Introduction	593
1. Corporations Without E&P	593
Problem 25-8	593
2. Corporations With E&P	594
a. Impact	594
b. Election to Purge Earnings and Profits	595
c. The Accumulated Adjustments Account ("AAA") Revisited	595
Problem 25-9	595

	Page
3. Distributions of Property	596
4. Post-Termination Distributions	597
Problem 25-10	598
I. Relationship of Subchapter S to Rest of Code	598
1. Interactions of Subchapter S and Subchapter C	599
a. Liquidations	599
Priv. Ltr. Rul. 9218019	599
b. S Corporation as a Shareholder	602
Priv. Ltr. Rul. 9245004	602
Notes	609
Problem 25-11	610
c. Dividends-Received Deduction	610
Naporano v. United States	610
Notes	618
d. Fringe Benefits	619
e. At-Risk Rules	619
f. Hobby-Loss Rules	619
g. Passive Activity Loss Rules	619
h. Alternative Minimum Tax	620
i. Transactions with Related Taxpayers	620
j. Audits of S Corporations	620
2. Multiform S Corporations	620
Priv. Ltr. Rul. 9017057	621
Notes	622
Outside Readings	623
CHAPTER 26. LIMITED LIABILITY COMPANIES	625
A. Background	625
B. The Wyoming Response	625
Rev. Rul. 93-38	625
C. Current Status	631
Priv. Ltr. Rul. 9029019	631
Problem 26-1	634
D. Selected Complications	634
E. Possible Optional Federal Income Tax Classification of Unincorporated Entities	635
Outside Readings	637
CHAPTER 27. TAX POLICY: ISSUES IN THE TAXATION OF CORPORATIONS AND OTHER BUSINESS ENTITIES	639
A. The Problem of Corporate and Individual Income Tax	639
B. Corporate Tax Incidence	643
C. Possible Justifications for a Separate Corporate Income Tax	646
D. Incorporating the Corporate and Individual Income Taxes: Possible Techniques	647
E. The January 1992 U.S. Treasury Department Study	658
F. The December 1992 U.S. Treasury Legislative Recommendations	664

	Page
G. The May 1993 American Law Institute "Reporter's Study"	667
H. Evaluation of the Merits and Deficiencies of the A.L.I. and Treasury Proposals	674
1. The Integration Ideal	674
2. The A.L.I. and Treasury Proposals Compared	674
I. Important Themes: Rate Relationships and Stock Basis	679
1. Tax Rate Relationships	679
2. Basis Adjustments in Shares	681
J. Corporate Tax Integration While Retaining Two Taxes	683
K. The Superiority of Complete Integration, Partnership or S Corporation Style Over Other Methods	686

Appendix. IRS Forms 693
   1. Form 1065: U.S. Partnership Return of Income 694
   2. Schedule K-1: Partner's Share of Income, Credits, Deductions, etc. . . . 698
   2. Form 2553: Election by a Small Business Corporation 700
Table of Cases 703
Table of Authorities 707
Index 731

Chapter 1
THE TAX CHARACTER OF PARTNERSHIPS

A. INTRODUCTION

1. STATE LAW CHARACTERISTICS

Partnerships are in essence contractually-based relationships among members of an enterprise organized for a profit. Partnerships fall into two categories, general partnerships and limited partnerships. General partnerships can arise orally and may be informal, although most operate under a written partnership agreement, which is to say a glorified contract between or among the members. The vital aspect of general partnerships is that each partner bears unlimited personal liability to third parties for the partnership's obligations. By contrast, limited partnerships are creatures of state law that must satisfy filing requirements, usually with a secretary of state, in order to come into being, and that must have at least one general partner. The limited partners, like shareholders in a corporation, are liable to third parties only to the extent of their actual contributions to the limited partnership, plus any promised additional contributions. Limited partners are generally precluded from managing the partnership. Limited partnership interests are fairly easy to market, whereas it is difficult to market general partnership interests. Finally, there is the concept of the joint venture. This is nontax terminology for a state law partnership that has a limited purpose, such as to build and sell a single apartment project.

2. TAX BACKGROUND

The partnership tax rules appear in §§ 701-761 of the Code, known as Subchapter K. Subchapter K was enacted in 1954 after careful study and in the hope of avoiding the confusion that arose under earlier tax laws. The Senate Finance Committee Report in support of the new framework provided:

> The existing tax treatment of partners and partnerships is among the most confused in the entire income tax field. The present statutory provisions are wholly inadequate. The published regulations, rulings, and court decisions are incomplete and frequently contradictory. As a result, partners today cannot form, operate or dissolve a partnership with any assurance as to tax consequences.
> This confusion is particularly unfortunate in view of the great number of business enterprises and ventures carried on in partnership form. It should also be noted that the partnership form of organization is much more

commonly employed by small businesses and in farming operations than the corporate form.

Because of the vital need for clarification, the House and our committee have undertaken the first comprehensive statutory treatment of partners and partnerships in the history of the income tax laws. In establishing a broad pattern applicable to partnerships generally, the principal objectives have been simplicity, flexibility, and equity as between partners.[1]

Little did the 1954 legislators imagine how deep the conflict between simplicity and flexibility could go, and how complicated Subchapter K would turn out to be in practice. Professor Bittker seems to feel it a failure. B. Bittker, Federal Taxation of Income, Estates and Gifts, Vol. 3 at ¶ 85.1.2 (1981).

It may help your confidence during this study to take a look at the annual partnership return (Form 1065) sometime; it appears as Appendix A to this Part. No tax payment accompanies the Form 1065, which is why it is called an *information* return. However, each Form 1065 is accompanied by at least two Forms K-1; this is the form on which a report of the individualized results of a partnership's year is made for each partner. The partnership's tax return preparer transmits a completed K-1 to each partner at the end of the partnership's taxable year, and it is used by each partner in preparing his, her, or its personal return. A Schedule K-1 appears immediately after the Form 1065 as Appendix B.

There is a tension that runs through Subchapter K, in that partnerships are both aggregates of partners who pay taxes directly on their share of the partnership's profits, and must, at the same time, be treated as separate entities for a variety of purposes, such as filing the tax return, having a distinct taxable year, and adopting an accounting method to compute their profits or losses. The former is referred to as the "aggregate theory"; the latter is known as the "entity theory." The tax law in some instances treats a partnership as if it were an entity and in others as if it were an aggregation of individuals.

If the forms appear straightforward enough and the Code provisions are sufficiently few, why is this not a simple study? The answer lies in the fact that clever or devious (you decide which) tax advisors predictably have exploited the rules of Subchapter K so as to minimize their clients' taxes, often doing so by taking rules that presumed rather simple-minded transactions and applying those rules to complicated tax-driven transactional formats. In equally predictable fashion, Congress and the Internal Revenue Service have responded with complex, if not sometimes paranoid, reactions that have eliminated the simplicity of Subchapter K.

---

[1] S. Rep. No. 1622, 83d Cong., 2d Sess. 89 (1954).

B. THE GROWING POPULARITY OF PARTNERSHIPS

The partnership form of doing business is often favored over incorporation. In large measure one can attribute this preference to recent changes in federal tax law which are relatively disadvantageous to corporations. The Internal Revenue Code of 1986 inverted the historic relationship between individual and corporate marginal tax rates in which top individual income tax rates used to exceed top corporate rates. As a result, the corporate form naturally became less desirable than previously. In more recent years, the rate inversion is slipping away in that individual rates have gradually crept upwards, but that is not a reason to return to preferring the corporate form, because there is still the problem of the double tax. A partnership itself is not subject to the separate U.S. income tax on corporations; all partnership items of income deduction or credit pass through to the partners.

Because corporations are separate legal and taxable entities in the United States, doing business in corporate form presents a "double tax" problem, in the sense that the corporation pays a tax on its income and shareholders pay taxes on earnings the corporation distributes to them. This disadvantage was mitigated when corporate rates were substantially lower than individual rates (before 1986), however, because corporate investors would have greater after-tax capital available within their corporate entity than would remain after taxes from comparable profits of a proprietorship or partnership. Now that corporate tax rates are similar to individual rates, that is no longer the case. Also, with the repeal of the *General Utilities*[2] doctrine in 1986, corporations must now pay federal income taxes on the appreciation in property they distribute. Consequently, there are major tax costs associated with incorporation versus forming a partnership. What is more, the corporation and the partnership generally offer the same tax benefits for pension plan purposes, although not for certain fringe benefits in employment. Finally, deductible costs, losses, and other tax-reducing items pass through a partnership and take effect, pro rata, in the partners' individual tax returns, where they can be of immediate benefit.

Although limited liability would seem to remain a major reason for favoring incorporation over partnership formation, essentially the same limited liability advantages can be gained through a limited partnership. Insulation against personal liability can be especially effective by using a corporation to act as the general partner of a limited partnership. Also, a new form of organization, the "limited liability company," offers limited liability to its owners or members and also is subject to the Subchapter K tax regime — no double tax. Limited liability

---

[2] *General Utils. & Oper. Co. v. Helvering*, 296 U.S. 200 (1935).

companies will be studied later, in Chapter 26. All you learn here about partnership taxation will apply to them.[3]

C. PARTNERSHIP STATUS

The first major inquiry is whether an entity organized as a partnership under local law stands up as such, or whether it has to be reclassified as another form of organization for federal income tax purposes. For federal income tax purposes all business entities fall into one of the following classifications: corporation; trust; or partnership. Reg. §§ 301.7701-2 through -4. Thus, for example, even the most obscure or novel foreign entity must be forced into one of these three pigeonholes for U.S. federal income tax purposes, assuming it somehow becomes ensnarled with the IRS. Conversely, many relationships that appear to involve no entity at all, such as landlord and tenant or debtor and creditor, have the potential for inadvertently producing a partnership for federal income tax purposes.

The Supreme Court shaped the process of classifying entities for federal income tax purposes in *Morrissey v. Commissioner*, 296 U.S. 344 (1935). The facts involved a trust that was organized to form and operate a golf course for a profit. The Court evaluated the question in terms of whether the trust more closely resembled a corporation or a traditional trust. Finding a preponderance of corporate characteristics, it declared the entity to be taxable as a corporation. In later years, physicians took advantage of the tendency of the case law to treat a state law limited partnership as a corporation if it had a "preponderance of corporate characteristics," thereby allowing them to get the benefit of the more generous pension plan arrangements formerly available only to corporations. The Treasury Department counterattacked with the so-called Kintner Regulations, named after the *Kintner* case, which strove to assure that a limited partnership would be treated as a partnership and not as a corporation. Tax shelter promoters in turn latched onto the generously pro-limited partnership rules and marketed their wares as limited partnership interests, with deductions passing through to the limited partners. Rather than amend the regulations, the government parried with a litigating position that limited partnerships are generally taxable as corporations, as the *Larson* case (next) exemplifies, and with the (lack of) success *Larson* shows.

LARSON v. COMMISSIONER
66 T.C. 159 (1976)

[The taxpayers owned limited partnership interests in two real estate syndications (Mai Kai and Soumis) organized under the California Uniform

---

[3] Some closely-held corporations are permitted to make a federal income tax election to be taxed as (Subchapter) S corporations. No separate corporate income tax applies to them, and they are taxed much like, but not the same as, Subchapter K partnerships.

C. PARTNERSHIP STATUS

Limited Partnership Act. The general partner in each partnership was a corporation (GHL) that was independent of the limited partners and was organized for the purpose of promoting and managing the syndications. Under California law the partnerships could be dissolved by the bankruptcy of the general partner. The general partner invested no money in the partnerships and held interests that were subordinated to those of the limited partners. The limited partners could vote to remove the general partner. The limited partners could transfer their income rights with the consent of the general partner, which consent could not unreasonably be withheld. A transferee of a limited partner's capital interest, if the transfer was at fair market value, had the right to become a substituted limited partner without the consent of any member.]

TANNENWALD, J.

....

Opinion

Petitioners owned limited partnership interests in Mai-Kai and Somis, two real estate ventures organized under the California Uniform Limited Partnership Act, Cal. Corp. Code secs. 15501 et seq.... (hereinafter referred to as CULPA). The partnerships incurred losses during the years in issue, and petitioners deducted their distributive shares of such losses on their individual tax returns. Respondent disallowed those deductions on the ground that the partnerships were associations taxable as corporations, as defined in section 7701(a)(3), and not partnerships as defined in section 7701(a)(2). Petitioners allege that the partnerships fail all of the tests of corporate resemblance established by respondent's regulations (sec. 301.7701-2, Proced. & Admin. Regs.); respondent contends that all those tests are satisfied. Both sides agree that the regulations apply and are controlling, and our opinion and decision are consequently framed in that context; the validity of respondent's regulations is not before us. In our previous (now withdrawn) opinion dated October 21, 1975, we concluded that respondent should prevail. Upon reconsideration, we have come to the opposite conclusion and hold for petitioners.

The starting point of the regulations' definition of an "association" is the principle applied in *Morrissey v. Commissioner*, 296 U.S. 344 (1935), that the term includes entities which resemble corporations although they are not formally organized as such. *Morrissey* identified several characteristics of the corporate form which the regulations adopt as a test of corporate resemblance. For the purpose of comparing corporations with partnerships, the significant characteristics are: continuity of life; centralization of management; limited liability; and free transferability of interests. Other corporate or noncorporate characteristics may also be considered if appropriate in a particular case. An organization will be taxed as a corporation if, taking all relevant characteristics into account, it more nearly resembles a corporation than some other entity. [Reg.] Sec.

301.7701-2(a)(1).... This will be true only if it possesses more corporate than noncorporate characteristics.

The regulations discuss each major corporate characteristic separately, and each apparently bears equal weight in the final balancing.... This apparently mechanical approach may perhaps be explained as an attempt to impart a degree of certainty to a subject otherwise fraught with imponderables. In most instances, the regulations also make separate provision for the classification of limited partnerships. Petitioners rely heavily on those provisions, while respondent seeks to distinguish them or to minimize their importance.

1. *Continuity of Life*

Pertinent provisions of the regulation concerning this characteristic are set forth below. A corporation possesses a greater degree of continuity of life than a partnership, since its existence is not dependent upon events personally affecting its separate members. Because of their more intimate legal and financial ties, partners are given a continuing right to choose their associates which is denied to corporate shareholders. A material alteration in the makeup of the partnership, as through the death or incapacity of a partner, either dissolves the partnership relation by operation of law or permits dissolution by order of court. Uniform Partnership Act, secs. 31 and 32 (hereinafter referred to as UPA). Partners are then free to withdraw their shares from the business, though they may agree to form a new partnership to continue it. A partner is also given the right to dissolve the partnership and withdraw his capital (either specific property or the value of his interest) at will at any time (UPA sec. 31(2)), although he may be unable to cause the winding up of the business and may be answerable in damages to other partners if his act breaches an agreement among them (UPA secs. 37 and 38(2)). The significant difference between a corporation and a partnership as regards continuity of life, then, is that a partner can always opt out of continued participation in and exposure to the risks of the enterprise. A corporate shareholder's investment is locked in unless liquidation is voted or he can find a purchaser to buy him out.

In a partnership subject to the Uniform Limited Partnership Act (hereinafter referred to as ULPA), this right of withdrawal is modified. A limited partner can withdraw his interest on dissolution (ULPA sec. 16), but he can neither dissolve the partnership at will (ULPA sec. 10) nor force dissolution at the retirement, death, or insanity of a general partner if the remaining general partners agree to continue the business in accordance with a right granted in the partnership certificate (ULPA sec. 20). CULPA section 15520 further provides that a new general partner can be elected to continue the business without causing dissolution, if the certificate permits.

The sole general partner in the limited partnerships involved herein was a corporation, whose business was the promotion and management of real estate ventures. As a practical matter, it is unlikely that either Mai-Kai or Somis would have been dissolved midstream and the partners afforded an opportunity to

C. PARTNERSHIP STATUS

withdraw their investments. Petitioners argue that the partnerships nevertheless lacked continuity of life because they could be dissolved either at will by, or on the bankruptcy of, the general partner. We turn first to the effect of bankruptcy of GHL.

California Uniform Partnership Act ... (hereinafter referred to as CUPA) provides that a partnership is dissolved on the bankruptcy of a partner. CUPA ... makes that act applicable to limited partnerships unless inconsistent with statutes relating to them. CULPA nowhere provides for dissolution or nondissolution in the event of bankruptcy. Section 15520, which merely covers dissolution and countervailing action by the remaining partners under certain circumstances, does not provide for such event. CUPA ... therefore applies. Since the bankruptcy of GHL would bring about dissolution by operation of law, each limited partner would be entitled to demand the return of his contribution (CULPA sec. 15516). Somis and Mai-Kai simply do not satisfy the regulations' test of continuity, which requires that the "bankruptcy ... of *any member* will not cause a dissolution of the organization." (Emphasis supplied.)[4]

The fact that under the agreements involved herein a new general partner might be chosen to continue the business does not affect this conclusion.... [I]f GHL became bankrupt while it was the general partner of Somis and Mai-Kai, there would at best be a hiatus between the event of bankruptcy and the entry of a new general partner so that, from a legal point of view, the old partnerships would have been dissolved. Moreover, at least in the case of Mai-Kai, a vote of 100 percent of the limited partners was required to elect a new general partner. *Glensder Textile Co.*, 46 B.T.A. 176 (1942), held that such contingent continuity of life did not resemble that of a corporation. Respondent's regulations ... incorporate this conclusion.

... We recognize that our application of respondent's existing regulations to the event of bankruptcy results in a situation where it is unlikely that a limited partnership will ever satisfy the "continuity of life" requirement of those regulations. But the fact that the regulations are so clearly keyed to "dissolution" (a term encompassing the legal relationships between the partners) rather than "termination of the business" (a phrase capable of more pragmatic interpretation encompassing the life of the business enterprise) leaves us with no viable alternative. In this connection, we note that respondent is not without power to alter the impact of our application of his existing regulations....

---

[4] In light of our conclusion, *infra* at pp. 177-179, that GHL has not been shown to have had a substantial interest in the partnerships, it may be argued that it was not a "member" for the purpose of the regulations. Such an argument, however, we find to be structurally incompatible with the regulations, which consider the substantiality of a partner's interest in the partnership only in connection with centralization of management and transferability of interests. *Cf.* sec. 301.7701-2(d)(2), Proced. & Admin. Regs., n. 19 *infra* (fourth sentence).

2. Centralized Management

In the corporate form, management is centralized in the officers and directors; the involvement of shareholders as such in ordinary operations is limited to choosing these representatives. In a general partnership, authority is decentralized and any partner has the power to make binding decisions in the ordinary course.... In a limited partnership, however, this authority exists only in the general partners (ULPA secs. 9 and 10), and a limited partner who takes part in the control of the business loses his limited liability status.... From a practical standpoint, it is clear that the management of both Mai-Kai and Somis was centralized in GHL. The sole general partner was empowered by law as well as by the partnership agreements to administer the partnership affairs. However, respondent's regulations specify that —

> In addition, limited partnerships subject to a statute corresponding to the Uniform Limited Partnership Act, generally do not have centralized management, but centralized management ordinarily does exist in such a limited partnership if substantially all the interests in the partnership are owned by the limited partners....

In specifying this additional condition, respondent has adopted the theory of *Glensder Textile Co., supra,* that managing partners with ... interests in the business are not "analogous to directors of a corporation" because they act in their own interests "and not *merely* in a representative capacity for a body of persons having a limited investment and a limited liability."

....

[P]etitioners herein have failed to show that the limited partners did not own all or substantially all the interests in the partnerships involved herein within the meaning of the regulations. GHL's interests in Mai-Kai and Somis were subordinated to those of the limited partners. Petitioners have not attempted to demonstrate that GHL's capital interests had any present value during the years in issue, and it is clear that, because of the subordination provisions, it had no present right to income during those years. Petitioners would have us look to the anticipated return on the partnership properties in future years to determine that GHL had a substantial proprietary stake in the business independent of its management role. They have not, however, proved by competent evidence that such a return could in fact be expected, relying instead on unsupported projections; nor have they shown that any such future profit would be reflected in the present value of GHL's interest. Although there was testimony that GHL expected profits from the subordinated interests when the limited partnerships were liquidated, we are not convinced that the possibility of such income at an indefinite future date had value during the years at issue. GHL reported gross income of $906,930.89 from fiscal 1969 to fiscal 1974, out of which only $118 represented a partnership distribution (from a partnership not involved herein).

C. PARTNERSHIP STATUS

Furthermore, the limited partners in Somis and Mai-Kai possessed the right to remove GHL as the general partner. Thus, GHL's right to participate in future growth and profits was wholly contingent on satisfactory performance of its management role, and not at all analogous to the independent proprietary interest of a typical general partner. In *Glensder Textile Co.*, *supra*, our conclusion that centralization of management was lacking rested not only on the fact that management retained a proprietary interest but also on the fact that the limited partners could not "remove the general partners and control them as agents, as stockholders may control directors."...

Petitioners argue that such power of removal and control could be given to limited partners under ULPA.... In our opinion, the regulation was not intended to provide a blanket exemption from association status for ULPA limited partnerships, regardless of the extent to which the partners by agreement deviate from the statutory scheme.... We have repeatedly held that an organization is to be classified by reference to the rights and duties created by agreement as well as those existing under State law.... The effect of such organic laws as ULPA (and CULPA) is to provide a rule which governs in the absence of contrary agreement. Where the theme is obscured by the variations, it is the latter which set the tone of the composition. Neither ULPA nor CULPA requires that the limited partners be given the right to remove the general partner; in fact, ULPA does not even mention such a possibility. By reserving that right, the limited partners in Mai-Kai and Somis took themselves out of the basic framework of ULPA and hence out of the shelter of the regulation, which is based on *Glensder*....

We conclude that Somis and Mai-Kai had centralized management within the meaning of respondent's regulations.

3. *Limited Liability*

Unless some member is personally liable for debts of, and claims against, an entity ... the entity possesses the corporate characteristic of limited liability. The regulation provides that "in the case of a limited partnership subject to a statute corresponding to the Uniform Limited Partnership Act, personal liability exists with respect to each general partner, except as provided in subparagraph (2) of this paragraph." The first sentence of subparagraph (2) establishes a conjunctive test, under which a general partner is considered not to have personal liability only "when he has no substantial assets (other than his interest in the partnership) which could be reached by a creditor of the organization and when he is merely a 'dummy' acting as the agent of the limited partners." (Emphasis added.) In other words, personal liability exists if the general partner either has substantial assets or is not a dummy for the limited partners.... Although the purpose of subparagraph (2) was ostensibly to delineate the conditions under which personal liability of a general partner does not exist, practically all the remaining material in the subparagraph outlines the conditions under which such personal liability does exist. In several examples, personal liability is said to exist, either because the general partner has substantial assets or because he is not a dummy for the limited partners. *See Zuckman v. United States, supra.* In no instance is there a suggestion that both conditions established by the first sentence of subparagraph (2) need not be satisfied.

In so concluding, we are mindful that in *Glensder Textile Co., supra,* the apparent source of the language in the regulations, the term "dummy" was arguably considered applicable to any general partner without substantial assets risked in the business. The opinion in *Glensder* states ... :

> If, for instance, the general partners were not men with substantial assets risked in the business but were mere dummies without real means acting as the agents of the limited partners, whose investments made possible the business, there would be something approaching the corporate form of stockholders and directors.... [Emphasis added.]

Thus, lack of substantial assets seems to be considered the equivalent of being a dummy — an equivalence which respondent apparently sought to avoid by using the word "and" in his existing regulations.

While it may be doubtful that GHL could be considered to have had substantial assets during the years in issue, we find it unnecessary to resolve this question since it is clear that GHL was not a dummy for the limited partners of Somis and Mai-Kai. Respondent contends that GHL fell within the "dummy" concept because it was subject to removal by the limited partners, and thus was subject to their ultimate control. While it is true that a mere "dummy" would be totally under the control of the limited partners, it does not follow that the presence of some control by virtue of the power to remove necessarily makes the general partner a "dummy." It seems clear that the limited partners' rights to remove the general partner were designed to give the limited partners a measure of control over their investment without involving them in the "control of the business"; the rights were not designed to render GHL a mere dummy or to empower the limited partners "to direct the business actively through the general partners." *Glensder Textile Co.,* 46 B.T.A. at 183. Moreover, the record indicates that the limited partners did not use GHL as a screen to conceal their own active involvement in the conduct of the business; far from being a rubber stamp, GHL was the moving force in these enterprises. With a minor exception, the persons controlling GHL were independent of and unrelated to the limited partners.

In view of the foregoing we conclude that personal liability existed with respect to GHL, and the partnerships lack the corporate characteristic of limited liability.

4. *Transferability of Interests*

A stockholder's rights and interest in a corporate venture are, absent consensual restrictions, freely transferable by the owner without reference to the wishes of other members. A partner, on the other hand, can unilaterally transfer

C. PARTNERSHIP STATUS 11

only his interest in partnership "profits and surplus," and cannot confer on the assignee the other attributes of membership without the consent of all partners.... Respondent's regulations recognize and rely upon this distinction.

The regulations state that if substantially all interests are freely transferable, the corporate characteristic of free transferability of interests is present. Since we have concluded, for the purposes of this case, that the limited partners should be considered as owning substantially all the interests in Mai-Kai and Somis ... , we turn our attention to the question whether their interests were so transferable....

Both partnership agreements permit the assignment of a limited partner's income interest with the consent of the general partner, which may not unreasonably be withheld. Petitioners have not suggested any ground on which consent could be withheld. The requirement of consent, circumscribed by a standard of reasonableness, is not such a restriction on transfer as is typical of partnership agreements; nor is it the sort referred to by the regulations....

Petitioners also argue that transferability is limited by the requirement that in the event of a proposed assignment, a limited partner's capital interest first be offered to other members under certain circumstances. While an assignment for less than fair market value could be prevented in this manner, there was no requirement that such an offer be made if an interest was to be sold to a third party at fair market value. Thus, there was no "effort on the part of the parties to select their business associates," as is characteristic of the usual partnership arrangement.... We think that these interests possessed considerably more than the "modified" form of free transferability referred to in subparagraph (2) of the regulation.

In sum, an assignee for fair consideration of a limited partner's interest in Somis or Mai-Kai could acquire all of the rights of a substituted limited partner within the framework of the agreement and governing State law, without discretionary consent of any other member. Any restrictions or conditions on such a transfer were procedural rather than substantive. The right of assignment more closely resembles that attending corporate shares than that typically associated with partnership interests. Mai-Kai and Somis therefore possessed the corporate characteristic of free transferability of interests.

5. *Other Characteristics*

Both parties have identified other characteristics of Mai-Kai and Somis which they allege are relevant to the determination whether those entities more closely resemble partnerships or corporations.... Petitioners point to the fact that, unlike a corporate board of directors, GHL as manager lacked the discretionary right to retain or distribute profits according to the needs of the business. This argument is in reality directed to the issue of centralized management. The same is true of respondent's analogy between the limited partners' voting rights and those of corporate shareholders. To be sure the partnership interests were not represented by certificates but this factor conceivably is more properly subsumed in the transferability issue.... Moreover, those interests were divided into units or shares and were promoted and marketed in a manner similar to corporate securities — an additional "characteristic" which we have not ignored, (*see Outlaw v. United States, supra*), but which we do not deem of critical significance under the circumstances herein. Similarly, we do not assign any particular additional importance to the facts that the partnerships have not observed corporate formalities and procedures ... or that, unlike general partners, limited partners were not required personally to sign the partnership certificates. Finally, respondent argues that the limited partnerships resemble corporations because they provide a means of pooling investments while limiting the liability of the participants.... As it relates to the facts of this case, this point is subsumed in our earlier discussion. To the extent that it presages an attempt to classify all limited partnerships as corporations, it is in irreconcilable conflict with respondent's own regulations.

6. *Conclusion*

The regulations provide that an entity will be taxed as a corporation if it more closely resembles a corporation than any other form of organization. They further state that such a resemblance does not exist unless the entity possesses more corporate than noncorporate characteristics. If every characteristic bears equal weight, then Mai-Kai and Somis are partnerships for tax purposes.... On the other hand, if the overall corporate resemblance test, espoused by *Morrissey* and adhered to by the regulations, permits us to weigh each factor according to the degree of corporate similarity it provides, we would be inclined to find that these entities were taxable as corporations. Each possessed a degree of centralized management indistinguishable from that of a pure corporation; the other major factors lie somewhere on the continuum between corporate and partnership resemblance. Were not the regulations' thumb upon the scales, it appears to us that the practical continuity and limited liability of both entities would decisively tip the balance in respondent's favor. However, we can find no warrant for such refined balancing in the regulations or in cases which have considered them.... Only in connection with free transferability of interests do the regulations recognize a modified and less significant form of a particular characteristic.

Our task herein is to apply the provisions of respondent's regulations as we find them and not as we think they might or ought to have been written.... On this basis, petitioners must prevail.

Decisions will be entered under Rule 155.

[The concurrence by Dawson and Goffe is omitted, as are the dissents of Raum, Drennen, Scott, and Quealy.]

SIMPSON, J., dissenting:
The majority has presented a careful analysis of the complex matters involved in this case. However, I respectfully suggest that, while becoming involved with the intricacies of the regulations, they have lost sight of the ultimate objective of the regulations, which is to decide whether Mai-Kai and Somis more nearly

C. PARTNERSHIP STATUS

resemble corporations or partnerships. For sake of emphasis, let me reiterate the matter to be decided: This case arose because the Commissioner disallowed the losses claimed by the members of those organizations. Congress has decided that such losses are deductible if, and only if, the organizations constitute partnerships for tax purposes. What we must decide is how the organizations are to be classified. Both parties have asked that we make such decision based on the present regulations so that our task is merely to interpret those regulations, and we are not asked to pass upon their validity.

1. *Other Significant Characteristics*

... The regulations enumerate the major characteristics of a corporation ... and set forth many rules to assist in applying those criteria. The regulations also recognize that there may be other characteristics which should be taken into consideration.... Since under both the cases and the regulations, the ultimate test is to decide whether an organization more nearly resembles a corporation or a partnership, we must consider all characteristics which have any relevancy in making that judgment. The even-split rule of the regulations applies only when there are no other significant characteristics....

The interests in the limited partnerships are securities under California and Federal law, just as is corporate stock.... Further, such interests were sold through licensed brokers just as corporate stock. GHL prepared and distributed offering circulars which advertised the interests as "tax-sheltered real estate investments." Thus, the method of raising capital and marketing the interests in the organizations was very similar, if not identical, to the methods customarily used by corporations....

Moreover, Mai-Kai and Somis possess another significant characteristic which also increases their resemblance to corporations.... CULPA provides that the limited partners may possess and exercise voting rights with respect to any matter "affecting the basic structure" of the limited partnership. Such rights include the right of the limited partners to remove the general partner at any time and to select a replacement and the right to vote on the sale of all, or substantially all, of the assets of the partnership. The certificates of Mai-Kai and Somis provided that the limited partners in each organization had the rights to remove the general partner and to select a replacement. Such rights could not be conferred upon limited partners under ULPA....

By conferring such rights on limited partners, California has created greater democracy in limited partnerships. It has thus enabled the limited partners to exercise control over the affairs of the enterprise in much the same manner as shareholders can control the affairs of a corporation....

Even if we assume, as does the majority, that there is an even split among the major characteristics, the method of marketing the interests in the organizations and the control conferred upon the limited partners are surely significant characteristics, and when they are taken into consideration, they establish a clear preponderance in favor of association classification.

2. *Limited Liability*

I also disagree with the majority's conclusion that Mai-Kai and Somis do not possess the characteristic of limited liability. The issue as to whether such organizations possess the characteristic of limited liability depends entirely on whether their sole general partner, GHL, possesses such characteristic. Whether GHL has personal or limited liability turns on the proper interpretation of section 301.7701-2(d)(2), Proced. & Admin. Regs., which provides, in part:

> (2) In the case of an organization formed as a limited partnership, personal liability does not exist, for purposes of this paragraph, with respect to a general partner when he has no substantial assets (other than his interest in the partnership) which could be reached by a creditor of the organization and when he is merely a "dummy" acting as the agent of the limited partners....

I am in complete agreement with the majority that limited liability exists only when the general partner lacks substantial assets and also is "merely a 'dummy' acting as the agent of the limited partners."... The majority finds that GHL was not a "dummy" since "the limited partners did not use GHL as a screen to conceal their own active involvement in the conduct of the business; far from being a rubber stamp, GHL was the moving force in these enterprises." I disagree with that construction of the term "dummy" and conclude that GHL was a "dummy" within the meaning of the regulations.

I have two reasons for my disagreement: In the first place, the majority's construction of the regulations will render the provision meaningless.... The regulations surely contemplate that under some situations, an organization formed as a limited partnership may have limited liability, but the construction of the regulations adopted by the Court of Claims, and now by a majority of this Court, will result in limited partnerships never possessing such characteristic....

Unfortunately, the term "dummy" has no precise meaning, but as the majority recognizes, the regulations adopted the language from *Glensder Textile Co.*... [W]hen the Board spoke of "mere dummies ... acting as the agents of the limited partners," they did not have in mind a private understanding in which the general partners were merely straw men for the limited partners. The Board had in mind the relationship between a board of directors and the shareholders of a corporation and was looking to State law to ascertain what powers were conferred upon the limited partners....

It is true that GHL was not a mere straw man for the limited partners in Mai-Kai and Somis, but it is also true that the limited partners in those organizations possessed rights very similar to those of shareholders in a corporation. As in the case of a board of directors of a corporation and the corporate officers chosen by it, GHL was expected to exercise its discretion in the management of the day-to-day affairs of the enterprises, but the limited partners, through their power to remove GHL, could exercise general control

C. PARTNERSHIP STATUS

over the policies of the enterprises. In other respects, the limited partners possess the powers with which the Board was concerned in *Glensder*.

3. *Continuity of Life*

Although I agree with the majority's conclusion that Mai-Kai and Somis lacked continuity of life within the meaning of the regulations, I do not agree with their reasons for that conclusion. Their conclusion is based on the finding that bankruptcy of the general partner would cause a dissolution of each of the organizations....

Under *Glensder*, there is no continuity of life whenever an organization's continuity is contingent, and if its continuity depends upon the agreement of remaining partners, it is contingent, irrespective of whether all, or merely a majority, of the remaining partners must agree.... In the case of Mai-Kai, dissolution could be avoided by an agreement of 100 percent of the limited partners, and in the case of Somis, a majority of the limited partners could prevent dissolution. In either event, the continuation of the organization depended upon the agreement of some or all of the limited partners, and consequently, continuity was contingent. For this reason, both organizations lack continuity of life within the meaning of the regulations and *Glensder*.

NOTES

1. *The IRS acquiesces.* In Rev. Rul. 79-106, 1979-1 C.B. 448, the Service accepted the outcome in *Larson* and in effect gave up the fight. It has not since made any apparent effort to change the regulations.

2. *But state law changes.* The Revised Uniform Limited Partnership Act (RULPA) is not the same as the UPA contemplated by the *Larson* court. *See* RULPA §§ 402, 801. It is now possible to have the partners agree that the partnership continue despite the bankruptcy of a general partner by means of selecting a new general partner within a ninety-day window period.

3. *Trusts.* In general, if a trust has the power to conduct business, it will be treated as a corporation. This is because, in addition to having a business purpose and associates (the beneficiaries, the grantor, or both combined), generally centralized management, and limited liability, free transferability and unlimited life are common to trusts; hence, they are generally doomed to corporate status. *See* Reg. §§ 301.7701-2(a)-(e), -3(a)-(b)(1) and -4(a)-(b).

4. *Associates in a testamentary trust setting. Bedell v. Commissioner*, 86 T.C. 1207 (1986), which is alluded to in the prior case, held that a testamentary trust that operated a bedding factory for profit was *not* to be treated as a corporation, on the theory that there were no "associates." The beneficiaries, who were heirs of the decedent, had no managerial authority and had no hand in forming the trust. The case may offer a blueprint for the wicked.

5. *Liquidating trusts.* There is another group of trusts that can qualify as trusts despite a business flavor. These consist of liquidating trusts which are used temporarily to take control of the assets of a corporation that is in the process of being dismantled, and bondholders' protective trusts, which are vehicles by which bondholders take temporary claim to a debtor's assets pursuant to powers granted them by the terms of the debt instrument. As long as their primary purposes are not submerged by the conduct of business, bondholders' trusts and liquidating trusts can retain their income-tax status as trusts, despite their possible profitability. Reg. § 301.7701-4(d). Likewise, investment trusts that hold portfolios of income-producing assets can retain their status as long as their reinvestment powers are highly circumscribed. Reg. § 301.7701-4(c). These are commonly referred to as "unit investment trusts" and are frequently advertised in business sections of newspapers.

6. *A proposal for simplified characterization of entities.* In late Spring 1995, there emerged a fascinating new development in the modern history of Internal Revenue Service administration of the entity-classification rules and problem. On March 29, 1995, the IRS announced that, rather than continuing to apply the current cumbersome classification rules for deciding whether a business should be treated as a partnership or a corporation for tax purposes, it and the Treasury Department are considering a simplified process.[5] Under this approach, an *unincorporated* business would be required only to make an *election* regarding its tax status, sometimes called a "check-the-box" method of entity classification.[6]

The press release issued with the notice stated that the "I.R.S. and thousands of taxpayers spend considerable resources in determining the classification of unincorporated business organizations under the current tax rules." The proposal would aid numerous unincorporated businesses that "cannot afford" to commit the financial resources needed to hire outside experts to cope with the current complexity. Incorporated businesses would not be eligible to make this election and would conclusively be subject to the corporate income tax (unless they made a Subchapter S election). After holding a July 20, 1995, hearing on the subject, the IRS and the Treasury will decide whether to propose regulations to implement a simplified election by which an *unincorporated* business simply may choose to be treated either as a partnership or as an association taxable as a corporation. The IRS observed that the existing classification regulations are based on "historical differences under local law between partnerships and corporations." It added that many states have revised their statutes — such as by enacting limited liability laws — to provide that partnerships and other unincorporated organizations may possess characteristics that have traditionally been associated with corporations. According to the notice, one consequence of the narrowing of the differences under state law between corporations and partnerships is that taxpayers can achieve partnership tax status for a non-publicly

---

[5] *See* Notice 95-14, 1995-14 I.R.B., together with a press release designated IR- 95-29, 3/29/95.
[6] *See* Tax Notes, May 29, 1995, p. 1139.

C. PARTNERSHIP STATUS

traded organization that is "indistinguishable from a corporation." Under the proposal, taxpayers could elect to have any domestic unincorporated business treated as a partnership or an association taxable as a corporation, at the taxpayer's option, unless the organization's classification is determined under another Internal Revenue Code provision. For instance, an entity that is treated as a partnership, but which is publicly traded and is taxed as a corporation under I.R.C. § 7704 would continue to be taxed as a corporation. As for entities that do not make an election, the "default classification" would be for the entity to be treated as a partnership for federal income tax purposes. The Service and Treasury indicated that they believe "domestic unincorporated business organizations typically are formed to obtain partnership classification." All elections would be prospective from the date the election is filed; retroactive elections would not be permitted.

PROBLEM 1-1

A Canadian real estate tax shelter promoter — Mr. Slick — wants to peddle interests in Florida apartment buildings to Canadian investors. The investors would claim large depreciation deductions with respect to the buildings under the Canadian tax laws. Assume further that American state laws forcing disclosure of Canadians' identity would make a U.S. partnership unattractive to jittery Canadians, but that a Florida corporation would work fine in this respect. Mr. Slick would like you to tell him if you could design a U.S. *corporation* that would be taxed as a partnership under U.S. law using the "corporate resemblance test." He believes that if that can be done, the entity can buy U.S. real property and the stock can in turn be sold to Canadian customers via a Canadian partnership. Can you design such a corporation. How? Assume there is nothing unique about Florida corporate law and that the mere fact of formal "incorporation" does not determine the issue for federal tax purposes.

Partner or Lender?

It is sometimes difficult to distinguish common commercial relationships from partnerships for federal income tax purposes. The following early case deals with the knotty question of sorting a lending arrangement from a partnership.

DORZBACK v. COLLISON
195 F.2d 69 (3d Cir. 1952),
aff'g 93 F. Supp. 935 (D. Del. 1950)

MARIS, CIRCUIT JUDGE.

This is an appeal from a judgment for the plaintiff taxpayer in an action brought in the United States District Court for the District of Delaware for the recovery of income taxes and interest paid to the defendant Collector pursuant to deficiency assessments made by the Commissioner of Internal Revenue for the years 1943, 1944 and 1945.

The facts are these. On May 14, 1941 the taxpayer's wife loaned to the taxpayer from her own funds the sum of $8,500 to pay off an existing indebtedness of his in that amount and to evidence his resulting indebtedness to her the taxpayer gave her his bond in that amount bearing interest at 5% per annum. On January 4, 1943 the taxpayer and his wife entered into a written agreement in which they agreed that in lieu of the interest she had been receiving on this indebtedness she should share in the net profits derived from the taxpayer's retail business by receiving 25% of the net profits after the payment of an annual salary of $4,000 to the taxpayer. It was further agreed that the wife should continue to be a creditor and not a partner of the taxpayer but that her standing as a creditor should be subordinated to the rights of all general business creditors of the taxpayer.

Under this agreement the taxpayer's wife received $6,892.33 for 1943, $7,681.63 for 1944 and $10,346.32 for 1945. In computing their taxable net incomes for these years these amounts were reported as income by the wife and deducted by the taxpayer as interest paid. The Commissioner of Internal Revenue disallowed taxpayer's interest deductions of 25% of net profits, allowing deductions only in the amount of 5% of the principal sum of $8,500. The present action was instituted to recover the deficiencies assessed and paid by reason of the disallowance of these deductions.

At the trial, the district judge directed the jury to bring in a verdict for the taxpayer on the ground that there was no evidence of lack of a bona fide debtor-creditor relationship between the taxpayer and his wife as a result of the agreement of January 4, 1943. The question whether or not the 25% share of net profits could legally be construed as a payment of interest was reserved and decided, as a matter of law, in favor of the taxpayer by the district judge. Alternatively, the district judge concluded that the taxpayer and his wife were joint adventurers and accordingly taxable on their respective shares in the profits of the business for the years involved. The defendant's motions for judgment n.o.v. and for a new trial were accordingly denied. D.C., 93 F. Supp. 935. This appeal followed.

The defendant contends that the district judge erred in not submitting to the jury the question whether a debtor-creditor relationship existed between the taxpayer and his wife and in concluding that the payments made by the taxpayer to his wife in 1943, 1944 and 1945 were deductible interest payments.

Section 23(b) of the Internal Revenue Code provides that in computing net income there shall be allowed as a deduction "All interest paid or accrued within the taxable year on indebtedness." The taxpayer contends that under the express terms of this section he is entitled to the whole of the deductions which he claimed. For, he says, he was indebted to his wife and the amounts he paid her were interest on that indebtedness. The defendant contends, on the other hand, that there was evidence from which the jury might have found that the 1943

C. PARTNERSHIP STATUS

agreement did not create a debtor-creditor relationship but was merely a scheme to reallocate family income and that therefore the taxpayer was not entitled to deduct as interest the amounts paid his wife during 1943, 1944 and 1945.

The defendant points to the following facts to which the taxpayer testified: The year 1942 had been fairly profitable for the taxpayer; the arrangement agreed upon would be advantageous to him in reporting his income; his wife desired a larger return on her money than 5%; he felt grateful to her because of the fact that in 1932, when his bank was pressing him for payment of his debt in the amount of $25,000, she had endorsed his note to provide additional security. The defendant urges that these circumstances surrounding the 1943 agreement show the arrangement to be a device to reallocate income among the family group and therefore raised an issue as to the bona fides of the agreement and whether a bona fide debtor-creditor relationship resulted from it. The defendant, however, does not deny that prior to January 4, 1943 the taxpayer was unconditionally indebted to his wife in the amount of $8,500. Nor does he contend that the controlling state law does not recognize inter-spouse indebtedness. The agreement of January 4, 1943 expressly provided that the wife should continue to be a creditor of the taxpayer. We think that the evidence would support no other finding than that the indebtedness which resulted from the wife's loaning of her own money to her husband in 1941 continued after the agreement of 1943.

We have not overlooked the principle that transactions between husband and wife calculated to reallocate family income or reduce family taxes are subject to careful scrutiny. But here, as we have pointed out, the wife had a personal stake of her own, the $8,500 of her own money which she had loaned the taxpayer, upon which she was entitled to a return. Indeed the defendant concedes this since the Commissioner allowed the deduction of interest at 5% for the years in question, a position clearly inconsistent with the denial of any debtor-creditor relationship.

We think that the district judge rightly held that the agreement of 1943 did not change that relationship. For that agreement concerned only the return which the wife was to receive on her loan. It did not change her status as a creditor. Nor did it affect her relationship as a creditor when she agreed to subordinate her claim to the claims of the general business creditors. *Commissioner of Internal Revenue v. O.P.P. Holding Corp.*, 2 Cir., 1935, 76 F.2d 11, 12. And even if the 1943 agreement had operated to change the wife's status from creditor to partner or joint adventurer the result, taxwise, would have been the same, as the district judge concluded. For in that situation the wife would still have been taxable on her 25% share of the profits of the business. We accordingly conclude that the district judge rightly held that the evidence established the existence of a bona fide debtor-creditor relationship between the taxpayer and his wife during the years in question.

The other question to be determined is whether the taxpayer was entitled to deduct the payments made under the 1943 agreement "in lieu of interest" as interest payments under Section 23(b). The defendant contends that the payments of 25% of net profits, which amounted almost to the amount of the principal in 1943 and 1944 and in 1945 were greater than the actual indebtedness, could not be considered to be interest under that section. He claims that it was error for the district judge to determine as a matter of law that payments of a share in the net profits of the business made in lieu of interest were deductible as interest payments.

Interest on indebtedness has been defined to mean "compensation for the use or forbearance of money." *Deputy v. Du Pont*, 308 U.S. 488, 498, (1940). The word must be given the "usual, ordinary and everyday meaning of the term." *Old Colony R. Co. v. Commissioner*, 1932(a), 284 U.S. 552, (a). In the *Old Colony* case the Supreme Court said [284 U.S. at page 560]: "And as respects 'interest,' the usual import of the term is the amount which one has contracted to pay for the use of borrowed money. He who pays and he who receives payment of the stipulated amount conceives that the whole is interest."

The defendant contends that although Section 23(b) provides that "All interest paid" shall be deductible, yet when payments are made in lieu of interest at such high rates as are present in this case they are so unreasonable that they must be held not to be allowable interest deductions but rather a subterfuge to reallocate business profits. We are not, however, persuaded that a payment made "in lieu of interest" is not the equivalent of "interest." The phrase "in lieu of" means "instead of." Webster's New International Dictionary, 2d Ed., p. 1427. In *Kena, Inc., v. Commissioner*, 1941, 44 B.T.A. 217, 219-220, 221, the Board of Tax Appeals said:

> It is axiomatic that the language used to describe a thing does not determine its character. The contract of December 13, 1932, denominated the amount to be paid to the petitioner as "an additional sum in lieu of interest." The word "lieu" means "place or stead." It does not imply that the character of the payment was different from interest but indicates that the method of computation was not in accord with the usual method of computing interest, the percentage of profit being employed as a substitute. The contract itself must be examined to determine whether the sum so designated was actual interest or was something else....
>
> It is not essential that interest be computed at a stated rate, but only that a sum definitely ascertainable shall be paid for the use of borrowed money, pursuant to the agreement of the lender and borrower.

Generally speaking, payments made for the use of money "in lieu of interest" are deductible as interest under Section 23(b).

Throughout the ages lenders have exacted all they could from borrowers for the use of money. How much has been exacted has depended upon the desperation of the borrower and the exigency of the moment. There is no requirement in Section 23(b) that deductible interest be ordinary and necessary or even that it be reasonable. Hence the phrase "All interest paid" contained in that section must be taken in its plain and literal meaning to include whatever

C. PARTNERSHIP STATUS 21

sums the taxpayer has actually had to pay for the use of money which he has borrowed. *Arthur R. Jones Syndicate v. Commissioner of Internal Revenue*, 7 Cir., 1927, 23 F.2d 833. We conclude that the district judge did not err in holding that the payments made by the taxpayer to his wife in 1943, 1944 and 1945 were interest paid on indebtedness and deductible under Section 23(b) of the Internal Revenue Code.

The judgment of the district court will be affirmed.

NOTES

1. *Bifurcation of debt and equity.* In *Farley Realty Corp. v. Commissioner*, 279 F.2d 701 (2d Cir. 1960), the court held that what the taxpayer claimed was "contingent interest," payable out of the appreciation in value of a building the taxpayer financed, was not interest at all, but instead reflected an equity (ownership) interest in the building. The court stopped short of declaring the arrangement a partnership, but it did deny interest expense deductions with respect to the equity component. The case is commonly seen as the first major pruning back of *Dorzback v. Collison*.

2. *The IRS's position on shared appreciation mortgages.* *Farley Realty* is an early example of an effort to create a shared appreciation mortgage (SAM). Such mortgages became popular in the 1970s when interest rates and inflation were especially high and lenders sought to share in the increases in property values caused by high rates of inflation that made lending money a more difficult business than in more stable times. In Rev. Rul. 83-51, 1983-1 C.B. 48, the IRS stated that a borrower's obligation to pay the lender a portion of the increase in value of the taxpayer's principal residence constituted deductible interest under § 163. The ruling is limited to the underlying situation, namely a fixed date for payment of both the contingent interest and the principal amount, a method for calculating the interest specified in the mortgage contract, an intent to create a debtor-creditor relationship, and payment that is made in cash or with funds borrowed from a different lender. The ruling is limited to residential loans, leaving commercial lenders in the dark as to the IRS's position on this important matter.

3. *Other relationships.* There are numerous other arrangements that may produce a partnership for federal income tax purposes. For some nondefinitive definitions, see I.R.C. §§ 761(a), 6231, 6031(a), 7701(a)(2). It is difficult to generalize about the factors that will cause a court to characterize the arrangement one way or another, but one important factor to keep in mind is that there need not be a sharing of losses in order to classify a person as a member of a partnership. *See McDougal v. Commissioner*, 62 T.C. 720 (1974), *acq*. Note also that even though there is a valid partnership, some alleged partners may not qualify as such for federal income tax purposes and other people may be cast as partners, even though it might be illegal for them to be partners under local law. *See* Rev. Rul. 77-332, 1977-2 C.B. 484 (even though such arrangements are illegal under state law, a nonaccountant may be treated as a member of an accounting partnership for federal income tax purposes).

Publicly Traded Partnerships

In the late 1980s a number of major partnerships began trading on national stock exchanges. This novel trend was motivated by two events. One was the declining attractiveness of operating in the corporate form; the other was a trend in favor of combining tax-shelter partnerships into larger enterprises. Congress became mildly alarmed at the potential revenue loss, and responded by including in the Revenue Act of 1987 a new § 7704, which treats certain publicly traded partnerships as corporations. As the name implies, a publicly traded partnership is any partnership whose interests are traded on an established securities market or readily tradable on a secondary market (or its equivalent). § 7704(b). There is a major exception for partnerships at least 90% of whose income is from passive investment sources or from certain natural resource related activities, or from both combined. § 7704(c). The exception is best explained as a lobbying triumph.

Election Against Partnership Status

Read § 761(a) and Reg. § 1.761-2(a)-(b).

Section 761(a) and the Regulations thereunder allow a partnership that is teetering on the brink of being a mere collection of individuals to elect out of Subchapter K, hence eliminating partnership status for purposes of that part of the Code. The statute identifies three situations where this can be done: (1) where the entity operates solely as an investment vehicle, (2) where it operates solely for the joint extraction or joint use of property, or (3) where securities dealers join forces to engage in a particular underwriting transaction. The first and third cases are easy to understand. The second case is designed to assist passive co-owners of oil, gas or mineral properties who depend on an active operating company for their revenues. This avoids the need to file partnership tax returns and permits the co-owners to make specialized individual elections. The congressional *quid pro quo* is that in all cases it must be possible to calculate each member's individual tax liability without the need to compute "partnership taxable income." Conversely, it is possible for an enterprise that is a partnership for tax purposes to be a co-ownership arrangement for state law purposes. Such entities are known as "tax partnerships," as the next case illustrates.

C. PARTNERSHIP STATUS

MADISON GAS & ELECTRIC CO. v. COMMISSIONER
72 T.C. 521 (1979),
aff'd 633 F.2d 512 (7th Cir. 1980)

SCOTT, JUDGE:

[The taxpayer is a regulated public utility that entered into a cooperative effort to build a nuclear power plant and to share the plant's output among its three principals. There was no agreement to share profits, only to take a share of the electric output.]

....

The second issue in this case involves deductions claimed by petitioner as ordinary and necessary business expenses under section 162(a) for certain training costs and other expenses paid in connection with its interest in Plant 2, the nuclear power plant.

Petitioner takes the position that the amounts paid in connection with its interest in the nuclear power plant for which it claims a deduction meet all the requirements of section 162(a) for deductible ordinary and necessary business expenses and are not capital expenditures within the meaning of section 263. Petitioner argues that these expenses were incurred in carrying on its trade or business and were not "start-up costs of a new business." Petitioner's primary position is that its agreement of joint ownership of its nuclear plant with WPS and WPL does not create a partnership and that even if it does the expenses which it paid are ordinary and necessary business expenses of the partnership.

Respondent takes the position that although the expenses which petitioner seeks to deduct would be ordinary and necessary expenses in its production of electricity if the construction of the nuclear plant were solely for use in its own business, these expenses are not deductible since they were incurred as pre-operating expenses of a partnership formed through petitioner's agreement with WPS and WPL....

Thus, the determination of whether expenses are related to an existing trade or business of the taxpayer is essential. Although the taxpayer may actively be engaged in a trade or business, the start-up costs or pre-operating expenses of another activity, not a part of such trade or business are not deductible under section 162(a) as they are not incurred in the carrying on of a trade or business.

It initially appears that all additional expenses involved in the present case were expended in the conduct of Petitioner's existing trade or business, the production of electricity. Although the means of production in the case of the nuclear facility may be radically different from conventional methods, the end product, electricity, is the same.

However, closer analysis reveals that all additional expenses claimed are in fact incurred in the initial activity of the partnership formed through Petitioner's agreement with WPS and WPL.

Respondent argues that the fact that the partners have elected under section 761(a) of the Code and section 1.761-1(a)(2), Income Tax Regs., for the partnership to be excluded from the application of subchapter K of the Code is an admission that petitioner's arrangement with WPS and WPL is a partnership. Respondent argues that irrespective of this election the agreement and relationship between petitioner, WPS and WPL creates a partnership within the meaning of section 7701(a)(2). Respondent contends that the expenses which petitioner claims to be deductible are start-up costs which must be capitalized and not expenses, relying primarily on *Richmond Television Corp. v. United States, supra.*

The question on which the parties initially join issue is whether the arrangement between petitioner, WPS and WPL creates a partnership as defined in section 7701. While we agree with petitioner that the fact that the partners elected under section 761(a) not to be subject to the provisions of subchapter K is not an admission that the arrangement is a partnership, the definition of partnership contained in sections 761(a) and 7701(a)(2) are the same.[7] It is therefore necessary for us to decide whether the arrangement between petitioner, WPS and WPL is a partnership as defined by section 7701(a)(2).

While petitioner denies that filing an election out under section 761(a) is an admission that a partnership exists for tax purposes, it does not contend that because of this election under section 761(a) no partnership exists for the purposes of determining what constitutes deductible expenses under section 162. The clear import of petitioner's brief is that if we conclude that its arrangement with WPS and WLP is a partnership as defined in section 7701, then the deductibility of the expenses here involved is dependent upon whether those expenses are deductible by the partnership. Respondent makes no argument with respect to the election-out of the partnership under section 761(a) but merely cites his Rev. Rul. 65-118, 1965-1 C.B. 30. Respondent does not cite or discuss *Bryant v. Commissioner*, 46 T.C. 848 (1966), *affd.* 399 F.2d 800 (5th Cir. 1968), although in that case we in effect approved Rev. Rul. 65-118, *supra*, specifically pointing to the definition of partnership in section 7701(a)(2) "when used in this title" and the fact that section 48(c)(2)(D) (involved in the *Bryant* case and the revenue ruling) contained a specific provision with respect to limitations in the case of a partnership. We have found no case dealing with an election-out under section 761(a) when the controlling statute outside of subchapter K makes no reference to partnerships. In texts on partnerships we have found statements which indicate that an election-out in such a situation is

---

[7] Respondent in Rev. Rul. 68-344, 1968-1 C.B. 569, concludes that a venture formed by four electrical power companies substantially similar to the arrangement here of petitioner, WPS and WPL is properly classified as a partnership for Federal tax purposes. The ruling then proceeds to discuss the provision of section 761(a) and concludes that the members of the venture may elect under section 761(a) to have the venture excluded from the application of subchapter K. The parties stipulated in this case that it was the intention of the co-tenants — petitioner, WPS and WPL — that they create only a co-tenancy and not a partnership and that they be taxed as co-tenants and not partners. This stipulation is followed by the stipulated statement: To that end WPS filed a federal partnership return, form 1065, and an election out of the provisions of subchapter K of the Internal Revenue Code of 1954.

C. PARTNERSHIP STATUS

not controlled by the *Bryant* decision and other indications in the same text that it is....

Since petitioner here makes no contention that an election-out under section 761(a) causes the unincorporated group not to be a partnership except for purposes of those statutes which contain a specific reference to "partnerships," we have not considered and do not here decide such a possible issue even though a question in this respect is raised by writers of texts on partnerships and a number of law review articles dealing with partnership problems.

It is petitioner's position that a profit motive of the partnership as an entity is a requirement of partnership status and that such a motive is lacking from the arrangement present in this case. Petitioner argues that only a co-ownership and expense-sharing arrangement was created from its agreement with WPS and WPL.

Petitioner notes that section 1.761-1(a), Income Tax Regs., and section 301.7701-3(a), Proced. & Admin. Regs., provide that "a joint undertaking merely to share expense is not a partnership" and that mere co-ownership of property is not a partnership. Petitioner also points out that these regulations provide that "Tenants in common, however, may be partners if they actively carry on a trade, business, financial operation, or venture and divide the profits thereof." Petitioner relies, in support of its position of the necessity of a profit motive by the entity for partnership status, on *Cooperative Power Plant v. Commissioner*, 41 B.T.A. 1143 (1940), and *Co-operative Insurance v. Commissioner*, 41 B.T.A. 1151 (1940), in which arrangements somewhat similar to those in the instant case were held not to be associations taxable as corporations because gain was not an objective of the arrangement. In our view, these cases have no bearing on whether the arrangement here involved created a partnership under the definition of section 7701(a)(2).

In addition, petitioner cites Wisconsin State law to support his view that the arrangement in this case is not a partnership. It is clear, however, that state law is in no way controlling on the question of whether an unincorporated activity is a partnership for Federal tax purposes. *Luna v. Commissioner*, 42 T.C. 1067, 1077 (1964).

Petitioner argues that respondent's Rev. Rul. 68-344, 1968-1 C.B. 569, is erroneous in concluding that an arrangement similar to the one here is a partnership. The essence of petitioner's argument is that the construction and operation of the nuclear power plant in this case is equivalent to a joint undertaking to share expenses such as that described in the regulations and therefore does not constitute a partnership. Section 1.761-1(a) and section 301.7701-3(a), Income Tax Regs., declare that "if two or more persons jointly construct a ditch merely to drain surface water from their properties, they are not partners." In our view, petitioner's arrangement with WPS and WPL is in no way comparable to the joint construction of a drainage ditch.

Prior to 1954, the following definition of a partnership for Federal tax purposes was found in section 3797(a)(2), I.R.C. 1939:

(2) Partnership and Partner. — The term "partnership" includes a syndicate, group, pool, joint venture, or other unincorporated organization, through or by means of which any business, financial operation, or venture is carried on, and which is not, within the meaning of this title, a trust or estate or a corporation; and the term "partner" includes a member in such a syndicate, group, pool, joint venture, or organization....[8]

As petitioner points out, it has long been recognized that mere co-ownership of property will not create a partnership. *Estate of Appleby v. Commissioner*, 41 B.T.A. 18 (1940). In that case co-owners of inherited property, at the suggestion of automotive dealers, erected a garage on the property and rented the space to defray the expenses of owning the inherited property, primarily real estate taxes. We held that the erection and renting of the garage was not a group, joint venture or other organization within the partnership definition of the 1939 Code. Whether co-ownership of property gives rise to a partnership for Federal tax purposes is determined by "the degree of business activities of the co-owners or their agents."... *See Hahn v. Commissioner*, 22 T.C. 212 (1954), which held the requisite activities not to be present. The regulations set forth this test in slightly different words and it is the wording of the regulations as interpreted by petitioner, which it would have us follow in equating the construction of a drainage ditch with the construction and operation of a nuclear power plant. Section 1.761-1(a), Income Tax Regs., and section 301.7701-3(a), Proced. & Admin. Regs., as noted above declare that "Tenants in common, however, may be partners if they actively carry on a trade, business, financial operation, or venture and divide the profits thereof." Petitioner, relying on this regulation, contends that a partnership must have a profit motive for the partnership entity and that, because petitioner received the electricity from the nuclear power plant in kind, such a profit motive did not exist in its arrangement with WPL and WPS. We do not agree.

First, the statute does not require a profit motive; rather it merely requires "an unincorporated organization, through or by means of which any business, financial operation, or venture is carried on...." The business activity or profit motive test is important in distinguishing partnerships from the mere co-ownership of property. However, this test is not the only test for what constitutes a partnership for Federal tax purposes. Second, the test of business activity or profit motive for purposes of finding a Federal tax partnership is clearly met in the situation at hand where a group of business organizations decide to band

---

[8] The definition was first placed in the Code by sec. 1111(a)(3) of the Revenue Act of 1932. The purpose of this provision was to broaden the Federal partnership definitions to include therein a number of arrangements that under state law were not partnerships, such as joint ventures. *See* S. Rept. No. 665, 72nd Cong., 1st Sess. (1932), 1939-1 (Part 2) C.B. 496, 538. In the 1954 Code, this definition of partnership was unchanged and is contained in two sections, section 761(a) and section 7701(a)(2).

C. PARTNERSHIP STATUS 27

together to produce with economies of scale a common product to be distributed to the members of the venture in kind. In *Bentex Oil Corp. v. Commissioner*, 20 T.C. 565, 571 (1953), we found without any extended discussion that an organization formed to extract oil under an operating agreement which called for distribution of the oil in kind was a partnership for Federal tax purposes. The agreement in the *Bentex* case was analogous to the agreement in the instant case. That an agreement such as the one here under consideration creates a partnership is implicit in the holdings in *Cooperative Power Plant, supra,* and *Cooperative Insurance, supra....* Joint construction of a drainage ditch simply does not require the business activity or contain the profit motive found in the joint extraction of oil or the joint production of electricity by a nuclear power plant.

Following the *Cooperative* cases and the *Bentex* case, Congress reenacted the definition of partnership in the 1954 Code. In addition to carrying the definition forward in section 7701(a)(2) without change, Congress also placed the definition within subchapter K, section 761(a), with the added caveat allowing certain organizations to elect to be excluded from the application of subchapter K. Section 761(a) reads as follows:

> (a) Partnership. — For purposes of this subtitle, the term "partnership" includes a syndicate, group, pool, joint venture, or other unincorporated organization through or by means of which any business, financial operation, or venture is carried on, and which is not, within the meaning of this title, a corporation or a trust or estate. Under regulations the Secretary may, at the election of all the members of an unincorporated organization, exclude such organization from the application of all or part of this subchapter, if it is availed of —
> (1) for investment purposes only and not for the active conduct of a business, or
> (2) for the joint production, extraction, or use of property, but not for the purpose of selling services or property produced or extracted, if the income of the members of the organization may be adequately determined without the computation of partnership taxable income.

If distribution in kind of jointly produced property was enough to avoid partnership status, we do not see how such distribution could be used as a test for allowing an election to be excluded from the partnership provisions of subchapter K. Although there is no discussion of the reason for the "election-out" provision of section 761(a) in the legislative history of the section it has been generally considered that this provision was enacted as Congressional approval of the *Bentex* case coupled with a recognition of the hardships caused by that decision[9]....

In sum, we hold that petitioner's arrangement with WPS and WPL was an unincorporated organization carrying on a business, financial operation or venture. To the extent a profit motive may be required for an unincorporated organization to be a partnership for Federal tax purposes, we hold that it is present in this case with the in kind distribution of electricity produced by the nuclear power plant.

....

NOTES

1. *IRS position*. The IRS continues to believe that joint production for separate sale is the same as "joint profit." *See* Flower & Holbrook, *Partners and Co-owners: The Use of Undivided Interests in Equipment Leasing*, 41 Tax Law. 733 (1988). Naturally, this conclusion has no bearing on whether there is a partnership for state law purposes.

2. *The "tax partnership."* Note that the product of the *Madison Gas* case is a so-called tax partnership, an entity that is a co-ownership at state law, but a partnership for federal income tax purposes. These are common in the oil patch, where they are used in connection with joint operating agreements. The advantages are: no need to negotiate a partnership agreement; a simple (often one page) agreement as to allocations; ability of each owner to encumber his or her own interest (as opposed to the difficult process of encumbering a partnership interest); and no participant with unlimited liability. If the partnership had managed to elect out of subchapter K, it would then have been a co-ownership for federal income tax purposes as well.

3. *Expense sharing*. What if the taxpayer's deal with the other two utilities had merely involved sharing expenses for maintaining a common facility? Clearly, there would be no partnership because there would be no sharing of revenues in cash or in kind. Reg. § 301.7701-3(a). What if they shared revenues from a commonly-owned rental property? Now it is getting more difficult. However, the same regulation tells us that there is still no partnership, but that

---

[9] Thus, Congress afforded such organizations an election to be excluded from the provisions of subchapter K. Petitioner makes some interesting arguments as to the policy reasons for not penalizing it because economies of scale have forced it to combine forces with other utilities to enjoy the advantages of nuclear power. These arguments, however, are misplaced with respect to the question of the definition of a partnership. Instead, they should have been addressed with respect to the effect of the sec. 761(a) election to be excluded from the application of subchapter K. In other words, the treatment of petitioner flows from the organization status as a sec. 761(a) electing organization; but petitioner does not argue that favorable treatment flows therefrom and, as discussed supra ..., we are making no decision on that question in this case.

C. PARTNERSHIP STATUS

if the co-owners provide services to the tenants in connection with renting the property, there is a partnership. *Id.*

4. *Failure to file by small partnerships.* Small partnerships often fail to file their federal income tax forms. Section 6698 of the Code imposes a $50 per partner penalty on failure to file a partnership return, but contains a built-in loophole in that it excuses the penalty if there is reasonable cause for nonfiling. Rev. Proc. 84-35, 1984-1 C.B. 509 presumes the existence of reasonable cause if the miscreant is a domestic partnership with not over ten partners, all of whom are U.S. persons who have adequately reported their shares of the partnership's profits or losses. That probably wipes thousands of partnership returns off the tax rolls.

5. *Lack of coordination with Subchapter K.* The entity-aggregate distinction can be a serious problem when partnership tax issues overlap with nonpartnership tax law questions. The explanation is fairly simple. Congress does not always consider the impact on the partnership rules when a new tax provision is added or an old one is tampered with. Indeed, it may take years for the lack of coordination between the partnership tax law and some other part of the tax law to show up. In general, it is usually best to apply the aggregate approach to partnerships outside of Subchapter K unless there are strong policy reasons not to do so. The lack of coordination between Subchapter K and the rest of the Code is chronic.

To take just a few simple examples, under § 453A there is an interest charge when a non-dealer sells property on the installment obligation for a price exceeding $150,000 if the seller also has total installment obligations outstanding at year end in excess of $5 million. § 453A(b)(1)-(2). The IRS *asserts* that the $5 million threshold is applied at the partner level. Notice 88-81, 1988-2 C.B. 397. By contrast under § 179(d)(8), annual expensing of $17,500 under § 179 is explicitly limited at both the partner and partnership levels. (Here, the IRS does not have to assert, it *knows*.) Thus, if a ten-person equal partnership had $20,000 of § 179 expenses, the partners would each report only $1,750.

PROBLEM 1-2

Assume the Oilbug family owns a productive oil and gas property operated by an unrelated oil company, and that the family elects out under § 761(a) and Regs. § 1.761-2(b). Assume that the family members own the property in joint tenancy and that they are legally free to dispose of their individual interests.

1. Can each owner use his or her own taxable year to report the profits or losses from the property? *See* § 706(b)(1)(A).

2. Can a family member make a tax-free exchange of her interest in the real estate under § 1031?

3. In Rev. Rul. 58-465, 1958-2 C.B. 376, the IRS ruled that an election out could not affect the limitation found in § 704(d). Is the ruling still viable?

Retroactive Amendments of Partnership Agreement

The partnership agreement generally controls the tax incidents associated with being a partner, but what if the agreement is amended? Can the amendment have retroactive force? Perhaps surprisingly, § 761(c) declares that the controlling agreement can be amended as late as the prescribed filing date for the entity's federal tax return, as long as the amendment is valid under local law. This means that the partners can wait up to the filing date to modify the agreement and, subject to some limits to be discussed later in this part, have the modifications stick for the year reported on the tax return. Reg. § 1.761-1(c). However, extensions of time granted to extend the filing date cannot extend the mandatory cut-off date for amending the partnership agreement.

D. IRS AUDITS

Prior to the enactment of §§ 6621-6632 in 1982, partnerships posed serious examination and collection problems for the IRS because the Service had to investigate and dispose of the liabilities of the partners one-by-one. Nowadays, they are disposed of as a group, except for partnerships with ten or fewer partners.

There are three key features to the new system. The first is that each partnership that is subject to "unified audit proceedings" must have a so-called "tax matters partner." That is the general partner identified as the tax matters partner in the partnership agreement, or, if no partner is designated, the partner with the largest profits interest. § 6231(a)(7). The tax matters partner faces off against the IRS in the audit process. The second key feature is the opportunity for minority partners who collectively have at least 5% of the profits to gang up and form their own group, which then becomes a separate force in dealing with the audit. § 6223(b). The third factor is that each partner is obligated to report items that appear on the partnership tax return consistently on their personal tax returns, unless the partner notifies the IRS of the inconsistency. § 6222. The details are ornate; this is only a thumbnail sketch.

OUTSIDE READINGS

F. Peel, *Definition of a Partnership: New Suggestions on an Old Issue*, 1979 Wis. L. Rev. 989 (1979).

D. Weidner, *The Existence of State and Tax Partnerships: A Primer*, 11 Fla. St. U. L. Rev. 1, (1983).

Chapter 2
PARTNERSHIP FORMATION

A. CONTRIBUTIONS OF CAPITAL

Read §§ 721, 722, and 723.

The essence of a new business in partnership form involves two or more persons who pool some combination of their services, goods, real estate, or cash for a mutual business objective. Each will make some contribution to the enterprise, even if it is just a promise of future services. In exchange, each will receive an interest in the enterprise; the interest in a partnership itself is personal property for nontax purposes. *See* UPA § 26; RULPA § 701. In a partnership setting, the initial income tax issues are whether a partner's contribution of property will result in a taxable gain or a deductible loss to the contributor, the partnership, or the other partners, and whether the receipt of a partnership interest in exchange for a partner's contribution of services will produce taxable income to the service provider, the partnership, or the other partners. If so, or if not, what basis will each side take in contributed property?

1. NONRECOGNITION OF GAIN

As a basic matter of tax policy, it is desirable to have a tax environment that does not impede business start-ups or changes in the form of doing business. Section 721(a) implements that policy with respect to partnerships by providing that no gain or loss is recognized by a partnership or its partners when a "contribution of property [is made] to the partnership in exchange for an interest in the partnership." This nonrecognition treatment is available for a partner's contributions to newly-formed partnerships and existing partnerships alike. As you will see later, § 351 performs much the same function with respect to corporations.

The grant of nonrecognition applies only to contributions of *property* (in the tax sense), rather than services.[1] Cash, tangible personal and real property, and intangibles such as patents and copyrights, as well as accounts receivable that have been accrued in income, have all been regarded as "property" at one time or another for purposes of § 721. The term "property" is not restricted to the category of "capital assets" as defined in § 1221. This discrepancy opens the door to conversions of ordinary income into capital gain via contributions of non-

---

[1] The nonrecognition exception does not apply to contributions to foreign partnerships. § 1491.

capital assets in exchange for a partnership interest, which itself is considered to be a capital asset.

UNITED STATES v. STAFFORD
727 F.2d 1043 (11th Cir 1984),
rev'g 552 F. Supp. 311 (M.D. Ga. 1982)

Before ANDERSON and CLARK, CIRCUIT JUDGES and DUMBAULD, DISTRICT JUDGE.

ANDERSON, CIRCUIT JUDGE:

Taxpayers DeNean and Flora Stafford appeal the district court's summary judgment in favor of the government on their refund action for allegedly overpaid taxes. The refund action involves the Staffords' 1969 tax return, in which they did not account for their receipt of a limited partnership interest valued at $100,000. The taxpayers argue that the partnership share qualified for nonrecognition treatment under I.R.C. § 721(a) because it was received in "exchange" for "property" they contributed to the partnership. The district court held that nonrecognition was not available because the taxpayers' contribution of a letter of intent to the partnership did not meet the exchange and property requirements of the statute....

2. *History of the Case*

[Mr. Stafford, the taxpayer, was a real estate developer who obtained an (unenforceable) letter of intent from Life of Georgia (LOG) written to him, promising a favorable interest rate and lease terms in connection with a hotel project. Stafford and his associates thereafter formed a partnership of which Stafford was the sole general partner. He bought two partnership shares and received a third share for contributing the letter of intent to the partnership. He claims it was a contribution of property, protected from taxation by § 721.] ...

4. *Exchange and Property Requirements*

....

1. *The Exchange Requirement*

   B. *Generally*

The district court held that Stafford's contribution of the letter of intent to the limited partnership was not an "exchange" for purposes of § 721. The court defined exchange as "a mutual or reciprocal transfer of one thing for another" and suggested that each side to the transaction must have a choice as to whether or not they desire the transfer.... Because transfer of the letter of intent to the partnership was part of the partnership agreement as drafted by the taxpayers' attorneys, the court found that the limited partners never had a choice as to whether or not the transfer would take place....

A. CONTRIBUTIONS OF CAPITAL 33

The district court's opinion on this element lacks support in the language and principles of § 721. The regulations under § 721 specify that each partner "is entitled to be repaid his contributions of money or other property to the partnership (at the value placed upon such property by the partnership at the time of the contribution) whether made at the formation of the partnership or subsequent thereto." Treas. Reg. § 1.721-l(b)(1). That Stafford's contribution of the letter of intent was part of the partnership agreement at formation in no way undermines his argument that the contribution was part of an exchange with the partnership under § 721.

Furthermore, the purpose of § 721 is to facilitate the flow of property from individuals to partnerships that will use the property productively.... By analogy § 351 of the Internal Revenue Code allows nonrecognition for individuals transferring property to corporations. Indeed, post-transfer control of the transferee corporation by the contributing shareholder is a prerequisite to tax-free treatment under § 351. We therefore reject the district court's assumption that individual members of the transferee limited partnership must agree to the transfer before an exchange can occur under § 721.

The district court opinion focused on the lack of agreement between Stafford and the limited partners. Viewed properly, the exchange that took place was between Stafford and the partnership, not the limited partners as individuals.... The assignment of January 21, 1969, tends to establish that such an exchange occurred. Stafford contributed the letter of intent and other items; the partnership issued the third share to Stafford. Again, that this exchange occurred at the formation of the partnership and without a formal partnership vote does not alter our conclusion that an exchange took place.

[The discussion of whether Stafford owned the letter of intent is omitted. That issue was decided in Stafford's favor.]

2. *The Property Requirement*

The district court alternatively held that Stafford had not received his third partnership share as the result of a contribution of "property." The court correctly stated that "the key to the benefit of nonrecognition afforded by I.R.C. § 721(a) is that *property* must be exchanged for an interest in the partnership." 552 F. Supp. at 314 (emphasis in original). The district court then stated as its test for property under § 721:

> "After having carefully considered the arguments of counsel in conjunction with the opinion of the court of appeals, it is the opinion of the court that both value and enforceability are necessary to a conclusion that a document is "property" for purposes of § 721."...

Finding as a matter of law that the letter of intent was not enforceable, the court concluded that it was not property and the taxpayers were not eligible for nonrecognition under § 721.

We agree with the district court's conclusion that the letter of intent was not enforceable. Under Georgia law an agreement becomes enforceable when there is a meeting of the parties' minds "at the same time, upon the same subject matter, and in the same sense." *Cox Broadcasting v. National Collegiate Athletic Ass'n*, 250 Ga. 391, 297 S.E.2d 733, 737, (1982). In the present case, the July 2 letter of intent and Stafford's subsequent acceptance on August 30 did reflect an agreement on many essential terms; in particular, the parties were in agreement on the interest rate for the loan and the formula for calculating lease terms. However, the July 2, 1968, letter of intent acknowledged that: "there were many details to be worked out" and stated only that "we [LOG] would like to continue our negotiations along the following general lines." The July 3 letter from LOG may have converted the proposal to negotiate to a firm proposal of major terms, but Stafford's response again made the execution of final lease and loan agreements expressly "subject to further negotiations" on several items. "Where it is evident from a written instrument, that the parties contemplated that it was incomplete, and that a binding agreement would be made subsequently, there is no agreement."

. . . .

The agreement in the present case unambiguously contemplated resolution of additional items before execution of the final contract. "An agreement to reach an agreement is a contradiction in terms and imposes no obligations on the parties thereto," *Well v. H.W. Lay Co.*, 78 Ga. App. 364, 50 S.E.2d 755, 758 (1949); as such, the agreement between Stafford and LOG embodied in the letter of intent and acceptance letter was unenforceable.... Stafford's contention that the parties intended to carry through with the terms of agreement set forth in the letter of intent is unavailing. Where, as here, the parties' written documents clearly and definitely make final agreement subject to mutually satisfactory future negotiations, we must decide as a matter of Georgia law that "the parties did not intend the letter agreement to be a binding, enforceable contract." *Dumas v. First Federal Savings & Loan Ass'n*, 654 F.2d 359, 361 (5th Cir. 1981) (applying Georgia contract law).

Nevertheless, notwithstanding its lack of legal enforceability, we still must determine whether the letter of intent was "property" within the meaning of § 721. The previous panel opinion stated that "enforceability of any agreement evidenced by the letter of intent, while perhaps not dispositive of the question, is important and material." 611 F.2d at 996 n. 6. We agree. An enforceable contract would perhaps be assured of property status; but the absence of enforceability does not necessarily preclude a finding that document, substantially committing the parties to the major terms of a development project, is property.

Several nonenforceable obligations may rise to the level of property for purposes of § 721 or § 351. Unpatented know-how, which results from services and is not enforceable, nevertheless can be deemed property.... (Rev. Rul. 64-56, 1964-1 (Part 1) C.B. 133 (the term property under § 351 includes unpatented

A. CONTRIBUTIONS OF CAPITAL 35

secret processes and formulas); Rev. Rul. 71-564, 1972-2 C.B. 179 (transfer of exclusive right to use trade secret is property under § 351)).

The instant transfer of the letter of intent outlining the major terms of a proposed loan and lease agreement to which both parties felt morally bound is closely analogous to a transfer of goodwill, which although clearly unenforceable, nevertheless has been treated as property. *See* Taxation of Partnerships, *supra* note 10, P4.02[1], n.18:

> "If goodwill is associated with a going business that is transferred to a partnership, there should be no question about the applicability of § 721. Furthermore, even if goodwill is associated with an individual who will remain active in the transferred business, an effective contribution of goodwill may be made. Citing Rev. Rul. 70-45, 1970-1 C.B. 17 (for the proposition that a professional person realizes capital gain on partial sale of goodwill to newly admitted partner); *see also* Rev. Rul. 79-288, 1979-2 C.B. 139 (transfer of trade name and goodwill to newly formed foreign corporation is transfer of property for purposes of § 351); Rev. Rul. 70-45, 1970-1 C.B. 17 (goodwill of a one-man personal service business can be capital asset; whether it is an anticipatory assignment of income or a transfer of goodwill is a question of fact)."

Thus, we conclude that the district court's requirement of legal enforceability as an absolute prerequisite to finding property status under § 721 was improper.

For purposes of our discussion as to whether the instant letter of intent is "property," we will assume arguendo that the factfinder on remand determines that the letter had value. Under the appropriate legal standard and under the circumstances peculiar to this case, we conclude that the letter of intent encompassed a sufficient bundle of rights to constitute "property" within the meaning of § 721.

Although the Internal Revenue Code does not define property for purposes of § 721 or § 351, the courts have given the term rather broad application. *See E.I. DuPont de Nemours & Co. v. United States*, ... 471 F.2d 1211, 1218, 200 Ct. Cl. 391 (1973). In *Hempt Bros., Inc. v. United States*, *aff'd*, 490 F.2d 1172 (3d Cir.), ... the court stated "that the term [property for purposes of § 351] encompasses whatever may be transferred."

The transfer of a taxpayer's full interest in a venture further supports a conclusion that the transferred item was property. *Cf.* Rev. Rul. 64-56, 1964-1 C.B. 133, 137 (evaluating the transfer of technical know-how from a United States corporation to a newly organized foreign corporation and stating that "[t]he transfer of all substantial rights and property of the kind hereinbefore specified [technical know-how] will be treated as a transfer or property for purposes of § 351 of the code"). *See also* 3 J. Mertens, supra P20.47 at 165.

... A conclusion that the letter of intent is "property" under the instant circumstances comports with the purpose of § 721. Stafford exerted personal efforts on his own behalf in negotiating with LOG. When LOG and Stafford exchanged the letter of intent and acceptance in 1968, the government had not suggested that Stafford recognized taxable income. He could have completed the project as a sole proprietor without recognition of income based on his receipt of the letter. The purpose of §§ 721 and 351 is to permit the taxpayer to change his individual business into partnership or corporate form; the Code is designed to prevent the mere change in form from precipitating taxation. In keeping with this purpose, we can discern no reason to exclude Stafford's transfer of the letter of intent from the protective characterization as "property."

Stafford through his business reputation and work efforts was able to negotiate a very promising development project with LOG. He obtained from LOG officials a written document, morally, if not legally, committing LOG to the major terms of a proposed loan and lease. The transferability of the letter is undisputed and Stafford transferred his full interest in the project to the partnership. We conclude that the letter encompassed a sufficient bundle of rights and obligations to be deemed property for purposes of § 721.

For the foregoing reasons, we have concluded that Stafford's transfer of the letter of intent to the partnership met both the "exchange" and "property" requirements of § 721. However, the factual dispute identified by the previous panel remains unresolved on the record before us and, accordingly, we must remand.

5. The Quid Pro Quo for Stafford's Receipt of the Partnership Share

The previous panel remanded for the factfinder to determine: "what was the quid pro quo for Stafford's receipt of the twenty-first partnership interest?" ... The panel was concerned that a jury might find that Stafford received the partnership share wholly or partially in exchange for the services he was to provide as general partner. *Id.* Thus, even though Stafford contributed the letter to the partnership, the panel was unable to conclude that Stafford's contribution of the letter was responsible for his receipt of the third partnership share. This dispute remains; from the record we cannot ascertain whether the partnership was compensating Stafford for services to be rendered or for contribution of the letter of intent, or partially for both.

Another factor also tends to support a finding that Stafford's partnership share was received in part for services. Officers from LOG have testified that much of their certainty that the development would take place was based on their confidence in DeNean Stafford....

The factfinder thus might conclude that Stafford received this third partnership interest partially in anticipation of the services he was to provide as general partner in consummating the deal.

Conversely, the assignment letter of January 21, 1969, unambiguously states that Stafford received the partnership share in exchange for property, namely the letter and other items. Mr. Irby's original affidavit supports that conclusion. Mr. Williams, another limited partner, also testified that the partnership share was

A. CONTRIBUTIONS OF CAPITAL

given in exchange for Stafford's property contribution. *Stafford v. United States*, 611 F.2d at 994. The district court, in a hearing held prior to summary judgment for the government, heard testimony from a third limited partner, Mr. Jenson, who only vaguely remembered the transaction and whose testimony would support both the property and the services explanation for Stafford's receipt of the third partnership share.

On remand the factfinder could determine that Stafford received the partnership share wholly in exchange for the letter of intent he contributed to the partnership. If so, the nonrecognition principles of § 721 apply and Stafford is entitled to his refund. *See Ungar v. Commissioner*, 22 T.C.M. 766 (1963) (the taxpayer had negotiated contracts embodying the sale, financing and leasing of real property and he transferred those contracts to a newly formed corporation in exchange for stock; the court held that the stock received in exchange for the contracts qualified for nonrecognition treatment under § 351). To support such a finding in this case, the jury necessarily must conclude that the letter of intent was worth at least $100,000 to the partnership.

On the other hand, it might be determined on remand that Stafford received the partnership share wholly as compensation for services, in which case the government's tax assessment was proper. *See* Treas. Reg. § 1.721-1(b)(1) ("the value of an interest in such partnership capital so transferred to a partner as compensation for services constitutes income to the partner under § 61").

Stafford's argument, however, misstates the assets of the partnership on the date of formation. In addition to the $2,000,000 in equity and the letter of intent, the partnership also had the value of Stafford's obligation as general partner to work toward completion of the project on behalf of Center Investments. This continuing service obligation would include the value of LOG's confidence in Stafford's ability to consummate the venture.

Finally, the factfinder might conclude the Stafford's receipt of the partnership share was partly in compensation for services and partly in exchange for property. If this is the case, the factfinder should determine the value of the property element (i.e., the letter of intent) and the value of the services element (i.e., the services to be rendered to the partnership by Stafford after formation of the partnership, including any value inherent in Stafford's continuing service obligation due to LOG's confidence in him, ... but excluding any salary paid to Stafford for such services), and allocate the $100,000 value of the third partnership share accordingly. *See Stafford v. United States*, 611 F.2d at 993 n. 5; *United States v. Frazell*, 335 F.2d at 490-91 (receipt of interest in partnership by taxpayer held partly in exchange for services and partly in exchange for property; remanded for determination of value of the property, 269 F. Supp. 885 (W.D. La. 1967); Rev. Rul. 64-56, 1964-1 C.B. 133, 134 ("[w]here both property and services are furnished as consideration for the receipt of stock in a § 351 transfer] ... a reasonable allocation is to be made"). Thus, if the factfinder determines that Stafford's receipt of the partnership share was partly in exchange for the letter and partly as service compensation, then he should prevail in his refund claim as to so much of the $100,000 share as was properly allocable to his letter of intent.

The district court's summary judgment in favor of the government is reversed and remanded for disposition not inconsistent with this opinion.

Reversed and *remanded*.

NOTES

1. *Sorting out the rulings.* The *Stafford* decision referred to a number of revenue rulings involving transfers of intangible assets to partnerships and corporations, but the judge did not describe the facts in detail. Here is a brief summary of some of those rulings. In Rev. Rul. 64-56, technical "know how" in the form of a secret process transferred to a new corporation along with a patent was treated as property, provided the secret process enjoyed "substantial legal protection against unauthorized disclosure." The ruling went on to permit taxpayers to treat services that are merely incidental to the transfer of property as "property." Rev. Rul. 71-564 treated the transfer of an exclusive right to use a trade secret for its legally protected life as a transfer of property, by analogy to the general rule for patent transfers. Finally, in Rev. Rul. 79-288 a corporation transferred its registered name to a new corporation, along with a document reciting that the new corporation would get all the goodwill associated with the name, in exchange for stock of the new corporation. The IRS ruled that the name and goodwill were property for Federal Income Tax purposes, provided the rights were legally protectible.

2. *Swap funds.* Taxable gain will occur on the contribution of property to a partnership if § 721(b) applies. The purpose of that subsection is to prevent the nontaxable formation of what are commonly known as "swap funds," i.e., partnerships formed by investors who pool their assets so as to stabilize and diversify the values of their investment portfolios. Section 721(b) seems to have stamped them out.

2. BASIS EFFECTS

Read §§ 705, 722 and 723.

In order to assure that nonrecognition treatment results in tax postponement rather than an exemption, § 722 declares that the contributing partner's basis in his or her partnership interest (generally known by its less awkward term "outside basis") will be the same as the basis of the property contributed by that partner. This leaves the partner facing an identical potential gain or loss on any later taxable disposition of the partnership interest. The amount of the partner's gain or loss from such a disposition will be the same, at least initially, as was inherent in the property he contributed to the partnership.

Likewise, § 723 makes the partnership's basis in the property which it receives (a.k.a. "inside basis") the same as the contributing partner's basis in that

A. CONTRIBUTIONS OF CAPITAL

property. If the partnership promptly sold the property, it would recognize gain (or loss) in the same amounts as each of the contributing partners potentially faced before making their contributions of property to the partnership. If, as, and when the partnership recognizes this gain or loss, the outside basis of each of the respective contributing partners will be adjusted up or down, respectively, to prevent a double counting of the same gain or loss on any later sale of a partnership interest. Section 705 also tells one that the partner's basis in the partnership will rise with partnership profits (which are taxable to the partners, *pro rata*) and fall with partnership losses (which are deductible) and distributions (returns of capital up to outside basis) from the partnership, among other factors. The symmetry between inside and outside basis is discussed in more detail in Chapter 3.

a. Impact of Section 704(c) on Contributed Property

Read § 704(c).

Consider the situation where one partner contributes appreciated property as to which there is a substantial paper gain waiting to be recognized, while another partner contributes cash or property with a basis equal to its value. Under these typical circumstances, even if the pretax value of each partner's contribution is the same, there will be a significant difference in the net after-tax values of their contributions.

The partners might want to strike a balance between the respective fractional interests and distributive shares they each receive in the partnership, so as to account for the net after-tax values of their contributions. If the appreciated property is unlikely to be sold in the foreseeable future, perhaps little if any account should be taken of the tax costs that would be incurred upon its sale. On the other hand, suppose a piece of highly appreciated contributed property were in fact promptly sold by the partnership. It is not hard to decide which of the partners ought to be taxed on the gain recognized in that sale.

Unless the Code provided some remedial mechanism, anyone with potentially taxable gains in the offing might transfer appreciated property to a partnership and thereby partly shift the tax burden to his or her partners, some of whom might have losses they could use to eliminate such gains. In order to block this ploy, § 704(c) requires that the partnership allocate all precontribution gain (or loss) on each piece of property to the partner who actually contributed that property.

> *To illustrate*: A and B are equal partners in the AB partnership. A contributes property with a basis of $60 and a fair market value of $100 at the time of contribution. B contributes $100 in cash. Assuming that A's contribution gets nonrecognition treatment, A's basis of $60 in the contributed property under § 722 becomes A's "outside basis" in the partnership interest that A receives in

exchange therefor. The partnership's "inside basis" in the property received from A under § 723 is likewise $60 (carried over from A). Now assume that shortly thereafter the partnership sells this property for $100. The partnership recognizes $40 of gain — the same amount of gain that A potentially faced as owner of the property. Note that at the same time as the partnership recognized its $40 of gain, under § 704(c) A's "outside basis" in the partnership will be increased to $100. This immediate step-up in A's outside basis results from the mandatory *allocation* (i.e., attribution) to A of all precontribution gain recognized by the partnership — a result required by assignment of income principles that are statutorily enforced by § 704(c). If, instead, it were sold a few years later for $120, $50 of gain would be taxed to A and $10 to B.

Note that § 704(c) does not work in reverse. That is, when a new partner contributes cash to an ongoing partnership which already holds appreciated or depreciated property, § 704(c) does not address the case.

b. Holding Periods

Read § 1223(1) and (2).

Partnership's. Consistent with the theory that "nothing happened" for federal income tax purposes when the partner contributed property to the partnership, the partnership will take over the holding period of the partner who contributed that property. § 1223(2).

Partner's. Each partner's interest in the partnership must also be assigned a holding period. A partner's holding period does not necessarily begin when the partnership is formed. Literally speaking, it is impossible for a partnership interest to exist before formation of the partnership, but it is logical for the partner's holding period to be derived from the holding period that the partner had in property which he or she contributed to the partnership in exchange for a partnership interest. Although a partnership interest is considered to be a single capital asset,[2] the partner will only tack the holding period from capital assets and section 1231 "quasi-capital" assets which he or she contributed to the partnership. See § 1221(1). Thus, a partner who contributed only cash or other noncapital assets will begin the holding period in his or her partnership interest on the day it was received in exchange for such property.

Suppose a given partner contributes several properties, some of them capital assets or § 1231 assets and others not. Even if all were capital assets, the partner may have held each of them for a different period of time. How is the partner's

---

[2] *See* Rev. Rul. 84-52, 1984-1 C.B. 157.

A. CONTRIBUTIONS OF CAPITAL

holding period in his or her single partnership interest then determined? In all likelihood, the partner's interest in the partnership will have a fragmented holding period in proportion to the relative values of the properties he or she contributed. A. Willis, J. Pennell & P. Postlewaite, Partnership Taxation ¶ 43.08 (4th ed. 1993). The partner would tack the holding period from each capital or § 1231 asset, and start afresh with that portion of the partnership interest which is seen to be received in exchange for cash or noncapital assets. Fortunately, there is rarely a need to determine the holding periods of partnership interests, because they are rarely disposed of before actually having been held for the long-term capital gain or loss period.

3. IMPACT OF DEBT ON OUTSIDE BASIS

Read § 752.

Section 752 allocates partnership liabilities among the partners. If § 752 causes an increase in a partner's share of partnership liabilities, that increase is treated as a contribution of cash by the partner, thereby increasing her outside basis. For example, if a 50:50 partnership borrowed $100 from a bank, each partner's outside basis would rise by $50. Conversely, if the partnership assumed the partner's liabilities, or accepts a contribution that was subject to a nonrecourse debt, the partner would be deemed to have received a distribution of cash, correspondingly reducing her outside basis. At the same time, § 752 apportions part of the debt to the contributing partner, which correspondingly increases her basis, but in an amount smaller than the initial hypothetical distribution. The balance of the liabilities is apportioned to the other partners, who are deemed to have contributed an equal amount of cash, thereby increasing their outside bases. Just how one apportions debt among the partners is taken up later in this part.

PROBLEM 2-1

The AB Partnership was formed on January 1, 199x. A contributed factory equipment for his one-half interest. A's adjusted basis in the equipment was $50,000. It was worth $150,000 at the time of transfer, and was subject to a mortgage of $15,000, which the AB partnership assumed. What is A's basis in his interest in the AB Partnership? *See* §§ 705(a)(2), 722, 733 and 752.

4. CAPITAL ACCOUNTS

The term "capital account" crops up constantly in the partnership tax area, but it is not formally defined.[3] It basically represents the partner's equity. The

---

[3] The § 704(b) regulations, which are discussed later in these materials, contain a comprehensive methodology for establishing and maintaining capital accounts, but it is only part of a complex safe harbor system established for the limited purpose of validating (or invalidating) special allocations of partnership income and loss among partners. *See* Reg. § 1.704-1(b)(2)(u).

federal income tax form presented by the government demands that the account be maintained.[4] It will generally consist of contributions which the partner made to the partnership in cash or kind (either using fair market values or tax basis) adjusted for the partner's share of profits and losses over the years, and reduced by distributions to the partner.[5] A common shorthand way of thinking of the capital account is that it is the same as the partner's basis in the partnership interest, shorn of allocable liabilities. Because the § 704(b) allocation rules use fair market values in fixing capital accounts under specialized safe haven rules, practitioners are getting used to the idea of value-oriented capital accounts. (So used, the capital account measures what the partner would be entitled to receive if the partnership liquidated.) The Tax Court seems laconically to accept the taxpayer's definition of the term as it appears in the partnership agreement, thus making it possible to use tax basis as the foundation for the partnership's capital accounts. *See Frink v. Commissioner*, 49 T.C.M. 386 (1984).

5. SECTION 724: CLOSING LOOPHOLES

Partnerships can potentially operate as a tax laundromat, turning dirty assets (such as appreciated inventory) in the hands of a contributing partner into clean ones (such as capital assets) that the partnership can sell on favorable tax terms. Read § 724(a)-(c) and you will get the flavor of how Congress solved the problem, including the way unrealized receivables (such as accounts receivable of a cash-method grocery store) are forever damned. Section 735 parallels § 724 for distributed property, branding the inventory for five years and unrealized receivables forever. Chapter 8 considers § 735 in depth, so § 724 gets short shrift here. After you master § 735, § 724 will feel comfortable.

B. CONTRIBUTIONS OF SERVICES

It is common for partners to receive partnership interests for past or future services (remember the IRS arguments in *Stafford, supra*) performed for the partnership. These transactions have to be carefully analyzed and monitored by the partnership's tax advisor to assure that there are no surprises.

1. CAPITAL INTEREST RECEIVED FOR SERVICES

Every partner has two interests, one in the partnership's future profits and one in the partnership's capital. An interest in profits is self-explanatory; an interest in capital refers to what the partner would receive if the partnership were liquidated and the partner received his share of the net assets of the enterprise. Reg. § 1.704-1(e)(1)(v). It also refers to the net proceeds of a liquidation of the

---

[4] *See* Form 1065, Schedule K-1, line I, reproduced in the Appendix to this book.

[5] Taxpayers who use tax basis rather than fair market values will have to add § 704(c) items to the capital account.

B. CONTRIBUTIONS OF SERVICES

partner's interest on withdrawal from the partnership. There is generally no difference between the net proceeds on withdrawal, as opposed to liquidation of the partnership.[6] As you will soon see, the simpler tax case arises where the services are compensated with an interest in partnership capital (with its concomitant share of future profits), as opposed to a mere interest in future profits.

a. Impact on the Service Partner

McDOUGAL v. COMMISSIONER
62 T.C. 720 (1974), *acq.* 1975-2 C.B. 2

FAY, JUDGE:

....

Findings of Fact

Certain facts have been stipulated by the parties and are found accordingly. The stipulation of facts and exhibits attached thereto are incorporated herein by this reference.

F. C. and Frankie McDougal are husband and wife, as are Gilbert and Jackie McClanahan. Each couple filed joint Federal income tax returns for the years 1968 and 1969 with the district director of internal revenue in Austin, Texas. Petitioners were all residents of Berino, New Mexico, when they filed their petitions with this Court.

F. C. and Frankie McDougal maintained farms at Lamesa, Texas, where they were engaged in the business of breeding and racing horses. Gilbert McClanahan was a licensed public horse trainer who rendered his services to various horse owners for a standard fee. He had numbered the McDougals among his clientele since 1965.

On February 21, 1965, a horse of exceptional pedigree, Iron Card, had been foaled at the Anthony Ranch in Florida. Title to Iron Card was acquired in January of 1967 by one Frank Ratliff, Jr., who in turn transferred title to himself, M. H. Ratliff, and John V. Burnett (Burnett). The Ratliffs and Burnett entered Iron Card in several races as a two-year-old; and although the horse enjoyed some success in these contests, it soon became evident that he was suffering from a condition diagnosed by a veterinarian as a protein allergy.

When, due to a dispute among themselves, the Ratliffs and Burnett decided to sell Iron Card for whatever price he could attract, McClanahan (who had trained the horse for the Ratliffs and Burnett) advised the McDougals to make the purchase. He made this recommendation because, despite the veterinarian's prognosis to the contrary, McClanahan believed that by the use of home remedy

---

[6] Some partnership agreements provide that distributions before liquidation of the partnership must be reduced by minority discounts, which tends to force the partners to stay together.

Iron Card could be restored to full racing vigor. Furthermore, McClanahan felt that as Iron Card's allergy was not genetic and as his pedigree was impressive, he would be valuable in the future as a stud even if further attempts to race him proved unsuccessful.

The McDougals purchased Iron Card for $10,000 on January 1, 1968. At the time of the purchase McDougal promised that if McClanahan trained and attended to Iron Card, a half interest in the horse would be his once the McDougals had recovered the costs and expenses of acquisition. This promise was not made in lieu of payment of the standard trainer's fee; for from January 1, 1968, until the date of the transfer, McClanahan was paid $2,910 as compensation for services rendered as Iron Card's trainer.

McClanahan's home remedy proved so effective in relieving Iron Card of his allergy that the horse began to race with success, and his reputation consequently grew to such proportion that he attracted a succession of offers to purchase, one of which reached $60,000. The McDougals decided, however, to keep the horse and by October 4, 1968, had recovered out of their winnings the costs of acquiring him. It was therefore on that date that they transferred a half interest in the horse to McClanahan in accordance with the promise which McDougal had made to the trainer. A document entitled "Bill of Sale," wherein the transfer was described as a gift, was executed on the following day.

On November 1, 1968, petitioners had concluded a partnership agreement by parol to effectuate their design of racing the horse for as long as that proved feasible and of offering him out as a stud thereafter.

....

Though the partnership initially filed no return for its first brief taxable year ended December 31, 1968, petitioners did make the computations which such a return would show and reported the results in their individual returns. The partnership was considered to have earned $1,314, against which was deducted depreciation in the amount of $278. Other deductions left the partnership with taxable income for the year of $737, which was allocated to the extent of $405 to the McDougals and to the extent of $332 to the McClanahans.

On their joint return for the year 1968 the McDougals reported, inter alia, gross income of $22,891 from their Lamesa farms. Against this income they deducted $1,390 representing depreciation on Iron Card for the first 10 months of 1968 and $9,213 in training fees. The McDougals appear, however, to have initially claimed no deduction by reason of the transfer to McClanahan of the half interest in Iron Card.

....

We shall now turn our attention to those returns and amended returns filed in April of 1970. The McDougals explicitly claimed by way of amendment to have transferred the half interest in Iron Card to McClanahan as compensation for services rendered and thus to be entitled to a $30,000 business expense deduction, computed by reference to the last offer to purchase Iron Card received prior to October 4, 1968. Furthermore, the McDougals acknowledged that they

B. CONTRIBUTIONS OF SERVICES

had recognized a gain on the aforesaid transfer. By charging the entire depreciation deduction of $1,390 against the portion of their unadjusted cost basis allocable to the half interest in Iron Card which they retained, the McDougals computed this *gain* to be $25,000 *and* characterized it as a long-term capital gain under section 1231(a) of the Internal Revenue Code of 1954.

The McClanahans simultaneously increased their income arising out of the transfer from $5,000 to $30,000. They could thus claim to have a tax cost basis of $30,000 in their half interest in the horse. Finally, purporting to have transferred the horse to a partnership in concert on November 1, 1968, petitioners computed the partnership's basis in the horse to be $33,610 under section 723.[7] This increase in basis led the partnership to claim a depreciation deduction of $934 for 1968 instead of $278 and to report only $81 of taxable income for that year. The McDougals thereupon reduced their distributive share of partnership income for 1968 from $405 to $40, while the McClanahans reduced their share from $332 to $41. For the year 1969 the partnership claimed a deduction for depreciation on Iron Card in the amount of $5,602, closing the year with a loss of $8,911. This loss was allocated in its entirety to the McDougals, pursuant to the partnership agreement.

....

Ultimate Findings of Fact

The transfer of October 4, 1968, gave rise to a joint venture to which the McDougals are deemed to have contributed Iron Card and in which they are deemed to have granted McClanahan an interest in the capital and profits thereof, equal to their own, as compensation for his having trained Iron Card.

....

Opinion

Respondent contends that the McDougals did not recognize a $25,000 gain on the transaction of October 4, 1968, and that they were not entitled to claim a $30,000 business expense deduction by reason thereof. He further contends that were Iron Card to be contributed to a partnership or joint venture under the circumstances obtaining in the instant case, its basis in Iron Card at the time of contribution would have been limited by McDougals' cost basis in the horse, as adjusted. Respondent justifies these contentions by arguing that the transfer of October 4, 1968, constituted a gift.

---

[7] Having charged the entire amount of the depreciation which they had claimed ($1,390) against their unadjusted cost basis of $5,000 in the half interest in Iron Card which they retained, the McDougals considered themselves to have an adjusted basis of $3,610 in that retained half. The McClanahans claimed a $30,000 tax cost basis in the half interest which they had just received. Under sec. 723 the contribution of the two halves to a partnership would therefore result in the partnership's having a basis of $33,610 in Iron Card.

In the alternative, respondent has urged us to find that at some point in time no later than the transfer of October 4, 1968, McDougal and McClanahan entered into a partnership or joint venture to which the McDougals contributed Iron Card and McClanahan contributed services. Respondent contends that such a finding would require our holding that the McDougals did not recognize a gain on the transfer of October 4, 1968, by reason of section 721, and that under section 723 the joint venture's basis in Iron Card at the time of the contribution was equal to the McDougals' adjusted basis in the horse as of that time.

....

A joint venture is deemed to arise when two or more persons agree, expressly or impliedly, to enter actively upon a specific business enterprise, the purpose of which is the pursuit of profit; the ownership of whose productive assets and of the profits generated by them is shared; the parties to which all bear the burden of any loss; and the management of which is not confined to a single participant.

While in the case at bar the risk of loss was to be borne by the McDougals alone, all the other elements of a joint venture were present once the transfer of October 4, 1968, had been effected. Accordingly, we hold that the aforesaid transfer constituted the formation of a joint venture to which the McDougals contributed capital in the form of the horse, Iron Card, and in which they granted McClanahan an interest equal to their own in capital and profits as compensation for his having trained Iron Card. We further hold that the agreement formally entered into on November 1, 1968, and reduced to writing in April of 1970, constituted a continuation of the original joint venture under section 708(b)(2)(A). Furthermore, that McClanahan continued to receive a fee for serving as Iron Card's trainer after October 4, 1968, in no way militates against the soundness of this holding. *See* section 707(c) and section 1.707-l(c), example 1, Income Tax Regs. However, this holding does not result in the tax consequences which respondent has contended would follow from it. *See* section 1.721-l(b)(1), Income Tax Regs.

When on the formation of a joint venture a party contributing appreciated assets satisfies an obligation by granting his obligee a capital interest in the venture, he is deemed first to have transferred to the obligee an undivided interest in the assets contributed, equal in value to the amount of the obligation so satisfied. He and the obligee are deemed thereafter and in concert to have contributed those assets to the joint venture.

The contributing obligor will recognize gain on the transaction to the extent that the value of the undivided interest which he is deemed to have transferred exceeds his basis therein. The obligee is considered to have realized an amount equal to the fair market value of the interest which he receives in the venture and will recognize income depending upon the character of the obligation satisfied. The joint venture's basis in the assets will be determined under section 723 in accordance with the foregoing assumptions. Accordingly, we hold that the

B. CONTRIBUTIONS OF SERVICES

transaction under consideration constituted an exchange in which the McDougals realized $30,000.

....

In determining the basis offset to which the McDougals are entitled with respect to the transfer of October 4, 1968, we note the following: that the McDougals had an unadjusted cost basis in Iron Card of $10,000; that they had claimed $1,390 in depreciation on the entire horse for the period January 1 to October 31, 1968; and that after an agreement of partnership was concluded on November 1, 1968, depreciation on Iron Card was deducted by the partnership exclusively.

Section 704(c) allows partners and joint venturers some freedom in determining who is to claim the deductions for depreciation on contributed property. As is permissible under the statute, petitioners clearly intended the depreciation to be claimed by the common enterprise once it had come into existence, an event which they considered to have occurred on November 1, 1968. Consistent with their intent and with our own holding that a joint venture arose on October 4, 1968, we now further hold that the McDougals were entitled to claim depreciation on Iron Card only until the transfer of October 4, 1968. Thereafter depreciation on Iron Card ought to have been deducted by the joint venture in the computation of its taxable income.

In determining their adjusted basis in the portion of Iron Card on whose disposition they are required to recognize gain, the McDougals charged all the depreciation which they had taken on the horse against their basis in the half in which they retained an interest. This procedure was improper. As in accordance with section 1.167(g)-1, Income Tax Regs., we have allowed the McDougals a depreciation deduction with respect to Iron Card for the period January 1 to October 4, 1968, computed on their entire cost basis in the horse of $10,000; so also do we require that the said deduction be charged against that entire cost basis under section 1016(a)(2)(A)....

The joint venture's basis in Iron Card as of October 4, 1968, must be determined under section 723 in accordance with the principles of law set forth earlier in this opinion. In the half interest in the horse which it is deemed to have received from the McDougals, the joint venture had a basis equal to one half of the McDougals' adjusted cost basis in Iron Card as of October 4, 1968, i.e., the excess of $5,000 over one half of the depreciation which the McDougals were entitled to claim on Iron Card for the period January 1 to October 4, 1968. In the half interest which the venture is considered to have received from McClanahan, it can claim to have had a basis equal to the amount which McClanahan is considered to have realized on the transaction, $30,000. The joint venture's deductions for depreciation on Iron Card for the years 1968 and 1969 are to be determined on the basis computed in the above-described manner.

When an interest in a joint venture is transferred as compensation for services rendered, any deduction which may be authorized under section 162(a)(1) by reason of that transfer is properly claimed by the party to whose benefit the services accrued, be that party the venture itself or one or more venturers, section 1.721-l(b)(2), Income Tax Regs. Prior to McClanahan's receipt of his interest, a joint venture did not exist under the facts of the case at bar; the McDougals were the sole owners of Iron Card and recipients of his earnings. Therefore, they alone could have benefited from the services rendered by McClanahan prior to October 4, 1968, for which he was compensated by the transaction of that date. Accordingly, we hold that the McDougals are entitled to a business expense deduction of $30,000, that amount being the value of the interest which McClanahan received.

....

Decision will be entered under Rule 155.

---

b. Impact on the Partnership

In *McDougal*, the transfer in fact preceded the formation of the partnership. The case does not precisely reach the more common situation in which a stranger to the partnership exchanges services for a partnership interest.

The exchange of services for a capital interest in an existing partnership is reconstructed as the partnership's payment to a third party, using partnership assets as the consideration. That implies gains or losses on the deemed sales of such partnership assets and potential section 162 or 212 deductions for the partners whose capital interests were diminished by the payment. Section 706(d)(1) and (2) imply that only the capital-providing partners will share the deduction, but prudence dictates embodying the understanding in the partnership agreement. This understanding may constitute a so-called special allocation, a matter taken up later in this part. Note that the expense may have to be capitalized under § 263. For example, if the payment to the service partner were for overseeing the construction of a building, the payment would be capitalized into the partnership's basis in the property. *See* Reg. § 1.721-l(b). *See also Stevens v. Commissioner*, 46 T.C. 492 (1966), *aff'd per cur.*, 388 F.2d 298 (6th Cir. 1968) (expenses of training racehorse consititued part of acquisition cost of horse, adding to cost basis). Finally, observe that § 83(h) insists that the partnership claim no deduction unless and until the service partner reports income from the receipt of the partnership interest. *See generally* W. McKee, W. Nelson, & R. Whitmire, Federal Taxation of Partnerships and Partners ¶ 5.03[2] (1978).

2. RECEIPT OF A PROFITS INTEREST FOR SERVICES

The treatment of partners who contribute a promise of services for an interest in profits is trickier than the transfer of a capital interest for services. This is an area dominated by case law. The primary issue is whether the partner has income on at the time of receiving the profit share, or whether there is income only if

B. CONTRIBUTIONS OF SERVICES

and when the partnership makes money. The leading decision in the area is *Diamond v. Commissioner*, 492 F.2d 286 (7th Cir. 1974), *aff'g* 56 T.C. 530 (1971). The facts involved an individual, Sol Diamond, who agreed to obtain major financing for a real estate partnership in exchange for a 60% profit and loss share if he arranged the financing. He did. Thereafter, one Liederman agreed to buy Diamond's interest for $40,000 and to become a 50:50 partner. Within two months of receiving his partnership interest, Diamond sold out to Liederman for $40,000. The courts held Diamond to have received compensation for services in the amount of $40,000 (the value of the partnership interest) when the lender provided the financing. The exact limits of the *Diamond* decision were unclear, but the courts seemed impressed by the facts that (1) Diamond's profit share was for services rendered prior to admission as a partner, and (2) the interest was capable of valuation (because it was sold in the same year it was received). The courts acknowledged that the *Diamond* result could cause double taxation — once when the profits interest is received and again when profits are earned — but suggested that the right solution was to allow the partner to amortize the value of the profits interest to reverse the double counting.

In G.C.M. 36346 (July 23, 1975) the IRS suggested that the *Diamond* case should be repudiated in favor of a more general rule that the receipt of an interest in future profits does not constitute immediate income to the recipient. The following excerpt is the lynchpin to the proposal:

> As you may be aware this Office has been considering the proper treatment of the receipt of a profits interest in a partnership as compensation for services. This consideration stems from the decision in *Sol Diamond*, 56 T.C. 530 (1971), *aff'd*, 492 F.2d 286 (7th Cir. 1974), holding that the fair market value of an interest in partnership profits received as compensation for services is taxable under Int. Rev. Code of 1954, § 61(a)(1).... This decision has been widely criticized as being contrary to Treas. Reg. § 1.721-1, as creating severe valuation problems and as resulting in double taxation to the recipient partner.... This approach was found unacceptable because it seemed to place a premium on whether the partnership is formed before or after the services are rendered....
>
> Arguably the only rationale for not taxing a profits interest received as compensation is that Treas. Reg. § 1.721-1(b) was apparently designed to reach such a result. *See* A. Willis, *supra* at § 11.01. It is difficult to quarrel with the Tax Court's finding that such an interest is property under Treas. Reg. § 1.61-2(d)(1). When a profits interest is defined to preclude any interest in partnership assets, as is done in the proposed revenue ruling, such an interest becomes analogous to an unfunded, unsecured promise to pay deferred compensation. Such a promise is not taxable upon receipt and, in fact, is not considered to be property. *See* Treas. Reg. § 1.83-3(e). An analogy of a partnership profits interest to an unfunded, unsecured promise to pay deferred compensation is imperfect, however, because amounts

received pursuant to or upon assignment of such a promise are taxable as compensation whereas the character of partnership profits or the character of the gain on a sale of a profits interest is determined under Code § 702(b) and Code § 741.

It must be emphasized that in holding that the receipt of a "profits" interest is not taxable, the proposed revenue ruling is limited to interests that give the holder no rights to existing partnership assets upon the liquidation of his interest. Correspondingly, a "capital" interest, which is taxable, includes an interest in earned but unrealized gains. This broad definition of a capital interest is simply an extension of the rule in Treas. Reg. § 1.61-2(d)(1) that property received as compensation is taxed at its fair market value....

The timing of income recognition is unfortunately convoluted because of § 83, which has a sweeping scope, but never comes to grips with partnership interests. Be that as it may, § 83 generally applies by its terms. In the interest of avoiding a treatise on the subject, the topic has been highly condensed in the following paragraphs.

Section 83 applies to transfers of property in connection with the performance of services as an employee or independent contractor. If a taxpayer receives an unrestricted right to property — and a partnership interest is generally a form of property — the value of the property is taxable when received. (This is the *Diamond* rule. However, if the interest is appropriately restricted, taxation is deferred until the interest is transferable or is not subject to a substantial risk of forfeiture. Read § 83(a) through (c) and Reg. §§ 1.83-3(c), 1.83-6(b).

A partial solution to the problem of being taxed on a partnership interest is to elect under § 83(b) to include the value of a restricted interest in income when it is received. "Restricted" means it is both nontransferable and subject to a substantial risk of forfeiture. The advantage of the § 83(b) election is that if the interest has only a small value when it is received but will likely have a much greater value when the restrictions lapse, the difference is subject to preferential long-term capital gains treatment and will not be taxed until the taxpayer disposes of the property. The disadvantages are that the value of the interest is taxed at once as ordinary income and that if the taxpayer forfeits the interest, there is no deduction beyond what she paid for the interest. § 83(b)(1).

One decision baldly accepted a profits interest as property for purposes of § 83, but found it to have no value, theorizing that a liquidation of the partnership would have yielded the taxpayer nothing. *St. John v. United States*, 84-1 USTC ¶ 9158 (C.D. Ill. 1984). Perhaps the court was confused by the difference between state law, which does recognize the interest as "property," and § 1.83-3(a), which treats "an unfunded and unsecured promise to pay money in the future" as not property.

One group of commentators consider that § 83 should simply be banished from Subchapter K, on the theory that Congress never intended § 83 to reach

B. CONTRIBUTIONS OF SERVICES

partnership situations. A. Willis, J. Pennell, & P. Postlewaite, Partnership Taxation §§ 45.04 and 46.09. Be that as it may, Reg. § 1.721-1(b)(1) says that § 721 does not apply to the extent any partner gives up the right to be repaid a part of his capital contribution as compensation for services and that § 83 instead applies.

Cf. United States v. Frazell, 335 F.2d 487 (5th Cir. 1964) (when a partnership was incorporated, the value of shares received was taxable under Reg. § 1.721-1(b) as compensation to a partner who had contributed services to the partnership in return for a partnership interest, because he was not transferring "property" to the corporation in a § 351 exchange.

CAMPBELL v. COMMISSIONER
943 F.2d 815 (8th Cir. 1991)

BEAM, CIRCUIT JUDGE.

[Mr. Campbell received profits interest in partnerships that he helped promote in exchange for services that he rendered to a different partnership, Summa T. Realty, that was in the business of forming and syndicating tax shelter limited partnerships. The interests in the tax shelter partnerships were readily marketable, and were valued by Campbell in part on the basis of the tax benefits they offered, and in part on the basis of the eventual value of the real estate they held. The Tax Court ruled him taxable, which set off a firestorm of controversy in the tax bar. Many felt the case could be reconciled as one in which the partner received an interest in another partnership. The petitioner sought the advice of two tax lawyers before taking the interests; both assured him there would be no tax.]

Campbell argues on appeal, as he did unsuccessfully in the Tax Court, that a service partner (i.e., a partner who receives his partnership interest in exchange for services provided to the partnership) who receives a profits interest (i.e., a right to share in profits and losses only, as opposed to an interest in the capital assets of a partnership) in a partnership does not realize income upon receipt of that interest, and, therefore, no taxable event occurs. In the alternative, he argues that the interests he received had no value at the time he received them and, thus, he should not have been taxed.

At this point, the Commissioner concedes that the Tax Court erred in holding that the receipt of a profits interest in exchange for services to the partnership should be considered ordinary income to the service provider.... However, for the first time, the Commissioner now asserts that Campbell actually received the partnership interests in exchange for services he provided to his employer, rather than services he provided to the partnerships. According to the Commissioner, the Tax Court held that Campbell received the interests as compensation from his employer. Thus, he is not a service partner; the principles of partnership taxation do not apply; and Campbell's receipt of compensation from his employer was taxable upon receipt.

A. *Employee or Partner*

We make short work of the Commissioner's alternate argument.... The Commissioner's argument, at best, requires that we resolve a disputed question of fact. Contrary to the Commissioner's belief, the Tax Court did not hold that Campbell received his partnership interests for services he performed for his employer rather than services performed for the partnerships.... In any event, we decline to address this factual matter and we disregard the argument.

B. *Taxing Profits Interests*

Although the Commissioner concedes the Tax Court's error in taxing a service partner's profits interest, the Tax Court's holding is not without support. In fact, the only circuit court to address the issue arrived at the same conclusion. *See Diamond*, 492 F.2d 286.... Thus, we are reluctant to accept the Commissioner's concession without substantive review.

....

The Tax Court's holding was based principally on *Diamond*, and that case is analogous. However, to fully understand the concerns raised, we must review several prior cases and the underlying statutory provisions. When a service partner receives an interest in partnership capital, the cases clearly hold that a taxable event has occurred. The receipt of the capital interest must be included in the service partner's income. *See, e.g., United States v. Frazell*, 335 F.2d 487, 489 (5th Cir. 1964).... As an interest in intangible personal property, the receipt of a capital interest appears to be taxable under the authority of section 83 of the Internal Revenue Code....

As noted, however, when the service partner receives solely a profits interest, the tax consequences are unclear. In contrast to *Diamond*, the Tax Court has held, and the Commissioner has conceded in some cases, that receipt of a profits interest by a service partner creates no tax liability. *See National Oil Co. v. Commissioner*, 52 T.C.M. (CCH) 1223, 1228 (1986) (Commissioner conceded that if taxpayer received only profits interest, no taxable event had occurred); *Renroy, Inc. v. Commissioner*, 47 T.C.M. (CCH) 1749, 1756-59 (1984) (profits interest had no fair market value, thus no tax liability upon receipt); *Hale v. Commissioner*, 24 T.C.M. (CCH) 1497, 1502 (1965) ("Under the regulations, the mere receipt of a partnership interest in future profits does not create any tax liability. Sec. 1.721-(l)(b), Income Tax Regs.").

The code does not expressly exempt from taxation a service partner's receipt of a profits interest, and the courts that have held that it is not taxed upon receipt do not appear to have closely analyzed the issue. However, commentators have developed three interrelated theories in support of the proposition that it is not a taxable event: 1) based upon regulation 1-721.1(b), a profits interest is not property for purposes of sections 61 and 83; 2) a profits interest may have no fair market value; and 3) the nonrealization concepts governing transactions between partner and partnership preclude taxation....

B. CONTRIBUTIONS OF SERVICES

The Tax Court and the Seventh Circuit rejected at least the first two of these theories in *Diamond*....

The commentators generally agree that the nonrecognition principles of section 721 do not apply to a service partner because a service partner does not contribute property in exchange for his partnership interest.... We also agree. However, the section 721 regulations are relied upon to tax a service partner's receipt of a capital interest. And, as with a profits interest, a service partner who receives a capital interest has not contributed property in exchange for his partnership interest. Thus, the section 721 regulations provide some guidance when reviewing whether general principles of partnership taxation provide for nonrealization in this case.

Section 721 codified the rule that a partner who contributes property to a partnership recognizes no income.... And, regulation 1.721-l(b)(1) simply clarified that the nonrecognition principles no longer apply when the right to return of that capital asset is given up by transferring it to another partner. At that time, the property has been disposed of and gain or loss, if realized, must be recognized. As a corollary, section 1.721-l(b)(1) outlines the tax treatment of the partner who receives that capital interest. A substantial distinction, however, exists between a service partner who receives a capital interest and one who receives a profits interest. When one receives a capital interest in exchange for services performed, a shift in capital occurs between the service provider and the individual partners.... The same is not true when a service partner receives a profits interest. In the latter situation, prior contributions of capital are not transferred from existing partners' capital accounts to the service provider's capital account. Receipt of a profits interest does not create the same concerns because no transfer of capital assets is involved. That is, the receipt of a profits interest never affects the nonrecognition principles of section 721. Thus, some justification exists for treating service partners who receive profits interests differently than those who receive capital interests.

Probably more relevant to our analysis, however, is section 707 of the Internal Revenue Code, which supports Campbell's argument.... Generally, a partner receives a distributive share of income instead of compensation from his partnership. *See Pratt v. Commissioner*, 550 F.2d 1023, 1026 (5th Cir. 1977) (salary payments to a partner treated as a distributive share of income); .... Except under certain circumstances, "the general statutory policy for treating partnerships for tax purposes contemplated that the income of a partnership would flow through to the individual partners." *Pratt*, 550 F.2d at 1026. Only when the transaction is treated as one between the partnership and a partner acting in a nonpartner capacity is the payment received by the partner not considered a distributive share....

Section 707 provides that when a partner engages in a transaction with a partnership in a nonpartner capacity that transaction will be treated as between the partnership and one who is not a partner. I.R.C. § 707(a)(1). When a partner receives payment for services performed for the partnership, that transaction falls under section 707(a)(1) if "the performance of such services ... and the allocation and distribution, when viewed together, are properly characterized as a transaction occurring between the partnership and a partner acting other than in his capacity as a member of the partnership." *Id.* § 707(a)(2)(A)(iii). This exception was enacted to prevent partnerships from using direct allocations of income to individuals, disguised as service partners, to avoid the requirement that certain expenses be capitalized.... Arguably, section 707(a) would be unnecessary if compensatory transfers of profits interests were taxable upon receipt because, if so, every such transfer would be taxed without this section....

In *Diamond*, where the service provider became a partner solely to avoid receiving ordinary income, we have no doubt that the receipt of the profits interest was for services provided other than in a partner capacity. That is, Diamond was likely to (and in fact did) receive money equal to the value of his services and apparently did not intend to function as or remain a partner. Thus, the receipt of his partnership profits interest was properly taxable as easily calculable compensation for services performed. Campbell's case, however, is not so clear. Campbell's interests were not transferable and were not likely to provide immediate returns. Thus, we doubt that the Tax Court correctly held that Campbell's profits interests were taxable upon receipt.

More troubling, however, is Campbell's argument that the profits interests he received had only speculative, if any, value. We fully agree with this contention and we reverse the Tax Court. As noted by the Tax Court, "fair market value is 'the price at which property would change hands in a transaction between a willing buyer and a willing seller, neither being under compulsion to buy nor to sell and both being informed' of all the relevant circumstances."...

The Tax Court relied too heavily on the fact that Class A limited partners were willing to pay substantial sums for their interests at the same time Campbell received his interest. Because of the difference in the nature of the investments, we believe that this fact is not relevant. The Class A limited partners had superior rights to cash distributions and return of capital, as well as some rights of participation. Further, the court should not have disregarded the expert's belief that the tax benefits were speculative in nature. The partnerships were taking untested positions in regard to deductions and all of them were likely to be challenged and disallowed by the IRS. In fact, many of the deductions were ultimately disallowed. Further, the predictions contained in the offering memoranda were just that — predictions. The partnerships had no track record. Any predictions as to the ultimate success of the operations were speculative. Thus, we hold that Campbell's profits interests in Phillips House, The Grand and Airport were without fair market value at the time he received them and should not have been included in his income for the years in issue.

....

B. CONTRIBUTIONS OF SERVICES

REV. PROC. 93-27

1993-24 I.R.B. 63

....

SEC. 3. BACKGROUND

Under section 1.721-1(b)(1) of the Income Tax Regulations, the receipt of a partnership capital interest for services provided to or for the benefit of the partnership is taxable as compensation. On the other hand, the issue of whether the receipt of a partnership profits interest for services is taxable has been the subject of litigation. Most recently, in *Campbell v. Commissioner*, 943 F.2d 815 (8th Cir. 1991), the Eighth Circuit in dictum suggested that the taxpayer's receipt of a partnership profits interest received for services was not taxable, but decided the case on valuation. Other courts have determined that in certain circumstances the receipt of a partnership profits interest for services is a taxable event under section 83 of the Internal Revenue Code. *See, e.g., Campbell v. Commissioner*, T.C.M. 1990-236, *rev'd*, 943 F.2d 815 (8th Cir. 1991); *St. John v. United States*, No. 82-1134 (C.D. Ill. Nov. 16, 1983). The courts have also found that typically the profits interest received has speculative or no determinable value at the time of receipt. *See Campbell*, 943 F.2d at 823; *St. John*. In *Diamond v. Commissioner*, 56 T.C. 530 (1971), *aff'd*, 492 F.2d 286 (7th Cir. 1974), however, the court assumed that the interest received by the taxpayer was a partnership profits interest and found the value of the interest was readily determinable. In that case, the interest was sold soon after receipt.

SEC. 4. APPLICATION

.01 Other than as provided below, if a person receives a profits interest for the provision of services to or for the benefit of a partnership in a partner capacity or in anticipation of being a partner, the Internal Revenue Service will not treat the receipt of such an interest as a taxable event for the partner or the partnership.

.02 This revenue procedure does not apply:

(1) If the profits interest relates to a substantially certain and predictable stream of income from partnership assets, such as income from high-quality debt securities or a high-quality net lease;

(2) If within two years of receipt, the partner disposes of the profits interest; or

(3) If the profits interest is a limited partnership interest in a "publicly traded partnership" within the meaning of section 7704(b) of the Internal Revenue Code.

....

PROBLEM 2-2

X, Y and Z plan to form the XYZ partnership to sell auto parts at a mall. Z has no money to speak of, but a considerable amount of useful experience, for which the partners anticipate giving him a 20% interest in profits in addition to a salary of $10,000 per year. What methods could the partnership employ to compensate Z for services to be provided, without risking the imposition of an income tax on Z when he receives his profits interest in the partnership?

C. ASSIGNMENT OF INCOME PRINCIPLES

One can fairly argue that when a cash method taxpayer contributes accounts receivable to a partnership of which he is a member, the cash eventually received should be taxed to that taxpayer under traditional assignment of income principles. On the other hand, § 721 suggests that there should be an amnesty, and assignment of income principles should not apply, at least if the taxpayer has a good business reason for contributing the receivables, and is not just trying to pull a fast one on the government. The part of this book dealing with incorporation addresses that subject in connection with *Hempt Bros. v. United States*, 490 F.2d 1172 (3d Cir.), *cert. denied*, 419 U.S. 826 (1974). There is, however, a special twist in the partnership area in that § 704(c) will tax the contributing partner to the extent of the difference between the receivables' bases and their values when the debtors pay off their debts, which in effect prevents the assignment of income to other partners.

D. FOREIGN PARTNERSHIPS

Partnerships may be formed under foreign laws. The U.S. view is that if one wishes one's partnership to be foreign, one need only include in the partnership agreement a statement that the partnership is organized under the laws of a particular foreign country. Doing so may lead to some surprises. For one thing, § 1491 imposes a 35% tax on the gain a U.S. person realizes when he contributes appreciated property to a foreign partnership. Also, some countries treat partnerships as taxable entities. Mexico is a leading example.

OUTSIDE READINGS

L. Cunningham, *Colloquium on Partnership Taxation: Taxing Partnership Interests Exchanged for Services*, 47 Tax L. Rev. 247 (1991).

M. Gergen, *Reforming Subchapter K: Compensating Service Partners*, 48 Tax L. Rev. 69 (1992).

C. Nachmias, *Using Profits to Compensate a Service Provider-Potential Partnership*, 21 Fla. St. U.L. Rev. 1125 (1994).

D. FOREIGN PARTNERSHIPS

L. Schmolka, *Colloquium on Partnership Taxation: Commentary: Taxing Partnership Interests Exchanged for Services: Let Diamond/Campbell Quietly Die*, 47 Tax L. Rev. 287 (1991).

W. Schwidetsky, *Partnership Taxation: Restructuring Partnership Debt — Life Is Change*, 11 Va. Tax Rev. 523 (1992).

Chapter 3
PARTNERSHIP OPERATIONS

A. TAXATION OF PARTNERSHIP OPERATIONS

Read §§ 702(a)-(c), 703 and 704(a)-(c).

1. COMPUTING PARTNERSHIP INCOME

The key tax feature of the partnership is that it operates as a conduit that flows its income or losses through to its owners without paying income tax itself. This is the aggregate theory in full bloom. The partnership's return filing obligations are directed at assuring that the partnership's annual operating results are recorded and carved up partner-by-partner, by means of the Schedule K-1. The partnership reports these results, misleadingly referred to as the "taxable income of the partnership" in § 703(a), on the basis of *its* taxable year and *its* accounting method, and in general, on the basis of tax elections made at the partnership level. The results themselves are determined as of the *end* of the partnership's taxable year. The partners' years may not exactly overlap with the partnership's. For example, if the partnership has a fiscal year that ends on June 30, partners preparing their 1995 calendar-year tax returns will use only the information on the partnership return filed for June 30, 1995. The partnership's operating results later in 1995 will not affect the partners' calendar year 1995 taxable income but will instead appear on their 1996 returns. Consider what chaos would result if the partners were free each to choose the taxable year or accounting method of the partnership income by which each would have his or her income attributed; this necessitates using something like the concept the "taxable income of the partnership." The concept is essential in order to centralize the measurement of income.

In a simple world the partnership's accountant could simply compute this "taxable income" and apportion it to each partner via the Schedule K-1. Section 703(a) tells us that the partnership's income or loss is "computed in the same manner as in the case of an individual" and then goes on to serve up a variety of modifications. The statutory thread then moves to § 702(a)(8), which in effect tell us that this "taxable income" is shared by the partners. Section 704(a) tells us that the partnership agreement dictates just how the sharing is accomplished. Flipping back to § 702(a)(1)-(7), we find a list of items that have to be separately stated because they may affect each partner differently, due to his or her tax status or circumstances; these are excluded from the calculation of the partnership's taxable income, but flow through to the partners anyway as distinct items. In effect, nothing is lost to the partners. The effect of this segregation is only to force the partners to report these items in separate locations on their own tax returns. Each time such an item is lifted out and segregated, the "partnership taxable income" rises or falls correspondingly.

a. Separately Stated Items

Because § 702(a)(1)-(7) is not an exclusive list, the courts are sometimes called on to see if anything else belongs on the list of separately stated items.

GERSHKOWITZ v. COMMISSIONER
88 T.C. 984 (1987)

WRIGHT, JUDGE.

[The taxpayer was a limited partner in four limited partnerships which marketed computer programs for income tax preparation, estate planning and financial planning. The partnerships bought the programs with nonrecourse notes and received nonrecourse loans from various entities, including Prentice-Hall. The partnerships liquidated in 1977, at which time each partnership was insolvent. The partners were solvent during 1977. The partnerships' loans were discharged by the lenders either by (1) forgiveness of indebtedness, or (2) conveyance of the security for the loan. The earlier *Stackhouse* case held that cancellation of indebtedness income is deemed a distribution under § 752(d). As a result, a reduction in debt that exceeded the partner's outside basis could produce a capital gain under § 731(a). Take a look at § 731(a)(1) and the last sentence of § 731(a), beginning "Any gain or loss ..." before reading this case.]

Opinion 1. Prentice-Hall Transactions

The first issue for consideration is whether petitioners must recognize a gain on the Prentice-Hall transaction. Each partnership received loans in the aggregate amount of $250,000 from Prentice-Hall. Those loans were nonrecourse, and were secured by the 40,000 shares of COAP common stock owned by each partnership and by the account receivable of each partnership. Prentice-Hall also had subordinate security interest in the computer programs purchased by each partnership from Digitax Associates and COAP Planning, Inc. On June 20, 1977, Prentice-Hall released its security interest in the COAP stock, the computer programs and the accounts receivable of the Digitax partnerships and extinguished the $250,000 debt owed by each partnership. In exchange, each partnership paid Prentice-Hall $40,000 in cash. The fair market value of the COAP stock at that time was $2,500. The partnerships were insolvent both before and after the transaction.

In determining whether petitioners in the instant case must recognize a gain on the discharge of the Prentice-Hall indebtedness, two sets of rules must be considered. First, the general provisions of section 61(a)(12) dealing with income from discharge of indebtedness, and secondly the distribution provision of section 752(b) relating to a decrease in partnership liabilities.

A. TAXATION OF PARTNERSHIP OPERATIONS   61

In general, gross income includes income from the discharge of indebtedness. Sec. 61(a)(12); *United States v. Kirby Lumber Co.*, 284 U.S. 1 (1931). Income realized by a partnership on the discharge of indebtedness is passed through to each partner under section 702, and the partner's basis in his partnership interest is increased by his distributive share of such income. Sec. 705(a)(1). Under a judicially-created exception to this rule, however, a debtor will not recognize income under section 61(a)(12) if he is insolvent following the discharge of indebtedness. *Dallas Transfer and Terminal Warehouse Co. v. Commissioner*, 70 F.2d 95 (5th Cir. 1934); *Astoria Marine Construction Co. v. Commissioner*, 12 T.C. 798 (1949).[1]

Under Section 752(a), at the time a partnership assumes a liability, an individual partner's share of such liability is treated as a contribution of money by the partner to the partnership and increases the partner's basis in his partnership interest. Sec. 722. Conversely, any decrease in the partner's share of the partnership liabilities is treated as a distribution of money by the partnership to the partner under section 752(b) and results in the recognition of gain by the partner to the extent that such a distribution exceeds his adjusted basis in his partnership interest. Sec. 731(a)(1). The gain recognized is characterized as gain from the sale or exchange by the partner of his partnership interest, and is taken into income under section 61(a)(3) (gains derived from dealing in property).

Under section 61(a)(12), the Digitax partnerships realized income from the discharge of indebtedness when Prentice-Hall discharged the loans. This income was then passed through to the individual partners pursuant to section 702(a)(8). Petitioners argue that although income was realized, it should not be recognized in the instant case due to the insolvency exception to the discharge of indebtedness doctrine. In support of their position, petitioners cite *Stackhouse v. United States*, 441 F.2d 465 (5th Cir. 1971). *Stackhouse* involved an insolvent partnership which settled a debt of $126,882.86 with a payment of $30,000. The Commissioner determined that the individual partners had income from the discharge of indebtedness to the extent of their solvency following the transaction. The District Court found that the partners had ordinary income under section 61(a)(12) to the extent of their solvency. *Stackhouse v. United States*, an unreported case (W.D. Tex. 1970, 27 AFTR 2d 71-414, 71-1 USTC par. 9128). The taxpayers appealed, alleging that the transaction was governed by the partnership distribution provisions of section 731 and 733. The Fifth Circuit Court of Appeals in *Stackhouse* attempted to reconcile the rules requiring recognition of discharge of indebtedness income with the partnership provisions providing for the treatment of partners on the discharge of a partnership liability. The court found that the discharge of partnership indebtedness resulted in a distribution to the partners under section 752(b) which resulted in a recognition

---

[1] Now see § 108(a)(1)(B). — Eds.

of gain by each partner under section 731(a) to the extent that the amount distributed exceeded each partner's adjusted basis in his partnership interest. The court stated that "[s]ection 731(a) merely prescribes the rules for determining the amount of income derived from this discharge of indebtedness to be included in the taxpayers' gross income under section 61(a)(12). In a sense then we are giving effect to both sections of the Code."...

Petitioners maintain that the opinion in *Stackhouse* stands for the proposition that income from the discharge of indebtedness should be recognized at the partnership, rather than the partner, level, and that the insolvency exception to the discharge of indebtedness doctrine applies, therefore, to the partnership. The solvency of the individual partner is immaterial under petitioners' analysis. Petitioners fail to note, however, that the court in *Stackhouse* was not faced with the issue of whether income should be recognized at the partner or the partnership level, but rather whether such income should be treated as ordinary income under section 61(a)(12) or capital gain under section 731(a). The court noted that "[t]he United States concedes ... that because the partnership had been insolvent before the settlement (its liabilities exceeded its assets), the gain to each partner should be recognized only to the extent of his solvency immediately after the settlement." 441 F.2d at 468. Thus, the parties in *Stackhouse* did not dispute, and the court did not consider, the level at which the insolvency exception applied, but rather the character of the partners' income.

Petitioners allege that their interpretation of *Stackhouse* is supported by the legislative history of the Bankruptcy Tax Act of 1980 (Pub. L. 96-589, December 24, 1980) ("the Act"). Section 2(a) of the Act amended section 108 of the Code to provide that the application of the code section providing for nonrecognition of discharge of indebtedness income when the taxpayer is insolvent should take place at the partner, rather than the partnership, level. Specifically, the legislative history states:

> "The bill provides that the rules of exclusion from gross income and reduction of tax attributes in section 108 of the Code (as amended by the bill) are to be applied at the partner level and not at the partnership level. S. Rept. No. 96-1035, 96th Cong., 2d Sess. 21 (1980)."

Based on this footnote, petitioners argue that Congress perceived that, prior to the Act, the insolvency exception to the recognition of discharge of indebtedness income was to be applied at the partnership level. Other than *Stackhouse*, however, petitioners cite no authority in support of this proposition, nor have we found any. As stated above, this issue was not addressed in *Stackhouse*. Further, by requiring recognition at the partner level, Congress provided for the inclusion of discharge of indebtedness income as a separately stated income item under section 702(a)(7) which would trigger an increase in each partner's basis under section 705. The court in *Stackhouse*, which treated such income as a distribution under section 731, ignored these provisions. Thus, Congress' intent to overturn *Stackhouse* related to application of sections 702 and 705 to discharge of

A. TAXATION OF PARTNERSHIP OPERATIONS

indebtedness income, rather than to the level at which such income is recognized. The legislative history indicates that the purpose of the amendment to section 108 was to clarify the requirement that discharge of indebtedness income was considered income to the individual partners under section 702 rather than solely as a partnership distribution under section 731. To the extent that the result of such treatment results in ordinary income, rather than capital gain as the court held in *Stackhouse*, Congress chose to overrule that case.

Even if we were to assume, however, that petitioners' analysis of the legislative history of the Act was correct, we would still decline to follow the opinion of the Fifth Circuit in *Stackhouse*. While the analysis used by the Fifth Circuit is appealing in that it purports to integrate the two sets of rules dealing with the discharge of indebtedness, the court failed to recognize that income recognized by a partner pursuant to section 731(a) is included in that partner's gross income under section 61(a)(3) rather than under section 61(a)(12). Income realized by a partnership under section 61(a)(12) must be recognized by the partners as ordinary income under section 702. The recognition of such income provides each partner with an increase in the adjusted basis of his partnership interest under section 705. The distribution provision of section 752(b) serves to offset the basis increase received by each partner when the indebtedness was incurred and does not provide for the distribution of section 61(a)(12) income. Distributions under section 752(b) result in capital gain under section 731(a). The two sets of rules operate independently and simultaneously. The Fifth Circuit, in *Stackhouse*, failed to consider the ordinary income character of the income from the discharge of indebtedness under section 61(a)(12) as opposed to the capital gain recognized under section 731(a).

For the above-stated reasons, petitioners' reliance on *Stackhouse* is misplaced. The application of the insolvency exception to the discharge of indebtedness income should be made at the partner, not the partnership, level. Because each petitioner herein was solvent at the time the debts were discharged, each must recognize ordinary income with respect to his share of the partnership's income under section 702(a)(8). This income will provide each partner with an increase in basis under section 705(a)(1)(A). At the same time, each partner will receive a distribution from the partnership in an amount equal to his share of the partnership indebtedness. Sec. 752(b). This distribution will offset each partner's basis under section 733(1). Thus, the increase in basis under section 705, coupled with the distribution and decrease in basis under sections 752 and 733 result in a net change of zero in each partner's basis. The optional adjustments to basis enacted by the Bankruptcy Tax Act of 1980 were intended to change this result. S. Rept. No. 96-1035, 96th Cong., 2d Sess. 21 (1980).

Respondent argues, on brief, that the partners should not be entitled to a basis increase under section 705(a)(1)(A) because of the realization of discharge of indebtedness income. Respondent asserts that the basis increase would provide an opportunity for limited partners to bail out of crossover tax shelter partnerships without the recognition of the "phantom gain" inherent in their partnership interests, citing McKee, Nelson and Whitmire, Federal Taxation of Partnerships and Partners, par. 9.06[3] n.144 (1977). We agree with respondent that, if the insolvency exception were to apply at the partnership level, such a step-up in basis would be abusive. In the instant case, however, we have determined that this exception must be applied at the partner level. When the loan proceeds were received by the partnerships, each partner increased his basis in his partnership interest by his distributive share of the liability. Sec. 722. This basis increase allowed the partners to deduct their distributive shares of partnership losses and deductions prior to the discharge of the loans. If the partnerships had received ordinary income instead of loan proceeds in the years 1972-74, the partners would have increased their bases in their partnership interests. Secs. 702(a)(8), 705(a)(1)(A). Because we are requiring the partners to recognize the same amounts as income in 1977, they should receive a basis increase in that year. While the partners were able to take advantage of the original basis increase on receipt of the loan proceeds in order to offset deductions during the intervening years, the mechanism for recognition of the use of such basis is contained in sections 752(b), 731(a) and 733, not in section 705. We note that because we have decided that the insolvency exception applies at the partner, not the partnership, level, we need not address respondent's contention that discharge of indebtedness income which is not recognized because the recipient of such income is insolvent does not constitute "tax-exempt receipts" for purposes of section 705(a)(1)(B).

[The court went on to conclude that each partnership realized income of $210,000 (liability of $250,000 less payment of $40,000).]

To reflect the foregoing, Decisions will be entered under Rule 155.

Reviewed by the Court.

---

b. Disallowed Deductions

Section 703(a)(2) bars a partnership itself from deducting foreign income taxes, charitable gifts, net operating losses and depletion in determining its taxable income. This is more bark than bite, since these items will nevertheless appear on the K-1 and the partners will pick these items up on their personal returns. In addition, the same subsection disallows personal exemptions and other items that have no business on a partnership return in the first place. The reason for eliminating these deductions from the computation of "partnership taxable income" is that deductions for these items may be uniquely limited, depending on the facts and circumstances of each partner.

c. Organization, Syndication and Start-Up Expenditures

Read § 709.

A. TAXATION OF PARTNERSHIP OPERATIONS

Section 709(a) generally denies deductions for costs of organizing and financing a partnership. However, § 709(b) relaxes the prohibition by allowing sixty-month amortization of organization, but not syndication, expenditures. (Section 248 is a clone provision for corporations.) Read § 709 and Reg. § 1.709-2, then try the following straightforward problem.

PROBLEM 3-1

L, M, and N formed the LMN limited partnership on December 1, 1994. The partnership incurred the following costs in 1994, before beginning business on January 15, 1995:

Legal fees for drafting partnership agreement	$6,000.00
State filing fee	2,000.00
Notice in newspaper, required by state	500.00
Commissions paid to broker to sell interests in the partnership	20,000.00
Legal fee paid for a tax opinion in the tax section of the prospectus	5,000.00

To what extent can the partnership deduct organizational costs under § 709(b) in 1994? In 1995?

Regardless of whether the partnership or corporate form is chosen, § 195 permits the sixty-month amortization of selected "start-up" costs incurred after the decision to acquire or establish a business, and prior to its commencing operations. The partnership makes the election. Start-up costs eligible for this amortization election include those paid or incurred in connection with:

(i) investigating the creation or acquisition of an active trade or business, or

(ii) creating an active trade or business, or

(iii) any activity engaged in for profit and for the production of income before the day on which the active trade or business begins, in anticipation of such activity becoming an active trade or business, and which, if paid or incurred in connection with the operation of an existing active trade or business (in the same field as the trade or business referred to in paragraph "(i)"), would be allowable as a deduction for the taxable year in which paid or incurred. You likely studied § 195 in the introductory tax course. It will not be dwelt upon here.

2. PARTNERSHIP LEVEL ELECTIONS

Partnerships are treated as separate entities for a variety of tax purposes. This flows naturally from the concept that a partnership has its own so-called taxable income even though it is not taxable on that amount. Section 703(b) lays the duty to make most elections affecting taxable income at the feet of the partnership.

a. Accounting Method

Section 703(b) implicitly obligates the partnership to select its own accounting method. Section 448 forces it on to the accrual method if it is a tax shelter or has a C corporation as a partner. Yes, a corporation can be a partner in a partnership. Likewise, a partnership can be a partner in another partnership. Other Code provisions may also force it onto a specified accounting method (including the accrual method), but this subject falls under the general heading of tax accounting and not partnership taxation.

b. Selection of Taxable Year

Read § 706(b).

The partnership generally selects its own taxable year. However, the Code sharply restricts its ability to use this generality to avoid taxes of its partners by clever choices of tax year. Section 706(b) places major restrictions on the choice of taxable year. The following is a description of the 1986 Act changes, as reported by the Staff of the Joint Committee on Taxation.[2] The materials cover partnerships, S corporations, and personal service corporations.

> G. Taxable Years of Partnerships, S Corporations, and Personal Service Corporations (... secs. 706, 1378, 441, and 267 of the Code)
>
> *Prior Law*
>
> *Partnerships.* — Prior law required a partnership adopting or changing a taxable year to use the same taxable year as all of its principal partners (or the calendar year, if all of the partnership's principal partners do not have the same taxable year and the partnership is adopting a taxable year), unless the partnership established to the satisfaction of the Secretary of the Treasury a business purpose for selecting a different taxable year (sec. 706).
>
> ....
>
> *Deferral of income.* — Under present law, partners in a partnership take into account their allocable share of income, gain, loss, deduction or credit of the partnership for their taxable year in which the partnership's taxable year ends. The items of income, gain, loss, deduction or credit are computed at the partnership level and reflect the partnership's (not the partner's) taxable year. To the extent that the partner's and the partnership's taxable years are not the same, a deferral of income can result. For example, assume a partnership has a taxable year ending in June, while an individual partner has a calendar year. The partner will include in his

---

[2] Joint Comm. on Tax'n, General Explanation of the Tax Reform Act of 1986, 100th Cong., 1st Sess. 533 (1987).

A. TAXATION OF PARTNERSHIP OPERATIONS

income tax return for the current calendar year his distributive share of partnership items that arose in the first six months of the current calendar year and his share of such items that arose in the last six months of the prior calendar year. Partnership items arising in the last six months of the current calendar year will not be included in the partner's return until the following calendar year. Thus, the recognition of six months' of partnership income has been deferred by the partner until the following taxable year.

A similar deferral may be accomplished through the use of a personal service corporation. For example, assume a personal service corporation with a taxable year ending in January pays its calendar year employee-owners a minimal salary during the year and, immediately prior to the close of the corporation's taxable year (during January), declares a bonus to the employee-owners equal to the profits of the corporation. The corporation obtains a deduction for the bonus paid (reducing its current year taxable income to zero) and the employee-owners report the bonus income as part of their income for the taxable year that ends eleven months later. The effect is to defer taxation on eleven months of income earned in one year until the following year.

Reasons for Change

The Congress believed that the prior law allowed an improper deferral of income for certain partners, shareholders in S corporations, and owners of personal service corporations. Where prior law allowed income earned by a partnership, S corporation or personal service corporation to be subjected to Federal income tax in a taxable year later than that in which it was earned, the value of the income earned is understated. This deferral of income was normally available only to certain types of taxpayers, resulting in preferential treatment of certain taxpayers at the overall expense of others. The Congress believed that requiring a partnership, S corporation, or personal service corporation to change its taxable year would impose less of a burden on the taxpaying public than other methods of eliminating the deferral.

Explanation of Provision

In general, the Act requires that all partnerships, S corporations, and personal service corporations conform their taxable years to the taxable years of their owners. An exception to the rule is made in the case where the partnership, S corporation, or personal service corporation establishes to the satisfaction of the Secretary of the Treasury a business purpose for having a different taxable year. The deferral of income to owners for a limited period of time, such as the three months or less rule of present law, is not to be treated as a business purpose.

The Act provides that a partnership may not have a taxable year other than the taxable year of the partners owning a majority interest in partnership profits and capital. If partners owning a majority of partnership profits and capital do not have the same taxable year, the partnership must adopt the same taxable year as its principal [5% of capital or profits] partners. If the principal partners of the partnership do not have the same taxable year and no majority of its partners have the same taxable year, the partnership must adopt a calendar year as its taxable year unless a different taxable year is provided by regulations. In each case, the partnership may use a different taxable year if it establishes to the satisfaction of the Secretary of the Treasury a business purpose therefor.

For example, assume a partnership has one principal partner which is a fiscal year corporation owning an interest of 10 percent in partnership profits and capital. The remainder of the partners are individuals on a calendar taxable year; none of these individuals owns a sufficient interest in the partnership to be a principal partner. Under prior law, the partnership would have been required to adopt the fiscal taxable year of the corporate partner (i.e., the taxable year of its principal partner). Under the Act, the partnership is required to adopt a calendar taxable year (i.e., the taxable year of the majority of its partners).

....

An exception to the rules requiring a certain taxable year is provided in each case where the partnership, S corporation, or personal service corporation establishes to the satisfaction of the Secretary of the Treasury a business purpose for having a different taxable year.''

To illustrate: The two partners of the AB general partnership consist of two partnerships, A and B. Each has an equal interest in the AB partnership. A consists of the Jones family, all of whom use the calendar year. The B partnership consists of two corporations, each of which is on the June 30 fiscal year. Unless it has a business reason for using a fiscal year, the AB partnership must use the calendar year. That is because there is no majority in interest, and because the principal partners (A and B) are not on the same taxable year

NOTES

As the legislative history indicates, unless the bulk of the partnership interests are owned by fiscal year taxpayers, the partnership is stuck with the calendar year, but as always, there are exceptions. The primary exception is for partnerships with a good business purpose for selecting a different year. For example, a ski resort might rightfully choose to close its books after ski season ends in the Spring. The other option is to make the so-called "Section 444 election," which permits a deferral of up to three months, but the price is that the partnership has to pay the government for the benefit of the deferral.

A. TAXATION OF PARTNERSHIP OPERATIONS

PROBLEM 3-2

C and D are the members of a prosperous law partnership, which uses the cash method and calendar year, as do the partners. The partnership has a pool of assets that the partners manage. The CD partnership had the following income during this year:

Gross fees	$800,000
Current § 162 deductions	180,000
Dividends from US corporations	1,000
Interest from corporate bonds	5,000
Net long-term capital gains	500
Net short-term capital gains	800
Rental income from investment property	6,000

What is the CD *partnership's* "taxable income" under § 702 for this year?

3. TAX CONSEQUENCES TO PARTNERS

Once the partnership's annual income or loss has been determined, one must attribute the results to each partner. § 704. This calls for determining each partner's so-called distributive share for the partnership's tax year. The term "distributive share" is carefully chosen, because the term concerns what is *imputed* to the partner, not what is *distributed* to the partner. In general, the partnership agreement controls the partner's distributive share of both partnership "taxable income" and of the items excluded from the computation of that figure.

a. Timing of Distributive Shares

In the following case, focus on the significance of the years 1933 and 1944-45.

COMMISSIONER v. GOLDBERGER'S ESTATE
213 F.2d 78 (3d Cir. 1954),
aff'g in part and rev'g in part 18 T.C. 1233 (1952),
acq. 1955-2 C.B. 6, 9

STALEY, CIRCUIT JUDGE.

In 1944 the estate of Norman S. Goldberger received $108,453.59 as a result of a judgment recovered in the United States District Court for the Southern District of New York. That receipt gave rise to these cases, the Commissioner having assessed income tax deficiencies for the year 1944 against both the estate and the beneficiary of a trust set up by Goldberger's will. The Tax Court held that there was no deficiency as to the estate but that the recovery, minus certain deductions, was income to the beneficiary.

The facts were stipulated and were found accordingly by the Tax Court.

In 1933 Goldberger entered into a joint venture with Bauer, Pogue & Co., Inc., a brokerage company, and George E. Tribble. The purpose of the venture was to trade in the stock of Fidelio Brewery, Inc. Each of the venturers contributed a substantial number of Fidelio shares, and Bauer, Pogue & Co., Inc., were the managers of the trading account. By the terms of the agreement, Goldberger was to receive 50/115ths of the net profits of the venture, which was active from June 8 to August 2, 1933. In September of that year, an accounting was rendered to Goldberger which showed that his share of the net profits of the venture was $71,847.58. This sum was paid to him. He died in 1936, believing that the accounting rendered in 1933 was correct. In 1939 his executrix, petitioner Trounstine, discovered that Bauer, Pogue & Co., Inc., had not dealt honestly with Goldberger in 1933. Trounstine brought suit in New York against Bauer, Pogue & Co., Inc., and Bauer, individually, for an accounting of the joint venture profits. Following removal of the suit, the district court found that, during the operation of the joint venture and in violation of its terms, Bauer, Pogue & Co., Inc., and Bauer and Pogue, individually, secretly traded in Fidelio shares and failed to account to Goldberger for the profits of those sales. After an accounting before a special master, the court found that in addition to the sum paid to Goldberger in 1933, he should have received $60,163.73. Final judgment was then entered in favor of the estate. In 1944 the estate received, in satisfaction of the judgment, $108,453.59, which included the $60,163.73 which Goldberger should have received in 1933, plus interest from August 11, 1933, and costs and disbursements. Expenses of the litigation amounted to $64,855.02, leaving a net recovery of $43,598.57.

Petitioner Trounstine is Goldberger's widow and the executrix of his estate. His will left his entire residuary estate in trust for his widow. The trustees were to pay to her all income from the *res* (with an irrelevant exception), and, if any year's income was less than $12,000, a sufficient amount from corpus to make a total annual payment of $12,000. Prior to receipt of the proceeds of the judgment, Goldberger's entire residuary estate, aggregating $79,272.61, had been paid over to her as trust beneficiary. The net recovery was deposited in an account maintained by her as ancillary executrix between December, 1944, and February, 1945. Between February and May of 1945, that amount was transferred to her domiciliary executrix account, and was transferred to her, individually, between March and May of 1945.

The estate did not file a return for 1944, and Trounstine's 1944 return did not report any of the amount received on the recovery. The Commissioner assessed deficiencies against both the estate and Trounstine and a 25 per cent penalty against the estate for failure to file a return. On petitions for redetermination the Tax Court held that the recovery was gross income to the estate in 1944 but that it was entitled to deduct the litigation expenses and the net amount of the recovery, the latter because it was held to be currently distributable to Trounstine as trust beneficiary. This left no net income to the estate and taxed the net recovery to Trounstine. The result was a determination of no deficiency against the estate, rendering moot the penalty for failure to file, but a deficiency as to Trounstine larger than that assessed....

A. TAXATION OF PARTNERSHIP OPERATIONS

The Commissioner supports his deficiency assessments by pointing to the general rule that the taxability of the principal amount of recovery in a law suit depends upon the nature of the claim and the basis of recovery. If the claim is for lost profits, the recovery is a taxable gain because it is in lieu of what would have been taxable had it been received without a law suit. If the claim is for loss of, or damage to, capital, the recovery is nontaxable because it is a return of capital. Here, the principal sum recovered was the amount of joint-venture profits wrongfully withheld from Goldberger and, therefore, we are told, there was taxable income. The taxpayers argue, correctly we believe, that the principal sum was taxable income to Goldberger in 1933 and is now beyond reach of the fisc because of the statute of limitations.

The Revenue Act of 1932 governs this phase of the case. [It] ... includes a joint venture within the meaning of the term "partnership." Thus, for simplicity's sake, we will use partnership language here. That Act treated the firm and the individual partners substantially as does the present Code. That is, for income tax purposes, the common law, aggregate theory prevailed. The firm was not a taxable entity; its return was informational only.... Its net income was computed, except as to the deduction for charitable contributions, in the same manner as that of an individual.... The tax was imposed upon the individual partner, who must include, in computing his net income, his distributive share of the firm's net income, whether or not distributed to him. That is the determinative point here. The joint venture made certain profits in 1933, but Goldberger did not receive his entire share. Nonreceipt makes no difference, taxwise.... Once the joint venture realized net income, Goldberger became taxable upon his distributive share, in spite of the fact that he did not actually receive it in that year.

Finally, we think the Commissioner distorts the nature of the 1944 judgment. He argues that what the estate recovered in 1944 never became joint-venture profits in 1933 but were the profits of the individual wrongdoers, made in breach of their fiduciary duty. The opinion and findings of fact in the 1944 action, which are part of the stipulated facts here, and the Tax Court's opinion show, however, that joint-venture profits, made in 1933 but wrongfully withheld from Goldberger in that year, are exactly what the estate recovered in 1944. The fact of their nonappearance on the books of the venture, if it is a fact, is not determinative here, for book entries are "no more than evidential, being neither indispensable nor conclusive."

....

NOTES

Statute of limitations and facts. Cases like *Goldberger's Estate* raise the contrast between tax deficiencies, which generally terminate after three years under the statute of limitations found in § 6501, and facts, as to which there is no statute of limitations. Section 705 determines the partner's outside basis, which should be treated as a fact. Thus, even though Mr. Goldberger never reported the income that he was swindled out of, that income should have increased his outside basis. That would set the stage for a diminished gain (or enlarged loss) if he had sold his partnership interest or a nontaxable distribution under § 731.

b. Character of Distributive Shares

Section 702(a) assures that the tax character of each item of income, expense, deduction, and credit that the partnership generates retains the same character in the hands of the partners.

c. Adjustments to Basis

It is a basic theme of partnership taxation that there is generally no taxable gain when property is either contributed to the partnership or distributed from it. §§ 721 and 731. However a partner is taxed annually on his distributive share, regardless of whether he receives a distribution. The pent-up paper gains or losses on the contributed or distributed property remain latent in the partnership interest. When a partner dies, of course, the magic of § 1014 takes over, largely eradicating pending gains and losses by changing the basis in the partnership interest to its fair market value at the partner's death. But there is always § 691 (income in respect of a decendent) to reckon with, especially as to recent income of, or from, the partnership.

(1) Partner's (Outside) Basis and Partnership's (Inside) Basis

Perhaps the most important technical lesson of Subchapter K is that one has to keep an eye on two accounts at the same time. One is the partner's basis in his or her partnership interest, which is generally referred to as the "outside basis." *See* § 705. A partner's interest in the partnership can be analogized to a block of stock in a corporation, but the basis of a partnership interest is far more dynamic; it increases and decreases regularly to reflect undistributed partnership income and losses. The determination of the partner's outside basis is of great importance. For example, current distributions of cash from the partnership are nontaxable when received until they exceed the distributee partner's outside basis. § 732. Outside basis is subtracted from the amount realized in calculating the gain or loss on the sale or exchange of a partnership interest. §§ 741, 1001. The partner can deduct her share of partnership losses only to the extent of her outside basis. § 704(d). When the partnership liquidates, the partner's basis in the distributed assets will generally equal her outside basis. § 732(b).

The other account is the partnership's basis in its own properties, which is generally referred to as the "inside basis." One can think of the inside basis as existing on the opposite side of a legal membrane that separates the partnership from its owners. Inside basis will commonly diverge sharply from the *value* of assets the partnership owns; by the same token, the value of a partner's interest

A. TAXATION OF PARTNERSHIP OPERATIONS

in the partnership is also apt to be quite different from the partner's outside basis. The partnership's basis in properties that its partners contribute to it is the transferor-partner's basis. *See* § 723. The "outside basis" of a partner and the "inside basis" of the partnership start out the same, but the inside-outside symmetry tends to deteriorate over time for various technical reasons.

(2) Impact of Income and Loss on a Partner's Basis

The notion that a partnership is a conduit (or "aggregate" of partners) for tax purposes does not mean that there will necessarily be any actual distributions to the partners. Allocations of partnership income, which the partners must report and on which they each will be taxed, may well involve income that the partnership retains. The managing partner typically controls distributions, making them only when the enterprise does not need surplus cash or property. If a partner is allocated partnership income, the partner's outside basis in the partnership interest will be correspondingly increased. § 705(a)(1). Absent this upward adjustment to outside basis, if the partner were to sell her interest before an actual distribution of the retained income, there could be a *second* tax on the same income that was earlier taxed to the selling partner as his or her share of partnership income. Conversely, the partner who is allocated a partnership loss deduction must reduce outside basis. § 705(a)(2)(A). Whenever the partnership makes an actual distribution to a partner, the partner's "outside basis" in his or her partnership interest is correspondingly decreased. § 705(a)(2).

An example involving money may drive home the point here. Assume that the partnership allocates a dollar of partnership income to each partner in accordance with the distributive shares of the respective partners as set out in their partnership agreement. Each partner will then be taxed on a dollar of income. The partner's taxability ensues regardless of whether any actual distribution of cash is made to that partner. Absent any actual distribution of the dollar, however, it naturally follows that a dollar-higher price will be realized on a sale of the partner's interest. After all, given the fact of undistributed partnership income, there is an additional dollar for each of the partners in the partnership's coffers. Unless each partner's outside basis in the partnership interest increases, there would be a dollar more of gain realized from the sale of any partner's interest in the partnership. Conversely, when a dollar is distributed, the partner's outside basis (and sales price) declines, symmetrically, by one dollar.

> *To illustrate*: A is a newly admitted equal partner in the ABC business partnership, which is on the calendar year. His admission took place on January 1 of this year. A's basis in his partnership interest at the time of admission was zero. Assume the ABC partnership earned a net profit of $150,000, all of which the partnership retained in its bank account. If his share of partnership income for the year is $50,000, his outside basis becomes also $50,000. If, in contrast, the tax law made A's outside basis

zero and he sold his partnership interest for its cash value of $50,000, he would suffer a double tax, once for the year the partnership earned the $50,000 allocable to A, and then a gain of $50,000 when A sold the partnership interest.

(3) Impact of Distributions on a Partner's Basis

Distributions also reduce the partner's basis in her partnership interest. Cash distributions reduce basis. § 705(a)(2). If and to the extent cash distributions exceed basis, the excess is treated as a gain on the sale of the partnership interest. § 731. Congress could have chosen to defer the tax by allowing negative basis, but, consistent with its handling of comparable issues throughout the Code, it did not. Property distributions are more complex and are discussed in detail in Chapter 7.

(4) Outside Basis Adjustments for Partnership Income That Is Tax-Exempt

When tax exempt income, such as interest on tax-free municipal bonds,[3] is allocated, each partner's "outside basis" must be correspondingly increased. § 705(a)(1)(B). If there were no increase in outside basis, eventually an income tax would fall on that supposedly exempt income when it was realized upon a distribution of cash or property to the partner or (especially) in the form of a greater amount realized from the sale of any partner's interest in the partnership. Of course, a partnership distribution of tax-exempt income dollars requires a lowering of each distributee-partner's outside basis, just as does any other cash distribution.

(5) Basis Adjustments for Partnership Expenses That Are Nondeductible

Partnership expenditures that are nondeductible for tax purposes are nonetheless allocated among the partners in accordance with the partners' distributive shares. The partner whose distributive share is a dollar of nondeductible partnership expenses must reduce outside basis by a dollar, despite the nondeductible nature of the dollar so allocated. § 705(a)(2)(B). Otherwise, the partner could convert the nondeductible expenditure into a deduction by selling her partnership interest and thereby realizing a dollar less of gain (or a dollar more of loss).

(6) Basis Adjustments for Partnership Expenditures That Are Capitalized

If the partnership's outlay is nondeductible because it has to be capitalized, it will obviously produce no deduction at the partner level until the capitalized amount produces a depreciation or amortization deduction. The capitalized sum

---

[3] See § 103.

A. TAXATION OF PARTNERSHIP OPERATIONS

naturally is reflected in the basis of the partnership's asset with reference to which the outlay was made. For example, if property having a basis of $100 is the subject of a $10 capital improvement, its basis is adjusted to $110, but the *aggregate* inside basis remains unchanged because the cash on hand prior to this outlay was already included in the aggregate inside basis amount; hence, no change in outside basis is needed to maintain order.

(7) Symmetry Between Inside and Outside Basis

Note how each dollar of income which the partnership earns increases both inside and outside basis by a dollar. Conversely, each dollar of loss *generally* affects inside and outside basis. As will be seen later, the symmetry breaks when the losses exceed the partner's outside basis.

d. General Deferral Limitation on Flow-Through of Losses

Read § 704(d).

As you saw, § 704(d) limits each partner's annual losses, including capital losses, to his or her outside basis, determined at the end of the partnership year in which the loss occurred. To accelerate a loss that is blocked by the § 704(d) limit, the partner can make a pre-year-end contribution, or do nothing and hope that there will be later profits that the suspended losses will offset, or make a contribution to the partnership in a later year, which will also revive the loss in that later year to the extent of the contribution. Because the partnership's borrowings increase the partners' outside bases, a common solution to the § 704(d) limitation is for the partnership to borrow enough money to insure that § 704(d) never becomes a problem; however, that in turn draws in the at-risk rules of § 465, which operate as a backstop to § 704(d).

SENNETT v. COMMISSIONER
752 F.2d 428 (9th Cir. 1985)

PER CURIAM: Taxpayers William and Sandra Sennett claimed an ordinary loss deduction of $109,061 on their 1969 tax return. This loss represented William Sennett's share of the ordinary losses incurred in 1968 by Professional Properties Partnership ("PPP") when it repurchased his interest in the partnership. The Commissioner of Internal Revenue disallowed the deduction asserting inter alia that in 1969 Sennett had no basis in an interest in PPP since he had left the partnership in 1968 and is precluded by 26 U.S.C. § 704(d) and Treas. Reg. § 1.704-1(d) from claiming any loss. The Tax Court ruled against petitioners. It held that a former partner may not claim a share of a loss that is incurred by the partnership after the withdrawal from the partnership of that partner. We agree and affirm.

Facts

Sennett entered PPP as a limited partner in December 1967. PPP's total capital at that time was approximately $402,000. Sennett contributed $135,000 and received a 33.5% interest in the partnership. In 1967 PPP reported an ordinary loss of $405,329, and Sennett reported his allowable distributive share of $135,000.

Sennett sold his interest in PPP on November 26, 1968, with an effective date of December 1, 1968. The contract provided that PPP would pay Sennett $250,000, in annual installments with interest. Sennett agreed to pay PPP within one year the total loss allocated to Sennett's surrendered interest. PPP then sold twenty percent of Sennett's interest to a third party. PPP's return in 1968 reported a negative capital account of $109,061, corresponding to the eighty percent portion of the partnership interest PPP bought from Sennett and retained.

On May 15, 1969, Sennett and PPP executed an amended agreement which reduced PPP's obligation to $240,000, without interest if paid in full by December 31, 1969, or if paid one-half in 1969 and the rest in 1970, at seven percent interest. PPP executed a promissory note to Sennett for $240,000, which Sennett signed as paid in full. Sennett meanwhile paid PPP $109,061, which was eighty percent of his share of PPP's losses. On his 1969 return Sennett reported $240,000 long-term capital gain and $109,061 as his distributive share of PPP's ordinary loss. The Commissioner disallowed the ordinary loss and maintained that, instead, there should be a long-term capital gain reported of $130,939 ($240,000 - $109,061). The Tax Court agreed and the Sennetts took this appeal.

Analysis

....

In deciding whether Sennett can deduct a $109,061 loss, we must look to 26 U.S.C. § 704(d). The statute provides:

> LIMITATION ON ALLOWANCE OF LOSSES. — A partner's distributive share of partnership loss (including capital loss) shall be allowed only to the extent of the adjusted basis of such partner's interest in the partnership at the end of the partnership year in which such loss occurred. Any excess of such loss over such basis shall be allowed as a deduction at the end of the partnership year in which said excess is repaid to the partnership....

Treas. Reg. § 1.704-1(d) — in force in 1969 and having substantively the same effect now — interprets the statute as allowing only a partner to benefit from the carryover allowed by subsection 704(d). The Commissioner relies upon this regulation in disallowing the deduction, since Sennett was not a partner in the year he repaid the excess. Sennett does not deny this. Nor does he deny that his basis was zero when PPP purchased his interest and incurred the loss in 1968. Sennett argues instead that the regulation is merely an "interpretive regulation," and entitled to little or no weight. Sennett points to statutory language which

A. TAXATION OF PARTNERSHIP OPERATIONS

allows the taxpayer to claim a deduction in the amount of the excess of basis in the partnership. He claims he repaid the loss in 1969 and is entitled to the deduction regardless of his lack of partner status.

This circuit has held that an interpretive regulation will be given effect if "it is a reasonable interpretation of the statute's plain language, its origin, and its purpose." *First Charter Financial Corp. v. United States*, 669 F.2d 1342, 1348 (9th Cir. 1982). "[A] Treasury regulation 'is not invalid simply because the statutory language will support a contrary interpretation.'" *Id.* (*quoting United States v. Vogel Fertilizer Co.*, 455 U.S. 16, 26, 70 L. Ed. 2d 792, 102 S. Ct. 821 (1982)). As will be explained below, restricting carryover to partners is a reasonable interpretation in light of the wording of the statute and the legislative history.

Statutory language supports the Treasury Regulation. For example, the presence of the word "partner" at the beginning of subsection 704(d) strongly implies that a taxpayer must be a partner to take advantage of the carryover.

The Treasury Regulation's interpretation is also supported by a review of the legislative history of the statute. Section 704(d), as initially adopted by the House, allowed for deduction of the distributive share to the extent of adjusted basis. There was no provision for a carryover of the excess loss until the excess was repaid. H.R. Rep. No. 1337, 83d Cong., 2d Sess. 1, reprinted in 1954 U.S. Code Cong. & Ad. News 4017, 4364. The bill the Senate passed, which was the version Congress enacted, provided for carryover. The accompanying Senate Report sums up both sentences of subsection 704(d) in a fashion that demonstrates the committee felt the subsection limited carryover to partners. It states:

> Your committee has revised subsection (d) of the House bill to provide that any loss in excess of the basis of a partner's partnership interest may be allowed as a deduction only at the end of the partnership year in which the loss is repaid, either directly, or out of future profits.
>
> Subsection (d), as amended, may be illustrated as follows. Assume that a partner has a basis of $50 for his interest, and his distributive share of partnership loss is $100. Under the subsection, the partner's distributive share of the loss would be limited to $50, thereby decreasing the basis of his interest to zero. The remaining $50 loss would not be recognized, unless the partner makes a further contribution of $50. If, however, the partner repays the $50 loss to the partnership out of his share of partnership income for the following year, then the additional $50 loss will be recognized at the end of the year in which such repayment is made. S. Rep. No. 1622, 83d Cong., 2d Sess. 1, reprinted in 1954 U.S. Code Cong. & Ad. News 4621, 5025....

Limiting carryovers to those who are partners at the time of repayment, as Treas. Reg. § 1.704-1(d) does, effectuates congressional intent to allow deductions only to the extent of adjusted basis. When a partner repays the excess loss, it is, as the Senate Report notes, "a further contribution" to the partnership. The partner thereby increases his basis by an amount equal to the loss and reduces it to zero by taking the loss. Nor is the partnership element merely a formal distinction, since the partner repaying the excess loss increases his interest in the partnership and his exposure to loss. Sennett's position, in contrast, was that of a debtor with rights superior to those of partners.

Conclusion

Since Sennett was not a member of the partnership and, therefore, had no basis in the partnership at the time of the loss, he was not entitled to deduct a portion of PPP's putative loss. The decision of the Tax Court rejecting the $109,061 deduction and setting taxpayer's long-term capital gain for the 1969 taxable year at $130,939 is affirmed.

QUESTIONS

1. What deduction would Sennett have been allowed if he did not repay his share of the loss to the partnership? Remember the basis loss-limitation rule of § 704(d). Why did he agree to repay that amount?

2. According to *Oden v. Commissioner*, T.C.M. 1981-184, *aff'd in an unpublished opinion*, 679 F.2d 885 (4th Cir. 1982), a cash-method taxpayer's note takes a zero basis in the partnership's hands. But what happens if the partnership sells the note and the partner later pays it off? Will the partnership have income on the sale? Will the profit on the sale of the note be attributed to the contributing partner? When the partner pays off the note, what basis is there for claiming a deduction for those payments?

e. Other Restrictions on Losses

A familiar grouping of other limitations that arise outside Subchapter K operates simultaneously with the general § 704(d) limitation.

(1) At-Risk Rules

The at-risk rules of § 465 are apt to restrict a partner's losses when § 704(d) will not. The key target will be nonrecourse debt that the partnership has incurred; such debt increases basis under § 752, but does not add at-risk amounts. Like § 704(d), the at-risk rules suspend losses pending further contributions or earnings. Unlike § 704(d), the at-risk rules apply at the partner, not the partnership level. § 465(a)(1). Thus, one must evaluate the extent to which the individual partner is at risk. § 465(b)(1). A favorable factor from the partners' perspective is that the obligation to make further capital contributions to the partnership is included in the amount at risk, provided outside creditors can force such contributions to be made. Prop. Reg. § 1.465-24.

The key exception to the general rule of § 465 is a special interest rule for the real estate industry, the core concept of which is that nonrecourse nonpurchase

A. TAXATION OF PARTNERSHIP OPERATIONS 79

money debt secured by real estate and obtained from an unrelated person is counted as being at-risk. *See* § 465(b)(6) (qualified nonrecourse financing treated as amount at risk). Interestingly, real estate is the one kind of asset that has historically been able to attract nonrecourse financing, so this is no small loophole. Space limitations prevent embellishing on these statements.

(2) Hobby Losses

Although the passive-activity loss rules have generally come to overshadow the hobby loss rules as a weapon against the syndication of tax-oriented investments, § 183 remains a potent force.[4] The government has had a string of litigating successes arguing its position that § 183 must be applied at the partnership level, such that, no matter how serious about making a profit the investor limited partners may have been when they contributed to enterprise, the partnership's right to claim deductions for operating losses depends on the promoter-general partner's motives. *Brannen v. Commissioner*, 722 F.2d 695 (11th Cir. 1984), seems to be the seminal decision here. Moreover, the courts have closed ranks behind the government and denied embezzlement or theft losses to such investors for their cash investments in tax shelters unless the investors were just completely naive. *See, e.g., Viehweg v. Commissioner*, 90 T.C. 1248 (1988) and Rev. Rul. 70-333, 1970-1 C.B. 38.

(3) Passive Activity Losses

The so-called passive loss rules of § 469 apply after the at-risk and hobby-loss rules. The passive loss rules have special consequences when applied to a partnership setting. The rules themselves are simply designed to prevent taxpayers from offsetting losses and credits from so-called passive trades or business against income from portfolio investments and personal services. The general approach of the passive loss rules is to make such losses and credits available only against income from passive trades or businesses, unless and until the taxpayer disposes of his or her entire interest in the passive activity in a fully taxable transaction. The details of § 469 are for another course.

It is natural that the PAL provisions apply to partnerships, because tax shelters (the primary targets of § 469) have historically been packaged and sold in limited partnership form, with the investors (often, in fact, victims of hyperbolic claims of promoters) buying in as limited partners. This area is so thorny that it seems best to hold down the size of this treatise by listing the primary rules and having done with the topic. The following, then, are the primary rules insofar as they affect partnerships:

---

[4] Curiously, § 183 is actually an allowance provision (permitting the use of deductions up to the amount of gross income from an income-generating hobby), but it is seen as a threat because it contains the regulations that are most often used to sort hobbies from real businesses.

1. The PAL rules apply after the § 704(d) basis limit and the at-risk rules of § 465. Staff of the Joint Committee on Tax'n, General Explanation of the Tax Reform Act of 1986, 100th Cong., 1st Sess. 223 (1987).
2. The PAL rules are applied partner-by-partner. § 469(a)(2)(A).
3. Any partner who "materially participates" is exempt from the PAL limits. (This calls for regular, continuous and substantial activity by the partner, or meeting certain more mechanical tests that operate as surrogates for the general standard.) This means a limited partner is not *per se* foreclosed from claiming loss deductions from a limited partnership. *See* Temp. Reg. § 1.469-5T(e)(2).
4. Investment income derived from a partnership is culled out and cannot be used to reduce the partnership's passive activity losses. § 469(e)(1). Service income earned from a partnership is treated the same way. § 469(e)(3).
5. Partnerships may have multiple activities; if so, each is broken out and tortured separately.

Enough said.

PROBLEM 3-3

Individuals X and Y form the XY partnership. Both the individuals and the partnership use the cash method and calendar year. X and Y each contribute $100,000 to the partnership, which it uses to buy a building costing $200,000. XY properly claims $5,000 of straight-line depreciation deductions and operating expenses of $7,000 for this year, which are its only expenses. Its only income is $13,000 of rents. In addition, XY pays an illegal bribe of $500. X and Y are active in the business.

(1) Assuming that X and Y are equal partners, how much net income or loss should each report?

(2) What is the year-end outside basis of X?

OUTSIDE READINGS

C. Berger, *Colloquium on Partnership Taxation: W(h)ither Partnership Taxation?*, 47 Tax L. Rev. 105 (1991).

N. Cunningham, *Colloquium on Partnership Taxation: Commentary: Needed Reform: Tending the Sick Rose*, 47 Tax L. Rev. 77 (1991).

R. Rudnick, *Enforcing the Fundamental Premises of Partnership Taxation*, 22 Hofstra L. Rev. __ (1993).

Chapter 4
TRANSACTIONS BETWEEN PARTNERS AND PARTNERSHIPS

Read § 707.

Partners can act as third parties "wearing different hats" when dealing with partnerships in which they are members. Section 707 is specifically designed to accommodate such relationships, but also to restrict the benefits of overdoing it. Briefly, § 707(a)(1) recognizes the partner acting as a stranger to the partnership, but § 707(a)(2) intervenes to recharacterize some potentially *male fide* dealings. Section 707(b) restricts losses and deductions between partners and their partnerships (related taxpayers as in § 267), without regard to motive, and § 707(c) creates a special hybrid, the guaranteed payment, referring to transactions in which a partner gets an assured payment for capital or services provided in his or her capacity as a partner.

A. LIMITATIONS ON LOSSES IN TRANSACTIONS BETWEEN PARTNERS AND PARTNERSHIPS

Section 707(b) prevents the recognition of losses between a partner and a partnership controlled by the transferor, or between commonly-controlled partnerships. The provision is logical in the sense that without these limits, taxpayers could claim losses with respect to transfers of property that they continue to control. This prohibition applies if:

1. The partner directly or indirectly owns over 50% of partnership capital *or* profits, or
2. The transaction is between two partnerships in which the same persons directly or indirectly own over 50% of partnership capital *or* profits. The powerful constructive ownership rules of § 267(c)(1), (2), (4) and (5) apply. Reg. § 1.707-1 (b)(3). Those rules deem owners of entities to own the portion of the partnership reflected by the owner's share of the entity (e.g., of a trust that owns a partnership interest). Individuals constructively own partnership interests owned by spouses, ancestors, siblings, and descendants.

The transferee of the property can offset future gains with the disallowed loss when it later sells the property. §§ 707(b)(1), 267(d). Because the transferee may sell the property for less than the original basis in the asset, the loss may never produce a tax benefit.

To illustrate: A sells his dog to the AB partnership. The dog has a basis of $20 and a fair market value of $10. A owns 60% of the capital of the AB partnership. The loss is disallowed. If the partnership later sells the dog for $11, AB will not be taxed on the $1 of gain, but the remaining $9 of disallowed loss is gone forever. Conversely, if the partnership later sells the dog for $8.00, the loss will never produce a tax benefit.

B. CONVERSION OF CHARACTER OF ASSETS

Read § 707(b)(2).

Section 707(b)(2) converts gains on assets sold to a controlled partnership (or between controlled partnerships) into ordinary gains if the property is an ordinary asset in the transferee-partnership's hands. This provision is buttressed by § 1239(a), which applies if the property is depreciable in the partnership's hands.

To illustrate: A, a dog fancier but not a dealer, sells his pet dachshund to the ABC partnership, a dealer in dogs. A has a 50.1% interest in ABC's profits. A's gain on this sale is taxable as ordinary income because A directly controls the ABC partnership.

Note how § 707(b)(2) only applies to gains. It cannot, therefore, be manipulated to turn capital losses into ordinary losses.

C. LIMITATIONS ON CURRENT DEDUCTIONS ON TRANSACTIONS BETWEEN PARTNERS AND PARTNERSHIPS

Section 267(a)(2) defers deductions from transactions with partners until the partner takes the payment into gross income. It also sweeps in transactions between the partnership and persons who are *related* to the partner. § 267(e). There is no minimum ownership level, but the deferral is proportionate to the related partner's interest in the partnership. Reg. § 1.267(b)-1(b).

PROBLEM 4-1

A is an equal member of the accrual-method ABC partnership. A owns X Corp., a cash-method taxpayer, which lent ABC some money last year. ABC owes interest of $300 to X Corp. as of the end of its year. To what extent can ABC deduct this interest? What is the effect on A's outside basis? *See* § 705(a)(2)(B).

Conversely, if X Corp. were on the accrual method and borrowed money from the ABC partnership and ABC were on the cash method, X Corp's interest expense deductions would be deferred in proportion to A's interest in ABC (i.e., one-third). Reg. § 1.267(b)-1(b), Examples (1) and (2).

D. GUARANTEED PAYMENT

A partnership implies risks. It is often necessary to offer assured income to certain partners in order to induce them to do what they would otherwise be expected to do as partners. For example, a partner in a real estate venture might insist on being paid a fixed sum for collecting and depositing the monthly rents. With this in mind, read § 707(c) and Reg. § 1.707-1(c).

1. IMPACT ON RECIPIENT

PRATT v. COMMISSIONER
64 T.C. 203 (1975),
aff'd in part and rev'd in part,
550 F.2d 1023 (5th Cir. 1977)

SCOTT, JUDGE:

....

The issue for decision is whether management fees for services performed by petitioners for, and interest earned on, loans made by petitioners to two limited partnerships, of which petitioners were general partners, are deductible by the partnerships, and, if so, whether these amounts are includable in the income of petitioners who report income on the cash basis in the year accrued and deducted as business expenses by the partnerships which report on an accrual basis, even though petitioners did not receive payment of the amounts in the years of accrual by the partnerships....

Each of the limited partnership agreements contained the following provisions:

> Such General Partners shall contribute their time and managerial abilities to this partnership, and each such General Partner shall expend his best effort to the management of and for the purpose for which this partnership was formed. That for such managerial services and abilities contributed by the said General Partners, they shall receive a fee of five (5%) per cent of the Gross Base Lease Rentals of the said leases, and then the said General Partners shall receive ten (10%) per cent of all overrides and/or percentage rentals provided for in said leases as a fee for such managerial services.
>
> The General Partners shall give their personal services to the Partnership and shall devote thereto such time as they may deem necessary, without compensation other than the managerial fees as hereinbefore set out. Any of the Partners, General or Limited, may engage in other business ventures of every nature and description, independently or with others, ...

The general partners had agreed that the management fees would be divided equally among the general partners who performed managerial services.

Petitioners contributed managerial services to the two partnerships and management fees were credited to accounts payable to them. These fees were accrued and deducted annually by each of the partnerships.... The amount of management fees accrued by each of the partnerships in each of the years indicated is a reasonable and proper fee to pay for the services of managing a shopping center of the type of Parker Plaza and Stephenville. A like amount of fees would have had to have been paid to a third party, not a general partner, as a fee for managing the shopping centers had such shopping centers been managed by a third party.

These management fees were not paid to petitioners, and petitioners did not report their respective management fees on their respective income tax returns for the years 1967, 1968, and 1969....

It was the intent of all the partners in Parker Plaza and Stephenville that the management fees and interest were to be expenses to the partnerships.

In his notice of deficiency mailed to each petitioner, respondent increased the income of each of them for each of the years 1968 and 1969 and each of them except Jack for 1967 by amounts equal to his portion of management fees and by the amounts of interest credited to his account by each partnership with the following explanation:

> It is determined that in computing the ordinary net income of the partnerships Plaza Shopping Center, Ltd. and Stephenville Shopping Center, Ltd. claimed management fees and interest are not allowed, such amounts being determined a division of partnership profits. Accordingly, your distributive share of the partnerships income is increased for 1967, 1968, and 1969 returns as ordinary income....

Petitioners stated that without question each of the partnerships could accrue and deduct the amounts of management fees and interest credited to petitioners' accounts had the amount been due and credited to third parties rather than partners, citing *Liflans Corp. v. United States*, 390 F.2d 965 (Ct. Cl. 1968), and that such third parties would not be required to include these amounts in their income if they reported their income on a cash basis until the amounts were actually or constructively received by them.

....

Petitioners contend that the management fees credited to them fall within the provisions of either 707(a) or 707(c) and under either section are properly deductible by the partnership but not includable in their income for the years accrued by the partnership and credited to their accounts. Petitioners point to no provisions of the statute other than sections 707(a) and 707(c) under which management fees to partners for services to the partnership might be treated differently than such items were treated under the law prior to the enactment of the 1954 Code. Prior to the enactment of the provisions of section 707 of the 1954 Code, credits or payments to a partner for services, whether designated as fees or as salary, were not deductible by the partnership in computing the partnership income but were considered as part of the distributive share of partnership income of the partner to whom the credit or payment was made pursuant to the partnership agreement. *Frederick S. Klein*, 25 T.C. 1045 (1956).

D. GUARANTEED PAYMENT

Therefore, if the management fees credited to petitioners do not qualify as transactions between a partner and a partnership, covered by section 707(a) or as guaranteed payments under section 707(c), they are part of the partners' distributive income from the partnership, includable in their distributive shares of profit or loss under section 706 for their taxable year in which the taxable year of the partnership ends and not proper deductions by the partnership in computing distributive partnership income.

In our view the management fees credited to petitioners were not "guaranteed payments" under section 707(c) even though, for reasons hereinafter discussed, we would not agree with petitioners' position that they were not required to include the amounts of the fees in their income for the years here in issue even if they were to be so considered.

Section 707(c) refers to payments "determined without regard to the income." The parties make some argument as to whether payments based on "gross rentals" as provided in the partnership agreements should be considered as payments based on "income." In our view there is no merit to such a distinction. The amounts of the management fees are based on a fixed percentage of the partnership's gross rentals which in turn constitute partnership income. To us it follows that the payments are not determined without regard to the income of the partnership as required by section 707(c) for a payment to a partner for services to be a guaranteed payment.

Since we conclude that the management fees are not guaranteed payments under section 707(c), we must decide whether the provisions for such fees in the partnership agreement might be considered as a "transaction" engaged in by petitioners with the partnership in a capacity other than as a partner within the meaning of section 707(a). Initially, it might be noted that since section 707(c) deals specifically with continuing payments to a partner for services such as salary payments or the management fees here in issue, it is far from clear that such continuing payments were ever intended to come within the provisions of section 707(a). Section 707(a) refers to "transactions" between a partner and a partnership and is susceptible of being interpreted as covering only those services rendered by a partner to the partnership in a specific transaction as distinguished from continuing services of the partner which would either fall within section 707(c) or be in effect a partner's withdrawal of partnership profits. *See F. A. Falconer*, 40 T.C. 1011, 1015 (1963), where we stated as follows with respect to section 707(c):

> Section 707(c) has no counterpart in the Internal Revenue Code of 1939. It initially appeared in the Internal Revenue Code of 1954. Since we have been unable to locate in our research any court decisions pertaining directly to the issue here presented, we approach the problem as one of the first impression. *But compare Foster v. United States*, (S.D.N.Y. 1963, 12 A.F.T.R. 2d, par. 63-5058, 63-2 U.S.T.C. par. 9588). The legislative history of section 707(c) reveals that it was specifically intended to require ordinary

income treatment to the partner receiving guaranteed salary payments and to give a deduction at the partnership level.

The touchstone for determining "guaranteed payments" is whether they are payable without regard to partnership income. And, in determining whether in a particular case an amount paid by a partnership to a partner is a "drawing" or a "guaranteed payment," the substance of the transaction, rather than its form, must govern. *See* sec. 1.707-1(a), Income Tax Regs. These are both factual matters to be judged from all the circumstances. S. Rept. No. 1622 to accompany H.R. 8300, 83d Cong., 2d sess., p. 387 (1954), contains the following explanation:

> "Subsection (c) provides a rule with respect to guaranteed payments to members of a partnership. A partner who renders services to the partnership for a fixed salary, payable without regard to partnership income, shall be treated, to the extent of such amount, as one who is not a partner, and the partnership shall be allowed a deduction for a business expense. The amount of such payment shall be included in the partner's gross income, and shall not be considered a distributive share of partnership income or gain. A partner who is guaranteed a minimum annual amount for his services shall be treated as receiving a fixed payment in that amount."

However, we need not decide whether a continuing payment to a partner for services was ever contemplated as being within the provisions of section 707(a).

Section 1.707-1(a) of the Income Tax Regulations with respect to a "partner not acting in capacity as partner" states that, "In all cases, the substance of the transaction will govern rather than its form." Here, the record indicates that in managing the partnership petitioners were acting in their capacity as partners. They were performing basic duties of the partnership business pursuant to the partnership agreement. Although we have been unable to find cases arising under the 1954 Code concerning when a partner is acting within his capacity as such, a few cases arising under the provisions of the 1939 Code dealt with whether a payment to a partner should be considered as paid to him in a capacity other than as a partner. *See Leif J. Sverdrup*, 14 T.C. 859, 866 (1950); *Wegener v. Commissioner*, 119 F.2d 49 (5th Cir. 1941), *affg.* 41 B.T.A. 857 (1940), *cert. denied* 314 U.S. 643 (1941). In *Wegener*, a joint venture was treated as a partnership for limited purposes, and the taxpayer-partner was found to be acting outside the scope of his partnership duties and in an individual capacity as an oil well drilling contractor, so that payments he received from the "partnership" for carrying out this separate and distinct activity were income to him individually as if he were an outsider. In the *Sverdrup* case, we recognized a payment to a taxpayer by a joint venture between a partnership of which the taxpayer was a member and a third party as compensation for work done on contracts being performed by the joint venture since "This sum was not a part of the income of

D. GUARANTEED PAYMENT

the partnership of which he was a member, but was paid to him as an individual for services rendered to the joint venture."

Petitioners in this case were to receive the management fees for performing services within the normal scope of their duties as general partners and pursuant to the partnership agreement. There is no indication that any one of the petitioners was engaged in a transaction with the partnership other than in his capacity as a partner. We therefore hold that the management fees were not deductible business expenses of the partnership under section 707(a). Instead, in our view the net partnership income is not reduced by these amounts and each petitioner's respective share of partnership profit is increased or loss is reduced by his credited portion of the management fees in each year here in issue. *Frederick S. Klein, supra.*

Respondent on brief argues that the interest accrued by the partnership on the promissory notes evidencing loans by each petitioner to the partnerships are "guaranteed payments" under section 707(c) includable in petitioners' income for the year accrued by the partnership under section 706(a) and section 1.707-1(c), Income Tax Regs. Petitioners agree with respondent that under section 707(c) the interest on the notes are guaranteed payments but argue that these amounts are includable in their income only when received, and that the regulation making such payments includable in income by the partners in the year paid or accrued by the partnership (section 1.707-1(c), Income Tax Regs.), is "an overextension of Respondent's authority."

In our view respondent's regulation is a reasonable interpretation of section 707(c) and carries out the express intention of Congress as reflected in the legislative history of section 707(c). S. Rept. No. 1622, to accompany H.R. 8300 (Pub. L. No. 591), 83d Cong., 2d Sess. 387 (1954), states in part as follows:

> It should be noted that such payments, whether for services or for the use of capital, will be includable in the recipient's return for the taxable year with or within which the partnership year in which the payment was made, or accrued, ends.

This language leaves no doubt that Congress intended to foreclose the possibility that a partnership might accrue salary and interest expenses, which expenses would reduce each partner's distributive share of net partnership income or increase his loss therefrom, while the salaried partner might never receive the payments and therefore never include the amounts in income. As we pointed out in *Andrew O. Miller, Jr.*, 52 T.C. 752, 762 (1969)

> These words ("but only for the purpose of section 61(a) ... and section 162(a) ...") were added to section 707(c) by the Senate which at the same time also amended section 706 to provide that guaranteed payments received by a partner are to be included in his income for his taxable year in which the partnership's taxable year ends. In connection with section 707(c), the Senate committee report indicates that the reason for the change was to

provide that guaranteed payments are to be included in income at the same time as a partner's distributive share — not at the time when compensation would ordinarily be included in income. This is the only example in the legislative history of the need for the "but only" words.

See also Thomas Browne Foster, 42 T.C. 974, 980 (1964). In our view, section 1.707-1(c), Income Tax Regs., is valid and in accordance with the provisions of section 707(c).

Decisions will be entered for the respondent.

NOTE

Capitalized guaranteed payments. Section 707(c) is explicit that a guaranteed payment used to compensate a partner must be capitalized if the services create a capital asset. After the *Pratt* decision came down, tax lawyers noted a loophole. If the service partner were compensated with an allocation, there could be no capitalization; one never capitalizes allocations. That meant that by using the blueprint mapped out in *Pratt* and applying it to a case where the service partner was, for example, devoting his time to the building of an apartment complex, the other partners would take a smaller allocation of profits instead of a larger allocation of profits plus a nondeductible service fee.

To illustrate: Murray is a member of the Murray, Moe & Jack building partnership. His profit share is so small we will ignore it. The partnership agreement states that he is entitled to receive 10% of gross rents as compensation for overseeing the staged development of a building. Rents are $100, and he receives $10 this year. If this were an allocation, he would report $10, and the other partners would report $90. If it were a guaranteed payment, the other partners would report $100 as their distributive share, and Murray would report § 707(c) income of $10. The § 707(c) payment would be capitalized, so the partners could not reduce their distributive shares by the guaranteed payment. Murray would get $10 under either structure, but Moe and Jack are better off with an allocation.

Presumably, the planning implication upset the IRS and provoked the following ruling

REV. RUL. 81-300
1981-2 C.B. 143

Issue

Are the management fees paid to partners under the circumstances described below distributive shares of partnership income or guaranteed payments under section 707(c) of the Internal Revenue Code?

D. GUARANTEED PAYMENT

Facts

The taxpayers are the general partners in a limited partnership formed to purchase, develop and operate a shopping center. The partnership agreement specifies the taxpayers' shares of the profit and loss of the partnership. The general partners have a ten percent interest in each item of partnership income, gain, loss, deduction, or credit. In addition, the partnership agreement provides that the general partners must contribute their time, managerial abilities and best efforts to the partnership and that in return for their managerial services each will receive a fee of five percent of the gross rentals received by the partnership. These amounts will be paid to the general partners in all events.

Pursuant to the partnership agreement, the taxpayers carried out their duties as general partners and provided the management services required in the operation of the shopping centers. The management fee of five percent of gross rentals were reasonable in amount for the services rendered.

Law and Analysis

Section 707(a) of the Code provides that if a partner engages in a transaction with a partnership other than in the capacity of a member of such partnership, the transaction shall, except as otherwise provided in this section, be considered as occurring between the partnership and one who is not a partner.

Section 1.707-1(a) of the Income Tax Regulations provides that a partner who engages in a transaction with a partnership other than in the capacity of a partner shall be treated as if the partner were not a member of the partnership with respect to such transaction. The regulation's section further states that such transaction [sic] include the rendering of services by the partner to the partnership and that the substance of the transaction will govern rather than its form.

Section 707(c) of the Code provides that to the extent determined without regard to the income of the partnership, payments to a partner for services, termed "guaranteed payments," shall be considered as made to one who is not a member of the partnership, but only for purposes of section 61(a) and, subject to section 263, for purposes of section 162(a).

In *Pratt v. Commissioner*, 64 T.C. 203 (1975), *aff'd in part, rev'd in part*, 550 F.2d 1023 (5th Cir. 1977), under substantially similar facts to those in this case, both the United States Tax Court and the United States Court of Appeals for the Fifth Circuit held that management fees based on a percentage of gross rentals were not payments described in section 707(a) of the Code. The courts found that the terms of the partnership agreement and the actions of the parties indicated that the taxpayers were performing the management services in their capacities as general partners. *Compare* Rev. Rul. 81-301, this page, this Bulletin.

When a determination is made that a partner is performing services in the capacity of a partner, a question arises whether the compensation for the services is a guaranteed payment under section 707(c) of the Code or a distributive share of partnership income under section 704. In *Pratt*, the Tax Court held that the management fees were not guaranteed payments because they were computed as a percentage of gross rental income received by the partnership. The court reasoned that the gross rental income was "income" of the partnerships and, thus, the statutory test for a guaranteed payment, that it be "determined without regard to the income of the partnership," was not satisfied. On appeal, the taxpayer's argument was limited to the section 707(a) issue and the Fifth Circuit found it unnecessary to consider the application of section 707(c).

The legislative history of the Internal Revenue Code of 1954 indicates the intent of Congress to treat partnerships as entities in the case of certain transactions between partners and their partnerships. *See* S. Rep. No. 1622, 83d Cong., 2d Sess. 92 (1954). The Internal Revenue Code of 1939 and prior Revenue Acts contain no comparable provision and the courts had split on the question of whether a partner could deal with the partnership as an outsider. *Compare Lloyd v. Commissioner*, 15 B.T.A. 82 (1929) and *Wegener v. Commissioner*, 119 F.2d 49 (5th Cir. 1941), *aff'g* 41 B.T.A. 857 (1940), *cert. denied* 314 U.S. 643 (1941). This resulted both in uncertainty and in substantial computational problems when an aggregate theory was applied and the payment to a partner exceeded the partnership income. In such situations, the fixed salary was treated as a withdrawal of capital, taxable to the salaried partner to the extent that the withdrawal was made from the capital of other partners. *See*, for example, Rev. Rul. 55-30, 1955-1 C.B. 430. Terming such treatment as unrealistic and unnecessarily complicated, Congress enacted section 707(a) and (c) of the Code of 1954. Under section 707(a) the partnership is considered an unrelated entity for all purposes. Under section 707(c), the partnership is considered an unrelated entity for purposes of sections 61 and 162 to the extent that it makes a guaranteed payment for services or for the use of capital.

Although a fixed amount is the most obvious form of guaranteed payment, there are situations in which compensation for services is determined by reference to an item of gross income. For example, it is not unusual to compensate a manager of real property by reference to the gross rental income that the property produces. Such compensation arrangements do not give the provider of the service a share in the profits of the enterprise, but are designed to accurately measure the value of the services that are provided.

Thus, and in view of the legislative history and the purpose underlying section 707 of the Code, the term "guaranteed payment" should not be limited to fixed amounts. A payment for services determined by reference to an item of gross income will be a guaranteed payment if, on the basis of all of the facts and circumstances, the payment is compensation rather than a share of partnership profits. Relevant facts would include the reasonableness of the payment for the services provided and whether the method used to determine the amount of the payment would have been used to compensate an unrelated party for the services.

It is the position of the Internal Revenue Service that in *Pratt* the management fees were guaranteed payments under section 707(c) of the Code. On the facts presented, the payments were not disguised distributions of partnership net

D. GUARANTEED PAYMENT

income, but were compensation for services payable without regard to partnership income.

Holding

The management fees are guaranteed payments under section 707(c) of the Code.

. . . .

NOTES

1. *Taxation of the receipt of a guaranteed payment.* We know that the beneficiary of the guaranteed payment is taxed in the year the partnership reports the deduction (whether by payment or accrual). *See* Reg. § 1.707-1(c). Presumably, there is no second tax when the beneficiary is on the cash method and the accrual method partnership pays the receivable in a later year. There is, however, no clear authority for this obvious proposition. *Cf.* Reg. § 1.704-1(b)(2)(iv)(o).

2. *Legislative history.* The legislative history of the Deficit Reduction Act of 1984 attempted to narrow § 707(c) in favor of § 707(a) in close cases. *See* S. Rep. 98-169, 98th Cong., 2d Sess. 226 (1984). This issue is discussed later in the chapter in connection with § 707(a)(2)(A).

PROBLEM 4-2

Pursuant to the partnership agreement, A manages the ABC partnership's apartment building for 10% of gross rents. What is the nature of the payment under Subchapter K?

2. GUARANTEED PAYMENT PLUS ALLOCATION

A guaranteed payment can be combined with a profit-sharing allocation. In such cases, the allocation reduces the guaranteed payment; the net positive figure, if any, is the guaranteed payment for § 707(c) purposes

To illustrate: A is a member of the AB partnership. He has a 30% distributive share, subject to a guarantee that it will never be less than $100. The partnership agreement says if the 30% share is less than $100, the guaranteed amount is to be treated as a partnership expense. Assume the partnership earns $200 this year before paying A. A's guaranteed payment is $40, viz.:

Guarantee	$100
less 30% distributive share of $200	60
Section 707(c) payment	$40

The partnership's income for the year, after deducting the guaranteed payment, is $160. The $60 is an allocation of profits to A. The remaining $100 is B's distributive share. The partners will share each item of partnership income in a 6:10 ratio, based on the $60 allocation to A and the $100 allocation to B. Rev. Rul. 69-180, 1969-1 C.B. 183. To put it in easier terms, as long as the distributive share at least equals the guaranteed minimum, the entire amount received by the beneficiary of the guaranteed payment is a distributive share.

PROBLEM 4-3

A and B each contributed $25,000 to the newly formed AB partnership to operate an existing clothing store. The partnership is on the accrual method. Their agreement provides that, in connection with A's duties as a partner, A is entitled to an annual payment of $10,000 regardless of the income of the partnership. Any profit or loss, after deducting A's guaranteed amount, shall be shared equally between A and B. The first year's operation resulted in a loss of $15,000 after deducting A's guarantee. What net income or loss from the partnership should A report on her individual income tax return, assuming she was a material participant in the business? *See* Reg. § 1.707-1(c).

3. IMPACT ON THE PARTNERSHIP

The partnership reports guaranteed payments in accordance with its method of accounting, but there is no assurance of a current deduction, given the explicit reference to § 263 in § 707(c). The classic situation in which a partner's § 707(c) payments must be capitalized occurs where a service partner oversees a real estate construction project.

E. DISGUISED TRANSACTIONS

1. COMPENSATION DISGUISED AS A DISTRIBUTION

Read § 707(a)(2)(A).

Section 707(a)(2)(A) has an interesting background. Following *Cagle v. Comm'r, supra,* tax advisors realized that guaranteed payments had to be capitalized if the services for which the guaranteed payment was made would have to be capitalized if performed by an outsider, so they parried with the device of using "allocations" of distributive shares of partnership income, plus "distributions" of money to their hard-working service partners, in place of § 707(a) or 707(c) payments. The scheme was to let the investor partners avoid the capitalization requirement and get a *de facto* deduction in the form of a reduced allocation of profits. Congress responded with § 707(a)(2)(A), turning such patterns of allocations and distributions into § 707(a)(1) payments, thereby indirectly forcing their capitalization. Congress identified some factors that eventual regulations would use in order to sort disguised service contracts from good-faith allocations. The primary factor is whether the service provider bears any real economic risk of nonpayment. The second most important factor is

E. DISGUISED TRANSACTIONS

whether the putative partner is a long-term member or is expected to withdraw once the services have been provided. There are further factors, but they are not worth dwelling on. It is better to point out that this section does not depend on taxpayer motivations, which means that the innocent can be punished along with the guilty, and stop there.

PROBLEM 4-4

A commercial office building constructed by a partnership is projected to generate gross income of at least $100,000 per year indefinitely. Its architect, whose normal fee for such services is $40,000, contributes cash for a 25% interest in the partnership and receives both a 25% distributive share of net income for the life of the partnership and an allocation of $20,000 of partnership gross income for the first two years of partnership operations after lease-up. The partnership is expected to have sufficient cash available to distribute $20,000 to the architect in each of the first two years, and the agreement requires such distributions.

How would you treat the architect's income from the partnership?

Now read § 707(a)(2)(B) and consider the following imaginary transaction:

PROBLEM 4-5

A is a member of the AB partnership. A contributes a building with a value of $10,000 and a basis of $6,000 to the partnership. A year later, she gets a cash distribution of $10,000. Can the two transactions "properly be characterized as a sale" of the building to the partnership? Skim Reg. § 1.707-3(b)(2) for a list of facts and read Reg. § 1.707-3(c), and then draw your own conclusions.

2. PROPERTY PURCHASES DISGUISED AS DISTRIBUTIONS

The game of cops and robbers never ends in the land of taxes. To prevent laundering exchanges of property via partnerships, § 707(a)(2)(B) declares that a matched contribution of one item of property to a partnership, combined with a distribution of another item of property, may in substance be a sale between the partners. Alternatively, they may in substance be sales or exchanges between the partners and the partnership. These disguised exchanges hiding behind a partnership are known as "mixing-bowl" transactions and have been used to undertake complex corporate restructurings. A special presumption in the Regulations matches contributions and distributions made within two years of each other. Congress has buttressed § 707(a)(2) with § 737.

Section 737, which was added to the Code in 1992, requires a partner to recognize her precontribution gains during the five years following her contribution, but only to the extent the value of the property distributed to her exceeds its inside basis, or, if less, to the extent of her net built-in gains under § 704(c). Distributions of her own property are not taxed. § 737(d)(1). Motives are irrelevant. This puts another restriction on mixing-bowl transactions, in effect forcing taxpayers to wait five years before they can take their stab at disguised exchanges via the manipulation of the general rules that permit tax-free contributions and tax-free distributions of property into and out of partnerships. *See also* § 704(c)(1)(B), which can in effect cause a contributor of property to be deemed to have sold such property.

F. FRINGE BENEFITS

The Code grants a number of nontaxable benefits to *employees*. Examples include premiums on up to $50,000 of group-term life insurance coverage under § 79 and certain meals and lodging under § 119. Because partners are not employees, such benefits are unavailable to partners. Thus, even though some benefits, such as group legal service plan arrangements, are available to partners because such plans' tax benefits can extend to nonemployees, no one will choose the partnership form of doing business for its fringe benefit advantage.

OUTSIDE READINGS

K. Burke, *Disquised Sales Between Partners and Partnerships: Section 707 and the Forthcoming Regulations*, 63 Ind. L.J. 489 (1988).

P. Postlewaite & D. Cameron, *Twisting Slowly in the Wind: Guaranteed Payments After the Tax Reform Act of 1984*, 40 Tax Law. 649 (1987).

Chapter 5
PARTNERSHIP ALLOCATIONS

A. ALLOCATION OF PROFITS AND LOSSES GENERALLY

Read § 704(b).

Tax lawyers involved in structuring a partnership often have to address two key issues, recognition of the partnership as such and the validity of the allocations among the partners of overall profits and losses or of specific items. To the extent an allocation is invalid, the tax law requires that it be adjusted to take account of the real economics of the partnership. If that occurs as a result of an IRS audit, the remedial adjustments may cause major additional taxes as well as interest and possible penalties.

Section 704(a) declares that each partner's distributive share of the partnership's income, gain, loss, deduction, and credit is generally determined by the partnership agreement unless the allocation of those items in the agreement lacks "substantial economic effect." "The agreement" includes amendments made up to the filing date for the partnership's tax return. § 761(c). Subchapter K's unique flexibility invites manipulation by structuring the partnership agreement to include devices such as allocating a disproportionate amount of tax-exempt income or depreciation deductions to high-bracket partners while allocating the taxable income to low-bracket partners. The government's previous approach to such abuses was to invalidate allocations that were designed to avoid taxes. The core idea under the current regulations is that the partners' agreement as to how income or deductions are allocated must be accompanied by real economic impacts, or be disregarded. *See* Reg. § 1.704-1(b)(2)(ii)(a). Taxpayer motivations no longer count.

This chapter concentrates heavily on the concept of the capital account to measure the viability of allocations of gains and losses, or particular items, to the partners. It used to be safe to say that each partner's capital account is essentially his or her outside basis, shorn of liabilities. For more recently formed partnerships, it is more likely to be the value of the partner's share of the partnership's assets, minus allocable liabilities.

> *To illustrate*: A contributes cash of $10, and B contributes property worth $10 and having a basis of $5 to the newly-formed AB partnership. If the partners ground their capital accounts on basis, the capital accounts will look like this:

	A	B
Initial Contribution	$10	$5
Plus:		
Partner's share of:		
- partnership taxable income	0	0
- tax-exempt income	0	0
- depletion in excess of basis	0	0
Minus:		
Partner's share of:		
- partnership losses	0	0
- non-capitalized, non-deductible expenses	0	0
- depletion not in excess of basis	0	0

Thereafter, the capital accounts will fluctuate with partners' shares of the profits (increase) and losses (decrease) of the partnership and the other items on the above list, all as directed by § 705. One important result is that if the partnership has significant losses, capital accounts can become negative because the losses are often based on money that the partnership borrowed. That is the essence of the typical old fashioned tax shelter.

If the partners adhere to the capital-account rules now found in the Regulations, they will use fair-market values (not basis) to report contributions (and distributions). Finally, the allocation provisions in the § 704(b) Regulations dictate that in order to assure that allocations are viable, the capital accounts must be maintained using fair-market values. Many commentators now assume that all partnership capital accounts use fair-market values.

Here is how the capital accounts of the AB partnership from the prior illustration would look when they are based on fair market values:

	A	B
Initial Contribution	$10	$10
Plus:		
Partner's share of:		
- partnership taxable income	0	0
- tax-exempt income	0	0
- depletion in excess of basis	0	0
Minus:		
Partner's share of:		
- partnership losses	0	0
- non-capitalized, non-deductible expenses	0	0
- depletion not in excess of basis	0	0

A. ALLOCATION OF PROFITS AND LOSSES GENERALLY

Whether the partnership uses basis or value to establish capital accounts, there is no doubt that one does not count partnership liabilities in the capital account. Given the growing use of fair-market value to gauge capital accounts, you can see that the statement that the capital account is outside basis less the partner's share of partnership liabilities is a dangerous oversimplification. It also makes business sense to use fair-market values to value capital accounts. That is because partnership agreements commonly provide that a partner's claim on the partnership's assets when the partnership liquidates (or when the partner withdraws) turns on the value of the partner's capital account. Knowing all this, you can see that the partner's capital account represents his equity investment in the venture.

Now, back to allocations. If an allocation does fail, then one must determine the "real" allocation by evaluating what the Regulations refer to as the "partner's interest in the partnership," essentially meaning the real economics that underlie the partnership agreement. The following case was decided under the old Regulations, but read it carefully and try to understand it, because its ghost rides again and again through the materials that follow.

Before launching into the case, you need to know about so-called gain chargebacks. These are special allocations of gain on the sale of partnership assets, the purpose of which is to attribute depreciation deductions back to partners who disproportionately enjoyed such deductions. In the typical case, wealthier partners find such chargebacks economically acceptable because the tax benefit of current depreciation deductions is not truly offset by the burden of subsequent identical gains because of the time value of money.

ORRISCH v. COMMISSIONER
55 T.C. 395 (1970),
aff'd per curiam in unpublished opinion
(9th Cir. 1973)

FEATHERSTON, JUDGE:

[The Orrisches and the Cristafis were partners in a partnership that owned depreciable real estate. They orally agreed to allocate all the depreciation to the Orrisches, provided that when the property was sold the Orrisches would be allocated an amount of gain on sale equal to their extra measure of depreciation (a form of "gain charge back"). There was no evidence as to how the parties would share an economic loss on the disposition of the properties. The special allocation of losses offered the parties an overall tax benefit, as the court explains herein.]

Opinion

The only issue presented for decision is whether tax effect can be given the agreement between petitioners and the Crisafis that, beginning with 1966, all the partnership's depreciation deductions were to be allocated to petitioners for their use in computing their individual income tax liabilities. In our view, the answer must be in the negative, and the amounts of each of the partners' deductions for the depreciation of partnership property must be determined in accordance with the ratio used generally in computing their distributive shares of the partnership's profits and losses.

Among the important innovations of the 1954 Code are limited provisions for flexibility in arrangements for the sharing of income, losses, and deductions arising from business activities conducted through partnerships. The authority for special allocations of such items appears in section 704(a), which provides that a partner's share of any item of income, gain, loss, deduction, or credit shall be determined by the partnership agreement. That rule is coupled with a limitation in section 704(b), however, which states that a special allocation of an item will be disregarded if its "principal purpose" is the avoidance or evasion of Federal income tax. *See Smith v. Commissioner*, 331 F.2d 298 (C.A. 7, 1964), affirming a Memorandum Opinion of this Court; *Jean V. Kresser*, 54 T.C. 1621 (1970). In case a special allocation is disregarded, the partner's share of the item is to be determined in accordance with the ratio by which the partners divide the general profits or losses of the partnership. Sec. 1.704-1(b)(2), Income Tax Regs.

The report of the Senate Committee on Finance accompanying the bill finally enacted as the 1954 Code (S. Rept. No. 1622, to accompany H.R. 8300 (Pub. L. No. 591), 83d Cong., 2d Sess., p. 379 (1954)) explained the tax-avoidance restriction prescribed by section 704(b) as follows:

> Subsection (b) ... provides that if the principal purpose of any provision in the partnership agreement dealing with a partner's distributive share of a particular item is to avoid or evade the Federal income tax, the partner's distributive share of that item shall be redetermined in accordance with his distributive share of partnership income or loss described in section 702(a)(9) [i.e., the ratio used by the partners for dividing general profits or losses]....
>
> Where, however, a provision in a partnership agreement for a special allocation of certain items has substantial economic effect and is not merely a device for reducing the taxes of certain partners without actually affecting their shares of partnership income, then such a provision will be recognized for tax purposes....

This reference to "substantial economic effect" did not appear in the House Ways and Means Committee report (H. Rept. No. 1337, to accompany H.R. 8300 (Pub. L. No. 591), 83d Cong., 2d Sess., p. A223 (1954)) discussing section 704(b), and was apparently added in the Senate Finance Committee to allay fears that special allocations of income or deductions would be denied effect in every case where the allocation resulted in a reduction in the income tax liabilities of one or more of the partners. The statement is an affirmation that special allocations are ordinarily to be recognized if they have business validity

A. ALLOCATION OF PROFITS AND LOSSES GENERALLY

apart from their tax consequences. Driscoll, "Tax Problems of Partnerships - Special Allocation of Specific Items," 1958 So. Cal. Tax Inst. 421, 426.

In resolving the question whether the principal purpose of a provision in a partnership agreement is the avoidance or evasion of Federal income tax, all the facts and circumstances in relation to the provision must be taken into account. Section 1.704-1(b)(2), Income Tax Regs., lists the following as relevant circumstances to be considered:

> Whether the partnership or a partner individually has a business purpose for the allocation; whether the allocation has "substantial economic effect," that is, whether the allocation may actually affect the dollar amount of the partners' shares of the total partnership income or loss independently of tax consequences; whether related items of income, gain, loss, deduction, or credit from the same source are subject to the same allocation; whether the allocation was made without recognition of normal business factors and only after the amount of the specially allocated item could reasonably be estimated; the duration of the allocation; and the overall tax consequences of the allocation....

Applying these standards, we do not think the special allocation of depreciation in the present case can be given effect.

The evidence is persuasive that the special allocation of depreciation was adopted for a tax-avoidance rather than a business purpose. Depreciation was the only item which was adjusted by the parties; both the income from the buildings and the expenses incurred in their operation, maintenance, and repair were allocated to the partners equally. Since the deduction for depreciation does not vary from year to year with the fortunes of the business, the parties obviously knew what the tax effect of the special allocation would be at the time they adopted it. Furthermore, as shown by our Findings, petitioners had large amounts of income which would be offset by the additional deduction for depreciation; the Crisafis, in contrast, had no taxable income from which to subtract the partnership depreciation deductions, and, due to depreciation deductions which they were obtaining with respect to other housing projects, could expect to have no taxable income in the near future. On the other hand, the insulation of the Crisafis from at least part of a potential capital gains tax was an obvious tax advantage. The inference is unmistakably clear that the agreement did not reflect normal business considerations but was designed primarily to minimize the overall tax liabilities of the partners.

Petitioners urge that the special allocation of the depreciation deduction was adopted in order to equalize the capital accounts of the partners, correcting a disparity ($14,000) in the amounts initially contributed to the partnership by them ($26,500) and the Crisafis ($12,500). But the evidence does not support this contention. Under the special allocation agreement, petitioners were to be entitled, in computing their individual income tax liabilities, to deduct the full amount of the depreciation realized on the partnership property. For 1966, as an example, petitioners were allocated a sum ($18,904) equal to the depreciation on the partnership property ($18,412) plus one-half of the net loss computed without regard to depreciation ($492). The other one-half of the net loss was, of course, allocated to the Crisafis. Petitioners' allocation ($18,904) was then applied to reduce their capital account. The depreciation specially allocated to petitioners ($18,412) in 1966 alone exceeded the amount of the disparity in the contributions. Indeed, at the end of 1967, petitioners' capital account showed a deficit of $25,187.11 compared with a positive balance of $405.65 in the Crisafis' account. By the time the partnership's properties are fully depreciated, the amount of the reduction in petitioners' capital account will approximate the remaining basis for the buildings as of the end of 1967. The Crisafis' capital account will be adjusted only for contributions, withdrawals, gain or loss, without regard to depreciation, and similar adjustments for these factors will also be made in petitioners' capital account. Thus, rather than correcting an imbalance in the capital accounts of the partners, the special allocation of depreciation will create a vastly greater imbalance than existed at the end of 1966. In the light of these facts, we find it incredible that equalization of the capital accounts was the objective of the special allocation.

This case is to be distinguished from situations where one partner contributed property and the other cash; in such cases sec. 704(c) may allow a special allocation of income and expenses in order to reflect the tax consequences inherent in the original contributions.

Petitioners rely primarily on the argument that the allocation has "substantial economic effect" in that it is reflected in the capital accounts of the partners. Referring to the material quoted above from the report of the Senate Committee on Finance, they contend that this alone is sufficient to show that the special allocation served a business rather than a tax-avoidance purpose.

According to the regulations, an allocation has economic effect if it "may actually affect the dollar amount of the partners' shares of the total partnership income or loss independently of tax consequences." The agreement in this case provided not only for the allocation of depreciation to petitioners but also for gain on the sale of the partnership property to be "charged back" to them. The charge back would cause the gain, for tax purposes, to be allocated on the books entirely to petitioners to the extent of the special allocation of depreciation, and their capital account would be correspondingly increased. The remainder of the gain, if any, would be shared equally by the partners. If the gain on the sale were to equal or exceed the depreciation specially allocated to petitioners, the increase in their capital account caused by the charge back would exactly equal the depreciation deductions previously allowed to them and the proceeds of the sale of the property would be divided equally. In such circumstances, the only effect of the allocation would be a trade of tax consequences, i.e., the Crisafis would relinquish a current depreciation deduction in exchange for exoneration from all or part of the capital gains tax when the property is sold, and petitioners would enjoy a larger current depreciation deduction but would assume a larger

A. ALLOCATION OF PROFITS AND LOSSES GENERALLY

ultimate capital gains tax liability. Quite clearly, if the property is sold at a gain, the special allocation will affect only the tax liabilities of the partners and will have no other economic effect.

To find any economic effect of the special allocation agreement aside from its tax consequences, we must, therefore, look to see who is to bear the economic burden of the depreciation if the buildings should be sold for a sum less than their original cost. There is not one syllable of evidence bearing directly on this crucial point. We have noted, however, that when the buildings are fully depreciated, petitioners' capital account will have a deficit, or there will be a disparity in the capital accounts, approximately equal to the undepreciated basis of the buildings as of the beginning of 1966. Under normal accounting procedures, if the building were sold at a gain less than the amount of such disparity petitioners would either be required to contribute to the partnership a sum equal to the remaining deficit in their capital account after the gain on the sale had been added back or would be entitled to receive a proportionately smaller share of the partnership assets on liquidation. Based on the record as a whole, we do not think the partners ever agreed to such an arrangement. On dissolution, we think the partners contemplated an equal division of the partnership assets which would be adjusted only for disparities in cash contributions or withdrawals. Certainly there is no evidence to show otherwise. That being true, the special allocation does not "actually affect the dollar amount of the partners' share of the total partnership income or loss independently of tax consequences" within the meaning of the regulation referred to above.

In the light of all the evidence we have found as an ultimate fact that the "principal purpose" of the special allocation agreement was tax avoidance within the meaning of section 704(b). Accordingly, the deduction for depreciation for 1966 and 1967 must be allocated between the parties in the same manner as other deductions.

Decision will be entered for the respondent.

NOTE

Here is a simplified model of the capital account analysis that the Orrisch court was struggling with:

To illustrate: The Orriches and the Cristafis contribute $10 each and borrow $80 on a nonrecourse basis from the Friendly Bank. The building is written off to $0, with the Orriches taking all the depreciation. If it is sold for $0, the $80 loan still encumbers the property, so there is an $80 *Tufts* gain, which is charged in full to the Orriches:

Capital Accounts

	Orrisches	Cristafis
Contribution	$10	$10
Deductions	(100)	-0-
Capital account	(90)	10
Gain on sale	80	-0-
Balance	($10)	$10

If the Orrisches had been obligated to contribute $10 to eliminate their deficit and to pay the Cristafis their capital account, the court might have been satisfied with the result, but there was no such duty. There was only a chargeback of the $80 gain, with liquidating distributions made without reference to the post-chargeback capital accounts. Another way to put it is that the allocations were not felt in cash.

1. SPECIAL ALLOCATIONS VERSUS "BOTTOM-LINE" ALLOCATIONS

A "bottom-line allocation" is an allocation of a partner's gross share of partnership profit or loss, exclusive of partnership items that have to be separately stated under § 702(a). Reg. § 1.704-1(b)(1)(vii). By contrast, a "special allocation" is an allocation of some particular item, such as tax-exempt interest, the partnership earns or spends and which differs from the division of profits and losses generally. Reg. § 1.704-1(a)(8)(i).

What you are about to read is novel and intricate. You must keep your sense of perspective about this topic. The subject matter is whether a particular allocation — whether special or "bottom-line" — to a partner reported on a Form K-1 for a particular year is valid in the sense of deserving enough economic respect to let the partner report the allocation on her personal tax return. If it is not, then one must divine and retrofit the "true" allocation based on the economic realities of partnership. There is almost no authority on how to go about this, except a statement in Reg. § 1.704-1(b)(3) to the effect that one uses "the partner's interest in the partnership," based on all the facts and circumstances, and a virtually useless presumption that everyone is an equal partner. The overarching idea is that tax allocations are good only if they follow economic reality; that generally calls for matching the tax allocation with an actual flow of cash and other property into and out of the partnership. The following materials contain a fairly large number of footnotes. It is best not to study them when you read this material for the first time. They may, however, be helpful for later readings.

2. POST-1985 APPROACH TO PARTNERSHIP ALLOCATIONS

The Treasury Department greatly modified the § 704(b) regulations for post-1985 years, moving away from a search for motives and substituting a

A. ALLOCATION OF PROFITS AND LOSSES GENERALLY

complicated economic analysis. The essential effect of the new rules is to disregard either special or "bottom-line" allocations if they lack "substantial economic effect." In such cases, the partners' distributive shares are instead allocated in accordance with their "interests in the partnership." Again, the new standards for disallowing allocations are objective, and do not depend on taxpayers' motives.

The approach of the new Regulations is to apply a dual test at the end of each partnership taxable year. The first test requires that the allocation have "economic effect." Reg. 1.704-1(b)(2)(i). The second test requires the economic effect to be "substantial." *Id.* If the allocation satisfies the rigorous standards imposed by the Regulations by both having economic effect *and* being substantial, it is definitely validated. Hence, the new Regulations in effect offer a safe harbor. If an allocation cannot find its way into the safe harbor, it may still be valid on the theory that it reflects the partner's interest in the partnership. For many small partnerships, the safe-harbor Regulations are too costly to bother trying to comply with, largely because of the requirement that certain tax records be maintained on the basis of fair-market values as opposed to historical costs. Thus, the small partnership will likely try to satisfy the looser "reflects the partner's interest" test.

a. Economic Effect

The fundamental concept is that any allocation must reflect the economic arrangement of the partners, i.e., generally have a realistic chance of being felt in cash. To do so, Reg. § 1.704-1(b)(2)(ii)(b) applies a cumulative three-step test, which is commonly referred to as the three-part mechanical test.

Three-part mechanical test: this powerful test grants an allocation "economic effect" if, throughout the life of the partnership, the partnership agreement (including all side agreements) assures that:

1. The partners' capital accounts will be determined and maintained under the usual rules for determining outside basis,[1] except that one uses fair-market values (minus associated encumbrances) in connection with computing contributions[2] and distributions of property[3]; *and*

---

[1] *See* Chapter 3.

[2] For example, if a partner contributed property with a gross fair market value of $500, a basis of $200, subject to a debt of $100, one would increase the partner's capital account by $400 ($500 - $100).

[3] The partnership may restate its assets and capital accounts in three specific situations, if the partnership agreement so requires. Reg. § 1.704-1(b)(2)(iv)(f). The most notable situation is when a partner is admitted or withdraws. The thoughtful tax advisor will provide for this adjustment in order to prevent capital shifts with possible immediate tax consequences. *See* B. Bittker & L. Lokken, Federal Taxation of Income, Estates and Gifts Vol. 3 ¶ 86.2.4 (1991).

104   CH. 5: PARTNERSHIP ALLOCATIONS

2. On the liquidation of the partnership (or of a partner's interest in the partnership) distributions will be made exclusively in accordance with the positive capital account balances of each partner[4]; *and*
3. If a partner has a deficit capital account balance after all adjustments for the year of the liquidation, he or she must restore the deficit[5] in order to pay partnership creditors or partners with positive capital account balances. This requirement is often referred to as a "deficit make-up" or "deficit restoration" provision.

Think back to how the taxpayer's agreement in *Orrisch* failed to meet these tests.

Alternative economic effect test: If a partnership allocation fails only the third part of the three-part mechanical test, the allocation may still have economic effect if it satisfies the "alternate economic effect test." Reg. § 1.704-1(b)(2)(ii)(d). This requires that the partnership agreement contain a "qualified income offset" (QIO). A QIO is an allocation of items of income and gain in an amount sufficient to eliminate, as quickly as possible, any deficit balance caused by *unexpected* adjustments, allocations, or distributions. (An example of an expected adjustment would be a depreciation deduction; an easy example of an unexpected adjustment would be a casualty loss.[6]) This dictates that every partnership agreement without a deficit restoration clause contain a QIO. Note that the QIO is a highly legalistic concept. It only works as long as there are no deficits; it does not validate an allocation that produces a deficit.[7] The following QIO language was extracted from an actual partnership agreement:

"(v) Prior to any allocations for a fiscal year under [a prior section of the agreement], in the event any partner unexpectedly receives any adjustments, allocations or distributions described in Treasury

---

[4] If this were not the case, the business deal would be unrealistic; any reasonable partner who is leaving the partnership will want her share of the *value* of the partnership, not her share of its basis. Only her tax lawyer and CPA care about basis at this juncture.

[5] To the extent the partner has a limited duty to restore the deficit, this test is met to the extent of the duty to restore. State law may impose such an obligation. One affirmative way to generate a limited duty is to contribute one's own promissory note. Reg.§ 1.704-1(b)(2)(iv)(d)(2).

[6] The motive behind the requirement that the adjustment be unexpected is to prevent taxpayers from playing timing games. The most obvious example would be holding off on a distribution until the following year so as to allocate sufficient losses to a partner to wipe out his capital account (resulting in a delicious tax deduction for the partner), followed by a distribution in the following year (taxable at the genteel 28% rate applicable to capital gains, as effectively directed by § 741). As the regulations now stand, the partnership reduces the partner's capital account by the anticipated distribution. This makes it more likely that the allocation of the expected amount will produce a deficit. Once there is a deficit, the allocation is controlled by the partner's interest in the partnership. Reg. § 1.704-1(b)(3)(iii) and -1(b)(5), Example 1(iv)-(vi).

[7] There may be some other solution, especially in connection with deductions founded on nonrecourse debt, which is discussed below.

A. ALLOCATION OF PROFITS AND LOSSES GENERALLY

Regulations Section 1.704-1(b)(2)(ii)(d)(4), (5) or (6) and such adjustment, allocation or distribution results in any partner having a deficit in his or her capital account, then items of income and gain shall be specially allocated to each such partner in an amount and manner sufficient to eliminate, as quickly as possible, to the extent required by Treasury Regulations, the deficit of such partner. This provision is intended to comply with the "qualified income offset" requirement in Treasury Regulations Section 1.704-1(b)(2)(ii)(d)(3), and shall be interpreted consistently therewith."

If there is a QIO, limited obligations of a partner to restore his deficit will be respected. Reg. § 1.704-2(b)(2)(ii)(f).

Economic effect equivalency test: If the partnership agreement fails both the three-part mechanical test *and* the alternate test for economic effect, allocations made to partners pursuant to the partnership agreement may nevertheless be treated as having economic effect if the partnership agreement ensures that a liquidation of the partnership as of the end of each partnership taxable year will produce the same economic results to the partners as would occur if:

1. Capital accounts were maintained for the partners;
2. Liquidation proceeds were distributed in accordance with such capital accounts; and
3. All partners had an unconditional obligation to restore deficits remaining in their capital accounts at the time of such liquidation.

This back-up protection is likely to be important if there is no deficit make-up provision in the partnership agreement, but state law in effect supplies such a provision. *See* Reg. § 1.704-1(b)(2)(ii)(i). This is the one and only reference you will see to the economic effect equivalency test in this book.

b. Illustration of an Economic Effect

The following example is from Reg. § 1.704-1(b)(5). It illustrates a number of points: (1) use of the safe harbor means books using adjusted basis must be kept to determine partnership income, while using another set of books based on fair-market values for allocation purposes; and, (2) the role of § 704(c) in allocating precontribution gain or loss to contributing partners:

Example 13. (i) Y and Z form a brokerage general partnership for the purpose of investing and trading in marketable securities. Y contributes cash of $10,000, and Z contributes securities of P corporation, which have an adjusted basis of $3,000 and a fair market value of $10,000.... The partnership agreement provides that the partners' capital accounts will be determined and maintained [on a fair market value basis, in accordance with the economic effect regulations], distributions in liquidation of the partnership (or any partner's interest) will be made in accordance with the partners' positive capital account balances, and any partner with a deficit balance in his capital account following the liquidation of his interest must restore that deficit to the partnership.... The initial capital accounts of Y and Z are fixed at $10,000 each. The agreement further provides that all partnership distributions, income, gain, loss, deduction, and credit will be shared equally between Y and Z, except that the taxable gain attributable to the precontribution appreciation in the value of the securities of P corporation will be allocated to Z in accordance with section 704(c). During the partnership's first taxable year, it sells the securities of P corporation for $12,000, resulting in a $2,000 book gain ($12,000 less $10,000 book value) and a $9,000 taxable gain ($12,000 less $3,000 adjusted tax basis). The partnership has no other income, gain, loss, or deductions for the taxable year. The gain from the sale of the securities is allocated as follows:

	Y		Z	
	Tax	Book	Tax	Book
Capital Account upon formation	$10,000	$10,000	$3,000	$10,000
Plus: gain	1,000	1,000	8,000	1,000
Capital Account at end of year 1	$11,000	$11,000	$11,000	$11,000

The allocation of the $2,000 book gain, $1,000 each to Y and Z, has substantial economic effect. Furthermore, under section 704(c) the partners' distributive shares of the $9,000 taxable gain are $1,000 to Y and $8,000 to Z.

c. Substantial

(1) General Rule

If an allocation is found to have economic effect, the next step is to determine whether that effect is also "substantial." If not, the allocation fails and must be retrofitted in light of the partner's interest in the partnership. Generally, the economic effect of an allocation is substantial if there is a reasonable possibility that the allocation will significantly affect the dollar amounts or value of property to be received by partners from the partnership independent of tax consequences. Reg. § 1.704-1(b)(2)(iii)(a). Conversely, the Regulations contain a general rule that stabs tax arbitrage in the heart; specifically, an allocation cannot be substantial if:

1. The after-tax economic consequences of at least one partner may, in present value terms, be enhanced by the allocation; and
2. There is a "strong likelihood" that the after-tax economic consequences of no partner will, in present value terms, be substantially diminished by the allocation.

A. ALLOCATION OF PROFITS AND LOSSES GENERALLY

"In present value terms" means that one uses discounting techniques to take account of futurity.[8] The Regulations do not tell one what interest rate to use when discounting future receipts or disbursements. The Regulations tell one to apply this test in light of each partner's tax situation outside the partnership. In the real world this is hard to do. It may be that the foregoing is largely an *in terrorem* clause which prevents marketing structures which are based on tax arbitrage.

(2) Shifting and Transitory Allocations

The regulations attack specific types of allocations for lack of substantiality, namely "shifting allocations" and "transitory allocations."

(a) Shifting Allocations

A shifting allocation is one which, when put in the partnership agreement, creates a strong likelihood that (1) the net increases and decreases in the partners' capital accounts within a single taxable year will not differ substantially from the net increases and decreases if the allocation were not part of the partnership agreement, *and* (2) the total tax liability of the partners will decline as a result of the allocation. For this purpose, one takes into account the impact of the partners' nonpartnership tax items. Reg. § 1.704-1(b)(2)(iii)(b) and (c).

PROBLEM 5-1

A and B are equal members of the AB partnership. The partnership is expected to report a $100 ordinary income and $80 of tax-exempt income. Assume that A is in the 40% tax bracket and B has a $100 net operating loss carryover this year, which loss will expire unless he can find income to offset it with. Knowing this, the partners amend the agreement for the year to provide that A will get all the tax-exempt income and B will get the $100 of operating income. Assume the partnership agreement satisfies the economic effect requirements.
1. Is this year's allocation valid?
2. Would it matter if A and B were unaware of each other's tax situations?

(b) Transitory Allocations

These are multi-year variants of the shifting allocation. The sin here is creating an allocation this year that will likely be offset by a countervailing allocation within five years, plus a tax saving. More precisely, the Regulations find a transitory allocation if there is a strong likelihood, at the time the allocations became part of the partnership agreement, that the net increases and decreases

---

[8] This simply refers to the fact that a dollar today is worth less than a dollar tomorrow because one can earn interest on the dollar received today.

in the partners' capital accounts as a result of allocations over several years will not differ substantially from the net increases and decreases that would have occurred had the allocations not been made, *and* the partners' total tax liability declines. If these two conditions are met, the regulations rebuttably presume the likelihood that these events would occur. Reg. § 1.704-1(b)(2)(iii)(c).[9] An example of a transitory allocation would be a two-person partnership which specially allocated all its income in one year to a partner with an expiring net operating loss deduction, with an agreement that in the following year(s) the other partner would be allocated an offsetting amount of income; the effect is to stabilize the capital account balances over time while reducing aggregate tax liability of the conspiring partners. Because the allocation is "transitory," it is disregarded and restructured in accordance with the partner's interest in the partnership. Think back to *Orrisch* and consider whether it fits this model.

The "transitory allocation" rules create the possibility that any extra claim to depreciation deductions will be invalidated if the partnership agreement contains a "gain chargeback" under which the partner who claimed an extra measure of depreciation is allocated a gain equal to the extra depreciation previously claimed when the property is sold. Reg. § 1.704-1(b)(2)(iii)(c)(2) comes to the partners' rescue by conclusively (and unrealistically) presuming that cost recovery deductions are matched by an equal decrease in the property's value, thereby obliterating the risk that the initial allocation of gain will be invalidated because it creates a legal fiction that the gain chargeback will never apply. That, by legal magic, renders the special allocation of depreciation "permanent" rather than transitory. This can be boon for the real estate industry, where tax depreciation is an all-important factor and investors generally assume that the property will not really decline in market value. As you will see later, this favorable rule is not enough to salvage *Orrisch* if it were to be reconsidered under the current regulations.

PROBLEM 5-2

C has invented a new industrial process that is in need of development. C thinks $200,000 is needed to bring it to market. The partnership agreement satisfies the mechanical three-part test. D is willing to invest $200,000 in cash to become a 50:50 partner. D insists that all losses be allocated to him, and that once the partnership becomes profitable, he be allocated enough profit to restore his capital account up to $200, after which profits will be shared 50:50. (Because

---

[9] Although the "likelihood" is often within the subjective control of the partners (such as a decision to sell property in the future), the Regulations avoid the search for intentions by providing that if the two conditions (no big capital account change *plus* tax saving) are met, the likelihood is rebuttably presumed to have existed from the outset. Offsetting allocations that are separated by over five years are released from the presumption that they are intertwined and are presumed innocent.

A. ALLOCATION OF PROFITS AND LOSSES GENERALLY

the three-part test was met, C could have been allocated a share of the losses because they would be covered by his deficit make-up obligation.) As expected, the partnership spends $200,000 and then, four years later, begins making money. Is the allocation invalid by virtue of being "transitory"? See Reg. § 1.704-1(b)(2)(c)(iii)(2) and -1(b)(5), Ex. (3).

d. Amendment of the Partnership Agreement

The Regulations assume that one is dealing with "the" partnership agreement, but we have already seen that § 761 generously allows amendments to the agreement, as long as they are made before the original due date of the partnership's tax return. This flexibility means there is always a risk that the partners have an unwritten agreement to change the partnership document at a crucial moment and in a way that subverts the allocation provisions. For example, the partners may presently have a viable allocation of depreciation with the correct gain chargebacks on sale of the property in anticipation of liquidation, but they may secretly agree that at that future date they will amend the partnership agreement to eliminate the deficit make-up provision. Reg. § 1.704-1(b)(4)(vi) contains a menacing statement that the prior allocations will be modified retroactively in such cases; the weakness of the threat is that the IRS can rarely go back beyond the three-year statute of limitations period. If the partnership existed for many years, the threat of reallocation may only be a paper tiger.

e. Partner's Interest in the Partnership

If an allocation does not pass the substantial economic effect test, it will be reallocated in accordance with the partner's interest in the partnership. One determines a partner's interest in the partnership by reference to the real economics dictated by the partnership agreement. Reg. § 1.704-1(b)(3)(i). This generally calls for evaluating the partner's contributions to the partnership, his or her share of current cash flow, and claims to distributions of cash and property (by value) during the partnership's operating life and when the partnership liquidates. Think back to how empty the *Orrisch* deal was in this respect, i.e., how the Tax Court realized in truth that the Orrisches and the Cristafis really split all cash income and losses, causing the attempted special allocation of depreciation to fail.

The following elaborate problem poses an allocation that does not smell right and asks you to determine for yourself what the partners' interest in the partnership really is. The problem is challenging. Do not despair if you cannot solve it, but do appreciate how even a fairly basic issue in this area calls for intensive analysis.

PROBLEM 5-3

Money Partner (MP), skeptical of Development Partner's (DP) grandiose claims with respect to the marketability of a building which DP proposes to build with MP's funds, negotiates the following agreement: Profits and losses will be allocated equally,[10] although MP will contribute $100 and DP only $1. MP's claim to cash distributions will grow at a rate of 10% simple interest for each year that any part of his capital remains unrecovered. They agree that the preferential distributions to MP will not reduce MP's capital account. No cash distribution will be made to DP until MP's claim to preferential distributions is satisfied, after which cash will be shared in accordance with the partners' relative capital accounts, provided that in all events MP will be paid in full before DP shares in cash flow. The unpaid accumulated claims against future cash flow, which grow at interest, are to be recorded in a memorandum account off the formal tax or financial records. What this means is that, if DP's claims about the building are true, he will get a lot of cash; if not, MP will have a preferential position with respect to whatever cash may grow out of the investment, with compensation for delay. NB: There is no deficit make-up provision, nor does state law impose one.

At the beginning of Year 1, the partners' capital accounts are as follows:

Money Partner	Development Partner
$100	$1

During Year 1, the partnership loses $2. The loss is shared equally, and the capital accounts will appear as follows:

	Money Partner	Development Partner
Opening	$100	$1
Loss	(1)	(1)
Year-end	$99	$0

For the next decade, the partnership is inexplicably inert, as a consequence of which MP's memorandum account shows a preferential claim to distributions of $109, based on $100 outstanding for one year and $99 for ten years at 10% simple interest.

At the beginning of Year 12, the partnership sells the property for $399 cash. Assume that the adjusted basis of the property sold by the partnership is $99. Accordingly, the partnership has a recognized gain of $300, and $399 in cash to be shared. The partners' capital accounts appear as follows:

---

[10] The agreement would also provide that if the allocated loss exceeds a partner's outside basis for federal income tax purposes, the resulting unusable loss will be allocated to the other partner. The provision would never actually be used, on the facts of this example.

B. APPORTIONING PARTNERSHIP LIABILITIES

	Money Partner	*Development Partner*
Opening	$99	$0
Gain	*150*	*150*
Year-end	$249	$150

Because of their agreement as to cash distributions, MP will get the lion's share of the $399. First, he gets a $109 preferential distribution, which is *not* viewed as reducing his claims against his capital account balance for purposes of the agreement; accordingly, he is entitled to a further $249, which in combination leaves $41 for DP, punishing DP for delay. Thus, MP will have netted $259 in cash as a consequence of participating in the venture ($358 *less* his $99 investment, treating the $1 loss as reducing his investment) and will report a capital gain on termination of the partnership of $109 (his cash receipts of $249 *plus* $109 *less* his $249 capital account).[11]

DP will net $41 in cash (termination proceeds, ignoring his $1 investment because of the offsetting $1 loss) and will claim a $109 capital loss, the difference between his closing capital account of $150 and the $41 he actually received on termination.[12]

What is your analysis of this complicated transaction? Specifically, does MP have a generous distribution, a guaranteed payment, interest income, or an allocation of profits as a result of the "preferential distribution" of cash?

B. APPORTIONING PARTNERSHIP LIABILITIES

Attribution of partnership debt to particular partners is crucial to any taxpayer who plans to invest in a partnership that may operate at a loss. Section § 704(d) limits the pass-through effect of each partner's share of the losses to his or her outside basis, with any excess carried forward to future years. To the extent a partner is attributed a share of partnership debt, her outside basis increases as if she had contributed cash to the partnership. §§ 722 and 752. As you will see, apportioning partnership liabilities among the partners is an involved process. Section 752 purports to apportion liabilities among the partners, but the real authority in the area is found in the regulations under § 752 and companion provisions in the § 704 Regulations. Note that one must work simultaneously with the § 704 and § 752 Regulations, as they are interdependent.

1. APPORTIONING RECOURSE LIABILITIES

The core idea of the Regulations is to allocate recourse liabilities to partners who bear the economic risk of loss associated with each particular liability. The Regulations take the view that a partner bears the economic risk of loss for a

---

[11] §§ 731(a)(1) and 741.
[12] §§ 731(a)(2) and 741.

partnership liability to the extent that the partner (or someone related to the partner) would bear the economic burden of discharging the obligation created by the liability if the partnership were financially unable to discharge it. This forces an evaluation of how the parties agreed to share economic losses arising out of partnership liabilities.[13]

A liability is recourse to the extent at least one partner[14] bears the economic risk of loss for the liability. Reg. § 1.752-1(a). The Regulations find an economic risk if and to the extent the partner has a personal duty to make a net payment to a creditor or other person, or to make a net contribution to the partnership in the event of liquidation, or if the partner is the lender and the liability is nonrecourse to the partnership.[15]

To determine whether any partner bears the economic risk of loss, one applies a hypothetical liquidation test in which one evaluates the effect of a sudden end of the partnership. In running through this imaginary doomsday liquidation of the partnership, one presumes the following things will occur: the partnership's assets become worthless; all liabilities fall due; the partnership surrenders its assets to its creditors; and the partnership allocates all of its operating results as of that moment among the partners per the partnership agreement and then liquidates. Reg. § 1.752-1(a), (b)(1). Moreover, each partner is generally presumed solvent and able to pay any liability he or she is allocated, even if the facts indicate otherwise, a simplifying assumption to put it mildly. Reg. § 1.752-1(b)(6). A key factor is that each encumbered property's disposition will produce a loss because there will be no amount realized. The losses will then be apportioned according to the directives in the partnership agreement. Reg. § 1.752-1(b)(2)(ii). For example, if the partners are equal members of a general partnership, they share partnership recourse liabilities equally, absent some other agreement. Generally, limited partners are never liable for recourse debt, unless they somehow manufacture personal liability by such acts as signing guarantees[16] or other side agreements. See R.U.L.P.A. § 303. The general result of this elaborate system is to allocate recourse debt in accordance with the proportions in which the partners share partnership losses.

---

[13] This analysis also applies to tiered partnerships. If an upper-tier partnership is a partner in a subsidiary partnership, the liabilities of the sub to outsiders are apportioned to the upper-tier partnership for purposes of applying § 752 to the partners in the upper-tier partnership. Reg. § 1.752-1T(j)(1).

[14] The Regulations regularly refer to partners or persons related to the partner. The text overlooks this complication.

[15] A partner's contribution of his own note is considered part of his net capital contribution for § 752 purposes. Reg. § 1.752-2(h)(4). A loan is also recourse to the extent of the fair market value of assets pledged to secure a loan or contributed to the partnership solely in order to provide security for a partnership liability. Reg. § 1.752-2(h)(1)-(2).

[16] A limited partner's guaranty is effective only if she waives her right of subrogation. See Reg. § 1.752-2(f), example (4).

B. APPORTIONING PARTNERSHIP LIABILITIES

PROBLEM 5-4

M and D organize the MD general partnership. The initial contributions will be $20,000 from M and $20,000 from D. The partnership will then borrow $60,000 from an unrelated lender, with recourse, to buy a property for $100,000. The allocation provisions will satisfy the § 704(b) regulations, including an obligation to restore capital account deficits. M, your client, wants to be allocated 90% of the losses. D agrees to this. M wants to know his basis in the MD partnership. What is your opinion? *See* Reg. § 1.752-2(f), Example 1.

2. APPORTIONING NONRECOURSE LIABILITIES

Although commercial nonrecourse debt is a rarity in the present economy, Reg. § 1.752-3 nevertheless tells one how it is apportioned to each partner.[17] The general rule remains as it was under prior law; namely, it is generally apportioned in accordance with how the partners share profits,[18] the theory apparently being that the debt will only be paid off out of partnership profits. Moreover, there is a special option to specially apportion nonrecourse debt, by specifying the partner's interest in partnership profits for purposes of allocating nonrecourse liabilities in the partnership agreement. *See* Reg. § 1.752-3(a)(3). However, the Regulations put two rules ahead of the general rule.

1. One first apportions nonrecourse debt in accordance with each partner's share of partnership minimum gain, meaning the gain that the partnership would recognize if it sold the encumbered asset for the amount of the debt; this is the minimum gain that the partnership can realize if it abandoned the property.[19] This is a most interesting provision. It means that if a partner is allocated deductions based on someone else's money, she gets a share of the debt sufficient to cover such deductions. It is not often that the partnership allocation provisions are so generous. On the other hand, one must remember that the nonrecourse debt rules primarily benefit the real estate industry, and that industry has enormous lobbying power.

---

[17] It is common in noncommercial settings. People regularly lend each other cash on an unsecured basis or sell property to each other without security.

[18] Using the general profit-sharing ratio as the guiding principle has its shortcomings. There may in fact be no general profit-sharing ratio because the partnership agreement is nothing but a mass of special allocations, or there may be a general profit-sharing ratio, but it may be subject to change if and when some specified level of profitability occurs. The Regulations acknowledge this problem and attempt to adapt to it by declaring that special allocations of profit for this purpose are valid if, *inter alia*, they are consistent with some significant items of partnership income or gain. Reg. § 1.752-3(a)(3).

[19] Note how this protects a partner who contributes appreciated property subject to nonrecourse debt from recognizing gain on that contribution.

To illustrate: Assume A is a limited partner with an 80% profit-and-loss-sharing ratio and that B is the general partner with the remaining 20% interest in the cash-method AB limited partnership, which has not made a special allocation of nonrecourse liabilities. Assume the AB partnership borrows $1,000 on a nonrecourse basis in order to buy a building, which it depreciates at the rate of $100 per year. Assume the $1,000 was the sole consideration for the purchase. Further assume that the building and the partnership generate no other receipts or disbursements and that at the end of the partnership's first taxable year it has claimed $100 of depreciation and, therefore, has a $900 basis in the building. If the partnership abandoned the building, it would have a gain of $100, the excess of the loan over the partnership's basis in the building. This is the minimum gain. Because A claimed an $80 depreciation deduction, A has an $80 minimum gain and is apportioned $80 of the "first" $100 of partnership debt; B has a $20 minimum gain. The $900 balance is shared in accordance with the partners' profit-sharing ratios, which is again 80:20, so A is apportioned a total of $80 plus $720, for a total of $800. B is apportioned the remaining $200. Note that A's claim to depreciation deductions depends on the partnership agreement's containing a "minimum gain chargeback." That matter is taken up shortly under the heading "Allocating Deductions Attributable to Nonrecourse Debt."

2. One next apportions gain in accordance with the partner's share of § 704(c) gain. This is the share of gain that the contributing partner must report as a result of contributing property with a value in excess of basis. Reg. § 1.752-3(a)(2). This coordinates the general rule of § 704(c) with the debt apportionment rules. You will not see it referred to again in this treatise or in the problems.

Liabilities that are not attributed to partners under rules "1" and "2" are referred to as "excess nonrecourse liabilities," and are shared in accordance with profit-sharing ratios or pursuant to a special allocation of nonrecourse debt if consistent with the allocation of some other significant deduction attributable to such debt. Reg. § 1.752-3(a)(3).

PROBLEM 5-5

X and Y become partners, X as the general partner and Y as the limited partner. X contributes $10 and Y contributes $90. XY then buys a building for $1,000, encumbered by $900 of nonrecourse debt, which calls for no principal

B. APPORTIONING PARTNERSHIP LIABILITIES

payments until maturity. Assume that the allocation provisions are valid (they are discussed under the next heading) and that they call for allocating 90% of the profits and losses in favor of Y, but a special 50:50 allocation of the nonrecourse debt. The partnership agreement contains a "flip-flop" provision that changes the overall allocations to 50:50 after Y has recovered his capital. Some years later, but before the "flip-flop" occurs, there is a $50 minimum gain because the property has a basis of $750 but is subject to a debt of $800. According to their partnership agreement, X and Y have a $5/$45 share of the minimum gain, respectively. The partners believe this means the debt is apportioned as follows:

	X	Y
Minimum Gain	5	45
§ 704(c) allocation	0	0
Excess nonrecourse liabilities	375	375
TOTAL	380	420

Do you agree with their analysis? *See* Reg. § 1.752-3.

3. ALLOCATING DEDUCTIONS ATTRIBUTABLE TO NONRECOURSE DEBT

The partners will not in fact bargain over how to allocate nonrecourse debt. They will argue over allocating deductions and refinancing proceeds that are founded on nonrecourse debt. The results of that bargaining will determine how nonrecourse liabilities are allocated.

So far, one can see that a partner can get outside basis as a result of the partnership's borrowing money on a nonrecourse basis, and the partners can bargain over how the debt will be apportioned. The next question is how partners can claim deductions on the strength of such debt. The two issues are intertwined.

a. Background

The Regulations resolve this enigma by validating the allocation of nonrecourse deductions any way the partners agree, provided the allocation meets a four-part test, a key aspect of which is that there must be a so-called "minimum-gain chargeback." Reg. § 1.704-2(e)(3)(f). The basic problem in this area is that, in reality, no allocation of a deduction based on nonrecourse debt is borne by the partner claiming the deduction. It is borne by the lender. The Treasury Department, therefore, could have written regulations requiring the partners to share such deductions in accordance with their relative capital accounts, or just equally. Either would be equally lacking in economic substance. At the opposite extreme, the Treasury Department might have permitted deductions of such items willy nilly, on the theory that the entire area lacked substance. In fact, it chose a middle ground which does not require economic substance (by dropping a firm deficit make-up requirement from the partnership agreement), but does require that, when the property is sold, any deductions based on the lender's debt be allocated to the partners who got those gains resulting from those deductions.[20] This pattern creates "tax substance," in the sense that the tax benefit of the prior deductions will be reversed in the form of an extra measure of gain when the property is disposed of, but only to the extent the gain was based on depreciation deductions that, in a more normal world, would have been deducted by the lender, because it bears the real economic risk of loss of value of the property. This is favorable to taxpayers because it allows them the benefit of the time value of money; that is, it allows current cost recovery deductions which are later repaid (in the form of a later tax burden) without indexing the repayment for inflation or interest.

The amount of gain that is charged back to the partners collectively at the time of disposition is referred to as the "minimum gain." *See* Reg. § 1.704-1(b)(4)(iv)(c). It is the minimum gain, in the sense that it represents what the partnership would report as gain if the partnership allowed the lender to foreclose and take back the property. For example, if a partnership received contributions of $100 and borrowed $900 to buy a depreciable building, the first $100 of depreciation deductions would be seen as coming out of the partners' capital. Any further depreciation will produce minimum gain, and that minimum gain will grow in amount as the years pass. Henceforth, in the interest of economy of language this book refers only to depreciation deductions; in fact the analysis refers to other deductions based on nonrecourse debt, such as operating expenses.

b. The Four-Part Test

The Regulations allow the partnership to allocate this depreciation any way the partners care to, but only if four rigorous tests are met. If they are not met, such depreciation deductions are shared in accordance with the partners' overall interests in the partnership, which calls for an *ad hoc* analysis. Reg. § 1.704-2(b)(1). NB: These rules apply only to allocations of "nonrecourse deductions," meaning deductions built on the partnership's minimum gain.

First, the allocation agreement on all material tax items *other than* the nonrecourse deductions must have substantial economic effect, under the general or alternative economic effect tests. Reg. § 1.704-2(e)(4). This is just an extra barrier erected by the Treasury Department. Note how difficult it is for smaller partnerships to comply.

---

[20] There is also required, discussed below, that the nonrecourse deductions be consistent with some other material item relating to the property secured by the debt. This tends to import a further measure of realism into the allocation of nonrecourse deductions.

B. APPORTIONING PARTNERSHIP LIABILITIES

Second, the allocation of nonrecourse deductions must be "reasonably consistent" with some other significant partnership item attributable to the property securing the nonrecourse liabilities of the partnership. Reg. § 1.704-2(e)(2). Presumably, such items would include maintenance costs, local property taxes or interest expenses attributable to the secured property. This is not quite as bad as it sounds, partly because the "other significant items" can be realized by the partnership in future years. For example, if interest or operating expenses with respect to the encumbered property are allocated in the same proportions, this test should be met. This puts a mild damper on truly flamboyant allocations of deductions based on nonrecourse debt. The regulations also treat the present or future overall profit- and loss-sharing ratio as a significant item. Reg. § 1.704-2(m), Ex.(1)(ii).

Third, the partnership agreement must satisfy the first two prongs of the three-part mechanical test or the alternative economic effect test, except as to nonrecourse liabilities. This requires inclusion in the partnership agreement of either a deficit make-up provision or a QIO. Reg. § 1.704-2(e)(1). In *Orrisch*, there was neither. Requiring only a QIO seems the equivalent of twenty lashes with a wet noodle, because in substance a QIO is just legal "boilerplate" language grafted onto the partnership agreement.

Fourth, starting when there are nonrecourse deductions (or distributions of the proceeds of nonrecourse liabilities),[21] there must be a minimum gain chargeback in the partnership agreement. The following language addresses the need for a minimum gain chargeback. The language was excerpted from the same partnership agreement as was quoted before:

> "(vi) After the application of (v) above [the QIO], but prior to the application for such fiscal year of any other provision of this section, if there is a net decrease in partnership minimum gain attributable to a partner nonrecourse debt during a fiscal year, then any partner with a share of the partnership minimum gain attributable to such debt at the beginning of such year shall be allocated items of income and gain for such year (and, if necessary, subsequent years) in the amount and proportions necessary to satisfy the provisions of Treasury Regulation Sections 1.704-2(b)(2) and 1.704-2(j)."

A reduction in minimum gain will typically occur when the partnership pays down principal on the nonrecourse debt or when the secured property is sold. The following is an example of a nonrecourse allocation that works:

> *To illustrate*: A is a general partner with a 10% profit share and B is a limited partner with a 90% share of profits. They agree that once B recoups his investment, they will share profits 50:50.

---

[21]The concept operates this way: if the partnership refinances its nonrecourse debt so as to get extra cash, any following partnership deductions are treated as nonrecourse deductions.

Assuming there is a "reasonable likelihood" that 90:10 and 50:50 provisions will in fact apply to "significant amounts of income,"[22] any allocation of nonrecourse items to B from 9:1 to 1:1 will be valid, provided the 9:1 and 1:1 allocations themselves have substantial economic effect. *See* Reg. § 1.704-2(m), Example (1)(ii).

C. VARYING INTRA-YEAR CAPITAL SHARES

The partners can retroactively change their distributive shares by means of amending the partnership agreement. In such cases, the only question is whether the allocation has substantial economic effect. By contrast, if a partner changes his *capital interest*, a more rigorous set of rules crops up under § 706. The thrust of the rules is to assure that the changes are only prospective.

1. VARYING CAPITAL INTERESTS

Read § 706(c) and (d)(1).

If the partner's proportionate interest in capital changed but was not eliminated, the distributive share is determined as if the partnership earned its income or loss at exactly the same daily rate over the course of the year. § 706(c)(1), (d)(1); Reg. § 1.706-1(c)(4). That makes the allocation process easy.

To illustrate: The equal AB partnership is on the cash method and uses the calendar year. It earned a net profit of $100 in 1994. Partner A sold half of his one-half interest to B on June 30, 1994. As a result, A reports $37.50 for the year (i.e., $25 for the first half of the year and $12.50 for the balance of the year), regardless of when the AB partnership earned the income. This would be true even if the partnership earned $100 in the first half of its year and nothing in the second half.

If, instead, the profit share were changed for the whole year by simply amending the partnership agreement after the end of the year with no sale or exchange, § 706(c) would not apply, because there was no intra-year change of ownership of capital interests.[23] By legal magic, the interest is retroactively rendered constant. This scenario is common in service partnerships in which profit shares are worked out around the end of the year and based on the partners' relative performances.

---

[22] This is a virtual certainty unless the partnership agreement contains a mass of special allocations such that the bottom-line allocations are an illusion.

[23] *See* Joint Comm. on Tax'n, General Explanation of the Tax Reform Act of 1984, 98th Cong, 2d Sess 219 (1984).

C. VARYING INTRA-YEAR CAPITAL SHARES

2. ADMISSION OF NEW PARTNER

A new partner may be admitted by making a contribution to the partnership. In such cases, the "varying interests" approach described above applies where there has been an intra-year change of proportionate capital interests. § 706(d)(1). The power to amend the agreement under § 761 may trump the fluctuating interest rules of § 706[24]. This is an area in need of regulations and Congressional action on the relationship of § 706 to § 761.

3. SALE, EXCHANGE, OR LIQUIDATION OF ENTIRE INTEREST

The daily proration approach does not apply — and instead there is an imaginary closing of the books which results in two tax years — if the partner sells the entire interest, or if the entire interest is liquidated (i.e., the interest is bought back by the partnership). The closing is solely as to the affected partner.

To illustrate: The equal AB partnership had a $100 profit for the first half of 1995 and a $100 loss for the second half. If A sold his entire interest to C in the middle of the year, A would report income of $50, even though the partnership broke even for the year.

Note the tax planning that can result; hold back a tiny share of a partnership interest and there is an automatic daily proration — dispose of it all and there are two synthetic taxable years as to the selling partner. Note also that *if all the partners agree*, the partnership can elect to use the daily proration approach instead of an interim closing. Reg. § 1.706-1(c)(2)(ii) contains the details.

PROBLEM 5-6

The calendar year, accrual method ABCD partnership lost $13,000 by the beginning of December 1995. It will make $1,000 in December. If D sells his interest to E and the partnership admits E as a new one-fourth partner on December 1, to what extent can E share in the $12,000 loss for 1995?

4. CASH-METHOD ITEMS LIMIT

Read § 706(d)(2).

In the interest of preventing tax manipulation by accelerating or deferring certain payments, § 706(d)(2) puts cash-method partnerships on the accrual method for purposes of calculating daily prorations. As a result, each partner is allocated, on a daily basis, his or her prorata share of various items economically accrued during his or her days of membership. This only applies to so-called "allocable cash basis items." These are items Congress considers prone to being

---

[24] This is the view of W. McKee, W. Nelson & R. Whitmire, Federal Taxation of Partnerships and Partners Vol. 1, § 11.05[2].

manipulated, namely interest, taxes, payments for services or the use of property, and any similar item to be specified in regulations that may have a material distorting effect. This proviso applies both to income and deductions, and it applies whether the partnership used a level proration or interim closing method. The practical effect is that these items must be prorated over the year. As a result, a partner who sells or liquidates her entire interest can neither shift these items to an incoming partner nor hoard them, and it limits abuses of the interim closing method. For example, if in the preceding problem the partnership delayed paying a $4,000 interest expense until December 15, E's deduction would not be $1,000 but would instead be $83.33, (i.e., $1,000 ÷ 12).

D. FAMILY PARTNERSHIPS

Read § 704(e)(1).

In principle, there is no reason why family members should not be able to form partnerships to conduct business or to make investments. In fact, there is good reason for the IRS to be leery of them, because family partnerships invite shifting income to members who are in relatively low tax brackets, thereby minimizing the family's overall federal income tax burden.

1. RECOGNITION OF THE FAMILY PARTNERSHIP

If capital is a material income-producing factor, the safe-harbor rule of § 704(e)(1) recognizes the partnership as long as the transfer of partnership interest is genuine. This will call for adequate protection of a particularly young or malleable donee, by such means as a guardianship or a trust for the donee. Reg. § 1.704-1(e)(2)(viii). In the case of a service partnership, however, there is no such safe harbor and the partnership will be validated only if it is a bona fide venture. *See Commissioner v. Culbertson*, 337 U.S. 733 (1949).

BALLOU v. UNITED STATES
64-2 U.S. Tax Cas.
(CCH) P9591; 15 A.F.T.R.2d
(P-H) 886 (S.D.Ohio 1964)

PECK, D.J.:

THE COURT: Ladies and gentlemen of the jury, in accordance with certain requests that have been received from counsel for the parties the Court will first read to you requested instructions which are in written form and which will accompany you to the jury room.

Special Instruction Number 1. "The Internal Revenue Code, which is the law governing this case, provides that a person shall be recognized as a partner if he owns a capital interest in a partnership in which capital is a material income-producing factor, whether or not such interest was derived by gift from

D. FAMILY PARTNERSHIPS

any other person. A trust may be a partner in a partnership as well as an individual. If you find that the three trusts for the respective benefit of James D. Ballou, Jr., Edward Wayne Ballou and Mary Ruth Ballou owned a capital interest in Ballou Services in 1956, 1957 and 1958 and if you find that capital was a material income-producing factor in the business of Ballou Services, then you will return a verdict for the plaintiffs.

"In determining whether capital is a material income-producing factor in Ballou Services, you may consider whether the partnership in the operation of its business owned typewriters, adding machines and office furniture and equipment; whether the partnership maintained an inventory of raw materials and manufactured parts; whether the partnership paid salaries to its employees; whether the partnership carried accounts receivable representing monies owed to it by customers; whether the partnership incurred liabilities of substantial amounts such as for advertising, which it required money to pay; and whether the partnership had capital invested in corporations owned by it. If you find a reasonable combination of any of the above facts to have existed in 1956, 1957 and 1958, then capital was an income-producing factor of the partnership Ballou Services. However, in general, capital is not a material income-producing factor when the income of the business is mainly derived from payments made for personal services performed by employees of the partnership."

Number 2. "If you determine that Ballou Services was a valid partnership composed of James D. Ballou, Sarah L. Ballou and James D. Ballou in his capacity as trustee of each of the three trusts for his children, James D. Ballou, Jr., Edward Wayne Ballou and Mary Ruth Ballou, that the distributive share of the partnership income owned by the three trusts has been determined in 1956, 1957 and 1958 after an allowance of reasonable compensation for services rendered to the partnership by James D. Ballou, and that the share of the partnership income attributable to the capital of the trusts is not proportionately greater than the share of the partnership income attributable to the capital of Mr. Ballou and Mrs. Ballou, then you will return a verdict for the plaintiffs."

Number 3. "A father and mother may, if they want to, make gifts of their property to their children, or to a trustee for their children. They may give cash, an automobile, real estate or an interest in a business which is being conducted in the form of a partnership. If a parent actually gives away an interest in a partnership business to his sons and daughters or a trustee for them, thereafter the proportionate share of the earnings of that business attributable to the interest given to the children's trustee belongs to the children's trustee and should be taxed to him. If you find that Mr. and Mrs. Ballou made such gifts to the trustee for their minor children, you will return a verdict for the plaintiffs."

Special Charge Number 4. "You are instructed that the Commissioner of Internal Revenue has made a determination that the three trusts involved in this case were not genuine owners of a capital interest in Ballou Services. I instruct you as a matter of law that this determination by the Commissioner is presumed to be correct. This does not mean that you ladies and gentlemen must accept the determination as correct. However, it does mean that the plaintiffs, Mr. and Mrs. Ballou, have the burden of proving that the Commissioner was wrong by a preponderance of the evidence."

Number 5. "I charge you that in determining whether partnership interests among members of a family are genuine, bona fide and valid, there must be a careful scrutiny made of the transactions and all surrounding circumstances."

Number 6. "The basic requirements for recognition of a partnership as bona fide, valid and genuine, are: (1) The existence of a genuine intent on the part of the participants to actually carry on business together as partners, wherein each is the true owner of capital used in the business or furnishes services useful to the partnership business; and, (2) having such intent that they conduct the business in accordance with a genuine partnership relationship."

Number 7. "Whether the trusts shall be recognized as owners of genuine partnership interests is to be ascertained from all of the facts and circumstances of the case. The reality of the trust ownership is to be determined in the light of the transactions as a whole and not from isolated facts. The execution of legally sufficient documents under State law is a factor to be considered but is not determinative of the reality of the alleged partnership interests."

Number 8. "One of the important factors, ladies and gentlemen, to be taken into account in deciding whether the trust actually owned a capital interest in Ballou Services is the extent to which the creator of the trust retained controls over the alleged trust property. In other words, one of the important factors in this case is the extent to which Mr. and Mrs. Ballou retained control over the partnership interests which they allegedly gave to the trusts.

"If you find that the creators of the trusts retained such controls that they, in effect, remained the substantial owners of the trust property, then you must not recognize the trusts as genuine partners in Ballou Services."

Number 9 and finally: "I charge you that one may be recognized as a partner only if his alleged partnership interest was acquired in a bona fide transaction, not as a sham for tax avoidance purposes."...

Immediately upon your retirement to the jury room you will elect one of your number as foreman or forelady to preside over your deliberations, and when a verdict has been reached you will indicate that fact to the Court through the bailiff.

Gentlemen, are there any specific requests?

MR. VOGELER: May I approach the Bench?

THE COURT: Yes.

(The following took place at the Bench out of the hearing of the jury:)

MR. VOGELER: In connection with the special charge which was presented by the defendant, which I think is number 8, which contains the language that the partnership is not valid if it was created for tax avoidance you did not insert the word "solely." In other words, tax considerations made by a party; tax avoidance and tax evasion, your Honor, are two different things.

D. FAMILY PARTNERSHIPS

MR. ZAPRUDER: I would hardly characterize it as solely either. I think "principally tax evasion."

MR. VOGELER: I think, your Honor, I have the wrong number.

MR. GARBIS: The instruction does say it is a mere sham. That would indicate that it would be solely for the purpose, the idea of mere sham.

MR. VOGELER: Requested that the words "not solely for tax avoidance purpose — "

MR. ZAPRUDER: We agreed on "principal," didn't we?

MR. VOGELER: There is nothing wrong, your Honor, as to avoid the greatest amount of tax. The Court has so stated.

MR. ZAPRUDER: The Supreme Court has also indicated —

THE COURT: I will put in the words "not principally or solely."

MR. VOGELER: All right.

MR. ZAPRUDER: Your Honor, in the first special charge the concluding clause is "If you find a reasonable combination of any of the events." We believe that the test is consideration of all of the facts in the case. They have specified certain facts; that there are other facts to be considered, which are not.

THE COURT: You may have an exception to that.

MR. VOGELER: I would like to raise one further question, your Honor, and that is in your statement of the general charge you instructed the jury that there were three elements on which we had the burden of proof. We claim and we allege that the third element is an alternative and not a concomitant of the first two, the third element being the capital as a material income-producing factor.

The Code Section, 704(e)(1) talks about capital as a material income-producing factor. The Code Section 704(e)(2) does not. The general heading of Section 704 is "Family partnerships." The 704(e)(1) speaks of capital as a material income-producing factor. Section 704(e)(2) is entirely separate, stands on its own feet and does not require capital as a material income-producing factor. All it requires is -

MR. ZAPRUDER: Your Honor, I don't have the Code with me.

THE COURT: Do you agree with that or disagree?

MR. ZAPRUDER: I disagree.

THE COURT: That's my understanding of the law and, Mr. Vogeler, the record may show your exception to that.

MR. GARBIS: Your Honor, may I make a formal exception to the charges which the Court has renumbered 12, 13, 14, 15, 16, 17 and 18, which are the defendant's requested instructions respectively 17, 16, 15, 14, 12, 7 and 6, and the Government will specifically note that there is no objection to the Court's refusal to grant the charges which the Court has renumbered 19 through 22.

(End of conference at Bench.)

THE COURT: Ladies and gentlemen of the jury, an amendment has been made to one of the special charges which has been read to you. It is special charge number 9 and the amendment has been made by long-hand interlineation on the charge. So there may be no misunderstanding concerning it, special charge number 9 as amended reads as follows:

> "One may be recognized as a partner only if his alleged partnership interest was acquired in a bona fide transaction, not principally or solely for tax avoidance purposes."

The jury may be excused.
(Thereupon, at 10:11 o'clock A.M., the jury retired from the courtroom.)

Special Interrogatories for the Jury

The defendant, United States of America, respectfully requests the Court to submit the following Special Interrogatories to the jury pursuant to Rule 49(a) of the Federal Rules of Civil Procedure:

1. Have the plaintiffs proven by a preponderance of the evidence that each of the three trusts which they created for their children genuinely owned a fifteen per cent capital interest in Ballou Services?

No / (Yes or No)

[Because] the answer to Question No. 1 is "No," there is no need to answer any further questions....

NOTES

1. *When is capital a material income-producing factor?* Reg. § 1.704-1(e)(1)(iv) considers that "substantial inventories" or a "substantial investment in plant, machinery and equipment" are generally required, but the courts have been more liberal, even going so far as to hold that a partnership's goodwill can qualify as long as it is a substantial source of the partnership's revenues. *Bateman v. United States*, 490 F.2d 549 (9th Cir. 1973).

2. *Competent minors.* Minors can be partners for federal income tax purposes if they are competent to fend for themselves. Reg. § 1.704-1(e)(2)(viii). If they cannot fend for themselves, their partnership interests will have to be held by trustees, custodians, or guardians.

3. *Distributions of partnership interests from trusts.* If a trust distributes appreciated assets to a beneficiary, there is generally no tax to the trust. Rev. Rul. 55-117, 1955-1 C.B. 233. There is a tax if the distribution satisfies a specific pecuniary amount (say $10,000). *Id.* As a result, a trust can hold a partnership interest, which it can generally distribute tax-free to the beneficiary or beneficiaries. The price paid is that the beneficiary will take the trust's basis in the partnership interest.

2. LIMITS ON ALLOCATIONS

Read § 704(e)(2).

D. FAMILY PARTNERSHIPS

Assuming that the family partnership is viable, the donee or family buyer is taxed on his or her distributive share of partnership income, but § 704(e)(2) imposes two important limits:

1. The donor and every other service provider must be reasonably compensated *before* partnership profits can be allocated, and
2. The donee's or related buyer's distributive share of partnership profits cannot be proportionately greater, by reference to capital interests, than the distributive share allocated to the donor or related seller.

PROBLEM 5-7

Mom runs a general store. She sold a one-third interest in the capital of the store operation to her husband, as a full-time employee of another company, for $30,000 on January 1 of the present year. They agree to share profits and losses 50:50. The store is a cash-method, calendar-year partnership. Her services are worth $40,000 per year. The store earned a net profit of $100,000 this year, before compensation to Mom. She took no compensation for services this year. What is her husband's distributive share of partnership profits this year?

OUTSIDE READINGS

H. Abrams, *Long-Awaited Regulations Under Section 752 Provide Wrong Answers*, 44 Tax L. Rev. 627 (1989).

B. Bittker & L. Lokken, Federal Taxation of Income, Estates and Gifts Ch. 86 (2d ed. 1989).

S. Boyer, *Family Partnerships: Who Must Recognize the Income*, 44 Mo. L. Rev. 217 (1979).

M. Burke & M. Friel, *Allocating Partnership Liabilities*, 41 Tax L. Rev. 173 (1986).

L. Lokken, *Partnership Allocations*, 41 Tax L. Rev. 547 (1986).

J. Steines, *Partnership Allocations of Built-In Gain or Loss*, 45 Tax L. Rev. 615 (1990).

S. Utz, *Partnership Taxation in Transition: Of Form, Substance and Economic Risk*, 44 Tax Law. 693 (1990).

Chapter 6
SALES AND EXCHANGES OF PARTNERSHIP INTERESTS

Read §§ 741 and 751(a)-(d).

If one were building a tax system from scratch, one would almost surely be puzzled as to how one ought to treat the sale of a partnership interest. If one believed that the aggregate concept should predominate over the entity concept, one would prefer to treat the sale of the partnership interest as a *de facto* sale of a share of each partnership asset. This is how sole proprietorships are taxed when they are sold. *See Williams v. McGowan*, 152 F.2d 570 (2d Cir. 1945). At the opposite extreme, one might prefer to use the entity model, taxing the sale of the interest as if it were a share of corporate stock. This is the view reflected in RULPA at § 704 for transfers of limited partnership interests.

Early judicial decisions echoed the entity concept embodied in state law and treated the sale of a partnership interest much like the sale of common stock. *See, e.g., Long v. Commissioner*, 173 F.2d 471 (5th Cir. 1949). This effectively let partners convert unrealized ordinary income into long-term capital gains. Even the income the partnership earned during the year in which the interest was sold was converted into capital gain. *Swiren v. Commissioner*, 183 F.2d 656 (7th Cir. 1950).

In enacting § 741, the 1954 Congress continued the basic analogy to the sale of common stock. Once Congress established that the sale of a partnership interest involved the transfer of a single asset rather than of a ratable share of each portion of the "mixed grill" of partnership assets, the transaction fitted neatly into the usual rules of § 1001 involving sales of property of any sort. However, Congress also attempted to plug the loopholes of prior law. It did so by means of § 751, which selectively converts gain based on unrealized ordinary income in the hands of the partnership into ordinary income in the hands of the partner, and § 706, which requires a sharing of the income for the year of sale between the buyer and the seller.

This chapter assumes that the sale is aboveboard, and not a matched liquidation of one partner's interest combined with the admission of a new partner. Section 707(a)(2)(B) rightly treats the matched liquidation-admission as a taxable sale of a partnership interest from the withdrawing partner to the newly admitted partner, rather than two tax-deferred transactions. Chapter 4 discussed § 707(a)(2)(B).

A. TAXATION OF THE SELLER: THE GENERAL RULE

Read §§ 706(c)-(d).

The vital Code provision here is § 741, which at heart declares that a partner who transfers a partnership interest must recognize a gain or loss on the transaction. More significantly, the section goes on to say that the transaction is deemed a sale or exchange of a capital asset, a unique provision, but probably not much of a loophole, since there are few dealers in partnership interests.[1]

Section 741 has a broad sway. It covers sales to strangers, sales to fellow partners, sales by the partners as a group to a third person, and even the sale of one partner's interest to the one remaining partner. Reg. § 1.741-1(b).

One uses familiar principles to determine the partner's gain or loss. The amount realized includes the cash or fair market value of other consideration received by the selling partner plus the selling partner's share of partnership liabilities, as defined by § 752(d). The seller's adjusted basis in the partnership interest is outside basis, adjusted to reflect the seller's pro rata share of partnership income or loss from the start of the current taxable year up to the date of sale. *See* § 705(a).

> *To illustrate:* C is a one-third member of the ABC partnership, which uses the cash method and is on the calendar year. C is a calendar-year, cash-method taxpayer and has a prior-year-end basis of $100 in her partnership interest. She sells her interest to D for $150 on June 30. ABC earns $300 in the January 1-June 30 period. She will report $100 as her interim distributive share of partnership income and will, therefore, increase her basis to $200. Ignoring any § 751 issues, she will report a $50 capital loss on the sale to D.

PROBLEM 6-1

Assume that X and Y are individuals who form the XY general partnership, in which they are equal members. The individuals and the partnership use the cash method and calendar year. Assume that XY has recourse liabilities of $50,000 and that X sells his interest to Z for $30,000 in cash at a time when X has an outside basis of $40,000. Assume that Z assumes X's share of the partnership's liabilities. What is X's gain or loss?

---

[1] There may be dealers in publicly-traded partnerships, but most of those partnerships are taxed as corporations.

Because one must adjust the seller's outside basis to reflect the seller's share of partnership income or loss up to the date of sale, one must know how to do the proration. The applicable rule here is that the partnership's taxable year closes as to the partner who sells her entire interest, unless all the partners agree to a level proration which treats every day as equally profitably or unprofitable, as the case may be. § 706(c)(2)(A); Reg. § 1.706-1(c)(2)(ii). If the partner sells only part of her interest, the year does not close as to her, but instead the share of partnership's income or loss for the whole year attributable to the portion of the interest she sold is prorated to her on a daily basis. *See* T. Gutierrez, *When Does the Period For Allocating Partnership And S Corp. Items Begin?*, Tax Notes, June 19, 1995, p. 1659.

B. EXCEPTION FOR § 751

If taxpayers could simply sell their partnership interests like a share of stock in a C corporation, there would be a potential tax loophole. Partners could sell their interests after the partnership had developed ordinary-income producing assets such as inventories, service contracts, or unrealized receivables. (The latter would be of concern in the case of cash-method partnerships. Accrual method partnerships would already have reported income from receivables and service contracts after the services had been performed.) Though the gain realized by a selling partner under such circumstances would be based on ordinary-income producing assets, the profit would stand to be taxed at favorable long-term capital gains rates. Enter § 751, which is designed to interdict these potential conversions of ordinary income into capital gain.

Section 751 works by selectively recharacterizing gains on the disposition of the partnership interest. The exceptions under § 751 apply only if and to the extent the consideration received in the sale reflects *unrealized receivables* or *substantially appreciated inventory items*, or both combined, as those terms are specially defined in § 751(c) and (d). This has the effect of allocating sale proceeds to particular items of partnership property as if they had been sold separately in the marketplace. Thus, § 751, when applicable, results in taxing proceeds from the sale of a partnership interest in much the same way that the sale of a proprietorship would be addressed, but with one major difference; thanks to § 741, there is a capital asset backdrop for all the sale proceeds not captured by § 751.

1. CONTRACT INTERESTS AS UNREALIZED RECEIVABLES

Reread § 751(c) and (d) and then decide for yourself if the following case reaches a reasonable result.

LEDOUX v. COMMISSIONER
77 T.C. 293 (1981),
aff'd, 695 F.2d 1320 (11th Cir. 1983)

STERRETT, JUDGE.

After concessions, the sole issue remaining for our decision is whether any portion of the amount received by petitioner John W. Ledoux pursuant to an agreement for the sale of a partnership interest was attributable to an unrealized receivable of the partnership and thus was required to be characterized as ordinary income under section 751, I.R.C. 1954.

Findings of Fact

[The petitioner was partner in the Collins-Ledoux partnership, the purpose of which was to manage and operate a dog racing track in Florida. The track itself was the property of an unrelated taxpayer, the Sanford-Orlando Kennel Club, Inc. The Collins-Ledoux partnership was obligated to pay the first $200,000 of annual net profits to Sanford-Orlando. The track was highly profitable.]

After the 1972 racing season two of the partners, Jerry Collins and Jack Collins, decided to purchase petitioner's 25-percent partnership interest. They agreed to allow Ledoux to propose a fair selling price for his interest. Ledoux set a price based on a price-earnings multiple of 5 times his share of the Partnership's 1972 earnings. This resulted in a total value for his 25-percent interest of $800,000. There was no valuation or appraisal of specific assets at the time, and the sales price included his interest in all of the assets of the Partnership....

On his 1972 Federal income tax return, petitioner properly elected to report the gain from the sale of his partnership interest under the installment method as prescribed in section 453. Petitioner calculated the total gain on such sale to be as follows:

Sales price	$ 800,000.00
Basis in partnership interest	62,658.70
Total gain on sale	$ 737,341.30

During 1972, 1973 and 1974 petitioner received payments in accordance with the October 17, 1972 Agreement of Sale. In each of those years, he characterized the reported gain, calculated pursuant to the installment sales method, as capital gain.

After consummation of the sale of petitioner's interest in the Collins-Ledoux Partnership, the remaining partners continued to operate the dog track under the Agreement of July 9, 1955 as amended.

Respondent, in his notice of deficiency, did not disagree with petitioner's calculation of the total gain. However, he determined that $ 575,392.50 of the

B. EXCEPTION FOR § 751

gain was related to petitioner's interest in the Dog Track Agreement and should be subject to ordinary income treatment pursuant to section 751.[2]

Opinion

The sole issue presented is whether a portion of the amount received by petitioner on the sale of his 25-percent partnership interest is taxable as ordinary income and not as capital gain. More specifically, we must decide whether any portion of the sales price is attributable to "unrealized receivables" of the Partnership.

Generally, gain or loss on the sale or exchange of a partnership interest is treated as capital gain or loss. Sec. 741. Prior to 1954, a partner could escape ordinary income tax treatment on his portion of the partnership's unrealized receivables by selling or exchanging his interest in the partnership and treating the gain or loss therefrom as capital gain or loss. To curb such abuses, section 751 was enacted to deal with the problem of the so-called "collapsible partnership." *See* S. Rept. 1622, 83d Cong., 2d Sess. 98 (1954)....

Petitioner contends that the Dog Track Agreement gave the Collins-Ledoux Partnership the right to manage and operate the dog track. According to petitioner, the Agreement did not give the Partnership any contractual rights to receive future payments and did not impose any obligation on the Partnership to perform services. Rather, the Agreement merely gave the Partnership the right to occupy and use all of the Corporation's properties (including the racetrack facilities and the racing permit) in operating its dog track business; if the Partnership exercised such right, it would be obligated to make annual payments to the Corporation based upon specified percentages of the annual mutuel handle. Thus, because the Dog Track Agreement was in the nature of a leasehold agreement rather than an employment contract, it did not create the type of "unrealized receivables" referred to in section 751.

Respondent, on the other hand, contends that the Partnership operated the racetrack for the Corporation and was paid a portion of the profits for its efforts. As such, the Agreement was in the nature of a management employment

---

[2] Respondent determined that the value of petitioner's proportionate share of partnership assets other than the Dog Track Agreement was as follows:

Asset	Value
Escrow deposit	$12,500.00
Sanford-Seminole Development Company stock	1,000.00
Fixed Assets	*211,107.50*
	$224,607.50

The difference between this value and the total purchase price ($800,000) was treated by respondent as having been received by petitioner in exchange for his rights in the Dog Track Agreement.

contract. When petitioner sold his partnership interest to the Collinses in 1972, the main right that he sold was a contract right to receive income in the future for yet-to-be-rendered personal services. This, respondent asserts, is supported by the fact that petitioner determined the sales price for his partnership interest by capitalizing his 1972 annual income (approximately $160,000) by a factor of 5. Therefore, respondent contends that the portion of the gain realized by petitioner that is attributable to the management contract should be characterized as an amount received for unrealized receivables of the Partnership. Consequently, such gain should be characterized as ordinary income under section 751.

The legislative history is not wholly clear with respect to the type of assets that Congress intended to place under the umbrella of "unrealized receivables." The House Report states:

> The term "unrealized receivables or fees" is used to apply to any rights to income which have not been included in gross income under the method of accounting employed by the partnership. The provision is applicable mainly to cash basis partnerships which have acquired a contractual or other legal right to income for goods or services.... [H. Rept. 1337, 83d Cong., 2d Sess. 71 (1954).]

Essentially the same language appears in the report of the Senate Committee. S. Rept. 1622, 83d Cong., 2d Sess. 98 (1954). In addition, the Regulations elaborate on the meaning of "unrealized receivables" as used in section 751. Section 1.751-1(c), Income Tax Regs., provides:

> (c) Unrealized receivables. (1) The term "unrealized receivables," ... means any rights (contractual or otherwise) to payment for —
>
> (i) Goods delivered or to be delivered (to the extent that such payment would be treated as received for property other than a capital asset), or
>
> (ii) Services rendered or to be rendered, to the extent that income arising from such rights to payment was not previously includable in income under the method of accounting employed by the partnership. Such rights must have arisen under contracts or agreements in existence at the time of sale or distribution, although the partnership may not be able to enforce payment until a later time. For example, the term includes trade accounts receivable of a cash method taxpayer, and rights to payment for work or goods begun but incomplete at the time of the sale or distribution.
>
> (3) In determining the amount of the sale price attributable to such unrealized receivables, or their value in a distribution treated as a sale or exchange, any arm's length agreement between the buyer and the seller, or between the partnership and the distributee partner, will generally establish the amount or value. In the absence of such an agreement, full account shall be taken not only of the estimated cost of completing performance of the

B. EXCEPTION FOR § 751

contract or agreement, but also of the time between the sale or distribution and the time of payment.

The language of the legislative history and the Regulations indicates that the term "unrealized receivables" includes any contractual or other right to payment for goods delivered or to be delivered or services rendered or to be rendered. Therefore, an analysis of the nature of the rights under the Dog Track Agreement, in the context of the aforementioned legal framework, becomes appropriate. A number of cases have dealt with the meaning of "unrealized receivables" and thereby have helped to define the scope of the term. Courts that have considered the term "unrealized receivables" generally have said that it should be given a broad interpretation. *Cf. Corn Products Co. v. Commissioner*, 350 U.S. 46, 52 (1955) (the term "capital asset" is to be construed narrowly, but exclusions from the definition thereof are to be broadly and liberally construed). For instance, in *Logan v. Commissioner*, 51 T.C. 482, 486 (1968), we held that a partnership's right in quantum meruit to payment for work in progress constituted an unrealized receivable even though there was no express agreement between the partnership and its clients requiring payment.

In *Roth v. Commissioner*, 321 F.2d 607 (9th Cir. 1963), *affg.* 38 T.C. 171 (1962), the Ninth Circuit dealt with the sale of an interest in a partnership which produced a movie and then gave a 10-year distribution right to Paramount Pictures Corporation in return for a percentage of the gross receipts. The selling partner claimed that his right to a portion of the payments expected under the partnership's contract with Paramount did not constitute an unrealized receivable. The court rejected this view, however, reasoning that Congress "meant to exclude from capital gains treatment any receipts which would have been treated as ordinary income to the partner if no transfer of the partnership interest had occurred." 321 F.2d at 611. Therefore, the partnership's right to payments under the distribution contract was in the nature of an unrealized receivable.

A third example of the broad interpretation given to the term "unrealized receivable" is *United States v. Edison*, 310 F.2d 111 (5th Cir. 1962), revg. an unreported opinion (W.D. Tex. 1961). The court there considered the nature of a management contract which was similar to the one at issue in the instant case. The case arose in the context of a sale by a partnership of all of its rights to operate and manage a mutual insurance company. The selling partnership received $170,000 for the rights it held under the management contract, and the government asserted that the total amount should be treated as ordinary income. The Court of Appeals agreed with the government's view on the ground that what was being assigned was not a capital asset whose value had accrued over a period of years; rather, the right to operate the company and receive profits therefrom during the remaining life of the contract was the real subject of the assignment. 310 F.2d at 116. The Fifth Circuit found the Supreme Court's holding in *Commissioner v. P.G. Lake, Inc.*, 356 U.S. 260 (1958), to be conclusive:

The substance of what was assigned was the right to receive future income. The substance of what was received was the present value of income which the recipient would otherwise obtain in the future. In short, consideration was paid for the right to receive future income, not for an increase in the value of the income-producing property. [356 U.S. at 266, cited in 310 F.2d at 115.]

In *United States v. Woolsey*, 326 F.2d 287 (5th Cir. 1963), *revg.* 208 F. Supp. 325 (S.D. Texas 1962), the Fifth Circuit again faced a situation similar to the one that we face herein. The Fifth Circuit considered whether proceeds received by taxpayers on the sale of their partnership interests were to be treated as ordinary income or capital gain. There, the court was faced with the sale of interests in a partnership which held, as one of its assets, a 25-year contract to manage a mutual insurance company. As in the instant case, the contract gave the partners the right to render services for the term of the contract and to earn ordinary income in the future. In holding that the partnership's management contract constituted an unrealized receivable, the court stated:

> When we look at the underlying right assigned in this case, we cannot escape the conclusion that so much of the consideration which relates to the right to earn ordinary income in the future under the "management contract," taxable to the assignee as ordinary income, is likewise taxable to the assignor as ordinary income although such income must be earned. Section 751 has defined "unrealized receivables" to include any rights, contractual or otherwise, to ordinary income from "services rendered, or to be rendered," (emphasis added) to the extent that the same were not previously includable in income by the partnership, with the result that capital gains rates cannot be applied to the rights to income under the facts of this case, which would constitute ordinary income had the same been received in due course by the partnership.... It is our conclusion that such portion of the consideration received by the taxpayers in this case as properly should be allocated to the present value of their right to earn ordinary income in the future under the "management contract" is subject to taxation as ordinary income.... [326 F.2d at 291.]

Petitioner attempts to distinguish *United States v. Woolsey, supra*, and *United States v. Edison, supra*, from the instant case by arguing that those cases involved a sale or termination of contracts to manage mutual insurance companies in Texas and that the management contracts therein were in the nature of employment agreements. After closely scrutinizing the facts in those cases, we conclude that petitioner's position has no merit. The fact that the *Woolsey* case involved sale of 100 percent of the partnership interests, as opposed to a sale of only a 25-percent partnership interest herein, is of no consequence. In addition, the fact that Edison involved the surrender of the partnership's contract right to

B. EXCEPTION FOR § 751 135

manage the insurance company, as opposed to the continued partnership operation in the instant case, also is not a material factual distinction.

The Dog Track Agreement at issue in the instant case is similar to the management contract considered by the Fifth Circuit in *Woolsey*. Each gives the respective partnership the right to operate a business for a period of years and to earn ordinary income in return for payments of specified amounts to the corporation that holds the state charter. Therefore, based on our analysis of the statutory language, the legislative history and the regulations and relevant case law, we are compelled to find that the Dog Track Agreement gave the petitioner an interest that amounted to an "unrealized receivable" within the meaning of section 751(c).

Petitioner further contends that the Dog Track Agreement does not represent an unrealized receivable because it does not require or obligate the Partnership to perform personal services in the future. The Agreement only gives, the argument continues, the Collins-Ledoux Partnership the right to engage in a business.

We find this argument to be unpersuasive. The words of section 751(c), providing that the term "unrealized receivable" includes the right to payment for "services rendered, or to be rendered," do not preclude that section's application to a situation where, as here, the performance of services is not required by the Agreement. As the Fifth Circuit said in *United States v. Edison, supra*:

> The fact that ... income would not be received by the [partnership] unless they performed the services which the contract required of them, that is, actively managed the affairs of the insurance company in a manner that would produce a profit after all of the necessary expenditures, does not, it seems clear, affect the nature of this payment. It affects only the amount. This is, the fact that the taxpayers would have to spend their time and energies in performing services for which the compensation would be received merely affects the price at which they would be willing to assign or transfer the contract.... [310 F.2d at 115.]

Consequently, a portion of the consideration received by Ledoux on the sale of his partnership interest is subject to taxation as ordinary income.

Having established that the Dog Track Agreement qualifies as an unrealized receivable, we next consider whether all or only part of petitioner's gain in excess of the amount attributable to his share of tangible partnership assets should be treated as ordinary income. Petitioner argues that this excess gain was attributable to goodwill or the value of a going concern.

With respect to goodwill, we note that petitioner's attorney drafted, and petitioner signed, the Agreement for Sale of Partnership Interest, dated October 17, 1972 which contains the following statement in paragraph 7:

7. In the determination of the purchase price set forth in this agreement, the parties acknowledge no consideration has been given to any item of goodwill.

The meaning of the words "no consideration" is not entirely free from doubt. They could mean that no thought was given to an allocation of any of the sales price to goodwill, or they could indicate that the parties agreed that no part of the purchase price was allocated to goodwill. The testimony of the attorney who prepared the document indicates, however, that he did consider the implications of the sale of goodwill and even did research on the subject. He testified that he believed, albeit incorrectly, that, if goodwill were part of the purchase price, his client would not be entitled to capital gains treatment.

Petitioner attempts to justify this misstatement of the tax implications of an allocation to goodwill not by asserting mistake, but by pointing out that his attorney "is not a tax lawyer but is primarily involved with commercial law and real estate." We find as a fact that petitioner agreed at arm's length with the purchasers of his partnership interest that no part of the purchase price should be attributable to goodwill. The Tax Court long has adhered to the view that, absent "strong proof," a taxpayer cannot challenge an express allocation in an arm's-length sales contract to which he had agreed. *See, e.g., Major v. Commissioner*, 76 T.C. 239, 249 (1981), *appeal pending* (7th Cir. July 7, 1981); *Lucas v. Commissioner*, 58 T.C. 1022, 1032 (1972). In *Spector v. Commissioner*, 641 F.2d 376 (5th Cir. 1981), *revg.* 71 T.C. 1017 (1979), the Fifth Circuit, to which an appeal in this case will lie, appeared to step away from its prior adherence to the "strong proof" standard and move toward the stricter standard enunciated in *Commissioner v. Danielson*, 378 F.2d 771, 775 (3d Cir. 1967), *remanding* 44 T.C. 549 (1965), *cert. denied* 389 U.S. 858 (1967). However, in this case, we need not measure the length of the step since we hold that petitioner has failed to introduce sufficient evidence to satisfy even the more lenient "strong proof" standard.

We next turn to petitioner's contention that part or all of the purchase price received in excess of the value of tangible assets is attributable to value of a going concern. In *VGS Corp. v. Commissioner*, 68 T.C. 563 (1977), we stated that —

> Going-concern value is, in essence, the additional element of value which attaches to property by reason of its existence as an integral part of a going concern.... [T]he ability of a business to continue to function and generate income without interruption as a consequence of the change in ownership, is a vital part of the value of a going concern.... [Cites omitted; 68 T.C. at 591-592.]

However, in the instant case, the ability of the dog-racing track to continue to function after the sale of Ledoux's partnership interest was due to the remaining partners' retention of rights to operate under the Dog Track Agreement. Without

B. EXCEPTION FOR § 751

such Agreement, there would have been no continuing right to operate a business and no right to continue to earn income. Thus, the amount paid in excess of the value of Ledoux's share of the tangible assets was not for the intangible value of the business as a going concern but rather for Ledoux's rights under the Dog Track Agreement.

Finally, we turn to petitioner's claim that a determination of the value of rights arising from the Dog Track Agreement has never been made and no evidence of the value of such rights was submitted in this case. We note that the $800,000 purchase price was proposed by petitioner and was accepted by Jack Collins and Jerry Collins in an arm's-length agreement of sale evidenced in the Memorandum of Agreement of July 19, 1972 and the Agreement for Sale of Partnership interest of October 17, 1972. In addition, the October 17, 1972 sales agreement, written by petitioner's attorney, provided in paragraph 1 that the "[s]eller [Ledoux] sells to buyer [Jerry Collins and Jack Collins] all of his interest in [the partnership] ... including but not limited to, the seller's right to income and to acquire the capital stock of The Sanford-Orlando Kennel Club, Inc."... Section 1.751-1(c)(3), Income Tax Regs., provides that an arm's-length agreement between the buyer and the seller generally will establish the value attributable to unrealized receivables.

Based on the provision in the Agreement that no part of the consideration was attributable to goodwill, it is clear to us that the parties were aware that they could, if they so desired, have provided that no part of the consideration was attributable to the Dog Track Agreement. No such provision was made.[3] Furthermore, the Agreement clearly stated that one of the assets purchased was Ledoux's rights to future income. Considering that petitioner calculated the purchase price by capitalizing future earnings expected under the Dog Track Agreement, we conclude that the portion of Ledoux's gain in excess of the amount attributable to tangible assets was attributable to an unrealized receivable as reflected by the Dog Track Agreement.

Decision will be entered for the respondent.

NOTE

The question of apportioning part of the sales price of a partnership interest to goodwill is taken up in a later chapter.

PROBLEM 6-2

Assume a partnership sold land it formerly held for a $1 million gain, payable in four equal installments of $500,000 cash, such that $250,000 of each installment was taxable as a § 1231 gain, and that there were no other § 1231

---

[3] We do not mean to imply that an opposite holding would automatically pertain if a provision had been made with respect to the Dog Track Agreement.

transactions. No payment has yet been made under the installment obligation. Now assume a 50% partner sold his interest to a third party. What would be the character of the gain on his sale of his partnership interest, assuming the installment obligation was the partnership's sole asset? *See* Reg. § 1.751-1(c)(1)(i).

2. TRADITIONAL RECAPTURE ITEMS

The second type of "unrealized receivable" involves traditional recapture items that would have produced ordinary income when the associated property is sold. Referring to these as unrealized receivables is obviously a misnomer, but the theory for including them under § 751 is sound because a partner could otherwise convert her ordinary gain into capital gain. Examples include recapture of accelerated depreciation on real estate (§ 1250), depreciation of personal property (§ 1245), and intangible drilling and development costs (§ 1254). *See* § 751(c).

3. SUBSTANTIALLY APPRECIATED INVENTORY

Unless certain tests, described below, are met, the portion of the gain attributable to appreciated inventory is swallowed up and taxed as part of the overall capital gain (or loss) in the sale of the partnership interest. For this purpose, the term "inventory" includes traditional inventory as well as stock in trade, property primarily held for sale to customers in the ordinary course of business, and any other similar property that would not be a capital asset or § 1231 asset if sold by the selling partner or the partnership. § 751(b)(2)(D). Inventory is "substantially appreciated" only if its value exceeds its basis by at least 20%.

The search for the thresholds is stacked against the selling partner, because unrealized receivables and inventory items are combined in applying the 20% test. *See, e.g.,* Reg. § 1.751-1(d)(2)(ii). This is potentially unfair, if only because in the hands of a cash-method taxpayer unpaid service contracts are apt to have a zero basis, so that their entire value is considered to be "appreciated." On the bright side, once the unrealized receivables have been factored into the equation for purposes of determining whether the percentage test was met, they are withdrawn and counted only once — as unrealized receivables — which is to the taxpayer's advantage. Assuming the "inventory" is sufficiently appreciated, it is not further broken down into appreciated and depreciated items.

Now try to answer the following problem.

PROBLEM 6-3

The ABC partnership is on the cash method, and has the following assets on its balance sheet. Assume the partnership bought the equipment for $10,000 and wrote it all off:

B. EXCEPTION FOR § 751

Asset	Adjusted Basis	FMV
Accounts Receivable	$ 0	$20,000
Equipment	0	10,000
Inventory	20,000	20,000
Land	50,000	50,000
Cash	70,000	70,000
	$140,000	$170,000

Does a partner in the ABC partnership who decides to sell his or her partnership interest have a § 751 problem, or is the entire gain taxed under § 741 alone?

4. CALCULATING GAINS AND LOSSES FROM SALE OR EXCHANGE OF PARTNERSHIP INTERESTS

Read Reg. § 1.751-1(a), (b).

When § 751 does apply, there usually will be a mix of capital and ordinary gain or loss results. But how much of each? The trick here is to understand how the entire amount realized is apportioned between § 751 assets and the § 741 assets.

Because the buyer and seller of a partnership interest are ordinarily on opposite sides of the tax fence — so that an allocation of the sales price to particular assets that might be most favorable towards the one of them will generally be most adverse towards the other — the IRS will generally accept an allocation by contract between the parties. Failing a viable apportionment agreement by the parties, either because there is none or the Service prevails in having it set aside, one apportions the amount realized by reference to the proportionate values of the two classes of assets. As to the basis of § 751 assets, **Reg. § 1.751-1(a)(2)** provides an important mechanical rule that the § 751 properties are first deemed distributed to the selling partner; § 732(c) generally assures that the basis of such properties will be the same as their bases in the partnership's hands and that accounts receivable of a cash method partnership will have a zero basis.

> *To illustrate*: C, a one-third member of the cash-method ABC partnership, will sell his interest to D for $100. He has an outside basis of $50. The partnership has two assets, receivables worth $150 with an adjusted basis of $0, and a parcel of land with a value and basis of $150. As a result of the relative values of the ABC partnership's assets, one-half (or $50) of C's proceeds from the sale are allocable to the receivables and half (also $50) to the land. Now C's outside basis is allocated to the § 751 assets as if his ratable portion of these partnership assets were distributed to him before the sale. This results in C taking a basis in the receivables which is equal to the partnership's inside basis in

that property ($0).[4] § 732(a). Subtracting the $0 basis just arrived at in § 751 assets from the amount realized with reference to receivables ($50, being 1/3rd of $150) produces the selling partner's ordinary gain or loss (i.e., $50).

Once the § 751 gain has been established, the remaining basis in the partnership interest is subtracted from the remainder of the amount realized, and is reported as a capital gain or loss under § 741. (Note the possibility of a gain in one grouping and a loss in the other.) Following through with the immediately preceding example, we know C has a $50 ordinary gain. After C has completed the § 751 calculation, revealing that the full $50 gain is recharacterized as ordinary income, the remaining $50 of amount realized will be apportioned to the partnership interest as such. As to that portion of the sale there is no gain or loss, because the residual amount realized ($50) equals his "post-distribution-of-§ 751-assets" outside basis. Note that under §§ 705 and 733, the initial imaginary distribution did not reduce C's outside basis, because the receivables had a $0 basis.

C. TAX IMPACT ON BUYER

Read §§ 754 and 743(b), (c).

1. INTRODUCTION

The buyer of the partnership interest will take a cost basis in the interest. §§ 742, 1011 and 1012. The incoming partner will include his or her allocable share of partnership liabilities under § 752(d), and will generally inherit the transferor's capital account. Reg. § 1.704-1(b)(2)(iv)(1).

2. SECTION 743(b) OPTIONAL BASIS ADJUSTMENT

Sales and exchanges of partnership interests tend to obliterate the symmetry between inside and outside basis. The problem is that a partner will rarely sell the partnership interest for an amount equal to his or her share of inside basis because inside basis does not reflect market value. At the same time, the partner's sale has no impact on inside basis.

To illustrate: C has a $100 basis in her 33% share of the ABC partnership, which is on the calendar year and uses the cash method. ABC's total inside basis is $300. The sole asset is a tract of unencumbered raw land, worth $330. She sells her interest to D on December 31 for $110, as a result of which D has a $110

---

[4] Special basis adjustments may be called for by §§ 704(c), 732(a)(2), (d) or 743(b). The partnership may take the occasion to adjust the partners' capital accounts for allocation purposes under § 704(b).

C. TAX IMPACT ON BUYER

outside basis. If ABD sells the land for $330 soon after D buys, D will be taxed on $10, her share of the $30 gain. This seems unfair to D. However, when the partnership is liquidated and the remaining cash is distributed, D will show a $10 loss because her liquidation proceeds ($110) will be $10 less than her outside basis. § 731(a)(2). If the transactions all occur in the same year, D will likely not care, but if the proceeds from the sale of the land are not distributed, she may become distraught.

Enter § 754 (a procedural provision granting powers of election to the partnership)[5] and § 743 (the guts of the system). If the partnership makes the § 754 election, *it can adjust its basis in assets allocable to the incoming partner.* A sale of a partnership interest is not the only event that triggers § 754, but it is the most obvious. For example, § 743 also applies to the death of a partner. In essence, § 754 is an imprecise effort to equate a partner's outside basis with his share of inside values. If a § 754 election is in effect, the relationship between aggregate inside bases and outside bases remains intact transfer-by-transfer. If the election is in force from the outset, aggregate inside and outside bases can remain identical, due to the mechanical adjustments that § 743 or § 734 imposes.

As applied to the ABC partnership example, ABD would increase its basis in the raw land by $10 *but only as to D*. As a result, ABD will report only a $20 gain on the sale of the land, and the $20 will be allocated to A and B alone. Now, when the partnership liquidates, D will also report no gain or loss, because the cash she receives will exactly equal her outside basis. Thanks to the election, D will be in the same overall position, in that she will not ultimately be taxed on the $10 but, thanks to § 743, freedom from taxation will occur by preventing the gain in the first instance rather than by combining an exaggerated gain with a later exaggerated loss.

The implications of the § 754 election can be formidable. It ties up all subsequent incoming partners, and it also forces the partnership to apply a companion provision (§ 734) to distributions from the partnership. Electing under § 754 means that partners who buy partnership interests at a discount must watch with dismay as their allocable shares of inside basis are *reduced*.[6] Moreover, the

---

[5] The election must be made on a timely tax return for the partnership, and can be revoked only with IRS consent. If the facts involve a multi-tiered partnership pattern, selling an interest in an upper-tier partnership causes an adjustment to the basis of lower-tier partnership property only if both partnerships elect. Rev. Rul. 87-115, 19872 C.B. 163.

[6] Partners in this kind of a bind who can force a § 754 election may prefer to avoid the election and instead have the partnership distribute assets to them so that they can make separate elections under § 732(d) to adjust the basis of assets in their hands. Note that in these discount situations the seller may be forced to accept a depressed price to account for the eroded inside basis, so it is not just the buyer's problem.

adjustment implicates the new partner's share of depreciation, amortization, and depletion, as well as gains and losses. Reg. § 1.743-1(b).

PROBLEM 6-4

A contributes $1,000 in cash and B contributes a popcorn-making machine with a value of $1,000 and a basis of $0 to the AB Popcorn Partnership, which makes the § 754 election in its partnership agreement. After years of breaking even, B tires of the deal and sells his interest to C for $1,000. We know that under § 704(c), the first $1,000 of gain on the sale of the popcorn machine has to be allocated to B. Can C's admission cause a step-up in basis of the machine to $1,000? *See* § 743(b)(1) and Reg. § 1.743-1(b)(2)(i), Ex. 2. Do the Regulations come to the right conclusion?

The § 754 election is especially important when one sells an interest in a service partnership holding large amounts of receivables. Absent the election, the buying partner will be taxed when the receivables are paid. Also, note that the single § 754 election causes basis adjustments under both § 743 and its companion provision, § 734, which relates to distributions and is discussed in Chapter 7. One must accept neither or both, and once made the election is irrevocable, unless the government consents to a revocation.[7]

3. SECTION 755: ALLOCATING SECTION 743 BASIS ADJUSTMENT

Section 755 tells one how to allocate the disparity between inside and outside basis. For convenience, we call a built-in gain that has to be allocated a "positive adjustment." If the subject is a built-in loss, we refer to it as a "negative adjustment." The allocation process works in three stages and is performed solely with respect to the partner who is affected by § 743, namely the buyer or heir.

First, divide the affected partner's share of all the assets into two classes: (1) § 1231 and capital assets; (2) all other assets.

Second, determine the net appreciation or depreciation in each such class. If only one class of assets appreciated, allocate a positive adjustment to that class; if only one class lost value, allocate the negative adjustment to that class. Reg. § 1.755-1(a)(1) and -1(b). If both classes moved in the same direction, prorate the positive or negative adjustment between the classes in proportion to the net appreciation or depreciation in each class. *Id.*

---

[7] There is another option; the partnership can be put through a technical termination under § 708, thereby creating a "new" partnership that can make "new" elections. That subject is discussed in a later chapter.

C. TAX IMPACT ON BUYER

Third, allocate the adjustment within a class among the assets in the class in proportion to the net appreciation or depreciation in value of each asset in the class. One cannot increase the basis of an asset that has declined in value or decrease the basis of an asset that has gained value. Section 755 moves the basis of assets closer to their values; thus, only appreciated assets gain basis, and only loss assets lose basis.

To illustrate: The ABC Partnership has three assets: X, a capital asset with an adjusted basis of $1,000 and a value of $1,500; Y, a depreciable § 1231 asset with an adjusted basis of $1,000 and a value of $900; and Z, inventory items with an adjusted basis of $700 and a value of $600. A sells his interest to D (when a basis adjustment election is in effect) for $1,000 (one-third of $3,000, the total value of partnership assets). D's share of the adjusted basis of partnership property is $900 (one-third of $2,700). Therefore, D has a basis adjustment of $100 ($1,000 - $900). This adjustment must be allocated entirely to property X, since such an allocation will have the effect of reducing the difference between the value and basis of the asset. Therefore, D has a basis increase of $100 with respect to property X, which now has a basis to him of $1,100. None of the (positive) adjustment is made to depreciable property Y or inventory items Z, since any such adjustment would increase the difference between the basis and value of each such asset. Reg. § 1.755-1(c), Example (1).

To sum up this area, over thirty years ago an esteemed tax commentator wrote that he hoped the Treasury Department would find some sensible way to avoid potentially being forced to list, consider, and potentially adjust the basis of each asset when a partner sells its partnership interest.[8] He died. We are still waiting for that sensible action.

PROBLEM 6-5

Assume a three-person cash-method partnership consisting of A,B and C, with each partner having identical interests in ABC. Assume it owns a building held for investment.

Partnership Asset	Value	Basis
Building	$1,200	$3,000
Accounts Receivable	400	-0-

---

[8] A. Willis, Handbook of Partnership Taxation p. 238 (1957). It is still an exceptionally good book.

Now assume that C sells her interest (which has a basis of $1,000) to D for $533.33 (one third of the total value of $1,600).

(1) What is the amount and character of C's gain or loss if she has an outside basis of $1,000? *See* §§ 741 and 751.

(2) What is D's basis in her share of the partnership's assets if the § 754 election is in force? *See* Reg. § 1.755-1(a), (b).

(3) If shortly after the purchase, and with a § 754 election in force, D receives an undivided one-third interest in the building in a nonliquidating distribution, what should D's basis be in that one-third interest? *See* Reg. § 1.743-1(b)(2)(ii).

Chapter 7
OPERATING DISTRIBUTIONS

A. EFFECT ON PARTNER

Read §§ 705, 731, 732(a) and 733.

1. INTRODUCTION

The subject of this disagreeably arithmetical chapter is the treatment of *nonliquidating* distributions of cash and property from ongoing partnerships to their ongoing partners. Because the distribution received from a partnership generally emanates from either capital contributed by the partner or from previously-taxed profits, it is appropriately given tax-free treatment up to outside basis. Section 731(a) generally assures that a current distribution is tax-free to the distributee partner because the partner takes the partnership's basis in the distributed property, so long as the partnerships's basis in the property does not exceed the partner's outside basis. § 732(a)(2). In effect, the distribution merely depletes the partnership's pool of assets to the extent of the partnership's basis in the distributed asset. Inasmuch as the distributee partner remains a partner, the distribution does not close out the investment relationship. Consequently, *nonliquidating* distributions reduce the partner's outside basis, but *never* produce losses to the distributee partner. They produce gains to the partner only if and to the extent more money is distributed than the partner has outside basis. § 731(a).

Distributions are usually easy to spot. When the partners, or at very least the managing partners, periodically review the partnership's finances and agree to distribute money or property to the partners, there is an obvious "constructive" distribution. Some distributions may be less obvious: for example, when a partner's share of partnership liabilities declines, there is a "constructive" distribution. *See* § 752(b). In other instances, while there may be a transfer of money or property from the partnership to a partner, it will not be a distribution in substance. Disguised sales provide typical examples of such *non*distributions.

> *To illustrate*: A and B form the AB partnership by having A contribute raw land and B contribute a car. Not much later AB liquidates; A gets the car and B gets the land. Substance-over-form principles assure that the overall transaction is a mere taxable exchange of property in disguise if the various steps can fairly be combined. *See* § 707(a)(2)(B).

If the contribution and distribution of property cannot be matched, § 704(c)(1)(B) provides a frightening rule that if the contributed property as to which there is a § 704(c) adjustment is merely distributed within five years of its contribution, it is deemed distributed, with the result that the contributing partner must recognize the gain or loss from his or her § 704(c) adjustment on the spot. The five-year period reflects a common congressional view that no taxpayer is patient enough to wait five years to complete a tax scam. The result is either a taxable gain or loss on the § 704(c) amount, as if the contributing partner had sold the property.

2. DISTRIBUTIONS OF CASH

A partner has a taxable gain if and to the extent she receives cash in excess of her basis in her partnership interest immediately before the distribution. § 731(a). Again, for this purpose, a distribution of cash includes a reduction in a partner's liabilities by the partnership or in the partner's share of partnership liabilities. § 752(b). Section 741 deems the gain to be from the sale of the partnership interest, so it will typically be a capital gain. This is virtually inevitable, because, to avoid absurd results, cash always takes basis equal to its face amount. Since there cannot be negative basis, the only solution is to tax cash in excess of outside basis as gains. Section 733's refusal to allow negative basis forces the result.

PROBLEM 7-1

A has a $2,000 basis in her partnership interest at the end of the year, at which time her share of the ABC partnership's liabilities declines by $7,000. What are the income and basis effects to A and the partnership?

Treatment of Partnership Draws. Partners in professional firms can rarely wait until year-end to take their profits out in cash, yet they will not know until year-end how prosperous the partnership will be. The Regulations have provided a solution for the treatment of midstream withdrawals; a "draw" against a distributive share of partnership income is treated as an interim loan followed by a year-end distribution which is used to repay the loan, *provided* the partner is obligated to restore amounts taken out during the year that exceed the partner's distributive share for the partnership's taxable year. Reg. § 1.731(a)(1)(ii). If there is no duty to repay, the draw is a current distribution.

Cancellations of Partnership Debt Distinguished. A creditor's cancellation of a partnership's debt is not a distribution. It is a form of gross income to the partnership, which is allocable to the partners in accordance with their partnership distributive shares. *See Gershkowitz v. Commissioner*, 88 T.C. 984 (1987), *supra*. It is up to each partner to find a justification outside Subchapter

A. EFFECT ON PARTNER

K for excluding the cancellation of indebtedness income from gross income. *See* § 108.

3. DISTRIBUTIONS OF PROPERTY

One of the striking features of partnership taxation is that distributions of property are generally tax-free both to the partner and the partnership. § 731(a), (b). By contrast, a corporation is taxed when it distributes appreciated assets. §§ 311 and 336. The shareholder also will probably be taxable. *See* § 301. One of the rationales for this favorable treatment of partnerships is that good economics dictate that there be no tax impediment to moving assets in and out of business or investment partnerships. The same argument should apply with equal force to corporations, but does not for questionable reasons. A distribution requires the partner to allocate outside basis between the distributed property and his interest in the partnership. § 733. In extreme cases, outside basis will be reduced to zero, but never below zero. § 733. By contrast, a distribution reduces the capital account without limit, and can quickly produce a negative number, especially if the partnership is loaded with depreciable property.

a. Distributee's Basis in Distributed Property and Partnership Interest

In the usual *non-liquidating distribution*, the partner simply reduces her basis in her partnership interest by the sum of the cash distributed and the *partnership's* basis in the distributed property. § 732(a). This has the practical effect of splitting the partner's outside basis between the property received and her remaining outside basis in her partnership interest. If cash and property are distributed at the same time, one calculates the tax implications of the cash distribution first. Reg. § 1.732-1(a). This rule favors taxpayers by minimizing the taxability of distributions.

The distributee takes the partnership's basis in the distributed property. Section 732(a)(1) thus shifts basis in the distributed asset from the partnership to the partner and defers gain or loss until the partner disposes of the asset. However, § 732(a)(2) imperiously declares that the carryover of the partnership's basis in its assets cannot exceed the partner's basis in his partnership interest.

> *To illustrate*: A is an equal partner in the AB partnership. She has an outside basis of $10. The partnership distributes $5 in cash plus an asset with a basis (to the partnership) of $10. Section 732(a)(2) assures that her basis in the asset will be $5, her original outside basis minus the $5 of cash. Section 733 will reduce her outside basis to $0.

If there were no § 732(a)(2) limit and no tax on the distribution of property, there would have to be negative basis in the partnership interest. Negative basis is apostasy throughout the Code, so § 732(a)(2) is not so imperious after all. Note how distributions *generally* maintain the equality between inside and outside basis. Each distribution reduces each account equally. The exception occurs if the distributee partner's outside basis is insufficient to absorb the partnership's basis in the property (cash or noncash) which it distributes. If the surfeit is caused by cash, the result is a gain. If it is caused by property, the result is a reduction in the basis of the distributed property.

PROBLEM 7-2

The ABC partnership has decided to distribute $100 in cash plus a tract of land with a value and an inside basis of $100 to A. A's basis in her partnership interest is $180. What are the income and basis effects to A?

The definition of property for purposes of §§ 731-732 is not entirely clear. Nevertheless, it does seem to include highly liquid assets such as short-term Treasury notes and interests in money-market mutual funds. This invites tax planning by turning leftover cash into such liquid assets, and distributing them in lieu of cash, thereby deferring any gain. Rider 150. However, new § 731(c) heads this off by turning "marketable securities" (including mutual fund stock) into "money."

There needs to be a way to assure that the partner will recognize the same amount of gain as the partnership would have if the partnership itself had sold receivables and inventory. Section 732(c)(1) saves the day by providing a rule that if the inside basis of distributed property exceeds outside basis, outside basis not absorbed by money is allocated first to unrealized receivables and inventory items (whether or not substantially appreciated) in proportion to the partnership's basis in such assets. This humane rule helps prevent the distributee partners from getting a step-down in the basis of these "hot assets," while at the same time preventing a windfall in the from of giving distributees an artificially high basis, which could trigger unrealistic ordinary losses if the partner later sells them; to put it another way, § 732(c)(1) strains to assure that the partner will recognize the same amount of ordinary income as the partnership would have recognized on its sale of receivables and inventory items. Whatever outside basis remains is next allocated to other properties in proportion to their bases in the partnership's hands. § 732(c)(1).

b. Character and Holding Period of Distributed Property

Potential depreciation recapture under § 1245 or § 1250 inherent in distributed property carries over into the distributee partner's hands and converts part of any later gain on its sale into ordinary income. §§ 1245(b)(3) and 1250(d)(3). If the distributed property is a capital asset or § 1231 asset, the partner tacks the partnership's holding period to her own holding period. § 1223(2). If the asset is an *unrealized receivable*, the property retains its ordinary income character

A. EFFECT ON PARTNER

forever. § 735(a)(1). If it is an *inventory item*, it only retains its ordinary character for five subsequent years, after which it loses its taint unless the taxpayer in fact holds it in inventory. § 735(a)(2). These rules assure that the character of so-called "hot assets" (especially receivables and inventory) is generally preserved after their distribution.

PROBLEM 7-3

A is a cash-method calendar-year equal member in the ABC partnership. She has an outside basis of $100. At year-end, she receives cash of $50, a tract of raw land with an inside basis of $40, inventory with a basis of $20, and unrealized receivables with a basis of $10. What are the income and basis effects to A? What is the holding period of the properties in A's hands? How long will A have to hold the assets in order to recognize a capital gain or capital loss on their later sale? Assume the partnership held the land for investment several years before distributing it.

c. Section 732(d) Election

Read § 732(d).

Recall that a § 754 election triggers § 743, and that under § 743 a person who purchases a partnership interest takes "look through" basis in his or her share of the partnership's assets. Section 732(d) lets the taxpayer elect to make a "mini" § 754 election as to himself alone with respect to property the partnership distributes. The effect of the election is to hypothesize that a § 754/743 election was in force when the taxpayer acquired the partnership interest. The § 732(d) election is available only if the distribution took place within two years of the time a partner acquired his interest and there was in fact no § 754 election in force when the taxpayer acquired the interest. The IRS reserves the right to impose the "election" on people who receive distributions of appreciated assets. *Id.*

There is great practical significance in making the election; taxes can be deferred via stepping up the bases of assets.

To illustrate: A year and a half ago, D paid $200 to buy out B's 33% interest in the ABC partnership. D's one-third of the ABC's partnership's assets at the time of purchase consisted of inventory worth $50, with a basis of $20, and a tract of investment land worth $150, with a basis of only $100. There was no § 754 election in force when D bought in, but if there had been, D's allocable share of inside basis would have risen from $120 to $200 as to D. Assuming the partnership will distribute those assets pro rata in the very near future and that D makes the § 732(d) election, he will have a $50 basis in inventory and a $150 basis in the land, whatever their value when he gets them.

Assuming his share of the tract is worth $155 when he receives it from the partnership, he can sell it immediately for a gain of $5 as opposed to $55.

d. Distributions of Encumbered Property

The distribution rules and the debt rules are not properly coordinated in the Code. The IRS has helped out with an important ruling in which the Service provided the necessary supplemental rules.

REV. RUL. 79-205
1979-2 C.B. 255

Distribution by partnership; property subject to liability. Increases in two partners' individual liabilities and decreases in their shares of partnership liabilities resulting from a transaction involving nonliquidating distributions to each partner of partnership properties subject to liabilities will be treated as occurring simultaneously for purposes of determining the amount of money considered distributed or contributed. The computation is shown of each partner's recognized gain or loss (if any), basis in the distributed property, and the new adjusted basis in the partnership interest.

Issues

When a partnership makes a nonliquidating distribution of property, (1) is a partner permitted to offset the increase in the partner's liabilities against the decrease in the partner's liabilities in determining the extent of recognition of gain or loss, and (2) is partnership basis adjusted before or after the property distribution?

Facts

A and B are general partners in M, a general partnership, which was formed for the purposes of owning and operating shopping centers.

On December 31, 1977, M made nonliquidating distributions in a single transaction of a portion of its property to A and B. A and B are equal partners in M. M, A and B are calendar year taxpayers. No assets of the type described in § 751(a) of the Internal Revenue Code of 1954 were distributed by M to either A or B.

Immediately prior to the distribution A had an adjusted basis for A's interest in M of 1,000x dollars, and B had an adjusted basis for B's interest in M of 1,500x dollars. The property distributed to A had an adjusted basis to M of 2,000x dollars, and was subject to liabilities of 1,600x dollars. The property distributed to B had an adjusted basis to M of 3,200x dollars and was subject to liabilities of 2,800x dollars. A's individual liabilities increased by 1,600x dollars by reason of the distribution to A. B's individual liabilities increased by 2,800x dollars by reason of the distribution to B. A's share and B's share of the

A. EFFECT ON PARTNER 151

liabilities of M each decreased by 2,200x dollars (1/2 of 1,600x + 1/2 of 2,800x dollars) by reason of the distributions. The basis and fair market value of the properties distributed were greater than the liabilities to which they were subject.

Law

Section 705(a) of the Code provides, in part, that the adjusted basis of a partner's interest in a partnership shall be the basis of such interest determined under § 722 decreased (but not below zero) by partnership distributions as provided in § 733.

Section 722 of the Code provides, in part, that the basis of a partnership interest acquired by a contribution of money shall be the amount of such money.

Section 731(a)(1) of the Code provides that in the case of a distribution by a partnership to a partner gain shall not be recognized to such partner, except to the extent that any money distributed exceeds the adjusted basis of such partner's interest in the partnership immediately before the distribution.

Section 732(a)(1) of the Code provides that the basis of property (other than money) distributed by a partnership to a partner other than in liquidation of the partner's interest shall, except as provided in § 732(a)(2), be its adjusted basis to the partnership immediately before such distribution.

Section 732(a)(2) of the Code provides that the basis to the distributee partner of property to which § 732(a)(1) is applicable shall not exceed the adjusted basis of such partner's interest in the partnership reduced by any money distributed in the same transaction.

Section 733 of the Code provides that in the case of a distribution by a partnership to a partner other than in liquidation of a partner's interest, the adjusted basis to such partner of the interest in the partnership shall be reduced (but not below zero) by the amount of any money distributed to such partner and the amount of the basis to such partner of distributed property other than money, as determined under § 732.

Section 752(a) of the Code provides that any increase in a partner's share of the liabilities of a partnership, or any increase in a partner's individual liabilities by reason of the assumption by such partner of partnership liabilities, shall be considered as a contribution of money by such partner to the partnership.

Section 752(b) of the Code provides that any decrease in a partner's share of the liabilities of a partnership, or any decrease in a partner's individual liabilities by reason of the assumption by the partnership of such individual liabilities, shall be considered as a distribution of money to the partner by the partnership.

Section 752(c) of the Code provides that for purposes of § 752 a liability to which property is subject shall, to the extent of the fair market value of such property, be considered as a liability of the owner of the property.

Analysis & Holding

In general, partnership distributions are taxable under § 731(a)(1) of the Code only to the extent that the amount of money distributed exceeds the distributee partner's basis for the partner's partnership interest. This rule reflects the Congressional intent to limit narrowly the area in which gain or loss is recognized upon a distribution so as to remove deterrents to property being moved in and out of partnerships as business reasons dictate. *See* S. Rep. No. 1622, 83rd Cong., 2nd Sess., page 96 (1954). Here, since partner liabilities are both increasing and decreasing in the same transaction offsetting the increases and decreases tends to limit recognition of gain, thereby giving effect to the Congressional intent. Consequently, in a distribution of encumbered property, the resulting liability adjustments will be treated as occurring simultaneously, rather than occurring in a particular order. Therefore, on a distribution of encumbered property, the amount of money considered distributed to a partner for purposes of § 731(a)(1) is the amount (if any) by which the decrease in the partner's share of the liabilities of the partnership under § 752(b) exceeds the increase in the partner's individual liabilities under § 752(a). The amount of money considered contributed by a partner for purposes of § 722 is the amount (if any) by which the increase in the partner's individual liabilities under § 752(a) exceeds the decrease in the partner's share of the liabilities of the partnership under § 752(b). The increase in the partner's individual liabilities occurs by reason of the assumption by the partner of partnership liabilities, or by reason of a distribution of property subject to a liability, to the extent of the fair market value of such property.

Because the distribution was part of a single transaction, the two properties are treated as having been distributed simultaneously to A and B. Therefore, all resulting liability adjustments relating to the distribution of the two properties will be treated as occurring simultaneously, rather than occurring in a particular order.

Treatment of Partner A

A will be deemed to have received a net distribution of 600x dollars in money, that is, the amount by which the amount of money considered distributed to A (2,200x dollars) exceeds the amount of money considered contributed by A (1,600x dollars). Since 600x dollars does not exceed A's basis for A's interest in M immediately before the distribution (1,000x dollars), no gain is recognized to A.

Under § 732(a) of the Code, the basis to A of the property distributed to A is the lesser of (i) the adjusted basis of the property to the partnership (2,000x dollars), or (ii) the adjusted basis of A's partnership interest (1,000x dollars) reduced by the amount of money deemed distributed to A (600x dollars). Therefore, the basis of the property in A's hands is 400x dollars. Under § 733, the adjusted basis of A's partnership interest (1,000x dollars) is reduced by the amount of money deemed distributed to A (600x dollars) and by the basis to A of the distributed property (400x dollars) . The adjusted basis of A's partnership interest is therefore reduced to zero.

B. EFFECT ON PARTNERSHIP

Treatment of Partner B

B will be deemed to have made a net contribution of 600x dollars, that is, the amount by which the amount of money considered contributed by B (2,800x dollars) exceeds the amount of money considered distributed to B $2,200x dollars). In applying § 732(a) and 733 of the Code to B, the adjustment to B's basis in B's partnership interest attributable to the liability adjustments resulting from the distributions will be treated as occurring first, and the distribution of property to B as occurring second. By so doing, B's basis for the distributed property is increased and B's basis in B's partnership interest is decreased. This allocation gives greater effect to the general rule of § 732(a)(1), which provides for the partner to have the same basis in distributed property as the partnership had for that property.

Therefore, the first step is that B's basis for B's partnership interest (1,500x dollars) is increased under §§ 722 and 705(a) by the amount of the net contribution deemed made by B (600x dollars), and is equal to 2,100x dollars. Next, under § 732(a) of the Code, the basis to B of the property distributed to B is the lesser of (i) the adjusted basis of the property to the partnership (3,200x dollars), or (ii) the adjusted basis of B's partnership interest (2,100x dollars) reduced by the amount of money deemed distributed to B (zero). Therefore, the basis of the property in B's hands is 2,100x dollars. Under § 733, the adjusted basis of B's partnership interest (2,100x dollars) is reduced by the amount of money deemed distributed to B (zero) and by the basis to B of the distributed property (2,100x dollars). The adjusted basis of B's partnership interest is therefore zero.

B. EFFECT ON PARTNERSHIP

Read § 731(b).

The partnership is not taxed when it distributes appreciated property, nor can it claim a loss deduction when it distributes property that has lost value. § 731(b). Nor is there depreciation recapture. §§ 1245(b)(3) and 1250(d)(6).[1] The view is that "nothing happened." Income and loss are deferred via frozen basis of property in the partner's hands. Things are equally straightforward for the partnership. The partnership simply reduces its inside basis by its predistribution basis in the property, not because of some special Code provision, but because it no longer owns the property. The only exception to the rule against taxation involves disproportionate distributions of "hot assets," which is discussed later in this Chapter.

---

[1] *But see* § 751(b) involving disproportionate distributions of "hot assets," discussed later in this chapter.

1. SECTION 734 ELECTION

Read § 754 and § 734(a) and (b).

Distributions of partnership property implicate the partnership's right to make a § 734(b) election, enabling the partnership to modify its basis in its *retained* assets. The adjustment comes in two forms; one merely affects timing. The other prevents the apostasy of disappearing basis.

a. Timing: Section 734(b)(1)(A)

This provision allows the partnership to modify its basis in its retained assets by § 731 gain or loss recognized by a distributee partner as a result of a partnership distribution. The adjustment reflects the fact that the distributee has recognized some of the gain inherent in partnership assets caused by the appreciation of partnership assets. To understand the issue, you need to know that when a partnership completely liquidates a partner's interest in the partnership (or the partnership itself) and distributes only cash, a partner who receives less than her outside basis can report a tax loss, thanks to § 731(a)(2).

> *To illustrate*: A is an equal member of the ABC partnership. Like her partners, she has a $300 outside basis, but the partnership's major asset, a tract of raw land, has appreciated in value from $300 to $1,200. It is a capital asset. The partnership also has $600 in cash and no liabilities. The partners agree that A must retire. Accordingly, the partnership appropriately distributes $600 cash (a third of the partnership's value) to her in complete liquidation, leaving the same raw land, with the same inherent gain as ever, in the partnership's hands. She has a $300 taxable gain under § 731(a)(1) because she got cash in excess of her outside basis.

Here is the problem. If the BC partnership sells the land for $1,200, it will have a $900 gain ($1,200 less $300 basis). B and C will each be taxed on $450, increasing their outside bases to $750 each. If the partnership folds up at this point, the partners will in fact only get $600 each (i.e., half of the $1,200 sales proceeds). Section 731(a)(2) allows them to report to a $300 loss ($1,500 aggregate outside basis less $1,200 sales proceeds).

A recognized a $300 gain based on a distribution of $600 that was partly based on her share of the appreciation in value of the land, but if the partnership later sells that land, there still will be a $900 gain. This is multiple taxation. When the partnership liquidates, there will admittedly be an offsetting $300 capital loss under § 731(a)(2) that B and C will share, so the overtaxation will eventually come out in the wash. There are two policy choices. The first is to forget the issue, since it is just a timing problem; the other is to complicate the Code. Congress opted for the latter.

B. EFFECT ON PARTNERSHIP

The Congressional solution is to increase the basis in remaining partnership assets by gains recognized by the distributee and, conversely, to reduce inside basis by the distributee's recognized losses. Going back to the example, the partnership would increase its basis in the land by $300. This will reduce the later gain when the tract is sold to $300 each to B and C, and will prevent a § 731(a)(2) loss to the partners on liquidation of the partnership. This election is available only if the partnership makes the § 754 election.

b. Basis: Section 734(b)(1)(B)

This elective provision has a more serious purpose. It prevents the permanent disappearance of basis. It takes effect when a partnership distributes property to a partner and § 732(a)(2) limits the partner's basis in the distributed property to the partner's predistribution outside basis. The election causes an increase in the partnership's inside basis in its remaining assets by the reduction in the basis of the distributed assets.

To illustrate: A is an equal member of the AB partnership. Like B, she has a $750 outside basis. The partnership has cash and two capital assets:

	Inside Basis	Asset Fair Market Value
Cash	$300	$300
Capital Asset X	900	300
Capital Asset Y	300	900
Total	$1,500	$1,500

If the partnership distributes $300 in cash to B and capital asset X to A, § 732(a)(2) crimps A's basis in capital asset X down to $750, her outside basis. If she later sells it for its fair market value of $300, she will correctly report a $450 loss. The remaining $150 ($900 - $750) of loss disappears forever, and the full gain on capital asset Y remains intact. This evaporation of basis will not do.

The solution is to increase the basis of the partnership's *remaining* assets by the $150 of disappearing basis. This election is available only if the partnership makes the § 754 election. Returning to the example, the § 734(b)(1)(B) prong of the § 754 election increases the inside basis of capital asset Y from $300 to $450. Again, § 755 supplies the mechanical rules for attributing the otherwise lost basis to the remaining assets. The key principle is to attach the increase to the same type of assets as generated the problem, treating capital assets and § 1231 assets as a single class and all other assets as another class.

Things are not quite as nifty as they seem. Now that the adjustment has been made, namely increasing the basis of capital asset Y to $450, should A benefit from the adjustment, or should there be a special allocation in favor of the remaining partner? The answer should be "yes" to the latter. A has already gotten the benefit of one-third of the appreciation inherent in the assets via a step-up in basis ($750 basis vs. $300 value); the balance of the loss should go B, as a matter of common sense. You will probably have to reread this example to understand it.

PROBLEM 7-4

X's adjusted basis in her partnership interest was $60,000 before she recently received the following properties in a nonliquidating distribution. Assume that a § 754 election is in force. What is X's basis in the properties she receives? What is the effect of § 734(b)(1)(B)? Grab your hand calculator.

Properties Distributed to Partner X

	Inside Basis	Fair Market Value
Cash	$13,000	$13,000
Inventory	25,000	27,000
Tract A	20,000	25,000
Tract B	21,000	26,000
TOTAL	$79,000	$91,000

C. FOREIGN PARTNERS

Section 1446 and Reg. § 1.1441-3(f) require domestic partnerships to withhold U.S. income tax on amounts distributed to foreign partners during the taxable year from business and investment income, respectively. If the withholdings fall short of the foreign partner's tax liability, the partnership must remit additional withholding taxes, apparently at the end of the year. If the partnership overwithheld, the foreign partner can claim a refund or credit.

D. DISPROPORTIONATE DISTRIBUTIONS INVOLVING "HOT ASSETS"

If there were an election for worst section of the Code, no list of candidates would be complete without § 751(b). Its purpose is to prevent wicked partners from using partnership distributions to reshuffle proportionate interests in property with an ordinary income component, such as unrealized receivables, known in the trade as "hot assets." Humane instructors do no more than ask students to "spot the issue" on a final examination. Regrettably, § 751(b) applies

D. DISPROPORTIONATE DISTRIBUTIONS INVOLVING "HOT ASSETS"

both to current distributions and to those which terminate the partner's interest in the partnership.

Section 751 and Regs. § 1.751-1(b) & (c) employ a reconstructive model, which works as follows:

1. *To the extent a partner gets a disproportionately small interest in "hot assets,"* the partner is deemed to have received a distribution of a proportionate interest in each class of partnership assets, and to have exchanged his excessive share of the "hot assets" with the partnership in order to obtain extra regular assets from the partnership. (This rationalizes how she came to hold so few hot assets.) If the partnership has a gain or loss on the imaginary disposition of the additional regular assets, it is allocated only to the other partners. Basis in assets after the dust settles is determined on the assumption that the hypothetical transactions really took place. Thus, for example, the partner's basis in the disproportionate share of the regular assets will be based on cost; the rest will have a carryover basis. This reconstruction is supposed to prevent partnerships from cleverly shifting capital assets to higher bracket taxpayers.

2. *To the extent a partner gets a disproportionately large interest in "hot assets,"* the model starts by assuming[2] the distributee partner got his pro rata share of all the assets, but that he then exchanged a share of his regular assets for the extra share of "hot assets." This means the partner is likely to have a capital gain on the imaginary disposition of the regular assets and that the partnership will have ordinary gain on the disposition of the "hot assets"; the ordinary gain is allocated only to the other partners. The basis rules track the reconstruction. For example, the distributee partner's basis in the "hot assets" will be partly founded on the carryover rules and partly on cost. This reconstruction is supposed to prevent partnerships from shifting ordinary income to partners in low tax brackets.

Note the order of business. First, always assume a pro rata distribution was made. Then inspect the transaction for an imbalance in hot assets. Explain the imbalance by imagining a taxable exchange of part of the distributed property. Tag the other partners alone with the partnership's gain or loss on the exchange.

Section 751(b) has a major weakness. It is triggered by the relative disproportion in the *value* of § 751(b) assets, not the amount of ordinary income inherent in those assets. This still makes it possible to distribute such assets equally by value, but to shift the lion's share of the ordinary income in the hands of the lower-bracket taxpayer. While this invites obvious tax planning maneuvers, it may be difficult to justify the associated professional fees given that the ultimate

---

[2] Reg. 1.751-1(g) lets the partners specify by agreement property within the class of nondistributed assets. Absent agreement, the distribution is deemed pro rata.

benefit is generally just the bracket spread between ordinary income and capital gains.

PROBLEM 7-5

A, B, C and D are equal members of the ABCD Partnership. Each partner has the following basis in his or her partnership interest:

A: $2,000
B: $9,000
C: $4,000
D: $5,000

ABC makes a current distribution of $1,500 to each partner, and at the same time it distributes the following properties to the partners:

A: Raw land with an inside basis and value of $7,000.
B: A car with an inside basis and value of $7,000.
C: Furniture with an inside basis of $0 and a value of $7,000.
D: A check for $7,000, which is worth $7,000.

What is the basis of each property to each partner, and what is each partner's outside basis and income, if any? Disregard any § 751 effects, but in the case of A, consider (without calculations) the implications of a § 754\734(b)(1)(B) election or the § 732(d) alternative, and in the case of D, consider the effect of a § 754\734(b)(1)(A) election.

OUTSIDE READINGS

W. Andrews, *Inside Basis Adjustments and Hot Asset Exchanges in Partnership Distributions*, 47 Tax L. Rev. 3 (1991).

C. Hanna, *Partnership Distributions: Whatever Happened to Nonrecognition*, 82 Ky. L.J. 465 (1994).

Chapter 8
LIQUIDATION OF A PARTNERSHIP INTEREST

A. INTRODUCTION

Read §§ 761(d), 736 and Reg. § 1.761-1(d).

In life or after death, there are only three ways for a partner (or the partner's estate) to get out of an ongoing partnership, apart from abandoning it. One is by sale or gift to a third party. The second is by a sale to one or more of the other partners. The final way is for the partnership to buy out his entire interest, known as liquidating the partner's interest. The buyout may be immediate or in a prolonged series of redemptions. Sales to remaining partners have the same economic results as liquidations. Either way, the retiring or deceased partner gets paid for his interest, and the remaining partners use their money, directly out of their pockets or out of their share of partnership assets, to buy out the exiting partner. However, the tax results can differ sharply. As a result, tax considerations dominate this field.

Congress has deliberately made the tax results elective. From a policy perspective that is a good idea, because it means the elections are explicit rather than accessible only to wealthy people who alone can afford to hire the tax skills to find implicit elections. It is also efficient from a purely economic standpoint. Another good thing is that the retirement of a majority partner does not result in a termination of the partnership under § 708. Reg. § 1.736-1(a)(6).

For the time being, the important point is that we are now beginning the study of *liquidations* as opposed to sales of partnership interests. Do not underrate this section. Liquidations of partnership interests occur all the time, are complicated and call for skillful representation. They also tend to be emotionally charged events.

Note that a distribution that retires one partnership interest (e.g., as a limited partner) but leaves the partner holding another interest (e.g., as a general partner) is not a liquidating distribution. § 761(d).

B. SALE VERSUS LIQUIDATION

FOXMAN v. COMMISSIONER
352 F.2d 466 (3d Cir. 1965),
aff'g 41 T.C. 535 (1964), *acq.* 1966-2 C.B. 4, 5

SMITH, CIRCUIT JUDGE.

This matter is before the Court on petitions to review decisions of the Tax Court, 41 T.C. 535, in three related cases consolidated for the purpose of hearing. The petitions of Foxman and Grenell challenge the decision as erroneous only as it relates to them. The petition of the Commissioner seeks a review of the decision as it relates to Jacobowitz only if it is determined by us that the Tax Court erred in the other two cases....

As the result of agreements reached in February of 1955, and January of 1956, Foxman, Grenell and Jacobowitz became equal partners in a commercial enterprise which was then trading under the name of Abbey Record Manufacturing Company, hereinafter identified as the Company. They also became equal shareholders in a corporation known as Sound Plastics, Inc. When differences of opinion arose in the spring of 1956, efforts were made to persuade Jacobowitz to withdraw from the partnership. These efforts failed at that time but were resumed in March of 1957. Thereafter the parties entered into negotiations which, on May 21, 1957, culminated in a contract for the acquisition of Jacobowitz's interest in the partnership of Foxman and Grenell. The terms and conditions, except one not here material, were substantially in accord with an option to purchase offered earlier to Foxman and Grenell. The relevant portions of the final contract are set forth in the Tax Court's opinion.

The contract, prepared by an attorney representing Foxman and Grenell, referred to them as the "Second Party," and to Jacobowitz as the "First Party." We regard as particularly pertinent to the issue before us the following clauses:

"WHEREAS, the parties hereto are equal owners and the sole partners of ABBEY RECORD MFG. Co., a partnership, ..., and are also the sole stockholders, officers and directors of SOUND PLASTICS, INC., a corporation organized under the laws of the State of New York; and

"WHEREAS, the first party is desirous of selling, conveying, transferring and assigning all of his right, title and interest in and to his one-third share and interest in the said ABBEY to the second parties; and

"WHEREAS, the second parties are desirous of conveying, transferring and assigning all of their right, title and interest in and to their combined two-thirds shares and interest in SOUND PLASTICS, INC., to the first party;

"NOW, THEREFORE, IT IS MUTUALLY AGREED AS FOLLOWS:

"First: The second parties hereby purchase all the right, title, share and interest of the first party in ABBEY and the first party does hereby sell, transfer, convey and assign all of his right, title, interest and share in ABBEY and in the moneys in banks, trade names, accounts due, or to become due, and in all other assets of any kind whatsoever, belonging to said ABBEY, for and in consideration of the following...."

The stated consideration was cash in the sum of $242,500; the assignment by Foxman and Grenell of their stock in Sound Plastics; and the transfer of an automobile, title to which was held by the Company. The agreement provided for the payment of $67,500 upon consummation of the contract and payment of the balance as follows: $67,500 on January 2, 1958, and $90,000 in equal monthly installments, payable on the first of each month after January 30, 1958. This balance was evidenced by a series of promissory notes, payment of which was

B. SALE VERSUS LIQUIDATION

secured by a chattel mortgage on the assets of the Company. This mortgage, like the contract, referred to a sale by Jacobowitz of his partnership interest to Foxman and Grenell. The notes were executed in the name of the Company as the purported maker and were signed by Foxman and Grenell, who also endorsed them under a guarantee of payment.

The down payment of $67,500 was by a cashier's check which was issued in exchange for a check drawn on the account of the Company. The first note, in the amount of $67,500, which became due on January 2, 1958, was timely paid by a check drawn on the Company's account. Pursuant to the terms of an option reserved to Foxman and Grenell, they elected to prepay the balance of $90,000 on January 28, 1958, thereby relieving themselves of an obligation to pay Jacobowitz a further $17,550, designated in the contract as a consultant's fee. They delivered to Jacobowitz a cashier's check which was charged against the account of the Company.

In its partnership return for the fiscal year ending February 28, 1958, the Company treated the sum of $159,656.09, the consideration received by Jacobowitz less the value of his interest in partnership property, as a guaranteed payment made in liquidation of a retiring partner's interest under § 736(a)(2).... This treatment resulted in a substantial reduction of the distributive shares of Foxman and Grenell and consequently a proportionate decrease in their possible tax liability. In his income tax return Jacobowitz treated the sum of $164,356.09, the consideration less the value of his partnership interest, as a long term capital gain realized upon the sale of his interest. This, of course, resulted in a tax advantage favorable to him. The Commissioner determined deficiencies against each of the taxpayers in amounts not relevant to the issue before us and each filed separate petitions for redetermination.

The critical issue before the Tax Court was raised by the antithetical positions maintained by Foxman and Grenell on one side and Jacobowitz on the other. The former, relying on § 736(a)(2), *supra*, contended that the transaction, evidenced by the contract, constituted a liquidation of a retiring partner's interest and that the consideration paid was accorded correct treatment in the partnership return. The latter contended that the transaction constituted a sale of his partnership interest and, under § 741 of the Code, 26 U.S.C.A., the profit realized was correctly treated in his return as a capital gain. The Tax Court rejected the position of Foxman and Grenell and held that the deficiency determinations as to them were not erroneous; it sustained the position of Jacobowitz and held that the deficiency determination as to him was erroneous. The petitioners Foxman and Grenell challenge that decision as erroneous and not in accord with the law.

It appears from the evidence, which the Tax Court apparently found credible, that the negotiations which led to the consummation of the contract of May 21, 1957, related to a contemplated sale of Jacobowitz's partnership interest to Foxman and Grenell. The option offered to Foxman and Grenell early in May of 1957, referred to a sale and the execution of "a bill of sale" upon completion of the agreement. The relevant provisions of the contract were couched in terms of "purchase" and "sale." The contract was signed by Foxman and Grenell, individually, and by them on behalf of the Company, although the Company assumed no liability thereunder. The obligation to purchase Jacobowitz's interest was solely that of Foxman and Grenell. The chattel mortgage on the partnership assets was given to secure payment.

Notwithstanding these facts and the lack of any ambiguity in the contract, Foxman and Grenell argue that the factors unequivocally determinative of the substance of the transaction were: the initial payment of $67,500 by a cashier's check issued in exchange for a check drawn on the account of the Company; the second payment in a similar amount by check drawn on the Company's account; the execution of notes in the name of the Company as maker; and, the prepayment of the notes by cashier's check charged against the Company's account.

This argument unduly emphasizes form in preference to substance. While form may be relevant "[the] incidence of taxation depends upon the substance of a transaction." *Commissioner of Internal Revenue v. Court Holding Co.*, 324 U.S. 331, 334, 65 S. Ct. 707, 708, 89 L. Ed. 981 (1945); *United States v. Cumberland Pub. Serv. Co.*, 338 U.S. 451, 455, 70 S. Ct. 280, 94 L. Ed. 251 (1950). The "transaction must be viewed as a whole, and each step, from the commencement of negotiations" to consummation, is relevant. *Ibid.* Where, as here, there has been a transfer and an acquisition of property pursuant to a contract, the nature of the transaction does not depend solely on the means employed to effect payment. *Ibid.*

It is apparent from the opinion of the Tax Court that careful consideration was given to the factors relied upon by Foxman and Grenell. It is therein stated, 41 T.C. at page 553:

> "These notes were endorsed by Foxman and Grenell individually, and the liability of [the Company] thereon was merely in the nature of security for their primary obligation under the agreement of May 21, 1957. The fact that they utilized partnership resources to discharge their own individual liability in such manner can hardly convert into a section 736 'liquidation' what would otherwise qualify as a section 741 'sale.'"

> "... the payments received by Jacobowitz were in discharge of their [Foxman's and Grenell's] obligation under the agreement, and not that of [the Company.] It was they who procured those payments in their own behalf from the assets of the partnership which they controlled. The use of [the Company] to make payment was wholly within their discretion and of no concern to Jacobowitz; his only interest was payment."

We are of the opinion that the quoted statements represent a fair appraisal of the true significance of the notes and the means employed to effect payment.

When the members of the partnership decided that Jacobowitz would withdraw in the interest of harmony they had a choice of means by which his withdrawal

C. TAXING THE PARTNER: SECTION 736

could be effected. They could have agreed inter se on either liquidation or sale. On a consideration of the plain language of the contract, the negotiations which preceded its consummation, the intent of the parties as reflected by their conduct, and the circumstances surrounding the transaction, the Tax Court found that the transaction was in substance a sale and not a liquidation of a retiring partner's interest. This finding is amply supported by the evidence in the record. The partners having employed the sale method to achieve their objective, Foxman and Grenell cannot avoid the tax consequences by a hindsight application of principles they now find advantageous to them and disadvantageous to Jacobowitz.

The issue before the Tax Court was essentially one of fact and its decision thereon may not be reversed in the absence of a showing that its findings were not supported by substantial evidence or that its decision was not in accord with the law.... There has been no such showing in this case.

The decisions of the Tax Court will be affirmed.

....

NOTE

Basic tax principles are not entirely banished. For example, if the "liquidating" partner, A, sells the distributed assets to D, who in turn contributes them to the partnership, thereby becoming a partner in the BCD partnership, the step-transaction analysis will prevail and the transaction will rightly be classified a sale of the distributee partner's interest for tax purposes. *Crenshaw v. United States*, 450 F.2d 472 (5th Cir. 1971). Likewise, a sale of a partnership interest for a share of future partnership profits may result in the selling partner being taxed on partnership income under assignment of income theories. *Collins v. Commissioner*, 14 T.C. 301, 306 (1950), *acq.*

C. TAXING THE PARTNER: SECTION 736

1. MODIFIED DISTRIBUTION RULES FOR PARTNERSHIP LIQUIDATIONS

Read §§ 732(b),(c) and 731(a)(2).

The taxation of liquidating distributions differs from the treatment of current distributions. Because the ex-partner will, by definition, have a $0 basis in her entire partnership interest, § 732(b) requires the partner to allocate her *outside* basis to the distributed money and property. Again, money is of necessity considered first. By contrast, nonliquidating distributions generally call for using *inside* basis to measure the basis of the distributed property in the partner's hands. § 732(a).

Liquidating distributions of receivables and inventory are singled out for special punishment. Congress was concerned that a partner might achieve a step-up in the basis of such property from the partnership's inside basis to the partner's outside basis. For example, if a partner had an outside basis of $3,000 and the partner received $1,000 in cash plus inventory with an inside basis of $100, the $1,000 would first reduce the partner's basis to $2,000, and the remaining $2,000 might be carried over to the inventory. To block the step-up, § 732(c)(1) declares that *in the context of a liquidation*, the basis of distributed properties shall be allocated first to any unrealized receivables and inventory *in an amount equal to the basis of each such property to the partnership*, with the result that the inventory takes a $100 basis, and § 731(a)(2) dictates that the partner report a loss if one distributee received nothing other than cash and inventory. In this instance, the distributee partner reports a loss of $1,900. Section 741 twists the knife by making the loss on the distribution a capital loss; this forcefully prevents a distributee partner from reporting an ordinary loss on distributed ordinary-income-producing assets. If, in addition, the partner had received any other property, even a pencil, that asset would take a $1,900 basis, the loss would be deferred, and the partner would wind up with what may be the pencil with the highest basis in the history of the world. Reg. § 1.731-1(a)(2). To summarize the loss rules, partners do recognize losses only on liquidating distributions, and then only if the distribution consists only of cash and ordinary income property and the inside basis of the distributed property plus the distributed cash is less than the partner's outside basis.

Imagine that A wants to withdraw from a real estate partnership in exchange for cash and put the money to some other use. In a world without taxes she would not care if the money came from a stranger, or from her partners as buyers of her interest, or from the partnership itself. However, as *Foxman* shows, it can make a big difference in a world with taxes. Despite the identity of *economic* results, the *tax* implications of a liquidation are more subtle and complex than a sale.

2. ROLE OF § 736

A withdrawing partner may want to retain a stake in the business, or to gear his selling price to future profits. For instance, he may say, "I want to get 10% of the net profits for the next 10 years," or "I want $10,000 per year out of the partnership for the next 10 years." Most people on the street would say that the first kind of payment makes him a "silent partner." The second kind of payment is less clear, but the person on the street might say he is getting a stream of income like a salary more than a payment for his share of the partnership's property. Section 736 tries to sort out these various possiblities.

To put it another way, assuming that the transaction is a liquidation of the partner's interest in a continuing partnership and not a sale, the next step is to classify the cash proceeds which the partner receives. That subject area is monopolized by § 736. The discussion in this chapter makes the usual assumption that § 736 applies only to distributions of money. We will not reach combinations of cash and property.

C. TAXING THE PARTNER: SECTION 736

Section 736 is a procedural section whose sole function is to sort payments which the partner receives from the partnership into either of two pigeonholes. Other Code sections of a general character then come into play to determine the federal income tax implications of the sorting process.

The two pigeonholes are:

1. Payments for the partner's interest in partnership "property," other than, in the case of a general partner in service partnership, (i) unrealized receivables in the sense of unpaid bills and (ii) goodwill (*unless* the partnership agreement provides to the contrary), and

2. All other payments.

The first class of payments is treated as a liquidating distribution. § 736(b)(1). The second class is generally treated as producing a flow of ordinary income to the retiring partner, either as a guaranteed payment if *not* geared to partnership income, or as a distributive share of partnership income if geared to partnership income. § 736(a)(1). These characterizations stick whether the payments are made in a lump sum or over time. These two classes of payments often occur simultaneously with respect to the same partner.

3. PAYMENTS FOR PARTNER'S SHARE OF PROPERTY: SECTION 736(b)

These payments are considered distributions in complete liquidation of the partner's interest, and generate a capital gain or loss to the partner when paid in money. *See* § 731. The gain or loss is measured by the difference between the partner's outside basis and the amount paid the partner (or the partner's estate or successor in interest), and should generally be reported in the year paid. Reg. § 1.731-1(a)(2). For this purpose, one includes reductions in partnership liabilities as constructive distributions of money. § 752(d). Also, if there is a § 754 election in force, § 734(b) adjustments will occur.

To take a simple example, if the ABC partnership had three equal members, and had as its sole asset a parcel of raw land with a basis and value of $300,000, and equal partner A retired interest in exchange for a $100,000 payment from the partnership, it would be obvious that the payment would be for property and that under § 731(a) A would have a gain or loss on the distribution, depending on whether the $100,000 he received was more or less than his outside basis in his partnership interest.

Taxpayers have to be at least somewhat honest. If there is no allocation agreement between the retiring partner and the partnership, the partner will have to report the value of her share of the partnership's assets as distributions. If there is an agreement (and there usually is), the retiring partner cannot overstate the value of her share of the underlying property. Reg. § 1.736-1(b)(5)(iii). An account they can exploit powerfully is goodwill. For example, if a partner withdraws and is paid more than the value of his share of the assets because the partnership has a great future, the parties are free to characterize the payment for the great prospects as either for goodwill — hence creating a distribution — or to treat the payments as in consideration of the partnership's prospects for future income — hence creating a guaranteed payment or an allocation.

4. TREATMENT OF PAYMENTS FOR PARTNER'S SHARE OF UNREALIZED RECEIVABLES AND GOODWILL

Payments for a *general partner's* share of unstated goodwill and unrealized receivables are *not* for property, but only if the payee is a general partner in a service partnership. § 736(b). This can be most painful for retiring doctors and lawyers, because their share of these items (especially receivables) can produce significant amounts of ordinary income. In all other cases, payments for stated goodwill, unstated goodwill, and even receivables are considered to be for property.

5. TREATMENT OF PAYMENTS FOR PARTNER'S SHARE OF GOODWILL

Going back to payment for receivables and unstated goodwill for a moment, assume that A is a one-third general partner of the ABC law partnership, which has no assets but which others have been clamoring to buy for $300,000. Assume that ABC buys out A's interest in cash for 33% of the next three years' profits and that there is no provision for goodwill in the partnership agreement. This transaction has to involve a payment for goodwill, because there are no other assets or receivables. Assuming that A has an outside basis of $0, the proceeds A receives have to be treated as a § 736(a)(1) distributive share, taxable to A. Its composition will depend on the character of the income earned by ABC and may, for example, include tax-exempt income and capital gains. The chance to buy the remaining partner out for a share of the partnership's income may appeal greatly to the remaining partners, because it reduces their future income taxes, compared to having the partner sell his interest to the remaining partners, which produces no tax reductions for the buyers. The taxation of section 736(a) payments is discussed below.

By contrast, if the partnership agreement labelled the payments as having been made for goodwill, the tax result would be a deemed payment for property. As a result, A would be deemed to receive distributions staggered over three years. In this simple case, every dollar received would be taxed as a capital gain, because A has an outside basis of $0. §§ 736(b), 731(a) and 741.

6. TREATMENT OF § 736(a) PAYMENTS

Again, § 736(a) payments are those for unrealized receivables and unstated goodwill of general partners in service businesses, and those otherwise not in exchange for the withdrawing partner's interest in partnership property. Reg.

C. TAXING THE PARTNER: SECTION 736

§ 1.736-1(a)(3). Section 736(a) payments are treated as distributive shares of partnership income if they vary with partnership income, and § 707(c) guaranteed payments if they do not. Either way, the remaining partners avoid taxes because the money paid out will either reduce part of their distributive shares of income or produce a § 162(a) deduction for the partnership, which the remaining partners will enjoy. Think about a prosperous "name" partner who retires from a big law firm. He probably has only a relatively small amount of his money tied up in the firm, but his partners are willing to pay him well to retain his name and to keep him friendly. The Code provides great bargaining flexibility. The major alternatives are:

1. Amend the partnership agreement to provide for a payment for (stated) goodwill to the name partner. Treat the cash paid for it as a payment of a purchase price (to be capitalized) and thereby let A report a capital gain.

2. Do not provide for payments for goodwill in the partnership agreement. Treat the distributions/payments as being for unstated goodwill. The retiring partner will report the payout as income but in exchange will bargain for more cash than under "1" because he will be taxed on the ordinary income at rates that are currently higher than capital gains tax rates.[1]

The latter is a reasonable result, in the sense that the essence of the deal may be that the retiring partner is being paid a continuing "quasi-salary" taxed under § 707(c) or a cut of the firm's profits, taxable as if he were still a partner. This can be viewed as the retirement plan the partners expect.

7. TIMING OF A § 731(a) GAIN

The withdrawing partner generally recognizes gains only after cash distributed exceeds the retiring partner's outside basis. § 731(a)(1). This is a rare application of the open transaction doctrine described in *Burnet v. Logan,* 283 U.S. 404, 413 (1931). However, Reg. § 1.736-1(b)(6) permits an optional proration of the gain. Presumably, most retiring partners will select the general rule, thereby deferring their tax bills, rather than prorating the gain. Losses are deferred until the last payment is made, unless the partner elects to prorate the loss. *Id.*

Paying off a major partner at once can put a big strain on the partnership's cash flow, so it is common to schedule the payouts over a number of years. In such cases, each payment is apportioned between § 736(a) and § 736(b) in accordance with the partner's retirement agreement. For example, all payments

---

[1] There is no capital gains tax rate differential if the partner is a corporation. §§ 11 and 1201.

could first be attributed to property until exhausted, which can achieve a major tax deferral.[2]

If there is no apportionment provision in the retirement agreement and the payments are *not fixed*, the payments are deemed to be 100% for property until the property interest is fully paid for. The rest is a guaranteed payment or distributive share. Reg. § 1.736-1(b)(5)(ii).

> *To illustrate*: C is leaving the ABC partnership. It is agreed that her interest in property is worth $100,000. The retirement agreement just contains a bare bones statement that, "The ABC partnership agrees to pay C 35% of profits for three years, starting this year." Assume her resulting share turns out to be $50,000 per year for each of the three years. The Regulations treat the first two payments as being for property alone. The last $50,000 is a distributive share because it is tied to profits, taxable as ordinary income to C. It correspondingly reduces the distributive shares of A and B.

By contrast, if the payments are *fixed*, each payment is prorated between § 736(a) and § 736(b) payments by relative value.

> *To illustrate*: C is leaving the ABC partnership. This year he will be paid a total of $150,000, of which $100,000 is for his interest in partnership property. He will get $50,000 per year for the next three years. Each $50,000 has to be divided into two elements — $33,333 as a payment for property and $16,667 as a guaranteed payment. C can report the gain (if any) on the $33,333 installments under the open-transaction method, or he can prorate the gain under Reg. § 1.736-1(b)(6) as if the transaction were an installment sale. The former method defers gain until C has recovered his basis in the property, after which all § 736(b) receipts are fully taxed. § 731(a)(1) and Reg. §§ 1.731-1(a)(1), 1.736-1(b)(6)-(7), Example (1).

The difference between these two treatments was a large feature of the following case.

ESTATE OF THOMAS P. QUIRK v. COMMISSIONER
55 T.C.M. 1188 (1988)

CLAPP, JUDGE.

[Quirk was a member of the QLM engineering partnership until his withdrawal. There was no written partnership agreement, even though the partnership was

---

[2] Reg. § 1.736-1(b)(5)(iii) provides that the total amount allocated to § 736(b) cannot exceed the value of the partner's interest in partnership property when he died or retired.

C. TAXING THE PARTNER: SECTION 736

a large enterprise. The business thereafter continued as the LMS partnership. Quirk's share of the partnership at the time of his withdrawal consisted of a share of the receivables, a share of the cash, and a share of the liabilities owed to a bank. No agreement was reached about his retirement compensation. The partnership reported cash distributions to Quirk plus reductions of his share of partnership liabilities as guaranteed payments of about $119,000 in 1974 and $185,000 in 1975. Quirk reported about $112,000 in 1974 and none in 1975 (the correct numbers turned out to be much higher, as shown in the last paragraph of the decision. The court accepted the outside accountants' (Peat, Marwick) analysis of the value of Quirk's capital account, given the confused record.]

Opinion

....

At the outset, it must be noted that Quirk presented no evidence to controvert the figures contained in the Peat Marwick financial statements. No independent evaluation or financial statement prepared by qualified accountants was entered into evidence on behalf of Quirk, and no witnesses testified on behalf of Quirk as to an alternative valuation....

Where parties fail to agree as to the value of a retired partner's interest in partnership property, we will value the property based on a review of the facts and circumstances before us. Based on a review of the uncontroverted evidence before us, we will adopt Peat Marwick's financial statement as the basis for our conclusions of the issues of this case. Peat Marwick had been QLM's accountants from 1971 through 1974, and prior to the instant controversy, Quirk took no issue with their tax conclusions on partnership matters. Moreover, the testimony of Michael Manus, a partner at Peat Marwick and a certified public accountant, confirmed to our satisfaction that the statements were prepared in a professional manner and in accordance with generally accepted accounting principles. Finally, and foremost, Quirk presented no alternative financial statements for us to review, and accordingly, has not sustained his burden of proof with respect to the unreliability of the statements on which respondent bases his deficiencies. With this determined, we turn to the issues at hand.

Quirk and the remaining partners disagree as to the character and treatment of the distributions. We will discuss each in turn.

Section 736 applies to payments made to a 'retiring partner' by the partnership in liquidation of the partner's entire interest in the partnership ..., and provides the framework to determine the nature and character of such distributions.

Section 736 and the regulations thereunder state that payments made in liquidation of the entire interest of a retiring partner are considered as a distribution, and not as a distributive share or as a guaranteed payment, to the extent that the payments are made in exchange for the partner's entire interest in the partnership property, *except* unrealized receivables (and good will, not at issue here).... [S]ection 736 payments include items treated as distributions of money under section 752.

Unrealized receivables as defined by section 751(c), include any rights to payments for goods, which are not considered capital assets, or for services to the extent that the payments have not been taken into income by the taxpayer under his method of accounting. If the payments are made for unrealized receivables of the partnership, then they are taken into account in the income of the withdrawing partner as a distributive share under section 702 if they are determined with regard to the income of the partnership, or under section 61(a) as a guaranteed payment if they are determined without regard to the income of the partnership.... If a guaranteed payment is involved, the relevant amount would be deductible by the partnership if the requirements of section 162(a) have been satisfied.

If the payments are not made for partnership unrealized receivables, then the amounts are treated as made for the partner's interest in assets and as a distribution in complete liquidation under section 731. The remaining partners are not allowed any deduction for those payments since they represent either a distribution or a purchase of the withdrawing partner's capital interest by the partnership and the remaining partners.... The withdrawing partner does not recognize any gain except to the extent that any money distributed exceeds the adjusted basis of the partner's interest in the partnership. Section 731(a)(1). The gain to be recognized would be capital in nature.... [The regulations provide] that the distributions to a withdrawing partner must be allocated between section 736(a) and 736(b) payments. The regulations, after requiring the above allocations, then discuss how the allocation should be made when the amount to be paid is a 'fixed amount' or is not a fixed amount. We will address each of these....

In addition to the stipulated distributions, the parties **agree** that Quirk received a distribution in liquidation of his partnership interest by virtue of his release from the Chemical Bank note in 1974 and 1975, but disagree over whether Quirk's release from the Chemical Bank debt by the partnership's payment of Quirk's share of the Chemical Bank note liability constituted a deemed distribution of cash to him for his interest in unrealized receivables or rather for his interest in other partnership assets.

Respondent determined, and the remaining partners maintain, that the special rules under section 736(b)(2) are applicable to the distributions to Quirk to the extent the partnership's assets consisted of unrealized receivables, 89.45989 percent according to the stipulation among the parties. Therefore, they contend, 89.45989 percent of the distributions to Quirk are to be treated as guaranteed payments since the amounts were determined without regard to the income of the partnership. As guaranteed payments, they are ordinary income to Quirk and deductible by the partnership under section 162 by virtue of section 707(c). The balance of each distribution or 10.5401 percent is a nontaxable return of basis to Quirk to the extent of his basis and not deductible by the remaining partners. Finally, they contend that the overall distributions to Quirk include the $184,002 release of liability of the Chemical Bank note pursuant to sections 752 and 736.

C. TAXING THE PARTNER: SECTION 736　　　　　　　　　　　　　　　　　　171

Quirk, on the other hand, disputes this analysis, and characterizes the distributions to him by the partnership as payments in exchange for his partnership interest under section 736(b)(1). Quirk maintains that with respect to each disputed item of the state lawsuit there was a reasonable prospect that the asset valuation could be changed. Those areas included the value of Quirk's overall partnership interest, the method by which QLM computed and valued accounts receivable, doubtful accounts, and the omission from the QLM financial statement of computer tapes and programs. That being the case, distributions might very well be deemed as made for assets other than unrealized receivables, and, if the payments are not for partnership unrealized receivables, then the amounts paid are treated as made for the partner's interest in assets and as a distribution under section 731.

We find for respondent and the remaining partners on these issues despite Quirk's arguments. Quirk provided no evidence to support his contentions that the distributions made to him for his interest in the partnership represented for the most part partnership assets other than unrealized receivables, and for purposes of this analysis, we will adopt the amounts and figures in the Peat Marwick statements. To the extent the payments were made for unrealized receivables, 89.45989 percent, Quirk must take the payments into income as guaranteed payments because the payments to him were made according to percentage interest in the assets of the partnership. Moreover, as the $184,002 decrease in Quirk's individual liability on the Chemical Bank note is considered as a distribution of cash to him by the partnership under section 752(b), and 89.45989 percent of that distribution is accordingly treated as attributable to unrealized receivables, this amount must also be found to be a guaranteed payment.

Having determined the nature of the payments, we must now determine the proper allocation of the distributions and whether or not the distributions received by Quirk were fixed or contingent within the meaning of the regulations and section 736, to decide their proper tax treatment.

As previously stated, [the regulations provide] that when a partnership makes payments to retire a withdrawing partner's entire interest, the payments must be allocated between payments under section 736(a) and payments under section 736(b). Payments made to a retiring partner for the value of his interest in partnership property other than unrealized receivables are classified as 'section 736(b) payments,' whereas payments to the retiring partner for unrealized receivables are classified as 'section 736(a) payments.'... Depending upon the circumstances, payments for goodwill may be section 736(a) or section 736(b) payments.

The regulations, after requiring the above allocation, which was determined to be 89.45989 percent/10.5401 percent, based on the Peat Marwick financial statement, discuss how the allocation should be made when the amount to be paid to the retiring partner (1) is a fixed amount and (2) is not a fixed amount.

Payments which are fixed in amount — The discussion in the regulations regarding the payment of a fixed amount assumes that the fixed amount will be paid over a specific period of time and provides that if the fixed amount (*whether or not supplemented by any additional amounts*) is to be received over a fixed number of years, a portion of each payment is treated as a distribution in exchange for partnership property under section 736(b). The portion of each payment so treated is equal to the ratio of the total fixed agreed payments under section 736(b) to the total fixed agreed payments under sections 736(a) and (b). The balance of each payment is treated as a payment under section 736(a)(1) or (2)....

Payments which are not fixed in amount — When the retiring partner receives payments which are not fixed in amount, 'such payments shall first be treated as payments in exchange for his interest in partnership property under section 736(b) to the extent of the value of that interest and, thereafter, as payments under section 736(a).'... Payments which are not fixed in amount are payments such as those based on a percentage of partnership income earned over a period of future years....

It is respondent's and the remaining partner's position that the determination of the character of each distribution to Quirk (of cash, or of a release of liability under section 752) is to be determined pursuant to section 1.736-1(b)(5)(i), Income Tax Regs., because the payments are of a fixed amount. They contend that while there is a dispute over the value of the assets, there is no dispute that Quirk is entitled to his percentage of the partnership assets as of October 31, 1974. It is submitted that Quirk's share of these assets represents a fixed amount as that term is used in the regulations, and the fact that Quirk could receive more as a result of the litigation would merely represent the 'supplemental' amounts contemplated by the regulations.

Petitioner Quirk argues to the contrary. He contends these distributions can not be characterized as fixed amounts because they were contingent pursuant to section 1.736-1(b)(5)(ii), Income Tax Regs., and that any payments to him in 1974 and 1975 must be treated as payments under section 736(b)(1) to the extent of his partnership basis, and that no part of the payments would be treated as attributable to unrealized receivables until Quirk had received payment for his interest in partnership property. Quirk provides two reasons for classifying his distribution payments as contingent and, therefore, as payments for his interest in partnership property under section 736(b)(1).

First, Quirk argues that the regulations describe the requisite fixed amount in conjunction with its receipt over a fixed number of years because the language explicitly requires both the existence of a fixed sum and a certain pay out period before a fixed sum can qualify as a payment to which the allocation ratio should be applied. In the present case, he points out that even if it might be said that a fixed amount is present, there are no facts from which it can be determined the period of time payments were to be made....

C. TAXING THE PARTNER: SECTION 736

The second reason why Quirk believes that the distribution payments should be treated as made pursuant to section 736(b)(1) is that the language of the regulations requires the existence of an agreement between the parties with respect to the total of the fixed payments, which he reads as stemming from the phrase 'total fixed agreed payments' in section 1.736-1(b)(5)(i), Income Tax Regs. In this case, he continues, the parties have not agreed in any respect on the issue of the totality of the payments Quirk will receive. Furthermore, it is incorrect to suggest that because minimum total payments, pursuant to the Peat Marwick financial statement, may eventually be paid to Quirk, the regulatory requirements needed to establish the existence of fixed payments have been met. The regulation does not specify or call for the existence of such a minimum amount.

Once again, we cannot agree with Quirk's interpretation of the regulations ... and find that the distribution payments to Quirk in the instant case were of a 'fixed amount.'

First, we do not read the regulations as necessarily requiring payments of a fixed amount *and* over a fixed period of time. The legislative history of section 736 illustrates this point:

> Section 736. Payments to a retiring partner or a deceased partner's successor in interest. This section provides rules for the treatment of payments made to a retiring partner or to the estate, heir, or any other successor in interest of a deceased partner. The provisions are applicable only if the payments are in exchange for the liquidation of the partnership interest of the recipient. *It is immaterial whether such payments are based on a percentage of partnership income, or are fixed in amount and payable either in a lump sum or periodically over an interval of time.* Emphasis added.

If we were to adopt petitioner's interpretation, a lump-sum payment could never be deemed a 'fixed amount' because by its terms it would not be payable over a fixed period. A lump-sum payment could not, therefore, ever be allocated between section 736(a) and 736(b) payments. This is in contradiction to the legislative history, and clearly not what the regulations intended. Moreover, in section 1.736-1(b)(5)(ii), Income Tax Regs., which discusses contingent payments, contingent payments are described as not fixed in amount. There is no mention of the 'not received over a fixed number of years' aspect, the emphasis of Quirk's argument. The regulations and the legislative history highlight the fixed 'amount' and not the fixed number of payments....

Second, nowhere in the regulations is an agreement required between the parties with respect to a set number of payments in order to have a 'fixed amount.' Section 1.736-1(b)(5)(iii), Income Tax Regs., specifically states that:

> "In lieu of the rules provided in subdivisions (i) and (ii) of this subparagraph, the allocation of each annual payment between section 736(a) and (b)

may be made in any manner to which all the remaining partners and the withdrawing partner ... agree. Thus, in the *absence* of an agreement, subdivisions (i) and (ii) apply." [Emphasis added]

Finally, Quirk makes the argument that the possibility he might receive an amount in excess of the Peat Marwick valuation of his share of the partnership assets means that all distributions made to him must be treated as contingent payments and not as a fixed amount. We do not agree with this contention. Any excess would be an additional amount within the meaning of section 1.736-1(b)(5)(i), Income Tax Regs., and would not disrupt his entitlement to 30.667 percent of the partnership assets. To interpret otherwise would allow any withdrawing partner to have the ability to create contingent payments merely by initiating litigation, thereby circumventing the regulations and allocation sanctioned therein. Moreover, this specified minimum amount based on a fixed percentage of partnership assets is due Quirk without regard to partnership income and would satisfy the definition of fixed amount pursuant to section 736 regulations.

Because we find a fixed amount is due Quirk, the applicable regulation is section 1.736-1(b)(5)(i), Income Tax Regs., and Quirk's payments must be allocated according to its provisions. Thus, the payment must be allocated between unrealized receivables and other assets. Of each payment received, 89.45989 percent is to be treated as guaranteed payments and reportable as ordinary income to Quirk and deductible by the partnership. The balance, or 10.5401 percent of each distribution, is a recovery of basis and then capital gain.

The total payments to Quirk after October 31, 1974, in liquidation of his partnership interest amounted to $151,945 in 1974 and $207,372 in 1975 and 89.45989 percent of each payment represented a guaranteed payment deductible by the partnership in 1974 to the extent of $135,929.83 ($151,945 x 89.45989 percent) and $185,514.76 in 1975 ($207,372 x 89.45989 percent). The balance of the distributions, $16,015 in 1974 ($151,945 x 10.5401 percent) in 1974 and $21,857 in 1975 ($207,372 x 10.5401 percent) are to be applied against Quirk's adjusted basis of his interest in the partnership under sections 736(b) and 731(a)(1). Quirk must report capital gain only to the extent his distributions exceed his adjusted basis in the partnership. Section 736(b).

Decisions will be entered under Rule 155.

QUESTION

Is it clear to you what was at stake to each party in this case?

8. LOSSES ON DISTRIBUTION

Section 731(a)(2) prevents the partner from recognizing loss on the liquidation of his interest, unless the distribution consists solely of money, unrealized receivables, or inventory items (or some combination thereof), in which event a

C. TAXING THE PARTNER: SECTION 736

loss is recognized to the extent that his outside basis exceeds the money plus his basis in the receivables and inventory items. This is an important issue from both planning and conceptual perspectives.

The reasoning behind § 731(a)(2) is fairly straightforward. Congress generally defers gains and losses when a partner receives a distribution of property (even though he may have withdrawn as a partner) because the partner continues his investment via his ownership of the property. To carry out the thought, § 731(a) generally refuses to allow a loss, and § 732(b) gives the partner a basis in the property equal to his former outside basis. This is a plain example of a nonrecognition transaction. The nonrecognition approach collapses, however, if the partner got money alone, because there is no conceivable way to assign money a basis other than its face amount, so there is no escape from recognizing gains and losses when cash alone is distributed, and there is no reason to wait any longer; the partner has "cashed out." Section 731(a)(1) and (2) reflect that reality. The nonrecognition approach is unavailable for inventory and receivables because of congressional anxiety that the distributee might receive such assets with a basis higher than their inside basis, thereby causing an aggregate reduction in ordinary income, or increased ordinary losses. Section 732(c)(1) stops that by limiting the basis in distributed inventory and unrealized receivables to their inside bases. The trouble is that the partner's outside basis may be higher than the property's inside basis. In such a case, the distributee can recognize a loss, assuming there are no non-§ 751 assets to be allocated basis under § 732(c)(2). § 731(a)(2). Note again that the loss will be a capital loss. §§ 731(a) and 741. If the loss was triggered by depreciated inventory, it may be better to sell it, allocate the resulting ordinary loss among the partners, and distribute the cash proceeds.

Finally, observe that if the partnership distributes only cash (and perhaps unrealized receivables as well) and throws in any other asset (aside from accounts receivable and inventory items), there is no loss. Instead, there is a lonely asset with what may be a preposterously high basis.

PROBLEM 8-1

A, B, C and D are equal members of the ABCD Partnership. Each partner has the following basis in his or her partnership interest:

A: $2,000
B: $9,000
C: $4,000
D: $5,000

ABCD makes a liquidating distribution of $1,500 to each partner and at the same time it distributes the following properties to the partners:

To A: Raw land with an inside basis and value of $7,000.

To B: A car with an inside basis and value of $7,000. Assume alternatively that the car is or is not dealer property.

To C: Furniture with an inside basis of $0 and a value of $7,000. Assume alternatively that the furniture has been written off under § 168 and is subject to § 1245 recapture. In the case where the furniture is subject to recapture, consider what would happen if C got furniture worth $6,900 and a $100 bond that was a capital asset in ABCD's hands.

To D: A check for $7,000, or a $7,000 money market fund account at Merrill Lynch.

What is the basis of each property to each partner, and what is each partner's outside basis and income, if any? Disregard any § 751 effects except for purposes of defining hot assets, and disregard the effects of §§ 736 and 734 on the theory that they do not apply to liquidations of the entire partnership.

D. LIQUIDATING THE TWO-PERSON PARTNERSHIP

Section 736 assures that, as long as payouts are being made to the withdrawing partner (or her estate), the partnership continues for federal income tax purposes, even if it was originally just a two-person partnership such that the disappearance of one member terminates its existence at local law. *See* Reg. §§ 1.708-1(b)(1)(i)(b) and 1.736-1(a)(6). This means the partnership is deemed to continue even though the remaining partner may sell the assets and retire from the business during the § 736 payment period.[3] Except for this special case, § 736 does not apply when the partnership liquidates, because § 736 contemplates a continuing partnership, including the twilight case under Reg. § 1.736-1(a)(6) where a partner retires from a partnership leaving only a single remaining partner.

E. TAXATION OF THE PARTNERSHIP

The partnership is not taxed on the distribution of appreciated or depreciated assets to a withdrawing partner. § 731(b). This stands in stark distinction to corporate distributions.[4]

F. SELECTING BETWEEN A SALE OR A LIQUIDATION OF THE PARTNERSHIP INTEREST

If there are only two partners, one of whom plans to sell out to the other, it does not matter from an economic point of view whether the transaction is

---

[3] Q: If there is no business, is the guaranteed payment-type § 736 payment deductible on the theory it came from remaining partners' capital?

[4] However, § 751 might tax the partnership to the extent there is a disproportionately large distribution of inventory, with a resulting deemed purchase of inventory by the distributee partner.

F. SELECTING BETWEEN SALE OR LIQUIDATION

structured as a sale of a partnership interest or a liquidation of the selling partner's interest, followed by the liquidated partner's sale of the distributed assets to his former partner. It can, however, matter for federal income tax purposes.

KINNEY v. UNITED STATES
228 F. Supp. 656 (1964),
aff'd, 358 F.2d 738 (5th Cir. 1966)

HUNTER, DISTRICT JUDGE.

This is an action for the recovery of $10,679.37, plus interest, paid as income tax for the year 1958....

In the early part of 1958 disagreements arose between the two men and they began discussing the termination of their partnership association. Stine, who wanted to operate the mill as an individual, made an offer to buy out Kinney's interest and further proposed that they divide various land holdings in kind. Kinney wanted to get out of the mill and discussed selling his interest to Stine. The men negotiated for some time and ultimately each placed the matter in the hands of their respective attorneys for resolution. The taxpayer was represented by Norman F. Anderson and Stine was represented by Richard A. Anderson. Since the taxpayer wanted to get out of the mill, his attorney approached the negotiations with the view to sell out or liquidate the business. Conversely, since Mr. Stine wanted to acquire the mill and continue to operate it individually, he instructed his attorney to negotiate to purchase Mr. Kinney's interest....

Finally, on June 14, 1958, Richard Anderson, on behalf of Mr. Stine, proposed to buy Mr. Kinney's interest in the partnership in the following terms: The fixed assets were to be transferred to a Texas corporation, which would be formed, in exchange for all of the stock of the corporation which would be distributed equally to Messrs. Stine and Kinney; Mr. Stine was to have an option to purchase Mr. Kinney's stock for $110,000 on terms, or $85,000 in cash; Mr. Stine was to acquire Mr. Kinney's remaining interest in the business by cancelling certain obligations owed to it by the partners, assuming all of the liabilities, and paying Mr. Kinney an additional $172,000. In his capacity as the taxpayer's representative, Norman Anderson made a counter-proposal pertaining to a change in the form of security for the notes Mr. Stine was to give to the taxpayer, and further proposed that the purchase price for the taxpayer's interest in the partnership which would remain after the transfer to the corporation be allocated to the individual assets at book value with the loss being absorbed in the inventory.

This proposal was acceptable to both parties and the respective attorneys began drafting the various instruments for signature. Finally, on July 7, 1958, the parties executed five documents reciting:

1. That the land and improvements owned by the partnership were transferred to the newly formed corporation, Orange Rice Milling Company, Inc., in exchange for its stock, said stock divided equally between Stine and Kinney.

2. That the depreciable, movable property owned by the partnership was transferred to the newly formed corporation, Orange Rice Milling Company, Inc., in exchange for its stock, said stock divided equally between Stine and Kinney.

3. That the Orange Rice Milling Company partnership be dissolved as of June 30, 1958.

4. That Mr. Stine was granted an option to purchase the taxpayer's stock in the new corporation.

5. That the taxpayer conveyed his interest in all of the other assets of the partnership to Mr. Stine, for $172,000, plus the assumption by Mr. Stine of all of the liabilities of the partnership and the cancellation of certain debts owed by the partners.

The document reciting the sale of the taxpayer's remaining interest in the partnership after the transfer to the corporation allocated the purchase price to the individual assets on this basis:

Asset	Consideration
A. Cash, receivables, claims, securities:	Book value
B. Sublease, trade names, patents, goodwill:	Zero
C. Inventory:	Remaining selling price in excess of items denoted in A.

....

On July 31, 1958, Mr. Stine exercised the option and discount feature by purchasing the taxpayer's stock in the newly formed corporation for $85,000. In their income tax return for 1958 the taxpayers reported a long-term capital loss on the sale of the stock in the amount of $61,233.85 computed as follows:

Cost or other basis in stock determined by basis in assets	$171,233.85
Selling price	110,000.00
Loss	$ 61,233.85

They also reported an ordinary loss of $18,033.12 and claimed that it was sustained on the sale of inventory to Mr. Stine. This loss was computed as follows:

Sale of inventory received upon dissolution of Orange Rice Milling Co. (Partnership):

Acquired 6-30-58 at a cost of	$922,132.05
Sold 7-7-58 for	904,098.93
Loss	$18,033.12

F. SELECTING BETWEEN SALE OR LIQUIDATION

Upon audit of the return, the Internal Revenue Service contended that several errors had been made in reporting the items listed above. The taxpayer's basis in the stock was found to be $152,290.16, rather than $171,233.85, and the selling price was discovered to be $85,000, rather than $110,000. The result of these adjustments was to allow a capital loss of $67,290.16, rather than $61,233.85 as had been reported. The determination was also made that the taxpayers did not sustain an ordinary loss of $18,033.12 on the sale of inventory, as had been reported, but that instead, a long-term capital loss of $36,976.81 was sustained on the sale of his remaining partnership interest computed as follows:

Basis of Mr. Kinney's one-half interest in partnership	$208,976.81
Selling price	172,000.00
Long-term capital loss	$36,976.81

....

The Law

The issue to be decided by the Court is whether the loss of $36,976.81 claimed by the taxpayers in the transaction hereinabove described should be treated as an ordinary loss, as they contend, or as a capital loss, as the Government contends. We are not concerned with that part of the partnership assets (land and depreciable items) which were transferred to the Texas corporation. The loss here in controversy only stems from the sale covering the miscellaneous assets (principally receivables and inventories). Also, it is not the amount, but the character of this loss which is in controversy.

The economic consequences, apart from income taxes, would be the same to the parties irrespective of whether the sale was a partnership interest or of property received as a distribution from the partnership.

The taxpayers' argument is that Congress has provided for different tax consequences dependent upon which procedure and form is followed. Where a partnership interest is sold, Section 741 specifies capital gain or loss treatment with exceptions not here involved; but, says the taxpayer, under Section [735], the sale by a distributee of property received as a distribution from a partnership keeps its character as either a capital item, or ordinary income or loss items, as if the distribution had been made by the partnership itself.

It is the substance of a transaction rather than the form in which it is cast that governs the tax consequences. (*Weinert's Estate v. Commissioner*, 294 F.2d 750, 755, C.A. 5th). The record here reveals that the substance of the transaction which gave rise to this lawsuit is far more than the sale of items of inventory. The essence of the transaction was a sale by the taxpayer of his interest in a partnership to his partner who continued to carry on the business. All the testimony on the subject, including that of the taxpayer and his attorney, leads us to that conclusion. We consider this transaction in its entirety, for to fragment or otherwise isolate a minute segment of the transaction is diametrically opposed to the entire philosophy of our tax laws. The Court of Appeals for the Sixth

Circuit made this plain in very cogent language (*Mather v. Commissioner*, 149 F.2d 393, 397, *certiorari denied*, 326 U.S. 767):

"It has been said too often to warrant citation, that taxation is an intensely practical matter, and that the substance of the thing done and not the form it took, must govern, and the courts have recognized that where the essential nature of a transaction is the acquisition of property, it will be viewed as a whole, and closely related steps will not be separated either at the instance of the taxpayer or the taxing authority. *Commr. v. Ashland Oil & Refining Co.*, 99 F.2d 588, 591 (C.C.A. 6)...."

An examination of this transaction in its entirety leaves no doubt but that the taxpayer sold his interest in the partnership to Mr. Stine and that the latter continued to operate the business formerly conducted by the partnership. It is, of course, an elementary principle that the sale or exchange of a partnership interest in a going concern is a capital transaction resulting in either a capital gain or a capital loss. It can in no way give rise to an ordinary loss as claimed by the taxpayer. Section 741 of the Internal Revenue Code of 1954....

Here, Stine acquired more than a group of assets. He acquired the right to continue operating the business formerly conducted by the partnership using the same assets, owing the same creditors, and using the same brand names. The business operation did not cease even during the negotiations and was continued by Mr. Stine after the transaction was closed just as the parties always contemplated.

We conclude that in this case Mr. Stine purchased the going business of the partnership "lock, stock and barrel." In fact, the contract reciting the sale of the assets even recites that he bought the taxpayer's half-interest in the cash owned by the partnership.

The significance of the total sale of a partner's total interest in a partnership has been noted by the Court of Appeals for the Sixth Circuit in *Commissioner v. Shapiro, supra* (p. 535):

> It is fundamental in applying tax statutes that matters of substance are of first importance. The price paid for the property in question may have been based partly on assets excluded under the act from the phrase "capital assets" such as inventories of property held by the partnership primarily for sale to customers in the ordinary course of its trade or business, but the sale made by respondent was not a sale of those assets. It is a well settled rule of law that the joint effects of a partnership belong to the firm and not the partners and that a partner has no individual property in any specific assets of the firm, instead the interest of each partner in the partnership property is his share in the surplus, after the partnership debts are paid and after the partnership accounts are settled. *Blodgett v. Silberman*, 277 U.S. 1, 10. Respondent sold all of his interest in the partnership, tangible and intangible, as a going concern, which in all essentials is different from the ordinary assets of the partnership used in the usual course of its business.

F. SELECTING BETWEEN SALE OR LIQUIDATION

It was made clear in this decision that whether or not the selling price was based on property other than capital assets is of no significance since the sale was the sale of the partner's total interest in the partnership. Coincidentally, the Court of Appeals for the Eighth Circuit had the same question before it in a case involving a taxpayer with the same name. *United States v. Shapiro*, 178 F.2d 459....

The critical question here is whether in fact and in substance the petitioners actually sold their respective interests in the partnership, and the facts show that the substance of what occurred was a sale by the taxpayer of his entire interest in the partnership to his partner.

In arguing that the transaction requires ordinary loss treatment, taxpayer is arguing that the execution on July 7, 1958, of a document reciting the dissolution of the partnership and distribution of the assets actually accomplished both of these things on June 30, 1958, or seven days earlier. In truth and in fact neither occurred. The business did not terminate on June 30, 1958, for its operations were in progress through July 7, 1958, and there was no real distribution of assets. What really happened is that on July 7, 1958, the taxpayer sold his entire one-half partnership interest to Edward J. Stine. That the transaction was divided into two parts, one being the creation of a corporation, is of no consequence. The creation of the corporation and transfer to it of the fixed and depreciable assets in exchange for stock amounts to a partial distribution to the partners and was not a taxable transaction. Section 731 of the Internal Revenue Code of 1954.... Although the taxpayer refers to it as the sale of "miscellaneous assets" the second part of the transaction was a sale by him of what remained of his partnership interest. These same circumstances existed in *Long v. Commissioner*, 173 F.2d 471. In holding that there had been a capital transaction, the Court noted that there had been no cessation of business or complete liquidation and that there had merely been a sale of the partnership interest that remained after the distribution of some assets.

Moreover, the taxpayer erroneously states that the sale of the miscellaneous assets was preceded by the termination of the business on July 7, 1958, as of June 30, 1958. Section 708(b) of the Internal Revenue Code of 1954 ... sets forth the only two circumstances under which a partnership shall be considered terminated for tax purposes....

Conclusion

Judgment is entered in favor of the Government. Taxpayers' complaint is dismissed with prejudice.

NOTES

1. *Which is the controlling cliche?* The most popular bromide of the tax avoider is Learned Hand's famous quotation, "Any one may so arrange his affairs that his taxes shall be as low as possible; he is not bound to choose that pattern which will best pay the Treasury; there is not even a patriotic duty to increase one's taxes." *Helvering v. Gregory*, 69 F.2d 809, 810 (2d Cir. 1934), *aff'd*, 293 U.S. 465 (1935). Conversely, every law student who has had even one tax course knows that the courts love to lecture the parties in tax litigation that substance must prevail over mere forms. Did Hunter, J. get it right in the *Kinney* decision, or did he merely pick the more attractive cliche and recklessly apply it to the facts?

2. *The tax stakes in* **Kinney.** The tax stakes apparently were that if the partnership interest were sold, even though it was rich in inventory, it would not generate any ordinary loss, because § 751 only reaches gains. Thus, the parties (we presume) decided on a distribution (with carryover basis) followed by a sale at a loss. If the taxpayers had won, § 735(a) would have assured a continuance of the character of the distributed properties, especially inventory, without regard to whether it was substantially appreciated. This issue can take a more common form.

> *To illustrate*: A is an equal member of the ABC partnership, whose primary asset has a basis of $0 and a value of $90. A proposes to buy the asset from the partnership. Would you advise that the partnership first distribute the asset? The answer is "almost surely yes," because if A buys the asset, A will be taxed on the $30 gain attributable to her share. If A buys the asset (after it is distributed to the partners) from B and C, only they will pay a tax. Is this an example of a trap for the unwary? How ignorant do you have to be to be "unwary," as opposed to dull-witted?

3. *The "basis strip."* This is a good point to introduce the "basis strip" concept, which is used in advance of a sale of an asset. The idea is to use the § 734(b) election aggressively to increase the basis of undistributed assets, thereby reducing the gain (or increasing the loss) on the sale of the distributed asset. For example, if the ABC partnership planned to sell asset M, which had a basis of $1,000, it might distribute asset N, which also has a $1,000 basis, to a partner with a zero basis in his partnership interest. This could increase ABC's basis in M to $2,000, and could even produce a loss on its sale. Should this be denounced as a mere manipulation of forms, or does it stand up? This leads us to the next topic.

G. THE PARTNERSHIP ANTI-ABUSE RULE REGULATIONS

In 1994, the IRS issued final regulations establishing a broad anti-abuse rule for partnerships. Reg. § 1.701-2. These *in terrorem* regulations permit the IRS to take virtually any action, including overriding the literal words of a particular statutory or regulatory provision, if it deems any partnership-related transaction to be abusive. The breadth and subjectivity of the regulations and the lack of any

G. THE PARTNERSHIP ANTI-ABUSE REGULATIONS

safe harbors may mean that transactions the parties considered innocent may easily be abusive under the regulations.

General Anti-abuse Rule

The regulations consider a partnership transaction abusive if:

> "a partnership is formed or availed of in connection with a transaction a principal purpose of which is to reduce substantially the present value of the partners' aggregate federal income tax liability in a manner that is inconsistent with the intent of subchapter K."

According to the Regulations, the intent of Subchapter K is to let taxpayers conduct joint business and investment activities through a flexible economic arrangement without incurring an entity level tax. The Regulations set forth certain requirements for a partnership transaction or series of related transactions to be treated as being within the intent of Subchapter K.

- First, the partnership must be bona fide, and the transaction (or series of related transactions) must be entered into for a substantial business purpose.

- Second, the form of the transaction (or series of related transactions) must be respected under substance-over-form principles.

- Third, the tax consequences to each partner from partnership operations and transactions must accurately reflect the partners' economic agreement and clearly reflect the partners' income. However, the Regulations provide an exception to the last requirement where such tax consequences result from certain provisions of Subchapter K that were adopted to promote administrative convenience and other policy objectives and such tax consequences, taking into account all the relevant facts and circumstances, are clearly contemplated by such provisions.

If the IRS determines that a partnership transaction is abusive under the above-described rule, it is empowered to recast the transaction in almost any manner in order to achieve tax results that are consistent with Subchapter K. For example, the IRS may disregard the partnership, treat one or more of the purported partners as not being a partner, adjust the partnership's or a partner's method of accounting, reallocate the partnership's items of income, deductions, losses, and credits, or otherwise adjust or modify the claimed tax treatment.

In determining whether a partnership was formed or availed of for an abusive purpose, the IRS will look to all the surrounding facts and circumstances. In addition, the Regulations list a number of factors, the existence of which *may* indicate the presence of an abusive purpose:

(i) the present value of the partners' aggregate tax liability is substantially less than if the partnership did not exist and the partners conducted the partnership's activities directly;

(ii) the present value of the partners' aggregate tax liability is substantially less than if a series of purportedly separate transactions designed to achieve an end result were integrated and treated as steps in a single transaction;

(iii) one or more partners who are necessary to achieve the claimed tax treatment have nominal interests, are substantially protected from any risks of loss or have little or no participation in profits in excess of a preferred return for the use of their capital;

(iv) substantially all of the partners are related;

(v) partnership tax items are allocated in accordance with the literal language of the allocation rules but the allocations result in consequences inconsistent with the purpose of such rules — thereby rendering compliance with the (formidable) substantial economic effect regulations inadequate (!);

(vi) the benefits and burdens of property nominally contributed to the partnership are retained in substantial part by the contributing party; and

(vii) the benefits and burdens of partnership property are shifted in substantial part to the distributee partners before or after the actual distribution of such property is made to the distributee partners.

A transaction may be abusive if merely "a" principal purpose of the transaction, as opposed to "the" principal purpose of the transaction, is to reduce the partners' federal income tax liabilities in a proscribed manner. This means that even if the form of the partnership transaction is driven by business considerations, it may be deemed abusive if there is also a principal purpose to reduce the partners' tax liabilities.

Similarly, in order to determine whether a transaction causes a proscribed reduction of the partners' aggregate tax liability, it is necessary to identify the partners' baseline tax liability for purposes of comparison. The Regulations provide no guidance in this regard. Thus, for example, the baseline may be the tax liability that would have resulted if a party was not a partner, if the partnership did not engage in the transaction or if a corporation was used instead of a partnership.

It is also unclear how the general anti-abuse rule of the Regulations interacts with the other more specific (and often elaborate) anti-abuse provisions of Subchapter K, such as, for example, the "disguised sale" provisions, and it is uncertain whether a recasting of a transaction under the Regulations will lead to the imposition of penalties on the parties as a matter of course and whether penalties may be avoided by the disclosure of the transaction by the parties on their tax returns.

G. THE PARTNERSHIP ANTI-ABUSE REGULATIONS

Abuse of Entity Treatment

The Regulations provide in general that the IRS can treat a partnership for tax purposes as an aggregate of its partners, and not as an entity, in order to carry out the purposes of any provision of the Code or Regulations. For example, if a joint venture that includes corporate partners issues a high-yield discount obligation, under the Regulations, the corporate partners will be subject to the same restrictions on the deductibility of their allocable shares of interest deductions on such obligation as would apply to a corporate issuer of such an obligation, notwithstanding that the partnership issued the obligation and not the corporate partners.

The Regulations provide an exception to this rule to the extent a statutory or regulatory provision treats a partnership as an entity and that treatment and the ultimate tax results, taking into account all the relevant facts and circumstances, are "clearly contemplated" by the provision. The trouble is it may often be difficult to determine whether the particular tax consequences resulting from treating a partnership as an entity are clearly contemplated by a particular statutory or regulatory provision.

Now, how do you think the "basis strip" stands up under the new regulations?

Chapter 9
TERMINATION OF A PARTNERSHIP

A. INTRODUCTION

In this chapter the focus swings from the termination of a partner's interest in the partnership to the termination of the partnership itself. From the partner's perspective, the tax implications are generally the same as if the partner had liquidated his interest, except that § 736 is inapplicable. Thus, once again when property is distributed in complete liquidation, there is generally no taxable gain or loss to the partners or to the partnership. Instead, the tax deferral is reflected in an adjustment to the basis of the distributed property. However, the distribution of cash alone can produce a taxable gain, and the partner may recognize a loss if she receives *only* money, unrealized receivables, or inventory, or some combination of these items. § 731(a)(2). The loss is easy to compute if cash alone is distributed. One just subtracts the cash from predistribution outside basis; the shortfall is deemed a loss on the sale of the partnership interest. Moreover, no other result is plausible. One cannot defer gains and losses by tinkering with the basis of cash, because cash must take a basis equal to its face amount. Any other result would be absurd. Given that, there *must* be a recognized loss where cash alone is distributed. If, instead, only unrealized receivables or inventory items are distributed, there is a *capital* loss to the extent inside basis of the distributed property is less than the distributee partner's outside basis. This arises because § 732(b) insists that the partner take a basis in receivables and inventory equal to their inside bases. These tax outcomes are exactly the same as for the liquidation of a partner's interest, except that all the partners must perform these calculations. Note that in many instances the partnership first sells its assets, reports *ordinary* gain or loss and then distributes cash to the partners, greatly simplifying things for the partners.

The first step is to read § 708(a) and (b), observing that § 708 tells one nothing about the effect of a termination. Instead, one must look to other Code sections, primarily §§ 706, 731 and 732, concerning the taxable year of, and distributions from, the partnership, respectively.

B. TERMINATION BY CESSATION OF BUSINESS

Read § 708.

NEUBECKER v. COMMISSIONER
65 T.C. 577 (1975)

DRENNEN, JUDGE.

....

Findings of Fact

Some of the facts have been stipulated and are accordingly so found.

Petitioners were husband and wife during 1969, and at all times material hereto resided in Milwaukee, Wis. Petitioners' joint Federal income tax return for the taxable year 1969 was filed with the Director, Internal Revenue Service Center, Kansas City, Mo., on June 22, 1970.

Edward F. Neubecker (hereinafter referred to as Neubecker or petitioner) is an attorney-at-law who engaged in the practice of law in Milwaukee, Wis. From December 1, 1964, to February or March of 1969, petitioner practiced law as a partner in the firm of Frinzi, Catania, and Neubecker (hereinafter sometimes referred to as the partnership), of which Messrs. Frinzi, Catania, and Neubecker were the sole members. No formal written partnership agreement existed among the three partners although there was an informal understanding as to the partners' respective duties and the division of partnership profits. The partnership maintained a bank account on which each of the partners was authorized to draw.

At some time in either February or March of 1969, the partnership was dissolved upon oral agreement of all the partners, whereupon petitioner and Catania left the location of the partnership, acquired office facilities elsewhere in Milwaukee, and immediately thereafter formed a new partnership under the name of Catania and Neubecker. Petitioner and Catania did not execute a written agreement evidencing the new arrangement.

No formal accounting occurred among the three partners incident to the dissolution of Frinzi, Catania, and Neubecker. The partnership bank account, as well as whatever accounts receivable were then outstanding, were left with Frinzi who continued to occupy the offices previously maintained by the partnership. To the extent some fees had at the time of dissolution been received from clients, no attempt was made to allocate these payments among the partners. Although no formal division or assignment of clients and pending cases took place petitioner and Catania, as partners in Catania and Neubecker, retained certain clients and cases for which they had responsibility when practicing as partners in Frinzi, Catania, and Neubecker.

Upon the dissolution of Frinzi, Catania, and Neubecker, petitioner actually received the following:

B. TERMINATION BY CESSATION OF BUSINESS

Item on dissolution	Fair market value
Cash	— -
Accounts Receivable	— -
Inventory	— -
1 typewriter	$100
1 secretary chair	50
2 file cabinets	100
Miscellaneous books and pamphlets	100
1 waiting room chair	50
Office supplies	<u>15</u>
Total value	$415

The bulk of the equipment and property used in the conduct of the business of the partnership remained with Frinzi.

As of the date of dissolution of the partnership, petitioner's capital account had a balance of $2,425.57.

As calendar year taxpayers, petitioners were required to file their joint federal individual income tax return for 1969 on April 15, 1970. They obtained an extension until May 15, 1970, on which date they received an additional extension of time until June 15, 1970. Petitioners actually filed their 1969 return on June 22, 1970.

Under Part III of Schedule E attached to their return for 1969, petitioners reported as income from partnerships the amount of $13,258.49 from Catania and Neubecker and $3,521.01 from Frinzi, Catania, and Neubecker. The employer identification number listed thereon was the same for both partnerships.

On Schedule D, "Sales or Exchanges of Property," under Part I, "Short-term capital gains and losses," petitioners reflected a $2,425.57 loss on the partnership interest in Frinzi, Catania, and Neubecker. Of this amount, petitioners claimed a deduction of $1,000, which respondent has disallowed in its entirety.

Opinion

The principal issue remaining for decision is whether, incident to the dissolution of the partnership of Frinzi, Catania, and Neubecker, petitioners sustained a recognizable loss on Edward F. Neubecker's interest in the partnership. We must also determine whether petitioners are liable for the addition to tax asserted by respondent pursuant to section 6651(a).

With regard to the partnership loss issue, petitioners' position is predicated on the dissolution of the Frinzi, Catania, and Neubecker partnership. Since Neubecker had, at the time of dissolution, a capital account in the amount of $2,425.57, and in view of the fact that the items taken by Neubecker and Catania for use in their new office were of minimal value, petitioners concluded they sustained a deductible loss on said partnership interest. On brief, petitioners shift the thrust of their argument and characterize the value of Neubecker's share of the assets which remained with Frinzi as an abandonment or forfeiture loss, which theory is premised on petitioner's contention that the Code sections specifically relating to the taxation of partners and partnerships (subchapter K) fail to deal with the treatment to which petitioners are entitled.

Respondent, on the other hand, argues that petitioners sustained no deductible loss on the partnership interest because the Frinzi, Catania, and Neubecker partnership, albeit dissolved, did not terminate within the meaning of section 708, and thus, there was no event occasioning realization of loss. Further, if under section 708, Neubecker's interest remained in partnership solution and therefore not completely liquidated, section 731(a)(2) would operate to deny recognition of the loss. In the alternative, even if a termination and complete liquidation of Neubecker's interest did occur, respondent contends that petitioners nevertheless failed to satisfy the requirement of section 731(a)(2) as to the nature of the property distributed and are thereby precluded from recognizing any realized loss.

While it can be argued that the provisions of subchapter K did not envision such an informal splitting up of a partnership as occurred here, we must agree with respondent's analysis that the provisions of subchapter K do prevent the recognition of any loss to petitioners under the circumstances here present.

We note as a threshold matter that in the context of section 708 there is an implicit distinction drawn between dissolution and termination, which dispels the dispositive significance which petitioners would accord the dissolution of Frinzi, Catania, and Neubecker. *See Elaine Yagoda*, 39 T.C. 170, 183 (1962), *affd.* 331 F.2d 485, 591 n.5 (2d Cir. 1964), *cert. denied* 379 U.S. 842 (1964). Under the law there would appear to be no termination of Frinzi, Catania, and Neubecker but rather a continuation of that partnership in Catania and Neubecker with Frinzi being the withdrawing partner.

Section 708(a) provides that an existing partnership shall be considered as continuing if it is not terminated, and subsection (b)(1)(A) provides that a partnership shall be considered as terminated only if "(A) no part of any business, financial operation, or venture of the partnership continues to be carried on by any of its partners in a partnership, or...." Section 708(b)(2)(B) provides that:

> In the case of a division of a partnership into two or more partnerships, the resulting partnerships (other than any resulting partnership the members of which had an interest of 50 percent or less in the capital and profits of the prior partnership) shall, for purposes of this section, be considered a continuation of the prior partnership....

We believe that the extant facts warrant no other conclusion than that a sufficient part of the business conducted by Frinzi, Catania, and Neubecker continued to be carried on by the Catania and Neubecker partnership such that the former cannot be considered as terminated. Sec. 708(b)(1)(A).... Immediately upon dissolution of the partnership, Catania and Neubecker formed the Catania and Neubecker partnership. To the extent that petitioner and Catania, as partners

B. TERMINATION BY CESSATION OF BUSINESS

in Catania and Neubecker, retained certain clients and cases for which they had responsibility when practicing as partners in Frinzi, Catania, and Neubecker, the continuity of operation contemplated in section 708(b)(1)(A) is clearly established. Although petitioners have not argued, nor does the record demonstrate, that these cases and clients were taken by Neubecker and Catania incident to winding down and arriving at a final accounting in respect of Frinzi, Catania, and Neubecker, that partnership would nevertheless be considered as continuing while in the process of winding down since section 708(b)(1)(A) requires complete cessation of business in order to effect a termination....

The fact that the Catania and Neubecker partnership kept the same employer identification number further supports our determination as to the continuation of Frinzi, Catania, and Neubecker. Contrary to the emphasis placed by petitioners on the fact that Neubecker and Catania vacated the old premises and relocated in other office facilities, we attribute little significance to such fact which, although indicative of some physical interruption of operation, is irrelevant in terms of the criteria set forth in section 708.

If, then, Frinzi, Catania, and Neubecker continued by virtue of the fact that its business was in part carried on by its partners, Neubecker and Catania, in a partnership, it follows that the receipt of the few items of office equipment and supplies, to the extent characterized as a distribution to Neubecker, nevertheless did not constitute a distribution in liquidation of his partnership interest, which is the threshold requirement for recognition of loss pursuant to section 731(a)(2) and the regulations thereunder.

Section 731(a)(2) provides that in the case of a distribution to a partner loss shall not be recognized to such partner unless the distribution is in liquidation of his interest in the partnership and then only if the property distributed to him consists only of money, unrealized receivables, and inventory. Here the assets received by Catania and Neubecker were not received in liquidation of their interests in the partnership; they retained their interests in the continuing partnership. But even if the partnership did terminate within the meaning of section 708 and Neubecker's interest in the firm was completely liquidated, section 731(a)(2) would still operate to preclude recognition of a loss at that time. While we need not decide precisely what property comprised the liquidating distribution to Neubecker, clearly such distribution did not consist solely of money, unrealized receivables, or inventory as specified in section 731(a)(2)(A) and (B).

The record is devoid of any evidence indicating receipt of any of the prescribed items of property. Petitioner received no cash. Presumably the business of Frinzi, Catania, and Neubecker involved no inventory. Neubecker himself testified that no allocation of receivables, if any existed, occurred. And further, petitioners have presented no evidence that Neubecker was relieved of any partnership liabilities so as to constitute a distribution of money under section 752(b). Furthermore, even if we might infer from Neubecker's retention of certain cases and clients that he in fact acquired accounts receivable or money, petitioners fail to qualify for recognition of loss under section 731(a)(2) by virtue of Neubecker's receipt of the aforementioned proscribed property.

Thus, under either approach, section 731(a)(2) dictates nonrecognition of petitioners' claimed loss. Moreover, we find that the applicability of section 731(a)(2) renders petitioners' characterization of the loss as a forfeiture or an abandonment loss, deductible under section 165, unavailing. In respect of the relation of subchapter K to the more general provisions of the Code, "the specific language of Section 731 prevails over the general language of Section 165(a) as to a fact situation falling within the ambit of Section 731." *Estate of Dupree v. United States*, 391, F.2d 753, 757-758 (5th Cir. 1968).

Not only does section 731 itself operate to deny petitioners recourse under section 165, but our findings and analysis necessary to determine the applicability of section 731 also preclude, as a factual matter, characterization of the loss in issue as an abandonment or forfeiture loss, both of which characterizations must be predicated on the contention that Neubecker received nothing in respect of his partnership interest. The record, however, clearly disproves this premise in view of the fact that Neubecker did receive some property upon dissolution of the partnership.

Further, we do not find support for either characterization in *Gaius G. Gannon*, 16 T.C. 1134 (1951), *acq.* 1951-2 C.B. 2, and *Palmer Hutcheson*, 17 T.C. 14 (1951), upon which petitioners primarily rely. In these cases, the respective petitioners, who were partners in the same law firm, voluntarily withdrew from the partnership and, by application of explicit forfeiture provisions in the partnership agreement, were thereby denied any compensation for their respective interests in the firm. We held in both cases that the petitioner was entitled to a deductible loss by virtue of the forfeiture of the partnership interest.

Unlike the facts in *Gaius G. Gannon, supra*, and *Palmer Hutcheson, supra*, the Frinzi, Catania, and Neubecker partnership agreement contained no forfeiture provision or restriction on Neubecker's right to receive a return of his investment upon withdrawal from, or the dissolution or termination, of the partnership. And, as we have emphasized, Neubecker did in fact receive property upon dissolution of the partnership....

On the basis of the foregoing, we hold that petitioners did not sustain a deductible loss in 1969 in respect of Neubecker's interest in the Frinzi, Catania, and Neubecker partnership.

Decision will be entered under Rule 155.

PROBLEM 9-1

Assume that A and B are calendar year members of the profitable AB partnership, which has a March 1 fiscal year. On November 30 of this year there is a final liquidating distribution that results in a termination of the AB partnership. How many months of income of the partnership will A and B report as a consequence of the final distribution?

C. TECHNICAL TERMINATIONS

Section 708 is generally designed to counteract the brittleness of partnerships under state law, although it is easy to see § 708(b)(1)(B) as an ambush rather than an act of legislative grace. Moreover, it is technically flawed in that it begins with the words "for purposes of this subchapter" and not "for all purposes of the Code," something one hopes the IRS and the courts will forgive as an example of hasty drafting rather than a rigid guideline for interpretation.

Section 708(b) provides that a termination occurs if there is a sale or exchange of 50% or more of the total interest in partnership capital *and* profits within a twelve-month period. Multiple transfers of the same interest in that period are ignored. Reg. § 1.708-1(b)(1)(ii). Although one counts sales to other partners, one ignores gifts, bequests, or liquidations of partnership interests, as well as contributions of property to the firm by a new partner. Reg. § 1.708-1(b)(1)(ii). The results of a termination must be gleaned from other provisions, mainly §§ 706 and 736, concerning the partnership taxable year and liquidating distributions.

The implication of a technical termination is an imaginary liquidating distribution of the "old" partnership's assets, followed instantly by a recontribution of the same assets to the "new" partnership. This implies a termination of the "old" partnership's taxable year and the other consequences that flow naturally from a complete liquidation of a partnership.

Shrewd tax advisors sometimes recommend technical terminations as a planning device to achieve goals such as:
- Changing taxable years,
- Changing accounting methods,
- Eliminating § 754 elections, and
- Changing methods of depreciation.

These elections are all made possible by the fictional existence of a "new" partnership. Absent a termination, these elections would require the consent of the IRS. Thus, if one wants to achieve the change without begging from the IRS, a technical termination may be just what the doctor ordered. There may be negative side effects from the medicine, as the following case illustrates.

EVANS v. COMMISSIONER
54 T.C. 40 (1970), *acq.*, 1978-2 C.B. 2,
aff'd, 447 F.2d 547 (7th Cir. 1971)

ATKINS, JUDGE.

....

The parties having reached agreement as to certain issues, the issues remaining for determination are (1) whether a purported assignment by petitioner of all his interest in a partnership to a corporation of which he was the sole stockholder was effective to relieve him of tax upon the distributive share of partnership income attributable to such interest and (2) whether gain derived on a subsequent sale of such partnership interest is taxable to petitioner.

Findings of Fact

....

In 1949 the petitioner entered into an informal oral partnership agreement with his brother-in-law, Raymond Zeier, to operate a business known as Evans-Zeier Plastic Company. The business consisted of the manufacture of plastic products by a process of injection molding. The machinery involved in this process was quite elaborate. The labor involved consisted of putting material into the machinery and then removing the finished product. Prior to 1961 the most employees the partnership ever had were four, in addition to petitioner and his partner, Zeier.

Petitioner and Zeier each owned a one-half interest in the partnership and each was entitled to one-half of the profits. There was never any discussion or agreement between the partners concerning the admission of new members to the partnership and not until 1965 was there any discussion or agreement as to the conveyance, transfer, or assignment of either partner's interest in the partnership.

Decisions on how to conduct the business were reached as a result of discussions between petitioner and Zeier. Such decisions had to do with what products to manufacture and to whom to sell them, what prices to charge, and where to buy their raw materials.

The petitioner never did develop a close or friendly relationship with Zeier. Petitioner felt that he himself was outside the family circle and he and Zeier had very little conversation aside from their work. Petitioner sometimes felt that there were problems of communication between them and this was a drawback in their relationship. The relationship between them, while never good, deteriorated greatly over the years immediately preceding 1960. A major conflict arose because petitioner wanted to expand the business while Zeier did not. Since he did not think that there would be any expansion of the partnership business in the foreseeable future, petitioner wanted to make arrangements to accumulate capital so he could start his own business. Because of the strained nature of the relationship with Zeier, petitioner did not want him to know of his plans.

In 1960 petitioner decided to seek professional advice about his business problems from his accountant and from his attorney. Both the accountant and the attorney told petitioner that to accomplish his purpose it would be advisable to form a corporation and transfer his interest in the partnership to the corporation. Petitioner decided to use this means of starting his own business.

On December 30, 1960, petitioner caused to be incorporated, and became the sole shareholder of Don Evans, Inc., a Wisconsin corporation, which has continued to be a valid corporation in good standing. In order to qualify for

C. TECHNICAL TERMINATIONS

doing business under the State law, there had to be $500 capital and therefore petitioner contributed $500 and had issued to himself two shares of stock.

On January 2, 1961, petitioner executed to the corporation an "Assignment of Partnership Interest," which provided:

> That the said first party for and in consideration of the sum of Fifty-one Thousand Five Hundred Eighteen and 46/100 Dollars ($51,518.46), receipt of which is hereby acknowledged, does hereby give, sell, assign, transfer and convey to Don Evans, Inc., all interest that he owns in the co-partnership of the Evans-Zeier Plastic Company in the stock of goods, wares, merchandise, equipment, furniture and fixtures thereunto appertaining and all of the books and other debts or accounts now due and owing to the Evans-Zeier Plastic Company with offices located at Highway 51 in the Town of Burke, Dane County, Wisconsin. The business interest hereby conveyed consists of an undivided one-half interest in the Evans-Zeier Plastic Company partnership and a one-half interest in all of the profits and losses of the Evans-Zeier Plastic Company to which the undersigned, Donald L. Evans, would be entitled in the continued operation of said partnership business.

The amount of $51,518.46 set forth in the assignment represented the amount at which petitioner's interest was then carried on the partnership books. The petitioner did not receive cash from the corporation but, rather, received 206 shares of its no-par-value stock, documentary stamps in the amount of $51.50 being affixed. The partnership interest was entered on the corporation's books as an asset at the amount of $51,518.46. After this transaction, the corporation issued no more stock, and petitioner continued to be its sole stockholder. In executing the assignment it was the intention of petitioner to transfer his entire partnership interest to the corporation in exchange for stock and thereby meet the nonrecognition of gain or loss provisions of section 351 of the Internal Revenue Code.

The partnership's books were kept on an accrual method of accounting and on the basis of the calendar year. At the time of the above assignment the partnership's books reflected all income accrued to that time and such income was reported for tax purposes by the partnership.

Petitioner executed the "Assignment of Partnership Interest" without telling his partner Zeier or asking him about it. At that time, Zeier had no knowledge of the existence of the corporation or of such assignment. The first time that Zeier heard of the corporation and any purported transfer of an interest to it was in 1962 in connection with the filing of the 1961 partnership returns. The petitioner's wife prepared the returns of the partnership and the accountant advised her that, in preparing the partnership returns for 1961, she should list the corporation as a partner because of the above assignment. When this was done, Zeier questioned petitioner about it and petitioner told him that there had been no change. Zeier, before filing the returns, erased the word "Incorporated" so that both the Federal and the State returns were filed listing the petitioner as a partner. About 2 or 3 months later he told the petitioners of the erasures. Zeier heard nothing further about the corporation insofar as the plastics business was concerned until he and petitioner were engaged in the dissolution of the partnership in 1965.

On all subsequent partnership returns petitioner was listed as Zeier's partner in the Evans-Zeier Plastic Co. The accountant told petitioner's wife that it would be all right to do this to avoid worsening the relationship with Zeier since the corporation would report the income attributable to the interest assigned to it. All of the partnership returns, except the final return for 1965, were prepared by petitioner's wife, who gave them to petitioner for examination. Petitioner then gave them to Zeier who, after examining them, signed them for the partnership.

The accountant had also initially advised petitioners that checks of the partnership representing distributions attributable to the one-half interest should be made payable to the corporation, but that if this would create additional tension with Zeier, the petitioner should be shown as payee but that the checks should be deposited directly in the corporation's bank account. The latter procedure was adopted. The checks were signed at times by petitioner's wife and at times by Zeier. The petitioner's name remained on the bank's signature card, enabling him to sign partnership checks. On one occasion, in 1965, the petitioner signed a partnership check representing a withdrawal of partnership funds for himself. Petitioner's wife, on the advice of the accountant, continued to carry the investment and drawing accounts on the books of the partnership in the names of the petitioner and Zeier.

The petitioner did not inform persons dealing with the partnership, including the credit-rating agency to which the partnership supplied information and the insurance company which wrote the partnership's liability coverage, of the assignment or represent to them that he was no longer a partner.

The petitioner was president of the corporation. His wife was its secretary-treasurer and did all the accounting and book work. The petitioner continued to perform about one-half of the work carried on by the partnership as he had done before the assignment.

After the incorporation of Don Evans, Inc., petitioner sought to implement his plans to enable him to start his own plastic business. In order for the corporation to accumulate capital, it purchased two apartment buildings. These were subsequently sold when the corporation purchased some machinery. Petitioner investigated thermal set molding, a process different from that used by the partnership. He did this work in his home with equipment owned by the corporation. In 1962 the corporation sold some of the products resulting from this experimental work. In 1963 and 1964 it began regularly to sell plastic products.

In March 1965, the Security State Bank of Madison, Wis., made loans totaling about $49,000 to the corporation. In connection with the requests for the loans, the corporation submitted a balance sheet, indicating a net worth of about

C. TECHNICAL TERMINATIONS 197

$108,000. Listed among the assets was the one-half interest in the partnership, valued at $37,855.24. In making the loans, the bank relied upon the balance sheet and would not have loaned the corporation $49,000 if the assets shown had not included the partnership interest.

The corporation paid amounts to the petitioner and his wife as salaries. The amounts so paid to the petitioner were: 1961, $18,000; 1962, $19,250; 1963, $15,000; 1964, $12,000; and 1965, $15,000. The corporation withheld taxes on these amounts, filed the required employment tax returns reflecting the withholding of taxes, and complied with the depository receipts requirements.

By 1965, relations with Zeier had become so strained that petitioner decided that it was time to sever his business association with him. Negotiations were handled by their respective attorneys. On December 16, 1965, an agreement was executed between Zeier and petitioner which provides in part as follows:

> WHEREAS, the parties have carried on the business known as Evans-Zeier Plastic Company, as partners, pursuant to an oral partnership agreement, (and Evans advises his partnership interest has been assigned by Evans to Don Evans, Inc., a Wisconsin corporation), and whereas it has been orally agreed between the parties that the Evans-Zeier Plastic Company partnership shall stand dissolved as of the end of business on June 15, 1965 on the terms hereinafter set forth and that thereafter the business shall belong to and be carried on by Zeier, the continuing partner, solely, and that the share of Evans in the real estate occupied by the partnership and owned by the parties as co-partners, doing business as Evans-Zeier Plastic Company, and in the machinery, (except two (2) machine tools listed on Exhibit A which Evans is to receive), equipment, tools, molds, inventories of materials and of molded products, accounts receivable, office furniture, books, records and generally all assets of the partnership shall be assigned and made over to Zeier who will take upon himself all of the debts and liabilities of the partnership which were outstanding on the date of dissolution and that Zeier will pay to Evans for Evans one-half interest in all of such items. It is agreed that the parties hereby declare that the partnership shall be considered as terminated and hence stand dissolved as of the end of business on June 15, 1965 and Evans agrees that he will convey his one-half interest in the real estate to Zeier by warranty deed, free and clear of all encumbrances upon being paid the amount for said real estate set forth in Exhibit A, and that he will by bill of sale, transfer and convey to Zeier, all of his interest in the partnership's machinery (except said two (2) machine tools) and equipment, tools, molds, inventories and all other tangible personal property of the partnership upon being paid the amounts therefor as set out in Exhibit A. Evans hereby assigns to Zeier all of his interest in the partnership's accounts receivables as of the termination date above set forth and agrees that he will, on demand, execute and deliver one or more Powers of Attorney that may be deemed necessary or desirable

by Zeier to collect said receivables for the sole benefit of Zeier and at his sole risk.

The above agreement was signed by Zeier, the petitioner, and the petitioner's wife and by the corporation by the petitioner as president and his wife as secretary. The agreement explains the joinder of petitioner's wife and the corporation as follows:

> Joan Evans, wife of Donald Evans, joins in this agreement and hereby agrees that she will, if required, execute the deed to the real estate along with her husband.
>
> Don Evans, Inc., a Wisconsin corporation, joins in the execution of this agreement and agrees to effect all transfers of interest acquired by said corporation by reason of assignment of assets of the partnership by Donald Evans to Don Evans, Inc.

The corporation was made a party to the agreement because Zeier's attorney wanted to avoid any question of ownership of the partnership interest and because petitioner's attorney felt that it was a necessary party in view of the assignment to the corporation executed by petitioner on January 2, 1961.

The proceeds of the sale were deposited directly in the corporation's bank account. After the sale the two machine tools which Zeier did not receive were entered on the corporation's books and thereafter the corporation claimed depreciation deductions with respect thereto.

At no time did Zeier ever consent to have any individual or corporation, other than the petitioner, as his partner in the partnership. At no time did he ever recognize, or represent to anyone, that any person other than the petitioner was his partner in the partnership.

In its Federal income tax returns for the taxable years 1961 through 1965 the corporation reported and paid tax on the distributive share of partnership income attributable to the one-half interest in the partnership, namely, the respective amounts of $39,277.21, $47,076.46, $37,197.79, $40,285.32, and $39,103.53. In their joint income tax returns for such years the petitioner and his wife did not report any income from the partnership. Rather, they reported as income the amounts paid to them by the corporation as salaries.

In its Federal income tax return for the taxable year 1965 the corporation reported a long-term capital gain of $26,041.23 on the sale of the partnership interest to Zeier and paid the tax thereon. In their return for 1965 the petitioners did not report any gain on such sale.

In preliminary statements dated December 4, 1964, and November 16, 1965, the respondent proposed adjustments based upon the view that petitioner remained taxable as a partner. Thereafter, in the notices of deficiency the respondent determined that the above amounts reported by the corporation as income derived from the partnership constituted income to the petitioner and increased his reported income by those amounts. The respondent also increased

C. TECHNICAL TERMINATIONS

the petitioners' reported income for the taxable year 1965 by the amount of $16,728.80 as "Gain on Sale of Partnership" with the following explanation:

> It is determined that you realized a gain on the sale of the partnership known as Evans-Zeier Plastic Company, in the amount of $26,041.23, taxable to extent of $16,728.80. Accordingly your taxable income is increased in the amount of $16,728.80, computed as follows:
>
> | | |
> |---|---:|
> | Gross sales price | $75,000.00 |
> | Less: Basis in partnership | 48,958.77 |
> | Gain on sale | 26,041.23 |
> | Less: Ordinary gain on section 1245 assets | 7,416.37 |
> | Long-term capital gain | 18,624.86 |
> | Less: Long-term capital gain deduction | 9,312.43 |
> | Net long-term capital | 9,312.43 |
> | Add: Ordinary gain on section 1245 assets | 7,416.37 |
> | Net taxable gain | 16,728.80 |

Opinion

The respondent does not question the separate identities of the petitioner and the corporation, nor does he contend that the execution of the "Assignment of Partnership Interest" by petitioner on January 2, 1961, was a sham. However, he contends that since the petitioner did not obtain the consent of his partner, Zeier, to the assignment, such assignment did not effect a transfer to the corporation of petitioner's entire partnership interest, but effected no more than an assignment of the right to future income to which petitioner thus retained his partnership interest; and that he is taxable upon his distributive share of the partnership income under section 702(a) of the Internal Revenue Code of 1954. He relies principally upon *Burnet v. Leininger*, 285 U.S. 136.

The petitioner, on the other hand, contends that under Wisconsin law the assignment of January 2, 1961, was effective to transfer his capital interest in the partnership to the corporation. He therefore contends that the corporation, as owner of such capital interest, is taxable on the income from such interest, regardless of whether the corporation technically became a partner under State law. He argues that for Federal income tax purposes the transfer terminated the old partnership between him and Zeier by virtue of the provisions of section 708(b)(1)(B) of the Code and the regulations thereunder; that thereafter, for Federal income tax purposes, he was no longer taxable as a partner; that the corporation became a coowner with Zeier of the company; that as coowners the corporation and Zeier continued to carry on a business, petitioner acting as agent for the corporation; that under section 761(a) of the Code the relationship between Zeier and the corporation, for Federal income tax purposes, must be considered as that of a partnership; and further that section 704(e)(1) of the Code provides that a person shall be recognized as a partner if he owns a capital interest in a partnership in which capital is a material income-producing factor.

Both parties refer to the Uniform Partnership Act as enacted by the State of Wisconsin, the respondent contending that thereunder the assignment in question transferred to the corporation only a share of the future profits of the partnership and, as stated, the petitioner contending that thereunder the assignment effected a transfer of his capital interest in the partnership.

We think it clear that the assignment in question was intended to, and did, transfer all the petitioner's interest in the partnership to the corporation, and not merely the right to future income. Under Wisconsin law a partner's interest in the partnership is his share of the profits and surplus. This interest is personal property and is assignable. An assignment of a partnership interest entitles the assignee to receive the profits to which the assigning partner would otherwise be entitled and, in the case of a dissolution of the partnership, entitles the assignee to receive the assignor's interest. And it appears that there is no requirement that consent to the assignment be obtained from the other partners.

The Internal Revenue Code of 1954 recognizes that an interest in a partnership may be sold or exchanged and, with exceptions not here material, considers the gain or loss as being from the sale or exchange of a capital asset. Sec. 741, I.R.C. 1954. In enacting section 741 Congress gave recognition to existing decisions which held that the sale of a partnership interest was generally considered to be a sale of a capital asset. H. Rept. No. 1337, 83d Cong., 2d Sess., p. 70, and S. Rept. No. 1622, 83d Cong., 2d Sess., p. 96. These cases also clearly established that a partner's interest in the partnership is his share of the profits and surplus, and that he individually has no interest in the partnership assets except as they might figure in his share of the profits and surplus.... We therefore think it reasonable to conclude that Congress, in enacting the 1954 Code, used the term "partnership interest" in that sense, namely, that a partnership interest is a partner's interest in profits and surplus. Accordingly, within the meaning of the Code, the petitioner did transfer to the corporation his partnership interest. He transferred all the interest he owned.

While it is true that the transfer of petitioner's partnership interest did not serve to terminate the partnership under State law, it is clear that, since the assignment did effect a transfer of 50 percent of the total interest in the partnership capital and profits, the assignment did effect a termination of the partnership for Federal tax purposes, pursuant to the provisions of section 708 of the Code and the regulations thereunder. The regulations under section 708 further indicate that upon such a termination the transferee of the partnership interest is to be treated as a partner in a new partnership. It follows that the petitioner was, after the assignment, no longer to be regarded as a partner for Federal income tax purposes, even though for State purposes he remained a partner.

This view finds support in the provisions of section 704(e) of the Code. Although directed primarily toward "family partnerships," that section is broad in its scope and covers a situation such as the instant case which does not involve a "family partnership" (there being involved no members of a family as defined

C. TECHNICAL TERMINATIONS

in section 704(e)(3) of the Code). That section provides that a person shall be recognized as a partner if he owns a capital interest in a partnership in which capital is a material income-producing factor. In enacting the predecessor of section 704(e), Congress made it clear that, although "family partnership" situations offer great potential for abuse, recognition must be given the general principle of income taxation that income produced by capital is taxed to the owner of such capital.

The regulations under section 704(e) define "capital interest in a partnership" as an interest in the assets of the partnership which is distributable to the owner of the capital interest upon his withdrawal from the partnership or upon liquidation of the partnership, but states that the mere right to participate in the earnings and profits is not a capital interest in the partnership. As stated above, the assignment in question, under section 178.23 of the Wisconsin statutes, entitled the corporation to not only the earnings and profits, but also, upon dissolution, to the petitioner's share of surplus, that is, his share of the partnership assets after payment of partnership liabilities. There can be no doubt that capital was a material income-producing factor in the business. Therefore, section 704(e) requires the recognition of the corporation, rather than the petitioner, as a partner for Federal income tax purposes.

In view of the above provisions of the Internal Revenue Code of 1954, we are of the opinion that *Burnet v. Leininger, supra*, which arose under prior tax statutes, is not governing in the instant case. Furthermore, it appears that in the *Leininger* case there was not an assignment by the taxpayer of a capital interest in the partnership in which he was a member, as was true here. In *Leininger* it was found only that a written agreement confirmatory of a preexisting oral agreement was entered into between taxpayer and his wife wherein it was acknowledged that taxpayer's wife had been and was a full equal partner with him in his interest in the partnership, entitled to share equally in the profits and obligated to bear equally any losses. The court stated that upon the facts found the agreement amounted to no more than an equitable assignment of one-half of what the taxpayer should receive from the partnership.

The fact that the petitioner continued to be the nominal partner is not sufficient to subject him to tax on the income from the distributive share held in his name since, as stated above, he had assigned to the corporation his full beneficial interest. *See United States v. Atkins*, (C.A. 5) 191 F.2d 146, *rehearing denied* 191 F.2d 951, *certiorari denied* 343 U.S. 941, in which it was held that, where the taxpayer assigned capital interest in partnerships of which he was a member to a partnership consisting of himself and his son, the taxpayer was not liable for tax upon the income attributable to the interest which he transferred, even though the assignee did not become a member of the original partnerships. In that case the court stated in part:

> This is not a case of the taxpayer assigning fees, wages, salaries, or other income, to be earned by him in the future from work to be performed by

him in the future. Atco's income resulted from capital invested in operating partnerships, and from the services performed by managing partners. The taxpayer did not assign income from those operating partnerships: he assigned his share, his entire interest in those partnerships to a separate partnership (Atco Investment Company), the members of which firm were engaged in a joint venture....

Appellee was required to make such individual return as to each partnership of which he was a member whether or not distribution was made to him, but not if he retained no beneficial interest in the operating partnerships and was a partner in name only.... Though not a member of the operating partnerships, the Atco Investment Company was equitably entitled to receive the entire net income from the appellee's share in said operating partnerships, because Atco was the beneficial owner thereof, since appellee had not simply assigned income but had assigned his entire equitable interest therein. After this assignment was made, appellee retained only a naked legal title to said share.... An equitable interest in a partnership is a vendible asset, the income from which is computable in the same manner and on the same basis as any other property, the legal title to which is in a naked trustee. The partnership return may state the nominal partners only, but the individual return of any such member may disclose additional facts, and if the income from a share in the partnership is ultimately received by the equitable owner thereof, and all income taxes paid thereon by the real beneficiary thereof, the nominal partner is not also liable....

In view of the foregoing, we hold that the respondent erred in holding that the petitioner was taxable upon one-half of the partnership earnings for each of the taxable years 1961 through 1965, and in holding that the petitioner is taxable upon the gain realized upon the sale of the partnership interest in 1965.

Decisions will be entered under Rule 50.

NOTE

One piece of good news in this area is that, as we saw in an earlier chapter, relief from liabilities is netted against assumed liabilities, so that there should generally be no gain to any partner. The treatment of cash is not so favorable; if and to the extent a partner is deemed to have received more cash than he has outside basis, the result will be a capital gain under § 741. § 731(a)(1). Conversely, § 731(a)(2) may permit the recognition of a loss.

PROBLEM 9-2

X and Y are equal partners in the XY partnership, which has been in business for five years. XY's inside basis in its assets (none of which consist of inventory items or unrealized receivables) is $40,000, but their value is $80,000. Y sells

C. TECHNICAL TERMINATIONS

her interest to Z for $40,000 on December 31 of this year. X has an outside basis of $30,000. Please consider the following issues:

1. Assuming no § 754 election is in place, and once the dust has settled:
   a) What is Z's basis in his partnership interest?
   b) What is XZ's basis in its assets?
   c) What is X's outside basis?
   d) What would be the effect of a § 754 election being in force at the time of Z's purchase?
   e) How should gain on a subsequent sale of the XZ partnership's assets be allocated?
2. Assume the same facts as above, but that Y is retiring and is being paid out of partnership assets.
   a) Is there a § 708(b)(1)(B) termination? *See* Reg. § 1.708-1(b)(1)(b)(ii).
   b) Assume that shortly thereafter, Z contributes $40,000 to form a new partnership with X. Is there any change in result? *See* the same Regulations immediately above and Reg. § 1.731-1.

OUTSIDE READINGS

J. Birkeland & P. Postlewaite, *Constructive Termination of a Partnership — A Fresh Look*, 39 Tax Law. 701 (1986).

Chapter 10
MERGER AND DIVISION OF PARTNERSHIPS

A. MERGER OF PARTNERSHIPS

Section 708(b)(2)(A) provides an economical statement of what happens when partnerships merge. Read it. Congress obviously expected the subject to be a particularly simple one, and on the whole, they were right. The first major pronouncement (aside from the regulations) was consistent with the theme of simplicity and indifference to form.

REV. RUL. 68-289
1968-1 C.B. 314

Where three partnerships merged, the terminating partnerships are treated as having contributed all of their assets and transferred their liabilities to the continuing partnership in exchange for interests in such partnership that are distributed to the respective partners of the terminating partnerships in liquidation of their interests.

Basis of the partnership interests acquired in the resulting partnership is determined under section 732(b) of the Internal Revenue Code of 1954.

Advice has been requested whether, under the circumstances described below, assets and liabilities of terminating partnerships, P1 and P2, are treated as having been distributed to the respective partners in liquidation and such assets and liabilities considered as subsequently recontributed by the respective partners to P3, the resulting partnership.

As of December 31, 1965, P1, P2, and P3 were limited partnerships engaged in the oil and gas business.

A and B, the only general partners, each owns a 20 percent interest in capital and profits of the three partnerships. The limited partners in P1 and P2 are also the limited partners in P3.

On January 1, 1966, in accordance with a written agreement, the three existing partnerships merged into one partnership with P3 contributing the greatest dollar value of assets.

In accordance with section 708(b)(2)(A) of the Internal Revenue Code of 1954 and section 1.708-1(b)(2)(i) of the Income Tax Regulations, P3 is the resulting partnership and P1 and P2 are considered terminated.

Accordingly, P3 is the resulting partnership and P1 and P2 are treated as having contributed all of their respective assets and transferred their liabilities to P3 in exchange for a partnership interest. P1 and P2 are thereafter considered terminated and their respective partners are considered to have received in liquidation partnership interests in P3 with a basis to them as determined under section 732(b) of the Code.

NOTES

1. *Basis effects.* Thereafter, in Rev. Rul. 77-458, 1977-2 C.B. 220, the government in effect announced, unsurprisingly, that the continuing partnership takes a carryover basis in the disappearing partnerships' assets. Thus inside basis continues unchanged, consistent with the general theme that nothing happened except for a change of form.

2. *Is there always a surviving partnership?* Not necessarily. For example, if three law firms of identical size combined and there were no overlapping partners, there would be no surviving partnership, merely a new, resulting one. *See* Reg. § 1.708-1(b)(2)(i).

REV. RUL. 90-17

1990-1 C.B. 119

Issue

If a partnership resulting from a partnership merger is considered a continuation of one of the merging partnerships under section 708(b)(2)(A) of the Internal Revenue Code, do liquidating distributions by the other merging partnerships of 50 percent or more of the capital and profits interests in the resulting partnership cause the resulting partnership to terminate under section 708(b)(1)(B) because of the application of section 761(e)?

Facts

A and B each owned a 50 percent interest in RP, a partnership having assets worth $500x. B and C each owned a 50 percent interest in MP1, a partnership having assets worth $400x. D and E each owned a 50 percent interest in MP2, a partnership having assets worth $100x. For business reasons independent of federal income tax consequences, the parties agreed to merge RP, MP1, and MP2. The merger was effected by each merging partnership contributing its assets to the resulting partnership in exchange for an interest in the resulting partnership. With respect to the interests in the resulting partnership RP received 50 percent, MP1 received 40 percent, and MP2 received 10 percent. The interests in the resulting partnership were then distributed proportionately to the respective partners of RP, MP1 and MP2. After the merger transaction, the interests in the resulting partnership were held, 25 percent by A, 45 percent by B, 20 percent by C, and 5 percent each by D and by E.

A. MERGER OF PARTNERSHIPS

Law and Analysis

Section 708(a) of the Code provides that an existing partnership shall be considered as continuing until such time as it is deemed terminated under section 708(b).

Section 708(b)(1) of the Code provides rules of general application governing the termination of partnerships. Section 708(b)(1)(B) provides that a partnership shall be considered terminated if, within a 12-month period, there is a sale or exchange of 50 percent or more of the total interest in partnership capital and profits.

Section 708(b)(2) of the Code provides rules of special application governing the termination of partnerships involved in mergers, consolidations, and divisions. Section 708(b)(2)(A) provides that, in the case of a merger or consolidation of two or more partnerships, the resulting partnership shall be a continuation of any merging or consolidating partnership whose members own an interest of more than 50 percent in the capital and profits of the resulting partnership.

Section 1.708-1(b)(2)(i) of the Income Tax Regulations provides that, if a resulting partnership can, under section 708(b)(2)(A) of the Code, be considered a continuation of more than one of the merging or consolidating partnerships, it shall be considered the continuation of the partnership that is credited with the contribution of the greatest dollar value of assets to the resulting partnership. Any other merging or consolidating partnership shall be considered as terminated.

Section 761(e) of the Code, which was added by the Tax Reform Act of 1984, section 75(b), 1984-3 C.B. (Vol. 1) 1, 102, provides that, except as otherwise provided in regulations, for purposes of section 708, any distribution of an interest in a partnership (not otherwise treated as an exchange) shall be treated as an exchange.

In Rev. Rul. 68-289, 1968-1 C.B. 314, three partnerships, P1, P2, and P3 are merged. All three partnerships have the same partners and, therefore, under section 708(b)(2)(A) of the Code, the partnership resulting from the merger could be treated as the continuations of either P1, P2 or P3. However, because P3 contributes the greatest dollar value of assets, the resulting partnership is considered the continuation of P3, P1 and P2 are treated as having first transferred their assets and liabilities to P3 in exchange for partnership interests and then as having distributed the P3 interests in liquidation.

Rev. Rul. 77-458, 1977-2 C.B. 220, considers the proposed merger of ten partnerships, P1-P10. These partnerships all have the same equal partners, A and B. Under the plan of merger P2-P10 will transfer all of their assets and liabilities to P1 (the largest partnership by dollar value of assets) in exchange for partnership interests in P1. P2-P10 will then distribute their interests in P1 to A and B. Rev. Rul. 77-458 concludes that the partnership resulting from the merger of P1-P10 will be considered the continuation of P1 because P1 will contribute the greatest dollar value of assets to the resulting partnership.

Under section 708(b)(2)(A) of the Code, the partnership resulting from the merger of RP, MP1, and MP2 can be considered the continuation of either RP or MP1. This is because both the members of RP (A and B) and the members of MP1 (B and C) become the owners of more than 50 percent of the capital and profits interests in the resulting partnership. In accordance with section 1.708-1(b)(2)(i) of the regulations, however, the resulting partnership is the continuation of RP, the partnership that contributes the greatest dollar value of assets ($500x).

Consistent with the analysis in Rev. Rul. 68-289, MP1 and MP2 are considered to have contributed their assets to RP in exchange for ownership interests in RP. MP1 and MP2 then liquidate and distribute their assets, the RP interests, to their partners. Because the RP partnership interests are received 40 percent by MP1 and 10 percent by MP2, a total of 50 percent of the RP interests is distributed in the course of the merger. If section 761(e) of the Code causes the distributions to be treated as exchanges to which section 708(b)(1)(B) applies, RP will terminate.

The question thus presented is whether sections 761(e) and 708(b)(1)(B) of the Code have the effect of adding an additional requirement to section 708(b)(2)(A), namely, that fewer than 50 percent of the interests in the resulting partnership are distributed in the merger.

Section 708(b)(2)(A) of the Code applies only to mergers and consolidations. Together with section 1.708-1(b)(2)(i) of the regulations, it provides the exclusive means for deciding whether a partnership involved in a merger will terminate. Section 708(b)(2)(A) does not define the term "merger." However, as illustrated in Rev. Rul. 68-289 and Rev. Rul. 77-458, a merger includes the distribution by the terminating partnerships of interests in the resulting partnership. Thus, section 708(b)(2)(A) is a statute that creates a specific rule for a particular transaction, a merger, and that transaction includes the distribution of resulting partnership interests.

Paragraphs (1) and (2) of section 708(b) set forth, respectively, a general rule on the termination of partnerships and specific rules on partnership terminations where a partnership merger, consolidation, or division is involved. The specific rules are clearly exceptions to the general rule and intended to override the general rule in the limited circumstances to which they apply. Even if this relationship were not clear from the provisions themselves, a basic principle of statutory construction is that a specific statutory provision, like section 708(b)(2), is not controlled or nullified by a more general one, like section 708(b)(1), unless that result is clearly intended. *Bulova Watch Co. v. United States*, 365 U.S. 753 (1961).

The legislative history of section 708(b)(1)(B) neither states nor implies a congressional intent that the provisions of section 708(b)(1)(B) take precedence over the partnership merger rules under section 708(b)(2)(A). *See* S. Rep. No. 1622, 83d Cong., 2d Sess. 388 (1954), and H.R. Rep. No. 2543, 83d Cong., 2d Sess. 61 (1954). Nor does the legislative history of section 761(e) state or imply

A. MERGER OF PARTNERSHIPS

a congressional intent to change the relationship between the provisions of sections 708(b)(1)(B) and 708(b)(2)(A)....

In other words, the purpose of the exception contained in section 708(b)(2)(A) of the Code and section 1.708-1(b)(2)(i) of the regulations is to provide for the continuation of one of the merging partnerships as the resulting partnership if the 50 percent test of those provisions is met, notwithstanding the provisions of the general rule of section 708(b)(1). Consistent with this purpose, a resulting (continuing) partnership in a merger to which section 708(b)(2)(A) applies is, as to the elements of the merger itself, excepted from the application of the termination provisions of section 708(b)(1).

Since section 761(e) of the Code cannot cause a termination of a partnership except through its effect on the term "exchange" in section 708(b)(1)(B), and since a resulting partnership in a merger to which section 708(b)(2)(A) applies is excepted from the application of section 708(b)(1) as to the elements of the merger itself, section 761(e) cannot cause the termination of the resulting partnership merely by virtue of its section 708(b)(2) merger.

Thus, the distribution of a total of 50 percent of the RP interests by MP1 and MP2 during the course of the merger will not cause a termination of RP under section 708(b)(1)(B) of the Code.

Holding

In a partnership merger, if the resulting partnership is considered a continuation of one of the merging partnerships under section 708(b)(2)(A), liquidating distributions by the other merging partnerships of 50 percent or more of the capital and profits interest in the resulting partnership do not cause the resulting partnership to terminate under section 708(b)(1)(B).

NOTE

Observe how the taxable year of the terminating partnership ends on its termination, thereby dumping its income or loss into the partners' laps of the disappearing firm on the spot. Reg. § 1.708-1(b)(1)(iii). By contrast, the continuing partnership (if there is one) just steams along using its normal tax period. *Id.* This could result in bunching a good deal of income if the terminating partnership had a fiscal year such as January 31 and it terminated, say, on December 1 of the prior year.

PROBLEM 10-1

What would be the proper tax accounting result when a cash-method partnership merges into an accrual-method partnership at a time when the cash-method partnership had substantial accounts receivable? If this creates a problem, how might it be solved?

B. DIVISION OF A PARTNERSHIP

Reg. § 1.708-1(b)(2)(ii) provides the road map. The basic rule is that upon the division of a partnership into two or more partnerships, the greater resulting partnership is treated as the continuation of the former partnership, and is saddled with the elections the predecessor may have made as well as with the predecessor's inside basis in its remaining assets. The successor is considered a new partnership if its members had an interest of half or less of the former partnership's capital and profits. The partners who are considered to have joined up with the new partnership are deemed to have received their interests via a liquidating distribution from the former partnership, followed by their contribution of those assets to the new firm. This subject has drawn virtually no attention in the courts or via IRS audits.

To illustrate: The forty person law firm of Lust, Envy, Greed, Hatred & Sloth recently split up. The litigation department, which consisted of fourteen people but 60% of the profits, broke away. Sloth went into solo practice. The two resulting firms are Lust, Envy & Hatred (the business lawyers) and Greed & Savage (the litigators). Savage was a former partner of the original firm, but his name was never part of the firm's name, although he wanted it to be. We cannot tell which firm is the survivor. The partnership whose members had a more than 50% interest in the capital and profits is the continuing firm, which suggests it is Greed & Savage, but it may be that the 60% is not also true of capital. Note that there is no backstop rule about which firm contributed more value. If there is no survivor, both firms are new. If there is a surviving firm, the survivor continues, using its same elections and same taxable year. The partners who join a new firm are considered to have received liquidating distributions and to have contributed the distributed assets to the new partnership, à la § 708(b)(1)(B). The tax year closes for the old firm, and its income or loss is dumped into its partners' laps.

Chapter 11
DEATH OF A PARTNER

One of several things can happen to a partnership interest when one of the partners dies: the interest can pass automatically to a successor in interest, such as a joint tenant; the interest can pass to the estate; or, it can pass automatically to another person or persons under a buy-sell contract of some sort. In default of an affirmative action, it will pass to the decedent's estate by law, and the estate will step into the decedent's shoes. Thereafter, the estate may distribute the interest to an heir, sell the interest, or liquidate the interest in exchange for distributions from the partnership. Recall from your introductory tax course that a decedent's spouse can file a joint return with the decedent's executor or administrator for the year of death. § 6013(a)(3).

A. PARTNERSHIP INCOME

1. GENERALLY

Read § 706(c).

As a matter of state law, the death of a general partner dissolves a general partnership, but does not necessarily mean that it is obligated to wind up its affairs and go out of business. UPA § 31. The remaining partners can immediately reinstate the partnership, and in any event the technical dissolution will not cause a § 708 termination. The State law rules are more generous for limited partnerships. *See* RULPA § 801. Thus, in a partnership consisting of more than two partners, whether it is a general or limited partnership, the entity typically continues along, despite the funeral.

Moreover, the partnership's taxable year does not close because of the death of a partner. § 706(c)(2)(A)(ii). The deceased partner's final return generally reports the income or loss for partnership years ending before his or her death. § 706(c)(2)(A)(ii). If the partner dies before the end of the partnership's year, the year closes *as to that partner* on the date of death. For example, if a calendar year partner dies on August 5, 1994, and her partnership's year ended on June 30, 1994, her final return will include the partnership's income through June 30, 1994, because the partnership's 1993-1994 fiscal year ended within her 1994 calendar year. The deceased partner's distributive share will otherwise be included on the return of the decedent's estate or successor in interest, because the estate or successor is the owner of the partnership interest on the last day of the partnership's taxable year. Reg. § 1.706-1(c)(3)(ii). Returning to the example, the deceased partner's successor, administrator, or executor will report the remaining (post-June 30) income in its return.

To illustrate: A, who is unmarried, is a member of the ABC accounting partnership, which uses the cash method. She and the partnership are both calendar-year taxpayers. A dies on October 9, 1994. Although her estate succeeds to her interest (there being no provision for a buy-out of her interest), A's own final return will include none of the partnership's income for 1994. Rather, A's estate will report the partnership's 1994 income in full.

Where the partnership's tax year does not close as to the partner, the estate or distributee will report the last year's income as income in respect of a decedent ("IRD"). § 691. Absent an automatic successor, the estate will generally succeed to the partnership interest, and, therefore, it is the estate that will report the last year's income. However, if the estate is probated quickly, such that the heir gets the interest by the end of the partnership's tax year, the heir will report the last year's income.

To illustrate: A was a calendar-year member of the cash-method ABC law partnership, which is also on the calendar year. A was married. A died on March 31, 1994. The estate was wound up on November 30, 1994, at which time A's spouse, Dee, inherited A's partnership interest. Dee will report all the 1994 income from the partnership for 1994. Only the portion of the income attributable to the January 1 to March 31 period is IRD. It does not get a fair-market-value-at-death basis. Dee gets a § 691(c) deduction on her return if and to the extent the inclusion of the IRD resulted in increased federal estate taxes.

2. PROBLEM OF LOST DEDUCTIONS

If there is no advance planning, all the partnership income or loss for the last year appears on the estate's income tax return. If the partnership had a major loss, the loss is likely to be worthless on the estate's return because estates rarely have large amounts of income. With a little advance planning, these losses can be salvaged by making the spouse the successor to the interest (for example, by a designation in the partnership agreement shifting the interest to the spouse at the date of death) and having the interim loss reported on the spouse's joint return filed with the decedent partner, or by having an automatic buy-sell arrangement so that at death the interest passes instantly to the other partners. *See* Reg. § 1.706-1(c)(3)(iii). There might also be a termination of the entire partnership by prearrangement. The following example is a synopsis of *Hesse v. Commissioner*, 74 T.C. 1307 (1980).

To illustrate: A, who is married, is an equal member of the ABC real estate partnership. A and ABC are calendar-year taxpayers. A dies on July 16, 1970. The shelter has a $300,000 loss. Because the estate cannot file a joint return with Mrs. A, the estate alone, not A or his widow, gets the $100,000 loss from ABC. Had the interest been immediately sold to A and B, or had the partnership terminated on A's death, the loss would have been reported on his final return. Relief is available under § 642(h), which provides that if, on the termination of an estate or trust, there is an unused NOL carryover under § 172 or, for the last taxable year of the estate or trust, deductions exceed gross income, the carryover or excess deduction will be allowed to the beneficiary who succeeds to the property of the estate or trust. However, the NOL or excess deduction cannot be carried back.

B. ESTATE TAXES

The partnership interest is appraised and assigned a fair market value, not reduced by liabilities, as of the date of death for federal estate tax purposes. § 1014 (basis). Estate taxes are imposed net of liabilities, including partnership liabilities, for otherwise the estate tax would be exaggerated. § 2053(a)(4). The gross estate includes income in respect of a decedent (IRD), but IRD items are subtracted from basis to the extent they were previously included in valuing the partnership interest, consistent with the general principle that IRD items do not get a new basis at the date of death, even though they are included in the decedent's gross estate. § 1014(c). For income tax purposes, IRD items have a zero basis. Items of income in respect of a decedent are taxed to their actual payee, which may be the estate or some other distributee. Recognizing that estate *and* income taxation of the same dollars is too harsh, § 691(c) grants the recipient of the IRD an income tax deduction for the increase in estate taxes attributable to the inclusion of the IRD items in the gross estate.

To illustrate: If the cash-method ABC partnership accrued $99 of unpaid income in the year during which A's death occurred, so that A died with a right to $33 of IRD, the estate tax value of A's partnership interest would be augmented by that $33, and that value would be subject to federal estate taxation. However, as noted above, IRD items always have a zero basis, and § 1014 does not apply to them. It is therefore necessary to reduce the estate taxed appraised value of A's partnership interest by $33 when determining the basis of the partnership interest after A's death. Section 691(c) lets A deduct the estate taxes on the $33.

Section 753 assures that § 736(a) payments to a decedent's successor in interest are always IRD. That seems entirely reasonable, as they are clearly income when held by the decedent.

QUICK'S TRUST v. COMMISSIONER

54 T.C. 1336 (1971), *aff'd per curiam*, 444 F.2d 90 (8th Cir. 1971)

Opinion

When Quick died he was an equal partner in a partnership which had been in the business of providing architectural and engineering services. In 1957, the partnership had ceased all business activity except the collection of outstanding accounts receivable. These receivables, and some cash, were the only assets of the partnership. Since partnership income was reported on the cash basis, the receivables had a zero basis.

Upon Quick's death in 1960, the estate became a partner with Maguolo and remained a partner until 1965 when it was succeeded as a partner by petitioner herein [i.e., the trust. Eds.]. The outstanding accounts receivable were substantial in amount at that time. In its 1960 return, the partnership elected under section 754 to make the adjustment in the basis of the partnership property provided for in section 743(b) and to allocate that adjustment in accordance with section 755. On the facts of this case, the net result of this adjustment was to increase the basis of the accounts receivable to the partnership from zero to an amount slightly less than one-half of their face value. If such treatment was correct, it substantially reduced the amount of the taxable income to the partnership from the collection of the accounts receivable under section 743(b) and the estate and the petitioner herein were entitled to the benefit of that reduction.

The issue before us is whether the foregoing adjustment to basis was correctly made. Its resolution depends upon the determination of the basis to the estate of its interest in the partnership, since section 743(b)(1) allows only an "increase [in] the adjusted basis of the partnership property by the excess of the basis to the transferee partner of his interest in the partnership over his proportionate share of the adjusted basis of the partnership property." This in turn depends upon whether, to the extent that "the basis to the transferee partner" reflects an interest in underlying accounts receivable arising out of personal services of the deceased partner, such interest constitutes income in respect of a decedent under section 691(a)(1) and (3). In such event, section 1014(c) comes into play and prohibits equating the basis of Quick's partnership interest with the fair market value of that interest at the time of his death under section 1014(a).

Petitioner argues that the partnership provisions of the Internal Revenue Code of 1954 adopted the entity theory of partnership, that the plain meaning of those provisions, insofar as they relate to the question of basis, requires the conclusion that the inherited partnership interest is separate and distinct from the underlying assets of the partnership, and that, therefore, section 691, and consequently section 1014(c), has no application herein.

Respondent counters with the assertion that the basis of a partnership interest is determined under section 742 by reference to other sections of the Code. He claims that, by virtue of section 1014(c), section 1014(a) does not apply to property which is classified as a right to receive income in respect of a decedent

B. ESTATE TAXES 215

under section 691 and that the interest of the estate and of petitioner in the proceeds of the accounts receivable of the partnership falls within this classification. He emphasizes that, since the accounts receivable represent money earned by the performance of personal services, the collections thereon would have been taxable to the decedent, if the partnership had been on the accrual basis, or to the estate and to petitioner if the decedent had been a cash basis sole proprietor. Similarly, he points out that if the business had been conducted by a corporation, the collections on the accounts receivable would have been fully taxable, regardless of Quick's death. Respondent concludes that no different result should occur simply because a cash basis partnership is interposed.

The share of a general partner's successor in interest upon his death in the collections by a partnership on accounts receivable arising out of the rendition of personal services constituted income in respect of a decedent under the 1939 Code. *United States v. Ellis*, 264 F.2d 325 (C.A. 2, 1959); *Riegelman's Estate v. Commissioner*, 253 F.2d 315 (C.A. 2, 1958), *affirming* 27 T.C. 833 (1957). Petitioner ignores these decisions, apparently on the ground that the enactment of comprehensive provisions dealing with the taxation of partnerships in the 1954 Code and what it asserts is "the plain meaning" of those provisions render such decisions inapplicable in the instant case. We disagree.

The partnership provisions of the 1954 Code are comprehensive in the sense that they are detailed. But this does not mean that they are exclusive, especially where those provisions themselves recognize the interplay with other provisions of the Code. Section 742 specifies: "The basis of an interest in a partnership acquired other than by contribution shall be determined under part II of subchapter O (sec. 1011 and following)." With the exception of section 722, which deals with the basis of a contributing partner's interest and which has no applicability herein, this is the only section directed toward the question of the initial determination of the basis of a partnership interest. From the specification of section 742, one is thus led directly to section 1014 and by subsection (c) thereof directly to section 691. Since, insofar as this case is concerned, section 691 incorporates the provisions and legal underpinning of its predecessor (sec. 126 of the 1939 Code),[1] we are directed back to a recognition, under the 1954 Code, of the decisional effect of *United States v. Ellis, supra,* and *Riegelman's Estate v. Commissioner, supra.*

Thus, to the extent that a "plain meaning" can be distilled from the partnership provisions of the 1954 Code, we think that it is contrary to petitioner's position. In point of fact, however, we hesitate to rest our decision in an area such as is involved herein exclusively on such linguistic clarity and purity.... However, an examination of the legislative purpose reinforces our

---

[1] According to the House committee report at the time the 1954 Code was enacted, sec. 1014 (c) "makes explicit the rule of existing law." *See* H. Rept. No. 1337, 83d Cong., 2d Sess., p. A267 (1954).

reading of the statute. Section 751, dealing with unrealized receivables and inventory items, is included in subpart D of subchapter K, and is labeled "Provisions Common to Other Subparts." Both the House and Senate committee reports specifically state that income rights relating to unrealized receivables or fees are regarded "as severable from the partnership interest and as subject to the same tax consequences which would be accorded an individual entrepreneur." *See* H. Rept. No. 1337, 83d Cong., 2d Sess., p. 71 (1954); S. Rept. No. 1622, 83d Cong., 2d Sess., p. 99 (1954). And the Senate committee report adds the following significant language.

> The House bill provides that a decedent partner's share of unrealized receivables are [sic] to be treated as income in respect of a decedent. Such rights to income are to be taxed to the estate or heirs when collected, with an appropriate adjustment for estate taxes.... Your committee's bill agrees substantially with the House in the treatment described above but also provides that other income apart from unrealized receivables is to be treated as income in respect of a decedent. [*See* S. Rept. No. 1622, *supra* at 99; ...]

In light of the foregoing, the deletion of a provision in section 743 of the House bill which specifically provided that the optional adjustment to basis of partnership property should not be made with respect to unrealized receivables is of little, if any, significance. H.R. 8300, 83d Cong., 2d Sess., sec. 743(e) (1954) (introduced print). The fact that such deletion was made without comment either in the Senate or Conference Committee reports indicates that the problem was covered by other sections and that such a provision was therefore unnecessary. Similarly, the specific reference in section 753 to income in respect of a decedent cannot be given an exclusive characterization. That section merely states that certain distributions in liquidation under section 736(a) shall be treated as income in respect of a decedent. It does not state that no other amounts can be so treated.

Many of the assertions of the parties have dealt with the superstructure of the partnership provisions — assertions based upon a technical and involuted analysis of those provisions dealing with various adjustments and the treatment to be accorded to distributions after the basis of the partnership has been determined. But, as we have previously indicated (*see* pp. 1340-1341, *supra*), the question herein involves the foundation, not the superstructure, i.e., what is the basis of petitioner's partnership interest?

Petitioner asserts that a partnership interest is an "asset separate and apart from the individual assets of the partnership" and that the character of the accounts receivable disappears into the character of the partnership interest, with the result that such interest cannot, in whole or in part, represent a right to receive income in respect of a decedent. In making such an argument, petitioner has erroneously transmuted the so-called partnership "entity" approach into a rule of law which allegedly precludes fragmentation of a partnership interest. But

B. ESTATE TAXES

it is clear that even the "entity" approach should not be inexorably applied under all circumstances. *See* H. Rept. No. 2543, 83d Cong., 2d Sess., p. 59 (1954). Similarly, the fact that a rule of non-fragmentation of a partnership interest (except to the extent that the statute otherwise expressly provides) may govern sales of such an interest to third parties (*cf.* Donald L. Evans, 54 T.C. 40 (1970)) does not compel its application in all situations where such an interest is transferred. In short, a partnership interest is not, as petitioner suggests, a unitary res, incapable of further analysis.

A partnership interest is a property interest, and an intangible one at that. A property interest can often be appropriately viewed as a bundle of rights. Indeed, petitioner suggests this viewpoint by pointing out that the partnership interest herein is "merely a right to share in the profits and surplus of the Partnership." That partnership interest had value only insofar as it represented a right to receive the cash or other property of the partnership. Viewed as a bundle of rights, a major constituent element of that interest was the right to share in the proceeds of the accounts receivable as they were collected. This right was admittedly not the same as the right to collect the accounts receivable; only the partnership had the latter right. But it does not follow from this dichotomy that the right of the estate to share in the collections merged into the partnership interest. Nothing in the statute compels such a merger. Indeed, an analysis of the applicable statutory provisions points to the opposite conclusion.

Accordingly, we hold that section 691(a)(1) and (3) applies and that the right to share in the collections from the accounts receivable must be considered a right to receive income in respect of a decedent. Consequently, section 1014(c) also applies and the basis of the partnership interest must be reduced from the fair market value thereof at Quick's death. The measure of that reduction under section 1014 is the extent to which that value includes the fair market value of a one-half interest in the proceeds of the zero basis partnership accounts receivable. *See* sec. 1.742-1, Income Tax Regs. It follows that the optional adjustment to basis made by the partnership under section 743(b) must be modified accordingly and that respondent's determination as to the amount of additional income subject to the tax should be sustained. *See* Rev. Rul. 66-325, 1966-2 C.B. 249.

[The portion of the opinion concerning the issue of the taxability of the estate for the year 1961 is omitted. Eds.]

....

NOTES

Assuming the election was in force at the date of death, § 754 will cause a § 743(b) adjustment of the partnership's assets to reflect the § 1014 set-up or step-down in outside basis at death. However, this process becomes curious in a community property state if the surviving spouse already owns half the partnership interest under the local community property laws. In such cases,

§ 1014(b)(6) will automatically adjust the *survivor's* interest to a fair market value at death (or optional valuation date) basis. Will the survivor also share in the § 743(b) adjustment?

REV. RUL. 79-124
1979-1 C.B. 224

Issue

What is the effect of section 743(b) of the Internal Revenue Code of 1954 under the circumstances described below?

Facts

A, a domiciliary of a community property state, was a member of a partnership at the time of A's death. Under state law the interest in the partnership was community property of A and A's spouse, B, but B was not a member of the partnership under state law. The election provided by section 754 of the Code was in effect with respect to the partnership for 1976, the year in which A's death occurred.

One-half of the partnership interest that was owned by A and B as community property was transferred to A's estate at A's death and was included in A's gross estate for federal estate tax purposes. A's estate was substituted by the partnership as a successor partner for purposes of administering the estate. B was not substituted as a successor partner but continued to own one-half of the partnership [as] a member of the partnership under state law.

Law and Analysis

Section 754 of the Code provides, in part, that if a partnership files an election in accordance with regulations prescribed by the Secretary of Treasury, the basis of partnership property shall be adjusted in the case of a transfer of a partnership interest in the manner provided in section 743. Such election shall apply with respect to all transfers of interest in the partnership during the taxable year with respect to which such election was filed and for all subsequent years.

Section 743(b) of the Code provides that if the election under section 754 is in effect, in the case of a transfer of an interest in a partnership by sale or exchange or upon the death of a partner, the partnership shall (1) increase the adjusted basis of its property by the excess of the basis to the transferee partner of the partner's interest in the partnership over the partner's proportionate share of the adjusted basis of the partnership property, or (2) decrease the adjusted basis of its property by the excess of the transferee partner's proportionate share of the adjusted basis of partnership property over the basis of the partner's interest in the partnership. Such increase or decrease is an adjustment to the basis of partnership property with respect to the transferee partner only.

Section 1014(a) of the Code provides, in part, that the basis of property in the hands of a person acquiring the property from a decedent or to whom the property passed from a decedent shall, if not sold, exchanged, or otherwise disposed of before the decedent's death by such person, be the fair market value of the property at the date of the decedent's death.

Section 1014(b)(6) of the Code provides that property which represents the surviving spouse's one-half share of property held by the decedent and the surviving spouse under the community property laws of any state, or possession of the United States or of any foreign country, shall be considered to have been acquired from or to have passed from the decedent if at least one-half of the whole of the community interest in such property was includible in determining the value of the decedent's gross estate for purposes of the federal estate tax.

Because one-half of the partnership interest owned by A and B as community property was included in A's gross estate for federal estate tax purposes, B's share of the partnership interest is considered, under section 1014(b)(6) of the Code, to have been acquired from A upon A's death. A's half of the partnership interest was actually transferred to A's estate at A's death. Therefore, the basis of the entire partnership interest in the hands of A's estate and B is to be determined in accordance with section 1014(a). In addition, for purposes of section 743(b), both A's community interest and B's community interest in the partnership interest are considered to have been transferred, upon the death of A, to A's estate and to B respectively.

Holding

Adjustments to the basis of partnership properties under section 743(b) of the Code are to be made in respect of the portion of such properties that is allocable to the entire interest in the partnership that was owned by A and B as community property immediately preceding the death of A. Furthermore, the same result would apply if B predeceased A.

C. OTHER ESTATE TAX ISSUES

1. ESTATE FREEZE

The federal estate tax basically falls on the value of a deceased taxpayer's property held at death. § 2001. The estate tax is buttressed by a federal gift tax which falls on inter vivos transfers. § 2501.[2] (If there were no gift tax, people would avoid the estate tax by the simple expedient of making lavish gifts during their lives.) The taxes are integrated, and the rates of both taxes are now as high as 55%, so avoiding federal transfer taxes on interests in family businesses is a matter of great concern to business owners. An older partner's financial planners are likely to worry about the estate tax burdens that could arise if the partnership

---

[2] There is also a specialized tax on so-called generation-skipping transfers. It is basically designed to assure that gifts or inheritances that leapfrog a generation are subject to further taxation as if the property had in fact not skipped a generation. § 2601.

becomes lucrative. One instinctive reaction will be to try to devise ways to shift appreciation in value to members of a younger generation. The simplest planning idea has been to give away a volatile partnership interest while retaining a partnership interest which offers a preferred return.

The primary problem nowadays will be § 2701, which disregards retained interests in partnerships when a partner transfers property to a spouse, a lineal descendent, or a spouse of a lineal descendent, in effect treating the retained interest as also having been given away, with a possibly large immediate gift tax due. Section 2701 does not reach transfers to other people, such as nieces and nephews, nor does it reach cases where the retained interest's value is supported by "qualified payment rights," meaning payments at a fixed rate or tied to a market index of some sort, much like dividends on preferred stock. A transfer in which the transferor retains such rights is fairly easy to achieve in a corporate setting using preferred stock. It is not so easy in a partnership setting. Moreover, to use the qualified payments route, the recapitalization transactions must be sufficiently disclosed to the IRS, and the consent of other senior members must be obtained. §§ 2701(a)(3)(c)(3), 6051(c)(9), and Reg. § 25.2701-2(2)(4).

Another alternative is to wait until death and give a preferred interest to the surviving spouse and the regular interest to the beneficiaries to whom the decedent wants to shift appreciation. However, this is poor planning in the case of a large estate; the real trick is to shift value *before* death.

2. BUY-SELL AGREEMENT

When a partner dies and her interest cannot realistically be shifted to an heir, say in the case of a law partnership, there has to be a mechanism to compensate the deceased partner's estate. The Uniform Partnership Act generally grants the estate of a deceased partner a right to the net value of the partner's interest at death, with interest. UPA § 42. The estate of a deceased limited partner generally steps into the partner's shoes and can withdraw as a member and demand a similar distribution of its share of the partnership's properties. RULPA §§ 603, 604, and 705. The partners can trump this general rule with a specified agreement as to how the estate will be paid, e.g., net asset value plus the appraised value of goodwill, an arbitrated figure, or perhaps a fixed figure. The buyer can be either the other partner(s) or the partnership itself.

Because the federal estate tax falls on the value of the decedent's estate, family-business owners are motivated to minimize the fair market value[3] of their business interests. One obvious way to do so is by obligating the business to buy up the decedent's interest at a low price. The rest of the family will be indifferent

---

[3] The term fair-market value basically means what a willing buyer would pay a willing seller, assuming neither was under duress and both had a reasonable knowledge of the facts. Reg. § 20.2031-1(b). *See* Rev. Rul 59-60, 1959-1 C.B. 237 for a list of factors often used to fix such values.

C. OTHER ESTATE TAX ISSUES

to the bargain price, because they will not share the discount with outsiders. However, if the price is low enough, it is clear that the decedent indirectly transferred value to surviving owners, who may all be family members. Once again, the Congress, the courts, and the IRS have been forced to draw practical lines to resolve an essentially impossible question. Nevertheless, if there is a buy-sell agreement, the value it fixes *generally* determines the value of the interest for estate taxes as well. The following case indicates the state of the law concerning the use of buy-sell agreements to limit the value of partnership interests for federal estate tax purposes. Before reading the case, review Reg. § 20.2031-2(h). This requirement continues in force, despite the addition of § 703 to the Code, if a purchase price determined under a buy-sell agreement is to fix the value of an interest in a closely-held business.

ST. LOUIS COUNTY BANK, EXECUTOR v. UNITED STATES OF AMERICA
674 F.2d 1207 (8th Cir. 1982),
rev'g and rem'g 511 F. Supp. 653 (E.D. Mo. 1981)

Before LAY, CHIEF JUDGE, ARNOLD, CIRCUIT JUDGE, and WOODS, DISTRICT JUDGE.

ARNOLD, JUDGE.

The government appeals the District Court's entry of summary judgment in favor of St. Louis County Bank, executor of the estate of Lee J. Sloan, in a suit brought to recover an alleged overpayment of estate taxes.... The central question on the merits is the proper valuation of certain stock in L.J.S. Investment Company held by Mr. Sloan at the time of his death....

I.

As of December 24, 1956, Lee J. Sloan owned all but one of the 466 shares of Sloan's Moving & Storage Company. The one share not owned by him belonged to his wife. On that day he made five gifts of 38 shares each (190 shares in all) to the following persons: Nina Roth (his daughter); Karl Roth (his son-in-law); and in trust for the benefit of Nancy Lee, Judy Ann, and Joy Anita Roth (his granddaughters).

Sometime after the gifts were made Sloan became concerned about the possibility that the stock might pass to persons outside the family. Sloan asked Woodside to prepare an agreement restricting the transfer of the stock. In 1964 all the shareholders entered into such an agreement, restricting inter vivos transfers of the stock to persons outside of Lee Sloan's immediate family. Under the agreement, at the death of any shareholder or at any time a shareholder wished to transfer his or her stock to someone outside the family, the company and the other shareholders had the option to purchase the shares at a price determined by a formula set out in the agreement. If the company or other family members failed to exercise their option, the shares could then be sold to someone outside the family. The formula price provided for in the agreement was ten times the average annual net earnings per share for the five years preceding the offer, adjusted to eliminate gains or losses on real estate and the income-tax consequences of such gains or losses.

Until 1972 the company continued to engage in the moving, storage, and parcel-delivery business. In that year the company sold virtually all of its operating assets and changed its name to L.J.S. Investment Company. Thereafter it engaged primarily in the rental of real estate. This change in the nature of the business had a significant, adverse impact on the "value" of the stock of the company. While engaged in the moving business the company generated substantial yearly income as defined by the formula in the stock-purchase agreement. From the years 1964 to 1970 the value per share of the stock, as measured by the formula embodied in the agreement, fluctuated from a high of $1,061.15 in 1968 to a low of $597.00 in 1970. As a company engaged in the rental of real estate, however, the "value" of each share of L.J.S. Investment Company as determined by the formula went down to $0 per share in 1971, and remained at that level through 1975. This was so because L.J.S. began to show substantial net losses as defined in the stock-purchase agreement. The years after 1975 are not relevant to our discussion here.

During this time there was one death among the parties to the stock-purchase agreement, that of Karl Roth. Karl left his entire estate, including his stock, to his wife, Nina Roth, who also served as his executrix. She did not offer the shares to either the corporation or the surviving shareholders as called for in the agreement, and apparently there was no objection. At that time Karl Roth's shares could have been purchased pursuant to the agreement for $0 per share. For federal-estate-tax purposes his estate reported the shares at $850 per share, reflecting their adjusted book value.

At the date of Lee J. Sloan's death, May 8, 1976, he held 265 shares of L.J.S. Investment Company, a controlling interest in the company. Shortly after Sloan's death his estate offered his 265 shares to the company under the terms of the stock-purchase agreement at $0 per share. The company accepted. As a result, Sloan's daughter and granddaughters became the beneficial owners of all the stock.

Sloan's estate filed an estate-tax return in February of 1977 and paid the sum of $36,383.06. On the return the 265 shares of stock were valued at $0 per share. On March 26, 1979, the Internal Revenue Service assessed a deficiency of $23,179.35 based on a valuation of L.J.S. stock at $544.60 per share, their book value. At the time the total assets of L.J.S. were valued at approximately $256,000, of which $201,000 was in cash. The estate paid the deficiency, and this action followed.

C. OTHER ESTATE TAX ISSUES

II.

The government's principal argument for reversal is that the District Court erred in granting summary judgment because there were genuine issues of fact left unresolved. When considering a motion for summary judgment a court must view the facts in the light most favorable to the party opposing the motion, and it must afford that party the benefit of all favorable inferences which may be derived from the facts contained in the pleadings, depositions, and affidavits.... The granting of the motion is appropriate only where there is no genuine issue of material fact and where the moving party is entitled to a judgment as a matter of law. Fed. R. Civ. P. 56(c).... With these standards in mind we now look to the decision of the District Court.

The law of the tax consequences of restrictive agreements to purchase stock is, for the most part, well settled. Several courts of appeals have held that such agreements, if enforceable both at death and during a person's lifetime, establish the value of the stock for estate-tax purposes. *See Brodrick v. Gore*, 224 F.2d 892 (10th Cir. 1955).... Embodied in these decisions is the rule stated in Treas. Reg. § 20.2031-2(h) (1958), that

> (e)ven if the decedent is not free to dispose of the underlying securities at other than the option or contract price, such price will be disregarded in determining the value of the securities unless it is determined under the circumstances of the particular case that the agreement represents a bona fide business arrangement and not a device to pass the decedent's shares to the natural objects of his bounty for less than an adequate and full consideration in money or money's worth....[4]

In sum, the law is that a restrictive agreement may fix the value of property for estate-tax purposes if the agreement has a bona fide business purpose and if it was not used as a tax-avoidance testamentary device.

We have no problem with the District Court's findings that the stock-purchase agreement provided for a reasonable price at the time of its adoption, and that the agreement had a bona fide business purpose — the maintenance of family ownership and control of the business. Courts have recognized the validity of such a purpose. *See Estate of Bischoff v. Commissioner*, 69 T.C. 32 (1977).... Here the District Court concluded that the existence of a valid business purpose necessarily excluded the possibility that the agreement was a tax-avoidance testamentary device.... We disagree. The fact of a valid business purpose could, in some circumstances, completely negate the alleged existence of a tax-avoidance testamentary device as a matter of law, but those circumstances are not necessarily presented here.

---

[4] In *May v. McGowan, supra*, 194 F.2d at 397, the court noted that the trial court had found no tax-avoidance motive. And in *Wilson v. Bowers, supra*, one of the parties to the restrictive agreement seems to have been a non-family member.

At the time of the agreement Lee J. Sloan had a heart condition and had previously suffered two heart attacks in the early 1960's.... Given this fact and the fact of the family relationship between the parties to the agreement, a reasonable inference could be drawn that the agreement was testamentary in nature and a device for the avoidance of estate taxes. Similar facts were before the court in *Slocum v. United States, supra*. The court there recognized that varying inferences could be drawn from the facts surrounding the agreement, and thus left the drawing of those inferences to the trier of fact at trial....

We are also bothered by the fact that decedent's stock was valued by his estate for estate-tax purposes at $0 when its total book value was admittedly in excess of $200,000. Appellee argues that courts should look only to the adequacy of the consideration at the time the agreement was entered into, rather than the date of decedent's death, when considering whether the agreement is a testamentary device to avoid estate taxes. *Estate of Bischoff v. Commissioner, supra*, 69 T.C. at 41 n.9. This may well be the best rule of general applicability (although appellees cite no appellate authority, and we have found none), but we think it has no application in the case at bar.

In 1964 the parties to the stock-purchase agreement adopted a formula for valuation of the stock that was admittedly reasonable at the time. However, some seven years later the assets of the moving and storage business, which was generating substantial net income as defined by the formula, were liquidated, and the proceeds transferred to an investment company, which engaged primarily in the rental of real estate. As a result of this transformation in the nature of the business, the value of the stock as determined by the formula was reduced to zero. Moreover, from all indications the decision to sell the assets of Sloan's Moving and Storage was Lee J. Sloan's and his alone. He held a majority of the stock, and there is no evidence that any of the minority shareholders took an active part in the management of the company. In light of these facts it would be unreasonable to restrict the court's inquiry to the adequacy of consideration and the conduct of the parties at the time of the agreement. The contrary rule, urged by taxpayers, may have some appeal in a situation where a wide disparity in formula price and other valuation methods, such as book value, is a result of failure of the business to generate a profit or other economic conditions outside the control of the parties to the agreement. Presumably such events would be within the contemplation of the parties to the agreement. The same cannot be said here where the nature of the business was completely transformed several years down the line.

Finally, the record reveals that at the time of Karl Roth's death the provisions of the agreement were not invoked. Under the agreement, at his death, his stock was to be offered first to the company at the formula price, and if refused, then to the other shareholders. Instead, his interest in the company passed under his will to his wife, Nina. At this point Karl Roth's shares (then numbering 43) could have been purchased at the formula price of $0 per share, though their book value was $850 per share. These events could be the basis for an inference

C. OTHER ESTATE TAX ISSUES

that the agreement was being used for the purpose of passing property to members of the family other than Lee J. Sloan, and thus ultimately accomplishing a tax-avoidance purpose benefiting the estate of Lee J. Sloan.[5]

At this stage of the case we must afford the government the benefit of all favorable inferences which could have been derived from the underlying facts. The historical facts themselves were left unchallenged by the government, to be sure, but they are subject to more than one interpretation. The trier of fact at trial should decide which interpretation is more persuasive. The judgment of the District Court is reversed, and the cause is remanded for further proceedings consistent with this opinion.

It is so ordered.

NOTES

1. If continuing family control is so important to the decedent, could he not have taken care of the problem directly by bequeathing the business interest to his heirs?

2. The suppression of values has risen to a virtual art form. For a fascinating article on the subject, see Cooper, *A Voluntary Tax? New Perspectives on Sophisticated Estate Tax Avoidance*, 77 Colum. L. Rev. 161 (1977). Some favorite taxpayer theories for claiming low estate tax values are that: (i) the decedent held a minority interest, which has to be discounted because the interest was subject to being dominated by others in important voting matters affecting the firm; (ii) if the decedent held a large interest and it were sold, it would suffer a price discount because it would flood the market (known as the "blockage rule").

3. If the parties decide on a cross-purchase funded by insurance, the benefit is that the insurance proceeds will not be taxable to the policy owner or the decedent. § 101(a). Rev. Rul. 56-397, 1956-2 C.B. 599. If the partnership owns the policy, the proceeds are not directly includable in the insured's estate, but they do increase the value of the decedent's partnership interest by the decedent's ratable share of the insurance proceeds unless the proceeds are explicitly excluded from the buy-sell calculation and the agreement is effective in setting values for estate tax purposes. Any such proviso should appear in the buy-sell agreement. *See Newell v. Commissioner*, 66 F.2d 102 (7th Cir. 1933).

---

[5] The adverse inference here is not that the agreement was used to benefit Karl Roth's estate. Indeed, on his estate-tax return his holdings were valued at $850 per share, their book value. Had the formula been used, his interest in the company would have been valued at $0. Dennis K. Woodside, attorney for Roth's estate as well as Lee J. Sloan and the company, stated that "it did not occur to (him) that the Stock Purchase Agreement might be used in that fashion."... Of course, the trier of fact might think that the parties' conduct at the time of Roth's death shows there was no tax-avoidance purpose. Our point is that a contrary inference may reasonably be drawn.

PROBLEM 11-1

Review Reg. § 25.2703-1(b) and consider whether the restrictions in the *St. Louis Bank* case would be respected under present law for purposes of suppressing estate tax values.

OUTSIDE READINGS

P. Wallace, *Selected Post-Death Problems of Partnerships and Partners*, 33 U.S.C. Inst. on Fed. Tax'n Ch. 18 (1981).

Chapter 12
INTRODUCTION TO THE CORPORATE INCOME TAX

The U.S. corporate income tax taxes a corporation as a separate and taxable entity. It has not always been so. The first U.S. national corporate income taxes were enacted during the Civil War, as were the first individual income taxes, which imposed graduated rates of up to 10%. (The Confederacy also had an income tax and at higher rates than the Union's.) The 1864 version was designed to tax corporate profits only once, either to the corporation or to its shareholders, but not both. It imposed a flat 5% tax on the profits of certain kinds of corporations (mainly financial and transportation companies) but dividends from such companies were excludible by shareholders to the extent they came from previously taxed earnings. Most corporations paid no taxes, but their profits were taxed to shareholders at once, even if not distributed; the income of the corporation was treated as the income of its shareholders. This would now be called a pass-through or partnership approach.[1] [This was held constitutional in *Collector v. Hubbard*, 79 U.S. (12 Wall) 1 (1870), though later repudiated in *Eisner v. Macomber*, 252 U.S. 189 (1920).] This income tax was repealed after the Civil War, but in 1894 another national corporate tax was enacted, taking a different approach but it was also fully integrated with the personal income tax, which had been enacted at the same time. A flat 2% tax was imposed upon all individuals and corporations, and the integration was achieved by simply exempting from tax all dividends paid to individual shareholders. These taxes never went into effect because the Supreme Court held the 1894 income tax act to be unconstitutional as an unapportioned "direct tax" in *Pollack v. Farmers' Loan & Trust Co.*, 157 U.S. 429 (1895). Because the 1894 act was held unconstitutional in its entirety, the corporate tax was annulled as well.

In 1909, Congress enacted a tax of 1% of net earnings and imposed it solely upon corporations as an excise tax, for the privilege of conducting business in corporate form, measured by income. This time the tax was upheld, in *Flint v. Stone Tracy Co.*, 220 U.S. 107 (1911), in which the Supreme Court held the tax to be a legitimate excise tax rather than an unconstitutional direct tax. Thereafter, the Sixteenth Amendment was passed in order to insure the validity of the individual income tax, which became effective on February 25, 1913. *See Doyle v. Mitchell Bros.*, 247 U.S. 179 (1918). The 1909 tax, treating the corporation

---

[1] *See* E.R.A. Seligman, The Income Tax, N.Y.: Macmillan, Pt. II, Ch. 3 (1911); Magill, R., Taxable Income 337 (rev. ed. 1945).

as a taxpayer, to be taxed on its own income, set the pattern for future developments.

There was no problem of "integration" of the corporate and individual income taxes under the 1909 act because there was no individual income tax in effect at the time. After enactment of the individual tax in 1913, however, corporate income was in effect taxed twice, unlike the 1864 and 1894 acts, because individuals were taxed on corporate dividends which represented profits which had already been taxed to the corporation. The problem may have arisen because the two taxes were enacted at different times and Congress simply failed to consider how the two taxes would interact. It is certainly the case that two levels of taxation on corporate profits means that shareholders investing in corporate stock are put at considerable disadvantage compared to more direct investments, subject to one level of tax, everything else being equal. The problem remains with us today, exacerbated by the vastly higher rates of tax at both levels. As we have seen earlier in the book, there is no such problem of double taxation with partnerships, nor for S corporations or limited liability companies, which are considered elsewhere in this book. The integrated "double tax" on distributed corporate profits in the U.S. probably misallocates resources, induces overuse of debt and undercapitalization with equity (stock), causes excessive and inefficient retention of corporate profits, discourages the use of the incorporated form of doing business and contributes to arguable overtaxation of capital income.

Another anomaly concerns the taxation of capital gains. Shareholders are entitled under § 1(h) to the benefit of a limit (of 28%) on the top rate of tax on net capital gains (vs. 39.6% on ordinary income.) By contrast, corporations enjoy little or no benefit; § 1201(a) assures that the maximum rate of tax on capital gains of corporations is 35% (versus 34% or 35% on ordinary income). Moreover, corporations that incur large capital losses can only offset them against capital gains for the same taxable year and after that, they can carry them back three years and forward only up to five years. § 1212(a). This makes it risky for a corporation to incur a large *capital* loss because there is a possibility that it will never be fully deductible. By contrast, individual taxpayers can deduct up to $3,000 of capital losses against their other income for the year and then can carry their losses forward indefinitely under § 1212(d).

In 1993 Congress enacted a remarkably generous new provision that authorizes non-corporate taxpayers to exclude from their income 50% of the gain from the sale or exchange of so-called qualified (small) business stock if the stock was held for more than five years. § 1202(a). This new provision is riddled with fairly difficult definitions and limitations but the fundamental thrust is quite apparent. Congress intended to provide a major incentive for investment in the corporate form by small businesses by diminishing tax on disposition of stock in certain C corporations. The only catch is that half of the excluded gain is included in the alternative minimum tax base. *See* § 57(a)7. Because it is an exclusion preference, the resulting AMT burden cannot be credited in later years. *See* § 53(d)(1)(B).

A. INCIDENCE OF THE INCOME TAX

Assume a world in which there is no corporate income tax. If the legislature suddenly imposed such a tax there would be a number of possible outcomes in terms of who actually bears the burden of the tax. Under one scenario, the corporation might be able to pass the tax on to consumers by marking up the price of its products. In such a case, the incidence of the tax would be said to be on the consumer. Alternatively, the corporation might be able to avoid the tax by cutting the wages of its employees. In that case, the incidence of the tax would be on the employees. Finally, if it could not avoid the tax by either of these techniques, the incidence of the tax would fall on the shareholders and the burden would take the form of reduced value of the company's stock. Contrary to the beliefs of some men and women "in the street," the tax is not borne "by the corporation," since only individuals bear taxes, not artificial legal persons like corporate entities—because only individuals consume (things like bread, wine and haircutting services), so only the consumption of individuals can be reduced by a tax. In most cases, the incidence of the tax probably will be on some mix of consumers, shareholders and employees.

The problem is actually more complex. First, even if the corporation can mark up the price of its goods to cover the tax, it may wind up selling fewer goods, with the result that the drop in demand will be felt by either the shareholders, the employees, the consumers, or some combination of them. Also, there may be a considerable difference between the incidence of the tax in the short run as opposed to the long run. In general, it seems unlikely that the tax can be shifted in the short run to persons other than the shareholders, at least in a competitive industry, but in the long run the burden can be pushed off shareholders and onto consumers and employees in some proportion which depends on the circumstances of the particular corporation. It may be, as Harburger contends, that in the long run, the corporate income tax is shifted to all owners of capital in the economy.[2] There is extensive economic literature on this subject but a shortage of firm conclusions. *See* C. McLure, Must Corporate Income Be Taxed Twice? (Washington, D.C.: Brookings 1979); J.G. Ballentine, *Equity, Efficiency and the United States Corporation Income Tax*, AEI (1980); W. Klein, *Income Taxation and Legal Entities*, 20 UCLA L. Rev. 13 (1972).

B. INTEGRATION OF CORPORATE AND SHAREHOLDER LEVEL TAXES

Business corporations and their owners (and economists and tax theorists) have long complained about the corporate *double tax*, on fairness and efficiency grounds. The objection is that the corporation itself pays a federal income tax on

---

[2] *See* Harburger & Bailey, The Taxation of Income from Capital (1969).

its earnings, leaving a diminished amount for distribution to its owners. When the entity does distribute its profits, those profits are taxed a second time at the shareholder level. The problem is easy to illustrate.

> *To illustrate*: Mr. Big owns 100% of the stock of the Big Book Corporation. Last year Big Book Corporation earned net profits of $1,000. Assuming for convenience that it paid a tax of $340, that would leave over $660 for distribution to Mr. Big. Assuming Mr. Big is in the 36% bracket and that Big Corporation distributed all of the profits, Mr. Big would receive $660 and would pay a tax of $237.60. The total tax bill would be $577.60. To put it another way, the tax burden would be 57.76% of net profits. By contrast, if Mr. Big were instead a proprietor or partner, the total tax bill would be only $360 (36%).

Over many years, a number of proposals to remove or ameliorate this unintegrated double taxation have emerged. One proposal is simply to allow the corporation a deduction for its distributions of profits as dividends, thereby equating interest payments and dividends. Another possibility would be to exclude or exempt dividends from tax to shareholders. Still another proposal would grant shareholders the right to claim a credit against their tax for the amount of income taxes paid by the corporation. There are various other proposals in the literature. Chapter 27 of this book investigates these problems and possible solutions in greater depth. *See also* C. McLure, Must Corporate Income Be Taxed Twice? (Washington, D.C.: Brookings 1979); J. McNulty, *Corporate Income Tax Reform In the United States: Proposals For Integration Of The Corporate And Individual Income Taxes, and International Aspects*, 12 Int'l Tax & Bus. Law. No. 2, 161 (1994); U.S. Treas. Dept., Integration of the Individual and Corporate Tax Systems — Taxing Business Income Once (1992); Alvin J. Warren, American Law Institute, Federal Income Tax Project—Reporter's Study of Corporate Tax Integration (1993); U.S. Treas. Dept., Blueprints for Basic Tax Reform (1977).

The associated political pressure has materialized in a number of other forms. One is an initiative to enact a national consumption tax or value added tax ("VAT") and to scale back or eliminate the corporate income tax. This sits well with manufacturing businesses in the United States, which understand that a destination-based VAT is neutral from the point of view of international trade because it would allow the imposition of a U.S. VAT on imported merchandise and would allow U.S. manufacturers to receive back the VAT previously paid when their goods are exported (and presumably a foreign VAT would apply at the place of sale). VATs are used extensively in the European Union and Japan. Yet another approach is to expand the availability of the so-called S corporation election by various devices. The S corporation is discussed at length later in the book.

C. CORPORATE TAXES AND TAX RATES

Finally, the recently emerging "limited liability company" provides canny investors with an opportunity to put their money into a fascinating hybrid that combines the tax benefits of operating as a partnership with the advantages of operating with limited liability for state law purposes. Chapter 26 of this book covers limited liability companies.

C. CORPORATE TAXES AND TAX RATES

Read §§ 11, 55(a), (b)(1)(B) and (c), and 59A.

Business corporations are subject to graduated income tax rates in much the same way as individuals. Like an individual, the corporation files an annual federal income tax return (Form 1120). Often the corporation is the parent of a constellation of subsidiary corporations, in which case it may file a so-called consolidated return, which has the practical effect of treating the affiliated group as one big corporation.

The taxable income of a corporation is determined in much the same way as for individuals, with obvious exceptions, such as the lack of deductions for personal exemptions.[3] Sections 61 and 63 provide the base on which the tax is imposed, a corporation does not employ the § 62 "adjusted gross income" calculation used by individuals, and § 11 imposes the rates of tax, as follows:

Taxable Income	Tax Rates
First $50,000:	15%
$50,000-$75,000:	25%
$75,000- $10 million:	34%[4]
$100,000-$335,000	39%
$10 million - 15 million:	35%
$15 million - $18,333,333:	38%
Over $18,333,333:	35%

To illustrate: National Box Corporation has taxable income of $100,000 for the present taxable year. It calculates its taxable income as follows:

---

[3] Section 291(a) imposes some special reductions in deductions, known as corporate preference items. This provision is hard to explain except as a revenue measure.

[4] In the case of a corporation that has income in excess of $100,000 for the year, the amount of tax is increased by the lesser of 5% of such excess or $11,750, meaning a rate of 39% on corporate income from $100,000 to $335,000. This added tax recaptures the benefits of the lower rate brackets for higher income corporations.

Tax on first $50,000 of taxable
  income at 15%: $7,500
Tax on next $25,000 at 25%: 6,250
Tax on remaining $25,000 at 34%: 8,500
  TOTAL $22,250

If this corporation had another $50,000 of taxable income, the marginal rate on the top $50,000 would be 39%, for an added tax of $19,500. The marginal rate would fall back to 34% on income above $335,000 (and up to $10,000,000). The humped rate schedule means that corporations with income of $335,000 or more get no benefit from the lower graduated rates applicable to the first $75,000 of income.

Also, § 11(b)(2) dictates that a so-called "qualified personal service corporation" is taxed at a flat 35% rate on its taxable income. The term *qualified personal service corporation* is defined in § 448(d)(2), under the rules excepting those corporations from the general rule that C corporations must use the accrual method of accounting. Basically, the term means a corporation the employees of which spend the bulk of their time in a professional or scientific field (e.g., medicine or engineering) and "substantially all" of the stock of which is held, directly or indirectly, by present or former employees performing services in the corporation's field. The Regulations treat "substantially all" as 95%.

Corporations are also subject to a corporate alternative minimum tax, which is imposed at the rate of 20% to the extent it exceeds the § 11 tax for the year. § 55(b)(1)(B). The corporate AMT has two unique features. One is the so-called adjusted current earnings (ACE) adjustment under § 56(g) which forces the corporation to derive something roughly equivalent to economic income and then increase its AMT base by 75% of the excess of ACE over alternative minimum taxable income (computed without the ACE adjustment). Compliance with this enormous complexity is rewarded with a general rule that allows corporations a credit for their alternative minimum taxes in years in which the regular income tax applies. The credit is based on both deferral and exclusion preferences, whereas the AMT on individuals allows a credit only for deferral preferences. § 53(d)(1)(B)(iv).

Finally, § 59A imposes a special low-rate environmental tax on corporations that have a modified form of alternative minimum taxable income of over $2 million. The rate is 0.12%. There seems to be no good reason not to apply that tax to sole proprietorships and partnerships as well.

The top tax rate on individuals is now 39.6% for those who have taxable income of over $250,000. By contrast, capital gains rates on individuals are capped at 28%. As a consequence, the total federal income tax take on a $100 dividend (assuming a 35% corporate rate and a 39.6% individual rate) is $60.74, unless the potential dividends can somehow be turned into long-term capital gains. Even if they are, the corporate tax on $100 ($35) and the top individual capital gain rate (28%) applied to a $65 increase in the share value (because of retained $65 profits) or $18.20 would total $53.20, for an effective rate of 53.2%, far above the top rate legislated for any single taxpayer. That makes the Subchapter C (regular corporate) form relatively unattractive.[5]

D. OPERATING VIA OVERSEAS SUBSIDIARIES

U.S. corporations that operate overseas are said to operate via "branches." Income or losses from branches are included in the corporation's U.S. income tax base just as if the branch were in another state; that is, the operating results are included currently. By contrast, operating via a foreign subsidiary that retains its profits can result in major deferral of U.S. tax.

COMPARISON OF THE TAX SYSTEMS OF THE UNITED STATES, THE UNITED KINGDOM, GERMANY, AND JAPAN, July 20, 1992 [Joint Committee Print]; JCS-13-92

II. *Description of the United States Tax System*

....

U.S. Taxation of Income Earned Through Foreign Corporations

U.S. persons that conduct foreign operations through a foreign corporation generally pay no U.S. tax on the income from those operations until the foreign corporation repatriates or is deemed to have repatriated its earnings to the United States.[6] The income appears on the U.S. owner's tax return for the year that the repatriation or deemed repatriation occurs, and the United States imposes tax on it then, subject to allowance of a foreign tax credit.

....

Several existing regimes provide exceptions to the general rule under which U.S. tax on income earned indirectly through a foreign corporation is deferred. The primary anti-deferral regime involves rules applicable to controlled foreign corporations and their shareholders.... Anti-deferral regimes not discussed in this pamphlet include, among others, foreign personal holding company rules, passive foreign investment company rules, and rules applicable to foreign investment companies.[7]

---

[5] *See* Raby, *Multiple Corporations Now Worth $18,500 Each*, 61 Tax Notes 235 (1993), discussing the advantages of multiple corporations and IRS weapons to restrict such manipulation.

[6] The foreign corporation itself generally will not pay U.S. tax unless it has income effectively connected with a trade or business carried on in the United States, or has certain generally investment types of U.S. source income.

[7] The specialized corporations described in this sentence generally result in immediate taxation of the shareholder, despite the failure to distribute the entity's earnings. Nowadays, there should be added references to regimes for U.S.-owned "Passive Foreign Investment Companies" as well as to the Subpart-F rules for U.S.-controlled foreign corporations with certain kinds of "tainted" income. All of these are subjects of a course on the taxation of international transactions. Eds.

OUTSIDE READINGS

H. Ault, *Colloquium on Corporate Integration: Corporate Integration, Tax Treaties and the Division of the International Tax Base: Principles and Practices*, 47 Tax L. Rev. 565, (Spring 1992).

R. Doernberg, *The Taxation of Reinvested Corporate Earnings*, 24 Wm. & Mary L. Rev 1 (Fall 1982).

J. Kwall, *The Uncertain Case Against the Double Taxation of Corporate Income*, 68 N.C. L. Rev. 613 (April 1990).

E. Manning, *The Service Corporation — Who Is Taxable on Its Income: Reconciling Assignment of Income Principles, Section 482, and Section 351*, 37 U. Miami L. Rev. 657 (1983).

R. Shuldiner, *Colloquium on Corporate Integration: Commentary, Corporate Integration: Do the Uncertainties Outweigh the Benefits*, 47 Tax L. Rev. 653 (Spring 1992).

J. Snoe, *The Entity Tax and Corporate Integration: An Agency Cost Analysis and a Call for a Deferred Distribution Tax*, 48 U. Miami L. Rev. 1 (September 1993).

P. Stephan, *Disaggregation and Subchapter C: Rethinking Corporate Tax Reform*, 76 Va. L. Rev. 655 (May 1990).

S. Taylor, *Corporate Integration in the Federal Income Tax: Lessons from the Past and a Proposal for the Future*, 10 Va. Tax Rev. 237 (1990).

E. Zolt, *Corporate Taxation After the Tax Reform Act of 1986: A State of Disequilibrium*, 66 N.C. L. Rev. 839, (June 1988).

Chapter 13
RECOGNITION OF THE CORPORATE FORM

A. BACKGROUND

The corporation has been a convenient rabbit in the hat of the business lawyer for many decades. As one can imagine, perhaps, not every entity that is a properly organized corporation for state law purposes will pass muster for federal income tax purposes. Corporations have often been used in artificial arrangements whose sole purpose was tax minimization, and as the following chapters will show, corporate taxation is in some measure the study of substance versus form. In cases they consider abusive, the courts are apt to characterize the corporation as a sham and to disregard its existence. On the other hand, according to the Supreme Court in *Moline Props., Inc., v. Commissioner*, 319 U.S. 436 (1943), if the formation of the corporation has a business purpose or if the corporation engages in more than insignificant business activities, it will not be treated as a sham and its separate taxable identity will be respected. This has led to a number of close cases in which title-holding companies which were organized to avoid local usury laws have been respected or disregarded on the basis of narrowly different fact patterns involving the extent to which the corporation engaged in financial transactions. It is difficult to predict exactly how such cases will come out without a careful evaluation of the facts, but in general, as long as the corporate formalities are respected and the corporation is not completely inert, the likelihood is that it will be respected as a separate entity for income tax purposes.

For many years, it was generally conceded that if a corporation could not be disregarded as a sham, then it also could not be treated as a mere nominee or agent. That theory is inherently illogical, because individuals often act as agents for other persons to perform such functions as collecting rent, managing property, and executing leases. When these operations are taken over by individuals, there has not been any great difficulty respecting their status as agents; hence it is illogical to say that a corporation cannot occupy the same status.

Note that an agent and a nominee are not the same things. An agency is a contractual relationship under which one party, the agent, acts as a sort of delegate of another person — the principal. By contrast, a nominee is an entity that holds bare legal title to property of another party. The other party is the real party in interest, so that if a struggle over ownership were ever to break out, the nominee's effort to retain the property would fail. For an excellent article on this subject, see Miller, *The Nominee Conundrum; The Live Dummy Is Dead but the Dead Dummy Should Live*, 34 Tax L. Rev. 213 (1979).

COMMISSIONER v. BOLLINGER
485 U.S. 340, 108 S. Ct. 1173 (1988)

[The following is a modified version of the Supreme Court syllabus: Because Kentucky's usury law limited the annual interest rate for non-corporate borrowers, lenders willing to provide money only at higher rates required borrowers to use a corporate nominee as the nominal debtor and the record titleholder of mortgaged property. Accordingly respondents, who formed a series of partnerships to develop Kentucky apartment complexes, in each instance entered into an agreement with a corporation wholly owned by respondent Bollinger, which provided that the corporation would hold title to the property as the partnership's nominee and agent solely to secure financing, that the partnership would have sole control of and responsibility for the complex, and that the partnership was the principal and owner of the property during financing, construction, and operation. All parties who had contact with the complexes, including lenders, contractors, managers, employees, and tenants, regarded the partnerships as the real owners and knew that each corporation was merely the partnerships' agent, if they were aware of the corporation at all. Income and losses from the complexes were reported on the partnerships' tax returns, and respondents reported their distributive share of the income and losses on their individual returns. Although the IRS disallowed respondents' deductions for losses on the ground that they were attributable to the corporation as the owner of the property, the Tax Court held that the corporation was the partnerships' agent and should therefore be disregarded for tax purposes, and the Court of Appeals affirmed. The case then was taken to the Supreme Court.]

JUSTICE SCALIA delivered the opinion of the Court.

Petitioner, the Commissioner of Internal Revenue, challenges a decision by the United States Court of Appeals for the Sixth Circuit holding that a corporation which held record title to real property as agent for the corporation's shareholders was not the owner of the property for purposes of federal income taxation.... We granted certiorari, ... to resolve a conflict in the Courts of Appeals over the tax treatment of corporations purporting to be agents for their shareholders.

....

II

For federal income tax purposes, gain or loss from the sale or use of property is attributable to the owner of the property.... The problem we face here is that two different taxpayers can plausibly be regarded as the owner. Neither the Internal Revenue Code nor the Regulations promulgated by the Secretary of the Treasury provide significant guidance as to which should be selected. It is common ground between the parties, however, that if a corporation holds title to property as agent for a partnership, then for tax purposes the partnership and not the corporation is the owner. Given agreement on that premise, one would suppose that there would be agreement upon the conclusion as well. For each of

A. BACKGROUND

respondents' apartment complexes, an agency agreement expressly provided that the corporation would "hold such property as nominee and agent for" the partnership, App. to Pet. for Cert. 21a, n. 4, and that the partnership would have sole control of and responsibility for the apartment complex. The partnership in each instance was identified as the principal and owner of the property during financing, construction, and operation. The lenders, contractors, managers, employees, and tenants — all who had contact with the development — knew that the corporation was merely the agent of the partnership, if they knew of the existence of the corporation at all. In each instance the relationship between the corporation and the partnership was, in both form and substance, an agency with the partnership as principal.

The Commissioner contends, however, that the normal indicia of agency cannot suffice for tax purposes when, as here, the alleged principals are the controlling shareholders of the alleged agent corporation. That, it asserts, would undermine the principle of *Moline Properties v. Commissioner*, 319 U.S. 436, (1943), which held that a corporation is a separate taxable entity even if it has only one shareholder who exercises total control over its affairs. Obviously, *Moline's* separate-entity principle would be significantly compromised if shareholders of closely held corporations could, by clothing the corporation with some attributes of agency with respect to particular assets, leave themselves free at the end of the tax year to make a claim — perhaps even a good-faith claim — of either agent or owner status, depending upon which choice turns out to minimize their tax liability. The Commissioner does not have the resources to audit and litigate the many cases in which agency status could be thought debatable. Hence, the Commissioner argues, in this shareholder context he can reasonably demand that the taxpayer meet a prophylactically clear test of agency.

We agree with that principle, but the question remains whether the test the Commissioner proposes is appropriate. The parties have debated at length the significance of our opinion in *National Carbide Corp. v. Commissioner, supra*. In that case, three corporations that were wholly owned subsidiaries of another corporation agreed to operate their production plants as "agents" for the parent, transferring to it all profits except for a nominal sum. The subsidiaries reported as gross income only this sum, but the Commissioner concluded that they should be taxed on the entirety of the profits because they were not really agents. We agreed, reasoning first, that the mere fact of the parent's control over the subsidiaries did not establish the existence of an agency, since such control is typical of all shareholder-corporation relationships, ... and second, that the agreements to pay the parent all profits above a nominal amount were not determinative since income must be taxed to those who actually earn it without regard to anticipatory assignment, *id.*, at 435-436, 69 S. Ct., at 733-734. We acknowledged, however, that there was such a thing as "a true corporate agent ... of [an] owner-principal," *id.*, at 437, 69 S. Ct., at 734, and proceeded to set forth four indicia and two requirements of such status, the sum of which has become known in the lore of federal income tax law as the "six National Carbide factors": "[1] Whether the corporation operates in the name and for the account of the principal, [2] binds the principal by its actions, [3] transmits money received to the principal, and [4] whether receipt of income is attributable to the services of employees of the principal and to assets belonging to the principal are some of the relevant considerations in determining whether a true agency exists. [5] If the corporation is a true agent, its relations with its principal must not be dependent upon the fact that it is owned by the principal, if such is the case. [6] Its business purpose must be the carrying on of the normal duties of an agent." *Ibid.* (footnotes omitted).

We readily discerned that these factors led to a conclusion of nonagency in National Carbide itself. There each subsidiary had represented to its customers that it (not the parent) was the company manufacturing and selling its products; each had sought to shield the parent from service of legal process; and the operations had used thousands of the subsidiaries' employees and nearly $20 million worth of property and equipment listed as assets on the subsidiaries' books....

The Commissioner contends that the last two National Carbide factors are not satisfied in the present case. To take the last first: The Commissioner argues that here the corporation's business purpose with respect to the property at issue was not "the carrying on of the normal duties of an agent," since it was acting not as the agent but rather as the owner of the property for purposes of Kentucky's usury law. We do not agree. It assuredly was not acting as the owner in fact, since respondents represented themselves as the principals to all parties concerned with the loans. Indeed, it was the lenders themselves who required the use of a corporate nominee. Nor does it make any sense to adopt a contrary-to-fact legal presumption that the corporation was the principal, imposing a federal tax sanction for the apparent evasion of Kentucky's usury law. To begin with, the Commissioner has not established that these transactions were an evasion. Respondents assert without contradiction that use of agency arrangements in order to permit higher interest was common practice, and it is by no means clear that the practice violated the spirit of the Kentucky law, much less its letter. It might well be thought that the borrower does not generally require usury protection in a transaction sophisticated enough to employ a corporate agent — assuredly not the normal modus operandi of the loan shark. That the statute positively envisioned corporate nominees is suggested by a provision which forbids charging the higher corporate interest rates "to a corporation, the principal asset of which shall be the ownership of a one (1) or two (2) family dwelling," Ky. Rev. Stat. § 360.025(2) (1987) — which would seem to prevent use of the nominee device for ordinary home-mortgage loans. In any event, even if the transaction did run afoul of the usury law, Kentucky, like most States, regards only the lender as the usurer, and the borrower as the victim. *See* Ky. Rev. Stat. § 360.020 (1987) (lender liable to borrower for civil penalty), § 360.990 (lender guilty of misdemeanor). Since the Kentucky statute imposed no penalties upon the borrower for allowing himself to be victimized, nor treated him as in pari delicto, but to the contrary enabled him to pay back the principal without any interest, and to sue for double the amount of interest already paid (plus attorney's fees), *see* Ky. Rev. Stat. § 360.020 (1972), the United States would hardly be vindicating Kentucky law by depriving the usury victim of tax advantages he would otherwise enjoy. In sum, we see no basis in either fact or policy for holding that the corporation was the principal because of the nature of its participation in the loans.

Of more general importance is the Commissioner's contention that the arrangements here violate the fifth *National Carbide* factor — that the corporate agent's "relations with its principal must not be dependent upon the fact that it is owned by the principal." The Commissioner asserts that this cannot be satisfied unless the corporate agent and its shareholder principal have an "arm's-length relationship" that includes the payment of a fee for agency services. The meaning of *National Carbide*'s fifth factor is, at the risk of understatement, not entirely clear. Ultimately, the relations between a corporate agent and its owner-principal are always dependent upon the fact of ownership, in that the owner can cause the relations to be altered or terminated at any time. Plainly that is not what was meant, since on that interpretation all subsidiary-parent agencies would be invalid for tax purposes, a position which the *National Carbide* opinion specifically disavowed. We think the fifth *National Carbide* factor — so much more abstract than the others — was no more and no less than a generalized statement of the concern, expressed earlier in our own discussion, that the separate-entity doctrine of *Moline* not be subverted.

In any case, we decline to parse the text of *National Carbide* as though that were itself the governing statute. As noted earlier, it is uncontested that the law attributes tax consequences of property held by a genuine agent to the principal; and we agree that it is reasonable for the Commissioner to demand unequivocal evidence of genuineness in the corporation-shareholder context, in order to prevent evasion of *Moline*. We see no basis, however, for holding that unequivocal evidence can only consist of the rigid requirements (arm's-length dealing plus agency fee) that the Commissioner suggests. Neither of those is demanded by the law of agency, which permits agents to be unpaid family members, friends, or associates. *See* Restatement (Second) of Agency §§ 16, 21, 22 (1958). It seems to us that the genuineness of the agency relationship is adequately assured, and tax-avoiding manipulation adequately avoided, when the fact that the corporation is acting as agent for its shareholders with respect to a particular asset is set forth in a written agreement at the time the asset is acquired, the corporation functions as agent and not principal with respect to the asset for all purposes, and the corporation is held out as the agent and not principal in all dealings with third parties relating to the asset. Since these requirements were met here, the judgment of the Court of Appeals is

Affirmed.

NOTES AND QUESTIONS

1. *What is the Court saying?* Has the Supreme Court managed to sort out the distinction between an agent and a nominee? If not, does it matter?

2. *Applying the Theory.* The *Bollinger* decision opens the door to the use of nominees and agents. If you represented an investor who planned to use a corporation to hold title to property as a nominee or agent, what steps would you take to assure that the agency or nominee relationship would be respected?

B. OTHER BASES FOR ATTACKING THE CORPORATION FORM

Sham corporation theory takes the relatively primitive position that there is no corporation. It rarely works. The Commissioner has an extensive arsenal of alternative theories for attacking transactions in which he believes that the corporation is being manipulated for tax avoidance purposes. The following case illustrates these weapons in their most common setting, the closely held corporation dominated by family members. Before reading the next case, read §§ 482(a) and 269(a)(1). Note also § 269A, enacted after the tax years involved in the case.

ACHIRO v. COMMISSIONER
77 T.C. 881 (1981)

HALL, JUDGE:

[Achiro and Rossi each owned 50% of the stock of Tahoe City Disposal, and each owned 25% of the stock of Kings Beach Disposal. In 1974, Achiro and Rossi incorporated A & R for the purpose of providing management services to Tahoe City Disposal and Kings Beach Disposal. Achiro and Rossi each owned 24% of A & R's stock, and Renato Achiro, who happened to be Achiro's brother and Rossi's brother-in-law, held the remaining 52%. A & R contracted to provide management services to Tahoe City Disposal and Kings Beach Disposal in exchange for management fees. Achiro and Rossi entered into exclusive employment contracts with A & R, and, acting in their capacities as A & R's employees, rendered management services to Tahoe City Disposal and Kings Beach Disposal. A & R's books and records consisted of a bank statement, a checkbook, and a bankbook. In addition, A & R's accountants kept a record of receipts and disbursements, payroll records, a summary general ledger, workpapers, and tax information. A & R had no separate office, its name did not appear on any office door or building, it had no separate telephone number or listing, and it had no printed business cards bearing its name, but it did have stationery bearing its name on the letterhead. All three companies had profit-sharing plans, and A & R had a pension plan.]

. . . .

B. OTHER BASES FOR ATTACKING THE CORPORATION FORM 241

Opinion

[Part A, involving the burden of proof, is omitted.]

B. *Respondent's Reallocation of Income and Deductions*

Next, we turn to the substantive issues raised by respondent. His reliance on sections 482, 269, and 61 to reallocate all of A & R's income and deductions to Tahoe City Disposal and Kings Beach Disposal represents a frontal attack on a taxpayer's use of a personal service corporation. The impetus behind respondent's all-out attack on A & R stems from his apparent concern about the use of corporations for the principal purpose of obtaining the benefits associated with corporate retirement plans.

It is well known that operating a business in corporate form provides advantages not available to self-employed individuals. In recent years, however, the driving force behind an ever increasing use (particularly by professionals) of corporations is the advantage of the richer tax deferral obtained through establishment of a corporate retirement plan. For example, for taxable years beginning before 1982, an employee not otherwise covered by a retirement plan is limited to the use of an individual retirement account which permits qualified contributions not in excess of 15 percent of compensation or $1,500, whichever is less. Sec. 219. Also for taxable years beginning before 1982, the tax deferred contribution available to a self-employed individual under a Keogh Plan (also known as H.R. 10 plan) is limited to the lesser of $7,500 per year or 15 percent of earned income. Sec. 404(e)(1). For taxable years beginning after 1981, however, even active participants in employer-sponsored plans may contribute to an individual retirement account. Additionally, the maximum amount of a qualified contribution to an individual retirement account is increased to the lesser of $2,000 or 100 percent of compensation. The Economic Recovery Act of 1981, Pub. L. 97-34, sec. 311, 95 Stat. 274-283 (1981). Similarly, for taxable years beginning after 1981, the maximum contribution to a Keogh Plan is increased to the lesser of $15,000 or 15 percent of income, and the amount of income that can be taken into account when computing the deduction is increased from $100,000 to $200,000....

In contrast, under a qualified pension or profit-sharing plan, a corporate employee-shareholder can enjoy annual contributions on his behalf to defined contribution plans in an amount not exceeding $41,500. Sec. 415(c)(1)(A); IRS News Release 81-16, Feb. 4, 1981. Alternatively, under a qualified defined benefit pension plan, the maximum contribution is an amount that will provide him with an annuity of $124,500 or an annuity equal to his average compensation for his most remunerative 3 consecutive years. Sec. 415(b)(1); IRS News Release 81-16, Feb. 4, 1981. The corporate employee can also have a combination of benefits through contributions to both defined contribution plans and defined benefit plans subject to the rule of 1.4. Sec. 415(e).

Respondent's distaste for this use of the corporate form is not new. However, respondent has significantly altered his mode of attacking personal service corporations. Prior to August 8, 1969, respondent relied primarily on the so-called Kintner regulations[1] to attack professional service corporations. As a result of numerous successful taxpayer challenges to the Regulations, respondent announced on August 8, 1969, that he would no longer litigate the tax classification of professional service corporations formed under State professional corporations laws.

Since that time, the Service has accepted professional service corporations that have respected their corporate form in conducting their businesses. As a result, the use of professional service corporations and other personal service corporations has spiraled without any significant legislation from Congress intended to halt such use of the corporate form. In recognition of these facts, the Seventh Circuit recently stated: We think that our approach in this case of recognizing some vitality in personal service corporations accords with congressional intent. "A history of legislation targeted at personal service corporations, the absence of any special exclusion of such corporations from corporate taxation and the personal holding company tax provisions indicate that to some extent Congress has sanctioned the incorporation of service businesses for tax purposes."

The keynote in respondent's present position under sections 482, 269, and 61 is his contention that incorporation for the principal purpose of taking advantage of corporate pension and profit-sharing plans amounts to an evasion or avoidance of income taxes, an unclear reflection of income, and/or an assignment of income. We disagree. Of course, a mere corporate skeleton, standing alone and without any flesh on its bones, will not suffice to provide its shareholder-employees with corporate retirement benefits. *See Roubik v. Commissioner*, 53 T.C. 365, 382 (1969) (Tannenwald, J., concurring). Once incorporated, the personal service business must be run as a corporation. Its shareholder-employees must recognize, respect, and treat their personal service corporation as a corporation. The corporation must accept the disadvantages as well as advantages of incorporation. Once a corporation is formed and all organizational and operational requirements are met, it should be recognized for tax purposes regardless of the fact that it was formed to take advantage of the richer corporate retirement plans. In light of this general discussion, the following discussion of respondent's sections 482, 269, and 61 assertions will be directed at determining the existence of any specific or extenuating circumstances compelling the use of one of those sections.

---

[1] *See* §§ 301.7701-2(a)(5) and (h), Proced. & Admin. Regs., as they read prior to their revocation in 1977 by T.D. 7515, 1977-2 C.B. 482. The name attached to these regulations derives from the case *United States v. Kintner*, 216 F.2d 418 (9th Cir. 1954).

B. OTHER BASES FOR ATTACKING THE CORPORATION FORM

1. Section 482

The first substantive issue is whether respondent's allocations are justified under Section 482. Section 482 states: In any case of two or more organizations, trades, or businesses (whether or not incorporated, whether or not organized in the United States, and whether or not affiliated) owned or controlled directly or indirectly by the same interests, the Secretary or his delegate may distribute, apportion, or allocate gross income, deductions, credits, or allowances between or among such organizations, trades, or businesses, if he determines that such distribution, apportionment, or allocation is necessary in order to prevent evasion of taxes or clearly to reflect the income of any such organizations, trades, or businesses. Relying on this statute, respondent allocated all of A & R's income and deductions to Tahoe City Disposal and Kings Beach Disposal. In essence, respondent is attempting to utilize section 482 to ignore the corporate existence of A & R.

The purpose of Section 482 is set forth in the Regulations: (b) Scope and purpose. (1) The purpose of Section 482 is to place a controlled taxpayer on a tax parity with an uncontrolled taxpayer, by determining, according to the standard of an uncontrolled taxpayer, the true taxable income from the property and business of a controlled taxpayer. The interests controlling a group of controlled taxpayers are assumed to have complete power to cause each controlled taxpayer so to conduct its affairs that its transactions and accounting records truly reflect the taxable income from the property and business of each of the controlled taxpayers. If, however, this has not been done, and the taxable incomes are thereby understated, the district director shall intervene, and, by making such distributions, apportionments, or allocation as he may deem necessary of gross income, deductions, credits, or allowances, or of any item or element affecting taxable income, between or among the controlled taxpayers constituting the group, shall determine the true taxable income of each controlled taxpayer. The standard to be applied in every case is that of an uncontrolled taxpayer dealing at arm's length with another uncontrolled taxpayer.... 1.482-1(b)(1), Income Tax Regs.

Reg. § 1.482-2(b)(1), deals specifically with circumstances involving the performance of services by one corporation for the benefit of another similarly controlled corporation: Where one member of a group of controlled entities performs marketing, managerial, administrative, technical, or other services for the benefit of, or on behalf of another member of the group without charge, or at a charge which is not equal to an arm's length charge as defined in subparagraph (3) of this paragraph, the district director may make appropriate allocations to reflect an arm's length charge for such services. Reg. § 1.482-2(b)(3), defines an arm's-length charge: For the purpose of this paragraph an arm's length charge for services rendered shall be the amount which was charged or would have been charged for the same or similar services in independent transactions with or between unrelated parties under similar circumstances considering all relevant facts....

In the context of the present case, respondent may utilize Section 482 to insure that the charges among the controlled entities represent arm's-length amounts. Instead of making such an allocation, respondent chose to allocate all of A & R's income and deductions to Tahoe City Disposal and Kings Beach Disposal. The evidence in the present case indicates that A & R received the arm's-length value of the services it rendered to Tahoe City Disposal and Kings Beach Disposal. In addition, respondent has essentially conceded that the payments reflect arm's-length charges by agreeing that if the payments are not allowed as deductible management fees to A & R, they will be allowed almost in their entirety to Tahoe City Disposal and Kings Beach Disposal as deductible salary payments.

Moreover, the cases respondent relies on do not support his position that without showing an arm's-length price for the services rendered, he may reallocate the entire price of such services from one corporation to another. In *Ach v. Commissioner, supra,* the taxpayer transferred her profitable sole proprietorship to her son's defunct corporation in exchange for the corporation's non-interest-bearing note. As a result of this transfer, the taxpayer was able to offset the income of her dress business against the net operating loss carryovers from her son's corporation. In sustaining most of respondent's allocations under Section 482 we stated: Plainly, this was not an arm's length transaction. The corporation was hopelessly insolvent, and it is utterly beyond belief that any unrelated third party would have sold a prosperous business for a non-interest bearing $30,705.57 note of such an insolvent maker where the level of earnings of that business was about $30,000 a year and rising, and where the seller contemplated continued fulltime management of the business without compensation....

In *Borge v. Commissioner,* 405 F.2d 673 (2d Cir. 1968), ... entertainer Victor Borge formed a corporation to which he transferred the assets of an unprofitable poultry business. In addition, Borge entered into an employment agreement with the corporation pursuant to which he agreed to perform entertainment services for the corporation in exchange for an annual salary of $50,000. The $50,000 salary was far less than the amount Borge's entertainment activities produced each year, and it was found that Borge would not have made a similar agreement in an arm's-length transaction. Accordingly, respondent properly allocated a larger amount of Borge's entertainment earnings directly to him.

In *Rubin v. Commissioner,* 56 T.C. 1155 (1971), ... the taxpayer and his brothers owned during the relevant tax years all the stock of Park, a corporation which, pursuant to management contracts, provided management services to Dorman Mills and its subsidiaries, also corporations controlled by the taxpayer. The taxpayer's efforts accounted for all of Park's income from management services. The taxpayer apparently never entered into an employment contract with Park and during the time he performed services for Dorman Mills as an employee of Park, he also received salaries from other corporations to which he rendered services. The taxpayer received from Park a substantially lower salary for his services than the amount received by Park from Dorman Mills. In light of these facts, we held that respondent properly allocated a greater portion of Park's income directly to the taxpayer. Although we did not specifically mention the lack of arm's-length dealing between the taxpayer and Park, it is clear that the result reached was intended to reflect an arm's length approach to the transactions between them. The circumstances clearly indicated that the employment relationship between the taxpayer and Park did not resemble the type of relationship that would have resulted had the taxpayer been dealing at arm's length with an unrelated third party.

In *Jones v. Commissioner*, 64 T.C. 1066 (1975), the taxpayer was an official court reporter for a Federal District Court. He formed a personal service corporation to loan out his services despite the legal requirement that an official court reporter be an individual and not a corporation. Furthermore, the taxpayer never entered into an employment agreement with his corporation, remained under the control of the judge to whom he was assigned, and personally certified the transcripts. Holding that the transactions between the taxpayer and his corporation were not at arm's-length, we stated (p. 1078): In the situation here, an uncontrolled taxpayer could not have dealt with another uncontrolled taxpayer as Mr. Jones dealt with the corporation because the functions of Mr. Jones in reporting the proceedings by stenographic note taking and the functions of the corporation in producing, selling, and certifying the transcripts must, by statute, be performed by the official court reporter, who must be an individual.

The fact that petitioners in the present case chose to incorporate A & R for the primary purpose of obtaining the benefits of its retirement plans does not justify respondent's Section 482 allocations. In addition, none of the cases relied on by respondent support his sweeping reallocation of all service income from A & R to Tahoe City Disposal and Kings Beach Disposal. Accordingly, Section 482 is inapplicable. This is true regardless of where the burden of proof lies. Respondent's 100 percent reallocation in the present case is arbitrary, capricious, and unreasonable. To utilize Section 482 in the present context respondent's allocations must, at the least, be reasonable attempts to reflect arm's-length transactions among the related entities. We see no reasonableness in respondent's present allocations and find that the transactions, as structured, reflected arm's-length charges for the services performed.

2. *Section 269*

The second issue is whether respondent properly utilized his authority under Section 269 to allocate A & R's income and deductions to Tahoe City Disposal and Kings Beach Disposal.

The "principal purpose" for the acquisition of control of the corporation must have been the evasion or avoidance of Federal income tax by securing the benefit of a deduction, credit, or other allowance not otherwise available. In the present case, the principal purpose for the formation of A & R was to secure the tax benefits of its retirement plans. We have already held that as a general proposition, the formation of a corporation for the principal purpose of securing the tax benefits of retirement plans is not an evasion or avoidance of taxes. Accordingly, Section 269 does not apply.

Furthermore, even if the formation of a corporation for such a purpose were an evasion or avoidance of taxes, it would not be so in the present case because the benefits expected from A & R's plans are not available. (*See* the Sec. 414(b) discussion, *infra*.)

   3. *Section 61*

The third issue is whether section 61 applies to shift A & R's income and deductions. Respondent stated his position as follows: "[A & R] is a sham for tax purposes; it did not actually earn the management fees which it reported. Section 61." Without citing *Moline Properties v. Commissioner*, ... respondent apparently is asking us to disregard the corporate existence of A & R. This we decline to do. *Moline Properties v. Commissioner*, ... ; requires the recognition of a corporation as a separate entity if either (1) the purpose for the formation of the corporation is the equivalent of a business activity or (2) the incorporation is followed by the carrying on of business. In the present case, A & R carried on a business subsequent to its incorporation. It hired employees and entered into employment contracts with them. It entered into management service contracts with Tahoe City Disposal and Kings Beach Disposal. Its employees respected its separate identity. It filed separate tax returns, paid taxes, kept separate books, formed pension and profit-sharing plans, etc. It rendered services through its two employees to the disposal companies. These subsequent acts amount to the carrying on of the business of a management company. Accordingly, A & R must be recognized as a viable entity for tax purposes....

Under his Section 61 approach, respondent further asks us to attribute the employees of A & R (namely, Achiro and Rossi) to Tahoe City Disposal and Kings Beach Disposal on the basis that their actions as employees were controlled by those companies instead of A & R. To do this we must, among other things, disregard their employment contracts with A & R and A & R's management contracts with Tahoe City Disposal and Kings Beach Disposal. Respondent relies on *Jones v. Commissioner*, *supra*, and *Roubik v. Commissioner*, 53 T.C. 365 (1969).

In *Jones* (see discussion, *supra*), this Court found that the taxpayer's personal service corporation was not a sham and that it engaged in substantial business activity. We also found, however, that the taxpayer performed services in his individual capacity because by law his corporation could not perform such services. Accordingly, we held that he assigned his income to the corporation. The present case is distinguishable. Here, we have found that Achiro and Rossi functioned as employees of A & R under valid exclusive employment agreements. In their capacities as employees, they rendered services to Tahoe City

B. OTHER BASES FOR ATTACKING THE CORPORATION FORM

Disposal and Kings Beach Disposal pursuant to management contracts between A & R on the one hand and Tahoe City Disposal and Kings Beach Disposal on the other hand. Furthermore, the parties were not precluded by law from operating in corporate form as in *Jones*.

In *Roubik v. Commissioner*, 53 T.C. 365 (1969), four radiologists who had separate practices formed a personal service corporation ostensibly to carry on their practices. We found as a fact that the radiologists continued to carry on their prior separate practices and merely assigned their income to their corporation. *Lucas v. Earl*, 281 U.S. 111 (1930). Although they entered into employment agreements with their corporation, the corporation never entered into loan-out agreements with the hospitals or others for whom the radiologists performed their services. The doctors did not respect the corporate form after the personal service corporation was formed. That is not our situation here. Respondent, on whom the burden of proof rests, has not proved that A & R is not a viable corporation, or that the petitioners did not respect its separate existence and the contracts into which it entered with them and with others....

4. *Section 414(b)*

The final issue is whether the employees of A & R and the employees of Tahoe City Disposal should be aggregated pursuant to Section 414(b). Respondent asserts that once so aggregated, A & R's pension and profit-sharing plans (which cover only petitioners) discriminate in favor of officers, shareholders, and highly compensated persons because those plans do not include Tahoe City Disposal's employees and because the North Tahoe P-S Plan's contributions and benefits are not commensurate with A & R's plans. Accordingly, respondent contends that A & R's pension and profit-sharing plans are not qualified trusts under Section 401, and the contributions made to such plans should be treated as income to petitioners under the provisions of Sections 402(b) and 83(a). Petitioners agree that if the employees of A & R are aggregated with the employees of Tahoe City Disposal, then A & R's pension and profit-sharing plans are not qualified trusts, and the contributions to those plans should be income to petitioners. Petitioners contend, however, that Section 414(b) does not require the aggregation of the employees of A & R with the employees of Tahoe City Disposal.

Section 414(b) requires aggregation of the employees of all corporations which are members of a controlled group of corporations as defined in Section 1563(a). Section 1563(a) applies to both parent-subsidiary and brother-sister controlled groups. The brother-sister controlled group determination consists of two tests. Sec. 1563(a)(2). The 80 percent test requires that five or fewer persons alone or in combination have at least an 80 percent interest in each of two or more organizations. The 50 percent test requires that the same five or fewer persons have more than a 50 percent interest in each organization, taking into account the interests of each person only to the extent that such interests are identical with regard to each organization.

Reg. § 1.1563-1(a)(6), defines voting powers for purposes of Section 1563(a) as follows: in determining whether the stock owned by a person (or persons) possesses a certain percentage of the total combined voting power of all classes of stock entitled to vote of a corporation, consideration will be given to all the facts and circumstances of each case. A share of stock will generally be considered as possessing the voting power accorded to such share by the corporate charter, bylaws, or share certificate. On the other hand, if there is any agreement, whether express or implied, that a shareholder will not vote his stock in a corporation, the formal voting rights possessed by his stock may be disregarded in determining the percentage of the total combined voting power possessed by the stock owned by other shareholders in the corporation, if the result is that the corporation becomes a component member of a controlled group of corporations. Moreover, if a shareholder agrees to vote his stock in a corporation in the manner specified by another shareholder in the corporation, the voting rights possessed by the stock owned by the first shareholder may be considered to be possessed by the stock owned by such other shareholder if the result is that the corporation becomes a component member of a controlled group of corporations.

Achiro and Rossi each owned 50 percent of the voting stock of Tahoe City Disposal and each held record title to 24 percent of the stock of A & R. Renato Achiro, Achiro's brother and Rossi's brother-in-law, held record title to the remaining 52 percent of the voting stock of A & R. Considering only record title, Tahoe City Disposal and A & R were not a brother-sister controlled group under Section 1563(a)(2). However, we have found that **Renato implicitly agreed** that he would either not vote his stock in A & R or vote his stock in the manner specified by Achiro. Under the Regulations, the validity of which has not been challenged by the parties, Renato's voting rights may be disregarded or attributed to Achiro. Therefore, Achiro and Rossi are deemed each to have 50 percent interests in Tahoe City Disposal and A & R (or Achiro is deemed to have a 76 percent interest in A & R), and the corporations constitute a brother-sister controlled group.

Since the corporations form a controlled group, the employees of A & R and the employees of Tahoe City Disposal must be aggregated under Section 414(b) for purposes of Section 401. Such a holding complies with the intent of Congress in enacting Section 414(b) as expressed in H. Rept. 93-779, at 49 (1974), 1974-3 C.B. 292: The committee, by this provision, intends to make it clear that the coverage and antidiscrimination provisions cannot be avoided by operating through separate corporations instead of separate branches of one corporation. For example, if managerial functions were performed through one corporation employing highly compensated personnel, which has a generous pension plan, and assembly-line functions were performed through one or more other corporations employing lower-paid employees, which have less generous plans or no plans at all, this would generally constitute an impermissible discrimination....

B. OTHER BASES FOR ATTACKING THE CORPORATION FORM 249

A & R was formed for the express purpose of rendering managerial services to Tahoe City Disposal and Kings Beach Disposal. In 1975 and 1976, A & R's employees, Achiro and Rossi, were officers, shareholders, and highly compensated. Sec. 1.401-4(a)(1)(i), Income Tax Regs. The "assembly-line functions" of the day-to-day waste disposal and dump operations were carried on by the employees of Tahoe City Disposal and Kings Beach Disposal. This is the very kind of situation Congress had in mind when it enacted Section 414(b).

Accordingly, for the years 1975 and 1976, A & R's pension and profit-sharing plans were not qualified because they discriminated in favor of Achiro and Rossi who were officers, shareholders, and highly compensated. Sec. 401. Contributions made to such plans must be included in the gross income of Achiro and Rossi under Sections 402(b) and 83(a).

Petitioners contend that the prescribed relationship between the stockholders of A & R and the stockholders of Tahoe City Disposal did not exist in 1975 or 1976. Petitioners' contention rests squarely on their assertion that Renato's 52% interest in A & R is not attributable to them and must be considered as owned by an unrelated and uncontrolled party when determining whether A & R and Tahoe City Disposal are members of a controlled group of corporations. In support of this contention, petitioners list numerous reasons for the acquisition of a controlling interest in A & R by Renato and cite two recent decisions of this Court, *Garland v. Commissioner*, 73 T.C. 5 (1979), and *Kiddie v. Commissioner*, 69 T.C. 1055 (1978).

Petitioner's factual arguments are without merit. Renato testified that it was his brother's wish that he acquire a controlling interest in A & R and that was the only reason for his acquisition of A & R's stock. Achiro believed that benefits from increased contributions to A & R's pension and profit-sharing plans were possible if Renato owned 52 percent of A & R's voting stock. We have found as a fact that Renato implicitly agreed not to vote his stock or to vote as Achiro instructed him.

Petitioner's reliance on *Garland v. Commissioner*, *supra*, and *Kiddie v. Commissioner*, *supra*, is similarly misplaced. The *Kiddie* decision states that attribution of partnership characteristics to a partner does not occur unless the partner controls the partnership. In that case, we held that a corporate partner, who never owned more than a 50 percent interest in a partnership, is not attributed the employees of the partnership when determining whether the corporate partner's pension and profit-sharing plans are discriminatory. In *Garland*, the parties agreed that neither Section 414(b) nor Section 414(c) applied. Accordingly, our decision here, which rests on the applicability of Section 414(b), does not conflict with our *Kiddie* and *Garland* decisions.

Decisions will be entered under Rule 155.

PROBLEM 13-1

Bob and Ray are in the wholesale computer components business, operating as equal shareholders of Overbyte, Inc., whose office is located in Flyneck, N.J., convenient to the port. Recently, they have expanded their activities to selling overseas and Overbyte, Inc. has formed a 100%-owned Bahamas corporation, Overbyte International, to undertake foreign sales. The pattern is for Overbyte, Inc. to locate the overseas customer and then direct the customer to Overbyte International to close the deal. Overbyte International buys the product from Overbyte, Inc. at lower prices than Overbyte, Inc. charges its customers. Title to the goods changes hands at sea on the way to the foreign port. The customer calls a number in the Bahamas, which rings through on a different phone in the U.S., which is invariably answered by Bob, Ray, or one of their staff in Flyneck. Overbyte, Inc. has a name on an office door in the Bahamas, and has a part-time employee who completes the paperwork on these transactions and makes sure that Overbyte International is in compliance with Bahamian law. Income taxes are trivial in the Bahamas.

If you were an IRS Agent auditing Overbyte, Inc. and you believed that the Bahamas corporation was formed for tax avoidance purposes, what theories might you use to increase Overbyte, Inc.'s taxes? How do you appraise the likelihood of success of each theory?

OUTSIDE READINGS

H. Chapman, *The Future of Personal Service Corporations*, 24 Ariz. L. Rev. 503 (1982).

J. Lee, *Entity Classification and Integration: Publicly Traded Partnerships, Personal Service Corporations, and the Tax Legislative Process*, 8 Va. Tax Rev. 57 (Summer 1988).

N. Steuben, *The Treatment of Nominee Corporations for Income Tax Purposes*, 16 Puget Sound L. Rev. 571 (Winter 1993).

Chapter 14
ORGANIZATION OF A CORPORATION

A. INTRODUCTION

The legal requirements for forming a corporation vary from state to state. Even in the most relaxed, state some money or property must be contributed to the corporation (in return for stock) in connection with its organization. State laws vary as to the acceptability and appraisal of stock that is issued for property or services. From a practical point of view, the formation of a corporation will require the establishing of a bank account to accept the minimum required contribution. The account will be in the name of the corporation and will be drawn upon by one or more individuals identified in the corporation's organization document. In all events, stock will have to be issued to the founders and in addition the corporation may issue debt (known as "securities" in tax law parlance) and possibly hybrid instruments such as stock options or stock warrants.

These transactions require a determination of whether the corporation will pay income taxes on what it receives in return for issuing its shares, whether the shareholders will pay taxes when they exchange property or money for stock, and what the basis of the properties received by the corporation and the stock, or securities issued to the shareholders, will be. In addition, as will become apparent, decisions at the dawn of the enterprise about how its capital structure is arranged will be a matter of great importance for purposes of planning for its future tax liabilities.

B. TAXATION OF THE CORPORATION

Read § 1032.

The corporation will recognize neither gain nor loss when it issues stock for money or other property, even though it has *realized* gain. *See* § 1032. That is true even if the stock is treasury stock, i.e., stock that was previously issued by the corporation but which the corporation bought back. Curiously, this means that even if the corporation actively trades in its own stock and makes a healthy profit doing so, there is no income tax. There is also still no tax if the corporation transfers its own stock in compensation for services. Reg. § 1.1032-1(a).

As a consequence of not recognizing gain or loss on issuance of its stock to contributors of property, or money, at least if the exchange satisfies § 351 or amounts to a contribution to capital or of paid-in surplus, the general rule is that the corporation will take a basis in property it receives equal to the basis the property had in the hands of each transferor, increased by the amount of any gain recognized to the transferor on the transfer. *See* § 362(a). Save the variations in § 362(b) and (c) for later. In thinking about the nonrecognition and basis rules in this context, recall the parallel rules applicable in § 1031 (like-kind) exchanges. Be sure always to determine first gain or loss *realized* and then move to the question of the amount of each that is *recognized*.

PROBLEM 14-1

What is the basis of property in the hands of a corporation which issues stock in exchange for property when the exchange is not covered by § 351, in other words in a taxable transaction? *See* Reg. § 1.1032-1.

C. TAXATION OF THE SHAREHOLDER

Read § 351(a), (b), (d).

In the absence of § 351, the exchange of property by contributors for stock of the issuing corporation would constitute a sale or other disposition that would result in taxable gains or losses to the shareholder, subject to the risk that § 267(a) might disallow any loss if the shareholder (directly and by attribution), owned more than half of the corporation's outstanding stock by value. *See* § 267(b)(2). Section 351 grants nonrecognition treatment to contributing shareholders if, and only if, the conditions specified in § 351 are met. The basic rationale of § 351 is that incorporation is a mere change in form of an ongoing business. In fact, that is only sometimes true, because if there are transferors who were not previously in business together, the result is a diversification of the shareholders' investments. Section 351(e) removes the nonrecognition benefits of § 351 if there is a transfer of property to *an investment company*, but this is only true if the transfer is to a mutual fund, real estate investment trust or to a corporation more than 80% of whose assets, aside from cash and certain debt securities, are held for investment and consist of readily marketable stock or securities.

The time has now come to learn the definitional elements of § 351.

D. TRANSFER OF PROPERTY IN EXCHANGE FOR STOCK

Section 351 applies only if "property" is exchanged for stock. Usually "property" includes money. *See* § 317. For § 351 purposes, new § 351(d) makes it clear that "property" does *not* include services, or some specified indebtedness or interest. What else does or does not constitute "property"?

This issue is addressed in the *Stafford* decision in the partnership section of the book, and it is clear from that decision that the term "property" in § 351 is generally consistent with the term used in § 721 and that it is broadly defined. The question of whether there has been an *exchange* of property for stock should also be familiar. The most common problem is determining whether a transfer of intangible property such as a patent to controlled corporation qualifies as an exchange. If the transferor retains significant economic interest in the transferred property, the retained interest may be so extensive as to constitute the transfer a "license" rather than an exchange.

E. STOCK

Read Reg. § 1.351-1(a).

There is not much turmoil as to the meaning of the term "stock"; however, it is clear that the term does not include stock rights or stock warrants. Other terms in § 351 have required interpretation and have entailed controversy.

For many years and until fairly recently, § 351 granted nonrecognition to a transfer solely in exchange for stock *or securities* (debt instruments with certain characteristics) in the corporation, so some cases or rulings you read may involve both or either, but now § 351 applies only to a transfer solely in exchange for stock.

HAMRICK v. COMMISSIONER
43 T.C. 21 (1964)

BRUCE, JUDGE:

[The taxpayer and another investor patented a device which they transferred to a corporation (Jet), receiving as consideration over half of the issued stock plus the right to receive additional shares if the future earnings reached certain agreed goals, until the stock received by them amounted to two-thirds of the total shares issued. One inventor withdrew and sold his stock and rights to another stockholder. The stockholders formed a new agreement to allow the petitioner to receive up to 44 percent of the stock. After the three years had elapsed the petitioner duly received his 44 percent.]

Opinion

The principal issue involves the taxable status of shares of capital stock issued by Jet to Hamrick in 1958, 1959, and 1960 pursuant to the assignment of November 6, 1957, and the memorandum of agreement of November 24, 1958. The petitioner contends that the provisions of section 351(a) of the Internal Revenue Code of 1954 apply, that all the stock he received was received in exchange for property, and that no gain or loss is to be recognized upon such receipt.

It will facilitate discussion if we treat all the stock involved as of the par value of $1. On this basis, Hamrick received the following amounts at the time stated:

Year	Shares
1957	19,000
1958	4,070
1959	9,824
1960	14,429

Of the stock received in 1960, 8,106 shares brought the total issued to Hamrick up to one-third of the total issued by Jet, and the additional 6,143 brought his total up to 44 percent of the issued stock....

The respondent concedes that the shares petitioner received in 1957 were received in a nontaxable exchange, but takes the position that the next 22,000 shares, received in 1958, 1959, and 1960, bringing the petitioner's total to one-third of the issued stock, represented long-term capital gains under section 1235 of the Internal Revenue Code of 1954, to the extent of the fair market value of the stock, and that the last 6,143 shares received in 1960 are taxable as ordinary income.

The respondent contends that section 351(a) is not applicable because (1) the right to receive the additional shares was neither "stock" nor "securities," (2) the time limitation of "immediately after the exchange" is not satisfied, (3) part of the stock was issued for services to be rendered, and (4) application of section 351 to certain of the shares would result in a tax-free distribution of earnings.

The respondent's first argument is that the right of the petitioner to receive additional stock in Jet was neither stock nor securities within the meaning of section 351(a) but was "other property," which is to be recognized as gain to the extent of its fair market value. Respondent cites *Helvering v. Southwest Corp.*, 315 U.S. 194 (1942), in which assets were acquired in a reorganization for voting stock and warrants which allowed the holder to acquire shares of stock upon payment of specified sums. The issue was whether the assets were acquired in a reorganization within the definition in section 112(g)(1) of the Internal Revenue Code of 1939, solely for voting stock. The Court said that "solely" leaves no leeway and that voting stock plus some other consideration does not meet the requirements, and held that the warrants were not voting stock nor did they carry the rights of a shareholder. The respondent says that the petitioner's contract right to acquire Jet stock was not the equivalent of stock but had more of the characteristics of the warrants in the cited case.

The petitioner cites *Carlberg v. United States*, 281 F.2d 507 (C.A. 8, 1960), which involved an exchange of stock for stock and certificates of contingent interest. The issue was whether such certificates were "stock" within the meaning of section 354(a)(1) of the 1954 Code or "other property," within the meaning of section 356(a)(1). The case arose from the merger of two lumber companies, referred to as Maryland and Missouri, into International Paper Co. At the time, Missouri had pending substantial unsettled liabilities. To protect International, certain shares were reserved and certificates of contingent interest issued with respect to them. The stockholders of Maryland and Missouri received shares of International plus certificates. When the liabilities were settled, the reserved shares would be distributed in accordance with the certificates if settlement were made within 10 years. The purpose of the device was to place the ultimate burden of the liabilities on the Missouri stockholders. The court referred to the *Southwest* case, and observed that there were obvious differences between the warrants in that case and the certificates in *Carlberg*, as the warrants provided rights to purchase at stated prices during a stated time, the holders having only an option to purchase, while the certificate holders were immediately entitled to all the reserved shares to be distributed and need take no positive action nor provide further consideration. The court said that the certificates could produce nothing but stock, that the arrangement for reserved shares seemed an ideal and logical solution of the problem of the contingent liabilities, and that what the holder possessed was either stock or nothing. The court held that the property interest represented by the certificates was "stock" within the meaning of section 354(a)(1) rather than "other property" or "boot."

The contract here was a solution of a problem, as in *Carlberg*. The cash investors were willing to allow Hamrick and Hensley voting control of the corporation to be formed but were unwilling to put up $35,000 for only one-third of the shares in an untried invention. The inventors wanted one-third of the stock each. The arrangement for additional shares to be issued to them in the event the invention proved salable was a compromise and a good faith solution of their differences. There was a valid business purpose in the arrangement. If earnings were meager, the investors would receive in dividends nearly half of them. If the business was successful, they would be content with one-third of satisfactory earnings. The inventors were willing to take the hazard of the salability of their invention which, if successful, would result in their receiving eventually the interests they wanted.

The respondent concedes that the stock issued in 1957 was received in exchange for the transfer of property. The contract right to receive additional stock was also a part of the consideration for the transfer. The right, as in *Carlberg*, can produce nothing other than stock to the petitioner. While the exact number of shares is not specified, what the petitioner can receive is nothing other than stock. Applying the rule of substance over form, we must conclude that the substance of the contract provides for only a stockholder's interest. It does not represent current gain, but additional equity ownership.

In *Carlberg*, the certificates authorized the issue of additional stock if certain conditions were met within 10 years. Here the contract authorized the issue of additional stock if certain conditions were met within 7 years. The stock was authorized and available for issuance if the conditions were met. The principle of the *Carlberg* case is applicable here, and Hamrick's right under the agreement was the equivalent of stock. *See also Philip W. McAbee*, 5 T.C. 1130 (1945), *acq.* 1946-2 C.B. 4, in which certificates were issued for stock placed in escrow in a reorganization and we held that the stock was received pursuant to a plan of reorganization and at the time of the escrow.

The respondent next contends that the time limitation of section 351 is not met. Under that section gain is not to be recognized if "immediately after" the exchange the transferors are in control of the corporation. The respondent contends that if the transaction is prolonged and spread out over several years it becomes impossible to determine the fact of control within the time limitation of the statute, and that an interval of 7 years within which the petitioner's rights are in abeyance would make the tax effect indeterminable within a reasonable time after the exchange.

The required control is 80 percent of the voting stock. Sec. 368(c). In this case Hamrick and Hensley exchanged their patent rights for 38,000 shares ($1 par value), plus the right to receive additional shares; the cash investors exchanged money for 35,000 shares; and 2,000 shares were issued to others for services. Stock issued for services is not considered as issued in return for property. Sec. 351(a). "Property," for the purpose of section 351, includes "money." *George M. Holstein III*, 23 T.C. 923 (1955). "Immediately after the exchange" the persons who transferred the rights to the patent and the cash, both of which are property, to the corporation were in control of it to the required extent. Hamrick and Hensley and the cash investors held 73,000 shares and the rights to additional shares, while other persons who rendered services, that is, Newcombe and the attorneys, held 2,000 shares, or less than 3 percent. Momentary control is sufficient. *American Bantam Car Co.*, 11 T.C. 397 (1948), *aff'd.* 177 F.2d 513 (C.A. 3, 1949), *certiorari denied* 339 U.S. 920. The tax effect is determinable immediately. The conclusion is not affected by subsequent issues, even where such issues result in reducing the transferors' control to less than 80 percent, *Lodi Iron Works, Inc.*, 29 T.C. 696 (1958), and we may observe that the right of Hamrick and Hensley to receive additional shares in the future could not possibly reduce the degree of control of the transferors here.

The respondent next contends that at least a part of the additional shares was issued for services rendered or to be rendered by the petitioner, referring to the covenant by Hamrick and Hensley in the original assignment that they would disclose to the corporation and assign to it any and all improvements made by either of them in the invention and all rights under any patents pertaining to such improvements or inventions. The respondent says that this contemplates services by petitioner in working toward improving the invention and that this is a service to be rendered Jet in exchange for the consideration passing from it. Stock issued for services is not considered as issued in return for property, and gain on such stock is not entitled to nonrecognition under section 351(a).

It is an established practice in patent assignments to provide for the assignment of future improvements and similar inventions by the assignor in order to protect the assignee from having his acquisition made worthless by reason of such improvements. *Aspinwall Manuf'g Co. v. Gill*, 32 F.2d 697 (1887). This is not construed as a contract for services. Hamrick was separately employed by Jet as an officer and was separately compensated for services as such. No part of the stock to be issued to him was intended or may be regarded as compensation for

F. CONTROL IMMEDIATELY AFTER THE TRANSACTION

services. He was not hired to invent, as in *Arthur N. Blum*, 11 T.C. 101 (1948), *aff'd*. 183 F.2d 281 (C.A. 3, 1950). Nor was there a provision in the agreement for separate compensation for inventing or promoting and developing inventions, as in *Arthur C. Ruge*, 26 T.C. 138 (1956), nor a provision reasonably to be interpreted as providing for such compensation, as in *Spence v. United States*, 156 F. Supp. 556 (Ct. Cl. 1957). The agreement to assign a subsequent improvement does not have the effect of an assignment. *See Roland Chilton*, 40 T.C. 552 (1963). There is no indication that any such transfer was in fact made here.

[The court went on to conclude that the stock was received pursuant to an amendment of the original agreement, not a new contract, and that the stock was worth somewhat over $14. Certain other issues are also omitted.]

Decision will be entered under Rule 50.

F. CONTROL IMMEDIATELY AFTER THE TRANSACTION

The statute says that the transferors must be in control "immediately after the transaction." What does the "control requirement" of § 351 really mean? Who is it who must be in such "control"?

FAHS v. FLORIDA MACHINE & FOUNDRY CO.
168 F.2d 957 (5th Cir. 1948.)

McCord, Circuit Judge.

Appellee, Florida Machine and Foundry Company, filed suit to recover additional income and excess profits taxes, aggregating $19,089.44, paid for the years 1941 and 1942 under protest. From a judgment for appellee taxpayer, the Collector takes this appeal.

The only question presented is the proper cost basis to be used by taxpayer in computing gain or loss on the sale of certain land it owned in 1941, and in determining taxpayer's equity invested capital for the years 1941 and 1942.

[§ 351 provides]

Recognition of gain or loss- ....

(b) Exchanges solely in kind- ....

(5) Transfer to corporation controlled by transferor.

No gain or loss shall be recognized if property is transferred to a corporation by one or more persons solely in exchange for stock or securities in such corporation, and immediately after the exchange such person or persons are in control of the corporation; ....

[Section 368(c) defines the term "control," as used in the above quoted provision, as follows:

... Definition of control. As used in this section the term "control" means the ownership of stock possessing at least 80 per centum of the total combined voting power of all classes of stock entitled to vote and at least 80 per centum of the total number of shares of all other classes of stock of the corporation....

... The basis to be used for property acquired by a corporation after December 31, 1920, through the issuance of its stock for property in accordance with [Section 351], above, is the same as it would be in the hands of the transferor.... If, however, the issuance of the stock for property is not governed by [Section 351], the taxpayer's basis is the cost to it of such property, or the fair market value of the property on the date of acquisition....

The evidence reveals that for some years prior to 1912, Franklin G. Russell, Senior, as sole owner, operated a business known as Florida Machine Works on Riverside Avenue in Jacksonville, Florida. On May 31, 1912, he purchased a tract of land bordering on West Church Street in Jacksonville, to which location the plant was later moved.

About the year 1920, it was shown that the Senior Mr. Russell, who had little technical education for foundry and machine ship [sic] work, discussed with his son, Franklin G. Russell, Junior, the possibility of the son eventually succeeding him in the business. The son had graduated from college in 1916 with a degree in mechanical engineering and, with the exception of about two years spent as a soldier in World War I, had served since that time as an apprentice in the various departments of his father's plant, later becoming assistant manager. When the location of the business was changed from Riverside Avenue to West Church Street, the son himself had planned and laid out the new plant installations. In 1921 the father and son entered into an agreement whereby the son would eventually receive a one-half interest in the business, if he remained with it and continued to operate the plant. In pursuance of this agreement, the Florida Machine and Foundry Company, taxpayer, was organized and incorporated on July 16, 1924. At the organization meeting on that date, the Senior Russell conveyed to the corporation all of the assets of the business which he then owned individually, including the tract of land in question, for stock in the corporation, with the shares thereof to be issued directly to himself, his son, and one share each to three other persons. The father received 1181 shares and his son 1176 shares, the father thereby retaining only a bare majority of the stock issued.

In 1941, the corporation sold a parcel of the land on West Church Street for $15,000. The March 1, 1913, value of this tract was $7,522.60. On July 16, 1924, the date taxpayer corporation was organized, the fair market value of the tract sold was $13,164.55.

In its 1941 return, the taxpayer claimed a loss on the above sale in the sum of $11,270, using as its basis of value for the land sold, the amount $26,270, which was the proportionate fair market value of the land sold as compared with the fair market value of the entire tract as of July 16, 1924, the date of organization of

F. CONTROL IMMEDIATELY AFTER THE TRANSACTION

the corporation and acquisition of the land by taxpayer. The Commissioner denied the validity of the basis used, on the ground that the transfer to the corporation on July 16, 1924, was really a non-taxable exchange of property for stock, as described in [Section 351] of the Code, and ruled that, for the purpose of computing taxpayer's gain or loss under Sec. 113(a) (8), the proper basis of value [sic?] was the March 1, 1913 value in the hands of the transferor, Franklin G. Russell, Senior, or $7,824.53, so that instead of a loss of $11,270, as claimed by taxpayer, there was a taxable gain of $7,175.47; he further required the use of the same basis in computing taxpayer's equity invested capital under Sec. 718(a)(2), for the years 1941 and 1942.

We are of opinion the district court's finding that Franklin Russell, Senior, was not in "control" of taxpayer corporation "immediately after the transfer" on July 16, 1924, and therefore, that [Section 351] did not apply, is abundantly supported by the evidence....

Appellant's contention that the son, Franklin Russell, Junior, by virtue of the agreement with his father in 1921, acquired an equitable one-half interest in the land involved, which thereafter placed him and his father, as joint transferors, in "control" of taxpayer immediately after the transfer, is not borne out by the evidence. We further find no merit in the argument that taxpayer should be required to use the basis of its transferor, Franklin G. Russell, Senior, because of the latter's failure to report the transfer in 1924. There can be no estoppel against taxpayer for the act of its transferor, who was not in control of taxpayer corporation immediately after the transfer, and who was shown to have acted in good faith. *Cf. Portland Oil Co. v. Commissioner*, 1 Cir., 109 F.2d 479....

It follows that the proper basis for the land in question is its fair market value when acquired by taxpayer corporation on July 16, 1924.

We find no reversible error in the record, and the judgment is therefore affirmed.

PROBLEM 14-2

Mrs. Vermon owns all the stock of Bongo Corporation, to which she recently transferred a large quantity of inventory in return for all of its stock. The corporation in turn contributed the inventory to a newly formed partnership in exchange for a 50% profits and capital interest in the partnership. Bongo Corporation's subsidiary, Drum Corporation, contributed cash of equal value to the partnership.

1. Does the retransfer to the partnership conflict with any requirements of § 351?

2. Would your conclusion differ if, in turn, Bongo Corporation and Drum Corporation each wound up as 25% partners and an unrelated partner held 50% of the new partnership?

G. ACCOMMODATION TRANSFERORS

In order for § 351 to apply, the *transferor* person or persons must be in "control" of the corporation. So who is the *transferor*? Take the example of the corporation that already exists and which has invited in a new shareholder who wants to contribute some high-value, low-basis real estate. The new shareholder wants to make sure that there is no tax on her exchange, but she will wind up with only 25% of the stock after the proposed transfer. Assume that the only other shareholder, whose ownership will be reduced to 75% by the exchange, says, "Okay, I'll transfer in $1 and I will get one share of stock and you can transfer in your real estate which is worth $100,000, for 100,000 shares of stock and that way § 351 will apply because we are both *transferors*." Wrong. That transaction is a sham. *See* Rev. Rul. 79-194, 1979-1 C.B. 145. So how much is enough? According to the IRS, the existing shareholder who accommodates the transaction (in our example, the 100%-75% shareholder) must transfer property or cash worth at least 10% of her original stock ownership. Rev. Proc. 77-37, 1977-2 C.B. 568.

There are more complicated variants of this situation. Imagine a corporation that is about to be formed by two shareholders, one contributing property with a value of $100 and a basis of zero, and the other contributing only services which are worth $80. This transaction will not satisfy § 351 because there is only one *transferor* of *property* and he is not in control after the transaction. Now imagine that the service provider proposes to contribute cash of $20. Does this make the service provider a *transferor*? According to Rev. Proc. 77-37, *supra*, it does. The reasoning is that as long as the service provider transfers property that is not of relatively small value, the service provider will be viewed as a transferor. The property is *of relatively small value* if it does not equal at least 10% of the value of the stock received for services. In our example, the stock received for services is worth $80 and the $20 cash transferred equals 25% of the value of the stock received for services. The key is that we now have two transferors. Together they are in control, hence their exchanges are protected by § 351.

Keep in mind that even though this reasoning prevents the transfers of property from being taxable, the service provider will always be taxed on stock issued for services. Thus, in the example, the service provider will have $80 of ordinary income on receipt of the stock unless the service provider's stock is restricted in such a way that it is not taxable until the restrictions lapse. *See* § 83(a).

H. THE IMPACT OF "BOOT"

Read § 351(b).

If the transferor receives not only stock but also other property, including bonds or notes, § 351(b) requires the recognition of any realized gain to the extent of the value of such nonqualifying property. If you review the partnership

H. THE IMPACT OF "BOOT"

analog, namely § 721, you will notice that it does not contain similar words. But the result may well be the same, since only an interest in the partnership can be received tax-free under § 721.

Note that § 351(b)(2) prevents the recognition of unrealized losses, which makes § 351(b) a one-way street.

REV. RUL. 68-55
1968-1 C.B. 140

In determining the amount of gain recognized under section 351(b) of the Internal Revenue Code of 1954 where several assets were transferred to a corporation, each asset must be considered transferred separately in exchange for a portion of each category of consideration received. The fair market value of each category of consideration received is separately allocated to the transferred assets in proportion to the relative fair market values of the transferred assets. Where as a result of such allocation there is a realized loss with respect to any asset, such loss is not recognized under section 351(b)(2) of the Code.

Advice has been requested as to the correct method of determining the amount and character of the gain to be recognized by Corporation X under section 351(b) of the Internal Revenue Code of 1954 under the circumstances described below.

Corporation Y was organized by X and A, an individual who owned no stock in X. A transferred $20x$ dollars to Y in exchange for stock of Y having a fair market value of $20x$ dollars and X transferred to Y three separate assets and received in exchange stock of Y having a fair market value of $100x$ dollars plus cash of $10x$ dollars.

In accordance with the facts set forth in the table below if X had sold at fair market value each of the three assets it transferred to Y, the result would have been as follows:

	Asset I	Asset II	Asset III
Character of asset	Capital asset held more than 6 months.	Capital asset held not more than 6 months.	Section 1245 property.
Fair market value	$22x$	$33x$	$55x$
Adjusted basis	$40x$	$20x$	$25x$
Gain (loss)	($18x$)	$13x$	$30x$
Character of gain or loss	Long-term capital loss.	Short-term capital gain.	Ordinary income.

The facts in the instant case disclose that with respect to the section 1245 property the depreciation subject to recapture exceeds the amount of gain that would be recognized on a sale at fair market value. Therefore, all of such gain would be treated as ordinary income under section 1245(a)(1) of the Code.

Under section 351(a) of the Code, no gain or loss is recognized if property is transferred to a corporation solely in exchange for its stock and immediately after the exchange the transferor is in control of the corporation. If section 351(a) of the Code would apply to an exchange but for the fact that there is received, in addition to the property permitted to be received without recognition of gain, other property or money, then under section 351(b) of the Code gain (if any) to the recipient will be recognized, but in an amount not in excess of the sum of such money and the fair market value of such other property received, and no loss to the recipient will be recognized.

The first question presented is how to determine the amount of gain to be recognized under section 351(b) of the Code. The general rule is that each asset transferred must be considered to have been separately exchanged. See the authorities cited in Revenue Ruling 67-192, C.B. 1967-2, 140, and in Revenue Ruling 68-23, page 144, this Bulletin, which hold that there is no netting of gains and losses for purposes of applying sections 367 and 356(c) of the Code. Thus, for purposes of making computations under section 351(b) of the Code, it is not proper to total the bases of the various assets transferred and to subtract this total from the fair market value of the total consideration received in the exchange. Moreover, any treatment other than an asset-by-asset approach would have the effect of allowing losses that are specifically disallowed by section 351(b)(2) of the Code.

The second question presented is how, for purposes of making computations under section 351(b) of the Code, to allocate the cash and stock received to the amount realized as to each asset transferred in the exchange. The asset-by-asset approach for computing the amount of gain realized in the exchange requires that for this purpose the fair market value of each category of consideration received must be separately allocated to the transferred assets in proportion to the relative fair market values of the transferred assets. See section 1.1245-4(c)(1) of the Income Tax Regulations which, for the same reasons, requires that for purposes of computing the amount of gain to which section 1245 of the Code applies each category of consideration received must be allocated to the properties transferred in proportion to their relative fair market values.

Accordingly, the amount and character of the gain recognized in the exchange should be computed as follows:

I. ASSUMPTION OF LIABILITIES

	Total	Asset I	Asset II	Asset III
Fair market value of asset transferred	$110x	$22x	$33x	$55x
Percent of total fair market value		20%	30%	50%
Fair market value of Y stock received in exchange	$100x	$20x	$30x	$50x
Cash received in exchange	10x	2x	3x	5x
Amount realized	$110x	$22x	$33x	$55x
Adjusted basis		40x	20x	25x
Gain (loss) realized		($18x)	$13x	$30x

Under section 351(b)(2) of the Code the loss of 18x dollars realized on the exchange of Asset Number I is not recognized. Such loss may not be used to offset the gains realized on the exchanges of the other assets. Under section 351(b)(1) of the Code, the gain of 13x dollars realized on the exchange of Asset Number [big d] II will be recognized as short-term capital gain in the amount 3x dollars, the amount of cash received. Under sections 351(b)(1) and 1245(b)(3) of the Code, the gain of 30x dollars realized on the exchange of Asset Number III will be recognized as ordinary income in the amount of 5x dollars, the amount of cash received.

I. ASSUMPTION OF LIABILITIES

Read § 357(a)-(c).

As a general rule, a transfer of encumbered property to a corporation under Section 351 will not result in any tax liability to the transferor, even though the transferee corporation assumes the liability or takes the property subject to it. This is in contrast to the general rule of Regs. § 1.1001-2(a). This general rule and the exception found in § 357(b) (for tax-avoidance purposes) have been the law since 1939. Another exception was added in 1954; that exception is § 357(c).

To illustrate: A shareholder in the course of forming a new corporation contributes property with a basis of $50,000 and a value of $100,000. The property is subject to a mortgage of $30,000. The shareholder will receive stock worth $70,000 (the difference between the value of the property and the encumbrance). The shareholder will have a realized gain of $50,000 (the amount realized is $70,000 worth of stock plus $30,000 of debt relief or $100,000 minus the $50,000 basis). But the recognized gain is zero because of § 351 and § 357(a), which prevents the assumed liability from being treated as boot under § 351(b). The shareholder's basis in the stock will be equal to the basis of the property, $50,000, minus the assumed liability of $30,000, for a net figure of $20,000. *See* § 358(d).

Section 357(b) treats as money received (i.e., as boot) any liabilities which are assumed with a principal purpose to avoid tax or, if not such purpose, without a bona-fide business purpose. The Regulations suggest that there must be a business purpose for both the transferor and the corporation even though the statute speaks only of the transferor.

On top of that, if there is an improper purpose for *any* assumption of liability, must *all* the liabilities assumed from that transferor be treated as money received? If challenged by the IRS, the taxpayer is required to demonstrate her purity of motive "by the clear preponderance of the evidence," which is an abnormally high burden of proof.

The usual case to which § 357(b) is directed is where the taxpayer seeks to wring out some tax-free cash by encumbering an asset just before transferring it to the corporation. Section 357(b) would also apply to more remote situations where the transferee corporation assumes a personal liability of the transferor, such as alimony, and there is no business reason for doing so.[1]

Section 357(c) is the more common problem. Where the amount of liabilities transferred exceeds the aggregate basis of the assets transferred, the excess is treated as immediately taxable gain. Note that as in the case of § 357(b) this inquiry is posed shareholder-by-shareholder and not by considering the transferor group as a whole. Although § 357(c) may look harmless, it can be a painful trap because the taxpayer has received no cash or other property with which to pay the tax. The constitutionality of § 357(c) was upheld in *Wiebusch v. Commissioner*, 59 T.C. 777, *aff'd per curiam*, 487 F.2d 515 (8th Cir. 1973). [Note: There *was* gain realized in *Wiebusch* — it is impossible for § 357(c) to apply without gain in the form of offloaded liabilities and other consideration in excess of

---

[1] In order to obtain a ruling for a § 351 transaction, the taxpayer must represent (among a myriad of other things) that any liabilities to be assumed were incurred in the ordinary course of business, or if not, must state the business reason for such assumption. Rev. Proc. 83-59, 1983-2 C.B. 575, at ¶.03.b.(2).

I. ASSUMPTION OF LIABILITIES

basis.] Note that § 357(c) does not apply to liabilities that would be deductible if paid, in other words to most current account payables such as business rent, wages, insurance and the like. § 357(c)(3)(A)(i).

LESSINGER v. COMMISSIONER
872 F.2d 519 (2nd Cir. 1989)

Before OAKES, CHIEF JUDGE, KEARSE and CARDAMONE, CIRCUIT JUDGES.

OAKES, CHIEF JUDGE:

[Taxpayer Lessinger transferred assets to a controlled corporation pursuant to section 351. The problem was that the liabilities transferred to the corporation exceeded the basis of the assets he transferred. To resolve the problem, the taxpayer promised to pay additional money to the corporation, first on "open account" but later substantiated by a promissory note. This was done to increase his basis and to avoid § 357(c).]

Discussion

....

[W]e must determine whether the taxpayer's purported debt to his corporation would offset those liabilities and prevent a net excess of liabilities over assets. The obligation which the taxpayer owed to his wholly-owned corporation, it must quickly be conceded, was not as well documented as a debt to a third party would be....

The Tax Court refused to count the debt as "property" transferred in the transaction, although its reasoning is not explicit. First, the opinion says that the corporate accounting entry entitled "Loan receivable — [Sol Lessinger]" "merely represents the excess of the liabilities over the adjusted basis," noting that the debt was not at first represented by a promissory note and that Lessinger paid no interest on it. The Tax Court then cites a decision in which it had ignored an entry that the taxpayer had characterized as an "artificial receivable." 85 T.C. at 837 n. 8 (citing *Christopher v. Commissioner*, 48 Tax Ct. Mem. Dec. (CCH) 663 (1984)). The Tax Court opinion concludes that "[e]ven if [Lessinger] had executed a note, it would have a zero basis in the hands of the corporation." *Id.* at 837 (citing *Alderman v. Commissioner*, 55 T.C. 662 (1971)). The Tax Court thus apparently believed there were two independently sufficient reasons to ignore the debt: first, that it was artificial, and, second, that it would have had a zero basis.

We are unpersuaded by the argument that the obligation was artificial. The Commissioner argues:

> This open account was not so much a debt as it was an accommodation by the corporation to its president and sole shareholder, who was having liquidity problems. In effect, he caused the corporation to apply its assets to satisfy his personal obligations, including those owed to trade creditors

which were shortly to fall due, intending to pay the money back only as and when he found it convenient to do so.

The Commissioner points out that the receivable lacked a due date, interest, security, or "other accepted features of true debt," but this analysis begs the question we have before us. The Commissioner's argument is not aided by likening this case to *Carolina, Clinchfield and Ohio Railway v. Commissioner*, 823 F.2d 33 (2d Cir. 1987) (*per curiam*), where an existing debt was replaced by a new debt payable ten centuries later, the present value of which was two quadrillionths of a cent. We believe that the receivable was an enforceable demand obligation. The decisions that the Commissioner cites for the definition of "true debt" concern the advance of funds to a close corporation by its shareholders. *Gilbert v. Commissioner*, 248 F.2d 399, 402 (2d Cir. 1957); *see also Raymond v. United States*, 511 F.2d 185, 190 (6th Cir. 1975). A taxpayer in that setting may seek to mischaracterize a capital contribution as debt in order for the corporation to be able to treat the obligation in a way that would disguise nondeductible dividends as deductible interest payments. In that context, the courts have defined "classic debt" narrowly as "an unqualified obligation to pay a sum certain at a reasonably close fixed maturity date along with a fixed percentage in interest," although the essential factor is a "binding obligation." *Gilbert*, 248 F.2d at 402.

We believe, however, that a due date, interest, and security are not necessary to characterize Lessinger's obligation to his corporation as debt, and that his obligation was binding. The promissory note he signed in 1981, which the corporation endorsed to Marine Midland as collateral for a loan, is significant because it shows that Marine Midland depended on his personal responsibility. And, in general, it is obvious that the creditors of the corporation continued to do business with it on the strength of the taxpayer's personal credit (whether as evidenced by the liability on the books or by operation of New York law protecting creditors of a partnership that is succeeded by an alter ego corporation,).... Lessinger received consideration when he gave his promise to the corporation, and we have no doubt that any court would enforce that promise to protect the corporate creditors if the corporation failed, even in the absence of alter ego liability. We conclude that the taxpayer's obligation to the corporation was real, not artificial.

We now turn to the Tax Court's second reason for ignoring the debt. The Tax Court quoted *Alderman, supra*, which, like our case, involved the incorporation of an accrual basis proprietorship with a negative net worth. In *Alderman*, the Tax Court disregarded the taxpayers' personal promissory note to their corporation "because [t]he Aldermans incurred no cost in making the note, so its basis to them was zero. The basis to the corporation was the same as in the hands of the transferor, i.e., zero. Consequently, the application of section 357(c) is undisturbed by the creation and transfer of the personal note to the corporation." 55 T.C. at 665; *see also* Rev. Rul. 68-629, 1968-2 C.B. 154-55 (same).

I. ASSUMPTION OF LIABILITIES

Alderman purported to follow the literal language of the Tax Code. Section 357(c) does support the *Alderman* court's reliance on the concept of basis, but the statutory language is not addressed to a transaction such as Lessinger's, where the transferor's obligation has a value to the transferee corporation. The *Alderman* court did not consider the value of the obligation to the transferee.

Section 357(a) provides that generally, the corporation's assumption of the transferor's liabilities should cause no recognition of gain: Except as provided in subsection[ ] ... (c), if — (1) the taxpayer receives property which would be permitted to be received under section 351, ... without the recognition of gain if it were the sole consideration, and (2) as part of the consideration, another party to the exchange assumes a liability of the taxpayer, or acquires from the taxpayer property subject to a liability, then such assumption or acquisition shall not be treated as money or other property, and shall not prevent the exchange from being within the provisions of section 351.... I.R.C. § 357(a) (1982). Subsection (c)(1) then provides an exception: (c) Liabilities in excess of basis (1) In general in the case of an exchange — (A) to which section 351 applies, ... if the sum of the amount of the liabilities assumed, plus the amount of the liabilities to which the property is subject, exceeds the total of the *adjusted basis* of the property transferred pursuant to such exchange, then such excess shall be considered as a gain.... *Id.* § 357(c) (emphasis added). In general, then, the "adjusted basis" of the property transferred is crucial to the calculation.

"Basis," as used in tax law, refers to assets, not liabilities. Section 1012 provides that "[t]he basis of property shall be the cost of such property, except as otherwise provided." Liabilities by definition have no "basis" in tax law generally or in section 1012 terms specifically.[2] The concept of "basis" prevents double taxation of income by identifying amounts that have already been taxed or are exempt from tax. 3 J. Mertens, Law of Federal Income Taxation § 21.01, at 11 (1988). The taxpayer could, of course, have no "basis" in his own promise to pay the corporation $255,000, because that item is a liability for him. We would add parenthetically that to this extent *Alderman* was correct in describing the taxpayers' note there. But the corporation should have a basis in its obligation from Lessinger, because it incurred a cost in the transaction involving the transfer of the obligation by taking on the liabilities of the proprietorship that exceeded its assets, and because it would have to recognize income upon

---

[2] Basis is "the original cost of property used in computing capital gains or losses for income tax purposes." Webster's Third New International Dictionary 182 (1963). It is a "[t]erm used in accounting, especially in tax accounting, to describe the value of an asset for purpose [sic] of determining gain (or loss) on its sale or transfer or in determining value in the hands of a donee of a gift." Black's Law Dictionary 138 (5th ed. 1979). Derived from "[a]cquisition cost or some substitute therefor," it is the "amount assigned to an asset for income tax purposes." *Id.*

Lessinger's payment of the debt if it had no basis in the obligation.[3] Assets transferred under section 351 are taken by the corporation at the transferor's basis, to which is added any gain recognized in the transfer. § 362(a). Consideration of "adjusted basis" in section 357(c) therefore normally does not require determining whether the section refers to the "adjusted basis" in the hands of the transferor-shareholder or the transferee-corporation, because the basis does not change. But here, the "basis" in the hands of the corporation should be the face amount of the taxpayer's obligation. We now hold that in the situation presented here, where the transferor undertakes genuine personal liability to the transferee, "adjusted basis" in section 357(c) refers to the transferee's basis in the obligation, which is its face amount.[4]

Yet the Commissioner says that to reverse the Tax Court would, as *Alderman*, 55 T.C. at 665, suggested, "effectively eliminate section 357(c) from the Internal Revenue Code." Would it? The question of substance is whether the taxpayer in fact realized a gain from the transaction. He certainly did not do so by a cancellation of his indebtedness. If there was any cancellation, it was illusory: While his trade creditors at the time of the incorporation may have been paid off (or their accounts rolled over as a result of sales and payments by the corporation and further advances of credit by the trade creditors), the taxpayer's indebtedness to the corporation itself continued (except to the extent he paid it off). If Lessinger had a "gain" from the incorporation, it did not show up in his personal balance sheet, let alone by way of economic benefit in his pocket.

The purpose of section 357(c) is to provide a limited exception to section 351's nonrecognition treatment that operates, as the Commissioner reminds us here, "where the transferor realized economic benefit which, if not recognized, would otherwise go untaxed." Brief at 27 (quoting *Focht v. Commissioner*, 68 T.C. 223, 235 (1977)). Section 351 was intended to allow changes in business form without requiring the recognition of income. *Bongiovanni v. Commissioner*, 470

---

[3] Our approach requires acceptance of the fact that section 362(a), which requires a carryover basis for "property" transferred in nonrecognition transactions under section 351, cannot be applied to the corporation's valuation of its receivable from the taxpayer. The purpose of the predecessor to section 362 was to avoid allowing the corporation a new, stepped-up basis from which to deduct depreciation expenses ... (the purpose of special basis rules for nonrecognition transactions is, in general, to prevent the transferee from having a stepped-up basis). Another purpose of transferred bases generally is to defer recognition of gain or loss.... In Lessinger's transaction, there simply were no gains or losses to be deferred. The excess of liabilities over assets (which Lessinger's promise to the corporation remedied) was caused by the proprietorship's insolvency — the excess of current payables over current receivables — rather than by unrecognized gain in any asset's basis.

[4] Curiously, the Commissioner does not actually make Alderman's zero-basis argument. The taxpayer, on the other hand, attempts to convince us that, as an accrual basis taxpayer he had a "basis" in his personal obligations to the corporation. We note, however, that the fact that he would have had a liability on his books does not require the conclusion that he had a "basis" in it for tax purposes.

F.2d 921, 924 (2d Cir. 1972); *Raich v. Commissioner*, 46 T.C. 604, 608 (1966). The transferor-shareholder recognizes income only to the extent that he receives boot in the form of money or other property. § 351(b). In 1938, the Supreme Court held that under the predecessor of section 351, section 112 of the Revenue Act of 1928, any assumption of liability by the transferee would be considered a payment of money or property to the transferor, causing the transferor to recognize income. *United States v. Hendler*, 303 U.S. 564, 58 S. Ct. 655, 82 L. Ed. 1018 (1938). Congress reacted immediately by enacting section 112(k) of the Internal Revenue Code of 1939, the predecessor of section 357(a), which provided that the assumption of a liability should not be considered the payment of property or money and should not provoke the recognition of gain. *See Focht*, 68 T.C. at 232 & n. 21 (quoting section 112(k) and its legislative history).

Congress did not add section 357(c), which requires the recognition of gain when liabilities exceed assets, until 1954, when a House committee referred to the section as an "additional safeguard[ ] against tax avoidance not found in existing law." H.R. Rep. No. 1337, 83d Cong., 2d Sess. 40, reprinted in 1954 U.S. Code Cong. & Admin. News 4017, 4066 ("House Report"). Some provision was necessary to ensure that manipulations of credit and depreciation were not used to realize tax-free gains. *Focht*, 68 T.C. at 235. The House and Senate committees that approved section 357(c) both cited a single example of a transaction that the section was intended to govern: If a taxpayer transfers property with an adjusted basis of $20,000 subject to a $50,000 mortgage, he should recognize $30,000 gain. House Report at A129, reprinted in 1954 U.S. Code Cong. & Admin. News at 4267 (describing what was then called § 356); S.Rep. No. 1622, 83d Cong., 2d Sess. 270, reprinted in 1954 U.S. Code Cong. & Admin. News 4621, 4908. While some have argued that section 357(c) was designed to avoid a negative basis,[5] its application in the Congress's example is also quite reasonable. The transferor, who has already benefited by depreciating the property or holding it while its value appreciates, has income because he will never have to pay the mortgage. Forcing the taxpayer in our case to recognize a gain, however, would be contrary to Congress's intent because it would tax a truly phantom gain, because his liability to the corporation, as we have said, was real, continuing, and indirectly, at least, enforceable by the corporation's creditors.

That section 357(c)'s language can be construed to require unjust and economically unfounded results is clear from the continuing debate over other aspects of the section's operation. In *Rosen v. Commissioner*, 62 T.C. 11 (1974), *aff'd mem.*, 515 F.2d 507 (3d Cir. 1975), for example, the Tax Court held that a transferor had to recognize gain from the assumption of liabilities, even though

---

[5] E.g., Cooper, Negative Basis, 75 Harv. L. Rev. 1352, 1358-60 (1962) (arguing that Congress created section 357(c) only to prevent the transferor from accumulating a negative basis in his stock in the transferee-corporation).

he remained personally liable and, in fact, paid the obligations himself. The Tax Court commented on section 357(c)'s harshness, noting that it "may even result in the realization of a gain for tax purposes where none in fact exists." *Id.* at 19. After oral argument, counsel for the Commissioner directed us to a case upholding the constitutionality of section 357(c). The court in that case, however, was not confronted with an exception to its optimistic observation that "[i]t is only when some tax benefit occurs, for example depreciation or further indebtedness on the property which yields tax-free cash not included in cost, that the liabilities will exceed the adjusted basis therein." *Wiebusch v. Commissioner*, 59 T.C. 777, 781, *aff'd per curiam*, 487 F.2d 515 (8th Cir. 1973). While we do not rest our decision today on constitutional grounds, we note that *Wiebusch's* analysis would not apply here.

Section 357(c) was amended in 1978 to solve a problem that had forced the courts to fashion delicate constructions of the section's language in order to conform with legislative intent. A cash basis transferor has no basis in accounts receivable. The Tax Court originally held that such a transferor would have to recognize gain if, after counting her accounts payable as transferred liabilities, liabilities exceeded assets. *See Raich, supra.* This analysis meant that the owner of almost any ongoing business transferred liabilities exceeding assets when incorporating. The Tax Court later developed an approach that excluded accounts payable from liabilities, *see Focht, supra,* after this court and the Court of Appeals for the Ninth Circuit announced different interpretations that achieved this result. *See Bongiovanni, supra*; *Thatcher v. Commissioner*, 533 F.2d 1114 (9th Cir. 1976). Congress added section 357(c)(3) in 1978, and it now excludes from subsection (c)(1) "a liability the payment of which ... would give rise to a deduction." This history, while not directly relevant to Lessinger,[6] is instructive. In *Bongiovanni*, "a too literal reading of the words of the statute [would have] produce[d] an inequitable result which cannot be allowed to stand," 470 F.2d at 924, and "Congress certainly could not have intended such an inequitable result especially in light of its expressed purposes in enacting Sections 351 and 357(c)," *id.* at 925. We find those words equally applicable here.

We conclude that our holding will not "effectively eliminate section 357(c)." Lessinger experienced no enrichment and had no unrecognized gains whose recognition was appropriate at the time of the consolidation. Any logic that would tax him would certainly represent a "trap for the unwary." *Bongiovanni*, 470 F.2d at 924 (quoting the Commissioner's characterization of the Tax Court's early treatment of cash basis taxpayers under section 351). Lessinger could have achieved incorporation without taxation under the Commissioner's theory by borrowing $260,000 cash, transferring the cash to the corporation (or paying

---

[6] Section 357(c)(3) is inapplicable because Lessinger's proprietorship was on the accrual basis. None of the liabilities would have produced deductions if paid by the transferor because those expenses had been previously deducted when they were entered in the proprietorship's records. *See* 3A Stand. Fed. Tax Rep. (CCH ¶ 2530.04 (1989)).

J. THE CONTROL REQUIREMENT

some of the trade accounts payable personally), and later causing the corporation to buy his promissory note from the lender (or pay it off in consideration of his new promise to pay the corporation). If taxpayers who transfer liabilities exceeding assets to controlled corporations are willing to undertake genuine personal liability for the excess, we see no reason to require recognition of a gain, and we do not believe that Congress intended for any gain to be recognized.

PROBLEM 14-3

Landlord owns real estate that may be contaminated enough to create CERCLA liability, and that has a basis of $100,000 and a fair market value of $500,000. Landlord contributes the property to a new, wholly owned corporation, Shell, Inc.

(a) Assume the CERCLA liability in the amount of $400,000 ripened before formation of the corporation. What result under § 357?

(b) Now assume the CERCLA liability is merely contingent at the time of the transfer. What result?

J. THE CONTROL REQUIREMENT

Read § 368(c).

Unlike its partnership analog § 721, the corporate tax provisions require that the transferors of property to a corporation be "in control" as defined in § 368(c) immediately after the exchange. It is important to note that control need not arise as a result of the exchange itself. Section 351 also applies where the transferor or transferors were already in control of the corporation, so that § 351 applies to transfers to both preexisting and newly created corporations.

REV. RUL. 59-259
1959-2 C.B. 115

The term "control" as defined in section 368(c) of the Internal Revenue Code of 1954 requires the ownership of stock possessing at least 80 percent of the total combined voting power of all classes of voting stock and the ownership of at least 80 percent of the total number of shares of each class of outstanding non-voting stock.

Advice has been requested whether "control" as defined in section 368(c) of the Internal Revenue Code of 1954 requires ownership of at least 80 percent of the total number of shares of each class of nonvoting stock for the purposes of section 351 of the Code.

Certain persons transferred property to a corporation in exchange for voting and non-voting stock, i.e., 83 percent of the Class A voting common stock, 83 percent of the Class A non-voting common stock, and 22 percent of the non-voting preferred stock. However, due to the relative number of non-voting common and preferred shares outstanding, these persons owned more than 80 percent of the total number of shares of the outstanding non-voting stock.

Section 351 of the Code provides, in effect, that no gain or loss shall be recognized to the transferors of property to a corporation if immediately after the transfer, the transferors are in "control" of the corporation as defined by section 368(c) of the Code.

Section 368(c) of such Code in defining "control" states, in part, as follows:
... the term "control" means the ownership of stock possessing at least 80 percent of the total combined voting power of all classes of stock entitled to vote and at least 80 percent of the total number of shares of all other classes of stock of the corporation.

The legislative history of section 368(c) of the Code indicates a congressional intent that ownership of each class of non-voting stock is required. The provisions of what is now section 368(c) of the Code were first enacted into law as section 202(c)(3) of the Revenue Act of 1921. That section as originally passed by the House of Representatives (H.R. 8245, 67th Cong., ... (1921)), defined "control" as the ownership of:
... at least 80 per centum of the voting stock and 80 per centum of all other classes of stock of the corporation....

The section was reported out of the Senate and enacted into law in a form substantially identical to its present form, retaining the reference to classes of non-voting stock. It is apparent, therefore, that the words "classes of stock" as used in section 368(c) of the Code refers to ownership of 80 percent of the total number of shares of each class of non-voting stock, as there is no other logical reason for retaining the words "classes of stock" in section 202(c)(3) of the Revenue Act of 1921.

Moreover, percentage ownership of the number of non-voting shares outstanding, as contrasted to percentage ownership of each class of non-voting shares, is ordinarily of no significance and can lead to results which are inconsistent with the statutory scheme and clear congressional purpose. Ownership of large numbers of non-voting shares in a multi-class stock structure would not necessarily assure, in itself, the continuation of substantial proprietary interests in modified corporate forms as contemplated by the statute. *See* section 1.368-1 of the Income Tax Regulations.

In view of the foregoing, it is held that "control" as defined by section 368(c) requires ownership of stock possessing at least 80 percent of the total combined voting power of all classes of voting stock and the ownership of at least 80 percent of the total number of shares of each class of outstanding non-voting stock. Therefore, a transfer of property under the above circumstances does not constitute a transfer to a controlled corporation within the purview of section 351 of the Code.

J. THE CONTROL REQUIREMENT

Classes of Stock. A problem may arise when some transferors provide "hard" assets such as cash or appreciated property which is easily valued and convertible to cash, and others provide "softer" assets such as goodwill of a going business, intellectual property or services. The contributors of "hard" assets will often desire some guarantee of the safety of their capital in the form of a privileged return from earnings and or first rights to the corporate property upon liquidation of the new corporation if it fails. The provider of soft assets, on the other hand, will often want an equal voice in management and equal enjoyment of future growth of the business. These competing goals cannot easily be met by issuing a single class of common stock to all transferors. The problem could be solved by issuing corporate debt to providers of hard assets in addition to stock, thus giving them a preferred claim to the extent of the debt, but debt ("securities") does not qualify for tax-free treatment under § 351. Securities are "boot" and will trigger gain of appreciated property. Also, securities do not count toward the control requirement. One solution is to issue more than one class of stock. All stock, including preferred stock, may be received tax-free under § 351, and all classes of stock count toward the control requirement.

> *To illustrate*: Money, Brains, and Land wish to form a computer corporation by contributing their respective assets in exchange for stock. Brains will contribute sufficient cash to meet the 10% requirement as a transferor, but will contribute 90% services and goodwill from his former computer business. Money and Land will contribute property of equal value, but want a guaranteed return before any profits are paid to Brains, and want first call on the corporate assets in liquidation. Brains, on the other hand, wants a full third of the stock, which implies an equal share in profits and assets in liquidation. Both Brains and Land (whose property is appreciated) want the transfers to qualify under § 351. A solution: issue voting preferred stock to Money and Land which pays a guaranteed return before any dividend can be paid on the common and which enjoys preference in liquidation, and issue common stock to Brains.

PROBLEM 14-4

Assume that Mrs. Small is a cofounder of Newco, Inc. She expects to receive 5% of the stock when the corporation is formed. Assume that she plans to transfer her dump truck which has a basis of $10,000 and a value of $5,000 to the corporation and plans to report a loss on the transaction. How might you take advantage of Rev. Rul. 59-259 to allow her to report a loss? What if the other 95% of the stock were going to be issued to her sons and daughters?

K. PROPERTY TRANSFERRED IN EXCHANGE AND TRANSFERORS' CONTROL

Read Reg. § 1.351-1(a).

Section 351 is laconic in its description of how the exchange is expected to take place. The Regulations make it clear that the exchanges by several persons need not be simultaneous, as long as all the transfers are pursuant to a prearranged plan. This is an important relaxation of what might be a rigid set of rules and prevents panic over precise closing dates. Also, it has the benefit of protecting efficient taxpayers from their indolent colleagues. For example, if two shareholders plan to take over an existing company by making large contributions to it so that together they wind up with at least 80% control, the first shareholder can diligently make her contribution while waiting, at least for a little while, for her colleague to get around to it.

The term *immediately* after the exchange suggests that a transferor can dump stock immediately after receiving it without breaking the control requirement.

JAMES v. COMMISSIONER
53 T.C. 63 (1969)

SIMPSON, JUDGE.

....

The issue for decision is whether the transaction by which Mr. James and Mr. Talbot acquired stock in a corporation was taxable or whether such transaction was tax free under section 351 of the Internal Revenue Code of 1954. The answer to the question thus posed with respect to each person depends on the determination of whether Mr. James received his stock in exchange for a transfer of property or as compensation for services.

Findings of Fact

....

For many years, Mr. James was a builder, real estate promoter, and developer with offices in Myrtle Beach, S.C. He has held the office of vice president of the National Association of Home Builders and was chairman of the association's Senior Citizens Housing Committee. During 1963, the James Construction Co. was licensed by the State of South Carolina to engage in the business of general contracting.

On January 12, 1963, Mr. and Mrs. Talbot entered into an agreement with Mr. James for the promotion and construction of a rental apartment project.... The agreement provided that on completion of the project the parties would form a corporation to take title to the project. The voting stock in such corporation was to be distributed one-half to the Talbots and one-half to Mr. James.... The Talbots agreed to transfer to the corporation the land on which the apartment project was to be built, such land to be the only asset contributed by the Talbots

K. PROPERTY TRANSFERRED IN EXCHANGE AND TRANSFERORS' CONTROL 275

to the venture. Mr. James agreed "to promote the project ... and ... [to] be responsible for the planning, architectural work, construction, landscaping, legal fees, and loan processing of the entire project." The agreement gave him until January 1, 1964, to promote the project....

After the execution of the January 12 agreement, Mr. James began negotiations to fulfill his part of the contract. He made arrangements with an attorney and an architectural firm to perform the work necessary to meet FHA requirements — development of legal documents, preparation of architectural plans, and the like; and he obtained from United Mortgagee Service Corp. (United Mortgagee), a lender, its agreement to finance the project and a commitment by FHA to insure the financing.... The attorney's and architect's fees were not paid by Mr. James but were paid out of the proceeds of the construction loan by the corporation subsequently established....

On November 5, 1963, Chicora Apartments, Inc. (Chicora), was granted, upon application of Messrs. Talbot and James, a corporate charter, stating its authorized capital stock to consist of 20 no-par common shares. On the same date, the land on which the apartment project was to be constructed was conveyed to Chicora by Mrs. Talbot in consideration for 10 shares of stock.... Chicora's board of directors determined that on the date of this conveyance the value of the real property so transferred was $44,000. Also on November 5, 1963, 10 shares of stock were issued to Mr. James. The minutes of a meeting of Chicora's board of directors held on that date state that those 10 shares were issued to Mr. James in consideration of his "transfer" to the corporation of the "following described property":

1. FHA Commitment issued pursuant to Title 2, Section 207 of the National Housing Act, whereby the FHA agrees to insure a mortgage loan in the amount of $850,700.00, on a parcel of land in Myrtle Beach, South Carolina, more particularly described in Schedule "A" hereto attached, provided 66 apartment units are constructed thereon in accordance with plans and specifications as prepared by Lyles, Bissett, Carlisle & Wolff, Architects-Engineers, of Columbia, South Carolina.

2. Commitment from United Mortgagee Servicing Corp., agreeing to make a mortgage loan on said property in the amount of $850,700.00 and also commitment from said mortgagee to make an interim construction loan in an identical amount.

3. Certain contracts and agreements which W. A. James over the past two years have [sic] worked out and developed in connection with the architectural and construction services required for said project.

4. The use of the finances and credit of W. A. James during the past two years (and including the construction period) in order to make it possible to proceed with the project.

Thus, as a result of these transactions, Chicora had outstanding all 20 of its authorized shares of stock....

Both Mr. and Mrs. James and Mr. and Mrs. Talbot deemed their receipt of Chicora common stock to be in return for a transfer of property to a controlled corporation under section 351. Accordingly, neither family reported any income from such receipt on their respective income tax returns for 1963. In his statutory notice of deficiency, the respondent determined that Mr. James received such stock, with a value of $22,000, for services rendered and not in exchange for property, and thus received taxable income in that amount. He further determined that the Talbot's transfer of property to Chicora did not meet the requirements of section 351, with the result that they should have recognized a long-term capital gain of $14,675 — the difference between $7,325, the basis of the land transferred, and $22,000, the value of the stock received.

Opinion

The first, and critical, issue for our determination is whether Mr. James received his Chicora stock in exchange for the transfer of property or as compensation for services. The petitioners argue that he received such stock in consideration of his transfer to Chicora of the FHA and United Mortgagee commitments and that such commitments constituted "property" within the meaning of section 351. The respondent does not appear to challenge the petitioners' implicit assertion that Mr. James was not expected to render future services to the corporation in exchange for the issuance of stock to him. Although the accuracy of this assertion is subject to some question, the state of the record is such that we must decide the issues as the parties have presented them. Thus, the sole question on this issue is whether Mr. James' personal services, which the petitioners freely admit were rendered, resulted in the development of a property right which was transferred to Chicora, within the meaning of section 351....

According to the petitioners' argument, Mr. James, as a result of the services performed by him, acquired certain contract rights which constituted property and which he transferred to Chicora. The fact that such rights resulted from the performance of personal services does not, in their view, disqualify them from being treated as property for purposes of section 351. In support of this position, the petitioners refer to situations involving the transfer of patents and secret processes. *James C. Hamrick*, 43 T.C. 21 (1964); *Lanova Corporation*, 17 T.C. 1178 (1952); *Ralph L. Evans*, 8 B.T.A. 543 (1927); Rev. Rul. 64-56, 1964-1 C.B. (Part 1) 133. *Cf. Roberts Co.*, 5 T.C. 1 (1945).

It is altogether clear that for purposes of section 351, not every right is to be treated as property. The second sentence of such section indicates that, whatever may be considered as property for purposes of local law, the performance of services, or the agreement to perform services, is not to be treated as a transfer of property for purposes of section 351. Thus, if in this case we have merely an agreement to perform services in exchange for stock of the corporation to be created, the performance of such services does not constitute the transfer of property within the meaning of section 351.

K. PROPERTY TRANSFERRED IN EXCHANGE AND TRANSFERORS' CONTROL

Although patents and secret processes — the product of services — are treated as property for purposes of section 351, we have carefully analyzed the arrangement in this case and have concluded that Mr. James did not transfer any property essentially like a patent or secret process; he merely performed services for Chicora. In January of 1963, he entered into an agreement to perform services for the corporation to be created. He was to secure the necessary legal and architectural work and to arrange for the financing of the project, and these were the services performed by him. Although he secured the services of the lawyer and the architect, they were paid for by the corporation. He put in motion the wheels that led to the FHA commitment, but it was not a commitment to him — it was a commitment to United Mortgagee to insure a loan to Chicora, a project sponsored by Mr. James. It was stipulated that under the FHA regulations, a commitment would not be issued to an individual, but only to a corporation. Throughout these arrangements, it was contemplated that a corporation would be created and that the commitment would run to the corporation....

The facts of this case are substantially similar to those in *United States v. Frazell*, 335 F.2d 487 (C.A. 5, 1964), *rehearing denied* 339 F.2d 885 (C.A. 5, 1964), *certiorari denied* 380 U.S. 961 (1965). In that case, the taxpayer, a geologist, investigated certain oil and gas properties to be acquired by a joint venture, and he was to receive an interest in the joint venture. However, before any transfer was made to him, a corporation was formed to take over the assets of the joint venture, and part of the stock was transferred to the taxpayer. It was not clear whether the taxpayer acquired an interest in the joint venture which was then exchanged for his share of the stock or whether he acquired the stock directly in exchange for the services performed by him. The court found that, in either event, the taxpayer received compensation for his services. If he received the stock in return for the services performed by him, such stock was taxable as compensation; and he did not transfer any property to the corporation within the meaning of section 351. *See also Mailloux v. Commissioner*, 320 F.2d 60 (C.A. 5, 1963), affirming on this issue a Memorandum Opinion of this Court.

The next question is whether the Talbots are taxable on the gain realized from the exchange of their land for Chicora stock. Section 351(a) applies only if immediately after the transfer those who transferred property in exchange for stock owned at least 80 percent of Chicora's stock. Sec. 368(c). Since Mr. James is not to be treated as a transferor of property, he cannot be included among those in control for purposes of this test. *Fahs v. Florida Machine & Foundry Co.*, 168 F.2d 957 (C.A. 5, 1948); *Mojonnier & Sons, Inc.*, 12 T.C. 837 (1949).... The transferors of property, the Talbots, did not have the required 80-percent control of Chicora immediately after the transfer, and therefore, their gain must be recognized. This result is inconsistent with the apparent meaning of the second sentence from the committee report, but the statutory scheme does not permit any other conclusion....

Decision will be entered for the respondent.

NOTES

1. *So what?* What were the tax implications to both incorporators as a result of the lack of control in *James*?

2. *Commercial v. noncommercial transactions*. The courts seem more willing to tolerate intended abandonment of control where the actions are based on estate planning or other personal motives as opposed to commercial purposes. It is therefore generally possible to have the transferees receive all of the stock from the corporation and then reduce ownership to under 80% by giving away stock to family members. *See, e.g., Wilgard Realty Co. v. Commissioner*, 127 F.2d 514 (2d. Cir.), *cert. denied*, 317 U.S. 655 (1942).

3. *What about options?* In *American Bantam Car Co. v. Commissioner*, 11 T.C. 397 (1948), *aff'd per curiam*, 177 F.2d 513 (3rd cir. 1949), *cert. denied*, 339 U.S. 920 (1950), the Tax Court held that a loss of control due to the exercise by nontransferors of a contractual right to acquire shares did not remove the protection of § 351, reasoning that the incorporators retained the right to cancel the contract at any time, and that the incorporation itself would have taken place with or without the subsequent transfers. If the transferors are bound at the time of incorporation to dispose of stock divesting them of control, however, or there is a preconceived plan to do so without which the incorporation would not have taken place, the control test is not met. *See, e.g., Intermountain Lumber Co.*, 65 T.C. 1025, 1031-32 (1976). The approach taken in *American Bantam Car* has the approval of the leading commentators. *See* B. Bittker & J. Eustice, Federal Income Taxation of Corporations and Shareholders ¶ 3.09[2] (6th ed. 1994).

L. BASIS OF TRANSFEROR'S STOCK

Read § 358(a), (b).

In general, the basis of stock in the transferor's hands will be the same as the basis of the property in the corporation's hands. The result, as with partnerships, is that the amount of basis has doubled through legal magic, with the possibility for gain or loss also doubling. For instance, if the property had a basis in excess of its value, the corporation could sell the property at a loss and the shareholder could sell his stock at a loss. The potential for proliferation of gains and losses is serious. For example, if the corporate recipient just described promptly formed its own subsidiary using the very same property, that would triple the amount of potential loss.

If the shareholder also receives boot, § 358(a)(2) gives the boot a basis equal to its value. Money obviously has to take a basis exactly equal to its face amount. The general result of boot is that it causes recognition of gain which is taxed and converted into basis in the boot. Any remaining unrecognized gain in the contributed property is deferred in the form of built-in gain in the stock received.

Boot also requires adjusting the transferor's basis in the stock received. § 358(a)(1). Starting with the same basis as the transferred property, the stock

L. BASIS OF TRANSFEROR'S STOCK

basis is then *decreased* by the amount of boot received (because boot is a disinvestment from the continuing business) and *increased* by the amount of gain recognized (to prevent double taxation of the same gain to the same person).

> *To illustrate*: Mr. Small transfers property with a basis of $30 and a value of $50 to Newco in exchange for $40 worth of Newco stock plus $10 cash. The cash is boot and is fully taxed. The stock has a basis of $30 ($30 substituted basis less $10 boot plus $10 gain recognized). The adjustments will not always be equal. If Mr. Small had received $25 worth of stock plus $25 cash, only $20 of the $25 boot would be taxable, because Mr. Small's realized gain is only $20 ($50 amount realized less $30 basis). But under § 358(a)(1) the full amount of boot must be subtracted from basis, which therefore equals $25 ($30 substituted basis less $25 boot plus $20 gain recognized). This gives the correct result because the stock is presumably worth $25 (the $50 property less $25 boot paid for it), and if sold, it should not trigger any additional gain, because the original $20 of built-in gain has already been fully taxed through the receipt of boot.

Section 358(d) provides a logical way to handle liabilities of the transferors or encumbrances on the property transferred to the corporation. It requires the transferor to reduce basis in the stock received as if the transferor had received cash boot in the amount of the liabilities. If this did not happen, the basis of the stock would be exaggerated and opportunity for artificial losses would arise. Remember, however, that this transferred-liability-as-boot treatment is limited to basis calculations under § 358; receipt of the deemed boot is generally *not* taxable and is protected by § 357(a).

> *To illustrate*: Mr. Small transfers property with a basis of $30 to Newco. In exchange he gets back stock and the assumption of a $10 debt which is associated with the property. Section 358(d) makes Mr. Small's basis in the stock $20. Assuming that the property has a fair market value of $50, ignoring the mortgage, we know that the unrealized gain on the property is $20 (i.e. $50 value minus $30 basis). We have just seen that the basis of the stock will be $20. We know that if the corporation sells the land, and the land is the only asset, it will get a net amount of $40. That means that the stock must also be worth $40. Now, if Mr. Small sells the stock he will receive $40 but will have a basis of only $20. This means that he will report a $20 gain on his tax return in the year he sells the stock, and this is exactly correct; it is identical to the gain that he would have reported had he sold the land directly. But for § 358(d), his basis in the

stock would have been too high, and a loophole would have been created.

Stock basis is not reduced for the assumption of liabilities which would have been deductible, such as accounts payable. § 358(d)(2). This exception parallels the exception of § 357(c)(3), under which deductible liabilities do not count in determining whether the aggregate liabilities transferred exceed the aggregate basis of the assets transferred.

Holding period for stock. The holding period for stock received tax-free consists of its actual holding period from the date of the exchange plus the transferor's holding period for the transferred property which is "tacked" on if the property was a capital asset or § 1231 property. § 1223(1). If the transferred property consisted of a mix of capital assets, 1231 assets, and noncapital assets, which is usually the case when a proprietorship or partnership is incorporated, each share will have a divided holding period which is allocated according to the fair market value of the transferred property. Rev. Rul. 85-164, 1985-2 C.B. 117.

To illustrate: Return to Rev. Rul. 68-55, *supra* Section H, and observe that three different assets were exchanged for one class of stock (plus cash). Two of the assets were capital, of which only one had already been held long-term, and the third asset was noncapital. Each share of stock will have a split holding period in proportion to the fair market value of the assets, respectively 20%, 30%, and 50%. Thus, if any share is sold on the day after the exchange, 20% of the proceeds will be long-term and 80% will be taxable as ordinary income. When the short-term capital asset becomes long-term, the ratio will be 50-50.

M. CORPORATION'S BASIS FOR PROPERTY IT RECEIVES

Read § 362(a).

The corporation will generally take the shareholder's basis increased by the amount of gain that the shareholder recognizes on the transfer. If the corporation receives property subject to a liability or assumes liabilities, this will have no impact on the basis of the transferred property, except to the extent that the transferor recognizes gain under § 357.

PROBLEM 14-5

Two individuals, A and B, decide to form X Corporation. A transfers land worth $100,000 (basis $120,000) for 50 shares of stock in X corp. worth $100,000. B transfers a building worth $60,000 (basis $30,000) and cash of $40,000 for 50 shares of stock in X corp. worth $100,000. *See* § 351(a) and Reg. § 1.351-1.

M. CORPORATION'S BASIS FOR PROPERTY IT RECEIVES

a) How much gain or loss do A and B recognize under § 351?

b) What is the basis of the shares held by A? by B?

c) How much gain or loss does the X corporation recognize as a result of the transfer?

d) What is X's basis in the property it received?

e) What is X's holding period in the assets it received?

PROBLEM 14-6

C, an accrual method taxpayer, transfers equipment worth $65,000 (basis $35,000) and $25,000 of accounts receivable to her wholly owned corporation. In return, C receives stock in the corporation worth $50,000 and a note receivable from the corporation with a face amount and value of $40,000. C had used the property, for which she originally paid $100,000, in her sole proprietorship for several years before she incorporated.

a) How much gain or loss does C recognize as a result of the transfer, and what is the character of the gain or loss?

b) What is C's basis in the stock and note received as a result of the transfer, and what is the holding period?

c) How much gain or loss does the corporation recognize as a result of the transfer?

d) What is the corporation's basis in the equipment and accounts receivable received from C as a result of the transfer, and what is the holding period?

PROBLEM 14-7

D owns a rental building held for investment worth $200,000 (basis $150,000). The building is subject to a long-standing nonrecourse mortgage which has a balance of $100,000. D transfers the building, which he has owned for six months, to his wholly owned corporation in return for 1,000 shares of stock in the corporation worth $100,000.

a) How much gain or loss does D recognize as a result of the transfer?

b) What is D's basis in the stock received, and what is the holding period? *See* § 358(a) and (d) and Reg. § 1.358-3.

c) How much gain or loss does the corporation recognize as a result of the transfer?

d) What is the corporation's basis in the building received?

PROBLEM 14-8

E owns a rental building held for investment worth $200,000 (basis $110,000). The building, which he had held for six months, is subject to a mortgage which has a balance of $150,000. E transfers the building to his wholly owned corporation in return for 500 shares of stock in the corporation worth $50,000.

a) How much gain or loss does E recognize as a result of the transfer? What is the character of the gain or loss?

b) What is E's basis in the stock received, and what is the holding period? *See* § 358(a) and (d) and Reg. § 1.358-3.

c) How much gain or loss does the corporation recognize as a result of the transfer?

d) What is the corporation's basis in the building received?

N. SPECIAL PROBLEMS OF MIDSTREAM INCORPORATION

Corporations may be formed to begin a new business, but they also may be used to incorporate an existing business which was carried on as a proprietorship or partnership. In such cases, there would typically be unpaid accounts payable and receivable and a variety of other bookkeeping entries that have a potential for mischief.

HEMPT BROS., INC. v. UNITED STATES
490 F.2d 1172 (3d Cir. 1974)

ALDISERT, CIRCUIT JUDGE.

In this appeal by a corporate taxpayer from a grant of summary judgment in favor of the government in a claim for refund, we are called upon to decide the proper treatment of accounts receivable and of inventory transferred from a cash basis partnership to a corporation organized to continue the business under Section 351(a). This appeal illustrates the conflict between the statutory purpose of Section 351, postponement of recognition of gain or loss, and the assignment of income and tax benefit doctrines.

The facts were wholly stipulated; therefore, they may be summarized as set forth by the government in its brief: ...

From 1942 until February 28, 1957, a partnership comprised of Loy T. Hempt, J. F. Hempt, Max C. Hempt, and the George L. Hempt Estate was engaged in the business of quarrying and selling stone, sand, gravel, and slag; manufacturing and selling ready-mix concrete and bituminous material; constructing roads, highways, and streets, primarily for the Pennsylvania Department of Highways and various political subdivisions of Pennsylvania, and constructing driveways, parking lots, street and water lines, and related accessories.

The partnership maintained its books and records, and filed its partnership income tax returns, on the basis of a calendar year and on the cash method of accounting, so that no income was reported until actually received in cash. Accordingly, in computing its income for federal income tax purposes, the partnership did not take uncollected receivables into income, and inventories were not used in the calculation of its taxable income, although both accounts

N. SPECIAL PROBLEMS OF MIDSTREAM INCORPORATION

receivable reflecting sales already made and physical inventories existed to a substantial extent at the end of each of the partnership's taxable years. Rather than using the inventory method of accounting, the partnership deducted the costs of its physical inventories of sand, gravel, and stone as incurred.

On March 1, 1957, the partnership business and most of its assets were transferred to the taxpayer solely in exchange for taxpayer's capital stock, the 12,000 shares of which were issued to the four members of the partnership. These shares constituted 100% of the issued and outstanding shares of the taxpayer. This transfer was made pursuant to Section 351(a) of the Internal Revenue Code of 1954; .... Thereafter, the taxpayer conducted the business formerly conducted by the partnership.

Among the assets transferred by the partnership to the taxpayer for taxpayer's shares of stock were accounts receivable in the amount of $662,824.40 arising from performance of construction projects, sales of stone, sand, gravel, etc., and rental of equipment prior to March 1, 1957. Also among the assets transferred were physical inventories of sand, gravel, and stone, with respect to which the partnership had deducted costs of $351,266.05 and the value of which was no less than $351,266.05.

Commencing with its initial fiscal year (which) ended February 28, 1958, taxpayer maintained its books and filed its corporation income tax returns on the cash method of accounting and, accordingly, did not take uncollected receivables into income and did not use inventories in the calculation of its taxable income. In its taxable years ending in 1958, 1959, and 1960, taxpayer collected the respective amounts of $533,247.87, $125,326.71 and $4,249.72 of the accounts receivable in the aggregate amount of $662,824.40 (sic) that had been transferred to it, and included those amounts in income in computing its income for its federal income tax returns for those years, respectively....

The Commissioner of Internal Revenue assessed deficiencies in taxpayer's federal income taxes for its fiscal years ending February 28, 1958, and 1959. The taxpayer paid the amounts in 1964, and in 1965 filed claims for refund of $621,218.09 plus assessed interest. The claims were disallowed in full on September 24, 1968, and the district court action was timely instituted on December 5, 1968.

The district court held: (1) taxpayer was properly taxable upon collections made with respect to accounts receivable which were transferred to it in conjunction with the Section 351 incorporation, ...

I.

Taxpayer argues here, as it did in the district court, that because the term 'property' as used in Section 351 does not embrace accounts receivable, the Commissioner lacked statutory authority to apply principles associated with Section 351. The district court properly rejected the legal interpretation urged by the taxpayer.

The definition of Section 351 "property" has been extensively treated by the Court of Claims in *E.I. Du Pont de Nemours and Co. v. United States*, 471 F.2d 1211, 1218-1219 (Ct. Cl. 1973), describing the transfer of a non-exclusive license to make, use and sell area herbicides under French patents:

> Unless there is some special reason intrinsic to ... (Section 351) ... the general word "property" has a broad reach in tax law.... For section 351, in particular, courts have advocated a generous definition of "property, ... and it has been suggested in one capital gains case that nonexclusive licenses can be viewed as property though not as capital assets....

We see no adequate reason for refusing to follow these leads.

We fail to perceive any special reason why a restrictive meaning should be applied to accounts receivables so as to exclude them from the general meaning of "property." Receivables possess the usual capabilities and attributes associated with jurisprudential concepts of property law. They may be identified, valued, and transferred. Moreover, their role in an ongoing business must be viewed in the context of Section 351 application. The presence of accounts receivable is a normal, rather than an exceptional accoutrement of the type of business included by Congress in the transfer to a corporate form. They are "commonly thought of in the commercial world as a positive business asset." *Du Pont v. United States, supra*, at 1218. As aptly put by the district court: "There is a compelling reason to construe 'property' to include ... (accounts receivable): a new corporation needs working capital, and accounts receivable can be an important source of liquidity." *Hempt Bros., Inc. v. United States, supra*, at 1176. In any event, this court had no difficulty in characterizing a sale of receivables as "property" within the purview of the "no gain or loss" provision of Section 337 as a "qualified sale of property within a 12-month period." *Citizens Acceptance Corp. v. United States*, 462 F.2d 751, 756 (3d Cir. 1972).

The taxpayer next makes a strenuous argument that "the government is seeking to tax the wrong person." It contends that the assignment of income doctrine as developed by the Supreme Court applies to a Section 351 transfer of accounts receivable so that the transferor, not the transferee-corporation, bears the corresponding tax liability. It argues that the assignment of income doctrine dictates that where the right to receive income is transferred to another person in a transaction not giving rise to tax at the time of transfer, the transferor is taxed on the income when it is collected by the transferee; that the only requirement for its application is a transfer of a right to receive ordinary income; and that since the transferred accounts receivable are a present right to future income, the sole requirement for the application of the doctrine is squarely met. In essence, this is a contention that the nonrecognition provision of Section 351 is in conflict with the assignment of income doctrine and that Section 351 should be subordinated thereto. Taxpayer relies on the seminal case of *Lucas v. Earl*, 281 U.S. 111, 74 L. Ed. 731, 50 S. Ct. 241 (1930), and its progeny for support of its proposition that the application of the doctrine is mandated whenever one transfers a right to receive ordinary income.

On its part, the government concedes that a taxpayer may sell for value a claim to income otherwise his own and he will be taxable upon the proceeds of the sale. Such was the case in *Commissioner v. P. G. Lake, Inc.*, 356 U.S. 260, 2 L. Ed. 2d 743, 78 S. Ct. 691 (1958), in which the taxpayer-corporation assigned its oil payment right to its president in consideration for his cancellation of a $600,000 loan. Viewing the oil payment right as a right to receive future income, the Court applied the reasoning of the assignment of income doctrine, normally applicable to a gratuitous assignment, and held that the consideration received by the taxpayer-corporation was taxable as ordinary income since it essentially was a substitute for that which would otherwise be received at a future time as ordinary income.

Turning to the facts of this case, we note that here there was the transfer of accounts receivable from the partnership to the corporation pursuant to Section 351. We view these accounts receivable as a present right to receive future income. In consideration of the transfer of this right, the members of the partnership received stock — a valid consideration. The consideration, therefore, was essentially a substitute for that which would otherwise be received at a future time as ordinary income to the cash basis partnership. Consequently, the holding in *Lake* would normally apply, and income would ordinarily be realized, and thereby taxable, by the cash basis partnership-transferor at the time of receipt of the stock.

But the terms and purpose of Section 351 have to be reckoned with. By its explicit terms Section 351 expresses the Congressional intent that transfers of property for stock or securities will not result in recognition. It therefore becomes apparent that this case vividly illustrates how Section 351 sometimes comes into conflict with another provision of the Internal Revenue Code or a judicial doctrine, and requires a determination of which of two conflicting doctrines will control.

As we must, when we try to reconcile conflicting doctrines in the revenue law, we endeavor to ascertain a controlling Congressional mandate. Section 351 has been described as a deliberate attempt by Congress to facilitate the incorporation of ongoing businesses and to eliminate any technical constructions which are economically unsound.[7]

---

[7] "One of the purposes of this section (Section 202(c)(3) of the Revenue Act of 1921) was to permit changes in form (of business) involving no change in substance to be made without undue restriction from the tax laws." Note, Section 351 of the Internal Revenue Code and "Mid-Stream" Incorporations, 38 U. Cin. L. Rev. 96 (1969). *See*, S. Rep. No. 275, 67th Cong. 1st Sess. 11 (1921). This intention is also reflected in the report of the House of Representatives accompanying 351 of the Internal Revenue Code of 1954. H.R. Rep. No. 1337, 83rd Cong. 2d Sess. 34 (1954). The House Ways and Means Committee recommended that nonrecognition treatment be granted for incorporation, reorganization and certain other types of exchanges to "permit business to go

Appellant-taxpayer seems to recognize this and argues that application of the *Lake* rationale when accounts receivable are transferred would not create any undue hardship to an incorporating taxpayer. "All a taxpayer (transferor) need do is withhold the earned income items and collect them, transferring the net proceeds to the Corporation. Indeed ... the transferor should retain both accounts receivable and accounts payable to avoid income recognition at the time of transfer and to have sufficient funds with which to pay accounts payable. Where the taxpayer (transferor is on the cash method of accounting (as here)), the deduction of the accounts payable would be applied against the income generated by the accounts receivable."...

While we cannot fault the general principle "that income be taxed to him who earns it," to adopt taxpayer's argument would be to hamper the incorporation of ongoing businesses; additionally it would impose technical constructions which are economically and practically unsound. None of the cases cited by taxpayer, including *Lake* itself, persuades us otherwise. In *Lake* the Court was required to decide whether the proceeds from the assignment of the oil payment right were taxable as ordinary income or as long term capital gains. Observing that the provision for long term capital gains treatment "has always been narrowly construed so as to protect the revenue against artful devices," 356 U.S. at 265, 78 S. Ct. at 694, the Court predicated its holding upon an emphatic distinction between a conversion of a capital investment — "income-producing property" — and an assignment of income per se. "The substance of what was assigned was the right to receive future income. The substance of what was received was the present value of income which the recipient would otherwise obtain in the future." *Ibid.*, at 266, 78 S. Ct. at 695. A Section 351 issue was not presented in *Lake*. Therefore the case does not control in weighing the conflict between the general rule of assignment of income and the Congressional purpose of nonrecognition upon the incorporation of an ongoing business.

We are persuaded that, on balance, the teachings of *Lake* must give way in this case to the broad Congressional interest in facilitating the incorporation of ongoing businesses. As desirable as it is to afford symmetry in revenue law, we do not intend to promulgate a hard and fast rule. We believe that the problems posed by the clash of conflicting internal revenue doctrines are more properly determined by the circumstances of each case. Here we are influenced by the fact that the subject of the assignment was accounts receivable for partnership's goods and services sold in the regular course of business, that the change of business form from partnership to corporation had a basic business purpose and was not designed for the purpose of deliberate tax avoidance, and by the conviction that

---

forward with the readjustments required by existing conditions" and to prevent "taxpayers from taking colorable losses in wash sales and other fictitious exchanges." *See* H.R. Rep. 350 67th Cong., 1st Sess. 10 (1921). The Senate Finance Committee added that such treatment would eliminate "many technical constructions which are economically unsound." *See* S. Rep. 275, 67th Cong. 1st Sess. 12 (1921). *Weiss, supra* 41 Ind. L.J. 666 n.4 (1966).

N. SPECIAL PROBLEMS OF MIDSTREAM INCORPORATION

the totality of circumstances here presented fit the mold of the Congressional intent to give nonrecognition to a transfer of a total business from a non-corporate to a corporate form.

But this too must be said. Even though Section 351(a) immunizes the transferor from immediate tax consequences, Section 358 retains for the transferors a potential income tax liability to be realized and recognized upon a subsequent sale or exchange of the stock certificates received. As to the transferee-corporation, the tax basis of the receivables will be governed by Section 362.

[The other issues are omitted.]

We have carefully considered each of appellant's contentions and have concluded that the judgment of the district court will be affirmed.

NOTES

1. *Tax benefit rule.* In *Nash v. United States*, 398 U.S. 1 (1970), the Supreme Court resolved a long-standing uncertainty about how previously deducted reserves for bad debts should be treated when a business is transferred from a proprietorship to a corporation. The Supreme Court held that the taxpayer did not have to take his bad-debt reserves into income when he transferred his receivables, but instead was simply treated as having transferred only the net value of his receivables. For example, if a proprietor who has a $10 reserve for bad debts transfers $100 of receivables, the *Nash* case would allow him to treat the transfer as if he contributed $90 worth of receivable to the corporation rather than forcing him to report $10 of tax benefit income and a $100 transfer to the corporation.

2. *Some tax planning ideas.* One should not assume that tax advisors simply suggest their clients dump all of their business assets into a corporation. For example, they may suggest that the contributor engage in any one of the following planning devices:

(a) Retention of property that can be sold at a loss, or retention of nondepreciable real estate that can be leased to the corporation. This can permit the owners to drain off corporate income in a deductible manner and shift it to owners of the land, which might be a benefit to children who are in a low tax bracket.

(b) Sale (rather than contribution for stock) of property to the corporation at a loss, provided § 267(a) can be avoided.

(c) Sale of property to the corporation in exchange for a long-term debt obligation in order to drain off corporate income as interest.

(d) Sale of appreciated land to a corporation in exchange for an installment obligation, if the corporation then subdivides the land and generates ordinary income from sales. This may assure the transferor of a long-term capital gain while shifting ordinary income to the corporation which may be taxed in a lower bracket.

(e) Avoiding § 351 altogether, say by issuing too much stock in exchange for services.

3. *Is a business purpose required for a § 351 transaction?* The government's position is unsurprising: yes. *See* Rev. Rul. 70-140 1970-1 C.B. 73. The Tax Court agrees. *See West Coast Mktg. Corp. v. Commissioner*, 46 T.C. 32 (1966), in which a purported § 351 transaction was ignored for tax purposes and treated as a taxable sale because the transferors immediately disposed of the stock and because the acquirer promptly liquidated the controlled corporation, indicating that its sole purpose was to avoid taxation of the transferors' gain.

REV. RUL. 84-111
1984-2 C.B. 88

....

Issue

Does Rev. Rul. 70-239, 1970-1 C.B. 74, still represent the Service's position with respect to the three situations described therein?

Facts

The three situations described in Rev. Rul. 70-239 involve partnerships X, Y, and Z, respectively. Each partnership used the accrual method of accounting and had assets and liabilities consisting of cash, equipment, and accounts payable. The liabilities of each partnership did not exceed the adjusted basis of its assets. The three situations are as follows:

Situation 1

X transferred all of its assets to newly-formed corporation R in exchange for all the outstanding stock of R and the assumption by R of X's liabilities. X then terminated by distributing all the stock of R to X's partners in proportion to their partnership interests.

Situation 2

Y distributed all of its assets and liabilities to its partners in proportion to their partnership interests in a transaction that constituted a termination of Y under section 708(b)(1)(A) of the Code. The partners then transferred all the assets received from Y to newly-formed corporation S in exchange for all the outstanding stock of S and the assumption by S of Y's liabilities that had been assumed by the partners.

Situation 3

The partners of Z transferred their partnership interests in Z to newly-formed corporation T in exchange for all the outstanding stock of T. This exchange terminated Z and all of its assets and liabilities became assets and liabilities of T.

N. SPECIAL PROBLEMS OF MIDSTREAM INCORPORATION

In each situation, the steps taken by X, Y, and Z, and the partners of X, Y, and Z, were parts of a plan to transfer the partnership operations to a corporation organized for valid business reasons in exchange for its stock and were not devices to avoid or evade recognition of gain. Rev. Rul. 70-239 holds that because the federal income tax consequences of the three situations are the same, each partnership is considered to have transferred its assets and liabilities to a corporation in exchange for its stock under section 351 of the Internal Revenue Code, followed by a distribution of the stock to the partners in liquidation of the partnership.

Law and Analysis

Section 351(a) of the Code provides that no gain or loss will be recognized if property is transferred to a corporation by one or more persons solely in exchange for stock or securities in such corporation and immediately after the exchange such person or persons are in control (as defined in section 368(c)) of the corporation.

Section 1.351-1(a)(1) of the Income Tax Regulations provides that, as used in section 351 of the Code, the phrase "one or more persons" includes individuals, trusts, estates, partnerships, associations, companies, or corporations. To be in control of the transferee corporation, such person or persons must own immediately after the transfer stock possessing at least 80 percent of the total combined voting power of all classes of stock entitled to vote and at least 80 percent of the total number of shares of all other classes of stock of such corporation.

Section 358(a) of the Code provides that in the case of an exchange to which section 351 applies, the basis of the property permitted to be received under such section without the recognition of gain or loss will be the same as that of the property exchanged, decreased by the amount of any money received by the taxpayer.

Section 358(d) of the Code provides that where, as part of the consideration to the taxpayer, another party to the exchange assumed a liability of the taxpayer or acquired from the taxpayer property subject to a liability, such assumption or acquisition (in the amount of the liability) will, for purposes of section 358, be treated as money received by the taxpayer on the exchange.

Section 362(a) of the Code provides that a corporation's basis in property acquired in a transaction to which section 351 applies will be the same as it would be in the hands of the transferor.

Under section 708(b)(1)(A) of the Code, a partnership is terminated if no part of any business, financial operation, or venture of the partnership continues to be carried on by any of its partners in a partnership. Under section 708(b)(1)(B), a partnership terminates if within a 12-month period there is a sale or exchange of 50 percent or more of the total interest in partnership capital and profits.

Section 732(b) of the Code provides that the basis of property other than money distributed by a partnership in a liquidation of a partner's interest shall be an amount equal to the adjusted basis of the partner's interest in the partnership reduced by any money distributed. Section 732(c) of the Code provides rules for the allocation of a partner's basis in a partnership interest among the assets received in a liquidating distribution.

Section 735(b) of the Code provides that a partner's holding period for property received in a distribution from a partnership (other than with respect to certain inventory items defined in section 751(d)(2)) includes the partnership's holding period, as determined under section 1223, with respect to such property.

Section 1223(1) of the Code provides that where property received in an exchange acquires the same basis, in whole or in part, as the property surrendered in the exchange, the holding period of the property received includes the holding period of the property surrendered to the extent such surrendered property was a capital asset or property described in section 1231. Under section 1223(2), the holding period of a taxpayer's property, however acquired, includes the period during which the property was held by any other person if that property has the same basis, in whole or in part, in the taxpayer's hands as it would have in the hands of such other person.

Section 741 of the Code provides that in the case of a sale or exchange of an interest in a partnership, gain or loss shall be recognized to the transferor partner. Such gain or loss shall be considered as a gain or loss from the sale or exchange of a capital asset, except as otherwise provided in section 751.

Section 751(a) of the Code provides that the amount of money or the fair value of property received by a transferor partner in exchange for all or part of such partner's interest in the partnership attributable to unrealized receivables of the partnership, or to inventory items of the partnership that have appreciated substantially in value, shall be considered as an amount realized from the sale or exchange of property other than a capital asset.

Section 752(a) of the Code provides that any increase in a partner's share of the liabilities of a partnership, or any increase in a partner's individual liabilities by reason of the assumption by the partner of partnership liabilities, will be considered as a contribution of money by such partner to the partnership.

Section 752(b) of the Code provides that any decrease in a partner's share of the liabilities of a partnership, or any decrease in a partner's individual liabilities by reason of the assumption by the partnership of such individual liabilities, will be considered as a distribution of money to the partner by the partnership. Under section 733(1) of the Code, the basis of a partner's interest in the partnership is reduced by the amount of money received in a distribution that is not in liquidation of the partnership.

Section 752(d) of the Code provides that in the case of a sale or exchange of an interest in a partnership, liabilities shall be treated in the same manner as liabilities in connection with the sale or exchange of property not associated with partnerships.

The premise in Rev. Rul. 70-239 that the federal income tax consequences of the three situations described therein would be the same, without regard to which

N. SPECIAL PROBLEMS OF MIDSTREAM INCORPORATION

of the three transactions was entered into, is incorrect. As described below, depending on the format chosen for the transfer to a controlled corporation, the basis and holding periods of the various assets received by the corporation and the basis and holding periods of the stock received by the former partners can vary.

Additionally, Rev. Rul. 70-239 raises questions about potential adverse tax consequences to taxpayers in certain cases involving collapsible corporations defined in section 341 of the Code, personal holding companies described in section 542, small business corporations defined in section 1244, and electing small business corporations defined in section 1371. Recognition of the three possible methods to incorporate a partnership will enable taxpayers to avoid the above potential pitfalls and will facilitate flexibility with respect to the basis and holding periods of the assets received in the exchange.

Holding

[To recapitulate the facts for the benefit of readers who are confused by now:

In situation 1 the partnership transferred its assets to the corporation, and then terminated by distributing the corporate stock;

In situation 2 the partnership made a liquidating distribution of its assets to the partners, who in turn transferred the distributed assets to the corporation; and,

In situation 3 the partners contributed their partnership interests to the corporation in exchange for stock, with the partnership terminating its existence and the corporation winding up with the assets of the former partnership].

Rev. Rul. 70-239 no longer represents the Service's position. The Service's current position is set forth below, and for each situation, the methods described and the underlying assumptions and purposes must be satisfied for the conclusions of this revenue ruling to be applicable.

Situation 1

Under section 351 of the Code, gain or loss is not recognized by X on the transfer by X of all of its assets to R in exchange for R's stock and the assumption by R of X's liabilities.

Under section 362(a) of the Code, R's basis in the assets received from X equals their basis to X immediately before their transfer to R. Under section 358(a), the basis to X of the stock received from R is the same as the basis to X of the assets transferred to R, reduced by the liabilities assumed by R, which assumption is treated as a payment of money to X under section 358(d). In addition, the assumption by R of X's liabilities decreased each partner's share of the partnership liabilities, thus, decreasing the basis of each partner's partnership interest pursuant to sections 752 and 733.

On distribution of the stock to X's partners, X terminated under section 708(b)(1)(A) of the Code. Pursuant to section 732(b), the basis of the stock distributed to the partners in liquidation of their partnership interests is, with respect to each partner, equal to the adjusted basis of the partner's interest in the partnership.

Under section 1223(1) of the Code, X's holding period for the stock received in the exchange includes its holding period in the capital assets and section 1231 assets transferred (to the extent that the stock was received in exchange for such assets). To the extent the stock was received in exchange for neither capital nor section 1231 assets, X's holding period for such stock begins on the day following the date of the exchange. See Rev. Rul. 70-598, 1970-2 C.B. 168. Under section 1223(2), R's holding period in the assets transferred to it includes X's holding period. When X distributed the R stock to its partners, under sections 735(b) and 1223, the partners' holding periods included X's holding period of the stock. Furthermore, such distribution will not violate the control requirement of section 368 (c) of the Code.

Situation 2

On the transfer of all of Y's assets to its partners, Y terminated under section 708(b)(1)(A) of the Code, and, pursuant to section 732(b), the basis of the assets (other than money) distributed to the partners in liquidation of their partnership interests in Y was, with respect to each partner, equal to the adjusted basis of the partner's interest in Y, reduced by the money distributed. Under section 752, the decrease in Y's liabilities resulting from the transfer to Y's partners was offset by the partners' corresponding assumption of such liabilities so that the net effect on the basis of each partner's interest in Y, with respect to the liabilities transferred, was zero.

Under section 351 of the Code, gain or loss is not recognized by Y's former partners on the transfer to S in exchange for its stock and the assumption of Y's liabilities, of the assets of Y received by Y's partners in liquidation of Y.

Under section 358(a) of the Code, the basis to the former partners of Y in the stock received from S is the same as the section 732(b) basis to the former partners of Y in the assets received in liquidation of Y and transferred to S, reduced by the liabilities assumed by S, which assumption is treated as a payment of money to the partners under section 358(d).

Under section 362(a) of the Code, S's basis in the assets received from Y's former partners equals their basis to the former partners as determined under the section 732(c) immediately before the transfer to S.

Under section 735(b) of the Code, the partners' holding periods for the assets distributed to them by Y includes Y's holding period. Under section 1223(1), the partners' holding periods for the stock received in the exchange includes the partners' holding periods in the capital assets and section 1231 assets transferred to S (to the extent that the stock was received in exchange for such assets). However, to the extent that the stock received was in exchange for neither capital nor section 1231 assets, the holding period of the stock began on the day following the date of the exchange. Under section 1223(2), S's holding period of the Y assets received in the exchange includes the partner's holding periods.

O. CONTRIBUTIONS TO CAPITAL DISTINGUISHED

Situation 3

Under section 351 of the Code, gain or loss is not recognized by Z's partners on the transfer of the partnership interests to T in exchange for T's stock.

On the transfer of the partnership interests to the corporation, Z terminated under section 708(b)(1)(A) of the Code.

Under section 358(a) of the Code, the basis to the partners of Z of the stock received from T in exchange for their partnership interests equals the basis of their partnership interests transferred to T, reduced by Z's liabilities assumed by T, the release from which is treated as a payment of money to Z's partners under sections 752(d) and 358(d).

T's basis for the assets received in the exchange equals the basis of the partners in their partnership interests allocated in accordance with section 732(c). T's holding period includes Z's holding period in the assets.

Under section 1223(1) of the Code, the holding period of the T stock received by the former partners of Z includes each respective partner's holding period for the partnership interest transferred, except that the holding period of the T stock that was received by the partners of Z in exchange for their interests in section 751 assets of Z that are neither capital assets nor section 1231 assets begins on the day following the date of the exchange.

....

Thus although all three types of transaction may be tax-free under § 351, they will differ as to the basis and holding period of both stock received and property transferred depending upon the transactional form chosen.

O. CONTRIBUTIONS TO CAPITAL DISTINGUISHED

Read § 118.

SENATE REPORT NO. 1622
83d Congress, 2d Session; H.R. 8300

Part III. - Items Specifically Excluded from Gross Income

....

Section 118. Contributions to the capital of a corporation

This section (except for a change in a cross-reference) is identical with section 118 of the bill as passed by the House. It has no counterpart in the 1939 Code; however, the rule of this section, that contributions to the capital of a corporation are excluded from income, merely restates the existing law as developed through administration and court decisions. Determination of the basis of property contributed to the capital of a corporation is to be made under section 362.

NOTES

What is a "contribution to capital"? First of all, consider that there may be either shareholder or nonshareholder contributions to capital. The Regulations identify contributions by government units or civic groups which are designed to encourage the corporation to locate its business in a particular community or to expand its facilities, which do qualify under § 118, but it does not apply to payments for goods or services rendered or subsidies which are designed to limit its production. *See* Reg. § 1.118-1. Section 118(b) covers the ambiguous case of contributions by customers to regulated utilities. The approach to that subsection is to exempt the payments from the recipient corporation's tax base but also to prevent the corporation from claiming such tax benefits as investment credits and increases in basis.

The practical difference between § 118 and § 351 is that § 118 permits a nontaxable transfer to occur at the shareholder level even though no stock was issued and in spite of the fact that the transferor or group of transferors are not in control of the corporation. Although the language of the Regulations could be clearer, Reg. § 1.118-1 can only be interpreted to mean that shareholders can only increase the basis in their stock to the extent that they contribute additional assets to the corporation. The contribution can only be to the extent of the basis of the contributed property. If the contributor is an outsider who never had any stock in the corporation and does not get any stock, § 118 guarantees that the corporation will not be taxed, at that time, but again, the property takes a zero basis under § 362(c)(1).

P. ORGANIZATIONAL AND SYNDICATION EXPENDITURES

Read § 248.

These expenditures are treated the same way as for partnerships, and so they are given only passing reference here. Section 248 authorizes the elective amortization of organizational expenditures over a sixty-month period beginning with the month in which the corporation begins business. Reg. § 1.248-1(b)(ii) excludes expenditures in connection with issuing or selling stock. These include such items as commissions, professional fees, and printing costs for prospectuses. This is true for debt as well, but the expenditures for debt have to be amortized over the term of the loan as an interest expense whereas syndication expenses for equity are never deductible. If it were not for § 248, one could only deduct organizational expenses when a corporation liquidated.

OUTSIDE READINGS

J. Bankman, *The Structure of Silicon Valley Start-Ups*, 41 UCLA L. Rev. 1737 (1994).

J. Cummings, *The Silent Policies of Conservation and Cloning of Tax Basis and Their Corporate Applications*, 48 Tax L. Rev. 113 (1992).

P. ORGANIZATIONAL AND SYNDICATION EXPENDITURES

T. Evans, *The Taxation of Non-shareholder Contributions to Capital: An Economic Analysis*, 45 Vand. L. Rev. 1457 (Nov. 1992).

G. Griffith, *Realization and Recognition of Losses on Stock Surrenders: A Frolic Through Subchapter C*, 17 Fla. St. U. L. Rev. 49 (Winter 1989).

R. Jensen, *Of Form and Substance: Tax-Free Incorporations and Other Transactions Under Section 351*, 11 Va. Tax Rev. 349 (Fall 1991).

C. Johnson, *Tax Models for Non-Prorata Shareholder Contributions*, 3 Va. Tax Rev. 81 (Summer 1983).

N. Kyser, *The Long and Winding Road: Characterization of Boot Under Section 356(a)(2)*, 39 Tax L. Rev. 297 (Spring 1984).

Chapter 15
PLANNING THE CORPORATION'S CAPITAL STRUCTURE

In one sense, capitalizing a corporation means obtaining for it the assets and resources it will need. Alternatively, it means arranging its capital structure in the sense of determining what claims against the corporation (stock, debt, etc.) will be exchanged with providers of actual assets, financial or otherwise. Will the corporation issue only common stock (or other proprietary claims) or will it also issue debt instruments, that is, creditors' claims?

Even in a world free of income taxes the decision about how to capitalize the corporation can be a difficult one. At one extreme, the corporation might be in such a risky business that virtually no one will lend to it. In such a case, it will have no choice but to issue stock alone. On the other end, if the corporation has stable prospects, it may be able to raise money from lenders. Such loans will range all the way from long-term bonds — which are heavily ornamented promissory instruments running many pages and ordinarily held by institutional lenders — to short-term advances from trade creditors, notes from shareholders and others, and bank loans which may or may not be secured by the corporation's property. Sometimes some debt is subordinated to other claims. On top of that, the corporation may issue preferred stock, which is a kind of a hybrid equity lying between a bond and common stock. The usual features of preferred stock are that it has a preferred claim on the corporation's available cash flow, usually in the form of a right to some minimum dividend level, and a priority for distributions in liquidation. The dividend level is commonly a rate similar to the market rate of interest, and it may include a "kicker" which would allow the holder of the preferred stock to participate in further cash flow if the company does particularly well. On the other hand, if the company collapses, holders of preferred stock must wait in line until the creditors are first paid in full. Then the preferred stock shareholders will be paid their accumulated dividends and the face or par value of their stock according to the terms of their liquidation preference, if any, and only thereafter will the common shareholders get anything. It is often the case that if the company defaults on its dividends on nonvoting preferred stock the holders will become entitled to vote and may obtain a position on the Board of Directors as a result.

Even common stock may be broken down into several classes. For example, there may be a Class A that is entitled to one vote per share. There may be a Class B stock which does not vote but has the same claim on dividends and to assets in the event the corporation liquidates. The typical Class B shareholder will be a child of the founder of the corporation who cannot yet be trusted to vote the stock, but to whom the founder wishes to pass income. Beyond that, there may be options and warrants, a subject not further taken up here. Finally, there may be convertible obligations. For example, the holders of some of the corporation's debt may have the right to convert the debt into a certain number of shares of common stock. Even more common is the feature found in many issues of preferred stock that allows the holders to convert one share of preferred stock into a given number of shares of common stock. Such an arrangement can give the holders of preferred stock much greater "upside potential" (participation in future profits) than does regular preferred stock.

In short, this is a complex business that requires keeping an eye on the tax laws, state law restrictions and the interests of the various stakeholders in the corporation. Failure to appreciate the many risks and opportunities inherent in structuring the corporation's capital can be a basis for mortification and in the worse instance, a malpractice suit against a negligent advisor.

A. THE DEBT-EQUITY PROBLEM

Read § 385.

One of the most unstable areas of corporate tax law is whether a particular debt instrument constitutes equity rather than debt for federal income tax purposes. The distinction is crucial for several reasons, most especially: (1) The corporation can deduct interest expenses, but not dividends. *See* § 163. (2) If the company buys back stock from a shareholder, the shareholder may have a taxable dividend or capital gain. If it buys back or repays debt, that is generally treated as a nontaxable return of capital to the lender. Thus, debt furnishes a way for an investor to get back cash from the corporation with more favorable tax treatment than does equity. Sometimes hybrid instruments bear characteristics of both debt and equity; they wander near or over the line between the two. There is an endless stream of cases on the subject and rich literature from the commentators. The following discussion of the subject is from a document prepared by the Joint Committee on Taxation:

DISTINGUISHING DEBT FROM EQUITY

The characterization of an investment in a corporation as debt or equity for Federal income tax purposes is generally determined by the economic substance of the investor's interest in the corporation. The form of the instrument representing the investment and the taxpayer's characterization of the interest as debt or equity is not necessarily controlling. However, taxpayers have considerable latitude in structuring the terms of an instrument so that an interest in a corporation will be considered to be debt or equity, as so desired.

There is presently no definition in the Code or the Regulations which can be used to determine whether an interest in a corporation constitutes debt or equity for tax purposes. Such a determination must be made under principles

A. THE DEBT-EQUITY PROBLEM

developed in case law. Courts have approached the issue of distinguishing debt and equity by trying to determine whether the particular investment at issue in each case more closely resembles a pure debt interest or a pure equity interest. It is generally understood that a pure debt instrument is ordinarily represented by a written, unconditional promise to pay a principal sum certain, on demand or before a fixed maturity date not unreasonably far in the future, with interest payable in all events and not later than maturity.[1] Conversely, a pure equity interest is generally understood as an investment which places the funds contributed by the investor at the risk of the enterprise, provides for a share of any future profits, and carries with it rights to control or manage the enterprise.

The determination of whether an interest constitutes debt or equity is generally made by analyzing and weighing the relevant facts and circumstances of each case.[2] Some interests in a corporation can clearly be characterized, on their face, as either debt or equity. However, other interests may have features common to both debt and equity (known as "hybrid securities"), or underlying facts and circumstances may indicate that an interest has been inappropriately characterized as debt or equity (such as when purported debt is held by the corporation's shareholders on a pro rata basis, or when debt is held in a thinly capitalized corporation).

Various courts have determined that the following features, among others, are characteristic of debt:

(1) a written unconditional promise to pay on demand or on a specific date a sum certain in money in return for an adequate consideration in money or money's worth, and to pay a fixed rate of interest;

(2) a preference over, or lack of subordination to, other interests in the corporation;

(3) a relatively low corporate debt to equity ratio;

(4) the lack of convertibility into the stock of the corporation;

(5) independence between the holdings of the stock of the corporation and the holdings of the interest in question;

(6) an intent of the parties to create a creditor-debtor relationship;

(7) principal and interest payments that are not subject to the risks of the corporation's business;

(8) the existence of security to ensure the payment of interest and principal, including sinking fund arrangements, if appropriate;

(9) the existence of rights of enforcement and default remedies;

---

[1] See, e.g., *Farley Realty Corp. v. Comm'r*, 279 F.2d 701 (2d Cir. 1960), and B. Bittker & J. Eustice, Federal Income Taxation of Corporations and Shareholders, para. 4.03 (1979).

[2] In *John Kelley Co. v. Comm'r*, 326 U.S. 489 (1943), the Supreme Court stated that "[t]here is no one characteristic, not even the exclusion from management, which can be said to be decisive in the determination of whether the obligations are risk investments in the corporations or debts."

(10) an expectation of repayment;
(11) the holder's lack of voting and management rights (except in the case of default or similar circumstances);
(12) the availability of other credit sources at similar terms;
(13) the ability to freely transfer the interest;
(14) interest payments that are not contingent on or subject to management or board of directors' discretion; and
(15) the labelling and financial statement classification of the instrument as debt.

In 1969, in response to the increased level of corporate merger activity and the increased use of debt for corporate acquisition purposes, Congress enacted Code § 279 (disallowance of interest deductions incurred to acquire certain stock or assets) and § 385 (treatment of certain interests in corporations as stock or indebtedness). Section 385 granted the Secretary of the Treasury the authority to prescribe such regulations as may be necessary or appropriate to determine whether an interest in a corporation is to be treated as stock or as indebtedness for Federal income tax purposes. The regulations were to prescribe factors to be taken into account in determining, with respect to particular factual situations, whether a debtor-creditor relationship or a corporation-shareholder relationship existed. In addition, section 385 provided that the factors set forth in the regulations could include, among others, the first five of the fifteen factors listed above.

Proposed regulations under § 385 were issued on March 20, 1980, and became final on December 29 of that year. The final regulations originally had an effective date of May 1, 1981, but this date was subsequently postponed to January 1, 1982, and then to July 1, 1982. New proposed regulations were issued on December 30, 1981. However, these regulations never became effective and on July 6, 1983, all § 385 regulations were withdrawn and to date no additional regulations have been issued.

The § 385 regulations did not succeed in the attempt to develop objective standards for distinguishing debt from equity. For example, one feature of the regulations was the development of objective safe harbor tests which, if met, would classify an interest as debt. The use of such mechanical tests would have allowed corporations to create instruments which would be considered to be debt for Federal income tax purposes, but economically had many of the characteristics of equity.[3]

---

[3] Federal Income Tax Aspects of Corporate Financial Structures, January 18, 1989 [Joint Committee Print]; JCS-1-89; corrected by JCX-1-89] pp. 35-37.

A. THE DEBT-EQUITY PROBLEM

PLANTATION PATTERNS, INC. v. COMMISSIONER
462 F.2d 712 (5th Cir. 1972)

[Planation Patterns was a closely held corporation that made various types of metal chairs. For convenience, it was referred to as "Old Plantation." A tycoon investment banker by the name of Mr. Jemison, acting through his corporation, Jemison Investment Co. ("JIC"), agreed to form a new company ("New Plantation," for convenience). He promised that JIC would contribute $155,000 in cash to New Plantation, of which $150,000 would be in return for 6½% subordinated notes and $5,000 for common stock. The $5,000 was contributed for stock, but a third party — Bradford and Company, Inc. — lent the $150,000 on a subordinated basis at an interest rate of 6½%. Soon thereafter, New Plantation agreed to buy the stock of Old Plantation for about $650,000, consisting of $10,000 cash at the closing, and the rest in installment payments (evidenced by interest-bearing subordinated notes) in the total amount of $609,878.33 over about 10 years. JIC and the tycoon guaranteed the purchase obligations. This total amount consisted of two parts: $100,000 of 5½% guaranteed notes and $509,878.33 of partially subordinated notes. The IRS asserted that the substance of these deals was a hypothetical loan from an outsider to New Plantation, followed by a *contribution* from New to Old Plantation. If the IRS won, the alleged interest payment would be nondeductible distributions by New Plantation.]

SIMPSON, CIRCUIT JUDGE:

....

The Tax Court held that all steps taken by Mr. Jemison and the shareholders of Old Plantation were parts of a single transaction for the purchase by New Plantation of the wrought iron furniture business of Old Plantation, and, applying the relevant factors with respect to debt-equity situations to the facts here, one of which was found to be thin capitalization, that the guaranteed debt must be treated as an indirect contribution to New Plantation's capital by Mr. Jemison. Therefore, it held that New Plantation was not entitled to deductions claimed under Code Section 163 for interest on the 5½% serial notes in its taxable years ended September 30, 1963 to September 30, 1966 and that the Jemisons were taxable in 1963 under Code Sections 301 and 316 with the principal and interest payments on these guaranteed notes in that year.[4]

II. *The Issues on Appeal*

The issues presented for our consideration are these:
1. Whether $100,000 of guaranteed 5½% serial debentures issued by New Plantation to the sellers of Old Plantation are to be treated as debt for income tax

---

[4] The Tax Court allowed the Jemisons a deduction for interest paid the sellers by New Plantation.

purposes where the notes were not subordinated and were paid when due by New Plantation without recourse to other financing?

2. Whether $509,878.33 of guaranteed 5½% notes issued by New Plantation to the sellers of Old Plantation are to be treated as debt for income tax purposes where the notes were subordinated to general creditors but were senior to $150,000 of other debentures which the Tax Court did treat as debt for income tax purposes?

3. Whether Jemison Investment Company, a co-guarantor, rather than John S. Jemison, Jr., a co-guarantor, should be deemed to have made the contribution to the equity capital of New Plantation in the event that any of the $609,878.33 principal amount of 5½% notes is deemed to represent a contribution to the equity capital of New Plantation?

III. *The Relevant Law*

The criteria for adjudicating debt-equity cases were set forth most clearly by Judge Jones for this Court in 1963 in *Montclair, Inc. v. C.I.R.*, 5 Cir., 1963, 318 F.2d 38. At page 40 of Volume 318 F.2d the factors which bear most strongly on the determination of the label to be applied to the transaction are enunciated: "(1) the names given to the certificates evidencing the indebtedness; (2) the presence or absence of a maturity date; (3) the source of the payments; (4) the right to enforce the payment of principal and interest; (5) participation in management; (6) a status equal to or inferior to that of regular corporate creditors; (7) the intent of the parties; (8) 'thin' or adequate capitalization; (9) identity of interest between creditor and stockholder; (10) payment of interest only out of 'dividend' money; (11) the ability of the corporation to obtain loans from outside lending institutions."

Since *Montclair, Inc.* consideration of debt-equity cases has frequently demanded the attention of this Court.... In applying these factors, each case must be decided on its own facts, and no one standard is controlling. *See generally* the cases just cited, *supra*. The tests are not "talismans of magical power," and the most that can be said is that they are a source of helpful guidance. *Tyler v. Tomlinson, supra*. Thus we decide debt-equity issues by a case by case analysis, applying the *Montclair* rubrics as best we can to the facts at hand.

IV. *Treatment of the $100,000 Unsubordinated 5½% Debentures and the $509,878.33 Partially Subordinated 5½% Notes*

With regard to the $100,000 unsubordinated debentures, the taxpayers urge us to reverse the Tax Court for the following reasons: (1) There was a reasonable prospect of payment when due, (2) the notes were not subordinated to any other indebtedness of New Plantation, (3) the holders, along with general creditors, had first claim on more than $1,000,000 in assets of New Plantation, (4) the notes matured within two years, (5) the notes could have been paid by New Plantation's cash flow, and (6) the notes were paid when due without recourse to additional financing.

A. THE DEBT-EQUITY PROBLEM 303

Of these factors, taxpayers point first and foremost to the fact that the debentures were totally unsubordinated, and thus conferred on the holders the right to participate with general creditors. They further call to our attention that under the Code of Alabama had the creditors paid the notes their subrogation rights would have permitted them to participate in any insolvency proceeding as a general creditor. Section 87, Title 9, Code of Alabama of 1940, as amended.

Taxpayers also vigorously assert that the assets of the corporation were more than adequate to support the $100,000 unsubordinated notes because on September 30, 1962, New Plantation's assets had a fair market value of $1,261,327.81, Note 6, *supra*. Central to this appeal is the taxpayers' contention that the Tax Court erroneously concluded that New Plantation was thinly capitalized.

Additionally, with regard to the $100,000 of unsubordinated 5½% debentures, taxpayers emphasize that they were to mature within two years, a factor militating strongly against a conclusion that the money was put "at the risk" of the business. Bolstering this point, taxpayers state that the cash flow from depreciation in 1963 and 1964, the years of payment of the $100,000 notes, exceeded the principal payments of $50,000 due on the notes. They say that in view of the fact that the interest on the notes is deducted in determining net income, it was not necessary for New Plantation to have net income to pay these notes, and thus their repayment was not contingent on the profitability of the business.

Finally, the taxpayers criticize the Tax Court for not giving greater weight in assessing the economic realities of the situation to the fact that the notes were paid on time. Taxpayers claim that giving this development its proper weight will lead us to the conclusion that the Tax Court was clearly erroneous in its holding that when the notes were issued there was no reasonable expectation that New Plantation could pay the notes. In this regard taxpayers also insist that the Tax Court gave undue emphasis to the overall debt-equity ratio, which they assert bears slight relevance to the determination of the treatment given unsubordinated notes. Taxpayers argue that whether a corporation can pay all of its debts is irrelevant to the question whether it can pay its priority debts.

Turning to the remaining $509,878.33 of partially subordinated 5½% serial debentures, the taxpayers argue five points in support of their proposition that the Tax Court erred: (1) There was reasonable prospect of payment when due, (2) the notes, though partially subordinated, were senior to $150,000 of 6½% debentures and $5,000 of common stock, (3) the assets of New Plantation were sufficient to support the debt, (4) the cash flow was sufficient to pay the debt, and (5) the notes were paid when due without recourse to additional financing.

Many of the arguments made by the taxpayers in favor of debt treatment for the $100,000 unsubordinated debentures are equally applicable for the remaining $509,878.33 of partially subordinated notes, and the taxpayers have urged us to accord them equal vitality here. New arguments also are raised at this juncture, however. Taxpayers contend that it is anomalous and inconsistent for the Tax

Court to characterize the $509,878.33 partially subordinated debentures as equity while at the same time characterizing inferior fully subordinated debentures held by Bradford and Company as debt, arguing that if the fully subordinated 6½% notes held by Bradford and Company are equity, surely the $509,878.33 debentures are entitled to the same treatment.

Here the taxpayers protest vigorously against the Tax Court's determination of the proper debt-equity ratio to apply in assessing the nature of the transaction. The principal dispute with the Tax Court revolves about that Court's valuation of the intangible assets of New Plantation, with particular emphasis on the personal business skills of Mr. Jemison. The Tax Court did recognize that intangible assets not carried on the balance sheet might have a bearing on the ability of the corporation to pay its debts. *Murphy Logging Company v. United States*, 9 Cir. 1967, 378 F.2d 222. But the Tax Court held that the relationship of Mr. Jemison's business skills to the well-being of New Plantation was not demonstrated with the specificity requisite to alter the picture of the overall debt-paying potential of New Plantation. Relying heavily on *Murphy Logging, supra*, the taxpayers contend that the record amply demonstrates that Mr. Jemison was a veritable financial genius, commanding Jemison Investment Company, a company with control of assets valued at more than $11,000,000 and with annual gross receipts of over $10,000,000. They point to the record as reflecting that Mr. Jemison was successfully engaged in a broad variety of business ventures. He was a director of several successful corporations, a bank, and two insurance companies. More important, however, taxpayers assert, is Mr. Jemison's demonstrated close contact with several large department store chains which provided ideal outlets for New Plantation's products. Taxpayer on this account urges that a proper debt-equity ratio should take into account the financial skills of Mr. Jemison.

Without receding from their strong stand that the 5½% debentures constitute debt, the taxpayers alternatively argue that if the court should hold that such notes do not constitute debt, the same equity treatment should be given to the 6½% subordinated debentures held by Bradford and Company. Stated otherwise, they argue that if the 5½% *partially* subordinated debentures are to be regarded as equity, then the 6½% totally subordinated debentures should logically be deemed to constitute preferred stock in New Plantation. Taxpayers point out that long-term debt held by non-stockholders has been held to be an equity interest in the nature of preferred stock. *Foresun, Inc. v. Commissioner of Internal Revenue*, 6 Cir. 1965, 348 F.2d 1006, *affirming* 41 T.C. 706 (1964). Taxpayers claim that they were denied the right to further trial on this point in the Tax Court, and they contend that at the very least this Court should remand the case to the Tax Court to permit development of further evidence as to the treatment to be given the $150,000 in Bradford and Company notes. If these notes are regarded as equity, taxpayers argue that the debt-equity ratio of New Plantation would be approximately 4 to 1 ($609,878.33 to $155,000), and not the plus 125 to 1 ratio which the government asserts is the proper debt-equity ratio

A. THE DEBT-EQUITY PROBLEM

($759,878.33 to $5,000). This would effectively demolish the Tax Court finding of thin capitalization....

More specifically the Commissioner places primary emphasis on the Tax Court's findings that the assets of the new corporation vis-à-vis its debts were insufficient to give New Plantation viable independence as a corporation. The Tax Court found that the corporate assets of New Plantation were "wholly inadequate to sustain a debt of $609,878.33." The Commissioner suggests that *Murphy Logging, supra,* the keystone in appellants' argument, is distinguishable. The Commissioner argues that in *Murphy Logging,* the guarantee of a guarantor-stockholder was held not significant because the corporation had substantial ability to meet its debts without the aid of a guarantor, a factor absent in this case. Further distinction is noted in that in *Murphy Logging* the Ninth Circuit was not dealing with a thinly capitalized corporation, as is the case here. The Commissioner discounts the fact that New Plantation was in actuality able to pay its obligations without resort to its guarantors, pointing out that we must view the transaction on the basis of the economic realities as they existed at New Plantation's inception, and not in the light of later developments. As matters stood September 28, 1962, asserts the Commissioner, the deal had not set up a bona fide corporation reasonably to be expected to manage to go it alone, and later developments do not alter the nature of the transaction for tax purposes.

Making further use of the debt vs. equity criteria established by *Montclair* and later cases, the Commissioner notes particularly that the sellers took the unusual step of agreeing to subordinate all but $100,000 of the purchase money notes. The Commissioner asserts that this action was taken because the sellers looked first and foremost to the guarantee of Mr. Jemison, an obligation which was primary in nature.

The Commissioner also claims that no third party arm's-length creditors, because of New Plantation's paper thin capitalization, would have loaned the amount of money by which the corporation became indebted. Establishment of any indebtedness, argues the respondent, would have required Mr. Jemison's guarantee, and therefore for tax purposes the indebtedness should be regarded as that of the Jemisons.

Resolving these two conflicting views of this amorphous transaction is no easy task, but we are not persuaded that the taxpayers have successfully demonstrated the incorrectness of the position taken by the Tax Court. Certainly we recognize that this transaction was initially cast to have all of the outward appearances of a debt transaction, complete with instruments styled "debentures" which had fixed maturity dates. But these surface considerations do not end our examination. Closer scrutiny establishes that the other factors which would give the transaction the aura of debt are noticeable by their absence.

Of critical importance in determining whether financial input is debt or equity is whether or not the money is expended for capital assets. In the instant case the substantial portion of the $609,878.33 was directed to the purchase of capital assets and to finance initial operations. In contrast, only $5,000.00 was set up as equity to finance launching of the corporate venture.

Other equity factors exist. While the sellers were ostensibly to look to the corporation for payment of the debt, it is apparent from the meager capital position of the company that Mr. Jemison's guarantee was regarded as the real undergirding for the deal. Our conclusion is reinforced by noting that the sellers apparently considered financially acceptable the agreement to subordinate the great majority of the 5½% debentures to almost all other corporate indebtedness so long as the debentures were guaranteed by Mr. Jemison. Mr. Jemison's guarantee was, of course, an obligation primary in nature.

Further, while Mrs. Jemison was the stockholder of record, and Mr. Jemison on the surface was only a guarantor, surrounding circumstances clearly demonstrate that Mr. Jemison completely controlled the shares held by Mrs. Jemison. Mrs. Jemison seldom attended the meetings of the corporation, and took little active interest in it. In contrast, Mr. Jemison was intimately and continuously involved in the operations of New Plantation. Regarding Mr. Jemison as the "constructive" owner of the stock, we have an identity of interest between the stockholder and the guarantor — a factor which points strongly toward equity treatment.

The record cannot support a determination by us that the Tax Court's finding that New Plantation was thinly capitalized is "clearly erroneous." The balance sheet of the corporation showed that its quick assets (cash and accounts receivables) of $317,000 could not cover its current liabilities of approximately $490,000. This ratio is one of the acid test indicators used by businessmen to determine the health of a business. After the dissolution of Old Plantation the new corporation had tangible assets, at fair market value, of approximately $1,064,000 securing debts of approximately $1,078,000. We regard this as thin capitalization, as did the Tax Court.

The guarantee enabled Mr. Jemison to put a minimum amount of cash into New Plantation immediately, and to avoid any further cash investment in the corporation unless and until it should fall on hard times. At the same time he exercised total control over its management. Adding together the personal guarantee of Mr. Jemison to the guarantee of Jemison Investment Company, which was wholly owned by him and Mr. Jemison's control of New Plantation, we think that the result is that Mr. Jemison's guarantee simply amounted to a covert way of putting his money "at the risk of the business." Stated differently, the guarantee enabled Mr. Jemison to create borrowing power for the corporation which normally would have existed only through the presence of more adequate capitalization of New Plantation.

We do not regard as significant the fact that ultimately things progressed smoothly for New Plantation and that its debts were paid without additional financing. The question is not whether, looking back in time, the transaction was ultimately successful or not, but rather whether at its inception there was a reasonable expectation that the business would succeed on its own. The transaction must be judged on the conditions that existed when the deal was consummated, and not on conditions as they developed with the passage of time. When New Plantation was incorporated its prospects of business success were questionable indeed without the Jemison guarantees.

We hold also that the Tax Court was correct in refusing to give value to the intangible financial skills of Mr. Jemison for purposes of computing the corporation's debt-equity ratio....

We decide only this case. We do not assert that intangible assets are never a proper consideration in assessing debt-equity ratio....

Our holding does not require that we find the notes held by Bradford and Company to be equity interests. While the Bradford and Company notes were subordinated, subordination is far from the sole criterion for determining whether an interest is debt or equity. It is not controlling. Aside from this single factor this record is productive of nothing to indicate that this was not a bona fide loan made by Bradford with the primary motive of inducing New Plantation to employ young Bradford. We agree with the Tax Court that this was a legitimate loan.

V. *Should the Equity Contribution Be Deemed to Have Been Made by Jemison Investment Company Rather Than by Mr. Jemison?*

The Tax Court found that the equity contribution was to be attributed to Mr. Jemison and not to Jemison Investment Company. Although acknowledging that Jemison Investment Company received a fee of $15,000.00 for its guarantee on the notes, the Tax Court reasoned that inasmuch as Mr. Jemison controlled both Jemison Investment and New Plantation, the fee for the guarantee was either a matter of internal accounting or for cosmetic effect, and not an indication that the sellers of Old Plantation realistically looked to Jemison Investment Company for any security. It is uncontested that practically all of Mr. Jemison's assets consisted of stock in Jemison Investment Company. It owned the house he lived in and the automobile he drove, but he owned it in its entirety. Furthermore, the Tax Court found that the sellers of Old Plantation only investigated the credit of Mr. Jemison, and that the Messrs. Jernigans as sellers looked at all times to Mr. Jemison's guarantee as the real insurance for the notes.

Although the appellants cast some doubt on the Tax Court's finding that the sellers did not investigate the financial statements of the Jemison Investment Company, in no other respect have they demonstrated error in the Tax Court's conclusion that through all of the haze of corporate red tape, the real financial keystone supporting the entire deal, the person to whom the sellers ultimately looked for their protection in the event of the failure of New Plantation was Mr. John S. Jemison, Jr....

NOTES

1. *Is there a way out of this mess?* Maybe. Probably the most sensible proposal is the "objective" analysis proposed in *Scriptomatic, Inc. v. Commis-*

308   CH. 15: PLANNING THE CORPORATION'S CAPITAL STRUCTURE

sioner, 555 F.2d 364, 367-68 (3d Cir. 1977). In essence the case casts the debt versus equity question along the following lines:

> "If this instrument had been proposed to an independent outside lender would that lender consider it was making a loan?" Although this will not solve all cases it is an excellent first cut. As a lawyer planning a transaction it is especially useful because it forces the parties away from being entranced by their cleverness and into looking objectively into what they are doing. It tends to elicit the inevitable proposal, "well, lets talk to our banker and see what the banker thinks!" If the banker can be induced to go on the record as to the character of the obligation that will produce useful documentation in the event of a future IRS audit.

2. *Once classified, always classified?* No. It is clear that the character of the corporation and its capital may change. For example, a corporation may issue a reasonable amount of subordinated debt at the outset, but later on may issue so much further debt or run into such financial difficulties, that what in an earlier day was unquestionably debt for tax purposes may become equity for federal income tax purposes.

3. *Why doesn't the Treasury do something about it?* The answer, as you read above, is that the Treasury did write extensive regulations pursuant to § 385 to try to sort out the debt-equity imbroglio, but the regulations were hooted down by practitioners and the Treasury Department reluctantly withdrew them.

PROBLEM 15-1

The founders of the L&B Corporation each own half of the common stock. At present, the company has the following assets and liabilities to creditors.

Assets		*Liabilities*	
Cash	$22,000	Note due directors	$100,000
Building	-0-	Mortgage on land	50,000
Land	39,000	Working capital loan	50,000
Office Equipment	14,000	Total	$200,000
Total	$75,000		

The assets are stated on a "tax" basis, using adjusted historic costs. The founders think the building is probably worth something in the area of $75,000.

The founders think they have access to an exciting business opportunity, and their accountant has advised them to raise the money by having L&B sell convertible debentures with a face amount of $200,000 and a value of $100,000, bearing simple interest of 5%. They do not want to go through the complications of offering the debentures to the public, and they propose to buy half of the debentures each, and in any case, they doubt a bank would lend money on these terms. The debentures are unsecured, and are convertible into 100 shares of stock. The value of the stock is speculative.

1. What is your view of whether the debentures will qualify as debt? Assuming they do, how will interest deductions be calculated? What additional information do you need or would you want to ask for?

2. The founders wonder if L&B might not be able to pay a very high rate of interest and claim a large deduction therefor in order to disgorge corporate profits nontaxably. Glance at §§ 163(e)(5)(A) and 163(i)(1) for the issue and look at § 163(j) (the "interest-stripping" rules), but do not spend more than a few moments.

B. THE SECTION 1244 STOCK OPPORTUNITY

Read § 1244.

If corporate stock becomes worthless, the investor normally is forced to report a capital loss. *See* § 165(g). Because of the severe restrictions imposed on capital losses, the result can be an unhappy one. *See* § 1211(b). This unhappy outcome also applies if the investor owns "securities," which for federal income tax purposes generally means corporate debt obligations with a maturity of at least five years. If you have already read the partnership materials, you will probably think that the right solution is for the company to operate in partnership form during the early, risky years of its existence so that the losses can be passed through directly to its shareholders, and that is a reasonable reaction. However, § 1244 opens another door in that it allows individual investors to treat what would otherwise be capital losses on "section 1244 stock" as ordinary losses. (Section 1244 stock can now include preferred as well as common stock.) The difficulty with § 1244 is that it is ringed with restrictions, including an annual limitation of $100,000 (for spouses filing a joint return, or $50,000 for other taxpayers.) The excess loss cannot be carried forward. Instead the taxpayer is stuck with trying carefully to recognize exactly $100,000 or $50,000 per year, as the case may be, in the event of a major loss. One difficulty is if the corporation becomes worthless and the shareholder has a particularly large block of stock, only the first $100,000 stock loss on a joint return will be treated as an ordinary loss. Presumably, the remainder must be treated as a capital loss. Section 1244 used to require a specific election by the corporation in order for the stock to qualify, but that is no longer the case, and as a result § 1244 has lost its most diabolical feature.

PROBLEM 15-2

The local investment club recently decided to form a holding company ("Holdings, Inc.") in order to buy the stock of Dynamic Meter Corporaton

("DMC"). On May 1 of this year the ten investors placed $200,000 each in an escrow account established by their lawyer, Busby Bungle, Esq. He in turn took $200,000 from the account, formed Holdings, Inc., and issued the first stock certificates. He also tried to complete the first stage of the acquisition, but found the going to be slow. Bungle filed an S election form for Holdings on June 1, but the IRS rejected the Subchapter S election on July 30. He did not try to refile. The acquisition failed on December 1 when it was learned that DMC had agreed to be taken over by another company. Busby promptly returned the $1.8 million to the 10 investors.

Can the 10 investors claim § 1244 losses?

C. SECTION 1202 AND 1044 OPPORTUNITIES

Read § 1202(a), (b)(1)-(2) and (c)(1).

The following description of the new provision is from the House-Senate Conference Report in 1994:

> The conference agreement generally follows the House bill, which generally permits a noncorporate taxpayer who holds qualified small business stock for more than five years to exclude from income 50 percent of any gain on the sale or exchange of the stock. The amount of gain eligible for the 50-percent exclusion is limited to the greater of (1) 10 times the taxpayer's basis in the stock or (2) $10 million of gain from stock in that corporation. One-half of any exclusion claimed is treated as an alternative minimum tax preference item. The conference agreement modifies the House bill by basing the $50 million qualified small business size limitation on the issuer's gross assets (i.e., the sum of the cash and the adjusted bases of other assets held by the small business) without subtracting short-term indebtedness. In addition, for purposes of the size limitation, the conference agreement provides that corporations that are part of a parent-subsidiary controlled group are treated as a single corporation. Under the conference agreement, the provision applies to stock issued after the date of enactment.[5]

There is more. Under § 1044, taxpayers who have enjoyed major profits on the sale of publicly-traded securities can roll over the gain into a minority-oriented corporation and defer the gain:

> The conference agreement follows the House bill, which permits any corporation or individual to elect to defer the recognition of any capital gain realized upon the sale of publicly traded securities to the extent that the proceeds from the sale are used to buy an equity interest in a specialized

---

[5] Staff of the Joint Committee on Taxation, Overview of the Conference Agreement on the Revenue Provisions of the Omnibus Budget Reconciliation Act of 1993, [Joint Committee Print]; H.R. 2264; JCS-10-93 (August 3, 1993) pp. 2 & 3.

small business investment company within 60 days of the sale of the securities. The provision is limited, in the case of an individual, to $50,000 of gain per year and $500,000 of gain over a lifetime. In the case of a corporation, these limits are $250,000 and $1,000,000. The provision is effective for sales of publicly traded securities on or after the date of enactment.[6]

OUTSIDE READINGS

K. Pratt, *Shifting Biases: Troubled Company Debt Restructurings After the 1993 Tax Act*, 68 Am. Bankr. L.J. 23 (Winter 1994).

D. Schneider, *Internal Revenue Code Section 306 and Tax Avoidance*, 4 Va. Tax Rev. 287 (Winter 1985).

---

[6] *Id.* at p. 3.

Chapter 16
DISTRIBUTIONS FROM CORPORATIONS TO SHAREHOLDERS ("WITH RESPECT TO THEIR SHARES")

A. INTRODUCTION

The subject of this chapter is current distributions (of money or property) from corporations to their shareholders in their capacity as shareholders. The topic is sometimes intricate but reasonably logical. There are a number of legislative alternatives to the present regime. If one were sitting down to work out the taxation of corporate distributions from scratch one might choose from any number of alternatives but the primary ones seem to be the following:

1. Do not tax distributions to shareholders at all, on the ground that corporate profits have already been taxed to the corporation, but require shareholders to reduce basis in their shares;
2. Tax all distributions to shareholders on a presumption that the corporation makes distributions to its shareholders only out of profits;
3. Tax distributions to shareholders only to the extent that the distributions actually do come out of corporate profits;
4. Tax distributions only after the shareholder has recovered his basis in his stock (capital recovery first).

What we have in substance is a combination of the first, third and fourth alternatives but in a different order. The general rule is that distributions are taxed to shareholders on the assumption that all distributions come out of profits first. To the extent that distributions exceed profits, they are not taxable, but shareholders must then reduce stock basis, and to the extent distributions exceed basis, the shareholder is treated as if she had sold her stock for a gain equal to the excess. While the structure is reasonably coherent, it necessarily involves two levels of taxation, which is a feature of our tax system that many economists and commentators consider excessive. *See* Chapter 27. On the other hand, it is true that both corporate and individual tax rates have dropped substantially since their high points after World War II, so that the combined burden is much reduced.

Distributions by a corporation to a *corporate* shareholder are subject to the same basic system but with a special deduction (acting like an exclusion) to remove or soften what could be a triple (or higher) tax on distributed corporate profits. *See* §§ 243-45, 1501-04. Treatment of individual shareholders will be taken up first.

The subject of the remainder of this chapter will be distributions out of current operations as distinct from distributions resulting from a partial or total liquidation of the enterprise, which are discussed in Chapters 17 and 18, respectively.

B. BASIC STRUCTURE

Read §§ 301(a), 301(c) and 316.

In case there was any doubt about it, § 61(a)(7) specifically includes "dividends" distributed to shareholders as a form of gross income (to them). However, a distribution is only a dividend to the extent it is covered by current or post-1913 "earnings and profits," as provided in § 316. To the extent that a distribution exceeds such earnings and profits, § 301(c)(2) treats the excess as a return of capital to the shareholder which reduces the adjusted basis of his stock, and distributions in excess of basis are taxed as capital gains.

One of the great difficulties with this system is that while it makes perfectly good sense in the case of individuals who are founders, it is questionable in the case of people who buy from the founders or who acquire stock still further down the chain of purchase. For example, a founder might invest $10 in a corporation and watch it earn another $90 and sell the stock for $100 reporting a long-term capital gain. If the corporation then distributed $90 to the buyer, he would be taxed on $90 of ordinary income with no reduction in basis of the stock, despite the fact that he is none the wealthier for the distribution.

C. "DIVIDEND" DEFINED

Read § 316 and Reg. § 1.316-1(a).

First, observe that the term "dividend" for federal income tax purposes does not mean the same thing as a dividend for state corporation law purposes. For example, a distribution from a corporation may be a dividend for federal income tax purposes even though it unlawfully impairs capital for state law purposes. To make things even more confusing to people who may have an accounting background, what the corporation shows as its "earned surplus" — which is generally thought of as the measure of the corporation's historical profitability — is not the same as "earnings and profits."

Section 316 defines and identifies two sources of taxable dividends:

1. Distributions out of earnings and profits accumulated after February 28, 1913, and
2. Distributions out of earnings and profits for the current taxable year.

The second source, earnings and profits for the taxable year, probably ought to be repealed as having outlived is usefulness. It was enacted in 1936 in order to limit the sting of a special tax on undistributed profits by permitting corporations to deduct dividends that came out of current earnings.[1] The special tax itself was later repealed, but the rule that earnings and profits for the current year are always a source of taxable dividends was not, despite the fact that it no longer had any rationale. Be this as it may, § 316(b)(2) plays a central role by dictating that if a distribution is made to shareholders the first source is presumptively considered to be current earnings and profits. If those earnings and profits are at least as large as the distribution, then one need not look at the accumulated earnings and profits account. Most surprisingly, even if the corporation has a huge cumulative loss which dwarfs the current year's earnings and profits, any current earnings and profits nevertheless convert an equal amount of the distribution into a dividend. This is the so-called "nimble dividend" rule.

Assuming that distributions for the year exceed current earnings and profits, then one must look next at the cumulative (undistributed) earnings and profits since 1913 as the second source of potential dividend. The 1913 date was commendably designed to forgive earnings and profits accumulated before passage of the Sixteenth Amendment so that the new tax would not apply retroactively.

Most corporations have cautious dividend-paying practices because there is so much adverse publicity associated with being forced to cut a dividend. As a result, there is almost always more than enough current or accumulated earnings and profits to cover any distribution. However, while this is true for most publicly-held corporations it is not nearly so true for smaller closely-held corporations which are frequently viewed by their owners as private pocketbooks.

One important rule is that earnings and profits are calculated as of the close of the taxable year, undiminished by actual distributions during that year. As a result, it is often not until well after the end of the taxable year that the accountants can finally determine how much of the distributions made in the prior year have to be treated as dividends and how much as mere returns of capital. It also makes the payment of distributions early in the year risky because a corporation which expected a distribution to be nontaxable might discover that it was taxable after-all due to a surge in profits late in the year.

D. CHRONOLOGICAL ASPECTS OF DIVIDENDS

Read Reg. § 1.316-2(a).

One needs to master a few basic rules in order to handle complicated dividend patterns. The first rule is that current earnings and profits are drained off first and in proportion to the amount of the distributions paid over the year. For example, if a corporation had $3 of current earnings and profits but it distributed a total of $9 over the course of the year, of which $6 is paid on June 30 and $3

---

[1] *See* Lent, The Undistributed Profits Tax (Columbia Press 1948).

on December 30, $2 of the current earnings and profits would be deemed distributed on June 30, and the remaining $1 would be deemed distributed on December 30.

Second, accumulated earnings and profits are deemed paid out in chronological order. Thus, for example, in the above example, if in addition the corporation had another $3 of accumulated earnings and profits as of the beginning of the current year, all $3 would be deemed distributed on June 30 according to the "first-come, first-served" rule. It would not be pro-rated between the two distributions, and the final result would be a $5 dividend on June 30 and a $1 dividend on December 30.

Third, the accumulated earnings and profits account and the current earnings and profits accounts are combined at the very end of the year after taking into account all distributions for the year. Thus, for example, if a corporation had a large accumulated deficit in its earnings and profit account over the years since 1913 but had a profitable year, it would first reduce its current earnings and profits by any distributions made during the current year and only then combine whatever earnings and profits were left over with the deficit in its accumulated earnings account at the end of the year, leaving over a diminished deficit for the following year.

Fourth, a distribution cannot produce a deficit in the accumulated earnings and profit account. A loss experienced by the corporation, of course, can do so.

Fifth, the two § 316 sources of taxable dividends are *alternative* sources in a sense; if the corporation has enough of either source (or both together), the distribution will be entirely taxable as a dividend. Only if and to the extent *both* sources have been exhausted will the distribution be treated by § 301 as a return of capital, up to basis, or capital gain (to the extent it exceeds basis).

E. "EARNINGS AND PROFITS" EXPLAINED

Read § 312(a), (b), (k)(1), (n)(2)-(3), (5) and (6).

It is an extraordinary fact that the crucial term *earnings and profits* is not defined in the Code. Section 312 instead works backwards by prescribing adjustments to the corporation's taxable income to arrive at its earnings and profits. Roughly speaking, "earnings and profits" is designed to provide a measure of the corporation's ability to make cash distributions to shareholders without invading the corporation's capital. It is similar to the accounting concept of "earned surplus" insofar as paid-in capital is ignored, but it also differs in some fundamental ways. For example, distributions of stock of the distributing corporation do not reduce earnings and profits.

The adjustments to taxable income may be conveniently divided into two main categories. The first is a number of rules which reflect the corporation's actual cash flow more accurately than does taxable income. For example, many otherwise nondeductible items are subtracted from earnings and profits to reflect the cash outlay, such as fines and penalties, capital losses in excess of capital

E. "EARNINGS AND PROFITS" EXPLAINED

gains, and federal income tax liabilities. Similarly, a number items which are excludible or deductible for tax purposes must be included in earnings and profits to reflect the cash inflow. These include, for example, tax-free municipal-bond interest, life-insurance proceeds, and intercorporate dividends received.

The second main category of adjustments involve changes in accounting rules to conform more nearly to financial accounting and which forbid the use of certain favorable rules which are allowed for tax purposes. For example, installment-sale reporting is not permitted for purposes of calculating earnings and profits. Instead, the profit must be included in full in the year of sale. Inventory profits must be reported on the first-in-first-out (FIFO) method rather than the more favorable last-in-first-out (LIFO) method. Also, depreciation methods are slower than for purposes of calculating taxable income.

PROBLEM 16-1

Newton Steel Corporation's recent financial statements reported the following items from its profit and loss statement:

Income from operations: $120,000;
Administrative and sales expenses: $75,000;
Interest income from U.S. Treasury bonds: $15,000;
Dividends from 70%-owned corporation: $5,000;[2]
Tax-exempt interest income from State obligations: $5,000;
Gain recognizable in future years from current installment sale: $1,000;
Accelerated depreciation allowed: $17,500;[3]
Life insurance proceeds paid on death of president of the company: $20,000;
Net operating loss carried over from prior year and currently deducted: $5,000;
Federal income taxes paid: $8,940;
Capital gains: $500;
Capital loss: $1,000;
Penalty paid to city: $250;
Interest expense on working capital: $10,000;
Interest expense for production of income from state obligations: $500.

Consider the effect each of these items has on the corporation's taxable income for the year and on its current earnings and profits. *See* Regs. § 1.312-6 and -7.

PROBLEM 16-2

Angry Kennels, Inc. has $57,000 of accumulated earnings and profits at the beginning of the year and has current earnings and profits of $28,000. This year, Angry Kennels distributed $45,000 on April 15 and again on September 15. The

---

[2] [*See* § 243.]

[3] Straight-line depreciation would have been $12,000.

company is equally owned by Danny and Gertrude. As of the beginning of this year, Danny's basis in his stock was $3,000, and Gertrude's basis was $1,000. What is the amount of each distribution that is deemed to come from current year earnings and profits and from accumulated earnings and profits? *See* Reg. § 1.316-2(b) and (c).

F. DISGUISED AND CONSTRUCTIVE DISTRIBUTIONS

We have already seen that corporations and their shareholders suffer from a serious problem of double taxation, creating pressure on shareholders to devise ways to extract cash, property or other value from the corporation without triggering the double tax. Shareholders have shown great ingenuity in beating the system. Common devices include leasing property to the corporation at exorbitant rates, selling property to the corporation at unreasonably high prices, paying excessive compensation, or making loans to shareholders (directly or indirectly) that lack the usual features of genuine debtor-creditor relationships. These transactions are risky because they may be reconstructed as distributions taxable as dividends. Further, sometimes overly clever intercorporate transfers will create unintended dividends to shareholders who own stock in both corporations.

STINNETT'S PONTIAC SERVICE, INC. v. COMMISSIONER
730 F.2d 634 (11th Cir. 1984)

HATCHETT, CIRCUIT JUDGE:

In this case, we review the Tax Court's holdings regarding the tax consequences of transactions involving two corporations and their common shareholder, the taxpayer. We affirm.

Facts

Richard W. Stinnett is president of Pontiac, an automobile dealership, and he owns 74% of the stock in the company....

On or about July 2, 1973, Stinnett, Danford L. Sawyer (Sawyer), and Albert L. Bundy (Bundy) purchased the entire stock of Cargo Construction Company, Ltd. (Cargo), a Bahamian corporation. Cargo's principal business activity was commercial fishing, and its only asset was the lobster boat, R/V Victory. Stinnett owned 43%; Sawyer owned 35%; and Bundy owned 22% of Cargo's stock. Stinnett, Sawyer, and Bundy also purchased the R/V Victory for approximately $55,000. The three shareholders realized that Cargo would need additional capital to satisfy certain unforeseen initial costs and, therefore, agreed to contribute additional capital, in proportion to each shareholder's stock ownership in Cargo, to Cargo to meet its needs.

From 1973 to 1975, Sawyer and Bundy contributed funds to Cargo as required by the shareholders' agreement. Stinnett, however, failed to contribute to Cargo pursuant to the shareholders' agreement. Pontiac, the corporation which Stinnett controlled, contributed funds and boat parts to Cargo. In 1973, Pontiac

F. DISGUISED AND CONSTRUCTIVE DISTRIBUTIONS

transferred $12,969.86 to Cargo, and, in return, Cargo issued interest bearing unsecured demand notes to Pontiac. During this same period, Pontiac also purchased marine parts for Cargo. Although Pontiac usually sold marine parts at 100% markup, it sold the marine parts to Cargo at only a 10% markup. Pontiac also made additional payments of $12,000 to Cargo. Cargo failed to issue any notes to Pontiac for any part of this amount.

From 1974 to 1975, Pontiac transferred an additional $45,000 to Cargo. Pontiac did not obtain any financial statements from Cargo prior to making any of the transfers, nor were the amounts of the transfers secured. After realizing that Cargo's lobster venture was unsuccessful, the shareholders decided to sell the R/V Victory and recoup their investment. On February 23, 1976, therefore, they agreed to sell the boat for $80,000 with Pontiac receiving $20,000 from the sale. That sale never materialized, but the R/V Victory was eventually sold for $42,000, and Cargo paid Richard Stinnett $6,000 for the sale of the boat.

On its 1974 federal income tax return, pursuant to § 166(a), Pontiac deducted $56,388.63 as a partially worthless debt for its advances to Cargo. It computed this amount by subtracting $20,000, the anticipated amount Pontiac would have received from the sale of the R/V Victory, from $76,388.63, the total amount Pontiac claimed it had advanced Cargo. The Commissioner disallowed the partially worthless debt deduction, and determined that the contributions from Pontiac to Cargo constituted constructive dividends to Stinnett in 1973 and 1974. Therefore, these dividends were taxable to Stinnett pursuant to §§ 301, 316....

B. *Were Pontiac's Advances to Cargo Constructive Dividends to Stinnett?*

A corporate distribution to a shareholder is a dividend which the shareholder must include in his gross income if the distribution comes out of current and accumulated earnings and profits. §§ 61(a)(7); 301(c)(1). "[A] transfer of property from one corporation to another corporation may constitute a [constructive] dividend to an individual who has an ownership interest in both corporations." *Sammons v. Commissioner of Internal Revenue*, 472 F.2d 449, 451 (5th Cir. 1972).

In *Sammons*, the Fifth Circuit delineated the standard to determine whether a transfer of funds from one corporation to another corporation constitutes a dividend to an individual who owns shares in both corporations:

> In every case, the transfer must be measured by an objective test [the distribution test]: did the transfer cause funds or other property to leave the control of the transferor corporation and did it allow the stockholder to exercise control over such funds or property either directly or indirectly through some instrumentality other than the transferor corporation. If this first assay is satisfied by a transfer of funds from one corporation to another rather than by a transfer to the controlling shareholder, a second, subjective test of purpose must also be satisfied before dividend characterization results. Though a search for intent or purpose is not ordinarily prerequisite

to discovery of a dividend, such a subjective test must necessarily be utilized to differentiate between the normal business transactions of related corporations and those transactions designed primarily to benefit the stock-owner. *Id.* at 451.

The advances from Pontiac to Cargo satisfy the distribution test. Stinnett, the common owner of shares in Cargo and Pontiac, received the funds from Pontiac and transferred them to Cargo as a capital contribution. *Sammons*, 472 F.2d at 453. Such a distribution is effected on the theory "that the funds pass from the transferor to the common stockholder as a dividend and then to the transferee as a capital contribution." *Id.* The only question, therefore, is whether the purpose test has been met in this case.

In determining whether the primary purpose test has been met, we must determine not only whether a subjective intent to primarily benefit the shareholders exists, but also whether an actual primary economic benefit exists for the shareholders. *Kuper v. Commissioner of Internal Revenue*, 533 F.2d 152, 160 (5th Cir. 1976). The tax court's finding of the primary purposes for the transfers is a question of fact and may not be disturbed unless clearly erroneous. *Kuper*, 533 F.2d at 161; *Sammons*, 472 F.2d at 452. In this case, the tax court concluded that the transfers were motivated to primarily benefit Stinnett and not Pontiac. This finding is not clearly erroneous.

If Pontiac had not made the advances to Cargo on Stinnett's behalf, Stinnett would have forfeited his interest in Cargo. Moreover, when Cargo was liquidated, Stinnett received $6,000 in the distribution. If the advances had not been made, Stinnett would have been unable to recoup any of his investment. Additionally, Stinnett's ownership interest in Cargo increased from 43% to 55% because of these advances. The evidence indicates that the advances from Pontiac to Cargo benefitted Stinnett. We, therefore, must affirm the tax court's ruling. Since the contributions from Pontiac to Cargo satisfy the *Sammons* test, they constitute constructive dividends to Stinnett; and therefore, the tax court properly included the amount of the advances in Stinnett's income....

Affirmed.

PROBLEM 16-3

Consider the following fact pattern and how you would reconstruct it, if at all: Jr. and Sis own J & S, Inc., a cash-method calendar year corporation which is in the newspaper business. Sis is prim and proper and has grown up to be a powerful business executive. Jr. is a slob and an alcoholic. Sis has no children but Jr. has two, both of whom are minors and are beneficiaries of a trust fund established for them with a modest contribution by their grandparents five years ago. The grandparents have since died. J & S is owned equally by Jr. and Sis, and it pays both a salary. Jr. received a salary of $80,000 a year, which is lavish, and Sis received a salary of $120,000 a year, which is almost surely not enough for a woman of her extraordinary talents. Every year the siblings, acting as directors of J & S, have caused J & S, Inc. to contribute $20,000 to the trust fund for the children. Things have gone on like this for years, and it is unlikely that they are going to change for quite some time. J & S recently hired you to enter the scene and make an honest appraisal of the situation from a federal income tax perspective. What do you think?

G. DISTRIBUTIONS OF PROPERTY

Read § 311(a) and (b)(1)-(2).

The amount of a distribution of property in kind is its value. § 301(b)(1). That means the shareholder takes a fair-market-value basis in the property. § 301(d). If the property is encumbered, the amount of the distribution, but not the basis of the property, is correspondingly reduced. § 301(c).

If a corporation distributes property, other than its own stock or rights to acquire its own stock, to a shareholder and the value of the property exceeds the corporation's adjusted basis in the property, the corporation is treated as if it had sold the property at the time of the distribution. The corporation will recognize gain on the excess of the fair market value over the adjusted basis of the property. Moreover, its earnings and profits increase, thereby enhancing the likelihood that the distribution will produce a taxable dividend to the recipient(s) of the property. § 312(a), (b).

> *To illustrate*: Midwest Freight Lines, Inc. distributes a keg of beer to its sole shareholder, Sara. The keg of beer is worth $200, has a basis of $100 in the hands of the corporation, and is subject to a nonrecourse debt of $100. The corporation is taxed on $100 of gain, and its earnings and profits are increased by the same amount. The amount of the distribution to Sara is $100, and it is all a taxable dividend (because of the $100 e.&p. created by the distribution itself). Sara's basis in the keg becomes $200. If her basis were only $100, then she would pay a tax on a $100 gain if someone immediately bought the keg from her. That would result in total income of $200, even though she has clearly received only $100 of value.

If shareholders think they can receive nontaxable dividends and safely avoid adjusting their stock basis under § 301(c), they are wrong. The corporation must file Form 5452 if nontaxable dividends are paid to stockholders. The information called for by the form is extensive.

NOTES AND PROBLEMS

1. *How about losses?* Review § 311(b). Does it allow the corporation to report a loss on distributed property? If not, what should a corporation do instead of distributing loss property?

2. *Effect on earnings and profits.* A distribution of property in kind at a gain increases the corporation's earnings and profits, as noted above. The distribution also *reduces* earnings and profits (for future purposes) by the fair market value of the distributed property, just like a cash distribution. § 312(a)(3), (b)(2). In the case of a distribution of *loss* property, the corporation can reduce earnings and profits only by the full basis of the property, and thus cannot enjoy the full value of the loss for purposes of its earnings and profits account. § 312(a)(3).

3. *Tax planning.* The problem with § 311 is that if the corporation holds rapidly appreciating property that it plans to dispose of, it will pay a major tax whether it distributes the property or sells it. One popular proposal is to have the corporation contribute the property to a partnership that it forms with its shareholders and continue to have access to the property via a lease. The partnership would be structured to shift a hefty portion of the gain to the shareholders when the property is distributed. Section 704(c) will prevent allocating away pre-contribution gain, but not post-contribution gain. *See* Lemons & Child, *Using a Partnership Freeze to Shift Future Appreciation in Corporate Assets*, 69 J. Tax'n 84 (1988).

4. *Valuation.* Assigning a value to property is not easy if there is no ready market for the item. Can a corporation minimize its and its shareholders' tax liabilities by declaring that the property is not even worth the amount of the liabilities? *See* § 311(b)(2).

5. *The May Department Store ruling and its aftermath.* A partnership can be used as a screen for selling property.

This refers to a transaction involving the May Department Stores in the late 1980's. It ran as follows. May wanted to sell the stock of its real estate subsidiary. May and the prospective buyers formed a 50:50 partnership to which May contributed the stock of the real estate sub and the prospective buyers contributed $550 million in cash, being equal to the fair market value of the real estate sub. The new partnership then took the cash and bought $550 million of May common stock directly from May. (May had recently acquired the stock on the open market.) After a dignified period of time to avoid both the step transaction and disguised sale doctrines the partnership set to be terminated, with May receiving back its common stock and the buyer getting the stock of the real estate sub. If the deal worked, May would avoid the gain recognized under § 311(b) (when bought on the open market) or under § 1001 (when bought from May itself) on the appreciated property and the buyer would get a cost basis in the real estate sub under § 732(b). *See* Notice 89-37, 1989-13 IRB 7, issued under section 337(d). It in effect forces May to report a gain on the *redemption* and imposes § 311 (not 732) on the redemption.

G. DISTRIBUTIONS OF PROPERTY

REV. RUL. 84-71
1984-1 C.B. 106

The Internal Revenue Service has reconsidered Rev. Rul. 80-284, 1980-2 C.B. 117, and Rev. Rul. 80-285, 1980-2 C.B. 119, in which transfers that satisfied the technical requirements of section 351(a) of the Internal Revenue Code were nevertheless held to constitute taxable exchanges because they were part of larger acquisitive transactions that did not meet the continuity of interest test generally applicable to acquisitive reorganizations.

In Rev. Rul. 80-284, fourteen percent of T corporation's stock was held by A, president and chairman of the board, and eighty-six percent by the public. P, an unrelated, publicly held corporation wished to purchase the stock of T. All the T stockholders except A were willing to sell the T stock for cash. A wished to avoid recognition of gain.

In order to accommodate these wishes, the following transactions were carried out as part of an overall plan. First, P and A formed a new corporation, S. P transferred cash and other property to S in exchange solely for all of S's common stock; A transferred T stock to S solely in exchange for all of S's preferred stock. These transfers were intended to be tax-free under section 351 of the Code. Second, S organized a new corporation, D, and transferred to D the cash it had received from P in exchange for all the D common stock. Third, D was merged into T under state law. As a result of the merger, each share of T stock, except those shares held by S, were surrendered for cash equal to the stock's fair market value and each share of D stock was converted into T stock.

Rev. Rul. 80-284 concluded that if a purported section 351 exchange is an integral part of a larger transaction that fits a pattern common to acquisitive reorganizations, and if the continuity of shareholder interest requirement of section 1.368-1(b) of the Income Tax Regulations is not satisfied with respect to the larger transaction, then the transaction as a whole resembles a sale and the exchange cannot qualify under section 351 because that section is not intended to apply to sales. Rev. Rul. 80-285 reached a similar conclusion with respect to an asset, rather than stock, acquisition in which a purported section 351 exchange was also part of a larger acquisitive transaction.

Upon reconsideration, the Service has concluded that the fact that "larger acquisitive transactions," such as those described in Rev. Rul. 80-284 and Rev. Rul. 80-285, fail to meet the requirements for tax-free treatment under the reorganization provisions of the Code does not preclude the applicability of section 351(a) to transfers that may be described as part of such larger transactions, but also, either alone or in conjunction with other transfers, meet the requirements of section 351(a).

NOTES

1. *The importance of the ruling.* To appreciate the importance of the ruling, put yourself in the position of the 14% shareholder. What did he accomplish? In what respect did he come out ahead of his fellow shareholders?

2. *Assignment of income.* In *Commissioner v. The First State Bank of Stratford*, 168 F.2d 1004 (5th Cir.), *cert. denied*, 335 U.S. 867 (1948), a bank distributed third-party promissory notes to its shareholders. The notes had been written off as worthless in the past, but the bank thought they might be collectible at some time. The notes turned out to have some value and later were collected. The Fifth Circuit held that the collections were taxable to the bank rather than the shareholders on the theory that the distribution was an anticipatory assignment of income which should be taxed to the transferor. What tax consequences does this holding imply for the shareholders?

H. DISTRIBUTION OF CORPORATE OBLIGATIONS

A corporation may decide that it is cheaper to distribute its own promissory obligations rather than cash. In such cases, it seems clear that an individual shareholder would have to report the value of each obligation as income under § 301 to the extent of available earnings and profits. It is clear that the distributing corporation will not be taxed on the distribution under §§ 311(b) and 317. Importantly, the amount of earnings and profits that are eliminated as a result of the distribution is limited to the *value* of the obligation rather than its face amount. § 312(a)(2). If it were not for this rule, a gaping loophole would open. A corporation could distribute an obligation worth far less than its face amount, say because of a low or zero rate of interest, and still reduce its earnings and profits by the face amount. This would permit earnings and profits to be artificially eliminated, thereby making later distributions tax-free returns of capital.

> *To illustrate*: X Corp. distributes a ten-year bond with a value of $60 and a face amount of $100. The $40 difference is original-issue discount, which will be reported as income to the holder and as a deduction to the issuer, over the life of the bond. *See* §§ 1272-1273 (income) and § 163(e) (deduction). The corporation reduces its earnings and profits by $60, not $100.

I. DIVIDENDS RECEIVED DEDUCTION

Read § 243.

Each time a corporation pays a dividend to a higher tier corporation which owns stock in the payor, yet another layer of corporate income taxes is imposed on the distribution. As the number of tiers increases, the amount of tax on the original profit out of which the dividend was paid would approach 100%. The result would be hard to justify.

To address this problem, the Code grants a special dividends-received deduction for corporate shareholders. The general deduction is equal to 70% of the dividends received from a domestic corporation. A close reading of § 243 shows that there is a spectrum of rates applicable to the deduction which increases with the degree to which the distributing corporation is owned by the distributee corporation:

Ownership of Distributing Corp.	Percentage Of Dividend That Can Be Deducted
- less than 20%-owned	70%
- at least 20%-owned	80%
- at least 80%-owned	100%
- small business investment corporation	100%

Some affiliated corporations, such as a parent and subsidiary or subsidiaries, can qualify to file a consolidated income tax return under §§ 1501-1504. The effect is to eliminate tax on intercorporate transactions within the consolidated group, including dividends paid by a sub to its parent. The Regulations under these sections are renowned for their length and complexity. You need not study them now.

The dividends-received deduction offers a number of tax planning opportunities to crafty taxpayers. In order to foil these people, Congress has felt itself compelled to enact a series of statutory barriers which are discussed next.

J. LEVERAGED DIVIDENDS

Read § 246A.

A crafty taxpayer might conclude that it could borrow money at 10% and use it to purchase stock that produced dividends at a rate of 10% (highly unlikely but used for illustrative purposes). If so, then each time the corporation received $100 in dividends it could claim a deduction of $70 and would report only $30 of income because of the 70% dividends-received deduction. At a 35% tax rate, this would cost the corporation $10.50 in taxes. At the same time it would be entitled to claim an interest deduction of $100, which at a 35% tax rate is worth $35. As a result, the taxpayer would have manufactured an artificial gain of $24.50 entirely due to the tax arbitrage. The economic transaction is a complete wash of $100 income and outgo. This is obviously a preposterous outcome and needs to be blocked. Section 246A does so by limiting the dividends-received deduction in proportion to the extent to which it is leveraged.

K. HOLDING PERIODS

Read § 246(c).

A corporation is not entitled to claim any dividends-received deduction for stock that is held for forty-five days or less, and that period is extended to at least ninety-one days in the case of cumulative preferred stock with an arrearage in dividends if the corporate shareholder receives more than 366 days worth of dividends. Both of these rules are designed to prevent corporations from claiming the dividends received deduction when they really just popped in and out of the market long enough to claim the dividend, exclude the bulk of it from income, and then sell the stock at a loss that reflects the fact that the dividend was paid. The loss would not be a true economic loss because ordinarily it would be exactly equal to the dividend paid out, and again the provision is designed to prevent artificial losses due to tax arbitrage alone. Another minor proviso disallows the deduction to the extent that the taxpayer is obligated, pursuant to a short sale or otherwise, to make related payments with respect to positions in substantially similar or related property. § 246(c)(i)(B).

L. RESTRICTIONS ON DEDUCTIONS FOR EXTRAORDINARY DIVIDENDS

Read § 1059(a), (c), (e).

This provision captures people who held the stock long enough to claim the dividends-received deduction but not long enough to make Congress happy. In order to prevent tax arbitrage by means of receiving large dividends and then selling the stock in order to claim a deduction solely due to payment of the dividend, § 1059 requires a reduction in the basis of stock held by corporate shareholders when they receive such dividends. True to its purpose of preventing short-term tax arbitrage, this rule does not apply if the stock with respect to which the dividend is paid was held for at least two years *before* announcement of the dividend. Basis in the stock with respect to which the dividend was paid is reduced by the non-taxed portion of the dividend (i.e., the dividend-received deduction). This effectively eliminates the possibility of claiming a deduction for the "loss." To be "extraordinary," the dividend must exceed 5% of the shareholder's adjusted basis in preferred stock or 10% of its adjusted basis in other stock. As you can see from § 1059(e), there is an exception for dividends received within an 80% or more commonly-owned affiliated group of corporations, provided that the distributed earnings and profits were earned during the period of affiliation.

M. STOCK DIVIDENDS

Read § 305(a).

M. STOCK DIVIDENDS

Common stock of a corporation represents the owner's equity in the corporation, meaning the value of the corporation less the amount of its indebtedness. As far as the owners are concerned, it makes no difference for economic purposes whether additional shares of stock are issued to the same owners if exactly in proportion to their predistribution ownership shares, because the additional stock will have no effect on their proportionate share of the equity. However, companies often declare stock dividends in order to keep the price per share of the stock low so that it will be more attractive to the public and to stimulate excitement about the company. Stock dividends were held to be tax-free in the early Supreme Court decision *Eisner v. Macomber*, 252 U.S. 189 (1920). Complications later arose in situations other than the simple common-on-common shares distribution in *Macomber*, and it was not until 1969 that the tax law in this area was stabilized in the form of what is now § 305 of the Code. Stock "splits," in which the shareholder receives say one, two, or three shares for each share currently held are rightly treated in exactly the same way for tax purposes as stock "dividends" in which one typically receives fewer shares, say one for each ten shares currently held, and in connection with which state corporation law generally requires that surplus be capitalized.

The structure of § 305 is exceptionally tidy by Code standards. It opens with the general statement in § 305(a) that gross income does not include stock distributions (or distributions of stock rights), except as otherwise provided in § 305(b). Section 305(b) in turn describes five situations in which a stock distribution is taxable to the distributee by exception to the general rule, and § 305(c) contains a subtle definitional provision which embellishes on § 305(b)(2). The remainder of this section is given over to a study of § 305 using the problem method.

1. OPTIONAL DISTRIBUTIONS TO SHAREHOLDERS

Read § 305(b)(1).

This is a draconian section because if even one shareholder has the right to get a distribution of cash or property, all the other shareholders who received stock are deemed to have received cash distributions instead.

To illustrate: The Friendly Corporation has 1,500 shareholders and is registered on the American Stock Exchange. It has decided to issue a stock dividend in which shareholders of common stock are entitled to receive one additional share of common stock, subject to one proviso, namely that Mrs. Thelma Klotz, a long-time employee of the company, is entitled to take the value of the stock dividend ($1 in her case because she only had one share) in cash instead of in the form of an additional share of stock. The company has accumulated earnings and profits of three million dollars. What is the tax impact of the stock distribution on Mrs. Klotz? On the other shareholders? Do not concern yourself with basis or holding period questions. If your conclusion is that everybody has taxable income from the stock distribution how are they expected to pay the tax without any additional cash? The shareholders will collectively recognize up to $3 million of dividend income pursuant to § 305(b)(1)(A) and Reg. § 1.305-2 because one stock dividend could be paid in cash in lieu of stock at Mrs. Klotz's election, even if she elects to take the stock! The value of the distributed stock is half the value of the existing outstanding stock.

PROBLEM 16-4

Individual A purchases 1,000 shares of common stock in XYZ Corp. at $24 per share on September 1, 1992. On September 1, 1995, XYZ Corp. distributes a stock dividend of one share of common stock on every five shares of its common stock issued and outstanding. The fair market value of XYZ Corp.'s common stock on September 1, 1995 was $50 per share.

1) How much taxable income does A recognize as a result of the stock dividend?

2) What is A's total cost basis and basis per share in his XYZ common stock after the stock distribution? *See* § 307(a) and Reg. § 1.307-1.

3) What is A's holding period for the stock?

4) What if the number of shares held by each taxpayer was not evenly divisible by 5, and so it was provided that rights to fractional shares would be paid in cash?

2. DISTRIBUTIONS OF COMMON AND PREFERRED STOCK

Read § 305(b)(3).

PROBLEM 16-5

Polluting Enterprises, Inc. has 1,000 public shareholders and two classes of common stock, Class A and Class B. Its board of directors decides to issue a dividend on the Class A shares payable in preferred stock and a dividend on the B shares payable in additional shares of Class B common stock. Is this a taxable distribution under § 305?

3. DISTRIBUTIONS ON PREFERRED

Read § 305(b)(4).

M. STOCK DIVIDENDS

PROBLEM 16-6

Some years after the distribution discussed in Problem 16-5, in an unrelated transaction, the preferred shareholders of Polluting Enterprises, Inc. receive one share of newly issued preferred stock with respect to each share of preferred stock that they held as of a certain date. The fair market value of each share of the newly issued preferred stock is $100. Do the shareholders who receive the preferred stock have income and if so in what amount? Do the common shareholders have the right to claim a deduction for the diminution in their share of the equity of the corporation? If not, is that an unfair result?

4. DISTRIBUTIONS OF CONVERTIBLE PREFERRED STOCK

Read § 305(b)(5).

PROBLEM 16-7

The Friendly Corporation has three million shares of common stock outstanding at a time when it has an enormous amount of earnings and profits. It issues one share of convertible preferred stock as a stock dividend on each share of common stock presently outstanding, which means that it has issued three million shares of the new preferred stock. The convertible preferred stock has a face amount and value of $10 per share when it is issued, and each share is convertible into one share of common stock. At present, the common stock is traded at $5 per share. The preferred stock is convertible for the next 10 years, after which the conversion feature lapses. Is this distribution taxable? *See* Reg. § 1.305-6.

5. DISPROPORTIONATE DISTRIBUTIONS

Read § 305(b)(2).

This is the most difficult aspect of the 1969 amendments. The basic concept is that a distribution of stock or rights will be taxable if the distribution (or series of distributions) has the effect of receipt of cash or property by some shareholders and an increase in the proportionate equity interest held by the other shareholders. This calls for testing for disproportionality within each class and among all of the classes of stock.

PROBLEM 16-8

Dual Corp. has two classes of common stock outstanding, Class A common and Class B common. On August 31, 1995, Dual Corp. declared a cash dividend on its Class A stock of $2 per share and declared a stock dividend of one share of Class B common on every share of its Class B common issued and outstanding. Will the shareholders of Dual Corp.'s Class B stock recognize taxable income? *See* § 305(b)(2) and Reg. § 1.305-3(b)(2).

If there is a series of distributions, it will be treated as a single transaction if the steps indicate an overall plan. The Regulations provide a presumption that there is no such plan only if the distributions are separated by at least thirty-six months. Reg. § 1.305-3(b)(4).

6. CONSTRUCTIVE DISTRIBUTIONS

Section 305(c) authorizes the Treasury Department to issue regulations that cause various corporate transactions to be treated as constructive distributions with respect to any shareholder whose proportionate interest in the corporation's earnings and profits or assets is increased as a result of the transaction. This buttresses § 305(b)(2) by creating an array of imaginary distributions which one must consult in the search for changes in proportionate interest in order to determine if § 305(b)(2) applies. For example, the Regulations indicate that a forbidden disproportionate distribution can be accomplished by a plan for periodic stock redemptions as well as through stock dividends. Note that the Regulations insist that both the redeemed and nonredeemed shareholders can be taxed, even though the nonredeemed shareholders have received no actual distribution at all.[4]

PROBLEM 16-9

Small Corporation, Inc. has ten shareholders, one of whom is tired of the business and wants to sell. The Board of Directors agrees to redeem her stock — that is, buy back all her stock — in order to facilitate her retirement. Is this transaction a distribution within the meaning of § 305(b)(2)? *See* Reg. § 1.305-3(e), example (10).

PROBLEM 16-10

National Arm Chair Corp. is equally owned by ten shareholders, each of whom owns 10% of the stock in the company. Curiously, the names of the shareholders are A, B, C, D, E, F, G, H, I, and J. The Board of Directors of the company agrees to redeem half of the stock of A, B, and C this year, half of the stock of C, D, and E next year and all of the stock of I the following year. Who if anyone has enjoyed a distribution within the meaning of § 305?

---

[4] For an example, see Rev. Rul. 78-60, 1978-1 C.B. 80 (periodic redemption plan involving three of five shareholders; ruled: the nonredeemed shareholders have § 305(b)(2) stock dividends because of their proportionately increased positions in the company, citing Reg. § 1.305-3(e), examples (8) and (9)).

Section 305 and the Regulations go very far. The statute authorizes regulations under which, even *without any distribution of stock by the corporation*, the following transactions or events shall be treated as a distribution to which § 301 applies (a potentially taxable dividend) with respect to any shareholder whose proportionate interest in the earnings and profits or assets of the corporation is increased by such event: (a) a change in conversion ratio; (b) a change in redemption price; (c) a difference between redemption price and issue price; (d) a redemption that is treated as a distribution to which § 301 applies; or (e) any transaction (including a recapitalization) having a similar effect on the interest of any shareholder. The Regulations also are broad and scary. A "deemed" distribution under § 305(c) is taxable if it has a result described in § 305(b)(2)-(5). Read § 1.305-7(a).

N. BASIS AND HOLDING PERIOD OF STOCK

Read § 307(a) and Reg. § 1.307-1.

If a shareholder receives new stock tax-free under § 305(a), basis must be reallocated to the new stock from the old stock by reference to the relative values of the old and new stock. § 307. For example, if the old stock has a basis of $20 and was worth $40 after the distribution, and the new stock was worth $10 after the distribution, one-fifth of the basis ($10/$50 of total value), or $4, would be allocated to the new stock, and the old stock would have a basis of $16 ($40/$50). In addition, the holding period of the new stock will include the period during which the shareholder held the old stock. § 1223(5). The practical effect is to split the basis between the old and the new stock and to assign the new stock a "tacked" holding period. The corporation will not reduce its earnings and profits in connection with a nontaxable distribution of stock. *See* § 312(d)(1). This is logical because the distribution is not viewed as a dividend, it is viewed as a non-event, the only impact of which to require a reallocation of basis and holding period at the shareholder level.

By contrast, if the distribution is taxable, § 301 will apply. The amount of the distribution will, as usual, be its fair market value. Reg. § 1.305-2(b), example (1) and Reg. § 1.301-1(d). This is consistent with the usual rule for distributions of property. The corporation will reduce its earnings and profits by the fair market value of the stock or rights distributed. Reg. § 1.312-1(d). There is no § 307 reallocation of basis and no tacking of the holding period. This is the standard result whenever one receives property in a fully taxable transaction. Distributions of stock rights are generally taxed the same way as distributions of stock.

O. SECTION 306 STOCK

The double-tax model on which Subchapter C is founded and any tax-rate differential for capital gains guarantees that shareholders and their tax advisors will relentlessly search for ways to take money out of corporations at capital gains rates, but — to the extent possible — without surrendering their level of control of the corporation. Ingenuity and boldness were well rewarded in *Chamberlin v. Commissioner*, 207 F.2d 462 (6th Cir. 1953), *cert. denied*, 347 U.S. 918 (1954), a case that created a recipe for the wicked. The steps in *Chamberlin* were as follows:

1. Distribute nonvoting preferred stock pro rata to the shareholders of the common stock, allocating part of the basis of the common stock to the newly issued preferred stock, as directed by § 307;

2. The common shareholders sell their preferred stock to a life insurance company by prearranged plan;

3. Some years later, the insurance company has its preferred stock redeemed by the corporation. The result when the dust clears is that the original shareholders have not surrendered any control and they have cash in their pockets from the sale of the stock to the insurance company which is taxed at favorable capital gains rates with an offset for the allocated basis as well.

A less generous court might have concluded that the overall transaction was really a dividend and the insurance company little more than a well-paid puppet. Be that as it may, rather than risk further losses in litigation, the Treasury got its way in Congress instead when § 306 was enacted in 1954. This created a new type of stock known as "Section 306 stock." The magic of this stock is that when it is sold or otherwise disposed of some, or sometimes all, of the "amount realized" is taxable as ordinary income. Section 306 has its complications, and some important exceptions, but if you keep the *Chamberlin* pattern in mind, it is not difficult to see why § 306 operates as it does. Section 306 stock arises only if "stock other than common stock" is issued at a time when the corporation has earnings and profits. For this purpose, "common stock" is stock that has either unlimited dividend or liquidation rights. Rev. Rul. 79-163, 1979-1 C.B. 131. Thus, for example, nonvoting redeemable stock with no dividend or liquidating preference has been ruled common stock. Rev. Rul. 75-222, 1975-2 C.B. 105.

PROBLEM 16-11

L and M are the two sole shareholders of X Corp.; each owns 50% of X Corp.'s issued and outstanding common stock. During the current year, pursuant to a § 368(a)(1)(E) recapitalization, L and M each received preferred stock from X Corp. in a § 305 stock dividend which had an allocable basis of $15,000 under § 307(a). The value of the stock when distributed to both L and M is $30,000 ($15,000 each). The accumulated and current earnings and profits of X Corp. was $40,000 at the time of the distribution.

In the next year, X Corp. redeemed L's preferred stock for $35,000. X Corp.'s accumulated and current earnings and profits at the time of the redemption was $25,000.

O. SECTION 306 STOCK

In the following year, M sells his preferred stock to D for $20,000. X Corp.'s accumulated and current earnings and profits at the time of the sale is $5,000.

(a) Is the stock received by L and M "§ 306 stock"? *See* § 306(c)(1) and Reg. § 1.306-3.

(b) What are the tax consequences to L on his redemption of his preferred stock? *See* § 306(a)(1) and Reg. § 1.306-1.

(c) What are the tax consequences to M resulting from the sale of his preferred stock? *See* § 306(a)(1) and Reg. § 1.306-1.

(d) What prior planning do these rules suggest?

PROBLEM 16-12

A owns 1500 shares of Big Corp. common stock and 300 shares of Big Corp. preferred stock all of which is § 306 stock. A's basis in her common and preferred stock totals $30,000. A sells all of her Big Corp. common and preferred stock to B, an unrelated buyer, for $100,000. What are the tax consequences of the sale to A?

OUTSIDE READINGS

C. Crane, *Toward a Theory of the Corporate Tax Base: The Effect of a Corporate Distribution of Encumbered Property to Shareholders,"* 44 Tax L. Rev. 113 (Fall 1988).

N. Kyser, *The Long and Winding Road: Characterization of Boot Under Section 356(a)(2)*, 39 Tax L. Rev. 297 (Spring 1984).

G. Mundstock, *Taxation of Intercorporate Dividends Under an Unintegrated Regime*, 44 Tax L. Rev. 1 (Fall 1988).

Chapter 17
REDEMPTIONS OF CORPORATE STOCK

State law generally permits corporations to repurchase (redeem) their own stock, for cash or other property. For example, it is common for publicly-held corporations that have excess cash to buy back their own stock on the open market if they have no better use for the money. This is generally welcomed by investors and tends to support the price of the stock. The picture tends to be different for several reasons when one discusses redemptions of stock of closely-held corporations. For one thing, redemptions may tip the balance of power among the shareholders. For another, the redemption is likely to implicate some serious tax questions.

To understand the tax problem, consider the following two extreme cases. In one case, Mr. A owns all the stock of X Corp., 100 shares. If he causes X Corp. to buy back some of his stock (50 shares) in *exchange* for cash, it is obvious that the end result is no different from a distribution of cash *with respect to* his 100 shares, and deserves to be treated as such because his level of 100% ownership is completely unchanged by the redemption. Conversely, if a Mr. B, who owns 1% of the stock of X Corp., sells three-fourths of his stock to X Corp. in exchange for cash, it looks much more like a true sale, so that Mr. B should be entitled to sale or exchange treatment ensuring exchange gain (possibly capital gain) on the transaction, as if he had sold to an unrelated buyer. The Code will generally assure that result. The picture is further confused if Mr. B is Mr. A's uncle and is fond of Mr. A. In that case, if one views A and B as a group, the transaction looks more like a *distribution* than an *exchange*. A redemption is never *exactly* the same as a distribution, because the amount of stock outstanding does change.

A. CONSTRUCTIVE OWNERSHIP

Read § 318(a).

The attribution rules "consider" stock to be owned by certain related parties by virtue of their relationship to the actual owner. The rules are simple in concept, but tricky to apply. The key provisions attribute constructive ownership of stock from some family members to others, from some entities to their owners, and from some owners to entities. For this purpose, the term "owners" is used loosely to include beneficiaries of estates and trusts.

A few general comments about the constructive ownership rules are in order. First, they are somewhat arbitrary. For example, a grandchild is never deemed to own her grandparent's stock, but the grandparents are deemed to own her stock, presumably on the theory that a grandparent always controls the grandchildren. § 318(a)(1)(A)(ii). That usually makes sense, but not always. The rules do not apply to some family relationships for reasons difficult to discern. For example, siblings are not deemed to own each others' stock, nor does one count aunts, uncles, nieces and nephews. The rule against double family attribution in § 318(a)(5)(B) keeps it that way. For example, stock which is first attributed from a son to his father under § 318(a)(1)(A)(ii), cannot be attributed a second time from the father to his daughter under the same Code section. If the father holds an option to buy his son's shares, however, the shares can be double-deemed to daughter because of a special rule giving priority to constructive ownership through options over family attribution in the event that both rules apply. § 318(a)(5)(D).

> *To illustrate*: The family consists of Mom, Dad, Sis and Junior (who are siblings). Mom has an option to buy 1,000 shares of stock held by Sis. Mom is deemed to own the 1,000 shares of stock under either of two theories, namely that she is a family member and that she holds an option. The stock Mom holds constructively because of the option *can* be attributed to Junior, because § 318(a)(4)(D) says the option rule displaces the family ownership rule when they overlap.

Another interesting feature is that there is no "sideways" attribution. § 318(a)(5)(C). This means that stock attributed from an owner to an entity cannot be attributed again from the entity to another owner. By contrast, stock *actually* held by the entity is attributed proportionately to the owners of the entity.

> *To illustrate*: Partner A, who is an equal partner of the ABC Partnership, owns as an individual 300 shares of X Corp. All 300 shares of X Corp. are constructively owned by the ABC Partnership under § 318(a)(3)(A). The ABC Partnership actually owns 300 shares of Y Corp. Each of the partners is deemed to own 100 shares of Y Corp. under § 318(a)(2)(A), but partners B and C are *not* deemed to own 100 shares of X Corp. because that would violate the anti-sidewise attribution rule of § 318(a)(5)(C). Stock cannot be attributed to an entity from an owner and then attributed out again to a different owner.

Apart from the above two prohibitions against double-attribution, multiple-attribution is *required*. Thus if father A is a beneficiary of Estate E which owns stock in X Corp., the X Corp. stock *must* be attributed to A in proportion to his percentage interest in E; then A's constructively owned stock in X Corp. *must* be attributed to his son B, and again from son B to Partnership BC of which B is a partner, and yet again from Partnership BC to Y Corp. if BC owns 50% or more of the stock of Y Corp.

B. REDEMPTION NOT ESSENTIALLY EQUIVALENT TO A DIVIDEND

You will return to the constructive ownership rules frequently in this chapter in connection with analyzing the various Code sections that permit redemptions to be treated like sales, which is the principal subject of the remainder of this chapter.

The basic theme henceforth is that if the shareholder's percentage interest in the corporation is sufficiently reduced by the redemption, the result will be treated as a sale for federal income tax purposes; if not, it will be treated as a distribution. In general, the reduction is measured at the shareholder level. Measuring contraction of activity at the corporate level is important only for determining whether a distribution qualifies as a a so-called partial liquidation under § 302(b)(4) and (e) which is considered later in this chapter.

Most of the rest of this chapter is given over to identifying stock redemptions that qualify as exchanges (return of capital and exchange gain or loss) and therefore avoid dividend (ordinary income to extent of earnings and profits) treatment. Such redemptions are described in §§ 302 and 303 and consist of the following types, namely redemptions that are:

1. Not essentially equivalent to a dividend;
2. Substantially disproportionate in terms of shareholder ownership;
3. In complete termination of a shareholder's interest;
4. In partial liquidation of a corporation and made to a noncorporate shareholder;
5. To pay a shareholder's death taxes, funeral expenses, and costs of administering the estate.

B. REDEMPTION NOT ESSENTIALLY EQUIVALENT TO A DIVIDEND

Read § 302(a) and (b) and Reg. § 1.302-2.

The following case is the fountainhead of learning for interpreting § 302(b)(1).

UNITED STATES v. DAVIS
397 U.S. 301 (1970)

MARSHALL, J.

In 1945, taxpayer and E. B. Bradley organized a corporation. In exchange for property transferred to the new company, Bradley received 500 shares of common stock, and taxpayer and his wife similarly each received 250 such shares. Shortly thereafter, taxpayer made an additional contribution to the corporation, purchasing 1,000 shares of preferred stock at a par value of $25 per share.

The purpose of this latter transaction was to increase the company's working capital and thereby to qualify for a loan previously negotiated through the Reconstruction Finance Corporation. It was understood that the corporation would redeem the preferred stock when the RFC loan had been repaid. Although in the interim taxpayer bought Bradley's 500 shares and divided them between his son and daughter, the total capitalization of the company remained the same until 1963. That year, after the loan was fully repaid and in accordance with the original understanding, the company redeemed taxpayer's preferred stock.

In his 1963 personal income tax return taxpayer did not report the $25,000 received by him upon the redemption of his preferred stock as income. Rather, taxpayer considered the redemption as a sale of his preferred stock to the company—a capital gains transaction under § 302 of the Internal Revenue Code of 1954 resulting in no tax since taxpayer's basis in the stock equaled the amount he received for it. The Commissioner of Internal Revenue, however, did not approve this tax treatment. According to the Commissioner, the redemption of taxpayer's stock was essentially equivalent to a dividend and was thus taxable as ordinary income under §§ 301 and 316 of the Code. Taxpayer paid the resulting deficiency and brought this suit for a refund. The District Court ruled in his favor, 274 F. Supp. 466 (D.C.M.D. Tenn. 1967), and on appeal the Court of Appeals affirmed. 408 F.2d 1139 (C.A. 6th Cir. 1969).

The Court of Appeals held that the $25,000 received by taxpayer was "not essentially equivalent to a dividend" within the meaning of that phrase in § 302(b)(1) of the Code because the redemption was the final step in a course of action that had a legitimate business (as opposed to a tax avoidance) purpose. That holding represents only one of a variety of treatments accorded similar transactions under § 302(b)(1) in the circuit courts of appeals. We granted certiorari, 396 U.S. 815 (1969), in order to resolve this recurring tax question involving stock redemptions by closely held corporations. We reverse.

The Internal Revenue Code of 1954 provides generally in §§ 301 and 316 for the tax treatment of distributions by a corporation to its shareholders; under those provisions, a distribution is includable in a taxpayer's gross income as a dividend out of earnings and profits to the extent such earnings exist. There are exceptions to the application of these general provisions, however, and among them are those found in § 302 involving certain distributions for redeemed stock. The basic question in this case is whether the $25,000 distribution by the corporation to taxpayer falls under that section — more specifically, whether its legitimate business motivation qualifies the distribution under § 302(b)(1) of the Code. Preliminarily, however, we must consider the relationship between § 302(b)(1) and the rules regarding the attribution of stock ownership found in § 318(a) of the Code.

Under subsection (a) of § 302, a distribution is treated as "payment in exchange for the stock," thus qualifying for capital gains rather than ordinary income treatment, if the conditions contained in any one of the four paragraphs of subsection (b) are met. In addition to paragraph (1)'s "not essentially equivalent to a dividend" test, capital gains treatment is available where (2) the taxpayer's voting strength is substantially diminished, (3) his interest in the company is completely terminated, or (4) certain railroad stock is redeemed. Paragraph (4) is not involved here, and taxpayer admits that paragraphs (2) and

B. REDEMPTION NOT ESSENTIALLY EQUIVALENT TO A DIVIDEND 339

(3) do not apply. Moreover, taxpayer agrees that for the purposes of §§ 302(b)(2) and (3) the attribution rules of § 318(a) apply and he is considered to own the 750 outstanding shares of common stock held by his wife and children in addition to the 250 shares in his own name.

Taxpayer, however, argues that the attribution rules do not apply in considering whether a distribution is essentially equivalent to a dividend under § 302(b)(1). According to taxpayer, he should thus be considered to own only 25% of the corporation's common stock, and the distribution would then qualify under § 302(b)(1) since it was not pro rata or proportionate to his stock interest, the fundamental test of dividend equivalency. *See* Treas. Reg. 1.302-2(b). However, the plain language of the statute compels rejection of the argument. In subsection (c) of § 302, the attribution rules are made specifically applicable "in determining the ownership of stock for purposes of this section." Applying this language, both courts below held that § 318(a) applies to all of § 302, including § 302(b)(1) — a view in accord with the decisions of the other courts of appeals, a longstanding treasury regulation, and the opinion of the leading commentators.

Against this weight of authority, taxpayer argues that the result under paragraph (1) should be different because there is no explicit reference to stock ownership as there is in paragraphs (2) and (3). Neither that fact, however, nor the purpose and history of § 302(b)(1) support taxpayer's argument. The attribution rules — designed to provide a clear answer to what would otherwise be a difficult tax question — formed part of the tax bill that was subsequently enacted as the 1954 Code. As is discussed further, *infra*, the bill as passed by the House of Representatives contained no provision comparable to § 302(b)(1). When that provision was added in the Senate, no purpose was evidenced to restrict the applicability of § 318(a). Rather, the attribution rules continued to be made specifically applicable to the entire section, and we believe that Congress intended that they be taken into account wherever ownership of stock was relevant.

Indeed, it was necessary that the attribution rules apply to § 302(b)(1) unless they were to be effectively eliminated from consideration with regard to §§ 302(b)(2) and (3) also. For if a transaction failed to qualify under one of those sections solely because of the attribution rules, it would according to taxpayer's argument nonetheless qualify under § 302(b)(1). We cannot agree that Congress intended so to nullify its explicit directive. We conclude, therefore, that the attribution rules of § 318(a) do apply; and, for the purposes of deciding whether a distribution is "not essentially equivalent to a dividend" under § 302(b)(1), taxpayer must be deemed the owner of all 1,000 shares of the company's common stock.

II

After application of the stock ownership attribution rules, this case viewed most simply involves a sole stockholder who causes part of his shares to be redeemed by the corporation. We conclude that such a redemption is always "essentially equivalent to a dividend" within the meaning of that phrase in § 302(b)(1) and therefore do not reach the Government's alternative argument that in any event the distribution should not on the facts of this case qualify for capital gains treatment.

The predecessor of § 302(b)(1) came into the tax law as § 201(d) of the Revenue Act of 1921, 42 Stat. 228:

> "A stock dividend shall not be subject to tax but if after the distribution of any such dividend the corporation proceeds to cancel or redeem its stock at such time and in such manner as to make the distribution and cancellation or redemption essentially equivalent to the distribution of a taxable dividend, the amount received in redemption or cancellation of the stock shall be treated as a taxable dividend...."

Enacted in response to this Court's decision that pro rata stock dividends do not constitute taxable income, *Eisner v. Macomber*, 252 U.S. 189 (1920), the provision had the obvious purpose of preventing a corporation from avoiding dividend tax treatment by distributing earnings to its shareholders in two transactions — a pro rata stock dividend followed by a pro rata redemption — that would have the same economic consequences as a simple dividend. Congress, however, soon recognized that even without a prior stock dividend essentially the same result could be effected whereby any corporation, "especially one which has only a few stockholders, might be able to make a distribution to its stockholders which would have the same effect as a taxable dividend." H.R. Rep. No. 1, 69th Cong., 1st Sess., 5. In order to cover this situation, the law was amended to apply "(whether or not such stock was issued as a stock dividend)" whenever a distribution in redemption of stock was made "at such time and in such manner" that it was essentially equivalent to a taxable dividend. Revenue Act of 1926, § 201(g), 44 Stat. 11.

This provision of the 1926 Act was carried forward in each subsequent revenue act and finally became § 115(g)(1) of the Internal Revenue Code of 1939. Unfortunately, however, the policies encompassed within the general language of § 115(g)(1) and its predecessors were not clear, and there resulted much confusion in the tax law. At first, courts assumed that the provision was aimed at tax avoidance schemes and sought only to determine whether such a scheme existed. *See, e.g., Commissioner v. Quackenbos*, 78 F.2d 156 (C.A. 2d Cir. 1935). Although later the emphasis changed and the focus was more on the effect of the distribution, many courts continued to find that distributions otherwise like a dividend were not "essentially equivalent" if, for example, they were motivated by a sufficiently strong nontax business purpose.... There was general disagreement, however, about what would qualify as such a purpose, and the result was a case-by-case determination with each case decided "on the basis of the particular facts of the transaction in question." *Bains v. United States*, 153 Ct. Cl. 599, 603, 289 F.2d 644, 646 (1961).

B. REDEMPTION NOT ESSENTIALLY EQUIVALENT TO A DIVIDEND

By the time of the general revision resulting in the Internal Revenue Code of 1954, the draftsmen were faced with what has aptly been described as "the morass created by the decisions." *Ballenger v. United States*, 301 F.2d 192, 196 (C.A. 4th Cir. 1962). In an effort to eliminate "the considerable confusion which exists in this area" and thereby to facilitate tax planning, H.R. Rep. No. 1337, 83d Cong., 2d Sess., 35, the authors of the new Code sought to provide objective tests to govern the tax consequences of stock redemptions. Thus, the tax bill passed by the House of Representatives contained no "essentially equivalent" language. Rather, it provided for "safe harbors" where capital gains treatment would be accorded to corporate redemptions that met the conditions now found in §§ 302(b)(2) and (3) of the Code.

It was in the Senate Finance Committee's consideration of the tax bill that § 302(b)(1) was added, and Congress thereby provided that capital gains treatment should be available "if the redemption is not essentially equivalent to a dividend." Taxpayer argues that the purpose was to continue "existing law," and there is support in the legislative history that § 302(b)(1) reverted "in part" or "in general" to the "essentially equivalent" provision of § 115(g)(1) of the 1939 Code. According to the Government, even under the old law it would have been improper for the Court of Appeals to rely on "a business purpose for the redemption" and "an absence of the proscribed tax avoidance purpose to bail out dividends at favorable tax rates." *See Northup v. United States*, 240 F.2d 304, 307 (C.A. 2d Cir. 1957); *Smith v. United States*, 121 F.2d 692, 695 (C.A. 3d Cir. 1941); *cf. Commissioner v. Estate of Bedford*, 325 U.S. 283 (1945). However, we need not decide that question, for we find from the history of the 1954 revisions and the purpose of § 302(b)(1) that Congress intended more than merely to re-enact the prior law.

In explaining the reason for adding the "essentially equivalent" test, the Senate Committee stated that the House provisions "appeared unnecessarily restrictive, particularly, in the case of redemptions of preferred stock which might be called by the corporation without the shareholder having any control over when the redemption may take place." S. Rep. No. 1622, 83d Cong., 2d Sess., 44. This explanation gives no indication that the purpose behind the redemption should affect the result. Rather, in its more detailed technical evaluation of § 302(b)(1), the Senate Committee reported as follows:

> "The test intended to be incorporated in the interpretation of paragraph (1) is in general that currently employed under section 115(g)(1) of the 1939 Code. Your committee further intends that in applying this test for the future ... the inquiry will be devoted solely to the question of whether or not the transaction by its nature may properly be characterized as a sale of stock by the redeeming shareholder to the corporation. For this purpose the presence or absence of earnings and profits of the corporation is not material. Example: X, the sole shareholder of a corporation having no earnings or profits causes the corporation to redeem half of its stock.

Paragraph (1) does not apply to such redemption notwithstanding the absence of earnings and profits." S. Rep. No. 1622, *supra*, at 234.

The intended scope of § 302(b)(1) as revealed by this legislative history is certainly not free from doubt. However, we agree with the Government that by making the sole inquiry relevant for the future the narrow one whether the redemption could be characterized as a sale, Congress was apparently rejecting past court decisions that had also considered factors indicating the presence or absence of a tax-avoidance motive.[1] At least that is the implication of the example given. Congress clearly mandated that pro rata distributions be treated under the general rules laid down in §§ 301 and 316 rather than under § 302, and nothing suggests that there should be a different result if there were a "business purpose" for the redemption. Indeed, just the opposite inference must be drawn since there would not likely be a tax-avoidance purpose in a situation where there were no earnings or profits. We conclude that the Court of Appeals was therefore wrong in looking for a business purpose and considering it in deciding whether the redemption was equivalent to a dividend. Rather, we agree with the Court of Appeals for the Second Circuit that "the business purpose of a transaction is irrelevant in determining dividend equivalence" under § 302(b)(1). *Hasbrook v. United States*, 343 F.2d 811, 814 (1965).

Taxpayer strongly argues that to treat the redemption involved here as essentially equivalent to a dividend is to elevate form over substance. Thus, taxpayer argues, had he not bought Bradley's shares or had he made a subordinated loan to the company instead of buying preferred stock, he could have gotten back his $25,000 with favorable tax treatment. However, the difference between form and substance in the tax law is largely problematical, and taxpayer's complaints have little to do with whether a business purpose is relevant under § 302(b)(1). It was clearly proper for Congress to treat distributions generally as taxable dividends when made out of earnings and profits and then to prevent avoidance of that result without regard to motivation where the distribution is in exchange for redeemed stock.

We conclude that that is what Congress did when enacting § 302(b)(1). If a corporation distributes property as a simple dividend, the effect is to transfer the

---

[1] This rejection is confirmed by the Committee's acceptance of the House treatment of distributions involving corporate contractions — a factor present in many of the earlier "business purpose" redemptions. In describing its action, the Committee stated as follows:

> "Your committee, as did the House bill, separates into their significant elements the kind of transactions now incoherently aggregated in the definition of a partial liquidation. Those distributions which may have capital-gain characteristics *because they are not made pro rata* among the various shareholders would be subjected, at the shareholder level, to the separate tests described in [§§ 301 and 318]. On the other hand, those distributions characterized by what happens solely at the corporate level by reason of the assets distributed would be included as within the concept of a partial liquidation." S. Rep. No. 1622, *supra*, at 49. (Emphasis added.)

B. REDEMPTION NOT ESSENTIALLY EQUIVALENT TO A DIVIDEND

property from the company to its shareholders without a change in the relative economic interests or rights of the stockholders. Where a redemption has that same effect, it cannot be said to have satisfied the "not essentially equivalent to a dividend" requirement of § 302(b)(1). Rather, to qualify for preferred treatment under that section, a redemption must result in a meaningful reduction of the shareholder's proportionate interest in the corporation. Clearly, taxpayer here, who (after application of the attribution rules) was the sole shareholder of the corporation both before and after the redemption, did not qualify under this test. The decision of the Court of Appeals must therefore be reversed and the case remanded to the District Court for dismissal of the complaint.

It is so ordered.

MR. JUSTICE DOUGLAS, with whom the CHIEF JUSTICE and MR. JUSTICE BRENNAN concur, dissenting.

I agree with the District Court ... and with the Court of Appeals ... that respondent's contribution of working capital in the amount of $25,000 in exchange for 1,000 shares of preferred stock with a par value of $25 was made in order for the corporation to obtain a loan from the RFC and that the preferred stock was to be redeemed when the loan was repaid. For the reasons stated by the two lower courts, this redemption was not "essentially equivalent to a dividend," for the bona fide business purpose of the redemption belies the payment of a dividend. As stated by the Court of Appeals:

> "Although closely-held corporations call for close scrutiny under the tax law, we will not, under the facts and circumstances of this case, allow mechanical attribution rules to transform a legitimate corporate transaction into a tax avoidance scheme."...

When the Court holds it was a dividend, it effectively cancels § 302(b)(1) from the Code. This result is not a matter of conjecture, for the Court says that in the case of closely held or one-man corporations a redemption of stock is "always" equivalent to a dividend. I would leave such revision to the Congress.

NOTES AND QUESTIONS

1. *Attribution of stock ownership.* Do you agree with the Court that as a matter of statutory construction it is clear that one must apply the attribution rules in a § 302(b)(1) case? *See* § 302(c). If so, does that inject an excessive rigidity into the rules?

2. *Family hostility.* There is some room for eliminating family attribution if one can show "family hostility," but the authorities are in conflict. *See Robin Haft Trust v. Commissioner*, 510 F.2d 43 (1st Cir. 1975) (mitigation of § 318 allowed); Rev. Rul. 80-26, 1980-1 C.B. 66 (*contra*); *Metzger Trust v. Commissioner*, 76 T.C. 42 (1981), *aff'd*, 693 F.2d 459 (5th Cir. 1982), *cert. denied*, 463 U.S. 1207 (1983) (attribution principles must be applied in assessing a shareholder's post-redemption proportionate interest, but if a reduction has occurred, hostility will then be a factor in determining whether such reduction was meaningful). This is useless for a taxpayer who owns 100% by attribution before and after the redemption, as in *Davis*, but may be helpful in other situations. There is a downside to the softening role of taking family hostility into account, because it may induce the IRS to expand the attribution net to include family members who are not referred to in § 318 on a theory of family harmony.

3. *What factors count?* It is rarely easy to tell if a particular redemption meets the standards of § 302(b)(1). The IRS and the courts have developed a fairly large body of authorities on the subject, but as the authorities increase in number they come to look more and more like a vipers' tangle than an aid to navigation. The primary reason for the confusion is that while a variety of factors have emerged as important, they are unranked. Before looking at the vipers' tangle, one needs to know that a shareholder has three different interests in a corporation, namely: the right to vote and thereby exercise control; the right to participate in current earnings and accumulated surplus; and the right to share in net assets on liquidation. *See, e.g., Himmel v. Commissioner*, 338 F.2d 815 (2d Cir. 1964). Of these interests, voting power appears to be the most important one, in part at least because minority (or nonvoting) shareholders who lack control of the corporation are not in a position to engineer schemes to disguise dividends as redemptions. Consider the following examples:

(a) A redemption causing loss of super-majority voting control when a shareholder's interest dropped from 85% to 61.7% was held to be an exchange, not a distribution, in *Wright v. United States*, 482 F.2d 600 (8th Cir. 1973). *See also Rickey v. United States*, 427 F. Supp. 484 (D.C. La. 1976). *But see* Rev. Rul. 78-401, 1978-2 C.B. 127 (*contra*).

(b) Reduction of a shareholder's voting power from over 50% to under 50%. indicates the redemption should be treated as an exchange, not a distribution. *Estate of Squier v. Commissioner*, 35 T.C. 950 (1961). There are few cases on point, which may mean the IRS simply agrees and has decided not to fight the issue.

(c) The smaller the shareholder's original interest, the greater the likelihood that the redemption will be considered meaningful, given that a small shareholder can rarely influence corporate policy. For example, in Rev. Rul. 75-512, 1975-2 C.B. 112, a decline from 30% ownership to 24.3% was meaningful.

(d) A related issue is whether the shareholder can easily gang up with other major shareholders to exercise control. In Rev. Rul. 76-364, 1976-2 C.B. 91, the redeemed shareholder owned 27% of the outstanding stock, and each of three other shareholders owned 23.33%. The redemption reduced the redeemed shareholder's interest to 22.27% and the percentage of stock owned by each of the other shareholders increased to 25.91%. In ruling that the reduction was meaningful, the IRS observed that the redemption caused the redeemed shareholder to go from a position where he could control the corporation by

B. REDEMPTION NOT ESSENTIALLY EQUIVALENT TO A DIVIDEND

acting in concert with only one other shareholder to a position where that would not be possible.

(e) Reduction of a shareholder's voting power from over 50% to exactly 50% was held sufficient to qualify for exchange treatment in Rev. Rul. 75-502, 1975-2 C.B. 111. Note that in these cases the redemption causes the shareholder to lose the power to control the corporation's day to day affairs and gives the other shareholders a veto power over corporate actions.

(f) A particularly small interest before the redemption is a strongly favorable factor. For example, where the redeemed shareholder owned .0001118% of the shares of a public corporation's only class of stock before the redemption and .0001081% after the redemption, the reduction was meaningful, largely because the shareholder exercised no control over the corporation's affairs. Rev. Rul. 76-385, 1976-2 C.B. 92.

4. *Preferred stock redemptions*. Redemptions of nonvoting preferred stock always qualify for exchange treatment provided the redeemed shareholder holds no other class of stock. *See* Rev. Rul. 77-426, 1977-2 C.B. 87. Redemptions of preferred stock in other situations are more difficult to evaluate. One must analyze the impact on the shareholder's participation in the right to vote, the right to participate in current earnings and accumulated surplus and the right to share in net assets on liquidation.

5. *Impact of redemptions of other shareholders*. Meaningfulness of any alleged reduction in the redeemed shareholder's proportionate interest must be evaluated with respect to each redeemed shareholder separately. Rev. Rul. 81-289, 1981-2 C.B. 82. If several shareholders' stock is redeemed, one looks at each shareholder after the redemption plan has been completed.

6. *Reporting to the IRS*. If a shareholder transfers stock to the corporation which issued the stock in exchange for property, the facts and circumstances of the exchange must be reported on the shareholder's return. Regs. §§ 1.302-2(b), 1.331-1(d). Quaere: If a shareholder of IBM sells some of the shares on the New York Stock Exchange, and unbeknownst to him the buyer is IBM, do the Regulations apply, and if so, how?

7. *The problem of disappearing basis*. If a stock redemption is treated as a sale, the basis of the redeemed stock is offset against the proceeds of the redemption when calculating the shareholder's gain or loss. However, if the redemption is taxed as a dividend, the basis of the redeemed shares might seem to disappear. If it did the shareholder would not only incur the tax on a dividend, but also suffer an unfairly enlarged gain or diminished loss when the remaining stock is sold. To prevent this anomaly, Reg. § 1.302-2(c) provides that basis of the redeemed stock is allocated to the shareholder's unredeemed stock, and to the extent there is no unredeemed stock, it is allocated to the stock owned by those from whom it was attributed under the § 318 rules for constructive ownership. The problem can only arise if the shareholder owns stock constructively, because if the taxpayer disposed of all his holdings actual and constructive, exchange treatment is guaranteed under § 302(b)(3).

PROBLEM 17-1

A, B, and C are otherwise unrelated equal partners in the ABC partnership. The partnership holds half of the stock of X Corp., and each partner separately owns 1/6th of the stock of X Corp. Assume that all of the stock held by the shareholders directly is redeemed by X Corp. so that the partnership emerges as the sole shareholder of X Corp.

1. Should the redemption be treated as an exchange or a distribution?
2. What becomes of the shareholders' basis in the X Corp. stock that was redeemed?
3. Does this problem indicate that there may be a risk of double taxation? Consider what would happen if the partnership sold the remaining stock and distributed the cash proceeds.
4. Change the facts in (1) above to assume that A is only a 2% partner and that B and C are each 49% partners. Will the result to A differ this time?

C. SUBSTANTIALLY DISPROPORTIONATE REDEMPTIONS

Read § 302(b)(2) and Reg. § 1.302-3.

Section 302(b)(2) contains a safe harbor provision which provides a three-part brightline rule that guarantees exchange treatment provided that the requirements of all three parts are met. After the redemption the taxpayer must (1) own less than 50% of the voting stock, (2) the redemption must reduce his ownership of voting stock to less than 80% of the percentage of his preredemption holdings, and (3) it must also reduce his ownership of all classes of common stock by the same percentage, computed by aggregate value. The 50% rule refers to ownership of the *corporation's* outstanding stock, but both the 80% rules refer only to the degree of the *shareholder's* reduction of ownership, no matter whether it was large or small at the outset. In making both calculations, one must be sure to adjust for the fact that after the redemption there will be fewer shares outstanding.

To illustrate: Shareholder A owns 55% and shareholder B owns the remaining 45% of the outstanding shares of X Corp. common stock. If a redemption of A's shares brings his percentage ownership down to 49% of the shares outstanding after the redemption, he has met the first test by owning less than 50% of the voting stock. His ownership has not dropped to below 80% of the percentage of his former holdings, however, because 49% is 89% of his former 50% holdings (49/55 = 89%). To meet the 80% test, A must go below 44% ownership (80% of 55% equals 44%). If A had owned 5% of the stock before the redemption, he would automatically meet the first test, but

C. SUBSTANTIALLY DISPROPORTIONATE REDEMPTIONS

would still have to reduce his holdings to below 4% of the new, smaller number of shares outstanding in order to meet the second (80% of 5% is 4%).

If the taxpayer fails the brightline tests of § 302(b)(2), all is not lost, because he may still qualify for exchange treatment under § 302(b)(1) if the redemption is not essentially equivalent to a dividend. Thus if A has 5 of his 30 shares redeemed in the above example, he would very likely qualify for exchange treatment as a small minority shareholder despite failing the 80% test. Nevertheless, after the *Davis* case, *supra* Section B, and under the constructive ownership rules of § 302(c), it may be difficult to fit within § 302(b)(1)'s haven. See the next case.

PATTERSON TRUST v. UNITED STATES
729 F.2d 1089 (6th Cir. 1984)

KRUPANSKY, CIRCUIT JUDGE.

The United States of America appeals the decision of the United States District Court for the Northern District of Ohio, Eastern Division, in favor of plaintiff-appellee Henry T. Patterson Trust (Trust) in this action for a refund of federal income taxes with interest. The Trust, by its Trustee, the Reeves Banking & Trust Company (Reeves), instituted this action for a refund of $115,747.98 in federal income taxes paid by the Trust in 1979 for the year 1976, plus interest of $15,805.94 which had accrued as of 1979. The Internal Revenue Service had assessed such taxes on the basis that the amount paid to the Trust for the redemption of all of the Trust's shares in the Puritan Laundry and Dry Cleaning Company (Puritan) should be taxed as a dividend, and not as a sale of stock. The record reveals the following facts.

Prior to 1969, Henry Patterson, Sr. was the sole shareholder and chief executive officer of Puritan. In 1969, he gave forty shares of Puritan stock to each of his children — John, Hank and Ellen. At the time, Ellen was married to Bill Hicks (Hicks), who, along with Hank, was employed by Puritan. Henry Patterson retained 200 shares of Puritan stock.

Bill Hicks was apparently a skilled business manager, while Hank Patterson (Hank) lacked effectiveness. Through the years, a bitter tension between Hicks and Hank developed, resulting in numerous altercations, one of which ended with Hank's hospitalization. At one point, John Patterson (John) participated in the management of the business but, because of the Hank-Hicks rivalry, John resigned and pursued a teaching career.

At trial, there was testimony that Henry Patterson desired that Hicks operate the company after Patterson's retirement. In early 1970, Patterson suffered a broken hip which forced him to remain away from the company. He designated Hicks to act as Puritan's president and general manager in his absence. Patterson's health continued to deteriorate and he died in November 1971.

In June 1971, Hicks presented the Puritan directors with a demand for an increase in salary and a proposal that they place all of the Puritan shares in a voting trust which Hicks would then control. The directors demurred and Hicks resigned. He immediately staged a slowdown of Puritan employees and persuaded the company's most substantial commercial accounts to demand that Puritan rehire him. Within ten days of Hicks' resignation, Puritan was on the verge of collapse. John, who had since returned to the business, contacted Hicks and negotiated a five-year employment contract with him.

Hicks' contract provided an increased salary, a profit sharing arrangement, and a five-year option to acquire eighty shares of Puritan stock. Hicks acquired five of those shares and his option on the remaining seventy-five shares remained open. At the same time, Hank also received a five-year contract.

During the ensuing five years, Puritan performed well but problems between Hank and Hicks became increasingly aggravated; Hank, John, and Ella Patterson, their mother, often were at odds with Hicks and his wife, Ellen.

In the spring of 1976, the Patterson estate was closed. Henry Patterson had placed his 200 shares of Puritan stock in the Henry T. Patterson Trust (Trust) with his widow, Ella, as the beneficiary with the power to appoint the corpus at her death. Following the closing of the estate, the Puritan stock was thus distributed:

Henry T. Patterson Trust	200 shares
Ella Patterson	25 shares
Hank Patterson	40 shares
John Patterson	40 shares
Ellen (Patterson) Hicks	40 shares
Bill Hicks	5 shares
Lester Winkler	6 shares

Hicks devised a two-step plan whereby he and his wife could obtain control of Puritan. First, Puritan would redeem the Trust shares and, following the redemption, Hicks would exercise his option and acquire an additional seventy-five shares. As a result, Hicks and his spouse would own 120 shares and the remaining shareholders would control only 111 shares, thus Hicks would acquire a controlling interest in Puritan.

The Reeves Bank, as Trustee, determined that if it refused to redeem the shares, Hicks would leave the company and eventually the Trust corpus would be worthless. Thus, acting in what it perceived as the best interests of the Trust and the beneficiary, the Reeves Bank determined to accept the proposed redemption.

On April 2, 1976, the directors were presented with the proposal. The Trustee reported that it would be in Ella's best interest to redeem the shares and invest the proceeds. The minutes report:

C. SUBSTANTIALLY DISPROPORTIONATE REDEMPTIONS

After detailed discussion, it was moved by Wm. Hicks and seconded by [Hank] F. Patterson, that the company purchase the outstanding 200 shares held by the Reeves Banking and Trust Company, in trust for Mrs. Patterson upon the following terms: Price One Hundred Ninety Thousand and no/100 dollars (200 shares $950.00)

$47,500 Down Balance
$47,500 Due January 15, 1977
$47,500 Due January 15, 1978
$47,500 Due January 15, 1979

Following the redemption, on July 7, 1976 Hicks exercised his option and purchased seventy-five shares of Puritan stock from the company. Hicks thereafter forced a realignment of the Puritan Board of Directors. Prior to his attaining control, the Directors were:

Ella Patterson   Lester Winkler
Ellen Hicks   John Patterson
Hank Patterson

Following the consummation of Hicks' plan, the Directors were:

Bill Hicks
Ellen Hicks
Lester Winkler

The Trust reported the transaction as a capital gains sale. Upon review, the Commissioner determined that the amount received by the Trust in the redemption, $190,000.00, was a dividend taxable as ordinary income under § 301 of the Internal Revenue Code of 1954. A deficiency of $115,747.98 plus interest of $15,805.94 was assessed. The Trust paid the deficiency, and, as a result, netted $58,446.08 from the original transaction.

The Trust was denied a refund and instituted the within litigation. The district court rejected the Trust's argument that the transaction amounted to a termination of its interest in Puritan, but accepted the Trust's alternative argument that the transaction was not essentially equivalent to a dividend and was therefore entitled to capital gains treatment. This timely appeal by the United States followed.

The Internal Revenue Code of 1954, 26 U.S.C. § 301, as effective in 1976, provided that "a distribution of property ... made by a corporation to a shareholder" would be taxed as the ordinary income of that shareholder. Section 302 of the Code, 26 U.S.C. § 302, established, however, four exceptions to the general rule that proceeds from a redemption of stock by a corporation shall be treated, for tax purposes, "as a distribution of property to which § 301 applies." As relevant, the 1976 version of § 302 stated:

    (a) General Rule. — If a corporation redeems its stock ..., and if paragraph (1), (2), (3), or (4) of subsection (b) applies, such redemp-

tion shall be treated as a distribution in part or full payment in exchange for the stock.
(b) Redemptions Treated as Exchanges. —
  (1) Redemptions not equivalent to dividends. — Subsection (a) shall apply if the redemption is not essentially equivalent to a dividend.

  ....

  (3) Termination of shareholder's interest. — Subsection (a) shall apply if the redemption is in complete redemption of all of the stock of the corporation owned by the shareholder.

  ....

  (5) Application of paragraphs. — In determining whether a redemption meets the requirements of paragraph (1) the fact that such redemption fails to meet the requirements of paragraphs (2), (3), or (4) shall not be taken into account.

  ....

(d) Redemptions Treated as Distributions of Property. — Except as otherwise provided in this subchapter, if a corporation redeems its stock ..., and if subsection (a) of this section does not apply, such redemption shall be treated as a distribution of property to which § 301 applies.

Paragraphs (2) [dealing with substantially disproportionate redemptions] and (4) [dealing with railroad stocks] are not applicable. The district court rejected the Trust's arguments pursuant to paragraph (3), and the Trust admitted on appeal that paragraph (3) is not applicable to this redemption. Therefore, at issue here is the propriety, as a matter of law, of the district court's determination that the Trust's redemption was not essentially a dividend, as defined by § 302(b)(1).

In *United States v. Davis*, 397 U.S. 301, 90 S. Ct. 1041, 25 L. Ed. 2d 323 (1970), the Supreme Court evaluated the intended scope of § 302(b)(1). In that case, a sole shareholder caused part of his shares to be redeemed by the corporation; the Court concluded that such a redemption is always equivalent to a dividend and thus subject to ordinary income tax. However, the Court's examination of § 302(b)(1)'s history is germane to the analysis of this appeal:

> It was clearly proper for Congress to treat distributions generally as taxable dividends when made out of earnings and profits and then to prevent avoidance of that result without regard to motivation where the distribution is in exchange for redeemed stock.

We conclude that that is what Congress did when enacting § 302(b)(1). If a corporation distributes property as a simple dividend, the effect is to transfer the property from the company to its shareholders without a change in the relative economic interests or rights of the stockholders. Where a redemption has that same effect, it cannot be said to have satisfied the "not essentially equivalent to a dividend" requirement of § 302(b)(1). Rather, to qualify for preferred

C. SUBSTANTIALLY DISPROPORTIONATE REDEMPTIONS 351

treatment under that section, a redemption must result in a meaningful reduction of the shareholder's proportionate interest in the corporation. Clearly, taxpayer here, who (after application of the attribution rules) was the sole shareholder both before and after the redemption, did not qualify under this test. 397 U.S. at 313, 90 S. Ct. at 1048.

As explicated by the Supreme Court, § 302(b)(1) provides that corporate distributions which do not alter the shareholder's "relative economic interests or rights" will be taxed as a dividend, regardless of the form or nomenclature given the transactions. The test is to examine the change in the taxpayer's relationship to the corporation; § 302(b)(1) is satisfied, under this test, if the examination establishes a "meaningful reduction" of the taxpayer's relative interests or rights in the company.

Whether a distribution by redemption of stock was "essentially equivalent to a dividend" for the purposes of the 1954 Code is a question of fact. *Wright v. United States*, 482 F.2d 600 (8th Cir. 1973); *United States v. Fewell*, 255 F.2d 496 (5th Cir. 1958); 26 C.F.R. 1.302-2(b) (Treasury Regulations). The district court's factual determinations must be upheld on appeal if they are supported by substantial evidence within the record considered as a whole. Federal Rule of Civil Procedure 52(a).

To determine if the district court properly discerned a meaningful reduction in the Trust's interest and rights in Puritan, the starting point must be a comparison of the Trust's relative holdings prior to and after the redemption. As in *United States v. Davis*, *supra*, this comparison requires application of the attribution statutes.

Briefly stated, the 1954 Code provided that a trust constructively owned its shares plus the shares held by the beneficiary, including those shares which § 318 attributed to the beneficiary. 26 U.S.C. §§ 302(c), 318.

Applying this statute, it is readily apparent that prior to the redemption, the Trust constructively owned 345 shares of the Puritan company, computed from its own shares (200), Ella's holdings (25), and the shares owned by Ella's children (John—40, Hank—40, Ellen Hicks—40). Following the redemption, the Trust's constructive holdings were reduced to 145 shares (25 owned by Ella, 120 held by her children). Only 11 other shares remained actually outstanding (Hicks—5, Winkler—6); therefore, the Trust held 345/356 shares, or 97%, before and 145/156 shares, or 93%, immediately after the redemption.

When the district court made this comparison it included the seventy-five option shares held by Hicks. Accordingly, the district court determined that the Trust held 80% of the company before redemption (345/431), and 62.8% after redemption (145/231). Because the Trust no longer controlled the company after the redemption (holding less than two-thirds of the stock), the district court concluded that the "meaningful reduction" test had been satisfied. The district court included the Hicks option in its calculations pursuant to the plain language of the attribution statute, 26 U.S.C. § 318 (a)(4), which stated [emphasis added]:

If *any* person has an option to acquire stock, such stock shall be considered as owned by such person.

On appeal, the Government urges that § 318(a)(4) actually applies only to the taxpayer or to individuals whose shares are otherwise attributable to the taxpayer. The Government would therefore greatly narrow the scope of § 318(a)(4). Under the Government's view of the statute, the Trust's ownership interest in Puritan was reduced only 4% as a result of the redemption, from 97 to 93%, which, it contends, was not meaningful as a matter of law.

"In determining the scope of a statute, one is to look first at its language." *Dickerson v. New Banner Institute, Inc.*, 460 U.S. 103.... "Absent a clearly expressed legislative intention to the contrary, that language must ordinarily be regarded as conclusive." *Consumer Product Safety Comm'n v. GTE Sylvania, Inc.*, 447 U.S. 102.... Further, "it is axiomatic that where a statute is clear and unambiguous on its face, a court will not look to legislative history to alter the application of the statute except in rare and exceptional circumstances." *Pope v. Rollins Protective Services Co.*, 703 F.2d 197, 206 (5th Cir. 1983).... Finally, "Congress is presumed to use words in their ordinary sense unless it expressly indicates the contrary." *Davis Bros., Inc. v. Donovan*, 700 F.2d 1368, 1370 (11th Cir. 1983) *reh. and reh. en banc denied* (Eleventh Circuit refused to allow the Secretary of Labor to interpret "customarily furnished" meals as meaning "voluntarily accepted" meals for purposes of wage provisions in Fair Labor Standards Act)....

Nevertheless, the Government invites this court to examine the legislative history of § 318(a) (4) and conclude that "any person" actually means only those "parties in the line of attribution." *See* 26 U.S.C. §§ 318(a)(1)(A), 318 (a)(4). The Government relies on the commentary in the "Detailed Discussion of Bill" portion of the Senate Report relative to § 318(a)(3) [currently effective as § 318(a)(4)]. The commentary describes the operation of the relevant portions of the attributive statute in the following manner:

§ 318. Constructive ownership of stock

This section describes the area in which although in fact transactions related to stock ownership are in connection with a specific individual, ownership of stock is deemed to be in the hands of persons other than the person directly involved. Thus, for the purpose of determining whether a redemption of stock qualifies as a disproportionate redemption consideration is given not only to the stock held by such person but also to stock owned by members of his family....

The area of constructive ownership includes members of the family, persons having interests in ... trusts, ... such ... trusts, ... and stock held under an option.

In the family area (sec. 318(a) (1)) an individual is deemed to own stock owned by his parents, his children, and his grandchildren.... In the case of

C. SUBSTANTIALLY DISPROPORTIONATE REDEMPTIONS

trusts, ... the beneficiary or grantor is deemed to own his proportionate interest in the stock owned by the trust or estate and the trust or estate is deemed to own all of the stock owned by its beneficiaries or grantors.

In any of the cases above described where stock, though not owned, is subject to an option, the holder of such option is deemed to own such stock (sec. 318(a)(3)). S. Rep. No. 1622, 83d Cong., 2d Sess 45, reprinted in [1954] U.S. Code Cong. & Ad. News 4621, 4890-91.

The Government urges that as a result of the commentary's apparent limitation of the option attribution rule to "the cases above described," "the Senate indicated its intent that § 318(a)(3) (now § 318(a)(4)) should be limited to parties in the line of attribution." The Internal Revenue Service has consistently followed the reasoning herein argued by the Government, see, e.g., Rev. Rul. 68-601, and the tax court has adopted the Service's view as well. See *Sorem v. Commissioner*, 40 T.C. 206 (1963); *Northwestern Steel and Supply Co., Inc. v. Commissioner*, 60 T.C. 356 (1973). However, only two appeals courts have addressed the issue and they, without analysis, adopted diverse positions.

In *Friend v. United States*, 345 F.2d 761 (1st Cir. 1965), the First Circuit's dictum indicated that that court believed that "Congress intended that section to apply only where options are held by the person whose shares are being redeemed." 345 F.2d at 764. In *Sorem v. C.I.R.*, 334 F.2d 275, 280 (10th Cir. 1964), the court, again without analysis, applied the plain language of the options attribution provision of § 318(a), and rejected the Government's view.

The Government argues that this court should defer to the Service's consistently-applied interpretation of the Code. However, while it is axiomatic that where statutory language remains vague even when illuminated by the legislative history, the construction offered by the agency charged with the enforcement of the statute will often be accorded dispositive weight, it is an equal principle that the agency may not so interpret the statute as to controvert its plain and unambiguous language. Except in "rare and exceptional circumstances," *Rubin v. United States, supra*, such as where Congress "expressly indicates" its intent that the plain meaning of the statutory language be avoided, *Davis Bros., Inc. v. Donovan, supra*, unambiguous statutory language "is to be regarded as conclusive." *Dickerson v. New Banner Institute, supra*.

Instantly, the Government asserts only the commentary of the Senate Report, reprinted above, as support for its construction of "any person" in § 318(a)(4). The commentary falls short of a clear indication by Congress that the natural impact of the statutory language under review should be restrained. Accordingly, the district court appropriately included the option shares held by Hicks in determining the Trust's relative holdings prior to and following redemption.

It should be noted that, even if the Hicks shares were excluded, on the instant record the district court would have been entitled to enter the factual finding that the transaction under review was not essentially equivalent to a dividend and was therefore properly claimed as a capital gain. "The question whether a distribution in redemption of stock ... is not essentially equivalent to a dividend ... depends upon the facts and circumstances of each case." 26 C.F.R. § 1.302-3(b) (1983 Treasury Regulations); *United States v. Davis, supra.* Obviously, one of the pertinent facts would be the relative holdings of the taxpayer as computed under § 318's constructive stock ownership provisions, 26 C.F.R. [§ 1.302-3(b)], *United States v. Davis,* however, neither statutory enactment nor judicial construction would support the proposition that the resulting comparative calculation would become the exclusive and dispositive fact. In this case, the redemption effected "a change in the relative economic interests or rights" of all the stockholders of the Puritan company. Therefore, despite the fact that—excluding operation of § 318(a)(4)— the Trust's relative holdings fell only 4% after redemption, under the unique facts and circumstances of this case, such was a "meaningfuly reduction"[sic] and the distribution was therefore not a dividend.

Accordingly, because substantial evidence supports the district court's factual determination that the transaction was not essentially equivalent to a dividend, the judgment below is

Affirmed.

NOTES

1. *Planning incomplete redemptions.* In light of *Patterson Trust*, what is the "real world" planning advice to taxpayers in family-owned corporations in situations where the retiring shareholder cannot for some reason fully terminate her interest?

2. *What about nonvoting stock and preferred stock?* Section 302(b)(2) says a distribution is substantially disproportionate only if the shareholder's reduction in ownership of all common stock (whether voting or nonvoting) meets the 80% requirement, but Reg. § 1.302-3(a) says that § 302(b)(2) does not apply to redemptions of nonvoting stock alone, whether common or preferred. However, if nonvoting stock is redeemed at the same time as voting stock, and the voting stock qualifies for exchange treatment under § 302(b)(2), the nonvoting stock can be "piggy-backed" on the voting stock and will qualify for exchange treatment as well. *See* Rev. Rul. 77-237, 1977-2 C.B. 88.

3. *What if the preferred is voting stock?* The votes of the preferred stock must be counted in applying the first test under § 302(b)(2)(C), because clauses (i) and (ii) refer to "the voting stock of the corporation owned by the shareholder." For purposes of the second or 80% test, the voting preferred is simply ignored, because it refers only to "the shareholder's ownership of the *common stock* of the corporation." If the stockholder has only voting preferred stock, § 302(b)(2) cannot be met by its literal terms, and § 302(b)(1) would appear to be the only route to exchange treatment.

D. COMPLETE TERMINATION OF THE SHAREHOLDER'S INTEREST

PROBLEM 17-2

Big Corp. is a large publicly-traded corporation that has one class of voting common stock outstanding and has current and accumulated earnings and profits totalling $80,000,000. R owns 55% of Big Corp.'s 2,000,000 shares of outstanding voting common stock. R's basis in his Big Corp. stock is $11,000,000 (R owns 1,100,000 shares with basis of $10 per share). R is not related within the meaning of § 318 to any other shareholder of Big Corp. R decides to retire as Chief Executive Officer of Big Corp., and shortly thereafter Big Corp. redeems 225,000 shares of R's voting common stock for $2,250,000.

What are the tax consequences to R as a result of the redemption under § 302(b)(2) and (b)(1)?

PROBLEM 17-3

A owns 65% of the 1,000 shares of outstanding voting common stock of Z Corp. A is not related to any other Z Corp. shareholder. Z Corp. has current and accumulated earnings and profits of $700,000. Z Corp. redeems 350 shares of A's Z Corp. stock for $200,000. A's basis in the redeemed shares is $70,000 ($200 per share x 350 shares).

What are the tax consequences of the redemption to A under §§ 302(b)(1) and (b)(2)?

D. COMPLETE TERMINATION OF THE SHAREHOLDER'S INTEREST

Read § 302(b)(3) and (c)(2) and Reg. § 1.302-4.

If a redemption completely terminates a shareholder's interest in the corporation, exchange treatment is assured under the safe harbor. § 302(b)(3). Even if all shares actually held are redeemed, however, the safe harbor does not apply if the shareholder still owns stock constructively by attribution from related shareholders. Exchange treatment is still available in this situation under § 302(c)(2), however, which permits the shareholder to break the chain of attribution provided that the shareholder renounces for ten years any and all interest in the corporation except that of a creditor. This safe harbor is extremely useful in the common situation of a transfer of control of a family business from one generation to the next. If the founder and sole shareholder wishes to transfer the business to her daughter, she will ordinarily require funds from the business to fund her retirement. If the founder transfers a few shares to daughter and has the balance redeemed by the corporation, the daughter will own 100% of the stock, but by attribution the founder will still own 100% as well. This is where § 302(c)(2) comes to the rescue. The founder can avoid attribution from her daughter and enjoy exchange treatment if she waives all connection with the business for the following ten years. She may remain a creditor, however, in order to permit redemption by means of an installment sale to the corporation. This is very common because often the corporation does not have the cash to redeem the full value of the founder's stock (leaving the value of future growth to the daughter), and so the value usually must be paid out of the corporation's future earnings. This in turn creates a serious risk. If the waiver is not fully complied with and the founder remains a part-time paid consultant or derives other benefits from the corporation, which is a constant source of litigation, the redemption may be treated as a dividend. This could be a disaster in the case of an installment sale, because § 453 only applies to sales and not to dividends, with the result that the entire fair market value of the installment note would be taxable immediately despite the lack of any actual cash from the sale out of which to pay the tax.

Another frequently recurring problem in connection with decedents' estates is resolved by § 302(c)(2)(C). Suppose founder dies leaving shares of the family business in his estate, and the beneficiaries of the estate are all family members who own the rest of the stock in the family corporation. If it is decided that the estate should have all its shares redeemed from the family corporation, the estate cannot waive attribution from its beneficiaries under § 302(c)(2) because that section applies by its terms only to *family* attribution under § 318(a)(1), not to attribution from beneficiaries to estates § 318(a)(3), and so the estate will continue to own 100% of the stock after redemption. Exchange treatment is provided under § 302(c)(2)(C) if *both* the estate *and* all of the shareholder-beneficiaries from whom stock is attributable to the estate jointly make the waiver and terminate their actual interests. Note that this provision is of no use if one of the beneficiaries cannot divest himself of all his stock, say because he is the controlling shareholder. In such a case, he must terminate his beneficial interest in the estate instead if the waiver is to succeed.

The following Private Letter Ruling is a fairly complex example of §§ 302(b)(3) and (c)(2) at work in an estate planning context.

PRIV. LTR. RUL. 9041005
June 25, 1990

....

Company, a State X corporation operating as a personal holding company, has outstanding 758 shares of a single class of stock ("Company Stock"). Prior to taking step (i) below, Company Stock was held as follows:

"Estate = 237 shares

A = 266 shares

B = 123 shares

C = 82 shares

Trust I = 25 shares

D. COMPLETE TERMINATION OF THE SHAREHOLDER'S INTEREST

Trust II = 25 shares."

The Company Stock held by B, C, Trust I, and Trust II was received by these shareholders as a gift from D in 1983.

Estate is the estate of D, who was the husband of A. A and/or trusts for A's benefit are beneficiaries of Estate. B is the daughter of A and D. C is the son-in-law of A and D. Trusts I and II are trusts for the benefit of E and F, the granddaughters of A and D. Thus, directly or indirectly (through constructive ownership under section 318(a) of the Internal Revenue Code), A owns all the outstanding Company Stock, except for the stock owned by C.

It is desired to terminate Estate, to give complete ownership of Company to B, C, and the Trusts, and to provide A with assets other than Company Stock. Accordingly, pursuant to a Stock Sales Agreement and a Stock Redemption Agreement, steps have been, or will be, taken as follows:

"(Step i) Estate sold all 237 shares of its Company Stock to A in exchange for a note ("Note I") in the amount of $418,345.23 ($1,765.17 per share). The note is due in 10 years and bears interest at approximately 8% per annum.

(Step ii) Estate will be terminated and will distribute all its assets to its beneficiaries. Note I is being distributed to Trust III, a trust for A's benefit.

(Step iii) Prior to the redemption in the last step, A will execute a disclaimer of all her interest (if any) in each of Trust I and Trust II.

(Step iv) Company will redeem all 503 shares of Company Stock held by A (the 266 shares held by A originally and the 237 shares purchased by A from Estate) for an amount equal to their fair market value at the time of redemption which will probably total approximately $900,000. Approximately two-thirds of the redemption price will be paid in cash, certificates of deposit, Treasury Bills, and securities in unrelated corporations or similar items. Approximately one-third of the redemption price will be paid with a Company note ("Note II")."

Note II will be a 10-year unsecured promissory note of Company bearing interest at the applicable rate provided by section 1274(d) of the Internal Revenue Code. Interest is payable monthly. Principal may be paid prior to maturity. The entire principal and any unpaid interest must be paid no later than 10 years from the date of the note's issuance. In the event of default in any interest payment, the entire principal amount will become due and payable.

In connection with the proposed redemption, the following representations have been made:

"(a) There are no outstanding options or warrants to purchase Company Stock, nor are there any outstanding debentures or other obligations that are convertible into Company Stock or would be considered Company Stock.

(b) At the time of the exchange, the fair market value of the consideration to be received by A will be approximately equal to the fair market value of the

Company Stock to be surrendered in exchange therefor. The price to be paid for the Company Stock to be redeemed will not result in a loss with respect to those shares of stock.

(c) No shareholder of Company has been or will be obligated to purchase any of the Company Stock that is to be redeemed.

(d) In no event will the last payment on Note II (issued to A) be made more than 15 years after the date of issuance of the note.

(e) None of the consideration being received by A from Company, including interest, consists entirely or partly of Company's promise to pay an amount that is based on, or contingent on, future earnings of Company, an amount that is contingent on working capital being maintained at a certain level, or any other similar contingency.

(f) Note II will not be subordinated to the claims of general creditors of Company.

(g) In the event of default on any note or other obligation, no shares of stock will revert to or be received by A nor will A be permitted to purchase the stock at a public or private sale.

(h) The redemption described in this ruling request is an isolated transaction and is not related to any other past or future transaction.

(i) There have been no redemptions, issuances, or exchanges by Company of its stock in the past 5 years. Company has no plan or intention to issue, redeem, or exchange additional shares of its stock.

(j) On the date of the redemption, none of the stock redeemed will be entitled to declared but unpaid dividends.

(k) The disclaimer by A of any interests in Trusts I and II (which will have been made prior to the redemption in Step (iv)) is irrevocable and is effective to divest A of any interests in each of the trusts and is valid and binding under applicable local law. Therefore, after disclaimer by A of any interests in Trusts I and II, the Trustee of these trusts will not have authority to pay or distribute trust assets to or for the benefit of A.

(l) Following the transaction, A will hold no stock in Company or its subsidiaries either directly, or indirectly (within the meaning of section 318(a)), except that the stock held by the Trusts is attributable to E and F, and this stock plus the stock held by B would (absent a waiver of family attribution pursuant to section 302(c)(2)) be attributed to A under section 318(a)(1) (family attribution). In addition, following the transaction, A will have no interest (including an interest as officer, director, or employee) in Company or its subsidiaries, other than an interest as a creditor (as described in section 1.302-4(d) of the Income Tax Regulations).

D. COMPLETE TERMINATION OF THE SHAREHOLDER'S INTEREST

(m) A will execute and file the agreement described in section 302(c)(2)(A)(iii) of the Code in accordance with section 1.302-4(a) of the Regulations.

(n) Except for the acquisition (in Step (i)) of Company Stock from Estate, none of the Company Stock held by A will have been acquired from a related person within the meaning of section 318(a) of the Code in the 10-year period prior to Step (iv).

(o) Estate will have been terminated prior to Step (iv).

(p) Following the proposed transaction, no person who will own Company Stock will have directly or indirectly acquired any Company Stock from A.''

Based solely upon the information submitted and the representations set forth above, and provided that the disclaimer in Step (iii) is executed prior to the redemption in Step (iv) and is effective under local law to permanently divest A of any interest she may have in either Trust I or Trust II, it is held as follows:

"(1) The acquisition in Step (i) by A of Company Stock from Estate within the 10-year period prior to the proposed redemption in Step (iv) does not constitute an acquisition from a related person from whom stock ownership is attributable at the time of the proposed redemption (within the meaning of section 302(c)(2)(B)(i) of the Code) because Estate will have been terminated in Step (ii) prior to the redemption.

(2) Provided that A executes and files the agreement required by section 302(c)(2)(A)(iii) of the Code in accordance with section 1.302-4(a) of the Income Tax Regulations, section 318(a)(1) will be inapplicable in accord with section 302(c)(2) and the proposed redemption by Company of all its stock held by A will constitute a complete termination of A's interest in Company within the meaning of section 302(b)(3) of the Code. The redemption will be treated as in full payment in exchange for the stock redeemed, as provided in section 302(a). However, this ruling is subject to the conditions and limitations stated in section 302(c)(2)(A)(i) and (ii) and Rev. Rul. 71-211, 1971-1 C.B. 112.

(3) As provided by section 1001 of the Code, gain will be realized and recognized to A on the redemption of Company Stock, with this gain measured by the difference between the amount of cash and other consideration received by A for each share of Company Stock and the adjusted basis of the share of Company Stock surrendered as determined under section 1011. Provided section 341 (relating to collapsible corporations) is not applicable and the Company Stock is a capital asset in the hands of A, the gain, if any, will constitute capital gain subject to the provisions and limitations of Subchapter P of Chapter 1. Pursuant to the provisions of section 267, no loss will be allowable.

(4) No gain or loss will be recognized to Company on the distribution of cash and Note II (its own note) to A in redemption of Company Stock (section 311(a) and (b)(1)(A)). Gain (but not loss) will be recognized to Company on the

distributions of assets (other than cash and its own note) as provided by section 311(b) of the Code. For purposes of this computation of gain under section 311(b), the term "cash" does not include any item, such as a Treasury Bill or certificate of deposit, where the fair market value of such property exceeds adjusted basis (section 311(b)(1)(B)).

(5) The remaining shareholders of Company will not receive a constructive dividend as a result of the redemption by Company of its stock held by A (Rev. Rul. 58-614, 1958-2 C.B. 920)."

The rulings in this letter will be considered void as to A, if Note II is subsequently determined to be equity and not debt. No opinion is expressed as to whether any note distributed is debt or equity because that determination is primarily one of fact (section 4.02(1) of Rev. Proc. 90-3, 1990-1 I.R.B. 54, 59)....

NOTES

1. *What about redemptions of preferred stock?* Section 302(b)(3) relating to a complete termination of a stockholder's interest in the corporation apparently must include preferred stock, because the statute finds a complete termination if the redemption is "in complete redemption of all of the stock of the corporation owned by the shareholder."

2. *Impermissible intrafamily transfers in connection with a complete termination.* Clever taxpayers might attempt to bail out corporate earnings at capital gains rates by transferring stock to their spouses or children and then causing the corporation to redeem all the gifted stock. If the donee could waive family attribution under § 302(c)(2), an enormous loophole would be opened. Section 302(c)(2)(B) prevents this by denying the waiver where the redeeming party received stock from a related person, or gave stock to a related person, during the decade before the redemption if the prior transfer was motivated by tax avoidance. The provision does not apply to legitimate intergenerational transfers of control, such as where a founder gives stock to his son as successor and has the balance redeemed, because tax avoidance is not a principal purpose of such transactions.

3. *What if the redeeming shareholder is a corporation?* A corporation will usually prefer a dividend over exchange treatment in order to enjoy the dividends-received deduction. That can be arranged by making relatively small redemptions, but a series of small redemptions spread over time, each of which is too small to qualify as a sale, may be lumped together as a single integrated transaction and treated as an exchange. *See Bleily v. Commissioner*, 72 T.C. 751 (1979) (corporate shareholder whose interest was completely terminated via periodic redemptions over twenty-three months pursuant to a firm plan held to have engaged in a sale, hence not entitled to dividends-received deduction).

D. COMPLETE TERMINATION OF THE SHAREHOLDER'S INTEREST 361

4. *Bootstrap acquisitions.* Suppose that the taxpayer wishes to sell all the stock of a corporation but the buyer lacks the cash to pay its full value. If the corporation itself has enough cash, can the problem be solved by having the taxpayer first sell half of her stock to the buyer, and then subsequently cause the remaining half of the stock to be redeemed out of the corporation's cash? The answer is yes according to the seminal case of *Zenz v. Quinlivan*, 213 F.2d 914 (6th Cir. 1954), where the court found a complete termination of interest treatment under § 302(b)(3) on step-transaction principles. In *U.S. v. Carey*, 289 F.2d 531 (8th Cir. 1961), the steps were reversed but the conclusion was the same, namely a redemption treated as a sale under § 302(b)(3) where the shareholder first redeemed part of her stock and then sold the rest to the buyer as part of a single plan. The IRS agrees with the result. Rev. Rul. 75-447, 1975-2 C.B. 113. This is an extremely important doctrine from the perspective of purchasers and sellers of corporations and is often useful where the corporation has some assets which the buyer does not wish to purchase and which can be extracted by redemption to the seller.

5. *Effect on earnings and profits.* In *Zenz* the buyer did have the cash to make an outright purchase, but designed the bootstrap redemption method in order to reduce the corporation's earnings and profits account at no cost to either buyer or seller. Under current § 312(n)(7), a redemption removes a ratable share of earnings and profits in proportion to the amount of stock redeemed, but not in excess of the amount of the redemption. Thus if a corporation has $500 of earnings and profits and redeems 50% of its stock for $800, this will reduce the earnings and profits account by $250. If the redemption proceeds were $100, however, only $100 of earnings and profits would be removed.

6. *Buy-sell agreements.* In order to prevent stock in a closely held corporation from falling into the hands of strangers, and to make sure that surviving spouses can obtain cash and do not become helpless minority shareholders, it is common for the founders to agree that in the event of the death of either, the other may (or must) purchase the stock from the decedent's estate. Such agreements may be structured in many ways, one of the most convenient being redemption by the corporation itself of the stock from the decedent's estate which leaves the survivor as sole owner. There is a dangerous trap here. If the surviving shareholder in fact was under an unconditional obligation to purchase the decedent's stock but assigned the obligation to the corporation, which then redeemed the estate's stock, the IRS will assert that the corporation paid the redemption proceeds to satisfy a debt of the surviving shareholder who will then be treated as having received a constructive dividend. *See* Rev. Rul. 69-608, 1969-2 C.B. 42. The moral here is that the survivor should not alone be obligated to purchase the decedent's stock and should always have the right to assign the option or obligation to the corporation. Perhaps it is just safer to obligate the corporation and not the survivor.

7. *Redemption incident to divorce.* A further wrinkle is added when stock in a closely held corporation must be divided between spouses pursuant to a divorce. If the corporation redeems out one spouse, there is a risk that the other will be treated as having received a constructive dividend if the divorce agreement places an unconditional obligation upon him personally to buy the stock. Because his obligation was unconditional, the taxpayer lost in *Hayes v. Commissioner*, 101 T.C. 593 (1993). The opposite result was reached in *Arnes v. Commissioner*, 102 T.C. 522 (1994), where the taxpayer's obligation was found not to be primary and unconditional. In a companion case, the wife who received the redemption proceeds was not taxed on the ground that they were excluded under § 1041 as an indirect payment from her husband incident to divorce. *See Arnes v. Commissioner*, 981 F.2d 456 (9th Cir. 1992). Thus neither spouse paid any tax on the transaction.

GROVE v. COMMISSIONER
490 F.2d 241 (2d Cir. 1973)

KAUFMAN, CHIEF JUDGE:

[Mr. Grove, a wealthy engineer who graduated from Rensselaer Polytechnic Institute ("RPI") entered into a pattern of making gifts of stock in his closely-held corporation to RPI. The stock was held for a few years and then like clockwork redeemed by the corporation at RPI's request, pursuant to an agreement between the corporation and RPI which subjected the stock to a right of first refusal (i.e., before RPI could sell the stock, it had to offer the stock to Grove's corporation at book value) which could be different from fair market value. Other minority shareholders of the corporation signed similar agreements. RPI invested the redemption proceeds in income-producing securities and made quarterly disbursements to Grove of any income received, which Grove reported as income. The IRS asserted that Grove had used RPI as a tax-free conduit for withdrawing funds from the Corporation and that redemption payments by the Corporation to RPI were constructive dividend payments to Grove.]

. . . .

The Commissioner's view of this case is relatively simple. In essence, we are urged to disregard the actual form of the Grove-RPI-Corporation donations and redemptions and to rewrite the actual events so that Grove's tax liability is seen in a wholly different light. Support for this position, it is argued, flows from the Supreme Court's decision in *Commissioner v. Court Holding Co.*, 324 U.S. 331, 89 L. Ed. 981, 65 S. Ct. 707 (1945), which, in language familiar to law students, cautions that "the incidence of taxation depends upon the substance of a transaction.... To permit the true nature of a transaction to be disguised by mere formalisms, which exist solely to alter tax liabilities, would seriously impair the effective administration of the tax policies of Congress." *Id.* at 334. In an effort to bring the instant case within this language, the Commissioner insists that whatever the appearance of the transactions here under consideration, their "true nature" is quite different. He maintains that Grove, with the cooperation of RPI, withdrew substantial funds from the Corporation and manipulated them in a

D. COMPLETE TERMINATION OF THE SHAREHOLDER'S INTEREST

manner designed to produce income for his benefit. In the Commissioner's view, the transaction is properly characterized as a redemption by the Corporation of Grove's, not RPI's shares, followed by a cash gift to RPI by Grove. This result, it is said, more accurately reflects "economic reality."

The Commissioner's motives for insisting upon this formulation are easily understood once its tax consequences are examined. Although Grove reported taxable dividends and interest received from the Merrill Lynch account on his 1963 and 1964 tax returns, amounts paid by the Corporation to redeem the donated shares from RPI were not taxed upon distribution. If, however, the transactions are viewed in the manner suggested by the Commissioner, the redemption proceeds would be taxable as income to Grove. Moreover, because the redemptions did not in substance alter Grove's relationship to the Corporation—he continued throughout to control a majority of the outstanding shares—the entire proceeds would be taxed as a dividend payment at high, progressive ordinary-income rates, rather than as a sale of shares, at the fixed, and relatively low, capital gains rate....

Clearly, then, the stakes involved are high. We do not quarrel with the maxim that substance must prevail over form, but this proposition marks the beginning, not the end, of our inquiry. The court in *Sheppard v. United States*, 361 F.2d 972, 176 Ct. Cl. 244 (1966), perceptively remarked that "all such 'maxims' should rather be called 'minims' since they convey a minimum of information with a maximum of pretense." *Id.* at 977 n. 9. Each case requires detailed consideration of its unique facts. Here, our aim is to determine whether Grove's gifts of the Corporation's shares to RPI prior to redemption should be given independent significance or whether they should be regarded as meaningless intervening steps in a single, integrated transaction designed to avoid tax liability by the use of mere formalisms.

The guideposts for our analysis are well marked by earlier judicial encounters with this problem. "The law with respect to gifts of appreciated property is well established. A gift of appreciated property does not result in income to the donor so long as he gives the property away absolutely and parts with title thereto before the property gives rise to income by way of sale." *Carrington v. Commissioner*, 476 F.2d 704, 708 (5th Cir. 1973), *quoting Humacid Co.*, 42 T. C. 894, 913 (1964). As noted below by the Tax Court, the Commissioner here "does not contend that the gifts of stock by [Grove] to RPI in 1961 and 1962 were sham transactions, or that they were not completed gifts when made." If Grove made a valid, binding, and irrevocable gift of the Corporation's shares to RPI, it would be the purest fiction to treat the redemption proceeds as having actually been received by Grove. The Tax Court concluded that the gift was complete and irrevocable when made. The Commissioner conceded as much and we so find.

It is argued, however, that notwithstanding the conceded validity of the gifts, other circumstances establish that Grove employed RPI merely as a convenient conduit for withdrawing funds from the Corporation for his personal use without incurring tax liability. The Commissioner would have us infer from the systematic nature of the gift-redemption cycle that Grove and RPI reached a mutually beneficial understanding: RPI would permit Grove to use its tax-exempt status to drain funds from the Corporation in return for a donation of a future interest in such funds.

We are not persuaded by this argument and the totality of the facts and circumstances lead us to a contrary conclusion. Grove testified before the Tax Court concerning the circumstances of these gifts. The court, based on the evidence and the witnesses' credibility, specifically found that "there was no informal agreement between [Grove] and RPI that RPI would offer the stock in question to the corporation for redemption or that, if offered, the corporation would redeem it." Findings of fact by the Tax Court, like those of the district court, are binding upon us unless they are clearly erroneous, ... and "the rule ... applies also to factual inferences [drawn] from undisputed basic facts."... It cannot seriously be contended that the Tax Court's findings here are "clearly erroneous" and no tax liability can be predicated upon a nonexistent agreement between Grove and RPI or by a fictional one created by the Commissioner.

Grove, of course, owned a substantial majority of the Corporation's shares. His vote alone was sufficient to insure redemption of any shares offered by RPI. But such considerations, without more, are insufficient to permit the Commissioner to ride roughshod over the actual understanding found by the Tax Court to exist between the donor and the donee. *Behrend v. United States*, (4th Cir. 1972), 73-1 USTC ¶ 9123, is particularly instructive. There, two brothers donated preferred shares of a corporation jointly controlled by them to a charitable foundation over which they also exercised control. The preferred shares were subsequently redeemed from the foundation by the corporation and the Commissioner sought to tax the redemption as a corporate dividend payment to the brothers. The court, in denying liability, concluded that although "it was understood that the corporation would at intervals take up the preferred according to its financial ability ..., this factor did not convert into a constructive dividend the proceeds of the redemption ... [because] the gifts were absolutely perfected before the corporation redeemed the stock." *Id.*

Nothing in the December, 1954, minority shareholder agreement between the Corporation and RPI serves as a basis for disturbing the conclusion of the Tax Court. Although the Corporation desired a right of first refusal on minority shares — understandably so, in order to reduce the possibility of unrelated, outside ownership interests — it assumed no obligation to redeem any shares so offered. In the absence of such an obligation, the Commissioner's contention that Grove's initial donation was only the first step in a prearranged series of transactions is little more than wishful thinking grounded in a shaky foundation....

We are not so naive as to believe that tax considerations played no role in Grove's planning. But foresight and planning do not transform a non-taxable event into one that is taxable. Were we to adopt the Commissioner's view, we would be required to recast two actual transactions — a gift by Grove to RPI and a redemption from RPI by the Corporation — into two completely fictional transactions—a redemption from Grove by the Corporation and a gift by Grove to RPI. Based upon the facts as found by the Tax Court, we can discover no basis for elevating the Commissioner's "form" over that employed by the taxpayer in good faith. "Useful as the step transaction doctrine may be in the interpretation of equivocal contracts and ambiguous events, it cannot generate events which never took place just so an additional tax liability might be asserted." *Sheppard v. United States, supra,* at 978. In the absence of any supporting facts in the record we are unable to adopt the Commissioner's view; to do so would be to engage in a process of decision that is arbitrary, capricious and ultimately destructive of traditional notions of judicial review. We decline to embark on such a course.

Accordingly, the judgment of the Tax Court is affirmed.

[Judge Oakes dissented on the ground that the IRS's view of the substance of the transaction was correct.]

E. REDEMPTIONS IN PARTIAL LIQUIDATION OF THE CORPORATION

Read § 302(b)(4) and (e).

A redemption payment that results from a "corporate contraction" is given exchange treatment to noncorporate shareholders if it meets the conditions of § 302(e). If it does meet the conditions, no reduction in the shareholder's percentage ownership is required and even a pro rata distribution will be treated as an exchange. The distribution itself may be either in cash or in property. (Note, however, that if the distribution consists of appreciated property, the corporation will be taxed under § 311(b) despite the privileged treatment at the shareholder level.)

To qualify as a partial liquidation, the corporate contraction must meet one of two alternative tests. The first is the vague and uncertain language of § 302(e)(1)(A) that it must not be "essentially equivalent to a dividend (determined at the corporate level rather than at the shareholder level)." There is little authority as to what the essentially equivalent test means, but the leading examples are: the sale of a line of business and a distribution of the sales proceeds to shareholders; and, the destruction of two floors of a seven-story factory by fire, followed by a reduction in business and distribution of the insurance proceeds to shareholders. In order to obtain a private letter ruling to guarantee exchange treatment, the IRS requires that the distribution result in a 20% or greater reduction in corporate gross revenues, net market value of assets, and number of employees. Rev. Proc. 82-40, 1982-2 C.B. 761.

The other test for partial liquidation status is a safe harbor under § 302(e)(2) which can be met if the corporation ceases to conduct an entire trade or business which has been actively conducted for five years preceding the distribution and which was not purchased in a taxable transaction within that period. The evident reason for the latter rule is that otherwise a corporation with excess cash could purchase a trade or business with the intention of distributing it to shareholders in kind, or reselling it for cash to be distributed to shareholders as an alternative to distributing a dividend. This can still be done, but the corporation must age the purchased business for at least five years before the distribution. In addition, the corporation must continue to conduct at least one other trade of business.

A subtle piece of drafting in § 302(b)(4) assures that *corporate* shareholders are *precluded* from getting a partial liquidation result. That will generally be fine with them because they may get the benefit of the § 243 dividends-received reduction as a result.

PROBLEM 17-4

ZZ Corp. is a successful VCR manufacturing company that has been in operation for approximately twelve years. Because of ZZ Corp's success, the company in 1988 decided to purchase X Co., a company that has been manufacturing recordable compact disks since 1987. X Co. is set up as a division of ZZ Corp. Because the sales of recordable compact disks have at best been marginal, ZZ Corp., in 1994, sold X Co. to Mega Corporation, which continues to operate the company.

Because of your shrewdness as a business attorney for ZZ Corp., the sales price for X Co. has left a large amount of cash in the company's bank accounts. ZZ Corp. has adopted a plan to distribute the sales proceeds to the company's shareholders (all of whom are individuals) and thereby to redeem 10% of the company's stock, provided the shareholders will receive capital gains treatment. The chairman of ZZ Corp. has asked you to provide a legal opinion on the proposed distribution.

What is the analysis of the proposed transaction under § 302(b)(4) and § 302(e) with respect to ZZ's shareholders?

PROBLEM 17-5

Assume the same facts as in Problem 17-4 above except that instead ZZ Corp. acquired X Co. in 1993 in a tax-free merger under § 368(a)(1)(A) so that X Co. became a division of ZZ Corp.. Will the proposed distribution by ZZ Corp. of X Co.'s assets in partial redemption of its shares qualify under § 302(b)(4) and § 302(e)?

PROBLEM 17-6

Assume the same facts as in Problem 17-4 above, except that instead ZZ Corp. bought X Co. a year before the distribution.

PROBLEM 17-7

X Corp. is owned by the AB Partnership and Big Corp., each of which owns 50% of the 10,000 X Corp. shares outstanding. AB Partnership's basis in its shares is $50,000 ($10 per share), and Big Corp's basis in its shares is $100,000 ($20 per share), and both have held their shares for over five years. X Corp. has two lines of business that it has been engaged in for over five years, a publishing company and an amusement park company. X Corp. sold the amusement park company this year to Bubbly Brewing Co. As a result of the sale, X Corp. distributed cash from the sale to its shareholders in redemption of 10% of their stock in a transaction that qualified as a partial liquidation under §§ 302(b)(4) and 302(e). The total amount distributed was $200,000. X Corp. also has substantial current and accumulated earnings and profits.

What is the result to AB Partnership and to Big Corp. on the distribution in exchange for their shares under § 302(b)?

F. REDEMPTIONS TO PAY DEATH TAXES

Read § 303(a) and (b).

When a taxpayer dies, the basis of the stock he or she held is changed to fair market value at death (or as of the alternative valuation date six months following death) in the hands of the heirs. § 1014. That generally means that stock can be sold by the heirs (or the estate) to third parties with little or no subsequent gain or loss. However, if the stock cannot be sold to third parties and the estate holds a large block of which the corporation is willing to redeem only a small amount, the result to the estate is likely to be a taxable dividend. This could be a harsh result if the cash is needed to pay funeral expenses, death taxes, or the costs of administering the estate. Section 303 addresses that concern, but in a lavish way. The legislative history indicates that it is oriented toward assuring that family businesses are not destroyed by estate taxes, but § 303 in fact does much more than that. Section 303 is literally a once in a lifetime opportunity to obtain a guaranteed sale or exchange result for a redemption even if the estate owns 100% of the stock. To qualify, the estate must own a substantial percentage of the corportion whose shares are redeemed, and the favorable treatment extends only to an upper limit consisting of the amount of transfer taxes and funeral and administration expenses. The subject is generally a sideshow from the point of view of corporate tax planning (as opposed to estate planning), so it is covered here with a revenue ruling and one problem.

Section 303 redemptions entail a practical problem for some closely-held corporations, because the redemption of a deceased shareholder's voting stock results in a proportionate increase in the voting power of the remaining shareholders. If the business is owned by a parent and children, this may not create a hardship, but if there are also outsiders, maintaining the desired balance of voting power can be a problem, one that can often be solved, as the next ruling shows.

REV. RUL. 87-132
1987-2 C.B. 82

....

Issue

Whether the application of section 303 of the Internal Revenue Code to a stock redemption is precluded when the stock redeemed was newly distributed as part of the same transaction.

Facts

X corporation had outstanding 300 shares of voting common stock that were owned equally by an estate and by A, an individual, who had no interest in the estate under section 318 of the Code. The value of the X stock held by the estate exceeded the amount specified in section 303(b)(2)(A). The estate wanted to effect a redemption pursuant to section 303 to pay death taxes.

In order to maintain relative voting power and to preserve continuity of management, X undertook the following two steps. First, X issued 10 shares of a new class of nonvoting common stock on each share of common stock outstanding. Thus, the estate and A each received 1,500 shares of this stock. Immediately thereafter, 1,000 shares of the nonvoting common stock were redeemed by X from the estate in exchange for cash. The overall result of these two steps was that the estate obtained the cash it needed while giving up only nonvoting stock.

The redemption of the X nonvoting common stock occurred within the time limits prescribed by section 303(b)(1)(A) of the Code and did not exceed the amount permitted by section 303(a).

Law and Analysis

Section 303(a) of the Code provides that a distribution of property to a shareholder by a corporation in redemption of stock of the corporation, which (for federal estate tax purposes) is included in determining the gross estate of a decedent, is treated as a distribution in full payment in exchange for the stock redeemed to the extent of the sum of certain taxes and expenses. These taxes and expenses are the estate, inheritance, legacy and succession taxes plus the amount of funeral and administrative expenses allowable as deductions for federal estate tax purposes.

Section 303(c) of the Code provides that if a shareholder owns stock of a corporation (new stock) the basis of which is determined by reference to the basis of stock of a corporation (old stock) that was included in determining the gross estate of a decedent, and section 303(a) would apply to a distribution in

F. REDEMPTIONS TO PAY DEATH TAXES

redemption of the old stock, then section 303(a) applies to a distribution in redemption of the new stock. Section 1.303-2(d) of the Income Tax Regulations specifically provides that section 303 applies to a distribution in redemption of stock received by an estate in a distribution to which section 305(a) applies.

Section 305(a) of the Code provides that, generally, gross income does not include the amount of any distribution of the stock of a corporation made by the corporation to its shareholders with respect to its stock. Section 305(b)(1), however, provides that if the distribution is, at the election of any of the shareholders (whether exercised before or after the declaration of the distribution), payable either in its stock or in property, then the distribution of stock is treated as a distribution to which section 301 applies. Section 305(b)(2) provides that if the distribution has the result of the receipt of property by some shareholders and an increase in the proportionate interest of other shareholders in the assets or earnings and profits of the corporation, then the distribution of stock is treated as a distribution to which section 301 applies.

Section 307(a) of the Code provides that if a shareholder already owning stock in a corporation ("old stock") receives additional stock ("new stock") in a distribution to which section 305(a) applies, then the basis of the old stock prior to the distribution is allocated between the old stock and new stock subsequent to the distribution.

Here, 3,000 shares of nonvoting common stock were distributed and 1,000 shares were subsequently redeemed by X as part of a plan designed to allow the estate to avail itself of the benefits of section 303 of the Code. The intent of Congress in enacting the statutory predecessor of section 303 was to provide an effective means whereby the estate of a decedent owning an interest in a family enterprise could finance the estate tax without being required to dispose of its entire interest in the family business in order to avoid the imposition of an ordinary dividend tax. H.R. Rep. No. 2319, 81st Cong., 2d Sess. 63-64 (1950). Given this intent, it follows that the estate should be able to obtain the benefits of section 303 without a substantially adverse effect on the estate's ownership of the family business.

Moreover, section 303(c) of the Code is a remedial provision that was added to expand the application of section 303 to the redemption of stock which, despite a technical change in the form of ownership, represents the same stock as that owned at death. S. Rep. No. 1622, 83rd Cong., 2nd Sess. 239 (1954). The sole requirement for application of section 303 to the redemption, under section 303(c), is that the basis of the stock redeemed ("new stock") be determined by reference to the basis of the "old stock" included in the estate. Section 1.303-2(d) of the Regulations provides that stock received by an estate in a section 305(a) distribution is entitled to section 303 treatment. Rev. Rul. 83-68, 1983-1 C.B. 75, holds that a distribution of stock that is immediately redeemable at the option of a shareholder gives the shareholder an election to receive either stock or property within the meaning of section 305(b)(1) and, therefore, is a distribution to which section 301 applies. *See also* Rev. Rul. 76-258, 1976-2 C.B. 95.

The nature of section 303 of the Code and the limited time period for redemption provided in section 303(b)(1) are generally indicative of a Congressional intent that section 303 be applicable to stock issued as part of the same plan as the redemption. Consequently, for purposes of section 303 only, section 305 should be applied prior to, and without reference to, the subsequent redemption.

Holding

The exclusion from gross income provision of section 305(a) of the Code, and the carryover of basis provisions of section 307(a), apply to X's distribution of its new nonvoting common stock to A and the estate. Section 303(a) applies to X's distribution of cash to the estate in redemption of the 1,000 shares of its new nonvoting common stock. For the tax consequences to A (the nonredeeming shareholder) as a result of this transaction, see section 305.

. . . .

PROBLEM 17-8

A died with a gross estate of $1,200,000. The sum of death taxes and funeral and administration expenses was $300,000. Included in A's gross estate is A's 30% interest in Corp. X stock valued at $200,000 and A's 25% interest in Corp. Y stock valued at $180,000. One year after A's death, the Corp. X and Corp. Y stock is redeemed for $300,000 paid to A's son and sole legatee. What will be the tax treatment of the Corp. X and Corp. Y stock redemption under § 303?

G. REDEMPTIONS THROUGH RELATED CORPORATIONS

Read § 304(a) and (b)(1)-(2).

Suppose that a taxpayer owns all the stock of two prosperous corporations. A redemption by either company of some of its shares will result in an (unacceptable) dividend to her. Can the taxpayer obtain capital gain treatment simply by selling the stock of one company to the other? If so, most of the barbed wire in § 302 could be easily bypassed. Section 304 plugs this loophole by importing the rules of § 302 to apply to situations in which one or more shareholders have 50% or more control of both corporations, and it asks whether, following the sale, the taxpayer's direct and indirect interest in the corporation whose stock was sold (the "issuing" corporation) was reduced enough to justify treating the transaction as an exchange rather than as a distribution. The change in indirect ownership is measured by looking through the acquiring corporation and attributing an amount of the issuing corporation's stock to the shareholder which is proportional to the amount of stock owned in the acquiring corporation for purposes of § 302. In the case of two 100% owned corporations, the result is always a distribution.

G. REDEMPTIONS THROUGH RELATED CORPORATIONS 371

> *To illustrate*: A owns 80% of X Corp. and 60% of Y Corp., each of which has 100 shares outstanding. The minority shareholders are unrelated to A. A causes Y Corp. to purchase 20 shares of X Corp. stock from her for cash. As a result, A now owns 60 shares of X Corp. and Y Corp. owns 20 shares. A will have distribution rather than an exchange treatment, because her ownership in X Corp. has only declined from 80% to 72% computed as follows: A owns 60 shares outright, plus 12 shares attributed to him by looking through his 60% ownership of Y Corp.'s 20 shares (60% x 20 = 12).

Another feature of § 304 is that it maximizes the likelihood of a taxable § 301 dividend, because it amalgamates the earnings and profits of both companies for purposes of measuring the purchasing company's dividend-paying capacity. § 304(b)(2). This can help corporate stockholders, but from the point of view of individual shareholders it can be worse than the result of a direct redemption. That is because if there is a direct redemption, the corporation buying back its stock may not have enough earnings and profits to cover the distribution, in which case there is a partial return of capital under § 301(c)(2).

An intuitively easy way to apprehend the problem § 304 deals with, and how it does so, is to consider an example to which § 304(a)(2) applies.

> *To illustrate*: Individual B owns all the stock of X Corp., which has a wholly owned subsidiary, Y Corp. Both corporations have "ample" earnings and profits. If X Corp. redeems any shares from B, the proceeds will be taxable to B as a dividend. What if Y Corp. purchases some of B's stock in X Corp. from B? How should the proceeds be taxable to B? *See* § 304(b)(2) (taxable dividend).
>
> Now consider what happens if the parent corporation has ample earnings and profits at the time of its purchase of X Corp. stock from B, but the subsidiary does not, in light of § 304(b)(2) (taxable dividend).

A § 304 transaction can be one whose facts also would fit, or nearly fit, § 351, and thus invoke the corollary rules of § 357 and § 358. Do you see how this could happen? Section 304(b)(3) coordinates § 304 with § 351 by specifying that § 304 will preempt § 351, and so it, not § 351, will apply to any property received in a distribution described in § 304(a).

PROBLEM 17-9

Sam owns 80% of the 1,000 outstanding shares of voting common stock of X Corp. Sam also owns 50% of the 1,000 outstanding shares of voting common stock of Y Corp. Sam's basis in the X Corp. stock is $80,000, and his basis in the Y Corp. stock is $35,000. Sam is not related to any other shareholder of X Corp. or Y Corp. X Corp. has earnings and profits of $20,000, and Y Corp. has earnings and profits of $50,000.

Sam sells 200 of his shares in X Corp. to Y Corp. for $70,000.

(a) What are the tax consequences of this transaction to Sam? *See* Reg. § 1.304-2.

(b) What if, instead, Sam owned 600 of the 1,000 shares of X Corp. and X Corp. owns 600 of the 1,000 shares of Y Corp., and Sam sells 400 shares of his X stock to Y Corp.? Is the transfer of the shares to Y Corp. an exchange or a distribution under § 302?

OUTSIDE READINGS

M. Lang, *Dividends Essentially Equivalent to Redemptions: The Taxation of Bootstrap Stock Acquisitions*, 41 Tax L. Rev. 309 (Winter 1986).

F. Royal, *Recovery of Basis in Non-Qualifying Stock Redemptions Under Sections 302 and 304*, 4 Va. Tax Rev. 85 (Summer 1984).

Chapter 18
LIQUIDATIONS

A. STATE LAW BACKGROUND

The legal termination and disappearance of a corporation results from a *dissolution*, which usually occurs via the voluntary filing of a certificate of dissolution with the State authority responsible for corporate documents, or involuntarily for failure to pay state income or franchise taxes. The process in which the corporation disgorges its assets, paying creditors and distributing assets to shareholders in exchange for their shares, is known as a *liquidation*. Since the federal income tax is concerned with economic realities rather than state law legalisms, the term "dissolution" does not rear its head in Subchapter C and the question of whether a corporation has come to an end for federal income tax purposes depends on whether it has liquidated. It may liquidate "in kind" or by selling some or all of its assets first and then distributing the proceeds.

The corporation is considered to have been liquidated for federal income tax purposes when it has ceased operating as a going concern and exists solely to wind up its affairs. *See* Reg. § 1.332-2(c).

Liquidations are not as ghoulish as they might first appear, because in most cases the operating assets will continue to be used in someone's business. In fact, they may even find their way into an affiliate of the liquidating corporation.

B. COMPLETE LIQUIDATIONS

Although entering corporate form is generally tax-free, exiting is not and can be very expensive. Both the corporation and its shareholders are subject to federal income taxes as a result of a complete liquidation, except in the special case of liquidation of a controlled subsidiary into its corporate parent, which is treated in the last section of this chapter.

1. SHAREHOLDER LEVEL EFFECTS

Read § 331.

In a complete liquidation, the shareholder distributees of corporate assets (whether in cash or in kind) are treated as if they sold their stock back to the corporation, which means they report gain or loss, which is usually capital gain or loss (except for the unusual case of a dealer in stocks) under §§ 331 and 1001. Because the exchange is taxable, the shareholders take a fair-market-value basis in the property they receive in liquidation, undiminished by associated liabilities. § 334(a). If one did reduce the basis of distributed assets by the liabilities, there would be a gain on the later sale by a shareholder of the distributed asset, which would mean double taxation of a single gain to the taxpayer, which is clearly inappropriate.

If the shareholder has several blocks of stock, the gain or loss calculations must be performed for each block. Reg. § 1.331-1(e). If the liquidation proceeds are distributed in two or more years, the shareholder can use an open-transaction approach, meaning no gain is reported until the liquidating distributions exceed stock basis, after which all distributions are fully taxable. Rev. Rul. 85-48, 1985-1 C.B. 126. Similarly, if the shareholder receives a disputed claim, it apparently need not be treated as an amount realized until it is reduced to value. *See* Rev. Rul. 58-402, 1958-2 C.B. 15. Finally, if certain conditions are met, the shareholder can report installment proceeds of obligations that the corporation distributes to the shareholder on the installment method, as if the proceeds were paid for his stock. § 453(h)(1)(A) and (B).

To illustrate: Bob owns all the stock of Bobco. He originally contributed $100 to Bobco, which used the money to buy inventory. Some years later, Bobco undertook a liquidation in which it sold the inventory on the installment method to one buyer for $200. It then distributed the installment note to Bob. The result is that Bob is taxed on a $100 gain (i.e., the $200 sales proceeds under the note minus his $100 stock basis), but he reports the gain as the note is paid, rather than when he receives it. Bobco itself is also taxable on the distribution of the installment obligation.[1] The taxation of distributed assets is discussed below.

Hold it! What if the final distribution in liquidation produced realization of a *loss* to the shareholder. Related persons usually cannot recognize losses when they sell or exchange property with each other. Can the shareholder recognize a loss on the liquidation even if he owns 100% of the stock of the corporation? The answer is "yes." *See* § 267(a)(1), second sentence. Otherwise, the loss would be permanently disallowed, not just deferred. However, the loss is deferred until the last and final liquidating distribution is made! Rev. Rul. 85-48, 1985-1 C.B. 126.

PROBLEM 18-1

You are a revenue agent examining the income tax returns of shareholders of a closely-held corporation that recently completed a protracted liquidation. The

---

[1] § 453B (not applicable to certain S corporations). In other words, Bobco is taxable on the gain in its inventory which it sold. Had it received cash, Bobco would have been taxable at once. Because it received an installment note, it will not be taxed until it connects or disposes of the note, which it does in the liquidation distribution to Bob.

B. COMPLETE LIQUIDATIONS

liquidation took an unduly long time as far as you are concerned, and you notice that the shareholders had a particularly low basis in their stock. How might you attack the liquidation? Why would the shareholders delay the liquidation, given the relatively flat individual federal income tax brackets we now have?

2. CORPORATE LEVEL EFFECTS

Read § 336(a)-(c).

The easiest way to understand the corporate-level effects of a complete liquidation and distribution of corporate assets in kind to shareholders is to imagine that the corporation sold each of its assets to strangers and then distributed the cash proceeds. The distributing corporation can recognize both gain and loss on the constructive sale of its various assets. Note that this rule is different from that of *current* distributions in kind where the distributing corporation recognizes gain but not loss under § 311.

Under pre-1987 law, there was generally no tax on a corporation going through a complete liquidation when it distributed appreciated assets to its shareholders. *See* former § 337 and *General Utils. & Oper. Co. v. Helvering*, 296 U.S. 200 (1935).[2] The *General Utilities* doctrine was legislatively reversed in 1986. *See* §§ 311, 336. One rationale for imposing a corporate level tax on the liquidating distribution is that the corporation *realizes* the inherent gain or loss in each property when it is distributed, and if it is not taxed at that point, it will never be taxed. (Remember that the shareholders take a fair-market-value basis in the property under § 334 and so the corporate-level accrued gain will not later be taxed to the shareholders). Do you agree? Did it really "cash in" its gain? If so, what consideration does the corporation receive in return? To look at another rationale, should the corporation be taxed just because it would have paid a tax if it had sold the assets to a third party?[3] Is it possible that the repeal of the *General Utilities* doctrine merely reflects a compulsive demand that the corporate double tax be completely unavoidable? In light of the spasmodic history of the double tax, is it a model we should honor?

PROBLEM 18-2

Harry and Sally each own 50 shares of the 100 shares of Movie, Inc. Harry's basis in his shares is $500,000, and Sally's basis in her shares is $200,000.

---

[2] The *General Utils.* case actually involved a current distribution, but it gave its name to the general principle under former law that a corporation did not recognize gain or loss upon a distribution of property to shareholders.

[3] *See* the formerly powerful issue of whether the corporation did sell the assets or whether it distributed them in kind to shareholders who made the sale, litigated in *Commissioner v. Court Holding Co.*, 324 U.S. 331 (1945) and *United States v. Cumberland Pub. Serv. Co.*, 338 U.S. 451 (1950), and former § 337.

Movie, Inc. has two assets, a completed motion picture, worth $1,000,000 and with a basis to the corporation of $500,000, and cash of $1,000,000. There is no creditor of the corporation.

(a) What will be the tax consequences to a third party, including basis, to the corporation and each shareholder if Movie, Inc. sells its movie to a third party for its fair market value and promptly distributes all its proceeds of sale and its cash (after payment of any corporate-level income tax) to its shareholders in a complete liquidation and repurchase of all their shares?

(b) What will be the tax consequences, including basis, to the corporation and each shareholder if Movie, Inc. distributes all its assets, in kind (after withholding for, or paying, any corporate-level tax), to its shareholders in complete liquidation, and they sell the movie to an outsider for its fair market value?

PRIV. LTR. RUL. 9428006
April 12, 1994

....

Corporation is a State X stock cooperative which holds fee simple title to various apartment buildings and owns (as part of the common elements) equipment, furniture, and reserve funds. On formation of Corporation, each member stockholder received shares of stock in an amount related to the original retail value of the apartment unit to which he received a proprietary lease. Shares are not transferable except on assignment of the lease to which the shares relate. Approximately 36% of Corporation's stock outstanding is held by tenant-stockholders, 63% is held by investor-stockholders, and 1% is held by Corporation because of foreclosures.

The cooperative structure makes it difficult to refinance a stockholder's interest in the cooperative. It is proposed that Corporation be converted to a condominium form of ownership and then be liquidated. To that end, Corporation will record a condominium declaration under which each apartment unit will become a separate condominium unit. Corporation will then adopt a plan of liquidation, distribute the deeds of legal title to the condominium units (and the undivided interest in the common elements appurtenant thereto) and its remaining property to its shareholders in cancellation of their shares of Corporation stock and their proprietary leases to the apartment units, and dissolve. Each shareholder will receive the deed to the particular apartment unit subject to his proprietary lease. Any stockholder who dissents to the conversion and liquidation will have his stock purchased for cash at fair market value by Corporation.

Based upon the facts and representations submitted, we hold as follows:

1. Provided that —
    (a) the transaction qualifies as a complete liquidation, and

B. COMPLETE LIQUIDATIONS 377

    (b) as part of the liquidation, Corporation distributes divided interests to the condominium units (and common elements) it owns because of foreclosures or purchases from dissenters, or sells such units and either distributes the proceeds of sale or applies the proceeds against its expenses (hereafter referred to as the remaining property), subject to the limitations of section 336 of the Code, Corporation will recognize gain or loss on the distribution of the deeds (and the undivided interests in the common elements) and the remaining property to its stockholders as if the distributed property were sold to the distributees at fair market value.

2. As provided in sections 216(e)[4] and 1034, Corporation will recognize no gain or loss on its distribution of a deed to a tenant-stockholder in exchange for the tenant-stockholder's stock, provided that the unit represented by the deed will have been the tenant-stockholder's principal residence for the period beginning 2 years before the day of the distribution, and will be the tenant-stockholder's principal residence for the period ending 2 years after the day of the distribution. Corporation will recognize gain or loss on the distribution of deeds to investor-stockholders whose exchange with Corporation will not qualify for nonrecognition under sections 216(e) and 1034. Sections 216(e) and 1034 will not apply to shield Corporation from recognizing gain or loss on the distribution of the remaining property to tenant-stockholders or investor-stockholders.

3. Any gain recognized by Corporation on the distributions to member stockholders will be income derived from transactions with members for purposes of computing net membership income under section 277. Therefore, Corporation may offset gain recognized on the distribution of deeds to member stockholders by the accumulated excess deductions, if any, arising from expenses in providing services, facilities, or goods to members during the taxable years 1988 through 1992. Furthermore, Corporation may offset such gain by the net operating loss carryovers, if any, arising from the excess of similar expenses over membership income for the taxable years 1981 through 1987, as permitted under section 172.

No opinion is expressed about the tax treatment of the transaction under other provisions of the Code and regulations or about the tax treatment of any conditions existing at the time of or effects resulting from the transaction that are not specifically covered by the above rulings. In particular, no opinion is

---

[4] Section 216(e) provides that no gain or loss is recognized on the distribution by a cooperative housing corporation of a dwelling unit to a shareholder if the distribution is in exchange for the stock and the exchange qualifies under § 1034 as an exchange of principal residences under § 1034(f). This protects the co-op from taxation. Section 1034(f) rounds out the picture by assuring that co-op shareholders are not precluded from benefitting from § 1034. [Eds.]

expressed about the amount of gain or loss recognized by Corporation under section 336. Also, no opinion is expressed as to the amount of Corporation's accumulated excess deductions or net operating loss carryovers available to offset gain recognized on the proposed transaction....

NOTES

1. § 446(b) power. The IRS often puts a liquidating corporation on the accrual method pursuant to an application of the § 446(b) power if its accounting method no longer clearly reflects income because of the liquidation. For example, it may be denied further use of the completed contract method of accounting. This usually has the effect of accelerating corporate income. *See* Bittker & Eustice, Federal Income Taxation of Corporations and Shareholders ¶ 10.06[2] (6th ed. 1994).

2. *Tax-benefit rule.* If the corporation previously deducted an item which it did not in fact consume or exhaust, e.g. expensed assets, the tax-benefit rule will force it to take that item back into income when it is distributed or when the bookkeeping entry is reversed. *Hillsboro Nat'l Bank v. Commissioner*, 460 U.S. 370 (1983).

3. *Anticipatory assignments of income.* Items of potential income that are ripe when distributed are taxable to the corporation even though they may be collected following liquidation. *See Wood Harmon Corp. v. United States*, 311 F.2d 918 (2d Cir. 1963).

4. *Tax returns.* A corporation going through liquidation must file federal income tax returns until the cessation of business and disposition of all its assets. Reg. § 1.6012-2(a)(2).

C. RECOGNITION OF LOSSES UNDER § 336

Read § 336(d)(1)-(2).

The 1986 repeal of former § 337 and the *General Utilities* doctrine for complete liquidations might have offered some opportunities to take advantage of the fact that liquidating corporations could enjoy tax losses for the first time. Shareholders might contribute loss property to a corporation with the intent of liquidating it and receiving the benefit of deductible losses realized at both the corporate and the shareholder levels. This possibility was anticipated by Congress and stymied in advance.

C. RECOGNITION OF LOSSES UNDER § 336

HOUSE OF REPRESENTATIVES REPORT NO. 841, 99th Congress, 2d Session, H.R. 3838[5]

RECOGNITION OF GAIN OR LOSS ON LIQUIDATING SALES AND DISTRIBUTIONS OF PROPERTY (GENERAL UTILITIES). P. L. 99-514

....

House Bill

In general

Under the House bill, gain or loss is recognized by a corporation on a liquidating distribution of its assets, as if the corporation had sold the assets to the distributee at fair market value, and on liquidating sales. In addition, the treatment of nonliquidating distribution is generally conformed to the treatment of liquidating distributions.

....

Conference Agreement

The conference agreement generally follows the House bill, with certain modifications and clarifications, thus repealing the *General Utilities* doctrine.

Thus, gain or loss is generally recognized by a corporation on a liquidating sale of its assets. Gain or loss is also generally recognized on a liquidating distribution of assets as if the corporation had sold the assets to the distributee at fair market value. Neither gain nor loss is recognized, however, with respect to any distribution of property by a corporation to the extent there is nonrecognition of gain or loss to the recipient under the tax-free reorganization provisions of the Code....

Limitations on the recognition of losses

The conferees are concerned that taxpayers may utilize various means to avoid the repeal of the *General Utilities* doctrine, or otherwise take advantage of the new provisions, to recognize losses in inappropriate situations or inflate the amount of losses actually sustained. For example, under the general rule permitting recognition of losses on liquidating distributions, taxpayers may be able to create artificial losses at the corporate level or to duplicate shareholder losses in corporate solution through contribution of built-in loss property. Consequently, the conference agreement includes two provisions intended to prevent the recognition of such corporate level losses.

First, the conference agreement provides generally that no loss is recognized by a liquidating corporation with respect to any distribution of property to a related person (within the meaning of section 267), unless the property is distributed to all shareholders on a pro rata basis and the property was not

---

[5] September 18, 1986.

acquired by the liquidating corporation in a section 351 transaction or as a contribution to capital during the five years preceding the distribution. Thus, for example, a liquidating corporation would not be permitted to recognize loss on a distribution of recently acquired property to a shareholder who, directly or indirectly, owns more than 50 percent in value of the stock of the corporation. Similarly, a liquidating corporation would not be permitted to recognize a loss on any property (regardless of when or how acquired) that is distributed to such a shareholder on a non-pro rata basis.

Second, the conference agreement generally provides that if a principal purpose of the contribution of property to a corporation in advance of its liquidation is to recognize a loss upon the sale or distribution of the property and thus eliminate or otherwise limit corporate level gain, then the basis (for purposes of determining loss) of any property acquired by such corporation in a section 351 transaction or as a contribution to capital will be reduced, but not below zero, by the excess of the basis of the property on the date of contribution over its fair market value on such date. For purposes of this rule, it is presumed, except to the extent provided in regulations, that any section 351 transaction or contribution to capital within the two-year period prior to the adoption of a plan to complete liquidation (or thereafter) has such a principal purpose. Although a contribution more than two years before the adoption of a plan of liquidation might be made with a prohibited purpose, the conferees expect that those rules will apply only in the most rare and unusual cases under such circumstances.

If the adoption of a plan of complete liquidation occurs in a taxable year following the date on which the tax return including the loss disallowed by this provision is filed, the conferees intend that, in appropriate cases, the liquidating corporation may recapture the disallowed loss on the tax return for the taxable year in which such plan of liquidation is adopted. In the alternative, the corporation could file an amended return for the taxable year in which the loss was reported.

The conferees intend that the Treasury Department will issue regulations generally providing that the presumed prohibited purpose for contributions of property two years in advance of the adoption of a plan of liquidation will be disregarded unless there is no clear and substantial relationship between the contributed property and the conduct of the corporation's current or future business enterprises. For example, assume that A owns Z Corporation which operates a widget business in New Jersey. That business operates exclusively in the northeastern region of the United States and there are no plans to expand those operations. In his individual capacity, A had acquired unimproved real estate in New Mexico that has declined in value. On March 22, 1988, A contributes such real estate to Z and six months later a plan of complete liquidation is adopted. Thereafter, all of Z's assets are sold to an unrelated party and the liquidation proceeds are distributed. A contributed no other property to Z during the two-year period prior to the adoption of the plan of liquidation. Because A contributed the property to Z less than two years prior to the adoption

C. RECOGNITION OF LOSSES UNDER § 336

of the plan of liquidation, it is presumed to have been contributed with a prohibited purpose. Moreover, because there is no clear and substantial relationship between the contributed property and the conduct of Z's business, the conferees do not expect that any loss arising from the disposition of the New Mexico real estate would be allowed under the Treasury regulations.

As another example, the conferees expect that such regulations would permit the allowance of any resulting loss from the disposition of any of the assets of a trade or business (or a line of business) that are contributed to a corporation. In such circumstance, application of the loss disallowance rule is inappropriate assuming there is a meaningful relationship between the contribution and the utilization of the corporate form to conduct a business enterprise, i.e., the contributed business, as distinguished from a portion of its assets, is not disposed of immediately after the contribution. The conferees also anticipate that the basis adjustment rules will generally not apply to a corporation's acquisition of property during its first two years of existence.

To illustrate the mechanical aspects of the basis adjustment rules, assume that on June 1, 1987, a shareholder who owns a 10-percent interest in X corporation ("X") contributes nondepreciable property with a basis of $1,000 and a value of $100 to X in exchange for additional stock; X is a calendar year taxpayer. Assume further that on September 30, 1987, X sells the property to an unrelated third party for $200, and includes the resulting $800 loss on its 1987 tax return. Finally, assume that X adopts a plan of liquidation on December 31, 1988. Thereafter, X could file an amended return reflecting the fact that the $800 loss was disallowed, because the property's basis would be reduced to $200. Alternatively, the conferees intend that X, under regulations, may be permitted to recapture the loss on its 1988 tax return. The amount of loss recapture in such circumstances would be limited to the lesser of the built-in loss ($900, or $1,000, the transferred basis under section 362, less $100, the value of the property on that date it was contributed to X) or the loss actually recognized on the disposition of such property ($800, or the $1,000 transferred basis less the $200 amount realized). Thus, unless X files an amended return, X must recapture $800 on its return for its taxable year ending December 31, 1988.

Now read again the "anti-stuffing" rules of § 336(d)(1) & (2).

PROBLEM 18-3

Terry owns 100% of the stock of Atlas Corp. Terry's basis in the stock is $100,000, and Terry has held the shares long-term. Atlas's only asset is a parcel of land it acquired seven years ago. The fair market value of the land is $90,000, and Atlas's basis is $100,000. Atlas adopts a plan of complete liquidation and distributes the land to Terry.

(a) What are the tax consequences including basis to Atlas and to Terry? *See* §§ 331, 336 and Reg. § 1.331-1.

(b) Assume the same facts, except that the land owned by Atlas was acquired by Atlas in a § 351 transaction two years before the complete liquidation of Atlas. How does this change the tax consequences to Atlas and Terry?

PROBLEM 18-4

Property with a fair market value of $20,000 and an adjusted basis of $30,000 is contributed to X Corp. by one of its shareholders. Nineteen months later, X Corp. liquidates. In connection with the liquidation, X Corp. sells the property for $18,000. How much loss is allowed on the liquidation?

PROBLEM 18-5

Same as Problem 18-4, except that the corporation sells the property for $22,000. What is the result?

PROBLEM 18-6

On June 1, Year 1, a shareholder of X Corp. (which is on the calendar year) contributes property to X Corp. with a fair market value of $10,000 and a basis of $100,000 in X Corp.'s hands immediately after the contribution. The contributed property is built-in loss property. On September 30 of the same year, X Corp. sells the property for $20,000 and reports an $80,000 loss on its tax return for Year 1. X adopts a plan of complete liquidation on Dec. 31, Year 2. What result?

D. SECTION 332 LIQUIDATIONS

Read §§ 332 and 337.

Although liquidations are generally taxable to both the corporation and the shareholder, §§ 332 and 337 provide an exception for liquidations of 80% owned subsidiaries into their parent corporations. Section § 332 protects the corporate parent from gain or loss on receipt of the assets from the controlled subsidiary, and § 337 protects the subsidiary against *General Utilities* gain or loss on distribution of its assets. The purpose of §§ 332 and 337 is to facilitate the simplification of complicated corporate financial structures by allowing the tax-free elimination of unnecessary subsidiaries. These liquidations may either involve dissolutions under state law or short-form mergers of subsidiaries into parent corporations under state law.[6] Assuming that such a restructuring is achieved — whether by merger or dissolution under state law — the parent

---

[6] In the latter case § 332 is not the controlling tax provision, but rather § 368(a)(1)(A), which is discussed in Chapter 21.

D. SECTION 332 LIQUIDATIONS

corporation normally obtains the liquidated subsidiary's tax attributes, including its earnings and profits account. *See* § 381(a)(1). Section 337(a) assures that the subsidiary is free of tax and § 334(b)(1) and (c)(2) force the recipient parent to take the assets with the bases that they had in the hands of the subsidiary. The result in effect is simply to ignore the corporate form of the subsidiary and treat its assets as if they had been owned by the controlling parent all along, which defers any gain or loss in those assets until the parent disposes of them. The curiosity of this arrangement is that the parent's basis in the stock of the subsidiary evaporates, which may be disadvantageous if the basis is particularly high.

1. REQUIREMENTS IMPOSED BY § 332

The requirements of § 332 are not subtle or treacherous.

First, the parent corporation must own 80% by vote and value of the stock of the corporation going through the liquidation, ignoring nonvoting, nonconvertible preferred stock. The difficulty is that this level of ownership has to be maintained *at all times* following the date on which the plan of the liquidation is adopted.

Second, the subsidiary is supposed to engage in "a complete cancellation or redemption of all of its stock." Although there is usually a state law dissolution, it is not mandatory and in fact the liquidating corporation can retain a few assets so as to continue its legal existence. Reg. § 1.332-2(c). This can save the parent corporation some legal fees and filing expenses in the event that it would like to have another corporation in storage for future use.

Third, the liquidation must be promptly completed — within one taxable year — in which case there need be no specified year in which the liquidation has to be performed. That leaves plenty of leeway for small corporations to dispose of their assets. For larger corporations, however, the plan of liquidation has to provide for the transfer of all of the properties within three years of the close of the taxable year in which the first distribution is made, and the transfers must be completed in this period.[7] If this requirement is not satisfied, the § 332 liquidation is retroactively disqualified, and the liquidation becomes fully taxable.

The protection of §§ 332 and 337 is available even if both the parent corporation and its controlled subsidiary liquidate, provided that the subsidiary is liquidated first so that the technical requirements of § 332 are met. *See* Rev. Rul. 69-172, 1969-1 C.B. 99; *Barkley Co. of Ariz.*, T.C. Memo 1988-324. This

---

[7] A solution to this problem may be to use a so-called liquidating trust. This contemplates that the corporation will constructively transfer its assets to its shareholders, who will in turn transfer the assets to a trust for their benefit. In the real world, the transfer is a direct flight to the trust, but for tax purposes, the assets are deemed to make a layover in the shareholders' hands.

can be very advantageous if the parent corporation has built-in gain in the subsidiary's stock because it eliminates that gain entirely.[8]

> *To illustrate*: Parent owns 100% of the stock of Sub, which is worth $100 and in which Parent has a basis of $10. Parent's other assets are worth $100, and Parent's basis in them is $50. Sub's own assets are also worth $100 and have a basis of $50 in Sub's hands. If Sub is liquidated into Parent under §§ 332/337, there will be no tax to either corporation, and Parent simply inherits Sub's assets with Sub's $50 basis. If Parent then liquidates, it will have gain of $100 under § 336 from the deemed sale of both its own and Sub's assets. If Parent liquidates first, however, it must recognize its gain of $90 in the Sub stock under § 336 in addition to its inside gain of $50, and when Sub is liquidated outside the protection of §§ 332/337, its own inside gain of $50 must be recognized. If Parent has a built-in *loss* in its Sub stock, the stakes are reversed and Parent has an incentive to flunk §§ 332/337 in order to deduct the loss which would otherwise evaporate.

2. MINORITY SHAREHOLDERS

Even if §§ 332 and 337 apply to liquidation of a controlled subsidiary, the protection of § 332 is not afforded to minority shareholders, and in addition, the liquidating subsidiary must recognize gain (but not loss) on any assets distributed to the minority shareholders. This is true even if the minority shareholder is itself a corporation. In effect, the minority shareholders and the liquidating subsidiary are treated as engaging in a separate §§ 331/336 taxable liquidation, except for the rule forbidding loss recognition under § 336(d). Section 336(d)(3) is designed to prevent "cherry-picking" of losses so that the liquidating subsidiary cannot distribute its gain assets tax free to its parent and at the same time enjoy a deduction by targeting its loss assets to minority shareholders.

Review Problem 18-2 and redetermine the tax consequences on the supposition that Movie, Inc. was 100% owned by a parent corporation that, in turn, was

---

[8] There was some judicial confusion surrounding the *Fairfield Steamship Corp. v. Commissioner* decision, 157 F.2d 321 (2d Cir. 1946), *cert. denied*, 329 U.S. 774 (1946), which indicated that the parent corporation must continue the business of the subsidiaries. While this authority is shaky at best, it is reasonably clear that if *both* parent and subsidiary go out of business, § 332 does not apply if the parent liquidates first or is no longer the controlling shareholder when the subsidiary is liquidated. For an example where § 332 did not apply because the parent distributed the stock of the subsidiary to the parent's shareholders, *see Kamis Eng'g Co. v. Commissioner*, 60 T.C. 763 (1973).

D. SECTION 332 LIQUIDATIONS

owned 50-50 by Harry and Sally, and that Movie, Inc. liquidated (both ways) this year, and soon afterwards the parent liquidated. *See* §§ 332, 337, 381, 334(b)(1).

REV. RUL. 70-106
1970-1 C.B. 70

....

Minority shareholders owned twenty-five percent of the capital stock of corporation X. The remaining seventy-five percent of the capital stock of X was owned by Corporation Y. Y desired to liquidate X in a transaction to which section 332 of the Internal Revenue Code of 1954 would apply in order that Y would recognize no gain on the transaction. The minority shareholders agreed to have their stock of X redeemed. Following the distribution to the minority shareholders, Y owned all the stock of X. Y then adopted a formal plan of complete liquidation of X and all of the remaining assets of X were distributed to Y.

Held, all of the shareholders of X received a distribution in liquidation under the provisions of section 331 of the Code, and the gain is recognized to Y and gain or loss is recognized to the minority shareholders under section 331 of the Code. The liquidation fails to meet the eighty percent stock ownership requirements of section 332(b)(1) of the Code since the plan of liquidation was adopted at the time Y reached the agreement with the minority shareholders and at such time, Y owned seventy-five percent of the stock of X.

NOTES

1. *Qualifying for § 332; is it quasi-elective?* Assume a corporation has two shareholders, an individual who owns twenty-one shares and an unrelated corporation that owns seventy-nine shares. If the individual redeems her shares before a plan of liquidation is adopted, the result can be a good § 332 liquidation. Does this make the system too elective? Despite Rev. Rul. 70-106, the courts have been very generous in upholding taxpayers' efforts to "back into" 80% control by prior redemptions and stock sales, and have not found a "plan" of liquidation until its official corporate adoption. *See George L. Riggs, Inc. v. Commissioner*, 64 T.C. 474 (1975), in which the court goes so far as to say that § 332 is elective for those who know how to structure the transaction properly.

2. *What about deliberately avoiding § 332 by first dumping some stock in order to get under the 80% threshold?* Here it has been held that even a good faith sale after adoption of the plan of liquidation will disqualify the plan. *Commissioner v. Day & Zimmerman, Inc.*, 151 F.2d 517 (3d Cir. 1945). Can you reconcile these results?

3. *What about debts of the subsidiary?* Parent corporations often lend generously to get their subsidiaries underway. If the subsidiary is a failure and is insolvent and the parent decides to liquidate it, then there is no *distribution with respect to stock* (the stock having no value) and § 332 does not apply, so the parent can claim a loss on the subsidiary's stock. If a liquidating subsidiary distributes property to its parent as repayment of its debt, the usual rule that gain or loss is recognized as if the property were sold to a stranger and the cash were used to pay the debt does not apply. Instead § 337(b)(1) treats the transfer as part of the §§ 332/337 liquidation with the result that no gain or loss is recognized to the subsidiary. The rule is designed to prevent the subsidiary from creating loss deductions by paying off its debts with loss property while transferring its gain property taxfree. On the parent's side of the transaction, however, any gain or loss is recognized if it receives payment *qua* creditor, say because it bought the subsidiary's debt at a discount and was repaid the full face amount. Reg. § 1.332-7.

PROBLEM 18-7

Grabber International, Inc. buys 100% of the stock of Target, Inc. on one day and liquidates it pursuant to § 332 three months later. Grabber paid $1 million for the stock. Target's assets have a basis of $100,000 and are worth $1 million. What gain or loss, if any, will Grabber and Target recognize? *See* §§ 332(a) and 337(a). What will be Grabber's basis in Target's assets?

PROBLEM 18-8

X Corp. owns 85% of the stock of its subsidiary, Y Corp. X Corp.'s basis in the stock of Y Corp. is $70,000. Individual M owns the remaining 15% of the stock of Y Corp. She has held the stock long-term, and her basis in the stock is $15,000. On June 1, 1993, Y Corp. adopts a plan of complete liquidation at which time it has the following assets:

	Fair Market Value	Y Corp.'s Basis
Cash	$30,000	$30,000
Inventory	80,000	100,000
Building	200,000	50,000

Pursuant to the plan of complete liquidation, Y Corp. distributes the $30,000 cash to M and the inventory and building to X Corp. What are the tax consequences to X Corp. and to M? *See* Regs. §§ 1.332-1, -2 and -5.

Chapter 19
TAXABLE ACQUISITIONS

A. INTRODUCTION

Business people and tax people tend to think differently. The business person wants a transaction that has business advantages, such as rounding out a product line. A tax person is brought in to optimize the tax results and may wind up suggesting transactions that are almost incomprehensible to the client, whose position is simply, "I want that business." Whether it is done as an acquisition of assets[1] — or as a stock acquisition[2] — is of no direct concern. The tax advisor will then review the important tax features of the target and of the acquiror and their owners and will suggest an optimal way to shape the transaction, usually on the assumption that the seller is well advised in tax matters. The advisor will study such issues as the bases of the target's assets, the existence of net operating losses, and earnings and profits accounts.

Once the advisor has ascertained the facts and the tax stakes, the next step is to try out the various specific kinds of transactions contemplated in the Code with an eye to achieving the optimum tax result. The transactions can include partial liquidations, preacquisitive distributions, nontaxable spinoffs of businesses of the target company in advance of a nontaxable acquisitive reorganization of the target company, and so forth. One of the deep issues in corporate taxation is whether the tax results of business acquisitions should be entirely elective, as opposed to relying on the manipulation of the "short list" of transactional forms meted out by the Code, which manipulation in effect produces elections visible only to the well-heeled.

In general, there are two basic ways for one corporation to acquire another. The simplest alternative is a taxable acquisition. Such an acquisition may be structured as a purchase of target assets or of target stock, either for cash or for any other consideration. A purchase of assets results in taxation at both the target and target shareholder levels. This benefits the acquiror if it can get a stepped-up basis in the acquired assets equal to their fair market value and the purchase price (cost) and wipes out the target company's earnings and profits. If the acquiror purchases the stock of the target, only the target shareholders are taxed on their capital gains and losses, but the price of avoiding a target-level tax is that the

---

[1] This may be achieved as a taxable asset purchase, on a current basis, on a deferred sale basis under § 453, or nontaxably under § 1031 (like kind exchanges) or perhaps by means of a joint contribution by buyer and seller to a new corporation under § 351 or to a partnership under § 721.

[2] This can be a taxable stock purchase or a nontaxable acquisitive reorganization using stock as consideration, the latter being the subject of Chapter 20.

target's assets keep their historic basis and all target's tax history survives. The target has merely changed owners with no effect upon its internal tax affairs.[3]

The other method is a tax-free corporate reorganization under § 368, in which the acquiror swaps stock for stock or assets of the target company. There will generally be no shareholder-level tax, but there will also be no step-up in basis of the target corporation's assets, much as under §§ 332/337 liquidations. Tax-free reorganizations are treated in Chapter 21.

To illustrate: Suppose Grabber, Inc., a large, publicly held corporation "on the make" wants to acquire the assets and business of Target Corp., a closely-held corporation (owned by the Mutt family) whose assets consist of real and personal property, some of it depreciable, some with low bases and some with high bases (but assume overall basis is far below value), cash, accounts receivable, some advantageous contracts, leases and intangibles, and cash. Consider how Grabber might acquire Target's business and the tax consequences, in broad outline, of each method.

Grabber can buy all the stock of Target Corp., if everyone will sell; if not, Grabber may be stuck with a troublesome minority shareholder. After buying all or most of the stock, it can continue Target as a subsidiary (with Target's internal tax characteristics unchanged). Or it can liquidate Target and run its business as a divsion of Grabber. Or it could merge Target up and into Grabber, or even merge Grabber into Target.

If Grabber buys all (or nearly all) the assets and assumes all (or nearly all) the liabilities of Target, it can run the business as a division, or it could "drop down" Target's assets and liabilities into a subsidiary, or distribute them to Graber's shareholders, who could then run the business separately and incorporate it. The Mutt family will have to liquidate Target Corp. to get their hands on the purchase price. Assume they have low bases in their shares. Or, Target could be liquidated in kind before the acquisition, in which event the Mutt family could then sell the assets to Grabber, Inc.

How many levels of recognition of gain or loss would each method involve? What basis and other advantages or disadvantages accompany each one? Vary your assumptions about gain or loss inherent in the assets in stock. Under what

---

[3] Except for problems of offsetting target loss carryforwards against future gains, which are treated in Chapter 23.

assumptions does one method or another seem most advantageous in terms of federal income tax treatment?

B. TYPES OF TAXABLE ACQUISITIONS

A corporate business may be acquired in one of two fundamental ways: by a purchase of the target corporation's stock from its shareholders, or by direct purchase of the assets from the target corporation itself. The differences between the two methods can be profound from both a business and a tax point of view. Cautious buyers prefer to buy assets because they wish to avoid hidden or contingent liabilities of the target corporation. The purchaser of stock buys the target's future lawsuits (against the corporation whose stock he has acquired). On the other hand, a purchase of assets is often very inconvenient or impossible if the target corporation has valuable contracts or licenses to do business that may be difficult to replace. In that case, it may be essential to obtain the target corporation itself, which can only be done through a purchase of stock. If business factors do not compel a choice, say because the seller is highly solvent and willing to indemnify the buyer against all liabilities, it is still rarely if ever the case that the tax law will be indifferent to whether an acquisition is structured as a purchase of assets or stock, although in a better world taxes would not intrude upon the business decision as to which form is most convenient. To complicate matters, an acquisition of either stock or assets may be accomplished through a bewildering variety of tax-free reorganizations, which is the subject of Chapter 21. The tax stakes may be very high for both buyer and seller, and as a result structuring the sale of a business is the tax lawyer's bread and butter.

In a taxable acquisition the basic tax stakes are familiar ones: whether the seller is taxed at ordinary or capital gains rates, and whether the buyer will inherit the target's tax history including the basis and depreciation schedules of its assets, net operating losses, and earnings and profits, or will begin afresh with a cost basis and a fresh slate. In addition, after the *General Utilities* repeal the target itself will be taxed if it sells its assets or liquidates. The picture becomes rapidly complicated where there are multiple parties to the transaction who may have conflicting interests, and/or where the buyer(s) wish to acquire some but not all of the seller's business. Accommodating the business and tax needs of all parties can become an extremely sophisticated and demanding task. Given the immense variety of possible tax structurings of what may be essentially the same business deal, and the high stakes involved, it should not be surprising that the craftiness and creativity of tax lawyers have produced a body of law that is unrivalled for its complexity.

If a purchaser (P) buys all the target corporation's (T's) assets and T is left with cash or notes, the sellers then have the choice of liquidating T under § 331 and getting a capital gain or loss result at the shareholder level. If T sold assets on the installment method in the course of the takeover of its properties, its shareholders can report their stock sale on the same method, which provides some deferral of the double tax burden.

A purchase of assets may be inconvenient for both parties because the cost of changing titles to property can be high. It is often easier to structure the transaction as a taxable merger. In a merger under state law, two corporations are legally combined and only the acquiring corporation survives (the target is automatically dissolved as a matter of state law). The surviving corporation becomes the owner of the target's assets as a matter of law. This does not solve the problem of avoiding the target's hidden or contingent liabilities, however, because under state law the surviving corporation of a merger acquires all the target's assets *and liabilities*.

A merger may be "triangular" in the sense that the acquiring corporation forms a subsidiary to do the dirty work of taking over the other company. A triangular merger can be made in two directions: either the target is merged into the new subsidiary, or the new subsidiary may merge into the target. For tax purposes, the former kind of merger is treated as a purchase of the target's assets from the target followed by a liquidation of the target. The latter is known as a "reverse subsidiary merger" and is treated for tax purposes as a purchase of the target's stock. Subsidiary mergers do not avoid the target's liabilities, but they do at least quarantine them within the subsidiary and prevent them from becoming claims against the acquiror's other assets in just the same way as a purchase of target stock.

Corporate law lawyers tend to assume that all mergers are tax-free, but that is not the case. A merger can be taxable if the transaction fails to satisfy one of any number of conditions that the Code imposes, most importantly, if the consideration paid to the target shareholders consists of too much cash in relation to stock (of the acquiring corporation).

C. ASSET PURCHASES

Read § 1060(a) and (c).

A purchase of the assets of a business (as opposed to the acquisition of stock) is treated for tax purposes as a separate purchase and sale of each and every asset of the business, including its intangible assets. This rule applies both to a sale of all a corporation's assets and to a sale of any part, including the sale of a division which constitutes a separate line of business. Thus, both the buyer and the seller of a business must assign part of the purchase price to each and every asset in the business in order to compare that part to the asset's basis and separately to compute gain and loss, asset by asset. If the business is a substantial one, the burden of apportioning the sales proceeds can be daunting.

At this point, § 1060 enters the picture and imposes a number of important requirements. Section 1060 is triggered by the existence of an *applicable asset acquisition*, meaning a direct or indirect transfer of assets which constitute a trade or business, if the transferee's basis in the assets is determined on the basis

C. ASSET PURCHASES

of what the buyer paid (the acquisition may be in part a like-kind exchange under § 1031). § 1060(c). Once § 1060 is swept in, there are a number of obligations:

1. The buyer and seller must generally use Form 8594, which they prepare jointly, to report the part of the sales price attributable to each asset.[4]

2. The basis of the acquired assets must be determined under the "residual method," the effect of which is to assign consideration sequentially, first to the most easily valued assets (viz., cash and certain bank deposits, ("Class I assets") and last to the intangibles that are the most difficult to value, namely going concern value and goodwill,[5] known as "Class IV assets." The intermediate assets are Class II, meaning liquid assets such as CDs, federal securities and other easily marketable securities. Class III assets consist of other tangible and intangible assets exclusive of goodwill and going concern value. Going concern value refers to the addition to value that arises from the fact that the business can be continued despite a change of ownership, whereas goodwill is supposed to reflect the above average earnings expectations for the enterprise.

3. Ten-percent owners of businesses must report to the IRS on contracts that are related to the acquisition. § 1060(e). This commonly forces disclosure of covenants not to compete, employment agreements, and other transactions.

Under pre-1993 law, there was *no* amortization deduction for goodwill or going concern value. As a result, buyers of assets were tempted to allocate as little of the purchase price as possible to goodwill, and as much as possible to depreciable assets or amortizable intangibles such as noncompete agreements. This process led to frequent claims that hitherto unknown forms of intangibles were amortizable and distinguishable from goodwill.

Section 1060 and its accompanying Regulations[6] were unable to cope with intangibles issues. For one thing, they failed to define goodwill, which allowed taxpayers to devise artful claims that new forms of intangibles had a limited useful life and a definitely ascertainable value. Taxpayers have long strained to show that what might otherwise appear to be a large amount of undifferentiated goodwill can be broken down into particular elements, at least some of which have limited useful lives and can therefore be separately amortized. Taxpayers did fairly well at that. For example, in Revenue Ruling 74-456, 1974-2 C.B. 65, the IRS capitulated and accepted the *Houston Chronicle* decision,[7] which no longer treated customer-related intangibles automatically as a mass asset and "indistinguishable from goodwill." The next major decision, which was

---

[4] If there is no written allocation agreement, the parties are still obligated to use the residual method (see below) of apportioning the purchase price to assets. Section 1060(b) authorizes this mandatory disclosure.

[5] For historical reasons that are touched on later in the book, the mechanical rules are found in Reg. § 1.338(b)-2T(b).

[6] Reg. §§ 1.1060-1(d) and 1.338(b)-2T.

[7] *Houston Chronicle Pub'g Co. v. United States*, 481 F.2d 1240 (5th Cir. 1973), *cert. denied*, 414 U.S. 1129 (1974).

overruled prospectively by enactment of § 197 in the same year, but which shows the problem with which the law attempts to deal, appears immediately below.

NEWARK MORNING LEDGER CO. v. UNITED STATES
113 S. Ct. 1670 (1993)

[The taxpayer was the successor to The Herald Company. When, in 1976, Herald bought the stock of Booth Newspapers, Inc., it allocated its adjusted income tax basis in the Booth shares among the assets it acquired in its merger with Booth. Among other things, it allocated $67.8 million to an intangible asset denominated "paid subscribers," a figure that was petitioner's estimate of future profits to be derived from identified subscribers to Booth's eight newspapers on the date of merger. On its federal income tax returns for 1977-1980, it claimed depreciation deductions based on the $67.8 million. The IRS asserted that the concept of "paid subscribers" was indistinguishable from goodwill and, therefore, was nondepreciable.]

JUSTICE BLACKMUN delivered the opinion of the Court....
Section 167(a) of the Code allows as a deduction for depreciation a reasonable allowance for the exhaustion and wear and tear, including obsolescence, of property used in a trade or business or of property held for the production of income.... This Court has held that "the primary purpose" of an annual depreciation deduction is "to further the integrity of periodic income statements by making a meaningful allocation of the cost entailed in the use (excluding maintenance expense) of the asset to the periods to which it contributes."

....

The Revenue Act of 1918, § 234(a)(7), authorized a "reasonable allowance for the exhaustion, wear and tear of property used in the trade or business, including a reasonable allowance for obsolescence." 40 Stat. 1057, 1078 (1919). Treas. Regs. 45 (1919), promulgated under the 1918 Act, explicitly recognized that intangible assets "may be the subject of a depreciation allowance." Art. 163. Thereafter, the Regulations governing the depreciation of intangible assets have remained essentially unchanged.

Since 1927, the IRS consistently has taken the position that "goodwill" is nondepreciable. One court has said specifically: "Indeed, this proposition is so well settled that the only question litigated in recent years regarding this area of the law is whether a particular asset is 'goodwill.'" *Houston Chronicle Publishing Co. v. United States*, 481 F.2d 1240, 1247 (CA5 1973)....

"Goodwill" is not defined in the Code or in any Treasury Department Regulations. There have been attempts, however, to devise workable definitions of the term. In *Metropolitan Bank v. St. Louis Dispatch Co.*, 149 U.S. 436, 13 S. Ct. 944, 37 L. Ed. 799 (1893), for example, this Court considered whether a newspaper's goodwill survived after it was purchased and ceased publishing under its old name. It ruled that the goodwill did not survive, relying on Justice Story's notable description of "goodwill" as

C. ASSET PURCHASES

"'the advantage or benefit, which is acquired by an establishment, beyond the mere value of the capital, stock, funds, or property employed therein, in consequence of the general public patronage and encouragement which it receives from constant or habitual customers, on account of its local position, or common celebrity, or reputation for skill or affluence, or punctuality, or from other accidental circumstances or necessities, or even from ancient partialities, or prejudices.'" *Id.*, at 446, 13 S. Ct., at 948, quoting J. Story, Partnerships § 99 (1841).

In *Des Moines Gas Co. v. Des Moines*, 238 U.S. 153 ... (1915), the Court described goodwill as "that element of value which inheres in the fixed and favorable consideration of customers, arising from an established and well-known and well-conducted business."

Although the definition of goodwill has taken different forms over the years, the short-hand description of goodwill as "the expectancy of continued patronage," *Boe v. Commissioner*, 307 F.2d 339 ... (CA 9 1962), provides a useful label with which to identify the total of all the imponderable qualities that attract customers to the business.... This definition, however, is of little assistance to a taxpayer trying to evaluate which of its intangible assets is subject to a depreciation allowance. The value of every intangible asset is related, to a greater or lesser degree, to the expectation that customers will continue their patronage.[8] But since 1918, at least some intangible assets have been depreciable. Because intangible assets do not exhaust or waste away in the same manner as tangible assets, taxpayers must establish that public taste or other socioeconomic forces will cause the intangible asset to be retired from service, and they must estimate a reasonable date by which this event will occur. *See* B. Bittker & M. McMahon, Federal Income Taxation of Individuals ¶ 12.4, p. 12-10 (1988). Intangibles such as patents and copyrights are depreciable over their "legal lives," which are specified by statute. Covenants not to compete, leaseholds, and life estates, for example, are depreciable over their useful lives that are expressly limited by contract.

The category of intangibles that has given the IRS and the courts difficulty is that group of assets sometimes denominated "customer-based intangibles." This group includes customer lists, insurance expirations, subscriber lists, bank

---

[8] We emphasize that while the "expectancy of continued patronage" is a serviceable description of what we generally mean when we describe an intangible asset that has no useful life and no ascertainable value, this shibboleth tells us nothing about whether the asset in question is depreciable. The dissent concedes that "the law concerning the depreciation of intangible assets related to goodwill has developed on a case-by-case basis," yet, inexplicably, it suggests that "[s]uch matters are not at issue in this case, however, because the asset that Ledger seeks to depreciate is indistinguishable from goodwill." As we demonstrate below, an intangible asset with an ascertainable value and a limited useful life, the duration of which can be ascertained with reasonable accuracy, is depreciable under § 167 of the Code. The fact that it may also be described as the "expectancy of continued patronage" is entirely beside the point.

deposits, cleaning-service accounts, drugstore-prescription files, and any other identifiable asset the value of which obviously depends on the continued and voluntary patronage of customers. The question has been whether these intangibles can be depreciated notwithstanding their relationship to "the expectancy of continued patronage."

When considering whether a particular customer-based intangible asset may be depreciated, courts often have turned to a "mass asset" or "indivisible asset" rule. The rule provides that certain kinds of intangible assets are properly grouped and considered as a single entity; even though the individual components of the asset may expire or terminate over time, they are replaced by new components, thereby causing only minimal fluctuations and no measurable loss in the value of the whole. The following is the usually accepted description of a mass-asset:

> "[A] purchased terminable-at-will type of customer list is an indivisible business property with an indefinite, nondepreciable life, indistinguishable from—and the principal element of—goodwill, whose ultimate value lies in the expectancy of continued patronage through public acceptance. It is subject to temporary attrition as well as expansion through departure of some customers, acquisition of others, and increase or decrease in the requirements of individual customers. A normal turnover of customers represents merely the ebb and flow of a continuing property status in this species, and does not within ordinary limits give rise to the right to deduct for tax purposes the loss of individual customers. The whole is equal to the sum of its fluctuating parts at any given time, but each individual part enjoys no separate capital standing independent of the whole, for its disappearance affects but does not interrupt or destroy the continued existence of the whole." *Golden State Towel & Linen Service, Ltd. v. United States*, 179 Ct. Cl. 300 ... (1967).

The mass-asset rule prohibits the depreciation of certain customer-based intangibles because they constitute self-regenerating assets that may change but never waste. Although there may have been some doubt prior to 1973 as to whether the mass-asset rule required that any asset related to the expectancy of continued patronage always be treated as nondepreciable goodwill as a matter of law, that doubt was put to rest by the Fifth Circuit in the *Houston Chronicle* case. The court there considered whether subscription lists, acquired as part of the taxpayer's purchase of The Houston Press, were depreciable. The taxpayer had no intention of continuing publication of the purchased paper, so there was no question of the lists being self-regenerating; they had value only to the extent that they furnished names and addresses of prospective subscribers to the taxpayer's newspaper. After reviewing the history of the mass-asset rule, the court concluded that there was no per se rule that an intangible asset is nondepreciable whenever it is related to goodwill. On the contrary, the rule does not prevent taking a depreciation allowance

C. ASSET PURCHASES

"if the taxpayer properly carries his dual burden of proving that the intangible asset involved (1) has an ascertainable value separate and distinct from goodwill, and (2) has a limited useful life, the duration of which can be ascertained with reasonable accuracy." *Id.*, at 1250.

Following the decision in *Houston Chronicle*, the IRS issued a new ruling, modifying prior rulings "to remove any implication that customer and subscription lists, location contracts, insurance expirations, etc., are, as a matter of law, indistinguishable from goodwill possessing no determinable useful life." Rev. Rul. 74-456, 1974-2 C.B. 65, 66. The IRS continued to claim that customer-based intangibles generally are in the nature of goodwill, representing "the customer structure of a business, their value lasting until an indeterminate time in the future." Nonetheless, it acknowledged that, "in an unusual case," the taxpayer may prove that the "asset or a portion thereof does not possess the characteristics of goodwill, is susceptible of valuation, and is of use to the taxpayer in its trade or business for only a limited period of time." *Ibid.* Under these circumstances, the IRS recognized the possibility that the customer-based intangible asset could be depreciated over its useful life.

Despite the suggestion by the Court of Appeals in this case that the mass-asset rule is "now outdated," 945 F.2d at 561, it continues to guide the decisions of the Tax Court with respect to certain intangible assets. In *Ithaca Industries, Inc. v. Commissioner*, 97 T.C. 253 (1991), for example, the Tax Court recently considered whether a taxpayer could depreciate the value allocated to the trained work force of a purchased going concern over the length of time each employee remained with the purchasing company. The court acknowledged that "whether the assembled work force is an intangible asset with an ascertainable value and a limited useful life separate from goodwill or going-concern value is a question of fact." *Id.*, at 263-264. After reviewing the record, it concluded that the mass-asset rule applied to prohibit the depreciation of the cost of acquiring the assembled work force:

"Although the assembled work force is used to produce income, this record fails to show that its value diminishes as a result of the passing of time or through use. As an employee terminated his or her employment, another would be hired and trained to take his or her place. While the assembled work force might be subject to temporary attrition as well as expansion through departure of some employees and the hiring of others, it would not be depleted due to the passage of time or as a result of use. The turnover rate of employees represents merely the ebb and flow of a continuing work force. An employee's leaving does not interrupt or destroy the continued existence of the whole." *Id.*, at 267.

As a factual matter, the Tax Court found that the taxpayer hired a new worker only so he could replace a worker "who resigned, retired, or was fired." *Id.*, at 268. The court found that the "assembled work force" was a nondiminishing asset; new employees were trained in order to keep the "assembled work force" unchanged, and the cost of the training was a deductible expense. *Id.*, at 271.

Since 1973, when *Houston Chronicle* clarified that the availability of the depreciation allowance was primarily a question of fact, taxpayers have sought to depreciate a wide variety of customer-based intangibles. The courts that have found these assets depreciable have based their conclusions on carefully developed factual records. In *Richard S. Miller & Sons, Inc. v. United States*, 210 Ct. Cl. 431, 537 F.2d 446 (1976), for example, the court considered whether a taxpayer was entitled to a depreciation deduction for 1,383 insurance expirations that it had purchased from another insurer.[9] The court concluded that the taxpayer had carried its heavy burden of proving that the expirations had an ascertainable value separate and distinct from goodwill and had a limited useful life, the duration of which could be ascertained with reasonable accuracy. The court acknowledged that the insurance expirations constituted a "mass asset" the useful life of which had to be "determined from facts relative to the whole, and not from experience with any particular policy or account involved." *Id.*, at 443.... The court also noted, however, that the mass-asset rule does not prevent a depreciation deduction "where the expirations as a single asset can be valued separately and the requisite showing made that the useful life of the information contained in the intangible asset as a whole is of limited duration." *Id.*, at 439, 537 F.2d at 452. All the policies were scheduled to expire within three years, but their continuing value lay in their being renewable. Based on statistics gathered over a 5-year period, the taxpayer was able to estimate that the mass asset had a useful life of not more than 10 years from the date of purchase. Any renewals after that time would be attributable to the skill, integrity, and reputation of the taxpayer rather than to the value of the original expirations. "The package of expirations demonstrably was a wasting asset." *Id.*, at 444, 537 F.2d at 455. The court ruled that the taxpayer could depreciate the cost of the collection of insurance expirations over the useful life of the mass asset.

In *Citizens & Southern Corp. v. Commissioner*, 91 T.C. 463 (1988), *aff'd*, 919 F.2d 1492 (CA 11 1990), the taxpayer argued that it was entitled to depreciate the bank-deposit base acquired in the purchase of nine separate banks.[10] The taxpayer sought to depreciate the present value of the income it expected to

---

[9] An "expiration" is a copy of the face of an insurance policy made when the policy is issued. It shows the name of the insured, the type of insurance, the premium, the covered property, and the expiration date. "Its principal value in the insurance business is its indication of the most advantageous time to solicit a renewal." *Richard S. Miller & Sons, Inc. v. United States*, 210 Ct. Cl. at 436, 537 F.2d at 450.

[10] The term "deposit base" describes "the intangible asset that arises in a purchase transaction representing the present value of the future stream of income to be derived from employing the purchased core deposits of a bank." *Citizens & Southern Corp. v. Commissioner*, 91 T.C., at 465. The value of the deposit base rests upon the "ascertainable probability that inertia will cause depositors to leave their funds on deposit for predictable periods of time." *Id.*, at 500.

C. ASSET PURCHASES

derive from the use of the balances of deposit accounts existing at the time of the bank purchases. The Commissioner argued that the value of the core deposits was inextricably related to the value of the overall customer relationship, that is, to goodwill. The Commissioner also argued that the deposit base consisted of purchased, terminable-at-will customer relationships that are equivalent to goodwill as a matter of law. The Tax Court rejected the Commissioner's position, concluding that the taxpayer had demonstrated with sufficient evidence that the economic value attributable to the opportunity to invest the core deposits could be (and, indeed, was) valued and that the fact that new accounts were opened as old accounts closed did not make the original purchased deposit base self-regenerating. *Id.*, at 499.

The court also concluded that, based on "lifing studies" estimating the percentage of accounts that would close over a given period of time, the taxpayer established that the deposit base had a limited useful life, the duration of which could be ascertained with reasonable accuracy. The taxpayer had established the value of the intangible asset using the cost-savings method, entitling it to depreciate that portion of the purchase price attributable to the present value of the difference between the ongoing costs associated with maintaining the core deposits and the cost of the market alternative for funding its loans and other investments. *Id.*, at 510.

The Tax Court reached the same result in *Colorado National Bankshares, Inc. v. Commissioner*, 60 TCM (CCH) 771 (1970), *aff'd* 984 F.2d 383 (CA 10 1993). The Tax Court concluded that

> "the value of the deposit base does not depend upon a vague hope that customers will patronize the bank for some unspecified length of time in the future. The value of the deposit base rests upon the ascertainable probability that inertia will cause depositors to leave their funds on deposit for predictable periods of time." *Id.*, at 789.

The court specifically found that the deposit accounts could be identified; that they had limited lives that could be estimated with reasonable accuracy; and that they could be valued with a fair degree of accuracy. They were also not self-regenerating. "It is these characteristics which separate them from general goodwill and permits separate valuation." *Ibid....*

Although acknowledging the "analytic force" of cases [such as those discussed above] the Court of Appeals in the present case characterized them as "no more than a minority strand amid the phalanx of cases" that have adopted the Government's position on the meaning of goodwill. 945 F.2d at 565. "In any case, consistent with the prevailing case law, we believe that the IRS is correct in asserting that, for tax purposes, there are some intangible assets that, notwithstanding that they have wasting lives that can be estimated with reasonable accuracy and ascertainable values, are nonetheless goodwill and nondepreciable." *Id.*, at 568. The Court of Appeals concluded further that in "the context of the sale of a going concern, it is simply often too difficult for the taxpayer and the court to separate the value of the list qua list from the goodwill value of the customer relationships/structure." *Ibid*. We agree with that general observation. It is often too difficult for taxpayers to separate depreciable intangible assets from goodwill. But sometimes they manage to do it. And whether or not they have been successful in any particular case is a question of fact.

The Government concedes: "The premise of the regulatory prohibition against the depreciation of goodwill is that, like stock in a corporation, a work of art, or raw land, goodwill has no determinate useful life of specific duration." Brief for United States 13. *See also Richard S. Miller & Sons, Inc. v. United States*, 210 Ct. Cl. at 437, 537 F.2d at 450 ("Goodwill is a concept that embraces many intangible elements and is presumed to have a useful life of indefinite duration"). The entire justification for refusing to permit the depreciation of goodwill evaporates, however, when the taxpayer demonstrates that the asset in question wastes over an ascertainable period of time. It is more faithful to the purposes of the Code to allow the depreciation deduction under these circumstances, for "the Code endeavors to match expenses with the revenues of the taxable period to which they are properly attributable, thereby resulting in a more accurate calculation of net income for tax purposes." *INDOPCO, Inc. v. Commissioner*, 503 U.S. [79], (1992).

In the case that first established the principle that goodwill was not depreciable, the Eighth Circuit recognized that the reason for treating goodwill differently was simple and direct: "'As good will does not suffer wear and tear, does not become obsolescent, is not used up in the operation of the business, depreciation, as such, cannot be charged against it.'" *Red Wing Malting Co. v. Willcuts*, 15 F.2d 626, 633 (1926) ... It must follow that if a taxpayer can prove with reasonable accuracy that an asset used in the trade or business or held for the production of income has a value that wastes over an ascertainable period of time, that asset is depreciable under § 167, regardless of the fact that its value is related to the expectancy of continued patronage. The significant question for purposes of depreciation is not whether the asset falls "within the core of the concept of goodwill," Brief for United States 19, but whether the asset is capable of being valued and whether that value diminishes over time. In a different context, the IRS itself succinctly articulated the relevant principle: "Whether or not an intangible asset, or a tangible asset, is depreciable for Federal income tax purposes depends upon the determination that the asset is actually exhausting, and that such exhaustion is susceptible of measurement." Rev. Rul. 68-483, 1968-2 Cum. Bull. 91-92....

Petitioner has borne successfully its substantial burden of proving that "paid subscribers" constitutes an intangible asset with an ascertainable value and a limited useful life, the duration of which can be ascertained with reasonable accuracy. It has proved that the asset is not self-regenerating but rather wastes as the finite number of component subscriptions are canceled over a reasonably predictable period of time. The relationship this asset may have to the expectancy of continued patronage is irrelevant, for it satisfies all the necessary conditions to qualify for the depreciation allowance under § 167 of the Code.

The judgment of the Court of Appeals is reversed, and the case is remanded for further proceedings consistent with this opinion.

It is so ordered.

[Judge Souter's dissent is omitted.]

NOTE

This decision invited a potential flood of litigation that would depend on exhaustive appraisals of fact. For example, assume you planned to buy a health club for a price well in excess of the cost of its hardware. The club enjoys a good reputation, has a well known name, reliable employees, and has a loyal customer base which the company regularly bombards with mailings. How would you go about sorting out how much of the premium in excess of the value of the hardware was paid for the intangibles and what each component consisted of? The only realistic solution was new legislation, which Congress delivered in the form of § 197, discussed below.

The 1993 Act prospectively changed the longstanding rule against writing off goodwill and going concern value prospectively, by making purchased goodwill and going concern value amortizable on the straight-line method over fifteen years. § 197. That was a major change,[11] likely for the better. However, the 1993 Act went beyond that simple goal and, among other things, lengthened the amortization periods of many short-lived intangibles to fifteen years. The latter is obviously to taxpayers' disadvantage.

D. OVERVIEW OF § 197

Read § 197(a)-(d).

Section 197 divides intangibles into four groups:

— Those always subject to fifteen-year amortization under § 197;
— Those never subject to § 197;
— Those subject to § 197 if transferred in the acquisition of all or a substantial part of a trade or business;
— Covenants not to compete, which are covered by § 197 only if there is a related acquisition of a business by a purchase of either assets or stock.

Intangibles that are always subject to § 197. This group consists of customer-based intangibles, governmental licenses, franchises, trademarks, trade names, and know-how.

---

[11] *See* Reg. § 1.167(a)-3, which provided, "No deduction for depreciation is allowable with respect to goodwill."

Intangibles that are never subject to § 197. These include off-the-shelf computer software, interests in tangible property leases, and interests in debt obligations. These are subject to the usual write-offs. For example, self-produced goodwill is not an *amortizable section 197 intangible*, so it is outside § 197 and not amortizable.

Intangibles that are subject to § 197 if transferred in connection with all or a substantial part of a business. These consist of customized computer software, contract rights to receive tangible property or services, patents, copyrights, films, and mortgage servicing rights. This grouping is the primary target of § 197.

Covenants not to compete. These are subject to § 197 where there is a related acquisition of a business by a purchase of either assets or stock. This is a big change and highly disadvantageous to taxpayers compared to prior law.

To illustrate: P Corp. buys T Corp.'s seed business for $10 million. The parties properly allocated the purchase price on a Form 8594 as follows:

Trademark	$1.5M
Goodwill	3.0M
Nonsection 197 assets	5.5M
Total	$10.0M

Section 197 allows P Corp. annual amortization deductions of $100,000 for fifteen years with respect to the trademark and of $200,000 with respect to the goodwill. If the president of the company also enters into a covenant not to compete, it will be written off over fifteen years rather than over the life of the covenant, which commonly was approximately five years.

Abandonment of Intangibles

Aside from lengthening the amortization lives of many intangibles, § 197 carries a heavy stick in that it prevents deductions for abandonments of intangibles unless and until the taxpayer disposes of all its § 197 intangibles in the acquired business. If there is an abandonment, there is no loss and the "disappearing basis" is assigned to the remaining intangibles.

To illustrate: At the end of the fourth year following the acquisition, when P's remaining basis in the trademark is $1.1 million, P abandons the trademark. P cannot claim a $1.1 million loss for the abandonment of the trademark unless P establishes that the goodwill acquired from T has become entirely worthless. P will continue to amortize the cost of the abandoned trademark over § 197's fifteen-year amortization period.

D. OVERVIEW OF § 197

To illustrate: P buys all of T's stock for $9 million and also pays T's sole shareholder $1 million for a three-year covenant not to compete. Under § 197, P is allowed amortization deductions for fifteen years of only $66,667 per year with respect to the covenant. At the end of three years when the covenant expires, P cannot deduct the unamortized balance of the covenant's purchase price unless P also disposes of its entire interest in T's business (assets and stock); rather, P would continue to amortize the price of the expired covenant over the remainder of § 197's fifteen-year amortization period (or, if earlier, when P disposes of its entire interest in T's business).

The following thoughts of two practitioners[12] are worth considering:

Because § 197 amortizes both purchased goodwill and a noncompete over 15 years, from a tax standpoint buyer no longer benefits from allocating purchase price to a noncompete rather than to goodwill in a [taxable] acquisition. Moreover, depending on the circumstances, there are two potential benefits to allocating purchase price to goodwill rather than to a noncompete:

First, seller's gain on the sale of goodwill generally is taxable as LTCG, whereas a noncompete payment is taxed as ordinary income ("OI"). Given the difference between the new highest marginal OI rate (39.6 percent) and the LTCG rate (28 percent) for individuals, **the tax savings can be significant where seller is an S corporation, a partnership of individuals, or a sole proprietor**. However, where seller is a C corporation, it may still prefer a noncompete payment to its shareholders (although taxed to the shareholders as OI) rather than a goodwill payment to the corporate seller, because the noncompete payment would be taxed only at the shareholder level and thus avoid corporate-level tax.

Because a C corporation is taxed at the same rate on LTCG and OI, a C corporation receiving a noncompete payment often will be indifferent to this issue, unless it has an available capital loss which can only be used against CG.

Second, for GAAP purposes, [the] buyer can amortize goodwill over a period of up to 40 years, whereas a noncompete payment is amortized for GAAP purposes over the life of the noncompete agreement. Therefore, goodwill has a less adverse impact on GAAP earnings in the early years, and hence, is a more attractive GAAP asset than a short-lived noncompete agreement. The favorable GAAP earnings result produced by goodwill is

---

[12] Levin & Rocap, *A Transactional Guide to New Code Section 197*, 61 Tax Notes 461 (1993). The examples are from the same article. G.A.A.P. stands for "Generally Accepted Accounting Principles."

particularly important for a publicly traded buyer (or a buyer which anticipates an IPO).

Given the high level of goodwill in the balance sheets of U.S. corporations, there is a chance to amortize or depreciate a large part of the purchase price of a corporation, making the taxable acquisition much more attractive (compared with a tax-free reorganization). One can project that § 197 will increase the demand for high-intangible businesses, and the associated deductions will partially offset the initial tax cost of choosing a taxable acquisition. The only apparent disadvantage of § 197 is the length of the amortization period. It will be interesting to see if lobbying forces arise to press for a shortening of the § 197 lives. A strong counter argument to allowing such a shortening is that the expenses of developing goodwill are often currently deductible, the most important of which is advertising expenses.[13]

Allocation agreements between buyer and seller. Assuming that the buyer and seller prepare their Form 8594 as required, can the IRS knock it over by quarrelling with the allocations? Section 1060(b) suggests so, but cooler heads believe the IRS will be loath to attack taxpayers' allocations except in fairly extreme cases, given the historical willingness of the IRS and the courts to accept agreed allocations. *See* B. Bittker & J. Eustice, Federal Income Taxation of Corporations and Shareholders ¶ 10.40[1] (6th ed. 1994).

PROBLEM 19-1

Eastern Enterprises is a corporation which operates various businesses including a retail store. Mr. Pimm is a minority shareholder of Eastern. In complete redemption of Pimm's stock within the meaning of § 302(b)(3), Eastern distributes to Pimm all of the assets of its retail store, which is not a trade or business in Pimm's hands, but was a separate trade or business in Eastern's hands. The assets have a gross value of $3 million. Is this an "applicable asset acquisition"? *See* Reg. § 1.1060-1T(b)(3), example (3).

PROBLEM 19-2

Acquiring Corp. pays $3,000 to Dolman Corporation for its dart board division. The division consists of various assets which comprise the dart board business. The fair market values of Dolman's Class II and III assets are:

---

[13] *See* Calvin Johnson, *The Mass Asset Rule Is Not the Blob That Ate Los Angeles,* 15 Tax Notes 1603 (1992), and Calvin Johnson, *Newark Morning Ledger: Intangibles Are Not Amortizable,* 57 Tax Notes 691 (1992).

E. STOCK PURCHASES

Asset Class	Assets	Fair Market Value
II	Portfolio of marketable securities	$400
III	Furniture and fixtures	800
III	Building	800
III	Land	200
III	Equipment	400
III	Accounts receivable	100
III	Covenant not to compete	100
	TOTAL	$2,800

(a) How is the purchase price allocated among the assets of the dart board business?

(b) Will this allocation also control Dolman's gain or loss on the sale of the division?

(c) Would there be any change in the allocations if the properties were subject to a debt of $1,000, and Acquiring Corp. paid $2,000 cash for them and assumed the $1,000 liability?

PROBLEM 19-3

(a) Over what period can the taxpayer in Problem 19-2 above write off his covenant not to compete?

(b) What if the party with whom the covenant was entered into dies? Can the covenant be written off at that time?

(c) Would the result be different if the intangibles were customer lists and technical know-how which became worthless?

(d) Assume the company developed its own patent. Would it be allowed to write off the patent over its legal life (twenty years)?

E. STOCK PURCHASES

1. THE SECTION 338 ELECTION

Suppose that a buyer is compelled for business reasons to acquire assets but the seller is only willing to sell stock. Under pre-1983 law, if the corporate buyer bought 80% control of the target's stock and then liquidated the target within a short period of time, the rules of §§ 332/337 did not apply, and the buyer could (or was required to) step up the basis of the target's assets to fair market value just as if it had bought the assets of the liquidating corporation (even though it was not taxed on the liquidating distribution, under then § 337). Unfortunately, these rules were of no avail to a buyer who could not liquidate the target, say because the target owned irreplaceable franchises or other licenses to do business. This seemed unfair, and as a result Congress enacted § 338, which enabled a corporate buyer in this situation to elect to step up the basis of assets owned by a newly-purchased controlled subsidiary without the necessity of actually liquidating the subsidiary. This was very welcome to taxpayers because the election produced a cost basis for the target's assets for purposes of depreciation and avoided tax on resale of unwanted assets owned by the target, all at no tax cost whatever. If the target's assets had built-in loss rather than gain, the buyer simply did not make the election and preserved the subsidiary's inside losses.[14]

As a result of the legislative repeal of *General Utilities* in 1986, however, § 338 is probably one of the largest pieces of deadwood in the Internal Revenue Code. It was passed as part of the Tax Equity and Fiscal Responsibility Act of 1982, at a time when distributions of assets of liquidating corporations were not taxed to the corporation, that is, while the *General Utilities* doctrine was in full bloom. Since the passage of § 338, we have witnessed the repeal of the doctrine, with the result that § 338 is now much more a trap for the unwary than the act of legislative grace that it was supposed to be when it was passed.

The heart of § 338 is an election whereby a corporation, the control of which was recently purchased, can electively hypothesize that it went through a complete liquidation in which it distributed all its assets to its shareholders at midnight of day one and repurchased those assets on the dawn of the following day at fair market value. This avoids all the problems inherent in making actual transfers of assets as part of an actual liquidation, and as such it is a great improvement over prior law. The difficulty is that § 338 rarely offers an appetizing outcome because of the repeal of the *General Utilities* doctrine, which exposes the gains that the corporation recognizes in the course of its liquidation to taxation. It makes no sense for the target to pay tax on its built-in gains now in order to obtain depreciation in the same amount later. In some situations the election may still be valuable, however, such as where the target has a large loss carryforward which can soak up the *General Utilities* tax imposed by § 336.

The mechanics of § 338 can be extremely elaborate, but the basic idea is that an acquiring corporation can elect to treat the purchase price of the stock (which

---

[14] As mentioned earlier, one of the deep issues in corporate taxation is whether the tax results of business acquisitions should be entirely elective, as opposed to relying on the manipulation of the "short list" of transactional forms meted out by the Code which in effect produces elections visible only to the well-heeled. An explicitly elective system has a number of advantages: it makes the complex "elections" hidden in the Code apparent to those who cannot afford expensive tax advice and it simplifies tax administration. On the other hand, the problem of conflicting interests of multiple parties cannot be solved by elections where the parties must jointly agree upon the election.

E. STOCK PURCHASES

may have been bought in different batches at different times) as the purchase price of the assets of the acquired corporation.

Section 338 applies only if certain preconditions are satisfied. The basic requirement is that a corporate purchaser must, within a twelve-month period beginning with its first purchase of stock, buy at least 80% of the target corporation's stock by vote and by value. This produces a "qualified stock purchase." In turn, § 338(g) allows the purchasing corporation to elect the deemed liquidation. The Government has graciously produced Form 8203, which the corporation files to make the election. The corporation must file the form not later than the fifteenth day of the ninth month following the acquisition date, meaning the date when the acquiring corporation got 80% control of the target corporation. § 338(g). The election is irrevocable.

2. DEEMED ELECTIONS UNDER § 338

Section 338(e) provides that there is a *deemed § 338 election* if the purchasing corporation (or any of its affiliates) bought any of the target (or target affiliate) assets before, or in addition to, buying the target's stock. This was designed to prevent acquirors from selectively purchasing some assets and enjoying a cost basis in them while taking the rest of the target's assets with carryover basis by not electing a § 338 deemed sale. All or nothing was the rule, and if any asset was purchased at cost, all were pursuant to the deemed election. This was capable of producing catastrophic results. Fortunately the final regulations issued in 1994 have eliminated the former deemed § 338 election by providing that a deemed election generally cannot arise as a result of the asset consistency rules. Reg. § 1.338-4(a)(1). Rather, if an asset is acquired from a target which is a member of a consolidated group, the acquiring corporation gets a carryover basis in that asset. In other situations the buyer does get a cost basis for purchase of a target asset.

PROBLEM 19-4

(a) Grabber buys all the stock of Target for $1 million. Target has a basis of $100,000 in its assets which are worth $1 million. Grabber makes the § 338(g) election on behalf of Target. What are the tax results to Grabber and Target?

(b) Does the residual method of allocating the deemed purchase price apply to Target's assets? *See* § 1060(a) and Reg. § 1.338(b)-2T.

(c) What difference, if any, would there be if, one month before the § 338(g) election, Grabber's parent (Dynamic Corp.) bought Target's fleet of trucks for $200,000? The trucks have a basis of only $25,000. *See* Reg. § 1.338-4(a)(1)-(3). Assume Target is a subsidiary that is a member of a group of affiliated corporations that file a consolidated tax return.

3. SECTION 338(h)(10) ELECTION

Read § 338(h)(10).

What you are about to read is important for several reasons. One reason is that it reflects a progressive approach to the taxation of corporate restructurings by means of elections as opposed to actual transactions. Second, the materials operate as a review of concepts you have already read.

Now, a word about consolidated returns. An affiliated group of corporations may elect to file a single *consolidated tax return* under the authority of § 1501 and its legislative regulations. The possible advantages include offsetting capital or operating losses of one corporation against the gains or operating profits of another, and of deferring income on intercompany transactions. An *affiliated group* is a parent-subsidiary chain or brother-sister group (with a common parent) of corporations in which at least 80% of the combined voting power *and* at least 80% of the total value of stock (except plain nonvoting preferred stock) are owned by so-called "includible corporations." (This limit assures that foreign corporations, insurance companies, and charities cannot file consolidated returns with business corporations.) This book pays little attention to consolidated returns and it is largely the domain of accountants, but it is in fact of great importance in practice.

Now, assume Parent owns all the stock of Target, and that they file a consolidated return. Assume that Acquiror wants to buy the stock of Target. If Parent and Acquiror elect[15] under § 338(h)(10) and Acquiror's purchase of stock was a qualified stock purchase,[16] the transaction is treated for tax purposes as if:

1. Target is first liquidated tax-free into Parent under §§ 332 and 337;
2. Parent then sells the assets of Target to Acquiror recognizing any gain or loss which was built into Target's assets;
3. Acquiror creates New Target, to which it contributes the assets of Target.

Note that although Parent reports a gain or loss on the imaginary sale of assets to Acquiror, *it will report no gain or loss on the sale of Target stock*. That is the point of the § 338(h)(10) election. It permits buyer and seller to agree that the tax results are the same as steps 1-3 above but without having to go through the trouble of an actual liquidation and sale of assets. This also preserves the Target's corporate existence.

Assuming this model, where should the earnings and profits and other tax attributes of Target come to rest?

---

[15] The election must be made not later than the fifteenth day of the ninth month beginning after the month in which the acquisition date occurs. Reg. § 1.338(h)(10)-1(d)(2).

[16] This requires that Acquiror buy 80% of Target's stock by vote and value in a twelve-month acquisition period.

E. STOCK PURCHASES

4. SECTION 336(e) ELECTION

Read § 336(e).

This is the country cousin of § 338(h)(10). It appears to be intended to produce the same tax result as § 338(h)(10) and simply extends it to situations where the subsidiary was 80%-owned by the seller corporation but did *not* file a consolidated return. This is sensible because the seller could have avoided gain on the sale of stock by liquidating the controlled subsidiary first under § 332 and then selling the target's assets in order to recognize that gain instead. A mystifying difference from § 338(h)(10) is that the seller can elect § 336(e) unilaterally. This apparently means that the seller can control the buyer's tax treatment even after the sale is completed. There is opportunity here for an unpleasant surprise, so if the buyer wants the target's tax history and asset basis to survive, the buyer presumably must bind the seller not to make a § 336(e) election as part of the sales contract. Thus for sophisticated taxpayers the § 336(e) election is *de facto* a joint one, and Congress might have done better to make it *de jure* joint to protect the unwary. The buyer bears no tax on the sale, but the statute does not specify who does.[17] Presumably it is the seller corporation.

Review of some options. An acquiring corporation has a number of choices of what to do with a recently purchased controlled subsidiary:

— It can do nothing, and perhaps file a consolidated return with the new subsidiary;

— It can liquidate the target company under §§ 332/337 and take a carryover basis in the assets, along with the target's tax attributes. This is nontaxable to both corporations;

— It can make the § 338(g) election on the subsidiary's behalf and, in most cases, cause it to pay taxes. That does not prevent it from buying assets from the sub and getting a cost basis in them, unless the sub had been a member of a consolidated group;

— If the subsidiary was a member of a consolidated group, the acquiring corporation can elect § 338(h)(10) together with the seller, which produces the equivalent of a taxable transaction to the target, thus stepping up the basis of the target's assets and extinguishing its tax history, and any taxes due are borne by the seller of target; and it can achieve the same result even if the target was not such a member but was 80% owned by the seller, by inducing the seller to make the § 336(e) election.

---

[17] By analogy § 338(h)(10). *See* B. Bittker & J. Eustice, Federal Income Taxation of Corporations and Shareholders ¶ 10.42[7] (6th ed. 1994).

If the buyer acquires less than 80% control of the sub's stock by vote or by value, it can put the subsidiary through a taxable liquidation and §§ 331 and 336 would apply to buyer and subsidiary, respectively.

F. ANTI-LOSS REALIZATION RULE FOR CONSOLIDATED SUBSIDIARIES

A member of a consolidated group is not allowed to deduct any loss recognized on disposition of stock of a consolidated subsidiary. Reg. § 1.1502-20(a)(1). To prevent evasion, a companion rule provides that if a share of stock of a subsidiary is deconsolidated, the basis of that share is reduced to its fair market value, thereby precluding any loss. Reg. § 1.1502-20(b)(1). The problem generally arises because the basis of a subsidiary can be artificially increased as a result of certain rigidities in the consolidated return rules. These anomalies are best described by example.

> *To illustrate*: P buys all the stock of T for $1,000, and T becomes a member of the P consolidated group. At that time, T's sole asset, in which T has a zero basis, is worth $1,000. T sells its asset for $1,000. Under the investment adjustment rules, P's basis in the T stock is increased to $2,000. Reg. § 1.1502-32. Some years later, P sells all the T stock to an unrelated person outside the group for $1,000, recognizing a loss of $1,000. Under the loss disallowance rule, P is not allowed any deduction for that loss. Reg. § 1.1502-20(a)(5), example (1).

The loss disallowance rules are a proper subject for a course in advanced corporate taxation, and deserve only passing reference in this course, but one should be aware of the issue since it presents a potentially serious trap for the unwary.

PROBLEM 19-5

Assume that Parent owns 100% of Target Corporation stock. Target has assets with a basis of $85 and a value of $100. Assume that Parent has a $10 basis in its Target stock, and it files a consolidated return with Target. What are the tax results to Parent and Target if the value of Target stock is $100 under the following circumstances:

(a) Grabber buys all the stock of Target, and Acquiror and Parent agree to make a § 338(h)(10) election?

(b) What result if Acquiror buys Target's stock and causes it to liquidate into Acquiror? Note what a bad deal for Parent this is.

(c) What result if Parent liquidates Target under §§ 332 and 337 and then sells the assets of Target to Acquiror? Note how much better than a stock sale this is.

OUTSIDE READINGS

J. Bogdanski, *Allocations of Price in Sales of Businesses*, 15 J. Corp. Tax'n. 99 (1988).

P. Bryan, *Leveraged Buyouts and Tax Policy*, 65 N.C. L. Rev. 1039 (1987).

G. Schwartz, *Liquidation-Reincorporation: A Sensible Approach Consistent with Congressional Policy*, 38 U. Miami L. Rev. 231 (1984).

Chapter 20
TAX-FREE CORPORATE DIVISIONS

There are many sound business reasons for dividing up a single corporation's lines of business into several corporations. For example, it may be good business judgment to separate a risky enterprise from a more stable one so that if a lawsuit is brought against the risky enterprise the other corporation will be free of liability. Another reason to break up a company might be to put an end to warfare between different groups of shareholders, or one might want to separate one division in connection with preparing for a sale of that or another division. Sometimes it is necessary to spin off newly-formed divisions of subsidiaries in order to comply with anti-trust decrees. These corporate separations may be done solely at the corporate level and on a pro-rata basis or they may be specially targeted so that only one group of shareholders winds up with the stock of a particular corporation at the shareholder (ownership) level by having some of the shareholders redeem their stock in exchange for receiving the stock of an incorporated line of business.

Tax-free corporate divisions break down into three groupings;

1. *A spin-off.* This is a distribution by one corporation of the stock of its subsidiary corporation to the parent's shareholders with respect to their shares, much like a stock dividend. The subsidiary may already be in existence or may be newly created to accommodate the transaction;

2. *A split-off.* This is the same as the spin-off, except that the shareholders of the parent corporation give up part of their stock in the parent corporation in exchange for stock of the subsidiary, much like a redemption or partial liquidation;

3. *A split-up.* Here the parent corporation distributes the stock of two or more of its subsidiaries, whether newly created or previously existing, in complete liquidation of the parent corporation.

Technically speaking, there are two categories of tax-free corporate separations: (a) the so-called corporate "divisions" involving a spin-off, split-off or split-up of pre-existing subsidiaries, using the rules of §§ 355, 356, and 358 alone; and (b) the "divisive reorganizations" that involve two steps under § 368(a)(1)(D), namely the formation or transfer of assets to one or more subsidiaries (as under § 351) and the distribution of that stock as in the pure corporate divisions. This two-step division is called a "D" reorganization. This chapter emphasizes the corporate divisions; the two-step divisive reorganization uses this law plus the law of tax-free acquisitive reorganizations covered in Chapter 21.

ILLUSTRATIVE PROBLEM

The basic outline of a § 355 corporate division reveals the pattern of fundamental income tax issues it produces and the statutory rules they invoke.

Suppose individuals A and B are equal shareholders of X Corporation, which has conducted two active businesses for more than five years, one of them as a division and one in a wholly-owned subsidary, Y Corporation. A and B want to go separate ways, or at least, and first, to make Y Corporation a sister (not a subsidiary) of X Corporation, owned directly by A and B.

A. To this end, X Corporation distributes all its stock in Y Corporation to A and B, pro-rata. If that is all, it amounts to a spin-off, a distribution of the sub's stock to the two shareholders of X Corporation with respect to their shares (not in exchange for anything). Now, X and Y are brother-sister corporations directly (and jointly) owned by A and B. A and B can sell either one to an outsider while retaining the other. There has been a separation at the corporate level only. What are the tax issues and answers? Suppose the stock in Y Corporation had a basis to X Corporation of $150x$ but was worth $300x$ at the time of distribution.

1. Will gain or loss be recognized to the distributing corporation (X Corporation)? While gain is *realized* by X Corporation, it is not *recognized*. See § 311(a). (Section 361 would apply only if this were part of a "D Reorganization," as defined in § 368 and to be a subject of study in Chapter 21.)

2. Will gain or loss be recognized to the distributee shareholders A and B? No, if everything is done right, by virtue of § 355. If X Corporation also distributed "boot" (other property), § 356 would require recognition, perhaps as a dividend, of gain up to the amount of boot, to the extent § 301 would provide. And see § 357 if liabilities were assumed or property taken subject to them by A and B.

3. What basis do A and B take in the Y Corporation shares distributed to them? The answer is that their basis is determined under § 358 by allocating the appropriate amount (according to relative fair market values) of A and B's basis in their X Corporation shares to their newly-received Y Corporation shares. See § 358(b), (c).

4. What basis effects will the division have on the distributing corporation? In a way, none; however, X Corporation no longer owns $300x$ worth of shares in Y Corporation and no longer has any basis in those shares (formerly it had a $150x$ basis in them).

5. What are the collateral consequences? The earnings and profits and other tax characteristics internal to Y Corporation will continue with it in the hands of its new owners. The holding periods for A and B in

their Y Corporation shares will include (tack on) the holding periods of X Corporation shares they held before (and still hold). See § 1223(1).

It is useful to determine how these same events would be taxed if the key nonrecognition sections and their correlative basis rules were not in the Code. In other words, what gain (or loss) was realized by each party (and what basis results would normally follow if all realized gain were recognized), and then how do the nonrecognition rules (and their basis correlates) change those results?

B. Now suppose, as a simple variant based on the original facts of this illustration, that A and B knew that they wanted to go their separate ways and A wanted to take with him the X Corp. division's assets and business and B wanted the Y Corp. subsidiary's assets and business. To that end, suppose X Corp. distributed all its shares in Y Corp. to B in return for all his shares in X Corp. B merely remained the holder of his shares (now 100%) of X Corp. This is a split-off. Now each individual has the business he or she wants, in separate corporate form. There has been a separation at both the corporate and shareholder levels. Assume each of A and B has a basis of $50x in his shares in X Corp. before transaction. What gain or loss is *realized* by each party? What gain or loss must be *recognized* by each, and what are the basis consequences, and how do they differ from the result if none of the nonrecognition rules and basis correlates was in the Code?

1. Must gain or loss be recognized by the distributing corporation, X Corp.? No. *See* § 311 (§ 336(c) if this were a split-up). If this were also part of a D reorganization, § 361 could apply.

2. Must gain or loss be recognized to the distributee shareholders, A and B? No; *see* § 354. Exceptions for boot, of which there is none here, are to be found, as before, in § 356, and other limitations in § 357 (liabilities). A simply rides through this transaction, maybe not even *realizing* gain or loss.

3. What basis do A and B have in their shares? A's basis remains the same in his shares in X Corp., which merely remain in his hands. B's basis in his X Corp. shares (which he surrendered in the exchange) becomes his basis in his Y Corp. shares which he received in the tax-free exchange. *See* § 358.

4. What are the basis effects to X Corp.? Again it no longer owns stock in Y Corp. and therefore has lost its basis in those shares. Its basis in other assets that it retains does not change.

5. What collateral tax issues ensue? Again there isn't much change because X Corp. and Y Corp. both preexisted the split-off and also survive it. B's basis and holding period (tacked) in Y shares will equal what he had in the X Corp. shares he formerly owned. *See* §§ 358, 1223(1). The earnings and profits of each corporation stay with it.

C. If Y Corp. had not preexisted and if its business had been conducted by X Corp. as a division instead, it would have been necessary to incorporate that division (or the other division, or both) in a separate subsidiary, which § 351 would have allowed tax-free and with carryover basis. In fact, that incorporation, if coupled with the division distribution, would qualify as a "D reorganization" under § 368(a)(1)(D), with the same *operative* nonrecognition and basis rules applying, namely §§ 355-57, 358, and 361 as to X Corp.

D. If X Corp. had formed or had owned the subsidiaries, as in ¶ C, above, and distributed their stock (and any other assets) to A and B in exchange for all their shares in X, that would have been a split-up (alone, or as part of a D Reorganization) subject to the same sets of nonrecognition rules.

The law prior to 1954 was generous with respect to spin-offs, allowing them to occur tax-free as long as property was passed from one corporation to another and the first corporation, its shareholders, or both combined, controlled the second corporation. If these conditions were met the shareholders of the first corporation paid no tax when they received the stock of the second corporation in connection with the plan of reorganization.[1] The tax policy presupposition was that the corporate rearrangement was a mere change in the form of ownership of the same assets by the same owners (continuity of proprietary interest and of business enterprise) and therefore was entitled to nonrecognition treatment — much as in the case of a plain § 351 incorporation. This unusually generous provision virtually invited shareholders to put liquid assets into newly-formed corporations and then distribute the stock of the newly formed corporations to shareholders, leaving the shareholders free to claim that the whole transaction was a tax-free reorganization, rather than a taxable dividend. Those shareholders could then liquidate the recently distributed corporation and take out the cash or liquid assets at long-term capital gain rates under the predecessor of § 331(a). The following landmark decision considered such a transaction and in so doing added an important judicial limitation to the corporate acquisition and the division rules. It is such an important case that it is known to most tax lawyers by name.

---

[1] *See* Revenue Act of 1924, Pub. L. No. 176, § 203(c), 43 Stat. 253, 256.

GREGORY v. HELVERING
293 U.S. 465 (1935)

MR. JUSTICE SUTHERLAND delivered the opinion of the Court.

Petitioner in 1928 was the owner of all the stock of United Mortgage Corporation. That corporation held among its assets 1,000 shares of the Monitor Securities Corporation. For the sole purpose of procuring a transfer of these shares to herself in order to sell them for her individual profit, and, at the same time, diminish the amount of income tax which would result from a direct transfer by way of dividend, she sought to bring about a "reorganization" under section § 368 of the Revenue Act of 1928, set forth later in this opinion. To that end, she caused the Averill Corporation to be organized under the laws of Delaware on September 18, 1928. Three days later, the United Mortgage Corporation transferred to the Averill Corporation the 1,000 shares of Monitor stock, for which all the shares of the Averill Corporation were issued to the petitioner. On September 24, the Averill Corporation was dissolved, and liquidated by distributing all its assets, namely, the Monitor shares, to the petitioner. No other business was ever transacted, or intended to be transacted, by that company. Petitioner immediately sold the Monitor shares for $133,333.33. She returned [reported] for taxation, as capital net gain, the sum of $76,007.88, based upon an apportioned cost of $57,325.45. Further details are unnecessary. It is not disputed that if the interposition of the so-called reorganization was ineffective, petitioner became liable for a much larger tax as a result of the transaction.

The Commissioner of Internal Revenue, being of opinion that the reorganization attempted was without substance and must be disregarded, held that petitioner was liable for a tax as though the United corporation had paid her a dividend consisting of the amount realized from the sale of the Monitor shares. In a proceeding before the Board of Tax Appeals, that body rejected the commissioner's view and upheld that of petitioner. 27 B.T.A. 223. Upon a review of the latter decision, the Circuit Court of Appeals sustained the commissioner and reversed the board, holding that there had been no "reorganization" within the meaning of the statute. 69 F.(2d) 809. Petitioner applied to this court for a writ of certiorari, which the government, considering the question one of importance, did not oppose. We granted the writ....

[T]he Revenue Act of 1928 ... deals with the subject of gain or loss resulting from the sale or exchange of property. Such gain or loss is to be recognized in computing the tax, except as provided in that section. The provisions of the section, so far as they are pertinent to the question here presented, follow:

> ... [The predecessor of § 354(a)] Distribution of Stock on Reorganization. If there is distributed, in pursuance of a plan of reorganization, to a shareholder in a corporation a party to the reorganization, stock or securities in such corporation or in another corporation a party to the reorganization, without the surrender by such shareholder of stock or securities in such a

corporation, no gain to the distributee from the receipt of such stock of securities shall be recognized....

Definition of Reorganization. As used in this section ...

The term "reorganization" under ... [§ 368(a)(1)(D)] means a transfer by a corporation of all or a part of its assets to another corporation if immediately after the transfer the transferor or its stockholders or both are in control of the corporation to which the assets are transferred.

....

It is earnestly contended on behalf of the taxpayer that since every element required by [§ 368(a)(1)(D)] is to be found in what was done, a statutory reorganization was effected; and that the motive of the taxpayer thereby to escape payment of a tax will not alter the result or make unlawful what the statute allows. It is quite true that if a reorganization in reality was effected ..., the ulterior purpose mentioned will be disregarded. The legal right of a taxpayer to decrease the amount of what otherwise would be his taxes, or altogether avoid them, by means which the law permits, cannot be doubted.

... But the question for determination is whether what was done, apart from the tax motive, was the thing which the statute intended. The reasoning of the court below in justification of a negative answer leaves little to be said.

When [§ 368(a)(1)(D)] speaks of a transfer of assets by one corporation to another, it means a transfer made "in pursuance of a plan of reorganization" ... of corporate business; and not a transfer of assets by one corporation to another in pursuance of a plan having no relation to the business of either, as plainly is the case here. Putting aside, then, the question of motive in respect of taxation altogether, and fixing the character of the proceeding by what actually occurred, what do we find? Simply an operation having no business or corporate purpose — a mere device which put on the form of a corporate reorganization as a disguise for concealing its real character, and the sole object and accomplishment of which was the consummation of a preconceived plan, not to reorganize a business or any part of a business, but to transfer a parcel of corporate shares to the petitioner. No doubt, a new and valid corporation was created. But that corporation was nothing more than a contrivance to the end last described. It was brought into existence for no other purpose; it performed, as it was intended from the beginning it should perform, no other function. When that limited function had been exercised, it immediately was put to death.

In these circumstances, the facts speak for themselves and are susceptible of but one interpretation. The whole undertaking, though conducted according to the terms of [§ 368(a)(1)(D)], was in fact an elaborate and devious form of conveyance masquerading as a corporate reorganization, and nothing else. The rule which excludes from consideration the motive of tax avoidance is not pertinent to the situation, because the transaction upon its face lies outside the plain intent of the statute. To hold otherwise would be to exalt artifice above reality and to deprive the statutory provision in question of all serious purpose.

Judgment affirmed.

A. TAX-FREE CORPORATE DIVISIONS UNDER CURRENT LAW

Read § 355(a), (b)(1).

Achieving a tax-free corporate division requires satisfying a cumulative set of tests. If all the tests are met the tax law allows a tax-free distribution by one corporation — known as the "distributing corporation" — of stock or securities of another corporation known as the "controlled corporation" — to shareholders of the distributing corporation with respect to (or in exchange for) their stock, or to security (debt) holders of the distributing corporation in exchange for their securities. Those requirements are discussed under the following headings.

1. CONTROL

Read § 368(c).

The distributing corporation must control the corporation whose stock or securities are being distributed. Section 368(c). It is the same definition of "control" as is used in connection with § 351. Control need exist only immediately before the distribution, and the IRS has been generous in allowing predistribution restructurings to meet the control requirement.[2]

2. DISTRIBUTION THRESHOLD

The distributing corporation must distribute all of its stock and securities in the controlled corporation, or failing that, distribute enough stock to constitute control. In the latter case the distributing corporation must satisfy the Treasury Department that the retention of stock or securities of the controlled corporation did not occur for reasons having to do with tax avoidance. Presumably the concern is that the distributing corporation might make occasional distributions of modest amounts of retained stock and securities instead of paying ordinary dividends. Another rationale is that retention can be used to satisfy obligations such as those arising under a stock option plan. *See* Rev. Proc. 91-62, 1991-2 C.B. 864, which facilitates private letter ruling requests with respect to retentions of stock.

---

[2] *See, e.g.,* Rev. Rul. 70-18, 1970-1 C.B. 74 (merger of sibling corporations to assure that the survivor got control).

3. BUSINESS PURPOSE

Read Reg. § 1.355-2(b)(1)(2).

The Regulations under § 355 demand a business purpose for the distribution at the corporate level. The difficulty in this realm is that in the case of closely-held corporations it is often difficult to differentiate the interests of the corporation from those of its shareholders.

RAFFERTY v. COMMISSIONER
452 F.2d 767 (1st Cir. 1971),
cert. denied, 408 U.S. 922 (1972)

MCENTEE, CIRCUIT JUDGE.

Taxpayers, Joseph V. Rafferty and wife, appeal from a decision of the Tax Court, which held that a distribution to them of all the outstanding stock of a real estate holding corporation did not meet the requirements of § 355 of the Internal Revenue Code of 1954 and therefore was taxable as a dividend. Our opinion requires a construction of § 355 and the regulations thereunder.

The facts, some of which have been stipulated, are relatively simple. The taxpayers own all the outstanding shares of Rafferty Brown Steel Co., Inc. (hereinafter RBS), a Massachusetts corporation engaged in the processing and distribution of cold rolled sheet and strip steel in Longmeadow, Massachusetts. In May 1960, at the suggestion of his accountant, Rafferty organized Teragram Realty Co., Inc., also a Massachusetts corporation. In June of that year RBS transferred its Longmeadow real estate to Teragram in exchange for all of the latter's outstanding stock. Thereupon Teragram leased back this real estate to RBS for ten years at an annual rent of $42,000. In 1962 the taxpayers also organized Rafferty Brown Steel Co., Inc., of Connecticut (RBS Conn.), which corporation acquired the assets of Hawkridge Brothers, a general steel products warehouse in Waterbury, Connecticut. Since its inception the taxpayers have owned all of the outstanding stock in RBS Conn. From 1962 to 1965 Hawkridge leased its real estate in Waterbury to RBS Conn. In 1965 Teragram purchased some unimproved real estate in Waterbury and built a plant there. In the same year it leased this plant to RBS Conn. for a term of fourteen years. Teragram has continued to own and lease the Waterbury real estate to RBS Conn. and the Longmeadow realty to RBS, which companies have continued up to the present time to operate their businesses at these locations.[3]

During the period from 1960 through 1965 Teragram derived all of its income from rent paid by RBS and RBS Conn. Its earned surplus increased from $4,119.05 as of March 31, 1961, to $46,743.35 as of March 31, 1965. The earned surplus of RBS increased from $331,117.97 as of June 30, 1959, to $535,395.77 as of June 30, 1965. In August 1965, RBS distributed its Teragram

---

[3] Both properties are also suitable for use by other companies in other types of business.

A. TAX-FREE CORPORATE DIVISIONS UNDER CURRENT LAW

stock to the taxpayers. Other than this distribution, neither RBS nor Teragram has paid any dividends.

Joseph V. Rafferty has been the guiding force behind all three corporations, RBS, RBS Conn., and Teragram. He is the president and treasurer of Teragram which, while it has no office or employees, keeps separate books and records and filed separate tax returns for the years in question.

On various occasions Rafferty consulted his accountant about estate planning, particularly about the orderly disposition of RBS. While he anticipated that his sons would join him at RBS, he wanted to exclude his daughters (and/or his future sons-in-law) from the active management of the steel business. He wished, however, to provide them with property which would produce a steady income. The accountant recommended the formation of Teragram, the distribution of its stock, and the eventual use of this stock as future gifts to the Rafferty daughters. The taxpayers acted on this advice and also on the accountant's opinion that the distribution of Teragram stock would meet the requirements of § 355.

In their 1965 return the taxpayers treated the distribution of Teragram stock as a nontaxable transaction under § 355. The Commissioner viewed it, however, as a taxable dividend and assessed a deficiency. He claimed (a) that the distribution was used primarily as a device for the distribution of the earnings and profits of RBS or Teragram or both, and (b) that Teragram did not meet the active business requirements of § 355.

We turn first, to the Tax Court's finding that there was no device because there was an adequate business purpose for the separation and distribution of Teragram stock. In examining this finding we are guided by the rule that the taxpayer has the burden of proving that the transaction was not used principally as a device. *Wilson v. Commissioner*, 42 T.C. 914, 922 (1964), *rev'd on other grounds*, 353 F.2d 184 (9th Cir. 1965). Initially, we are disturbed by the somewhat uncritical nature of the Tax Court's finding of a business purpose. Viewing the transaction from the standpoint of RBS, RBS Conn., or Teragram, no immediate business reason existed for the distribution of Teragram's stock to the taxpayers. Over the years the businesses had been profitable, as witnessed by the substantial increase of the earned surplus of every component, yet none had paid dividends. The primary purpose for the distribution found by the Tax Court was to facilitate Rafferty's desire to make bequests to his children in accordance with an estate plan. This was a personal motive. Taxpayers seek to put it in terms relevant to the corporation by speaking of avoidance of possible interference with the operation of the steel business by future sons-in-law, pointing to *Coady v. Commissioner*, 33 T.C. 771 (1960)....

In *Coady*, however, the separation was in response to a seemingly irreconcilable falling-out between the owners of a business. This falling-out had already occurred and, manifestly, the separation was designed to save the business from a substantial, present problem.... In the case at bar there was, at best, only an envisaged possibility of future debilitating nepotism. If avoidance of this danger could be thought a viable business purpose at all, it was so remote and so completely under the taxpayers' control that if, in other respects the transaction was a "device," that purpose could not satisfy the taxpayers' burden of proving that it was not being used "principally as a device" within the meaning of the statute.

Our question, therefore, must be whether taxpayers' desire to put their stockholdings into such form as would facilitate their estate planning, viewed in the circumstances of the case, was a sufficient personal business purpose to prevent the transaction at bar from being a device for the distribution of earnings and profits. While we remain of the view, which we first expressed in *Lewis v. Commissioner*, 176 F.2d 646 (1st Cir. 1949), that a purpose of a shareholder, qua shareholder, may in some cases save a transaction from condemnation as a device, we do not agree with the putative suggestion in *Estate of Parshelsky v. Commissioner*, 303 F.2d 14, 19 (2d Cir. 1962), that any investment purpose of the shareholders is sufficient. Indeed, in Lewis, although we deprecated the distinction between shareholder and corporate purpose, we were careful to limit that observation to the facts of that case, and to caution that the business purpose formula "must not become a substitute for independent analysis." 176 F.2d at 650. For that reason we based our decision on the Tax Court's finding that the transaction was "undertaken for reasons germane to the continuance of the corporate business." *Id.* at 647.

This is not to say that a taxpayer's personal motives cannot be considered, but only that a distribution which has considerable potential for use as a device for distributing earnings and profits should not qualify for tax-free treatment on the basis of personal motives unless those motives are germane to the continuance of the corporate business. *Cf. Commissioner v. Wilson*, 353 F.2d 184 (9th Cir., 1965); Treas. Reg. § 1.355-2 (c). We prefer this approach over reliance upon formulations such as "business purpose," and "active business." *See generally* Whitman, *Draining the Serbonian Bog: A New Approach to Corporate Separations Under the 1954 Code*, 81 Harv. L. Rev. 1194 (1968). The facts of the instant case illustrate the reason for considering substance. Dividends are normally taxable to shareholders upon receipt. Had the taxpayers received cash dividends and made investments to provide for their female descendants, an income tax would, of course, have resulted. Accordingly, once the stock was distributed, if it could potentially be converted into cash without thereby impairing taxpayers' equity interest in RBS, the transaction could easily be used to avoid taxes. The business purpose here alleged, which could be fully satisfied by a bail-out of dividends, is not sufficient to prove that the transaction was not being principally so used.

Given such a purpose, the only question remaining is whether the substance of the transaction is such as to leave the taxpayer in a position to distribute the earnings and profits of the corporation away from, or out of the business. The first factor to be considered is how easily the taxpayer would be able, were he so to choose, to liquidate or sell the spun-off corporation. Even if both corporations are actively engaged in their respective trades, if one of them is a

A. TAX-FREE CORPORATE DIVISIONS UNDER CURRENT LAW

business based principally on highly liquid investment-type, passive assets, the potential for a bail-out is real. The question here is whether the property transferred to the newly organized corporation had a readily realizable value, so that the distributee-shareholders could, if they ever wished, "obtain such cash or property or the cash equivalent thereof, either by selling the distributed stock or liquidating the corporation, thereby converting what would otherwise be dividends taxable as ordinary income into capital gain...." *Wilson v. Commissioner, supra*, 42 T.C. at 923. In this connection we note that the Tax Court found that a sale of Teragram's real estate properties could be "easily arranged."... Indeed, taxpayers themselves stressed the fact that the buildings were capable of multiple use.

There must, however, be a further question. If the taxpayers could not effect a bail-out without thereby impairing their control over the on-going business, the fact that a bail-out is theoretically possible should not be enough to demonstrate a device because the likelihood of it ever being so used is slight. "[A] bail-out ordinarily means that earnings and profits have been drawn off without impairing the shareholder's residual equity interest in the corporation's earning power, growth potential, or voting control." B. Bittker & J. Eustice, Federal Income Taxation of Corporations and Shareholders (3d ed. 1971) § 13.06. If sale would adversely affect the shareholders of the on-going company, the assets cannot be said to be sufficiently separated from the corporate solution and the gain sufficiently crystallized as to be taxable. *See Lewis v. Commissioner, supra* 176 F.2d at 650. In this case, there was no evidence that the land and buildings at which RBS carried on its steel operations were so distinctive that the sale of Teragram stock would impair the continued operation of RBS, or that the sale of those buildings would in any other way impair Rafferty's control and other equity interests in RBS.[4]

In the absence of any direct benefit to the business of the original company, and on a showing that the spin-off put saleable assets in the hands of the taxpayers, the continued retention of which was not needed to continue the business enterprise, or to accomplish taxpayers' purposes, we find no sufficient factor to overcome the Commissioner's determination that the distribution was principally a device to distribute earnings and profits.

[The portion of the decision addressing the need for an active trade or business is limited to the following paragraph.]

It is our view that in order to be an active trade or business under § 355 a corporation must engage in entrepreneurial endeavors of such a nature and to such an extent as to qualitatively distinguish its operations from mere investments. Moreover, there should be objective indicia of such corporate operations. Prior to 1965 Teragram's sole venture was the leasing back to its

---

[4] Our conclusion is reinforced by the fact that RBS and RBS Conn. were guaranteed occupancy of Teragram property under long term leases at fixed rents.

parent of its only asset for a fixed return, an activity, in economic terms, almost indistinguishable from an investment in securities. Standing by itself this activity is the type of "passive investment" which Congress intended to exclude from § 355 treatment. Furthermore, there are hardly any indicia of corporate operations. Prior to 1965 Teragram paid neither salaries nor rent. It did not employ independent contractors, and its only activity appears to have been collecting rent, paying taxes, and keeping separate books. Prior to 1965 it failed to meet either set of criteria for an active trade or business. We need not reach the more difficult question of whether its activities in 1965 constituted an active trade or business.

Affirmed.

NOTES

1. Rafferty *now embodied in the Regulations.* Reg. § 1.355-2(d)(ii) in essence says that if a distribution serves a corporate business purpose, there is evidence that the prohibited device is lacking, but if the distribution also indicated the presence of a device, one must weigh the business purpose against the evidence of a device in order to determine whether the prohibited device exists or not. Is this the same standard as the one *Rafferty* developed?

2. *The IRS concedes.* In Rev. Rul. 75-337, 1975-2 C.B. 124, the IRS ruled that estate planning which had the effect of preserving a business constituted a business purpose under § 355.

3. *Scope of business purpose requirement.* According to Reg. § 1.355-2(b)(5), example 3, the business purpose requirement covers both the formation of the new corporation which is about to be distributed *and also* the distribution of the stock of the controlled corporation. For example, as indicated in the regulation, although it may make good sense to form a new subsidiary to insulate the parent company from risks associated with the subsidiary, that does not necessarily mean that it makes sense to distribute the controlled corporation's stock to the shareholders of the distributing company. An independent business purpose is required for that second step.

4. *Realty companies.* These corporations are often organized for the purpose of draining off income from an affiliated corporation that has retained so much of its earnings that it might become liable for the confiscatory accumulated earnings tax (§§ 531-537). Realty companies are also used to generate compensation which can be bled off the realty company, thereby limiting the burden of the corporate double tax. By contrast, if the same total compensation were paid by one corporation, some of it might more likely be regarded as unreasonable compensation.

5. *Owner-occupied real estate.* *Rafferty* held that the passive warehouse operation was not an active trade or business, but it seems that owner-occupied real estate can qualify as an active business if there are sufficient activities connected with the real estate. *See, especially, Gada v. U.S.*, 460 F. Supp. 859

(D. Conn. 1978) which held that the absence of rents from third parties was merely "some evidence" that a corporation has not engaged in a separate active trade or business. The corporation obtained almost all of its income from rentals to a sister corporation. Because there were no significant activities connected with the real estate, the District Court found no active trade or business. But see the threats of careful IRS scrutiny with respect to the independent "device" issue as well in Reg. § 1.355-2(d)(2)(iv)(C).

4. DEVICE FOR DISTRIBUTING EARNINGS AND PROFITS

Read Reg. § 1.355-2(d)(2)(ii), -(iii)(A), and (E)(iv).

The corporate division must not be principally a "device" for the distribution of earnings and profits of the distributing corporation or of the controlled corporation or of both. The Code takes a hostile view of prearranged sales of stock of the distributing or controlling corporation following the division. § 355(a)(1)(B). Regulations identify various other evidences of a "device" or a "bailout" of earnings and profits. One obvious factor is that if the distribution is pro-rata, evidence of the existence of a "device" is enhanced. It looks like a dividend. The same is true if either the controlled or distributing corporation winds up particularly rich with liquid assets that can easily be sold off. This kind of search for factors is a common outgrowth of a tax statute that metes out its results on the basis of taxpayer's motives. Because it is impossible to know what is occurring in their minds, we have to infer their motives from external factors. Moreover, even if the facts indicate the presence of a prohibited device, the taxpayer may nevertheless have a legitimate business purpose for undertaking the transaction as well. What then?

If no one directly or indirectly owns over 5% of a publicly-traded corporation, that is evidence of the absence of a device. Reg. § 1.355-2(d)(3)(C)(iii). There is also counterevidence of a device if the distributees are all corporations which can use the benefits of the dividends-received deduction. Reg. § 1.355-2(d)(3)(C)(iv). The same is true if the distributing and control corporations lack earnings and profits and are low on appreciated assets. Reg. § 1.355-2(d)(5)(ii). In addition, if in the absence of § 355 all of the distributees would have qualified for sale or exchange treatment under § 302(a) or 303(a), that is also evidence of lack of a device. Reg. § 1.355-2(d)(5)(iii) and (iv).

5. ACTIVE TRADE OR BUSINESS REQUIREMENT

Read § 355(b) and Reg. § 1.355-3(b)(2).

To qualify for nonreorganization treatment, the parent distributing corporation and the subsidiary must each be engaged in the active conduct of a trade or business immediately after the distribution. The untrained eye can see whether this requirement has been met. A more difficult issue is determining whether each trade or business has been actively conducted throughout the five-year period prior to the distribution. In addition, the active trade or business must not have been acquired by either the parent or subsidiary in a taxable transaction during that five-year period. Note that these requirements echo those of § 302(e) governing partial liquidations and distributions of *assets* as opposed to *stock*.

For this purpose, the Regulations require that a trade or business include every operation that forms part of the process of earning income or profit, including the collection of income and the payment of expenses. To be "active" the corporation must perform "active and substantial management and operational functions." This excludes activities undertaken by outside contractors, or the mere holding of stock, securities, royalties, land, or other passive investment activities with respect to owning or leasing property used in the trade or business unless the owner of the property performs significant services with respect to the operation and management of the property. For example, a taxpayer who owns and operates her own hotel or motel business on a full time basis would be engaged in the active conduct of a trade or business, whereas someone who leases a warehouse to a manufacturing company almost surely would not be if the management of the warehouse were the obligation of the tenant under a net lease.

PROBLEM 20-1

X Corporation owns all the stock of Y Corporation. X Corporation has no activity other than being a partner in the X-M general partnership. M is an unrelated entity which is in the business of manufacturing hubcaps. Assume that X wants to spin off Y and that after the spin-off has occurred Y will be actively engaged in a trade or business and that X will continue to be a general partner in the X-M partnership. Is the active conduct of a trade or business test satisfied here? What are the considerations?

6. VERTICAL DIVISION OF A SINGLE BUSINESS

Although one might imagine that § 355 contemplates the existence of two different businesses prior to the breakup, the opposite is true. In fact, a single active business can be divided in half (or theoretically even into smaller groupings) as long as each half is a free-standing business. The leading case is *Coady v. Commissioner*, 289 F.2d 490 (6th Cir. 1961). The facts involved a construction business held by two feuding owners. As a result of the corporate division, each was allowed to walk away tax-free with a separate, freestanding construction business consisting of several ongoing projects. The original business had been active in the construction industry for over five years. The Court held that the five-year active business test was met, in effect tacking the five-year history of the whole to each of the parts. The Regulations confirm that this is a viable approach. *See* Reg. § 1.355-3(c), example 4. *Coady* is the leading example of a so-called "vertical division" of one business and company into two smaller twins.

A. TAX-FREE CORPORATE DIVISIONS UNDER CURRENT LAW

It is even possible to move a supporting function of a business into a separate corporation and to have the separation meet the five-year active business test. The trouble is that such a division may be evidence of a device to avoid tax. *See* Reg. § 1.355-2(d)(2)(iv)(C). The Regulations provide an example of a separation of a research department into a newly-formed subsidiary which continued its research activities under contract with the company from which it was spun off or with that company and outside organizations as well. *See* Reg. § 1.355-3(c), example (9).

7. HORIZONAL DIVISION OF A SINGLE BUSINESS

Successful businesses often expand geographically as well as by expanding their product lines. On occasion they may decide that it is desirable to spin off a recently-opened store or to incorporate a new product line into a separate company and distribute it to its shareholders. These ideas raise the question of whether a new location or product line constitutes a new business or whether it is instead merely an expansion of an existing business which can be divided under *Coady* so that each part inherits the maturity of the original business. A leading example is *Lockwood's Estate v. Commissioner*, 350 F.2d 712 (8th Cir. 1965). There, one corporation sold portable potato-sorting machines in various potato-producing states in the West. Later it went into the business of selling other kinds of farming equipment. In 1954 it established a branch in Maine which it incorporated and spun off to its shareholders in 1956. The Court was faced with the question of whether to apply a geographical test to determine the existence and duration of a business (which was rejected), or a functional test, which was accepted. Under the functional test the corporation was viewed as having carried on a farm equipment sales business since the late 1940's and the business in Maine was merely an extension of that same business. As a result, the five-year test was met, and the spin-off was treated as the nontaxable *division* of a single business as under *Coady*. The Regulations treat even the taxable acquisition of a new branch as an expansion of a pre-existing business unless the acquisition so changes the character of the business that it constitutes the acquisition of a new or different business. *See* Reg. § 1.355-3(b)(3)(ii).

NIELSEN v. COMMISSIONER
61 T.C. 311 (1973)

IRWIN, JUDGE....

The partnership of Riener C. Nielsen and Gene E. Moffatt was located in Los Angeles, Calif., and filed Forms 1065, U.S. Partnership Return of Income, for the taxable years ending 1964 and 1965.

Oak Park Community Hospital, Inc. (Oak Park), a California corporation, was organized on November 8, 1956, for the purpose of conducting a hospital business. From its inception until its dissolution on March 31, 1964, the 7 outstanding shares of Oak Park were held by the following individuals:

	Shares
Riener C. Neilsen, Los Angeles, Calif	1
Gene E. Moffatt, Los Angeles, Calif	1
Michael F. LoPresti, North Hollywood, Calif	1
L. W. Gaertner, North Hollywood, Calif	1
Lloyd Boettger, Stockton, Calif	1
Theodore P. Pulas, Stockton, Calif	1
John A. Cook, Stockton, Calif	1
total	7

A successful and profitable hospital business was actively conducted by Oak Park in Stockton, Calif., from its organization in 1956 until August 14, 1961, when it acquired an additional hospital in Los Angeles, Calif. Prior to August 14, 1961, South Side Community Hospital, Inc., a corporation, owned and operated a hospital business located in Los Angeles, Calif. The owners of this corporation were not related in any manner to any of the seven individuals who owned the stock of Oak Park.

On August 14, 1961, Oak Park, in a taxable transaction, purchased all the assets and properties, both real and personal, of every kind and character, of South Side Community Hospital, Inc. The assets acquired by Oak Park included the hospital building, furniture, fixtures and equipment therein, stock in trade including drugs, medicine and surgical supplies, goodwill, accounts receivable, books of account, and existing licenses and permits, and the right to conduct the business of operating a hospital in and/or upon the acquired property.

Oak Park's acquisition of these assets was made from its corporate funds and no outside capital was employed. After this purchase, Oak Park Community Hospital, Inc., took over the operation of South Side Community Hospital, Inc., at 7 a.m. on August 15, 1961.

During the 2½-year period, August 15, 1961, to March 31, 1964, Oak Park operated the hospital in Stockton and the hospital in Los Angeles. This operation included the following details:

a. The Stockton hospital primarily served the medical needs of the Stockton region and its patients came mainly from that area, whereas the Los Angeles hospital served primarily the medical needs of the central Los Angeles region and its patients came mainly from that area.

b. Each hospital had a separate staff of doctors who performed services for patients.

c. The same accounting firm and the same attorney represented Oak Park in all its accounting and legal matters with respect to both hospitals.

d. The same insurance company wrote the hospital malpractice insurance and hospital employee dishonesty insurance policies for both hospitals.

e. Nonperishable food served to patients and employees in both hospitals was obtained from the same institutional supplier; however, no common warehouse

A. TAX-FREE CORPORATE DIVISIONS UNDER CURRENT LAW 427

or supply of food was maintained for the two hospitals and the food was ordered by the hospital administrator as needed, pursuant to an old contract with the institutional supplier.

f. Oak Park consistently presented financial statements to respective creditors on a consolidated basis without differentiating the Stockton hospital from the Los Angeles hospital; however, separate profit-and-loss statements were prepared monthly for each hospital.

g. Ethel G. George was the administrator of Oak Park and in this capacity she served as the administrator for both the Stockton and the Los Angeles hospitals, commuting between them in order to perform her duties.

h. Patient accounts were maintained at each hospital by employees thereof; also, each hospital maintained subsidiary invoice records relating to its own expenses; however, Ethel G. George supervised the maintenance of the patient accounts at both hospitals and expenditures at each hospital were required to be approved by her.

i. Each hospital maintained a separate commercial bank account; however, only Ethel G. George, as president and secretary-treasurer of Oak Park, had authority to sign checks on these bank accounts; also, Ethel G. George reconciled the bank accounts.

j. Separate profit-and-loss statements were prepared monthly for each hospital. The operations of the Stockton hospital were generally profitable, whereas the operations of the Los Angeles hospital were initially unprofitable. The operations of the Los Angeles hospital thereafter became profitable but substantially less than operations of the Stockton hospital. After the corporate split-up the operation of the Los Angeles hospital again became unprofitable.

k. The board of directors of Oak Park met alternately in the cities of Stockton and Los Angeles from the fall of 1961 until March 31, 1964.

The cities of Los Angeles, Calif., and Stockton, Calif., are 344 miles apart.

During the course of Oak Park's operation of the two hospitals, a dispute arose among the stockholders concerning matters relating to the Los Angeles hospital. In this dispute, Riener C. Nielsen, Gene E. Moffatt, and Michael F. LoPresti maintained one position, while the other four stockholders maintained another. As a result of this dispute, the stockholders agreed to split up the Los Angeles hospital business and the Stockton hospital business into two separate corporations. In order to accomplish this purpose the stockholders of Oak Park negotiated an agreement regarding the split-up. This dispute became bitter and at one point legal action was threatened to resolve it. By a letter dated January 10, 1964, the three dissident shareholders (Riener C. Nielsen, Gene E. Moffatt, and Michael F. LoPresti) offered in effect that they would take the Los Angeles hospital while Lloyd Boettger, Theodore P. Pulas, John A. Cook, and L. W. Gaertner would take the Stockton hospital. Based on this letter offer, an "agreement" regarding split-up (hereinafter referred to as the agreement) was executed by the stockholders of Oak Park.

Pursuant to the agreement two new California corporations were formed, Oak Park Community Hospital, Inc., of Northern California (hereinafter referred to as Oak Park North) and Germ Hospital, Inc. (hereinafter referred to as Germ). Thereafter, Oak Park transferred the assets of the Stockton hospital to Oak Park North in exchange for its stock and transferred the assets related to the Los Angeles hospital to Germ in exchange for all its stock.

....

On March 31, 1964, pursuant to the agreement, Oak Park Community Hospital, Inc., distributed the stock of Germ Hospital, Inc., pro rata to Riener C. Nielsen, Gene E. Moffatt, and Michael F. LoPresti in return for and respect to their stock in Oak Park. Oak Park controlled Oak Park North and Germ immediately before the distribution described above. At this time Oak Park had owned no assets other than the stock of these two corporations.

Pursuant to section 355 a distribution of the stock of a controlled corporation enjoys tax-free status if the following conditions are met: (1) The distributing corporation distributes stock of corporations of which it has, immediately prior to the distribution, 80-percent control; (2) the distribution is not principally a device for distributing earnings and profits of either the distributing or controlled corporations; (3) the 5-year active business requirements of section 355(b) are satisfied; and (4) the distributing corporation distributes all the stock it has of the controlled corporation. *Albert W. Badanes*, 39 T.C. 410 (1962); *Edmund P. Coady*, 33 T.C. 771 (1960), *affd.* 289 F.2d 490 (C.A. 6, 1961).

The only dispute between the parties is whether the distribution of the stock of Germ to petitioners satisfied the 5-year active business requirement of section 355(b). Generally, section 355(b) requires in the case of a corporate split-up that each of the corporations resulting from the split-up be actively engaged in the conduct of a trade or business immediately after the split-up and that such trade or business have been conducted actively for the 5-year period immediately preceding the split-up. The 5-year period only includes the active conduct of the business by the distriuting corporation; by a corporation controlled by the distributing corporation, or by a person from whom the business was acquired by the distributing corporation in a transaction in which gain or loss was not recognized in whole or in part.

Petitioner contends that for more than 5 years preceding the March 31, 1964, distribution Oak Park conducted a single hospital business of which the Los Angeles hospital was a part. It is well established that a corporation engaged in a single business may be divided into two corporations without recognition of gain under section 355 as long as the two resulting corporations continue to engage in the same business carried on by their predecessor. *Edmund P. Coady*, supra; *United States v. Marett*, 325 F.2d 28 (C.A. 5, 1963); Rev. Rul. 64-147, 1964-1 C.B. (Part 1) 136. The 5-year active-business requirement is even satisfied where a corporation expands its business by purchasing assets within the 5-year period preceding the division and these assets become the principal assets of one of the corporations resulting from the division. *Patricia W. Burke*, 42

A. TAX-FREE CORPORATE DIVISIONS UNDER CURRENT LAW

T.C. 1021 (1964); *Lockwood's Estate v. Commissioner*, 350 F.2d 713 (C.A. 8, 1965).

Respondent claims that Oak Park did not conduct a single business as of March 31, 1964, but two distinct hospital businesses of which only one, the Stockton hospital, had the requisite 5-year history. If a corporation engaged in the conduct of two separate businesses, both must have a 5-year history at the time of a corporate division in order to qualify under section 355. *Isabel A. Elliott*, 32 T.C. 283 (1959). After careful consideration of all of the facts in the stipulated record, we are of the opinion that the operations of Stockton and Los Angeles hospitals constituted two separate businesses. Accordingly, the distribution of the stock of Germ to petitioners pursuant to the agreement to split up Oak Park failed to meet the 5-year active-business requirement of section 355(b) because the Los Angeles hospital business was acquired by purchase only 2½ years prior to the distribution.

Although the two hospitals shared the same top management, there was no integration of the income-producing activities of each hospital. The medical staff and patients of each hospital were mutually exclusive. One hospital could hardly be called the branch operation of the other. We think this fact distinguishes the present case from *Patricia W. Burke, supra,* and *Lockwood's Estate v. Commissioner, supra,* upon which petitioners rely. Each hospital had the requisite assets and employees for the production of income, and each was a self-sufficient operation. *See* sec. 1.355-1(c), Income Tax Regs. The things which the hospitals had in common — representation by the same attorneys and accountants and the use of the same insurance company and the same suppliers for some items — might have been shared by any two totally dissimilar businesses owned by one person. Accordingly, we hold that as of March 31, 1964, Oak Park was engaged in the conduct of two separate businesses of which only one, the Stockton Hospital, had been conducted actively for 5 years preceding that date as required by section 355(b).

We have noted that in *Lloyd Boettger, supra,* we also considered the application of section 355 to the split-up of Oak Park with respect to the distributions received by shareholders other than petitioners. Although we have reached the same result that obtained in *Boettger*, we admit that our analysis of section 355 is somewhat different. Irrespective of the rationale of *Boettger*, we believe our analysis of section 355 is well founded on cases like *Patricia W. Burke, supra,* and *Lockwood's Estate v. Commissioner, supra.*

In view of the foregoing,

Decisions will be entered for the respondent.

NOTES AND QUESTIONS

1. *What were the facts again?* Is it true that the only things the hospitals had in common were the same lawyers, accountants, insurance company, and some suppliers? In *Boettger*, cited in *Nielsen*, the Tax Court held that, on exactly the same facts, another of the individuals involved in the same investments and transactions also was taxable on the distribution to him of Oak Park North stock worth $67,937.59 as a dividend, without any offset for his basis of $9,700 in the stock he surrendered in the parent corporation. The Court decided that the acquired hospital was a business that had not been actively conducted for the required five-year period and so the distribution was not entitled to tax-free treatment. The statutory terms had not been met, so the distribution was taxable even though it did not constitute a purposeful attempt to "bail out" earnings by acquisition of a business for later distribution. The record established a valid business purpose for the distribution, and the IRS made no argument that it was a device for distributing earnings and profits.

2. How would the Regulations (as revised in 1989) treat these cases? *See* especially Reg. § 1.355-3(c), example 8 and § 1.355-3(b)(3)(ii) (last sentence).

3. If there were a single business in *Boettger*, could one reconcile the case with *Lockwood?*

4. Which rationale strikes you as preferable, the one in *Nielsen* or the one in *Boettger?*

PROBLEM 20-2

X Corp. has two lines of businesses, an electronics manufacturing company and a gasoline refining company, which have been operating since 1975. Both businesses are equal in value. The outstanding stock of X Corp. is owned equally by A and B. Because A is more interested in running only the electronics company, and B is more interested in running only the refining company, they decide to split up the company in order that each may devote substantially all his time to his own company. Also, A and B have been having disputes in the past about running the companies.

How can A and B structure the transaction to meet the nonrecognition requirements of § 355? Provide an analysis of the requirements of § 355. *See* Reg. § 1.355-1(b), 2(a) and (b)(1)-(4).

PROBLEM 20-3

Y Corp. has two lines of businesses, a telecommunications company which was purchased by Y Corp. from ICM in 1993 and a gas pipeline company which Y Corp. has been operating since 1975. Both businesses are equal in value. The outstanding stock of Y Corp. is owned equally by A and B. The in-house counsel has drawn up a plan that he believes qualifies under § 355 in order to divide the two business into separate distinct companies, wherein Y Corp. transfers the telecommunications company assets to a newly formed subsidiary, Sub Co., and will distribute the Sub Co. Stock to A in exchange for his Y Corp. stock. A will run the telecommunications company and B will run the gas pipeline company. Before the plan is implemented, A sells all his Y Corp. stock to C, an unrelated party. After the plan to divide the companies is carried out, C sells all the Sub Co. stock he acquired pursuant to the plan and recognizes a substantial gain.

Based on the above facts, will the transaction meet the nonrecognition requirements of § 355? Provide an analysis of the § 355 requirements and the effect on A, B, C, and Y Corp. *See* Reg. § 1.355-2(d)(iii).

8. SPIN-OFF OF UNWANTED ASSETS FOLLOWED BY TAX-FREE ACQUISITION

Read §§ 368(a)(1)(D) and 354(a) and (b)(1).

An acquiring corporation may refuse to accept certain assets of the target corporation and insist that the target dispose of them before the tax-free acquisition. In such a case, the target's shareholders may be forced to retain the unwanted assets, and the question arises how to do so at the smallest tax cost. Basically there are two choices, one of which is to spin off the unwanted assets and then combine the remaining (original) corporation with the acquiring company. The other is to spin off the wanted assets into a new corporation and to combine the new corporation with the acquiring corporation. Although the business and economic effects of these two choices are identical, the tax results are vastly different.

COMMISSIONER v. MORRIS TRUST
367 F.2d 794 (9th. Cir. 1966)

HAYNSWORTH, CHIEF JUDGE.

Its nubility impaired by the existence of an insurance department it had operated for many years, a state bank divested itself of that business before merging with a national bank. The divestiture was in the form of a traditional "spin-off," but, because it was a preliminary step to the merger of the banks, the Commissioner treated their receipt of stock of the insurance company as ordinary income to the stockholders of the state bank. We agree with the Tax Court, that gain to the stockholders of the state bank was not recognizable under § 355 of the 1954 Code.

In 1960, a merger agreement was negotiated by the directors of American Commercial Bank, a North Carolina corporation with its principal office in Charlotte, and Security National Bank of Greensboro, a national bank. American was the product of an earlier merger of American Trust Company and a national bank, the Commercial National Bank of Charlotte. This time, however, though American was slightly larger than Security, it was found desirable to operate the merged institutions under Security's national charter, after changing the name to North Carolina National Bank. It was contemplated that the merged institution would open branches in other cities.

For many years, American had operated an insurance department. This was a substantial impediment to the accomplishment of the merger, for a national bank is prohibited from operating an insurance department except in towns having a population of not more than 5000 inhabitants. To avoid a violation of the national banking laws, therefore, and to accomplish the merger under Security's national charter, it was prerequisite that American rid itself of its insurance business.

The required step to make it nubile was accomplished by American's organization of a new corporation, American Commercial Agency, Inc., to which American transferred its insurance business assets in exchange for Agency's stock which was immediately distributed to American's stockholders. At the same time, American paid a cash dividend fully taxable to its stockholders. The merger of the two banks was then accomplished.

Though American's spin-off of its insurance business was a "D" reorganization, as defined in § 368(a) (1), provided the distribution of Agency's stock qualified for non-recognition of gain under § 355, the Commissioner contended that the active business requirements of § 355(b)(1)(A) were not met, since American's banking business was not continued in unaltered corporate form. He also finds an inherent incompatibility in substantially simultaneous divisive and amalgamating reorganizations.

Section 355(b) (1) (A) requires that both the distributing corporation and the controlled corporation be "engaged immediately after the distribution in the active conduct of a trade or business." There was literal compliance with that requirement, for the spin-off, including the distribution of Agency's stock to American's stockholders, preceded the merger. The Commissioner asks that we look at both steps together, contending that North Carolina National Bank was not the distributing corporation and that its subsequent conduct of American's banking business does not satisfy the requirement.

A brief look at an earlier history may clarify the problem.

Initially, the active business requirement was one of several judicial innovations designed to limit nonrecognition of gain to the implicit, but unelucidated, intention of earlier Congresses.

Nonrecognition of gain in "spin-offs" was introduced by the Revenue Act of 1924. Its § 203(b)(3), as earlier Revenue Acts, provided for nonrecognition of gain at the corporate level when one corporate party to a reorganization exchanged property solely for stock or securities of another, but it added a provision in subsection (c) extending the nonrecognition of gain to a stockholder of a corporate party to a reorganization who received stock of another party without surrendering any of his old stock. Thus, with respect to the nonrecognition of gain, treatment previously extended to "split-offs" was extended to the economically indistinguishable "spin-off."

The only limitation upon those provisions extending nonrecognition to spin-offs was contained in § 203(h) and (i) defining reorganizations. The definition required that immediately after the transfer, the transferor or its stockholders or both be in control of the corporation to which the assets had been transferred, and "control" was defined as being the ownership of not less than eighty per

A. TAX-FREE CORPORATE DIVISIONS UNDER CURRENT LAW

cent of the voting stock and eighty per cent of the total number of shares of all other classes of stock.

With no restriction other than the requirement of control of the transferee, these provisions were a fertile source of tax avoidance schemes. By spinning-off liquid assets or all productive assets, they provided the means by which ordinary distributions of earnings could be cast in the form of a reorganization within their literal language.

The renowned case of *Gregory v. Helvering*, 293 U.S. 465, 55 S. Ct. 266, 79 L. Ed. 596, brought the problem to the Supreme Court. The taxpayer there owned all of the stock of United Mortgage Corporation which, in turn, owned 1000 shares of Monitor Securities Corporation. She wished to sell the Monitor stock and possess herself of the proceeds. If the sale were effected by United Mortgage, gain would be recognized to it, and its subsequent distribution of the net proceeds of the sale would have been a dividend to the taxpayer, taxable as ordinary income. If the Monitor stock were distributed to the taxpayer before sale, its full value would have been taxable to her as ordinary income. In order materially to reduce that tax cost, United Mortgage spun-off the Monitor stock to a new corporation, Averill, the stock of which was distributed to the taxpayer. Averill was then liquidated, and the taxpayer sold the Monitor stock. She contended that she was taxable only on the proceeds of the sale, reduced by an allocated part of her cost basis of United Mortgage, and at capital gain rates.

The Supreme Court found the transaction quite foreign to the congressional purpose. It limited the statute's definition of a reorganization to a reorganization of a corporate business or businesses motivated by a business purpose. It was never intended that Averill engage in any business, and it had not. Its creation, the distribution of its stock and its liquidation, the court concluded, was only a masquerade for the distribution of an ordinary dividend, as, of course, it was.

In a similar vein, it was held that the interposition of new corporations of fleeting duration, though the transactions were literally within the congressional definition of a reorganization and the language of a nonrecognition section, would not avail in the achievement of the tax avoidance purpose when it was only a mask for a transaction which was essentially and substantively the payment of a liquidating dividend, a sale for cash, or a taxable exchange.

Such cases exposed a number of fundamental principles which limited the application of the nonrecognition of gain sections of the reorganization provisions of the Code. Mertens defines them in terms of permanence, which encompasses the concepts of business purpose and a purpose to continue an active business in altered corporate form. As concomitants to the primary principle and supplements of it, there were other requirements that the transferor, or its stockholders, retain a common stock interest and that a substantial part of the value of the properties transferred be represented by equity securities.

Underlying such judicially developed rules limiting the scope of the nonrecognition provisions of the Code, was an acceptance of a general congressional purpose to facilitate the reorganization of businesses, not to exalt economically meaningless formalisms and diversions through corporate structures hastily created and as hastily demolished. Continuation of a business in altered corporate form was to be encouraged, but immunization of taxable transactions through the interposition of short-lived, empty, corporate entities was never intended and ought not to be allowed.

While these judicial principles were evolving and before the Supreme Court declared itself in *Gregory v. Helvering*, an alarmed Congress withdrew nonrecognition of gain to a stockholder receiving securities in a spin-off. It did so by omitting from the Revenue Act of 1934, a provision comparable to § 203(c) of the Revenue Act of 1924.

Nonrecognition of gain to the stockholder in spin-off situations, however, was again extended by § 317(a) of the Revenue Act of 1951, amending the 1939 Code by adding § 112(b) (11). This time, the judicially developed restrictions upon the application of the earlier statutes were partially codified. Nonrecognition of gain was extended "unless it appears that (A) any corporation which is a party to such reorganization was not intended to continue the active conduct of a trade or business after such reorganization, or (B) the corporation whose stock is distributed was used principally as a device for the distribution of earnings and profits to the shareholders of any corporation a party to the reorganization."

If this transaction were governed by the 1939 Code, as amended in 1951, the Commissioner would have had the support of a literal reading of the A limitation, for it was not intended that American, in its then corporate form, should continue the active conduct of the banking business. From the prior history, however, it would appear that the intention of the A limitation was to withhold the statute's benefits from schemes of the *Gregory v. Helvering* type. It effectively reached those situations in which one of the parties to the reorganization was left only with liquid assets not intended for use in the acquisition of an active business or in which the early demise of one of the parties was contemplated, particularly, if its only office was a conduit for the transmission of title. The B limitation was an additional precaution intended to encompass any other possible use of the device for the masquerading of a dividend distribution.

The 1954 Code was the product of a careful attempt to codify the judicial limiting principles in a more particularized form. The congressional particularization extended the principles in some areas, as in the requirement that a business, to be considered an active one, must have been conducted for a period of at least five years ending on the distribution date and must not have been acquired in a taxable transaction during the five-year period.[5] In other areas, it relaxed and ameliorated them, as in its express sanction of non-pro/rata distributions. While there are such particularized variations, the 1954 Code is a legislative re-expression of generally established principles developed in response

---

[5] Section 355(b)(2).

A. TAX-FREE CORPORATE DIVISIONS UNDER CURRENT LAW   435

to definite classes of abuses which had manifested themselves many years earlier. The perversions of the general congressional purpose and the principles the courts had developed to thwart them, as revealed in the earlier cases, are still an enlightening history with which an interpretation of the reorganization sections of the 1954 Code should be approached.

Section 355(b) requires that the distributing corporation be engaged in the active conduct of a trade or business "immediately after the distribution." This is in contrast to the provisions of the 1951 Act, which, as we have noted, required an intention that the parent, as well as the other corporate parties to the reorganization, continue the conduct of an active business. It is in marked contrast to § 355(b)'s highly particularized requirements respecting the duration of the active business prior to the reorganization and the methods by which it was acquired. These contrasts suggest a literal reading of the post-reorganization requirement and a holding that the Congress intended to restrict it to the situation existing "immediately after the distribution."

Such a reading is quite consistent with the prior history. It quite adequately meets the problem posed by the *Gregory v. Helvering* situation in which, immediately after the distribution, one of the corporations held only liquid or investment assets. It sufficiently serves the requirements of permanence and of continuity, for as long as an active business is being conducted immediately after the distribution, there is no substantial opportunity for the stockholders to sever their interest in the business except through a separable, taxable transaction. If the corporation proceeds to withdraw assets from the conduct of the active business and to abandon it, the Commissioner has recourse to the back-up provisions of § 355(a)(1)(B) and to the limitations of the underlying principles. At the same time, the limitation, so construed, will not inhibit continued stockholder conduct of the active business through altered corporate form and with further changes in corporate structure, the very thing the reorganization sections were intended to facilitate.

Applied to this case, there is no violation of any of the underlying limiting principles. There was no empty formalism, no utilization of empty corporate structures, no attempt to recast a taxable transaction in nontaxable form and no withdrawal of liquid assets. There is no question but that American's insurance and banking businesses met all of the active business requirements of § 355(b)(2). It was intended that both businesses be continued indefinitely, and each has been. American's merger with Security, in no sense, was a discontinuance of American's banking business, which opened the day after the merger with the same employees, the same depositors and customers. There was clearly the requisite continuity of stockholder interest, for American's former stockholders remained in 100% control of the insurance company, while, in the merger, they received 54.385% of the common stock of North Carolina National Bank, the remainder going to Security's former stockholders. There was a strong business purpose for both the spin-off and the merger, and tax avoidance by American's stockholders was neither a predominant nor a subordinate purpose.

In short, though both of the transactions be viewed together, there were none of the evils or misuses which the limiting principles and the statutory limitations were designed to exclude.

We are thus led to the conclusion that this carefully drawn statute should not be read more broadly than it was written to deny nonrecognition of gain to reorganizations of real businesses of the type which Congress clearly intended to facilitate by according to them nonrecognition of present gain.

The Commissioner, indeed, concedes that American's stockholders would have realized no gain had American not been merged into Security after, but substantially contemporaneously with, Agency's spin-off. Insofar as it is contended that § 355(b) (1) (A) requires the distributing corporation to continue the conduct of an active business, recognition of gain to American's stockholders on their receipt of Agency's stock would depend upon the economically irrelevant technicality of the identity of the surviving corporation in the merger. Had American been the survivor, it would in every literal and substantive sense have continued the conduct of its banking business.

Surely, the Congress which drafted these comprehensive provisions did not intend the incidence of taxation to turn upon so insubstantial a technicality. Its differentiation on the basis of the economic substance of transactions is too evident to permit such a conclusion.

This, too, the Commissioner seems to recognize, at least conditionally, for he says that gain to the stockholders would have been recognized even if American had been the surviving corporation. This would necessitate our reading into § 355(b)(1) (A) an implicit requirement that the distributing corporation, without undergoing any reorganization whatever, whether or not it resulted in a change in its corporate identity, continue the conduct of its active business.

We cannot read this broader limitation into the statute for the same reasons we cannot read into it the narrower one of maintenance of the same corporate identity. The congressional limitation of the post-distribution active business requirement to the situation existing "immediately after the distribution" was deliberate. Consistent with the general statutory scheme, it is quite inconsistent with the Commissioner's contention.

The requirement of § 368(a)(1)(D) that the transferor or its stockholders be in control of the spun-off corporation immediately after the transfer is of no assistance to the Commissioner. It is directed solely to control of the transferee, and was fully met here. It contains no requirement of continuing control of the transferor. Though a subsequent sale of the transferor's stock, under some circumstances, might form the basis of a contention that the transaction was the equivalent of a dividend within the meaning of § 355(a) (1) (B) and the underlying principles, the control requirements imply no limitation upon subsequent reorganizations of the transferor.

There is no distinction in the statute between subsequent amalgamating reorganizations in which the stockholders of the spin-off transferor would own 80% or more of the relevant classes of stock of the reorganized transferor, and

A. TAX-FREE CORPORATE DIVISIONS UNDER CURRENT LAW 437

those in which they would not. The statute draws no line between major and minor amalgamations in prospect at the time of the spin-off. Nothing of the sort is suggested by the detailed control-active business requirements in the five-year predistribution period, for there the distinction is between taxable and nontaxable acquisitions, and a tax free exchange within the five-year period does not violate the active business-control requirement whether it was a major or a minor acquisition. Reorganizations in which no gain or loss is recognized, sanctioned by the statute's control provision when occurring in the five years preceding the spin-off, are not prohibited in the post-distribution period.

As we have noticed above, the merger cannot by any stretch of imagination be said to have affected the continuity of interest of American's stockholders or to have constituted a violation of the principle underlying the statutory control requirement. The view is the same whether it be directed to each of the successive steps severally or to the whole.

Nor can we find elsewhere in the Code any support for the Commissioner's suggestion of incompatibility between substantially contemporaneous divisive and amalgamating reorganizations. The 1954 Code contains no inkling of it; nor does its immediate legislative history. The difficulties encountered under the 1924 Code and its successors, in dealing with formalistic distortions of taxable transactions into the spin-off shape, contain no implication of any such incompatibility. Section 317 of the Revenue Act of 1951 and the Senate Committee Report, to which we have referred, did require an intention that the distributing corporation continue the conduct of its active business, but that transitory requirement is of slight relevance to an interpretation of the very different provisions of the 1954 Code and is devoid of any implication of incompatibility. If that provision, during the years it was in effect, would have resulted in recognition of gain in a spin-off if the distributing corporation later, but substantially simultaneously, was a party to a merger in which it lost its identity, a question we do not decide, it would not inhibit successive reorganizations if the merger preceded the spin-off.

The Congress intended to encourage six types of reorganizations. They are defined in § 368 and designated by the letters "A" through "F." The "A" merger, the "B" exchange of stock for stock and the "C" exchange of stock for substantially all of the properties of another are all amalgamating reorganizations. The "D" reorganization is the divisive spin-off, while the "E" and "F" reorganizations, recapitalizations and reincorporations, are neither amalgamating nor divisive. All are sanctioned equally, however. Recognition of gain is withheld from each and successively so. Merger may follow merger, and an "A" reorganization by which Y is merged into X corporation may proceed substantially simultaneously with a "C" reorganization by which X acquires substantially all of the properties of Z and with an "F" reorganization by which X is reincorporated in another state. The "D" reorganization has no lesser standing. It is on the same plane as the others and, provided all of the "D" requirements are met, is as available as the others in successive reorganizations.

We have not placed our reliance upon that provision of the National Banking Act which continues the identity of each merging bank in the consolidated banking association which is deemed the same bank as each of the merging constituents. We have not done so, for, at best, it would supply an answer only to the Commissioner's most limited contention. Moreover, we have had previous occasion to point out the narrow purpose of that statute. It was enacted to secure the continuing efficacy of previous fiduciary appointments of each of the constituent banks. It was not intended, as we held in Fidelity-Baltimore, to exempt merging banks from stamp taxes to which all other merging corporations are subject. Nor do we think it was intended, when enacted in 1959, to amend the reorganization sections of the 1954 Code or to accord to the stockholders of reorganizing banks more favorable tax treatment than that accorded the stockholders of other corporations undergoing comparable reorganizations. The comprehensive scheme of the 1954 Code was intended to have a uniform application. The courts should not import artificial distinctions into it.

Our conclusion that gain was not recognizable to American's stockholders as a result of the spin-off, therefore, is uninfluenced by the fact that the subsequent merger was under the National Banking Act. It would have been the same if the merger had been accomplished under state laws.

In a substantive sense, however, in every merger there is a continuation of each constituent. Each makes its contribution to the continuing combination, and the substantiality of that contribution is unaffected by such technicalities as a choice to operate under the charter of one constituent rather than that of another. After the merger, North Carolina National Bank was as much American as Security. It was not one or the other, except in the sense of the most technical of legalisms; it was both, and with respect to the Charlotte operation, old American's business, it was almost entirely American. North Carolina National Bank's business in the Charlotte area after the merger was American's business conducted by American's employees in American's banking houses for the service of American's customers. Probably the only change immediately noticeable was the new name.

While we reject the technical provision of the National Banking Act as a basis for decision, therefore, it is important to the result that, as in every merger, there was substantive continuity of each constituent and its business. In framing the 1954 Code, the Congress was concerned with substance, not formalisms. Its approach was that of the courts in the *Gregory v. Helvering* series of cases. Ours must be the same. The technicalities of corporate structure cannot obscure the continuity of American's business, its employees, its customers, its locations or the substantive fact that North Carolina National Bank was both American and Security.

A. TAX-FREE CORPORATE DIVISIONS UNDER CURRENT LAW 439

A decision of the Sixth Circuit[6] appears to be at odds with our conclusion. In *Curtis*, it appears that one corporation was merged into another after spinning-off a warehouse building which was an unwanted asset because the negotiators could not agree upon its value. The Court of Appeals for the Sixth Circuit affirmed a District Court judgment holding that the value of the warehouse company shares was taxable as ordinary income to the stockholders of the first corporation.

A possible distinction may lie between the spin-off of an asset unwanted by the acquiring corporation in an "A" reorganization solely because of disagreement as to its value and the preliminary spin-off of an active business which the acquiring corporation is prohibited by law from operating. We cannot stand upon so nebulous a distinction, however. We simply take a different view. The reliance in *Curtis* upon the Report of the Senate Committee explaining § 317 of the Revenue Act of 1951, quite dissimilar to the 1954 Code, reinforces our appraisal of the relevant materials....

For the reasons which we have canvassed, we think the Tax Court, which had before it the opinion of the District Court in Curtis, though not that of the affirming Court of Appeals, correctly decided that American's stockholders realized no recognizable taxable gain upon their receipt in the "D" reorganization of the stock of Agency.

Affirmed.

NOTE

The IRS concedes. In Rev. Rul. 68-603, 1968-2 C.B. 148, the IRS accepted the decision in *Morris Trust* to the extent that it held that a merger of the distributing corporation into the acquiring corporation after the division does not fail the "active business" test or the control test of § 368(a)(1)(D). Reg. § 1.355-2(d)(2)(iii)(E), issued in 1989, states that a spin-off followed by a sale indicates a device, but a spin-off followed by a reorganization does not, thus validating *Morris Trust* and opening the door to a wide variety of transactions.

9. SPIN-OFF OF WANTED ASSETS FOLLOWED BY TAX-FREE ACQUISITION

Before you launch into this ruling, you need to know that a type B reorganization is one in which the acquiring corporation issues its voting stock in exchange for stock of the target company and afterwards has 80% control of the target. § 368(a)(1)(B).

---

[6] *Curtis v. United States*, 6 Cir., 336 F.2d 714.

REV. RUL. 70-225
1970-1 C.B. 80

Advice has been requested whether the transactions described below qualify as (1) a reorganization under section 368(a)(1)(D) of the Internal Revenue Code of 1954, (2) a distribution of stock of a controlled corporation under section 355 of the Code, and (3) a reorganization under section 368(a)(1)(B) of the Code.

R, a corporation with one shareholder, A, for many years has operated a taxicab business and a car rental business. T, an unrelated widely held corporation, desired to acquire R's car rental business. Pursuant to a plan, R transferred the assets of its car rental business to a newly formed corporation, S, in exchange for all the stock of S and distributed the stock of S to its sole shareholder (A) in a transaction intended to qualify under sections 368(a)(1)(D) and 355 of the Code. As part of the prearranged plan, A immediately exchanged all his S stock for some of the outstanding voting stock of T in an exchange intended to meet the requirements of section 368(a)(1)(B) of the Code.

Section 368(a)(1)(D) of the Code defines a "reorganization" to include a transfer by a corporation of all or a part of its assets to another corporation if immediately after the transfer the transferor, or one or more of its shareholders (including persons who were shareholders immediately before the transfer), or any combination thereof is in control of the corporation to which the assets are transferred; but only if, in pursuance of the plan, stock or securities of the corporation to which the assets are transferred are distributed in a transaction which qualifies under sections 354, 355, or 356 of the Code.

Section 368(c) of the Code defines the term "control" as ownership of stock possessing at least 80 percent of the total combined voting power of all classes of stock entitled to vote and at least 80 percent of the total number of shares of each other class of stock of the corporation.

Section 355 of the Code provides rules for the distribution, without recognition of gain or loss to the shareholders, of stock of a corporation controlled by the distributing corporation.

Section 368(a)(1)(B) of the Code provides that the term "reorganization" includes the acquisition by one corporation, in exchange solely for all or a part of its voting stock, of stock of another corporation if, immediately after the acquisition, the acquiring corporation has control of such corporation.

Revenue Ruling 54-96, C.B. 1954-1, 111, as modified by Revenue Ruling 56-100, C.B. 1956-1, 624, discusses a situation where X corporation organized a new corporation, Y, to which X transferred one of two separate businesses X had operated in exchange for all the stock of Y. As part of a prearranged plan X transferred all the stock of Y to an unrelated corporation, Z, in exchange for 20 percent of the outstanding voting stock of Z. That Revenue Ruling holds that since the two steps were part of a prearranged, integrated, plan they may not be considered independently of each other. Consequently, since X was not in control of Y after transferring a part of its assets to that corporation, the transfer did not

B. SPIN-OFF FOLLOWED BY A TAXABLE ACQUISITION

constitute a reorganization as defined in the predecessor of section 368(a)(1)(D) of the Code nor did it constitute a tax-free transfer under the predecessor of section 351 of the Code. That Revenue Ruling also holds that the predecessor of section 368(a)(1)(B) of the Code was not applicable, for in net effect X transferred part of its assets to Z in exchange for a part of the Z stock, rather than all the stock of a previously existing corporation.

Similarly, in the instant case, the transfer by R of part of its assets to S in exchange for all the stock of S followed by the distribution of the S stock to A and by the transfer of the S stock to T by A in exchange for T stock is a series of integrated steps which likewise may not be considered independently of each other. Accordingly, neither R nor its sole shareholder A is in control of S after the transfer and the transaction does not constitute a reorganization under section 368(a)(1)(D) of the Code nor a transfer under section 351 of the Code. Section 368(a)(1)(B) of the Code is not applicable to the transaction, since in effect R transferred part of its assets to T in exchange for a part of the T stock, rather than T having acquired all the stock of a previously existing corporation solely in exchange for its own voting stock.

Accordingly, the receipt by A of the stock of T is not a distribution to which section 355 of the Code applies. The fair market value of the stock of T is taxable to A as a distribution by R under section 301 of the Code. In addition, gain or loss is recognized by R on the transaction.

QUESTIONS

1. *Section 311 effects.* Will the gain to R increase its earnings and profits, thereby increasing the dividend to the shareholders?

2. *Spin-off of preexisting subsidiary.* In Rev. Rul. 75-406, 1975-2 C.B. 125, the IRS ruled that if the wanted assets were already held in an eight-year-old subsidiary which was spun off and then merged with an unrelated corporation pursuant to a single plan the transaction did not violate the continuity-of-interest or device tests and was a good § 355 distribution and a good type A reorganization (do not worry about this alphabet soup yet, just focus on the § 335 issue). How can one reconcile these disparate results?

3. *Substance and form.* Why should the spin-off and retention of unwanted assets work, but not the reverse transaction? Is this a triumph of form over substance?

B. SPIN-OFF FOLLOWED BY A TAXABLE ACQUISITION

Whereas the law has developed favorably toward combining divisive transactions with taxfree acquisitive ones, the same cannot be said where the second step is a taxable *sale* of either the distributing or spun-off company's stock. First, the taxable transaction is evidence of a device under Reg. § 1.355-2(d)(ii). Also, the divisive transaction is taxable because there is a lack of continuity of proprietary interest on the part of the shareholders of whichever entity is sold. This violates the requirement that the historic shareholders of the original corporation must continue to have a major equity stake in both companies after the corporate division. *See* Reg. § 1.355-2(c).

C. TAX TREATMENT OF DISTRIBUTEES IN A CORPORATE DIVISION

If done right, the shareholders and the securities holders of the distributing corporation will recognize no gain or loss when they receive stock or securities of the spun-off corporation. Instead, they will allocate their basis in the distributing corporation stock between that stock and the stock of the subsidiary in proportion to their relative fair market values, just as in the case of a tax-free stock dividend. Similarly, they can "tack" the holding period of their old stock on to the new stock. *See* §§ 358(a) and 1223(1).

If "boot" is distributed, § 356 steps in. Taxable boot includes cash, and the fair market value of any distributed property other than stock and securities of the corporation, as well as stock rights and warrants, and any stock of the controlled corporation which was acquired by the distributing corporation in a taxable transaction within the past five years. *See* § 355(a)(3)(B). If the corporation distributes securities with a principal amount (meaning face amount) which is greater than the total principal amount of the securities that the taxpayer gave up, the *fair market value* of the difference between the principal amount of the distributed securities and the principal amount of the securities (if any) constitutes boot. § 355(a)(3) and § 356(d).

> *To illustrate*: An individual shareholder exchanges a security in the principal amount of $1,000 for another security in the principal amount of $1,200 with fair market value of $1,080. The fair market value of the $200 excess principal amount is $180, and that is the amount of taxable boot. This figure is obtained by multiplying the ratio of fair market value to face amount ($1080\$1200 = 90%) of the new security by the excess face amount (90% of $200 = $180). Reg. § 1.356-3(b), example (5).

It is worth going through this small technical detour now because one uses the same calculation of boot in connection with the distribution of additional principal amounts of debt as part of acquisitive reorganizations treated in the following Chapter.

No losses are recognized in otherwise qualifying the tax-free distributions under § 355. *See* § 356(c).

C. TAX TREATMENT OF DISTRIBUTEES IN A CORPORATE DIVISION

1. BOOT IN A SPIN-OFF

In a spin-off, boot is treated as a § 301 distribution regardless of the shareholder's realized gain. This will result in a dividend to the extent of the distributing corporation's earnings and profits, and any excess of the distribution above earnings and profits first reduces basis and then produces capital gain. §§ 356(b) and 301(c).

2. SPLIT-OFF OR SPLIT-UP

In a split-off or split-up, however, an exchange of stock for boot resembles a redemption under § 302. Under § 356(a)(1) and (2), boot in such transactions is given sale or exchange treatment unless it "has the effect of the distribution of a dividend." Even then there are two limitations to the dividend: (1) it is limited to the amount of gain recognized, and (2) it is limited to the recipient shareholder's ratable share of earnings and profits of the distributing corporation. The remainder of recognized gain, if any, is capital gain under § 356(a)(1). Whether the boot has "the effect of a dividend" is determined under the principles of § 302(b) as shown in Rev. Rul. 93-62 below.

> *To illustrate*: In a qualifying § 355 split-off shareholder A receives all the stock of Sub Corp. plus $200 cash from Distributing Corp. in exchange for all of A's 50% shareholdings in Distributing. Distributing has $100 of earnings & profits, of which A's ratable share is thus $50. The Sub stock is worth $800, and A's basis in his Distributing stock was $900. A's gain realized is $100 (total consideration of $1,000 less basis of $900) all of which must be recognized because he has received $200 of boot. However, even if the distribution has the effect of a dividend, no more than $50 of the boot (A's ratable share of earnings and profits) will be treated as a dividend. Of the remaining $150 of boot, $50 will be capital gain and $100 a tax-free return of capital.

REV. RUL. 93-62
1993-30 I.R.B. 10

....

Facts

Distributing is a corporation with 1,000 shares of a single class of stock outstanding. Each share has a fair market value of $1x. A, one of five unrelated individual shareholders, owns 400 shares of Distributing stock. Distributing owns all of the outstanding stock of a subsidiary corporation, Controlled. The Controlled stock has a fair market value of $200x.

Distributing distributes all the stock of Controlled plus $200x cash to A in exchange for all of A's Distributing stock. The exchange satisfies the requirements of section 355 but for the receipt of the cash.

Law and Analysis

Section 355(a)(1) of the Code provides, in general, that the shareholders of a distributing corporation will not recognize gain or loss on the exchange of the distributing corporation's stock or securities solely for stock or securities of a controlled subsidiary if the requirements of section 355 are satisfied.

Section 356(a)(1) of the Code provides for recognition of gain on exchanges in which gain would otherwise not be recognized under section 354 (relating to tax-free acquisitive reorganizations) or section 355 if the property received in the exchange consists of property permitted to be received without gain recognition and other property or money ("boot"). The amount of gain recognized is limited to the sum of the money and the fair market value of the other property.

Under section 356(a)(2) of the Code, gain recognized in an exchange described in section 356(a)(1) that "has the effect of the distribution of a dividend" is treated as a dividend to the extent of the distributee's ratable share of the undistributed earnings and profits accumulated after February 28, 1913. Any remaining gain is treated as gain from the exchange of property.

Determinations of whether the receipt of boot has the effect of a dividend are made by applying the principles of section 302 of the Code. *Commissioner v. Clark*, 489 U.S. 726 (1989), 1989-2 C.B. 68. Section 302 contains rules for determining whether payments in redemption of stock are treated as payments in exchange for the stock or as distributions to which section 301 applies.

Under section 302(a) of the Code, a redemption will be treated as an exchange if it satisfies one of the tests of section 302(b). Section 302(b)(2) provides exchange treatment for substantially disproportionate redemptions of stock. A distribution is substantially disproportionate if (1) the shareholder's voting stock interest and common stock interest in the corporation immediately after the redemption are each less than 80 percent of those interests immediately before the redemption, and (2) the shareholder owns less than 50 percent of the voting power of all classes of stock immediately after the redemption.

In *Clark*, the Supreme Court determined whether gain recognized under section 356 of the Code on the receipt of boot in an acquisitive reorganization under section 368(a)(1)(A) and (a)(2)(D) should be treated as a dividend distribution. In that case, the sole shareholder of the target corporation exchanged his target stock for stock of the acquiring corporation and cash. In applying section 302 to determine whether the boot payment had the effect of a dividend distribution, the Court considered whether section 302 should be applied to the boot payment as if it were made (i) by the target corporation in a pre-reorganization hypothetical redemption of a portion of the shareholder's target stock, or (ii) by the acquiring corporation in a post-reorganization hypothetical redemption of the acquiring

C. TAX TREATMENT OF DISTRIBUTEES IN A CORPORATE DIVISION

corporation stock that the shareholder would have received in the reorganization exchange if there had been no boot distribution.

The Supreme Court stated that the treatment of boot under section 356(a)(2) of the Code should be determined "by examining the effect of the exchange as a whole," and concluded that treating the boot as received in a redemption of target stock would improperly isolate the boot payment from the overall reorganization by disregarding the effect of the subsequent merger. Consequently, the Court tested whether the boot payment had the effect of a dividend distribution by comparing the interest the taxpayer actually received in the acquiring corporation with the interest the taxpayer would have had if solely stock in the acquiring corporation had been received in the reorganization exchange.

Prior to the decision in *Clark*, the Service considered the facts and issue presented in this revenue ruling in Rev. Rul. 74-516, 1974-2 C.B. 121. The determination of whether the exchange of Distributing stock for Controlled stock and boot under section 355 of the Code had the effect of a dividend distribution under section 356(a)(2) was made by comparing A's interest in Distributing prior to the exchange with the interest A would have retained if A had not received Controlled stock and had only surrendered the Distributing stock equal in value to the boot. The Court's decision in *Clark* does not change the conclusion in Rev. Rul. 74-516, because, like *Clark*, the ruling determined whether the exchange in question had the effect of a dividend distribution based on an analysis of the overall transaction.

The exchange of A's Distributing stock for stock of Controlled qualifies for non-recognition treatment under section 355 of the Code in part because the overall effect of the exchange is an adjustment of A's continuing interest in Distributing in a modified corporate form. *See* section 1.355-2(c) of the Income Tax Regulations. The Controlled stock received by A represents a continuing interest in a portion of Distributing's assets that were formerly held by A as an indirect equity interest. The boot payment has reduced A's proportionate interest in the overall corporate enterprise that includes both Distributing and Controlled. Thus, the boot is treated as received in redemption of A's Distributing stock, and A's interest in Distributing immediately before the exchange is compared to the interest A would have retained if A had surrendered only the Distributing shares equal in value to the boot.

Under the facts presented here, before the exchange, A owned 400 of the 1,000 shares, or 40 percent, of the outstanding Distributing stock. If A had surrendered only the 200 shares for which A received boot, A would still hold 200 of the 800 shares, or 25 percent, of the Distributing stock outstanding after the exchange. This 25 percent stock interest would represent 62.5 percent of A's pre-exchange stock interest in Distributing. Therefore, the deemed redemption would be treated as an exchange because it qualifies as substantially disproportionate under section 302(b)(2) of the Code.

Holding

In an exchange of stock that otherwise qualifies under section 355 of the Code, whether the payment of boot is treated as a dividend distribution under section 356(a)(2) is determined prior to the exchange. This determination is made by treating the recipient shareholder as if the shareholder had retained the distributing corporation stock actually exchanged for controlled corporation stock and received the boot in exchange for distributing corporation stock equal in value to the boot.

NOTE

Boot always takes a fair market value basis and its holding period will begin on the date of the exchange. § 358(a)(2). The presence of boot does not affect the favorable tax treatment of qualifying stock and securities received in the transaction.

PROBLEM 20-4

X Corp.'s stock is owned equally by two shareholders A and B and has two lines of business, Hardware worth $1300 and Pizza worth $700. X Corp. has ample earnings and profits. Due to management disagreements, A and B decide to split X Corp. up into two corporations. In a valid split-up under §§ 368(a)(1)(D) and 355, X Corp. first forms Y Corp. and transfers to it the Pizza division, and then in exchange for all of A's stock in X Corp., it distributes all the Y Corp. stock to A. As part of the transaction, X Corp. also distributes $300 cash to A as an equalization payment. What is the tax result to A from receipt of the $300 boot?

D. TAX TREATMENT OF DISTRIBUTING CORPORATION

The outcome is the same no matter whether the distribution is a simple § 355 transaction involving a preexisting subsidiary which is "old and cold," or the distribution is part of a type D reorganization in which the assets of a line of business are first incorporated into a controlled subsidiary. In both cases the distributing corporation recognizes no gain or loss on the distribution of subsidiary stock or subsidiary obligations (known as "qualified property") to its shareholders. §§ 361(c)(1), 355(c)(1). In both cases the distributing corporation will recognize a gain if it distributes appreciated boot but will not be entitled to recognize any loss. §§ 361(c)(2), 355(c)(2).

In 1990 Congress added § 355(d), pursuant to which the distributing corporation must recognize gain on the distribution of certain "disqualified stock."[7] The reason for the change was a congressional belief that the following kind of transaction was running rampant.

> *To illustrate*: A group of corporate raiders recently bought 55% of the stock of Creaky Co., which owns a silver mine that the raiders think to be worth $1.5 million. The purchase price of the 55% interest in Creaky was only $1 million. The basis of the mine is only $100,000, and it has been in Creaky's hands for over fifty years. To get rid of the raiders, Creaky incorporates the mine into Mines, Inc., distributes its stock to the raiders, and in exchange the raiders hand back their Creaky stock. The raiders claim that the exchange is a tax-free split-off under § 355 and assign a $1 million basis to the Mines, Inc. stock. The raiders sell the Mines, Inc. stock to another party for $1.5 million and report a $500,000 long-term capital gain when the combined holding periods of the Creaky and Mines, Inc. stock exceeds one year. The transaction resembles an outright sale of a newly formed mining subsidiary but with no corporate level tax paid by the seller.
>
> In the terminology of the Code, the distributing corporation — Creaky Co. — is subject to taxes on its "disqualified distributions" of stock or securities of the Mines, Inc. subsidiary. § 355(d)(1).

Impact on Tax Attributes

The distributing corporation in a § 355 transaction which is part of a qualifying D reorganization divides its earnings and profits between itself and the controlled corporation in proportion to relative fair market value of the assets that each holds after the distribution. Reg. § 1.312-10(a). In the case of a stand-alone § 355 distribution, the adjustment may be smaller. Reg. § 1.312-10(b). However, the distributing corporation retains all its other tax attributes such as net operating losses and does not share them with the controlled corporation. Note that in a split-up the distributing corporation is liquidated and its tax attributes disappear entirely.

E. DISTRIBUTIONS IN CONNECTION WITH TAXABLE DIVISIONS

There is some irony in this subject. It is clear that a spin-off that falls outside § 355 will constitute a distribution of property under § 301 with the result that

---

[7] The distributee shareholders do not recognize any gain as long as the remaining requirements of § 355 are satisfied.

there can be a tax to the distributing corporation under § 311(b) and a dividend to the recipient under § 301.

A nonqualifying split-off should be treated as a redemption of the stock of the distributing corporation which is taxable to the distributing corporation under § 311(b) and to the shareholders under § 302. This would force one to consult § 302 in order to determine whether the distribution qualifies as an exchange or as a distribution under § 301.

A nonqualifying split-up, however, looks like a complete liquidation under §§ 331(a) and 336, which means that although the liquidating corporation would owe a *General Utilities* tax, the shareholders would be in the luxurious position of reporting capital gains or losses to the extent that the value of what they receive exceeds the basis of their stock in the distributing corporation that they surrender. A nonqualifying split-up ought to be taxed as a regular liquidation under § 331 even if the subsidiaries were recently formed.[8]

---

[8] For a skeptical analysis, see B. Bittker & J. Eustice, Federal Income Taxation of Corporations and Shareholders ¶ 11.15[3] (6th Ed. 1994).

Chapter 21
CORPORATE REORGANIZATIONS

A. INTRODUCTION

The corporate reorganization rules are an exception to the general rule that realized gains and losses from exchanges of stock for stock as assets must be recognized. The corporate reorganization provisions — §§ 354-368 — carve out a major exception for transactions involving corporate stock or corporate property, provided the transactions fit into one of several highly particularized molds dictated by the Code, all of which are determined at the corporate level. An individual shareholder cannot make a tax-free exchange of stock in one corporation for stock of another unless the transaction qualifies at the corporate level as a reorganization. The operative nonrecognition rules keyed to § 368's definitional rules transform what would be taxable acquisitions (Chapter 19 above) (and divisions) into nontaxable ones.

The tax policy assumption underlying these non-recognition provisions appears in Reg. § 1.1002-1(c), namely that the tax-free exchange provisions apply in cases where "the new property is substantially a continuation of the old investment, still unliquidated; and, in the case of reorganizations that the new enterprise, the new corporate structure and the new property are substantially continuations of the old still unliquidated." This is consistent with other tax-deferral provisions in the Code that depend on the fundamental assumption that the taxpayer's investment has not been cashed out. The reorganization provisions grant tax deferral by requiring the unrealized gains and losses to remain embedded in the taxpayer's property for future taxation. To do this, various basis rules, particularly in §§ 358 and 362, are employed as correlatives of the nonrecognition rules of §§ 354-57, § 361 and § 1032. As usual, this principle is thwarted in the case of stock held until the taxpayer's death, because at death the stock receives a fair market value basis under § 1014.

The earliest reorganization provisions were enacted as part of the Revenue Act of 1918, in anticipation of the end of World War I and of the need to restructure American industry from its wartime footing to a world at peace. As the Senate Finance Committee put it, the legislation would "negative the assertion of tax in the case of certain purely paper transactions."[1] Under prior law, an exchange which was purely technical could be held taxable, such as where a New Jersey corporation did nothing more than reincorporate itself as a Delaware corporation

---

[1] S. Rep. No. 617, 65th Cong., 3d Sess. 4-5 (1918) (Senate Finance Committee report on § 202(b) of the Revenue Act of 1918).

and issued new Delaware shares to its shareholders in exchange for their old New Jersey shares in the same company. *See Marr v. U.S.*, 268 U.S. 536 (1925).[2]

The legislative history of the 1918 Act provided little guidance as to what the term "reorganization" might mean. As a result, the courts were forced to develop some of the most important doctrines in the area. Subsequent Revenue Acts provided more fine-grained definitions of the term "reorganization" and expanded the kinds of transactions that could qualify, but did not explicitly incorporate these judicial doctrines. Even today the definition of a "reorganization" consists of two elements. One is the mechanical description of various types of qualifying exchanges of stock and assets in § 368 of the Code. The other is three substance-over-form requirements derived from case law which operate independently of the definitions in § 368, namely:

1. The reorganization must have a corporate business purpose;

2. The target company's business must continue to some minimum extent after the reorganization, known as the "continuity of business enterprise" requirement; and

3. The owners of the target company must have a continuing stake in the acquiring company, known as the "continuity of proprietary interest" requirement.

These requirements are still not all in the Code, and were not all included in the Regulations until 1980. *See* Reg. § 1.368-1. Their fundamental purpose is to assure that the reorganization provisions are limited to *bona fide* cases, and above all to prevent "astute tax lawyers" from converting what is in substance a taxable sale into a tax-free reorganization by skillful maneuverings of form. *See, e.g.*, H.R. Rep. No. 179, 68th Cong., 1st Sess. (1924), *reprinted in* 1939-1 C.B. (Pt. 2), 142, 252 and 554, 556.

B. CODE STRUCTURE

Read §§ 368(a)(1), 354(a) and 361(a).

If a transaction meets both the statutory definition of a "reorganization" under § 368(a)(1) and the three judicial requirements discussed above, the transaction will generally be tax-free at both the shareholder and corporate levels. At the shareholder level, § 354 assures that gain or loss will go unrecognized if stock or securities in a corporation that is "a party to a reorganization" (as defined in § 368(b)), is exchanged solely for stock or securities in that same corporation or in another corporation which is a party to the reorganization. This provision protects shareholders and security holders from current taxation. If "boot" property or liabilities are involved, there may be some recognition of gain under

---

[2] Such an exchange would now be tax-free under § 368(a)(1)(F) as a "mere change in identity, form, or place of organization of one corporation."

C. STATUTORY MERGERS AND CONSOLIDATIONS 451

§§ 356-57. The basis rules of §§ 358 and 362 produce deferral, not forgiveness, of recognition. Corporate parties to the reorganization are protected by § 361 and § 1032, which also provides for nonrecognition of gains *or losses* on a corporate exchange of property solely for stock or securities of another corporation that is a party to the reorganization. These provisions are not elective, so that a taxpayer who desires to recognize a loss for tax purposes may discover to his disappointment that the loss is barred because it arose in the context of an unexpected "reorganization." On the other hand, large corporations almost always seek an advance ruling from the IRS to assure the expected tax treatment.

C. STATUTORY MERGERS AND CONSOLIDATIONS

Read § 368(a)(1)(A).

Section 368(a)(1)(A) contemplates two similar kinds of transactions, a statutory merger or a consolidation. A merger arises under specific state statutes pursuant to which one corporation absorbs another corporation and becomes the sole survivor, comprising the assets and liabilities of both. The absorbed corporation goes out of existence. In a merger, under state law the acquiring corporation obtains all the assets and liabilities of the target corporation automatically by operation of law, which greatly diminishes the need for deeds and other transfer documents. A consolidation occurs when two (or more) free-standing corporations combine and become a third corporation. The old corporations disappear but the shareholders and creditors of the disappearing corporations automatically become the shareholders and creditors of the new corporation by operation of state law.

The statutory merger was the first form of reorganization to be explicitly recognized in the Code. It is also the most popular form due to its great flexibility. For example, unlike the other forms of reorganization under § 368(a), it freely allows the use of nonvoting stock or preferred stock of the acquiring corporation as consideration paid to the shareholders of the target, and it is generous in its permission to use money or other "boot" as consideration as well.

Minimum Continuity of Proprietary Interest

The riskiest feature of the Type A reorganization concerns the minimum amount of equity that must be issued in connection with the reorganization. The question presented by this issue is how much of the consideration paid by the acquiring corporation to the shareholders of the target corporation must be in the form of equity of the acquiring corporation? The rule of thumb for practitioners is 50%, and this is derived from the fact that the IRS will not issue a ruling in advance unless this 50% requirement is met. Rev. Proc. 77-37, 1977- 2 C.B. 568. Note that the 50%-rule has nothing to do with percentage ownership of the acquiring corporation or with the relative sizes of the two corporations. A minnow may swallow a whale in a valid A reorganization just as a whale may swallow a minnow.

> *To illustrate*: X Corporation is a target of a takeover by P Corporation by means of a merger under state law. X Corporation is owned by one shareholder, Mr. A. He owns stock with a value of $10.00 and holds $90.00 of X Corporation Bonds. As long as he receives at least $5.00 worth of P Corporation stock in the merger, the continuity of proprietary interest test will be considered met. The size of P is irrelevant, and it does not matter whether A's $5.00 worth of P stock represents .001% of P or 99%. If X had several shareholders the question would be whether *as a group* they received at least $5.00 worth of P Corporation stock. The particular distribution of the P stock among the X Corp. shareholders does not matter and need not be pro rata.

The courts, at least in some older cases, have allowed much lower percentages. In *Miller v. Commissioner*, 84 F.2d 415 (6th Cir. 1936), 25% was held to be sufficient. Any kind of stock of the acquiror (but not warrants or other rights) counts toward continuity of interest, including even nonvoting preferred which has no interest in future growth and is this respect more like debt than equity. In *John A. Nelson Corp. v. Helvering*, 296 U.S. 374 (1935), the Supreme Court decided that continuity of interest was present where the consideration paid for the target's voting common stock consisted of 38% nonvoting preferred stock and 62% cash. At the other end of the spectrum, the highest reported level of continuity that failed to qualify appears to be that in *Kass v. Commissioner*, 60 T.C. 218 (1973), *aff'd* 491 F.2d 749 (3d. Cir. 1974), holding that 16% in the form of voting common stock is not "tantalizingly high."

According to Rev. Proc. 77-37, the continuity of interest requirement applies to the historic shareholders of the target, and therefore sales and redemptions of target stock before the acquisition must be taken into account as well as sales of the acquiror's stock after the acquisition, to determine whether the target's historic shareholders have the required 50% continuity.

G.C.M. 39404
September 4, 1985

....

Issues

1. Does the statutory merger of S into P result in sufficient continuity of interest to constitute a "reorganization" within the meaning of section 368(a)(1)(A) if P owns a 70 percent "old and cold" stock interest in S?

C. STATUTORY MERGERS AND CONSOLIDATIONS

2. If the statutory merger does qualify as an "A" reorganization, does P recognize gain or loss on the transaction?

Facts

....

P, a publicly owned corporation, owns 70 percent of the only class of stock of S corporation. All of the S stock owned by P was purchased in the over-the-counter market more than twenty years ago. The remaining 30 percent of S stock is owned by M corporation. In order to achieve a result that was advantageous to P and M a plan of reorganization was adopted under which S was merged into P in a statutory merger pursuant to state law. Under the plan M received 400x dollars and 100 shares of P stock trading at 1x dollars per share, in a value-for-value exchange, for the S stock held by M. Thereafter, P used the assets of S in its business.

Analysis

The proposed revenue ruling is based on the facts of a private letter ruling considered by this office in G.C. M. 31228, ... (May 14, 1959). Following G.C.M. 31228, the proposed ruling concludes that the upstream merger of a less than 80 percent subsidiary does not qualify as a reorganization. The transaction is viewed instead as a complete liquidation of S in which P recognizes gain or loss pursuant to section 331(a)(1).

I. *The Statutory Merger of S into P Constitutes a Section 368(a)(1)(A) Reorganization.*

  A. *Section 332*

Section 332 provides that no gain or loss will be recognized where an 80 percent subsidiary is liquidated into its parent corporation. The flush language of section 332(b) states that this result will not be affected by the fact that assets are transferred to the taxpayer corporation (parent) in an exchange described in section 361, and by the fact that shares not owned by the taxpayer (parent corporation) are surrendered in an exchange described in section 354. Section 332 overrides the reorganization rules to the extent that the two overlap. *But see Eastern Color Printing Co. v. Commissioner*, 63 T.C. 27 (1974) *acq.*, 1975-1 C.B. 1, and cases cited therein holding that an "F" reorganization that met the provisions of section 332 could nonetheless be excluded from section 381(b)(3); Rev. Rul. 75-561, 1975-2 C.B. 129. This means that a transaction may qualify as a reorganization as to minority shareholders while still being treated as a section 332 liquidation for purposes of the controlling parent. *See* Treas. Reg. §§ 1.332-2(d) and (e), 1.332-5. If the acquiring corporation owns less than 80 per cent of the acquired corporation at the time of the adoption of the plan of merger, section 332 is inapplicable. However, nothing in section 332 or the

Regulations thereunder requires that a transfer of assets from a less than 80 percent subsidiary to be characterized as a liquidation.

In addition, the legislative history of section 332 does not indicate that Congress intended to preclude tax-free treatment in an upstream merger of a less than 80 percent subsidiary into its parent. "[T]he statutory predecessor of section 332 was adopted to encourage the simplification of corporate structures and the elimination of holding companies." Testimony before the Committee on Finance disclosed that there was some uncertainty in the business community as to the tax-free status of a liquidation of a subsidiary into its parent by merger, thus inhibiting desirable corporate restructuring.... It was felt that the clarifying legislation would cure the uncertainty in the area. Nowhere does it appear, however, that Congress intended to limit the scope of the definitions relating to corporate reorganizations, or to foreclose the possibility that an upstream merger could qualify for reorganization treatment.

In summary, the legislative history of the predecessor of section 332 indicates that Congress was aware that the liquidation of a subsidiary into its parent by merger might qualify as a tax-free reorganization under existing law and desired to insure this nonrecognition for 80 percent controlled subsidiaries.

B. *Continuity of Interest*

In view of the above, where the acquiring corporation's interest in the acquired corporation is old and cold and the merger is pursuant to state law, as in the instant case, the question arises whether the merger should be treated as a section 368(a)(1)(A) reorganization, rather than a liquidation to which section 331(a)(1) is applicable. Treas. Reg. § 1.368-1(b) provides that requisite to a reorganization is a continuity of interest in the new corporation on the part of those persons who directly or indirectly were the owners of the enterprise prior to the reorganization. Treas. Reg. § 1.368-2(a)) provides that the term "reorganization" does not embrace the mere purchase by one corporation of the properties of another. These regulations embody a well-developed judicial gloss on the statutory definition of reorganizations, the purpose of which is to exclude from the scope of the reorganization provisions those transactions that are in fact sales....

The court in *Southwest Natural Gas Company* summarized the continuity of interest test as follows:

> While no precise formula has been expressed for determining whether there has been retention of the requisite interest, it seems clear that ... [there must be] a showing: (1) that the transferor corporation or its shareholders retained a substantial proprietary stake in the enterprise represented by a material interest in the affairs of the transferee corporation, and, (2) that such retained interest represents a substantial part of the value of the property transferred. 189 F.2d at 334 (footnote omitted).

The court held that the continuity of interest test was applicable to an "A" reorganization although not specifically mandated by the statute.

C. STATUTORY MERGERS AND CONSOLIDATIONS 455

In G.C.M. 31228, we disagreed with your proposed conclusion and held that the statutory merger of a 66 percent subsidiary into its parent fails to qualify as a section 368(a)(1)(A) reorganization because the transaction does not meet the continuity of interest requirement. Continuity was analyzed by looking solely to the consideration received by the minority shareholders of the subsidiary, and since the parent's stock received by the minority shareholders represented less than 15 percent in value of the stock surrendered by such shareholders, continuity of interest was lacking. The instant cases require reconsideration of that position.

In an upstream merger, the indirect stock interest of the parent in its subsidiary is converted into a direct interest in the subsidiary's assets, assuming the parent's prior stock interest is old and cold, as in the instant case since the parent's original investment remains at the risk of the business.

The historic purpose of the continuity of interest requirement is to distinguish sales from reorganizations. In an upstream merger only the form of the parent's investment has been changed, and is prior equity interest has been intensified and not "cashed out." Although the previous corporate relationship has been terminated, this is not the same as a cash sale of the subsidiary's assets. We believe that denying the existence of continuity of interest under such circumstances misapprehends the purpose of the rule. Additional support for counting the parent's "old and cold" interest may be found in B. Bittker and J. Eustice, Federal Income Taxation of Corporations and Shareholders, P14.12, p. 14-36 (4th ed. 1979), in which the authors comment on the same factual situation as here under consideration: "[I]f the initial steps [previous acquisitions of stock] are 'old and cold' (i.e., separate from the subsequent merger of the acquired into the acquiring corporation), reorganization treatment of the second transaction probably should prevail."...

Including the parent's "old and cold" interest for purposes of measuring continuity is supported by *Kass v. Commissioner*, 60 T.C. 218 (1973), *aff'd without opinion*, 491 F.2d 749 (3rd Cir. 1974). In *Kass*, as part of an integrated transaction TRACK (corporation), which was organized and controlled by a group owning 10.23 percent of the stock of ACRA (corporation), purchased 83.95 percent of ACRA's stock and then merged ACRA into itself. The taxpayer, Kass, was one of the ACRA's stockholders (holding 5.82 percent of ACRA stock) who did not sell their stock to TRACK prior to the merger. Upon the statutory merger of ACRA into TRACK, taxpayer received shares of TRACK in exchange for her shares of ACRA. The Tax Court held that the transaction constituted a taxable liquidation to minority shareholders because the parent's stock was purchased as part of the plan to acquire assets in section a 334(b)(2) liquidation.[3] The court stated:

---

[3] Section 334(b)(1) was the statutory predecessor of § 338, under which a corporate buyer of a controlling stock interest in a target corporation could liquidate the target within two years of the purchase and step up the basis of the target's assets to the price paid for the stock. There was no

In short, where the parent's stock interest is "old and cold," it may contribute to continuity-of-interest. Where the parent's interest is not "old and cold," the sale of shares by the majority of shareholders actually detracts from continuity-of-interest.

In petitioner's case, TRACK's stock in ACRA was acquired as part of an integrated plan to obtain control over ACRA's business. The plan called for, first, the purchase of stock and, second, the subsidiary into parent merger. Accordingly, continuity-of-interest must be measured by looking to all the pre-tender offer stockholders rather than to the parent (TRACK) and the nontendering stockholders only; and by that measure the merger fails and the petitioner must recognize her gain. 60 T.C. at 223 (footnote omitted)....

Published positions of the Service do not resolve whether the continuity of interest requirement is satisfied under the facts of the instant case, because the minority shareholders do not receive a sufficient amount of parent stock....

More recently the Service concluded that the statutory merger of a 79 percent subsidiary into its parent constituted a reorganization under section 368(a)(1)(A) and (a)(2)(C) in Rev. Rul. 58-93, 1958-1 C.B. 188, considered in ... (May 4, 1955). In this ruling X corporation held 79 percent of Y corporation; Y transferred its assets to newly formed Z corporation in exchange for all the stock of Z. Y was then merged into X in a statutory merger. The minority shareholders of Y received X stock in exchange for their Y shares. The transaction was characterized as a merger of Y into X under section 368(a)(1)(A) followed by a transfer of the acquired Y assets to Z pursuant to section 368(a)(2)(C), and the ruling concludes that gain or loss will not be recognized by X, Y, or Z, or the minority shareholders of Y. Because the minority shareholders of Y received only X stock continuity of interest is satisfied under the standard of G.C.M. 31228.

The Regulations under section 332 stated that a transaction may be treated as a liquidation of an 80 percent subsidiary with respect to the parent corporation, and yet be a reorganization with respect to minority shareholders. Treas. Reg. § 1.332-2(d) states:

> If a transaction constitutes a distribution in complete liquidation within the meaning of the Internal Revenue Code of 1954 and satisfies the requirements of section 332, it is not material that it is otherwise described under the local law. If a liquidating corporation distributes all of its property in complete liquidation and if pursuant to the plan for such complete liquidation a corporation owning the specified amount of stock in the liquidating corporation received property constituting amounts distributed in complete liquidation within the meaning of the Code and also receives other property

---

target-level tax because under former § 336 liquidations were taxfree until the 1986 repeal of the General Utilities doctrine. Eds.

C. STATUTORY MERGERS AND CONSOLIDATIONS

attributable to shares not owned by it, the transfer of the property to the recipient corporation shall not be treated, by reason of the receipt of such other property as not being a distribution (or one of a series of distributions) in complete cancellation or redemption of all of the stock of the liquidating corporation within the meaning of section 332, even though for purposes of those provisions relating to corporate reorganizations the amount received by the recipient corporation in excess of its ratable share is regarded as acquired upon the issuance of its stock or securities in a tax-free exchange as described in section 361 and the cancellation or redemption of the stock not owned by the recipient corporation is treated as occurring as a result of a tax-free exchange described in section 354.

Since in a section 332 liquidation by merger no more than twenty percent of the total value of the acquired corporation can be acquired for stock of the acquiring (parent) corporation, it follows that continuity is preserved in this situation by ownership of assets. We do not believe it is reasonable to consider a parent's eighty percent indirect interest to be continuity preserving while treating a lesser percentage indirect interest as not continuity preserving....

II. *Nonrecognition to Parent Corporation*

The Service has argued on at least two occasions that although an upstream merger could qualify as a reorganization, the parent's acquisition is not tax-free, because there is no provision that literally provides nonrecognition treatment to exchanges by a corporation of stock in another corporation for property of such other corporation. In *Rogan v. Starr Piano Company*, 139 F.2d 671 (9th Cir. 1943), *cert. denied*, 322 U.S. 728 (1944), the court accepted this position and rejected the parent's argument that a statutory merger could not be both a reorganization and a liquidation. Thus the court held that although the statutory merger of a wholly-owned subsidiary into its parent constituted a reorganization under section 112(g)(1)(A) of the Revenue Act of 1934, gain should be recognized to the parent as on a distribution in complete liquidation. The predecessors to sections 354(a) and 361(a) were inapplicable since there had been no actual exchange of stock or securities for stock or securities, and no exchange by a corporation of property for stock or securities in another corporation. The court refused to find a constructive exchange of parent stock for subsidiary assets sufficient for purposes of qualifying the acquisition under the predecessor to section 354(a).

The Second Circuit arrived at a contrary result in *Gutbro Holding Company v. Commissioner*, 138 F.2d 16 (2d Cir. 1943). There, a parent and its wholly-owned subsidiary were consolidated under state law, pursuant to a plan providing that upon consolidation, the stock of the parent should represent the stock of the consolidated corporation. The court held that the substance of the transaction was a reorganization, and it did not possess the characteristics of a liquidation. Although acquisition of the subsidiary's assets did not literally fall within the reorganization nonrecognition provisions, the court was willing to view the transaction as constructively involving an exchange within the meaning of the predecessor to section 354(a), since a formal stock-for-stock exchange under these circumstances would have been an "idle act."...

> On reconsideration of this question it is our opinion that, since the [parent] exchanged the stock which it owned in the [subsidiary] for shares of its own stock held by the latter company in pursuance of a plan of reorganization to which reorganization both corporations were parties, the transaction comes within the express language of [the predecessor of section 354(a)(1)] and the profit derived is not recognizable for tax purposes. 29 B.T.A. 905, 909 nonacq., XIII-1 C.B. 32 (1934).

We do not believe the absence of a section 1032 exchange preceding the merger [is the right way to dispose of the *Starr Piano* problem because] [s]uch an exchange is a purely formal transaction, an "idle act" ..., so that to insist upon it as a condition for nonrecognition would serve only to set a trap for the unwary. Moreover, the strict requirement of a stock-for-stock exchange would be contrary to the characterization of the transaction in Rev. Rul. 58-93....

NOTES

1. *Impact on tax attributes.* If this were a taxable liquidation, the subsidiary's tax attributes could disappear, and both corporations would be taxed under §§ 336 and 331. That could be a very high price to pay. Under some circumstances, taxable treatment might be acceptable. For example the subsidiary might have sufficient losses from other sources to offset its own § 336 gain, and the parent may have losses to offset its § 331 gain recognized in the taxable liquidation. By contrast, both a § 332 liquidation and a Type A reorganization result no tax to either corporation and the parent takes over the tax attributes of the target. Take a glance at § 381(a)(1) to confirm this.

2. *The idle act theory.* If you think back to the first stock redemption case you read, *Davis v. Commissioner*, you will recall that the taxpayer failed to engage in proper tax planning and the Supreme Court refused to rescue him on the ground that the statute must be read closely and applied rigorously. In this General Counsel Memorandum the IRS displays some willingness to overlook failures to engage in tax planning. Which is the better view in your opinion?

3. *Downstream mergers.* In G.C.M. 39404 the inquiry involves the merger of a subsidiary into a parent. What about the merger of a parent into a subsidiary company? In *Edwards Motor Transit Co. v. Commissioner*, T.C. Memo 1964-317 (1964), a parent company merged into its subsidiary in a transaction which formally met the requirements of § 368(a)(1)(A). The case does not seem surprising unless you ask yourself whether the practical result is not really a liquidation of the parent company. In *Edwards Motor Transit* the parent was a mere holding company and it is difficult to see what distinguished the transaction from a liquidation other than the fact that it met the technical definition of a

C. STATUTORY MERGERS AND CONSOLIDATIONS

reorganization. On the other hand, reorganization treatment promotes the simplification of corporate structures by eliminating unnecessary layers of corporations on a tax-deferred basis.

4. *Dropdowns.* Section 368(a)(2)(C) allows the acquiring corporation in a Type A, B, or C reorganization to drop down the acquired stock or assets to a corporation which it controls. In Rev. Rul. 64-73, 1964-1 C.B. 142 (in connection with a Type C reorganization) the IRS interpreted "control" as allowing a drop-down to a second-tier or presumably lower-tier corporation as long as the acquiring corporation directly or indirectly controls the lowest-tier subsidiary within the meaning of § 368(c).

5. *"Creeping" mergers.* Any acquisition can be made either in a single transaction or over time by gradual acquisitions of stock followed by a final stock or asset acquisition which resembles a reorganization. It is often difficult to determine whether such creeping acquisitions qualify partly or wholly as reorganizations because of the lack of Congressional attention to them. One of the big problems, already addressed, is whether a stock purchase followed by a liquidation in a state-law merger can constitute a Type A reorganization or whether it is necessarily a taxable purchase combined with a taxable liquidation. An analysis of creeping reorganizations depends primarily on whether each step of the acquisition is respected as a separate transaction or is treated as part of a single "plan" so that all the steps are collapsed into a single transaction. For example, if pursuant to a plan an acquiring company buys all of the stock of a target company for cash and then immediately merges the target subsidiary into itself, it is fairly obvious that there is no "reorganization" because the target shareholders lack any continuing proprietary stake in the continuing former business. By contrast, if the upstream merger takes place after the cash acquisition is "old and cold," the parent corporation has become the historic shareholder and the merger will qualify as an A reorganization. It will not matter whether the initial step is "old and cold" if the consideration paid to the target shareholders contains sufficient continuity of interest (i.e., sufficient stock of the acquiring corporation) because continuity of interest will be present in either case.

6. *What is an equity interest?* Warrants and rights to purchase stock do not carry continuity of interest, nor does debt which is convertible into stock until it is actually converted. However, if the corporation is insolvent, there is authority for the position that the debt holders should be treated as having become de facto the equity shareholders. *See Helvering v. Alabama Asphaltic Limestone Co.*, 315 U.S. 179 (1942).

7. *Accounting treatment of mergers and acquisitions.* The accounting treatment for these transactions is not consistent with the tax results. The accounting analog of a nontaxable corporate restructuring is a *pooling of interests*. The result is that the acquiring company picks up the Target's assets, liabilities and net worth at the same book values as they had on the target's balance sheet and is entitled to report the target's earnings as its own. However, it is hard to achieve a pooling result because, in highly simplified terms it generally requires that:

— At least 90% of the consideration received by Target (T) shareholders is voting common stock of the acquiror (P) (however, no continuity of owners is required so the T shareholders are free to sell their P stock immediately afterwards);
— Before the acquisition P and T must be autonomous entities;
— P and T did not engage in stock redemptions of voting stock spin-offs, or any other changes in capital stock in connection with the P-T plan of combination;
— The consideration paid by T is fixed in amount;
— P will not dispose of T assets or reacquire P stock from T shareholders.

If any requirement is not met, the result is a *purchase*, which results in P taking a cost basis in T's assets and treating the excess of the purchase price over the value of the assets as goodwill to be amortized over forty years. This is generally undesirable, because amortization of goodwill creates an annual financial expense on P's books which reduces P's reported earnings.

McDONALD'S RESTAURANTS OF ILLINOIS, INC. v. COMMISSIONER
688 F.2d 520 (7th Cir. 1982)

CUMMING, CHIEF JUDGE.

....

The pertinent facts as found by the Tax Court and supplemented by the record are not in dispute. In June 1977, when they filed their petitions in the Tax Court to review the deficiency assessments, taxpayers were 27 wholly-owned subsidiaries of McDonald's Corporation, the Delaware corporation that franchises and operated fast-food restaurants. The taxpayers all had their principal places of business in Oak Brook, Illinois. They maintained their books and records on the accrual method and filed their tax returns on a calendar-year basis.

On the opposite end of the transaction at issue here were Melvin Garb, Harold Stern and Lewis Imerman (known collectively as the Garb-Stern group). The group had begun with a single McDonald's franchise in Saginaw, Michigan, in the late 1950's and expanded its holdings to include McDonald's restaurants elsewhere in Michigan and in Oklahoma, Wisconsin, Nevada and California. After 1968 relations between the Garb-Stern group and McDonald's deteriorated. In 1971 McDonald's considered buying some of the group's restaurants in Oklahoma, but abandoned the idea when it became clear that the acquisition could not be treated as a "pooling of interests" for accounting purposes unless all of the Garb-Stern group's restaurants were acquired simultaneously. In November 1972, however, negotiations resumed, McDonald's having decided that total acquisition was necessary to eliminate the Garb-Stern group's friction.

C. STATUTORY MERGERS AND CONSOLIDATIONS 461

The sticking point in the negotiations was that the Garb-Stern group wanted cash for its operations, while McDonald's wanted to acquire the Garb-Stern group's holdings for stock, consistent with its earlier expressed preference for treating the transaction as a "pooling of interests" for accounting purposes. McDonald's proposed a plan to satisfy both sides: it would acquire the Garb-Stern companies for McDonald's common stock, but it would include the common stock in a planned June 1973 registration so that the Garb-Stern group could sell it promptly.

Final agreement was not reached until March 1973. Negotiations then were hectic; for a variety of accounting and securities-law reasons, the acquisition had to be consummated not before and not after April 1, 1973. The final deal was substantially what had been proposed earlier. The Garb-Stern companies would be merged in stages into McDonald's, which would in turn transfer the restaurant assets to the 27 subsidiaries that are the taxpayers here. In return the Garb-Stern group would receive 361,235 shares of unregistered common stock. The agreement provided that the Garb-Stern group could participate in McDonald's planned June 1973 registration and underwriting or in any other registration and underwriting McDonald's might undertake within six years (Art. 7.4); the group also had a one-time right to demand registration in the event that McDonald's did not seek registration within the first year (Art. 7.5). The Garb-Stern group was not obligated by contract to sell its McDonald's stock but fully intended to do so.

After the April 1 closing, both parties proceeded on the assumption that the Garb-Stern group's shares would be included in the June 1973 "piggyback" registration. In mid-June a widely publicized negative report about McDonald's stock caused the price to drop from $60 to $52 a share in two weeks, and McDonald's therefore decided to postpone the registration and sale of additional stock. The Garb-Stern group acquiesced, although it had made no effort to withdraw from the registration before McDonald's decided to cancel it.

Through the rest of the summer, the price of McDonald's stock staged a recovery. In late August McDonald's decided to proceed with the registration, and the Garb-Stern group asked to have its shares included. The registration was announced on September 17 and completed on October 3, 1973. The Garb-Stern group thereupon sold virtually all of the stock it had acquired in the transaction at a price of more that $71 per share.

In its financial statements McDonald's treated the transaction as a "pooling of interests." In its tax returns for 1973, however, it treated it as a purchase. Consistent with that characterization, McDonald's gave itself a stepped-up basis in the assets acquired from the Garb-Stern group to reflect their cost ($29,029,000, representing the value of the common stock transferred and a $1-2 million "nuisance premium" paid to eliminate the Garb-Stern group from the McDonald's organization). It allocated that basis among various Garb-Stern assets, then dropped the restaurant assets to the 27 taxpayer subsidiaries pursuant to Section 351 of the Internal Revenue Code governing transfers to corporations controlled by the transferor. The subsidiaries used the stepped-up basis allocable to them to compute depreciation and amortization deductions in their own 1973 tax returns.

It is those deductions by the subsidiary taxpayers that the Commissioner reduced. He ruled that the transfer of the Garb-Stern group's assets to McDonald's was not a taxable acquisition but a statutory merger or consolidation under Section 368(a)(1)(A) of the Code, and that under Section 362(b) McDonald's was required to assume the Garb-Stern group's basis in the assets acquired. In turn, the subsidiaries were required to compute depreciation and amortization deductions on this lower, carryover basis. With properly computed deductions the subsidiary taxpayers owed an additional $566,403 in 1973 income taxes. the Tax Court upheld the Commissioner's deficiency assessments, and this appeal is the result.

The Code distinguishes between taxable acquisitions and nontaxable (or more accurately tax-deferrable) acquisitive reorganizations under Sections 368(a)(1)(A)-(C) and 354(a)(1) for the following common-sense reason: If acquired shareholders exchange stock in the acquired company for stock in the acquiring company, they have simply readjusted the form of their equity holdings. They have continued an investment rather than liquidating one, and the response of the tax system is to adjust their basis to reflect the transaction but postpone tax liability until they have more tangible gain or loss.

To ensure that the tax treatment of acquisitive reorganizations corresponds to the rationale that justifies it, the courts have engrafted a "continuity of interest" requirement onto the Code's provisions. *See, e.g., Helvering v. Alabama Asphaltic Limestone Co.*, 315 U.S. 179, 86 L. Ed. 775, 62 S. Ct. 540; *LeTulle v. Scofield*, 308 U.S. 415, 84 L. Ed. 335, 60 S. Ct. 313. That test examines the acquired shareholders' proprietary interest before and after the reorganization to see if "the acquired shareholders' investment remains sufficiently 'at risk' after the merger to justify the nonrecognition tax treatment," 76 T.C. at 997.

The taxpayers, the Commissioner, and the Tax Court all agree that the Garb-Stern group holdings were acquired by statutory merger. They also all agree that the "continuity of interest" test is determinative of the tax treatment of the transaction of which the statutory merger was a part. But the taxpayers on the one hand, and the Commissioner and the Tax Court on the other, part company over how the test is to be applied, and what result it should have produced. In affirming the Commissioner, the Tax Court recognized that the Garb-Stern group had a settled and firm determination to sell their McDonald's shares at the first possible opportunity rather than continue as investors, 76 T.C. at 989. It nonetheless concluded that because the Garb-Stern group was not contractually bound to sell, the merger and the sale could be treated as entirely separate transactions and the continuity-of-interest test applied in the narrow time-frame of the April transaction only. Thus tested, the transaction was in Judge Hall's view a nontaxable reorganization, and the taxpayer subsidiaries were therefore saddled with the Garb-Stern group's basis in taking depreciation and amortization deductions. The taxpayers by contrast argue that the step-transaction doctrine

C. STATUTORY MERGERS AND CONSOLIDATIONS

should have been applied to treat the April merger and stock transfer and the October sale as one taxable transaction. They also argue that the Tax Court's extremely narrow view of both the step-transaction doctrine and the continuity-of-interest test in this case is not consonant with appellate court case law, the Tax Court's own precedents, or the Service's practice hitherto. We agree with the taxpayers.

The Step-Transaction Doctrine

The step-transaction doctrine is a particular manifestation of the more general tax law principle that purely formal distinctions cannot obscure the substance of a transaction. *See e.g., Redding v. Commissioner*, 630 F.2d 1169, 1175 (7th Cir. 1980). As our Court there noted: The commentators have attempted to synthesize from judicial decisions several tests to determine whether the step-transaction doctrine is applicable to a particular set of circumstances.... Unfortunately, these tests are notably abstruse — even for such an abstruse field as tax law.

Nonetheless, under any of the tests devised — including the intermediate one nominally adopted by the Tax Court and the most restrictive one actually applied in its decision — the transactions here would be stepped together. For example, under the "end result test," "purportedly separate transactions will be amalgamated with a single transaction when it appears that they were really component parts of a single transaction intended from the outset to be taken for the purpose of reaching the ultimate result." 76 T.C. at 994, *citing King Enterprises, Inc. v. United States*, 418 F.2d 511, 516 (Ct. Cl. 1969) and referring to *Redding, supra*, 630 F.2d at 1175. Here there can be little doubt that all the steps were taken to cash out the Garb-Stern group, although McDonald's sought to do so in a way that would enable it to use certain accounting procedures. Admittedly, not every transaction would be as pellucid as this one, but here the history of the parties' relationships, the abortive attempt to buy some of the group's holding, the final comprehensive deal, and the Garb-Stern group's determination to sell out even in the face of falling prices in the stock all are consistent and probative.

A second test is the "interdependence" test, which focuses on whether "the steps are so interdependent that the legal relations created by one transaction would have been fruitless without a completion of the series." *Redding, supra*, at 1177, *quoting with approval* Paul, Selected Studies in Federal Taxation (2d Series 1938) 200, 254. This is the test the Tax Court purported to apply, 76 T.C. at 997-999, although its version of the test is indistinguishable from yet another formulation, the "binding commitment" test. That is, the Tax Court would have found interdependence only if the Garb-Stern group had itself been legally bound to sell its stock. In fact, the "interdependence" test is more practical and less legalistic than that. It concentrates on the relationship between the steps, rather than on the "end result" (*cf.* p. 524 *supra*). Here it would ask whether the merger would have taken place without the guarantees of saleability, and the answer is certainly no. The Garb-Stern group's insistence on this point is demonstrated both by its historic stance in these negotiations and by the hammered-out terms of the agreement. Although the Tax Court emphasized the permissive terms about "piggyback" registration, it glossed over the Garb-Stern group's one time right to force registration — and hence sale — under the agreement. The very detail of the provisions about how McDonald's would ensure free transferability of the Garb-Stern group's McDonald's stock shows that they were the quid pro quo of the merger agreement.

Finally, the "binding commitment" test most restricts the application of the step-transaction doctrine, and is the test the Tax Court actually applied despite its statements otherwise. The "binding commitment" test forbids use of the step-transaction doctrine unless "if one transaction is to be characterized as a 'first step' there [is] a binding commitment to take the later steps." *Redding, supra*, at 1178 *quoting Commissioner v. Gordon*, 391 U.S. 83, 96, 20 L. Ed. 2d 448, 88 S. Ct. 1517. The Tax Court found the test unsatisfied because the Garb-Stern group was not legally obliged to sell its McDonald's stock. We think it misconceived the purpose of the test and misapplied it to the facts of this case.

In the first place, the "binding commitment" test is the most rigorous limitation on the step-transaction doctrine because it was formulated to deal with the characterization of a transaction that in fact spanned several tax years and could have remained "not only indeterminable but unfixed for an indefinite and unlimited period in the future, awaiting events that might or might not happen." *Gordon, supra*, 391 U.S. at 96. By contrast this transaction was complete in six months and fell entirely within a single tax year. The degree of uncertainty that worried the Gordon court is absent here, and a strong antidote for uncertainty is accordingly not needed.

In the second place, the Tax Court underestimated the extent to which the parties were bound to take the later steps. The registration and underwriting provisions in the parties' agreement did not just enhance salability; they were essential to it. Unless and until McDonald's registered the stock, it was essentially untransferable. 76 T.C. at 981-982. Second, although McDonald's had the choice of when during the first year after the merger it would seek registration, if it did nothing the Garb-Stern group could make a legally enforceable demand for registration in either year two or year three. On the other hand, if McDonald's did register stock during the first year but the Garb-Stern group chose not to "piggyback," the group's demand registration rights would be lost. These limitations made it extremely likely that the sale would — as it did — take place promptly. They are enough to satisfy the spirit, if not the letter, of the "binding commitment" test.

Under any of the three applicable criteria, then, the merger and subsequent sale should have been stepped together. Substance over form is the key (*Kuper v. Commissioner*, 533 F.2d 152, 155 (5th Cir. 1976)). Had the Tax Court taken a pragmatic view of the actions of the Garb-Stern group, it would have found that they clearly failed to satisfy the continuity-of-interest requirement that has been engrafted onto the Code provisions governing nonrecognition treatment for acquisitive reorganizations.

Statutory Merger Precedents

Quite apart from the proper application of the step-transaction doctrine, the available precedents dealing with statutory mergers — though scanty — strongly support the taxpayers. No case supports the myopic position adopted below that although "the crux of the continuity-of-interest test lies in the continuation of the acquired shareholders' proprietary interest" (76 T.C. at 997), the test "by itself does not require any length of post merger retention" (*id.*)....

The taxpayers rely on, and the Tax Court was unsuccessful in distinguishing, *Heintz v. Commissioner*, 25 T.C. 132 (1955). The *Heintz* case differs from this case only in focusing on the tax liability of the acquired shareholder rather than the acquiring corporation[4]....

As in the present case, the taxpayers' wishes to sell were clear and the transaction was designed to accommodate them. As in the present case, the acquiring corporation's promise was to facilitate the sale, not to guarantee it. As in the present case, the acquiring corporation did not require a reciprocal commitment from the acquired shareholders — for all that appears, Heintz and Jack were free to retain their equity interest in Precision. As in the present case, these understandings of the parties were not reflected in the written agreement. There is no principled way to distinguish the two cases, and the Tax Court's efforts to do so here (76 T.C. at 1001) are unsuccessful....

Additional Considerations

Part of the reason that there is so little litigation about statutory mergers and the effect of post-merger events on tax treatment is that people involved in nontaxable reorganizations usually seek advice in the form of private letter rulings beforehand. *See* McDonald Br. 25-27; *cf. also* Bittker & Eustice Federal Income Taxation of Corporations and Shareholders (4th Ed. 1979) P14.01 at 14-7-8 ("Rarely do the participants deliberately invite a test of strength in the courts, even if they feel a good deal of confidence in the outcome. As a result, the Service can make 'law' in this area by a lifted eyebrow.")

The Commissioner's usual position in this context is not the one adopted by the Tax Court, namely, that the intent of the acquired shareholders is irrelevant and no period of post-merger retention is required. 76 T.C. at 990, 992, 997. *See*, for example, Rev. Proc. 77-37, 1977-2 C.B. 568, 569:

> The "continuity of interest" requirement of section 1.368-1(b) of the Income Tax Regulations is satisfied if there is a continuing interest through stock ownership in the acquiring or transferee corporation (or a corporation

---

[4][The *Heintz* decision found the transactions, which were similar to the present case, taxable. Eds.]

in "control" thereof within the meaning of section 368(c) of the Code) on the part of the former shareholders of the acquired or transferor corporation which is equal in value, as of the effective date of the reorganization, to at last 50 percent of the value of all of the formerly outstanding stock of the acquired or transferor corporation as of the same date.... Sales redemptions, and other dispositions of stock occurring prior or subsequent to the exchange which are part of the plan of reorganization will be considered in determining whether there is a 50 percent continuing interest through stock ownership as of the effective date of the reorganization....

... Moreover, the Commissioner usually does not limit his scrutiny to explicit contemporaneous commitments to sell out. Rev. Rul. 77-479, 1977-2 C.B. 119; Rev. Rul. 66-23, 1966-1 C.B. 67. In fact, taxpayers who seek a ruling in advance of the reorganization must represent that there is "no plan or intention on the part of the Acquired shareholders to [reduce their new holdings] to a number of shares having, in the aggregate a value of less than 50 percent of the total value of the Acquired stock outstanding immediately prior to the proposed transaction." McDonald Br. ....

Against this background, the Commissioner's treatment of the McDonald's transaction — as affirmed by the Tax Court — seems opportunistic. The agency's practice, described above, suggests that if McDonald's had laid its plan before the Internal Revenue Service ahead of time, it would not have been deemed a nontaxable reorganization. Furthermore the Garb-Stern group has already been fully taxed because of its relatively prompt disposition; the Internal Revenue Service has had all the benefits of sale treatment on that end of the transaction. *See* Prusiecki, *Continuity of Interest in Tax-free Mergers: New Opportunities After McDonald's of Zion*, 55 J. Tax. 378, 380 (1981). Now the Service seeks to saddle the taxpayers with the disadvantageously low basis that goes with the "reorganization" label. On the other hand, as the taxpayers note (Reply Br. 14) if the Garb-Stern group's basis had been higher than the fair market price of the McDonald's shares exchanged, the Commissioner could, consistently with his prior positions, have refused reorganization status and forced the taxpayers to accept a lower cost basis for depreciation and amortization purposes. This is heads-I-win, tails-you-lose law.

If, on the other hand, the treatment here represents a considered change in the Service's treatment of reorganizations, then the Commission's victory in the Tax Court was Pyrrhic and he should welcome reversal. The Tax Court's decision was barely six months old before tax planners were publicizing the possibilities for manipulating it. Prusiecki, op. cit., at 380-381, notes nine new types of tax avoidance that the case opens up, all taking advantage of the new-found ability to obtain reorganization status without constraining post-merger sales. The key to all of them is the extraordinary rigidity of the "binding commitment" test and the ephemeral continuity of interest the Tax Court seems to require.

C. STATUTORY MERGERS AND CONSOLIDATIONS

The decisions appealed from are reversed, with instructions to enter fresh decisions in the taxpayers' favor.

NOTES

1. *The stakes.* Just exactly what were the stakes to the shareholders in the case?

2. *Applying the step-transaction doctrine.* The *McDonald's* discussion of the step-transaction doctrine is explicit about the fact that there are three alternative definitions. Not every court has been so forthright. The difficulty in this area is that if the court has prejudged the case, it can simply choose whichever formulation of the step-transaction doctrine fits the desired outcome and decide the case according to an apparently neutral principle of law. Does the *McDonald's* case mean that if any one of the formulations applies the transactions must be combined? Should the courts have discretion to decide which formulation to use? Is this an area in which it would be best for Congress to intervene with one formulation?

3. *The step-transaction doctrine as a taxpayer's sword.* In *King Enters. v. United States*, 418 F.2d 511 (Ct. Cl. 1969), the acquiring corporation paid cash for approximately 49% of target company's stock and its own stock for the balance, and in a later but prearranged second step then merged the newly-acquired subsidiary into itself. The upstream merger was held a Type A reorganization and the initial acquisition was held to be part of the same transaction so that the target shareholders were entitled to reorganization treatment on the exchange of stock (the cash was taxable boot). The target shareholders employed the step-transaction doctrine to salvage a potentially taxable stock acquisition (a failed "B" reorganization) and turned it into a nontaxable "A" reorganization.[5]

ESTATE OF MOSE SILVERMAN v. COMMISSIONER
98 T.C. 54 (1992)

RUWE, JUDGE:

....

[In 1982, pursuant to a plan of merger the taxpayers exchanged their shares of stock in a State-chartered stock S&L for passbook savings accounts and

---

[5] In a wonderful example of whipsaw, the acquiring corporation obtained a step-up in the basis of the target's assets because it was protected by a private letter ruling which guaranteed (former) § 334(b)(2) treatment of the transaction as a purchase of assets. Thus the two sides of the transaction were given inconsistent treatment and each side got the best of both worlds: it was a *taxable* transaction on the buyer's side (before *General Utilities* repeal, so without tax to the target corporation), but a *tax-free reorganization* to the sellers. To top it all off, the sellers were corporations, and the boot was treated as a dividend qualifying for the § 243 dividends received deduction!

certificates of deposit in the acquiring federally chartered mutual S&L. No part of the principal of the certificates of deposit could be withdrawn for 6 years. The taxpayer treated the gain realized on the transaction as the nontaxable proceeds of a § 368(a)(1)(A) reorganization. In 1985, the U.S. Supreme Court decided *Paulsen v. Commissioner*, 469 U.S. 131 (1985), holding that exchanges of this type did not qualify as tax-free reorganizations, so the taxpayers filed an amended federal income tax return for 1982, treating the exchange as an installment sale. They paid taxes on the gain attributable to passbook savings accounts received, but treated the certificates of deposit as delayed payment obligations. The IRS claimed the transaction did not qualify for installment sale treatment.]

Opinion

Respondent contends that Mr. and Mrs. Silverman were required to include the entire gain on disposition of their Olympic stock in their 1982 income. Petitioners concede that the exchange is not entitled to treatment as a tax-free reorganization. They argue, however, that the gain on the exchange may be reported on the installment method. We must decide whether the Silvermans were entitled to report the exchange under the installment method.

Section 1001(a) provides that the gain from the sale of property[6] shall be the excess of the amount realized therefrom over the adjusted basis. Amount realized is defined as the sum of any money received plus the fair market value of property (other than money) received. Sec. 1001(b). All gain realized under section 1001 must be recognized absent a statutory exception. Sec. 1001(c).

Section 453 provides such an exception. It allows income from an installment sale to be reported in the year "payment" is received. The amount of income to be recognized for any taxable year is the "proportion of the payments received in that year which the gross profit (realized or to be realized when payment is completed) bears to the total contract price." Sec. 453(c).

An "installment sale" is defined as "a disposition of property where at least 1 payment is to be received after the close of the taxable year in which the disposition occurs." Sec. 453(b)(1). Generally, and for purposes of this case, the term "'payment' does not include the receipt of evidences of indebtedness of the person acquiring the property." Sec. 453(f)(3).

Mr. and Mrs. Silverman disposed of property (Olympic stock) to Coast [the acquiring S&L]. Coast was thus "the person acquiring the property." In return, the Silvermans received withdrawable statement savings accounts and term accounts that could not be withdrawn for 6 years. If the Coast term accounts which Mr. and Mrs. Silverman received in the exchange are "evidences of indebtedness of the person acquiring the property," then Mr. and Mrs.

---

[6] There is no question that the term accounts in the instant case constitute property within the meaning of § 1001.

C. STATUTORY MERGERS AND CONSOLIDATIONS

Silverman's receipt of the term accounts would not constitute "payment" for purposes of section 453, and they would therefore be entitled to report the disposition of their Olympic stock on the installment method.

Whether certificates of deposit are "evidences of indebtedness" of the issuing savings and loan association was answered by the Supreme Court in *Paulsen v. Commissioner*, 469 U.S. 131 (1985). In that case, involving practically identical facts, the Court was called upon to determine whether a transaction wherein the taxpayer received savings accounts and certificates of deposit from a federally chartered mutual savings and loan association in exchange for stock in a State-chartered savings and loan association, qualified as a tax-free reorganization under sections 354(a)(1) and 368(a)(1)(A). One requirement for such a tax-free exchange was that the taxpayer's ownership in the prior organization must continue in a meaningful fashion in the reorganized enterprise, i.e., "the seller must acquire an interest in the affairs of the purchasing company more definite than that incident to ownership of its short-term purchase-money notes." *Pinellas Ice & Cold Storage Co. v. Commissioner*, 287 U.S. 462, 470 (1933); *Paulsen v. Commissioner*, 469 U.S. at 136. In *Paulsen*, the Court recognized that the certificates of deposit had both "equity and debt characteristics," *Paulsen*, 469 U.S. at 138, but found that the debt characteristics predominated, and that the equity characteristics were insubstantial.

> "There are substantial debt characteristics to the Citizens shares that predominate. Petitioners' passbook accounts and certificates of deposit are not subordinated to the claims of creditors, and their deposits are not considered permanent contributions to capital. Shareholders have a right on 30 days' notice to withdraw their deposits, which right Citizens is obligated to respect. While petitioners were unable to withdraw their funds for one year following the merger, this restriction can be viewed as akin to a delayed payment rather than a material alteration in the nature of the instruments received as payment....
>
> In our view, the debt characteristics of Citizens' shares greatly outweigh the equity characteristics. The face value of petitioners' passbook accounts and certificates of deposit was $210,000. Petitioners have stipulated that they had a right to withdraw the face amount of the deposits in cash, on demand after one year or at stated intervals thereafter. Their investment was virtually risk free and the dividends received were equivalent to prevailing interest rates for savings accounts in other types of savings institutions. The debt value of the shares was the same as the face value, $210,000; because no one would pay more than this for the shares, the incremental value attributable to the equity features was, practically, zero...."

We perceive no meaningful distinction between the certificates of deposit in *Paulsen* and those involved here. The certificates of deposit received by Mr. and Mrs. Silverman represent "evidences of indebtedness" of the person acquiring their property. Petitioners meet all of the literal statutory requirements of section 453 so as to entitle them to report income from the disposition of Olympic stock using the installment method.

Respondent argues that the term accounts are "cash equivalents" and therefore must be included in income in the year of sale. Respondent points out that the Court in *Paulsen* characterized the accounts as cash equivalents....

Petitioners do not dispute that gain was realized in 1982. Such realized gain under section 1001 must be recognized absent a statutory exception, but, as previously pointed out, section 453 provides such an exception. A finding that a transaction may be reported under section 453 assumes there has been a realization event and makes any further consideration of the cash equivalence doctrine redundant. *See Warren Jones Co. v. Commissioner*, 68 T.C. 837 (1977), *affd.* 617 F.2d 536 (9th Cir. 1980). Thus, despite the inclusion of the value of the buyer's obligation in the amount realized under section 1001(b), a taxpayer is entitled to report gain from the transaction under the installment method. *Warren Jones Co. v. Commissioner*, 524 F.2d 788 (9th Cir. 1975)....

The legislative history of section 453 indicates that Congress believed that the cash equivalence characteristics of certain types of debt instruments made it inappropriate to allow them to be reported under the installment method. As a result, it enacted specific provisions to preclude certain debt instruments from being reported under the installment method. *See* S. Rept. 91-552 (1969), 1969-3 C.B. 423, 515. These provisions, section 453(f)(4) and (5), first became part of the installment sale section in 1969 as paragraph 453(b)(3). These paragraphs provide:

> "(3) Payment. — Except as provided in paragraph (4), the term "payment" does not include the receipt of evidences of indebtedness of the person acquiring the property (whether or not payment of such indebtedness is guaranteed by another person).
>
> (4) Purchaser evidences of indebtedness payable on demand or readily tradable. — Receipt of a bond or other evidence of indebtedness which
>
> (A) is payable on demand, or
>
> (B) is issued by a corporation or a government or political subdivision thereof and is readily tradable, shall be treated as receipt of payment.
>
> (5) Readily tradable defined. — For purposes of paragraph (4), the term "readily tradable" means a bond or other evidence of indebtedness which is issued —
>
> (A) with interest coupons attached or in registered form (other than one in registered form which the taxpayer establishes will not be readily tradable in an established securities market), or

C. STATUTORY MERGERS AND CONSOLIDATIONS 471

(B) in any other form designed to render such bond or other evidence of indebtedness readily tradable in an established securities market."

These provisions were a Congressional response to the increasing number of acquisitive corporate reorganizations in which shareholders received corporate debentures for shares. Such an exchange was not exempt from taxation under the sections of the Code governing reorganizations, but tax deferral could otherwise be secured under section 453.

The Senate Finance Committee report stated:

> "Debentures, however, in most cases can be readily traded on the market and therefore are a close approximation of cash. Thus, the problem of the seller not having the cash with which to pay the tax due would not appear to be present where he receives debentures or other readily marketable securities. [S. Rept. 91-552 (1969), 1969-3 C.B. 423, 515.] Consequently, Congress directed that certain types of indebtedness be treated as payment received in the year of sale." S. Rept. 91-552 at 516.

The type of indebtedness to be treated in this manner are bonds or debentures with interest coupons attached, in registered form, or in any other form designed to make it possible to readily trade them in an established securities market.... [S. Rept. 91-552 at 516.]

However, the report goes on to state that:

> "The committee amendments also provide that bonds in registered form which the taxpayer establishes will not be readily tradeable [sic] in an established securities market are not to be treated as payments received in the year of sale, since because of their lack of ready marketability they do not possess the characteristics which would render them essentially similar to cash." [S. Rept. 91-552 at 516.]

Therefore, while Congress has created an exception to installment reporting based on the cash equivalence characteristics of certain obligations, it specifically enumerated the type of debt obligations which fell within the exception. We conclude that cash equivalence is not an exception to the installment method except as specifically provided in the statute. The term accounts in issue in this case were not readily tradable in an established securities market, and, thus, were not within the aforementioned statutory exception.

During 1982, the Silvermans never possessed the right to receive payment of the amounts represented by the term accounts. The term accounts were not withdrawable until 1988, were not readily tradable in an established securities market, and were not assignable except upon the death of a joint owner, in which case title could only be vested in the decedent's personal representative or the surviving joint owner. The passbooks evidencing the accounts stated on their face that transferability was limited. In short, it is difficult to see how the Silvermans received the economic benefits of payment when the term accounts could not be withdrawn, sold, or borrowed against during the year in issue....

Decision will be entered for petitioners.

NOTE

Installment sale treatment in a valid reorganization. Silverman involved a fully taxable merger (not a § 368(a)(1) "reorganization" for tax purposes). What if the transaction were a "reorganization" and the target company shareholder got paid "boot" in the form of an installment obligation payable over time? The answer is that as long as the obligation is taxed as a gain (and not as a dividend), the boot can be reported under § 453. This means that the shareholder is assured of being able to match his tax bill with his cash proceeds, which is the purpose of § 453.

D. TYPE B REORGANIZATIONS

Read § 368(a)(1)(B).

A Type B reorganization, as defined in § 368(a)(1)(B), is an acquisition by one corporation, in exchange solely for its voting stock (or stock of its parent) of stock of another corporation, if the requiror thereafter has "control" of the acquired corporation. It is a stock-for-stock exchange, but only if the requiror is a corporation.

The Type B reorganization is fairly uncommon. It is most frequently seen in the form of the so-called tender offers in which an acquiring company publicly invites the shareholders of a target company to tender (deliver) their stock to a particular institutional agent by a certain deadline. If the shareholders of the target company acquiesce by mailing in their certificates in a sufficient volume, the deal closes, and they receive stock of the acquiring company. If they do not tender enough stock, the offer is typically terminated, and the tendered shares are returned to the target company shareholders who responded to the offer. The acquiring company may use common or preferred stock, but it must be voting stock and cannot, for example include warrants or stock options. *See Helvering v. Southwest Consol. Corp.*, 315 U.S. 194 (1942).

The most formidable difficulty with using a B reorganization is that no boot of any kind may be paid to the target shareholders directly or indirectly to acquire their shares. The acquisition must be made "solely" for voting stock of the acquiring corporation (or its controlling parent). There is plenty of room here for disastrous accidents, especially when all transactions which precede and follow the acquisition of control are considered together.

D. TYPE B REORGANIZATIONS

NOTES

1. *Cash payments that can be made without destroying a Type B reorganization.* The acquiring company can pay cash for a target company shareholders' fractional shares. Rev. Rul. 55-59, 1955-1 C.B. 35. For example, if the acquiring company stock were worth only $10.00 a share and it had to acquire the stock of a particular shareholder who held only one share worth $12.00, in a perfect world the acquiring company would issue one and one-fifth of its shares to the target company's shareholder in exchange for her share. The ruling allows her to take $2.00 in cash in lieu of the fractional share without disqualifying the B reorganization.

Dissenting shareholders of the target cannot be bought out for cash or other property by the acquiring company, but the target company can redeem stock from such shareholders for cash or other property without upsetting the Type B reorganization, provided the cash does not derive from the acquiring corporation. *See* Rev. Rul. 68-285 1968-1 C.B. 147.

The acquiring company may safely buy bonds or notes issued by the target corporation because that does not entail a provision of boot in exchange for *stock. See Stockton Harbor Indus. Co. v. Commissioner*, 216 F.2d 638 (9th Cir. 1954), *cert. denied,* 349 U.S. 904 (1955).

Obviously, the acquiring company cannot pay for the target company shareholders' personal expenses in connection with the reorganization, but the IRS has ruled that it can pay the target corporation's expenses, provided they are directly related to the reorganization. Rev. Rul. 73-54, 1973-1 C.B. 187 (involving an acquisition of target assets for acquiring corporation stock).

2. *Issuance of additional shares.* Sometimes an acquiring company will promise to issue more stock to the sellers in the event that the target company performs especially well. In such cases, the "solely for voting stock" requirement is not considered violated unless the target company shareholders receive a negotiable instrument evidencing their rights. Rev. Proc. 84-42, 1984-1 C.B. 521.

3. *Overlap with other transactions.* Assume that all of Tiny Corporation's stock is held by Mr. A. A large corporation contributes a very large amount of its voting stock to Tiny Corp. in exchange for 80% or more of the voting stock of Tiny, thus giving it control of Tiny. Is this is a § 368(a)(1)(B) transaction, or is it a § 351 transaction?

4. *Triangular Type B reorganization.* The parenthetical language in the definition of a Type B reorganization clearly allows the acquiring company to use its parent corporation's stock. As a result, when the dust settles, there will be a three-tier structure in which the target company will be in the third tier and the former shareholders of the target company will own stock of the corporation in the top tier. Note that one cannot use the stock of both corporations. *See* Reg. § 1.368-2(c).

5. Dropdowns. Section 368(a)(2)(C) specifically allows the acquiring corporation to take the target company's stock and to drop it into a subsidiary producing the same three-tier structure described above. Likewise, the acquiror can be a first-tier subsidiary, using its parent's stock. § 368(a)(2)(C). It can then drop down sub stock to a lower tier.

1. CREEPING "B" REORGANIZATIONS

The "solely for voting stock" (or no boot) requirement makes it difficult for the acquiring corporation to acquire the stock of the target over time in a "creeping B" reorganization if doing so involves paying cash or other nonstock consideration to any seller. If the acquiring company previously acquired *any* of the target company stock for consideration other than the acquiror's own voting stock, the exchange after which the acquiror meets the 80% control requirement will not qualify as a Type B reorganization unless the prior acquisition is "old and cold."

As in a § 351 transaction, it is not necessary to acquire control in qualifying B reorganization; it is only necessary for the acquiror to *have* control immediately after the exchange. Thus the acquiring corporation may already own some or even a controlling stock interest before a valid B reorganization provided the earlier stock acquisitions — if for other than stock of the acquiror — were not made by purchase as part of the same plan.

Even if the acquiror obtains 80% control of the target solely for voting stock in a single transaction, if any other stock was obtained by purchase and can be linked to an overall plan the B reorganization is invalid. *See Chapman v. Commissioner*, 618 F.2d 856 (1st Cir. 1980). There International Telephone and Telegraph Corporation purchased 8% of Hartford Fire Insurance Company's common stock for nonstock consideration. Fourteen months later, it attempted to acquire the rest of Hartford's stock in exchange for its own voting stock in a B reorganization. Before the exchange, ITT sold the previously-purchased 8% interest to a third party in order to comply with a condition of its private letter ruling. The shareholders of Hartford tendered the requisite 80% amount, but sometime later the IRS asserted that the previously-purchased 8% had been "parked" in friendly hands and never fully disposed of, and that the attempted B reorganization was invalid. In a proceeding for summary judgment which did not decide the facts, ITT argued that even if the previously-purchased stock formed part of the larger acquisition, there was still a valid B reorganization because it obtained control (80%) of Hartford solely in exchange for its voting stock, and that it did not matter whether it also acquired additional shares by purchase. The court ruled that as a matter of law if the initial cash purchase and the later stock-for-stock exchange were part of a single integrated series of transactions, the B reorganization was defective. That laid to rest one of the intriguing issues about the Type B reorganization that Congress had never fully clarified.

D. TYPE B REORGANIZATIONS

The effect of a failed B reorganization is a taxable exchange of stock.

If the prior taxable transaction is "old and cold," a later stock-for-stock swap can qualify as a Type B reorganization as long as the acquiror has control immediately after the exchange.

> *To illustrate*: If ITT had purchased 30% of Hartford as an investment and then 10 years later decided to take over Hartford, it could engage in the following tax-deferred transaction. ITT would issue voting (preferred or common) stock to Hartford shareholders, obtaining at least another 50% of the outstanding Hartford stock. This second transaction would qualify as a Type B reorganization, because ITT had control immediately after the exchange and did not transfer any consideration to ITT's shareholders other than voting stock. If instead ITT had purchased 90% of Hartford stock for cash, it could obtain the remaining 10% in a later unrelated B reorganization because it need not obtain control in the transaction.

PROBLEM 21-1

(a) Country Music, Inc. (CMI) is 100% owned by Mel Gilley. Gilley recently agreed to exchange his CMI stock (all of which is voting stock) for voting stock of an unrelated publicly-owned corporation, Bronx Recording Corporation (BRC). The parties entered into the deal because they felt that by combining companies, they could develop a new musical art form, "country rap." As it turned out, CMI is so valuable that Gilley wound up owning 82% by vote and value of BRC. CMI stays in the same business as before. What is the nature of this transaction?

(b) Assume Gilley wound up owning only 40% of BRC's stock, but BRC then contributed the stock to a partnership consisting of BRC and an unrelated party. Would the transfer to the partnership disturb the "B" reorganization? Consider § 368(a)(2)(C).

PROBLEM 21-2

Acquiring Corporation engaged in the following unrelated transactions in which it swapped its voting stock for stock of Target Corporation. The sequence was as follows:

Five years ago	25%
Four years ago	30%
Three years ago	35%
This year	10%

(a) Which of these transactions, if any, would qualify as a Type B reorganization?

(b) What if all the transactions were bound together as a single plan?

2. ACQUIRING COMPANY'S BASIS IN TARGET COMPANY STOCK

Read § 362(b).

The acquiring company takes as its basis in the target company's stock the same basis as the target company shareholders had in the stock. *See* § 362(b). This presents difficulties if the target company is widely held and the target company shareholders do not cooperate in providing information as to their stock basis. The IRS has sensibly allowed acquiring corporations to use statistical sampling techniques in order to determine a reasonable approximation to be used as the acquiring company's basis in the target company stock. Rev. Proc. 81-70, 1981-2 C.B. 729.

PROBLEM 21-3

Parent Corporation owns 100% of the stock of Subsidiary Corporation. Parent wants to acquire all of the stock of Target Company and wishes to place it in a subsidiary of Subsidiary. Assume that Parent contributes Parent stock to Subsidiary and that Subsidiary uses that stock to acquire all of the stock of Target in a Type B reorganization.

(a) Can Subsidiary form its own subsidiary to which the stock of Target is contributed without disqualifying the reorganization?

(b) Assume that after the reorganization Subsidiary owns all of the stock of Target. What is Parent's basis in Subsidiary? *See* Prop. Reg. § 1.358-6(b).

PROBLEM 21-4

Acquiso Corp. wants to acquire Target Corp. in order to expand its product line, but the shareholders of Target will agree to the acquisition only if the transaction will be nontaxable to them. Because of the desires of Target's shareholders, Acquiso Corp. offers Target's shareholders one share of Acquiso Corp. voting common stock for each share of Target common stock (the only class of stock) they hold as of the date of the reorganization. All of the shareholders of Target Corp. agree to the offer by Acquiso Corp.

(a) Will the exchange of Target's stock for Acquiso Corp. stock meet the requirement of § 368(a)(1)(B)?

(b) Assume the same facts except that the offer by Acquiso Corp. allows the shareholders of Target Corp. to receive for their Target Corp. stock either one share of Acquiso Corp. voting common stock or $250. 90% of the Target Corp. shareholders elect to take the Acquiso Corp. stock in exchange for their Target Corp. stock, while the remaining Target Corp. shareholders elect to receive cash. Will the exchange of Target's stock for Acquiso Corp. stock under this fact situation meet the requirements of § 368(a)(1)(B)?

E. TYPE C REORGANIZATIONS

(c) Assume the same facts except that Acquiso Corp. exchanges its voting stock for 90% of the stock of Target Corp. and exchanges Acquiso Corp. warrants for the remaining Target Corp. stock. Will the exchange of Target's stock for Acquiso Corp. stock and warrants under this fact situation meet the requirements of § 368(a)(1)(B)?

PROBLEM 21-5

(a) Various reorganization expenses are incurred pursuant to a valid Type B reorganization between P Corp. and T Corp. T incurs the following expenses due to the reorganization: legal and accounting fees; appraisal fees; administrative costs; underwriting and SEC registration fees; transfer taxes; and transfer agent's fees. If P Corp. pays the above reorganization expenses of T Corp., will the reorganization still qualify as a Type B reorganization?

(b) Assume the same facts except that P Corp. also agrees to pay the additional following expenses: shareholder's investment expenses; legal and tax advice for the shareholders; estate planning fees; and any transfer taxes which only the shareholders are obliged to pay. Does the transaction qualify as a B reorganization?

E. TYPE C REORGANIZATIONS

Read §§ 368(a)(1)(C) and 368(a)2(B).

In a "C" reorganization the acquiring corporation must obtain "substantially all the properties" of the target corporation in exchange solely for voting stock of the acquiring company or its parent. These transactions are often called "practical mergers" because the effects of a merger and a Type C reorganization are so similar. As a taxable form, this model would be a stock for assets acquisition.

1. SUBSTANTIALLY ALL THE PROPERTIES

Failure to acquire substantially all of the target's assets implies that the transaction may be divisive in character. If the transaction is divisive, it should be tested under the Type D reorganization rules and § 355, which is highly restrictive. By contrast, if substantially all of the properties are acquired, it is logical to use standards that are more similar to those that apply in a merger. For purposes of obtaining a private letter ruling, the IRS requires that the acquiring company obtain at least 70% of the target's gross assets and 90% of the net assets. Also, the taxpayer must represent that it intends no prereorganization spin-offs, sales or redemptions which are related to the acquisition and might deplete T's assets for purposes of the 70%/90% rule. Rev. Proc. 77-37, 1977-2 C.B. 568.

REV. RUL. 57-518
1957-2 C.B. 253

Where one corporation transfers 70 percent of its assets to another corporation in exchange solely for part of the latter's voting stock and then liquidates pursuant to a plan of reorganization, the properties to be transferred constitute "substantially all" of the properties of the transferor and the transaction qualifies as a reorganization under section 368(a)(1)(C) of the Internal Revenue Code of 1954, where the properties retained are approximately equal in value to the amount of the liabilities paid and are confined to cash, accounts receivable, notes, and three percent of its total inventory....

Advice has been requested as to the Federal income tax consequences of a reorganization between two corporations under the circumstances described below.

The M and N corporations were engaged in the fabrication and sale of various items of steel products. For sound and legitimate business reasons, N corporation acquired most of M corporation's business and operating assets. Under a plan of reorganization, M corporation transferred to N corporation (1) all of its fixed assets (plant and equipment) at net book values, (2) 97 percent of all its inventories at book values, and (3) insurance policies and other properties pertaining to the business. In exchange therefor, N corporation issued shares of its voting common stock to M corporation.

The properties retained by M corporation include cash, accounts receivable, notes, and three percent of its total inventory. The fair market value of the assets retained by M was roughly equivalent to the amount of its liabilities. M corporation proceeded to liquidate its retained properties as expeditiously as possible and applied the proceeds to its outstanding debts. The property remaining after the discharge of all its liabilities was turned over to N corporation, and M corporation was liquidated.

Section 368 of the Internal Revenue Code of 1954, in defining corporate reorganizations, provides in part:

> (a) REORGANIZATION. - (1) IN GENERAL. - ... the term "reorganization" means - ... (C) The acquisition by one corporation, in exchange solely for all or a part of its voting stock (or in exchange solely for all or a part of the voting stock of a corporation which is in control of the acquiring corporation), of substantially all of the properties of another corporation, ...

The specific question presented is what constitutes "substantially all of the properties" as defined in the above section of the Code. The answer will depend upon the facts and circumstances in each case rather than upon any particular percentage. Among the elements of importance that are to be considered in arriving at the conclusion are the nature of the properties retained by the transferor, the purpose of the retention, and the amount thereof. In *Milton Smith, et al. v. Commissioner*, 34 B.T.A. 702, *acquiescence*, page 7, this Bulletin,

E. TYPE C REORGANIZATIONS

withdrawing nonacquiescence, C.B. XV-2, 46 (1936), a corporation transferred 71 percent of its gross assets. It retained assets having a value of $52,000, the major portion of which was in cash and accounts receivable. It was stated that the assets were retained in order to liquidate liabilities of approximately $46,000. Thus, after discharging its liabilities, the outside figure of assets remaining with the petitioner would have been $6,000, which the court stated was not an excessive margin to allow for the collection of receivables with which to meet its liabilities. No assets were retained for the purpose of engaging in any business or for distribution to stockholders. In those circumstances, the court held that there had been a transfer of "substantially all of the assets" of the corporation. The court very definitely indicated that a different conclusion would probably have been reached if the amount retained was clearly in excess of a reasonable amount necessary to liquidate liabilities. Furthermore, the court intimated that transfer of all of the net assets of a corporation would not qualify if the percentage of gross assets transferred was too low. Thus, it stated that, if a corporation having gross assets of $1,000,000 and liabilities of $900,000 transferred only the net assets of $100,000, the result would probably not come within the intent of Congress in its use of the words "substantially all."

The instant case, of the assets not transferred to the corporation, no portion was retained by M corporation for its own continued use inasmuch as the plan of reorganization contemplated M's liquidation. Furthermore, the assets retained were for the purpose of meeting liabilities, and these assets at fair market values, approximately equaled the amount of such liabilities. Thus, the facts in this case meet the requirements established in the case of *Milton Smith*, *supra*.

The instant case is not in conflict with I.T. 2373, C.B. VI-2 19 (1927), which holds that, where one corporation transferred approximately three-fourths of its properties to another corporation for a consideration of bonds and cash, it did not dispose of "substantially all the properties" owned by it at the time and, therefore, no corporate reorganization took place, so that the transaction constituted an exchange of property resulting in a gain or loss to the transferor for income tax purposes. I.T. 2372, *supra*, is obsolete to the extent that it implies that a corporate reorganization could have occurred where there was no continuity of interest. However, that ruling is still valid with regard to its discussion of the question of what constitutes "substantially all of the properties." From the facts as stated in that case, it appears that a major part of the 25 percent of the assets retained were operating assets, and it does not appear that they were retained for the purpose of liquidating the liabilities of the corporation. On the contrary, it seems likely that the corporation may have contemplated continuation of its business or the sale of the remainder of its operating assets to another purchaser. As a result, I.T. 2373, *supra*, is clearly distinguishable from the instant case.

Accordingly, since the assets transferred by M to N constitute "substantially all" of the assets of the transferor corporation within the meaning of that statutory phrase, the acquisition by N corporation, in exchange solely for part of its voting common stock, of the properties of M corporation pursuant to the plan will constitute a reorganization within the purview of section 368(a)(1)(C) of the Code. No gain or loss is recognized to the transferor as a result of the exchange of its property for common stock of the transferee under section 361 of the Code; and no gain or loss is recognized to the shareholders of M corporation, under section 354(a)(1) of such Code, as the result of their receipt of N common stock.

2. PERMISSIBLE CONSIDERATION

Stock of the acquiring company's parent company stock can be used as consideration instead of its own. Section 368(a)(1)(C), parenthetical language. In addition, the acquiring company can assume any amount of the transferor's liabilities and any amount of property subject to liabilities without violating the "solely for voting stock" rule. Unlike a B reorganization, a C reorganization does permit the acquiring corporation to pay boot in addition to voting stock under the under the so-called boot relaxation rule of § 368(a)(2)(B). The amount of permissible boot is a maximum of 20% of the fair market value of all the target's property, and the remainder must be paid for with voting stock. This concession is more apparent than real however, and it is extremely dangerous to rely upon it. The reason is that if the acquiring company pays any form of boot, any liabilities it assumes or takes subject to are also treated as boot. It is the combination of liabilities and boot that creates the greatest anxiety for tax planners.

To illustrate: Target corporation has property with a total value of $100,000, and the property is subject to liabilities of $15,000. This means that the acquiring corporation can pay not more than $5,000 in money or other boot in addition to assuming the liabilities or taking the properties subject to the liabilities. *See* § 368(a)(2)(B), last sentence.

There is another element of peril with respect to the 80% rule. Because at least 80% of the value of all of the properties of the transferor corporation must be acquired for voting stock, it follows that any retained property reduces the amount of money or other boot that can be paid by the acquiring corporation.

To illustrate: Target corporation has properties with a total value of $100,000. It plans to retain $18,000 of the properties. Because the acquiror must pay stock for at least $80,000 worth of property, this means that only $2,000 worth of transferred assets can be acquired for boot.

Note the high risks involved here. One must be accurate and precise about the $100,000 value of the Target's assets and the $15,000 amount of its liabilities. If it turns out that the assets are worth less, or that the liabilities are greater than

F. TRIANGULAR MERGERS

anticipated, the transaction does not qualify as a Type C reorganization because the 20% test was violated.

The acquiring corporation can use its parent's stock but not both the stock of itself and of its parents. Reg. § 1.368-2(d)1. However, if the 80% standard is met it seems likely that one could use parent company stock as if it were cash under the boot relaxation rule.

In addition to all the other requirements, the target company must liquidate and distribute whatever consideration it received in the reorganization and all the rest of its assets. § 368(a)(2)(G)(i).

3. OVERLAPS

Suppose that one corporation acquires another in a valid B reorganization and then promptly liquidates the target into itself. According to Rev. Rul. 67-274, 1967-2 C.B. 141, this is a C reorganization. This has positive and negative features. The positive is that some boot can apparently be transferred, and thus an attempted B reorganization which has failed due to a minimal transfer of boot can be saved from taxability by a related liquidation and conversion to a C reorganization. The negative is that in a B reorganization nothing prevents the target from disposing of unwanted assets by sale, redemption, or otherwise in preparation for the acquisition, but if it does so and is later liquidated by the acquiror, it may fail the "substantially all the properties" rule when the transaction is tested as a C reorganization.

PROBLEM 21-6

Mega Corp. seeks to acquire the assets of one of its customers Seller Corp., which has a dominant share of the market for selling Mega Corp's products. Mega Corp. proposes to exchange its voting stock for the assets of Seller Corp. Seller Corp. owns assets with a value of $500,000 and a basis of $300,000, along with liabilities of $100,000. Mega Corp., after acceptance by shareholders of Seller Corp., exchanges its voting stock worth $400,000 for all the assets of Seller Corp., subject to or assuming liabilities, as part of a plan of reorganization. Will the exchange of Seller Corp's assets for Mega Corp. stock under the plan of reorganization meet the requirements of § 368(a)(1)(C)?

F. TRIANGULAR MERGERS

See § 368(a)(2)(D) and (E).

In a forward triangular merger, the target corporation merges into a subsidiary of a parent company, and the shareholders of the target receive stock of the parent company. In a reverse triangular merger the subsidiary disappears into the target company by means of a merger. The practical results are the same, because in both transactions the target company shareholders wind up holding parent company stock and the parent owns either all of the stock of the target itself (reverse merger) or of the acquisition subsidiary which has become the target's alter ego (forward merger). The advantage of the reverse merger is that it assures that the name of the target company is unchanged, it prevents any debate with creditors about the continuation of the target's liabilities and otherwise leaves the target intact just as in a B reorganization.

If minority shareholders of the company protest, state law generally limits their rights to an appraisal proceeding pursuant to which they are entitled to the cash value of their stock of the target company. These are called dissenters' rights. In order to simplify the process for all concerned, triangular mergers often provide for a "cash option" pursuant to which the target company's shareholders can elect to take cash in lieu of stock. As you already know from your previous readings, if too many target shareholders elect to take cash the merger will be unable to qualify as a Type A reorganization. As a result, cash options are often restricted to some fraction of the total consideration, 50% being a traditional number in the case of a forward merger. A reverse merger is more restrictive in the amount of boot which may be paid.

Both of these forms of acquisition reorganizations are highly popular with corporate planners. Not only does the use of a subsidiary insulate the parent from the target's hidden liabilities, but also it is extremely clumsy to use the parent as the acquiror if it is publicly held. State corporate law generally requires either a majority or a super-majority vote of all the shareholders before a corporation may engage in a merger. This is clearly impractical for a large diversified corporation which may engage in many acquisitions each year. By the use of acquisition subsidiaries such a corporation can engage in acquisitions by the decision of management alone.

1. FORWARD TRIANGULAR MERGERS

A forward triangular merger requires the same 50% continuity of interest as for mergers under § 368(a)(1)(A) but has two additional restrictions which are not applicable to plain A reorganizations. The first is borrowed from the C reorganization. Under § 368(a)(2)(D) the acquisition subsidiary (S) (which may be a newly-formed shell or a preexisting S) must obtain "substantially all the properties" of the target corporation (T), which has the usual 90%/70% meaning for ruling purposes. Just as for a C reorganization, premerger spin-offs, sales or redemptions of assets from T may upset compliance with this requirement. The second restriction (the reason for which is far from apparent) is that no stock of S can be used as consideration. The parent (P) of S can issue its stock directly to T shareholders; it does have to contribute the stock to its subsidiary first. P.L.R. 8925087 (March 30, 1989). As in an A reorganization, there is no limit on the amount of T's liabilities that S can assume. This is a substantial improvement over the baroque rules governing C reorganizations.

To illustrate: P forms wholly-owned S and contributes P stock to S. T (worth $100) merges into S under state law, and S transfers to the T

F. TRIANGULAR MERGERS

shareholders P stock worth $100 in exchange for all their shares of T. The transaction is a valid forward triangular merger under § 368(a)(2)(D), provided S receives substantially all T's assets. If instead the consideration consisted of $90 worth of P stock and $10 worth of S stock, the transaction would be taxable despite an apparent 100% continuity of interest. Overlap with A reorganization: if the consideration were $40 worth of P stock and $60 worth of S stock the transaction would not qualify under § 368(a)(2)(D), but should nevertheless qualify as an A reorganization directly into S with the P stock treated as permissible boot.

P's basis in the T stock will consist of its premerger basis in S stock plus the net basis of assets that P transfers to S and which S retains, plus T's basis in its own assets after the merger (reduced by the value of any consideration that T independently paid its shareholders). P's basis in its S stock is reduced by any liabilities assumed by S in the merger, just as if P first acquired T's assets and then dropped them down to S, in order to prevent an artificial loss on a later sale of S stock. Prop. Reg. § 1.358-6(c)(4), example 1(e).

T shareholders will be taxed as if they went through a standard A merger or consolidation. That means shareholders will take a basis in P stock that equals their basis in their T stock, modified for the impact of boot. § 358.

2. REVERSE TRIANGULAR MERGERS

A reverse triangular merger strongly resembles a B reorganization, because the result in both cases is that T becomes a controlled subsidiary of P, and T's shareholders receive P voting stock in exchange. It is useful in situations where it is necessary to preserve the corporate existence of T. Although its mechanical requirements are more stringent than those of a forward triangular merger, they are somewhat more flexible than for a B reorganization.

Section 368(a)(2)(E) requires that, (1) the shareholders of T transfer control of T solely for voting stock of S's controlling parent P and (2) that after the transaction T hold substantially all the properties of both T and S (except for any P stock which S transferred to T's shareholders in the exchange). These two requirements are borrowed from the rules for C reorganizations: up to 20% boot may be paid to T's shareholders (but without the C-reorganization concern that permissible boot is reduced by assumption of T's liabilities), and the "substantially all the properties" rule. Unlike a B reorganization, 80% control of T must be obtained in the transaction. Thus preexisting ownership by S or P of more than 20% of T's stock will prevent the use of § 368(a)(2)(E). There is little if anything to justify these complications.

It is not necessary for P to transfer its stock to S so that S can distribute the P stock to T's shareholders. The IRS has allowed a direct transfer from P to the shareholders of T in P.L.R. 9125013 (March 21, 1991).

P's basis in the T stock is calculated in precisely the same way as for a forward triangular merger, except that if P acquires less than 100% of S, a corresponding basis reduction is made to reflect the fact. *See* Prop. Reg. § 1.358-6(c)(4), examples 2 (d) and (e).

As in all reorganizations, T's shareholders will take a substituted basis in the P stock that equals their former basis in their T stock, modified for the impact of boot. § 358.

Forced B Reorganization

If an attempted reverse triangular merger fails to meet one or more of the technical requirements of § 368(a)(2)(E), it may nevertheless qualify as a B reorganization. For example, suppose that in connection with an otherwise valid reverse triangular merger using 100% P stock as consideration, T disposes of operating assets immediately before the merger so that T fails the "substantially all" rule. If the transaction had been structured as a B reorganization it would have been tax-free because there is no "substantially all" rule in a B reorganization. Before enactment of § 368(a)(2)(e), the IRS applied the step-transaction doctrine to such a transaction in Revenue Ruling 67-488, 1967-2 C.B. 144, to the taxpayers' advantage and held that the intervening merger could be ignored because the end result was a valid B reorganization. Note that the forced B reorganization facilitates squeeze outs of minority shareholders, so it is not a source of pleasure to everyone.

PROBLEM 21-7

T has 10,000 shares of voting common stock outstanding, all in one class. Assume that P bought 2,000 shares of T in December of 1990. In an unrelated transaction in June of 1995, P merged transitory S into T and received 7,900 shares (out of the total of 8,000 remaining shares) of T. The shareholders of T received as consideration solely voting stock of P. In connection with the merger the directors of T acquiesced to the demands of some angry shareholders and agreed that T would buy their 100 shares of stock at a fair price.

(a) Is this a successful reverse triangular merger?

(b) Can this qualify as a Type B reorganization? *See* Reg. § 1.368-2(j)(7), example (5).

G. ACQUISITIVE TYPE D REORGANIZATIONS AND § 356(b)

Read § 368(a)(1)(D).

A D reorganization can be either divisive or acquisitive in form and in result. In Chapter 20 you saw that § 368(a)(1)(D) comprehends a divisive reorganization in which the distributing corporation first forms a controlled subsidiary (or subsidiaries) to which it transfers *part* of its assets and then distributes the stock of subsidiary to its shareholders with respect to their shares, under § 355. If the distributing corporation transfers *substantially all* its assets to a corporation which it thereafter controls and then distributes the stock together with all its other properties, however, it is a reorganization under § 368(a)(1)(D) without being divisive at all. If an exchange of the distributing company's stock for stock in it or in another corporation is involved, the transaction is governed by § 354 instead of § 355. The required level of control of the transferee corporation is reduced from the usual 80% standard to the 50% standard (using the § 318(a) attribution rules) of § 304(c). See § 368(a)(2)(H).

Acquisitive D reorganizations are uncommon in practice but they are frequently imposed on taxpayers by the Government in its effort to combat the liquidation-reincorporation abuse in which a corporation's owners attempt to withdraw cash from the business without paying taxes on dividends at ordinary income rates. To accomplish this, the owners choose the alternative path of liquidating the corporation with a view to retaining some of the proceeds of the liquidation, typically cash, and later contributing the operating assets to another operating company which they control. The practice can take various forms. In the simple case of an abusive liquidation with a major retention of cash by the shareholder-taxpayer, the taxpayer benefits by what amounts to a withdrawal of cash from a going concern at long-term capital gains rates and enjoying the secondary benefits of a stepped-up basis in reincorporated assets together with the elimination of the earnings and profits account. The IRS is aware of the revenue loss resulting from these practices, and has fashioned two primary counterattacks. The first is that the steps, taken together, constitute a corporate reorganization of some sort (usually a D reorganization), with the result that the withdrawn cash is taxable at ordinary income rates, and the second is that there was no *bona fide* complete liquidation.[7]

> *To illustrate*: National Accumulator Corporation has a long history of profitability and has accumulated cash. The founders would like to extract the cash at long-term capital gain rates. To carry out their wishes, the corporation liquidates and distributes all of its

---

[7] *See generally* Westin, *In Like a Lion and Out Like a Lamb: The 98th Congress and the Liquidation-Reincorporation Abuse*, Tax Notes, February 20, 1989, at 997.

assets to the founders. The founders in turn report capital gain under § 331 when they receive the assets of the corporation. The founders next contribute the manufacturing assets plus a small amount of cash to a newly formed corporation (Newco) which carries on National Accumulator Corporation's business and changes its name to National Accumulator Corporation. If this scheme works, the founders will manage to extract a large amount of cash and claim the benefit of long-term capital gain rates.

Section 368(a)(1)(D) has become the weapon of choice for combatting the liquidation reincorporation abuse. In the above illustration, the IRS is likely to argue that the transaction is not a liquidation at all, but rather a D reorganization with the result that the liquid assets constitute boot which is taxable as a dividend, the operating assets retain their original basis as if they had never left corporate solution, and the old earnings and profits account is similarly carried over to the new corporation.

The IRS would win in the above illustration. But suppose the newly-reincorporated Newco's shareholders are not identical to the former shareholders of National because 21% of Newco shares are purchased by newcomers in the reincorporation? Before the 1984 enactment of § 368(a)(2)(H) this would succeed because Newco would not be controlled by National or its former shareholders at the 80% level then required for a D reorganization. *See Berghash v. Commissioner*, 43 T.C. 743 (1965), *aff'd* 361 F.2d 257 (2d Cir. 1966). Under current law, the former shareholders of National must own less than 50% of Newco (after applying the § 318 attribution rules) for the transaction to avoid being a D reorganization.

The courts have generally ignored the other requirements of § 368(a)(1)(D) in their eagerness to squelch abusive liquidation-reincorporations. For example, in *Smothers v. U.S.*, 642 F.2d 894 (5th Cir. 1981), the "substantially all" rule was held to be met by a sale of only 15% of the assets of one corporation to a commonly-controlled sister corporation followed by liquidation of the transferor on the ground that the assets constituted substantially all the operating assets of a service business, and because the sister corporation hired the former employees of the liquidated corporation. The requirement of a distribution of all the stock of the transferee corporation under § 354(b)(1)(B) was held unnecessary on the ground that the shareholders of the transferor already owned all the stock of the transferee.

The reorganization and liquidation sections have generally been held to be mutually exclusive. A transaction is either one or the other. The IRS has occasionally argued to the contrary in order to combat liquidation-reincorporations on a theory of "incomplete liquidation." The courts have generally refused to accept this doctrine, except for the Tax Court's decision (of uncertain reach) in *Telephone Answering Serv. Co. v. Commissioner*, 63 T.C. 423 (1974), *aff'd*

G. ACQUISITIVE TYPE D REORGANIZATIONS AND § 356(b)

by order, 546 F.2d 423 (4th Cir. 1967), *cert. denied*, 431 U.S. 914 (1977) ("TASCO"). In TASCO a shell parent corporation transferred its operating assets to an alter ego subsidiary and liquidated. The court held that the putative liquidation of the parent was "incomplete" because the parent's business continued in the form of another corporation.

Although it is was once a bloody battlefield, the area became much calmer after the 1986 Tax Reform Act repealed *General Utilities* and narrowed the spread between capital gains and ordinary income rates. The above illustration looks far less enticing now that the liquidating corporation must pay taxes on its own gains under current § 336 and the difference between ordinary income and capital gain rates is 11.6 percentage points rather than 30 points as it was in 1985 (or 50 points before 1969).

PROBLEM 21-8

Dr. deSoto incorporates HoldCo (H), which in turn incorporates Subco (S). S is an operating company which accumulates cash over the years from deSoto's practice and passes that cash up to H from time to time. H eventually liquidates, distributing its assets (cash and the stock of S) to deSoto. After a decent interval, S forms a new holding company and the process begins anew. What abuse lurks in this transaction? Does the IRS have any tools to combat the abuse?

PROBLEM 21-9

(a) Teleco Corp. seeks to acquire Regulated Corp., one of its largest customers, but due to statutory restrictions, Regulated Corp. must be the surviving corporation. In order to comply with the statutory restrictions, Teleco. Corp. transfers all its assets to Regulated Corp. in exchange for 10,000 shares of Regulated Corp. which is 51% of the total issued and outstanding stock of Regulated Corp., measured after their issuance. Teleco Corp. then liquidates by transferring all the Regulated Corp. stock to its shareholders in exchange for their Teleco Corp. stock. Will this transaction qualify as a Type D reorganization?

(b) X Corporation issues $1 million worth of its voting common stock to Y Corporation. Y distributes the X stock to its shareholders and then transfers all its assets to X and liquidates. Next, X contributes the assets it received from Y to a newly organized subsidiary. How does one characterize this transaction?

NOTES

1. *Alter ego theory.* The so-called alter ego theory is best illustrated in *Telephone Answering Serv. Co. v. Commissioner*, 63 T.C. 423 (1974), *aff'd*, 546 F. 423 (4th Cir. 1976), *cert. denied*, 431 U.S. 914 (1977), which was briefly described above. Parts of this case were quite dramatic. A telephone answering company went through a split-up in which all of its assets found their way into a second corporation which was identical in every respect to the first corporation, including the name. The only difference that one could detect was the legal event of dissolution of the first corporation and a new bank account. The government successfully asserted that there was in effect no liquidation and that the surviving corporation was merely an alter ego of the allegedly liquidated corporation.

2. *Overlap*. Assume that a parent corporation contributes all of its assets to a wholly-owned subsidiary, and in exchange it receives stock of the subsidiary. This looks like a § 351 exchange. To qualify under § 354(b) as a D reorganization the subsidiary must receive all of the parent's assets (achieved) and the parent company must distribute all of its properties, including the stock of the subsidiary, in pursuance of the plan of reorganization. Is this a D reorganization or § 351 exchange? If it is a reorganization, § 381 applies and the tax attributes of the parent company will be shifted to the subsidiary company. These would include such things as its earnings and profits account, net operating losses and capital loss carryovers. By contrast, if it is a § 351 exchange, there will be no carryover of tax attributes.

3. *More overlap questions*. Assume the same facts given immediately above. Why is this not also a C reorganization? The subsidiary acquired all of the assets of the transferor in exchange for voting stock. *See* § 368(a)(2)(G)(i). This transaction qualifies as *both* a C and a D reorganization, but a special rule covering this situation requires that it must be treated as a D reorganization. § 368(a)(2)(A).

H. TYPE E REORGANIZATIONS

Read § 368(a)(1)(E).

An E reorganization is simply stated to be a "recapitalization." § 368(a)(1)(C). There are numerous reasons to engage in a recapitalization. Probably the most common reason is to shift control of a closely-held corporation from the older generation to the next generation by a recapitalization exchange of common stock for preferred stock. The older generation then gives away a generous amount of the common stock to the children. If this is done shrewdly, the common stock will have little immediate value, but it will represent the value of the corporation's future growth if the younger generation can manage the corporation effectively. The lack of any clear definition of the E reorganization other than a "recapitalization" has caused some difficulties, but it is clear that not every reshuffling of the corporation's capital structure will result in a tax-free reorganization.

BAZLEY v. COMMISSIONER
331 U.S. 737, 67 S. Ct. 1489 (1947)

MR. JUSTICE FRANKFURTER delivered the opinion of the Court:

....

H. TYPE E REORGANIZATIONS

The Commissioner of Internal Revenue assessed an income tax deficiency against the taxpayer for the year 1939. Its validity depends on the legal significance of the recapitalization in that year of a family corporation in which the taxpayer and his wife owned all but one of the Company's one thousand shares. These had a par value of $100. Under the plan of reorganization the taxpayer, his wife, and the holder of the additional share were to turn in their old shares and receive in exchange for each old share five new shares of no par value, but of a stated value of $60, and new debenture bonds, having a total face value of $400,000, payable in ten years but callable at any time. Accordingly, the taxpayer received 3,990 shares of the new stock for the 798 shares of his old holding and debentures in the amount of $319,200. At the time of these transactions the earned surplus of the corporation was $855,783.82.

The Commissioner charged to the taxpayer as income the full value of the debentures. The Tax Court affirmed the Commissioner's determination, against the taxpayer's contention that as a "recapitalization" the transaction was a tax-free "reorganization" and that the debentures were "securities in a corporation a party to a reorganization," "exchanged solely for stock or securities in such corporation" "in pursuance of a plan of reorganization," and as such no gain is recognized for income tax purposes. Internal Revenue Code, [§ 368(a)(1)(E)]. The Tax Court found that the recapitalization had "no legitimate corporate business purpose" and was therefore not a "reorganization" within the statute. The distribution of debentures, it concluded, was a disguised dividend, taxable as earned income under [§§ 61(a)(7), 301 and 302]. The Circuit Court of Appeals for the Third Circuit, sitting en banc, affirmed, two judges dissenting. 155 F.2d 237.

Unless a transaction is a reorganization contemplated by [§ 368(a)(1)], any exchange of "stock or securities" in connection with such transaction, cannot be "in pursuance of the plan of reorganization" under [§ 368(a)(1)]. While [§ 368(a)(1)] informs us that "reorganization" means, among other things, "a recapitalization," it does not inform us what "recapitalization" means. "Recapitalization" in connection with the income tax has been part of the revenue laws since 1921.... Congress has never defined it and the Treasury Regulations shed only limited light. One thing is certain. Congress did not incorporate some technical concept, whether that of accountants or of other specialists, into § 368, assuming that there is agreement among specialists as to the meaning of recapitalization. And so, recapitalization as used in [§ 368(a)(1)(E)] must draw its meaning from its function in that section. It is one of the forms of reorganization which obtains the privileges afforded by [§ 354(a)(1)] Therefore, "recapitalization" must be construed with reference to the presuppositions and purpose of [the reorganization rules]. It was not the purpose of the reorganization provision to exempt from payment of a tax what as a practical matter is realized gain. Normally, a distribution by a corporation, whatever form it takes, is a definite and rather unambiguous event. It furnishes the proper occasion for the determination and taxation of gain. But there are circumstances where a formal distribution, directly or through exchange of securities, represents merely a new form of the previous participation in an enterprise, involving no change of substance in the rights and relations of the interested parties one to another or to the corporate assets. As to these, Congress has said that they are not to be deemed significant occasions for determining taxable gain.

These considerations underlie [§ 368] and they should dominate the scope to be given to the various sections, all of which converge toward a common purpose. Application of the language of such a revenue provision is not an exercise in framing abstract definitions. In a series of cases this Court has withheld the benefits of the reorganization provision in situations which might have satisfied provisions of the section treated as inert language, because they were not reorganizations of the kind with which [§ 368], in its purpose and particulars, concerns itself.

Congress has not attempted a definition of what is recapitalization and we shall follow its example. The search for relevant meaning is often satisfied not by a futile attempt at abstract definition but by pricking a line through concrete applications. Meaning frequently is built up by assured recognition of what does not come within a concept the content of which is in controversy. Since a recapitalization within the scope of [§ 368] is an aspect of reorganization, nothing can be a recapitalization for this purpose unless it partakes of those characteristics of a reorganization which underlie the purpose of Congress in postponing the tax liability.

No doubt there was a recapitalization of the Bazley corporation in the sense that the symbols that represented its capital were changed, so that the fiscal basis of its operations would appear very differently on its books. But the form of a transaction as reflected by correct corporate accounting opens questions as to the proper application of a taxing statute; it does not close them. Corporate accounting may represent that correspondence between change in the form of capital structure and essential identity in fact which is of the essence of a transaction relieved from taxation as a reorganization. What is controlling is that a new arrangement intrinsically partake of the elements of reorganization which underlie the Congressional exemption and not merely give the appearance of it to accomplish a distribution of earnings. In the case of a corporation which has undistributed earnings, the creation of new corporate obligations which are transferred to stockholders in relation to their former holdings, so as to produce, for all practical purposes, the same result as a distribution of cash earnings of equivalent value, cannot obtain tax immunity because cast in the form of a recapitalization-reorganization. The governing legal rule can hardly be stated more narrowly. To attempt to do so would only challenge astuteness in evading it. And so it is hard to escape the conclusion that whether in a particular case a paper recapitalization is no more than an admissible attempt to avoid the consequences of an outright distribution of earnings turns on details of corporate

H. TYPE E REORGANIZATIONS

affairs, judgment on which must be left to the Tax Court. *See Dobson v. Commissioner*, 320 U.S. 489.

What have we here? No doubt, if the Bazley corporation had issued the debentures to Bazley and his wife without any recapitalization, it would have made a taxable distribution. Instead, these debentures were issued as part of a family arrangement, the only additional ingredient being an unrelated modification of the capital account. The debentures were found to be worth at least their principal amount, and they were virtually cash because they were callable at the will of the corporation which in this case was the will of the taxpayer. One does not have to pursue the motives behind actions, even in the more ascertainable forms of purpose, to find, as did the Tax Court, that the whole arrangement took this form instead of an outright distribution of cash or debentures, because the latter would undoubtedly have been taxable income whereas what was done could, with a show of reason, claim the shelter of the immunity of a recapitalization-reorganization.

The Commission, the Tax Court and the Circuit Court of Appeals agree that nothing was accomplished that would not have been accomplished by an outright debenture dividend. And since we find no misconception of law on the part of the Tax Court and the Circuit Court of Appeals, whatever may have been their choice of phrasing, their application of the law to the facts of this case must stand. A "reorganization" which is merely a vehicle, however elaborate or elegant, for conveying earnings from accumulations to the stockholders is not a reorganization under [§ 368]. This disposes of the case as a matter of law, since the facts as found by the Tax Court bring them within it. And even if this transaction were deemed a reorganization, the facts would equally sustain the imposition of the tax on the debentures under [§ 356(a)(1) and (2)]....

NOTES

1. *The impact of § 354(a)(2).* Bazley was decided before the passage of § 354(a)(2). If that section had been in force when *Bazley* was decided, would it have made any difference? If there is no reorganization, what Code section applies to the receipt of additional consideration, including additional securities?

2. *Impact of § 453(f)(6).* This commonly-overlooked provision permits installment-sale treatment for securities received in a reorganization that are treated as boot, so that gain is recognized only when the obligations are actually paid or when the installment obligation itself is disposed of. This means shareholders can defer the recognition of gain until their securities are redeemed or sold. Installment-sale treatment is not available for readily tradable securities, so it will generally only be beneficial for closely-held corporations. *See* § 453(f)(4). Note also that installment-sale reporting is not available if the boot is treated as a dividend. Would the installment-sale method be available if *Bazley* were decided today?

3. Bond for bond exchanges. A corporation may choose to redeem old bonds and substitute new ones if interest rates have changed. This can be a complex area because it implicates § 108 and the original issue discount rules.

4. Continuity of interest. Assume that a taxpayer exchanges common stock for a combination of bonds and common stock in the same corporation. Does the recapitalization fail if the 50% continuity of proprietary interest standard is not satisfied? The answer is "no." Continuity of interest is not required in a recapitalization exchange. *See* Rev. Rul. 77-415, 1977-2 C.B. 311 and Rev. Rul. 77-479, 1977-2 C.B. 119.

5. Relationship to § 305. A transaction might be an E reorganization and also fit within the list of taxable transactions under § 305(b). If that is the case, what are the results? Is it a nontaxable reorganization or a taxable stock distribution? The answer appears to be a taxable stock distribution except in a "classic recapitalization" in which an older generation of founders swaps its common stock for newly preferred stock while the younger generation of executives correspondingly increase their share of common stock. The underlying basis for this is a statement by Senator Long in the course of the Senate Floor Debate on the Bill Incorporating Session § 305. *See* 115 Cong. Rec. 37902 (1969). *See also* Reg. § 1.305-3(e), example 12, which formalizes the statement.

REV. RUL. 55-112
1955-1 C.B. 344

Six stockholders owning 54 percent of the common stock of a corporation (which had only common then outstanding) surrendered all of their common stock for newly issued nonvoting preferred stock of the same book value and same fair market value. After the exchange, none of the preferred stockholders was an officer, director, or employee of the corporation, and none of such stockholders had any direct or indirect economic interest in the affairs of the corporation except that evidenced by his preferred stock, Held, the transaction is a nontaxable reorganization (recapitalization) within the terms of section 112(g)(1)(E) of the Internal Revenue Code of 1939.

Advice has been requested with respect to the tax consequences, for Federal income tax purposes, of a change in the capital structure of M Corporation.

All the stock of the M Corporation (which had only common stock outstanding) was held by 5 men interested in its management and operation and by the wives of these individuals. Three of these men, due to ill-health and other reasons, desired to cease all activity in connection with the corporate business, while the other 2 desired to remain active in the business. The 2 who wished to remain active wanted complete control of the corporation and the others were willing to let them have such control.

Accordingly, all the interested parties agreed that the stockholders who did not wish to remain active would exchange their common stock for preferred stock. Therefore, the corporate charter was amended to authorize the issuance of

H. TYPE E REORGANIZATIONS

nonvoting stock, preferred as to dividends and on liquidation, having no pre-emptive rights and redeemable at the option of the corporation. The 3 stockholders who desired to cease being active, and their wives, surrendered all their common stock (totalling 54 percent of all the stock) and received in exchange preferred stock of equal fair market value and of equal book value (such book value being determined by the corporation's basis for its assets for tax purposes). The corporation redeemed and cancelled all the common stock received by it in the exchange. After the transaction all the preferred stockholders owned no common stock, and were not officers, directors or employees of the corporation. None of the preferred stockholders was related by blood or marriage to any common stockholder, or to any officer, director or employee of the corporation, and no preferred stockholder had any economic interest whatever in the affairs of the corporation except that evidenced by his preferred stock shares.

Section 112(a) of the Internal Revenue Code of 1939 provides, in effect, that upon the sale or exchange of property, the entire amount of the gain or loss resulting shall be recognized, unless the results of such exchanges are expressly exempted by the provisions of section 112(b) of such Code. Among the exchanges, the results of which are exempted, is an exchange in connection with a recapitalization (reorganization).

Section 112(b)(3) provides:

> (b) EXCHANGES SOLELY IN KIND. -
>
> ....
>
> (3) STOCK FOR STOCK ON REORGANIZATION. - No gain or loss shall be recognized if stock or securities in a corporation, a party to a reorganization, are, in pursuance of the plan of reorganization, exchanged solely for stock or securities in such corporation or in another corporation, a party to the reorganization.

Section 39.112(g)-1(b) of Regulations 118 provides that the purpose of the reorganization provisions of the Internal Revenue Code is to except from the general rule certain specifically described exchanges incident to such readjustments of corporate structures, made in one of the particular ways specified in the Code, as are required by business exigencies, and which effect only a readjustment of continuing interests in property under modified corporate forms. The same subsection also provides that a continuity of the business enterprise under the modified corporate form, and a continuity of interest therein on the part of those persons who were the owners of the enterprise prior to the transaction, are requisite to a reorganization under the Code.

Section 39.112(e) of Regulations 118 provides that a recapitalization and therefore a reorganization, takes place if, for example; a corporation issues preferred stock, previously authorized but unissued, for outstanding common stock.

Accordingly, the described transaction is a recapitalization as defined by section 112(g)(1)(E) of the Internal Revenue Code of 1939 and under section 112(b)(3) no gain or loss is recognized to the stockholders upon the exchanges by them of their common stock for new preferred stock. The basis of the preferred stock received by each shareholder is the same as the cost or other basis of the common stock surrendered by him. The exchanges of common stock for preferred stock have no effect upon the accumulated earnings and profits....

NOTES

1. *Section 306 effect.* Assuming the corporation had earnings and profits at the time of this transaction, is the preferred stock § 306 stock?

2. *The burden of § 306.* What result if the senior shareholders were to cause some of their stock to be redeemed? The older shareholders might decide to give away their § 306 stock so as to strip their estates. If so, the corporation can redeem their stock in full at death, and the § 306 taint will not apply, if the redemption is complete. § 306(b)(1). The donees might later be able to persuade the corporate to recapitalize the preferred back into common, thereby eliminating the § 306 taint entirely.

Wait a minute! What if the person holding the preferred agreed to convert it to common and then promptly redeemed the common. Would that not open up a loophole? The answer is "yes." What is more, the IRS is aware of it. In Rev. Rul. 76-387, 1976-2 C.B. 96, a recapitalization exchange of all the outstanding § 306 stock for nonvoting common was ruled to qualify under § 368(a)(1)(E), all *provided there was no plan to redeem the common.*

3. *The § 1036 alternative.* Read § 1036 and note how it overlaps with the recapitalization provisions. However it is narrow because it only extends to exchanges of the same grade of stock (common for common or preferred for preferred).

I. TYPE F REORGANIZATIONS

Read § 368(a)(1)(F).

This form of reorganization is typically used when a corporation wishes to move from one state to another. It will normally do so by forming a new corporation with the same name in a different state and then transferring all its assets and liabilities to the new corporation in exchange for stock of the new corporation, after which the old corporation liquidates. Even though this involves two corporations, as long as only one of them is active there can still be a nontaxable Type F reorganization. [Except for this situation (where there is only one active corporation), the F reorganization does not apply if more than one corporation is involved.] The advantage of an F reorganization is that the survival of tax attributes in the hands of the surviving corporation is granted far more generously than for reorganizations under A,B,C, and D.

K. TREATMENT OF THE PARTIES TO A REORGANIZATION

NOTES

1. *The need for keeping multiple operating companies from benefitting from the F reorganization rules.* In *National Tea Co. v. Commissioner*, 83 T.C. 8 (1984), the Tax Court held that a corporation that went through an Type F reorganization with its subsidiary corporation could not apply its post-reorganization net operating losses against the prereorganization income of the subsidiary under § 381. The Court reasoned that the exception for F reorganizations from the loss-tracing requirements of § 381(b)(3) was founded upon the assumption that an F reorganization would involve only one operating corporation. Accordingly, the Tax Court upheld Rev. Rul. 75-561, 1975-2 C.B. 129, which required loss-tracing when an F reorganization involves two or more operating corporations, as consistent with legislative intent.

2. *Another trust case.* In Rev. Rul. 67-376, 1967-2 C.B. 142, a domestic corporation wanting to conduct its business as a trust proposed to form a new domestic trust qualifying as a corporation within the meaning of § 7701(a)(3). The trust then acquired all the assets of the corporation, subject to all its liabilities, in exchange for transferable certificates of beneficial interest. Thereafter, the corporation distributed the certificates of beneficial interest in exchange for its stock and dissolved. The IRS ruled that the trust was a corporation for purposes of § 368, and therefore the transaction qualified as a reorganization within the meaning of § 368(a)(1)(F). *See also* PLR 9121049 (February 26, 1991) (same result, and in addition the corporation's S election was preserved).

J. TYPE G REORGANIZATIONS

Read § 368(a)(1)(G).

This class of reorganization was recently added in order to accommodate the needs of corporations going through restructurings in bankruptcy. The key feature of § 368(a)(1)(G) is that it opens the door to treating creditors who receive stock as persons with respect to whom there is continuity of proprietary interest. If it were not for this provision, a corporation whose net worth was wiped out could never go through a reorganization because as a practical matter its shareholders would never receive enough stock to constitute continuity of proprietary interest under the general meaning of that term. Section 368(a)(1)(G) is rarely used in practice and is only alluded to here.

K. TREATMENT OF THE PARTIES TO A REORGANIZATION

Read §§ 354(a), 361, 362(a) and (b).

In a qualifying reorganization §§ 354, 361, and 362 dictate the bulk of the outcomes at the corporate and the shareholder levels. The result is generally that income taxes are deferred by means of a continuation of basis similarly under § 1223 there will also be a continuation of holding periods. The problem is that §§ 354, 361, and 362 are not well organized and use unfamiliar language to express Congress' intent. Because the initial steps in a reorganization generally occur at the corporate level, the corporate-level effects appear first below.

1. IMPACT ON CORPORATIONS

The central feature of the acquisitive reorganization is that the stock or assets of one corporation are transferred to another corporation. The Code uses the term of a "transferor" generally to mean the target corporation, viz. the company that transfers its assets to the acquiring "transferee."

a. As to the Transferor ("Target") Corporation

Section 361(a) prevents the transferor from recognizing gain or loss on the transfer of assets to the acquiring corporation and thus overrides §§ 311 and 336. The same is true for the target's transfer of both the acquiring corporation's stock and boot to its shareholders under § 361(b), but only if the entire boot is either distributed to its shareholders or used to pay creditors, or both combined. § 361(b)(1)(B). Note that the transferor is not permitted to recognize any loss in the exchange even if it is due to boot received from the transferee. § 361(b)(2). Gain (but not loss) is recognized by the transferor, however, if it distributes boot to its shareholders which does *not* derive from the transferee, such as its own appreciated property. § 361(c). Basis issues are a bit complicated, and are discussed separately below.

b. As to the Transferee (Acquiring) Corporation

The acquiring corporation does not recognize gain on the issuance of stock for assets. § 1032. However, if the acquiring corporation transfers boot in kind, its gain or loss in the boot *is* recognized under § 1001 as a taxable exchange even though the exchange arises in the context of an otherwise nontaxable reorganization. The acquiror's transfer of cash boot would not be taxed because the basis of cash is always equal to its face amount.

It is generally not a problem if the acquiring company assumes the liabilities of the target company. § 357(a). However, if tax avoidance motives were at work, § 357(b) turns all liabilities into boot. Also, if total liabilities assumed or taken subject to exceed the basis of the target's property, § 357(c) forces the target to recognize gain but only in a Type D reorganization. *See* Rev. Rul. 75-161, 1975-1 C.B. 114.

Section 358 governs the basis results for the target company, but these are marginal issues, because the target generally liquidates as part of the plan of reorganization.

K. TREATMENT OF THE PARTIES TO A REORGANIZATION

What if the parent corporation's stock is used by a subsidiary to acquire the assets of the target in a merger? Does § 1032 apply? Formally, the answer is "no," but in Rev. Rul. 57-278, 1957-1 C.B. 124, the IRS ruled that the subsidiary recognizes no gain or loss on the theory that there would have been none had there been a merger at the parent level followed by a drop down to the subsidiary. This is an admirable example of the application of common sense to Subchapter C.

c. The Acquiring Company's Basis in Acquired Assets

Section 362(b) says that property which a corporation acquires "in connection with a reorganization" normally takes a basis equal to the transferor's (target company's) basis plus any gain that the target company recognized on the transfer. Thus in the relatively infrequent situations where the target's distribution of boot may cause it to recognize gain, the acquiring corporation apparently benefits from an upward adjustment to basis. If the transaction is not a reorganization, the acquiring company takes a cost basis in the target's assets as, for example, in a cash merger where most of the target company stock is exchanged for boot.

d. Foreign Corporations

If a reorganization or incorporation involves a transfer of appreciated assets to a foreign corporation, Congress is understandably concerned that such assets might escape tax permanently and has installed two key safeguards. First, § 367 generally taxes gains (but not losses) on such "outbound" (i.e., to a foreign country) transfers by the curious mechanism of declaring the transferee corporation *not a corporation*. Therefore, the nonrecognition rules of §§ 354-356, § 361, § 1032, and the definitions of § 368 will not apply because they require transfers to and from a "corporation." There are various exceptions for transfers of assets that will be used in an active business, and the Treasury has regulatory authority to relax the rules even further. The other safeguard is § 1491, which imposes a 35% excise tax on certain otherwise tax-free transfers to foreign entities, an excise tax that can be escaped by making a § 1057 election — that the transferor be taxable under the income tax.

2. TAXATION OF SHAREHOLDERS AND SECURITY HOLDERS

Read §§ 354(a), 356, and 358.

Section 354(a)(1) and § 355(a)(1) generally prevent recognition of gain to the target's shareholders on exchanges or distributions in a qualifying reorganization, but if boot is distributed, § 354(a)(3) directs the reader to § 356, which requires the distributee to recognize any realized gain to the extent of the amount of the boot received. No loss may be recognized by target shareholders who participate in the reorganization. § 356(c). Securities are boot except to the extent that securities of the target are given up in the same face amount in the exchange. If a greater face amount is received than given up, the *value* of the excess face amount is boot. § 356(a)(2).

> *To illustrate*: Mrs. Klinger owns one share of T stock with a basis of $105 and a value of $175. T merges into P in an A reorganization in which she receives stock of T stock worth $100, $50 in cash and a note with face amount and value of $25 in exchange for her one share of stock. Assume the exchange does not have the flavor of a distribution, so that there is no dividend issue. Her realized gain is $70 ($175 total consideration received less her basis of $105). The recognized gain is also $70 (the note is boot), because § 356(a)(1) necessarily limits recognized gain to realized gain.[8]

The gain is treated as from a sale or exchange unless the boot distribution "has the effect of the distribution of a dividend," but even then dividend treatment is imposed only to the extent of the distributee's ratable share of earnings and profits. § 356(a)(2). The *Clark* case explores the problem of when boot "has the effect of a dividend."

Section 358 describes the basis of property received by shareholders in a reorganization, and it is identical to the rules for § 351 exchanges. The basis of the shareholder's stock received is the same as that of the target stock given up, less any boot received and plus any gain recognized. Boot receives a fair market value basis.

COMMISSIONER OF INTERNAL REVENUE v. CLARK
489 U.S. 726 (1989)

[In 1979 taxpayer, the sole shareholder of Basin Surveys, Inc. (Basin), entered into a triangular merger agreement with NL Industries, Inc. (NL), pursuant to which he transferred all of Basin's stock to NL's wholly owned subsidiary in exchange for 300,000 NL shares, being approximately 0.92% of NL's outstanding common stock, and a significant amount of cash. Taxpayer reported the cash as a capital gain, but the IRS asserted that the result was a distribution.]

JUSTICE STEVENS delivered the opinion of the Court.

This is the third case in which the Government has asked us to decide that a shareholder's receipt of a cash payment in exchange for a portion of his stock was taxable as a dividend. In the two earlier cases, *Commissioner v. Estate of Bedford*, 325 U.S. 283 (1945), and *United States v. Davis*, 397 U.S. 301 (1970), we agreed with the Government largely because the transactions involved

---

[8] As long as neither the T stock nor the note is "readily tradable," she can report the gain on the installment method. *See* § 453(f)(6).

K. TREATMENT OF THE PARTIES TO A REORGANIZATION

redemptions of stock by single corporations that did not "result in a meaningful reduction of the shareholder's proportionate interest in the corporation." *Id.*, at 313. In the case we decide today, however, the taxpayer in an arm's-length transaction exchanged his interest in the acquired corporation for less than 1% of the stock of the acquiring corporation and a substantial cash payment. The taxpayer held no interest in the acquiring corporation prior to the reorganization. Viewing the exchange as a whole, we conclude that the cash payment is not appropriately characterized as a dividend. We accordingly agree with the Tax Court and with the Court of Appeals that the taxpayer is entitled to capital gains treatment of the cash payment.

I

In determining tax liability under the Internal Revenue Code of 1954, gain resulting from the sale or exchange of property is generally treated as capital gain, whereas the receipt of cash dividends is treated as ordinary income. The Code, however, imposes no current tax on certain stock-for-stock exchanges. In particular, § 354(a)(1) provides, subject to various limitations, for nonrecognition of gain resulting from the exchange of stock or securities solely for other stock or securities, provided that the exchange is pursuant to a plan of corporate reorganization and that the stock or securities are those of a party to the reorganization. 26 U.S.C. § 354(a)(1).

Under § 356(a)(1) of the Code, if such a stock-for-stock exchange is accompanied by additional consideration in the form of a cash payment or other property — something that tax practitioners refer to as "boot" — "then the gain, if any, to the recipient shall be recognized, but in an amount not in excess of the sum of such money and the fair market value of such other property." 26 U.S.C. § 356(a)(1). That is, if the shareholder receives boot, he or she must recognize the gain on the exchange up to the value of the boot. Boot is accordingly generally treated as a gain from the sale or exchange of property and is recognized in the current tax year.

Section 356(a)(2), which controls the decision in this case, creates an exception to that general rule. It provided in 1979:

> "If an exchange is described in paragraph (1) but has the effect of the distribution of a dividend, then there shall be treated as a dividend to each distributee such an amount of the gain recognized under paragraph (1) as is not in excess of his ratable share of the undistributed earnings and profits of the corporation accumulated after February 28, 1913. The remainder, if any, of the gain recognized under paragraph (1) shall be treated as gain from the exchange of property." 26 U.S.C. § 356 (a)(2) (1976 ed.).

Thus, if the "exchange ... has the effect of the distribution of a dividend," the boot must be treated as a dividend and is therefore appropriately taxed as ordinary income to the extent that gain is realized. In contrast, if the exchange does not have "the effect of the distribution of a dividend," the boot must be treated as a payment in exchange for property and, insofar as gain is realized, accorded capital gains treatment. The question in this case is thus whether the exchange between the taxpayer and the acquiring corporation had "the effect of the distribution of a dividend" within the meaning of § 356(a)(2).

The relevant facts are easily summarized. For approximately 15 years prior to April 1979, the taxpayer was the president of Basin Surveys, Inc. (Basin). In January 1978, he became sole shareholder in Basin, a company in which he had invested approximately $85,000. The corporation operated a successful business providing various technical services to the petroleum industry. In 1978, N. L. Industries, Inc. (NL), a publicly owned corporation engaged in the manufacture and supply of petroleum equipment and services, initiated negotiations with the taxpayer regarding the possible acquisition of Basin. On April 3, 1979, after months of negotiations, the taxpayer and NL entered into a contract.

The agreement provided for a "triangular merger," whereby Basin was merged into a wholly owned subsidiary of NL. In exchange for transferring all of the outstanding shares in Basin to NL's subsidiary, the taxpayer elected to receive 300,000 shares of NL common stock and cash boot of $3,250,000, passing up an alternative offer of 425,000 shares of NL common stock. The 300,000 shares of NL issued to the taxpayer amounted to approximately 0.92% of the outstanding common shares of NL. If the taxpayer had instead accepted the pure stock-for-stock offer, he would have held approximately 1.3% of the outstanding common shares. The Commissioner and the taxpayer agree that the merger at issue qualifies as a reorganization under §§ 368(a)(1)(A) and (a)(2)(D).

Respondents filed a joint federal income tax return for 1979. As required by § 356(a)(1), they reported the cash boot as taxable gain. In calculating the tax owed, respondents characterized the payment as long-term capital gain. The Commissioner on audit disagreed with this characterization. In his view, the payment had "the effect of the distribution of a dividend" and was thus taxable as ordinary income up to $2,319,611, the amount of Basin's accumulated earnings and profits at the time of the merger. The Commissioner assessed a deficiency of $972,504.74.

Respondents petitioned for review in the Tax Court, which, in a reviewed decision, held in their favor. 86 T.C. 138 (1986). The court started from the premise that the question whether the boot payment had "the effect of the distribution of a dividend" turns on the choice between "two judicially articulated tests." *Id.*, at 140. Under the test advocated by the Commissioner and given voice in *Shimberg v. United States*, 577 F.2d 283 (CA5 1978), *cert. denied*, 439 U.S. 1115 (1979), the boot payment is treated as though it were made in a hypothetical redemption by the acquired corporation (Basin) immediately prior to the reorganization. Under this test, the cash payment received by the taxpayer indisputably would have been treated as a dividend. The second test, urged by the taxpayer and finding support in *Wright v. United States*, 482 F.2d 600 (CA8 1973), proposes an alternative hypothetical redemption. Rather than concentrating on the taxpayer's prereorganization

K. TREATMENT OF THE PARTIES TO A REORGANIZATION

interest in the acquired corporation, this test requires that one imagine a pure stock-for-stock exchange, followed immediately by a postreorganization redemption of a portion of the taxpayer's shares in the acquiring corporation (NL) in return for a payment in an amount equal to the boot. Under § 302 of the Code, which defines when a redemption of stock should be treated as a distribution of dividend, NL's redemption of 125,000 shares of its stock from the taxpayer in exchange for the $3,250,000 boot payment would have been treated as capital gain.

The Tax Court rejected the prereorganization test favored by the Commissioner because it considered it improper "to view the cash payment as an isolated event totally separate from the reorganization." 86 T.C., at 151. Indeed, it suggested that this test requires that courts make the "determination of dividend equivalency fantasizing that the reorganization does not exist." *Id.*, at 150 (footnote omitted). The court then acknowledged that a similar criticism could be made of the taxpayer's contention that the cash payment should be viewed as a postreorganization redemption. It concluded, however, that since it was perfectly clear that the cash payment would not have taken place without the reorganization, it was better to treat the boot "as the equivalent of a redemption in the course of implementing the reorganization," than "as having occurred prior to and separate from the reorganization." *Id.*, at 152....

The Court of Appeals for the Fourth Circuit affirmed. 828 F.2d 221 (1987). Like the Tax Court, it concluded that although "[s]ection 302 does not explicitly apply in the reorganization context," *id.*, at 223, and although § 302 differs from § 356 in important respects, *id.*, at 224, it nonetheless provides "the appropriate test for determining whether boot is ordinary income or a capital gain," *id.*, at 223. Thus, as explicated in § 302(b)(2), if the taxpayer relinquished more than 20% of his corporate control and retained less than 50% of the voting shares after the distribution, the boot would be treated as capital gain. However, as the Court of Appeals recognized, "[b]ecause § 302 was designed to deal with a stock redemption by a single corporation, rather than a reorganization involving two companies, the section does not indicate which corporation [the taxpayer] lost interest in." *Id.*, at 224. Thus, like the Tax Court, the Court of Appeals was left to consider whether the hypothetical redemption should be treated as a prereorganization distribution coming from the acquired corporation or as a postreorganization distribution coming from the acquiring corporation. It concluded:

> "Based on the language and legislative history of § 356, the change-in-ownership principle of § 302, and the need to review the reorganization as an integrated transaction, we conclude that the boot should be characterized as a post-reorganization stock redemption by N. L. that affected [the taxpayer's] interest in the new corporation. Because this redemption reduced [the taxpayer's] N. L. holdings by more than 20%, the boot should be taxed as a capital gain." *Id.*, at 224-225.

This decision by the Court of Appeals for the Fourth Circuit is in conflict with the decision of the Fifth Circuit in *Shimberg v. United States*, 577 F.2d 283 (1978), in two important respects. In *Shimberg*, the court concluded that it was inappropriate to apply stock redemption principles in reorganization cases "on a wholesale basis." *Id.*, at 287; *see also ibid.*, n.13. In addition, the court adopted the prereorganization test, holding that "§ 356(a)(2) requires a determination of whether the distribution would have been taxed as a dividend if made prior to the reorganization or if no reorganization had occurred." *Id.*, at 288.

To resolve this conflict on a question of importance to the administration of the federal tax laws, we granted certiorari. 485 U.S. 933 (1988).

II

We agree with the Tax Court and the Court of Appeals for the Fourth Circuit that the question under § 356(a)(2) whether an "exchange ... has the effect of the distribution of a dividend" should be answered by examining the effect of the exchange as a whole. We think the language and history of the statute, as well as a commonsense understanding of the economic substance of the transaction at issue, support this approach.

The language of § 356(a) strongly supports our understanding that the transaction should be treated as an integrated whole. Section 356(a)(2) asks whether "an exchange is described in paragraph (1)" that "has the effect of the distribution of a dividend."... The statute does not provide that boot shall be treated as a dividend if its payment has the effect of the distribution of a dividend. Rather, the inquiry turns on whether the "exchange" has that effect. Moreover, paragraph (1), in turn, looks to whether "the property received in the exchange consists not only of property permitted by section 354 or 355 to be received without the recognition of gain but also of other property or money."... Again, the statute plainly refers to one integrated transaction and, again, makes clear that we are to look to the character of the exchange as a whole and not simply its component parts. Finally, it is significant that § 356 expressly limits the extent to which boot may be taxed to the amount of gain realized in the reorganization. This limitation suggests that Congress intended that boot not be treated in isolation from the overall reorganization. *See* Levin, Adess, & McGaffey, *Boot Distributions in Corporate Reorganizations — Determination of Dividend Equivalency*, 30 Tax Lawyer 287, 303 (1977).

Our reading of the statute as requiring that the transaction be treated as a unified whole is reinforced by the well-established "step-transaction" doctrine, a doctrine that the Government has applied in related contexts, *see, e.g.*, Rev. Rul. 75-447, 1975-2 Cum. Bull. 113, and that we have expressly sanctioned, *see Minnesota Tea Co. v. Helvering*, 302 U.S. 609, 613 (1938); *Commissioner v. Court Holding Co.*, 324 U.S. 331, 334 (1945). Under this doctrine, interrelated yet formally distinct steps in an integrated transaction may not be considered independently of the overall transaction. By thus "linking together all interdepen-

K. TREATMENT OF THE PARTIES TO A REORGANIZATION

dent steps with legal or business significance, rather than taking them in isolation," federal tax liability may be based "on a realistic view of the entire transaction." 1 B. Bittker, Federal Taxation of Income, Estates and Gifts para. 4.3.5, p. 4-52 (1981).

Viewing the exchange in this case as an integrated whole, we are unable to accept the Commissioner's prereorganization analogy. The analogy severs the payment of boot from the context of the reorganization. Indeed, only by straining to abstract the payment of boot from the context of the overall exchange, and thus imagining that Basin made a distribution to the taxpayer independently of NL's planned acquisition, can we reach the rather counterintuitive conclusion urged by the Commissioner — that the taxpayer suffered no meaningful reduction in his ownership interest as a result of the cash payment. We conclude that such a limited view of the transaction is plainly inconsistent with the statute's direction that we look to the effect of the entire exchange.

The prereorganization analogy is further flawed in that it adopts an overly expansive reading of § 356(a)(2). As the Court of Appeals recognized, adoption of the prereorganization approach would "result in ordinary income treatment in most reorganizations because corporate boot is usually distributed pro rata to the shareholders of the target corporation." 828 F.2d, at 227; *see also* Golub, *"Boot" in Reorganizations — The Dividend Equivalency Test of Section 356(a)(2),* 58 Taxes 904, 911 (1980); Note, 20 Boston College L. Rev. 601, 612 (1979). Such a reading of the statute would not simply constitute a return to the widely criticized "automatic dividend rule" (at least as to cases involving a pro rata payment to the shareholders of the acquired corporation), *see* n.8, *supra*, but also would be contrary to our standard approach to construing such provisions. The requirement of § 356(a)(2) that boot be treated as dividend in some circumstances is an exception from the general rule authorizing capital gains treatment for boot. In construing provisions such as § 356, in which a general statement of policy is qualified by an exception, we usually read the exception narrowly in order to preserve the primary operation of the provision. *See Phillips, Inc. v. Walling,* 324 U.S. 490, 493 (1945) ("To extend an exemption to other than those plainly and unmistakably within its terms and spirit is to abuse the interpretative process and to frustrate the announced will of the people"). Given that Congress has enacted a general rule that treats boot as capital gain, we should not eviscerate that legislative judgment through an expansive reading of a somewhat ambiguous exception.

The postreorganization approach adopted by the Tax Court and the Court of Appeals is, in our view, preferable to the Commissioner's approach. Most significantly, this approach does a far better job of treating the payment of boot as a component of the overall exchange. Unlike the prereorganization view, this approach acknowledges that there would have been no cash payment absent the exchange and also that, by accepting the cash payment, the taxpayer experienced a meaningful reduction in his potential ownership interest.

Once the postreorganization approach is adopted, the result in this case is pellucidly clear. Section 302(a) of the Code provides that if a redemption fits within any one of the four categories set out in § 302(b), the redemption "shall be treated as a distribution in part or full payment in exchange for the stock," and thus not regarded as a dividend. As the Tax Court and the Court of Appeals correctly determined, the hypothetical postreorganization redemption by NL of a portion of the taxpayer's shares satisfies at least one of the subsections of § 302(b). In particular, the safe harbor provisions of subsection (b)(2) provide that redemptions in which the taxpayer relinquishes more than 20% of his or her share of the corporation's voting stock and retains less than 50% of the voting stock after the redemption shall not be treated as distributions of a dividend. *See* n.6, *supra.* Here, we treat the transaction as though NL redeemed 125,000 shares of its common stock (i.e., the number of shares of NL common stock forgone in favor of the boot) in return for a cash payment to the taxpayer of $3,250,000 (i.e., the amount of the boot). As a result of this redemption, the taxpayer's interest in NL was reduced from 1.3% of the outstanding common stock to 0.9%. See 86 T.C., at 153. Thus, the taxpayer relinquished approximately 29% of his interest in NL and retained less than a 1% voting interest in the corporation after the transaction, easily satisfying the "substantially disproportionate" standards of § 302(b)(2). We accordingly conclude that the boot payment did not have the effect of a dividend and that the payment was properly treated as capital gain.

III

The Commissioner objects to this "recasting [of] the merger transaction into a form different from that entered into by the parties," Brief for Petitioner 11, and argues that the Court of Appeals' formal adherence to the principles embodied in § 302 forced the court to stretch to "find a redemption to which to apply them, since the merger transaction entered into by the parties did not involve a redemption," *id.*, at 28. There are a number of sufficient responses to this argument. We think it first worth emphasizing that the Commissioner overstates the extent to which the redemption is imagined. As the Court of Appeals for the Fifth Circuit noted in *Shimberg*, "[t]he theory behind tax-free corporate reorganizations is that the transaction is merely 'a continuance of the proprietary interests in the continuing enterprise under modified corporate form.' *Lewis v. Commissioner of Internal Revenue*, 176 F.2d 646, 648 (CA1 1949); Treas. Reg. § 1.368-1(b). *See generally* Cohen, *Conglomerate Mergers and Taxation*, 55 A.B.A. J. 40 (1969)." 577 F.2d, at 288. As a result, the boot-for-stock transaction can be viewed as a partial repurchase of stock by the continuing corporate enterprise — i.e., as a redemption. It is, of course, true that both the prereorganization and postreorganization analogies are somewhat artificial in that they imagine that the redemption occurred outside the confines of the actual reorganization. However, if forced to choose between the two analogies, the postreorganization view is the less artificial. Although both

K. TREATMENT OF THE PARTIES TO A REORGANIZATION 505

analogies "recast the merger transaction," the postreorganization view recognizes that a reorganization has taken place, while the prereorganization approach recasts the transaction to the exclusion of the overall exchange.

Moreover, we doubt that abandoning the prereorganization and postreorganization analogies and the principles of § 302 in favor of a less artificial understanding of the transaction would lead to a result different from that reached by the Court of Appeals. Although the statute is admittedly ambiguous and the legislative history sparse, we are persuaded — even without relying on § 302 — that Congress did not intend to except reorganizations such as that at issue here from the general rule allowing capital gains treatment for cash boot. 26 U. S. C. § 356(a)(1). The legislative history of § 356(a)(2), although perhaps generally "not illuminating," Estate of Bedford, 325 U.S., at 290, suggests that Congress was primarily concerned with preventing corporations from "siphon[ing] off" accumulated earnings and profits at a capital gains rate through the ruse of a reorganization. See Golub, 58 Taxes, at 905. This purpose is not served by denying capital gains treatment in a case such as this in which the taxpayer entered into an arm's-length transaction with a corporation in which he had no prior interest, exchanging his stock in the acquired corporation for less than a 1% interest in the acquiring corporation and a substantial cash boot.

Section 356(a)(2) finds its genesis in § 203(d)(2) of the Revenue Act of 1924. See 43 Stat. 257. Although modified slightly over the years, the provisions are in relevant substance identical. The accompanying House Report asserts that § 203(d)(2) was designed to "preven[t] evasion." H. R. Rep. No. 179, 68th Cong., 1st Sess., 15 (1924). Without further explication, both the House and Senate Reports simply rely on an example to explain, in the words of both Reports, "[t]he necessity for this provision." Ibid.; S. Rep. No. 398, 68th Cong., 1st Sess., 16 (1924). Significantly, the example describes a situation in which there was no change in the stockholders' relative ownership interests, but merely the creation of a wholly owned subsidiary as a mechanism for making a cash distribution to the shareholders:

> "Corporation A has capital stock of $100,000, and earnings and profits accumulated since March 1, 1913, of $50,000. If it distributes the $50,000 as a dividend to its stockholders, the amount distributed will be taxed at the full surtax rates.
>
> "On the other hand, Corporation A may organize Corporation B, to which it transfers all its assets, the consideration for the transfer being the issuance by B of all its stock and $50,000 in cash to the stockholders of Corporation A in exchange for their stock in Corporation A. Under the existing law, the $50,000 distributed with the stock of Corporation B would be taxed, not as a dividend, but as a capital gain, subject only to the 12½ per cent rate. The effect of such a distribution is obviously the same as if the corporation had declared out as a dividend its $50,000 earnings and profits. If dividends are to be subject to the full surtax rates, then such an amount so distributed

should also be subject to the surtax rates and not to the 12½ per cent rate on capital gain." *Ibid.*; H.R. Rep. No. 179, at 15.

The "effect" of the transaction in this example is to transfer accumulated earnings and profits to the shareholders without altering their respective ownership interests in the continuing enterprise.

Of course, this example should not be understood as exhaustive of the proper applications of § 356(a)(2). It is nonetheless noteworthy that neither the example, nor any other legislative source, evinces a congressional intent to tax boot accompanying a transaction that involves a bona fide exchange between unrelated parties in the context of a reorganization as though the payment was in fact a dividend. To the contrary, the purpose of avoiding tax evasion suggests that Congress did not intend to impose an ordinary income tax in such cases. Moreover, the legislative history of § 302 supports this reading of § 356(a)(2) as well. In explaining the "essentially equivalent to a dividend" language of § 302(b)(1) — language that is certainly similar to the "has the effect ... of a dividend" language of § 356(a)(2) — the Senate Finance Committee made clear that the relevant inquiry is "whether or not the transaction by its nature may properly be characterized as a sale of stock...." S. Rep. No. 1622, 83d Cong., 2d Sess., 234 (1954); *cf. United States v. Davis*, 397 U.S., at 311.

Examining the instant transaction in light of the purpose of § 356(a)(2), the boot-for-stock exchange in this case "may properly be characterized as a sale of stock." Significantly, unlike traditional single corporation redemptions and unlike reorganizations involving commonly owned corporations, there is little risk that the reorganization at issue was used as a ruse to distribute a dividend. Rather, the transaction appears in all respects relevant to the narrow issue before us to have been comparable to an arm's-length sale by the taxpayer to NL. This conclusion, moreover, is supported by the findings of the Tax Court. The court found that "[t]here is not the slightest evidence that the cash payment was a concealed distribution from BASIN." 86 T.C., at 155. As the Tax Court further noted, Basin lacked the funds to make such a distribution:

> "Indeed, it is hard to conceive that such a possibility could even have been considered, for a distribution of that amount was not only far in excess of the accumulated earnings and profits ($2,319,611), but also of the total assets of BASIN ($2,758,069). In fact, only if one takes into account unrealized appreciation in the value of BASIN's assets, including good will and/or going-concern value, can one possibly arrive at $3,250,000. Such a distribution could only be considered as the equivalent of a complete liquidation of BASIN...." *Ibid.*

In this context, even without relying on § 302 and the post-reorganization analogy, we conclude that the boot is better characterized as a part of the proceeds of a sale of stock than as a proxy for a dividend. As such, the payment qualifies for capital gains treatment.

L. CONTINGENT PAYOUTS

The judgment of the Court of Appeals is accordingly

Affirmed.

[Justice White's dissent is omitted. Eds.]

NOTES

1. *Consider the choices.* The *Wright* decision evaluated the effect of a hypothetical redemption of stock of the acquiring corporation *after* the reorganization. *Shimberg* considered whether a hypothetical redemption from the target corporation would have been taxed as a dividend if it had been made *before* the reorganization. The third possibility is to compare the taxpayer's level of ownership of the target company with her level of ownership of the acquiring company. The last theory is most likely to find a redemption treated as an exchange. The *Shimberg* theory is least likely to find a redemption treated as an exchange and the *Wright* lies somewhere in between. Congress should have specified what § 356(a)(2) means instead of leaving the issue to the courts.

2. *Application.* Going back to the example of Mrs. Klinger before the *Clark* case, if the distribution of the cash and note were in the nature of a dividend because the merger was into a shell corporation such that her ownership interest did not decline, only $70 of the $75 boot would be treated as gain and/or as a dividend to her. Why not tax her on the full $75?

L. CONTINGENT PAYOUTS

It is fairly common business practice to provide for further consideration if the target corporation is especially prosperous in the post-reorganization. The IRS and the courts have accommodated these needs.

REV. PROC. 77-37
1977-2 C.B. 568

SECTION 1. PURPOSE

.01 The purpose of this Revenue Procedure is to update Rev. Proc. 74-26, 1974-2 C.B. 478, which sets forth certain operating rules of the Internal Revenue Service pertaining to issuing ruling letters and in determining whether it should decline to issue ruling letters.

....

SEC. 3. OPERATING RULES FOR ISSUING RULING LETTERS

....

.03 In reorganizations under sections 368(a)(1)(A), 368(a)(1)(B), and 368(a)(1)(C) of the Code where the requisite stock or property has been acquired, it is not necessary that all of the stock of the acquiring corporation or a corporation in "control" thereof, which is to be issued in exchange therefor, be issued immediately provided (1) that all of the stock will be issued within five years from the date of the transfer of assets in the case of reorganizations under sections 368(a)(1)(A) and 368(a)(1)(C), or within five years from the date of the initial distribution in the case of reorganization under section 368(a)(1)(B); (2) there is a valid business reason for not issuing all of the stock immediately, such as the difficulty in determining the value of one or both of the corporations involved in the reorganization; (3) the maximum number of shares which may be issued in the exchange is stated; (4) at least fifty percent of the maximum number of shares of each class of stock which may be issued is issued in the initial distribution; (5) the agreement evidencing the right to receive stock in the future prohibits assignment (except by operation of law) or, in the alternative, if the agreement does not prohibit assignments, the right must not be evidenced by negotiable certificates of any kind and must not be readily marketable; and (6) such right can give rise to the receipt of only additional stock of the acquiring corporation or a corporation in "control" thereof, as the case may be. Stock issued as compensation, royalties or any other consideration other than in exchange for stock or assets will not be considered to have been received in the exchange. Until the final distribution of the total number of shares of stock to be issued in the exchange is made, the interim basis of the stock of the acquiring corporation received in the exchange by the shareholders of the acquired corporation (not including that portion of each share representing interest) will be determined, pursuant to section 358(a), as though the maximum number of shares to be issued (not including that portion of each share representing interest) had been received by the shareholders....

.06 In reorganizations under sections 368(a)(1)(A), 368(a)(1)(B), and 368(a)(1)(C) of the Code where the requisite stock or property has been acquired, a portion of the stock of the acquiring corporation, or a corporation in "control" thereof, that is issued in the exchange may be placed in escrow by the exchanging shareholders, or may otherwise be made subject to a condition pursuant to the agreement or plan of reorganization, for possible return to the acquiring corporation under specified conditions provided (1) there is a valid business reason for establishing the arrangement; (2) the stock subject to such arrangement appears as issued and outstanding on the balance sheet of the acquiring corporation and such stock is, in fact, legally outstanding under applicable state law; (3) all dividends paid on such stock will be distributed currently to the exchanging shareholders; (4) all voting rights of such stock (if any) are exercisable by or on behalf of the shareholders or their authorized agent; (5) no shares of such stock are subject to restrictions requiring their return to the issuing corporation because of death, failure to continue employment or similar restrictions; (6) all such stock is released from the arrangement within 5 years from the date of consummation of the reorganization (except where there is a bona fide dispute as to whom the stock should be released to); and (7) at least 50 percent of the number of shares of each class of stock issued initially to the shareholders (exclusive of shares of stock to be issued at a later date as described in .03 above) is not subject to the arrangement.

OUTSIDE READINGS

D. Posin, *Taxing Corporate Reorganizations: Purging Penelope's Web*, 133 U. Pa. L. Rev. 1335 (1985).

W. Rands, *Section 356(a)(2): A Study of Uncertainty in Corporate Taxation*, 38 U. Miami L. Rev. 75 (1983).

Chapter 22
CARRYOVERS OF TAX ATTRIBUTES AND RESTRICTIONS ON CARRYOVERS

Read § 381(a), (b)(3), and (c)(2).

The basic theme of a tax-free asset acquisition, whether it be a § 368(a)(1) "reorganization or a § 332 subsidiary liquidation," is that it is a mere reshuffling of continuing businesses within corporate form which should not be interrupted by taxes. Consistent with that approach, § 381(a) states the general rule that the acquiring corporation "shall succeed to and take into account the tax attributes of the acquired corporation specified in § 387(c), including earnings and profits, accounting methods, capital-loss carryovers, and net operating loss carryovers. Section 381 provides an extensive list of mechanical directions to make sure that the target corporation's (or liquidated subsidiary's) tax attributes shift to the acquiring corporation, just as the tax history of the assets themselves is transferred by means of the carryover basis rules of § 362 and the holding period rules of § 1223. Both the earnings and profits account of the target and its net operating losses (NOLs) are carried over to the acquiror by operation of § 381(c).

The fact that NOLs carry over to the acquiror (together with built-in losses in assets) has caused considerable friction between taxpayers and the government. Acquirors have been quick to see opportunities to shelter their own income by means of offsetting losses of the target against them, and if it were not for the elaborate safeguards Congress has enacted, would acquire failed corporations (even corporate "shells") for no other reason than to enjoy this sheltering. This was called "trafficking" in NDIs.

Sheltering in the opposite direction is restricted as well, so that losses of the acquiring corporation are often ineligible for offset against target corporation's gains. After all, Gainco can merge into Lossco just as easily as the other way around. Some safeguards are built directly into § 381 itself, and a variety of other hurdles may be found in §§ 269 and 382-384, which are the subject of this Chapter.

Section § 381 generally forbids offsets in both directions for gains and losses of either corporation that occurred *before* the acquisition. Section 381(c)(1) prevents the target's preexisting NOLs from offsetting profits of the acquiring corporation which accrued before the acquisition, and thus the target's NOLs can only be used to offset *post-acquisition* earnings of the acquiror. Similarly, § 381(b)(3) forbids an acquiring corporation to carry back its NOLs to offset the target's earnings from years prior to the acquisition (except in an F reorganization). This overrides the usual rules of § 172 which generally permit a corporation to carry its *own* losses back for three years to offset its prior gains and to obtain a refund of tax. There are similar barriers against using deficits in earnings and profits of either corporation to offset positive earnings and profits from preacquisition years. *See* § 381(c)(2).

A. SECTION 269: THE SUBJECTIVE APPROACH TO DENYING LOSSES

Read § 269.

Section 269 permits the IRS to disallow any deduction or other tax benefit that may flow from an acquisition of 50% or more control of a corporation (or its assets in a tax-free transaction) if the "principal purpose for which such acquisition was made is evasion or avoidance of Federal income tax." The provision applies potentially to all A and C reorganizations, as well as to B reorganizations in which the acquiror had less than 50% control before the exchange. It also applies to taxable purchases of stock (but not of assets).

On its face this rule confers very broad power upon the IRS, but in practice it is limited by the need to demonstrate the taxpayer's forbidden state of mind. There are nearly always multiple reasons for acquiring a corporation or its assets, and § 269 applies only if the "principal purpose" was to secure tax benefits not otherwise available. The following case presses the question of how bad one has to be to suffer a tax forfeiture under § 269.

CANAVERAL INTERNATIONAL CORP. v. COMMISSIONER
61 T.C. 520 (1974), *acq.*, 1974-2 C.B. 1

[Canaveral International Corp., the publicly-traded parent of an affiliated group of corporations, negotiated to swap some of its stock for a yacht which could be converted to business use as a charter vessel. On learning that Norango, Inc. owned the yacht and that the yacht had an undepreciated basis of $769,632.75, Canaveral instead acquired all of Norango's stock in exchange for some of Canaveral's nonvoting preferred stock. Thereafter, Norango improved the yacht and unsuccessfully tried to charter it for commercial purposes until Norango finally sold it for $250,000. On its consolidated return, Canaveral reported depreciation deductions and an ordinary loss under § 1231 on the sale computed with reference to Norango's undepreciated basis.]

FEATHERSTON, JUDGE.

Respondent determined a deficiency in petitioner's Federal income tax and that of its affiliated companies for the taxable year ended September 30, 1966, in the amount of $159,431.48. By stipulation the parties have settled most of the issues outlined in the notice of deficiency, leaving for decision the following questions:

(1) Whether the principal purpose motivating petitioner's acquisition of the stock of Norango, Inc., was the evasion or avoidance of Federal income tax within the meaning of section 269; ...

Opinion

1. *The Applicability of Section 269 to the Acquisition of the Stock of Norango, Inc.*

(a) *Tax-avoidance purpose.* — Section 269(a) provides, in pertinent part, that if any person acquires control of a corporation, and the "principal purpose" for which such acquisition is made is evasion or avoidance of Federal income tax by securing the benefit of a deduction, credit, or other allowance which such person or corporation would not otherwise enjoy, such deduction, credit, or other allowance shall not be allowed. More simply, the section "states in effect that, if A acquires B for the principal purpose of tax avoidance, then A cannot have the tax benefit which the ownership of B would otherwise entail." *Bobsee Corporation v. United States*, 411 F. 2d 231, 234 (C.A. 5, 1969).

For the section to be operative, the tax evasion or avoidance purpose must outrank, or exceed in importance, any other one purpose. S. Rept. No. 627, 78th Cong., 1st Sess. (1943), 1944 C.B. 1017. The determination of the purpose of an acquisition requires a scrutiny of the entire circumstances in which the transaction or course of conduct occurred, including the relationship of the transaction to the claimed consequent tax result. Sec. 1.269-3(a), Income Tax Regs. The burden of proof rests with petitioner. "Theoretically the question of purpose is purely subjective; pragmatically, however, the trier of fact can only determine purpose from objective facts." *Bobsee Corporation v. United States*, *supra* at 238.

The enactment in 1943 of the predecessor of section 269(a) was prompted by a desire to curb a growing market for defunct corporate shells with a history of large amounts of invested capital coupled with subsequent net operating losses. Such characteristics were effective income and excess profits tax shields for booming war enterprises. H. Rept. No. 871, 78th Cong., 1st Sess. (1943), 1944 C.B. 938; S. Rept. No. 627, 78th Cong., 1st Sess. (1943), 1944 C.B. 1016. But the section was intended to be broader in concept than a measure merely to prevent the trafficking in loss corporations. Its grander design, as expressed by Congress, was —

> "to codify and emphasize the general principle set forth in *Higgins v. Smith* (308 U.S., 473 ...), and in other judicial decisions, as to the ineffectiveness of arrangements distorting or perverting deductions, credits, or allowances so that they no longer bear a reasonable business relationship to the interests or enterprises which produced them and for the benefit of which they were provided." S. Rept. No. 627, 1944 C.B. at 1016.

We think the evidence in the instant case, weighed in the light of the foregoing principles, requires a holding that petitioner's principal purpose in acquiring Norango's stock was to receive the tax benefits of the vessel's sizable basis which otherwise would not have been enjoyed by petitioner and its affiliated group. Legitimate business reasons may have motivated petitioner to seek a vessel suitable for oceanographic and geodetic charter purposes. However, once petitioner's representatives became aware of Norango's corporate existence, viewed Norango's books, and discovered the yacht's underpreciated $769,632.75 cost basis, we think the overriding reason for acquiring Norango's stock was to reduce petitioner's consolidated income tax liability, present and prospective. *See Industrial Suppliers, Inc.*, 50 T.C. 635, 646 (1968); *Temple Square Mfg. Co.*, 36 T.C. 88, 94 (1961).

The evidence is unmistakably clear that petitioner's representatives, not the Woolworth estate, were responsible for casting the transaction in the form of an acquisition of Norango's stock. The evidence shows that Woolworth had advertised a yacht for sale, not a corporation owning a yacht, and that petitioner had decided to acquire a vessel for use in an oceanographic and geodetic charter business, not a corporation engaged in such business. There is some dispute as to whether Woolworth, prior to his death, had agreed to a stock-for-stock exchange. But the evidence is clear that after examining Norango's books, petitioner's representatives, including a New York attorney-accountant versed in tax matters, proposed to Malcolm, the representative of the Woolworth estate, that the transaction be cast in the form of an exchange of some of petitioner's stock for Norango's stock and the notes payable to Woolworth.[1]

Petitioner's representatives made this proposal notwithstanding the risk of undisclosed liabilities ordinarily attendant upon the acquisition of the stock of a small corporation. Also, the notes payable in the amount of $961,484.89, recorded on Norango's books, ordinarily would have dictated that only the corporation's assets be acquired. However, by purchasing Norango's notes payable and stock and contributing the notes to the capital of the corporation,

---

[1] Malcolm, representative of the Woolworth estate, testified that petitioner's representatives proposed that the transaction take the form of a sale of stock:

Q. Did you bring up the possibility of selling the stock of Norango, Inc.?

A. I didn't bring it up.

Q. Did you suggest that?

A. I didn't bring it up. They asked me for it.

Though Henry Dubbin's testimony on the issue is evasive, he testified at one point:

"[Mr. Field, the New York attorney-accountant who assisted in the negotiations] may have been called in on tax matters. I don't really recall him being called in specifically on tax matters. I recall him being — discussing them with our comptroller and our auditing division."

petitioner tailored the transaction to make the purchase of Norango's stock economically feasible. It would have been simpler to have acquired the yacht directly, and petitioner has given no worthwhile explanation as to why the more roundabout route was taken. The most reasonable inference is that petitioner's representatives wanted the transaction cast in this form for tax-avoidance reasons.

The potential tax benefits from the stock acquisition were so disproportionate in relation to the consideration paid for the stock as to cause a major distortion in petitioner's income. For the Norango stock, petitioner traded 949 shares of its non-dividend-bearing, non-voting preferred stock which were convertible to 20,878 shares of petitioner's common shares. The conversion could not take place until sometime between December 31, 1966, and February 1, 1967. On the day of the closing of the sale, petitioner's common stock was selling at a high of 11 1/4 and a low of 10 3/4. Due to the restrictions on the preferred stock's convertibility, the non-dividend-bearing character of the preferred stock, and the uncertainty of the number of shares of preferred stock allocable to the notes acquired in the transaction, we have found that the value of the yacht and of the shares of stock petitioner exchanged for the Norango stock was $177,500.[2]

For this outlay of property worth $177,500, petitioner's consolidated group obtained potential tax deductions in the form of depreciation over the life of the vessel or a loss on a subsequent sale, computed by use of an adjusted basis of $769,632.75 (the cost of the yacht and furniture and fixtures as carried over from the books of Norango). At the prevailing corporate tax rates, the tax windfall from Norango's high basis in the yacht so far exceeded petitioner's investment in Norango's stock that the consolidated group could have realized a net profit even if the newly acquired yacht had sunk on its first voyage. This is the kind of subversion of the basis-loss provisions to distort income that section 269 was enacted to prevent. Sec. 1.269-2(b), Income Tax Regs.; *Scroll, Inc. v. Commissioner*, 447 F. 2d 612, 618-619 and fn. 15 (C.A. 5, 1971).

Petitioner hammers away on the point that it intended to, and did, use the vessel for business purposes. However, the fact that petitioner would have acquired the yacht in the absence of a tax-avoidance motive is not determinative. Sec. 1.269-3(a), Income Tax Regs. *See F. C. Publication Liquidating Corporation v. Commissioner*, 304 F. 2d 779, 780-781 (C.A. 2, 1962), *affirming* 36 T.C. 836 (1961); *Industrial Suppliers, Inc.*, 50 T.C. at 646. Section 269 is directed to the principal purpose for the acquisition of control of a corporation, not the absence of a business purpose in acquiring a corporation's assets. That petitioner

---

[2] We have found the value of the yacht at the time of petitioner's acquisition of the Worango [sic] stock in August 1962 was $177,500, the value of the stock given in the exchange. We recognize that petitioner sold the yacht in December 1963 for $250,000. However, this sale followed extensive renovations and refurbishment and a demonstration of the feasibility of the use of the vessel — described by one of the witnesses as a "white elephant" — for commercial purposes.

planned to use the yacht for business reasons does not alone explain the principal purpose underlying its acquisition of the stock.

In *Industrial Suppliers, Inc., supra*, Caldwell and associates acquired for $20,000 the stock of a corporation which had a merchandise inventory with a book value of $165,475 and which had a long history of net operating losses. The purchasers thereupon used the corporation in carrying out a highly profitable joint venture. Rejecting a contention that section 269 was not applicable because the purchasers' principal purpose was to acquire the corporation's inventory, this Court said (50 T.C. at 646):

> We have no doubt that Caldwell was interested in acquiring petitioner's inventory at what he considered to be a bargain price and, on first impression, this would appear to be a valid, business purpose for the acquisition of petitioner's stock. We are not convinced, however, that the tax benefits to be derived from the carryover of previous net operating losses was not the principal purpose for acquiring the inventory through the purchase of petitioner's stock rather than by a simple purchase of the inventory itself. The purchase of the stock and the various manipulations which this involved, as well as the subsequent utilization of petitioner in the ... [joint] venture, thereby creating additional profits against which the loss carryovers could be applied, belies Caldwell's testimony that the tax benefits were not a consideration for the purchase of the stock.

Similarly, in *Bobsee Corporation v. United States*, 411 F. 2d at 239, the court dismissed an argument that section 269 did not apply because each of seven corporations was created for a business purpose, stating: "To establish a principal non-tax motive ... [the owner of the taxpayer] had to justify the creation of seven corporations; however, the reason she gave would only justify the formation of a single corporation." By analogy, that petitioner wanted to acquire a vessel for business purposes does not show that its principal reason for acquiring the stock of Norango was not tax avoidance.

Petitioner argues that the claimed loss on the sale of the yacht occurred after the Norango stock was acquired and that there is substantial disagreement among the Courts of Appeals as to whether section 269 is applicable at all to postacquisition losses. The disagreement petitioner refers to is whether section 269 applies to losses which accrue economically after affiliation. *Compare Herculite Protective Fabrics Corp. v. Commissioner*, 387 F.2d 475 (C.A. 3, 1968); *and Zanesville Investment Co. v. Commissioner*, 335 F.2d 507 (C.A. 6, 1964); *with Hall Paving Co. v. United States*, 471 F.2d 261 (C.A. 5, 1973); *Borge v. Commissioner*, 405 F.2d 673 (C.A. 2, 1968) (and cases cited therein), *certiorari denied sub nom. Danica Enterprises, Inc. v. Commissioner*, 395 U.S. 933 (1969); *Temple Square Mfg. Co.*, 36 T.C. 88 (1961). The economic loss in the instant case, i.e., the difference between the basis of the yacht carried on Norango's books and the value of the consideration exchanged by petitioner for Norango's stock, had already accrued at the time of Norango's affiliation, and the Courts of Appeals all agree that section 269 may be used to disallow such "built-in" losses.

In holding against petitioner, we do not suggest that section 269 requires a taxpayer to acquire a corporation's assets rather than its stock merely because a stock acquisition produces more favorable tax results. In given cases, the courts have recognized that acquiring the stock of a corporation may be the only, or the most feasible, way of handling the transaction. *Hawaiian Trust Co., Ltd. v. United States*, 291 F.2d 761 (C.A. 9, 1961). *See, e.g., Glen Raven Mills, Inc.*, 59 T.C. 1, 15 (1972); *Clarksdale Rubber Co.*, 45 T.C. 234, 240-241 (1965); *Baton Rouge Supply Co.*, 36 T.C. 1, 13 (1961). But when section 269 is placed in issue, it does require a showing that the most favorable tax route, when that route involves the acquisition of a corporation, was principally motivated by non-tax-related business reasons. Petitioner has shown no substantial business reasons for acquiring Norango's stock rather than the yacht. The evidence is persuasive that the transaction was so cast in an effort to obtain the tax benefits of the yacht's high basis which petitioner otherwise would not have enjoyed.

In cases where the purchase price paid for the stock of a corporation is substantially less than the aggregate basis of the corporation's assets, the burden of proof imposed on the taxpayer can be difficult to sustain. *See* sec. 269(c); *Scroll, Inc. v. Commissioner*, 447 F.2d at 618. In the instant case, petitioner exchanged preferred stock worth $177,500 for stock in a corporation with assets having a $769,632.75 basis. Through such use of Norango's basis, unrelated to petitioner's cost, petitioner sought, among other things, to reduce its consolidated tax liability by taking excessive depreciation deductions and by converting an economic gain on the sale of the yacht into a deductible tax loss. The practical effect of the transaction, if section 269 does not apply, was to enable petitioner's consolidated group to offset current business earnings from other sources against a preacquisition economic loss suffered by Norango while the yacht was used for nonbusiness purposes. *See Scroll, Inc. v. Commissioner, supra* at 617. Such a distortion of petitioner's tax liability is by itself prima facie evidence of the principal purpose of tax evasion or avoidance, and petitioner has failed to produce convincing evidence proving otherwise.

QUESTION

Whom does § 269 scare? Is it possible that § 269 does as much harm as good by scaring off well-intentioned taxpayers? Do we really need such *in terrorem* rules?

B. SECTION 382: THE OBJECTIVE APPROACH TO LOSSES

Read § 382(a), (b)(1)-(2).

1. INTRODUCTION

The purpose of § 382 is to prevent "trafficking" in loss corporations. Section 382 is designed to limit the extent to which corporate loss carryovers (NOLs) may be enjoyed after a change of an ownership of a "loss corporation." The fundamental idea is quite simple: if more than 50% of the stock of any corporation changes hands within a three-year period, that corporation's NOLs survive but they are restricted so as to offset income only at an annual rate which is limited to the value of the loss corporation multiplied by a given rate of interest, namely the federal "long-term tax exempt rate." § 382(f). In addition, the business enterprise must be continued for two years; otherwise, the NOLs are disallowed altogether. § 382(c). The intended effect is to allow the NOLs to offset no more income than the corporate assets would earn if they were sold and the proceeds invested in treasury bills or notes.

This ownership-based approach is in some respects a radical departure from pre-1986 law, which was chiefly concerned with preventing losses from one business from offsetting gains from another. To the extent current § 382 is applied to business combinations of two or more corporations, it is generally a reasonable solution, if perhaps arbitrary and overly complex. If X Corporation, owned by A and B, is profitable and it acquires unrelated Y Corporation (a loss corporation) by an A, C, nondivisive D or F reorganization, (or by a subsidiary liquidation under § 382 if Y had been X Corp.'s subsidiary) § 382 will limit the extent that X Corporation can use Y Corp.'s NOLs from preacquisition (change of ownership) years — compared to what Y Corp. could have done if left alone and if it became profitable.

However, a simple change of ownership of a single loss corporation will trigger the § 382 limitation even if the new owner(s) do not combine the loss corporation with any other business. So if A and B, the shareholders of X Corporation, sell their shares to C and D, this change of ownership of a single, unchanged corporation, will limit the extent to which it can carry forward and use its NOLs from pre-change of ownership years to post-change years, compared to what X Corp. could have done if it had not changed hands. If the new owners turn the loss corporation around with new management and/or infusion of additional capital, § 382 applies despite the fact that the NOLs would offset income derived solely from the same business which produced the losses. In such a case the NOLs would merely perform their intended income-averaging function. It is difficult to see any policy reason for subjecting the new owners to worse tax treatment than the original owners. In fact, a loss corporation which has been successfully turned around under new ownership may have greater value if it is resold again, because if § 382 is deliberately triggered a second time, the increased sales price will free up the remaining NOLs at a faster rate.

B. SECTION 382: THE OBJECTIVE APPROACH TO LOSSES

a. Ownership Change

The annual "section 382 limitation" of § 382(b) is triggered by an "ownership change" as defined under § 382(g)(1). There are two ways in which an ownership change may occur. The first is through an "owner shift" involving one or more 5% shareholders. § 382(g)(2). The second is through an "equity structure shift." § 382(g)(3).

b. Owner Shift Involving 5% Shareholders

An ownership change occurs if the percentage of stock owned by one or more 5% shareholders increases more than fifty percentage points above their lowest percentage ownership during the testing period. § 382(g)(1). A "5% shareholder" is any person holding 5% or more of the loss corporation during the testing period. § 382(k)(7). The "testing period" consists of the three years ending on the day of a 5% shareholder or equity structure shift. § 382(i)(1). The testing period begins immediately after an "owner shift," which is any change in ownership, no matter how large or small, of a 5% shareholder. § 382(g)(2).

> *To illustrate*: If A owns 100% of the stock of L Corp. and on January 1, 1996, A sells 51% to B, two "owner shifts" occur on that date, because A and B are both 5% shareholders immediately after the sale, and both have altered their holdings. B's owner shift causes an "ownership change" triggering the § 382 limitation, because B's ownership of L Corp. has increased by more than fifty percentage points (from zero to 51%) within the three-year period ending immediately after the sale.

If an ownership change has already occurred within the preceding three years, the testing period begins immediately after the most recent ownership change. § 382(i)(2). The stock ownership percentage of a shareholder is determined by the value of the shares owned by the shareholder, not the number of shares. § 382(k)(6)(C). Nonvoting, nonconvertible preferred shares are not treated as "stock." § 382(k)(6)(A). On the other hand warrants, options, and convertible debt are generally treated as "stock." § 382(k)(6)(B). A strikingly one-sided rule provides that such rights to acquire stock are treated as "stock" only if it will result in an ownership change — i.e., only when it benefits the Government. § 382(l)(3)(A)(iv).

For the purpose of testing whether an ownership change has occurred, all less than 5% shareholders are treated as a single 5% shareholder. § 382(g)(4)(A). The result is that changes in ownership of less than 5% shareholders are not normally counted, except where such shareholders are acting in concert. This rule avoids the problem of keeping track of all purchases and sales of publicly-traded stock, and prevents accidental triggering of an ownership change if 50% of the stock changes hands over a three-year period through countless anonymous sales on a public exchange. If all the public shareholders are less than 5% shareholders, no matter how many sales take place, the public shareholders count as a single 5% shareholder and their (its) aggregate ownership remains unchanged.

All stock owned by any members of the same family (as defined by § 318(a)(1)) is treated as owned by a single individual. Thus sales and other transfers within a family are ignored. § 382(l)(3)(A)(i). Similarly, gifts, bequests, and transfers of stock between spouses or incident to divorce are also ignored. § 382(l)(3)(B).

> *To illustrate*: A has owned all 100 Shares of Loss Corp. for four years and sells 45 shares to B on July 1, 1996. Both A and B are 5% shareholders whose ownership has changed on July 1, 1996, and that date becomes the testing date to determine whether an ownership change has occurred. The sale does not result in an ownership change because B did not increase his percentage of stock in the loss corporation by more than 50% over his lowest percentage of ownership during the three-year testing period. B has increased his ownership only 45% (from zero to 45% of the value of all shares). Note that subsequent stock transactions may become risky as a result. If, on January 1, 1997, A sells 30 shares to C., January 1, 1997 becomes a new testing date, and the testing period is again three years because the previous transaction on July 1, 1996 did not result in an ownership change. The sale to C results in an ownership change, because both B and C are 5% shareholders and their combined ownership in Loss Corp. increased from zero to 75% during the three-year testing period. The use of Loss Corp.'s NOLs by the "New Loss" Corp. is subject to the annual limitation of § 382.

In the above illustration, if any two of the three shareholders A, B, and C are related as family members, no ownership change occurs, and the same would be true if any of the transfers were by gift, bequest, or pursuant to divorce.

c. Equity Structure Shift

An ownership change also occurs if there is an "equity structure shift" resulting in an increase of more than 50% ownership within the testing period. An equity structure shift is a tax-free reorganization under § 368 (except for reorganizations under § 368(a)(1)(D) or (G), unless the requirements of § 354(b)(1) are met, and reorganizations under § 368(a)(1)(F) involving a mere change in form). § 382(g)(3)(A). Equity structure shifts also include taxable reorganizations, public offerings and similar transactions. § 382(g)(3)(B). Any combination of equity structure shift(s) and/or owner shifts within the testing period will trigger an ownership change if the total new ownership increases by more than 50%.

B. SECTION 382: THE OBJECTIVE APPROACH TO LOSSES

When an equity structure shift occurs, the less than 5% shareholders of each corporation which was a party to the reorganization are treated as a separate less-than-5% shareholder. § 382(g)(4)(B)(i). Whether an ownership change has occurred is measured by comparing the ownership of the loss corporation (whether it is the target or the acquirer) before and after the reorganization. The surviving corporation possessing the NOLs is a "new loss corporation." § 382(k)(3).

> *To illustrate*: If Loss Corp. is merged into Gain Corp. and the former shareholders of Loss Corp. receive 25% of Gain Corp. stock, an ownership change occurs which subjects Gain Corp. (the "new loss" corporation) to the § 382 limitation. The Gain Corp. shareholder group, considered as a single less-than-5% shareholder, has increased its ownership in Loss Corp. from zero to 75%. If the acquisition of Loss Corp. were effected through an exchange of 25% of Gain Corp. stock for all the stock of Loss Corp. in a "B" reorganization, the § 382 result would be the same.

Absent the rule of § 382(g)(4)(B) which separates the less than 5% shareholders of each corporation into two different groups, most reorganizations would escape the grasp of § 382. In the above illustration, if no shareholder of either corporation is a 5% shareholder, and the less-than-5% shareholders of both Loss Corp. and Gain Corp. were treated as a single less-than-5% shareholder, that less than 5% shareholder's holdings would be unchanged by the merger.

d. Constructive Ownership

Stock held by partnership, estate, trust, or corporation is considered to be held by the partners, beneficiaries, or shareholders, respectively, in proportion to their interest in the entity, and the 50% corporate ownership interest required by § 318 does not apply. § 382(l)(3)(A)(ii). In effect, these rules look through entities to treat all stock as owned by individuals. Only ultimate ownership by individuals matters. This may require looking through a maze of entities to determine the individual ownership of all shares of stock.

One purpose of these look-through rules is to prevent easy avoidance of § 382 by interposition of an entity owner of a loss corporation's stock. Consider a variation of the above illustration of the acquisition of Loss Corp. by means of a "B" reorganization. If the Loss Corp. stock is held by Holding Co. and Holding Co. stock is exchanged for 25% of Gain Corp. stock, Loss Corp. is 100% owned by Holding Co. both before and after the exchange. The look-through rules appropriately treat the Gain Corp. shareholders as proportionate owners of Loss Corp. stock, however, and because their indirect ownership has increased from zero to 75%, § 382 applies.

The look-through rules can also prevent § 382 from applying where it otherwise might. If loss corporation stock is transferred to another corporation which has the same owner(s), common ownership will prevent application of § 382.

2. LIMITS ON THE USE OF NOL AFTER AN OWNERSHIP CHANGE

a. Business Continuity Requirement

The new loss corporation must continue the business enterprise of the old loss corporation at all times for the two-year period after the ownership change. § 382(c). The "continuity of business enterprise" requirement is satisfied if the new loss corporation continues the old loss corporation's historic business or if it uses a significant portion of the old loss corporation's assets in some other line of business. If this requirement is not met, the loss corporation's NOLs are completely eliminated and the § 382 annual limitation for any post-change year is zero. There is an exception under which certain recognized built-in gains (discussed below) may still be offset against the NOLs despite lack of business continuity. § 382(c)(2).

b. Annual Income Limitation

If an ownership change occurs, the "Section 382 limitation" then applies to restrict the new loss corporation's NOLs by allowing them to offset post-change income only to the extent of a formula: the value of the old loss corporation multiplied by the "long-term tax-exempt rate." § 382(b)(1) and (f). The value of the old loss corporation is the fair market value of its stock immediately before the ownership change, including the value of any nonvoting preferred stock which was omitted in determining whether a change of ownership occurred. § 382(e)(1).

> *To illustrate*: Loss Corp. has $1,000,000 of NOLs at the change date when all its stock is sold to new owners. The stock is sold for $200,000, which is its fair market value. The applicable long-term tax-exempt interest rate is 10%. The § 382 annual limitation is thus $200,000 times 10%, or $20,000 per year. Loss Corp. will be permitted to use its NOLs to offset post-change income at a maximum rate of $20,000 per year.

It should be noted that nothing in § 382 extends the fifteen-year statutory life of NOLs under § 172(b)(1)(ii), and thus in the above example most of the NOLs will be lost altogether. Multiplying $20,000 per year by the maximum fifteen-year life yields a total of $300,000, so that at least $700,000 of the $1 million of NOLs is in effect disallowed.

If Loss Corp. does not have sufficient income in a post-change year to use the entire $20,000 allowable deduction, the remainder may be carried over and

B. SECTION 382: THE OBJECTIVE APPROACH TO LOSSES

increases the following year's § 382 annual limitation. Using the above example, if Loss Co. has only $10,000 of income and cannot use the full $20,000 allowable deduction, the $10,000 unused amount is added to the following year's limitation which is increased to $30,000. § 382(b)(2).

If the ownership change occurs in mid-year, the § 382 limitation applies only to income of the post-change portion of the taxable year, calculated on a ratable daily basis. As a result, income which is allocable to the pre-change portion of the year may be offset by the pre-change NOLs without limitation. § 382(b)(3)(A). Post-change income may be offset only by a prorated amount of the § 382 annual limitation which is proportional to the number of days remaining after the change. § 382(b)(3)(B). Thus if the change occurs precisely at mid-year, precisely half of the $20,000 limitation, or $10,000, will become the allowable § 382 limitation for the post-change period of the year. Finally, it should be remembered that the § 382 limitation applies only to NOLs which were in existence on the change date. Losses incurred subsequent to a change of ownership are fully deductible and may create NOLs which are unrestricted by § 382.

> *To illustrate*: Continuing the previous example, suppose Loss Corp.'s change date is April 1, 1997 and that at the end of 1997, Loss Corp. has a $40,000 loss for the year. This amount is separated into the prechange and postchange years on a pro rata daily basis. Because the change date occurs after 1/4 of the year, 1/4 of the $40,000 loss, or $10,000, would be added to the prechange NOL resulting in a carryforward of $1,010,000 which is subject to the § 382 annual limitation of $20,000. The remaining $30,000 of the 1997 loss allocable to the last 3/4 of 1997 is attributed to the post-change tax year and is not subject to the § 382 annual limitation. The unused portion of the § 382 annual limitation for 1997 is $15,000 (3/4 times the $20,000 § 382 annual limitation). This $15,000 carries forward to 1998 and increases the § 382 annual limitation for 1998 to $35,000.
>
> If, instead, Loss Corp. had $400,000 of taxable income for 1997, 1/4 of the income ($100,000) allocable to the prechange portion of the year would be fully offset by the prechange NOLs without limitation. This reduces the NOLs from $1 million to $900,000 as of the change date. The remaining 3/4 of Loss Corp.'s 1997 income ($300,000) is subject to the § 382 annual limitation, which is 3/4 of $20,000, or $15,000. Thus only $15,000 of the postchange NOLs may be used to offset the $300,000 postchange income for 1997. Loss Corp.'s remaining NOLs will be $885,000 at the beginning of 1998, and the § 382 annual limitation on their use will be $20,000.

c. Anti-Stuffing Rules

Because the § 382 limitation is dependent upon the value of the loss corporation at the change date, taxpayers might be tempted to increase its value in order to increase the limitation. Again using the example of Loss Corp., if the original owners were to contribute $800,000 worth of Treasury bonds to its capital before selling Loss Corp.'s stock, the stock would be worth $1 million, and the § 382 annual limitation would become $100,000 (10% times $1 million) rather than $20,000. This ploy is forestalled by an "anti-stuffing" rule, however. Section 382(l)(1) requires the value of any capital contributions to be disregarded if they are made pursuant to a plan to increase the § 382 annual limitation, and presumes such a forbidden plan if the contributions are made within two years before the change date. Another anti-stuffing rule requires reduction of the value of the loss corporation if at least one-third of the value of its assets consist of nonbusiness (investment) assets, regardless of when or why such assets were acquired. § 382(l)(4)(B)(i). The loss corporation's value must then be reduced by the value of its nonbusiness assets, less an allocable portion of loss corporation's indebtedness. § 382(l)(4)(A). Under either or both the anti-stuffing rules, the contribution of $800,000 worth of Treasury bonds to Loss Corp. would not increase the § 382 annual limitation.

d. Built-in Gains and Losses

Section 382(h) provides that if a loss corporation has "net unrealized built-in gain" on the change date, the § 382 limitation amount is increased by any "recognized built-in gain" during the five-year "recognition period" following the change date. In effect, the loss corporation is given credit for unrealized gains which accrued before the change date, and if such gains are later recognized through a taxable sale or other disposition, they may be fully offset by pre-change NOLs despite the § 382 annual limitation. § 382(h)(1)(A). When a pre-change appreciated asset is sold during the recognition period, only the pre-change built-in gain qualifies for offset by increasing the § 382 limitation. § 382(h)(2)(A). Thus any taxable profit due to further post-change appreciation does not increase the § 382 limitation.

Conversely, "net unrealized built-in losses" which are recognized during the five-year post-change period are treated in the same way as pre-change NOLs, and their deductibility is subject to the § 382 limitation. § 382(h)(1)(B). This rule reflects Congress' concern that a corporation with unrealized losses in its assets might be an attractive acquisition for tax purposes for the same reason as a corporation with NOLs. The acquiring corporation could offset its own gains against such built-in losses by causing them to be recognized after the acquisition.

However, there is a "threshold requirement" before either of the above gain or loss rules can apply. The "net unrealized built-in gain" (or loss) must exceed the lesser of: (1) 15% of the fair market value of the loss corporations assets

B. SECTION 382: THE OBJECTIVE APPROACH TO LOSSES

immediately prior to the ownership change, or (2) $10 million. § 382(h)(3)(B). "Net unrealized built-in gain" (or loss) means the amount by which the fair market value of all the assets is more (or less, respectively) than their aggregate basis immediately before the change date. § 382(h)(3)(A)(i). If the threshold is not met, the net unrealized gain (or loss) is treated as zero. § 382(h)(3)(B). The effect of this *de minimis* rule is that recognized built-in gains would not increase the § 382 limitation, and losses would not be subject to it (i.e., they would be freely deductible).

> *To illustrate*: Again using the Loss Corp. example, suppose that the pre-change aggregate value of its assets is $200,000 and the aggregate basis is $250,000. There is a net aggregate built-in loss of $50,000 which exceeds the threshold requirement of $30,000 (15% of FMV of Loss Corp.'s $200,000 of assets). The threshold is met. If Loss Corp. sells asset A within the five-year recognition period and recognizes a $20,000 loss, and asset A as of the change date had a value of $50,000 and basis of $70,000, the loss deduction is subject in its entirety to the § 382 annual limitation. This would use up Loss Corp.'s entire $20,000 annual limitation. If the change date value of asset A had been $60,000 instead, only $10,000 of the loss (the amount of loss built in at the change date) would reduce the annual limitation, and the remaining $10,000 of loss would be freely deductible.

PROBLEM 22-1

(a) On January 1, 1994 Sam purchased 49% of X Corp. from its sole shareholder, Ted. Ted died, and Corp. X redeemed the 51% of Corp. X stock held by Ted's estate for $550,000 cash on January 1, 1995. At the date of the redemption, X had a $300,000 NOL carryforward, and none of the NOL will expire before the year 2000. Immediately before the redemption, the value of Corp. X was $1,000,000. In 1995, X has taxable income of $75,000. Assume the Federal long-term tax-exempt rate on January 1, 1993 is 10%. What is the § 382 limitation, and how much of X Corp.'s 1995 taxable income can be offset by its NOL carryforward? *See* § 382(b), (c)(1), (e)(2), and (g)(1).

(b) Assume the same facts as in (a), except that X Corp. had $25,000 of taxable income in 1995. How does this change the § 382 limitation?

(c) Assume the same facts as in (a), except that Sam made a $300,000 capital contribution to X Corp. on December 1, 1994, in order to increase the value of X before the corporation redeemed its stock from Ted's estate on January 1, 1995. What are the tax implications of Sam's capital contribution with respect to the § 382 limitation? *See* § 382(l).

PROBLEM 22-2

X Corp. acquired all the stock of Y Corp. on January 1, 1994. Y had a $200,000 NOL carryforward at January 1, 1994, and none of the NOL carryforward would expire before the year 2000. At the date of acquisition, the § 382 limitation was determined to be $100,000. For 1994, Y had taxable income of $50,000, which was fully offset against Y's $200,000 NOL carryforward, because the § 382 limitation was $100,000. On April 1, 1995, X Corp. decides to discontinue Y Corp.'s business and sells Y's historic operating assets. What are the tax implications of the sale? *See* § 382(c).

PROBLEM 22-3

(a) Sid was the sole shareholder of Loss Corp. On January 1. 1993, Sid sold his stock in Loss Corp. to Big Corp. for $3,000,000, at which time Loss Corp. had a $1,000,000 loss carryforward and the federal long-term tax exempt rate was 10%. At the acquisition date, Loss Corp's assets, excluding cash and cash equivalents, had an aggregate fair market value of $3,500,000 and an aggregate basis of $2,500,000. Loss Corp. had held all of its assets for more than two years before the January 1, 1993, acquisition date. On January 1, 1993, Loss Corp. owned a manufacturing plant with a fair market value of $400,000 and a basis of $300,000. Loss Corp. sold the manufacturing plant on June 1, 1995, when its fair market value was $400,000 and its adjusted basis was $250,000. What is the tax implication of the sale? *See* § 382(h)(1).

(b) Assume the same facts as in (a), except that Loss Corp.'s assets had an aggregate basis of $5,000,000 and the plant had a basis of $500,000 on January 1, 1993, and on June 1, 1993, $500,000.

C. SECTION 384: LIMITATION ON USE OF PREACQUISITION LOSSES TO OFFSET BUILT-IN GAINS

Section 384 further restricts the ability of a corporation to acquire another corporation or its assets in order to offset the preacquisition losses of one corporation against the built-in gains of the other. The principal purpose of § 384 is to foreclose "trafficking" in *gain* corporations; i.e., acquisition by a loss corporation of a corporation with built-in gains. Section 382 would not cover this situation because there is no ownership change of the loss corporation. which meets the threshold requirement of Section 382(h). If § 384(a) applies, built-in gains of a "gain corporation" may not be offset by preacquisition losses of the other corporation. The gain corporation remains entitled to offset its own preacquisition losses against its post-acquisition gains.

Two kinds of acquisitions activate § 384: (1) a corporation acquires directly, or through one or more other corporations, control of another corporation, or (2) the assets of a corporation are acquired by another corporation in a Type A, C,

C. SECTION 384: LIMITATION ON USE OF PREACQUISTION LOSSES

or D reorganization under § 368(a)(1). In either type of acquisition, one of the corporations must be a "gain corporation." § 384(a). A "gain corporation" is a corporation with built-in gains on the acquisition date which are large enough to meet the threshold requirement of § 382(h)(3)(B). § 384(c)(4), (8).

It does not matter whether the loss corporation acquires the gain corporation or the gain corporation acquires the loss corporation. In either event § 384 may apply. Also, if there is an ownership change of the loss corporation, both §§ 382 and 384 may apply at the same time.

Section 384 mercifully does not apply if both corporations were members of a "controlled group" at all times during the five-year period prior to the acquisition date. § 384(b). "Controlled group" is defined as in § 1563(a), but modified to lower the ownership requirement from 80% to "over 50%" of both the voting power and the value of the stock. This reflects the 50% rule for an ownership change under § 382. If one or both of the corporations has been in existence less than five years, the shorter period of existence will be substituted for the five-year requirement.

PROBLEM 22-4

(a) Mr. A has owned all the stock of P for over ten years. Early this year, when P has a $5,000 NOL, P bought all of T's outstanding stock from unrelated parties. Just before the acquisition, the total value of T's assets (aside from cash and some marketable securities it owned) was $10,000, and their total basis amounted to $6,000. Does § 384 apply to this acquisition? If so, what is the effect of its application?

(b) Same as (a), but P acquired 80% of T's stock (all of which is voting common stock) in a Type B reorganization, in which T's shareholders received 40% of P's stock in the exchange. Does § 384 apply to this acquisition? If so, what is the effect of its application?

PROBLEM 22-5

Loss Co. (Loss), which has NOLs that are soon to expire, obtains all the assets of the landholding partnership (LHP) in a § 351 transaction. LHP expects large profits, perhaps large enough to fully offset the expiring NOLs of Loss. In exchange, Loss issues 35% of its stock for the land. The existing shareholders of Loss Co. contribute enough cash to constitute 10% of the stock they previously owned, so that they become contributors under the accommodation transfer rules. The shareholders of Loss are unrelated to the partners LHP.

Is this transaction vulnerable to attack under § 269, 382, 384, or 482?

PROBLEM 22-6

Beta Boat Corporation sold its assets and went out of business about three months ago; its sole remaining asset is a $3 million NOL. Mr. Lomax owns

100% of Beta and is keeping the company alive to prevent the inadvertent loss of the NOL. He also owns 55% of Delta Boat Corporation, which owns three ferries, each of which has a basis of $100,000 and a value of $1 million. He was the founder of both corporations, and has been a dominant figure for twenty years. The other 45% is owned by Leona Lomax, his daughter and current CEO of Beta Boat. Offshore Rigs, Inc. ("Offshore") has signed a letter of intent with Delta to buy two of Delta's ferries at $1 million each. All three corporations are on the calendar year and use the accrual method of accounting. Realizing that Beta Boat's loss is an asset that should be used to offset the $900,000 gain on each boat, the accounting firm of Andrew Andrewson has advised the Lomax family to merge Delta into Beta as soon as possible so that Beta can be the seller of the boats. The deal is about to close. Leona thinks there is something fishy about the deal and wants your advice on whether the deal will work. Make sure to mention the effect, if any, of § 384.

OUTSIDE READINGS

D. Simmons, *Net Operating Losses and Section 382: Searching for a Limitation on Loss Carryovers*, 63 Tul. L. Rev. 1045 (1989).

Chapter 23
SPECIAL CORPORATE PENALTY OR REGULATORY TAXES

A. INTRODUCTION

This chapter briefly covers three sets of Code provisions that perform a policeman's role, namely:

- The accumulated earnings tax;
- The personal holding company tax; and
- The collapsible corporation rules.

The first two provisions patrol for corporations that retain their profits in a corporation instead of distributing them. The third prevents the use of corporations to convert ordinary income into capital gains.

B. ACCUMULATED EARNINGS TAX

Read §§ 531, 532(a), and 533(a).

Congress has imposed on the undistributed income of some corporations, in addition to the regular corporate income tax and the corporate alternative minimum tax, the accumulated earnings surtax of § 531. Its purpose is to penalize a corporation that excessively accumulates its earnings, beyond the reasonable needs of its business, and (presumably) to defer or avoid the shareholder income tax on distributed corporate earnings. When individual rates ranged much higher than corporate rates, a corporation that accumulated its earnings beyond the needs of its business could advantageously shelter income by retaining it, but now that top individual and corporate rates are closely aligned, this penalty tax has become of lesser importance. Rate relationship changes could alter that condition. Meanwhile, the § 531 tax is still on the books and is enforced even against publicly-held corporations. It has an exemption-equivalent (of $250,000) and some legitimate escape routes, thus room for argument in many instances.

As you can see, if the taxpayer can show that the accumulation is *not* unreasonable, then the IRS loses, and vice versa. As a result, these cases tend to revolve around the *bona fides* of the accumulation. The following case is an old favorite. (The author of the opinion is a former distinguished tax law professor.) The tax bite if § 531 applies is horrendous, because the tax itself is nondeductible. § 275(A)(4). Note that if the corporation is organized outside the United States, it may seek to accumulate its business profits indefinitely, but it must battle a special network of rules designed to prevent shifting income from intercorporate activities into low tax countries and to prevent the accumulation of investment income in foreign corporations in an attempt to defer application of the U.S. (perhaps higher) regular corporate income tax.

MYRON'S ENTERPRISES v. UNITED STATES
548 F.2d 331 (9th Cir. 1977)

SNEED, CIRCUIT JUDGE:

Taxpayer-corporations sued in district court below for a refund of accumulated earnings taxes imposed by the Commissioner. The Commissioner had based the tax on his determination that for taxpayers' fiscal years 1966 through 1968 the reasonable needs of the business stemmed entirely from working capital needs and never exceeded $21,272. The taxpayers contended that their retained earnings for the years in question of $316,000, $374,316, and $415,766 respectively were needed to cover both working capital requirements of $100,000 and the planned purchase and remodeling of the ballroom operated by taxpayers, at an estimated cost of $375,000.

The district court, in *Myron's Ballroom v. United States*, 382 F. Supp. 582 (C.D. Cal. 1974), held that taxpayers had accumulated earnings in excess of the reasonable needs of their business, but not to the extent claimed by the Commissioner. The court also found that the taxpayers had been availed of for the purpose of avoiding income taxes. Thus, the court upheld the surtax, but required a partial refund in light of the Commissioner's underestimation of taxpayers' reasonable business needs.

The taxpayers argue on appeal that they are entitled to a full refund (i) because all of the retained earnings in the years in question were required to meet the reasonable needs of their business, and (ii) because they proved by the preponderance of the evidence that they were not availed of to avoid taxes, despite the contrary finding by the district court. The Government argues, in response, that taxpayers were not even entitled to a partial refund — that the Commissioner's initial determination of the reasonable needs of the business was correct and that taxpayers failed to prove lack of tax-avoidance motivation. We conclude that the taxpayers are entitled to the full refund they seek. Therefore, we reverse and remand for such necessary proceedings as are consistent with this opinion.

I.

Taxpayer-corporations operate a ballroom and adjoining cocktail lounge. At all times since taxpayers were formed, they have leased their operating premises from Miss Pearl Rose, an elderly lady who has owned the property for approximately 30 years. The taxpayers began inquiring into the possibilities of purchasing the property in 1957, in part because they did not wish to make needed improvements unless they owned the building. Taxpayers made offers to

B. ACCUMULATED EARNINGS TAX

Miss Rose of $100,000 and $150,000 for the property in the late 1950s — early 1960s, neither of which was accepted. However, at the time of the second offer, Miss Rose told taxpayers that they would have "first choice" if and when she decided to sell the ballroom.

In 1963, taxpayers learned that Russ Morgan, a former orchestra leader at the ballroom, had offered Miss Rose $300,000 cash for the property, in an attempt apparently to take over the ballroom operation. The price offered by Morgan probably reflected the goodwill that taxpayers had built up in their operations and therefore was considerably higher than the value of the ballroom property by itself. Morgan's actions convinced taxpayers that their business could be involuntarily "acquired" by someone purchasing the ballroom from Miss Rose,[1] taxpayers, therefore, promptly offered Miss Rose the identical sum of $300,000. This offer was renewed in 1964, 1965, 1966, 1967, 1968 and 1970. While Miss Rose never objected to the terms of the offers, she never sold and still owned the ballroom at the time of trial.

As the Government points out, Miss Rose was never particularly clear as to when and if she would sell her building. Nevertheless, the district court found (a) that taxpayers "expected at any time during the years 1966, 1967 and 1968 that [they] would be able to purchase the ballroom property from Pearl Rose for a price of $300,000 cash, no less than that amount, and maybe more," 382 F. Supp. at 587, and moreover (b) that the "expectation that the ballroom property would be acquired at any time during the years in issue was a reasonable expectation," *id.* at 588. Thus, During the years in issue, the acquisition of the ballroom property and the planned improvements and repairs were reasonably anticipated business needs of [taxpayers], and said needs were directly connected with the business of the corporations." *Id.*

The district court further concluded that "[c]onsidering the reasonably anticipated business need of the corporations to purchase the ballroom property. The corporations combined required at least $375,000, in addition to their combined working capital needs of $100,000." *Id.* However, the court went on to hold that in light of taxpayers' sole-shareholder Mrs. Myrna Myron's willingness to loan up to $200,000 to her corporations for purchase of the ballroom "if the corporations did not have sufficient funds to consummate the transactions, ... a reasonable accumulation [for the purchase] would be $250,000, with Mrs. Myron loaning the balance of funds required," *id.*, thus leading to an excess accumulation in 1967 and 1968.

---

[1] While taxpayers had a lease and an option to renew on the ballroom property at the time Morgan made his $300,000 offer to Miss Rose, there was always the possibility that the lease could be broken or evaded. According to Mrs. Myron, Morgan had asked his attorney and Miss Roses agent "to review [the lease] line by line to see if there was some way or some word-something that could break the lease." F.T. at 73. This possibility of a loophole in the lease left the door open for involuntary "acquisition."

II.

Section 537 of the Internal Revenue Code provides that the reasonable needs of a business, for purposes of determining whether there has been an excess accumulation of earnings, include "the reasonably anticipated needs of the business." Treas. Reg. § 1.537-1(b)(1) provides that to justify an accumulation of earnings on grounds of reasonably anticipated business needs, a corporation must have "specific, definite, and feasible plans for the use of such accumulation" and must not postpone execution of the plan "indefinitely."

The Government contends that the district court erred in concluding that the taxpayers had a "specific, definite, and feasible plan" to acquire and remodel the ballroom. The Government notes that Miss Rose never agreed to sell the ballroom and argues that taxpayers could not have reasonably expected Miss Rose to so agree within the taxable years in question after nearly a decade of unsuccessful negotiations.

We agree with other circuits that a determination by the trial court of the reasonably anticipated business needs of a corporation is a finding of fact which must be sustained unless clearly erroneous.... A court should be particularly wary of overturning a finding of a trial court supporting the taxpayer's determination of its anticipated business needs, since, in the first instance, the "reasonableness of the needs is necessarily for determination by those concerned with the management of the particular enterprise. This determination must prevail unless the facts show clearly the accumulations were for prohibited purposes." *Henry Van Hummell, Inc. v. Commissioner of Internal Revenue*, 364 F.2d 746, 749 (10th Cir. 1966), *cert. denied*, 386 U.S. 956, 87 S. Ct. 1019, 18 L. Ed. 2d 102 (1967). We conclude that the district court was not clearly erroneous in finding that taxpayers' expected purchase and remodeling of the ballroom for $375,000 was a "reasonably anticipated need of the business."

The Government argues that if the instant plan to purchase the ballroom is held to be a reasonably anticipated business need, "any individual could organize a one-man corporation, lease a building and discuss with the lessor the purchase of the building at some future time, and then assert that in the meantime business needs required accumulation of corporate earnings." *I.A. Dress Co. v. Commissioner of Internal Revenue*, 273 F.2d 543, 544 (2d Cir.), *cert. denied*, 362 U.S. 976, 80 S. Ct. 1060, 4 L. Ed. 2d 1011 (1960).

Such fears of artificially constructed needs were well-founded in the quoted case of *I.A. Dress Co.*; there, the owner of the building that the taxpayer sought to purchase "was willing to sell but at a price some $300,000 more than the taxpayer was willing to pay." *Id.* The offer of the taxpayer lacked substance and could easily have been a facade. In the instant case, however, the taxpayers were extremely diligent in their attempts to purchase the ballroom; the taxpayers agreed to all of Miss Rose's stated terms — including payment in all cash; the

B. ACCUMULATED EARNINGS TAX

price offered, far from being criticized by Miss Rose as too low, was apparently in excess of the property's fair market value.[2]

Neither do we have a situation where taxpayers' planned purchase of the ballroom was clearly infeasible. *See Colonial Amusement Corp.*, 1948 Tax. Ct. Me. Dec. (P-H) P 48,149 (building restrictions and priorities prevented carrying out of expansion plans). Here, as in *Universal Steel Co.*, 5 T.C. 627 (1945) (war priority restrictions temporarily blocked purchase of pickling plant), the taxpayers "had a right to hope, if not expect," *id.* at 638, that Miss Rose would sell to them in the near future. Miss Rose never foreclosed the possibility of sale on the terms offered by taxpayers; she merely wanted to "think it over some more." As expressed by Miss Rose's agent at one point during the negotiations, Miss Rose "was an elderly lady and had a very definite mind"; her answers, according to the agent, would differ depending on how she felt on getting up in the morning. Taxpayers were encouraged at several points in the negotiations; in 1965, Miss Rose's agent had told taxpayers, "Be prepared and ready to go." In light of the reasonable possibility that Miss Rose might have decided to accept the offer at any time during the taxable years in issue, calling for quick collection of $375,000 in cash, it would have been unreasonable to force taxpayers to pay out all of their earnings in dividends. Section 537 allows taxpayers to provide for "reasonably anticipated needs," not merely for certainties.

The district court's finding is supported by several tax court cases. In *Magic Mart, Inc.*, 51 T.C. 775 (1969), *acq.*, 1969-2 C.B. xxiv, the Tax Court held that the taxpayer's accumulation of earnings for 1959 through 1962 was reasonable in light of taxpayer's plan to acquire enlarged and expanded facilities, even though it had tried unsuccessfully to buy larger facilities since 1957 and was not able to close a deal until 1967, five years after the taxable years in question. In *Breitfeller Sales, Inc.*, 28 T.C. 1164 (1957), *acq.*, 1958-2 C.B. 4, the Tax Court held that a General Motors dealership's accumulation of earnings was justified, inter alia, by "the continuing possibility that it might [to avoid harmful competition] be required to finance a new dealership in [a neighboring community]." *Id.* at 1168.... *See also Universal Steel Co., supra.*

---

[2] The Government argues that in addition to these steps the taxpayers also should have investigated purchasing other property in the general area, once Miss Rose did not prove totally disposing. *Cf. Magic Mart., Inc.*, 51 T.C. 775 (1969), *acq.*, 1969-2 C.B. xxiv. We agree that the failure of a taxpayer to look into the possibility of purchasing alternative properties generally will be a relevant factor in determining whether the taxpayer actually had a reasonably anticipated business need to purchase the sought-after property. However, other factors also must be considered, including the uniqueness of the sought property. However, other factors also must be considered, including the uniqueness of the sough property. Here, as was testified to at trial, a substantial amount of good will was tied up in the ballroom occupied by taxpayers; given that this value would have been lost if taxpayer had moved to another location, we do not believe that taxpayers' failure to pursue other possible properties (if other ballrooms even existed) calls for reversing the finding of the district court.

III.

The Government rests its entire case upon the argued lack of a specific, definite, and feasible plan. No attempt is made to support the trial court's use of Mrs. Myrna Myron's capacity to loan to the taxpayers to reduce the amount of the reasonable accumulation. The Government thus agrees with taxpayers that, assuming a feasible plan, the district court, in determining whether taxpayers unreasonably accumulated earnings, erred in subtracting from the cash needed to purchase the ballroom an amount that Mrs. Myron stated that she would be willing to loan to the taxpayers if necessary. We also agree. Having found that the reasonably anticipated business need of the taxpayers to purchase the ballroom property required at least $375,000 in cash, the district court erred in concluding that a reasonable accumulation was any less.[3]

Having determined that the reasonable business needs of taxpayers, within the meaning of section 535, equalled or exceeded the accumulated earnings of taxpayers for the taxable years in question, it is unnecessary for us to consider whether the district court was correct in holding that taxpayers had been availed of to avoid taxes within the meaning of section 531.[4] Taxpayers are entitled to

---

[3] That the reasonableness of accumulations should be judged without regard to the borrowing capabilities of the corporation-taxpayer is well established by the case law. *See, e.g., General Smelting Co.*, 4 T.C. 313, 323 (1944), *acq.*, 1945 C.B. 3; B. Bittker & J. Eustice, Federal Income Taxation of Corporations and Shareholders 8-20 to 8-21 & n. 42 (3rd ed. 1971). In computing "accumulated taxable income," which forms the base for the accumulated earnings tax, I.R.C. § 535 provides that a credit will be provided for the amount "retained for the reasonable needs of the business." There is no authority for reducing the credit to reflect the lending capacity of taxpayer's shareholders. If the reasonable business needs of taxpayer equal or outstrip the retained earnings, no surtax can be imposed, even though the needs could be financed by borrowing from outside — such financing decisions are for the taxpayer not the courts to make.

The district court's logic could conceivably be extended to the point of totally nullifying Congress' expressed policy of allowing corporate taxpayers to accumulate earnings necessary for reasonable business needs. A sole shareholder can always loan back any cash distributed by his corporation in dividends if the corporation later needs the money (minus, of course, any income taxes paid). Therefore, to take into account the ability of a shareholder to loan money to the corporation could be construed as virtual authority "for denying all sole stockholder corporations the right ever to maintain accumulations even for reasonable needs. The test expressed by the statute would then be completely abandoned." *Smoot Sand & Gravel Corp. v. Commissioner of Internal Revenue*, 241 F.2d 197, 206 (4th Cir.), *cert. denied*, 354 U.S. 922, 77 S. Ct. 1383, 1 L. Ed. 2d 1437 (1957).

[4] The Government, before oral argument, withdrew its attack on the district court's computation of working capital, recognizing that, if the district court was correct in concluding that the reasonable business needs of taxpayers included $375,000 for their planned purchase of the ballroom, this justified taxpayers' accumulation of earnings for the years in issue. *See* Appendix A (net liquid assets of taxpayers for 1966-1968 never exceeds $375,000 plus Government's $21,172 estimate of working capital needs). Therefore we do not consider the issue of whether the district court was correct in its determination of the working capital needs of the taxpayers.

C. CALCULATING THE TAX

The basis for the accumulated earnings tax is so-called accumulated taxable income, which is determined under § 535. One begins with taxable income and then makes various adjustments, such as the elimination of the dividends-received deduction, in order to arrive at something in the nature of real economic income. The tax is then offset by a credit. The credit amounts to a minimum exemption of $250,000 for most corporations.[5] That amount increases to the extent the corporation can tell a good story to justify its further accumulations, and verify it. Note that a controlled group of corporations is entitled to only one credit, that the tax is nondeductible, and that it is imposed in addition to the regular corporate income tax.

PROBLEM 23-1

PSC Corp. is a personal service company solely owned by Adam. The principal purpose of PSC Corp. is to provide architecture services. PSC Corp. is a calendar year taxpayer. PSC Corp. filed its 1994 corporate income tax return in January 1995. In February 1995, the IRS audited PSC Corp's 1994 tax return and the agent determined that the company had accumulated earnings beyond the reasonable needs of the business. PSC Corp's accumulated taxable income as of December 31, 1994 was $1,000,000.

1. How can PSC Corp. avoid the accumulated earnings tax? *See* §§ 561(a), 563(a) and 565.
2. Can PSC Corp. deduct a deficiency dividend paid to PSC Corp.'s sole shareholder Adam under § 547(a)?
3. Explain how the accumulated earnings credit is applied to these facts. *See* § 535(c).

D. PERSONAL HOLDING COMPANIES

1. INTRODUCTION

Read § 541.

The Personal Holding Company Tax ("PHC") provisions are supposed to prevent taxpayers from shifting income to closely-held corporations (perhaps taxable at lower rates) in lieu of having the shareholder (or his or her invest-

---

[5] The figure is $150,000 for personal service corporations and $250,000 for holding or investment corporations (capped at the same figure, i.e., not a penny more). § 535(c)(2)-(3).

ments) earn the money directly. One can avoid the tax by having the corporation pay dividends. The tax is directed at three sins, which are often described in terms of the following memorable characterizations:

1. The incorporated talent;
2. The incorporated pocketbook;
3. The incorporated yacht.

The federal income tax return forces the tax return preparer to disclose whether the corporation is a PHC. If it is, it is subject to a separate tax under § 543. The tax is calculated under § 545, a key feature of which is that it exempts long-term capital gains. Like the accumulated earnings tax, the PHC tax is nondeductible and can be mitigated by paying dividends, including deficiency dividends.

2. DETERMINATION OF PERSONAL HOLDING COMPANY STATUS

The Code imposes a special tax on the undistributed income of a personal holding company (PHC), a company controlled by a limited number of shareholders and deriving a large percentage of its income from specified sources. In order to be treated as a PHC, a corporation must meet a tainted-income test under § 543(a), and a stock-ownership test under § 542(a)(2).

[In determining whether the tainted income test is met under current law, the aggregate partnership theory applies so that a corporate partner takes into account its distributive share of income from a partnership. However, for purposes of ascertaining whether the stock ownership test is met, each partner, through attribution rules, is deemed to own all of the stock held by the partnership, and not simply that partner's allocable share.]

Under § 542(a)(1) the tainted income test requires that at least 60% of the corporation's adjusted ordinary gross income for a taxable year constitute PHC income, as defined in § 543(a). [The IRS ruled in PLR 8043098 (July 19, 1980) that because a limited partnership interest is not one of the items enumerated in § 543(a) as comprising PHC income, and because a limited partnership interest represents the limited partner's distributive share of the partnership's income, it is the nature of the underlying income generated by the partnership that determines whether there is PHC income — a "look-through" rule.]

The stock ownership test is met if, "at any time during the last half of the taxable year, more than fifty percent in value [of the corporation's] outstanding stock is owned, directly or indirectly, by or for not more than five individuals." § 542(a)(2). A specific set of attribution rules applies in determining whether the stock ownership test is met. [Under § 544(a)(1), each partner is considered to own a proportionate share of the stock held by his partnership.] Under § 544(a)(2), an individual is considered to own the stock owned, directly or indirectly, by or for his family or by or for his partners; and § 544(a)(5) provides reattribution rules. [As a result of the attribution rules, a partner is always deemed to own all of the stock held by his partnership and any other stock held by his fellow partners outside the partnership.]

a. The Incorporated Talent

Read § 543(a)(7).

The following ruling illustrates the § 541 tax issues when the income arises from rendering personal services.

REV. RUL. 75-67
1975-1 C.B. 169

Advice has been requested whether, under the circumstances described below, a corporation will be considered to have received personal holding company income within the meaning of section 543(a)(7) of the Internal Revenue Code of 1954.

B, a doctor specializing in a certain area of medical services, owns 80 percent of the outstanding stock of L, a domestic professional service corporation. B is the only officer of L who is active in the production of income for L, and he is the only medical doctor presently employed by L. B performs medical services under an employment contract with L. L furnishes office quarters and equipment, and employs a receptionist to assist B. P, a patient, solicited the services of and was treated by B.

Section 543(a)(7) of the Code provides, in part, that the term personal holding company income includes amounts received under a contract whereby a corporation is to furnish personal services if some person other than the corporation has the right to designate, by name or description, the individual who is to perform the services, or if the individual who is to perform the services is designated, by name or description, in the contract.

In dealing with a professional service corporation providing medical services, an individual will customarily solicit and expect to receive the services of a particular physician, and he will usually be treated by the physician sought.

A physician-patient relationship arises from such a general agreement of treatment. Either party may terminate the relationship at will, although the physician must give the patient reasonable notice of his withdrawal and may not abandon the patient until a replacement, if necessary, can be obtained. C. Morris & A. Mortiz, Doctor and Patient and the Law 135 (5th ed. 1971). Moreover, if a physician who has entered into a general agreement of treatment is unable to treat the patient when his services are needed, he may provide a qualified and competent substitute physician to render the services. C. Morris & A. Moritz, *supra*, at 138, 374-75.

Thus, when an individual solicits, and expects, the services of a particular physician and that physician accepts the individual as a patient and treats him, the relationship of physician-patient established in this manner does not constitute a designation of the individual who is to perform the services under a contract for personal services within the meaning of section 543(a)(7) of the Code.

If, however, the physician or the professional service corporation contracts with the patient that the physician personally will perform particular services for the patient, and he has no right to substitute another physician to perform such services, there is a designation of that physician as the individual to perform services under a contract for personal services within the meaning of section 543(a)(7) of the Code.

The designation of a physician as an individual to perform services can be accomplished by either an oral or written contract. *See* Rev. Rul. 69-299, 1969-1 C.B. 165.

Moreover, if L agreed to perform the type of services that are so unique as to preclude substitution of another physician to perform such services, there is also a designation.

Accordingly, since in the instant case there is no indication that L has contracted that B will personally perform the services or that the services are so unique as to preclude substitution, it is held that income earned by L from providing medical service contracts will not be considered income from personal service contracts within the meaning of section 543(a)(7) of the Code.

b. The Incorporated Pocketbook

The notion here is that taxpayers should not be allowed to generate investment income and hide it in a low-bracket corporation, where it is split off from the taxpayer's other income, losses, expenses, and tax-filing characteristics. The trouble is that some special purpose corporations, such as those formed to hold real estate or oil and gas interests, are formed for legitimate nontax reasons. How does one sort them out? The answer is that § 543(a)(2)-(6) describe a series of corporations that are rich with some special type of passive income, but low on other passive income, and purge their income by classifying it as *not* personal holding company income. Now scan § 543(a)(2)-(6) to see how the concept is applied, and note that there is another test relating to the extent to which the corporation has § 162 deductions. Congress views the existence of such deductions as evidence that there really is a business under the microscope.

c. The Incorporated Yacht

Read § 543(a)(6).

The sin here is putting a yacht, or some other property, into the hands of a corporation and then personally renting it from the corporation. The fiscal scheme would be to generate tax deductions (for business or profit-seeking costs, such as depreciation of a hunting lodge) where none would otherwise be available (for personal consumption expenditures or costs). Section 543(a)(6) comes to the Treasury's rescue by turning such income into personal holding company income.

E. COLLAPSIBLE CORPORATIONS 539

d. Miscellany

(1) In the Foreign Sphere

The *foreign* personal holding company is basically a foreign corporation that fits the same form as a domestic personal holding company. The punishment associated with such companies is that the U.S. *shareholders* may be taxed on undistributed income of the foreign PHC even if they never receive the funds. That takes the fun out of a large number of shady tax plans. Section 551 is not a penalty tax on the corporation, like § 541; it is an early tax on shareholders. infamous Subpart F (§§ 951-964) does a similar thing also in the international context. There is more to it than this, but the unique feature of this provision is that it levies a tax on the owner of stock with respect to distributions that were never received. Devotees of a strict reading of the Sixteenth Amendment may find this startling. (Compare the P.F.I.C. [Passive Foreign Investment Company] rules of §§ 1291-1297.)

(2) Overlap

If a corporation is subject to both the accumulated earnings tax and the personal holding company tax, the personal holding company tax rules prevail. § 532(b)(1).

(3) Deficiency Dividends

Look at the deficiency dividend rules in § 547. Do they mean that the § 541 tax should never be paid, or is never paid? The tax is designed not to raise revenue but rather to regulate conduct and to force offending corporations to make distributions to shareholders, so that the right kind of tax will be collected and not deferred or ultimately escaped. If § 541 is sometimes a trap for the unwary, § 547 is the escape for the unwary who have become wary.

E. COLLAPSIBLE CORPORATIONS

Scan § 341.

Section 341 converts capital gain from the sale of corporate stock into ordinary income if the corporation was interposed to generate income and to be sold or liquidated before it realized or could be taxed on such income. Consider a corporation formed to build a track of houses or to create a movie which is sold or liquidated before it sells the houses (inventory) or licenses or distributes the movie. Were it not for § 341 *et seq.*, the entrepreneurs would be taxed on capital gain, and the buyers, having a high cost basis in the assets, would have little (ordinary) income to report. Remember your study of liquidations and taxable or tax-free acquisitions. The definitions are intricate, and the whole system is undercut by an election under § 341(f) that allows the shareholders to report capital gains if the corporation consents to recognize its own gains on "subsection (f) assets." This provision now has little effect at the corporate level after the repeal of *General Utilities*, because corporations must recognize such gains in any event.

F. LIMITATIONS ON THE USE OF MULTIPLE CORPORATIONS

Corporations pay graduated income taxes. In theory, a single business could fragment itself into a large number of corporations in order to pay taxes in lower brackets. Section 1561 pinches off this strategy by treating a group of commonly controlled corporations as a single taxpayer. Section 1563(a) defines the key term "controlled group of corporations" as including both parent-subsidiary and brother-sister groups. Various other Code provisions strive to assure the same result on an ad hoc basis. *See*, for example, § 179(d)(6).

Although Congress is hostile to fragmenting income among multiple corporations to reduce overall taxes, it is generally receptive to allowing affiliated corporations to file a single consolidated federal income tax return. This calls for preparing a separate imaginary or tentative return for each member corporation and then, among other things, eliminating intercompany transactions and deferring their recognition until one of the parties to the transaction leaves the group, say because the common parent corporation sold the stock of a member which sold property to another member, or until an asset is sold or services are rendered or profits are distributed to someone outside the group.

PROBLEM 23-2

(a) A common parent corporation ("X Corporation") owns 100% of two subsidiaries, Sub One and Sub Two. The parent and both subsidiaries are "includible corporations." The two subsidiaries are equal partners in a partnership that owns all of the stock of Sub Three, which is also an includible corporation. Can the Corporation file a consolidated return with Sub One, Sub Two, and Sub Three? *See* Reg. § 1.1502-1(b).

(b) Assume that Sub Three cannot be included in a consolidated return, and it pays a dividend to the partnership. Would that dividend qualify for the 100% dividends-received deduction? *See* § 243(a)(3).

Chapter 24
S CORPORATIONS: DEFINITION AND QUALIFICATIONS

A. INTRODUCTION

Most tax practitioners would tell you that an S corporation is basically a regular domestic corporation (formed under the ordinary incorporation law of one of the fifty states) that makes an election to be taxed much like a partnership, with the result that S corporations are treated as conduits and that taxable income or loss of an S corporation, as well as the tax credits it generates, "pass through" the corporation and are subject to a single shareholder level tax. They will also tell you that the "S" stands for the subchapter of the Code that contains the specialized rules relating to these corporations. (These statements are helpful in a general way, but dangerously misleading in their details, hence much of this chapter will concentrate on the areas of divergence from the supposedly simple "pure conduit" model of Subchapter K.)

The practitioner will point out that S corporations have the advantage of not being subject to the personal holding company tax or the tax on unreasonable accumulations, or the alternative minimum tax. The practitioner might pause and point out that there is no guarantee that there would not be a significant state income or franchise tax.

The practitioner might even point out that the entity can use the cash method of taxation, unless it is a tax shelter as defined in § 448, and that his wealthy clients who act only as investors have been gratified to learn that profitable S corporations can generate passive income which can be used to offset passive losses under § 469. Taxpayers holding tax shelter investments have a great interest in "passive-income generators" (PIGs) because a PIG can produce income that is absorbed by otherwise suspended passive-activity losses and credits. This makes the S corporation extraordinary, as it permits a passive investor in an S corporation to generate income that can sop up suspended losses arising out of tax shelter investments, something § 469 generally strives to avoid. Conversely, if the investor is passive and the S corporation loses money, § 469 applies and the investor's losses may be put on ice. If the investor becomes inpatient and sells his stock, the sale frees up the suspended losses for deduction; and any losses on the stock *may* qualify for ordinary loss treatment under § 1244.

When top individual income tax rates were far higher than corporate tax rates, it was a common business strategy to run a new businesses as an S corporation while it lost money, and then drop the election once the corporation operated in the black. With the present rate structure, it now makes sense never to drop the

S election. Thus, a great many corporations owned by small groups of shareholders operate as S corporations. Some of them are mammoth enterprises.

The S corporation is a fairly recent arrival on the tax scene. In 1954, the Senate made a legislative initiative to allow small corporations to be taxed as partnerships, partly to eliminate the influence of taxes on the choice of business form. S. Rept. No. 1622, 83th Cong., 2d Sess., 119 (1954). The initiative failed in 1954, but succeeded in 1958. The 1958 rationales included a desire to allow small business people to be taxed at their rate brackets rather than the frequently higher rates imposed on their corporations and to allow them to flow their losses through to their owners so that the owners could offset them against their personal income. S. Rept. No. 1983, 85th Cong., 2d Sess., 87 (1958).[1] There was yet another major revision in 1982, which eliminated many defects in the 1958 legislation, as a result of which the more general goal of equating the federal income taxation of S corporations with partnerships has largely been achieved. However, like the partnership, the S corporation is far from a pure conduit. It is an entity for a variety of purposes and makes almost all the tax elections that affect the preparation of its (information) tax return.[2] Like a partnership it pays its own excise and employment taxes.

We will look at the significant disparities between S corporations and partnerships later in this and the following chapters. The primary examples are that whereas partnership status is readily achieved, one can only achieve S corporation status via an election procedure that is ringed with restrictions. Also, corporate liabilities are not included in a shareholder's basis in the company's stock, and special allocations are not a feature of S corporations. Moreover, a transferee of S corporation stock cannot modify the basis of his or her stock to reflect the value of the share of the entity's assets in order to take account of the disparity between the purchase price of the stock and the corporation's basis in its assets. Compare this to § 754, which allows a periodic realignment of inside and outside basis in a partnership. Worse, from the owner's perspective, S corporations that used to be C corporations may have to pay a specialized income tax on excessive passive investment income as well as a major tax on certain built-in gains that existed at the time of making the S election. These are discussed in detail later in the chapter. There are also two minor taxes that are merely alluded to here and never again. One is the tax from recomputing a prior-year investment tax credit (ITC), and the other is a LIFO recapture tax. *See* Reg. § 1.47-4(a)(1) for ITC recapture. The LIFO recapture amount is computed and included in the gross income of the corporation's last taxable year as a C

---

[1] In 1958 the Congress also enacted legislation whereby a partnership could elect to be taxed as a corporation. Because it was so little used, this legislation was repealed just a very few years later.

[2] The shareholders elect only as to the treatment of certain mining exploration costs under § 617, and as to deducting or crediting of foreign taxes. § 1363(c)(2)(A).

B. ELIGIBILITY TO ELECT STATUS

corporation. § 1363(d)(1). In light of the purposes of this book, it is not worth looking up those Code sections.

B. ELIGIBILITY TO ELECT STATUS

Read § 1361.

Section 1361(a)(1) contains an easy generic rule that:

> [T]the term "S corporation" means, with respect to any year, *a small business corporation* for which an *election* under section 1362(a) is in effect for such year.

Subsection (b) in turn defines a small business corporation as a domestic (i.e., U.S.) corporation that is not an *ineligible corporation* (more on that shortly) and which does not violate a series of standards. The concept of an ineligible corporation generally concerns the industry the corporation is in. Section 1362(b)(2) operates to exclude a bank, financial institution, member of an affiliated group,[3] a company electing the possessions tax credit under § 936, or a DISC or former DISC.[4]

1. AFFILIATED GROUPS

Section 1361(b)(2)(A)'s prohibition against being a member of an affiliated group is confusing. It does not refer to the presence of a consolidated return; rather, it refers to not letting the S corporation own 80% of the stock of another corporation by vote and value. § 1504(a)(2). There are no attribution rules under § 1504.

The prohibition does not apply if the subsidiary is inactive, meaning a corporation that, during any period in a tax year has not begun business at any time on or before the close of that period, and has no gross income for that period. § 1361(d)(6). This enables S corporations to protect their corporate names in other states by forming inactive subsidiaries.

Because § 1504 prevents a foreign corporation from being a member of an affiliated group, it might seem that an S corporation can, for example, own any amount of stock of a foreign corporation. In fact, that is not so. If you read § 1361(b) carefully, you will see that the definition of an affiliated corporation does not take into account the exceptions under § 1504(b). As a result, the only question that counts is the level of ownership.

---

[3] This prevents a corporation from being a member of a group of corporations filing a consolidated return and also prevents an S corporation from being a member of 80% parent-subsidiary chain.

[4] These are export promotion companies that are all but defunct now. They have been replaced by foreign international sales corporations ("FSCs"), which cannot be S corporations because they must be foreign.

PROBLEM 24-1

An S corporation that you operate wants to buy 50% of the stock of two C corporations, whose names are T1 and T2. T1 and T2 already own 50% of each other. The plan is that T1 and T2 will each issue enough stock to the S corporation to give it 50% control of each C corporation. Will this violate the rule against affiliated group membership?

2. THIRTY-FIVE SHAREHOLDER LIMIT

Over the years the availability of the S corporation has gradually expanded via a progressive growth in the number of people who can be shareholders. The present limit of thirty-five is coordinated with the private placement exemption under § 4(2) of the Securities Act of 1933.[5] Going over the thirty-five shareholder limit results in instantaneous termination of the Subchapter S election and therefore instant C corporation status. The same "sudden death rule" applies to any other event that violates the requirements for getting or keeping S corporation status. § 1362(d)(2).

Defining "a shareholder" is not a cut-and-dried matter. When counting shareholders, the Code imposes the following rules, not because they are particularly clever, but because some definitional clarification is needed.

— Count each beneficiary of a voting trust as a shareholder.
— Treat the grantor of a grantor trust as the shareholder.[6] This is consistent with the concept of ignoring the existence of these trusts for federal income tax purposes.
— Count a husband and wife, and their estates, as one shareholder, even if they own stock separately.
— Otherwise, count everyone who owns any stock, even if the stock is owned jointly with another person.[7]

3. LIMITS ON TYPES OF SHAREHOLDERS

a. Nonresident Aliens

A nonresident alien is an alien who is not a resident of the United States. Reg. §§ 1.871-2 and 301.7701-5. An alien becomes a resident alien either by obtaining a so-called "green card," which is formal admission to the U.S. as a resident, or by being present in the U.S. for a significant period of time. § 7701(b)(1)(A).

---

[5] The private placement exemption allows issuing corporations to sell their own securities without the expense of registering the securities with the SEC. The § 4(2) exemption also admits certain sophisticated investors and insiders, so the parallel between § 4(2) and § 1362 is imperfect.

[6] Likewise, one treats a § 678 beneficiary as an owner. § 1362(c)(2)(A)(i), (B)(i).

[7] Proposed legislation would revise some of these rules so as to allow more persons to have an interest in an S corporation under whatever numerical rule (non-thirty-five shareholders) prevails.

B. ELIGIBILITY TO ELECT STATUS

A nonresident alien cannot be a shareholder of an S corporation. § 1361(b)(1)(C). One strategy for dropping S corporation status in a hurry is to sell to just such a person. Conversely, one can avoid the problem by inserting language on the stock certificates to state that the charter or by-laws of the company treat such transfers (as well as other disqualifying transfers) as void. Naturally, the charter or bylaws should bear out the threat.

No legislative history accompanies this discriminatory provision. Perhaps Congress thought that nonresident aliens could too easily avoid taxes on their share of the corporations's profits.[8]

b. Trusts

(1) Trusts Other Than Qualified Subchapter S Trusts

The following domestic trusts can be shareholders of an S corporation under § 1361(c):[9]

— A trust may continue to be an S corporation shareholder of stock held by the trust when the owner died, but not for more than 60 days. However, if the entire corpus of a grantor trust is included in the owner's gross estate, the sixty-day period becomes a two-year period. The owner's estate is treated as the shareholder.
— A trust created primarily to exercise the voting power of stock transferred to it. Each beneficiary of the trust is treated as a shareholder.
— Any trust to which stock is transferred according to the terms of a will, but only for sixty days, beginning with the day the stock was transferred to the trust under the will. The estate of the person leaving the will is treated as the shareholder.

(2) Qualified Subchapter S Trusts

The beneficiaries of so-called qualified Subchapter S trusts (QSSTs, pronounced like "twists") can elect to have their trusts qualify as shareholders. A qualified Subchapter S trust is a trust described in § 1361(d). Review the requirements on your own. It is an important provision. As you read it, you might want to imagine a closely-held S corporation the stock of which has to date been owned by the founder, who has two minor children. Consider the power of the QSSTs as a tax planning device, given that it can enable the founder to shift an S corporation's profits to the QSSTs, thence to the children, with no need to make corporate distributions to cover the profits attributed, and taxed, to the

---

[8] *See* B. Bittker & L. Lokken, Federal Taxation of Income, Estates and Gifts, Vol. 3 ¶ 95.6.2 (2d ed. 1991). One might well wonder if this rule creates discrimination problems under double-tax treaties.

[9] § 1361(c)(2).

children via their QSSTs. To avoid his children's wrath, the founder can exercise his power over the corporation to make sure the children will be distributed enough cash to cover the income taxes the QSSTs burden them with. Of course, the kiddie tax of I.R.C. § 1(g) will limit the tax-reducing advantages of splitting income with minor children.

c. Estates

Estates, including bankruptcy estates,[10] can be shareholders. § 1361(b)(1)(B), (c)(3). In fact the surviving spouse and the estate of the decedent count as one shareholder under § 1361(c)(1).

4. ONE CLASS OF STOCK

a. General Rule

One of the most troubling provisions is the so-called "one class of stock rule" under § 1361(b)(1)(D). One class of stock generally means that the outstanding shares of the corporation must be identical with respect to the rights of the holders in the profits and in the assets of the corporation. Stock can have differences in voting rights and still be considered one class of stock. For example, one might have Class A voting stock owned by the adults and Class A nonvoting stock held by trusts for their children.

Authorized but unissued stock and treasury stock are not considered in determining if a corporation has more than one class of stock. The existence of outstanding options, warrants to acquire stock, or convertible debentures do not in themselves constitute a second class of stock. Once they are exercised into a novel class of stock, however, the risk of a second class becomes immediate and potentially catastrophic from a tax perspective.

Note the downside; if the corporation in fact had two classes of stock from the time it was formed, it is a C corporation *ab initio*. The following cases exemplify and explore some of the policies underlying the single-class-of stock rule.

PAIGE v. UNITED STATES
580 F.2d 960 (9th Cir. 1978),
aff'g 75-2 USTC P9587 (C.D. Cal. 1975)

SKOPIL, DISTRICT JUDGE:

Plaintiff-taxpayers appeal from the denial of their claim for a tax refund. The issue involved is whether taxpayers' corporation qualified for the subchapter S election provided in 26 U.S.C. § 1371 (1954).[11] We hold that it did not....

---

[10] As a result, a corporation's S election is not terminated because of the commencement of a bankruptcy case involving an individual who is a shareholder in the corporation.

[11] The statute as it read in 1965 is controlling here. It was slightly amended in 1976. Pub. L. No. 94-455 § 902, 90 Stat. 1608, 1609.

B. ELIGIBILITY TO ELECT STATUS

Tackmer made the subchapter S election in 1965. The government now contends that Tackmer Corporation had more than one class of stock.

Tackmer is a small California company that was first incorporated in 1965. When Tackmer first issued stock, it received two different kinds of consideration. Plaintiffs and another party assigned their rights to an exclusive license agreement in exchange for Tackmer stock ("property shareholders"). Eight other parties paid cash ("cash shareholders").

The Articles of Incorporation state that "No distinction shall exist between the shares of the corporation (or) the holders thereof."... The applicable California Corporation Code, § 304 (West 1949),[12] stated that there could be no distinction between shares unless specified in the Articles.

Before Tackmer could issue any stock, it was required to obtain a permit from the California Department of Corporations. The California Corporation Code gave the Department authority to impose conditions on corporations for the protection of the public.[13] Pursuant to this authority the Department had a policy of imposing certain conditions on small corporations such as Tackmer which were capitalized with both cash and property that had an indeterminate value. The purpose of the conditions was to protect the shareholders who paid with cash from having their interests diluted by overissue of stock to the shareholders who paid with property.

The conditions imposed by the Department of Corporations were as follows:

(a) The stock had to be deposited in escrow and could not be sold without the Department's consent;
(b) If the company defaulted on dividend payments for two years, the cash shareholders would have irrevocable power of attorney to vote the property shareholders' shares for the board of directors;
(c) On dissolution, the property shareholders had to waive their rights to the distribution of assets until the cash shareholders had received the full amount of their purchase price plus any unpaid accumulated dividends at 5% per year;
(d) The property shareholders had to waive their rights to any dividends until the cash shareholders annually received cumulative dividends equal to 5% of the purchase price per share;
(e) The conditions were to remain in effect until the shares were released from escrow.... The conditions were in effect from 1965 to 1970.

---

[12] Now codified in Cal. Corp. Code § 203 (West 1977).

[13] Cal. Corp. Code § 25508 (West 1949) provided: "AUTHORITY TO IMPOSE CONDITIONS FOR PROTECTION OF PUBLIC. The commissioner may impose conditions requiring the deposit in escrow of securities ..., the waiver of assets and dividends by holders of promotional securities, and such other conditions as he deems reasonable and necessary or advisable for the protection of the securities." This section was repealed by 1968 Cal. Stat. c. 88 p. 243, § 1 (1969). Former § 25508 is similar to Cal. Corp. Code § 25141 (West 1977).

The property shareholders signed an agreement with the company stating that they would abide by the conditions. The taxpayers admit that the conditions could have been waived by the cash shareholders.... Notwithstanding the conditions, the differences between the two kinds of shareholders were never taken into account and all dividends were distributed on a pro rata basis.

A corporation must meet six requirements in order to qualify for subchapter S tax treatment. The applicable statute reads: "For purposes of ... subchapter (S, a qualifying corporation is) a domestic corporation which is not a member of an affiliated group ... and which does not "(1) have more than [35] shareholders; (2) have as a shareholder a person (other than an estate) who is not an individual; (3) have a nonresident alien as a shareholder; and (4) have more than one class of stock." 26 U.S.C. § 1371 (1954)....

The taxpayers filed a timely joint tax return in 1970.... On January 14, 1973, the Commissioner of Internal Revenue ... assessed additional taxes of $244.64 plus $37.30 interest (total: $281.94). The reason stated for the disallowance was that the conditions imposed by the California Department of Corporations created more than one class of stock, disqualifying Tackmer for subchapter S treatment.

On October 25, 1973, the taxpayers prepaid the tax and filed a timely claim for refund. On December 7, 1973, the government sent taxpayers a Notice of Disallowance of the claim. On December 12 the taxpayer filed this action. The issue was submitted to the District Court for the Central District of California on cross motions for summary judgment. The court entered judgment for the United States.

The taxpayers contend that because the Articles and state law authorized only one class of stock, there can be only one class for subchapter S purposes. We hold, however, that the interpretation of subchapter S qualifications is a federal question. *Kean v. Commissioner of Internal Revenue*, 469 F.2d 1183 (9th Cir. 1972).

Treas. Reg. § 1.1371-1(g) provides that "If the outstanding shares of stock of the corporation are not identical with respect to the rights and interests which they convey in the control, profits, and assets of the corporation, then the corporation is considered to have more than one class of stock."... The cash shareholders had preferred rights over property shareholders, notwithstanding that the cash shareholders chose not to exercise those rights. The possibility of the exercise of differing rights is enough to disqualify a corporation for subchapter S tax treatment.

Taxpayers' assertion that Tackmer in fact made all distributions on a pro rata basis is irrelevant. A corporation's qualifications for subchapter S status is judged at the date of election. *See, Barnes Motor & Parts Co. v. United States*, 309 F. Supp. 298 (E.D.N.C. 1970). The court may not consider Tackmer's actual distributions after its election. The language in the statute is clear. Tax planners must be able to assume that the court will give it its plain meaning.

Taxpayers assert that Treas. Reg. § 1.1371-1(g) has been overturned as applied to them by *Parker Oil Company*, 58 T.C. 985 (1972) and the Service's

B. ELIGIBILITY TO ELECT STATUS

acquiescence in Rev. Rul. 73-611, 1973-2 C.B. 312. Taxpayers contend that the Regulation was found to be inconsistent with the basic purpose of the requirement that there be one class of stock. We disagree. *Parker Oil* involved only voting rights arising out of shareholder agreements. It did not involve distributions from the corporations. Control of distributions is at the heart of the one class of stock requirement. This aspect of Treas. Reg. § 1.1371-1(g) was untouched by *Parker Oil*.

....

There is a strong policy behind the requirement that subchapter S corporations have only one class of stock. The corporations themselves pay no corporate income tax. The shareholders pay individual income tax on a pro rata share of all corporate income, regardless of whether any money or property has actually been distributed to the shareholder. If the statute allowed more than one class of stock, complicated allocation problems could arise....

This would introduce substantial complexity in the administration of subchapter S. It was this type of potential difficulty which Congress sought to avoid by limiting subchapter S corporations to one class of stock.

We agree with the taxpayers that the purpose of subchapter S is to benefit small corporations such as the one here. It is unfortunate that a requirement of state law has caused a result that no one intended. However, the taxpayers' subjective intent to create one class of stock cannot be allowed to override statutory requirements. *Cf. Gamman v. Commissioner of Internal Revenue*, 46 T.C. 1 (1966). Congress has set forth specific objective requirements for subchapter S qualification, and we must follow the mandate of the statute.

We affirm.

PORTAGE PLASTICS CO. v. UNITED STATES
486 F.2d 632 (7th Cir. 1973)

CUMMINGS, CIRCUIT JUDGE.

This appeal presents the question whether plaintiff qualified as a small business corporation within the meaning of Section 1371(a) of the Internal Revenue Code, thus supporting its timely elections under Section 1372(a) not to be subject to corporate income taxes for the fiscal years 1961, 1962 and 1963. The district court upheld plaintiff's qualification (301 F. Supp. 684), but a panel of this Court reversed by divided vote (470 F.2d 308). On en banc consideration, we now affirm the district court's refund judgment.

The facts were largely stipulated, but other facts were found after a bench trial. There is no dispute as to the facts, and only the essential ones reflected in the testimony or found by the district court will be stated in this opinion.

Plaintiff, a plastics manufacturer, is a Wisconsin corporation with its principal place of business in Portage, Wisconsin. It adopted the accrual method of accounting, with its fiscal year ending May 31. It was organized on June 1, 1957, and its Articles of Incorporation authorized 1,000 shares of common stock with a par value of $10 per share. Effective January 23, 1962, the Articles were amended to increase the authorized shares to 20,000 shares of common stock of the same par value. No other class of common stock was authorized.

During the first of the fiscal years in question, plaintiff's stockholders were William G. Hamilton, Ann Hamilton Kirk, Eugene Palmbach and William Hamilton, Jr., and in the latter two fiscal years, Armand Cimaroli was an additional stockholder.

According to the testimony of the secretary-treasurer of plaintiff, its organizers "did not want to sacrifice any of the equity of the corporation" to obtain working capital but found a very unfavorable reception from banks in regard to loans. As a result, on June 1, 1957, William G. Hamilton's mother, Mrs. Elizabeth Berst, and his aunt, Miss Sara Garnett, agreed to advance the plaintiff $12,500 each and in exchange received standard business note forms. These instruments obligated plaintiff to pay Mrs. Berst and Miss Garnett $12,500 apiece on June 1, 1962, in Portage, Wisconsin, and contained the following provision for "Interest: 5% of the net profit before taxes." At the time of issuance, the parties verbally agreed that on June 1, 1962, either or both of the ladies could renew the June 1, 1957, instruments at their request for a similar 5-year period. Both ladies exercised their renewal options, and accordingly, on June 1, 1962, two identical renewal instruments were executed. In June of 1963, Mrs. Berst and Miss Garnett exchanged those instruments for 245 shares each of common stock of plaintiff.

There was no oral or written agreement for the repayment of the $25,000 advanced by the ladies in the event of default in payment of the stipulated "interest." Plaintiff did not establish a sinking fund to provide for the retirement of the obligations within the time periods provided.

Mrs. Berst and Miss Garnett executed separate agreements in June 1959, subordinating for a year all their rights pertaining to the instruments in favor of the City Bank of Portage, Wisconsin, a lender to plaintiff. On February 8 and March 26, 1962, respectively, they agreed to subordinate their rights in the instruments in favor of the First National Bank of Chicago, another lender to plaintiff.

The original and renewal instruments were recorded as Notes Payable on the books and records of the corporation and were shown as Long-term Debt and as Notes Payable on the annual audit reports prepared by its certified public accountants and on financial statements furnished to banks and other creditors. The accrual and payment of the amounts denoted as "interest" in the instruments were recorded on the books and records of the corporation in the Accrued Interest Payable account. The payments to each lady were as follows: $957.87 in 1959; $4,916.05 in 1960; $4,737.31 in 1961; $3,323.79 in 1962; and $2,245.03 in 1963. These payments reflected the unexpectedly fast growth of the corporation.

In the first year of operation, plaintiff lost $13,485.08, but thereafter earned substantial sums in each fiscal year. During the years in question, plaintiff had

B. ELIGIBILITY TO ELECT STATUS

a relatively high debt to equity ratio because it found it necessary to borrow funds to fulfill the increasing needs for capital engendered by rapid expansion. No actual distributions were made with respect to the common stock until fiscal year 1962, when $40,000 was distributed, and in fiscal year 1963, when $36,000 was distributed. The primary reason for such distributions was to enable the shareholders to meet their tax obligations brought about as a result of plaintiff's timely election to be taxed pursuant to the provisions of Subchapter S of the Internal Revenue Code for the fiscal years ending in 1961, 1962 and 1963.

The Commissioner of Internal Revenue determined that plaintiff was ineligible to make the statutory election not to be subject to corporate income taxes for these three fiscal years on the ground that it had more than one class of stock and was therefore not a small business corporation as defined in Subchapter S. Accordingly, in January 1965, the Commissioner first notified plaintiff that he was claiming deficiencies in the amount of what he decided was the proper corporate income tax for the years 1961 through 1963. Plaintiff paid the deficiencies asserted and thereafter sued to recover income taxes and statutory interest in the amount of $164,733.13, plus interest. The district court held that plaintiff was entitled to such a refund because it "qualified as a small business corporation within the meaning of Section 1371(a) so as to be eligible to elect under Section 1372(a) not to be subject to corporate income taxes for its fiscal years 1961, 1962 and 1963." 301 F. Supp. at 694. We affirm.

Section 1371(a) of the Internal Revenue Code provides as follows:

> "Small business corporation. — For purposes of this subchapter, the term 'small business corporation' means a domestic corporation which is not a member of an affiliated group (as defined in section 1504) and which does not — "(1) have more than 10 shareholders; "(2) have as a shareholder a person (other than an estate) who is not an individual; "(3) have a nonresident alien as a shareholder; and "(4) have more than one class of stock." (26 U.S.C. § 1371(a)).

It is conceded that plaintiff met the first three requirements of the statute, but the Commissioner contends that the instruments issued to Mrs. Berst and Miss Garnett in exchange for their advances of $12,500 apiece were contributions to plaintiff's capital rather than loans and constituted a second class of stock, thus disqualifying plaintiff as a small business corporation. On the other hand, plaintiff contends that the advances were loans, but in any event did not constitute another class of stock within the meaning of the statute.

Applying the traditional tests of the thin capitalization doctrine, the district court held that the advances in question constituted contributions to capital. The court was impressed by the fact that the rate of interest was fixed at a percentage of net profits, thus placing the risks of the venture upon Mrs. Berst and Miss Garnett. The court was also impressed by the following factors: on two occasions their rights under the instruments were subordinated to bank loans; plaintiff had a comparatively high ratio of debt to equity; there was no provision for acceleration of payment of principal in case of default in interest payments; and plaintiff's plastics business had been a marginal operation, rendering its anticipated returns speculative in nature. In the aggregate, these factors were found clearly to outweigh those suggesting that the advances constituted loans. The entire panel of this Court agreed with the district court's conclusion that the advances were contributions to capital rather than loans under the criteria of the thin capitalization doctrine, but that decision is unnecessary to review here. The point at issue is whether the criteria heretofore developed to determine the debt versus equity question in other contexts are determinative of the question whether another "class of stock" exists within the meaning of Section 1371(a)(4).

Both in the district court and here, the Government relied on Treasury Regulation § 1.1371-1(g), which provides in pertinent part:

> "Obligations which purport to represent debt but which actually represent equity capital will generally constitute a second class of stock. However, if such purported debt obligations are owned solely by the owners of the nominal stock of the corporation in substantially the same proportion as they own such nominal stock, such purported debt obligations will be treated as contributions to capital rather than a second class of stock." D. 6904, 1967-1 Cum. Bull. 219).

The Government of course points to the inapplicability of the second sentence of the Regulation because Mrs. Berst and Miss Garnett were then not stockholders of the plaintiff corporation, so that the proportionality exception of the Regulation was inapplicable. It is the Government's position that the tests of the thin capitalization doctrine determine the existence of a second class of stock if the instruments in question do not come within the exception of the Regulation's second sentence. The underlying argument does little more than postulate the ubiquitous utility of those tests. Then the Government simply states:

> "Every instrument representing an advance to a corporation is either stock or debt. There is no such thing as non-stock equity. Corporate obligations that have been recharacterized as equity, are preferred stock for tax purposes."[14]

---

[14] Principal appellate brief for the United States, p. 28 (footnote omitted). Although Treasury Regulation § 1.1371-1(g) states that obligations actually representing equity capital will "generally" constitute a second class of stock, the Government has not argued that the regulation admits of any exception other than that set forth in its second sentence. On the contrary, as the Fifth Circuit also found in *Amory Cotton Oil Co. v. United States*, 468 F.2d 1046, 1054 (5th Cir. 1972), "... the construction advanced, in fact insisted upon, by the Commissioner is that the regulation is mandatory in operation unless the specific exception of proportionality is applicable." *Accord*: *Shores Realty Co., Inc. v. United States*, 468 F.2d 572, 576-578 (5th Cir. 1972). The proportionality exception adds to, rather than detracts from, the regulation's arbitrariness since the fact that debt is held proportionately by the shareholders is a factor traditionally considered to militate in favor of recharacterization as equity. *See, e.g., Henderson v. United States*, 245 F.

B. ELIGIBILITY TO ELECT STATUS

While holding that these advances constituted contributions to capital rather than loans, the district court concluded that "it does not appear that the traditional debt-equity tests applied in other areas of tax litigation are relevant to the general purpose of Subchapter S or to the two conceivable purposes of the one class of stock requirement ..." (301 F. Supp. at 692). Consequently, the court analyzed the instruments in question in the light of the statutory purposes to ascertain whether they would be served by a conclusion that they constituted a second class of stock, disqualifying plaintiff from eligibility for Subchapter S status. The judge's perceptive analysis led him to conclude: "... that the general purpose of Subchapter S to permit small businesses to select a form of organization without regard to tax consequences would be served by a conclusion that plaintiff was eligible to elect to be taxed as a small business corporation during the years in question. It further appears that the purposes of the one class of stock requirement, to avoid administrative complexities and to limit the advantages of Subchapter S status to small corporations, would not be served by a conclusion that the instruments in question constituted a second class of stock within the meaning of § 1371(a)(4)." ... at 694).

In the panel's prior opinion herein, the majority was of the view that the criteria heretofore developed to determine the debt versus equity question under the thin capitalization doctrine and used by the district court to conclude that the advances by Mrs. Berst and Miss Garnett were contributions to capital rather than loans were determinative of the existence of a second class of stock. Thus the majority upheld the validity of Treasury Regulation § 1.1371-1(g) and held that thereunder, once the district court had concluded the advances were contributions to capital, that ipso facto meant they constituted a class of stock, the proportionality exception being inapplicable.

For the reasons detailed in the dissenting opinion ..., incorporated herein by reference, we conclude that the traditional thin capitalization doctrine tests for determining whether a purported loan should be treated as an equity contribution in order to prevent improper tax avoidance in other contexts are not suitable for determining whether a purported loan constitutes a second class of stock within the meaning of Section 1371(a)(4).[15]...

As can best be divined, the purpose of the single class of stock requirement was none other than to avoid the administrative complexity in the allocation of income which would result with more than one class of stock when preferred dividends were paid in excess of current earnings from undistributed but taxed

---

Supp. 782 (M.D. Ala.1965); *Cataline Homes, Inc.*, 23 CCH Tax Ct. Mem. 1361, 1367 (1964); Caplin, *The Caloric Count of a Thin Incorporation*, 43 Marq. L. Rev. 31, 57, 69 (1959).

[15] As emphasized in the prior dissenting opinion, this conclusion in no way forecloses use of the thin capitalization doctrine tests to recharacterize purported debt as equity where appropriate to deny particular tax benefits wrongfully taken in those cases where tax avoidance through the use of debt is still available in the Subchapter S context and in those cases where it is peculiarly available within the confines of Subchapter S. 470 F.2d at 318.

prior earnings.[16] Because the shareholders of a Subchapter S corporation are pro rata taxed on the corporation's undistributed taxable income for any year, if in a subsequent year dividends in excess of current earnings are distributed to preferred shareholders, the common stockholders will have already been taxed on the excess going to the preferred shareholders. But under the existing provisions of the Code, the common shareholders could only receive a capital loss benefit for the previously taxed income which they did not receive. Section 1376(a). Consequently, some sort of refund mechanism would be necessary to prevent the inequity to the common shareholders, and this is the administrative problem Congress evidently sought to avoid through the single class of stock requirement.

Although the district court accurately pointed out that this problem could not occur in the instant case because "interest" on the advances was to be paid only out of net profits before taxes, it further appears that the problem is not encountered in any case so long as interest is treated as interest. This is because shareholders are permitted a deduction for the excess of interest payments over earnings in any year, and hence they are adequately compensated for having been previously taxed on the earnings out of which interest payments may later be made.[17] 26 U.S.C. § 1374(a), (d)(1); *see* 26 U.S.C. § 1376(b). Indeed, assuming that the general problem of allocation of earnings and losses between various classes of stock was a Congressional concern in enacting the single class of stock requirement, the district court recognized that the problem arises only if the interest payments are first recharacterized as dividends.... The same principle applies to the particular administrative problem which occurs when dividends are paid to preferred shareholders in excess of current earnings — it is a problem only if the payments are recharacterized as dividends in the first place. The Government concedes as much when it states,

> "Once the notes have been recharacterized as equity, they present the same tax accounting problems with respect to the Subchapter S treatment of the corporation's undistributed taxable income and net operating loss as are presented by preferred stock."

(Principal appellate brief for the United States, p. 13....

The earlier dissenting opinion in this cause and the Fifth Circuit's opinion in *Shores Realty, supra,* have demonstrated that just because the purported loans come out on the capital contribution end on the thin capitalization test scale is not a sufficient reason to make that initial recharacterization. In enacting the single

---

[16] S. Rep. No. 1622, 83d Cong., 2d Sess. 453-454 (1954).

[17] Whatever problems that exist with "leakage" of previously taxed but undistributed earnings when a shareholder transfers stock before interest is paid out of them in a year giving rise to a net operating loss, these problems are inherent in the provisions of Subchapter S and exist regardless of the nature of the loan. *See* Note, 41 N.Y.U. L. Rev. 1012, 1018-1019 (1966); Note, 67 Colum. L. Rev. 494, 513-514 (1967).

B. ELIGIBILITY TO ELECT STATUS

class of stock requirement, there is no evidence of a Congressional design to ensure that what is debt for corporate purposes be insulated from the risks of the business venture to such an extent that the doctrine's tests would not recharacterize it as equity if used for tax avoidance. And generally, in enacting Subchapter S, Congress has evinced no concern with the manner in which a small business corporation is capitalized in terms of how the contributors furnish money or property to the corporation. Quite the contrary, for the primary policy underlying the enactment of Subchapter S is "to permit businesses to select the form of business organization desired without the necessity of taking into account major differences in tax consequences."[18] Moreover, in seeking to approximate partnership tax treatment, it is difficult to understand why Congress would view differentiation among participants in the venture as to the form and extent of their participation as inherently bad from an economic policy standpoint.

The Government argues that if the taxpayer's denomination of the advances is to control, the corporation can avoid the single class of stock requirement by simply attaching a label of debt to any instruments different from the common stock of the corporation. But this argument is nothing else than a contention that a corporation should not be able to secure Subchapter S treatment through a sham in a scheme of improper tax avoidance. Assuming the advantage of Subchapter S election itself can properly be considered improper tax avoidance,[19] this case hardly fits the Government's hypothetical. It does not exemplify an instance of masquerading instruments as debt in order to evade any qualification requirement for Subchapter S status. The capital structure of the plaintiff was established and its common stock and the instruments in question were issued in 1957 when Subchapter S did not exist.[20] Even considering Mrs. Berst and Miss Garnett as shareholders, plaintiff would have had no more than seven shareholders during any of the taxable years in question, would not have had a corporation, trust, or partnership as a shareholder, and would have had no alien shareholders. Section 1371(a)(1)-(3). The existence of a business purpose for the issuance of debt instruments to Mrs. Berst and Miss Garnett is not questioned. And, simply stated, the Commissioner has never contended that the capital structure of the plaintiff was adopted with a view toward taking advantage of Subchapter S by evading the requirements for qualification thereunder.

Furthermore, it ill suits the Government to argue that the tests of the thin capitalization doctrine are justified to prevent the above, hypothetical "evasion"

---

[18] S. Rep. No. 1983, 85th Cong., 2d Sess. 87 (1958), U.S. Code Cong. & Admin. News 1958, p. 4791; *see* S. Rep. No. 830, 88th Cong., 2d Sess. 146 (1964), U.S. Code Cong. & Admin. News 1964, p. 1313.

[19] For the argument contra, *see* Bravenec, *The One Class of Stock Requirement of Subchapter S — A Round Peg in a Pentagonal Hole*, 6 Houston L. Rev. 215, 260-261 (1958); Note, 41 N.Y.U. L. Rev. 1012, 1017 (1966).

[20] The Subchapter S provisions were enacted in 1958 as part of The Technical Amendments Act of 1958.

because those tests were designed to prevent tax avoidance through the use of debt in contexts where treatment as debt would subvert underlying congressional policy to afford benefits for debt when "the funds were advanced with reasonable expectations of repayment regardless of the success of the venture ... [and were not] placed at the risk of the business...." *Gilbert v. Commissioner*, 248 F.2d 399, 406 (2d Cir. 1957).... The Government does not have a comparable economic policy underlying its desire to thwart supposed spurious labeling through use of the thin capitalization doctrine tests. Apparently the Government is concerned solely with a nefarious tax avoidance motive in denominating certain advances as debt, but if that is a justifiable concern, it would seem only logical to attack the problem directly, instead of through the blunderbuss application of the thin capitalization doctrine tests. Moreover, it seems that Treasury Regulation § 1.1371-1(g) cannot be justified on the Government's argument, since that Regulation would apparently allow a corporation seeking to qualify for or retain Subchapter S status deliberately to put a label of debt on instruments that otherwise would have been denominated preferred stock in order to evade the single class of stock requirement — so long as the purported debt obligations were held by the shareholders in substantially the same proportion that they owned the nominal stock.

Finally, it is unnecessary to decide whether the advances in question were properly recharacterized as equity contributions under the tests of the thin capitalization doctrine, for in determining whether the instruments held by these ladies constituted a second class of stock, there is no occasion to utilize those tests. Even if they constituted contributions to capital according to those criteria, the Commissioner has not persuaded us that they must be considered as a second class of stock within the meaning of the statute. To the extent that Treasury Regulation 1.1371-1(g) calls for a contrary result, it is arbitrary and beyond the power of the Commissioner.

Affirmed.

b. Straight Debt Safe Harbor

As we have seen, the big problem with issuing debt is the perpetual risk that the IRS might attempt to reclassify debt as equity, thereby potentially creating a prohibited second class of stock. There is a special safe-harbor rule for so-called "straight debt," which assures that even if such debt is found to be equity, it will not be a second class of stock. § 1361(c)(5).

"Straight debt" means any written unconditional promise to pay a fixed amount on demand or on a specific date, with three special features. First, the interest rate and interest payment dates are not contingent on profits, the borrower's discretion, or similar factors. Second, the debt cannot be converted directly or indirectly into stock. Third, the creditor must be an individual, estate, or trust eligible to hold stock in an S corporation. This means that a simple bank loan is outside the safe harbor. On the other hand, in the unlikely event that the

B. ELIGIBILITY TO ELECT STATUS

debt provided by a bank turned out to be equity, the S election would fail because of the existence of a corporate shareholder, so the limit on who can make a loan that fits inside the safe harbor is apparently not absurd, just redundant.

c. Treasury Views on Debt and Hybrid Instruments

The IRS and practitioners are persistently troubled by the one-class-of-stock rule. From the taxpayer's point of view, the provision causes needless restrictions on the company's ability to finance itself creatively. As you know already, from the Treasury Department's point of view, a relaxation of the rules would lead to complexity. S. Rep. No. 1622, 83d Cong. 2d Sess. 453 (1954).

The following Notice of Proposed Rule Making appeared in the Federal Register in mid-1991 as an attempt to calm down a hornet's nest of angry reactions of practitioners to a previous set of proposed regulations on the second-class-of-stock issue.[21] What follows is an edited form of the notice of proposed regulations and some comments, set off in brackets, as to how the final (November 1992) regulations came out:

Explanation of Provisions

General Rules

> Under the proposed regulations, a corporation is treated as having only one class of stock if all outstanding shares of stock of the corporation confer identical rights to distribution and liquidation proceeds and if the corporation has not issued any instrument or obligation, or entered into any arrangement, that is treated as a second class of stock.
>
> The determination of whether all outstanding shares of stock confer identical rights to distribution and liquidation proceeds is based on the corporate charter, articles of incorporation, bylaws, applicable State law, and any binding agreements relating to distribution or liquidation proceeds (collectively, the "governing provisions"). It is the rights conferred by the governing provisions that are taken into account in determining whether the corporation has more than one class of stock. A [...] commercial contractual arrangement such as a lease, employment agreement, or loan agreement is not a "binding agreement relating to distribution and liquidation proceeds" and thus is not a governing provision, unless such an agreement is entered into [with a principal purpose] to circumvent the one class of stock requirement of § 1361(b)(1)(D) and this regulation.
>
> Although a corporation is not treated as having more than one class of stock if the governing provisions provide for identical distribution and liquidation rights, any distributions (including actual, constructive, or

---

[21] 26 C.F.R. Part 1, [PS-4-73], RIN 1545-AC37, 56 Fed. Reg. 38,391 (August 13, 1991).

deemed distributions) that differ in timing or amount are to be given appropriate tax effect in accordance with the facts and circumstances. For example, a payment of excessive compensation may be recharacterized as a distribution by the corporation for which no deduction is allowed; however, neither the payment nor the distribution created by the recharacterization results in a second class of stock. Similarly, a distribution may be recharacterized in whole or in part as deductible compensation (on which FICA and FUTA taxes may be due), but any difference in distribution rights resulting from such a recharacterization will not result in a second class of stock.

Exceptions to General Rules

The proposed regulations provide that certain types of state laws and binding agreements are disregarded in determining all of a corporation's outstanding shares of stock confer identical rights to distribution and liquidation proceeds. State laws that require a corporation to pay or withhold state income taxes on behalf of some or all of the corporation's shareholders are disregarded, provided that, when the constructive distributions resulting from the payment or withholding of taxes by the corporation are taken into account, the outstanding shares confer identical rights to the distribution and liquidation proceeds. The difference in timing between the constructive distributions and the actual distributions to the other shareholders does not create a second class of stock.

Agreements to redeem or purchase stock at the time of death, disability, [divorce] or termination of employment are disregarded in determining whether a corporation's outstanding shares of stock confer identical distribution and liquidation rights [regardless of the stock price or other terms of the agreement]. In addition, bona fide buy-sell agreements among shareholders, agreements to restrict the transferability of stock, and certain redemption agreements are disregarded in determining whether a corporation's outstanding shares of stock confer identical distribution and liquidation rights unless (i) the agreement is entered into to circumvent the one class of stock requirement of § 1361(b)(1)(D) and the proposed regulations and (ii) the agreement establishes a redemption or purchase price that, at the time the agreement is entered into, is significantly in excess of or below the fair market value of the stock. Under the proposed regulations, agreements described in the preceding sentence that provide for the purchase or redemption of stock at book value or at a price between fair market value and book value are disregarded.

The proposed regulations also address situations in which there has been a change of stock ownership and the corporation determines the amount of its post-change distributions to its shareholders based on the allocation of income in the immediately preceding year. Agreements that provide for distributions in this manner do not result in a second class of stock. If

B. ELIGIBILITY TO ELECT STATUS 559

distributions pursuant to the agreement are not made within a reasonable time after the close of the taxable year in which the ownership change occurs, however, the distributions may be recharacterized depending on the facts and circumstances.

Shares Taken into Account

Under the proposed regulations, all outstanding shares of stock are taken into account in determining whether a corporation has a second class of stock. The proposed regulations provide that, for purposes of subchapter S, stock that is substantially nonvested within the meaning of § 1.83-3(b) is not treated as outstanding stock unless the holder makes an election with respect to the stock under § 83(b). Substantially nonvested stock with respect to which an election under § 83(b) has been made, however, is taken into account in determining whether a corporation has a second class of stock. Such stock is not treated as a second class of stock if the stock confers rights to distribution and liquidation proceeds that are identical to rights conferred by the other outstanding shares of stock....

Rules Relating to Debt Obligations, Call Options, and Similar Instruments

In General

Under the proposed regulations, instruments, obligations, or arrangements may be treated as a second class of stock in certain circumstances. The proposed regulations provide a number of safe harbors or exceptions for certain ordinary business arrangements entered into by S corporations and their shareholders.

Obligations Designated as Debt

The proposed regulations generally provide that an obligation (whether or not designated as debt) is not treated as a second class of stock unless two conditions are met: (1) The obligation constitutes equity or otherwise results in the holder being treated as the owner of stock under general principles of Federal tax law, and (2) the obligation is used to contravene the rights conferred by the corporation's outstanding stock with regard to distribution or liquidation proceeds or to contravene the limitation on eligible shareholders contained in this subchapter. This rule is consistent with case law holding that purported debt which would ordinarily be recharacterized as equity does not always constitute a second class of stock for purposes of subchapter S.

Certain Safe Harbors for Obligations Designated as Debt

The proposed regulations also set forth certain safe harbors for obligations issued by a corporation. First, unwritten advances from a shareholder that do not exceed $10,000 in the aggregate at any time, are treated as debt by the parties, and are expected to be repaid within a reasonable time are not treated as a second class of stock, even if the advances are considered equity under general principles of Federal tax law. Second, proportionately-held obligations are not treated as a second class of stock. Proportionately-held obligations are any class of obligations that are considered equity under general principles of Federal tax law, but are owned solely by the owners of, and in the same proportion as, the outstanding stock of the corporation. Obligations owned by the sole shareholder of a corporation are always held proportionately to the corporation's outstanding stock.

The failure of an obligation to meet either of these safe harbors will not necessarily result in a second class of stock. As stated above, an unwritten advance or another obligation will not be treated as a second class of stock unless it is considered equity under general principles of Federal tax law and is used to contravene the rights conferred by the outstanding stock or the limitation on eligible shareholders.

Safe Harbor for Call Options

The proposed regulations also provide that a call option (or similar instrument) is not treated as a second class of stock unless, taking into account all the facts and circumstances, the call option is substantially certain to be exercised and has a strike price substantially below the fair market value of the underlying stock[22] on the date that the call option is issued, transferred [by an eligible shareholder] to a person who is not an eligible shareholder, or materially modified. For purposes of this rule, if an option is issued in connection with a loan and the time period in which the option may be exercised is extended in connection with (and consistent with) a modification of that loan, with the loan the extension of the time period in which the option may be exercised is not a material modification. The determination of whether an option is substantially certain to be exercised takes into account not only the likelihood that the holder may exercise the option, but also the likelihood that a subsequent transferee may exercise the option. For example, a corporate holder may be unlikely (or unable) to exercise an option, but the option would still be substantially certain to be exercised if it could be transferred to an individual who would be substantially certain to exercise the option. A call option does not have a strike price substantially below fair market value if the price at the time of exercise cannot, pursuant to the terms of the instrument, be substantially below the fair market value of the underlying stock at that time.

---

[22] See Reg. § 1.1361-1(l)(4)(iii)(C) for an objective definition of "substantially below fair market value."

B. ELIGIBILITY TO ELECT STATUS 561

If a convertible debt instrument embodies rights equivalent to those of a call option, it is evaluated both as debt and as a call option under the proposed regulations.

Exceptions for Certain Call Options

The proposed regulations set forth two exceptions for call options. First, a call option is not treated as a second class of stock if it is issued by a corporation to a person that is actively and regularly engaged in the business of lending and is issued in connection with a loan to the corporation that is commercially reasonable. [A transfer of a call option from one lender to another, along with the loan, qualifies for the lender exemption.] Second, a call option that is issued to an individual who is an employee or an independent contractor in connection with the performance of services (and that is not excessive by reference to the services performed) is not treated as a second class of stock if the call option is nontransferable within the meaning of § 1.83-3(d) and the call option does not have a readily ascertainable fair market value as defined in § 1.83-7(b) at the time the option is issued. If the call option becomes transferable, however, the exception ceases to apply. In this event, the option is tested under the general option rule if and when it is transferred to a person who is not an eligible shareholder or is materially modified.

Safe Harbor for Call Options

The proposed regulations also provide a safe harbor for certain call options issued by a corporation. A call option is not treated as a second class of stock if, on the date the call option is issued, transferred to a person who is not an eligible shareholder, or materially modified, the strike price of the call option is at least 90 percent of the fair market value of the underlying stock on that date. For purposes of this safe harbor, a good faith determination of fair market value by the corporation will ordinarily be respected.

....

PROBLEM 24-2

You are an associate at a law firm that has a new client by the name of Jiffy Products, Inc. You have driven out to visit the offices of Jiffy Products to prepare it for the filing of an S election. So far, you have learned that Jiffy Products is an accrual-method, calendar-year C corporation that has been around for thirty years. It has accumulated "earnings and profits" (*see* § 316) of $150,000 and is owned by four shareholders, including the ABC partnership, which holds 15% of the common stock. A and B are U.S. citizens, both of whom reside in Jiffy's home state, but C only recently arrived in the USA. Jiffy has issued some warrants to its executives and has a shadow stock plan that gives executives extra money if the company's stock performs well. Jiffy has two classes of common stock, which differ only in that one class votes and the other does not. Jiffy's liabilities and capital account, which you were just shown, look like this:

Accounts payable	$300,000
Note due to president	$30,000
Long-term bonds	$800,000
Paid-in-capital for common stock	$10,000
Paid-in-capital for preferred stock	$40,000
Retained earnings	$150,000
Paid-in capital for warrants (convertible into common stock)	$1,000

What steps need to be taken to assure Jiffy's effort to become an S corporation can be achieved, starting next year? Assume it is now October 15. As to the warrants, see Reg. § 1.1361-1(l)(4)(iii)(B)(2) and (C).

5. ELECTION PROCEDURE

Read § 1362(a)-(c).

a. Effect of Election

The S election is not a taxable event to the corporation making the election.[23] Accordingly, all the attributes of a C corporation that existed prior to the election continue after the election. The big exception is that net operating losses of the C corporation are suspended and cannot be used again until the corporation reverts to C corporation status, although the clock continues to run on them.

b. Shareholder Consents For Obtaining S Corporation Status

The corporation's election of S corporation status is valid only if all shareholders consent to the election. The process of gathering up the consents is much simplified by IRS Form 2553, to which one adds the consent as a separate page.[24] The difficulty is timely filing. An election made during the first 2½ months of the tax year can be effective for the full year in which it was made. (However, if the consent is filed after the beginning of the year for which it is to be effective, all shareholders in the corporation who held stock *on any day* in the election year but *before* the election is made must also consent, no matter where they might reside at the moment. Reg. § 1.1362-6(b)(3)(i). This puts tax

---

[23] This ignores the comparatively trivial LIFO and ITC recapture taxes mentioned earlier on. By the way, legislation has been proposed to make the selection a (taxable) constructive liquidation of the preceding C corporation.

[24] Reg. § 1.1362-6(b)(3)(i). *See* Form 2553, which is reproduced in the Appendix to this book.

advisors in the position of warning clients teetering on the brink of making an S election against exotic travel by any of the shareholders, including those who sold their stock early in the year.) In addition, the entity itself must have been a "small business corporation" for the part of the year preceding the election. § 1362(a)(2). The corporation's S election is invalid if any consent is filed late, except that a late-filing shareholder may apply to the Internal Revenue Service Center for an extension of time to file the consent. Reg. § 1.1363-6(b)(3)(A).

c. Corporate Election

The shareholders consent; the corporation elects. This qualification process is again simplified by the existence of Form 2553, which in a gesture of rare efficiency also includes the place to indicate the corporation's election, and a means for selecting the taxable year. Having elected, the corporation must file the form at a time when it qualifies for the election. § 1361(b); § 1362(b)(1). This can be a challenging problem because of the number of requirements that must be met in order to be an S corporation.[25] Also, there is something about forms and filing dates that some taxpayers just cannot seem to cope with.

C. LOSS OF STATUS VIA TERMINATION OR REVOCATION OF THE ELECTION

1. REVOCATION

Read § 1362(d)(1).

The corporation can revoke its S election for any taxable year. This process requires that shareholders who collectively own more than 50% of the outstanding stock in the S corporation consent to the revocation. The consenting shareholders must own their stock in the S corporation at the time the corporation makes the revocation. The corporation must provide the IRS with a statement to that effect and, if the corporation wants to pick a particular revocation date that will take effect in the future, must specify the date the revocation will take effect. The corporation is supposed to attach a statement of consent, signed by each shareholder who consents to the revocation to its statement.[26]

---

[25] The S election corporation status is effective for a tax year if Form 2553 is filed any time during the previous tax year, or by the fifteenth day of the third month of the tax year to which the election is to apply, e.g., by March 15 for a calendar-year S corporation, as most are. Once the election and consents are perfected, the enterprise can continue as an S corporation indefinitely. If the election to claim S corporation status is otherwise valid, and it is made before the sixteenth day of the third month of the taxable year, but the election or consent is flawed, the election is treated as made for the next taxable year. § 1362(b)(2).

[26] If the corporation does not specify a prospective revocation date, the revocation is effective on the first day of the tax year if the revocation is made during the first 2½ months of the same tax year. If the corporation waits past that deadline, the revocation is effective on the first day of

2. TERMINATION

Read § 1362(d)(2).

Revocation is a voluntary act. Termination is not, unless the corporation deliberately uses a termination as a short cut for a revocation. There are several ways a termination of a valid S election can come about.

a. By Cessation of Small Business Corporation Status

S corporation status terminates the moment the corporation ceases to qualify as an S corporation. If the corporation inadvertently ceases to qualify, there is a chance the IRS will, with appropriate begging and pleading from the taxpayer, relent and disregard the fault.

There is no shortage of ways to lose S corporation status. For example, there might be more than thirty-five shareholders; a shareholder might transfer stock to a nonresident alien, to a corporation or to a partnership; or the company might issue a second class of stock, or might acquire a domestic subsidiary, other than a nonoperating subsidiary.

A termination of S corporation status is effective as of the date the terminating event occurred. If this occurs other than on the first day of the tax year, the result is an "S termination year." There will be more on that later.

If a corporation does terminate its status as an S corporation, it generally must wait five tax years before it can again become an S corporation, although if it gets the permission of the IRS, the waiting period may be shortened. § 1362(g). One might wonder if the owners could form a new company and cause the tormented S corporation to be acquired by merger or purchase so as to let the new company make the S election. The answer is negative. The Treasury has identified the scam and has promulgated a regulation that treats the successor corporation as the continuation of the old S corporation. Reg. § 1.1362-5.[27]

PROBLEM 24-3

The president of an incorporated client recently called to say that the company was expecting to have a very bad year next year. The client wondered if, assuming it met the requirements to be an S corporation, it could make the S election, flow the losses through to its owners, and then drop the election for the

---

the following taxable year, unless the revocation specifies some particular future date that the revocation will take effect. If the corporation specifies a prospective date for revocation that is other than the first day of the tax year, the result will be a so-called "S termination year," a matter taken up later in this Chapter.

[27] A successor corporation is one that acquires a substantial part of the S corporation assets or whose assets were in large measure owned by the S corporation, provided at least half its stock is directly or indirectly owned by persons who owned at least half of the S corporation's stock when the termination became effective. Prop. Reg. § 1.1362-6(b); Reg. § 1.1362-5(b) (prior law).

C. LOSS OF STATUS VIA TERMINATION OR REVOCATION OF ELECTION 565

following year. The client also wondered if it could do the same thing again in the future. How would you answer? *See* § 1362(g).

b. By Violating Passive Income Limitation

Read § 1362(d)(3).

This way of losing S corporation status is fairly easy to bumble into because there are few obvious signals of a problem. Under § 1362(d)(3), an S corporation's status terminates if both of the following conditions occur for three consecutive taxable years:

— The corporation has pre-S corporation earnings and profits at the end of each such taxable year, *and*
— Its passive investment income for each such year is more than 25% of its gross receipts. The terms "passive investment income" and "gross receipts" are discussed later under the heading "Tax on Excess Net Passive Income."

This rule is evidently intended to prevent a regular C corporation from electing S status and converting into a passive investment company, rather than liquidating and incurring an income tax at the shareholder level on liquidation proceeds from the period that it operated as a C corporation.

It is important to not lose sight of the converse. If there are no earnings and profits from pre-S corporation years, then the S corporation can act as an investment company without losing its status as an S corporation, and without paying federal income taxes. The income tax on passive investment income only applies if it has earnings and profits ("e&p") from a time when it operated as a C corporation (or obtained the e&p in a reorganization) is discussed later. In other words, a corporation that has been an S corporation since its formation (a "virgin" S corporation in the lingo of the trade) is not susceptible to termination for excessive passive income.

3. S TERMINATION YEAR

Read § 1362(e)(1)-(4).

A termination that takes effect on any day other than the first day of the taxable year creates an S termination year. The part of the S termination year ending on the day before the effective date of the termination is an 1120S (S corporation) short tax year. The part of the S termination year beginning on the next day is an 1120 (C corporation) short tax year. § 1362(e)(1). After the S termination year is divided into an 1120S short year and an 1120 short year, the corporation's income and deductions are generally prorated on a daily basis between the two years, unless it elects an imaginary closing of the books, as with partnerships.[28]

4. RELIEF FOR INADVERTENT TERMINATIONS

Read § 1362(f).

Imagine an S corporation whose accountants concluded that it had no accumulated pre-S corporation earnings and profits, and that the corporation was audited by the IRS some years later. In the course of the audit it turned out that the corporation did indeed have undistributed earnings and profits left over from its years as a C corporation. Given the right facts, that could easily lead to a conclusion that the corporation had violated the passive investment income test of § 1362(d)(3). As you will see later, it can also result in the imposition of a tax on the corporation under § 1375. In that case, the company would owe corporate taxes, plus interest and perhaps penalties, and the shareholders would have to amend their returns to remove income or losses flowed through to them in past years, a messy proposition for all concerned.[29]

Section 1362(f) provides that if the corporation inadvertently terminated its election because it ceased to qualify as an S corporation or because it violated the restriction on passive investment income, the IRS may waive the termination if it concludes that the termination was inadvertent, the corporation takes steps to correct the event within a reasonable period of time, and the corporation and its shareholders agree to be treated as if the event had not occurred.[30]

OUTSIDE READINGS

L. Bravenec & D. Gray, *Shareholders Agreements Can Preserve the S Election and Remedy its Termination*, 63 J. Tax'n 130 (1985).

---

[28] § 1362(e)(2), (3). One must use the exact method if one-half or more of the corporation's stock is sold or exchanged during the S termination year. § 1362(e)(6)(D). The S termination year counts as only one tax year for figuring carrybacks and carryforwards, even though two returns are filed for the year. The result is favorable to taxpayers, because it reduces the risk that suspended net operating losses (NOLs) will be obliterated. The problem with NOLs is that they die of old age, in general, after fifteen tax years following the year they arose in. § 172(b)(1)(A)(ii).

[29] This problem is worsened by the possibility that come of their years might be closed and that the mitigation provisions of § 1311 *et seq.* do not extend to S corporations and their shareholders. § 1313(c).

[30] The format for asking for this help is apparently to seek a private letter ruling from the National Office of the IRS, using Revenue Procedure 91-1, 1991-1 C.B. 321 as the template. The request should state all relevant facts pertaining to the terminating event, including when the corporation's election to be an S corporation took place, a detailed explanation of the event causing termination, when and how the event was discovered, and what steps were taken to return the corporation to S corporation status.

Chapter 25
TAXATION OF THE ENTITY AND ITS OWNERS

A. CONDUIT MODEL

Read § 1366(a)-(c).

The *basic* model of pass-through taxation of an S corporation and its shareholders is generally the same as that for partnerships. Each shareholder reports a pro rata share of each item of income, loss, deduction, or credit that is separately stated on the information return filed by the entity and a pro rata share of nonseparately stated income or loss on his or her income tax return, with the character of each item flowing through to the shareholder. This is taxed to the shareholder, using the corporation's accounting method. § 1366(a)(1); Reg. § 1.1363-1(b). The shareholder's stock basis rises with corporate profits and shareholder contributions, and declines with corporate losses and distributions. § 1367.

However, do not be fooled into thinking the S corporation is as pure a conduit as a partnership. Instead, as with C corporations, regular and liquidating distributions of appreciated property are recognition events and the appreciation is taxable to the owners, and in the case of S corporations with earnings and profits accumulated from C corporation years, there is a risk of incurring a corporate-level tax on excessive passive investment income under § 1375, and on sales and distributions of property with built-in gains (a.k.a., "the BIG tax") under § 1374. The shareholders alone pay the tax on distributions, unless the BIG tax of § 1374 applies, in which case the corporation pays a separate tax. Sections 1374 and 1375 are discussed later in the text.

B. COMPUTATION OF CORPORATE TAX BASE

1. ACCOUNTING METHOD

An S corporation can use the cash method unless it is a tax shelter. § 448. Congress considers use of the cash method a privilege, and to some extent it is. If it prefers, the S corporation is free to use the accrual method. In either case, the corporation will calculate its income on the basis of its selected accounting method, and the choice may have a major impact on the shareholders. To take a simple example, if the company can accrue a large interest expense deduction, the result may be significant tax savings for the shareholders. Conversely, shareholders of an engineering firm with a big backlog of receivables may incur an undue amount of taxes, subject to later bad-debt deductions in the event of nonpayment.

2. TAXABLE YEAR

Congress has made a general effort to force S corporations onto the calendar year. In form, one can still choose between a calendar year or a fiscal year. § 1378. However, a fiscal year will have to be a so-called "permitted year," for which the corporation establishes a substantial business purpose to the satisfaction of the IRS. Otherwise, the corporation can elect under § 444 to have a tax year other than a permitted tax year, but in that case it will have to pay a toll charge in the form of accelerated payments of income taxes that rob the company of the benefit of making a fiscal year election; this puts S corporations and partnerships in the same boat.

The shareholder will report the corporation's results in the shareholder's year in which, or with which, the corporation's tax year ends. If the years overlap, the shareholder reports the results of the overlapping year. § 1366(a)(1). Nowadays, the corporation and its shareholders will normally both be on the calendar year.

3. TAXABLE INCOME AND DISTRIBUTIVE SHARES

To calculate an S corporation's income, one divides its items of income, loss, expense, and credit into two groups: separately stated items, and items used to figure non-separately stated income or loss. Both groups are often called "pass thru items" [sic] because they are passed through to the shareholders on a pro rata basis. §§ 1363(b), 1366. This is the same rule as applies for partnerships.

The concept here is the same as for partnerships under § 702(a), namely that one must separately state items of income, loss, expense, and credit to the extent that, when separately treated on the shareholder's income tax return, they could affect the shareholder's tax liability. Examples include interest income, dividend income, short-term capital gain or loss, long-term capital gain or loss, and items needed to calculate the shareholder's alternative minimum tax.

As with partnerships, the entity prepares its own return and a Schedule K-1 for each shareholder. The share of income attributable to each owner depends on his or her proportionate ownership of the company's common stock, using a daily per-share proration to apportion the results.

C. ELECTIONS

Read § 1363(c).

Most tax elections are made by the entity. Note that there is no analog to § 754, so stock transfers cannot affect the S corporation's basis in its assets in any way.

D. BUILT-IN GAINS TAX ON S CORPORATIONS THAT FORMERLY WERE C CORPORATIONS

This is a *critical* problem with respect to the S election. The legislative purpose of the BIG tax is to remove the benefit of using S corporations to duck the anti-*General Utilities* rules enacted in 1986. If it were not for the BIG tax, a C corporation could launder gains from property that had appreciated during the C corporation years by making the S election, promptly selling or distributing appreciated property, and thereby shifting the gain to the shareholders alone, with no corporate-level tax. Consistent with the Congressional concern, the BIG tax does not reach a corporation that has been an S corporation all its life; practitioners sometimes refer to the latter kind of entity as a "virgin S" corporation. The following description is from a Joint Committee document summarizing the BIG tax:

> [P]resent law (as modified by the 1986 Act) also provides that a corporate-level tax is imposed on certain gains of an S corporation that was formerly a C corporation. The corporate-level tax applies to any gain that arose prior to the conversion of the corporation to S status ("built-in gain") and is recognized by the S corporation, through sale, distribution or other disposition within ten years after the date on which the S election took effect (sec. 1374). The total amount of gain subject to corporate-level tax, however, is limited to the aggregate net built-in gain of the corporation at the time of conversion to S corporation status.

The Code taxes built-in gains at the *top* corporate rate of 35%. Congress hit hard with the BIG tax, in that it imposed an immediate tax on *both* the S corporation and on the shareholder (whose tax base or inclusion is reduced by the tax the corporation paid). By contrast, if a C corporation distributes appreciated property,[1] although the corporation will be taxable on the appreciation, there is no assurance of a shareholder level gain; it might well be that the distribution constituted a return of capital because the corporation had no e&p (hence no dividend) and the shareholder had a high enough stock basis that the distribution would not be taxable under § 301. Moreover, if the C corporation merely sells an appreciated asset there is, of course, no shareholder level tax until a distribution is made.

The amount of net recognized built-in gain for any taxable year is limited to the amount that would be taxable income of the corporation if it were not an S corporation. § 1374(d)(2). For this purpose, taxable income means gross income of the corporation minus most deductions, including the amortization deduction for corporate organization costs allowed a corporation, but not the net operating

---

[1] The same result occurs if the C corporation sells the asset and then distributes the sales proceeds to its shareholders.

loss deduction or other special deductions for corporations, e.g., the dividends-received deduction. Although this limit assures that the BIG tax will not kick economically weak companies when they are down, the BIG tax reapplies when they get back up. That is because under § 1374 the suspended amount is treated as recognized built-in gain in the following tax year, unless the corporation elected S status before April 1988. § 1374(d)(2)(B).

Any BIG tax (i.e., the check written to the IRS) is passed through to the shareholders as a loss for the year in which the tax arises. § 1366(f)(2). The character of the loss depends on the character of the built-in gain on which the BIG tax was imposed. Consider the inequity if the tax did not flow out as a deduction and the shareholder later sold stock.

Here is a simple example of the BIG tax:

> *To illustrate*: C Corp. elected to be an S corporation this year, at a time when it had one asset, having a value of $10,000 and a basis of $0. It soon thereafter sold the asset, incurring a corporate tax of 35% of $10,000, or $3,500. The shareholder was also taxed on $10,000 gain, less the $3,500 tax; thus, the shareholder's federal income tax base (the amount to be included in income) is $6,500. Assuming a 40% tax rate, the shareholder pays a tax of $2,600. Total taxes are $6,100.

Now read § 1374(a), (b)(1)-(2), and (c)(1)-8(a), and § 1375(a).
You might want to try this as a self-test:

Suppose XXX Corporation is a small business corporation which qualifies for and elects S corporation status for its first tax year beginning after 199x, having operated as a C corporation since its inception in 1990. All of its outstanding shares of common stock are owned equally by mother and daughter, Anne and Marie, each of whom has a basis of $25,000 in her stock. In its first S corporation year XXX earns $250,000, $100,000 of which is long-term capital gain, and $100,000 of which is rental income. XXX Corp. incurred no capital loss. It does not distribute anything to its shareholder. Consider these questions, with minimum concern for the numbers.

(1) Will XXX Corporation have to pay a tax for this year? *See* §§ 1363, 1374, 1375.
(2) What amounts will Anne and Marie each have to include in income? *See* § 1366(a). Could the fact that Anne worked full-time as a rental property manager for XXX and received $2,500 annual salary from the corporation affect the allocation of income to the shareholders? *See* § 1366(e).

Answers:

(1) XXX Corporation will not have to pay any tax on ordinary corporate income (§ 1363), but would be subject to an entity-level tax if any of its income were from realizing built-in gain, which at least part of the

$100,000 gain is, since it has not always been an S corporation (§ 1374) or excess passive investment income (§ 1375, if it had any leftover Subchapter C earnings and profits). If the entire $100,000 were subject to the BIG tax, the bill would be $35,000.

(2) Anne and Marie would each have to include her pro-rata share of the corporation's income, with the long-term capital gain (less the BIG tax) and (possibly passive) rental income. § 1366. The rates of tax on each type of income (with its character passed through) will depend on the individual circumstances of each shareholder. § 1366. The salaries can reduce the corporation's taxable income, thereby deferring the BIG tax.

PROBLEM 25-1

Xeno Corp. is a prosperous cash-method incorporated architectural firm that elects to be an S corporation. It has $10,000 of receivables from clients at the beginning of its first tax year as an S corporation, which was last year. Are the receivables built-in gain items? *See* § 1374(a), (d).

PROBLEM 25-2

Alpha Corp. is a cash-method, calendar-year S corporation that recently elected S corporation status. At the time of the election, it had two assets, one with a value of $20,000 and an adjusted basis of $0, and the other with a value of $0 and an adjusted basis of $10,000. There are no other assets. In its first year as an S corporation, it sold both assets for their fair market values. Alpha also had a $10,000 loss from other activities after it became an S corporation.

(a) Is Alpha subject to the BIG tax?

(b) Would the result differ if Alpha's loss arose during its prior existence as a C corporation and it has no income for the year? *See* § 1374(b)(2).

(c) Reconsider part "(a)." Now assume that in the next taxable year Alpha had taxable income of $20,000, none of which is attributable to recognized built-in gains. Is it subject to the BIG tax?

Although one can defer the date of payment of the tax. one cannot beat the BIG tax by selling assets on the installment method, with the first payment beginning after the ten-year "recognition period." *See* Notice 90-27, 1990-1 C.B. 336.

Pre-1987 S elections. Corporations that made the S election before 1987 are grandfathered and made subject to an older and far milder form of § 1374.[2] It is now largely irrelevant. Former § 1374(c)(3).

E. TAX ON EXCESS NET PASSIVE INCOME

Read § 1375.

An S corporation that has earnings and profits at the end of a taxable year may be subject to a tax on its excess net passive income. § 1375. Moreover, if passive investment income is more than 25% of gross receipts for three consecutive taxable years and the corporation has earnings and profits at the end of each of those years, the corporation's S corporation status terminates, and the corporation would not be able to reelect S status for five years. § 1362(d)(3).

There is no minimum amount of earnings and profits; it appears that one cent would do. Note that earnings and profits can only exist for a former C corporation that elected S corporation status or one that reorganized with a C corporation that had e&p. It could not arise in a "virgin" S corporation. Thus, virgin S corporations make handy investment companies.

The base on which the tax is imposed is "excess passive net income." § 1375(a). The tax rate is the top corporate rate, currently 35%. § 11(b).

Section 1375(b)(3) indirectly defines the term "gross receipts" as the total amount an S corporation receives or accrues under its method of tax accounting, including the proceeds of sales or exchanges of most property.[3]

The term "passive investment income" includes gross receipts from royalties, rents, dividends, interest, annuities, and sales or exchanges of stock or securities. § 1362(d)(3)(D)(i). Each of the listed terms has its own definition, but the details are beyond the scope of a book such as this. "Net passive income" is passive investment income minus allowable deductions directly connected with the production of the income. § 1375(b)(2). The net operating loss deduction and special deductions under §§ 241-250 are not allowed. § 1375(b)(2)(B). There are some further esoteric restrictions.

Calculating the tax. The 35% tax falls on excess net passive income for the taxable year. To compute the amount of excess net passive income, one must

---

[2] The gist of the old rule is that S corporations which make a "one shot" sale of appreciated assets are taxable as if they were C corporations. The rule only applies if the corporation sold or distributed an asset in the first three years of its life as an S corporation. The old rules are generally deadwood now, because 1987 is more than three years in the past. There is a parallel provision for small S corporations that elected before 1989.

[3] Proceeds from the sale or exchange of stock or securities are included in gross receipts only to the extent of net gain; losses are disregarded. § 1375(b)(3); § 1362(d)(3)(D)(i). Certain amounts received in exchange for stock in a corporate liquidation are also disregarded if the S corporation owned over one-half of each class of the liquidating corporation's stock as of the first distribution with respect to the liquidation. § 1362(d)(3)(D)(iv).

E. TAX ON EXCESS NET PASSIVE INCOME

multiply net passive income by a fraction consisting of passive investment income minus 25% of gross receipts over passive investment income. Once this jumble of words is turned into a formula, it is much less daunting:

net passive investment income for the year × (passive investment income in excess of 25% of gross receipts for the year) / passive investment income for the year

The tax is softened three ways. First, excess net passive income cannot be more than the S corporation's taxable income for the year, as determined without allowance for dividends-received deductions and net operating loss deductions. § 1375(b)(1)(B). Second, the S corporation may be able to talk its way out of the tax if it can show that it believed it did not in fact have earnings and profits at the end of the taxable year and it disgorges its earnings and profits within a reasonable time after discovering the error. Reg. § 1.1375-1A. Third, the tax reduces the amount of passive investment income that is taxed to the shareholders, thereby modestly reducing shareholder level taxes. § 1366(f)(3).

The following problems illustrate the application of the tax.

PROBLEM 25-3

The Gilmore Corporation, a cash-method calendar-year taxpayer, has operated a profitable warehouse business since 1957 in Big City, USA. Its books clearly show that it has earnings and profits of $800,000 as of the end of this year. It made the S election two years ago. It has rented out one of its properties on a net lease basis (i.e., the tenant pays local taxes, etc.) to be used as a parking lot. At the same time, it is only breaking even on the warehouse business. The net lease income is $1 million this year. Its gross receipts from the warehouse business were $1 million, but its related expenses were also $1 million. The corporation incurred $250,000 of professional fees in connection with a dispute with the net-lease tenant this year.
(a) What, if anything, is its § 1375 tax?
(b) What defenses or limitations can the corporation raise to the tax?
(c) Is the S election forfeited?

PROBLEM 25-4

X Corporation is an S corporation that owns one-fourth of the profits and capital interests of the X-N partnership as a limited partner and one-fourth of the same interests as a general partner. The partnership is actively engaged in a plumbing repair business which has no passive investment income. Under Rev.

Rul.71-455[4] an S corporation's allocable share of income from a partnership retains its character for passive investment income purposes.

(a) If X sells its interest as a general partner, how will that gain be treated? *See* Reg. § 1.1362-2(c)(4)(ii)(B).

(b) How is the sale of the limited-partnership interest treated? *See* Reg. § 1.1362-2(c)(4)(ii)(B)(3), (4).

F. PASS-THROUGH OF INCOME AND LOSS: TIMING OF PASS-THROUGH AND CHARACTER OF INCOME

1. PRO RATA SHARE RULE

Read §§ 1366(a) and 1377(a).

The general rule is that every shareholder reports a daily pro-rata share of the S corporation's annual net income or loss, except to the extent components of net income or loss are separately stated because of their possible differential effect on the tax liability of any shareholder. Those separately stated items are also includable on a pro rata, per-day basis. This is the same pattern as applies for partnerships.

Earnings or losses from an S corporation are normally apportioned among shareholders on a daily per-share basis. However, if any shareholder terminated his or her interest in an S corporation during a taxable year, and if all persons who were shareholders in the corporation at any time during that taxable year sign consents, the taxable year of the corporation is treated as if it were composed of two taxable years, the first of which ends on the date the shareholder's interest in the corporation terminates. This opens powerful tax planning opportunities. For example, a high-bracket shareholder can sell all her stock just before the company turns profitable and, via the election, repel all future income and dump it in the lap of a low-bracket buyer. *See* § 1377(a)(2). Note that whether or not the § 1377(a)(2) election is made, the seller's tax liability for the part of the year when she held her stock will be affected by the way the corporation's tax return is prepared by the buyer at the end of the year. This exposure increases if the election is not made, because the buyers may be able to exaggerate income in the year of the sale so as to ascribe as much income as possible to the sellers.

PROBLEM 25-5

S Corporation was organized two years ago. It is on the cash method and uses the calendar year. Its shareholders are all U.S. citizens. A owns 60% of the stock

---

[4] 1961-2 C.B. 318.

F. PASS-THROUGH OF INCOME AND LOSS

and has a May 31 year-end. B, who is on the calendar year, used to own 40%, but he sold his stock to C (also a U.S. citizen) on June 30 of year two. S Corporation had $20,000 of ordinary income in year two, and it distributed $1,500 to A and B on February 1 of year two. S Corporation did not elect to close its tax year as to B on his sale to C. How much income should A, B, and C report for year two?

PROBLEM 25-6

Mrs. Friendly is a 33% shareholder in the Dynamo Corporation, which, like her, uses the cash method and the calendar year. Dynamo has $1 million of accounts receivable and very little other income and few expenses. Dynamo is an S corporation. She is just about to sell her stock to Edward ("Fast Eddy") Zapp for $400,000. Fast Eddy will take over as CEO and will be able to do just about anything he wants to do once he has the stock. Mrs. Friendly is a bit worried that Eddy might sell the receivables and somehow harm her thereby. She wants your advice as to what to do. Assume the sales price of the stock and the closing date are negotiable.

PRIV. LTR. RUL. 9026005
(March 9, 1990)

District Director
... District Office
National Office
Internal Revenue Service
...

Issue

Has X, an S corporation that intended to elect to treat the tax year at issue as if it consisted of two tax years pursuant to section 1377(a)(2) of the Internal Revenue Code, substantially complied with the election requirements of section 18.1377-1 of the Temporary Income Tax Regulations, even though it did not include a statement of election with the tax return for the tax year at issue?

Facts

X, a subchapter S corporation, had two fifty percent shareholders during 1985, A and B. X was on a fiscal year ending February 28. On April 1, 1985, A sold all of his stock in X to B for $1,300,000. On January 27, 1986, X sold all its assets to another corporation and completely liquidated to the sole remaining shareholder, B.

The Form 1120S tax return for X for the tax year ending January 27, 1986, stated ordinary income of $655,810 and a net long-term capital gain of $2,786,466. The Schedule K-1 for B, attached to X's tax return, stated $666,430 of ordinary income and $2,786,466 of net long-term capital gain. The Schedule

K-1 for A, attached to X's tax return, stated an ordinary loss of $10,620. However, no statement of election with accompanying statement of consent as specified in section 18.1377-1 of the temporary regulations was included with X's tax return.

On A's individual income tax return, he reported the $10,620 ordinary loss from the Schedule K-1 attached to X's tax return. On B's individual income tax return, he reported the $666,430 of ordinary income and the $2,786,466 of net long-term capital gain from the Schedule K-1 attached to X's tax return.

Law and Analysis

Section 1377(a)(1) of the Code provides that for purposes of subchapter S, except as provided in section 1377(a)(2), each shareholder's pro rata share of any item for any tax year shall be the sum of the amounts determined with respect to the shareholder (A) by assigning an equal portion of such item to each day of the tax year, and (B) then by dividing that portion pro rata among the shares outstanding on such day.

Section 1377(a)(2) of the Code provides that under regulations prescribed by the Secretary, if any shareholder terminates his interest in the corporation during the tax year and all persons who are shareholders during the tax year agree to the application of this paragraph, section 1377(a)(1) shall be applied as if the tax year consisted of two tax years the first of which ends on the date of the termination.

Section 18.1377-1 of the temporary regulations provides that in the case of a tax year of an S corporation during which any shareholder terminates his or her entire shareholder interest in the corporation, the corporation may elect under section 1377(a)(2) to have the rules in section 1377(a)(1) applied as if the tax year consisted of two tax years. The election can be made only with the consent of all persons who are or were shareholders in the corporation at any time during such tax year. Such election shall be made by the corporation by filing a statement that the corporation elects under section 1377(a)(2) to have the rules provided in section 1377(a)(1) applied as if the tax year consisted of two tax years, which statement shall set forth the manner of the termination (e.g., the sale of a shareholder's entire shareholder interest) and the date thereof and shall be filed with the return for such tax year. The statement to be filed with the return for such tax year shall be signed by any person authorized to sign the return required to be filed under section 6037. In addition, there shall be attached to the statement of election a statement of consent, signed by each person who is or was a shareholder in the corporation at any time during the tax year, in which each such shareholder consents to the corporation making the election under section 1377(a)(2).

Because X did not include the statement of election required by section 18.1377-1 of the temporary regulations, we must determine if the filing of the Form 1120S with accompanying Schedules K-1 together the X's shareholders filing their individual tax returns consistent with the Schedules K-1 is enough to "substantially comply" with section 18.1377-1 of the temporary regulations.

F. PASS-THROUGH OF INCOME AND LOSS

Literal compliance with procedural directions in Treasury regulations is not always required. "[S]ubstantial compliance may be sufficient if the regulatory requirements in dispute are procedural or directory in that they are not of the essence of the thing to be done but are given with a view to the orderly and prompt conduct of business, and if the omission of the required material has not operated to the Commissioner's prejudice." *Tipps v. Commissioner*, 74 T.C. 458 at 468 (1980), *acq.*, 1981-2 C.B. 2 (Citations omitted).

For substantial compliance to exist one need not comply with all the formal requirements set forth in the Code and regulations; however, it must be clear from the return as filed that the election is being made, what the election covers, and that the taxpayers understand and accept the consequences of the election. *Tipps v. Commissioner, supra*. The taxpayer must not be left room to argue later that he had never intended to make the election and must not be permitted to "wait and see" or use hindsight to the Commissioner's disadvantage. *Young v. Commissioner*, 83 T.C. 831, 839 (1984), *and Taylor v. Commissioner*, 67 T.C. 1071, 1080 (1977); *acq.* 1979-2 C.B. 2.

The doctrine of substantial compliance applies to the present case because the requirements in section 18.1377-1 of the temporary regulations are "procedural and directory" and not the essence of the thing to be done. The statement of election required by section 18.1377-1 facilitates the conduct of business in a prompt and orderly manner by stating that the section 1377(a)(2) election is being made, stating the manner and date of the terminating event, and providing a statement of consent for each shareholder. However, it is not the essence of the statutory and regulatory scheme. The essence of section 1377(a)(2) of the Code and accompanying regulations is to have the shareholders agree to treat the tax year as if it consisted of two tax years, the first of which ends on the date of the termination of the shareholder's interest. If the taxpayers indicate from the return, accompanying schedules, and in the case of an S corporation, their corresponding individual returns, that they have agreed to treat the tax year as if it consisted of two tax years, then the essence of the statutory and regulatory scheme has been satisfied.

The failure to file the election and consent statement as set forth in section 18.1377-1 of the temporary regulations has not operated to the Commissioner's prejudice because an examination of the return, accompanying Schedules K-1, and the shareholders' corresponding individual returns would indicate that the election was made, what the election covered, and that the shareholders understood and accepted the consequences of the election. There was not an opportunity to use hindsight to the Commissioner's prejudice because the shareholders indicated their intent to be bound by the election. If the taxpayers did not intend to make the section 1377(a)(2) election, the Schedules K-1 for A and B would have stated ordinary income and capital gain for both shareholders because under section 1377(a)(1) of the Code each shareholder would have been assigned a pro rata portion of the S corporation items that would have been assigned equally to each day of the tax year. Thus, neither shareholder would have been allocated a loss for the tax year because for the tax year as a whole there was ordinary income and net long-term capital gain. If the shareholders did not agree to be bound by the section 1377(a)(2) election, they would not have reported the items from the Schedules K-1 attached to X's tax return consistently on their individual returns.

Conclusion

Although X failed to file a statement of election with the tax return for the tax year at issue in the precise manner required by section 18.1377-1 of the temporary regulations, X has substantially complied with the requirements of section 18.1377-1 of the temporary regulations.

NOTES

Some compliance is substantial, some is not. As usual, the courts are dragged in and asked to draw lines. Judges must feel as if they are being forced to handle the Greek paradox of the heap.[5]

Rockwell Inn, Ltd. v. Commissioner, 65 T.C.M. 2374 (1993), is more challenging. There, the Tax Court ruled the S election invalid where the corporation failed to file its Form 2553 on time, even though the corporation filed its tax return indicating that it had previously elected to be treated as an S corporation and issued a Schedule K-1 to each of its shareholders, showing each shareholder's distributive share of the corporation's income, and each shareholder reported the information shown on the K-1 on his or her individual tax return. The court rejected the taxpayer's assertion that Form 2553 is not mandatory in order to make the S election. It also rejected the contention that the corporation and its shareholders had substantially complied with the requirements for making an S election since the corporation's federal income tax return, including the Schedules K-1, contained essentially all the information sought by Form 2553. The court said that the corporate income tax return did not clearly and firmly elect S status, and therefore the corporation did not substantially comply with the essence of the statute. Can you reconcile *Rockwell* with Private Letter Ruling 9026005? Is there some difference in the risk of prejudice to the IRS in the two cases? Is there a difference in the degree of notice provided by taxpayers in the two cases? Can one articulate what substantial compliance means? Might it be a good idea to leave the concept of substantial compliance vague to prevent taxpayers from playing fast and loose with their obligations?

---

[5] The paradox goes like this: Imagine a modest sized heap of sand. Now take away a grain of sand from the heap. It is still a heap. Now remove another grain of sand, and then another. There is still a heap. If you keep doing it long enough, you know there will be only one grain of sand left. Is that grain a heap? If it is not, when did it stop being a heap?

F. PASS-THROUGH OF INCOME AND LOSS

Read Reg. § 18.1377-1. Does it seem to you that there would be any difference between a redemption of the shareholder's stock by the corporation as opposed to a sale to another person?

2. BASIS OF STOCK

Read §§ 1367(a), (b) and 1366(a)-(b).

The Code readings should seem fairly familiar if you have already completed the materials on partnership taxation. If not, be expecially sure to give them a good reading. Now consider the following problem.

PROBLEM 25-7

Gamma Corp. is a calendar-year, cash-method S corporation. It has the following items of income, credit and deductions. Assume Gamma has one shareholder who has a basis of $10,000 in her stock as of the end of the prior year. What is her basis in Gamma's stock after the following adjustments are made?

Operating revenues	$10,000
Business deductions	5,000
Nondeductible expenses	1,000
Income tax credits	2,000
Tax-exempt interest	7,000

3. REALLOCATION AMONG FAMILY GROUPS

Read § 1366(e).

Misallocations of income and losses from S corporations require great ingenuity because Subchapter S contains no equivalent of § 704(b). There are several reasons to do so, aside from merely shifting income to low-bracket family members. For example, one might use an S corporation to convert compensation income that is otherwise subject to Social Security taxes into investment earnings that can be used to sop up losses from a tax shelter investment that are otherwise suspended by the passive loss rules of § 469. This both dodges Social Security taxes on employee-shareholders and generates nontaxable income, thanks to the passive loss rules.

Section 704(e) requires appropriate allocations with respect to services and capital in family partnership settings. Section 1366(e) performs a similar job, but unlike § 704(e), it is not self-executing.

DAVIS v. COMMISSIONER
64 T.C. 1034 (1975)

GOFFE, JUDGE:

....

The petitioner, Dr. Davis, is an orthopedic surgeon who was engaged in a complete medical practice in that specialty. In his diagnostic work he relied upon x-rays made in his office and in cases where treatment was administered, the physical therapy was performed in his office. He organized two corporations, one of which performed the x-ray function and the other carried out physical therapy treatment which he prescribed. He made gifts of 90 percent of the stock of each of the corporations to his three minor children and they and the corporations elected to be taxed as small business corporations under the provisions of Subchapter S.

The Commissioner determined that the income of the corporations should be taxed to Dr. Davis under three distinct principles: (1) that under section 61 Dr. Davis attempted to assign the income or "fruit of the tree" when, in reality, Dr. Davis earned the income reported by the corporations; (2) section 482 required allocation of the income from the corporations to Dr. Davis in order to prevent avoidance of tax; and (3) Dr. Davis performed services for the corporations and section [1366(e)], therefore, required allocation back to him of the income reported by the corporations.

Respondent has limited the scope of his challenge to the reporting of the income by apparently conceding that X-Ray and Therapy were not "'shams' or 'fictions' in the purest sense." Likewise, respondent concedes that Dr. Davis' transfer of the stock to his children had substance and should, therefore, be recognized.... We are urged, on the authority of *Gregory v. Helvering*, 293 U.S. 465, 470 (1935); *Commissioner v. Court Holding Co.*, 324 U.S. 331, 334 (1945); *Kimbrell v. Commissioner*, 371 F.2d 897, 902 (5th Cir. 1967), to find that the economic practicalities and substance of the arrangement requires taxation of the income to Dr. Davis rather than to the corporations.

Respondent further submits that the transfer of the x-ray and therapy facilities by Dr. Davis to the corporations followed by his transfer of the stock to his children constituted an anticipatory assignment of a portion of his future income. *See, e.g., Lucas v. Earl*, 281 U.S. 111 (1930); *Helvering v. Clifford*, 309 U.S. 331, 335 (1940); *Commissioner v. Sunnen*, 333 U.S. 591 (1948). Alternatively, respondent advocates an allocation of the entire net taxable income of the corporations to Dr. Davis on the theory that the corporate contributions to the earning of the net taxable income were de minimis as compared to the services rendered by Dr. Davis. In this regard, he relies on the presumption accorded his determination under section 482, *Grenada Industries, Inc.*, 17 T.C. 231 (1951), affd. 202 F.2d 873 (5th Cir. 1953), cert. denied 346 U.S. 819 (1953), and, in the main, upon the inferences that may be drawn from all the circumstances where income is generated by a controlled business activity dependent upon the

F. PASS-THROUGH OF INCOME AND LOSS

direction of patients, clients or consumers from a controlling business activity which is closely related. Respondent also contends that the net taxable income of the corporations should be allocated to Dr. Davis pursuant to section [1366(e)] to reflect the value of his services to the corporations.

Respondent does not contend that X-Ray and Therapy were not viable business entities. Instead, respondent relies upon *Gregory v. Helvering*, 293 U.S. 465 (1935), and challenges taxation of the income to the corporations rather than to Dr. Davis on the grounds that his purpose in organizing the corporations was solely tax motivated. The primary reasons given by Dr. Davis for the transfers of the x-ray and physical therapy functions to the corporations and gifts of the stock to his children were as follows:

1. To provide security for his children in view of his marital difficulties and his personal health problems;

2. To insulate him personally from damage suits arising from negligent use of the potentially dangerous x-ray and physical therapy equipment; and

3. To separate the personnel problems into the x-ray and physical therapy functions and away from the personnel problems of his medical practice. Respondent counters with alternative remedies to the concerns of Dr. Davis. He could have made cash gifts to his children; he could have purchased liability insurance to insulate him from liability arising from the negligent use of the x-ray and physical therapy equipment; and he could have issued mandates to resolve the personnel problems.

We do not agree with respondent that Dr. Davis' purposes were tenuous. The transfer of valuable property rights with a known potential to produce income seems a logical reason to establish the corporations and give the stock to his children instead of giving cash which would have to be invested. Using the corporate form to insulate the taxpayer from liability has long been recognized as a valid reason for incorporating. *Sam Siegel*, 45 T.C. 566 (1966). It is especially applicable here because Dr. Davis had recently experienced the possibility of liability caused by serious burns received by a patient who was receiving heat therapy. We find Dr. Davis' explanation of resolving personnel differences by separation of the operations a plausible and satisfactory reason.

Respondent's reliance upon *Kimbrell, supra*, is unavailing. In that case the corporations merely executed contracts, hired employees, negotiated loans and collected interest thereon, and filed income tax returns. In the instant case the corporations x-rayed patients and administered physical therapy to patients.

Moreover, a taxpayer is not required to continue one form of business organization which results in the maximum tax on business income. *Polak's Frutal Works, Inc.*, 21 T.C. 953, 974-975 (1954).

Respondent contends that the earnings of the corporations should be taxed to Dr. Davis because he had control over the earning of the profits by performing the services. The facts are otherwise. Dr. Davis prescribed the type of x-ray or x-rays to be made for each patient and he prescribed the physical therapy to be administered. The x-ray prescriptions to the corporation were no different than were those to a radiologist he referred patients to before he owned x-ray equipment or those given to the hospital when he would prescribe x-rays for a patient who was admitted to the emergency room. We see little difference in prescribing x-rays or physical therapy and prescribing drugs to be compounded by a pharmacist. Dr. Davis' division of his endeavors is not particularly unusual. It is common knowledge that an orthopedic surgeon does not himself normally take x-rays nor does he administer physical therapy. If, on the other hand, Dr. Davis attempted to separate his diagnostic work from his surgery, this would be unusual because a doctor personally performs both of these services for a patient. The income of the corporations was generated by the services of persons employed by the corporations not by the services performed by Dr. Davis. Dr. Davis' direct services to the corporations were minimal. Under section 61, we conclude that the corporations controlled the capacity to produce the income through their employees and they, not Dr. Davis, are taxable on that income. *Ronan State Bank*, 62 T.C. 27 (1974).

Section 482 authorizes the Commissioner to allocate income and other items among related taxpayers in order to clearly reflect income or to prevent evasion of taxes.[6]

In his notices of deficiency the Commissioner allocated the net taxable income of the corporations to Dr. Davis. In his brief the Commissioner contends that the corporate employees were adequately compensated for the services they performed and that he advocates allocation only of the net taxable income of the corporations to Dr. Davis because the corporations' contributions of earning that portion of the income were minimal. This line of reasoning is fallacious. The corporations were paid fees comparable to those charged by other x-ray laboratories and physical therapists in the community and those fees were received by the corporations for the services performed by their employees, not Dr. Davis. Again, the analogy to the pharmacist is appropriate. The x-ray technician, the physical therapist and the pharmacist all carry out prescriptions made by the doctor. Respondent's blanket characterization of the tasks of the employees of the corporations which include the x-ray technician and the physical therapist as "routine" is not warranted. Both are specialists trained to carry out a doctor's order just as a pharmacist fills a prescription. As pointed out above in our discussion of section 61, the division of Dr. Davis' practice into medical practice, x-ray and physical therapy is not unusual in that the different endeavors are frequently engaged in by separate persons or entities. It is also not unusual in the respect that x-ray laboratories and physical therapists rely on referrals for their business. Again, we see a close analogy to the better known relationship of doctor and pharmacist. The entire arrangement was comparable to others in the

---

[6] Petitioner seeks to distinguish management and control by directing our attention to a series of decisions which are concerned with the assignment of income question under *Lucas v. Earl*, 281 U.S. 111 (1930). Accordingly, we find those decisions distinguishable. We find the reality of control obvious. Sec. 1.482-1(a)(3)(4), Income Tax Regs.

F. PASS-THROUGH OF INCOME AND LOSS 583

community except that Dr. Davis was in a position to forward business to the corporations. For example, before he owned x-ray equipment, he referred his patients to a radiologist which did not give him a referral fee in return. The radiologist performed no service for the patient different from what the X-Ray corporation now performs; i.e., in both instances the x-rays were interpreted and acted upon by Dr. Davis. Based on all the evidence we conclude that petitioners have made an adequate showing that the Commissioner abused the discretion granted to him by section 482 in allocating the net taxable income of the corporations to Dr. Davis.

Respondent relies upon *Pauline W. Ach*, 42 T.C. 114 (1964), *affd.* 358 F.2d 342 (6th Cir. 1966). That case is factually distinguishable. Ach involved the transfer of a lucrative dress shop business from one member of a family to a related family-owned corporation which had operated a losing dairy business. The transfer was for a promissory note equal to the book value of the assets of the dress shop business. The income of the dress shop business was absorbed by net operating loss carryovers of the dairy business. We sustained disallowance of the net operating loss carryovers under the provisions of section 269 and we approved allocation under section 482 of 70 percent of the dress business profits to Pauline Ach because that portion was attributable to her services. In the instant case we have found as a fact that the gross income of the corporations was not generated by Dr. Davis but, instead, by the employees of the corporations. The referrals, because they are not unusual as explained above, do not constitute services rendered by Dr. Davis to the corporations.

Respondent points to the failure of Dr. Davis to charge rent for the first six months of 1966, the failure to charge Dr. Davis for use of the x-ray machine and the failure to share common overhead expenses as indicative that his reallocation was proper. As explained above, we have held the reallocation of the Commissioner to be unreasonable. Respondent has not pleaded in the alternative that the specific items described above should be allocated nor did he request amendment of his pleadings following the trial to conform them to the proof. It is obvious that there is some basis for reallocation of the three items, minimal as they are. We will not voluntarily attempt to make such an allocation at this point because the pleadings never apprised petitioners of that issue in order that they could offer proof of the proper allocation of those specific items. The issue presented at trial was allocation of net taxable income upon the broad concept that Dr. Davis generated the income. The size of these three items in relation to the gross income and other expenses cannot justify allocation of the entire net taxable income to Dr. Davis.

As a final "string to his bow" the Commissioner relies upon section [1366(e)] which permits him to allocate from one shareholder in a "Small Business Corporation" (Subchapter S corporation) amounts treated as dividends which should be allocated to other shareholders who are members of the shareholders' family to reflect the value of services rendered to the corporation by such shareholders. The purpose of section [1366(e)] is to tax each shareholder of a

Subchapter S corporation on the full value of the income he earns. No deflection of that income is to be permitted through artificial salary or dividend payments. S. Rept. No. 1983, 85th Cong., 2d Sess. (1958), 1958-3 C.B. 1143-1144; *Charles Rocco*, 57 T.C. 826, 831 (1972).

> In determining the value of services rendered by a shareholder, consideration shall be given to all the facts and circumstances of the business, including the managerial responsibilities of the shareholder, and the amount that would ordinarily be paid in order to obtain comparable services from a person not having an interest in the corporation.... [Sec. 1.1375-3(a), Income Tax Regs.[7]]
>
> The determination is factual and tests applied to ascertain the value of the shareholder's services include "the nature of the services performed, the responsibilities involved, the time spent, the size and complexity of the business, prevailing economic conditions, compensation paid by comparable firms for comparable services, and salary paid to company officers in prior years...." *Walter J. Roob*, 50 T.C. 891, 898, 899 (1968).

As in *Charles Rocco, supra*, at 832, we need not decide whether section [1366(e)] requires petitioner to merely overcome the presumptive correctness of the Commissioner's determination or requires him to prove that the Commissioner abused his discretion (if section [1366(e)] provides the Commissioner with the same authority he possesses under section 482) because here we find that petitioners have satisfied both tests.

The Commissioner allocated 100 percent of the net taxable income of the Subchapter S corporations to Dr. Davis. The undisputed testimony is that he did not actually spend more than 20 hours per year in direct duties to the corporations, which is minimal.

Respondent would have us consider the referral activities of Dr. Davis as being personal services rendered by him to the corporations. This we will not do. As stated above, one of the tests we enumerated above from *Roob, supra*, is compensation paid by comparable firms for comparable services. When Dr. Davis referred x-ray patients to a radiologist before he acquired x-ray equipment, the radiologist did not pay him a fee. The same is true as to referrals to a physical therapist. The fees earned by the corporations were the result of the use of the equipment which they owned and the services of their employees, not as a result of services performed by Dr. Davis for the corporations. Respondent's theory, therefore, fails under the comparability test and our holding under section [1366(e)] is consistent with our holdings under section 61 and 482. The Commissioner erred in allocating the net taxable income of the corporations to Dr. Davis under section [1366(e)].

---

[7] This provision continues to appear in the Regulations beginning "1.1375," but the Code has been reshuffled to put the subject in 1366(e), at least until the next reshuffling.

Accordingly, we find that none of the net taxable income of X-Ray and Therapy was taxable to Petitioners Edwin D. Davis and Sandra W. Davis for the taxable years 1966 and 1967.

Decisions will be entered under Rule 155.

....

NOTES

Assuming the transactions with the related corporations are at arm's length, what has Dr. Davis achieved from an income tax perspective? Assuming it is desirable to coordinate Subchapter S and Subchapter K, should § 1366(e) be made self-executing, or should § 704(e) perhaps be made not self-executing?

Note that if one successfully shifts income to children, even if the children pay taxes at income tax rates as high as their parents' on income from the S corporation, the parent will still have saved federal estate or gift taxes compared to being taxed on the S corporation's income and making gifts of the net proceeds to children, if federal transfer taxes apply to the gifts. Because transfer tax rates peak at 55%, they are an important planning consideration for the owner of a prosperous business.

Another important point is that a share of profits from an S corporation is not subject to Social Security ("payroll") taxes.[8] Because Social Security taxes on income from self-employment now exceed 14%, this is a serious consideration. *See* § 1401.

Observe that § 704(e) only covers cases where interests in the partnership have been shifted by gift or sale to family members. There is no such limit upon § 1366(e). On the other hand, § 1366(e) only allows reallocation within the family, whereas § 704(e) allows reallocations between donor and donee, regardless of their relationship.

G. LIMITS ON USE OF LOSSES AND DEDUCTIONS

1. GENERAL LIMITATION

Read §§ 1366(d)(1) and (2) and 1367(b)(2).

The amount of losses and deductions a shareholder of an S corporation can claim is limited to the adjusted basis of the shareholder's stock, plus any loans the shareholder has made to the corporation. § 1366(d)(1). To compute these limits, a shareholder computes the adjusted basis of the shareholder's stock at year-end, first reducing basis in the stock for deductions taken. Once the basis in the S corporation stock is reduced to zero, the shareholder then reduces her

---

[8] Rev. Rul. 59-221, 1959-1 C.B. 225.

basis in the debt, if necessary, for further pass-through deductions taken. § 1366(a)(2), (d)(1)(B).[9]

When the rule limiting shareholder deduction of pass-through items to stock and debt basis actually operates to limit a shareholder's loss or deduction, the excess deduction is suspended and deemed incurred by the S corporation in the *next* taxable year for that shareholder and carries forward until that shareholder uses up the suspended amount. § 1366(d)(2). The loss may be further limited by some other restriction, such as the "at-risk" restriction of § 465. Thus, several restrictions may operate at once.

2. MANIPULATION OF DEBT AND GUARANTEES

One can easily see that shareholders have an incentive to strain for tax purposes to classify business debt as their own obligation and not the corporation's, because they get no "outside" basis in the company's debt, quite unlike the case for partnerships (under § 752). This has led to a lot of tax planning and occasional major blunders by taxpayers and their advisors.

ESTATE OF LEAVITT v. COMMISSIONER
875 F.2d 420 (4th Cir. 1989),
cert. denied, 493 U.S. 958 (1989)

MURNAGHAN, CIRCUIT JUDGE.

The appellants, Anthony D. and Marjorie F. Cuzzocrea and the Estate of Daniel Leavitt, Deceased, et al., appeal the Tax Court's decision holding them liable for tax deficiencies for the tax years 1979, 1980 and 1981. Finding the appellants' arguments unpersuasive, we affirm the Tax Court.

I.

As shareholders of VAFLA Corporation, a subchapter S corporation during the years at issue, the appellants claimed deductions under § 1374 of the Internal Revenue Code of 1954 to reflect the corporation's operating losses during the three years in question. The Commissioner disallowed deductions above the $10,000 bases each appellant had from their original investments.

The appellants contend, however, that the adjusted bases in their stock should be increased to reflect a $300,000 loan which VAFLA obtained from the Bank of Virginia ("Bank") on September 12, 1979, after the appellants, along with

---

[9] There is a trap here with respect to debt, namely that if the holder of the debt sells it before its basis is replenished, the holder will suffer a taxable gain if the debt is sold for an amount greater than its basis. Another trap is that if the corporation makes a distribution with respect to its stock at a time when the holder's basis in the debt has not been replenished, the result is a gain with respect to the stock, because the stock has a zero basis. *See* § 1368(b)(2). This problem could arise if the tax advisor forgot that S corporation income replenishes basis first in debt, then stock, not vice-versa.

G. LIMITS ON USE OF LOSSES AND DEDUCTIONS

five other shareholders ("Shareholders-Guarantors"), had signed guarantee agreements whereby each agreed to be jointly and severally liable for all indebtedness of the corporation to the Bank. At the time of the loan, VAFLA's liability exceeded its assets, it could not meet its cash flow requirements and it had virtually no assets to use as collateral. The appellants assert that the Bank would not have lent the $300,000 without their personal guarantees.

VAFLA's financial statements and tax returns indicated that the bank loan was a loan from the Shareholders-Guarantors. Despite the representation to that effect, VAFLA made all of the loan payments, principal and interest, to the Bank. The appellants made no such payments. In addition, neither VAFLA nor the Shareholders-Guarantors treated the corporate payments on the loan as constructive income taxable to the Shareholders-Guarantors.

The appellants present the question whether the $300,000 bank loan is really, despite its form as a borrowing from the Bank, a capital contribution from the appellants to VAFLA. They contend that if the bank loan is characterized as equity, they are entitled to add a pro rata share of the $300,000 bank loan to their adjusted bases, thereby increasing the size of their operating loss deductions. Implicit in the appellants' characterization of the bank loan as equity in VAFLA is a determination that the Bank lent the $300,000 to the Shareholders-Guarantors who then contributed the funds to the corporation. The appellants' approach fails to realize that the $300,000 transaction, regardless of whether it is equity or debt, would permit them to adjust the bases in their stock if, indeed, the appellants, and not the Bank, had advanced VAFLA the money. The more precise question, which the appellants fail initially to ask, is whether the guaranteed loan from the Bank to VAFLA is an economic outlay of any kind by the Shareholders-Guarantors. To decide this question, we must determine whether the transaction involving the $300,000 was a loan from the Bank to VAFLA or was it instead a loan to the Shareholders-Guarantors who then gave it to VAFLA, as either a loan or a capital contribution.

Finding no economic outlay, we need not address the question, which is extensively addressed in the briefs, of whether the characterization of the $300,000 was debt or equity.

II.

To increase the basis in the stock of a subchapter S corporation, there must be an economic outlay on the part of the shareholder. *See Brown v. Commissioner*, 706 F.2d 755, 756 (6th Cir. 1983), *affg.* T.C. Memo 1981-608 (1981) ("In similar cases, the courts have consistently required some economic outlay by the guarantor in order to convert a mere loan guarantee into an investment."); *Blum v. Commissioner*, 59 T.C. 436, 440 (1972) (bank expected repayment of its loan from the corporation and not the taxpayers, i.e., no economic outlay from taxpayers).[10] A guarantee, in and of itself, cannot fulfill that requirement. The guarantee is merely a promise to pay in the future if certain unfortunate events should occur. At the present time, the appellants have experienced no such call as guarantors, have engaged in no economic outlay, and have suffered no cost.

The situation would be different if VAFLA had defaulted on the loan payments and the Shareholders-Guarantors had made actual disbursements on the corporate indebtedness. Those payments would represent corporate indebtedness to the shareholders which would increase their bases for the purpose of deducting net operating losses under § 1374(c)(2)(B). *Brown*, 706 F.2d at 757. *See also Raynor v. Commissioner*, 50 T.C. 762, 770-71 (1968) ("No form of indirect borrowing, be it guaranty, surety, accommodation, comaking or otherwise, gives rise to indebtedness from the corporation to the shareholders until and unless the shareholders pay part or all of the obligation.").

The appellants accuse the Tax Court of not recognizing the critical distinction between § 1374(c)(2)(A) (adjusted basis in stock) and § 1374(c)(2)(B) (adjusted basis in indebtedness of corporation to shareholder). They argue that the "loan" is not really a loan, but is a capital contribution (equity). Therefore, they conclude, § 1374(c)(2)(A) applies and § 1374(c)(2)(B) is irrelevant. However, the appellants once again fail to distinguish between the initial question of economic outlay and the secondary issue of debt or equity. Only if the first question had an affirmative answer, would the second arise.

The majority opinion of the Tax Court, focusing on the first issue of economic outlay, determined that a guarantee, in and of itself, is not an event for which basis can be adjusted. It distinguished the situation presented to it from one where the guarantee is triggered and actual payments are made. In the latter scenario, the first question of economic outlay is answered affirmatively (and the second issue is apparent on its face, i.e., the payments represent indebtedness from the corporation to the shareholder as opposed to capital contribution from the shareholder to the corporation). To the contrary is the situation presented here. The Tax Court, far from confusing the issue by discussing irrelevant matters, was comprehensively explaining why the transaction before it could not represent any kind of economic outlay by the appellants.

The Tax Court correctly determined that the appellants' guarantees, unaccompanied by further acts, in and of themselves, have not constituted contributions of cash or other property which might increase the bases of the appellants' stock in the corporation.

The appellants, while they do not disagree with the Tax Court that the guarantees, standing alone, cannot adjust their bases in the stock, nevertheless argue that the "loan" to VAFLA was in its "true sense" a loan to the

---

[10] Even the Eleventh Circuit case on which the appellants heavily rely applies this first step. *See Selfe v. United States*, 778 F.2d 769, 772 (11th Cir. 1985) ("We agree with *Brown* inasmuch as that court reaffirms that economic outlay is required before a stockholder in a Subchapter S corporation may increase her basis.").

G. LIMITS ON USE OF LOSSES AND DEDUCTIONS

Shareholders-Guarantors who then theoretically advanced the $300,000 to the corporation as a capital contribution. The Tax Court declined the invitation to treat a loan and its uncalled-on security, the guarantee, as identical and to adopt the appellants' view of the "substance" of the transaction over the "form" of the transaction they took. The Tax Court did not err in doing so.

Generally, taxpayers are liable for the tax consequences of the transaction they actually execute and may not reap the benefit of recasting the transaction into another one substantially different in economic effect that they might have made. They are bound by the "form" of their transaction and may not argue that the "substance" of their transaction triggers different tax consequences. *Don E. Williams Co. v. Commissioner*, 429 U.S. 569, 579-80, 51 L. Ed. 2d 48, 97 S. Ct. 850 (1977); *Commissioner v. National Alfalfa Dehydrating & Milling Co.*, 417 U.S. 134, 149, 40 L. Ed. 2d 717, 94 S. Ct. 2129 (1974).[11] In the situation of guaranteed corporate debt, where the form of the transaction may not be so clear, courts have permitted the taxpayer to argue that the substance of the transaction was in actuality a loan to the shareholder. *See Blum*, 59 T.C. at 440. However, the burden is on the taxpayer and it has been a difficult one to meet. That is especially so where, as here, the transaction is cast in sufficiently ambiguous terms to permit an argument either way depending on which is subsequently advantageous from a tax point of view.

In the case before us, the Tax Court found that the "form" and "substance" of the transaction was a loan from the Bank to VAFLA and not to the appellants:

> The Bank of Virginia loaned the money to the corporation and not to petitioners. The proceeds of the loan were to be used in the operation of the corporation's business. Petitioners submitted no evidence that they were free to dispose of the proceeds of the loan as they wished. Nor were the payments on the loan reported as constructive dividends on the corporation's Federal income tax returns or on the petitioners' Federal income tax returns

---

[11] On the other hand, the Commissioner is not so bound and may recharacterize the nature of the transaction according to its substance while overlooking the form selected by the taxpayer. *Higgins v. Smith*, 308 U.S. 473, 477, 84 L. Ed. 406, 60 S. Ct. 355 (1940). In doing so, the Commissioner usually applies debt-equity principles to determine the true nature of the transaction. As the Selfe court noted:

> This principle is particularly evident where characterization of capital as debt or equity will have different tax consequences. Thus in Plantation Patterns the court held that interest payments by a corporation on debentures were constructive stockholder dividends and could not be deducted by the corporation as interest payments. There, the former Fifth Circuit recharacterized debt as equity at the insistence of the Commissioner.

Selfe, 778 F.2d at 773.

It is important to note that those cases did not involve the question posed here of whether an economic outlay existed because it clearly did. Actual payments were made. The only question was what was the nature of the payments, debt or equity.

during the years in issue. Accordingly, we find that the transaction was in fact a loan by the bank to the corporation guaranteed by the shareholders.

Whether the $300,000 was lent to the corporation or to the Shareholders/Guarantors is a factual issue which should not be disturbed unless clearly erroneous. Finding no error, we affirm.

It must be borne in mind that we do not merely encounter naive taxpayers caught in a complex trap for the unwary. They sought to claim deductions because the corporation lost money. If, however, VAFLA had been profitable, they would be arguing that the loan was in reality from the Bank to the corporation, and not to them, for that would then lessen their taxes. Under that description of the transaction, the loan repayments made by VAFLA would not be on the appellants' behalf, and, consequently, would not be taxed as constructive income to them. *See Old Colony Trust Co. v. Commissioner*, 279 U.S. 716, 73 L. Ed. 918, 49 S. Ct. 499 (1929) (payment by a corporation of a personal expense or debt of a shareholder is considered as the receipt of a taxable benefit). It came down in effect to an ambiguity as to which way the appellants would jump, an effort to play both ends against the middle, until it should be determined whether VAFLA was a profitable or money-losing proposition. At that point, the appellants attempted to treat the transaction as cloaked in the guise having the more beneficial tax consequences for them.

Finally, the appellants complain that the Tax Court erred by failing to apply debt-equity principles[12] to determine the "form" of the loan. We believe that the Tax Court correctly refused to apply debt-equity principles here, a methodology which is only relevant, if at all, to resolution of the second inquiry — what is the nature of the economic outlay. Of course, the second inquiry cannot be reached unless the first question concerning whether an economic outlay exists is answered affirmatively. Here it is not.

The appellants, in effect, attempt to collapse a two-step analysis into a one-step inquiry which would eliminate the initial determination of economic outlay by first concluding that the proceeds were a capital contribution (equity). Obviously,

---

[12] The appellants correctly state that the First, Fifth and Ninth Circuits have all applied traditional debt-equity principles in determining whether a shareholder's guarantee of a corporate debt was in substance a capital contribution. *See Casco Bank & Trust Co. v. United States*, 544 F.2d 528 (1st Cir. 1976), *cert. denied*, 430 U.S. 907, 97 S. Ct. 1176, 51 L. Ed. 2d 582 (1977); *Plantation Patterns v. Commissioner*, 462 F.2d 712 (5th Cir. 1971), *cert. denied*, 409 U.S. 1076, 93 S. Ct. 683, 34 L. Ed. 2d 664 (1972); *Murphy Logging Co. v. United States*, 378 F.2d 222 (9th Cir. 1967). What the appellants fail to point out, however, is that those cases each involved activated guarantees, i.e., actual advances or payments on defaults. Therefore, the issue in those cases was not whether the taxpayer had made an "investment" — an economic outlay — in the corporation. The investment was admitted. The issue in those cases asked what was the nature of the investment — equity or debt. None of those cases involved the disallowance of deductions claimed by a shareholder pursuant to § 1374 for his or her share of an electing corporation's operating losses where there had simply been no economic outlay by the shareholder under the guarantee.

G. LIMITS ON USE OF LOSSES AND DEDUCTIONS

a capital contribution is an economic outlay so the basis in the stock would be adjusted accordingly. But such an approach simply ignores the factual determination by the Tax Court that the Bank lent the $300,000 to the corporation and not to the Shareholders-Guarantors.

The appellants rely on *Blum v. Commissioner*, 59 T.C. 436 (1972), and *Selfe v. United States*, 778 F.2d 769 (11th Cir. 1985), to support their position. However, the appellants have misread those cases. In *Blum*, the Tax Court declined to apply debt-equity principles to determine whether the taxpayer's guarantee of a loan from a bank to a corporation was an indirect capital contribution. The Tax Court held that the taxpayer had failed to carry his burden of proving that the transaction was in "substance" a loan from the bank to the shareholder rather than a loan to the corporation. The *Blum* court found dispositive the fact that "the bank expected repayment of its loan from the corporation and not the petitioner." *Blum*, 59 T.C. at 440.

With regard to *Selfe*, the Tax Court stated:

> the Eleventh Circuit applied a debt-equity analysis and held that a shareholder's guarantee of a loan made to a subchapter S corporation may be treated for tax purposes as an equity investment in the corporation where the lender looks to the shareholder as the primary obligor. We respectfully disagree with the Eleventh Circuit and hold that a shareholder's guarantee of a loan to a subchapter S corporation may not be treated as an equity investment in the corporation absent an economic outlay by the shareholder.

The Tax Court then distinguished *Plantation Patterns*, 462 F.2d 712 (5th Cir. 1972), relied on by *Selfe*, because that case involved a C corporation, reasoning that the application of debt-equity principles to subchapter S corporations would defeat Congress' intent to limit a shareholder's pass-through deduction to the amount he or she has actually invested in the corporation.

The Tax Court also distinguished *In re Lane*, 742 F.2d 1311 (11th Cir. 1984), relied on by the *Selfe* court, on the basis that the shareholder had actually paid the amounts he had guaranteed, i.e., there was an economic outlay. In *Lane*, which involved a subchapter S corporation, the issue was "whether advances made by a shareholder to a corporation constitute debt or equity...." *Id.* at 1313. If the advances were debt, then Lane could deduct them as bad debts. On the other hand, if the advances were capital, no bad debt deduction would be permitted. Thus, the issue of adjusted basis for purposes of flow-through deductions from net operating losses of the corporation was not at issue. There was no question of whether there had been an economic outlay.

Although *Selfe* does refer to debt-equity principles, the specific issue before it was whether any material facts existed making summary judgment inappropriate. The Eleventh Circuit said:

> At issue here, however, is not whether the taxpayer's contribution was either a loan to or an equity investment in Jane Simon, Inc. The issue is

whether the taxpayer's guarantee of the corporate loan was in itself a contribution to the corporation [as opposed to a loan from the bank] sufficient to increase the taxpayer's basis in the corporation.

The *Selfe* court found that there was evidence that the bank primarily looked to the taxpayer and not the corporation for repayment of the loan. Therefore, it remanded for "a determination of whether or not the bank primarily looked to Jane Selfe [taxpayer] for repayment [the first inquiry] and for the court to apply the factors set out in *In re Lane* and I.R.C. section 385 to determine if the taxpayer's guarantee amounted to either an equity investment in or shareholder loan to Jane Simon, Inc. [the second inquiry]." *Id*. at 775. The implications are that there is still a two-step analysis and that the debt-equity principles apply only to the determination of the characterization of the economic outlay, once one is found.

Granted, that conclusion is clouded by the next and final statement of the *Selfe* court: "In short, we remand for the district court to apply *Plantation Patterns* and determine if the bank loan to Jane Simon, Inc. was in reality a loan to the taxpayer." *Id*. To the degree that the *Selfe* court agreed with *Brown* that an economic outlay is required before a shareholder may increase her basis in a subchapter S corporation, *Selfe* does not contradict current law or our resolution of the case before us. Furthermore, to the extent that the *Selfe* court remanded because material facts existed by which the taxpayer could show that the bank actually lent the money to her rather than the corporation, we are still able to agree. It is because of the *Selfe* court's suggestion that debt-equity principles must be applied to resolve the question of whether the bank actually lent the money to the taxpayer/shareholder or the corporation, that we must part company with the Eleventh Circuit for the reasons stated above.

In conclusion, the Tax Court correctly focused on the initial inquiry of whether an economic outlay existed. Finding none, the issue of whether debt-equity principles ought to apply to determine the nature of the economic outlay was not before the Tax Court. The Tax Court is

Affirmed.

QUESTIONS

Does it make sense to deny a shareholder-guarantor basis for a loan made by a third party to the S corporation, especially if the lender is really looking to the guarantor's credit and not the corporation's? Does this rigidity not trap the unwary who use guarantees, while forcing those who can afford good tax advice to go through the extra step of borrowing the money and then lending it on to the S corporation? Also, why deny a guarantor basis for an S corporation debt, but grant basis in nonrecourse debt if a partnership is the borrower?

H. CURRENT DISTRIBUTIONS: INTRODUCTION

Read § 1368(a) and (b).

A shareholder is generally not subject to tax on actual distributions of cash or property by the S corporation to them unless the distributions exceed the shareholder's basis in the corporation's stock or, in general, unless the corporation was formerly a C corporation and still has earnings and profits. § 1368. The details in this area are not simple, but not overwhelmingly difficult either.

1. CORPORATIONS WITHOUT E&P

Read § 1368(a) and (b).

At the end of an S corporation's taxable year, the shareholder first must adjust his or her basis in the S corporation stock for all increases and decreases that pass through and produce adjustments to basis of his or her shareholder's stock, except for distributions made during the S corporation's tax year.

Next, the shareholder uses this adjusted basis to determine the tax treatment of any distributions actually received during the entity's taxable year. Any distribution a shareholder receives from an S corporation which has no earnings and profits reduces the adjusted basis of the shareholder's stock in the S corporation. If the distribution does not exceed the adjusted basis, it is treated as a nontaxable return of capital and the resulting adjusted basis of the shareholder's stock is next year's opening adjusted basis. (A shareholder's basis in debt cannot be used to affect tax on distributions; it can be used to affect the allowance of losses passed through.)

If and to the extent the distributions exceed the adjusted basis of the shareholder's stock, the excess is treated as a gain from the sale or exchange of stock. Thus, the gain is generally long- or short-term capital gain. The next year's opening adjusted basis for shareholder's stock is zero.

> *To illustrate*: Monica Wharton owns all the stock of S Corp. It has no e&p. Her year-end stock basis is $60,000, before adjustments for income, losses, and distributions. S Corp. incurs a $60,000 loss this year and distributes $10,000 to her at the end of the year. As a result, she can deduct the $60,000 loss, but doing so reduces her predistribution stock basis to $0, and the $10,000 distributed produces a currently taxable gain under § 1368 of $10,000. Her stock basis remains $0 after the distribution.

PROBLEM 25-8

You are the sole shareholder of an S corporation that is faring poorly. You invested $10,000 of cash and loaned the company $30,000. It then lost $40,000.

However, it is now the very end of the year and the company has recently borrowed $10,000, which you want and need. How would you characterize the $10,000 you are about to get so as to minimize your tax burden? Assume alternatively that you were the lender or that a bank was the lender.

2. CORPORATIONS WITH E&P

Read § 1368(c) through (e)(2).

Some S corporations will have e&p, usually because they operated as C corporations in the past and generated profits which they did not disgorge. These S corporations have more complicated tax lives than those without e&p. The key issue is that the existence of earnings and profits can turn distributions into taxable dividends.

a. Impact

Although S corporations cannot generate or reduce earnings and profits for taxable years beginning after 1982 in which they were S corporations, an S corporation can still have earnings and profits from various sources, including:

— liquidations and redemptions governed by Subchapter C;
— taxable years when the corporation was a C corporation;
— a corporate acquisition that caused a carryover of earnings and profits under § 381.

To determine the source of a distribution the Code sets forth a priority list of sources in § 1368(c). If the corporation has accumulated earnings and profits, it must maintain separate accounts for three separate sources of distributions, namely: (1) the accumulated adjustments account (AAA), which is post-1982 earnings of an S corporation that have been taxed to shareholders; (2) previously taxed income (PTI), which is undistributed income of an S corporation that was taxed to shareholders under pre-1983 law; and (3) accumulated earnings and profits.

The ordering rules tend to favor basis reductions instead of producing ordinary income. A distribution is deemed first to come out of the accumulated adjustments account (AAA). Such a distribution reduces the shareholder's adjusted basis in his or her stock and is not taxable up to that amount. A distribution out of AAA which exceeds the shareholder's adjusted basis in the stock is gain from the sale or exchange of property, unless there are further sources, as described in the following sentences.

If and to the extent distributions in the taxable year exceed the AAA at the end of the taxable year (calculated before the distributions), the AAA is generally allocated to each distribution made during the year in proportion to the amount of each distribution. If the S corporation has previously taxed income (PTI), the PTI is the next source for distributions. Any distribution out of PTI reduces the

H. CURRENT DISTRIBUTIONS: INTRODUCTION 595

shareholder's basis in his or her stock and is not taxable up to that basis. A distribution out of PTI in excess of the shareholder's stock basis is also deemed a gain from the sale or exchange of property, unless there are also earnings and profits. Third, after the prior two sources are exhausted, a distribution is deemed to come from the S corporation's e&p, if any. Any such distribution is a taxable dividend up to the amount of the corporation's earnings and profits; these distributions do not reduce stock basis. § 1367(a)(2)(A). Fourth, after the prior three sources are exhausted, a distribution is applied against and reduces the shareholder's basis in stock. Finally, any further distribution is deemed taxable as from a sale or exchange of property. (Stock basis is never reduced below zero by these rules.)

b. Election to Purge Earnings and Profits

An S corporation can always elect to treat its distributions as coming *first* from e&p, if all shareholders who receive a distribution during the taxable year consent to the S corporation election. § 1368(e)(3).

The effect of the election is that each shareholder reports a taxable dividend in the amount of the distribution that is treated as coming from e&p. Once earnings and profits are fully disgorged, subsequent distributions are generally treated as having been paid by an S corporation without earnings and profits. The benefits can be significant; if the corporation has no e&p, there will be no § 1375 tax on excess passive income and no loss of S corporation status because of having too much such income.

c. The Accumulated Adjustments Account ("AAA") Revisited

Read §§ 1367(a)(2)(D) and 1368(e)(1)(A).

The AAA begins at zero (unless the company is the product of a reorganization that resulted in picking up another firm's AAA account) and is adjusted annually for income, losses, and expenses. On the first day of an S corporation's first tax year that begins after 1982, the balance of its AAA is zero. This accommodates the law that created the concept of the AAA. One makes no adjustment to the AAA for tax-exempt income or related expenses, whereas such amounts do entail adjustments to the basis of the stock. *See* § 1367(a)(2)(D) and § 1368(e)(1)(A).

The AAA can be negative, in which case later income will make the account positive, but only after the negative balance has been restored.

PROBLEM 25-9

Assume that Bob owns 60% and Ray owns 40% of the stock of Einbinder Flypaper Corporation, which is an S corporation. The stock constitutes a capital asset in each of their hands. As of the end of the year, Bob's basis for his stock was $80,000, and Ray's basis for his stock was $30,000, because he recently bought the stock on the cheap from Bob's nephew. At a time when it had accumulated e&p from a C corporation year of $10,000, Einbinder Flypaper Corporation distributed cash of $90,000 to Bob and $60,000 to Ray. The following items were allocated to Einbinder Flypaper Corporation's shareholders during its period of operating as an S corporation: (1) Tax-exempt interest of $40,000; (2) § 1231 gains of $30,000; (3) nonseparately computed income from domestic sources of $110,000; (4) short-term capital losses of $10,000; (5) long-term capital losses of $15,000; (6) foreign losses of $25,000. Assume that all these amounts were already accounted for in computing Bob and Ray's basis in their stock.

(1) What is Einbinder Flypaper Corporation's AAA account?
(2) What is the post-distribution basis of the stock held by Bob? By Ray?
(3) How are the distributions to Bob and Ray taxed?
(4) How is the tax-exempt income accounted for? *See* §§ 1367(a) and 1366(a).

3. DISTRIBUTIONS OF PROPERTY

Read § 1371(a)(1).

If an S corporation distributes property, currently or in liquidation, the "amount of the distribution" is its fair market value. If it distributes property with a value in excess of basis, the S corporation is treated as if it had sold the property to its shareholders at fair market value. § 311, § 1371(a)(l). The corporation must recognize the gain (it does not recognize a loss) and it will pass that gain through to its shareholders. § 311. Thus, the corporation *generally* does not actually pay a tax; the shareholders do. The key exception is the § 1374 BIG tax, which falls on the corporation itself.

The shareholder uses that same hypothetical fair-market-value sales price to report the tax treatment of the property distribution.

> *To illustrate*: Sam Shareholder owns all the stock of S Corp. His basis in his stock is $2,000. S Corp. owns an asset with a basis of $0 and a fair market value of $1,000. S Corp. distributes the asset to Sam. Assume the asset has been held for eleven years, so the BIG tax does not apply. The results are that S Corp. pays no tax, but it does report that Sam had a $1,000 gain. This momentarily increases Sam's stock basis to $3,000. The $1,000 distribution, however, reduces his basis back down to $2,000.

If it is a current distribution, the corporation will be forced to recognize gains, but will not be allowed to report losses. S. Rep. No. 445, 100th Cong, 2d Sess. 78 (1988). The shrewd S corporation will of course sell depreciated assets rather than distribute them. Again, unless the BIG tax of § 1374 applies, the practical effect is that the corporation as such pays no tax; rather, the gain flows through to its shareholders. If § 1374 applies, the story is quite different. The corporation will in fact pay tax at top corporate rates.

H. CURRENT DISTRIBUTIONS: INTRODUCTION

If the distribution is part of a liquidation, § 336 applies, and the company reports gains *and losses* on its constructive sale of appreciated or diminished-value property, which will in turn flow through to its shareholders. Again, if § 1374 applies, there may be a corporate level tax. If the distribution occurred in liquidation, § 331 treats shareholders as if they sold their stock; thus the shareholder's gain is almost invariably a capital gain.

Returning to the example of a current liquidation, if the BIG tax applied, the differences are dramatic. Sam will get soaked.

> *To illustrate*: The facts are the same, except that the asset was contributed nine years ago. This time S Corp. will pay a tax of, say, 35% of $1,000, viz. $350. Sam also pays a tax on the gain under § 1363(f)(2), but it is only on the amount deemed distributed after taxes, $650 over the property's basis ($0), because the S corporation's payment of the § 1374 BIG tax gives rise to a loss deduction under § 1366(f)(2). Sam's stock basis will increase by the gain recognized under § 1367(a)(1)(A) ($1,000), and the distribution of $1,000 will reduce it in equal measure. § 1367(b)(2)(A).

4. POST-TERMINATION DISTRIBUTIONS

Read §§ 1366(d)(3), 1371.

When an S corporation becomes a C corporation, its AAA devolves into an earnings and profits account. § 301. One might have thought that post-termination distributions of profits generated while an S corporation should be capable of being distributed as returns of capital, thereby reducing stock basis. Instead of so providing, Congress halfheartedly granted a post-termination distribution rule that allows some breathing room during which the company can disgorge funds from the AAA despite the termination. It is somewhat as if Cinderella were given an extra few hours after midnight to put away the pumpkin and get to bed.

Moving away from metaphors, the effect of § 1371 is that distributions of money by a former S corporation to its shareholders during a so-called post-termination transition period merely reduce the shareholders' adjusted bases in their stock to the extent of the AAA. All other distributions are taxed under § 301. Moreover, the former S corporation may elect, with the consent of all its shareholders to whom distributions are made during this period, to have all cash distributions treated as dividends to the extent of the corporation's earnings and profits. § 1371(e)(2). Just why they would bother to do so is unclear unless the shareholders are in a particularly low tax bracket or have losses that year or the shareholder is a C corporation that just bought all the stock of the S corporation.

Another advantage of the post-termination transition period is that shareholders whose losses were suspended as a result of not having sufficient debt and equity in prior periods can infuse the corporation with extra equity (but not debt), and thereby salvage their losses. §§ 1366(d)(3) and 1377(b).

The "post-termination transition period" begins the day after losing S corporation status and ends on the *later* of one year after the last day as an S corporation, or the due date for filing the return for the last year as an S corporation, including extensions. Also, in the interest of helping putative S corporations caught in controversies over their status, the post-termination transition period is a 120-day period beginning on the date of a determination that the corporation's election of S corporation status had terminated for a previous tax year. For this purpose, a "determination" means: (1) a court decision that becomes final; (2) a closing agreement; or (3) an agreement between the corporation and the IRS that the corporation did not qualify as an S corporation.

PROBLEM 25-10

Sal owns all the stock of S Corp. Her basis in the stock is $12,000. It has a $9,000 AAA. She causes S Corp. to revoke its S election as of the beginning of this year. She also causes it to distribute $8,000 in cash nine months later.

(1) How is the $8,000 taxed? What is her stock basis after the distribution?

(2) What is S Corp.'s (now a C corporation) e&p after the distribution?

(3) Assume S Corp. also earned $1,000 of tax-exempt income. Could it be withdrawn tax-free?

I. RELATIONSHIP OF SUBCHAPTER S TO REST OF CODE

Read §§ 1363(a) and 1371(a).

Subchapter S occupies only a small corner of the Internal Revenue Code. S corporations regularly have to contend with a mass of issues raised by the remainder of the Code, including the definition of gross income, availability of deductions, timing rules, capital gains versus ordinary income and merger and acquisition effects, to name just a few. Unfortunately, as one might expect, Subchapter S is not entirely coordinated with the rest of the Code.

One area of interaction between Subchapter S and Subchapter C that is well-coordinated concerns net operating losses (NOLs). A C corporation that becomes an S corporation passes its post-election NOLs through to its shareholders. The corporation cannot apply carryovers or carrybacks from tax years when it was not an S corporation to years when it is an S corporation. § 1371(b)(1). NOLs generally expire after fifteen years. § 172(b)(1)(A)(ii). The fifteen-year carryforward is preceded by a three-year carryback. § 172(b)(1)(A). By making the S election, NOLs are put on a kind of death row and can be reinstated only if and when the corporation reverts to being a C corporation. Each year of operation as an S corporation shortens the life of the C corporation NOLs by one year. Conversely, an S corporation's losses cannot be used by the corporation after it terminates its S election. The only relief is that during the magical post-

I. RELATIONSHIP OF SUBCHAPTER S TO REST OF CODE

termination transition period shareholders may use up the corporation's suspended loss carryovers by contributing to equity. § 1366(d)(3).

1. INTERACTIONS OF SUBCHAPTER S AND SUBCHAPTER C

Except to the extent that Subchapter S contains a specific corporate tax rule, one must generally consult Subchapter C. *See* § 1371(a), which makes it clear that, except as otherwise provided or as inconsistent with Subchapter S, Subchapter C shall apply to an S corporation and its shareholders. Thus, for example, one looks to § 351 to see how to perform a tax-deferred incorporation, § 331 for the impact of liquidations on shareholders, § 368(a) and its compatriots to determine the implications of mergers and acquisitions, § 355 and § 368(a)(1)(D) for divestitures, and so forth. Again, the rules are not fully coordinated, but the basic congressional directive is clear. The materials that follow illustrate the issues taxpayers must face in this area.

a. Liquidations

PRIV. LTR. RUL. 9218019

(May 1, 1992)

Dear [Taxpayer]

We received your letter on July 30, 1991, requesting a ruling on behalf of A about the tax consequences to a shareholder on a sale by an S corporation of its assets followed by a liquidating distribution of the proceeds of the sale in the same taxable year as the sale. This letter is in reply to your request.

In 1969, X was incorporated under the laws of Z. X elected S corporation status under section 1362(a) of the Internal Revenue Code on December 23, 1986, for its January 1, 1987, taxable year. Since 1969, X has owned, as its sole capital asset, a commercial building located in Z. On December 31, 1990, X's adjusted basis for the commercial building was about $100,000. Depreciation on X's commercial building has been calculated on the straight line method.

At the time of death, B owned all of X corporation's stock. On B's death, B's estate, A, became the owner of all X corporation's stock. C, who is B's only beneficiary, does not wish to operate the commercial building that is the sole asset of X. Thus, the executors of A propose to sell the commercial building owned by X, and to distribute the cash proceeds to A in complete liquidation of X.

In connection with the proposed transaction, the taxpayer represents the following: (a) No formal or informal plan of liquidation has ever been adopted by X, except for the proposed plan in which the sale of the building is contemplated. (b) The liquidation of X will not be preceded or followed by the reincorporation in, or transfer or sale to, a recipient corporation (Recipient) of any of the business or assets of X, if persons holding more than 20 percent in value of the stock in X also hold more than 20 percent in value of the stock in

Recipient. For purposes of this representation, ownership has been determined by application of the constructive ownership rules of section 318 of the Internal Revenue Code as modified by section 304(c)(3). (c) All assets of X will be distributed in complete liquidation of X within the 12-month period beginning on the date of adoption of the plan of liquidation. (d) No part of the consideration to be received by any shareholder of X will be received by the shareholder as a creditor, employee, or in some capacity other than that of a shareholder of X. (e) Pursuant to the proposed plan of liquidation, X will cease to be a going concern and its activities will be limited to the winding up of its affairs, paying its debts, and distributing any balance of its assets to its shareholders. (f) The fair market value of X's assets will exceed its liabilities both on the date of adoption of the plan of liquidation and at the time the first liquidating distribution is made. (g) No distribution of assets representing earned but unreported income will be made by X to its shareholders in the liquidation. (h) The liquidating distribution described in this ruling request is an isolated transaction and is not related to any other past or future transaction. (i) X does not maintain a reserve for bad debts.

Section 1014(a) of the Code provides, generally, that the basis of property in the hands of a person acquiring the property from a decedent is the fair market value of the property at the date of the decedent's death. Section 1001(a) of the Code provides, generally, that the gain from the sale or other disposition of property is the excess of the amount realized from the sale or disposition over the adjusted basis of the property.

Section 1367(a) of the Code provides, generally, that the basis of each shareholder's stock in an S corporation is increased for any period by the sum of items of income described in section 1366(a)(1)(A) and (B) of the Code.

Section 1374(a) of the Code provides, generally, that if an S corporation has a net recognized built-in gain for any taxable year beginning in an S corporation's recognition period, a tax is imposed on the income of such corporation for such taxable year.

Section 1371(a)(1) of the Code provides, generally, that except as otherwise provided in the Internal Revenue Code, and except to the extent inconsistent with subchapter S, subchapter C applies to S corporations and S corporation shareholders. Section 1.1372-1(c) of the Income Tax Regulations provides, generally, that to the extent the provisions of subchapter C of the Code are not inconsistent with the provisions and regulations under subchapter S such provisions will apply to an S corporation and its shareholders.

Section 336(a) requires, generally, that a liquidating corporation recognize gain or loss on the distribution of property in complete liquidation as if the property were sold to a distributee at its fair market value.

Section 331(a) of the Code provides that amounts received by a shareholder in a distribution in complete liquidation of a corporation are treated as in full payment in exchange for stock.

Based on the information submitted and the above representations made by the taxpayer, we reach the following conclusions.

Under section 1014(a), A's basis in the stock of X will be stepped-up to the fair market value of the property as of the date of B's death. Under section 1001(a), X's gain from the sale of its commercial building will be measured by the difference between the amount realized on the sale of the building and X's adjusted basis in the building.

Section 1366 requires all items of an S corporation's income to pass-through to the S corporation shareholders. Thus, we conclude that the gain realized by X on the sale of its commercial building will pass-through to and be recognized by A, its sole shareholder. Further, we conclude that under section 1367(a)(1), A's stepped-up basis under section 1014(a) will be increased by the amount realized and passed-through to A on X's sale of its building.

Under section 336(a) of the Code, a liquidating corporation recognizes gain or loss on the distribution of property in complete liquidation. However, X is not a taxable entity under section 1363(a)(1), and any gain or loss recognized would be recognized by X's shareholder. In addition, X is distributing cash not appreciated assets. Thus, we conclude that section 336(a) does not require recognition of gain or loss on the distribution of cash in complete liquidation of X.

In addition, assuming the liquidation of X qualifies as a complete liquidation under section 331(a) of the Code, we conclude that the amounts received by A in the distribution in complete liquidation of X are treated as in full payment in exchange for A's stock in accordance with section 331(a). We further conclude that A's gain or loss, under section 1001, will be measured by the difference between the amount of cash received and A's adjusted basis in its X stock surrendered.

Finally, assuming X has been continuously an S corporation, within the meaning of section 1361(a)(1) of the Code, as of the effective date of its above-described S corporation election, and further assuming that X's election is not subject to a terminating event, within the meaning of section 1362(d) of the Code, prior to the date of the complete liquidation, we reach the following conclusion.

X will not be subject to the tax on net built-in gains imposed by section 1374 of the Code, ... for assets held by X on December 31, 1986.... The provisions of section 1374 of the Code will apply to X for any asset held by X that was acquired after December 31, 1986, and is described in section 1374(d)(8) of the Code....

Except as specifically ruled on above, we express no other opinion about the federal tax consequences of any aspects of the above-described transaction. More specifically, no opinion is expressed about whether X met the requirements of section 1361(b) of the Code, or whether its S election was terminated under section 1362(d) as a result of any events not specifically addressed and ruled on by this letter ruling....

Sincerely,

William P. O'Shea
Chief, Branch 3
Office of the Assistant
Chief Counsel
(Passthroughs and Special Industries)

b. S Corporation as a Shareholder

For purposes of Subchapter C, if an S corporation is a shareholder in another corporation, the S corporation is treated as an individual. § 1371(a)(2). This seemingly simple statement has engendered a good deal of confusion.[13]

PRIV. LTR. RUL. 9245004
(July 28, 1992)

....

Issues

(1) Does the fact that section 1371(a)(2) of the Internal Revenue Code treats a subchapter S corporation (S), in its capacity as a shareholder of another corporation, as an individual mean that (i) S's purchase of the stock of a subchapter C corporation (T) was not a qualified stock purchase under section 338(d)(3) and (ii) the subsequent dissolution of T into S was not a section 332 liquidation, because sections 338 and 332 only apply to acquisitions by corporations?

(2) Will the purchase by small business corporation S of all the stock of T followed by the immediate liquidation of T terminate S's election to be taxed as a subchapter S corporation under section 1362(d)(2)?

Facts

T, a subchapter C corporation, was engaged in the trade or business of a. T used the FIFO method of valuing its inventory. As of Date 1, the stock ownership of T was as follows:

---

[13] See S. Bonovitz, *S Corporations and Section 332*, 48 Tax Notes 1545 (1990).

I. RELATIONSHIP OF SUBCHAPTER S TO REST OF CODE

Percentage Owned	Owner
60 percent	X, a wholly owned subsidiary of W
23 percent	Y, an unrelated corporation
7 percent	by Mr. A

On Date 2, S purchased all the T shares owned by A, X and Y and became the 100 percent owner of T.[14] Immediately thereafter, S caused T to dissolve and distribute all of its assets to S. The name of S was then changed to T (New T).

Issue 1

Applicable Law

Section 1371(a)(1) of the Code provides that, except as otherwise provided, and except to the extent inconsistent with subchapter S, subchapter C applies to an S corporation and its shareholders. Section 1371(a)(2) provides that, for purposes of subchapter C, an S corporation in its capacity as a shareholder of another corporation is treated as an individual.

Section 332 generally provides that no gain or loss is recognized on the receipt by a corporation of property distributed in complete liquidation of another corporation if (1) the corporation receiving the property is the owner of 80 percent of both the voting power and value of the liquidating corporation's stock, and (2) the distribution of property is in complete cancellation or redemption of the stock of the liquidating corporation. Section 337 further provides that, in general, no gain or loss shall be recognized to the liquidating corporation on the distribution of property in a complete liquidation to an 80 percent distributee to which section 332 applies.

Section 338 of the Code provides that an acquiring corporation may elect, in the case of a qualified stock purchase of a target corporation, to treat the target corporation (1) as if it sold all of its assets at fair market value and (2) as a new corporation which purchased all the assets. A qualified stock purchase is defined in section 338(d) as the acquisition of stock of a target corporation (representing 80 percent of both the vote and value of the target's stock) by an acquiring corporation by purchase during a 12 month acquisition period.

Analysis

Only a corporation can make a "qualified stock purchase" under section 338(d)(3) of the Code and only a corporate distributee can qualify for section 332(a) nonrecognition treatment. Therefore, if section 1371(a)(2) applies to treat S as an individual for section 338 and 332 purposes then (1) S's purchase of the

---

[14] [Presumably, there is a mistake, as the three figures amount to only 90%. Readers can ignore this and assume that T bought 100%. Eds.]

T stock would not be a section 338(d)(3) stock purchase, and (2) the dissolution of T into S would not be a section 332 liquidation.

Section 1371(a)(2) of the Code was enacted in the Subchapter S Revision Act of 1982 (SSRA 1982), Sec. 1, 1982-2 C.B. 2, 708. The legislative history to section 1371(a)(2) does not address section 338 qualified stock purchases or corporate liquidations, but refers only to the taxation of an S corporation as a distributee under section 301....

Summarizing this point, in our view, section 1371(a)(2) of the Code was enacted to deal with section 301 distributions. Clearly, the legislative history to section 1371(a)(2) is devoid of any suggestion that Congress intended to prevent S corporations from making qualified stock purchases under section 338 or receiving property in section 332 liquidations.

The prototype of section 332 of the Code was enacted in 1935. *See* Revenue Bill of 1935, Sec. 110, 7. *See also* section 112(b)(6) of the 1939 Code. Under the predecessors to sections 332 and 334 the parent corporation could take a carryover basis in the property received from the liquidating corporation. Sections 112(b)(6) and 113(a)(6) of the 1939 Code. As a result, dramatically different tax results could arise from transactions that were substantively similar. For example, in a case where the basis in a target corporation's assets was greater than their fair market value, if an acquiring corporation purchased the target assets directly, its basis would have been stepped-down to their fair market value pursuant to the predecessor of section 1012. Section 113(a) of the 1939 Code. Instead, in such a case, the acquiring corporation would have generally preferred to purchase the stock of the target, liquidate the target tax-free under section 112(b)(6) of the 1939 Code, and take the higher carryover basis in the target's assets under section 113(a)(6) of the 1939 Code. Before 1954, there were instances where the Service sought to apply the step-transaction doctrine so that the acquiring corporation in such cases would be treated as purchasing the target's assets directly.

In *Kimbell-Diamond Milling Co. v. Commissioner*, 14 T.C. 74 *aff'd per curiam*, 187 F.2d 718 (5th Cir. 1951), *cert. denied*, 342 U.S. 827 (1951), the court held that the purchase of the stock of a target corporation for the purposes of acquiring its assets through a prompt liquidation should be treated by the purchaser as one transaction, namely a purchase of the target's assets with the purchaser receiving a cost basis in the assets. The focus of the *Kimbell-Diamond* line of cases was whether the stock acquisition of a target corporation was affected in contemplation of a complete liquidation of the target. Former section 334(b)(2) of the Code was added in 1954 to codify the principles of *Kimbell-Diamond*. *See* S. Rep. No. 1622, 83d Cong. 2d Sess. 257 (1954). However, the application of former section 334(b)(2) was based upon objective factors rather than attempting to determine the acquiring corporation's intent at the time of the stock acquisition. Thus, section 334(b)(2) of the 1954 Code was an improvement to the *Kimbell-Diamond* doctrine because it provided predictable results.

I. RELATIONSHIP OF SUBCHAPTER S TO REST OF CODE

Prior to the enactment of section 1371(a)(2) of the Code in SSRA 1982, the Service's published position was that an acquiring S corporation's purchase of the stock of a target corporation followed by the dissolution of the target was a transaction under former sections 332(b)(2) and 334(b)(2) of the 1954 Code, pursuant to which the acquiring corporation took a basis in the target assets generally equal to the purchase price of the target stock. *See* Rev. Rul 73-496, 1973-2 C.B. 312.

In 1982 Congress repealed former section 334(b)(2) of the 1954 Code and enacted section 338. Tax Equity and Fiscal Responsibility Act of 1982 (TEFRA 1982), Sec. 224, 1982-2 C.B. 501, 503. Section 338 was "intended to replace any nonstatutory treatment of a stock purchase as an asset purchase under the *Kimbell-Diamond* doctrine." H.R. Conf. Rep. No. 760, 97th Cong., 2d Sess. 536 (1982), 1982-2 C.B. 600, 632. Under section 338, in the case of any qualified stock purchase, an acquiring corporation may either allow the target corporation to retain the target's basis in its assets or the acquiring corporation can elect to treat the stock purchase as a purchase of the target's assets with the result that the target corporation can obtain a cost/fair market value basis in the target's assets. For this purpose, it does not matter whether the target corporation is liquidated.

Rev. Rul. 90-95, 1990-2 C.B. 67, holds that if an acquiring corporation organizes a subsidiary solely for the purpose of acquiring the stock of a target corporation in a reverse subsidiary cash merger, the acquiring corporation is treated as having acquired the stock of the target in a qualified stock purchase under section 338 of the Code. In addition, the revenue ruling holds that if the acquiring corporation makes a qualified stock purchase of the target stock and immediately liquidates the target as part of the plan to acquire the assets of the target, the acquiring corporation is treated as having acquired the stock in a qualified stock purchase under section 338, rather than having made an acquisition of assets pursuant to the *Kimbell-Diamond* doctrine. Rev. Rul. 90-95 therefore is consistent with Congress' intent to afford wide discretion to corporations to either make a section 338(g) election and obtain a cost basis in a target's assets or not make a section 338(g) election and obtain a carryover basis in target's assets.

Less than two months after the enactment of section 338 of the Code in TEFRA 1982, section 1371(a)(2) was enacted in SSRA 1982. We do not believe that Congress intended to return S corporations to the law as it existed before the 1954 Code, when it was necessary to ascertain the intent of the acquiring corporation at the time of the stock purchase in order to determine whether the transaction would be treated as an asset purchase. Moreover, we do not believe that Congress in enacting section 1371(a)(2) intended to limit the freedom of small business S corporations to structure their acquisitions in the most advantageous manner. For example, there often are legitimate business reasons for corporations to acquire the stock of a target corporation rather than its assets. In addition, if the basis of the assets of the target corporation exceed [sic] their fair market value, the acquiring corporation may seek to acquire the stock and liquidate under section 332, thereby preserving the high carryover basis. In addition, S corporations making a qualified stock purchase should also be afforded the flexibility to make a section 338(g) election or make a joint election with a selling consolidated group under section 338(h)(10). Under the section 338(h)(10) election, the target corporation is essentially treated as if it sold all of its assets while it was a member of the selling consolidated group. The selling group thus has the flexibility to recognize gain or loss on the transfer of target's assets rather than the transfer of target stock and retain target's tax attributes. *See generally* section 338(h)(10), 381(a)(1), and section 1.338(h)(10)-1T(e) of the temporary Income Tax Regulations. Absent an indication to the contrary in the legislative history to SSRA 1982, it is unlikely that Congress enacted section 1371(a)(2) to prohibit S corporations from benefitting from the flexibility that section 338 had just been enacted to create. Rather, pursuant to section 1371(a)(1), an acquiring S corporation should be given the same flexibility accorded subchapter C corporations.

The enactment of section 1371(a)(2) of the Code also raises an issue, similar to the issue presented in this technical advice memorandum, of whether S corporations can continue to engage in qualified corporate reorganizations. For example, in a divisive reorganization under section 368(a)(1)(D), a corporation transfers assets to another corporation that it controls immediately afterwards followed by a distribution of the stock of the controlled corporation that qualifies under section 355. Thus, if the transferor in this transaction is an S corporation, the S corporation will, for a moment, hold the stock of the controlled corporation. If section 1371(a)(2) is applied to treat the transferor S corporation as an individual, the transaction could not qualify for divisive reorganization treatment under sections 368(a)(1)(D) and 355, because the transaction would not involve a transfer of assets by one corporation to another corporation under section 368 and a distribution by a corporation of controlled stock under section 355. Section 361(a) would also not apply because the transferor S corporation would not be a corporate "party to the reorganization."

GCM 39768, I-130-88 (Dec. 1, 1988) concludes that section 1371(a)(2) of the Code does not prevent a transferor S corporation that momentarily holds the stock of a controlled or acquiring corporation from engaging in a divisive reorganization under sections 368(a)(1)(D) and 355. This conclusion is based on three factors that we believe support a similar interpretation of the applicability of section 1371(a)(2) with respect to sections 338 and 332. First, former section 1363(e) recognized that an S corporation can be a transferor in a reorganization. Second, prior to 1982, the Service held in several revenue rulings that an S corporation could be a transferor corporation in a reorganization. If Congress intended to overturn the Service's position and prevent transferor S corporations from engaging in reorganizations it would have done so only by explicitly stating such intent. There is no indication of such intent in the legislative history of section 1371. Third, the policy of allowing taxpayers to conduct their enterprises in modified corporate forms because of business exigencies, without recognition of gain or loss, dictates that reorganizations involving S corporations as transferors should be allowed. For the same reasons, section 1371(a)(2) should not be applied to preclude S corporations from obtaining the business and tax flexibility accorded by section 338.

In addition, it would make little sense to prevent an S corporation that has made a qualified stock purchase from applying section 332 of the Code to a liquidation of the target corporation that follows the stock acquisition. Under section 1361(b)(2), an S corporation cannot hold more than 80 percent of the vote and value of another corporation without losing its S corporation status. Therefore, in order to retain its S status, an S corporation that makes a qualified stock purchase must immediately liquidate the acquired target corporation. Consequently, the issue of whether a distribution to an S corporation can qualify for section 332(a) treatment arises in those situations where the S corporation has just acquired control of the target corporation and then liquidates the target corporation. If section 331 (and not 332) applies to the liquidation of target, the target corporation will always recognize gain or loss on its liquidation, the acquiring S corporation will always acquire a cost basis in the target's assets and the flexibility that Congress intended to have created by enacting section 338 will be significantly curtailed. As a result, the arguments in support of the position that Congress did not intend the enactment of section 1371(a)(2) to preclude S corporations from obtaining the benefits of section 338 also support the position that Congress did not intend to preclude S corporations from obtaining the benefits of section 332.

Permitting an S corporation to make a qualified stock purchase and to liquidate a subsidiary under section 332 of the Code does not conflict with any policy underlying subchapter S, nor does it give rise to any abuse under today's federal tax system, such as the avoidance of *General Utilities* gain. Neither section 338 nor section 332 provide [sic] a vehicle whereby *General Utilities* repeal can be avoided through a transfer of assets from a subchapter C corporation to a subchapter S corporation. After the enactment of the Tax Reform Act of 1986, a section 338(g) election requires the target corporation to recognize gain upon the deemed sale of its assets. Conversely, if a section 338(g) election is not made, the basis in the assets of the target will carry over to the acquiring corporation in a section 332 liquidation. Pursuant to section 1374(d)(8), any built-in gain in these assets will be subject to tax under section 1374.

In summary:

(1) The purpose of section 1371(a)(2) as manifested by its legislative history was to treat S corporation shareholders as individuals for section 301 purposes. As a result of subsequent amendments to sections 301 and 311, corporate shareholders and individual shareholders are now treated the same under those sections. The legislative history is devoid of any suggestion that Congress intended to preclude subchapter S acquiring corporations from making section

338 qualified stock purchases or liquidating target corporations under section 332(a).

(2) The history of *Kimbell-Diamond*, former section 334(b)(2), and section 338 demonstrates that Congress now intends that *Kimbell-Diamond* issues should be resolved by objective statutory standards according the acquiring corporation the maximum flexibility to elect between a cost basis or a carryover basis in the target assets.

(3) The legislative and ruling history concerning S corporations and the reorganization provisions demonstrate [sic] that Congress intends for S corporations to have the same business and tax flexibility in making corporate acquisitions as C corporations.

(4) Allowing S corporations to make qualified stock purchases and section 332 liquidations does not violate any policies represented by *General Utilities* repeal.

Conclusion

Section 1371(a)(2) does not prevent an S corporation from being treated as a corporation for purposes of sections 338 and 332 of the Code. Instead, under section 1371(a)(1), the rules of subchapter C should apply to S's purchase of the T stock and the dissolution of T into S. Therefore, S's purchase on Date 2 of the stock of T was a qualified stock purchase under section 338(d)(3) followed by a section 332 liquidation of T into S.

Issue 2

Applicable Law

Section 1361(b)(2) of the Code provides that a small business corporation is a corporation that, among other things, is not a member of an affiliated group (determined under section 1504 without regard to the exceptions contained in subsection (b) thereof).

Section 1362(a) of the Code allows a small business corporation, as defined in section 1361, to elect not to be subject to the taxes imposed by Chapter 1 of the Code, with certain exceptions, but to have all its income taxed directly to its shareholders. An election under this section shall be valid only if all persons who are shareholders in the corporation on the day on which the election is made consent to such election.

Section 1362(d)(2)(A) of the Code provides that an election under section 1362(a) shall be terminated whenever (at any time on or after the first tax year for which the corporation is an S corporation) the corporation ceases to be a small business corporation.

Rev. Rul. 72-320, 1972-1 C.B. 270, holds that the momentary ownership by an S corporation of all the stock in another corporation in connection with a divisive reorganization under section 368(a)(1)(D) of the Code does not terminate the corporation's election.

I. RELATIONSHIP OF SUBCHAPTER S TO REST OF CODE 609

Analysis

After S acquired the stock of T, on Date 2, S was in control of T (determined under section 1504 without regard to the exceptions contained in subsection (b) thereof). However, T was immediately liquidated after S purchased the T stock. Therefore, the exception provided in Rev. Rul. 72-320 to the requirements set forth in sections 1361(b)(2) and 1362(d)(2)(A) apply to S's momentary control of T prior to T's liquidation.

Conclusion

S's momentary ownership of the stock of T will not cause S to be an ineligible corporation under section 1361(b)(2)(A) of the Code, and therefore, will not terminate S's election to be taxed as an S corporation under section 1362(d)(2).

NOTES

1. *Who participates in Private Letter Rulings?* The foregoing ruling stakes out a strong position on Congressional intent. Even though taxpayers are formally not allowed to rely on other people's private letter rulings, these rulings are watched with great interest by the practicing bar, and an unexpected change of position on the government's part is likely to reverberate inside and outside the National Office of the IRS in Washington. So who participates in this process on the government's part? The answer is (1) tax experts in the Technical Branch of the IRS who specialize in the particular Code section or sections at issue, (2) and, if requested by "Technical," the people from the Interpretative, General Litigation, and Legislation and Regulations ("L&R") Divisions of the Office of the Chief Counsel of the IRS. *See* M. Saltzman, IRS Practice and Procedure para. 3.03[5]. This particular ruling is likely to have been the subject of broad participation. Note that PLR 9245004 is actually a Technical Advice Memorandum, meaning an opinion issued by the IRS National Office to a taxpayer and the IRS (in the field) to help resolve an audit issue. The same personnel participate in it as in a regular private letter ruling.

2. *How long stock of an active subsidiary of an S corporation can be held.* Rev. Rul. 73-496, 1973-2 C.B. 312 provides that an S corporation can hold the stock of an active corporation for as long as thirty days, provided the holding of such stock is part of a larger restructuring plan, for example, holding the stock in anticipation of liquidating the subsidiary. As the foregoing letter ruling points out, in General Counsel Memorandum 39768 (Dec. 1, 1988) the IRS legal staff concluded that an S corporation that "momentarily has a C corporation shareholder in the course of a reorganization" does not lose its status as an S corporation, despite the seemingly strict language of § 1361(b)(1). This complements Rev. Rul. 73-496 nicely, but represents a weak authority to rely upon.

3. *Spin-offs involving S corporations.* In Private Letter Ruling 9321006 (Nov. 30, 1993) the IRS reviewed a divisive type D reorganization and ruled, among other things, that the newly-formed subsidiary would be subject to the BIG tax to the same extent the distributing parent corporation was, but with the favorable result that the parent's holding period for the built-in gain assets would be added to the subsidiary's holding period, as opposed to beginning anew. In the second ruling the IRS also found that, consistent with Reg. § 1.1368-2(d)(3), the AAA of the distributing corporation would be split between it and the controlled corporation(s).[15]

PROBLEM 25-11

The Friendly Corporation is a cash-method calendar-year S corporation. On June 30, 199X, for good business reasons, and not to avoid taxes, it acquired all the stock of the National Hatblocking Corporation, a C corporation that manufactures hat-shaping equipment, which is also on the cash method and uses the calendar year. The consideration for the acquisition was voting stock of Friendly Corporation. On the same day Friendly Corporation purported to make a § 338 election on National Hatblocking Corporation's behalf, and immediately liquidated National Hatblocking into itself in a § 332 liquidation. Prior to the merger, National Hatblocking redeemed all the stock of its founder, Harold Hatman, for $600,000 in cash it did not need. After the redemption, National Hatblocking had assets with a value of $5 million and a basis of $2 million and no liabilities. It also had a net-operating-loss carryover of $4 million. The time between the acquisition of the stock and the liquidation into Friendly Corporation was fourteen days.

(1) Does Friendly Corporation lose its S election?

(2) Are the §§ 332 and 338 elections valid?

(3) Assuming the election is valid, would gains on the hypothetical sales of the assets pursuant to § 338 of S corporation be taxable to the shareholders or to National Hatblocking? If so, when? *See* Reg. § 1.338-1T(f)(8).

(4) What is the character of the reorganization? *See* Rev. Rul. 76-123, 1976-1 C.B. 94, discussed in connection with type B reorganizations earlier in this book.

(5) What becomes of National Hatblocking's NOL? *See* § 338(a), (b) and (g)(3).

c. Dividends-Received Deduction

NAPORANO v. UNITED STATES
834 F. Supp. 694 (D.C. N.J. 1993)

LECHNER, DISTRICT JUDGE.

[The Naporano family owned two Subchapter S corporations, referred to as Naporano Iron & Metal Co. ("Naporano Iron & Metal") and Nimco Shredding

---

[15] This directive called for applying the principles of § 312(h), which generally relies on relative fair market values.

Co. ("Nimco Shredding"). In 1987 and 1988, Naporano Iron & Metal and Nimco Shredding received dividends (the "NFS Dividends") from Naporano Foreign Sales Corp. ("Naporano Foreign Sales"). Naporano Foreign Sales is a "foreign sales corporation."[16] The effect of being an FSC is that part of its income attributable to export sales is tax-exempt, and its dividends are deductible under § 245(c)(1)(A) when paid to a corporate shareholder. Until the Naporanos made an issue of it, the consensus was that S corporations could not deduct dividends from FSCs. The IRS disallowed the § 245(c)(1)(A) deductions taken by Naporano Iron & Metal and Nimco shredding.]

. . . .

The dispute between the parties in the present case rests on conflicting interpretations of the Code and of the IRS policy regarding S Corporations and dividends-received deductions[17] under section 245(c)(1)(A). Because the parties agree on the facts relevant to this dispute, see 12G Statement, the case is a particularly appropriate candidate for summary judgment analysis....

B. *Statutory Interpretation*

The dispute between the Taxpayers and the Government centers on an issue of statutory construction as to whether the term "domestic corporation" in 26 U.S.C. § 245(c)(1) includes S corporations. Section 245(c)(1)(A) provides:

> In the case of a domestic corporation, there shall be allowed as a deduction an amount equal to —
> (A) 100 percent of any dividend received from another corporation which is distributed out of earnings and profits attributable to foreign trade income for a period during which such other corporation was a FSC.... 26 U.S.C. § 245(c)(1)(A).

The Taxpayers argue that the word "corporation" in 26 U.S.C. § 245(c)(1) should be interpreted so as to include S corporations.... Under that interpretation, they argue, the dividends received by Naporano Iron & Metal and Nimco Shredding — both S Corporations — were deductible by those companies. *Id.*

---

[16] A foreign sales corporation ("FSC") is defined in 26 U.S.C. § 922(a) as any corporation which (1) is created or organized under the laws of a foreign country which is party to certain treaty agreements or under the laws of a United States possession, (2) has no more than 25 shareholders, (3) has no outstanding preferred stock, (4) maintains an office outside the United States, (5) has a board of directors which includes at least one non-U.S. resident and (6) is not a member of a controlled group of corporations which includes a domestic international sales corporation. *Id.* § 922(a)(1)(A)-(F); *see Polychrome Int'l Corp. v. Krigger*, Nos. 92-7509 and 92-7510, slip op. at 4-5, 1993 U.S. App. LEXIS 23287 (3d Cir. 10 Sept. 1993).

[17] Normally, shareholders are required to include as part of their taxable income any dividends they receive. The Code, however, allows shareholders which are corporations to deduct, in some instances, a percentage of the dividends they receive. *See, e.g.*, 26 U.S.C. §§ 243 (dividends of domestic corporations), 245 (dividends of foreign corporations), 247 (preferred stock of public utility companies). These deductions are generally referred to as dividends-received deductions.

They further argue this resulted in the Taxpayers being able to appropriately exclude the amount from their individual tax returns in 1987 and 1988.[18] *Id.* The Government, on the other hand, argues for a more literal interpretation of the word "corporation."... The Government contends this term includes only "C Corporations"[19] and excludes S Corporations and all other noncorporate entities.... The construction of section 245(c)(1)(A), as it applies to S Corporations, appears to be an issue of first impression.

"A court's objective in interpreting a Federal statute is to ascertain the intent of Congress and to give effect to its legislative will."... In determining the legislative intent of Congress, "'the starting point' should be 'the language itself.'"...

Under principles of statutory construction "where the terms of a statute are unambiguous, judicial inquiry is complete."... In such a case, where the plain meaning of a statute is evident from the face of the statute, "'the sole function of the courts is to enforce it according to its terms.'"... If the language is ambiguous, a court should consider the legislative history of the statute....

1. *Construction of Code Provisions*

Because Congress intends to tax all income except that which has been specifically exempted, there exists a long-standing rule that the terms of any provision allowing a deduction are to be strictly construed.

Under our system of Federal income taxation, ... every element of gross income of a person, corporate or individual, is subject to tax unless there is a statute or some rule of law that exempts that person or element....

2. *Overview of Subchapter S Corporations*

The relevant statutory provisions at issue in this case are: (1) the provisions in Subchapter S of the Code, particularly section 1363(b) and (2) section 245(c)(1)(A), a provision which allows a dividends-received deduction.

Subchapter S was enacted with the intention of "eliminat[ing] tax disadvantages that might dissuade small businesses from adopting the corporate form and

---

[18] The Taxpayers' interpretation of the Code would allow the dividends received from Naporano Foreign Sales to remain — untaxed until some future date to be solely determined by the Taxpayers. Specifically, Naporano Iron & Metal and Nimco Shredding would have at their disposal a significant sum of money (more than two million dollars) tax-free. *See* 12G Statement, P 5. The Taxpayers argue that the dividend income should only be subject to Federal taxation if and when Naporano Iron & Metal and Nimco Shredding choose to distribute the money to their shareholders. *See* Taxpayers Brief at 11. The Taxpayers, therefore, would have exclusive control over the decision whether the dividend income would ever be taxed. *See id.*

[19] For purposes of Subchapter S, corporations which are not S Corporations are called C Corporations. 26 U.S.C. § 1361(a)(1) ("the term 'C corporation' means ... a corporation which is not an S corporation"). Although, the term "C Corporation" is defined for purposes of Subchapter S, *id.*, in other areas of the Code, C Corporations are referred to simply as corporations.

I. RELATIONSHIP OF SUBCHAPTER S TO REST OF CODE

to lessen the tax burden on such businesses."... The Code accomplishes this purpose by means of a "pass-through" system under which corporate income, losses, deductions and credits are attributed to individual shareholders in a manner akin to the tax treatment of partnerships.... "Generally [S corporation) income is treated as ordinary income to the shareholder without the retention of any special characteristics it might have had in the hands of the corporation."[20] S. Rep. No. 1983, 85th Cong., 2d Sess. 86 (1958). Although S Corporations file informational tax returns in which they determine the amount of income to be allocated to their shareholders, only the shareholders pay tax on the income. *See Kelley*, 877 F.2d at 758; 26 U.S.C. § 1363 (a) and (b).[21]

As a matter of substantive corporate law, an S Corporation is organized and operated as any other corporation. The principal difference between S Corporations and other corporations is the pass-through nature in which its income is treated for tax purposes.... The hybrid nature of S Corporations has caused some confusion over whether S Corporations are more closely related to C Corporations or to partnerships. The answer appears to be S Corporations are corporations for many non-tax purposes but share the tax aspects of partnerships. *See Katz*, 791 F. Supp. at 984 ("'it is common for tax practitioners to refer to an S Corporation as a corporation which is taxed like a partnership'").... However, even for some tax purposes S Corporations are treated like C corporations. *See, e.g., id.* (recognized the corporate status of S Corporation for purpose of calculating the tax on net-earnings from self-employment).

Section 1371 of Subchapter S, for example, states: "Except to the extent inconsistent with this subchapter, subchapter C [which governs C Corporations] shall apply to an S Corporation and its shareholders."[22] 26 U.S.C. § 1371(a)(1).... Therefore, the determining factors in deciding how to treat an S Corporation appear to be (1) whether the situation involves a tax question and (2) whether the proposed tax treatment would be inconsistent with the pass-through nature of the provisions in Subchapter S.

---

[20] The individual tax treatment of S Corporation income is provided by section 1363(b). Section 1363(b) states: The taxable income of an S Corporation shall be computed in the same manner as in the case of an individual. 26 U.S.C. § 1363(b). Section 1363(b) also creates four exceptions to this rule; none of these exceptions applies in the instant case. *See* 26 U.S.C. § 1363(b)(1)-(4).

[21] In contrast, C Corporations are generally treated as entities separate and apart from their shareholders, so income earned by C Corporations is taxed twice; once at the corporate level, and again at the individual level when profits are distributed as dividends to the shareholders. *See* 26 U.S.C. §§ 61, 301.

[22] Because § 1371(a), by its language, restricts its application to the provisions in Subchapter C, it does not directly apply to the question presented in the instant case. Section 245(c)(1)(A), a dividends-received deduction provision, is not found in Subchapter S, but in Subchapter B.

C. *Whether S Corporations are "Domestic Corporations" Within the Meaning of Section 245(c)(1)(A)*

1. *Statutory Language*

As discussed, the starting point for the analysis of a statutory provision must be the language of that provision.... Section 245(c)(1)(A) allows a shareholder which is a corporation to take a deduction equal to one hundred percent of the dividends it receives from a FSC.

In the instant case, the text of the statute at issue is not entirely helpful because it is susceptible to competing reasonable interpretations. The Government argues the term "domestic corporation" includes only C Corporations and excludes S Corporations and all other non-corporate entities.... The Taxpayers contend the language of section 245 makes no such distinction between C Corporations and S Corporations, and, therefore, S Corporations are included within the section.... Because section 245(c)(1)(A) neither expressly includes nor excludes S Corporations, the issue cannot be resolved solely from its text.

2. *Legislative History*

Where the statutory language is ambiguous, the court must turn to the legislative history. *See Continental Airlines*, 932 F.2d at 287; *Victoria Station*, 875 F.2d at 1383. When the constructions urged by both the taxpayer and the Government in a tax refund case are reasonable interpretations of the statutory language, "the court should not disregard any expressions of legislative intent in the committee reports." *Greenville Steel Car Co. v. United States*, 222 Ct. Cl. 400, 615 F.2d 911, 912 (Ct. Cl. 1980).

The purpose of section 245 has been described as providing

> "that a portion of the export income of an eligible [FSC] will be exempt from Federal income tax. It will also allow a domestic corporation a 100 percent dividend-received deduction for dividends distributed from the FSC out of earnings attributable to certain foreign trade income. Thus, there will be no corporate level tax imposed on a portion of the income from exports."

Staff of the Joint Comm. of House and Senate on Taxation, General Explanation of Revenue Provision of the Deficit Reduction Act of 1984, H.R. Doc. No. 4170, 98th Cong., 2d Sess. 1042, 1059 (1984).

The legislative history of section 245(c)(1)(A) does not provide any further illumination on whether to construe the term "domestic corporation" to include S Corporations. Although the legislative history generally refers to the policies underlying the need to provide a special deduction for dividends attributable to foreign trade income, it provides no specific direction on determining whether S Corporations are precluded from eligibility under section 245(c)(1)(A).

I. RELATIONSHIP OF SUBCHAPTER S TO REST OF CODE

3. *Section 245(c)(1)(A) and its Relation to the Code as a Whole*

Because neither the language of section 245(c)(1)(A) nor its legislative history is helpful, a wider review of the policies underlying Subchapter S and other relevant provisions of the Code must be effected to decide the issue. Accordingly, "the overall statutory framework" of Subchapter S must be analyzed.... In this regard, the sections of the Code must be read so as to be consistent with one another....

As discussed, under section 1363(b) of the Code, all of the income of an S Corporation is passed through to the shareholders and taxed at the individual level. 26 U.S.C. § 1363(b). Section 245(c)(1)(A) was not in existence at the time section 1363 was enacted in 1958 or amended in 1982, so Congress never dealt specifically with the issue of whether section 1363(b) bars S Corporations from taking advantage of section 245(c)(1)(A). However, Congress did address the issue of whether a dividends received deduction under another provision of the Code applied to S Corporations. *See* S. Rep. No. 640 at 15. In that context, Congress concluded the dividends-received deduction did not apply to S Corporations.

As in the case of partnerships, deductions generally allowable to individuals will be allowed to [S Corporations], but provisions of the Code governing the computation of taxable income which are applicable only to corporations, such as the dividends received deduction (sec. 243)[23] or the special rules relating to corporate tax preferences (sec. 291) will not apply. *Id*.... The IRS has reiterated this conclusion:

> The preclusion of the [dividends-received deduction] falls under the purview of section 1363(b) of the Code which essentially provides that an S Corporation computes its earnings as if it were an individual. Under section 243, only corporations are allowed [dividends-received deductions].

Tech. Adv. Mem. 9245003, 9245004 (July 28, 1992) (citing legislative history of 1982 amendment of Subchapter S); *see United States v. Vogel Fertilizer Co.*, 455 U.S. 16, 24, 70 L. Ed. 2d 792, 102 S. Ct. 821 (1982) ("deference is ordinarily owing to the agency construction"); *Ford Motor Credit Co. v. Milhollin*, 444 U.S. 555, 565, 63 L. Ed. 2d 22, 100 S. Ct. 790 (1980) (same); *American Medical Ass'n v. United States*, 668 F. Supp. 1085, 1096-97 n.20 (N.D. Ill. 1987) (technical advice memoranda is instructive in interpreting Code), *aff'd in part rev'd in part on other grounds*, 887 F.2d 760 (7th Cir. 1989). In fact, the Taxpayers agree the dividends-received deduction under section 243 is not available to S Corporations. Taxpayers Reply Brief at 1.

---

[23] In the case of a corporation, there shall be allowed as a deduction an amount equal to the following percentages of the amount received as dividends from a domestic corporation which is subject to taxation under this chapter. 26 U.S.C. § 243(a). The section was enacted to eliminate the double taxation of dividends distributed to shareholders which are corporations....

Congress and the IRS have interpreted the language in section 243(a) as applying only to C Corporations. *See* S. Rep. No. 640 at 15; Tech. Adv. Mem. at 9245004. The operative language of section 245(c)(1)(A) is substantially the same as the language of section 243. Section 245(c)(1)(A) applies "in the case of a domestic corporation," and section 243 applies "in the case of a corporation." 26 U.S.C. §§ 243(a) and 245(c)(1)(A). Therefore, as argued by the Government, the intent of Congress and the IRS to proscribe the use of section 243 by S Corporations may be construed as an indication that the use of the deduction under section 245(c)(1)(A) is similarly proscribed.[24] *See Jordan v. Lyng*, 659 F. Supp. 1403, 1412 (E.D. Va. 1987) ("the legislature is presumed to intend the same result by using similar language in similar legislation"); *see also Lutz v. Chromatex, Inc.*, 730 F. Supp. 1328, 1332 (M.D. Pa. 1990) ("in determining the legislative intent of a particular statute, the court may look to other similar statutory provisions").

In addition, the dividends-received deduction is unnecessary in the context of S Corporations. Subchapter S eliminates the corporate level of taxation, *see* 26 U.S.C. § 1363(b), so it is redundant to apply provisions such as section 243 and 245(c)(1)(A) which were also enacted to eliminate, for the specified purposes, the corporate level of taxation. *See Georgia R.R. & Banking*, 348 F.2d at 282 (section 243 enacted to prevent double taxation of corporate profits) ... H.R. No. 4170 at 1059 (under section 245(c) "there will be no corporate level tax imposed on a portion of the income from exports").[25] A statute should not be interpreted in a way that would render any of its provisions superfluous....

---

[24] Commentators addressing the issue have also concluded that § 245(c)(1)(A) does not apply to S Corporations. *See* James S. Eustice & Joel D. Kuntz, Federal Income Taxation of S Corporations P 2.04[16][a] & n.280 (3d ed. 1993) ("the ... dividends-received deduction [under § 245(c)(1)) will not apply to dividends received from the FSC by the S Corporation and its shareholders"); Samuel P. Starr, S Corporations: Operations 731 Tax Management, A-130, A-142 (BNA 1992) ("FSC income is subject to tax when distributed to the S Corporation because the S Corporation's shareholders are not eligible for the dividends-received deduction"). In contrast, the Taxpayers have been unable to point to any authority which agrees with their interpretation of § 245(c)(1)(A).

[25] The following is an illustration of the redundancy of a dividends-received deduction in the context of S Corporations. In the absence of any dividends-received deduction rules, the profits earned by a corporation which is the subsidiary of another corporation would be subject to Federal income taxes at three different levels: (1) the subsidiary would be taxed on the profits it earned,

I. RELATIONSHIP OF SUBCHAPTER S TO REST OF CODE 617

The Taxpayers place significance on the fact that section 245(c)(1)(A) was enacted in 1984 and, therefore, was not in existence when Subchapter S was enacted in 1958 and amended in 1982.... However, merely because Congress did not specifically consider section 245(c)(1)(A) when it established the pass-through nature of Subchapter S, does not bar the application of Subchapter S to that provision. Where, as in the instant case, "Congress has made a choice of language which fairly brings a given situation within a statute, it is unimportant that the particular application may not have been contemplated by the legislators."... Similarly, in construing a tax statute, the court in *Pool v. Commissioner* stated:

> "The excellence of our jurisprudence is its flexibility. In applying general statutory language to particular situations, courts best conform to the tradition of growth of our system when they adapt realistically general principles to different or constantly changing situations." 251 F.2d 233, 237-38 (9th Cir. 1957), *cert. denied*, 356 U.S. 938 (1958).

As discussed, the Taxpayers have the burden of proving the propriety of their deductions. They have failed to come forward with a clearly applicable Code provision allowing their deduction. Each of the attempts by the Taxpayers to distinguish section 245(c)(1)(A) fails because each argument seeks an interpretation inconsistent with the pass-through nature of S Corporations. The argument of the Taxpayers that they are penalized by an interpretation of section 245(c)(1)(A) which excludes S Corporations ... is presented in the wrong forum; that argument is one better "addressed to Congress, not the courts."... Moreover, to the extent any ambiguity remains as to Congress' intent regarding

---

see 26 U.S.C. § 61; (2) the parent corporation would be taxed on any dividends it received from the subsidiary, see id. at § 301(c); and (3) the shareholders of the parent corporation would be taxed on any dividends they received from the parent corporation. *See id*. at § 301(c). The mechanics of section 245(c)(1)(A) are virtually identical, with the only significant difference being the subsidiary corporation is a FSC. *See id*. at § 245(c)(1)(A).

Substituting an S Corporation for the parent corporation in the above example illustrates that the dividends-received deduction is unnecessary in the context of S Corporations: (1) profits would be taxed at the subsidiary level; (2) when the dividend was distributed to the parent — which is an S Corporation — the dividend would pass through to the shareholders of the S Corporation without being taxed at that second level; and (3) the S Corporation shareholders would be taxed on the dividend. *See id*. at § 1363(b). It is therefore unnecessary for an S Corporation to deduct the dividend because S Corporations are not taxed on income at the corporate level.

the application of section 245(c)(1)(A) to S Corporations, that ambiguity is to be resolved in favor of the Government....

The approach adopted in this case construes section 245(c)(1)(A) so that the Code policies regarding the pass-through nature of S Corporations are consistently advanced. To adopt the approach advocated by the Taxpayers would create an inconsistency in the law.

Conclusion

For the reasons stated above, the Government motion for summary judgment is granted; the Taxpayers' cross motion for summary judgment is denied.

An order accompanies this opinion.

NOTES

The foreign sales corporation ("FSC") is a creature of the federal income tax laws designed to stimulate US exports of goods and certain services. The FSC itself is a foreign corporation, usually a subsidiary of a US parent and having only minor substance. In the typical case, the US parent sells its products to the FSC, which in turn resells the goods at a mark-up. Because of the FSC's activities in the US, it will typically be subject to US taxes, but § 921 exempts a portion of the FSC's income and § 245(c)(1)(A) grants corporate recipients of dividends from FSCs a major dividends-received deduction to the extent the dividend is from qualified export activities. Thus, the exempt part of the FSC's income is never subject to US tax and the nonexempt part is taxed only once. Smaller corporations can reduce the administrative costs of participating in this elegant federal subsidy program by forming "shared FSCs." *See* § 927(g).

If one accepts the *Naparano* decision, one will agree that an S corporation cannot get a dividends-received deduction, but what if the FSC stock is held by a founder's Keogh plan? Might that permit the deferral of taxation of distributions from the FSC? There are rumors in the tax bar that some taxpayers are using this planning technique. No comment.

In Rev. Rul. 93-36, 1993-19, I.R.B. 4, the IRS ruled that an S corporation must separately state its business and non-business bad-debt deductions. The theory was that, even though bad-debt deductions are not separately enumerated exceptions to the general rule of § 1366(b), § 166 applies the same way as it does for an individual when computing an S corporation's taxable income. Thus, an S corporation has to include any wholly worthless-nonbusiness bad debt in its separately-stated short-term capital loss.

What if an S corporation holds stock in other companies? Can the S corporation pass a § 1244 loss through to its shareholders? The answer is "no" according to *Rath v. Commissioner*, 101 T.C. 196 (1993), largely because of the Tax Court's view that Congress did not intend to extend the benefits of § 1244 that far. The court did note that § 1377(a)(2) could not apply because § 1244 is

I. RELATIONSHIP OF SUBCHAPTER S TO REST OF CODE 619

outside Subchapter C. The court declined to consider Rev. Rul. 93-36 because it considered it unauthoritative. Can you reconcile *Rath* and Rev. Rul. 93-36?

d. Fringe Benefits

Read § 1372.

No founder will organize an S corporation for its fringe benefit advantages; there are none. This is because people owning 2% or more of the common stock of an S corporation are treated like partners in a partnership. § 1372. This status arises if there is direct or indirect ownership on any day of the taxable year. The 2% refers either to voting stock or to total outstanding stock; thus, there is no hiding out from the rule by issuing a lot of nonvoting stock to third parties. The intended implication is that 2% shareholders cannot be employees. Because various fringe benefit plans are available only to employees, the result is fatal to some key fringe benefits, especially medical reimbursement plans. *See* §§ 105 and 106. Other examples include the exclusions for meals and lodging (§ 119) and certain life insurance coverage (§ 79) furnished by an employer.

e. At-Risk Rules

Losses that pass through to shareholders may be limited by the at-risk rules of § 465. The restriction is measured activity-by-activity at the shareholder level. § 465(a)(1)(A). A special rule combines businesses in which the taxpayer actively manages, provided at least 65% of the losses are allocated to active managers. § 465(c)(3)(B). The at-risk rules apply before the passive-loss rules. Reg. § 1.469-2T(d)(6)(i).

f. Hobby-Loss Rules

S corporations are subject to the hobby-loss rules at the corporate level. Reg. § 1.183-1(f).

g. Passive Activity Loss Rules

These apply at the shareholder level, activity-by-activity. Each shareholder who materially participates (or who actively participates, in the case of rental real estate) is free of the restrictions of § 469. Reg. § 1.469-2T(e)(1). Operating income earned by a shareholder in an S corporation is considered passive income, a good thing from the point of view of a shareholder with net passive losses, but losses the S corporation generates are suspended unless the shareholder is active in the business. Reg. § 1.469-2T(e)(1). Another advantage of being active in the business is that interest paid to buy the S corporation stock will be free of the § 163(d) limit on investment-interest expenses.[26]

h. Alternative Minimum Tax

This tax applies at the shareholder level. §§ 1363(a), 55. The entity reports the AMT items on the annual Form K-1 distributed to owners, and they in turn combine the AMT amounts from all sources for the year to determine whether the items generate an AMT liability.

i. Transactions with Related Taxpayers

S corporations can deal with their shareholders as if they were strangers to the entity, the same as with C corporations. There is no analog to the guaranteed payment by a partnership to a partner.

The same basic rules apply to denial of losses and deferral of deductions in dealings with shareholders as apply in the case of partnerships. There is no unique set of provisions under Subchapter S. Thus, one must look to § 267 for these limitations. They are discussed with respect to partnerships in the pertinent chapters of this book.

j. Audits of S Corporations

Section 6244 extends the TEFRA partnership audit procedures to Subchapter S corporations, with the bulk of the specific incorporation of the TEFRA procedures to S corporations left for Regulations. Some Regulations have been promulgated and most of the TEFRA partnership audit procedures have been incorporated for S corporation audits. The part of this book devoted to partnerships discusses the TEFRA audit procedures. The Form 1120S contains a place to designate the tax matters person. The TEFRA audit rules do not apply to S corporations with five or fewer shareholders, all of whom are people or estates. §§ 6241-6245.

2. MULTIFORM S CORPORATIONS

It should come as no surprise that practicing lawyers have found ways to combine S corporations with other entities. As you may recall, a partnership cannot hold stock in an S corporation. § 1361(b)(1). However, the reverse is not true. S corporations can combine to form partnerships.

---

[26] See § 163(d)(4)(D). Section 163(d) limits current interest-expense deductions to net current investment income, and defers the nondeductible portion to future years.

I. RELATIONSHIP OF SUBCHAPTER S TO REST OF CODE 621

PRIV. LTR. RUL. 9017057
January 30, 1990

This is in response to a request for a private letter ruling, dated September 22, 1989, submitted on your behalf by your authorized representative, regarding the treatment of the above-referenced corporations as small business corporations.

The information submitted states that X1, X2, X3, X4, X5, X6, X7, X8, X9, X10, X11, X12, X13, X14, X15, X16, X17, X18, and X19 are corporations, all of which were incorporated between 1979 and 1988. The shareholders of each corporation have filed an election, under section 1362(a) of the Internal Revenue Code, for the corporation to be treated as an S corporation for federal income tax purposes. Each S corporation election has been in effect since the inception of each corporation. Stock in the corporations is held by a total of 136 individuals, with several individuals holding stock in more than one corporation.

Each corporation owns one or two restaurant sites and in connection therewith owns the land, improvements, equipment and furnishings necessary for the operation of the restaurant or restaurants. None of the corporations have [sic] pledged assets to secure the indebtedness of another corporation, and no corporation has guaranteed or otherwise agreed to assume liability for the indebtedness of another corporation.

Each corporation entered into a management agreement with W, a corporation. W has not made an election to be treated as an S corporation for federal income tax purposes. Under the management agreement, W is responsible for providing bookkeeping, accounting and payroll services, personnel training, management services and direction, advertising and maintenance services. In return, W generally receives a fee for each of these management functions, based on a percentage of the corporation's gross receipts, or it bills the corporation directly for the cost of providing the services. The stock of W is wholly-owned by A, an individual.

The Corporations and W have proposed forming a limited partnership for the purpose of acquiring, owning and operating additional restaurants. W will be the general partner of the partnership and each of the corporations will be a limited partner. W will contribute organizational and management services for its interest in the partnership and each corporation will contribute cash. Each corporation will continue to own and operate the restaurant site or sites it currently owns, and will remain liable for its current liabilities. In certain cases, a corporation may acquire additional restaurant sites.

It has been represented that the partnership can acquire new restaurant sites more easily and economically by using cash contributed to the partnership, rather than raising the equity for each future restaurant from the proceeds of the sale of stock in newly-created corporations. In addition, the shareholders of the corporations wish to avoid the dilution of their ownership in their directly-held sites. Finally, the proposed limited partnership form will not subject the restaurants directly-held by the corporations to the liabilities associated with the restaurants acquired by the partnership.

Section 1361(a)(1) of the Code defines an "S corporation" as a small business corporation for which an election is in effect for the taxable year. Section 1361(b)(1) defines "small business corporation," in part, as a corporation that has no more than 35 shareholders and that has as shareholders no persons other than individuals, estates, or trusts described in section 1361(c)(2).

Rev. Rul. 71-455, 1971-2 C.B. 318, implies that an S corporation can own a partnership interest without losing its status as an S corporation. In Rev. Rul. 71-455, the S corporation owned and operated motion picture theaters and was also an equal partner with another in a joint venture that owned and operated a motion picture theater. However, in Rev. Rul. 77-220, 1977-1 C.B. 263, the Service announced that it would disregard a form of business organization that lacks economic substance and that is established principally to circumvent the provisions of subchapter S of the Code. In that ruling, thirty unrelated individuals who jointly operated a single business divided themselves into three groups of ten. Each group organized a separate corporation that held equal amounts of capital. The corporations then organized a partnership to carry on the joint business. The shareholders set up three separate corporations principally so that each corporation could elect to be taxed under subchapter S. The predecessor of section 1361 limited to ten the number of shareholders of a small business corporation. The ruling held that the separate corporations were in substance a single corporation that could not elect to be an S corporation.

Unlike the parties in Rev. Rul. 77-220, the parties in the present case are existing S Corporations who will contribute cash to the partnership while retaining their existing operating assets. Like Rev. Rul. 71-455, each corporation in the present case has valid business reasons for the transaction and each corporation will continue to operate its directly-owned restaurant or restaurants independently of the business of the partnership.

Based on the above, we conclude that the mere formation of partnership and the acquisition of interests therein by X1, X2, X3, X4, X5, X6, X7, X8, X9, X10, X11, X12, X13, X14, X15, X16, X17, X18, and X19 will not cause X1 to violate the 35 shareholder limitation contained in section 1361(b)(1)(A) of the Code....

NOTES

1. *Aggressive tax planning.* A more provocative model involves using an S corporation to operate a business at a loss and a low-bracket C corporation to lend money to it. One might imagine a yacht-leasing company that the owner actively manages, thereby avoiding the passive loss rules as to that owner. The leasing company loses money because of interest expense deductions and depreciation. The lending company reports interest income. This raises the specter of § 267(a)(2), but there is no deferral or disallowance of the interest expenses as long as the payments are made in a timely manner.

2. *De facto* § 754 results. Private Letter Ruling 9218019 (May 1, 1992), *supra*, states that S corporation stock takes a fair market value at death basis, with the result that if the corporation has appreciated assets, they can be sold at a taxable gain, increasing stock basis, but if the stock is then sold, the stock's basis (now exaggerated) will likely be more than the amount realized, with the result that the loss will offset the prior gain. This results in a *de facto* § 754 election at the S corporation level. The planning advice is to hang onto valuable assets in the S corporation and to sell the assets whose bases are greater than their values.

OUTSIDE READINGS

G. Coven, *Subchapter S Distributions and Pseudo Distributions: Proposals for Revising the Defective Blend of Entity and Conduit Concepts*, 42 Tax L. Rev. 381 (Winter 1987).

J. Eustice, *Subchapter S Corporations and Partnerships: A Search for the Pass Through Paradigm*, 39 Tax L. Rev. 345 (Summer 1984).

M. Ginsburg, *Colloquium on Corporate Integration: Maintaining Subchapter S in an Integrated Tax World*, 47 Tax L. Rev. 665 (Spring 1992).

A. Hess, *The Subchapter S Revision Act: An Analysis and Appraisal*, 50 Tenn. L. Rev. 569 (Summer 1983).

M. Oberst, *Reform of the Subchapter S Distribution Rules: Repudiation of Section 311(a)*, 38 Tax L. Rev. 79 (Fall 1992).

D. Shores, *The New Subchapter S Distribution Rules: A Half-Step Forward But a Full-Step Back*, 4 Va. Tax Rev. 49 (Summer 1984).

Chapter 26
LIMITED LIABILITY COMPANIES

A. BACKGROUND

For many years, sophisticated natural resource corporations used the *limitada*, a form of Hispanic or Brazilian law entity, to undertake risky projects here and abroad. The charm of the *limitada* is that its owners' liabilities are limited in the the same way as are those of typical shareholders, but that the enterprise is taxable as a partnership for federal income tax purposes, in effect achieving the flow-through benefits offered by S corporations (which are, of course, not available to corporate shareholders) without the usual restrictions.

B. THE WYOMING RESPONSE

The State of Wyoming was the first to recognize the opportunity to legislate a homegrown form of the *limitada*, the so-called limited liability company ("LLC"). In Rev. Rul. 88-76, 1988-2 C.B. 360, the IRS opened the flood gates of tax planning by conceding that a well-formed Wyoming LLC should be classified as a partnership for federal income tax purposes. As of mid-1995, forty-seven states and the District of Columbia had enacted limited liability company laws. The following is an illustrative case.

REV. RUL. 93-38
1993-1 C.B. 233

Issues

Are M and N, Delaware limited liability companies, classified for federal tax purposes as associations or as partnerships under section 7701 of the Internal Revenue Code?

Facts

Situation 1. M is organized as a limited liability company (LLC) pursuant to the provisions of the Delaware Limited Liability Company Act (Act), Del. Code Ann. tit. 6, §§ 18-101 through 18-1106 (1992). M is authorized under its articles of organization to engage in any and all business activity permitted by the laws of the State of Delaware. M has 25 members.

Section 18-402 of the Act provides that unless otherwise provided in a limited liability company agreement (LLC agreement), the management of an LLC is vested in its members in proportion to the current percentage or other interest of members in the profits of the LLC owned by all of the members. An LLC agreement may, however, provide for the management, in whole or in part, of an LLC by a manager who is chosen by the members in the manner provided in the LLC agreement. M's LLC agreement provides that M's management is vested in its members.

Section 18-303 of the Act provides that except as otherwise provided in the Act, the debts, obligations, and liabilities of an LLC, whether arising in contract, tort, or otherwise, are solely the debts, obligations, and liabilities of the LLC; and no member or manager of an LLC is obligated personally for any debt, obligation, or liability of the LLC solely by reason of being a member or acting as a manager of the LLC.

Section 18-701 of the Act provides that an LLC interest is personal property. Section 18-702(a) of the Act states that an LLC interest is assignable in whole or in part except as provided in an LLC agreement. The assignee of a member's LLC interest has no right to participate in the management of the business and affairs of an LLC except as provided in an LLC agreement and upon (1) the approval of all of the members of the LLC other than the member assigning the member's LLC interest, or (2) compliance with any procedure provided for in the LLC agreement. Section 18-702(b) of the Act provides that unless otherwise provided in an LLC agreement, (1) an assignment entitles the assignee to share in profits and losses, to receive distributions, and to receive an allocation of income, gain, loss, deduction, or credit or any similar item to which the assigner was entitled, to the extent assigned, and (2) a member ceases to be a member and to have the power to exercise any rights or powers of a member upon assignment of all of the member's LLC interest. Section 18-704(a) of the Act provides that the assignee of a member's LLC interest may become a member as provided in an LLC agreement and upon (1) the approval of all of the members of the LLC other than the member assigning the member's LLC interest, or (2) compliance with any procedure provided for in the LLC agreement. M's LLC agreement provides that an assignee must receive the unanimous consent of the remaining members to participate in the management of the business and affairs of M and to become a member of M.

Section 18-801 of the Act provides that an LLC is dissolved upon the first to occur of the following: (1) at the time specified in an LLC agreement or 30 years from the date of the formation of the LLC if no time is set forth in the LLC agreement, (2) upon the happening of events specified in an LLC agreement, (3) by the written consent of all members, (4) by the death, retirement, resignation, expulsion, bankruptcy, or dissolution of a member or the occurrence of any other event that terminates the continued membership of a member in the LLC unless the business of the LLC is continued either by the consent of all of the remaining members within 90 days following the occurrence of any terminating event or pursuant to a right to continue stated in the LLC agreement, or (5) by the entry of a decree of judicial dissolution under the Act. M's LLC agreement does not provide for a right to continue following the death, retirement, resignation, expulsion, bankruptcy, or dissolution of a member.

B. THE WYOMING RESPONSE 627

Situation 2. The facts for N are the same as for M except as follows: First, N's LLC agreement provides that management of N is vested in managers that are elected by the members on an annual basis. A, B, and C, who are members of N, are the elected managers. Second, N's LLC agreement provides that the assignee of a member's LLC interest may participate in the management of the business and affairs of N and become a member of N after the assignee provides N with written notice of the transfer. Consent of the remaining members to the assignment is not required. Third, N's LLC agreement provides that the entity shall continue following the death, retirement, resignation, expulsion, bankruptcy, or dissolution of a member, or the occurrence of any other event that terminates the continued membership of a member in N.

Law and Analysis

Section 7701(a)(2) of the Code provides that the term "partnership" includes a syndicate, group, pool, joint venture, or other unincorporated organization, through or by means of which any business, financial operation, or venture is carried on, and which is not a trust or estate or a corporation.

Section 301.7701-1(b) of the Procedure and Administration Regulations states that the Code prescribes certain categories, or classes, into which various organizations fall for purposes of taxation. These categories, or classes, include associations (which are taxable as corporations), partnerships, and trusts. The tests, or standards, that are to be applied in determining the classification in which an organization belongs are set forth in sections 301.7701-2 through 301.7701-4.

Section 301.7701-2(a)(1) of the regulations sets forth the following major characteristics of a corporation: (1) associates, (2) an objective to carry on business and divide the gains therefrom, (3) continuity of life, (4) centralization of management, (5) liability for corporate debts limited to corporate property, and (6) free transferability of interests. Whether a particular organization is to be classified as an association must be determined by taking into account the presence or absence of each of these corporate characteristics.

Section 301.7701-2(a)(2) of the regulations provides that an organization that has associates and an objective to carry on business and divide the gains therefrom is not classified as a trust, but rather as a partnership or association taxable as a corporation. It further provides that characteristics common to partnerships and corporations are not material in attempting to distinguish between an association and a partnership. Since associates and an objective to carry on business and divide the gains therefrom are generally common to corporations and partnerships, the determination of whether an organization that has these characteristics is to be treated for tax purposes as a partnership or as an association depends on whether there exist centralization of management, continuity of life, free transferability of interests, and limited liability.

Section 301.7701-2(a)(3) of the regulations provides that if an unincorporated organization possesses more corporate characteristics than noncorporate characteristics, it constitutes an association taxable as a corporation.

In interpreting section 301.7701-2 of the regulations, the Tax Court, in Larson v. Commissioner, 66 T.C. 159 (1976), acq., 1979-1 C.B. 1, concluded that equal weight must be given to each of the four corporate characteristics of continuity of life, centralization of management, limited liability, and free transferability of interests.

Situation 1. In this situation, M has associates and an objective to carry on business and divide the gains therefrom. Therefore, M must be classified as either an association or a partnership. M is classified as a partnership for federal tax purposes unless the organization has a preponderance of the remaining corporate characteristics of continuity of life, centralization of management, limited liability, and free transferability of interests.

Section 301.7701-2(b)(1) of the regulations provides that if the death, insanity, bankruptcy, retirement, resignation, or expulsion of any member will cause a dissolution of the organization, continuity of life does not exist. Section 301.7701-2(b)(2) provides that an agreement by which an organization is established may provide that the business will be continued by the remaining members in the event of the death or withdrawal of any member, but the agreement does not establish continuity of life if under local law the death or withdrawal of any member causes a dissolution of the organization.

Under the Act, unless the business of M is continued by the consent of all the remaining members or by a right to continue stated in the LLC agreement, M is dissolved upon the death, resignation, expulsion, bankruptcy, or dissolution of a member or the occurrence of any other event that terminates the continued membership of a member in the company. M's LLC agreement does not provide for any other right to continue. If a member of M ceases to be a member of M for any reason, the continuity of M is not assured because all remaining members must agree to continue the business. Consequently, M lacks the corporate characteristic of continuity of life.

Section 301.7701-2(c)(1) of the regulations provides that an organization has the corporate characteristic of centralized management if any person (or group of persons that does not include all of the members) has continuing exclusive authority to make management decisions necessary to the conduct of the business for which the organization was formed.

Section 301.7701-2(c)(2) of the regulations provides that the persons who have this authority may, or may not, be members of the organization and may hold office as a result of a selection by the members from time to time, or may be self perpetuating in office. Centralized management can be accomplished by election to office, by proxy appointment, or by any other means that has the effect of concentrating in a management group continuing exclusive authority to make management decisions.

B. THE WYOMING RESPONSE 629

Section 301.7701-2(c)(4) of the regulations provides that there is no centralization of continuing exclusive authority to make management decisions, unless the managers have sole authority to make the decisions. For example, in the case of a corporation or a trust, the concentration of management powers in a board of directors or trustees effectively prevents a stockholder or a trust beneficiary, simply because that person is a stockholder or beneficiary, from binding the corporation or the trust.

Under the Act, an LLC may be managed either by an elected manager or managers or by its members. Under the LLC agreement, M's management is vested in all of its members; therefore, M lacks the corporate characteristic of centralized management.

Section 301.7701-2(d)(1) of the regulations provides that an organization has the corporate characteristic of limited liability if under local law there is no member who is personally liable for the debts of, or claims against, the organization. Personal liability means that a creditor of an organization may seek personal satisfaction from a member of the organization to the extent that the assets of the organization are insufficient to satisfy the creditor's claim.

Under the Act, the members of M are not liable for M's debts, obligations, or liabilities. Consequently, M possesses the corporate characteristic of limited liability.

Section 301.7701-2(e)(1) of the regulations provides that an organization has the corporate characteristic of free transferability of interests if each of the members or those members owning substantially all of the interests in the organization have the power, without the consent of other members, to substitute for themselves in the same organization a person who is not a member of the organization. For this power of substitution to exist in the corporate sense, the member must be able, without the consent of other members, to confer upon the member's substitute all of the attributes of the member's interest in the organization. The characteristic of free transferability does not exist if each member can, without the consent of the other members, assign only the right to share in the profits but cannot assign the right to participate in the management of the organization.

Under the Act, a member of M can assign or transfer that member's interest to another person who is not a member of the organization. However, under M's LLC agreement, the assignee or transferee does not become a substitute member and does not acquire all of the attributes of the member's interest in M unless all of the remaining members approve the assignment or transfer. Therefore, M lacks the corporate characteristic of free transferability of interests.

M has associates and an objective to carry on business and divide the gains therefrom. In addition, M possesses the corporate characteristic of limited liability. M does not, however, possess the corporate characteristics of continuity of life, free transferability of interests, and centralized management.

Situation 2. N has associates and an objective to carry on business and divide the gains therefrom. Therefore, N must be classified as either an association or a partnership. N is classified as a partnership for federal tax purposes unless the organization has a preponderance of the remaining corporate characteristics of continuity of life, centralization of management, limited liability, and free transferability of interests.

Like M in Situation 1, N possesses the corporate characteristic of limited liability.

Section 301.7701-2(b)(1) of the regulations provides that an organization has continuity of life if the death, insanity, bankruptcy, retirement, resignation, or expulsion of any member will not cause a dissolution of the organization.

Under the Act, unless the business of N is continued by the consent of all of the remaining members or by a right to continue stated in the LLC agreement, N is dissolved upon the death, resignation, expulsion, bankruptcy, or dissolution of a member or the occurrence of any other event that terminates the continued membership of a member in the company. N's LLC agreement provides that N shall continue under all circumstances without the approval or consent of any member or manager. Consequently, N possesses the corporate characteristic of continuity of life.

Under the Act, an LLC may be managed either by an elected manager or managers or by its members. Under the LLC agreement, N is managed by its elected managers A, B and C; therefore, N possesses the corporate characteristic of centralized management.

Under the Act, a member of N can assign or transfer that member's interest to another person who is not a member of the organization. Moreover, under N's LLC agreement, an assignee of an interest in N becomes a substitute member and acquires all of the attributes of the member's interest in N by the assignee providing written notice to N. The approval or consent of any other member or manager is not required for the substitution to be effective. Therefore, N possesses the corporate characteristic of free transferability of interests.

N has associates and an objective to carry on business and divide the gains therefrom. In addition, N possesses the corporate characteristics of continuity of life, centralized management, limited liability, and free transferability of interests.

Holdings

The Delaware Limited Liability Company Act contains numerous provisions that can be modified by an LLC agreement; accordingly, depending on the provisions of the LLC agreement, a Delaware LLC can assume the characteristics either of a corporation or of a partnership for federal tax purposes. In the factual situations presented above:

(1) M has associates and an objective to carry on business and divide the gains therefrom but lacks a preponderance of the four remaining corporate characteristics. Accordingly, M is classified as a partnership for federal tax purposes.

(2) N has associates and an objective to carry on business and divide the gains therefrom and possesses all four of the remaining corporate characteristics. Accordingly, N is classified as an association for federal tax purposes.

C. CURRENT STATUS

Although called a "company," the LLC is an *unincorporated* form of business association formed under State (or D.C.) laws that are separate from state corporation laws. States have moved quickly to pass limited liability company acts, and the IRS has gracefully issued rulings on those acts. Some of the statutes are of a "bullet-proof" variety, meaning they assure a partnership result for an association validly formed under them. Others are broad enough that one can structure the entity so as more closely to resemble either a partnership or a corporation for federal income tax purposes. Moreover, the IRS is willing to issue rulings that classify entities as LLCs.

The various limited liability company acts diverge greatly in their details. For example, some permit a majority of the shareholders to reconstitute the company on the withdrawal of a shareholder; others require a unanimous approval. Some statutes, such as Delaware's,[1] permit mergers involving limited liability companies. Other statutes permit shareholders' agreements to control LLCs and permit disproportionate distributions.[2] One can expect state legislatures gradually to modify their limited liability statutes in light of the need to coordinate federal income tax statutes with the legal features of limited liability companies. For the time being, the coordination is partial and mysteries abound.

Authoritative pronouncements on the tax classification of LLCs (and guidelines for advance rulings) include Rev. Proc. 95-10, I.R.B. 1995-3 20 (Jan. 17, 1995).[3]

PRIV. LTR. RUL. 9029019
April 19, 1990

Dear [Taxpayer]:

This is in reply to your letter dated March 26, 1990, and prior correspondence, submitted on behalf of P, requesting rulings under sections 708 and 7701 of the Internal Revenue Code.

The information submitted states that P is a state of Z general partnership owned by individuals A, B, C, and D. The partnership began doing business in 1981, and currently operates four motels in the state of Z.

---

[1] Del. Code § 18-209.

[2] *See, e.g.*, Del. Code § 18-101(6) (shareholders' agreements) and Ga. Code § 14-11-404 (disproportionate distributions).

[3] *See* Wirtz & Harris, *Assessing the Long-Awaited LLC Classification Guidelines*, Taxes, Feb. 1995, p. 51.

P's partners propose to divide P into four state of Z general partnerships, Q, R, S and T. Subsequently, partnership R will be converted into a state of Z limited liability company and be known as X. The partners' proportionate interests in the Q, R, S and T partnerships and the limited liability company will be the same as their interests in P.

Section 708(a) of the Code provides that an existing partnership shall be considered as continuing if it is not terminated.

Section 708(b)(1) of the Code provides that a partnership shall be considered as terminated only if either (A) no part of any business, financial operation, or venture of the partnership continues to be carried on by any of its partners in a partnership, or (b) [sic] within a twelve-month period there is a sale or exchange of 50 percent or more of the total interest in partnership capital and profits.

Section 708(b)(2)(B) of the Code provides that in the case of a division of a partnership into two or more partnerships, the resulting partnerships (other than any resulting partnership the members of which had an interest of 50 percent or less in the capital and profits of the prior partnership) shall, for purposes of section 708, be considered a continuation of the prior partnership.

Section 1.708-1(b)(2)(ii) of the Income Tax Regulations provides, in part, that upon the division of a partnership into two or more partnerships, any resulting partnership or partnerships shall be considered a continuation of the prior partnership if its members had an interest of more than 50 percent in the capital and profits of the prior partnership.

In the transaction described above, all of P's partners will be the only partners of Q, R, S and T, and the partners will have the same percentage of ownership in Q, R, S and T as they had in P. Thus, members of P will own 100 percent of the capital and profits of Q, R, S and T. Accordingly, the division of P into four state of Z general partnerships will not cause a termination of P under section 708(b) of the Code.

Subsequent to the division of P into four state of Z general partnerships, R will convert to a state of Z limited liability company. After the conversion, it will be known as X.

X will have associates and an objective to carry on business and divide the gains therefrom. Section 301.7701-2(A)(2) of the Procedure and Administration Regulations. Therefore, in order to be classified as a partnership, X must lack at least two of the following corporate characteristics: continuity of life, centralization of management, limited liability, and free transferability of interests. Section 301.7701-2(a)(3) of the regulations.

Section 608.441 of the Act provides that a limited liability company shall be dissolved upon the death, retirement, resignation, expulsion, bankruptcy, or dissolution of a member or upon the occurrence of any other event which terminates the continued membership of a member in the limited liability company, unless the business of the limited liability company is continued by the consent of all the remaining members or under a right to continue stated in the articles of organization of the limited liability company. In this case, no right to

C. CURRRENT STATUS 633

continue the business of X upon a member ceasing to be a member of X is stated in the articles of organization or other documents submitted with the request apart from continuance of X's business upon the consent of all the remaining members. Therefore, if a member of X ceases to be a member of X for any reason, the continuity of X is not assured, because all remaining members must agree to continue the business. Consequently, X lacks the corporate characteristic of continuity of life. Section 301.7701-2(b) of the regulations.

Section 608.432 of the Act provides that an interest of a member in limited liability company may be transferred or assigned as provided in the operating agreement. However, if all of the other members of the limited liability company other than the member proposing to dispose of his or its interest do not approve of the proposed transfer or assignment by unanimous written consent, the transferee of the interest of the member shall have no right to participate in the management of the business and affairs of the limited liability company or to become a member. The transferee shall be entitled to receive only the share of profits or other compensation by way of income and the return of contributions to which that member otherwise would be entitled. Therefore, X lacks the corporate characteristic of free transferability of interests. Section 301.7701-2(e)(1) of the regulations.

X has associates and an objective to carry on business and divide the gains therefrom. In addition, X possesses the corporate characteristics of limited liability and centralized management. X does not, however, possess the corporate characteristics of continuity of life and free transferability of interests. Provided that X is organized and operated in accordance with the applicable state of Z statute pertaining to limited liability companies, X will be classified as a partnership for federal income tax purposes.

Section 721(a) of the Code provides that no gain or loss is recognized by a partnership or any of its partners upon the contribution of property to the partnership in exchange for an interest therein.

Rev. Rul. 84-52, 1984-1 C.B. 157, considers the federal income tax consequences of the conversion of a general partnership interest into a limited partnership interest in the same partnership. In Rev. Rul. 84-52, X was formed as a general partnership with equal partners A, B, C, and D. The partners propose to convert the general partnership into a limited partnership, with A and B as limited partners, and C and D as both general partners and limited partners. Each partner's total percent interest in the partnership's profits, losses, and capital will remain the same when the general partnership is converted into a limited partnership. The general partnership's business will continue after the conversion.

Rev. Rul. 84-52 treats the conversion as an exchange under section 721 of the Code and holds, in part, that because the business of X will continue after the conversion and because, under section 1.708-1(b)(1)(ii) of the regulations, a transaction governed by section 721 is not treated as a sale or exchange for purposes of section 708, X will not be terminated under section 708. Accordingly, the conversion of R from a state of Z general partnership into X, a state of Z limited liability company, will not result in a termination of R under section 708(b) of the Code.

Based on the information submitted we conclude:

(1) The division of P into four state of Z general partnerships, Q, R, S and T, will not cause a termination of P under section 708(b) of the Code.

(2) Provided that X is organized and operated in accordance with the applicable Z statute pertaining to limited liability companies, X will be classified as a partnership for federal income tax purposes. This conclusion is subject to the requirements set forth in Rev. Proc. 89-12, 1989-1 C.B. 798, and in particular subject to the condition that X continuously complies with the requirements set forth in sections 4.01 and 4.03 of Rev. Proc. 89-12. If the requirements of Rev. Proc. 89-12 fail to be met at any time, conclusion (2) will have no force or effect, retroactive to the date of its issuance.

(3) The conversion of R from a state of Z general partnership into X, a state of Z limited liability company, will not result in a termination of R under section 708(b) of the Code.

Except as specifically ruled upon above, no opinion is expressed concerning the federal income tax consequences of the transaction described above under any other provision of the Code.

A copy of this letter should be attached to the first tax return filed by the partnerships that participate in the transaction. A copy is enclosed for that purpose. This ruling is directed only to the taxpayer who requested it. Section 6110(j)(3) of the Code provides that it may not be used or cited as precedent.

In accordance with the power of attorney on file, we are forwarding a copy of this letter to P.

PROBLEM 26-1

Now, imagine for a moment that an accountant on the other end of the phone line tells you that she plans to have a client of yours form a corporation and make the S corporation election. You wish to point out some of the advantages of using the limited liability company approach. What particular benefits would you point out, in comparison to the S election?

D. SELECTED COMPLICATIONS

Coordinating the limited liability company acts and federal income tax laws, especially Subchapter K, is not easy.

1. What is the effect of changing the charter of an LLC which is presently taxed as a corporation in a way that makes it a partnership for federal income tax purposes?

2. Can a qualified income offset be installed in an LLC, and if so, how? How does one install a "minimum-gain chargeback provision"? If LLC liabilities are

E. POSSIBLE OPTIONAL CLASSIFICATION OF UNINCORPORATED ENTITIES

nonrecourse, this becomes an issue. This may be tied to the corporate law question of whether the Board of the LLC can differentiate among members when making distributions.

3. If there is to be a special allocation, in general each partner must have a duty to restore any deficit in his or her capital account after liquidation of the partnership or of the partnership interest. How does one accomplish this in an LLC, where the expectation is that there is no duty to make further contributions?

4. What would be the impact of a member of an LLC issuing a guarantee of an LLC debt?

E. POSSIBLE OPTIONAL FEDERAL INCOME TAX CLASSIFICATION OF UNINCORPORATED ENTITIES

Limited liability companies are becoming increasingly popular in the formation of new businesses, and some existing corporations or partnerships are converting to limited liability company status.[4] For the U.S. and foreign practitioner, the income tax and nontax characteristics of the limited liability company must carefully be compared with the general partnership, limited partnership, limited liability partnership (another new form, found only in a few states), corporation, S corporation, and proprietorship to determine which among the available forms will provide both tax and nontax optimal combinations.

In late Spring 1995, there emerged a fascinating new development in the modern history of Internal Revenue Service administration of the entity-classification rules and problem. This development certainly owes much to the development and proliferation of state limited liability company legislation and the fast-growing use of that, and the limited liability *partnership*, form of business association.

On March 29, 1995, the IRS announced that, rather than continuing to apply the current cumbersome classification rules for deciding whether an unincorporated business should be treated as a partnership or a corporation for tax purposes, it and the Treasury Department are considering a simplified process.[5] Under this approach, an *unincorporated* business would be required only to make an *election* regarding its tax status. This quickly was named a "check-the-box" system.

In the press release issued with the notice, IRS said that the "IRS and thousands of taxpayers spend considerable resources determining the classification of unincorporated business organizations under the current tax rules." The proposal would aid numerous unincorporated businesses that "cannot afford" to

---

[4] *See* D. Culpepper, *Tax Aspects of Limited Liability Companies*, 73 Or. L. Rev. 5 (1994); M. Goding, *Tax Aspects of Converting a Partnership or Corporation Into an Oregon Limited Liability Company*, 73 Or. L. Rev. 25 (1994).

[5] *See* Notice 95-14 1995-14 I.R.B., together with a press release designated IR-95-29, 8/29/95.

commit the financial resources needed to hire outside experts to cope with the current complexity. Incorporated businesses would not be eligible to make this election and would conclusively be subject to the corporate income tax (unless they made a Subchapter S election.)

After holding a July 20, 1995 hearing on the subject, the IRS and Treasury will decide whether to propose regulations to implement a simplified election by which an *unincorporated* business simply may choose to be treated either as a partnership or as an association taxable as a corporation for federal income tax purposes.

The IRS observed that the existing classification regulations are based on "historical differences under local law between partnerships and corporations." It added that many states have revised their statues — such as by enacting limited liability laws — to provide that partnerships and other unincorporated organizations may possess characteristics that have traditionally been associated with corporations. According to the notice, one consequence of the narrowing of the differences under state law between corporations and partnerships is that taxpayers can achieve partnership tax status for a non-publicly traded organization that is "indistinguishable from a corporation."

Treasury also said that the proposal would not have any revenue impact and went on to say that this simplification "should not have any appreciable effect on the corporate income tax base, since any taxpayer who is forming a new business venture who is not willing to pay corporate tax on any income from the venture is already able to avoid classification as a corporation under the current rules."

Under the proposal, taxpayers could elect to have any domestic unincorporated business treated as a partnership or an association taxable as a corporation, at the taxpayer's option, unless the organization's classification is determined under another Internal Revenue Code provision. For instance, an entity that is treated as a partnership, but which is publicly traded and is taxed as a corporation under I.R.C. § 7704, would continue to be taxed as a corporation.[6]

As for entities that do not make an election, the "default classification" would be for the entity to be treated as a partnership for federal income tax purposes. The Service and Treasury indicated that they believe "domestic unincorporated business organizations typically are formed to obtain partnership classification." All elections would be prospective from the date the election is filed; retroactive elections would not be permitted.

The IRS and Treasury are also considering simplifying the classification rules for *foreign organizations* in a manner consistent with the approach described for domestic organizations. However, several unique concerns arise in a foreign

---

[6] Under proposed regulations, the odds have increased that a business entity would become subject to the separate corporate tax because it is classified as a publicly-traded partnership under § 7704. *See* Notice 95-28, 1995-21 I.R.B. 9.

context, the IRS said, noting that there is no foreign entity analogous to a state-law corporation. "The Service and Treasury are considering the appropriateness and feasibility of identifying particular forms of foreign organizations that, like state-law corporations, would automatically be treated as corporations," the notice stated.

The IRS and Treasury also expressed concern about inconsistent treatment of an entity in a foreign context. Under such a scenario, a business could be treated as a taxable entity in one country, but as a flow-through entity under the tax laws of another country. Such a "hybrid" entity could prove very useful for sophisticated international tax planning.

If the IRS and Treasury decide that taxpayers may elect to classify their status, consideration must be given to the classification of foreign organizations that do not make the election. While domestic unincorporated organizations are typically formed to obtain partnership classification, the desired classification of foreign organizations is likely to be less uniform. Nonetheless, Treasury said that it believes that it would be appropriate to treat a foreign organization that fails to make an election as an association (taxable as a corporation), the opposite of the default rule for domestic, U.S. organizations. The reason given was that "this rule would avoid inadvertently subjecting taxpayers to the partnership compliance rules and excise tax provisions and is likely in many circumstances to coincide with taxpayers' desired classification," the notice stated.[7]

Congress may choose to examine the issue, if the IRS and Treasury decide to move ahead with the proposal. Rather than leaving the matter up to the Executive Branch, Congress may decide that the proposal seriously implicates integration of the corporate and income tax systems. For that reason, it might choose to take up the proposal, or integration itself, as a legislative matter.

The IRS and Treasury asked interested parties to comment on a variety of specific questions relating to domestic and foreign entities.

OUTSIDE READINGS

S. Kalinka, *The Limited Liability Company and Subchapter S: Classification Issues Revisited*, 60 U. Cin. L. Rev. 1083 (1992).

J. Kurtz, *The Limited Liablity Company and the Future of Business Taxation: A Comment on Professor Berger's Plan*, 47 Tax L. Rev. 815 (1992).

B. Wolfman, *Self-Help Integration (LLCs) or Otherwise*, 62 Tax Notes 769 (1994).

---

[7] Reg. § 301.7701-2 has been used to classify entities formed under the laws of a foreign country, and all foreign entities are considered to be "unincorporated organizations" under the corporate resemblance test for association status. *See* Rev. Rul. 88-8, 1988-1 C.B. 403; Rev. Rul. 93-4, 1993-1 C.B. 225.

Chapter 27
TAX POLICY: ISSUES IN THE TAXATION OF CORPORATIONS AND OTHER BUSINESS ENTITIES

There are significant and pressing corporate income tax issues on the tax policy agenda of the United States in the coming years. We still have a "classical," unintegrated corporate income tax and individual income system. It produces the so-called double taxation of distributed corporate earnings and incentives to avoid such over-taxation by choice of business firm, capital structure, distribution or retention policy and other tax-planning techniques. Most of the industrialized countries of the world, in Western Europe, East Asia, Australia, and New Zealand have reformed their income tax systems to remove or ameliorate this unintegrated structure and these problems. Important persons and institutions have recommended that the U.S. adapt similar reforms, but nothing has happened in Congress. The result is probably economic and fiscal inefficiency, unfairness as between taxpayers and overall loss of welfare.

Solving, or even evaluating, these problems involves thinking about the evidence and economic effects of the corporate income tax.

The following text introduces these and related issues for the noneconomist law student or policy analyst. It is taken, almost without change, from an article by one of the authors of this coursebook.*

A. THE PROBLEM OF CORPORATE AND INDIVIDUAL INCOME TAX

There has long been controversy in the United States and abroad over the method of taxation of corporate earnings.[1] The controversy has centered on the

---

*J.K. McNulty, *Corporate Income Tax Reform in the United States: Proposals for Integration of the Corporate and Individual Income Taxes, and International Aspects*, 12 INT'L TAX & BUS. LAW., 161-259 (1994), pp. 170-217. This material, somewhat modified, is reprinted here with permission. Its footnotes contain references to other readings on these subjects.

[1] *See* Charles E. McLure, Must Corporate Income Be Taxed Twice? (1979); Joseph A. Pechman, Federal Tax Policy (5th ed. 1987); U.S. Dep't of the Treasury, Vol.2 Tax Reform for Fairness, Simplicity, and Economic Growth — The Treasury Department Report to the President (1984) (hereinafter Treasury I); U.S. Dep't of the Treasury, Blueprints for Basic Tax Reform 68-75 (1977) (hereinafter Treasury Blueprints]; Alvin Warren, *The Relation and Integration of Individual and Corporate Income Taxes*, 94 Harv. L. Rev. 719 (1981); John K. McNulty, *Integrating the Corporate Tax?*, 31 Am. J. Corp. Law 661 (1983) (hereinafter McNulty, *Integrating?*); John K. McNulty, *Reform of the Individual Income Tax by Integration of the Corporate Income Tax*, 46 Tax Notes 1445 (1990) *reprinted* (in Japanese) *in* 63 Keio Hogaku-Kenku (Journal of Law, Politics, and Sociology) No. 12 at 373-400 (1991) (hereinafter McNulty, *Reform by Integration*).

alleged "double taxation" of corporate profits, in that the profits are taxed when earned by the corporation and "taxed again" when distributed in the form of dividends to the owners of the corporation, the shareholders. The question is whether there is sufficient justification for this "double taxation"?[2]

In 1954, the United States Congress provided a partial (4%) shareholder credit against tax and a $100 dollar annual exclusion from income for dividends in an effort to meet in part the "double taxation" argument.[3] The little credit, however, was repealed effective as to dividends received after December 31, 1964.[4] The small exclusion of dividends was repealed in 1986. (It could hardly have been said to have any substantial effect on the problem of "double taxation.")

The 1984, U.S. Treasury Proposals called for partial elimination of the second level of tax on distributed earnings by a deduction (allowable to the corporation) for 50% of earnings distributed to shareholders,[5] a proposal that was scaled down (in 1985) to 10%,[6] and never enacted into law.[7] A corporate-level deduction for dividends paid resembles, of course, the treatment of interest paid by a corporation to creditors.

Consider the familiar structure of the tax on corporate income in the United States. A corporation, a domestic one or a foreign one, is generally treated by U.S. income tax law as a separate entity, a separate taxpayer. So are the individual shareholders of the corporation. Both are subject to the general income tax.

If a corporation earns $100, it must pay tax of up to $35 (the top corporate rate for most purposes). When it wants to pay a dividend, a distribution of profits, to its investors, it consequently has only $65 left after taxes. If it distributes the $65 as a dividend, those shareholders who receive the payment are

---

[2] For a basic study of the economic effects of the corporate income taxes, see Richard Goode, The Corporation Income Tax (1951); J. Gregory Ballentine, Equity Efficiency and the United States Corporation Income Tax (1980); Gary Fromm & Paul Taubman, Public Economic Theory and Policy 89-139 (1973); Arnold C. Harberger, *Corporation Income Taxes*, 15 Int'l Encycl. Soc. Sci. 538 (1968); Pechman, *supra* note 1, at 179-88. For a recent, new proposal for Great Britain, see Capital Taxes Group, Institute for Fiscal Studies, Setting Savings Free (1994).

[3] I.R.C. §§ 34, 116 (1954).

[4] Pub. L. 99-514 § 612(a), 100 Stat. 2250 (1964).

[5] Treasury I, *supra* note 1, at 136.

[6] The President's Proposals to the Congress for Fairness, Growth, and Simplicity 122 (1985) (hereinafter Treasury II).

[7] Bittker & Eustice, Federal Income Taxation of Corporations and Shareholders (5th ed.), ¶ 1.08; see Kevin Buchanan, *The Dividend Paid Deduction Proposal: Separating Myth From Reality*, 28 Tax Notes 97 (1985); Karla W. Simon, *Comments on the Dividends Paid Deduction of H.R. 3838*, 31 Tax Notes 609 (1986).

In 1977, the U.S. Treasury Department recommended complete integration by direct attribution of corporate income to shareholders but admitted that there would be "potential administrative problems with this approach." Treasury Blueprints, *supra* note 2, at 69-75.

A. THE PROBLEM OF CORPORATE AND INDIVIDUAL INCOME TAX

taxed on their dividend income of $65, at a top normal rate of, let us say, 36% (rather than the very top or surtax rate of 39.6%).[8] So their tax will total $23.40. As a result of tax at the corporate level at a maximum rate of 35% on $100 and a shareholder income tax of 36% of the $65 dividend, a total tax of $58.40 will have been paid on $100 of distributed corporate income. That rate is 22.4 percentage points higher than the top rate the law usually applies to an individual's income of $100 ($36 or 36%). It is more than the top *corporate* rate (of 35%) by 23.4 percentage points. This is simply the consequence of a classical, unintegrated system of corporate and individual income taxation.

In contrast, if the $100 were earned by a partnership or proprietorship or limited liability company in the United States the total tax burden would be much lower. A partnership or limited liability company is *not* treated as a separate taxpayer by U.S. income tax law.[9] Its income is not taxed to the partnership, but is passed through to the partners. So, $100 of partnership income will be taxed once, at up to the 36% (or even 39.6%) rate, to the partners (whether or not the income is distributed to them). This is much lower than the 58.40% rate that applies to distributed corporate income (35% plus 23.40%). It is little more than the corporate rate on undistributed, retained corporate earnings (35%).

Similarly, if an individual proprietor or investor received $100 income directly, he or she would pay just 36% in tax, assuming the $100 were taxable at the usual top rate.

Why does the United States tax distributed *corporate* profits so much more heavily? Is it because the situation resembles that of an employer who earns $100, pays tax of $36, then pays his employee the remaining $64, in which event the employee is taxed (again) on the $64 wages at 36%? This cannot be the answer because, if the employee's wages are a cost of the business or profit-seeking activity, the employer can deduct the wages from his income. The deduction of $100 paid in wages leaves the employer with no tax liability to pay on the income from which the wages are paid out. The income is taxed once, to the employee, at a 36% rate.

Should not the corporation be allowed to deduct its dividend? Isn't the dividend a cost of capital or of funds used in the business? In fact, if the corporation has borrowed its funds and paid $100 of its income as interest to a creditor such as a bank, or even to a shareholder who lent funds to the corporation in an arms-length loan transaction, the corporation would be allowed to deduct the interest.[10] So, the $100 income of the corporation that it used to

---

[8] A top 39.6% rate applies to the very highest range. I.R.C. § 1.

[9] So long as it is not one of the new breed of "publicly-traded partnerships," as defined in I.R.C. § 7704, enacted in 1987, in which event it is taxed as a corporation. Bittker & Eustice, Federal Income Taxation of Corporations and Shareholders, ¶ 1.07.

[10] I.R.C. §§ 163, 162, 212.

pay the cost of borrowed funds would be taxed only once, to the lender, at that taxpayer's normal rate.

But the corporation cannot, under U.S. law, deduct its dividend payments. So, business planners often avoid the corporate form and, for tax reasons, use the sometimes less desirable partnership or limited liability company form.[11] Or, if a corporation is formed, it may borrow most of its capital, so as to pay interest, which is deductible, rather than dividends, which are not deductible, as a cost of its capital. This incentive causes the problem of "thin capitalization." Or, a corporation may refrain from distributing any dividends in order to save or postpone the second (shareholder) income tax. Also, U.S. corporations seek ways to make non-dividend distributions so as to avoid either the corporate-level or shareholder-level tax; they attempt to use stock redemptions, liquidations, stock sales or other transactions (including excessive compensation) to get assets out of corporate solution without a dividend tax.[12] Some U.S. corporations have recapitalized with increased debt or have used leveraged buyouts (or have been acquired in such transactions), in effect substituting debt for equity and thereby "eroding the corporate tax base."[13]

The U.S. income tax law treats the corporation that pays dividends like the employer who earns $100, pays $36 in tax, and then pays $64 in wages to a *personal* employee, a nonbusiness employee such as his gardener or barber or housekeeper. No deduction is allowed for such wages because they are a personal, consumption expenditure. And, the wages are taxed again to the employee, as wage income to him.

This result does not make sense when applied to corporate dividends. It discriminates between equity and debt capital, between corporations and partnerships, and between retained and distributed earnings. It "overtaxes" $100 of corporate income earned by low-income or tax-exempt shareholders by $35. It overtaxes the income of even a rich, high-income shareholder by $22.40. It leads to excessive corporate borrowing, undue retention of corporate profits for expansion, avoidance or deferral of shareholder tax, or to attempts to convert the income to capital gains (if and when a special, lower rate applies to capital gains)

---

[11] For eligible corporations having no more than 35 shareholders, it may be possible to elect S-corporation status, which means a single tax regime even on distributed corporate profits much as with a partnership, for Federal (and sometimes also for state) income tax purposes. *See id.* §§ 1361-1379; McNulty, Federal Income Taxation of S Corporations (1992); John K. McNulty, *Subchapter S and S Corporations*, in 2 Corporate Taxation §§ 10.01-.110 (James T. O'Hara et. al. eds., 1992) (hereinafter McNulty, *S Corporations*). As to the recently developed limited liability company form, see Ch. 26 of this book.

[12] *See* American Law Institute, Federal Income Tax Project, Subchapter C, Proposals of the American Law Institute on Corporate Acquisitions and Dispositions and Reporter's Study on Corporate Distributions, app. at 341-55 (1982) (hereinafter A.L.I., Subchapter C Study).

[13] American Law Institute, Federal Income Tax Project, Reporter's Study Draft — Subchapter C (Supplemental Study), 4-38 (1989) (hereinafter A.L.I., Reporter's Draft).

or to untaxed income under the fresh-start basis at death rule.[14] It also produces costly and inefficient under-investment in the corporate sector of the United States' economy.

Often, it is said that the United States has a classical, unintegrated system of corporate taxation.[15] More correctly put, the United States has that system plus an elective, complete, pass-through integration system for U.S. owned, single-class stock companies with thirty-five or fewer individual shareholders, or for limited liability companies.[16] Furthermore, the "corporate," second tax is imposed on publicly-traded limited partnerships, and on other noncorporate entities that resemble a corporation.[17]

Why does the United States have, and retain, this unintegrated tax regime?

B. CORPORATE TAX INCIDENCE

The U.S. separate corporate income tax probably is based on the (mistaken) notion that corporations are legal persons or aggregations of capital that can, do, and should pay taxes and bear tax burdens. That is a false idea, economists tell us.[18] Only humans bear taxes. Corporations do not. Only humans can consume, so only consumption by humans can be reduced by taxes. Corporations don't eat or drink, so tax burdens can't force them to eat or drink less. Corporations as such don't bear taxes and should not be taxed and cannot be taxed. Some humans must bear the corporate income tax. Who are they? The point is one of the incidence of the corporate income tax.

Traditional economic analysis concludes that no shifting occurs in the short run. Presumably, a rationally managed corporation will operate to maximize profits in an economy with no corporate income tax. At such a production level, the cost of producing an additional item (marginal cost) will just equal the additional revenue gained from selling that item (marginal revenue). The enactment of the tax should have no effect on the output of the already profit-maximizing firm. At each level of output, the amount of profit will be reduced by the same percentage, the corporate tax rate. Therefore, the output point of maximum profit will remain the same after the tax is imposed. To increase production would mean increasing marginal costs past marginal revenue, regardless of the tax. To decrease production would mean reducing profits, again regardless of the tax's effects. Furthermore, any pricing change (movement along

---

[14] I.R.C. § 1014.

[15] See, e.g., Malcolm Gammie, *Reforming Corporate Taxation: An Evaluation of the United States Treasury Integration Proposals and other Corporate Tax Systems in an International Context* (pts. 1 & 2), 1992 Brit. Tax Rev. 148, 243.

[16] See I.R.C. §§ 1361-1379.

[17] Id. §§ 7701(a)(3), 7704(a); Bittker & Eustice, *supra* note 7, ¶¶ 2.01-.06.

[18] See, e.g., McLure, *supra* 1, at 20; Ballentine, *supra* note ?, at 5-7; The Taxation of Income from Capital (Arnold C. Harberger & Martin J. Bailey eds., 1969).

the demand curve) would also presumably decrease profits. Therefore, the introduction of a corporate income tax will produce no change in production or pricing. In the short run, the corporation itself, and thus its shareholders, will bear the burden of any corporate income tax — according to the traditional analysis.

One school of thought, personified by Harberger, essentially agrees with this approach but adds a new dimension. *See* Arnold Harberger, *The Incidence of the Corporate Income Tax,* 70 J. Pol. Econ. 215 (1962). He asserts that there will be an absorption of the tax by the capital investors in the now-taxed corporate sector, or at least in its equity-financed portion.

In the longer run, Harberger's analysis continues, the necessary result of the imposition of a corporate income tax will be to shift capital away from the corporate sector, at least from the equity-intense corporate area. His view focuses on the rate of return to capital as the parameter by which to measure the effect of the incidence of a new corporate tax. Accordingly, Harberger contends that the elasticity of supply factors, that is, the substitutability of labor for capital, will heavily influence the future production in a newly-taxed field. Harberger's analysis implies an inefficient and artificial reallocation of resource capital from highly productive (efficient) investment to less productive (inefficient) investment. The result is an underallocation of investment in corporate equities and a loss in efficient production.

Another school, represented by Krzyzaniak and Musgrave, disagrees. *See, e.g.,* Marian Krzyzaniak & Richard A. Musgrave, Shifting of the Corporation Income Tax, An Empirical Study of Its Short Run Effect Upon the Rate of Return (1963). Beginning with the same traditional economic analytical framework, Krzyzaniak and Musgrave take a different path at the fork. They conclude that there is a short-run shifting of the burden of a corporate tax — to consumers. First, Krzyzaniak and Musgrave feel that many corporate enterprises do not presently maximize profits, whether to deter competition by not appearing overly prosperous or out of satisfaction with an already healthy rate of return. Those firms, desiring to maintain their previous profits, will, after the imposition of a tax, more actively engage in profit maximization than before. Once satisfied with their pricing because their rate of return was sufficient, such firms may find themselves needing more income for the same rate of return. Prices will rise. Furthermore, those firms that had not been exercising all the market muscle they had, those with monopolistic or oligopolistic control, will exercise a bit more of their market power to raise prices. Additional firms may be able to raise prices due to imperfect competition. Pricing, formerly regarded as optimal, may be reexamined, Krzyzaniak and Musgrave put stress on practical exceptions to the general rules of neo-classical economic *analysis.*

Goode sides with Harberger and adds to his analysis the contention that all prices will rise as a result of the corporate tax. The prices in taxed areas will rise, if a rate of return is to be maintained, and prices in nontaxed areas will rise as a result of the inflationary tendencies brought about by the price rises in the

B. CORPORATE TAX INCIDENCE

taxed areas. Richard Goode, *Who Bears the Corporation Income Tax?*, 1964-65 U. Chi. L. Rev. 410.

That corporations and capital investors bear some of the brunt of the tax burden seems likely; that consumers bear part of it also seems probable. Labor also may not escape unscathed. Frequently, labor union contracts are tied to, or at least affected by, after-tax profits. If these are decreased by a corporate income tax, labor may carry some of the tax burden as well.

This incidence question has troubled many economists, even after the meaning of the term "burden" in the question has been determined (no easy task).

Even if the justification for the U.S. corporate income tax is based on the idea that the shareholders bear the corporate tax, it does not make sense that they are taxed at much more than the maximum rate the law generally says individual taxpayers should pay on their income, namely 36%. There is no good reason why the effective rate of 58.40% applies to an individual's income from the corporate sector and 36% on all his other income.

Perhaps the U.S. Congress (or the public) thinks all shareholders are very rich people who should be taxed at especially high rates. Yet, statistics show that, in the United States, many corporate shares are held by, or on behalf of, low or middle-income persons or tax-exempt institutions such as charities or pension funds. They should not be taxed at extra high rates. And as to rich, high-income shareholders, there is no policy reason given why should they be taxed at 58.40% or more on only their income from investment in dividend-paying corporations, and not on their interest income, rents, wages, royalties, or capital gains. At best, this is a very crude and inefficient effort at enhancing progressivity.

Arguably, all U.S. corporations should be treated like partnerships, their income (or loss) passed through to shareholders, to be taken into account just like any other income in their individual income tax returns? (Or, should all partnerships and proprietorships be made taxable like corporations?[19])

To sum it up, economists *do not* convincingly tell us who actually pays the corporate income tax. It may not be shareholders at all but employees of corporations through lower wages. Or the corporate tax may be passed on to consumers of corporate products in the form of higher prices. Possibly, in the long run, the tax may be borne by all holders of capital in the economy, not just by those having capital invested in corporations. The economists do not agree or give us a definite answer.[20]

---

[19] Some "publicly-traded partnerships" in the United States are taxable as corporations. I.R.C. § 7704.

[20] *See generally* Ballentine, *supra* note ?; William A. Klein, *The Incidence of the Corporation Income Tax: A Lawyer's View of a Problem in Economics*, 1965 Wis. L. Rev. 576; Pechman, *supra* note 2, at 141-46.

C. POSSIBLE JUSTIFICATIONS FOR A SEPARATE CORPORATE INCOME TAX

Just as the question has been asked in other countries in recent years, we ask why the United States should retain a separate corporate income tax, if no one knows who bears it and if it over-taxes shareholders (if they do bear it), or becomes an erratic or arbitrary sales tax or payroll tax (in only the corporate sector) if it is shifted; and if it biases investment, financial structures, and distribution policy; or, if it taxes income from all capital, when the United States needs to encourage saving and investment?

One answer is simple: it produces revenue. And it produces revenue from an ultimately uncertain or unidentifiable source, so there is no self-aware, heavily-burdened person to complain about the legislators who enact it or who raise its rates. (Paradoxically, Congress lowered the top corporate rate from 46% to 34% in 1986 but raised it in 1993 by one point to 35%.)

In fact, the revenue from the U.S. corporate tax has been shrinking, as a result of lower rates and investment allowances such as the investment tax credit (now repealed) and accelerated depreciation. Also, debt finance and retention of earnings have contributed to the decline in revenue from the "double tax" system for distributed corporate profits. The deduction for interest has led to highly leveraged buy-outs of corporations, which shrink the base of the corporate income tax.[21] More corporations, if eligible, elect S corporation (conduit) treatment, to avoid higher rates and/or the double tax. New businesses often are formed as limited-liability companies, taxable as pass-through partnerships.

Another purpose served by the separate, entity-level corporate income tax is, in the international arena, to enable the country of residence or incorporation of a corporation to capture revenue from its enterprise when it is neither the country of source of the income nor the country of residence of the shareholders. For example, if a United States corporation is owned by foreign shareholders in Country X and it has income from sources only in Country Y, the United States nevertheless taxes the income of the corporation because it is a United States entity, as determined by the place of incorporation.[22] Not only that, the United States applies an income tax to the foreign shareholders on their dividends from this corporation, collected by a flat-rate withholding tax that the company must

---

[21] See Michael J. Graetz, *The Tax Aspects of Leveraged Buyouts and Other Corporate Financial Restructuring Transactions*, 42 Tax Notes 721, 721-22 (1989); Robert A. Jacobs & Rebecca S. Rudnick, *ABA Tax Section Task Force Looks at Passthrough Entities*, 42 Tax Notes 607 (1989); but see Michael C. Jensen et al., *Effects of LBOs on Tax Revenues of the United States' Treasury*, 42 Tax Notes 727 (1989) ("LBOs" refers to leveraged buy-outs).

[22] See Gammie, *supra* note 15. Even if it is the country of source and can tax corporate distributions of dividends or interest, it cannot reach capital gains realized by nonresident shareholders; the corporate level tax helps get at profits that otherwise could be taken off shore. *Id* at 167.

remit to the United States Treasury.[23] The United States asserts "jurisdiction" to tax the corporation's income even though the economic source of the income lies entirely outside United States borders. The artificial legal entity interposed between the source and the owners is a United States entity — whether or not any material benefits are received from such status. And the United States imposes income tax on the shareholders who receive a distribution of profits (or upon a foreign lender who receives an interest payment) from the corporation, regardless of the foreign location of the investor and the absence of economic activities within the United States.

Another good reason for retaining a separate corporate income tax is so that the law can use it to control corporate financial and economic behavior — by creating exceptions, allowances, rate differentials, and penalty provisions in the tax. And, the corporate income tax exerts some macroeconomic control and anti-cyclical influence. With progressive rates the corporate tax, like an individual income tax with graduated rates, soaks up more of profits in inflationary or profitable times and leaves more profits in private hands during a depression or recession.

D. INTEGRATING THE CORPORATE AND INDIVIDUAL INCOME TAXES: POSSIBLE TECHNIQUES

If it is desirable to leave the corporate income tax in place in the United States, what can be done to improve the situation?[24] Of course, the "double tax" aspect could be removed by eliminating the corporate tax entirely and taxing dividends when they are distributed to shareholders. Thus there would not be any tax imposed on corporate earnings until and unless distributed. But that would not only decrease or defer revenue, it would also permit investors to delay individual tax indefinitely by causing their corporations to retain profits, an intolerable unfairness. And it would forego the regulatory and stabilization functions of the corporate-level tax.

Instead, the individual tax on dividends could be abolished, at least to the extent tax had been borne at the corporate level, leaving only the corporate tax in effect.[25] (In fact, the United States had a very small dividends-received exclusion in its law at one time, but the exclusion was limited to just $100 per person, a tiny tax relief designed for small investors.)[26] However, corporate

---

[23] I.R.C. § 871.

[24] *See* John K. McNulty, *The United States' Individual and Corporate Income Tax: Future Reform Possibilities*, 1 Bond L. Rev. 52, 67-72 (1989) (Austl.), from which some parts of this section are taken (hereinafter McNulty, *Future Reform*).

[25] *See* Victor Thuronyi, *Tax Reform for 1989 and Beyond*, 42 Tax Notes 981, 984-85 (1989). Such a system is in place in Columbia, where dividends are exempt to the extent of 7/3 of the (30%) corporate tax paid. *Id.* at 985 n.8.

[26] *See* I.R.C. § 116 (1954).

taxation and complete dividend exclusion usually would mean taxing the income once but at the "wrong" rate. For example, the low-income or tax-exempt shareholder's share of corporate earnings would be taxed at 35% (if the top corporate rate applied), the same rate as that applied to the rich shareholder's share of corporate earnings. What rate actually applied would depend on the aggregate *corporate* income, not the total income of each shareholder. The rate would not systematically correspond to the income or ability to pay of the individuals who would actually bear the tax. The rates would be erratic and arbitrary. When corporate income tax rates are much lower or higher than individual income tax rates, this effect would become accentuated.

Alternatively, perhaps dividends should be deductible, like interest payments, by the corporation. This would make distributed corporate earnings taxable at the "correct" rate, that of each shareholder. But, while this approach would counteract the present debt/equity bias, it might induce corporate managers to "overdistribute" corporate earnings so as to get the largest deduction, please shareholders, and show maximum after-tax income. Retained profits, after all, would attract and "bear" the corporate tax. And they would continue to be taxed at the fixed corporate rate until they were distributed. A deduction for some (50% or 10%), or all, dividends paid has been recommended by the U.S. Treasury Department (in 1984) and other prominent sources in the United States (in 1989), but has never been enacted.[27]

There can occur a kind of "back-door integration" if capital gains on sales of stock are wholly or partially exempt from income tax. In the United States, capital gains realized upon the sale or exchange of stock in a corporation are in principle taxable as part of a shareholder's gross income, even if — in some years, particularly before 1986 — the rate of tax was reduced by deduction of some part of the gain. Presently, rate relief is provided by the 28% ceiling or maximum rate imposed under I.R.C. § 1(h) for individuals or the 35% ceiling of I.R.C. § 1201 (for corporations).

In some instances, however, the gain on sale or exchange of shares is exempted, wholly or partially, by a fresh-start basis rule, such as that of § 1014 (basis of property acquired from a decedent) or by an exclusion as in new § 1202 (50% of exclusion for gains from certain small business stock). Such a complete or partial exclusion provides "back-door integration" of the corporate and individual income tax in that corporate profits retained and having borne only the corporate-level tax are not taxed (to the extent of the exclusion) to the shareholder or his or her successor, when realized upon sale of the shares or redemption.

---

[27] *See supra* notes 5 and 6. The House of Representatives, in 1985, passed a partial deduction for dividends to be phased in, but the bill did not become law. *See* H.R. 3838, 99th Cong., 2d Sess. § 311 (1985); Bittker & Eustice, *supra* note 7, ¶ 1.08 n.76. A dividend deduction and a reduced rate of corporate tax for *distributed* corporate earnings (a split-rate system) are essentially equivalent.

D. INCORPORATING THE CORPORATE AND INDIVIDUAL INCOME TAXES 649

The buyer of the shares takes a cost basis in them and can liquidate or return the shares, or resell them, without further tax due to his or her high basis.

In other countries, capital gains upon the sale of stock are not taxed at all by the income tax, sometimes on the view that they do not constitute "income." Whatever the rationale, the exemption of such capital gain relieves the shareholder investor of the second level of tax, in a way paralleling an explicit integration mechanism such as a dividend exclusion. The higher the rate of individual income tax applicable to dividends, in relationship to the rate of tax on corporate earnings to the entity, the greater the savings, since it is the individual-level tax that this "back-door" integration relieves.

Another solution is the partnership or transparency method. This means taxing shareholders on corporate income, whether or not it is distributed, and not imposing any entity-level or corporate tax. This method actually is in use in the United States, on an elective basis, for corporations having no more than thirty-five shareholders. A regular corporation that is eligible can elect this treatment, under Subchapter S of the Internal Revenue Code, and become taxable as an "S corporation."[28]

This election for a small corporation to be taxed almost exactly the same as a partnership has worked very well. It gives small businesses the opportunity to combine the non-tax advantages of using a corporation (including limited liability) and the income tax advantages of a partnership, which avoids the double layer of corporate and shareholder taxes on distributed earnings.

Subchapter S could serve as a model for mandatory partnership tax treatment of small corporations, or for elective or mandatory treatment for large corporations in the United States.[29] For years when individual tax rates stood much

---

[28] *See* I.R.C. §§ 1361-1379 (Subchapter S). The U.S. Treasury Department in 1977 recommended that "the effect of subchapter S Corporation treatment... be extended to all corporations." Treasury Blueprints, *supra* note 1, at 69. Nothing came of this recommendation.

[29] *See* Kragen & McNulty, Federal Income Taxation (1985) at 995-1012, 1241-58 (1985); Thuronyi, *supra* note 25, at 984. The United States already has experience with mandatory transparency systems in the international arena. For controlled foreign corporations with "tainted" foreign income (§§ 951-964), and foreign personal holding companies (§§ 551-558), undistributed corporate income is taxable to controlling U.S. shareholders as constructive or "deemed" dividends. The U.S. international tax system also contains some *elective* or partly elective transparency systems, as with foreign investment companies (§§ 1246-1247), passive foreign investment companies (§§ 1291-1297) and domestic international sales corporations (DISCs) (§§ 991-994). The Foreign Sales Corporation (FSC) legislation (§§ 921-927) includes, in contrast, an exemption from U.S. tax for part of a FSC's foreign trade income and qualification for a 100% dividend received deduction when the FSC's parent receives a dividend distribution from the FSC.

Some authors recommend integration only for small or non-publicly traded corporations, to be taxed on a flow-through method or by excluding dividends from such companies if full corporate tax had been paid. *See, e.g.,* Thuronyi, *supra* note 25, at 984. They would repeal the corporate tax for publicly-traded corporations and would tax shareholders annually on any increase in value of their shares. Others would argue that, while integration makes sense for small, closely-held corporations, in a flat-tax world publicly-held corporations should pay the extra corporate income

above corporate rates, such transparency or partnership style taxation of shareholders would actually have increased tax revenues. However, in the case of large corporations many new complications and difficulties would be encountered, such as how to attribute corporate earnings to shareholders in complicated capital structures that include preferred stock, participating debentures, etc., or with affiliated corporate groups, or if tax audit adjustments must be made for prior years, or if shareholders bought and sold shares during the year. It is not entirely clear whether these problems can be solved satisfactorily in the United States. And, the partnership or Subchapter S method would create a liquidity problem; shareholders would request or demand actual distribution of corporate earnings in order to have funds with which to pay the tax. This makes the partnership method unattractive to corporate managers who want to retain earnings for expansion, and it worries economists who want the tax system to be neutral with respect to dividend distribution policies.

Probably a better solution for large corporations, or perhaps for all corporations, would be a shareholder imputation credit approach, perhaps along the lines of the system recently adopted in New Zealand or Australia. This method of integrating the corporate income tax with the individual income tax has been used, in one form or extent or another, not only in Australia, but also in parts of Asia, much of Europe, and elsewhere, and has been recommended in the United States.[30]

Under this method, familiar by now, U.S. corporate income tax would be collected on corporate income. When and if the after-tax corporate profits were distributed to shareholders, they would be taxable on the amount of the distribution, "grossed-up" by the amount of corporate tax paid, and they would be allowed to credit the corporate tax paid against their individual tax liability on "qualifying dividends."[31]

So the entire corporate earnings, say $100, would be imputed to the shareholders when the after-tax distribution, say $65 ($100 minus $35 corporate tax), was made. They then could credit the previously-paid corporate tax ($35) against their individual income tax liability. They would have to pay any balance

---

tax, without integration, because the demand for liquidity, which characterizes investment in them, is inelastic and hence the higher tax burden will not distort economic choices or allocations. *See, e.g.*, Rebecca S. Rudnick, *Corporate Tax Integration: Liquidity of Investment*, 42 Tax Notes 1107 (1989); *cf.* Gammie, *supra* note 15 (discussing a proposal to retain a separate corporate tax on the above-normal return on corporate equity but to allow a deduction for the "normal" imputed cost of equity capital).

[30] Somewhat similar imputation credit integration plans have been proposed in the United States, by the Treasury Department, by Congressman Al Ullman (former Chairman of the House Ways and Means Committee) and by scholars including economists and lawyers. McLure, *supra* note ?, at 143-50; *see* McNulty, *Integrating?*, *supra* note 1; Kragen & McNulty, *supra* note 29, at 1241-58; Warren, *supra* note 1; Alvin C. Warren, Jr., *Recent Corporate Restructuring and the Corporate Tax System*, 42 Tax Notes 715, 719 (1989).

[31] This system would track the post-1987 Australian system.

D. INCORPORATING THE CORPORATE AND INDIVIDUAL INCOME TAXES 651

owing or possibly get a refund if their shareholder credit (e.g., $35) exceeded their shareholder tax (e.g., $28).

Their creditable amount could be geared to the amount of corporate tax paid on the earnings out of which the dividend was paid, lest untaxed or tax-preference income carry too much credit relief to shareholders. (The system, in a way, would resemble the indirect foreign tax credit given in the United States to a U.S. corporate shareholder which receives dividends from a foreign subsidiary out of foreign earnings on which a foreign tax was paid by the subsidiary.)[32]

When top individual income tax rates in the United States were 91% or 70% (1940s-1960s), and corporate tax rates were 52% or 46%, this difference in rates would have discouraged actual dividend distributions by a corporation even if a shareholder imputation and credit system had been in effect, since distribution to relatively high-bracket investors would have caused a second tax much higher than the credit allowed for the corporate tax paid earlier.

The 1986 Tax Reform Act (temporarily) established a new rate relationship between top (or usual) corporate tax rates and top (or usual) individual rates in the United States. Between 1986 and 1993, with the U.S. top corporate rate higher (34%) than the usual top individual rate (28% or even 33%, with the 5% surtax to phase out exemptions and lower brackets) for the first time in U.S. history, a credit for corporate tax would not only have equalled, but would usually have exceeded, U.S. individual tax. So, shareholders would have been happy to receive dividends that were taxable at 28% to them but would give them a 34% tax credit, and hence a $6 refund (or an excess credit of $6 that could offset tax on their other income). Many of them would actually have preferred to invest in corporations that paid out all their profits each year as taxable dividends, or would have put pressure on their corporations to distribute all of their after-tax profits. As a consequence of an imputation credit that often would have *exceeded* shareholder tax, U.S. tax law would then have become biased *against* retention of earnings by a corporation.

One solution to this problem of a tax bias of a shareholder credit system in favor of actual distributions would be to give each corporation a right to elect to allocate, or attribute, its earnings to its shareholders, even if it did not actually distribute them to shareholders. Allocated earnings would be taxable to shareholders as if distributed, even if retained by the corporation for expansion or other reinvestment. Such "allocated" and taxable earnings would entitle the shareholders to whom they were attributed to take a credit for corporate income tax paid.

So long as the top corporate tax rate equalled or exceeded the top individual shareholder's tax rate, as it did between 1986 and 1993 in the United States, shareholders would not object to being taxed on corporate earnings that had not

---

[32] *See* I.R.C. § 902; *cf.* I.R.C. § 960.

actually been distributed to them. This would be true because the taxability to them would entitle them to a tax credit that, assuming the corporate income was fully "franked," would at least fully offset their individual tax burden and possibly or often exceed it. They would be happy to become eligible to get the excess as a refund, or only as a credit against tax on their other income.[33] This plan would leave the corporate income tax in place, for incentive or regulatory uses. When the key rate relationship between the top individual and top corporate rates was again reversed in 1993, the U.S. situation reverted somewhat to that in the pre-1986 years, but the top corporate and individual rates are still on nearly the same level.

To be sure, there are some difficult problems with either a mandatory or elective shareholder imputation credit approach to integration. They include the problems of corporate tax preferences, foreign shareholders, tax-exempt shareholders, audit adjustments, foreign income, and changes in shareholders during the year. Studies in the United States, and experience in Western Europe, Australia, and Asia, show that these problems probably can be solved satisfactorily, or at least tolerated, in the United States.[34] Admittedly, the solutions add some complexity to the system. A deduction (or split-rate of tax, as in Japan at one time, and in Germany) for dividends paid would be simpler — but also less complete and less fair.[35]

Some of the proposals for reform of Subchapter C contemplate that the separate corporate income tax will remain as a separate tax in a classical, nonintegrated income tax system and are incompatible with, or contradict, partial or complete "integration" of the two taxes. Some, however, are compatible with integration, or could serve as an intermediate step between a pure classical system and some form of integration.

A complete proposal that could substantially reform and perfect Subchapter C, and hence is offered as a policy alternative to integration, but which could also lead into integration, is the 1982 American Law Institute Reporter's set of proposals with respect to the taxation of corporate distributions.[36] To alleviate

---

[33] This voluntary allocation technique was an inventive part of the Carter commission in Canada in 1966. Royal Commission on Taxation, Report of the Royal Commission on Taxation (1966) (hereinafter Carter Commission Report). This technique became feasible or easy to adopt in the United States because of the new near parity between top corporate and individual rates created by the 1986 Tax Reform Act. See McNulty, *Reform by Integration*, supra note 1.

[34] See id.; Martin Norr, The Taxation of Corporations and Shareholders (1982); *Business Tax Reform: Ending the Double Tax on Company Dividends — Statement of the Treasurer of 10 December 1986* (Austl.), in 41 Bull. Int'l Bureau Fiscal Documentation 91 (1987).

[35] See Report of the Treasury on Integration of the Individual and Corporate Tax Systems — Taxing Business Revenue Once (1992) (hereinafter "Treasury Report"), app. at 172-76; Tax Bureau Ministry of Finance, An Outline of Japanese Taxes 1991 (1991) (Japan).

[36] See A.L.I., Subchapter C Study, supra note 12, at app. 356-513. For a comparison of this proposal with integration plans, see Warren, supra note 1 (commenting on A.L.I. Tentative Draft No. 2 (1979)).

D. INCORPORATING THE CORPORATE AND INDIVIDUAL INCOME TAXES 653

what it regarded as the excessive amount of taxation on corporate earnings distributed (sometimes called "double taxation"), the A.L.I. Reporter, Professor William D. Andrews, recommended that a deduction be given to corporations for dividends paid, but only for those on "new equity" (to prevent windfalls for shareholders who bought stock in a market that set a price that assumed the continued existence of a two-tier tax on distributed corporate earnings).[37] To make non-dividend distributions on stock (by redemption transactions and other distributions that now escape the ordinary income tax on dividends) carry a tax price equal to the tax on dividend distributions, the A.L.I. Reporter proposed a corporate excise tax on such non-dividend distributions on equity capital.[38] This tax would be imposed in addition to whatever shareholder level tax would apply.

Such non-dividend transactions (those that would carry the new excise tax to equate them with dividends) would include a purchase by a corporation of shares of stock in any corporation other than the purchaser itself. Such an exchange, like a cash dividend or a redemption of the purchasing corporation's own stock, can be viewed as consisting of a distribution of assets out of corporate solution into the hands of individuals (even though the individuals are not shareholders of the purchasing corporation). Hence the equalizing excise tax would apply to the purchase, much as if it were a redemption from, or a payment to, the purchasing corporation's own equity holders. The corporate level excise tax could be credited by shareholders, if any of these distributions were deemed to be a dividend for individual income tax purposes. (Sales and redemptions of appreciated corporate shares by individuals would continue to be taxed in a preferential manner.)[39]

This shareholder credit, like the corporate deduction for dividends on new equity, resembles shareholder imputation credit integration proposals in form. The resemblance is more than skin deep. The 1982 A.L.I. program and integration proposals both seek to remedy a perceived over-taxation of distributed corporate earnings, in comparison with retained earnings, and corporate earnings that somehow leak up to the individual shareholder level at a lower tax cost as return of capital, as capital gains, or as deductible interest, without bearing a tax burden comparable to that on outright dividends.

As such, the A.L.I. Reporter's recommendations should be considered as an alternative to integration, as well as a possible transition toward it (by broadening the corporate deduction for dividends or by enlarging the shareholder credit for tax paid by the corporation).[40] Professor Alvin Warren has made just such a

---

[37] A.L.I., Subchapter C Study, *supra* note 12, at 330-35, 356, 367-70; *see* A.L.I., Reporter's Draft, *supra* note 13, at 53; *cf.* Capital Taxes Group, *supra* note ? (describing ACE (Allowance for Corporate Equity) proposals); *see also* Gammie, *supra* note 15.

[38] A.L.I, Subchapter C Study, *supra* note 12, at 401.

[39] *Id.* at 401-86.

[40] *See* A.L.I., Reporter's Study Draft, *supra* note 13, at 49-53; A.L.I., Subchapter C Study, *supra* note 12, app. at 514-18.

comparison and has concluded that straightforward integration of some form would be preferable in theory and economic results and would be workable in practice.[41] In its 1984 Proposals, the Treasury Department recommended a deduction for 50% of the dividends paid by the corporation each year. This reform resembles the 1982 A.L.I. Reporter's suggestion, although not going as far, and also contains a limit geared to corporate taxes paid on underlying earnings.[42] As mentioned above, the 50% dividends-paid deduction was scaled back by Treasury (in "Treasury II") in 1985 to a 10% deduction that, although incorporated in a House Bill, never became law.[43]

Somewhat in the same tradition as the 1982 A.L.I. Reporter's proposal, the Summary of Final Report of the Capital Taxes Group of the (London based) Institute For Fiscal Studies (the "I.F.S.") entitled "Setting Savings Free" (Proposals for the Taxation of Savings and Profits) recommends a new allowance to be used by all corporations in computing their taxable profits. This allowance, termed the ACE (for "Allowance for Corporate Equity") allowance, would provide an annual deduction to be taken by a corporation when calculating its taxable profits. The allowance would be based on the amount invested and reinvested in the company by its shareholders. It would be calculated at an official rate based on the interest rate currently paid on medium-term government securities. The shareholders' funds, upon which the allowance would be calculated, would consist of the capital subscribed or contributed by shareholders plus retained post-taxed profits, less dividends paid and less amounts invested in another corporation.[44]

The allowance for corporate equity would more or less equalize the tax treatment of corporate income financed by equity or by debt,[45] since interest paid on corporate debt would remain deductible by the company and taxable to the recipients of its interest payment. Hence, the corporation tax system would be virtually neutral as between debt and equity. Because the ACE allowance would permit a corporation to accumulate corporate income free of tax up to the normal rate of return on shareholders' funds, it would be conducive to corporate investment in every profitable source (profitable up to the normal rate of return) and, of course, in *more* profitable sources, those producing economic rents or entrepreneurial profits. The ACE allowance ensures that pre- and post-tax rates

---

[41] *See* Warren, *supra* note 36; George K. Yin, *The Deficit Reduction Act of 1984: Some Small Steps Toward Corporate Reform*, 25 Tax Notes 73 (1984).

[42] *See* Treasury I, *supra* note 1, at 134.

[43] *See supra* note 27 and accompanying text.

[44] *See* Capital Taxes Group, *supra* note ?.

[45] In a way exactly opposite to the CBIT tax system proposed in 1992 by the U.S. Treasury. Gammie, *supra* note 15, at 266.

D. INCORPORATING THE CORPORATE AND INDIVIDUAL INCOME TAXES

of return on profits that are just barely viable in the absence of a tax (in that they would earn a normal market rate of return) would be the same.[46]

While the I.F.S. recommends the ACE allowance in the context of sweeping plans to make savings out of after-tax dollars free of tax, it is independent of these plans and worth separate consideration.[47]

An ACE allowance would eliminate corporate income tax on income consisting of a normal rate of return earned by the corporation. In this way, the treatment would equal present treatment of debt-financed normal income, the deductible interest cost of which offsets the gross income of the earnings, leaving no taxable income. The treatment of shareholder funds left in the corporation in an ACE tax world would exactly parallel reinvested (re-lent) interest in the present tax world. If the corporation earned more than such a normal rate, "economic rent" or "entrepreneurial income" (or the risk premium for invested equity), that extra income would be taxable to it. If this extra income, after tax, were left in the corporation, it would contribute to the "shareholder funds account" ("SFA") and increase the ACE allowance for the next tax period.

The ACE allowance would itself *reduce* the shareholder funds account (because it is a tax-free return on invested capital), as would taxes paid and dividends paid, with the consequence that the ACE allowance for the next period would be smaller.

One happy consequence of this interrelated series of adjustments is that it doesn't much matter to a corporation if it overstates or understates its income in any given period. If the corporation makes a mistake it and pays more tax than

---

[46] *See* Gammie, *supra* note 15.

[47] Under the broader proposals for "setting savings free," I.F.S. would nearly convert the realization or accrual-type income tax into a universal expenditure tax, by using tax-free savings accounts or arrangements called EXPEPs (Extended Personal Equity Plans). These would function like broad-gauge I.R.A.s or tax exempt-savings accounts. However, they would exempt savings from income tax and make the income tax into an expenditure in consumption-type income tax by a technique that reverses the I.R.A. and U.S. academic proposals.

They would require that qualifying savings come from taxed sources, for example out of current taxable income, would not allow any deduction or other relief upon contribution, but then would exempt the earnings on those invested savings from tax and also would exempt from income tax all withdrawals from the accounts. This is (more or less) the financial equivalent of allowing a deduction upon contribution, exempting earnings, and then taxing withdrawal. Use of an EXPEP could enable a shareholder who invests his or her after-tax earnings in a corporation to receive dividends tax free. Combined with the ACE allowance, dividends from a normal rate of return of corporate income would be free of corporate and individual income tax, by combining corporate tax integration with an exempt savings regime. Combining the ACE allowance and EXPEPs makes sense if one wants to exempt savings from (corporate and personal) income tax altogether. If one does not want to go so far, however, but only seeks to eliminate the double tax on savings in the corporate sector, the EXPEP or exempt savings part of the I.F.S. proposals can be put to one side and the ACE allowance considered in the context of an income tax system that would continue to tax income investments in corporate equities once, at the rates applicable to individual shareholders.

it should have, it also will have a higher shareholder funds account as a result and, consequently, it will be entitled to a higher ACE allowance in the future. If it understates income and tax, it will suffer for its acts by having a smaller shareholder funds account and ACE allowance in the future.[48] (And, assuming the company can fund the overpayment of tax at the ACE rate and can earn income on funds saved by reducing its tax at that rate, the ACE system is neutral as to the deferral effects.)[49] In general, the ACE system is neutral with regard to the timing of realization of profit.[50] Similarly, indexation of capital gains in the corporate sector would not be necessary to correct the taxation of capital gains for inflation because the ACE rate adjusts for inflation.

Moreover, the ACE system in effect achieves something tantamount to an accrual method of taxation for gain on assets. Since "shareholder funds" include taxable profits (minus tax) for previous periods, if the corporate taxpayer defers paying tax, it reduces the ACE allowance that it will receive in the future (it pays less tax early, but more later). If it realizes the income soon, it pays more tax then but less in the future because it will be entitled to a larger ACE allowance in the future.

What happens when a corporation living in an ACE system pays a dividend? At that point, shareholders would be taxable (so long as no EXPEP, IRA, KEOGH, qualified pension plan, or exempt shareholder were in the picture). The portion of the dividend paid out of ACE rate income ("normal return") would become taxed for the first and only time, at the shareholders' appropriate rates. The portion paid out of income above the ACE rate, which was taxed to the corporation, would be taxed again. Such tax would be collected by a withholding obligation imposed by the corporation. The distribution would reduce the future ACE allowance of the company because it would reduce the company's shareholder's funds account used to calculate its future ACE allowance.[51]

Thus the ACE system amounts, in a way, to taxing companies at a zero rate on an initial band of profits.[52] It is loosely similar in effect to a shareholder imputation credit system in which the tax credits are limited to the tax on a rate equal to the normal commercial rate on equity capital combined with a sort of dividend reinvestment plan for undistributed profits up to that limit.

The key is that the Shareholders' Funds Account measures the after-tax dollar investment of shareholders in the corporation, and the yield on that investment, the I.F.S. Capital Taxes Group thinks, should be forever exempt from *corporate* income tax. Only the *extra* profits that a company earns, after paying all its costs, including the (imputed) cost of its equity capital, should be taxable to the

---

[48] *See* Capital Taxes Group, *supra* note ?, at 34.
[49] Gammie, *supra* note 15, at 268 n.81.
[50] *Id.* at 268 n.80.
[51] *See* Capital Taxes Group, *supra* note ?, at 3.
[52] Gammie, *supra* note 15, at 266 n.74.

D. INCORPORATING THE CORPORATE AND INDIVIDUAL INCOME TAXES

corporation.[53] An unintegrated, separate corporate tax on economic *rents* is acceptable because it will not deter investment since it (by definition) is a level of profit higher than can be earned elsewhere.

None of these possible techniques for complete integration or for partial integration (dividend relief) was adopted inthe U.S. The integration movement in the U.S. gathered energy in the late 1970s, but then the movement diminished and lay relatively quiet, until the late 1980s. Concern about excessive use of debt and the failure of over-leveraged companies in the late 1980s and the early 1990s revived the question of how to tax corporate earnings that are distributed either as dividends or as interest, and whether to "integrate" the corporate income tax with the individual income tax.[54] In a country with a low rate of investment, there was concern that the unintegrated system discouraged new equity financing of corporate investments.

As of 1995, the United States federal income tax law continues to employ the so-called "classical system," which treats corporations and their investors as separate taxable entities and imposes tax at both the corporate and shareholder levels on earnings that are distributed by the corporation as dividends. There is no relief from this double tax on individual shareholders. Dividends are not deductible by the paying corporation. In contrast, corporate earnings that are distributed to lenders as interest are deductible by the corporation and taxable to the lender. Investors who choose noncorporate forms of business, such as the sole proprietorship or partnership, limited liability company, or closely-held corporations that qualify to elect to be taxed as "S corporations," are taxed on a pass-through method, and the undistributed as well as distributed earnings of the business are taxable, currently, to the shareholders, at their rates and according to their relevant individual tax characteristics. For the ordinary corporation, however, the corporate income tax is not "integrated" with the individual income tax.

The double-layered, unintegrated system works to (a) discourage incorporation; (b) encourage retention of corporate earnings indefinitely or until redemption or liquidation, especially until after the death of a shareholder; (c) reward use of debt rather than equity capitalization; (d) induce sale of shares (or tax-free reorganization) of corporations with retained earnings rather than distribution of dividends; (e) discourage multiple corporate layers, except where a 100% dividends secured deduction or income tax consolidation under §§ 1501-1504 can be achieved through concentration of corporate ownership; and (f) favor tax-exempt or foreign shareholders, insofar as only U.S. taxes are taken into account. Still, income tax incentives arise from the structure and relationship of the unintegrated corporate and individual taxes, rules, and rates.

---

[53] Capital Taxes Group, *supra* note ?, at 24.

[54] *See supra* note 21 and accompanying text.

It is non-neutralities, inequities and complications such as these that proposals for complex integration or for partial integration (dividend relief) have been designed to reduce or eliminate. The following sections describe and explore two of the most recent and important proposals, that of the U.S. Treasury Department and that of the American Law Institute Reporter.

E. THE JANUARY 1992 U.S. TREASURY DEPARTMENT STUDY

On January 6, 1992, the U.S. Treasury Department issued a report entitled "Integration of the Individual and Corporate Tax Systems, Taxing Business Income Once."[55] This report resulted from the revival of the integration debate and helped set the agenda for the policy discussion in the ensuing years. The Secretary of the Treasury had been instructed by the Tax Reform Act of 1986 to study reforms of the taxation of corporate income.[56] It was earlier expected that the study would consider less fundamental approaches to corporate income tax reform. The Treasury decided to undertake a more comprehensive study of integration of the corporate and individual tax and to address fundamental questions about how the corporate income tax might be restructured to reduce tax distortions of important corporate financial decisions and to achieve a more efficient system, especially given the prevalence of integrated corporate income tax systems elsewhere in the world.[57]

The Treasury study outlined four prototypes for integration, one of which was an imputation credit prototype, but the Treasury recommended against such form of integration for the U.S. tax system. It also recommended against a dividend deduction alternative.[58]

The Treasury study, under the direction of Michael Graetz, concentrated on three other integration prototypes. The first was a simple proposal to exclude dividends from the income taxable to shareholders, the "dividend-exclusion prototype."[59] The second was a "shareholder allocation" model, much like the partnership or transparency models discussed in many countries over the years and rather like the "Subchapter S" legislation in the United States. Under this model, corporate earnings would be allocated to shareholders, even though not distributed to them. The allocated earnings would be taxable to shareholders, either without a tax at the corporate level, or with a credit for any tax paid at the

---

[55] Treasury Report, *supra* note 35.
[56] Pub. L. No. 99-514, § 634, 100 Stat. 2282 (1986).
[57] *See id.* at ix.
[58] *See* Treasury Report, *supra* note 35, at 93, 107.
[59] *See id.* at 17.

E. THE JANUARY 1992 U.S. TREASURY DEPARTMENT STUDY

corporate level.[60] The Treasury Department recommended against this allocation approach as well.[61]

The final prototype was the "Comprehensive Business Income Tax" or "CBIT" prototype.[62] The CBIT model would impose a schedular or flat rate of tax on the business earnings of any entity, not only upon the income of corporations but also upon the income of proprietorships, and all other businesses or business associations. Distributions by such entities to shareholders or other investors would be excluded from income, much as dividends would be excluded under the dividend-exclusion prototype. Most remarkably, the CBIT proposal would deny a deduction at the business level for interest and would exclude interest from the income of recipients, just the way dividends would be nondeductible by the corporation and excluded from the income of shareholders. Interest and dividends, both viewed as costs of capital, to this extent would be treated alike.

---

[60] *See id.* at 27.

[61] *See id.* at viii. The shareholder allocation prototype that Treasury outlined and discussed, but, unfortunately, did not recommend for further study, differs from Subchapter S in some important respects. It retains a tax on the entity which is allocated to shareholders for credit against their personal tax liabilities. Furthermore, it denies a pass-through for losses. This prototype would not be limited to closely-held or one-class-of-stock entities. Treasury disavowed this allocation prototype because it would not invariably collect at least one tier of U.S. tax on foreign source income or tax-preferred corporate income. *Id.* at 27-37.

The Treasury Report in general probably was driven by a strong impulse to close the tax differences between equity and debt, and by the over-leveraging of the 1980s. Lee A. Sheppard, *Tax Officials Discuss Integration, Future Legislation at ABA Meeting*, 46 Tax Notes 756 (1990); *see generally* Graetz, *supra* note 21; J. Andrew Hoerner, *Tax Bar Prepares for Treasury's Corporate Integration Report*, 47 Tax Notes 778 (1990); Warren, *supra* note 30.

Probably also it was very concerned with the difference between taxation of dividends and of other, dividend-like, distributions, such as redemption of shares. *See generally* Anne L. Alstott & James B. Mackie, *Approaches to Corporate Integration: The Treasury Department Report, Where's the Beef? A Review and Critique of the Treasury Integration Study*, 54 Tax Notes 1391 (1992); Richard Goode, *Integration of Corporate and Individual Taxes: A Treasury Report*, 54 Tax Notes 1667 (1992); Gene Steuerle, *Two Cheers for the Treasury Integration Study*, 54 Tax Notes 331 (1992); Geraldine Gerardi et al., *Corporate Integration Puzzles*, 43 Nat'l Tax J. 307 (1990); McNulty, *Reform by Integration*, *supra* note 1; *see also* John K. McNulty, *The Basic Structure and Characteristics of the U.S. Income Tax and Future Reform Possibilities* (pts. 1 & 2), 1988 The Jurist 80, 90 (Japan) (on the corporate tax integration question).

A high regard for Subchapter S, and the notion that it might be well to retain it in a world of divided relief or anything less than complete, pass-through integration, can be found in McNulty, Taxation of S Corporations, *supra* note 11; McNulty, *S Corporations*, *supra* note 11, ¶ 10.06; *see also* Treasury Blueprints, *supra* note 1, at 68-69; Kragen & McNulty, *supra* note 29, at 995-1012; McNulty, *Integrating?*, *supra* note 1; McNulty, *Future Reform*, *supra* note 24; Willard B. Taylor & M. Bernard Aidinoff, *Approaches to Debt: Is Integration the Answer?*, 67 Taxes 931, 934 (1989) (listing arguments in favor of the shareholder credit method); Alvin C. Warren, Jr., *Taxing Corporate Income in the U.S. Twenty Years After the Carter Commission Report: Integration or Disintegration?*, 26 Osgoode Hall L.J. 313 (1988).

[62] *See* Treasury Report, *supra* note 35, at 39-60.

As Treasury recognized, the dividend-exclusion model would be relatively simple to legislate and put into place, whereas the CBIT proposal represents a long-term and more comprehensive method of taxing all business associations similarly and equalizing the tax treatment of debt and equity. Treasury suggested that full implementation of CBIT might well take ten years to bring into effect by a series of phases. Unlike the other proposals for integration, the CBIT proposal would be "self-financing," and in fact would generate additional revenue, which would permit lowering the corporate rate to the same level as the (1992) maximum individual income tax rate of 31%, without loss of revenue, even if capital gains on corporate stock were fully exempt from tax when realized by shareholders.[63]

The Treasury Department made a number of policy recommendations, which (unfortunately) acted as constraints on their study. These included the ideas that (i) integration should not result in the extension of corporate tax preferences to shareholders, (ii) integration should not reduce the total tax collected on corporate income allocable to tax-exempt investors, (iii) integration should be extended to foreign shareholders only through treaty negotiations, not by statute, and finally (iv) foreign taxes paid by U.S. corporations should not be treated by statute identically to taxes paid to the United States government.[64]

The January 1992 Treasury Department integration study examined and, for the near term, recommended a "dividend exclusion prototype" which could either stand alone or serve as a transition to the comprehensive business income tax (CBIT) prototype, which Treasury ultimately recommended.[65] The dividend exclusion prototype contemplated that U.S. corporations would continue to pay the usual corporate income tax on their income at the specified statutory rate. However, in contrast to present law, when dividends were distributed to shareholders, those dividends would be excluded from the taxable income of the shareholders. More or less the present definition of "dividend" would be retained, which incorporates the concept of "current or accumulated earnings and profits."[66] In other words, under the dividend exclusion approach, the corporate income tax as it stands now would substitute for the present combination of corporate and shareholder tax. The shareholder tax on distributed corporate income would be repealed.

This model tends to provide a secure source for collection of revenue, consisting of the single tax on all corporate source income. Thus the income is taxed when realized by the legal entity that earns it, namely the corporation. By

---

[63] *See id.* at viii, 111-52.

[64] *See id.* at viii-ix.

[65] *See id.* at viii, 17-27. The CBIT prototype includes a dividend exclusion within it and, therefore, can best be understood after a description and an examination of the dividend exclusion prototype itself.

[66] *See* I.R.C. § 316.

E. THE JANUARY 1992 U.S. TREASURY DEPARTMENT STUDY

leaving this tax in effect and repealing the shareholder income tax, Treasury would have an integration plan that avoids the exceptions to, and avoidance of, the shareholder level tax. However, the corporate income tax is not completely comprehensive because of corporate income tax preferences.

The Treasury dividend exclusion prototype would not allow the pass-through of any such corporate income tax preferences.[67] It would retain the current alternative minimum tax on corporations and would impose what amounts to a second minimum tax on preference income when it left corporate solution. To be specific, to the extent preference income was distributed as dividends, the distribution *would* be taxable to the recipient. This result is achieved by imposing on corporations the need to maintain an "Excludable Distributions Account" ("EDA") which would be the sum total of present and previously fully-taxed corporate income from which excludable dividends could be paid. If any dividends were distributed at a time when the EDA had a zero balance, they would be taxable to the shareholder-recipient as under current law.[68] This is the sense in which preferences would not be passed through to the shareholders.

Foreign source income that has been taxed abroad would not be treated as fully-taxed income and would not increase the EDA *unless* there were agreement to that effect by international tax treaty. In other words, integration would not extend to foreign source income, even if fully taxed abroad, unless a treaty so provided. In the absence of a treaty, a distribution of foreign source income would be taxed again by the United States at the shareholder level. The foreign tax credit would not flow-through in any way.[69]

Dividends would be excludable by corporate shareholders as well as to individual shareholders. The corporation receiving a dividend would increase its EDA by the amount of the excludable dividend, which then would allow a distribution of the same funds to its shareholders without further tax to them. The corporate shareholder would continue to be entitled to a dividends-received deduction, under I.R.C. § 243, if it received a taxable dividend.[70]

With respect to non-dividend distributions, Treasury's dividend exclusion prototype would retain present law.[71] This means that a distribution that was "essentially equivalent to a dividend" would be taxable as a dividend (to the extent of earnings and profits) and would be treated under the general rules for dividends outlined above. A non-dividend distribution that qualified as a redemption or payment in exchange for stock of the selling shareholder would be treated as a return of capital up to the shareholder's basis in his or her shares

---

[67] *See* Treasury Report, *supra* note 35, at 18.
[68] *See id.* at 19.
[69] *See id.* at 21.
[70] *See id.* at 20.
[71] *Id.* at 17, 24.

and as capital gain above that.[72] If the distribution were categorized as a non-dividend distribution, no part of it would be tax-free to the shareholder even if the corporation had a positive EDA balance at the time, and the corporation would not reduce its EDA by the amount of the distribution. In other words, for these purposes it might be much more favorable to treat a distribution as a dividend, rather than as a non-dividend distribution, contrary to the position under present law.

If a shareholder governed by the dividend exclusion prototype were to sell his or her shares, it appears (although the Treasury study is not entirely definite) that the principles of current law would apply.[73] Consequently, the sale of shares would be a taxable event, and any gain, amount realized above basis, would be taxable in full. Capital losses would be deductible. In effect, this could produce a second or shareholder tax upon retained corporate earnings, which seems inconsistent with the theory of the dividend exclusion prototype.

Apparently the only relief from this effect would be the prototype's elective "Dividend Reinvestment Plan" ("DRIP").[74] Under this plan the corporation could elect to declare a constructive dividend, which would be treated as a regular dividend followed by reinvestment by shareholders of an equal amount in the corporation. As a consequence, shareholders could increase their basis in their stock by the after-tax proceeds of corporate income that was retained but constructively distributed and recontributed. If all corporations made this election with respect to all their earnings, then the second tax upon the sale of all shareholders' shares would not apply to the amount of the gain resulting from retained earnings and would not reintroduce double taxation. The DRIP dividend would allow the corporation to treat the shareholders as if they had received excludable dividends up to the corporation's EDA balance, followed by a deemed recontribution of the distributed amount by the shareholders back to the corporation. The deemed distribution would not be taxable, although it would reduce the corporation's EDA balance, because the dividend would be an excludable one. It is the deemed recontribution that would entitle the shareholder to increase his or her stock basis, which then would have the effect of diminishing his or her capital gain on sale of the shares, or possibly of creating or increasing the amount of a capital loss on their sale.

The Treasury's dividend exclusion prototype was favored because Treasury believed that the most significant efficiency gains could be achieved by a schedular system in which all corporate income would be taxed at a uniform rate, at the corporate level, without regard to the tax rate of the corporate shareholder.[75] Treasury went on to say that the neutral taxation of capital income would

---

[72] *Id.* at 24.

[73] *Id.* at 17-27.

[74] *Id.* at 24.

[75] *See id.* at 12.

reduce distortions found in the present system.[76] Economic efficiency suggests, Treasury believed, that all capital income should be taxed at the same rate.[77]

Treasury also emphasized the simplification advantages of taxing corporate income only to the corporation and at corporate rates.[78] Income that had been fully taxed at the corporate level would be taxed just the same whether distributed or not and would be taxed in a uniform manner, regardless of the tax brackets of the individual shareholders. Consequently, the portions of corporate income attributable to tax-exempt or foreign shareholders or low-bracket shareholders would be taxed at the same rate as would the income attributed to fully-taxable high-bracket shareholders. Therefore, whatever progressivity would be found would be inherent in the *corporate* tax rate schedule. The progressivity would depend upon the amount of income of the corporation, in the aggregate, rather than on the income, from all sources, of each individual shareholder. In contrast, corporate preference income would be taxable to the shareholders at their individual rates, rather than at the corporate rate. The progressivity and other characteristics of this tax system have been worked out interestingly by Professor George Yin.[79]

The CBIT prototype was the most "comprehensive" of those developed by Treasury.[80] It would apply the same tax regime to unincorporated as well as to incorporated businesses. The income of all business entities would be taxable to the entity at a single rate, 31% in the Treasury example.[81] In other words, an entity-level corporate-like income tax would apply to all businesses, even partnerships or other "conduit" organizations, and the base would resemble the present corporate income tax. However, no deduction would be allowed to the corporation for interest or dividends paid; dividends and interest received by shareholders and lenders from CBIT entities would be excluded.[82] Neither dividends nor interest would be taxable when received by investors.[83] The CBIT model uses the dividend exclusion approach of Treasury's dividend exclusion prototype and expands this treatment to apply also to interest, which would no longer be deductible. Hence, corporate earnings would be taxable once, to the entity, at a single rate, whether distributed or not, and whether distributed as dividends or interest.

---

[76] *Id.*

[77] *Id.* at 12, 112, 128. But one difficulty flows from the fact that some corporate income, especially in small closely-held corporations, consists of labor or entrepreneurial income.

[78] *Id.* at viii, 93.

[79] *See* George K. Yin, *Corporate Tax Integration and the Search for the Pragmatic Ideal*, 47 Tax L. Rev. 431, 453-462 (1992).

[80] *See* Treasury Report, *supra* note 35, at 39.

[81] *Id.* at 40.

[82] *Id.* at 53.

[83] *See id.* at 39-60.

Treasury expected that such a new system would not fully be implemented at once, but perhaps would be phased in over ten years or so.[84] It would equalize debt and equity and eliminate the second level of tax of present law and would place all, or almost all, business organizations under the same tax regime. It has many of the merits and weaknesses of the dividend exclusion approach, and can be compared with other dividend relief and complete integration proposals in much the same terms, without — however — losing sight of its greater extent, difficulty of implementation and possibly greater economic neutrality.

F. THE DECEMBER 1992 U.S. TREASURY LEGISLATIVE RECOMMENDATIONS

Throughout 1992, tax scholars and expert groups studied the U.S. Treasury Department proposal, and the Treasury Department promised that, before the end of 1992, it would make a legislative recommendation and thus express a choice of which form of integration should be adopted. In a December 11, 1992, letter from Treasury Secretary Nicholas F. Brady to House Ways and Means Committee Chairman Dan Rostenkowski, the Treasury Department enclosed its recommendation.[85] This recommendation is very similar to the "dividend-exclusion prototype" first put forward by Treasury on January 6, 1992. In other words, Treasury again preferred the dividend-exclusion approach to a pass-through or shareholder imputation credit model. It also preferred, for the near term at least, the simple dividend-exclusion approach to the more sweeping "comprehensive business income tax" (CBIT) approach that was the strongest recommendation made in January. Treasury preferred the dividend-exclusion approach because of its simplicity, because it could be relatively easily inserted into the present legal framework of the corporate income tax and easily administered, and because it could be implemented at once, without any transition or phase-in period.[86] Also, Treasury stated that the dividend-exclusion approach was preferable to the shareholder allocation and imputation-credit prototypes because it was consistent with Treasury's policy view that, over the long term, it would be "desirable to move the tax system in the direction of a schedular tax on enterprise activity," such as a tax like the CBIT prototype or some version of a business cash-flow tax or a business transfer tax.[87]

Under the dividend exclusion model recommended on December 11, 1992, a corporation would compute its taxable income and pay tax as it does under

---

[84] See id.

[85] A Recommendation For Integration of the Individual and Corporate Tax Systems, accompanying a letter from Treasury Secretary Nicholas Brady to House Ways and Means Comm. Chairman Dan Rostenkowski, Released December 11, 1992, in Daily Tax Rept. (BNA) No. 240, at L-7 (Dec. 14, 1992) (hereinafter "Treasury Recommendation").

[86] See id.

[87] Id.

F. THE DECEMBER 1992 U.S. TREASURY LEGISLATIVE RECOMMENDATIONS

current law. Any distribution made to shareholders out of the corporation's income that remained after paying its tax and after making certain limited adjustments to "taxable income," adjustments that would produce the determination of "adjusted taxable income" or "ATI," would be treated as a dividend and would be excludable from gross income when received by the shareholders. Distributions in excess of ATI would be treated as a return of capital to the shareholders, or as capital gain to the extent the distributions exceeded their adjusted bases in their shares.[88]

ATI is defined by this new Treasury proposal as corporate taxable income that has been reduced by federal income taxes and creditable foreign taxes paid or accrued and increased by excludable dividends received and by any items of income that are permanently excluded from income under the present tax law (tax-exempt interest, percentage depletion in excess of basis, etc.).[89] It thus resembles the present concept of "earnings and profits."[90] Because distributions that exceed taxable income would to be treated as a return of capital to the shareholders, no distribution ever would be treated as a taxable dividend to shareholders. That is to say, a distribution would be one of the following: (1) an excludable dividend, up to ATI; (2) a return of capital; or (3) capital gain to the extent the distribution exceeded each shareholder's basis in his or her shares, which is taxable at rates that (sometimes) differ from the rates applicable to ordinary income.

The new Treasury proposal allows corporations to adopt a "dividend reinvestment plan" (again termed a "DRIP"), along the lines of the dividend reinvestment plan proposed by Treasury in January of 1992 and modeled on the "voluntary allocation" of the Carter Commission Report in Canada in 1966.[91] Under the dividend reinvestment plan, a corporation voluntarily could pretend that a cash dividend had been paid to its shareholders out of its adjusted taxable income and that such dividend was immediately reinvested by the shareholders. No money would change hands. Instead, earnings of the corporation retained by the company would be "deemed" to have been distributed and recontributed. The shareholders would not pay any tax on the constructive or "deemed" dividend (because all dividends would be excludable by shareholders), but they would increase their bases in their shares by the amount of the "deemed" dividend. The effect of this basis increase would be to reduce the capital gain, or increase any capital loss, that the shareholders would realize when they sell

---

[88] *Id.* at L-8, L-9, L-10. A shareholder's basis in the shares is a changing record of the shareholder's after-tax dollar or "capital" invested in the shares, not previously returned by corporate distributions or tax benefits. It resembles "adjusted historical cost" in Japan's income tax law.

[89] *Id.*

[90] *See* Treas. Reg. § 1.312-6 (1955).

[91] Treasury Recommendation, *supra* note 85, at L-12.

their shares. The gain would be reduced by an amount equal to the corporation's retained but previously taxed and "allocated" earnings.

Treasury's December ATI proposal differs in some important respects from the dividend exclusion prototype described earlier by Treasury in its integration study of January, 1992. The most important differences are the following: first, all distributions in excess of "adjusted taxable income" are treated as returns of capital to the shareholders, rather than as taxable dividends;[92] second, integration *is* extended to foreign source income, by "flowing through" creditable foreign taxes;[93] third, the proposal would have an immediate effective date with only limited, elective transition relief for corporate shareholders.[94]

The December 1992 Treasury proposal contained 23 recommendations.[95] One of the recommendations indicates that Treasury *would* retain the current U.S. treatment of "S corporations," partnerships and other pass-through entities, such as regulated investment companies, real estate investment trusts and real estate mortgage investment conduits.[96] This would mean that investors who would prefer to have a single layer of tax imposed on business earnings at the rates dictated by the individual income tax and by the income tax situations of the shareholders, could, subject to eligibility rules, form proprietorships or partnerships or other pass-through entities, or could cause their closely-held corporations, if otherwise qualified, to elect "Subchapter S" treatment.

The top individual rate of federal income tax specified in the United States is now (1995) 39.6% and the top corporate rate is 35%. It seems quite possible, though, that rate increases in one or both taxes will be enacted in the future, at least within some income ranges, and that the relatively equivalent relationship between the top rates, and the lower or intermediate rates, would cease to exist. If, for example, individual rates went far higher than the corporate rates, taxpayers might prefer to use a corporation subject to the new ATI proposal. Under this proposal, business income would be taxed once, at corporate rates, and not taxed a second time, even upon distribution to high-income shareholders. On the other hand, if top corporate rates went higher than top individual income tax rates or the rates applicable to particular shareholders, investors might prefer the pass-through treatment of partnerships and S corporations. This would result in one level of tax, at the individual shareholder rate, rather than the higher

---

[92] *Id.* at L-11.

[93] *Id.* at L-10.

[94] *Id.* at L-16. Like the dividend-exclusion proposal of January, the ATI proposal would not be extended to foreign shareholders by statute but Treasury contemplated that integration benefits might be granted to foreign shareholders by international income tax treaties. *Id.* at L-15.

[95] These recommendations constitute the ATI proposal itself. Some of them are relatively technical and explain the extent to which the proposal would allow the present corporate income tax to remain in place without modification, and others indicate that some, relatively minor, alterations would have to be made in the corporate tax legislation.

[96] *Id.* at L-14.

corporate rate. If taxpayers anticipate losses in their business, they might prefer the pass-through treatment of partnership or S corporation form, which would allow those losses to be deducted from other income on their individual shareholder returns.

Treasury recognized that retaining Subchapter S and partnership treatment for eligible businesses would be somewhat inconsistent with its long-term policy preference for a schedular tax on enterprise activity and with its goal of tax simplification. It recognized, however, that the partnership, Subchapter S and other alternative regimes are so deeply embedded in the U.S. income tax system that any other approach would prove exceedingly disruptive and would require elaborate transition rules. Treasury implied that conversion to a Comprehensive Business Income Tax (CBIT) later would be desirable and that it would entail repealing Subchapter S.[97]

G. THE MAY 1993 AMERICAN LAW INSTITUTE "REPORTER'S STUDY"

During the preceding years, the prestigious American Law Institute also had begun to undertake a study of integrating the corporate and individual income taxes. By October of 1992, a final draft of the A.L.I. "Reporter's Study" on "Integration of Individual and Corporate Income Taxes" was made available to the Council of the American Law Institute.[98] The A.L.I. "Reporter's Study" was completed and presented to the Institute at its Annual Meeting in May, 1993.[99]

The American Law Institute Reporter's Study proposed a shareholder imputation credit method of integration of the corporate and individual income tax for the United States in a form roughly resembling that recently enacted in New Zealand, and familiar in Australia and the European Community. Under this method of integration, the corporate income tax would remain in place, and dividends would be taxable to shareholders. The shareholders would, however, receive a credit for the corporate tax paid with respect to the earnings out of which distributions were made to them as dividends.[100]

The A.L.I. Reporter, Professor Alvin Warren of the Harvard Law School, produced an excellent analysis and proposal for shareholder imputation credit integration in the United States, thoughtfully argued and superbly worked out, although not cast in the form of legislation. The A.L.I. proposal benefitted from

---

[97] Id. at L-14.

[98] American Law Institute, Federal Income Tax Project, Council Draft No. 20 Reporter's Study — Integration of the Individual And Corporate Income Taxes (1992). Earlier drafts had been discussed by special study groups and consultants to the American Law Institute.

[99] See Alvin C. Warren, Jr., American Law Institute, Federal Income Tax Project — Reporter's Study of Corporate Tax Integration (1993) (hereinafter A.L.I. Reporter).

[100] Id. at 47.

the work of the "Carter Commission" of Canada, the Royal Commission which produced an attractive proposal for shareholder credit integration in 1966, including a plan for voluntary "allocation" of retained earnings.[101] In the United States, the income tax rate relationships newly established by the 1986 Tax Reform Act, relationships between the top individual income tax rate and the top corporate income tax, made the Carter Commission "allocation" idea, and the shareholder credit method of integration in general, especially feasible and desirable.[102] Taking into account the experience and legislative variations among shareholder credit integration systems in Western Europe and the rest of the world, the A.L.I. study could receive continued attention from policy analysts and the Congress of the United States.

The shareholder imputation credit model, as developed by the A.L.I. Reporter, and like that in use in many countries, comes very close to the results and virtues of a transparency or Subchapter S type integration system. It is probably the "second-best" alternative and should be adopted if true transparency integration is not feasible, for legal, economic or political reasons. The imputation credit model allows the corporate income tax to serve temporarily as the proxy for the shareholder level tax that would arise if there had been an allocation of corporate earnings to the shareholders.

However, the corporate tax is a very imperfect proxy, and it is not sensitive to the individual tax rates applicable to the owners of the corporation. It is therefore treated as a withholding tax, creditable to the account of the shareholders upon final reconciliation of their income tax liabilities. This reconciliation does not happen until there is a dividend distribution, in other words until there has been a "realization" of the income by the shareholder. Thus, it satisfies the "realization" requirement of the U.S. income tax. At the time of such a distribution, the shareholder must include the distribution in his or her income and recalculate the proper tax burden on that distribution. The shareholder is then viewed as having prepaid part or all of his tax by virtue of payment by the corporation of its corporate income tax for the account of the shareholder. This prepayment is credited to the distributee in the form of a (possibly refundable) tax credit. If the credit equals the shareholder's tax, no further payment must be made. If the corporate tax rate is higher, there would be a refund of the excess credit to the shareholder. If the corporate tax is insufficient, the shareholder must make an additional payment.[103]

The simple mechanism of the shareholder imputation tax credit system becomes much more complicated when it takes into account real world problems, particularly including those of "preference income" (income received by the corporation at a lower rate of tax, or tax-free, by virtue of legislative preferences

---

[101] Carter Commission Report, *supra* note 33.

[102] *See* McNulty, *Reform by Integration, supra* note 1, from which some of this text is taken.

[103] A.L.I. Reporter, *supra* note 99, at 50-57, 94-134.

G. THE MAY 1993 AMERICAN LAW INSTITUTE "REPORTER'S STUDY"

granted to corporations), foreign source income (corporate income arising in a foreign country and then repatriated to the United States), and tax-exempt and foreign shareholders.[104] It also becomes necessary to take into account the fact that shareholders can realize their proportionate amounts of corporate source income through means other than dividend distributions, means including non-dividend and redemption distributions by the corporation and sales of stock to third parties.[105] The American Law Institute Reporter's proposal intelligently and elegantly deals with these special "real world" problems.

As to corporate tax preferences, the question is whether those preferences should be passed through to the shareholders, thus allowing the eventual tax on individual shareholders upon their corporate source income to be determined with the benefit of the corporate tax preference. The transparency approach of integration would suggest allowing a complete pass-through with the preferences, as if the income had been earned in noncorporate form. This seems particularly allowable if the preference was intended as an inducement to investors to perform certain economic activity, regardless of the legal form of the investor. In contrast, it may be argued that some corporate tax preferences are granted only for the benefit of corporations, sometimes in an effort to reduce the double taxation of earnings taxable to a corporation. If that is the case, eliminating double taxation would seem to imply ending the preference, or "washing it out." At present, there is no pass-through of corporate preferences for normal "C" corporations because of the technical definition of corporate "earnings and profits," which does not take into account such preferences.[106]

The A.L.I. Reporter's Study passes through some preferences but washes out certain others. The washout is accomplished by imposing a "Dividend Withholding Tax" ("DWT"), at the regular corporate tax rate, on the distributing corporation when a dividend is distributed, to the extent the dividend consists of an untaxed portion of preference income.[107] In a complicated device, the Dividend Withholding Tax is imposed on the dividend distribution of *any* income, whether out of preference sources or otherwise, but the corporation would have maintained a "Taxes Paid Account" ("TPA") to keep track of taxes paid by the corporation, and it could use its positive balance in the TPA to satisfy its DWT liability. The result is to impose the DWT only upon the distribution of previously untaxed preference income.[108]

Preferences allowed to be passed through would be controlled by an "Exempt Income Account" ("EIA") to keep track of those preferences. Distributions of

---

[104] See id. at 108-13.
[105] See id. at 135-50.
[106] I.R.C. §§ 312, 316; Treas. Reg. § 1.312-6 (1955).
[107] A.L.I. Reporter, *supra* note 99, at 92-93, 98.
[108] See id. at 93.

amounts allowed from this account would not give rise to the DWT and would not be taxable to the recipient shareholder.[109]

As to foreign-source income, if the income has been taxed in the foreign country, and if the United States would normally allow a foreign tax credit for the foreign tax paid, the foreign source income would resemble "preference income" because it could be received by the U.S. corporation without payment of further U.S. tax unless the U.S. tax rate were higher than the foreign tax. The A.L.I. Reporter's Study treats foreign source income as exempt income that may be distributed tax free to the investors in the corporation.[110] The effect is to pass through the benefit of the foreign tax credit. However, the Reporter's study recommends that this pass-through be implemented only as part of a tax treaty with a foreign country, not by statute.[111] In other words, the United States would not unilaterally give up tax jurisdiction to the foreign country, to this extent, but would do so only as part of the negotiations of an international income tax treaty.

Tax-exempt and foreign shareholders present another problem. An allocation or transparency approach would seem to suggest that corporate source income that is allocable or distributable to a tax-exempt owner would not be taxed because of the tax-exempt status of that shareholder. Similarly, if a foreign shareholder would not be subject to U.S. income tax normally, he or she should not be taxable merely because the income takes the form of a dividend from a U.S. corporation. That probably is the correct theoretical result for tax-exempt and foreign shareholders.

The real world problem is complicated by the fact that tax-exempt shareholders in the United States presently are, in effect, indirectly subject to a corporate level tax when they receive dividends, even if they are not taxable on the dividends themselves.[112] This is because the corporation paying the dividend has been taxed on its own income, despite the tax-exempt status of the shareholder. The same thing is true of a foreign shareholder. Consequently, a change to what might be described as the theoretically correct result would involve a change in the current status of tax-exempt and foreign shareholders and would involve a revenue loss.

Also, it is important to note that if a tax-exempt owner earns income from a business enterprise directly, rather than through the vehicle of a corporation, the income is likely to be subjected to a tax called the "unrelated business income tax."[113] Arguably, the same tax burden should be imposed on dividend income

---

[109] *Id.* at 108.

[110] *Id.* at 198.

[111] *Id.*

[112] In contrast, in the United Kingdom the tax-exempt status of an institution holding shares frees it from the indirect corporate tax. *See* Gammie, *supra* note 15.

[113] I.R.C. §§ 511-513.

G. THE MAY 1993 AMERICAN LAW INSTITUTE "REPORTER'S STUDY"

as well, after integration, if the system is to disregard the corporate entity for tax purposes.[114]

As to foreign shareholders, there is a similar problem because they are affected by withholding taxes imposed on dividends paid to foreign shareholders.[115] And U.S. shareholders are subject to foreign withholding taxes on their dividend income paid by foreign corporations. The issue can be viewed as raising the

---

[114] Internal Revenue Code §§ 501-509 deals with organizations that are exempt from income tax. Section 501 proves a for a very comprehensive range of exemption, including in its scope charities, educational institutions, chambers of commerce, labor unions, trade associations, social clubs, and a score of other organizations. These organizations are required to file an application for exemption with the District Director of the Internal Revenue Service. With exceptions discussed *infra*, if the exemption is granted, the organizations are free from income tax liability as long as no substantial change takes place in their purposes, organization, or operation.

There is a general provision against exemption where any portion of the net earnings of an organization insures to the benefit of any private person (other than payments which carry out its exempt function, such as payments for the benefit of the poor). *See, e.g., Founding Church of Scientology v. United States*, 412 F.2d 1197 (Ct. Cl. 1969). Exemption has been denied to trade associations where a substantial portion of their activities was the rendering of services to individual members, such as obtaining credit information. *See United States v. Oklahoma Retailers Ass'n*, 331 F.2d 328 (10th Cir. 1964); *Indiana Retail Hardware Ass'n v. United States*, 366 F.2d 998 (Ct. Cl. 1966). However, activities conducted for the general benefit of the membership of a union or trade association do not preclude it from obtaining tax-exempt status.

The exemption from income taxation of organizations described in § 501(c) is somewhat limited. Most of such organizations are subject to the provisions of §§ 511-513 which subject to the corporation income tax *unrelated business taxable income*, that is income derived from an unrelated trade or business. An unrelated trade or business is any trade or business the conduct of which is not substantially related to the exercise or performance by an exempt organization of its exempt function. *See* § 513(a). Sections 511-513 were enacted to prevent the practice of exempt organizations acquiring businesses which they would then operate without income tax liability. (The most notorious example was the acquisition by New York University of the Mueller Macaroni Company.) A further result of the application of §§ 511-513 is that the expenses of conducting an organization's exempt-function activities may not be deducted from unrelated business taxable income. The effects of §§ 511-13 may make exemption unattractive to a membership organization rendering services to its members, such as a social club or a business league, if the costs of membership services are met in part by income derived from an unrelated trade or business.

With some modifications, organizations exempt under § 527 (political organizations) or § 528 (homeowners associations) are taxable under the usual rules affecting corporations on income which is not exempt-function income. The scope of exemptions is therefore much narrower than for organizations exempt under § 501(c).

The tax-exempt organizations that have attracted the greatest attention from Congress are those described in § 501(c)(3): organizations organized and operated exclusively for religious, charitable, scientific, testing for public safety, literary, or educational purposes, or to foster national or international amateur sports competition, or for the prevention of cruelty to children or animals. Section 170 also provides a tax deduction (within certain limits) for the amount of a gift made to a § 501(c)(3) organization, including publicly-supported churches, colleges and charities.

Otherwise "tax-exempt" institutions are subject to the tax of I.R.C. §§ 511-513 on their "unrelated business income," which does not include dividends on portfolio stock.

[115] I.R.C. §§ 871(a), 1441.

question whether pass-through integration is the goal or whether it is simply enough to eliminate "double taxation."

The A.L.I. Reporter's Study maintains the single level of tax on corporate income received by tax-exempt investors.[116] The study takes a similar approach to foreign investors.[117] The study recommends an explicit new tax on certain categories of investment income, including dividends and stock gains for tax-exempt and foreign shareholders.[118] When a distribution is made to such an investor, the integration credit (for dividend withholding tax) could be used to offset this new tax and any excess credit would be refundable to the distributee. For foreign shareholders, this new tax would replace the existing withholding tax. It would be subject to mutual reduction in tax treaties.[119]

Finally, there is the problem of corporate shareholders and parent-subsidiary situations. Distributions between corporations should not involve additional tax burdens. The A.L.I. Reporter's Study achieves this by including dividends in the income of the corporate recipient but allowing the recipient a refundable integration credit.[120] The tax rates at the time of the distribution would govern both the amount of the tax due and the amount of the credit. Therefore, the dividend could be distributed free of any tax. There would be a reduction in the distributing corporation's taxes-paid account and an increase in the corporate shareholder's taxes-paid account by the amount of the credit, comparable to how "earnings and profits" accounts might be affected by an intercorporate dividend under present law.

If preference income is distributed to a corporate shareholder, there would be a further problem of whether to wash out the preference or not, since the income remains "in corporate solution." The A.L.I. study would treat a distribution of preference income as in principle implicating a DWT liability for the distributing corporation even though the distribution were made to a corporate shareholder. But, if the corporate identity of the shareholder were known, the A.L.I. proposal will permit treatment of the dividend as exempt income to the recipient. In that case, it would not give rise to DWT or be taxable or creditable to the recipient, and it would not produce any change in the TPA of either corporation.[121]

The A.L.I. study also deals with the alternative means that corporate-source income can be realized by shareholders. It would distinguish between stock redemptions that are very similar to dividends, which would be taxable like dividends under the integration proposal,[122] and gains from the sale of corpo-

---

[116] A.L.I. Reporter, *supra* note 99, at 8.
[117] *Id.* at 8-9.
[118] *See id.* at 159-64 (exempt shareholders and creditors), 190-94 (foreign investors).
[119] *Id.* at 192-93.
[120] *Id.* at 151-58.
[121] *Id.* at 154.
[122] *See id.* at 143-44.

G. THE MAY 1993 AMERICAN LAW INSTITUTE "REPORTER'S STUDY" 673

rate equity securities that would be taxable at the (ordinary income) rate of the seller. Also, stock losses would be deductible, within certain ingenious limitations.[123]

If a shareholder were to sell his shares before a distribution had been made by the corporation, but after tax had been paid by it, or if the shareholder received a non-dividend distribution under such circumstances, there could be a double tax on retained corporate income. This is possible because the shareholder's basis in his shares would not reflect the previously taxed but undistributed income of the corporation. To solve this problem, the A.L.I. Reporter's Study recommends an elective constructive dividend procedure resembling that in the proposal of the Carter Commission in Canada, in 1966.[124] A corporation could declare any amount of its earnings as a constructive dividend, to be treated as followed by a constructive recontribution of such amount back to the corporation. In such event, the constructive dividend would be taxable to the shareholders, but they would be able to offset the tax with available refundable tax credits. The shareholders would also be entitled to increase their tax bases in their shares by the amount of income taxable to them, even though the tax was offset by available credits. The corporation would then record these constructive amounts in a "previously taxed dividend account." Actual distributions made from this account would be tax-free to the shareholders to the extent each distributee had sufficient stock basis.

To produce proper (parallel) treatment of interest payments by a corporation on corporate debt, the A.L.I. Reporter also recommended retaining the interest deduction but adding a new "interest withholding tax" ("IWT") at the corporate level on interest on other than trade credit. The credit for such interest withholding tax would be usable against U.S. tax liability and would be refundable to the same extent as the shareholder withholding credit.[125]

The A.L.I. Reporter's Study thus constructs and elaborates an excellent modern shareholder imputation credit model for integrating the U.S. individual and corporate income taxes by using a design essentially following that in use in the countries of the European Union, and in Australia and New Zealand. Unless a practical partnership-type or allocation model can be shown adequately to address the problems of tax-exempt and foreign shareholders, the A.L.I. imputation credit model seems the optimal course for U.S. policy and legislation to follow.

---

[123] See id. at 129-32.
[124] See id. at 126-29.
[125] See id. at 15, 90-92.

H. EVALUATION OF THE MERITS AND DEFICIENCIES OF THE A.L.I. AND TREASURY PROPOSALS

1. THE INTEGRATION IDEAL

The theoretically ideal model for corporate and individual income tax integration is the flow-through, partnership style, Subchapter S or "transparency" model. The Treasury Department study called this its "shareholder allocation prototype," although that model did not go nearly so far as does Subchapter S or true partnership-style integration.[126] Under such a system, the corporation is viewed merely as a conduit or vehicle for its owners. The corporate source income that is technically earned and retained or distributed by the corporation is treated as if earned by the owners of the enterprise, as it arises in the hands of the corporation. Such a transparency or conduit model provides the closest approximation between the taxation of income earned by a corporation and the taxation of the same income earned from the same business activity through an unincorporated form, such as a partnership or sole proprietorship.[127]

In the partnership model, a tax is imposed on corporate source income as it arises. The tax is determined by taking into account the tax rates of the owners of the income. And finally the income sourced in a corporation is subjected to neither more nor less than one level of taxation.

These characteristics are satisfied by partnership or Subchapter S style integration because the earnings or losses are passed through and taken into account by the individual partners or S corporation shareholders each year, whether or not distributed. The distribution of the burdens is sensitive to the individual tax paying abilities of those benefitting from the income. The income of a tax-exempt shareholder is not subjected to any tax. The income of a low-bracket shareholder is taxed at low rates. The income of a high-bracket shareholder is taxed at high rates. The income of a foreign shareholder would be taxable or not by the source jurisdiction depending upon its international tax rules for dividends or other income sourced within its borders and taxable to foreign investors.

2. THE A.L.I. AND TREASURY PROPOSALS COMPARED

Compared to the classical system presently in effect in the United States, both the A.L.I. and Treasury proposals have the effect of reducing or eliminating the "double" tax on distributed corporate source income. The Treasury proposal eliminates the shareholder tax entirely on fully-taxed corporate source income. The A.L.I. proposal eliminates the corporate level tax, by allowing payment of

---

[126] *See* Treasury Report, *supra* note 35, at 27-38.

[127] *See* James S. Eustice, *Subchapter S Corporations and Partnerships: A Search for the Pass-Through Paradigm*, 39 Tax L. Rev. 345, 346 (1984).

H. EVALUATION OF A.L.I. AND TREASURY PROPOSALS

the corporate tax to provide a credit when shareholders receive distributions and are taxable on them.

It is important to emphasize this point: the Treasury dividend exclusion prototype (and CBIT) and the A.L.I. proposal are *not* models of *complete* integration, they are models of partial integration or "dividend relief." They provide relief or proper shareholder taxation only for *distributed* corporate earnings. They are theoretically inferior to partnership (or Subchapter S or pass-through or transparency) integration, which would allow a pass-through of losses as well as gains and would produce taxation of the shareholders at the time the income or losses were realized by the corporation, at the shareholder rates applicable, and without waiting until a distribution had been made to shareholders. Such a system would also allow a basis increase for the interest of the partners or Subchapter S shareholders so that a sale or exchange of their shares would not implicate a second, unintegrated tax.

Also, compared to a pure transparency system, the January Treasury and A.L.I. proposals would not allow a complete pass-through of corporate preferences, including the foreign tax credit (if that is viewed as a preference), and would not allow foreign taxes to be treated as the equivalent of the payment of U.S. taxes. They also involve complicated withholding taxes and extra corporate level accounts in order to accomplish a variety of objectives.

As compared with each other, the A.L.I. shareholder imputation credit proposal seems quite superior to the Treasury dividend-exclusion prototype and the Treasury comprehensive income tax or "CBIT." The one advantage of the CBIT proposal over the dividend exclusion prototype is that it would treat interest just the same as dividends, by denying a corporate deduction for both and by excluding both from the income of shareholders. However, as Treasury recognized, the CBIT proposal would be difficult to phase in, would involve a schedular approach to the taxation of corporate sector income, and would not be sensitive to the individual rates and taxpaying status of various individual shareholders. The A.L.I. proposal would perpetuate and perfect the application of individualized rates. It would also partly equalize the tax treatment of debt with equity by its new interest withholding tax and lender credit paralleling the dividend withholding tax and credit, although interest payments would remain deductible as under present law.[128]

As to equating the tax treatment of interest and dividends, the key item in the A.L.I. proposal is that because interest payments would remain deductible, the earnings used to pay them would not generate any increase in the "taxes paid account" ("TPA"). Any balance in the TPA account would not satisfy the corporation's liability for the new interest withholding tax (IWT) imposed when interest was paid by the corporation. So this IWT would constitute a *new* tax liability on payment of interest but would be creditable by recipients of corporate

---

[128] A.L.I. Reporter, *supra* note 99, at 112-13.

interest payments against their various tax liabilities on receipt of the interest income. What would be left then, if the IWT rate equalled the corporate tax rate would be: corporate income ($X) reduced to $0 by interest deduction for interest paid; IWT tax on interest paid ($X × IWT rate); individual recipient's tax on $X interest received, partly or wholly offset by the IWT credit; so interest paid would ultimately be taxed once and at each creditor's rate, much as dividends would be taxed after distribution.[129]

The Treasury dividend exclusion prototype has the advantage of being relatively easy to phase in, merely by enacting a new exclusion for dividends in the Internal Revenue Code and then requiring the necessary corporate level accounts and special rules for the treatment of special preference income and foreign source income. Depending upon one's point of view, it also may be an advantage of the dividend exclusion prototype that it would provide a more uniform rate of tax on corporate source income across shareholder lines. However, Professor Yin has shown that the dividend exclusion prototype actually permits a wide range of tax burdens on corporate source income, ranging from a low of negative 17% to a high of 58%.[130] In fact, there would be a substantial loss of neutrality.

Secondly, both the dividend exclusion and CBIT prototypes are objectionable on grounds of horizontal and vertical equity. Neither one is a very fair system, if fairness is determined by the personal rates of tax of individual shareholders, given the total income and filing status of each. To put it another way, the fairness of an integration system may be viewed as depending upon whether it removes a uniform percentage of the additional tax burden represented by the *corporate* tax for all income classes. The Treasury dividend exclusion prototype (or CBIT) fails both of these tests. Both the dividend exclusion prototype and CBIT would give increasing amounts of relief to higher-bracket shareholders compared to low-bracket shareholders. This would leave in effect a high rate of tax on low-income and tax-exempt shareholders. Thus, low-income shareholders would be overtaxed and, by some standards, high-income shareholders would be undertaxed.

The dividend exclusion prototype also has some complexities of its own, those dealing with preference income and other matters. By making dividend distributions much more favorable than non-dividend distributions or capital gains on sales, the perverse posture of present law (which favors non-dividend distributions of corporate profits) generally would be turned upside down, rather than remedied. Nevertheless, in some instances remaining, some individual shareholders would prefer non-dividends over dividends. Above all, taxing dividend income, unlike other income from a corporation, would raise serious problems with closely-held corporations, where it is difficult to distinguish

---

[129] *See id.*

[130] *See* Yin, *supra* note 79, at 462.

H. EVALUATION OF A.L.I. AND TREASURY PROPOSALS 677

between dividend income (excludable by shareholders) and salary income, rents, royalties, and interest (deductible by corporation; includable by recipients). A great deal of tax planning and tax avoidance by converting labor income to capital income, or vice versa, would be invited by adoption of this proposal.

In contrast, the A.L.I. proposal deserves a relatively high score. Its adoption would leave corporate sector income taxed once, and — after distribution — at the rates and characteristics belonging to the individual shareholder recipients. Thus, it would provide considerably more neutrality as between investment and income in the corporate form and in noncorporate forms. It would allow the pass-through or washout of corporate tax preferences, as preferred by the legislature. It would be robust to possible tax rate relationship changes between the rates of corporate tax and the rates of individual income tax, something lacking in the Treasury's dividend exclusion prototype.

As to fairness, the A.L.I. proposal ranks very high. When it is compared with the theoretically preferable partnership or transparency complete integration model, the A.L.I. proposal would leave *distributed* corporate income taxed in the same way, that is at rates appropriate to the individual shareholders. Compared to the transparency model, the A.L.I. shareholder imputation credit would leave *undistributed* corporate earnings taxed at the corporate rates, inasmuch as the corporate income tax would remain in effect, and would serve to prevent undue deferral of income by incorporation, as well as serve as a tax tentatively collected from the business entity for the ultimate account of the individual shareholders. Compared to complete pass-through or Subchapter S integration, this means that the corporate income is taxed at the "wrong" rates (except by coincidence) for a period of time — until it is distributed to shareholders.

This could be cured by corporate elective constructive distribution of all retained earnings, and a deemed recontribution by the shareholders, envisioned by the A.L.I. Reporter. If the top individual income tax rate were the same as the applicable corporate rate, shareholders would be happy to receive such constructive dividends because the credit which would also be constructively distributed to them would at least offset their tax liability. In the case of lower-bracket shareholders, the excess credit would entitle them to a refund. However, this hope may be placing too much weight on the A.L.I. constructive dividend opportunity, just as the Treasury Department relies too much upon the DRIP proposal to solve some of its problems.

If the rate relationship between individual income tax and corporate income tax rates were to change in the direction of a much higher individual rate schedule, shareholders might resist constructive distributions (if the credit would be insufficient and they would have to pay tax without having received any cash in hand). Or, if corporate rates rose above individual rates, shareholders would clamor for constructive or actual distributions because a higher corporate tax rate and credit would provide even the highest individual tax bracket shareholders with substantial refunds.

In general, the A.L.I. proposal does the best job of providing partial integration or dividend relief because it accords with the fundamental philosophy of the U.S. income tax, which is to apply graduated rates to the global income of each shareholder, depending upon the personal filing status of that shareholder.

The A.L.I. proposal is more complex than Treasury's dividend exclusion prototype and perhaps more complex than the CBIT proposal, although that seems to be a problematic conclusion. As noted above, the Treasury proposals have their own complexity.[131] Also, the shareholder imputation tax credit model can build upon the experience of a number of other industrialized countries, and hence U.S. legislators and administrators will be better able to anticipate administrative and compliance problems and the kinds of legislation and regulatory promulgation necessary to deal with them.

The A.L.I. proposal is relatively neutral as to the ways in which income can be taken from a closely-held corporation, that is to say, as deductible salary, interest, rents or royalties, or nondeductible distributions or profits. (In *effect*, dividends (and interest) are deductible under the A.L.I. proposal, because the corporate tax on the corporate earnings is erased by the credit, and the final tax rate is the rate applicable to the individual recipient of the funds.)

The A.L.I. proposal is better than Treasury's CBIT proposal in a number of respects. CBIT would require distinguishing interest or borrowings from investors from interest paid to trade creditors and others. It would rigidly impose its schedular system on all corporations and all unincorporated businesses. It would not leave any room for a Subchapter S or partnership (or limited liability company) complete integration system for the kinds of businesses that now can use those regimes in the United States.

The economic shock from the nondeductibility of interest under the CBIT proposal would be a major problem for the economy and would require a very gradual phase-in. Interest rates on CBIT interest, in the international economy, would be tax-prepaid and exempt to the recipient, at least insofar as the U.S. federal income tax goes.[132] And finally, CBIT, like the dividend exclusion prototype which it incorporates, imposes a schedular tax system within the U.S. income tax which is definitely not schedular in its makeup and underlying theory.

For these reasons, and others, the shareholder imputation credit proposal of the American Law Institute seems distinctly preferable to both the dividend-exclusion and the CBIT prototypes proposed by Treasury. The A.L.I. proposal resembles New Zealand's legislation of recent years and builds upon experience

---

[131] *See supra* Sections E and F.

[132] *See* Gammie, *supra* note 15, at 258.

there and in Australia and in Western European nations.[133] It is reasonably fair and secure, much more fair and more economically neutral than the dividend exclusion and CBIT proposals. It comes close to the merits of transparency or a partnership-type integration, although only as to *distributed* corporate profits.

I. IMPORTANT THEMES: RATE RELATIONSHIPS AND STOCK BASIS

1. TAX RATE RELATIONSHIPS

One important theme that runs throughout an evaluation of proposals for corporate income tax integration is the importance of the relationship between certain tax rates. The most important relationship is that between the top or applicable *corporate* income tax rate and the top or applicable *individual* income tax rate. For example, if the corporate rate is much *lower* than the individual rate, the rate relationship establishes an incentive for taxpayers to incorporate their businesses, and even their passive investment assets, and to cause the corporation to retain earnings, sheltered from the higher individual tax rate until distribution or some other maneuver. It would seem, in other words, that such a rate relationship creates a disincentive for dividends. The retained earnings can be reinvested at the lower corporate income tax rate. Therefore, if the before-tax yield of investment by corporations is approximately equal to the before-tax yield of investment by individual shareholders, much more after-tax corporate income can be earned and retained over a period of years than would be true if the original earnings had been distributed to shareholders and reinvested by them.

If corporate rates are much *higher* than individual income tax rates, this inverted rate relationship may not necessarily reverse the incentive to distribute, because the distribution under a classical system will incur a second tax. However, under these conditions the distributed earnings can be reinvested by shareholders at a lower rate of tax in their hands than if the earnings are reinvested by the corporation, so an incentive to distribute may well be created. This again assumes the before-tax rate of return of investments by shareholders will be approximately the same as the before-tax rate of return on investments by corporations.

If the corporate tax rate is much *lower*, and a dividend exclusion or CBIT form of integration is adopted, corporate income will be taxed once and at a lower rate than the other income of individuals. This unequal schedular system

---

[133] *See* A.L.I. Reporter, *supra* note 99, at 72, 77, 84, 85; Treasury Report, *supra* note 35, app. at 159-84.

In 1993, the Tax Division of the American Institute of Certified Public Accountants also recommended integration by a shareholder-imputation credit method, partly on grounds of its ease and compatibility with generally accepted accounting principles and practices. *See* Tax Division, A.I.C.P.A., Integration of the Corporate and Shareholder Tax Systems (1993).

seems unfair, is far from neutral and very likely to induce tax avoidance planning. If the corporate rate is much *higher* than the applicable individual shareholder rates, there again will be an unfairness because corporate income will be taxed at higher rates than labor income and than the same income of individuals who use entities other than corporations, entities such as partnerships, Subchapter S corporations, limited liability companies, or proprietorships, to make their investments. If the comprehensive business income tax approach is adopted, all businesses would be subjected to the same regime.[134]

If the corporate rate is much *higher* than the individual shareholder rates, and the United States adopts a shareholder imputation credit system, along the lines of the A.L.I. proposal, the tax on retained corporate profits will be higher than that imposed upon final distribution to shareholders. At least one result will be tremendous pressure to distribute, or constructively distribute, corporate earnings so that the high credit for corporate tax can be enjoyed by the shareholders as soon as possible and so that distributed earnings can be reinvested at lower tax rates. If the corporate rate is much *lower* than the individual income rate applicable to shareholders in question, there probably will be a tendency to retain corporate profits, rather than to incur the higher shareholder tax soon, and make distributed earnings subject to higher tax rates upon investment outside the corporation. But the issue may be more complicated or doubtful than this.[135]

The rate relationship between ordinary income and capital gains will also matter a great deal. If capital gains are taxed at a much lower rate, and if distributions by corporations can be made in nondividend form, there will be an incentive for using such distributions and capital gain transactions (especially in the international economy) and for avoiding ordinary income. An extreme case is presented by the I.R.C. § 1014 fresh start basis at death rule. If dividends can be postponed and corporate profits realized in the form of the sale of shares after the death of the shareholder, the fresh start basis at death rule means that a sale of those shares can be made without any income (capital gains) tax. This is infinitely preferable to taxable dividends. It is not, however, preferable to dividends that are tax-free, if a dividend exclusion prototype or CBIT regime is in effect.

It also must be remembered that not all capital gains result from the retention of corporate profits. Appreciation in corporate assets, not yet realized by the

---

[134] Does that mean that individual, passive and portfolio investments would also be subject to a CBIT tax? If not, the distinction between businesses (including proprietorships) and investments would become crucial.

[135] *See*, however, the "new view" of dividend taxation, discussed, along with the "traditional view," in A.L.I. Reporter, *supra* note 99, Treasury Report, *supra* note 35, and in George R. Zodrow, *On The "Traditional" and "New" Views of Dividend Taxation*, 44 Nat'l Tax. J. 497 (1991); Alan J. Auerbach, *Tax Integration and the "New View" of the Corporate Tax: A 1980s Perspective*, Proceedings of the National Tax Association — Tax Institute of America, pp. 21-27 (1981).

corporation, and market factors — including an expectation of future corporate profits or unrealized appreciation at the corporate level — can produce a big increase in the fair market value of shares in the corporation.

If capital losses are deductible, with lower tax benefit and subject to greater limitations than ordinary losses, there will be an incentive to convert capital losses into ordinary losses or into short-term capital losses if such losses are treated like ordinary losses.

Not only are rate relationships such as these important to be taken into account in considering the merits of a particular integration plan, but also it is important to prefer an integration plan that is robust and will be stable and sensible even if present rate relationships change a great deal. It is better to have a corporate tax system in which the legislature can from time to time increase the rates of corporate tax or individual income tax, and even change the relationship of these rates, without upsetting the entire system or the pattern of tax planning incentives it creates. Also, any legislation of an integration plan must contemplate that some shareholders may be taxed at higher rates than others and some corporations at higher rates than others. Therefore, there may be a multiplicity of rate relationships between different corporations and shareholders, including tax-exempt shareholders, foreign shareholders, and high- and low-bracket shareholders. Particularly in an international economy, a nation's corporate tax rates may be hostage to prevailing international levels and to international tax policy (capital exporting, capital importing) and tax avoidance considerations.[136]

2. BASIS ADJUSTMENTS IN SHARES

A second, very important theme has to do with rules regulating the owner's basis in corporate shares. If the basis in a shareholder's shares is not appropriately altered as a result of taxable or tax-free distributions or taxable allocations, the result may be that corporate income is taxed twice, or is not even taxed once, rather than the one tax goal of integration plans.[137] Incentives may be created for shareholders to deal with each other in order to shift losses or gains.

In the Subchapter S and partnership regimes in the United States, "outside basis" of a partner's interest, or adjusted basis in a shareholder's shares, is adjusted to take account of income that is taxable to the partner or the shareholder even though it has not yet been distributed.[138] As a consequence, when an actual distribution is made, it is received tax-free up to the basis that has been created by the earlier taxation of those undistributed earnings to the investor. Or, if the investor sells his partnership interest or shares before actual distribution,

---

[136] *See* Gammie, *supra* note 15, at 253.

[137] *Cf.* I.R.C. § 1059 (providing for reduction in a corporate shareholder's basis by the nontaxed portion of an extraordinary dividend).

[138] *Id.* § 1367.

the higher basis in the shares resulting from the earlier imputation means that there will be less capital gain or there will be a deductible loss upon the sale of the shares, which is appropriate in view of the earlier taxation to the investor.

It is not so clear that appropriate basis adjustments will be made under the Treasury proposals and other integration plans. For example, under Treasury's Dividend Exclusion model, there is an important question whether "stock basis would be reduced by what economically amount to return-of-capital distributions."[139] If not, the result could be that corporate income would not be taxed at all.[140]

Suppose, for example, that a shareholder governed by the dividend exclusion prototype receives a dividend distribution from his corporation, one that is not taxable to him because there is sufficient balance in the EDA account. If his basis in his shares is not reduced by virtue of receiving this distribution, he could then sell the shares at a loss and take a loss deduction for the difference between the amount realized and his basis in the shares.

Or, suppose that in year one a corporation had earned and retained profits. Those profits now could be distributed tax-free to a shareholder under the dividend-exclusion prototype. Suppose a second person buys the shares from the first shareholder for a price that reflects the value of the retained profits. In year two that new shareholder could receive the dividends apparently tax-free (up to his high cost basis), and then could sell the shares for a lower price (deductible loss), reflecting the fact that the retained earnings now had been distributed and the shares were worth less as a consequence.

A related problem has to do with the role that tax-exempt institutions might play as intermediaries for taxable shareholders. Under a shareholder imputation credit system, the credit would not do much good to a tax-exempt institution. But if the institution sold the shares to a taxable shareholder, who then could receive a distribution and obtain a benefit from the shareholder imputation credit that flows out with the distribution, might there be some tax avoidance? Or, under some integration proposals, as under the classical system, would not tax-exempt institutions bid up the price of shares because dividends are inherently not taxable to those tax-exempt shareholders, even though taxable to other shareholders?

The ability to shift the refundable credit under a shareholder imputation credit model to a purchaser of stock might make it extremely difficult to insure in practice that all corporate income was in fact subject to a nonrefundable tax. Even if the credit were made nonrefundable, if it were still available for use against unrelated income of the shareholder, the effect would be much the same as that of a refundable credit. Practitioner Michael Schler has shown that clever tax practitioners would be very likely to find ways to avoid the one level of tax

---

[139] Michael Schler, *Taxing Corporate Income Once (Or Hopefully Not at All): A Practitioner's Comparison of the Treasury and A.L.I. Integration Models*, 47 Tax L. Rev. 509, 562 (1992).
[140] *Id.*

intended, or to shift taxability from high- to low-bracket taxpayers, under any integration proposal, particularly under the dividend exclusion models proposed by the Treasury Department.[141]

A related danger is that an integration proposal might nevertheless result in the double-taxation of corporate profits. This might happen if, for example, a corporation earned income that was taxable to it and retained the earnings. If the shares went up in value because of the retained earnings, under a system such as the dividend exclusion prototype, and if the shareholder sold the shares before an actual distribution was made, he or she would be taxable on the capital gain (a second tax, at the shareholder level), even though he or she could have received an excludable dividend distribution from the corporation. In other words, under such a system dividends would be much more attractive than nondividend distributions or gains from the sale of securities. The purchaser in such an example would not reduce the price paid for the shares to capitalize any tax burden because the purchaser presumably would be entitled to receive the dividends tax-free and because of the basic function of the dividend exclusion prototype. In these cases, it is observed that there can be a failure of integration and a double-taxation of corporate profits, even under an integration system that is designed to remove the double-taxation (or "over-taxation") of corporate profits.

J. CORPORATE TAX INTEGRATION WHILE RETAINING TWO TAXES

Another approach to the problem of over-taxation of corporate source income would be to retain both the corporate and shareholder income taxes and to relate the two taxes and tax rates so that the total burden on corporate source income would be the same as, or close to, that on noncorporate source income. This means using two relatively low-rate taxes.[142]

The United States had a system of this type for some years following the enactment of the income tax in 1913. At that time dividend income was exempt from the flat-rate basic income tax, called the "normal tax," that applied to all individuals.[143] However, to preserve progressivity, dividend income was not excluded from the tax base of the "additional tax" or surtax on individuals, a graduated tax that applied only to high-income persons.[144] For such taxpayers, at that time, corporate source income was taxed once at the corporate level, at a relatively low rate, and then again as part of the shareholder surtax, if the dividends were received by a relatively high-income individual. Taxpayers in

---

[141] Id.

[142] See Yin, supra note 79, at 481.

[143] Roy G. Blakey & Gladys C. Blakey, The Federal Income Tax 96-97 (1940).

[144] Yin, supra note 79, at 481.

lower income ranges, subject only to the "normal tax," had their corporate source income taxed only once, at the corporate level.[145] This system endured in the United States until 1936, when the tax system became unintegrated.[146]

To accomplish integration of the retained double taxes, the corporate tax rate could be reduced to the basic rate applicable to low-bracket investors, and thus the corporate tax would serve as a surrogate for the tax otherwise owed by those investors if they had earned the corporate source income directly, rather than through a corporation. As a result, dividends and other means by which such investors could realize the corporate source income, including gains realized upon the sale of equity securities, would be exempted from ordinary income tax. Because the corporate tax would be insufficient as a substitute for the total tax on higher bracket shareholders, they would be subject to a surtax, again no matter how they realized their corporate source income. Thus integration with the desired degree of progressivity could be accomplished roughly through a combination of the two taxes (or tax reliefs), each with relatively low marginal rates.[147]

It must be admitted that zero-bracket or tax-exempt shareholders, including low-income individuals, would still suffer overtaxation of their income realized through the corporation, because it would have been taxed at least at the relatively low corporate rate. To compensate, they could be given a refundable tax credit, one that would be eaten up if their overall incomes were higher. In general, the extremes of undertaxation and overtaxation that are entailed by the Treasury Department's dividend exclusion approach or CBIT approach would be minimized or eliminated. There would not be complete schedular taxation of corporate source income, but rather taxation largely geared to the individual income situations of the shareholders. While this approach does not match the accuracy and fairness of the Subchapter S pass-through model or the A.L.I. shareholder imputation credit model, it has some advantages and may deserve further exploration. However, its great and perhaps fatal weakness may lie in the ability of high-income shareholders to defer the application of higher tax rates and to shelter income by putting it into a corporation.

---

[145] *Id.*

[146] *See* Blakey & Blakey, *supra* note 143.

The Treasury dividend-exclusion and CBIT prototypes could be modified so as to make dividends excludable from only a low or other fixed rate of shareholder taxation and leave them taxable to the extent of the difference between this and higher marginal shareholder rates. But this would invite tax-rate arbitrage between taxpayers, and other income-shifting and tax-avoidance maneuvers.

[147] *See* Yin, *supra* note 79, at 482. In a way the linking of reductions in two taxes resembles the pre-1988 Japanese system's combination of a reduced corporate rate on distributed corporate profits and a low shareholder tax credit for a fixed percentage of gross dividends received. *See* Tax Bureau Ministry of Finance, An Outline of Japanese Taxes 1992 50 (1992) (Japan).

J. CORPORATE TAX INTEGRATION WHILE RETAINING TWO TAXES

Professor Yin, who has developed and analyzed a sophisticated version of the two-tax model, called "Integration Through Double-Taxation: The Surtax Approach,"[148] would let two low-rate taxes on the same income serve the function of a higher single rate of tax.[149] He has analyzed the problems of preference income, political considerations, the simplicity of the tax system and the security of tax, the treatment of tax-exempt and low-bracket shareholders, the flexibility of the legal system, and the problem of deferred shareholder-level tax. He concludes that there are many merits to the idea and that the difficulties can be dealt with intelligently.[150] He also suggests that perhaps the surtax or double tax approach should be confined to widely-held, perhaps publicly-traded corporations.[151] This, of course, resembles the situation in the United States at the present time, inasmuch as closely-held corporations can elect Subchapter S integration, or investors can use the partnership or limited liability company form. In fact, the limited liability company form may soon be extended to rather widely-held corporations as well. While Professor Yin acknowledges that the surtax approach is far from a perfect means of implementing integration, he intelligently argues for its merits, although he admits that the "tax shelter problem ... may be its fatal flaw."[152]

A related problem and solution has to do with the difference between the present U.S. tax system's treatment of corporate income that is financed by debt rather than by equity investments. It is this difference that seems to have driven the Treasury Department so far towards the dividend exclusion and CBIT approaches. If the classical system were retained, or if the rates were ameliorated somewhat to relieve the severity of the double-taxation of corporate income, the difference between debt and equity finance could be addressed to some extent by limiting or reducing the deductibility of interest paid on corporate debt. Another possibility would be to favor somewhat the distribution of dividends and to lower the tax burden upon distributed corporate earnings by a split-rate or dividend deduction system, perhaps with a shareholder tax credit as well (as in Japan before 1988).[153] While such a system might make it difficult to prevent extending the benefits to foreign shareholders or to tax-exempt institutions, it has the advantage of tremendous simplicity. As a distinguished Japanese financial expert said in a Tokyo conversation in 1979, "a deduction for dividends may be overall the best method of dividend relief and double-tax relief because it is the simplest." One might add that it is advantageous because it tends to reduce the difference between debt and equity finance. It could also be combined, as Japan

---

[148] Yin, *supra* note 79, at 480.
[149] *Id.* at 481.
[150] *See id.* at 505.
[151] *Id.* at 500.
[152] *Id.* at 501.
[153] *See supra* note 147.

for so many years combined its split-rate system, with a small credit given to shareholders for a percentage of the dividends they receive, a credit not based upon an imputation of the corporate income tax to the shareholders, but rather given merely as a blunt form of tax relief to taxable shareholders of corporations.

A study of the complexities and uncertainties entailed in the various integration proposals recently recommended in the United States, and proposed or studied over the years by tax scholars, may cause a tax theorist to say, as a Dutch tax adviser remarked in conversation a few years ago in Amsterdam, that "the classical system may not be such a bad system after all." In other words, one distinct policy alternative is to leave the classical system in place and to decide that integration or dividend relief is not worth the difficulties and costs involved, or to retain the double layer of tax but to minimize its economic and legal disadvantages.

Nevertheless, the benefits of complete, or partial, integration would be so great that it seems mistaken not to continue the effort.

K. THE SUPERIORITY OF COMPLETE INTEGRATION, PARTNERSHIP OR S CORPORATION STYLE OVER OTHER METHODS

Complete integration, in the "pass-through," or "partnership," or "S corporation" style, or the nearest thing to it, such as the Carter Commission or A.L.I. proposals, seems far superior to CBIT and dividend exclusion (or even dividend deduction/split rate versions, in use in Germany, in Japan from 1961 to 1989 and elsewhere,[154] and recommended by the U.S. Treasury in 1984[155] and the President of the United States in 1985[156]). Business income ultimately should be taxed to the *owners* of the business, at *their* rates, when they earn or benefit from it. This view embraces, in other words, the fundamental theory of the U.S. individual income tax. That tax is a *personal* tax, one that takes a global (not a schedular) approach to its base and rates, and, as a general principle, it is one that lumps all of a taxpayer's financial gains together in one quantity and then taxes that amount according to Congress' notions of "ability to pay" — the ability to pay of each individual taxpayer, as determined by his or her relevant financial, social, and tax characteristics.[157]

---

[154] *See, e.g.*, Treasury Report, *supra* note 35, app. at 172-76; Tax Bureau Ministry of Finance, *supra* note 147.

[155] Treasury I (1984), *supra* note 1, at 136-40. Recall that the U.S. Treasury Department at other times studied and advocated a pass-through integration model. *See* Treasury Blueprints, *supra* note 1.

[156] Treasury II (1985), *supra* note 6, at 122-26.

[157] *See* John K. McNulty, *Preserving the Virtues of Subchapter S in an Integrated World*, 47 Tax Law Rev. 681, 684, from which this section is derived (hereinafter McNulty, *Preserving Subchapter S*).

K. THE SUPERIORITY OF COMPLETE INTEGRATION, PARTNERSHIP, ETC.

As one author has put it, "... where under an income tax corporate tax rates diverge significantly from personal tax rates and the same *graduated* personal tax rates are intended to be applied to capital and labour income, the only satisfactory form of integration is a shareholder allocated method."[158] Because only individuals can consume, or benefit from consumption, only individuals bear the incidence or burden of any tax, and it is this burden that should be geared to ability to pay (somehow rightly conceived) of the individual bearers. Ideally, all income would and should be taxed ultimately to individuals, and only to individuals.

Thus, if one takes the basic philosophy, structure, and theory of the individual income tax seriously, one probably would prefer to tax undistributed corporate income to shareholders by taxing unrealized appreciation (and diminution) in the value of shares as an accretion to net worth, à la the von-Schanz/Haig-Simons[159] conceptions of income.[160] However, the realization rule, part of the U.S. income tax's "genetic code" and the practicalities it represents, make accretion taxation of unrealized share gains and losses apparently unworkable for most corporations.[161] Yet, if the corporation's earnings are not taxed to shareholders until distribution, the deferral or avoidance possibilities will be unacceptable. Consequently, a separate corporate income tax has evolved as a surrogate for (theoretically correct) current taxation of shareholders, lest undistributed corporate earnings go entirely untaxed for too long.[162]

This perspective emphasizes that the United States has an income tax on corporations in the classical mold largely because of the "rule of realization," without which there could be annual taxation of accretions or diminutions in value of shares, the theoretically correct way to tax shareholders. There is a

---

[158] Gammie, *supra* note 15, at 252.

[159] Robert M. Haig, *The Concept of Income — Economic and Legal Aspects*, in The Federal Income Tax (Robert M. Haig ed. 1921), *reprinted in* American Economic Association, Readings in the Economics of Taxation 54 (Richard A. Musgrave & Carl S. Shoup eds. 1959); Henry C. Simons, Personal Income Taxation 50 (1938); Georg van Schanz, *Der Einkommensbegriff und die Einkommensteuergesetze*, 13 Finanz-Archiv 1-87 (1896).

[160] McNulty, *Reform by Integration*, *supra* note 1, at 1450; *see* Leon Gabinet & Ronald J. Coffey, *The Implications of the Economic Concept of Income for Corporation-Shareholder Income Tax Systems*, 27 Case W. Res. L. Rev. 895, 912-18 (1977); *see also* Gammie, *supra* note 15, at 154-55; Noël B. Cunningham & Deborah H. Schenk, *Taxation Without Realization: A "Revolutionary Approach" to Ownership*, 47 Tax L. Rev. 725 (1992).

[161] *But see* David Slawson, *Taxing as Ordinary Income the Appreciation of Publicly Held Stock*, 76 Yale L.J. 623, 644-51 (1967); David J. Shakow, *Taxation Without Realization: A proposal for Accrual Taxation*, 134 U. Pa. L. Rev. 1111 (1986); Scott A. Taylor, *Corporate Integration in the Federal Income Tax: Lessons From the Past and a Proposal for the Future*, 10 Va. Tax Rev. 237, 298-301 (1990).

[162] Gammie, *supra* note 15, at 150. "The need to tax companies in some way or other can, therefore, be regarded as a measure of the extent to which the personal tax system *falls short* of achieving either the comprehensive income tax or the universal expenditure tax." *Id.*

separate tax on income received by corporations only as a kind of substitute tax because of the inability, or the unwillingness, to try to tax shareholders on an accretion basis. The corporate tax system serves as a "collection mechanism for the personal tax system."[163]

So, in this view, the corporate income tax is really just a tax designed to aid and perfect the *individual* income tax. It includes undistributed corporate sector earnings in the income tax base only in a crude and brute way, and, without integration, it overtaxes distributed corporate earnings.[164]

Consequently, the Subchapter S (or pass-through) integration model, which taxes business income of Subchapter S corporations the way it would be taxed if the business were a proprietorship or a partnership, serves best *as an integration model*, and as a desirable real world system operating wherever it can be used. It accords with U.S. values about individual income taxation. That is to say, it promotes progressivity, fairness and horizontal and vertical equity and takes a global rather than a schedular definition of income.[165] It is sensitive to rate, status and other individual characteristics of individual shareholders. These are some things the two main Treasury proposals do not do.[166] Subchapter S integration also provides, for these reasons and others, the *fairest* method of integration, regardless of assumptions about the incidence of the income tax, an aspect that receives little attention in the Treasury Report.

Depending on their basis rules and capital gain taxes,[167] the A.L.I. and Treasury models still may differentiate between the effective taxation of retained and distributed earnings in important ways. Consequently, either of these models would constitute a suboptimal improvement.

Subchapter S integration also should provide the most efficient *allocation of resources* between incorporated and unincorporated sections of the economy. It

---

[163] *Id.* at 157.

[164] To be sure, taxing a corporation's earnings to it at its rate does not do the same thing as taxing unrealized accretions or diminutions in share values, and dividends, to the shareholders at their rates. Nor is a pass-through approach to integration the same thing as taxing unrealized share gains and losses — because changes in share values do not exactly equal retained earnings, though the two values tend to move together. Among the tax substitutes for von Schanz-Haig-Simons accrual taxation, the Subchapter S approach seems far superior on theoretical grounds to either the unintegrated classical approach or to a schedular (Treasury) or other partial integration model.

[165] The models that Treasury recommended surreptitiously introduce a distinction between income from capital and income from labor. *See, e.g.*, Treasury Report, *supra* note 35, at 42. Doing so necessarily implicates the need systematically to distinguish one from the other. *See* Gammie, *supra* note 15, at 156, 253.

[166] The Treasury recommendations do not so much propose to integrated the two taxes, as that term usually means both ensuring that only a single tax will be applied and that it will be levied at the shareholders' marginal rates, as they simply tend to lay a flat rate tax on capital income that takes the form of corporate profits. Gammie, *supra* note 15, at 250. The A.L.I. proposal, in contrast, does attempt to attain both aspects of integration.

[167] For a comprehensive discussion of these issues, *see* Schler, *supra* note 139.

K. THE SUPERIORITY OF COMPLETE INTEGRATION, PARTNERSHIP, ETC. 689

would enhance neutrality and economic *efficiency*. It is close to neutral with respect to the distribution or retention of earnings and as to debt versus equity capitalization of firms.[168] It also is reasonably efficient *fiscally*. It is relatively neutral as between the choice of form: proprietorship, partnership, or corporation (or limited liability company, the coming phenomenon and a very important development on the choice-of-form scene[169]). Moreover, if there is not retention and expansion of Subchapter S, limited liability companies will probably come to substitute for S corporations. Treasury's CBIT plan would, presumably, override them, as it would override Subchapter S and the present proprietorship and partnership regimes,[170] but the dividend exclusion plan apparently would not do so.[171]

The United States has a long and valuable experience with pass-through systems, including Subchapter K for partnerships and Subchapter S for electing closely-held corporations, not only at the federal level, but also among the states. Many states have adopted a Subchapter S analogue in their state income tax systems.[172] Other states have learned how to operate their own systems in a world where corporations are able to elect Subchapter S at the national level, or in other states. That experience ought not lightly be set aside.[173]

---

[168] Treasury's CBIT would equalize debt and equity by denying a deduction for interest (just as dividends would be nondeductible), and excluding interest and dividends from recipients' income. Treasury Report, *supra* note 35, at 39.

A recent study by two Treasury economists indicates that A CBIT type integration would have a strong effect on overall foreign asset holdings in the United States, resulting in a drop in the U.S. capital stock. Because CBIT denies an interest deduction, interest rates paid on U.S. debt would be expected to fall, and foreign capital, being mobile, would flow elsewhere. The study indicates that a full integration or dividend credit approach, in contrast, would not have this overall effect; although these plans would induce a decline in foreign holdings of U.S. equity, there would be an increase in foreign holdings of U.S. debt. *Corporate Integration Options May Alter Mix, Level of Foreign Investment in U.S.*, Daily Tax Rep. (BNA) No. 198, at G-4 to G-5 (Oct. 13, 1992).

[169] Francis J. Wirtz & Kenneth L. Harris, *The Emerging Use of the Limited Liability Company*, 70 Taxes 377, 377-78 (1992); *see* Rev. Rul. 93-5, 1993-3 I.R.B. 6; Rev. Rul. 93-6, 1993-3 I.R.B. 8; Rev. Rul. 88-76, 1988-2 C.B. 360 (limited liability company taxable as a partnership); Edward J. Roche, Jr. et al., *Limited Liability Companies Offer Pass-Through Benefits Without S Corp. Restrictions*, 74 J. Tax'n 248 (1991).

[170] Treasury Report, *supra* note 35, at 39-43, 17-25.

[171] *See* Treasury Recommendation, *supra* note 85, at L-14.

[172] *See, e.g.*, Cal. Rev. & Tax. Code §§ 17087.5, 23800-23811 (West Supp. 1992); Ill. Ann. Stat. ch. 120, para. 2-205(c) (Smith-Hurd Supp. 1991).

[173] The U.S. also has experience, at the federal level, with other pass-through or allocation systems, including Subpart F, applicable to foreign subsidiaries. *See generally* James S. Eustice, *Subchapter S Corporations and Partnerships: A Search for the Pass Through Paradigm (Some Preliminary Proposals)*, 39 Tax L. Rev. 345 (1984). Moreover, proposed legislation would make the undistributed income of all subsidiaries of U.S. multinationals currently taxable by the United States. H.R. 5270, 102d Cong., 2d Sess. § 201 (1992).

In other words, Subchapter S-type pass-through correctly taxes all (realized) business income, including losses (negative income), on a comprehensive income tax approach, which is not true of the proposals of either the A.L.I. Reporter's Study or the Treasury Report. Subchapter S also provides a tremendously desirable form or model of integration, because it is robust as to income tax rate changes and rate relationship changes. The other integration prototypes under consideration are immensely vulnerable, in varying degrees, if rate relationships (for example, between top individual and corporate rates or between ordinary income and capital gains rates) change a good deal — or even a little.[174] As a consequence, the Treasury's two main models, and even the A.L.I. approach, might tend to lock in the existing rate relationships, a considerable loss of national public policy flexibility. Subchapter S-type integration, however, would preserve flexibility.

Also, compared to Treasury's integration models at least, Subchapter S provides outside (shareholder) basis adjustments for the pass-through of income and losses.[175] The system of basis and taxation of gains (or losses) is important when shareholders in an integrated system sell or dispose of their shares, in order to prevent "too much" or "too little" integration from resulting. In fact, it seems that some aspects of these problems have not been adequately worked out for other integration models,[176] but Subchapter S has a fine apparatus, and historical record, on this score. More particularly, under Subchapter S, when income (capital gains) tax is imposed upon the sale of shares, there is not double taxation of retained profits,[177] as would be the case under Treasury's dividend exclusion prototype or CBIT unless a dividend reinvestment plan, with basis consequences, were elected with respect to (exactly) all retained earnings. Consequently, pass-through type integration, as exemplified by Subchapter S or partnership taxation in the U.S., should continue to be the model for integration that applies to *all* corporations in the U.S. If that model cannot be universalized, the A.L.I. shareholder imputation credit model should be employed as the second best.[178]

Compared to pass-through Subchapter S type complete integration, the A.L.I. shareholder imputation credit is a good substitute, but the Treasury dividend

---

[174] Corporate tax rates, at least, are likely to change in response to rates in other countries, because of increasingly internationalized capital markets. Individual income tax rates can be set by each country more autonomously.

[175] *See* Prop. Reg. §§ 1.1367-0, -1, -2, -3, 57 Fed. Reg. 24,426 (1992); *cf.* I.R.C. § 1059.

[176] *See generally* Schler, *supra* note 139.

[177] Income of an S Corporation passes through and is reported by the shareholders whether or not it is distributed (I.R.C. § 1366(a)) and increases the basis of the shares (I.R.C. § 1367(a)), thus preventing further tax on the same gain when they are sold.

[178] *See* McNulty, *Preserving Subchapter S*, *supra* note 157, at 692-97; Martin Ginsburg, *Maintaining Subchapter S in an Integrated World*, 47 Tax L. Rev. 665 (1992); Deborah H. Schenk, *Complete Integration in a Partial Integration World*, 47 Tax L. Rev. 697 (1992).

K. THE SUPERIORITY OF COMPLETE INTEGRATION, PARTNERSHIP, ETC.

exclusion and CBIT prototypes, which also provide only dividend relief, not complete integration, are distinctly defective forms of relief from the classical system.[179] Even if complete integration were not possible, as some believe,[180] an exclusion for dividends, as in the Treasury's models, cannot measure up as a reform model for the United States. As Professor Sunley says, the realistic choice lies between a dividends-paid deduction at the corporation level or an imputation credit at the shareholder level.[181] As between these two approaches, the imputation credit model would be best. The A.L.I. Reporter's development of this model, building on extensive experience in many other countries, has shown how feasible and attractive, though admittedly complex, such an approach can be.[182]

---

[179] *See* Emil M. Sunley, *Corporate Integration: An Economic Perspective*, 47 Tax L. Rev. 621, 626 (1992).

[180] *Id.*; *see* Treasury Report, *supra* note 35, at 27, *passim*.

[181] Sunley, *supra* note 178, at 626.

[182] In contrast, the Treasury's CBIT model both goes too far and not far enough. *See* Sunley, *supra* note 179, at 631-35.

Appendix
IRS FORMS

	Page
1. Form 1065: U.S. Partnership Return of Income	694
2. Schedule K-1: Partner's Share of Income, Credits, Deductions, etc.	698
3. Form 2553: Election by a Small Business Corporation	700

1. FORM 1065: U.S. PARTNERSHIP RETURN OF INCOME

Form **1065**	**U.S. Partnership Return of Income**	OMB No. 1545-0099
Department of the Treasury Internal Revenue Service	For calendar year 1994, or tax year beginning ...., 1994, and ending ...., 19 .... ▶ See separate instructions.	**1994**

A Principal business activity	Use the IRS label. Other- wise, please print or type.	Name of partnership	D Employer identification number
B Principal product or service		Number, street, and room or suite no. (If a P.O. box, see page 9 of the instructions.)	E Date business started
C Business code number		City or town, state, and ZIP code	F Total assets (see Specific Instructions) $

G Check applicable boxes: (1) ☐ Initial return (2) ☐ Final return (3) ☐ Change in address (4) ☐ Amended return
H Check accounting method: (1) ☐ Cash (2) ☐ Accrual (3) ☐ Other (specify) ▶ ....
I Number of Schedules K-1. Attach one for each person who was a partner at any time during the tax year ▶ ....

Caution: Include **only** trade or business income and expenses on lines 1a through 22 below. See the instructions for more information.

Income
- 1a Gross receipts or sales 1a
- b Less returns and allowances 1b   1c
- 2 Cost of goods sold (Schedule A, line 8) 2
- 3 Gross profit. Subtract line 2 from line 1c 3
- 4 Ordinary income (loss) from other partnerships, estates, and trusts (attach schedule) . . . 4
- 5 Net farm profit (loss) (attach Schedule F (Form 1040)) . . . 5
- 6 Net gain (loss) from Form 4797, Part II, line 20 6
- 7 Other income (loss) (see instructions) (attach schedule) . . 7
- 8 **Total income (loss).** Combine lines 3 through 7 8

Deductions (see instructions for limitations)
- 9 Salaries and wages (other than to partners) (less employment credits) . . . 9
- 10 Guaranteed payments to partners 10
- 11 Repairs and maintenance 11
- 12 Bad debts 12
- 13 Rent 13
- 14 Taxes and licenses 14
- 15 Interest 15
- 16a Depreciation (see instructions) 16a
-   b Less depreciation reported on Schedule A and elsewhere on return 16b   16c
- 17 Depletion **(Do not deduct oil and gas depletion.)** . . . 17
- 18 Retirement plans, etc. 18
- 19 Employee benefit programs 19
- 20 Other deductions (attach schedule) 20
- 21 **Total deductions.** Add the amounts shown in the far right column for lines 9 through 20 . 21
- 22 **Ordinary income (loss)** from trade or business activities. Subtract line 21 from line 8 . 22

Please Sign Here
Under penalties of perjury, I declare that I have examined this return, including accompanying schedules and statements, and to the best of my knowledge and belief, it is true, correct, and complete. Declaration of preparer (other than general partner) is based on all information of which preparer has any knowledge.
▶ Signature of general partner or limited liability company member   ▶ Date

Paid Preparer's Use Only
Preparer's signature ▶	Date	Check if self-employed ▶ ☐	Preparer's social security no.
Firm's name (or yours if self-employed) and address ▶		E.I. No. ▶	
		ZIP code ▶	

For Paperwork Reduction Act Notice, see page 1 of separate instructions.   Cat. No. 11390Z   Form **1065** (1994)

1. FORM 1065: U.S. PARTNERSHIP RETURN OF INCOME

Form 1065 (1994)   Page **2**

Schedule A — Cost of Goods Sold

1	Inventory at beginning of year	1
2	Purchases less cost of items withdrawn for personal use	2
3	Cost of labor	3
4	Additional section 263A costs (see instructions) *(attach schedule)*	4
5	Other costs *(attach schedule)*	5
6	**Total.** Add lines 1 through 5	6
7	Inventory at end of year	7
8	**Cost of goods sold.** Subtract line 7 from line 6. Enter here and on page 1, line 2	8

9a Check all methods used for valuing closing inventory:
   (i) ☐ Cost
   (ii) ☐ Lower of cost or market as described in Regulations section 1.471-4
   (iii) ☐ Writedown of "subnormal" goods as described in Regulations section 1.471-2(c)
   (iv) ☐ Other (specify method used and attach explanation) ▶ ....

   b Check this box if the LIFO inventory method was adopted this tax year for any goods *(if checked, attach Form 970)* . ▶ ☐
   c Do the rules of section 263A (for property produced or acquired for resale) apply to the partnership? . . ☐ Yes ☐ No
   d Was there any change in determining quantities, cost, or valuations between opening and closing inventory? ☐ Yes ☐ No
   If "Yes," attach explanation.

Schedule B — Other Information

		Yes	No
1	What type of entity is filing this return? Check the applicable box ▶ ☐ General partnership ☐ Limited partnership ☐ Limited liability company		
2	Are any partners in this partnership also partnerships?		
3	Is this partnership a partner in another partnership?		
4	Is this partnership subject to the consolidated audit procedures of sections 6221 through 6233? If "Yes," see **Designation of Tax Matters Partner** below		
5	Does this partnership meet **ALL THREE** of the following requirements?		
a	The partnership's total receipts for the tax year were less than $250,000;		
b	The partnership's total assets at the end of the tax year were less than $600,000; **AND**		
c	Schedules K-1 are filed with the return and furnished to the partners on or before the due date (including extensions) for the partnership return. If "Yes," the partnership is not required to complete Schedules L, M-1, and M-2; Item F on page 1 of Form 1065; or Item J on Schedule K-1		
6	Does this partnership have any foreign partners?		
7	Is this partnership a publicly traded partnership as defined in section 469(k)(2)?		
8	Has this partnership filed, or is it required to file, **Form 8264**, Application for Registration of a Tax Shelter?		
9	At any time during calendar year 1994, did the partnership have an interest in or a signature or other authority over a financial account in a foreign country (such as a bank account, securities account, or other financial account)? (See the instructions for exceptions and filing requirements for Form TD F 90-22.1.) If "Yes," enter the name of the foreign country. ▶		
10	Was the partnership the grantor of, or transferor to, a foreign trust that existed during the current tax year, whether or not the partnership or any partner has any beneficial interest in it? If "Yes," you may have to file Forms 3520, 3520-A, or 926		
11	Was there a distribution of property or a transfer (e.g., by sale or death) of a partnership interest during the tax year? If "Yes," you may elect to adjust the basis of the partnership's assets under section 754 by attaching the statement described under **Elections Made By the Partnership**		

Designation of Tax Matters Partner (See instructions.)
Enter below the general partner designated as the tax matters partner (TMP) for the tax year of this return:

Name of designated TMP ▶

Identifying number of TMP ▶

Address of designated TMP ▶

APPENDIX: IRS FORMS

Form 1065 (1994)   Page 3

Schedule K   Partners' Shares of Income, Credits, Deductions, etc.

	(a) Distributive share items		(b) Total amount
Income (Loss)	1 Ordinary income (loss) from trade or business activities (page 1, line 22)	1	
	2 Net income (loss) from rental real estate activities *(attach Form 8825)*	2	
	3a Gross income from other rental activities 3a		
	b Expenses from other rental activities *(attach schedule)* . . . 3b		
	c Net income (loss) from other rental activities. Subtract line 3b from line 3a	3c	
	4 Portfolio income (loss) (see instructions): a Interest income	4a	
	b Dividend income	4b	
	c Royalty income	4c	
	d Net short-term capital gain (loss) *(attach Schedule D (Form 1065))*	4d	
	e Net long-term capital gain (loss) *(attach Schedule D (Form 1065))*	4e	
	f Other portfolio income (loss) *(attach schedule)*	4f	
	5 Guaranteed payments to partners	5	
	6 Net gain (loss) under section 1231 (other than due to casualty or theft) *(attach Form 4797)*	6	
	7 Other income (loss) *(attach schedule)*	7	
Deductions	8 Charitable contributions (see instructions) *(attach schedule)*	8	
	9 Section 179 expense deduction *(attach Form 4562)*	9	
	10 Deductions related to portfolio income (see instructions) (itemize)	10	
	11 Other deductions *(attach schedule)*	11	
Investment Interest	12a Interest expense on investment debts	12a	
	b (1) Investment income included on lines 4a, 4b, 4c, and 4f above	12b(1)	
	(2) Investment expenses included on line 10 above	12b(2)	
Credits	13a Credit for income tax withheld	13a	
	b Low-income housing credit (see instructions):		
	(1) From partnerships to which section 42(j)(5) applies for property placed in service before 1990	13b(1)	
	(2) Other than on line 13b(1) for property placed in service before 1990	13b(2)	
	(3) From partnerships to which section 42(j)(5) applies for property placed in service after 1989	13b(3)	
	(4) Other than on line 13b(3) for property placed in service after 1989	13b(4)	
	c Qualified rehabilitation expenditures related to rental real estate activities *(attach Form 3468)*	13c	
	d Credits (other than credits shown on lines 13b and 13c) related to rental real estate activities (see instructions)	13d	
	e Credits related to other rental activities (see instructions)	13e	
	14 Other credits (see instructions)	14	
Self-Employment	15a Net earnings (loss) from self-employment	15a	
	b Gross farming or fishing income	15b	
	c Gross nonfarm income	15c	
Adjustments and Tax Preference Items	16a Depreciation adjustment on property placed in service after 1986	16a	
	b Adjusted gain or loss	16b	
	c Depletion (other than oil and gas)	16c	
	d (1) Gross income from oil, gas, and geothermal properties	16d(1)	
	(2) Deductions allocable to oil, gas, and geothermal properties	16d(2)	
	e Other adjustments and tax preference items *(attach schedule)*	16e	
Foreign Taxes	17a Type of income ▶ .... b Foreign country or U.S. possession ▶		
	c Total gross income from sources outside the United States *(attach schedule)*	17c	
	d Total applicable deductions and losses *(attach schedule)*	17d	
	e Total foreign taxes (check one): ▶ ☐ Paid ☐ Accrued	17e	
	f Reduction in taxes available for credit *(attach schedule)*	17f	
	g Other foreign tax information *(attach schedule)*	17g	
Other	18a Total expenditures to which a section 59(e) election may apply	18a	
	b Type of expenditures ▶		
	19 Tax-exempt interest income	19	
	20 Other tax-exempt income	20	
	21 Nondeductible expenses	21	
	22 Other items and amounts required to be reported separately to partners (see instructions) *(attach schedule)*		
Analysis	23a Income (loss). Combine lines 1 through 7 in column (b). From the result, subtract the sum of lines 8 through 12a, 17e, and 18a	23a	

b Analysis by type of partner:	(a) Corporate	(b) Individual		(c) Partnership	(d) Exempt organization	(e) Nominee/Other
		i. Active	ii. Passive			
(1) General partners						
(2) Limited partners						

1. FORM 1065: U.S. PARTNERSHIP RETURN OF INCOME

Form 1065 (1994) — Page 4

Note: If Question 5 of Schedule B is answered "Yes," the partnership is not required to complete Schedules L, M-1, and M-2.

Schedule L — Balance Sheets

Assets	Beginning of tax year (a)	(b)	End of tax year (c)	(d)
1 Cash				
2a Trade notes and accounts receivable				
b Less allowance for bad debts				
3 Inventories				
4 U.S. government obligations				
5 Tax-exempt securities				
6 Other current assets (attach schedule)				
7 Mortgage and real estate loans				
8 Other investments (attach schedule)				
9a Buildings and other depreciable assets				
b Less accumulated depreciation				
10a Depletable assets				
b Less accumulated depletion				
11 Land (net of any amortization)				
12a Intangible assets (amortizable only)				
b Less accumulated amortization				
13 Other assets (attach schedule)				
14 **Total assets**				
Liabilities and Capital				
15 Accounts payable				
16 Mortgages, notes, bonds payable in less than 1 year				
17 Other current liabilities (attach schedule)				
18 All nonrecourse loans				
19 Mortgages, notes, bonds payable in 1 year or more				
20 Other liabilities (attach schedule)				
21 Partners' capital accounts				
22 **Total** liabilities and capital				

Schedule M-1 — Reconciliation of Income (Loss) per Books With Income (Loss) per Return (see instructions)

1 Net income (loss) per books
2 Income included on Schedule K, lines 1 through 4, 6, and 7, not recorded on books this year (itemize): ....
3 Guaranteed payments (other than health insurance)
4 Expenses recorded on books this year not included on Schedule K, lines 1 through 12a, 17e, and 18a (itemize):
  a Depreciation $ ....
  b Travel and entertainment $ ....
5 Add lines 1 through 4

6 Income recorded on books this year not included on Schedule K, lines 1 through 7 (itemize):
  a Tax-exempt interest $ ....
7 Deductions included on Schedule K, lines 1 through 12a, 17e, and 18a, not charged against book income this year (itemize):
  a Depreciation $ ....
8 Add lines 6 and 7
9 Income (loss) (Schedule K, line 23a). Subtract line 8 from line 5

Schedule M-2 — Analysis of Partners' Capital Accounts

1 Balance at beginning of year
2 Capital contributed during year
3 Net income (loss) per books
4 Other increases (itemize): ....
5 Add lines 1 through 4

6 Distributions: a Cash
  b Property
7 Other decreases (itemize): ....
8 Add lines 6 and 7
9 Balance at end of year. Subtract line 8 from line 5

2. SCHEDULE K-1: PARTNER'S SHARE OF INCOME, CREDITS, DEDUCTIONS, ETC.

SCHEDULE K-1 (Form 1065) Department of the Treasury Internal Revenue Service	Partner's Share of Income, Credits, Deductions, etc. ▶ See separate instructions. For calendar year 1994 or tax year beginning , 1994, and ending , 19	OMB No. 1545-0099 **1994**
Partner's identifying number ▶	Partnership's identifying number ▶	
Partner's name, address, and ZIP code	Partnership's name, address, and ZIP code	

A This partner is a ☐ general partner ☐ limited partner
☐ limited liability company member
B What type of entity is this partner? ▶ ....
C Is this partner a ☐ domestic or a ☐ foreign partner?
D Enter partner's percentage of: (i) Before change (ii) End of
or termination year
Profit sharing . . . . % .... %
Loss sharing . . . . % .... %
Ownership of capital . . . . % .... %
E IRS Center where partnership filed return: ....

F Partner's share of liabilities (see instructions):
Nonrecourse . . . . $ ....
Qualified nonrecourse financing . $ ....
Other . . . . $ ....
G Tax shelter registration number . ▶ ....
H Check here if this partnership is a publicly traded partnership as defined in section 469(k)(2) . . . . ☐
I Check applicable boxes: **(1)** ☐ Final K-1 **(2)** ☐ Amended K-1

J Analysis of partner's capital account:

(a) Capital account at beginning of year	(b) Capital contributed during year	(c) Partner's share of lines 3, 4, and 7, Form 1065, Schedule M-2	(d) Withdrawals and distributions	(e) Capital account at end of year (combine columns (a) through (d))
			( )	

		(a) Distributive share item		(b) Amount	(c) 1040 filers enter the amount in column (b) on:
Income (Loss)	1	Ordinary income (loss) from trade or business activities	1		
	2	Net income (loss) from rental real estate activities	2		See Partner's Instructions for Schedule K-1 (Form 1065).
	3	Net income (loss) from other rental activities	3		
	4	Portfolio income (loss):			
	a	Interest	4a		Sch. B, Part I, line 1
	b	Dividends	4b		Sch. B, Part II, line 5
	c	Royalties	4c		Sch. E, Part I, line 4
	d	Net short-term capital gain (loss)	4d		Sch. D, line 5, col. (f) or (g)
	e	Net long-term capital gain (loss)	4e		Sch. D, line 13, col. (f) or (g)
	f	Other portfolio income (loss) *(attach schedule)*	4f		Enter on applicable line of your return
	5	Guaranteed payments to partner	5		See Partner's Instructions for Schedule K-1 (Form 1065).
	6	Net gain (loss) under section 1231 (other than due to casualty or theft)	6		
	7	Other income (loss) *(attach schedule)*	7		Enter on applicable line of your return
Deductions	8	Charitable contributions (see instructions) *(attach schedule)*	8		Sch. A, line 15 or 16
	9	Section 179 expense deduction	9		
	10	Deductions related to portfolio income *(attach schedule)*	10		See Partner's Instructions for Schedule K-1 (Form 1065).
	11	Other deductions *(attach schedule)*	11		
Investment Interest	12a	Interest expense on investment debts	12a		Form 4952, line 1
	b	(1) Investment income included on lines 4a, 4b, 4c, and 4f above	b(1)		See Partner's Instructions for Schedule K-1 (Form 1065).
		(2) Investment expenses included on line 10 above	b(2)		
Credits	13a	Credit for income tax withheld	13a		See Partner's Instructions for Schedule K-1 (Form 1065).
	b	Low-income housing credit:			
		(1) From section 42(j)(5) partnerships for property placed in service before 1990	b(1)		⎫
		(2) Other than on line 13b(1) for property placed in service before 1990	b(2)		⎪ Form 8586, line 5
		(3) From section 42(j)(5) partnerships for property placed in service after 1989	b(3)		⎬
		(4) Other than on line 13b(3) for property placed in service after 1989	b(4)		⎭
	c	Qualified rehabilitation expenditures related to rental real estate activities (see instructions)	13c		
	d	Credits (other than credits shown on lines 13b and 13c) related to rental real estate activities (see instructions)	13d		See Partner's Instructions for Schedule K-1 (Form 1065).
	e	Credits related to other rental activities (see instructions)	13e		
	14	Other credits (see instructions)	14		

For Paperwork Reduction Act Notice, see Instructions for Form 1065. Cat. No. 11394R Schedule K-1 (Form 1065) 1994

2. SCHEDULE K-1: PARTNER'S SHARE OF INCOME, CREDITS, ETC.

Schedule K-1 (Form 1065) 1994 — Page 2

	(a) Distributive share item		(b) Amount	(c) 1040 filers enter the amount in column (b) on:
Self-employment	15a Net earnings (loss) from self-employment	15a		Sch. SE, Section A or B
	b Gross farming or fishing income.	15b		See Partner's Instructions for Schedule K-1 (Form 1065).
	c Gross nonfarm income.	15c		
Adjustments and Tax Preference Items	16a Depreciation adjustment on property placed in service after 1986	16a		
	b Adjusted gain or loss	16b		See Partner's Instructions for Schedule K-1 (Form 1065) and Instructions for Form 6251.
	c Depletion (other than oil and gas)	16c		
	d (1) Gross income from oil, gas, and geothermal properties . .	d(1)		
	(2) Deductions allocable to oil, gas, and geothermal properties	d(2)		
	e Other adjustments and tax preference items *(attach schedule)*	16e		
Foreign Taxes	17a Type of income ▶			Form 1116, check boxes
	b Name of foreign country or U.S. possession ▶			
	c Total gross income from sources outside the United States *(attach schedule)*	17c		Form 1116, Part I
	d Total applicable deductions and losses *(attach schedule)* . . .	17d		
	e Total foreign taxes (check one): ▶ ☐ Paid ☐ Accrued . . .	17e		Form 1116, Part II
	f Reduction in taxes available for credit *(attach schedule)* . . .	17f		Form 1116, Part III
	g Other foreign tax information *(attach schedule)*	17g		See Instructions for Form 1116.
Other	18a Total expenditures to which a section 59(e) election may apply	18a		See Partner's Instructions for Schedule K-1 (Form 1065).
	b Type of expenditures ▶			
	19 Tax-exempt interest income	19		Form 1040, line 8b
	20 Other tax-exempt income.	20		See Partner's Instructions for Schedule K-1 (Form 1065).
	21 Nondeductible expenses	21		
	22 Recapture of low-income housing credit:			
	a From section 42(j)(5) partnerships	22a		Form 8611, line 8
	b Other than on line 22a.	22b		

Supplemental Information

23 Supplemental information required to be reported separately to each partner *(attach additional schedules if more space is needed):*

....
....
....
....
....
....
....
....
....
....
....
....
....
....
....
....
....
....

3. FORM 2553: ELECTION BY A SMALL BUSINESS CORPORATION

Form **2553** (Rev. September 1993) Department of the Treasury Internal Revenue Service	**Election by a Small Business Corporation** (Under section 1362 of the Internal Revenue Code) ▶ For Paperwork Reduction Act Notice, see page 1 of instructions. ▶ See separate instructions.	OMB No. 1545-0146 Expires 8-31-96

Notes: 1. *This election, to be an "S corporation," can be accepted only if all the tests are met under **Who May Elect** on page 1 of the instructions; all signatures in Parts I and III are originals (no photocopies); and the exact name and address of the corporation and other required form information are provided.*

2. *Do not file Form 1120S, U.S. Income Tax Return for an S Corporation, until you are notified that your election is accepted.*

Part I Election Information

Please Type or Print	Name of corporation (see instructions)	**A** Employer identification number (EIN)
	Number, street, and room or suite no. (If a P.O. box, see instructions.)	**B** Date incorporated
	City or town, state, and ZIP code	**C** State of incorporation

D Election is to be effective for tax year beginning (month, day, year) . . . . ▶ __/__/__

E Name and title of officer or legal representative who the IRS may call for more information

F Telephone number of officer or legal representative ( )

G If the corporation changed its name or address after applying for the EIN shown in **A**, check this box . . . . ▶ ☐

H If this election takes effect for the first tax year the corporation exists, enter month, day, and year of the **earliest** of the following: (1) date the corporation first had shareholders, (2) date the corporation first had assets, or (3) date the corporation began doing business . . . . ▶ __/__/__

I Selected tax year: Annual return will be filed for tax year ending (month and day) ▶ ....

If the tax year ends on any date other than December 31, except for an automatic 52-53-week tax year ending with reference to the month of December, you **must** complete Part II on the back. If the date you enter is the ending date of an automatic 52-53-week tax year, write "52-53-week year" to the right of the date. See Temporary Regulations section 1.441-2T(e)(3).

J Name and address of each shareholder, shareholder's spouse having a community property interest in the corporation's stock, and each tenant in common, joint tenant, and tenant by the entirety. (A husband and wife (and their estates) are counted as one shareholder in determining the number of shareholders without regard to the manner in which the stock is owned.)	K Shareholders' Consent Statement. Under penalties of perjury, we declare that we consent to the election of the above-named corporation to be an "S corporation" under section 1362(a) and that we have examined this consent statement, including accompanying schedules and statements, and to the best of our knowledge and belief, it is true, correct, and complete. (Shareholders sign and date below.)*		L Stock owned		M Social security number or employer identification number (see instructions)	N Share-holder's tax year ends (month and day)
	Signature	Date	Number of shares	Dates acquired		

*For this election to be valid, the consent of each shareholder, shareholder's spouse having a community property interest in the corporation's stock, and each tenant in common, joint tenant, and tenant by the entirety must either appear above or be attached to this form. (See instructions for Column K if a continuation sheet or a separate consent statement is needed.)

Under penalties of perjury, I declare that I have examined this election, including accompanying schedules and statements, and to the best of my knowledge and belief, it is true, correct, and complete.

Signature of officer ▶ _____ Title ▶ _____ Date ▶ _____

See Parts II and III on back.   Cat. No. 18629R   Form **2553** (Rev. 9-93)

3. FORM 2553: ELECTION BY A SMALL BUSINESS CORPORATION

Form 2553 (Rev. 9-93)   Page **2**

Part II   Selection of Fiscal Tax Year (All corporations using this part must complete item O and one of items P, Q, or R.)

O   Check the applicable box below to indicate whether the corporation is:
     1. ☐ A new corporation adopting the tax year entered in item I, Part I.
     2. ☐ An existing corporation retaining the tax year entered in item I, Part I.
     3. ☐ An existing corporation changing to the tax year entered in item I, Part I.

P   Complete item P if the corporation is using the expeditious approval provisions of Revenue Procedure 87-32, 1987-2 C.B. 396, to request: **(1)** a natural business year (as defined in section 4.01(1) of Rev. Proc. 87-32), or **(2)** a year that satisfies the ownership tax year test in section 4.01(2) of Rev. Proc. 87-32. Check the applicable box below to indicate the representation statement the corporation is making as required under section 4 of Rev. Proc. 87-32.

     1. Natural Business Year ▶ ☐ I represent that the corporation is retaining or changing to a tax year that coincides with its natural business year as defined in section 4.01(1) of Rev. Proc. 87-32 and as verified by its satisfaction of the requirements of section 4.02(1) of Rev. Proc. 87-32. In addition, if the corporation is changing to a natural business year as defined in section 4.01(1), I further represent that such tax year results in less deferral of income to the owners than the corporation's present tax year. I also represent that the corporation is not described in section 3.01(2) of Rev. Proc. 87-32. (See instructions for additional information that must be attached.)

     2. Ownership Tax Year ▶ ☐ I represent that shareholders holding more than half of the shares of the stock (as of the first day of the tax year to which the request relates) of the corporation have the same tax year or are concurrently changing to the tax year that the corporation adopts, retains, or changes to per item I, Part I. I also represent that the corporation is not described in section 3.01(2) of Rev. Proc. 87-32.

Note: *If you do not use item P and the corporation wants a fiscal tax year, complete either item Q or R below. Item Q is used to request a fiscal tax year based on a business purpose and to make a back-up section 444 election. Item R is used to make a regular section 444 election.*

Q   Business Purpose—To request a fiscal tax year based on a business purpose, you must check box Q1 and pay a user fee. See instructions for details. You may also check box Q2 and/or box Q3.

     1. Check here ▶ ☐ if the fiscal year entered in item I, Part I, is requested under the provisions of section 6.03 of Rev. Proc. 87-32. Attach to Form 2553 a statement showing the business purpose for the requested fiscal year. See instructions for additional information that must be attached.

     2. Check here ▶ ☐ to show that the corporation intends to make a back-up section 444 election in the event the corporation's business purpose request is not approved by the IRS. (See instructions for more information.)

     3. Check here ▶ ☐ to show that the corporation agrees to adopt or change to a tax year ending December 31 if necessary for the IRS to accept this election for S corporation status in the event: (1) the corporation's business purpose request is not approved and the corporation makes a back-up section 444 election, but is ultimately not qualified to make a section 444 election, or (2) the corporation's business purpose request is not approved and the corporation did not make a back-up section 444 election.

R   Section 444 Election—To make a section 444 election, you must check box R1 and you may also check box R2.

     1. Check here ▶ ☐ to show the corporation will make, if qualified, a section 444 election to have the fiscal tax year shown in item I, Part I. To make the election, you must complete **Form 8716**, Election To Have a Tax Year Other Than a Required Tax Year, and either attach it to Form 2553 or file it separately.

     2. Check here ▶ ☐ to show that the corporation agrees to adopt or change to a tax year ending December 31 if necessary for the IRS to accept this election for S corporation status in the event the corporation is ultimately not qualified to make a section 444 election.

Part III   Qualified Subchapter S Trust (QSST) Election Under Section 1361(d)(2)**

Income beneficiary's name and address	Social security number
Trust's name and address	Employer identification number

Date on which stock of the corporation was transferred to the trust (month, day, year) . . . . ▶   /   /

In order for the trust named above to be a QSST and thus a qualifying shareholder of the S corporation for which this Form 2553 is filed, I hereby make the election under section 1361(d)(2). Under penalties of perjury, I certify that the trust meets the definitional requirements of section 1361(d)(3) and that all other information provided in Part III is true, correct, and complete.

Signature of income beneficiary or signature and title of legal representative or other qualified person making the election	Date

**Use of Part III to make the QSST election may be made only if stock of the corporation has been transferred to the trust on or before the date on which the corporation makes its election to be an S corporation. The QSST election must be made and filed separately if stock of the corporation is transferred to the trust after the date on which the corporation makes the S election.

Table of Cases

References are to page numbers. Principal cases and the pages where they appear are in italics.

A

Achiro v. Commissioner, 240
American Bantam Car Co. v. Commissioner, 278
Arnes v. Commissioner, 362

B

Ballou v. United States, 120
Barkley Co. of Ariz., 383
Bateman v. United States, 124
Bazley v. Commissioner, 488
Bedell v. Commissioner, 15
Berghash v. Commissioner, 486
Bleily v. Commissioner, 360
Brannen v. Commissioner, 79
Burnet v. Logan, 167

C

Campbell v. Commissioner, 51
Canaveral Int'l Corp. v. Commissioner, 512
Chamberlin v. Commissioner, 332
Chapman v. Commissioner, 474
Coady v. Commissioner, 424
Collector v. Hubbard, 227
Collins v. Commissioner, 163
Commissioner v. Bollinger, 236
Commissioner v. Culbertson, 120
Commissioner v. Day & Zimmerman, Inc., 385
Commissioner v. Goldberger's Estate, 69
Commissioner v. Morris Trust, 431
Commissioner v. The First State Bank of Stratford, 324
Commissioner of Internal Revenue v. Clark, 498
Crenshaw v. United States, 163

D

Davis v. Commissioner, 580
Diamond v. Commissioner, 49
Dorzback v. Collison, 17
Doyle v. Mitchell Bros., 227

E

Edwards Motor Transit Co. v. Commissioner, 458
Eisner v. Macomber, 227, 327
Estate of Leavitt v. Commissioner, 586
Estate of Mose Silverman v. Commissioner, 467
Estate of Squier v. Commissioner, 344
Estate of Thomas P. Quirk v. Commissioner, 168
Evans v. Commissioner, 193

F

Fahs v. Florida Mach. & Foundry Co., 257
Farley Realty Corp. v. Commissioner, 21
Flint v. Stone Tracy Co., 227
Foxman v. Commissioner, 159
Frink v. Commissioner, 42

G

Gada v. U.S., 422
General Utils. & Oper. Co. v. Helvering, 375
George L. Riggs, Inc. v. Commissioner, 385
Gershkowitz v. Commissioner, 60, 146
Gregory v. Helvering, 415
Grove v. Commissioner, 362

H

Hamrick v. Commissioner, 253
Hayes v. Commissioner, 362
Helvering v. Alabama Asphaltic Limestone Co., 459
Helvering v. Gregory, 182
Helvering v. Southwest Consol. Corp., 472
Hempt Bros., Inc. v. United States, 56, 282
Hillsboro Nat'l Bank v. Commissioner, 378
Himmel v. Commissioner, 344

I

Intermountain Lumber Co., 278

J

James v. Commissioner, 274
John A. Nelson Corp. v. Helvering, 452

K

Kass v. Commissioner, 452
King Enters. v. United States, 467
Kinney v. United States, 177

L

Larson v. Commissioner, 4
Ledoux v. Commissioner, 130
Lessinger v. Commissioner, 265
Lockwood's Estate v. Commissioner, 425
Long v. Commissioner, 127

M

Madison Gas & Elec. Co. v. Commissioner, 23
Marr v. U.S., 450
McDonald's Restaurants of Ill., Inc. v. Commissioner, 460

McDougal v. Commissioner, 21, *43*
Metzger Trust v. Commissioner, 343
Miller v. Commissioner, 452
Moline Props., Inc., v. Commissioner, 235
Morrissey v. Commissioner, 4
Myron's Enters. v. United States, 530

N

Naporano v. United States, 610
Nash v. United States, 287
National Tea Co. v. Commissioner, 495
Neubecker v. Commissioner, 188
Newark Morning Ledger Co. v. United States, 392
Nielsen v. Commissioner, 425

O

Oden v. Commissioner, 78
Orrisch v. Commissioner, 97

P

Paige v. United States, 546
Patterson Trust v. United States, 347
Plantation Patterns, Inc. v. Commissioner, 301
Pollack v. Farmers' Loan & Trust Co., 227
Portage Plastics Co. v. United States, 549
Pratt v. Commissioner, 83

Q

Quick's Trust v. Commissioner, 214

R

Rafferty v. Commissioner, 418
Rath v. Commissioner, 618
Rickey v. United States, 344
Robin Haft Trust v. Commissioner, 343
Rockwell Inn, Ltd. v. Commissioner, 578

TABLE OF CASES

S

St. John v. United States, 50
St. Louis Cty. Bank, Ex'r v. United States of Am., 221
Scriptomatic, Inc. v. Commissioner, 307
Sennett v. Commissioner, 75
Smothers v. U.S., 486
Stevens v. Commissioner, 48
Stinnett's Pontiac Serv., Inc. v. Commissioner, 318
Stockton Harbor Indus. Co. v. Commissioner, 473
Swiren v. Commissioner, 127

T

Telephone Answering Serv. Co. v. Commissioner, 486, 487

U

United States v. Davis, 337
United States v. Frazell, 51
United States v. Stafford, 32
U.S. v. Carey, 361

V

Viehweg v. Commissioner, 79

W

West Coast Mktg. Corp. v. Commissioner, 288
Wiebusch v. Commissioner, 264
Wilgard Realty Co. v. Commissioner, 278
Williams v. McGowan, 127
Wood Harmon Corp. v. United States, 378
Wright v. United States, 344

Z

Zenz v. Quinlivan, 361

Table of Authorities

References are to pages. Principal authorities and the pages where they appear are in italics.

Internal Revenue Code (I.R.C.)

§ 1 — 641
§ 1(g) — 546
§ 1(h) — 648
§ 11 — 167, 231
§ 11(b) — 572
§ 11(b)(2) — 232
§ 34 — 640
§ 53(d)(1)(B) — 228
§ 53(d)(1)(B)(iv) — 232
§ 55 — 620
§ 55(a), (b)(1)(B) and (c) — 231
§ 55(b)(1)(B) — 232
§ 56(g) — 232
§ 57(a)7 — 228
§ 59A — 231, 232
§ 61 — 231
§ 61(a)(7) — 314
§ 62 — 231
§ 63 — 231
§ 79 — 94, 619
§ 83 — 50
§ 83(a) — 260
§ 83(a) through (c) — 50
§ 83(b) — 50
§ 83(b)(1) — 50
§ 101(a) — 225
§ 103 — 74
§ 105 — 619
§ 106 — 619
§ 108 — 147, 492
§ 116 — 640, 647
§ 118 — 293, 294
§ 118(b) — 294
§ 119 — 94, 619
§ 162 — 48, 538, 641
§ 162(a) — 167
§ 163 — 21, 298, 641
§ 163(d) — 620

§ 163(d)(4)(D) — 620
§ 163(e) — 324
§ 163(e)(5)(A) — 309
§ 163(i)(1) — 309
§ 163(j) — 309
§ 165(g). — 309
§ 166 — 618
§ 168 — 176
§ 170 — 671
§ 172 — 213, 511
§ 172(b)(1)(A) — 598
§ 172(b)(1)(ii) — 522
§ 172(b)(1)(A)(ii) — 566, 598
§ 179 — 29
§ 179(d)(6) — 540
§ 179(d)(8) — 29
§ 183 — 79
§ 195 — 65
§ 197 — 392, 399
§ 197(a)-(d) — 399
§ 212 — 48, 641
§ 216(e) — 377
§§ 241-50 — 572
§ 243 — 317, 324, 366, 661
§§ 243-45 — 313
§ 243(a)(3) — 540
§ 245(c)(1)(A) — 618
§ 246(c) — 326
§ 246(c)(i)(B) — 326
§ 246A — 325
§ 248 — 65, 294
§ 263 — 48, 92
§ 267 — 81, 620
§ 267(a) — 252, 287
§ 267(a)(1) — 374
§ 267(a)(2) — 82, 623
§ 267(b)(2) — 252
§ 267(c)(1), (2), (4) and (5) — 81
§ 267(d) — 81
§ 267(e) — 82
§ 269 — 511, 512, 517, 527
§ 269(a)(1) — 240
§ 269A — 240
§ 275(A)(4) — 529
§ 279 — 300
§ 291(a) — 231
§ 301 — 147, 316, 324, 331, 371, 412, 443, 447, 569, 597

TABLE OF AUTHORITIES

§ 301(a) — 314
§ 301(b)(1) — 321
§ 301(c) — 314, 321, 443
§ 301(c)(2) — 314, 371
§ 301(d) — 321
§ 302 — 337, 370, 372, 443, 448
§ 302(a) — 423
§ 302(a) and (b) — 337, 367
§ 302(b) — 443
§ 302(b)(1) — 337, 343, 344, 347, 354, 355
§ 302(b)(1) and (b)(2) — 355
§ 302(b)(2) — 346, 347, 354, 355
§ 302(b)(2)(C) — 354
§ 302(b)(3) — 345, 355, 360, 361, 402
§ 302(b)(3) and (c)(2) — 356
§ 302(b)(4) — 337, 366, 367
§ 302(c) — 343, 347
§ 302(c)(2) — 355, 360
§ 302(c)(2)(B) — 360
§ 302(c)(2)(C) — 356
§ 302(e) — 365, 366, 367, 424
§ 302(e)(1)(A) — 365
§ 302(e)(2) — 365
§ 303 — 337, 367, 370
§ 303(a) — 423
§ 303(a) and (b) — 367
§ 304 — 370, 371
§ 304(a) — 370, 371
§ 304(a)(2) — 371
§ 304(b)(1)-(2) — 370
§ 304(b)(2) — 371
§ 304(b)(3) — 371
§ 304(c) — 485
§ 305 — 327, 328
§ 305(a) — 326, 331
§ 305(b) — 327, 492
§ 305(b)(1) — 327
§ 305(b)(1)(A) — 328
§ 305(b)(2) — 327, 329, 330
§ 305(b)(2)-(5) — 331
§ 305(b)(3) — 328
§ 305(b)(4) — 328
§ 305(b)(5) — 329
§ 305(c) — 330, 331
§ 306 — 331, 494
§ 306(a)(1) — 333
§ 306(b)(1) — 494

§ 306(c)(1) — 333
§ 307 — 331, 332
§ 307(a) — 328, 331, 332
§ 311 — 322
§ 311 — 375, 413, 441, 496, 596
§ 311(a) — 412
§ 311(a) and (b)(1)-(2) — 321
§ 311(b) — 322, 324, 365, 448
§ 311(b)(2) — 322
§ 312 — 316, 669
§ 312(a), (b) — 321
§ 312(a), (b), (k)(1), (n)(2)-(3),(5) and (6) — 316
§ 312(a)(2) — 324
§ 312(a)(3), (b)(2) — 322
§ 312(d)(1) — 331
§ 312(h) — 610
§ 312(n)(7) — 361
§ 316 — 314, 561, 660, 669
§ 316(b)(2) — 315
§ 317 — 252, 324
§ 318 — 343-45, 355, 486
§ 318(a) — 335, 485
§ 318(a)(1) — 356, 520
§ 318(a)(1)(A)(ii) — 336
§ 318(a)(2)(A) — 336
§ 318(a)(3) — 356
§ 318(a)(3)(A) — 336
§ 318(a)(4)(D) — 336
§ 318(a)(5)(B) — 336
§ 318(a)(5)(C) — 336
§ 318(a)(5)(D) — 336
§ 331 — 373, 382, 408, 448, 458, 486, 597, 599
§ 331(a) — 414, 448
§ 332 — 382, 383, 385, 386, 388, 403, 406, 407, 408, 458, 511, 610
§ 332(a) — 386
§ 334 — 375
§ 334(a) — 373
§ 334(b)(1) — 385
§ 334(b)(1) and (c)(2) — 383
§ 335 — 441
§ 336 — 375, 378, 382, 384, 404, 408, 448, 458, 496, 597
§ 336(a)-(c) — 375
§ 336(c) — 413
§ 336(d) — 384
§ 336(d)(1) and (2) — 378, 381
§ 336(d)(3) — 384
§ 336(e) — 407

§ 337 — 382, 385, 386, 388, 403, 406, 407, 408
§ 337(a) — 383, 386
§ 337(b)(1) — 386
§ 338 — 403, 405, 610
§ 338(a), (b) and (g)(3) — 610
§ 338(e) — 405
§ 338(g) — 405, 407
§ 338(h)(10) — 406-08
§ 341 — 539
§ 341(f) — 539
§ 351 — 31, 51
§ 351 — 251-53, 257, 259, 260, 263, 264, 271, 274, 288, 294, 371, 382, 387, 414, 417, 473, 474, 488, 498, 527, 599
§ 351(a) — 280
§ 351(a), (b), (d) — 252
§ 351(b) — 260, 264
§ 351(b)(2) — 261
§ 351(d) — 252
§ 351(e) — 252
§ 354 — 413, 450, 485, 496
§§ 354-56 — 497
§§ 354-57 — 449
§§ 354-68 — 449
§ 354(a) — 450, 495, 497
§ 354(a) and (b)(1) — 431
§ 354(a)(1) — 497
§ 354(a)(2) — 491
§ 354(a)(3) — 497
§ 354(b) — 488
§ 354(b)(1) — 520
§ 354(b)(1)(B) — 486
§ 355 — 411, 412, 418, 422-24, 441, 442, 443, 446, 477, 485, 599
§§ 355-57 — 414
§ 355(a), (b)(1) — 417
§ 355(a)(1) — 497
§ 355(a)(1)(B) — 423
§ 355(a)(3) — 442
§ 355(a)(3)(B) — 442
§ 355(b) — 423
§ 355(c)(1) — 446
§ 355(c)(2) — 446
§ 355(d) — 446
§ 355(d)(1) — 447
§ 356 — 411, 412, 413, 442, 497
§§ 356-57 — 451
§ 356(a)(1) — 443, 498
§ 356(a)(1) and (2) — 443

§ 356(a)(2) — 498, 507
§ 356(b) — 443, 485
§ 356(c) — 442, 497
§ 356(d) — 442
§ 357 — 271, 280, 371, 412, 413
§ 357(a) — 264, 279, 496
§ 357(a)-(c) — 263
§ 357(b) — 263, 264, 496
§ 357(c) — 263, 264, 496
§ 357(c)(3) — 280
§ 357(c)(3)(A)(i) — 265
§ 358 — 279, 371, 411, 412, 413, 414, 449, 451, 483, 484, 496, 497, 498
§ 358(a) — 442
§ 358(a), (b) — 278
§ 358(a) and (d) — 281, 282
§ 358(a)(1) — 278
§ 358(a)(2) — 278, 446
§ 358(b), (c) — 412
§ 358(d) — 264, 279
§ 358(d)(2) — 280
§ 361 — 412, 413, 414, 449, 451, 495, 496, 497
§ 361(a) — 450, 496
§ 361(b) — 496
§ 361(b)(1)(B) — 496
§ 361(b)(2) — 496
§ 361(c) — 496
§ 361(c)(1) — 446
§ 361(c)(2) — 446
§ 362 — 449, 451, 496, 511
§ 362(a) — 252, 280
§ 362(a) and (b) — 495
§ 362(b) — 476, 497
§ 362(b) and (c) — 252
§ 362(c)(1) — 294
§ 367 — 497
§ 368 — 388, 412, 450, 495, 497, 520
§ 368(a) — 451, 599
§ 368(a)(1) — 450, 472, 511, 527
§ 368(a)(1)(A) — 366, 382, 451, 458, 482
§ 368(a)(1)(B) — 439, 472, 473, 476
§ 368(a)(1)(C) — 477, 480, 481, 488
§ 368(a)(1)(D) — 414, 416, 431, 439, 446, 485, 486, 599
§ 368(a)(1)(D) or (G) — 520
§ 368(a)(1)(E) — 332, 488, 494
§ 368(a)(1)(F) — 450, 494, 495, 520
§ 368(a)(1)(G) — 495
§ 368(a)(2)(A) — 488

§ 368(a)(2)(B) — 477, 480
§ 368(a)(2)(C) — 459, 474, 475
§ 368(a)(2)(D) — 482, 483
§ 368(a)(2)(D) and (E) — 481
§ 368(a)(2)(E) — 483, 484
§ 368(a)(2)(G)(i) — 481, 488
§ 368(a)(2)(H) — 485, 486
§ 368(b) — 450
§ 368(c) — 271, 417, 459
§ 381 — 385, 488, 495, 511, 594
§ 381(a), (b)(3), and (c)(2) — 511
§ 381(a)(1) — 383, 458
§ 381(b)(3) — 495, 511
§ 381(c) — 511
§ 381(c)(1) — 511
§ 381(c)(2) — 512
§ 382 — 517, 527
§§ 382-84 — 511
§ 382(a), (b)(1)-(2) — 517
§ 382(b) — 519
§ 382(b), (c)(1), (e)(2), and (g)(1) — 525
§ 382(b)(1) and (f) — 522
§ 382(b)(2) — 523
§ 382(b)(3)(A) — 523
§ 382(b)(3)(B) — 523
§ 382(c) — 518, 522, 526
§ 382(c)(2) — 522
§ 382(e)(1) — 522
§ 382(f) — 518
§ 382(g)(1) — 519
§ 382(g)(2) — 519
§ 382(g)(3) — 519
§ 382(g)(3)(A) — 520
§ 382(g)(3)(B) — 520
§ 382(g)(4)(A) — 519
§ 382(g)(4)(B) — 521
§ 382(g)(4)(B)(i) — 521
§ 382(h) — 524, 526
§ 382(h)(1) — 526
§ 382(h)(1)(A) — 524
§ 382(h)(1)(B) — 524
§ 382(h)(2)(A) — 524
§ 382(h)(3)(A)(i) — 525
§ 382(h)(3)(B) — 525, 527
§ 382(i)(1) — 519
§ 382(i)(2) — 519
§ 382(k)(3) — 521

§ 382(k)(6)(A) — 519
§ 382(k)(6)(B) — 519
§ 382(k)(6)(C) — 519
§ 382(k)(7) — 519
§ 382(l) — 525
§ 382(l)(1) — 524
§ 382(l)(3)(A)(i) — 520
§ 382(l)(3)(A)(ii) — 521
§ 382(l)(3)(A)(iv) — 519
§ 382(l)(3)(B) — 520
§ 382(l)(4)(A) — 524
§ 382(l)(4)(B)(i) — 524
§ 384 — 526, 527
§ 384(a) — 526, 527
§ 384(b) — 527
§ 384(c)(4), (8) — 527
§ 385 — 298, 300, 308
§ 387(c) — 511
§ 444 — 568
§ 446(b) — 378
§ 448 — 66, 541, 567
§ 448(d)(2) — 232
§ 453 — 356, 387, 472
§ 453(f)(4) — 491
§ 453(f)(6) — 491, 498
§ 453(h)(1)(A) and (B) — 374
§ 453A — 29
§ 453A(b)(1)-(2) — 29
§ 453B — 374
§ 465 — 75, 78, 80, 586, 619
§ 465(a)(1) — 78
§ 465(a)(1)(A) — 619
§ 465(b)(1) — 78
§ 465(b)(6) — 79
§ 465(c)(3)(B) — 619
§ 469 — 79, 541, 579, 619
§ 469(a)(2)(A) — 80
§ 469(e)(1) — 80
§ 469(e)(3) — 80
§ 482 — 527
§ 482(a) — 240
§§ 501-09 — 671
§ 501(c) — 671
§ 501(c)(3) — 671
§§ 511-13 — 670, 671
§ 513(a) — 671
§ 527 — 671

TABLE OF AUTHORITIES

§ 531 — 529
§§ 531-37 — 422
§ 532(a) — 529
§ 532(b)(1) — 539
§ 533(a) — 529
§ 535 — 535
§ 535(c) — 535
§ 535(c)(2)-(3) — 535
§ 541 — 535, 537, 539
§ 542(a)(1) — 536
§ 542(a)(2) — 536
§ 543 — 536
§ 543(a) — 536
§ 543(a)(2)-(6) — 538
§ 543(a)(6) — 538
§ 543(a)(7). — 537
§ 544(a)(1) — 536
§ 544(a)(2) — 536
§ 544(a)(5) — 536
§ 545 — 536
§ 547 — 539
§ 547(a) — 535
§ 551 — 539
§§ 551-58 — 649
§§ 561(a) — 535
§ 563(a) — 535
§ 565 — 535
§ 642(h) — 213
§ 678 — 544
§ 691 — 72, 212
§ 691(c) — 212, 213
§§ 701-61. — 1
§ 702 — 69
§ 702(a) — 72, 102, 568
§ 702(a)-(c) — 59
§ 702(a)(1)-(7) — 59, 60
§ 702(a)(8) — 59
§ 703 — 59, 221
§ 703(a) — 59
§ 703(a)(2) — 64
§ 703(b) — 65, 66
§ 704 — 69, 111
§ 704(a) — 59, 95
§ 704(a)-(c) — 59
§ 704(b) — 41, 42, 95, 96, 102, 113, 140, 579
§ 704(c) — 39, 40, 56, 93, 105, 114, 140, 142, 146, 322
§ 704(c)(1)(B) — 94

§ 704(d) — 29, 72, 75, 78, 80, 111
§ 704(e) — 579, 585
§ 704(e)(1) — 120
§ 704(e)(2) — 124, 125
§ 705 — 38, 39, 71, 72, 96, 140, 145
§ 705(a) — 128
§ 705(a)(1) — 73
§ 705(a)(1)(B) — 74
§ 705(a)(2) — 41, 73, 74
§ 705(a)(2)(A) — 73
§ 705(a)(2)(B) — 74, 82
§ 706 — 118, 119, 127, 187, 193
§ 706(b) — 66
§ 706(b)(1)(A) — 29
§ 706(c) — 118, 211
§ 706(c)-(d) — 128
§ 706(c)(1), (d)(1) — 118
§ 706(c)(2)(A) — 129
§ 706(c)(2)(A)(ii) — 211
§ 706(d)(1) — 119
§ 706(d)(1) and (2) — 48
§ 706(d)(2) — 119
§ 707 — 81
§ 707(a) — 91, 92
§ 707(a)(1) — 81, 92
§ 707(a)(2) — 81, 93
§ 707(a)(2)(A) — 91, 92
§ 707(a)(2)(B) — 93, 127, 145
§ 707(b) — 81
§ 707(b)(1) — 81
§ 707(b)(2) — 82
§ 707(c) — 81, 83, 88, 91, 92, 167
§ 708 — 159, 187, 193, 211
§ 708(a) and (b) — 187
§ 708(b) — 193
§ 708(b)(1)(B) — 193, 203, 210
§ 708(b)(2)(A) — 205
§ 709 — 64, 65
§ 709(a) — 65
§ 709(b) — 65
§ 721 — 31, 51, 56, 72, 252, 261, 271, 387
§ 721(a) — 31
§ 721(b) — 38
§ 722 — 31, 38, 39, 41, 111
§ 723 — 31, 38, 40, 73
§ 724 — 42
§ 724(a)-(c) — 42

TABLE OF AUTHORITIES

§ 731 — 72, 74, 145, 154, 165, 187
§§ 731-32 — 148
§ 731(a) — 145, 146, 147, 165, 166, 167, 175
§ 731(a)(1) — 111, 154, 167, 168, 175, 202
§ 731(a)(2) — 111, 141, 154, 163, 164, 174, 175, 187, 202
§ 731(b) — 147, 153, 176
§ 731(c) — 148
§ 732 — 72, 187
§ 732(a) — 140, 145, 147, 163
§ 732(a)(1) — 147
§ 732(a)(2) — 140, 145, 147, 155
§ 732(b) — 72, 175, 187
§ 732(b),(c) — 163
§ 732(c) — 139
§ 732(c)(1) — 148, 164, 175
§ 732(c)(2) — 175
§ 732(d) — 140, 141, 149, 158
§ 733 — 41, 140, 145, 146, 147
§ 734 — 141, 154, 176
§ 734(a) — 154
§ 734(b) — 154, 165
§ 734(b)(1)(A) — 154, 158
§ 734(b)(1)(B) — 155, 158
§ 735 — 42
§ 735(a) — 182
§ 735(a)(1) — 149
§ 735(a)(2) — 149
§ 736 — 159, 163, 164, 176, 187, 193
§ 736(a) — 166, 167, 213
§ 736(a)(1) — 165, 166
§ 736(b) — 165, 166-68
§ 736(b)(1) — 165
§ 737 — 93
§ 741 — 72, 111, 127-29, 139, 140, 144, 146, 164, 166, 175, 202
§ 742 — 140
§ 743 — 141, 142, 149
§ 743(b) — 140, 217, 218
§ 743(b), (c) — 140
§ 743(b)(1) — 142
§ 751 — 127, 129, 139, 144, 157, 176, 182
§ 751(a)-(d) — 127
§ 751(b) — 153, 156, 157
§ 751(b)(2)(D) — 138
§ 751(c) — 129, 138
§ 751(d) — 129
§ 752 — 41, 78, 111, 112, 586
§ 752(b) — 145, 146

§ 752(d) — 128, 140, 165
§ 753 — 213
§ 754 — 140, 141, 144, 149, 154, 158, 165, 203, 217, 542, 568, 623
§ 755 — 142, 155
§ 761 — 109, 119
§ 761(a) — 21, 22, 29
§ 761(c) — 30, 95
§ 761(d) — 159
§ 871 — 647
§ 871(a) — 671
§ 902 — 651
§ 921 — 618
§§ 921-27 — 649
§ 927(g) — 618
§§ 951-64 — 539, 649
§ 960 — 651
§§ 991-94 — 649
§ 1001 — 72, 127, 373, 496
§ 1011 — 140
§ 1012 — 140
§ 1014 — 72, 213, 217, 367, 449, 648, 680
§ 1014(b)(6) — 218
§ 1014(c) — 213
§ 1031 — 29, 252, 387, 391
§ 1032 — 251, 449, 451, 496, 497
§ 1034 — 377
§ 1034(f) — 377
§ 1036 — 494
§ 1044 — 310
§ 1057 — 497
§ 1059 — 326, 681, 690
§ 1059(a), (c), (e) — 326
§ 1059(e) — 326
§ 1060 — 390
§ 1060(a) — 405
§ 1060(a) and (c) — 390
§ 1060(b) — 391, 402
§ 1060(c) — 391
§ 1060(e) — 391
§ 1201 — 167, 648
§ 1202 — 310
§ 1202(a) — 228
§ 1202(a), (b)(1)-(2) and (c)(1) — 310
§ 1211(b) — 309
§ 1212(a) — 228
§ 1212(d) — 228
§ 1221 — 31

§ 1221(1) — 40
§ 1223 — 496, 511
§ 1223(1) — 280, 413, 414, 442
§ 1223(1) and (2) — 40
§ 1223(2) — 148
§ 1223(5) — 331
§ 1231 — 40, 41, 137, 138, 142, 143, 148, 155, 280, 596
§ 1239(a) — 82
§ 1244 — 309, 541, 618
§ 1245 — 138, 148, 176
§ 1245(b)(3) — 148, 153
§§ 1246-47 — 649
§ 1250 — 138, 148
§ 1250(d)(3) — 148
§ 1250(d)(6) — 153
§ 1254 — 138
§§ 1272-73 — 324
§§ 1291-97 — 539, 649
§ 1311 — 566
§ 1313(c) — 566
§ 1361 — 543
§§ 1361-79 — 642, 643, 649
§ 1361(a)(1) — 543
§ 1361(b) — 543, 563
§ 1361(b)(1) — 609, 620
§ 1361(b)(1)(B), (c)(3) — 546
§ 1361(b)(1)(C) — 545
§ 1361(b)(1)(D) — 546
§ 1361(b)(2)(A) — 543
§ 1361(c) — 545
§ 1361(c)(1) — 546
§ 1361(c)(2) — 545
§ 1361(c)(5) — 556
§ 1361(d) — 545
§ 1361(d)(6) — 543
§ 1362(a)-(c) — 562
§ 1362(a)(2) — 563
§ 1362(b)(1) — 563
§ 1362(b)(2) — 543, 563
§ 1362(c)(2)(A)(i), (B)(i) — 544
§ 1362(d)(1) — 563
§ 1362(d)(2) — 544, 564
§ 1362(d)(3) — 565, 566, 572
§ 1362(d)(3)(D)(i) — 572
§ 1362(d)(3)(D)(iv) — 572
§ 1362(e)(1) — 565
§ 1362(e)(1)-(4) — 565

§ 1362(e)(2), (3) — 566
§ 1362(e)(6)(D) — 566
§ 1362(f) — 566
§ 1362(g) — 564, 565
§ 1363 — 570
§ 1363(a) — 598, 620
§ 1363(b) — 568
§ 1363(c) — 568
§ 1363(c)(2)(A) — 542
§ 1363(d)(1) — 543
§ 1363(f)(2) — 597
§ 1366 — 568, 571
§ 1366(a) — 570, 574, 596, 690
§ 1366(a)-(b) — 579
§ 1366(a)-(c) — 567
§ 1366(a)(1) — 567, 568
§ 1366(a)(2), (d)(1)(B) — 586
§ 1366(b) — 618
§ 1366(d)(1) and (2) — 585
§ 1366(d)(2) — 586
§ 1366(d)(3) — 597, 598, 599
§ 1366(e) — 570, 579, 585
§ 1366(f)(2) — 570, 597
§ 1366(f)(3) — 573
§ 1367 — 567, 681
§ 1367(a) — 596, 690
§ 1367(a), (b) — 579
§ 1367(a)(1)(A) — 597
§ 1367(a)(2)(A) — 595
§ 1367(a)(2)(D) — 595
§ 1367(b)(2) — 585
§ 1367(b)(2)(A) — 597
§ 1368 — 593
§ 1368(a) and (b) — 593
§ 1368(b)(2) — 586
§ 1368(c) — 594
§ 1368(c) through (e)(2) — 594
§ 1368(e)(1)(A) — 595
§ 1368(e)(3) — 595
§ 1371 — 597
§ 1371(a) — 598, 599
§ 1371(a)(1) — 596
§ 1371(a)(2) — 602
§ 1371(b)(1) — 598
§ 1371(e)(2) — 597
§ 1372 — 619
§ 1374 — 567, 570-72, 596, 597

TABLE OF AUTHORITIES

§ 1374(a), (b)(1)-(2), and (c)(1)-8(a) — 570
§ 1374(a), (d) — 571
§ 1374(b)(2) — 571
§ 1374(d)(2) — 569
§ 1374(d)(2)(B) — 570
§ 1375 — 566, 567, 570, 571-73, 595
§ 1375(a) — 570, 572
§ 1375(b)(1)(B) — 573
§ 1375(b)(2) — 572
§ 1375(b)(2)(B) — 572
§ 1375(b)(3) — 572
§ 1377(a) — 574
§ 1377(a)(2) — 574, 618
§ 1377(b) — 598
§ 1378 — 568
§ 1401 — 585
§ 1441 — 671
§ 1446 — 156
§ 1491 — 31, 56, 497
§ 1501 — 406
§§ 1501-04 — 313, 325, 657
§ 1504 — 543
§ 1504(a)(2) — 543
§ 1504(b) — 543
§ 1561 — 540
§ 1563(a) — 527, 540
§ 2001 — 219
§ 2053(a)(4) — 213
§ 2501 — 219
§ 2601 — 219
§ 2701 — 220
§ 2701(a)(3) — 220
§ 2701(c)(3) — 220
§ 6013(a)(3) — 211
§ 6031(a) — 21
§ 6051(c)(9) — 220
§§ 6621-32 — 30
§ 6222 — 30
§ 6223(b) — 30
§ 6231 — 21
§ 6231(a)(7) — 30
§§ 6241-45 — 620
§ 6244 — 620
§ 6501 — 71
§ 6698 — 29
§ 7701(a)(2) — 21
§ 7701(a)(3) — 495, 643

§ 7701(b)(1)(A) — 544
§ 7704 — 17, 22, 636, 641, 645
§ 7704(a) — 643
§ 7704(b) — 22
§ 7704(c) — 22

Treasury Regulations

Reg. § 1.47-4(a)(1) — 542
Reg. § 1.83-3(a) — 50
Reg. § 1.83-3(c) — 50
Reg. § 1.83-6(b) — 50
Reg. § 1.118-1 — 294
Reg. § 1.167(a)-3 — 399
Reg. § 1.183-1(f) — 619
Reg. § 1.248-1(b)(ii) — 294
Reg. § 1.267(b)-1(b) — 82
Reg. § 1.301-1(d) — 331
Reg. § 1.302-2 — 337
Reg. § 1.302-2(b) — 345
Reg. § 1.302-2(c) — 345
Reg. § 1.302-3 — 346
Reg. § 1.302-3(a) — 354
Reg. § 1.302-4 — 355
Reg. § 1.304-2 — 372
Reg. § 1.305-2 — 328
Reg. § 1.305-2(b) — 331
Reg. § 1.305-3(b)(2) — 329
Reg. § 1.305-3(b)(4) — 330
Reg. § 1.305-3(e) — 330, 492
Reg. § 1.305-6 — 329
Reg. § 1.305-7(a) — 331
Reg. § 1.306-1 — 333
Reg. § 1.306-3 — 333
Reg. § 1.307-1 — 328, 331
Reg. § 1.312-1(d) — 331
Reg. § 1.312-6 — 665, 669
Reg. §§ 1.312-6 and -7 — 317
Reg. § 1.312-10(a) — 447
Reg. § 1.312-10(b) — 447
Reg. § 1.316-1(a) — 314
Reg. § 1.316-2(a) — 315
Reg. § 1.316-2(b) and (c) — 318
Reg. § 1.331-1 — 382
Reg. § 1.331-1(d) — 345
Reg. § 1.331-1(e) — 374
Reg. §§ 1.332-1, -2 and -5 — 386

TABLE OF AUTHORITIES

Reg. § 1.332-2(c) — 373, 383
Reg. § 1.332-7 — 386
Reg. § 1.338(b)-2T — 391, 405
Reg. § 1.338(b)-2T(b) — 391
Reg. § 1.338(h)(10)-1(d)(2) — 406
Reg. § 1.338-1T(f)(8) — 610
Reg. § 1.338-4(a)(1) — 405
Reg. § 1.338-4(a)(1)-(3) — 405
Reg. § 1.351-1 — 280
Reg. § 1.351-1(a) — 253, 274
Reg. § 1.355-1(b), 2(a) and (b)(1)-(4) — 430
Reg. § 1.355-2(b)(1)(2) — 418
Reg. § 1.355-2(b)(5) — 422
Reg. § 1.355-2(c) — 442
Reg. § 1.355-2(d)(2)(ii), -(iii)(A), and (E)(iv) — 423
Reg. § 1.355-2(d)(2)(iii)(E) — 439
Reg. § 1.355-2(d)(2)(iv)(C) — 423, 425
Reg. § 1.355-2(d)(3)(C)(iii) — 423
Reg. § 1.355-2(d)(3)(C)(iv) — 423
Reg. § 1.355-2(d)(5)(ii) — 423
Reg. § 1.355-2(d)(5)(iii) and (iv) — 423
Reg. § 1.355-2(d)(ii) — 422, 441
Reg. § 1.355-2(d)(iii) — 431
Reg. § 1.355-3(b)(2) — 423
Reg. § 1.355-3(b)(3)(ii) — 425, 430
Reg. § 1.355-3(c) — 424, 425, 430
Reg. § 1.356-3(b) — 442
Reg. § 1.358-3 — 281, 282
Reg. § 1.368-1 — 450
Reg. § 1.368-2(c) — 473
Reg. § 1.368-2(d)1 — 481
Reg. § 1.368-2(j)(7) — 484
Reg. § 1.469-2T(d)(6)(i) — 619
Reg. § 1.469-2T(e)(1) — 619
Reg. § 1.701-2 — 182
Reg. § 1.704-1(a)(8)(i) — 102
Reg. § 1.704-1(b)(1)(vii) — 102
Reg. § 1.704-1(b)(2)(i) — 103
Reg. § 1.704-1(b)(2)(ii)(a) — 95
Reg. § 1.704-1(b)(2)(ii)(b) — 103
Reg. § 1.704-1(b)(2)(ii)(d) — 104
Reg. § 1.704-1(b)(2)(ii)(i) — 105
Reg. § 1.704-1(b)(2)(iii)(a) — 106
Reg. § 1.704-1(b)(2)(iii)(b) and (c) — 107
Reg. § 1.704-1(b)(2)(iii)(c) — 108
Reg. § 1.704-1(b)(2)(iii)(c)(2) — 108
Reg. § 1.704-1(b)(2)(iv)(1) — 140

Reg. § 1.704-1(b)(2)(iv)(d)(2) — 104
Reg. § 1.704-1(b)(2)(iv)(f) — 103
Reg. § 1.704-1(b)(2)(iv)(o) — 91
Reg. § 1.704-1(b)(2)(c)(iii)(2) and -1(b)(5) — 109
Reg. § 1.704-1(b)(2)(u) — 41
Reg. § 1.704-1(b)(3)(i) — 109
Reg. § 1.704-1(b)(3)(iii) and -1(b)(5) — 104
Reg. § 1.704-1(b)(4)(iv)(c) — 116
Reg. § 1.704-1(b)(4)(vi) — 109
Reg. § 1.704-1(b)(5) — 105
Reg. § 1.704-1(e)(1)(iv) — 124
Reg. § 1.704-l(e)(1)(v) — 42
Reg. § 1.704-1(e)(2)(viii) — 120, 124
Reg. § 1.704-2(b)(1) — 116
Reg. § 1.704-2(b)(2)(ii)(f) — 105
Reg. § 1.704-2(e)(1) — 117
Reg. § 1.704-2(e)(2) — 117
Reg. § 1.704-2(e)(3)(f) — 115
Reg. § 1.704-2(e)(4) — 116
Reg. § 1.704-2(m) — 117, 118
Reg. § 1.706-1(c)(2)(ii) — 119, 129
Reg. § 1.706-1(c)(3)(ii) — 211
Reg. § 1.706-1(c)(3)(iii) — 212
Reg. § 1.706-1(c)(4) — 118
Reg. § 1.707-1(b)(3) — 81
Reg. § 1.707-1(c) — 83, 91, 92
Reg. § 1.707-3(b)(2) — 93
Reg. § 1.707-3(c) — 93
Reg. § 1.708-1(b)(1)(b)(ii) — 203
Reg. § 1.708-1(b)(1)(i)(b) — 176
Reg. § 1.708-1(b)(1)(ii) — 193
Reg. § 1.708-1(b)(1)(iii) — 209
Reg. § 1.708-1(b)(2)(i) — 206
Reg. § 1.708-1(b)(2)(ii) — 210
Reg. § 1.709-2 — 65
Reg. § 1.721-1(b) — 48, 51
Reg. § 1.721-1(b)(1) — 51
Reg. § 1.731(a)(1)(ii) — 146
Reg. § 1.731-1 — 203
Reg. § 1.731-1(a)(1) — 168
Reg. § 1.731-1(a)(2) — 164, 165
Reg. § 1.732-1(a) — 147
Reg. § 1.736-1(a)(3) — 166
Reg. § 1.736-1(a)(6) — 159, 176
Reg. § 1.736-1(b)(5)(ii) — 168
Reg. § 1.736-1(b)(5)(iii) — 165, 168
Reg. § 1.736-1(b)(6) — 167, 168

TABLE OF AUTHORITIES

Reg. § 1.736-1(b)(6)-(7) — 168
Reg. § 1.741-1(b) — 128
Reg. § 1.743-1(b) — 142
Reg. § 1.743-1(b)(2)(i) — 142
Reg. § 1.743-1(b)(2)(ii) — 144
Reg. § 1.751-1(a), (b) — 139
Reg. § 1.751-1(a)(2) — 139
Reg. § 1.751-1(b) & (c) — 157
Reg. § 1.751-1(c)(1)(i) — 138
Reg. § 1.751-1(d)(2)(ii) — 138
Reg. § 1.751-1(g) — 157
Reg. § 1.752-1(a) — 112
Reg. § 1.752-1(a), (b)(1) — 112
Reg. § 1.752-1(b)(2)(ii) — 112
Reg. § 1.752-1(b)(6) — 112
Reg. § 1.752-1T(j)(1) — 112
Reg. § 1.752-2(f) — 112, 113
Reg. § 1.752-2(h)(1)-(2) — 112
Reg. § 1.752-2(h)(4) — 112
Reg. § 1.752-3 — 113, 115
Reg. § 1.752-3(a)(2) — 114
Reg. § 1.752-3(a)(3) — 113, 114
Reg. § 1.755-1(a), (b) — 144
Reg. § 1.755-1(a)(1) and -1(b) — 142
Reg. § 1.755-1(c) — 143
Reg. § 1.761-1(c) — 30
Reg. § 1.761-1(d) — 159
Reg. § 1.761-2(a)-(b) — 22
Reg. § 1.761-2(b) — 29
Reg. § 1.871-2 — 544
Reg. § 1.1001-2(a) — 263
Reg. § 1.1002-1(c) — 449
Reg. § 1.1032-1 — 252
Reg. § 1.1032-1(a) — 251
Reg. § 1.1060-1(d) — 391
Reg. § 1.1060-1T(b)(3) — 402
Reg. § 1.1361-1(l)(4)(iii)(B)(2) and (C) — 562
Reg. § 1.1362-2(c)(4)(ii)(B) — 574
Reg. § 1.1362-2(c)(4)(ii)(B)(3), (4) — 574
Reg. § 1.1362-5 — 564
Reg. § 1.1362-5(b) — 564
Reg. § 1.1362-6(b)(3)(i) — 562
Reg. § 1.1363-1(b) — 567
Reg. § 1.1363-6(b)(3)(A) — 563
Reg. § 1.1368-2(d)(3) — 610
Reg. § 1.1375-1A — 573
Reg. § 1.1441-3(f) — 156

Reg. § 1.1502-1(b) — 540
Reg. § 1.1502-20(a)(1) — 408
Reg. § 1.1502-20(a)(5) — 408
Reg. § 1.1502-20(b)(1) — 408
Reg. § 1.1502-32 — 408
Reg. § 1.6012-2(a)(2) — 378
Reg. § 18.1377-1 — 579
Reg. § 20.2031-1(b) — 220
Reg. § 20.2031-2(h) — 221
Reg. § 25.2701-2(2)(4) — 220
Reg. § 25.2703-1(b) — 226
Reg. § 301.7701-2 — 637
Reg. § 301.7701-2 through -4 — 4
Reg. § 301.7701-2(a)-(e), -3(a)-(b)(1) and -4(a)-(b) — 15
Reg. § 301.7701-3(a) — 28
Reg. § 301.7701-4(c) — 16
Reg. § 301.7701-4(d) — 16
Reg. § 301.7701-5 — 544

Revenue Rulings

Rev. Rul. 55-59, 1955-1 C.B. 35 — 473
Rev. Rul. 55-112, 1955-1 C.B. 344 — 492
Rev. Rul. 55-117, 1955-1 C.B. 233 — 124
Rev. Rul. 56-397, 1956-2 C.B. 599 — 225
Rev. Rul. 57-278, 1957-1 C.B. 124 — 497
Rev. Rul. 57-518, 1957-2 C.B. 253 — 478
Rev. Rul. 58-402, 1958-2 C.B. 15 — 374
Rev. Rul. 58-465, 1958-2 C.B. 376 — 29
Rev. Rul. 59-60, 1959-1 C.B. 237 — 220
Rev. Rul. 59-221, 1959-1 C.B. 225 — 585
Rev. Rul. 59-259, 1959-2 C.B. 115 — 271, 273
Rev. Rul. 64-56 — 38
Rev. Rul. 64-73, 1964-1 C.B. 142 — 459
Rev. Rul. 67-274, 1967-2 C.B. 141 — 481
Rev. Rul. 67-376, 1967-2 C.B. 142 — 495
Rev. Rul. 67-488, 1967-2 C.B. 144 — 484
Rev. Rul. 68-55, 1968-1 C.B. 140 — 261, 280
Rev. Rul. 68-285 1968-1 C.B. 147 — 473
Rev. Rul. 68-289, 1968-1 C.B. 314 — 205
Rev. Rul. 68-603, 1968-2 C.B. 148 — 439
Rev. Rul. 69-172, 1969-1 C.B. 99 — 383
Rev. Rul. 69-180, 1969-1 C.B. 183 — 92
Rev. Rul. 69-608, 1969-2 C.B. 42 — 361
Rev. Rul. 70-18, 1970-1 C.B. 74 — 417
Rev. Rul. 70-106, 1970-1 C.B. 70 — 385
Rev. Rul. 70-140 1970-1 C.B. 73 — 288
Rev. Rul. 70-225, 1970-1 C.B. 80 — 440

Rev. Rul. 70-333, 1970-1 C.B. 38 — 79
Rev. Rul. 71-455 — 573
Rev. Rul. 71-564 — 38
Rev. Rul. 73-54, 1973-1 C.B. 187 — 473
Rev. Rul. 73-496, 1973-2 C.B. 312 — 609
Rev. Rul. 74-456, 1974-2 C.B. 65 — 391
Rev. Rul. 75-67, 1975-1 C.B. 169 — 537
Rev. Rul. 75-161, 1975-1 C.B. 114 — 496
Rev. Rul. 75-222, 1975-2 C.B. 105 — 332
Rev. Rul. 75-337, 1975-2 C.B. 124 — 422
Rev. Rul. 75-406, 1975-2 C.B. 125 — 441
Rev. Rul. 75-447, 1975-2 C.B. 113 — 361
Rev. Rul. 75-502, 1975-2 C.B. 111 — 345
Rev. Rul. 75-512, 1975-2 C.B. 112 — 344
Rev. Rul. 75-561, 1975-2 C.B. 129 — 495
Rev. Rul. 76-123, 1976-1 C.B. 94 — 610
Rev. Rul. 76-364, 1976-2 C.B. 91 — 344
Rev. Rul. 76-385, 1976-2 C.B. 92 — 345
Rev. Rul. 76-387, 1976-2 C.B. 96 — 494
Rev. Rul. 77-237, 1977-2 C.B. 88 — 354
Rev. Rul. 77-332, 1977-2 C.B. 484 — 21
Rev. Rul. 77-415, 1977-2 C.B. 311 — 492
Rev. Rul. 77-426, 1977-2 C.B. 87 — 345
Rev. Rul. 77-458, 1977-2 C.B. 220 — 206
Rev. Rul. 77-479, 1977-2 C.B. 119 — 492
Rev. Rul. 78-60, 1978-1 C.B. 80 — 330
Rev. Rul. 78-401, 1978-2 C.B. 127 — 344
Rev. Rul. 79-106, 1979-1 C.B. 448 — 15
Rev. Rul. 79-124, 1979-1 C.B. 224 — 218
Rev. Rul. 79-163, 1979-1 C.B. 131 — 332
Rev. Rul. 79-194, 1979-1 C.B. 145 — 260
Rev. Rul. 79-205, 1979-2 C.B. 255 — 150
Rev. Rul. 79-288 — 38
Rev. Rul. 80-26, 1980-1 C.B. 66 9 — 343
Rev. Rul. 81-289, 1981-2 C.B. 82 — 345
Rev. Rul. 81-300, 1981-2 C.B. 143 — 88
Rev. Rul. 83-51, 1983-1 C.B. 48 — 21
Rev. Rul. 84-52, 1984-1 C.B. 157 — 40
Rev. Rul. 84-71, 1984-1 C.B. 106 — 323
Rev. Rul. 84-111, 1984-2 C.B. 88 — 288
Rev. Rul. 85-48, 1985-1 C.B. 126 — 374
Rev. Rul. 85-164, 1985-2 C.B. 117 — 280
Rev. Rul. 87-115, 1987-2 C.B. 163 — 141
Rev. Rul. 87-132, 1987-2 C.B. 82 — 368
Rev. Rul. 88-8, 1988-1 C.B. 403 — 637
Rev. Rul. 88-76, 1988-2 C.B. 360 — 625, 689
Rev. Rul. 90-17, 1990-1 C.B. 119 — 206

Rev. Rul. 93-4, 1993-1 C.B. 225 — 637
Rev. Rul. 93-5, 1993-3 I.R.B. 6 — 689
Rev. Rul. 93-6, 1993-3 I.R.B. 8 — 689
Rev. Rul. 93-36, 1993-19 I.R.B. 4 — 618, 619
Rev. Rul. 93-38, 1993-1 C.B. 233 — 625
Rev. Rul. 93-62, 1993-30 I.R.B. 10 — 443

Private Letter Rulings

Priv. Ltr. Rul. 8043098 (July 19, 1980) — 536
Priv. Ltr. Rul. 8925087 (March 30, 1989) — 482
Priv. Ltr. Rul. 9017057 (January 30, 1990) — 621
Priv. Ltr. Rul. 9026005 (March 9, 1990) — 575
Priv. Ltr. Rul. 9029019 (April 19, 1990) — 631
Priv. Ltr. Rul. 9041005 (June 25, 1990) — 356
Priv. Ltr. Rul. 9121049 (February 26, 1991) — 495
Priv. Ltr. Rul. 9125013 (March 21, 1991) — 484
Priv. Ltr. Rul. 9218019 (May 1, 1992) — 599, 623
Priv. Ltr. Rul. 9245004 (July 28, 1992) — 602
Priv. Ltr. Rul. 9321006 (Nov. 30, 1993) — 609
Priv. Ltr. Rul. 9428006 (April 12, 1994) — 376

Revenue Procedures

Rev. Proc. 77-37, 1977-2 C.B. 568 — 260, 451, 452, 477, *507*
Rev. Proc. 81-70, 1981-2 C.B. 729 — 476
Rev. Proc. 82-40, 1982-2 C.B. 761 — 365
Rev. Proc. 83-59, 1983-2 C.B. 575 — 264
Rev. Proc. 84-35, 1984-1 C.B. 509 — 29
Rev. Proc. 84-42, 1984-1 C.B. 521 — 473
Rev. Proc. 91-1, 1991-1 C.B. 321 — 566
Rev. Proc. 91-62, 1991-2 C.B. 864 — 417
Rev. Proc. 93-27, 1993-24 I.R.B. 63 — 55
Rev. Proc. 95-10, I.R.B. 1995-3 20 — 631

Property Regulations

Prop. Reg. § 1.358-6(b) — 476
Prop. Reg. § 1.358-6(c)(4), example 1(e) — 483
Prop. Reg. § 1.358-6(c)(4), examples 2 (d) and (e) — 484
Prop. Reg. § 1.465-24 — 78
Prop. Reg. § 1.1362-6(b) — 564
Prop. Reg. §§ 1.1367-0, -1, -2, -3 — 690

Notices

Notice 88-81, 1988-2 C.B. 397 — 29
Notice 90-27, 1990-1 C.B. 336 — 571

TABLE OF AUTHORITIES

Notice 95-14, 1995-14 I.R.B. — 16
Notice 95-28, 1995-21 I.R.B. 9 — 63

Uniform Partnership Act (UPA)

UPA § 26 — 31
UPA § 31 — 211
UPA § 42 — 220

Revised Uniform Limited Partnership Act (RULPA)

RULPA § 303 — 112
RULPA §§ 402, 801 — 15
RULPA §§ 603, 604, and 705 — 220
RULPA § 701 — 31
RULPA § 704 — 127
RULPA § 801 — 211

Miscellaneous Authorities

General Counsel Memoranda

G.C.M. 36346 (July 23, 1975) — 49
G.C.M. 39404 (September 4, 1985) — 452
G.C.M. 39768 (Dec. 1, 1988) — 609

Public Laws

Pub. L. 99-514, § 612(a), 100 Stat. 2250 (1964) — 640
Pub. L. 99-514, § 634, 100 Stat. 2282 (1986) — 658

Senate Report

S. Rep. No. 1622, 83d Cong., 2d Sess. 89 (1954) — 2, 293

House Reports

H.R. Rep. No. 841, 99th Cong., 2d Sess. — 379
H.R. Rep. No. 5270, 102d Cong., 2d Sess. § 201 (1992) — 689

Revenue Act of 1924

Revenue Act of 1924, Pub. L. No. 176, § 203(c), 43 Stat. 253, 256 — 414

Temporary Treasury Regulation

Temp. Reg. § 1.469-5T(e)(2) — 80

Index

A

ADMISSION OF NEW PARTNER.
Allocation of profits and losses.
  Varying intra-year capital shares, pp. 119, 120.
AMERICAN LAW INSTITUTE.
"Reporter's study," pp. 667 to 673.
  Evaluation of the merits and deficiencies, pp. 674 to 679.
ANTI-ABUSE RULE REGULATIONS.
Liquidation of a partnership interest, pp. 182 to 185.
ANTI-LOSS REALIZATION RULE.
Consolidated subsidiaries.
  Taxable acquisitions, p. 408.
ASSET PURCHASES.
Corporations.
  Taxable acquisitions, pp. 390 to 399.

B

BUY-SELL AGREEMENTS.
Partnerships.
  Death of a partner, pp. 220 to 226.

C

CORPORATIONS.
Accumulated earnings tax, pp. 529 to 535.
Capital structure planning.
  Debt-equity problem, pp. 298 to 309.
    Distinguishing debt from equity, pp. 298 to 300.
  Research aids, p. 311.
  §§1202 and 1044 opportunities, pp. 310, 311.
  §1244 stock opportunity, p. 309.
Carryovers of tax attributes.
  Basic theme, pp. 511, 512.
  Ownership-based approach, pp. 518 to 522.
    Constructive ownership, pp. 521, 522.
    Equity structure shift, pp. 520, 521.
    Owner shift involving five percent shareholders, pp. 519, 520.
    Ownership change, pp. 519 to 521.
  Research aids, p. 528.
  Tax-avoidance purpose, pp. 512 to 517.
  Use of NOL after an ownership change, pp. 522 to 526.
    Annual income limitation, pp. 522, 523.
    Anti-stuffing rules, p. 524.

CORPORATIONS—Cont'd
Carryovers of tax attributes—Cont'd
  Use of NOL after an ownership change—Cont'd
    Built-in gains and losses, pp. 524 to 526.
    Business continuity requirement, p. 522.
  Use of pre-acquisition losses to offset built-in gains, pp. 526 to 528.
Collapsible corporation rules, pp. 539, 540.
Controlled corporations as a single taxpayer, p. 540.
Corporate taxes, pp. 231 to 233.
Distributions from corporations to shareholders.
  Basic structure, p. 314.
  Basis and holding period of stock, p. 331.
  Chronological aspects of dividends, pp. 315, 316.
  Corporate obligations, p. 324.
  Disguised and constructive distributions, pp. 318 to 321.
  "Dividend" defined, pp. 314, 315.
  Dividends received deduction, pp. 324, 325.
  "Earnings and profits" explained, pp. 316 to 318.
  Extraordinary dividends.
    Restrictions on deductions, p. 326.
  Holding period, p. 326.
  Introduction, pp. 313, 314.
  Legislative alternatives to present regime, p. 313.
  Leveraged dividends, p. 325.
  Property distributions, pp. 321 to 324.
  Research aids, p. 333.
  Stock dividends, pp. 326 to 331.
    Common and preferred stock, p. 328.
    Constructive distributions, pp. 330, 331.
    Convertible preferred stock, p. 329.
    Disproportionate distributions, pp. 329, 330.
    Optional distributions to shareholders, pp. 327, 328.
    Preferred stock, pp. 328, 329.
  §306 stock, pp. 331 to 333.
Domestic overseas subsidiaries, p. 233.
Historical background, pp. 227, 228.
Incidents of the income tax, p. 229.
Individual income tax distinguished, p. 228.
Integration of corporate and shareholder level taxes, pp. 229 to 231.
Liquidations.
  Complete liquidations, pp. 373 to 378.
    Corporate level effects, pp. 375 to 378.
    Stockholder level effects, pp. 373 to 375.
  Recognition of losses §336, pp. 378 to 382.
  State law background, p. 373.
  §332 liquidations, pp. 382 to 386.
    Minority shareholders, pp. 384, 385.
    Requirements, pp. 383, 384.
Organization of a corporation.
  Accommodation transferors, p. 260.
  Assumption of liabilities, pp. 263 to 271.
  Basis for property corporation receives, pp. 280 to 282.
  Basis of transferor's stock, pp. 278 to 280.
  "Boot" impact, pp. 260 to 263.
  Contributions to capital distinguished, pp. 293, 294.
  Control immediately after the transaction, pp. 257 to 259.

INDEX

CORPORATIONS—Cont'd
Organization of a corporation—Cont'd
  "Control" requirement.
    Property transferred in exchange and transferors' control, pp. 274 to 278.
    Rev. Rul. 59-252, pp. 271 to 273.
  Organizational and syndication expenditures, p. 294.
  Partnerships.
    Incorporation, pp. 282 to 287.
    Rev. Rul. 84-11, pp. 288 to 293.
  Proprietorships.
    Incorporation, pp. 282 to 287.
  Research aids, pp. 294, 295.
  Stock.
    How defined, pp. 253 to 257.
  Taxation of corporate entity, pp. 251, 252.
  Taxation of shareholders, p. 252.
  Transfer of property in exchange for stock, pp. 252, 253.
  Variation of state law, p. 251.
Personal holding company tax, pp. 535 to 539.
Recognition of the corporate form.
  "Agent" and "nominee" distinguished, pp. 235 to 240.
  "Arm's-length relationship," p. 239.
  Kintner regulations, p. 242.
  Personal service corporations, pp. 240 to 250.
  Research aids, p. 250.
  Substantive attacks on the corporate entity, pp. 240 to 250.
Redemptions of corporate stock.
  Closely-held corporations.
    "Family hostility" doctrine, pp. 343, 344.
  Complete termination of shareholder's interest, pp. 355 to 365.
  Constructive ownership, pp. 335 to 337.
  Partial liquidation of corporation, pp. 365 to 367.
  Payment of death taxes, pp. 367 to 370.
  Redemption not essentially equivalent to a dividend, pp. 337 to 346.
  Related corporations, pp. 370 to 372.
  Research aids, p. 372.
  Substantially disproportionate redemptions, pp. 346 to 355.
Reorganizations.
  Acquisitive type D reorganizations.
    §356(b) considerations, pp. 485 to 488.
  Code structure, pp. 450, 451.
  Contingent payoffs, pp. 507 to 509.
  Forward triangular mergers, pp. 482, 483.
  Historical background, pp. 449, 450.
  Impact on corporations, pp. 496, 497.
  Impact on shareholders and security holders, pp. 497 to 507.
  "Reorganization" defined, p. 450.
  Research aids, p. 509.
  Reverse triangular mergers, pp. 483, 484.
  Statutory mergers and consolidations, pp. 451 to 472.
    Accounting treatment, pp. 459, 460.
    Continuity of interest, pp. 452 to 458.
    "Creeping" mergers, p. 459.
    Idle act theory, p. 458.
    Installment sale treatment, pp. 467 to 472.
    Pooling of interests, pp. 460 to 467.
    Step-transaction doctrine, pp. 463 to 467.

CORPORATIONS—Cont'd
Reorganizations—Cont'd
  Tax treatment of parties to a reorganization, pp. 495 to 507.
  Triangular mergers, pp. 481 to 484.
  Type B reorganizations, §§472 to 475.
    Acquiring company's basis in target company stock, pp. 476, 477.
    "Creeping" reorganizations, pp. 474 to 476.
  Type C reorganizations, pp. 477 to 481.
    Overlaps, p. 481.
    Permissible consideration, pp. 480, 481.
    Substantially all the properties, pp. 477 to 479.
  Type E reorganizations, pp. 488 to 494.
  Type F reorganizations, pp. 494, 496.
  Type G reorganizations, p. 495.
Research aids.
  Capital structure planning, p. 311.
  Carryovers of tax attributes, p. 528.
  Corporate reorganizations, p. 509.
  Distributions from corporations to shareholders, p. 333.
  Introduction to corporate income taxation, p. 234.
  Organization of a corporation, pp. 294, 295.
  Recognition of the corporate form, p. 250.
  Taxable acquisitions, p. 409.
Restrictions on carryovers.
  Ownership-based approach, pp. 518 to 522.
  Research aids, p. 528.
  Tax-avoidance purpose, pp. 512 to 517.
  Use of NOL after an ownership change.
    Limitations on use, pp. 522 to 526.
  Use of preacquisition losses to offset built-in gains.
    Limitation on use, pp. 526 to 528.
Sham corporation theory, p. 240.
Special corporate penalty or regulatory taxes, pp. 529 to 541.
  Accumulated earnings tax, pp. 529 to 535.
  Collapsible corporation rules, pp. 539, 540.
  Controlled corporations as a single taxpayer, p. 540.
  Personal holding company tax, pp. 535 to 539.
Taxable acquisitions.
  Abandonment of intangibles, pp. 399 to 403.
  Anti-loss realization rule.
    Consolidated subsidiaries, p. 408.
  Asset purchases, pp. 390 to 399.
  Introduction, pp. 387 to 389.
  Research aids, p. 409.
  Stock purchase elections, pp. 403 to 408.
  Tax-free corporate divisions.
    Spin-off followed by a taxable acquisition, pp. 441, 442.
  Types of taxable acquisitions, pp. 389, 390.
Tax-free corporate divisions.
  Active trade or business requirement, pp. 423, 424.
  Boot in a spin-off, p. 443.
  Business purpose, pp. 418 to 423.
  Categories of separations, p. 411.
  Control, p. 417.
  Device for distributing earnings and profits, p. 423.
  Distributions in connection with taxable divisions, pp. 447, 448.
  Distribution threshold, p. 417.

INDEX

CORPORATIONS—Cont'd
Tax-free corporate divisions—Cont'd
  Groupings of corporate divisions, p. 411.
  Illustrative problem, pp. 412 to 414.
  "Reorganization" construed, pp. 415 to 417.
  Requirements, pp. 417 to 441.
  Single business, pp. 424 to 431.
    Horizontal division, pp. 425 to 431.
    Vertical division, pp. 424, 425.
  Spin-off followed by a tax acquisition, pp. 441 to 442.
  Spin-off of unwanted assets.
    Followed by tax-free acquisition, pp. 431 to 439.
  Spin-off of wanted assets.
    Followed by tax-free acquisition, pp. 439 to 441.
  Split-off or split-up, pp. 443 to 446.
  Tax treatment of distributees in a corporate division, pp. 442 to 446.
  Tax treatment of distributing corporation, pp. 446, 447.
Tax policy issues.
  Corporate tax incidence, pp. 643 to 645.
  "Double taxation" of corporate profits, pp. 639 to 643.
  Incorporating the corporate and individual income taxes.
    Abolishment of individual tax on dividends, pp. 647, 648.
    A.L.I. proposals for reform of Subchapter C, pp. 652 to 654.
    Allowance for corporate equity (ACE), pp. 654 to 657.
    Corporate tax integration while retaining two taxes, pp. 683 to 686.
    Deductibility of dividends, p. 648.
    Partnership or transparency method, p. 649.
    Shareholder imputation credit approach, pp. 650 to 652.
    Superiority of complete integration over other methods, pp. 686 to 691.
    U.S treasury department study and recommendations, pp. 658 to 667.
      Evaluation of the merits and deficiencies, pp. 674 to 679.
      Integration of the individual and corporate tax systems, pp. 658 to 664.
  Intergrating the corporate and individual income taxes, pp. 647 to 658.
  Justifications for a separate corporate income tax, pp. 646, 647.
  Rate relationships and stock basis, pp. 679 to 683.
Tax rates, pp. 231 to 233.

D

DEATH TAXES.
Redemptions of corporate stock, pp. 367 to 370.

DISSOLUTION.
Corporations.
  Liquidations, pp. 373 to 386.
Partnerships, pp. 187 to 203.

DIVIDENDS.
Corporations.
  Distributions from corporations to shareholders.
    Generally, pp. 313 to 333.
    Stock dividends, pp. 326 to 331.

E

ESTATE TAXES.
Corporations.
  Redemptions to pay death taxes, pp. 367 to 370.

ESTATE TAXES—Cont'd
Partnerships.
  Death of a partner, pp. 213 to 226.

G

GOODWILL.
Liquidation of a partnership interest.
  Treatment of payments for partner's share of goodwill, pp. 166, 167.

H

HOBBY LOSSES.
Tax consequences to partners, p. 79.

HOT ASSETS.
Partnership operating distributions.
  Disproportionate distributions involving "Hot Assets," pp. 156 to 158.

I

IRS AUDITS.
Partnerships, p. 30.

L

LIMITED LIABILITY COMPANIES.
Background, p. 625.
Issues for consideration, pp. 634, 635.
Research aids, p. 637.
Tax classification status.
  Current status, pp. 631 to 634.
  Optional classification of unincorporated entities, pp. 635 to 637.
  Partnership, pp. 625 to 631.

LIMITED PARTNERSHIPS.
Tax character of partnerships, pp. 4 to 15.

M

MERGER.
Partnerships, pp. 205 to 209.

P

PARTNERSHIPS AND PARTNERS.
Admission of new partner.
  Allocation of profits and losses, pp. 119, 120.
Allocation of profits and losses, pp. 102 to 120.
  Alternative economic effect test, pp. 104, 105.
  Amendment of partnership agreement, p. 109.
  Apportioning partnership liabilities, pp. 111 to 117.
    Allocating deductions attributable to nonrecourse debt, pp. 115 to 118.
    Nonrecourse liabilities, pp. 113 to 115.
      Allocating deductions attributable to nonrecourse debt, pp. 115 to 118.
    Recourse liabilities, pp. 111 to 113.
  Bottom-line allocation, defined, p. 102.

INDEX 737

PARTNERSHIPS AND PARTNERS—Cont'd
Allocation of profits and losses—Cont'd
  Economic effect, pp. 103 to 106.
  Family partnerships, pp. 120 to 125.
  Generally, pp. 95 to 102.
  Partner's interest in partnership, pp. 109 to 111.
  Post-1985 approach, pp. 102 to 111.
  Research aids, p. 125.
  Special allocation, defined, p. 102.
  Substantial, pp. 106 to 109.
  Three-part mechanical test, pp. 103, 105.
  Varying intra-year capital shares, pp. 118 to 120.
    Admission of new partner, p. 119.
    Capital interests, p. 118.
    Cash-method items limit, pp. 119, 120.
    Sale, exchange or liquidation of entire interest, p. 119.
Anti-abuse rule regulations, pp. 183 to 185.
  Abuse of entity treatment, p. 185.
  General anti-abuse rule, pp. 183, 184.
Capital contributions, pp. 31 to 42.
  Capital accounts, pp. 41, 42.
  Closing loopholes, p. 42.
  Holding principles, pp. 40, 41.
  Impact of debt on outside basis, p. 41.
  Impact of §704(c) on contributed property, pp. 39, 40.
  Inside basis, pp. 38, 39.
  Nonrecognition of gain, pp. 31 to 38.
Cash distributions.
  Operating distributions, pp. 146, 147.
Computing partnership income, pp. 59 to 65.
  Disallowed deductions, p. 64.
  Organization, syndication and start-up expenditures, pp. 64, 65.
  Separately stated items, pp. 60 to 64.
Death of a partner, pp. 211 to 226.
  Buy-sell agreements, pp. 220 to 226.
  Estate freeze, pp. 219, 220.
  Estate taxes, pp. 213 to 219.
  Partnership income, pp. 211 to 213.
  Research aids, p. 226.
Distributive shares, pp. 69 to 80.
  Adjustments to basis, pp. 72 to 75.
    Basis adjustments for capitalized partnership expenditures, pp. 74, 75.
    Basis adjustments for nondeductible partnership expenses, p. 74.
    Impact of distributions on partner's basis, p. 74.
    Impact of income and laws on partner's basis, pp. 73, 74.
    Outside basis adjustments for tax-exempt partnership income, p. 74.
    Partner's (outside) basis and partnership's (inside) basis, pp. 72, 73.
    Symmetry between inside and outside basis, p. 75.
  Character of distributive shares, p. 72.
  Limitation on allowance of losses.
    At-risk rules, pp. 78, 79.
    General deferral limitation on flow-through of losses, pp. 75 to 78.
    Hobby losses, p. 79.
    Passive activity losses, pp. 79, 80.
  Timing of distributive shares, pp. 69 to 72.
    Statute of limitations, pp. 71, 72.
Division of a partnership, p. 210.

PARTNERSHIPS AND PARTNERS—Cont'd
Family partnerships.
   Allocation of profits and losses.
      Limits on allocations, pp. 124, 125.
      Recognition of partnership, pp. 120 to 124.
Formation of partnerships, pp. 31 to 57.
   Assignment of income principles, p. 56.
   Capital.
      Contributions, pp. 31 to 42.
   Foreign partnerships, p. 56.
   Research aids, p. 56.
   Service contributions, pp. 42 to 56.
Level elections, pp. 65 to 69.
   Accounting method, p. 66.
   Selection of taxable year, pp. 66 to 69.
Liquidation of a partnership interest.
   Anti-abuse rule regulations, pp. 182 to 185.
   Overview, p. 159.
   Sale or liquidation option, pp. 176 to 182.
   Sale vs. Liquidation, pp. 159 to 163.
   Taxability of partnership, p. 176.
   Tax treatment of partner's payments, pp. 163 to 175.
      Goodwill, pp. 166, 167.
      Losses on distribution, pp. 174 to 176.
      Modified distribution rules, pp. 163, 164.
      Role of §736.
         Property distributions, pp. 165, 166.
      Timing of payments, pp. 167 to 174.
      Unrealized receivables and goodwill, p. 166.
   Two-person partnership, p. 176.
   §736 partner tax treatment, pp. 163 to 175.
Merger of partnerships, pp. 205 to 209.
Operating distributions, pp. 145 to 156.
   Effect on partner, pp. 145 to 150.
      Cash distributions, pp. 146, 147.
      Overview, pp. 145, 146.
   Effect on partnership, pp. 153 to 156.
   Encumbered property distributions, pp. 150 to 153.
   Foreign partners, p. 156.
   "Hot Assets."
      Disproportionate distributions, pp. 156 to 158.
   Property distributions, pp. 147 to 153.
      §732(d) election, pp. 149, 150.
   Research aids, p. 158.
   §734 election, pp. 154 to 156.
Property distributions.
   Liquidation of a partnership interest, pp. 163 to 175.
   Operating distributions, pp. 147 to 153.
Research aids.
   Allocation of profits and losses, p. 125.
   Death of a partner, p. 226.
   Formation of partnerships, p. 56.
   Operating distributions, p. 158.
   Taxation of partnership operations, p. 80.
   Tax character of partnerships, p. 30.
   Termination of a partnership, p. 203.
   Transactions between partners and partnerships, p. 94.

PARTNERSHIPS AND PARTNERS—Cont'd
Sales and exchanges of partnership interests.
  Buyer's tax liability, pp. 140 to 144.
    Allocating optional basis adjustment, pp. 142, 143.
    Optional basis adjustment, pp. 140 to 144.
  Seller's tax liability, pp. 128 to 140.
    Calculating gains and losses, pp. 139, 140.
    Contract interests as unrealized receivables, pp. 129 to 138.
    Substantially appreciated inventory, pp. 138, 139.
    Traditional recapture items, p. 138.
Service contributions.
  Capital interest received for services, pp. 42 to 48.
  Receipt of profits interest for services, pp. 48 to 56.
Tax character of partnerships, pp. 1 to 30.
  IRS audits, p. 30.
  Limited partnerships, pp. 4 to 15.
  Partnership status, pp. 4 to 30.
    Debtor-creditor relationship, pp. 17 to 22.
    Expense sharing, pp. 28, 29.
    Joint ventures, pp. 23 to 28.
    Retroactive amendments of partnership agreement, p. 30.
  Popularity of partnerships, pp. 3, 4.
  Research aids, p. 30.
  State law characteristics, p. 1.
  Tax treatment background, pp. 1, 2.
Tax policy issues.
  Superiority of the partnership style over other methods, pp. 686 to 691.
Tax treatment of partner's payments.
  Open transaction doctrine, p. 167.
Termination of a partnership.
  Cessation of business, pp. 187 to 193.
  Overview, p. 187.
  Research aids, p. 203.
  Technical terminations, pp. 193 to 203.
Transactions between partners and partnerships, pp. 81 to 94.
  Compensation disguised as distribution, pp. 92, 93.
  Conversion of character of assets, p. 82.
  Disguised transactions, pp. 92 to 94.
  Fringe benefits, p. 94.
  Guaranteed payment, pp. 83 to 92.
  Guaranteed payment plus allocation, pp. 91, 92.
  Impact on partnership, p. 92.
  Limitations on current deductions, pp. 82, 83.
  Limitations on losses in transactions, pp. 81, 82.
  Property purchases disguised as distributions, pp. 93, 94.
  Research aids, p. 94.

R

REDEMPTIONS.
Corporate stock.
  Generally, pp. 335 to 372.

S

S CORPORATIONS.
Basic taxation model, p. 567.

S CORPORATIONS—Cont'd
Built-in gains tax.
  S corporations formerly C corporations, pp. 569 to 572.
Computation of corporate tax base, pp. 567, 568.
Conduit taxation model, p. 567.
Current distributions, pp. 593 to 598.
  Corporations with earnings and profits, pp. 594 to 596.
  Corporations without earnings and profits, pp. 593, 594.
  Post-termination distributions, pp. 597, 598.
  Property distributions, pp. 596, 597.
Elections, p. 568.
Eligibility to elect status, pp. 543 to 561.
  Affiliated groups, pp. 543, 544.
  Corporate election, p. 562.
  Debt and hybrid instruments.
    Treasury views, pp. 557 to 562.
  Election procedure, pp. 562, 563.
  General rule.
    One class of stock, pp. 546 to 556.
  Nonresident aliens, pp. 544, 545.
  One class of stock, pp. 546 to 562.
  Qualified Subchapter S trusts, pp. 545, 546.
  Shareholder consents, pp. 562, 563.
  Straight debt safe harbor, pp. 556, 557.
  Thirty-five shareholder limit, p. 544.
  Trusts, p. 545.
Excess passive net income tax, pp. 572 to 574.
Interactions of Subchapter S and Subchapter C.
  Alternative minimum tax, p. 620.
  At-risk rules, p. 619.
  Audits of S corporations, p. 620.
  Dividends-received deduction, pp. 610 to 619.
  Fringe benefits, p. 619.
  Hobby-loss rules, p. 619.
  Liquidations, pp. 599 to 602.
  Passive activity loss rules, pp. 619, 620.
  S corporation as a shareholder, pp. 602 to 610.
  Transactions with related taxpayers, p. 620.
Losses and deductions.
  General limitation, pp. 585, 586.
  Manipulation of debt and guarantees, pp. 586 to 592.
Loss of status.
  Relief from inadvertent terminations, p. 566.
  Revocation of the election, p. 563.
  S termination year, pp. 565, 566.
  Termination of the election, pp. 564, 565.
Multiform S corporations, pp. 620 to 623.
Overview, pp. 541, 542.
Pass-through of income and loss.
  Basis of stock, p. 579.
  Pro rata share rule, pp. 574 to 579.
  Reallocation among family groups, pp. 579 to 585.
  Timing of pass-through and character of income, pp. 574 to 585.
Research aids, p. 566.
  Taxation of the entity and its owners, p. 623.
Tax policy issues.
  Superiority of the S corporation style over other methods, pp. 686 to 691.

INDEX

STOCK PURCHASE ELECTIONS.
Corporations.
  Taxable acquisitions, pp. 403 to 408.

T

TRANSACTIONS BETWEEN PARTNERS AND PARTNERSHIPS, pp. 81 to 94.

TWO-PERSON PARTNERSHIP.
Liquidation of a partnership interest, p. 176.

U

U.S. TREASURY DEPARTMENT STUDY.
Integration of the individual and corporate tax systems.
  Evaluation of the merits and deficiencies, pp. 674 to 679.
  Treasury department legislative recommendations, pp. 664 to 667.